Readings in Jurisprudence and Legal Philosophy

Cohen and Cohen's

Readings in Jurisprudence
and Legal Philosophy

Philip Shuchman
Professor of Law, University of Connecticut

Little, Brown and Company   *Boston and Toronto*

Published simultaneously in Canada
by Little, Brown & Company (Canada) Limited

Printed in the United States of America

Contents

Contents

Chapter 2. **The Nature of the Judicial Process**   **235**

Contents

Chapter 7. **Problems of Knowledge in the Law**   667

Chapter 8. **Law and History**   713

Chapter 9. **Law and Anthropology**   755

Contents

x

Preface

I used the original edition of this book of readings with pleasure for several years. It is an elegant collection. I hope the revisions do not change the character of the book but take into account those publications of the past twenty-five years which the Cohens would have found noteworthy.

The contributions of Morris R. Cohen to so many fields of philosophy are, deservedly, still well known. He wrote with insight and great critical acumen in almost every area of philosophy and especially in philosophy of law. His son Felix had already done seminal work when his untimely death deprived us of much more in progress. I viewed as a compliment the invitation of the publisher to revise their book.

The scheme of the volume, as stated in the Preface to the First Edition, has not been significantly altered. The only omission is the first part of the original which contained the "materials of controversy," chiefly about private property, in the substantive fields of law: contract, tort, liability, crime and punishment. The development of theory in these areas has been intense and is today reflected in most casebooks and texts.

Felix Cohen had recommended as a single companion text the outstanding book of Julius Stone, The Province and Function of the Law. To that, of course, one can now add Stone's later works: Legal System and Lawyers' Reasonings (1964); Human Law and Human Justice (1965); Social Dimensions of Law and Justice (1966). Other useful recent general reference works include: J. Hall, Foundations of Jurisprudence; W. Friedmann, Legal Theory; E. Bodenheimer, Jurisprudence.

In the teacher's manual which is to accompany this anthology I provide some specific bibliographic references.

The state of contemporary jurisprudence, defined in conventional terms, is mixed. Some of it is mere analysis which usually takes the form of redefining, of restating the typology of our system of labels. Another large segment consists of exhortations. Vast elaborations on Bentham and Hobbes seem the prevailing ethical and social theories of contemporary jurisprudence.

The major recent works of H. L. A. Hart, John Rawls, and Robert Nozick have created veritable industries of commentary. Perhaps it has always been the case that when a dramatic work comes along its meaning is to be known only through the explications of critics, reviewers and commentators, and their respondents. That seems true of Wittgenstein and John Austin in recent memory.

To the extent that contemporary jurisprudence is philosophical— not adding new knowledge but performing Locke's underlabor functions, examining presuppositions, and clearing away the tangled notions of any substantive undertaking—it seems sterile. But philosophy in its critical role and inquiring mode does not seek the kind of information that is in law books. It accepts those propositions and suggests what they might mean when viewed from vantage points not familiar to lawyers and law students.

A derivative function of philosophy of law results in another kind of jurisprudential approach. For example, the critical posture of legal realism, broadly conceived has worked to foster the development of new disciplines in law such as those involving the use of economic and sociological theory and the investigative techniques of those disciplines to help explain the meaning of law in different contexts and, for some, even to redefine law.

New or newly applied techniques and new knowledge change the very premises with which any philosopher of law must start. It is not as though the student of jurisprudence must know the law any more than a philosopher of science need be a trained scientist. But some knowledge which informs one about the legal and legislative process is essential unless the philosopher of law retreats to his own internal system and is not concerned with whether his critical commentary is at all based on fact. One can, with suitable premises, come to extraordinary conclusions, wonderful in their logic, but entirely untrue in fact and therefore not useful for philosophical criticism. I urge all students to beware of that path named Logic Lane which, I am advised, does not necessarily go anywhere.

I am grateful to my secretary, Mildred Mobilia, and to my research assistants, Jomarie Theve Andrews, Jack Clarkson, William Matthews, and Joan Spignesi.

My wife has had to bear with the cutting and pasting of several versions of this anthology. She has been patient and gracious. For that and other reasons that count, this volume is dedicated to Hedvah.

Philip Shuchman

Hartford, Connecticut

Preface to First Edition

The Scheme of the Volume

A distinguished teacher once gave a series of lectures on law and ethics that made so deep an impression that the notes taken by his students are still being widely circulated. In his final lecture, this teacher commented on the prevailing notion of practical men that legal ideals are other-worldly or utopian, and made the ever-pertinent observation on the nature of ethical doctrine:

> It is not in heaven, that thou shouldest say, Who shall go up for us to heaven, and bring it unto us, and make us to hear it, that we may do it? Neither is it beyond the sea, that thou shouldest say, Who shall go over the sea for us, and bring it unto us, and make us to hear it, that we may do it? But the word is very nigh unto thee, in thy mouth, and in thy heart, that thou mayest do it.

It is with the thought that all of the ethical issues of the law are very near to us, in courtrooms, legislative halls, and city streets, that the materials of this book have been put together.

"To see so far as one may, and to feel, the great forces that are behind every detail," said Holmes, "makes all the difference between philosophy and gossip."[1] So conceived, legal philosophy is not an escape from reality to an easy world of irrefutable imaginings, but rather one of the most rigorous of intellectual disciplines. Abstract questions concern-

---

1. "The Class of '61" in O. W. Holmes, Jr., *Speeches* (privately printed, 1913), 95, 96.

ing the nature of law have significance only against a background of concrete controversies. . . .

The Vocation of Our Age for Jurisprudence and Legal Philosophy

Jurisprudence, as the jurist's quest for a systematic vision that will order and illumine the dark realities of the law, and legal philosophy, conceived as the philosopher's effort to understand the legal order and its role in human life, have come close enough together in our land and our generation to warrant a unified approach to these two overlapping fields. Such, at least, is the premise upon which this volume of readings has been prepared.

This effort at cross-fertilization between legal practicalities and philosophic understanding would be out of place or out of time in many lands today where rational criticism of existing institutions is unwelcome. But it is only as existing institutions are stripped of ancient cruelties by bold philosophical analysis that men escape from the barbaric servitudes of the past; and only as men learn to substitute rigorous reflective thought for hit-or-miss trial-and-error can they escape the barbarisms that the future pins to most human hopes. This is what gives pragmatic significance to the contemporary study of legal philosophy. . . .

There is still a powerful drive among many contemporary philosophers to keep their philosophies pure and unpolitical by avoiding contact with the realities of human controversy and social disorder. As strong, or even stronger, is the opposition of many practical men to critical reflection upon existing legal institutions. Both these views result in a view of jurisprudence as a maze of inert ideas, a museum of intellectual curiosities far removed from logic or practice. What follows is that analytical, historical, metaphysical, and sociological jurisprudences and their various hybrids and offshoots are exhibited before innocent students like a series of butterflies, all neatly labeled, pinned to their proper cards, and thoroughly dead. The history of law, its logical analysis, the scientific study of its social consequences, and the evaluation of those consequences, instead of being viewed as related problems posed by a common subject matter, come to be viewed as mutually exclusive objectives of conflicting "schools." The pejorative suffix "ism" is invoked to disparage interest in science by calling it "scientism," and interest in history or scholarship can be effectively discouraged by the use of such labels as "historicism" or "scholasticism." It is very easy to dismiss all our predecessors on the ground that they did not know about some recent discovery of psychiatry or sociology or never mastered some modern prestige-vocabulary. But what then? "The notion that we can dismiss the views of all previous thinkers surely leaves no basis for the hope that our own work will prove of any value to others."[2]

The teaching of jurisprudence, so conceived, commonly results only in the suppression of curiosity and the turning of clean-cutting minds into intellectual junk shops. The human product of this process, distrustful of all generalizations and abstractions, is likely to be quite incapable of projecting ideas into the future, since the future is itself an abstraction. But the long-range problems of a social order in competition with rival ideas can certainly not be solved by those who fail to understand the force of ideas. And it is ancient wisdom that in the long run nothing is so powerful as an idea when its time has come. In that moment the "proud men of action," as Heine remarked, "are nothing but unconscious instruments of the men of thought."

The disparagement of ideas by those who mistake short-sightedness for practicality is perhaps part of a "loss of nerve" which attacks the complacent when they face the unfamiliar. But there are many signs today that the pattern of complacency towards the familiar and of mistrust towards all unfamiliar accents and ideas is doomed, that the era of classificatory caricatures in jurisprudence is drawing to a close, and that the value of a multi-dimensional perspective upon legal realities and legal ideals is gradually winning acceptance. . . .

The Process of Selection

To select out of the writings of these men, and out of a much larger body of writings of other lands and ages, materials that can provide a useful introduction to the problems of legal philosophy is no easy task. A factor of selection unrelated to the merits of the works involved arises from the objective of this volume. Its editors have tried to present a wide selection of different viewpoints in a brief space. To accomplish this end it has been necessary to pass over many important works that are so solidly integrated that brief excerpts cannot possibly do justice to the viewpoints they develop. This has unfortunately been particularly true in the field of general philosophy, where, as in a system of geometry, no single fragment can reveal the whole. Thus contemporary thinkers such as Ralph Barton Perry and C. I. Lewis appear in the following pages only through the words of their students, as do such distinguished predecessors in philosophic paths as Plato and Spinoza. But even with the aid of such mechanical selectors the choice of materials has been a difficult one. Basically, the process of selection as carried out by the compilers of this

---

2. M. R. Cohen, *Reason and Nature* (1931), p. x.

volume has consisted in throwing a much larger mass of materials at their students and retaining those fragments that struck sparks. . . .

Introductions and Footnotes

The chief purpose of any anthology, I suppose, is to save its user the time and carfare that would otherwise be consumed in borrowing from friends or libraries the books he doesn't possess. Were that the only function of this volume, the intervention of an editor between the original authors and the reader would be an impertinence. But since this volume is intended not only for browsing but also for use as a course text and as a beginner's introduction to the main currents of legal thought, I have found it necessary to insert introductory notes at the start of each chapter and a considerable number of footnotes throughout the text. These are intended to clarify the relation of one author or excerpt to another by indicating the various perspectives of time and purpose that orient the works from which these selections have been taken. . . .

Acknowledgments

To my wife Lucy Kramer, who searched through hundreds of volumes with me to glean the fragments that are here bound together, . . . and to the many friends and associates who have aided along the way, I give my grateful thanks.

Epilogue

In completing alone what began as a joint enterprise, I am painfully aware of my many ineptitudes for the appointed task. I have neither the mastery of philosophic and scientific systems, the command of languages and intellectual history, the rich experience as a teacher, nor the many other talents that would be needed to complete this work with the comprehensive and penetrating vision that was present when the work was begun. I must therefore look to the criticisms of colleagues and students for aid in correcting errors of commission and omission in this volume, errors which might have been avoided if it had been possible to complete the task five years ago. But I can only say to my chief guide and collaborator that I have done my best, with clumsy hands, to finish what he began. And I find solace, as he did, in the words of an ancient seer: "The day is short and the task is great. It is not incumbent upon thee to complete the whole work, but neither art thou free to neglect it."

FELIX S. COHEN

WASHINGTON, D.C.

Readings in Jurisprudence and Legal Philosophy

Chapter 1

The Nature of Law

I. GENERAL AND HISTORICAL

Hobbes, Leviathan*

Chapter Thirteen. Of the Natural Condition of Mankind As Concerning Their Felicity and Misery

Men by nature equal. Nature has made men so equal in the faculties of the body and mind as that, though there be found one man sometimes manifestly stronger in body or of quicker mind than another, yet, when

* [(1651.) The *Leviathan* of Thomas Hobbes (1558-1679) represents the first comprehensive application of the approach to the field of law. Locke, in part, and to a much greater degree, Bentham, Austin, Holmes, Gray, and the later American realists, have pursued and developed the Hobbesian approach. Hobbes' views on the evils of civil strife in the absence of generally recognized authority were based upon considerable personal experience.

In 1640, alarmed at political developments in England, Hobbes fled to France where he remained in the company of English refugee aristocrats, serving even as tutor to the future Charles II for two years. *De Cive* (On the State), although published in 1647, was actually written ten years before the appearance of the *Leviathan,* Hobbes' most famous work. The latter book, having aroused the opposition of the French because of its attacks on the Catholic Church, forced Hobbes to return to London to make what peace he could with Cromwell. In spite of his notoriety as a materialist and suspected atheist, Hobbes was awarded a pension after the Restoration, although in fact it was never paid. After an investigation of atheistic writings by a committee of the House of Commons, Hobbes was forced to publish his works abroad in Amsterdam, a great center of publishing in the seventeenth and eighteenth centuries because of its tradition of freedom of press. There appeared the *Behemoth,* a less controversial work than the *Leviathan,* in 1688, and twenty years later, a century after Hobbes' birth but only nine after his death, the first collected edition appeared. Cairn's *Legal Philosophy from Plato to Hegel* contains an instructive chapter on Hobbes' legal views.]

1

all is reckoned together, the difference between man and man is not so considerable as that one man can thereupon claim to himself any benefit to which another may not pretend as well as he. For as to the strength of body, the weakest has strength enough to kill the strongest, either by secret machination or by confederacy with others that are in the same danger with himself.

And as to the faculties of the mind, setting aside the arts grounded upon words, and especially that skill of proceeding upon general and infallible rules called science—which very few have and but in few things, as being not a native faculty born with us, nor attained, as prudence, while we look after somewhat else—I find yet a greater equality among men than that of strength. For prudence is but experience, which equal time equally bestows on all men in those things they equally apply themselves unto. That which may perhaps make such equality incredible is but a vain conceit of one's own wisdom, which almost all men think they have in a greater degree than the vulgar–that is, than all men but themselves and a few others whom, by fame or for concurring with themselves, they approve. For such is the nature of men that howsoever they may acknowledge many others to be more witty or more eloquent or more learned, yet they will hardly believe there be many so wise as themselves; for they see their own wit at hand and other men's at a distance. But this proves rather that men are in that point equal than unequal. For there is not ordinarily a greater sign of the equal distribution of anything than that every man is contented with his share.

*From equality proceeds diffidence.*From this equality of ability arises equality of hope in the attaining of our ends. And therefore if any two men desire the same thing, which nevertheless they cannot both enjoy, they become enemies; and in the way to their end, which is principally their own conservation, and sometimes their delectation only, endeavor to destroy or subdue one another. And from hence it comes to pass that where an invader has no more to fear than another man's single power, if one plant, sow, build, or possess a convenient seat, others may probably be expected to come prepared with forces united to dispossess and deprive him, not only of the fruit of his labor, but also of his life or liberty. And the invader again is in the like danger of another.

From diffidence war. And from this diffidence of one another there is no way for any man to secure himself so reasonable as anticipation—that is, by force or wiles to master the persons of all men he can, so long till he see no other power great enough to endanger him; and this is no more than his own conservation requires, and is generally allowed. Also, because there be some that take pleasure in contemplating their own power in the acts of conquest, which they pursue farther than their security requires, if others that otherwise would be glad to be at ease within modest bounds should not by invasion increase their power, they would not be able, long time, by standing only on their defense, to subsist. And by consequence, such augmentation of dominion over men being necessary to a man's conservation, it ought to be allowed him.

Again, men have no pleasure, but on the contrary a great deal of grief, in keeping company where there is no power able to overawe them all. For every man looks that his companion should value him at the same rate he sets upon himself; and upon all signs of contempt or undervaluing naturally endeavors, as far as he dares (which among them that have no common power to keep them in quiet is far enough to make them destroy each other), to extort a greater value from his contemners by damage and from others by the example.

So that in the nature of man we find three principal causes of quarrel: first, competition; secondly, diffidence; thirdly, glory.

The first makes men invade for gain, the second for safety, and the third for reputation. The first use violence to make themselves masters of other men's persons, wives, children, and cattle; the second, to defend them; the third, for trifles, as a word, a smile, a different opinion, and any other sign of undervalue, either direct in their persons or by reflection in their kindred, their friends, their nation, their profession, or their name.

Out of civil states, there is always war of every one against every one. Hereby it is manifest that, during the time men live without a common power to keep them all in awe, they are in that condition which is called war, and such a war as is of every man against every man. For WAR consists not in battle only, or the act of fighting, but in a tract of time wherein the will to contend by battle is sufficiently known; and therefore the notion of *time* is to be considered in the nature of war as it is in the nature of weather. For as the nature of foul weather lies not in a shower or two of rain but in an inclination thereto of many days together, so the nature of war consists not in actual fighting but in the known disposition thereto during all the time there is no assurance to the contrary. All other time is PEACE.

The incommodities of such a war. Whatsoever, therefore, is consequent to a time of war where every man is enemy to every man, the same is consequent to the time wherein men live without other security than what their own strength and their own invention shall furnish them withal. In such condition there is no place for industry, because the fruit thereof is uncertain: and consequently no culture of the earth; no navigation nor use of the commodities that may be imported by sea; no commodious building; no instruments of moving and removing such things

3

as require much force; no knowledge of the face of the earth; no account of time; no arts; no letters; no society; and, which is worst of all, continual fear and danger of violent death; and the life of man solitary, poor, nasty, brutish, and short.

It may seem strange to some man that has not well weighed these things that nature should thus dissociate and render men apt to invade and destroy one another; and he may therefore, not trusting to this inference made from the passions, desire perhaps to have the same confirmed by experience. Let him therefore consider with himself—when taking a journey he arms himself and seeks to go well accompanied, when going to sleep he locks his doors, when even in his house he locks his chests, and this when he knows there be laws and public officers, armed, to revenge all injuries shall be done him—what opinion he has of his fellow subjects when he rides armed, of his fellow citizens when he locks his doors, and of his children and servants when he locks his chests. Does he not there as much accuse mankind by his actions as I do by my words? But neither of us accuse man's nature in it. The desires and other passions of man are in themselves no sin. No more are the actions that proceed from those passions till they know a law that forbids them, which, till laws be made, they cannot know, nor can any law be made till they have agreed upon the person that shall make it.

It may peradventure be thought there was never such a time nor condition of war as this, and I believe it was never generally so over all the world; but there are many places where they live so now. For the savage people in many places of America, except the government of small families, the concord whereof depends on natural lust, have no government at all and live at this day in that brutish manner as I said before. Howsoever, it may be perceived what manner of life there would be where there were no common power to fear by the manner of life which men that have formerly lived under a peaceful government use to degenerate into in a civil war.

But though there had never been any time wherein particular men were in a condition of war one against another, yet in all times kings and persons of sovereign authority, because of their independency, are in continual jealousies and in the state and posture of gladiators, having their weapons pointing and their eyes fixed on one another—that is, their forts, garrisons, and guns upon the frontiers of their kingdoms, and continual spies upon their neighbors—which is a posture of war. But because they uphold thereby the industry of their subjects, there does not follow from it that misery which accompanies the liberty of particular men.

In such a war nothing is unjust. To this war of every man against every man, this also is consequent: that nothing can be unjust. The notions of

4

right and wrong, justice and injustice, have there no place. Where there is no common power, there is no law; where no law, no injustice. Force and fraud are in war the two cardinal virtues. Justice and injustice are none of the faculties neither of the body nor mind. If they were, they might be in a man that were alone in the world, as well as his senses and passions. They are qualities that relate to men in society, not in solitude. It is consequent also to the same condition that there be no propriety, no dominion, no *mine* and *thine* distinct; but only that to be every man's that he can get, and for so long as he can keep it. And thus much for the ill condition which man by mere nature is actually placed in, though with a possibility to come out of it consisting partly in the passions, partly in his reason.

The passions that incline men to peace. The passions that incline men to peace are fear of death, desire of such things as are necessary to commodious living, and a hope by their industry to obtain them. And reason suggests convenient articles of peace, upon which men may be drawn to agreement. These articles are they which otherwise are called the Laws of Nature.

Savigny, Of the Vocation of Our Age For Legislation and Jurisprudence*

Preface to the Second Edition

The first edition of the present work appeared in 1814, at a time which can never be forgotten by any, who with full consciousness, have lived through it. For years the fetters which bound our country to the

---

*[The first edition of Savigny's famous tract against codification, *Vom Beruf unsrer Zeit für Gesetzgebung und Rechtswissenschaft,*was published in 1814. It was written in reply to a pamphlet by Thibaut, *Über die Nothwendigkeit eines allgemeinen bürgerlichen Rechts für Deutschland* (1814). The translation here given follows generally the translation by Hayward (1831).

Friedrich Carl von Savigny (1779-1861) published his first treatise, *Das Recht des Besitzes*(*The Law of Possession*) in 1803. In 1810 Savigny became Professor of Roman Law at the new University of Berlin, where he also served as tutor to the Crown Prince and lectured on government. His protest against the demand for codification in 1814 served as a model for similar protests in other lands against the movement for codification to which Bentham had given great impetus. In 1815 the first volume of Savigny's *Geschichte des römischen Rechts im Mittelalter* came out; the final volume in 1831. Savigny's famous work on the contemporary Roman law, *System des heutigen römischen Rechts* (1840-1849, 8 volumes) was supplemented in 1853 by a treatise on Contracts (*Das Obligationrecht*). Meanwhile Savigny had served from 1842 to 1848 as head of the Prussian legal system, which afforded the opportunity of recasting the law of commercial paper and the divorce statutes. After 1848 Savigny devoted himself entirely to theoretical jurisprudence.]

arbitrary rule of a foreigner had been drawing tighter and tighter, and it was plain that, when the designs of the oppressor came to be fully developed, our destiny must end in the annihilation of our nationality. The momentous events by which the foreign yoke was broken, averted this hard lot from our country; and the feeling of grateful joy, universally excited by this deliverance from the greatest of all dangers, might well be cherished as a sacred recollection by the whole nation. . . .

II. Origin of Positive Law

We first inquire of history, how law has actually developed amongst nations of the nobler races; the question—What may be good, or necessary, or, on the contrary, censurable herein,—will be not at all prejudiced by this method of proceeding.

In the earliest times to which authentic history extends, the law will be found to have already attained a fixed character, peculiar to the people, like their language, manners and constitutions. Nay, these phenomena have no separate existence, they are but the particular faculties and tendencies of an individual people, inseparably united in nature, and only wearing the semblance of distinct attributes to our view. That which binds them into one whole is the common conviction of the people, the kindred consciousness of an inward necessity, excluding all notion of an accidental and arbitrary origin.

In modern times the view has come to prevail that all life was at first of an animal character, passing through evolution step by step to a tolerable existence, until at length the height on which we now stand has been attained. . . .

But this organic connection of law with the being and character of the people, is also manifested in the progress of the times; and here, again, it may be compared with language. For law, as for language, there is no moment of absolute rest; it is subject to the same movement and development as every other popular tendency; and this very development remains under the same law of inward necessity, as in its earliest stages. Law grows with the growth, and strengthens with the strength of the people, and finally dies away as the nation loses its nationality. . . .

. . . With the progress of civilization, national tendencies become more and more distinct, and what otherwise would have remained common, becomes appropriated to particular classes. The jurists now become more and more a distinct class of the kind. Law perfects its language, takes a scientific direction, and, as formerly it existed in the consciousness of the community, it now devolves upon the jurists, who thus, in this respect, represent the community. . . .

. . . The sum, therefore, of this view is, that all law is originally formed in the manner in which, in ordinary but not quite correct language, customary law is said to have been formed: i.e. that it is first developed by custom and popular faith, next by jurisprudence,—everywhere, therefore, by internal silently-operating powers, not by the arbitrary will of a lawgiver. . . .

III. Laws and Law Books

Legislation, properly so called, not infrequently exercises an influence upon particular portions of the law; but the causes of this influence vary greatly. In the first place, the legislator, in altering the existing law, may be influenced by high political purposes. When, in our time, unprofessional men speak of the necessity of new legislation, they commonly mean only that of which the settlement of the rights of land-owners is one of the most striking examples.[1] The history of the Roman law, also, supplies examples of this kind,—a few in the free times of the republic, —the important *Lex Julia et Papia Poppaea,* in the time of Augustus,—and a great number since the Christian emperors. That enactments of this kind easily become a baneful corruption of the law, and that they should be most sparingly employed, must strike any one who consults history. . . .

Putting together what has been said above concerning the requisites of a really good code, it is clear that very few ages will be found qualified for it. Young nations, it is true, have the clearest perception of their law, but their codes are defective in language and logical skill, and they are generally incapable of expressing what is best, so that they frequently produce no individual image, whilst their matter is in the highest degree individual. The laws of the middle ages, already quoted, are examples of this; and had we the twelve tables complete before us, we should probably find something of the sort, only in a less degree. In declining ages, on the other hand, almost everything is wanting—knowledge of the matter, as well as language. There thus remains only a middle period; that which (as regards the law, although not necessarily in any other respect,) may be accounted the summit of civilization. But such an age has no need of a code for itself: it would merely compose one for a succeeding and less fortunate age, as we lay up provisions for winter. But an age is seldom disposed to be so provident for children and grandchildren.

---

1. The author, I believe, alludes to the law of 1810, enacting that all hereditary tenants of lands in Prussia might, by giving up a certain proportion of them to the landlord, become free proprietors of the rest.—TRANSL.

Austin, The Province of Jurisprudence Determined*

Laws proper, or properly so called, are commands; laws which are not commands, are laws improper or improperly so called. Laws properly so called, with laws improperly so called, may be aptly divided into the four following kinds.

1. The divine laws, or the laws of God: that is to say, the laws which are set by God to his human creatures.

2. Positive laws: that is to say, laws which are simply and strictly so called, and which form the appropriate matter of general and particular jurisprudence.

3. Positive morality, rules of positive morality, or positive moral rules.

4. Laws metaphorical or figurative, or merely metaphorical or figurative.

The divine laws and positive laws are laws properly so called. —Of positive moral rules, some are laws properly so called, but others are laws improper. The positive moral rules which are laws improperly so called, may be styled laws or rules set or imposed by opinion: for they are merely opinions or sentiments held or felt by men in regard to human conduct. A law set by opinion and a law imperative and proper are allied by analogy merely; although the analogy by which they are allied is strong or close. —Laws metaphorical or figurative, or merely metaphorical or figurative, are laws improperly so called. A law metaphorical or figurative and a law imperative and proper are allied by analogy merely; and the analogy by which they are allied is slender or remote.

Consequently, positive laws (the appropriate matter of jurisprudence) are related in the way of resemblance, or by close or remote analogies, to the following objects. 1. In the way of resemblance, they are related to the laws of God. 2. In the way of resemblance, they are related to those rules of positive morality which are laws properly so called: And by a close or strong analogy, they are related to those rules of positive mo-

---

* [*Analysis of Lectures* and *Lecture I* (1832).

John Austin's *Province of Jurisprudence* set a pattern in Anglo-American jurisprudence which has been closely followed, ever since, by most Anglo-American teachers and treatises in this field. Gray and Holmes in the United States, and Holland, Pollack, and Salmond in the United Kingdom were faithful followers of Austin's analytical approach. For Austin (1790-1859), as for his teacher, Jeremy Bentham, clear objective analysis of the law was not an end in itself but a necessary prelude to intelligent ethical criticism of actual rules.]

rality which are laws set by opinion. 3. By a remote or slender analogy, they are related to laws metaphorical, or laws merely metaphorical.

The principal purpose or scope of the six ensuing lectures, is to distinguish positive laws (the appropriate matter of jurisprudence) from the objects now enumerated: objects with which they are connected by ties of resemblance and analogy; with which they are further connected by the common name of "laws"; and with which, therefore, they often are blended and confounded. And, since such is the principal purpose of the six ensuing lectures, I style them, considered as a whole, "the province of jurisprudence determined." For, since such is their principal purpose, they affect to describe the boundary which severs the province of jurisprudence from the regions lying on its confines.

The way which I take in order to the accomplishment of that purpose, may be stated shortly thus.

I. I determine the essence or nature which is common to all laws that are laws properly so called: In other words, I determine the essence or nature of a law imperative and proper.

II. I determine the respective characters of the four several kinds into which laws may be aptly divided: Or (changing the phrase) I determine the appropriate marks by which laws of each kind are distinguished from laws of the others.

And here I remark, by the by, that examining the respective characters of those four several kinds, I found the following the order wherein I could explain them best: First, the characters or distinguishing marks of the laws of God; secondly, the characters or distinguishing marks of positive moral rules; thirdly, the characters or distinguishing marks of laws metaphorical or figurative; fourthly and lastly, the characters or distinguishing marks of positive law, or laws simply and strictly so called.

By determining the essence or nature of a law imperative and proper, and by determining the respective characters of those four several kinds, I determine positively and negatively the appropriate matter of jurisprudence. I determine positively what that matter is; and I distinguish it from various objects which are variously related to it, and with which it not unfrequently is blended and confounded. I show more over its affinities with those various related objects: affinities that ought to be conceived as precisely and clearly as may be, inasmuch as there are numerous portions of the *rationale* of positive law to which they are the only or principal key.

Having suggested the principal purpose of the following treatise, I now will indicate the topics with which it is chiefly concerned, and also the order wherein it presents them to the reader.

I. In the *first* of the six lectures which immediately follow, I state the essentials of a law or rule (taken with the largest signification that can be given to the term properly). In other words, I determine the essence or nature which is common to all laws that are laws properly so called.

Determining the essence or nature of a law imperative and proper, I determine implicitly the essence or nature of a command; and I distinguish such commands as are laws or rules from such commands as are merely occasional or particular. Determining the nature of a command, I fix the meanings of the terms which the term "command" implies: namely "sanction" or "enforcement of obedience"; "duty" or "obligation"; "superior and inferior."

II. (a) In the beginning of the *second* lecture, I briefly determine the characters or marks by which the laws of God are distinguished from other laws.

In the beginning of the same lecture, I briefly divide the laws, and the other commands of the Deity, into two kinds: the revealed or express, and the unrevealed or tacit.

Having briefly distinguished his revealed from his unrevealed commands, I pass to the nature of the signs or index through which the latter are manifested to Man. Now, concerning the nature of the index to the tacit commands of the Deity, there are three theories or three hypotheses: First, the pure hypothesis or theory of general utility; secondly, the pure hypothesis or theory of a moral sense; thirdly, a hypothesis or theory mixed or compounded of the others. And with a statement and explanation of the three hypotheses or theories, the greater portion of the *second* lecture, and the whole of the *third* and *fourth* lectures, are exclusively or chiefly occupied.

That exposition of the three hypotheses or theories may seem somewhat impertinent to the subject and scope of my Course. But in a chain of systematical lectures concerned with the *rationale* of jurisprudence, such an exposition is a necessary link.

Of the principles and distinctions involved by the *rationale* of jurisprudence, or of the principles and distinctions occurring in the writings of jurists, there are many which could not be expounded correctly and clearly, if the three hypotheses or theories had not been expounded previously. For example: Positive law and morality are distinguished by modern jurists into law natural and law positive: that is to say, into positive law and morality fashioned on the law of God, and positive law and morality of purely human origin.

[T]he divine law is the measure or test of positive law and morality: or (changing the phrase) law and morality, in so far as they *are* what they *ought* to be, conform, or are not repugnant, to the law of God. Consequently, an all-important object of the science of ethics (or, borrowing the language of Bentham, "the science of deontology") is to determine the nature of the index to the tacit commands of the Deity, or the nature of the signs or proofs through which those commands may be known. —I mean by "the science of ethics" (or by "the science of deontology"), the science of law and morality as they respectively *ought* to be: or (changing the phrase), the science of law and morality as they respectively *must* be *if they conform to their measure or test.* That department of the science of ethics, which is concerned especially with positive law as it ought to be, is styled the science of legislation: that department of the science of ethics, which is concerned especially with positive morality as it ought to be, has hardly gotten a name perfectly appropriate and distinctive. —Now, though the science of legislation (or of positive law as it *ought* to be) is not the science of jurisprudence (or of positive law as it *is*), still the sciences are connected by numerous and indissoluble ties. Since, then, the nature of the index to the tacit command of the Deity is an all-important object of the science of legislation, it is a fit and important object of the kindred science of jurisprudence.

There are certain current and important misconceptions of the theory of general utility: There are certain objections resting on those misconceptions, which frequently are urged against it: There are also considerable difficulties with which it really is embarrassed. Labouring to rectify those misconceptions, to answer those objections, and to solve or extenuate those difficulties, I probably dwell upon the theory somewhat longer than I ought. Deeply convinced of its truth and importance, and therefore earnestly intent on commending it to the minds of others, I probably wander into ethical disquisitions which are not precisely in keeping with the subject and scope of my Course. If I am guilty of this departure from the subject and scope of my Course, the absorbing interest of the purpose which leads me from my proper path, will excuse, to indulgent readers, my offense against rigorous logic.

II.   (b) At the beginning of the *fifth* lecture, I distribute laws or rules under two classes: First, laws properly so called, with such improper laws as are closely analogous to the proper; secondly, those improper laws which are remotely analogous to the proper, and which I style, therefore, laws metaphorical or figurative. —I also distribute laws proper with such improper laws as are closely analogous to the proper under three classes: namely, the laws properly so called which I style the laws of God; the laws properly so called which I style positive laws; and the laws properly so called, with the laws improperly so called, which I style positive morality or positive moral rules. —I assign moreover my reasons for marking those several classes with those respective names.

Having determined, in preceding lectures, the characters or distinguishing marks of the divine laws, I determine, in the fifth lecture, the characters or distinguishing marks of positive moral rules: that is to say, such of the laws or rules set by men to men as are not armed with legal sanctions; or such of those laws or rules as are not positive laws, or are not appropriate matter for general or particular jurisprudence. —Having determined the distinguishing marks of positive moral rules, I determine the respective characters of their two dissimilar kinds: namely, the positive moral rules which are laws imperative and proper, and the positive moral rules which are laws set by opinion.

The divine law, positive law, and positive morality, are mutually related in various ways. To illustrate their mutual relations, I advert, in the fifth lecture, to the cases wherein they agree, wherein they disagree without conflicting, and wherein they disagree and conflict.

I show, in the same lecture, that my distribution of laws proper, and of such improper laws as are closely analogous to the proper, tallies, in the main, with a division of laws which is given incidentally by Locke in his Essay on Human Understanding.

II. (c) At the end of the same lecture, I determine the characters or distinguishing marks of laws metaphorical or figurative. And I show that laws which are merely laws through metaphors, are blended and confounded, by writers of celebrity, with laws imperative and proper.

II. (d) In the *sixth* and *last* lecture, I determine the characters of laws positive: that is to say, laws which are simply and strictly so called, and which form the appropriate matter of general and particular jurisprudence.

Determining the characters of positive laws, I determine implicitly the notion of sovereignty, with the implied or correlative notion of independent political society. For the essential difference of a positive law (or the difference that severs it from a law which is not a positive law) may be stated generally in the following manner. Every positive law or every law simply and strictly so called, is set by a sovereign person, or a sovereign body of persons, to a member or members of the independent political society wherein that person or body is sovereign or supreme. Or (changing the phrase) it is set by a monarch, or sovereign number, to a person or persons in a state of subjection to its author.

To elucidate the nature of sovereignty, and of the independent political society that sovereignty implies, I examine various topics which I arrange under the following heads. First, the possible forms or shapes of supreme political government; secondly, the limits, real or imaginary, of supreme political power; thirdly, the origin or causes of political government and society. Examining those various topics, I complete my description of the limit or boundary by which positive law is severed from positive morality. For I distinguish them at certain points whereat they seemingly blend, or whereat the line which divides them is not easily perceptible.

The essential difference of a positive law (or the difference that severs it from a law which is not a positive law) may be stated generally as I have stated it above. But the foregoing general statement of that essential difference is open to certain correctives. And with a brief allusion to those correctives, I close the sixth and last lecture.

Lecture I.

The matter of jurisprudence is positive law: law, simply and strictly so called: or law set by political superiors to political inferiors. But positive law (or law, simply and strictly so called) is often confounded with objects to which it is related by *resemblance*, and with objects to which it is related in the way of *analogy:* with objects which are *also* signified, *properly* and *improperly,* by the large and vague expression *law*. To obviate the difficulties springing from that confusion, I begin my projected Course with determining the province of jurisprudence, or with distinguishing the matter of jurisprudence from those various related objects: trying to define the subject of which I intend to treat, before I endeavour to analyse its numerous and complicated parts.

A law, in the most general and comprehensive acceptation in which the term, in its literal meaning, is employed, may be said to be a rule laid down for the guidance of an intelligent being by an intelligent being having power over him. Under this definition are included, and without impropriety, several species. It is necessary to define accurately the line of demarcation which separates these species from one another, as much mistiness and intricacy has been infused into the science of jurisprudence by their being confounded or not clearly distinguished. In the comprehensive sense above indicated, or in the largest meaning which it has, without extension by metaphor or analogy, the term *law* embraces the following objects: Laws set by God to his human creatures, and laws set by men to men.

The whole or a portion of the laws set by God to men is frequently styled the law of nature, or natural law: being, in truth, the only natural law of which it is possible to speak without a metaphor, or without a blending of objects which ought to be distinguished broadly. But, rejecting the appellation Law of Nature as ambiguous and misleading, I name those laws or rules, as considered collectively or in a mass, the *Divine law,* or the *law of God.*

Laws set by men to men are of two leading or principal classes:

classes which are often blended, although they differ extremely; and which, for that reason, should be severed precisely, and opposed distinctly and conspicuously.

Of the laws or rules set by men to men, some are established by *political* superiors, sovereign and subject: by persons exercising supreme and subordinate *government,* in independent nations, or independent political societies. The aggregate of the rules thus established, or some aggregate forming a portion of that aggregate, is the appropriate matter of jurisprudence, general or particular. To the aggregate of the rules thus established, or to some aggregate forming a portion of that aggregate, the term *law,* as used simply and strictly, is exclusively applied. But, as contradistinguished to *natural* law, or to the law of *naᵢ ᵢre* (meaning, by those expressions, the law of God), the aggregate of the rules, established by political superiors, is frequently styled *positive* law, or law existing *by position.* As contradistinguished to the rules which I style *positive morality,* and on which I shall touch immediately, the aggregate of the rules, established by political superiors, may also be marked commodiously with the name of *positive law.* For the sake, then, of getting a name brief and distinctive at once, and agreeably to frequent usage, I style that aggregate of rules, or any portion of that aggregate, *positive law:* though rules, which are *not* established by political superiors, are also *positive,* or exist *by position,* if they be rules or laws, in the proper signification of the term.

Though *some* of the laws or rules, which are set by men to men, are established by political superiors, *others* are *not* established by political superiors, or are *not* established by political superiors, in that capacity or character.

Closely analogous to human laws of this second class, are a set of objects frequently but *improperly* termed *laws,* being rules set and enforced by *mere opinion,* that is, by the opinions or sentiments held or felt by an indeterminate body of men in regard to human conduct. Instances of such a use of the term *law* are the expressions —"The law of honour"; "The law set by fashion"; and rules of this species constitute much of what is usually termed "International law."

The aggregate of human laws properly so called belonging to the second of the classes above mentioned, with the aggregate of objects *improperly* but by *close analogy* termed laws, I place together in a common class, and denote them by the term *positive morality.* The name *morality* severs them from *positive law,* while the epithet *positive* disjoins them from the *law of God.* And to the end of obviating confusion, it is necessary or expedient that they *should* be disjoined from the latter by that distinguishing epithet. For the name *morality* (or *morals*), when standing unqualified or alone, denotes indifferently either of the following objects: namely, positive morality *as it is,* or without regard to its merits; and positive morality *as it would be,* if it conformed to the law of God, and were, therefore, deserving of *approbation.*

Besides the various sorts of rules which are included in the literal acceptation of the term law, and those which are by a close and striking analogy, though improperly, termed laws, there are numerous applications of the term law, which rest upon a slender analogy and are merely metaphorical or figurative. Such is the case when we talk of *laws* observed by the lower animals; of *laws* regulating the growth or decay of vegetables; of *laws* determining the movements of inanimate bodies or masses. For where *intelligence* is not, or where it is too bounded to take the name of *reason,* and, therefore, is too bounded to conceive the purpose of a law, there is not the *will* which law can work on, or which duty can incite or restrain. Yet through these misapplications of a *name,* flagrant as the metaphor is, has the field of jurisprudence and morals been deluged with muddy speculation.

Having suggested the *purpose* of my attempt to determine the province of jurisprudence: to distinguish positive law, the appropriate matter of jurisprudence, from the various objects to which it is related by resemblance, and to which it is related, nearly or remotely, by a strong or slender analogy: I shall now state the essentials of *a law* or *rule* (taken with the largest signification which can be given to the term *properly*).

Every *law* or *rule* (taken with the largest signification which can be given to the term *properly*) is a *command.* Or rather, laws or rules, properly so called are a *species* of commands.

Now, since the term *command* comprises the term *law,* the first is the simpler as well as the larger of the two. But simple as it is, it admits of explanation. And, since it is the *key* to the sciences of jurisprudence and morals, its meaning should be analysed with precision.

Accordingly, I shall endeavour, in the first instance, to analyse the meaning of *"command":* an analysis which, I fear, will task the patience of my hearers, but which they will bear with cheerfulness, or, at least, with resignation, if they consider the difficulty of performing it. The elements of a science are precisely the parts of it which are explained least easily. Terms that are the largest, and, therefore, the simplest of a series, are without equivalent expressions into which we can resolve them *concisely.* And when we endeavour to *define* them, or to translate them into terms which we suppose are better understood, we are forced upon awkward and tedious circumlocutions.

If you express or intimate a wish that I shall do or forbear from some act, and if you will visit me with an evil in case I comply not with your wish, the *expression* or *intimation* of your wish is a *command*. A command is distinguished from other significations of desire, not by the style in which the desire is signified, but by the power and the purpose of the party commanding to inflict an evil or pain in case the desire be disregarded. If you cannot or will not harm me in case I comply not with your wish, the expression of your wish is not a command, although you utter your wish in imperative phrase. If you are able and willing to harm me in case I comply not with your wish, the expression of your wish amounts to a command, although you are prompted by a spirit of courtesy to utter it in the shape of a request.

A command, then, is a signification of desire. But a command is distinguished from other significations of desire by this peculiarity: that the party to whom it is directed is liable to evil from the other, in case he comply not with the desire.

Being liable to evil from you if I comply not with a wish which you signify, I am *bound* or *obliged* by your command, or I lie under a *duty* to obey it. If, in spite of that evil in prospect, I comply not with the wish which you signify, I am said to disobey your command, or to violate the duty which it imposes.

Command and duty are, therefore, correlative terms: the meaning denoted by each being implied or supposed by the other. Or (changing the expression) wherever a duty lies, a command has been signified; and whenever a command is signified, a duty is imposed.

Concisely expressed, the meaning of the correlative expressions is this. He who will inflict an evil in case his desire be disregarded, utters a command by expressing or intimating his desire: He who is liable to the evil in case he disregard the desire, is bound or obliged by the command.

The evil which will probably be incurred in case a command be disobeyed or (to use an equivalent expression) in case a duty be broken, is frequently called a *sanction,* or *an enforcement of obedience.* Or (varying the phrase) the command or the duty is said to be *sanctioned* or *enforced* by the chance of incurring the evil.

Considered as thus abstracted from the command and the duty which it enforces, the evil to be incurred by disobedience is frequently styled a *punishment.* But, as punishments, strictly so called, are only a *class* of sanctions, the term is too narrow to express the meaning adequately.

I observe that Dr. Paley, in his analysis of the term *obligation,* lays much stress upon the *violence* of the motive to compliance. In so far as I can gather a meaning from his loose and inconsistent statement, his meaning appears to be this: that, unless the motive to compliance be *violent* or *intense,* the expression or intimation of a wish is not a *command,* nor does the party to whom it is directed lie under a *duty* to regard it.

If he means, by a *violent* motive, a motive operating with certainty, his proposition is manifestly false. The greater the evil to be incurred in case the wish be disregarded, and the greater the chance of incurring it on that same event, the greater, no doubt, is the *chance* that the wish will *not* be disregarded. But no conceivable motive will *certainly* determine to compliance, or no conceivable motive will render obedience inevitable. If Paley's proposition be true, in the sense which I have now ascribed to it, commands and duties are simply impossible. Or, reducing his proposition to absurdity by a consequence as manifestly false, commands and duties are possible, but are never disobeyed or broken.

If he means by a *violent* motive, an evil which inspires fear, his meaning is simply this: that the party bound by a command is bound by the prospect of an evil. For that which is not feared is not apprehended as an evil; or (changing the shape of the expression) is not an evil in prospect.

The truth is, that the magnitude of the eventual evil, and the magnitude of the chance of incurring it, are foreign to the matter in question. The greater the eventual evil, and the greater the chance of incurring it, the greater is the efficacy of the command, and the greater is the strength of the obligation: Or, (substituting expressions exactly equivalent) the greater is the *chance* that the command will be obeyed, and that the duty will not be broken. But where there is the smallest chance of incurring the smallest evil, the expression of a wish amounts to a command, and therefore, imposes a duty. The sanction, if you will, is feeble or insufficient; but still there *is* a sanction, and therefore, a duty and a command.

By some celebrated writers (by Locke, Bentham, and, I think, Paley), the term *sanction,* or *enforcement of obedience,* is applied to conditional good as well as to conditional evil: to reward as well as to punishment. But, with all my habitual veneration for the names of Locke and Bentham, I think that this extension of the term is pregnant with confusion and perplexity.

Rewards are, indisputably, *motives* to comply with the wishes of others. But to talk of commands and duties as *sanctioned* or *enforced* by rewards, or to talk of rewards as *obliging* or *constraining* to obedience, is surely a wide departure from the established meaning of the terms.

If *you* expressed a desire that *I* should render a service, and if you proffered a reward as the motive or inducement to render it, *you* would scarcely be said to *command* the service, nor should *I,* in ordinary language, be *obliged* to render it. In ordinary language, *you* would *promise* me a reward, on condition of my rendering the service, whilst *I* might be *incited* or *persuaded* to render it by the hope of obtaining the reward.

Again: If a law hold out a *reward* as an inducement to do some act, an eventual *right* is conferred, and not an *obligation* imposed, upon those who shall act accordingly: The *imperative* part of the law being addressed or directed to the party whom it requires to *render* the reward.

In short, I am determined or inclined to comply with the wish of another, by the fear of disadvantage or evil. I am also determined or inclined to comply with the wish of another, by the hope of advantage or good. But it is only by the chance of incurring *evil*, that I am *bound* or *obliged* to compliance. It is only by conditional *evil*, that duties are *sanctioned* or *enforced*. It is the power and the purpose of inflicting eventual *evil*, and *not* the power and the purpose of imparting eventual *good*, which gives to the expression of a wish the name of a *command*.

If we put *reward* into the import of the term *sanction*, we must engage in a toilsome struggle with the current of ordinary speech; and shall often slide unconsciously, notwithstanding our efforts to the contrary, into the narrower and customary meaning.

It appears then, from what has been premised, that the ideas or notions comprehended by the term *command:* are the following. 1. A wish or desire conceived by a rational being, that another rational being shall do or forbear. 2. An evil to proceed from the former, and to be incurred by the latter, in case the latter comply not with the wish. 3. An expression or intimation of the wish by words or other signs.

It also appears from what has been premised, that *command, duty,* and *sanction* are inseparably connected terms: that each embraces the same ideas as the others, though each denotes those ideas in a peculiar order or series.

"A wish conceived by one, and expressed or intimated to another, with an evil to be inflicted and incurred in case the wish be disregarded," are signified directly and indirectly by each of the three expressions. Each is the name of the same complex notion.

But when I am talking *directly* of the expression or intimation of the wish, I employ the term *command:* The expression or intimation of the wish being presented *prominently* to my hearer; whilst the evil to be incurred, with the chance of incurring it, are kept (if I may so express myself) in the background of my picture.

When I am talking *directly* of the chance of incurring the evil, or (changing the expression) of the liability or obnoxiousness to the evil, I employ the term *duty,* or the term *obligation:* The liability or obnoxiousness to the evil being put foremost, and the rest of the complex notion being signified implicitly.

When I am talking *immediately* of the evil itself, I employ the term *sanction,* or a term of the like import: The evil to be incurred being signified directly; whilst the obnoxiousness to that evil, with the expression or intimation of the wish, are indicated indirectly or obliquely.

To those who are familiar with the language of logicians (language unrivalled for brevity, distinctness, and precision), I can express my meaning accurately in a breath. —Each of the three terms *signifies* the same notion; but each *denotes* a different part of that notion, and *connotes* the residue.

Commands are of two species. Some are *laws* or *rules*. The others have not acquired an appropriate name, nor does language afford an expression which will mark them briefly and precisely. I must, therefore, note them as well as I can by the ambiguous name of *"occasional or particular* commands."

The term *laws* or *rules* being not unfrequently applied to occasional or particular commands, it is hardly possible to describe a line of separation which shall consist in every respect with established forms of speech. But the distinction between laws and particular commands may, I think, be stated in the following manner.

By every command, the party to whom it is directed is obliged to do or to forbear.

Now where it obliges *generally* to acts or forbearances of a class, a command is a law or rule. But where it obliges to a *specific* act or forbearance, or to acts or forbearances which it determines *specifically* or *individually* a command is occasional or particular. In other words, a class or description of acts is determined by a law or rule, and acts of that class or description are enjoined or forbidden generally. But where a command is occasional or particular, the act or acts, which the command enjoins or forbids, are assigned or determined by their specific or individual natures as well as by the class or description to which they belong.

The statement which I have given in abstract expressions I will now endeavour to illustrate by apt examples.

If you command your servant to go on a given errand, or *not* to leave your house on a given evening, or to rise at such an hour on such a morning, or to rise at that hour during the next week or month, the command is occasional or particular. For the act or acts enjoined or forbidden are specially determined or assigned.

But if you command him *simply* to rise at that hour, or to rise at that hour *always,* or to rise at that hour *till further orders,* it may be said, with propriety, that you lay down a *rule* for the guidance of your servant's conduct. For no specific act is assigned by the command, but the command obliges him generally to acts of a determined class.

If a regiment be ordered to attack or defend a post, or to quell a riot, or to march from their present quarters, the command is occasional or particular. But an order to exercise daily till further orders shall be given would be called a *general* order, and *might* be called a *rule.*

If Parliament prohibited simply the exportation of corn, either for a given period or indefinitely, it would establish a law or rule: a *kind* or *sort* of acts being determined by the command, and acts of that kind or sort being *generally* forbidden. But an order issued by Parliament to meet an impending scarcity, and stopping the exportation of corn *then shipped and in port,* would not be a law or rule, though issued by the sovereign legislature. The order regarding exclusively a specified quantity of corn, the negative acts or forbearances, enjoined by the command, would be determined specifically or individually by the determinate nature of their subject.

As issued by a sovereign legislature, and as wearing the form of a law, the order which I have now imagined would probably be *called* a law. And hence the difficulty of drawing a distinct boundary between laws and occasional commands.

Again: An act which is not an offence, according to the existing law, moves the sovereign to displeasure: and, though the authors of the act are legally innocent or unoffending, the sovereign commands that they shall be punished. As enjoining a specific punishment in that specific case, and as not enjoining generally acts or forbearances of a class, the order uttered by the sovereign is not a law or rule.

Whether such an order would be *called* a law, seems to depend upon circumstances which are purely immaterial: immaterial, that is, with reference to the present purpose, though material with reference to others. If made by a sovereign assembly, deliberately, and with the forms of legislation, it would probably be called a law. If uttered by an absolute monarch, without deliberation or ceremony, it would scarcely be confounded with acts of legislation, and would be styled an arbitrary command. Yet, on either of these suppositions, its nature would be the same. It would not be a law or rule, but an occasional or particular command of the sovereign One or Number.

To conclude with an example which best illustrates the distinction, and which shows the importance of the distinction most conspicuously, *judicial commands* are commonly occasional or particular, although the commands which they are calculated to enforce are commonly laws or rules.

For instance, the lawgiver commands that thieves shall be hanged. A specific theft and a specified thief being given, the judge commands that the thief shall be hanged, agreeably to the command of the lawgiver.

Now, the lawgiver determines a class or description of acts; prohibits acts of the class generally and indefinitely; and commands, with the like generality, that punishment shall follow transgression. The command of the lawgiver is, therefore, a law or rule. But the command of the judge is occasional or particular. For he orders a specific punishment, as the consequence of a specific offence.

According to the line of separation which I have now attempted to describe, a law and a particular command are distinguished thus. —Acts or forbearances of a *class* are enjoined *generally* by the former. Acts *determined specifically,* are enjoined or forbidden by the latter.

A different line of separation has been drawn by Blackstone and others. According to Blackstone and others, a law and a particular command are distinguished in the following manner. —A law obliges *generally* the members of the given community, or a law obliges *generally* persons of a given class. A particular command obliges a *single* person, or persons whom it determines *individually.*

That laws and particular commands are not to be distinguished thus, will appear on a moment's reflection.

For, *first,* commands which oblige generally the members of the given community, or commands which oblige generally persons of given classes, are not always laws or rules.

Thus, in the case already supposed; that in which the sovereign commands that all corn actually shipped for exportation be stopped and detained; the command is obligatory upon the whole community, but as it obliges them only to a set of acts individually assigned, it is not a law. Again, suppose the sovereign to issue an order enforced by penalties, for a general mourning, on occasion of a public calamity. Now, though it is addressed to the community at large, the order is scarcely a rule, in the usual acceptation of the term. For, though it obliges generally the members of the entire community, it obliges to acts which it assigns specifically, instead of obliging generally to acts or forbearances of a class. If the sovereign commanded that *black* should be the dress of his subjects, his command would amount to a law. But if he commanded them to wear it on a specified occasion, his command would be merely particular.

And, *secondly,* a command which obliges exclusively persons individually determined, may amount, notwithstanding, to a law or rule.

For example, A father may set a *rule* to his child or children: a guardian, to his ward: a master, to his slave or servant. And certain of God's *laws* were as binding on the first man, as they are binding at this hour on the millions who have sprung form his loins.

Most, indeed, of the laws which are established by political superiors, or most of the laws which are simply and strictly so called, oblige generally the members of the political community, or oblige generally persons of a class. To frame a system of duties for every individual of the community, were simply impossible: and if it were possible, it were utterly useless. Most of the laws established by political superiors are, therefore, *general* in a twofold manner: as enjoining or forbidding generally acts of kinds or sorts; and as binding the whole community, or, at least, whole classes of its members.

21

But if we suppose that Parliament creates and grants an office, and that Parliament binds the grantee to services of a given description, we suppose a law established by political superiors, and yet exclusively binding a specified or determinate person.

Laws established by political superiors, and exclusively binding specified or determinate persons are styled, in the language of the Roman jurists, *privilegia*. Though that, indeed, is a name which will hardly denote them distinctly: for, like most of the leading terms in actual systems of law, it is not the name of a definite class of objects, but of a heap of heterogeneous objects.

It appears from what has been premised, that a law, properly so called, may be defined in the following manner.

A law is a command which obliges a person or persons.

But, as contradistinguished or opposed to an occasional or particular command, a law is a command which obliges a person or persons, and obliges *generally* to acts or forbearances of a *class*.

In language more popular, but less distinct and precise, a law is a command which obliges a person or persons to a *course* of conduct.

Laws and other commands are said to proceed from *superiors,* and to bind or oblige *inferiors.* I will, therefore, analyse the meaning of those correlative expressions; and will try to strip them of a certain mystery, by which that simple meaning appears to be obscured.

Superiority is often synonymous with *precedence* or *excellence.* We talk of superiors in rank; of superiors in wealth; of superiors in virtue: comparing certain persons with certain other persons; and meaning that the former precede or excel the latter in rank, in wealth, or in virtue.

But taken with the meaning wherein I here understand it, the term *superiority* signifies *might:* the power of affecting others with evil or pain, and of forcing them, through fear of that evil, to fashion their conduct to one's wishes.

For example, God is emphatically the *superior* of Man. For his power of affecting us with pain, and of forcing us to comply with his will, is unbounded and resistless.

To a limited extent, the sovereign One or Number is the superior of the subject or citizen: the master, of his slave or servant: the father, of the child.

In short, whoever can *oblige* another to comply with his wishes, is the *superior* of that other, so far as the ability reaches: The party who is obnoxious to the impending evil, being, to that same extent, the *inferior*.

The might or superiority of God, is simple or absolute. But in all or most cases of human superiority, the relation of superior and inferior, and the relation of inferior and superior are reciprocal. Or (changing the expression) the party who is the superior as viewed from one aspect, is the inferior as viewed from another.

For example, To an indefinite, though limited extent, the monarch is the superior of the governed: his power being commonly sufficient to enforce compliance with his will. But the governed, collectively or in mass, are also the superior of the monarch: who is checked in the abuse of his might by his fear of exciting their anger; and of rousing to active resistance the might which slumbers in the multitude.

A member of a sovereign assembly is the superior of the judge: the judge being bound by the law which proceeds from that sovereign body. But, in his character of citizen or subject, he is the inferior of the judge: the judge being the minister of the law, and armed with the power of enforcing it.

It appears, then, that the term *superiority* (like the terms *duty* and *sanction*) is implied by the term *command*. For superiority is the power of enforcing compliance with a wish: and the expression or intimation of a wish, with the power and the purpose of enforcing it, are the constituent elements of a command.

"That *laws* emanate from *superiors*" is, therefore, an identical proposition. For the meaning which it affects to impart is contained in its subject.

If I mark the peculiar source of a given law, or if I mark the peculiar source of laws of a given class, it is possible that I am saying something which may instruct the hearer. But to affirm of laws universally "that they flow from *superiors*," or to affirm of laws universally "that *inferiors* are bound to obey them," is the merest tautology and trifling.

Like most of the leading terms in the sciences of jurisprudence and morals, the term *laws* is extremely ambiguous. Taken with the largest signification which can be given to the term properly, *laws* are a species of *commands*. But the term is improperly applied to various objects which have nothing of the imperative character: to objects which are *not* commands; and which, therefore, are *not* laws properly so called.

Accordingly, the proposition "that laws are commands" must be taken with limitations. Or, rather, we must distinguish the various meanings of the term *laws;* and must restrict the proposition to that class of objects which is embraced by the largest signification that can be given to the term properly.

I have already indicated, and shall hereafter more fully describe, the objects improperly termed laws, which are *not* within the province of jurisprudence (being either rules enforced by opinion and closely analogous to laws properly so called, or being laws so called by a metaphorical application of the term merely). There are other objects improperly termed laws (not being commands) which yet may properly be included within the province of jurisprudence. These I shall endeavour to particularise: —

1. Acts on the part of legislatures to *explain* positive law, can scarcely be called laws, in the proper signification of the term. Working no change in the actual duties of the governed, but simply declaring what those duties *are,* they properly are acts of *interpretation* by legislative authority. Or, to borrow an expression from the writers on the Roman Law, they are acts of *authentic* interpretation.

But, this notwithstanding, they are frequently styled laws; *declaratory* laws, or declaratory statutes. They must, therefore, be noted as forming an exception to the proposition "that laws are a species of commands."

It often, indeed, happens (as I shall show in the proper place), that laws declaratory in name are imperative in effect: Legislative, like judicial interpretation, being frequently deceptive; and establishing new law, under guise of expounding the old.

2. Laws to repeal laws, and to release from existing duties, must also be excepted from the proposition "that laws are a species of commands." In so far as they release from duties imposed by existing laws, they are not commands, but revocations of commands. They authorize or permit the parties to whom the repeal extends, to do or to forbear from acts which they were commanded to forbear from or to do. And, considered with regard to *this,* their immediate or direct purpose, they are often named *permissive laws,* or, more briefly and more properly, *permissions.*

Remotely and indirectly, indeed, permissive laws are often or always imperative. For the parties released from duties are restored to liberties or rights: and duties answering those rights are, therefore, created or revived.

But this is a matter which I shall examine with exactness, when I analyze the expressions "legal right," "permission by the sovereign or state," and "civil or political liberty."

3. Imperfect laws, or laws of imperfect obligation, must also be excepted from the proposition "that laws are a species of commands."

An imperfect law (with the sense wherein the term is used by the Roman jurists) is a law which wants a sanction, and which, therefore, is not binding. A law declaring that certain acts are crimes, but annexing no punishment to the commission of acts of the class, is the simplest and most obvious example.

Though the author of an imperfect law signifies a desire, he manifests no purpose of enforcing compliance with the desire. But where there is not a purpose of enforcing compliance with the desire, the expression of a desire is not a command. Consequently, an imperfect law is not so properly a law, as counsel, or exhortation, addressed by a superior to inferiors.

Examples of imperfect laws are cited by the Roman jurists. But with us in England, laws professedly imperative are always (I believe) perfect or obligatory. Where the English legislature affects to command, the English tribunals not unreasonably presume that the legislature exacts obedience. And, if no specific sanction be annexed to a given law, a sanction is supplied by the courts of justice, agreeably to a general maxim which obtains in cases of the kind.

The imperfect laws, of which I am now speaking, are laws which are imperfect, in the sense of *the Roman jurists:* that is to say, laws which speak the desires of political superiors, but which their authors (by oversight or design) have not provided with sanctions. Many of the writers on morals, and on the so called *law of nature,* have annexed a different meaning to the term *imperfect.* Speaking of imperfect obligations, they commonly mean duties which are *not legal:* duties imposed by commands of God, or duties imposed by positive morality, as contradistinguished to duties imposed by positive law. An imperfect obligation, in the sense of the Roman jurists, is exactly equivalent to no obligation at all. For the term *imperfect* denotes simply, that the law wants the sanction appropriate to laws of the kind. An imperfect obligation, in the other meaning of the expression, is a religious or a moral obligation. The term *imperfect* does not denote that the law imposing the duty wants the appropriate sanction. It denotes that the law imposing the duty is *not* a law established by a political superior: that it wants that *perfect,* or that surer or more cogent sanction, which is imparted by the sovereign or state.

I believe that I have now reviewed all the classes of objects to which the term *laws* is improperly applied. The laws (improperly so called) which I have here lastly enumerated are (I think) the only laws which are not commands, and which yet may be properly included within the province of jurisprudence. But though these, with the so called laws set by opinion and the objects metaphorically termed laws, are the only laws which *really* are not commands, there are certain laws (properly so called) which may *seem* not imperative. Accordingly, I will subjoin a few remarks upon laws of this dubious character.

1. There are laws, it may be said, which *merely* create *rights:* And, seeing that every command imposes a *duty,* laws of this nature are not imperative.

But, as I have intimated already, and shall show completely hereafter, there are no laws *merely* creating *rights.* There are laws, it is true, which *merely* create *duties:* duties not correlating with correlating rights, and which, therefore, may be styled *absolute.* But every law, really conferring a right, imposes expressly or tacitly a *relative* duty, or a duty correlating with the right. If it specify the remedy to be given, in case the right shall be infringed, it imposes the relative duty expressly. If the remedy to be given be not specified, it refers tacitly to pre-existing law, and clothes the right which it purports to create with a remedy provided by that law. Every law, really conferring a right, is, therefore, imperative: as imperative, as if its only purpose were the creation of a duty, or as if the relative duty, which it inevitably imposes were merely absolute.

The meanings of the term *right,* are various and perplexed; taken with its proper meaning, it comprises ideas which are numerous and complicated; and the searching and extensive analysis, which the term, therefore, requires, would occupy more room than could be given to it in the present lecture. It is not, however, necessary, that the analysis should be performed here. I purpose, in my earlier lectures, to determine the province of jurisprudence; or to distinguish the laws established by political superiors, from the various laws, proper and improper, with which they are frequently confounded. And this I may accomplish exactly enough, without a nice inquiry into the import of the term *right.*

2. According to an opinion which I must notice *incidentally* here, though the subject to which it relates will be treated *directly* hereafter, *customary laws* must be excepted from the proposition "that laws are a species of commands."

By many of the admirers of customary laws (and, especially, of their German admirers), they are thought to oblige legally (independently of the sovereign or state), *because* the citizens or subjects have observed or kept them. Agreeably to this opinion, they are not the *creatures* of the sovereign or state, although the sovereign or state may abolish them at pleasure. Agreeably to this opinion, they are positive law (or law, strictly so called), inasmuch as they are enforced by the courts of justice: But, that notwithstanding, they exist *as positive law* by the spontaneous adoption of the governed, and not by position or establishment on the part of political superiors. Consequently, customary laws, considered as positive law, are not commands. And, consequently, customary laws, considered as positive law, are not laws or rules properly so called.

An opinion less mysterious, but somewhat allied to this, is not uncommonly held by the adverse party: by the party which is strongly opposed to customary law; and to all law made judicially, or in the way of judicial legislation. According to the latter opinion, all judge-made law, or all judge-made law established by *subject* judges, is purely the creature of the judges by whom it is established immediately. To impute it to the sovereign legislature, or to suppose that it speaks the will of the sovereign legislature, is one of the foolish or knavish *fictions* with which law-yers, in every age and nation, have perplexed and darkened the simplest and clearest truths.

I think it will appear, on a moment's reflection, that each of these opinions is groundless: that customary law is *imperative,* in the proper signification of the term; and that all judge-made law is the creature of the sovereign or state.

At its origin, a custom is a rule of conduct which the governed ob-serve spontaneously, or not in pursuance of a law set by a political su-perior. The custom is transmuted into positive law, when it is adopted as such by the courts of justice, and when the judicial decisions fashioned upon it are enforced by the power of the state. But before it is adopted by the courts, and clothed with the legal sanction, it is merely a rule of positive morality: a rule generally observed by the citizens or subjects; but deriving the only force, which it can be said to possess, from the gen-eral disapprobation falling on those who transgress it.

Now when judges transmute a custom into a legal rule (or make a legal rule not suggested by a custom), the legal rule which they establish is established by the sovereign legislature. A subordinate or subject judge is merely a minister. The portion of the sovereign power which lies at his disposition is merely delegated. The rules which he makes de-rive their legal force from authority given by the state: an authority which the state may confer expressly, but which it commonly imparts in the way of acquiescence. For, since the state may reverse the rules which he makes, and yet permits him to enforce them by the power of the polit-ical community, its sovereign will "that his rules shall obtain as law" is clearly evinced by its conduct, though not by its express declaration.

The admirers of customary law love to trick out their idol with mys-terious and imposing attributes. But to those who can see the difference between positive law and morality, there is nothing of mystery about it. Considered as rules of positive morality, customary laws arise from the consent of the governed, and not from the position or establishment of political superiors. But, considered as moral rules turned into positive laws, customary laws are established by the state: established by the state directly, when the customs are promulged in its statutes; established by the state circuitously, when the customs are adopted by its tribunals.

The opinion of the party which abhors judge-made laws, springs from their inadequate conception of the nature of commands.

Like other significations of desire, a command is express or tacit. If the desire be signified by *words* (written or spoken), the command is express. If the desire be signified by conduct (or by any signs of desire which are not words), the command is tacit.

Now when customs are turned into legal rules by decisions of subject judges, the legal rules which emerge from the customs are *tacit* commands of the sovereign legislature. The state, which is able to abolish, permits its ministers to enforce them: and it, therefore, signifies its pleasure, by that its voluntary acquiescence, "that they shall serve as a law to the governed."

My present purpose is merely this: to prove that the positive law styled *customary* (and all positive law made judicially) is established by the state directly or circuitously, and, therefore, is *imperative*. I am far from disputing, that law made judicially (or in the way of improper legislation) and law made by statute (or in the properly legislative manner) are distinguished by weighty differences. I shall inquire, in future lectures, what those difference are; and why subject judges, who are properly ministers of the law, have commonly shared with the sovereign in the business of making it.

I assume, then, that the only laws which are not imperative, and which belong to the subject-matter of jurisprudence, are the following: —1. Declaratory laws, or laws explaining the import of existing positive law. 2. Laws abrogating or repealing existing positive law. 3. Imperfect laws, or laws of imperfect obligation (with the sense wherein the expression is used by the Roman jurists).

But the space occupied in the science by these improper laws is comparatively narrow and insignificant. Accordingly, although I shall take them into account so often as I refer to them directly, I shall throw them out of account on other occasions. Or (changing the expression) I shall limit the term *law* to laws which are imperative, unless I extend it expressly to laws which are not.

Morris, Verbal Disputes and the Legal Philosophy of John Austin*

. . . What sort of task is Austin engaged in when he inquires into "the nature of law"? Initially, we might describe it as a task of definition. He defines what he means by "law" at first in a general way. It is, for him, "a species of command." He next defines "command" and we learn that

*[7 *U.C.L.A.L. Rev.* 27, 29-36, 41-56 (1959). Copyright © 1959 by the U.C.L.A. Law Review. Reprinted by permission.

Herbert Morris (1928–) received an LL.B. from Yale (1954) and a D.Phil. from Oxford University. He is Professor of Law and Professor of Philosophy at the University of California School of Law, Los Angeles, where he has taught since 1956. He is the author of *Freedom and Responsibility* (1961), *Guilt and Shame* (1971), and *The Masked Citadel* (1968).]

the concept of "a command" encompasses such other concepts as "a sanction," "an obligation," and "a superior." He then refines his general definition of "law" by introducing the concepts of "a rule" and "a sovereign" and "an independent political society." The concepts of "a rule" and "a sovereign" are closely connected with commands. A rule is a "general command" and a sovereign is always characterized as a person or a group of persons. This characterization is derived from his view that a sovereign issues commands and only persons can command.

Put this way, the matter looks deceptively simple. Austin appears engaged in limiting the scope of inquiry in jurisprudence, and this requires defining what he means by "law," the subject matter of his study. But if this is so, why has there been dispute over Austin's "theories"? If "law is a species of command" is a definition, what sort of definition is it? Is it like saying, "Let's take 'Lorien' to mean 'star-bright' "? Or is it like looking in a dictionary for the meaning of "hobgoblin" and finding that it means "mischievous imp"? Or is it more like a judge deciding that "obscene" does not apply to a work where the primary intent of the creator of the work was "artistic"? Or is it a mixture, perhaps, of each of these? Was Austin engaged in the activity of arbitrarily laying down definitions? If it is "all a matter of definition how you define law," why do we refer, to raise the question again, to "Austin's theory of law"? Surely this is misleading. And should we not now refer to it as "Austin's definition of law" and thus avoid much confusion and much needless dispute? Are we to conclude that in Austin's legal theory, at least, definition and theory are much the same thing? But if we do not conclude this, other problems are raised. If a peculiarly "theoretical" task occupied Austin's attention, what was the nature of this task? Are all theories of one type? And how does a theory differ, if it does, from an empirical generalization like "all Harvard graduates drink sherry"? Was Austin defining or theorizing or generalizing or was he engaged in an activity which somehow combined some or all of these activities?

The answers which we are prepared to give to these questions are clearly relevant to the criticism which we may level at Austin. Some definitions are "true" or "false": "it is true that 'hobgoblin' means 'mischievous imp.' " Other definitions are "convenient" or "inconvenient": "it is inconvenient defining 'Lorien' as 'dullstar' when you have just defined it as 'star-bright.' " Other definitions may be labelled "wise" or "foolish": "it was foolish for the judge to regard such activities as unreasonable." When we turn to theories, we discover that some may be "true," "false," or "probable": "my theory is that Gandolf put the glove at the scene of the crime to mislead us." Other theories are "adequate" or "inadequate": "Copernicus' theory is more adequate than Ptolemy's in accounting for certain epicyclical phenomena." Generalizations about facts like the one about Harvard graduates are "true" or "false" or "probable" or "improbable."

An apparently simple statement, then, like "law is a species of command"—the statement one might regard as fundamental to Austin's jurisprudence and a type of statement common to a number of so-called "legal theories" inquiring into the nature of law—on slight probing reveals possibilities of great logical complexity. We will now move on and discuss the activities of defining and theorizing and generalizing. With this behind us we will determine the role, if any, played by each of these activities in Austin's inquiry.

We may categorize definitions as either stipulative, lexical, or explicative. When we introduce a new term and define it by terms which are already familiar, we stipulate a meaning for the new term. This is one type of stipulative definition. The new term may or may not have a homonym. It is new not because it is a novel sign, but because it has not been defined before in the way that it is now defined. There is a second type of definition or defining activity which we shall call stipulative. If we propose to take the meaning which a term already has in some context and utilize that meaning in a new context, we shall speak of "stipulating a meaning for the term." There are, then, at least two types of proposals, both of which we shall treat as stipulative. There is a proposal to give a new term meaning and a proposal to give a term meaning in a new context which it has in some other contexts. Stipulative definitions are proposals for the use of signs. Though there are several grammatical forms for such definitions, these forms all convey proposals.

Such definitions are not assertions of fact about what words are synonymous with what other words. They are not reports. Consequently, the predicates "true" and "false" are inappropriately applied to definitions of this type. When people have said, "definitions can't be false," they have usually been thinking of such definitions.

We do, however, criticize stipulative definitions. Criticism proceeds with regard to standards which we may broadly refer to as "standards of convenience." What are the background conditions of such criticism when it is made? We have an end-in-view; it may be playing a game, building a house, or developing a theory to account for a particular subject matter. Proposals are made concerning the tools to be used in achieving our end-in-view. In some cases the tools proposed are those intended to facilitate communication. If they are inadequate tools, we criticize them and may reject them. Even before we define our terms we may offer criticism. For example, we may propose to use a term for a task which we regard as necessary, but the term may be too difficult to handle; it may weigh heavily on our tongues when we need a term which is light, that may be quickly spoken, quickly grasped. We may criticize definitions because they too severly limit the scope of inquiry. Or when a meaning is stipulated, we may think that it is likely to cause confusion because a homonym has been given a different meaning in the same context. We do not think it arbitrary what meanings we give to signs that we introduce nor are the signs that we introduce always arbitrarily chosen. Words are introduced and defined with a purpose and criticism results if there is conflict with this purpose.

Another type of definition is used informatively. It is used to inform people that a particular word has been defined in a certain way. Sometimes, when there have been quite explicit stipulative definitions made, the task is simple. At other times, when reference must be had to "ordinary usage," the task may become difficult. The lexicographer's function is to compile such definitions and we can conveniently refer to them as "lexical definitions."

There are two types of reports that we may consider as lexical definitions. There is, first, simply a report of a stipulation that has been made. When Mr. X proposes that "Lorien" mean "star-bright," he has, as we have seen, offered a stipulative definition. Mr. Y when asked, "what does Mr. X mean by 'Lorien'?" provides us with a lexical definition when he reports that it means the same as "star-bright." Such a definition may be either true or false. Secondly, a lexical definition is provided when there is a report of usage. "Hobgoblin" means "mischievous imp." This, too, is a statement of fact and it may be false. Dictionaries may make mistakes. When someone invokes ordinary usage as a standard and seeks to comply with that usage in the definitions he offers, we may say, not simply that the definitions appear to us "inconvenient," which they may be for some of our purposes, but that it is a "wrong" or a "false" definition.

We will label our third type of definition "an explicative definition." The need for it arises in the following way. Each day we use terms with "loose edges." When does night become day and red become pink or pieces of stray wood a pile or a pamphlet a book? When we determine more precisely the application of terms like "night" and "red" by deciding that they are or are not applicable to new types of situations, we are defining them.

When we expand or narrow the application of a term by an explicative definition, we do not simply report a usage. The need for greater precision indicates that the usage to which we can appeal is not definite enough for our purposes. It is important to realize that while a stipulation is involved in such a definition, it is not *solely* a stipulative definition. The term is not new; it has meaning. Nor is it a proposal to employ the

31

meaning it has. The difficulty arises because the meaning is too vague. We have difficulty in classifying "borderline cases." The term, defined as it is, proves quite serviceable in a large number of contexts. A new context, however, demands a decision whether or not the term is to be applied to a new situation. After we have made more precise its meaning, by a stipulation, it carries, as it were, its old meaning and its new meaning. Future occasions may only rarely demand our employing the modified definition. To decide, then, that a term applies or does not apply to a new type of situation is to make its meaning more precise and is to provide an explicative definition.

What sorts of terms are in need of explicative definitions? We may categorize terms as "exactly defined," "ambiguous," and "vague." Terms in a discipline such as mathematics are the traditional examples of terms "exactly defined," terms like "a point" and "a straight line." About their meaning there is no doubt. There may be doubt, however, as to their physical application, for we may not be sure whether in a particular case the facts fit closely enough our concepts. A definition of a straight line or a point is quite exact; it clearly indicates what sorts of things are straight lines and points. In fact, however, because such definitions are "ideal," we never meet with straight lines and points as so defined. With such terms an explicative definition is not needed.

We categorize a term as "ambiguous" when in a particular context it has two or more quite distinct meanings and the context does not reveal which one is intended..When in such a situation we say, "be more precise, please," we are implying that we know of various meanings, that we are not sure which one is intended on this particular occasion, and we are asking "how are you using the word?" The answer is a lexical definition: "I am using 'X' to mean . . ." Told by Mr. Clearwater to save a boy that we both see drowning "because it is your duty," I may wish to know more "precisely" what Mr. Clearwater means by "duty." And if he provides me with a short reply like, "I mean your 'moral duty,'" this may be all my interests require. However, to settle such difficulties, an explicative definition is not required. Explicative definitions are not required when a term has several distinct meanings and we are not sure which one is intended.

Now let us turn to vagueness. Suppose a conversation with our French friend Mr. Politic. He calls a certain Frenchman "a radical." We are in difficulty. Does he mean "a member of the Radical Party" or "someone that advocates sudden and great changes in the social order"? But he soon clarifies the ambiguity; he means "a radical" in the latter sense. We then continue our conversation, employing the word in that sense, and find that we have difficulty in agreeing over the use of the word. The meaning it has, though quite adequate for us to handle the word with little, if any, difficulty in any number of stiuations is not sufficiently clear so that we can handle it with ease in "borderline cases." We agree that if the man advocates a forceful overthrow of the government that he is a radical. We agree, too, that if he never wants to change that which has existed since Napoleon I's time, he is not. Our trouble lies with the cases that fall between the extremes. "Radical" is a vague word. There are clearcut cases and for these there is no need to be more precise. We apply the term confidently. Deciding in such cases is almost mechanical. If a Ford and Buick are "vehicles" for purposes of a traffic regulation, then Austins and Bentleys are vehicles as well for purposes of that regulation. But what of a bicycle? Or a trailer? Or a person on roller-skates? Or a perambulator? Or a home-made wooden coaster with wooden wheels that travels as fast as an Austin downhill?

There are words which may always prove vague. We cannot "tighten" them up once and for all time. Waismann has coined the phrase "open texture" for such words. A new situation may always logically arise which brings out their vagueness. Words for empirical concepts are of this type and so also are words for legal concepts. Decisions on all the logically possible situations which may arise are impossible. And if we attempt to destroy the possibility of vagueness by some stipulative device such as "only cases identical with those decided as 'reasonable' are to be regarded as 'reasonable,'" we have exactly defined a word but also imposed a dogmatic restriction which destroys what often proves the desirable elasticity of such words.

When we make more precise the meaning of a word, we at least partly stipulate a meaning. Some misconceptions may arise here with regard to stipulation. First, stipulating a more precise meaning is only necessary when we must decide whether a familiar word covers a new type of case. "Define 'reasonable' exactly, please!" is a request that must be qualified to be understandable. "Exactness" is a concept varying with our purposes. Such terms as "reasonable," "table," "house," "pile," "rule"— there are obviously many more such words—are used without misunderstanding and are quite serviceable in many situations though they are all of open texture. Most affairs of life from telling the time of day to sewing a straight seam move smoothly along with varying criteria of exactness. Judges, limiting their decisions to the facts before them, reject the notion of "absolute exactness" and provide one with a meaning which is sufficiently definite to satisfy the needs of the situation.

Another misconception has a long philosophical history. The new type of situation, if we do decide that the word is applicable to it, need not have some "essential element" which it shares with situations of a different kind to which the term is applied. Words we use in everyday discourse and in legal situations acquire new meanings in a less systematic fashion. A general term is often applied to cases of widely differing sorts when these cases have, if anything in common, only an insignificant element, and when they differ with respect to elements which are significant. The way in which we employ words like "game," "law" and "rule" indicates that general terms prove quite serviceable where no essential element is shared. These general terms apply to types of situations which have "family resemblances." With a "family resemblance" we have a normal or standard case which exemplifies all the features partially exemplified by each case designated as a member of the family. "He's John's boy; look at his eyes, his mouth, his nose!" "She's John's girl; look at her smile, her hair, her complexion!" And brother and sister may not resemble each other in any respect.

Finally, when we stipulate a more precise meaning for a vague word, what we do is not arbitrary in the sense that no reasons can be offered in support of our decision. First, a word applied to a new type of situation is applied because we think there are elements which are shared by the new type of situation with a situation already so characterized. Second, whether we choose to regard the differences as significant depends on our purposes. Third, deciding one way or another has consequences. The consideration of the effect of our decision on our purposes guides our decision.

Explicative definitions are subject to criticism. We have just hinted at what some of the grounds for such criticism might be. And the discussion to follow on theory and definition will indicate other possible types of criticism. The issue is not so simple as might be thought by those who see only an issue of "covenience" in definition. Certainly, when a scientist takes a word employed in ordinary language and defines it more precisely, we do not usually say that the definition he proposes is "false" because it deviates from the way the word is customarily used. However, those defining more exactly words employed in ordinary language have sometimes chosen misleading language in describing their procedure. There has been reference to "real" meaning and "true" or "proper" definition.

Of most interest to us is the relation which definitions have to analysis. Russell's words concerning definition at the beginning of *Principia Mathematica* indicate how analysis of a concept ("definition" in a way we have not yet discussed) affects a stipulative definition:

> . . . . when what is defined is (as often occurs) something already familiar, such as cardinal or ordinal numbers, the definition contains an

analysis of a common idea, and may therefore express a notable advance. Cantor's definition of the continuum illustrates this: his definition amounts to the statement that what he is defining is the object which has the properties commonly associated with the word "continuum" though what precisely constitutes these properties had not before been known. In such cases a definition is an idea which had previously been more or less vague.

The consequence of a new theory (a word which we shall use, among other things, for the formulated result of a philosophical analysis) is a new proposal with regard to the meaning of a term.

The connection between a definition of a word and a theory reflecting the results of an analysis requires at least some brief discussion of theories. Statements like "law is a species of command" or "courage is staying at one's post and not fleeing an approaching enemy" may perform the function of a stipulative definition such as "let 'ore' mean 'evil one'" or they may be broad generalities such as "all Englishmen eat fish." On the other hand, they may resemble theories such as those developed by the detective to account for the evidence he uncovers, by Copernicus to account for certain astronomical observations, or a theory of causality developed to account for the meaning of a statement such as "x caused y." Indeed, such a statement may be used (in ways we shall have to discuss) for a combination of these functions. If it is so used, we can regard it as a "Janus statement," one facing in more than one direction, performing more than one task. Perhaps we can learn something about this interrelation between theory and definition by a consideration of the works of some of the classical philosophers. . . .

When Austin writes, "law is a species of command," do we have a "Janus statement" and if so, what role is played by definition, theory and generalization? There are two notions that require our attention, the notions of "a command" and "law." What follows is a study in the logic of Austin's task and not a study in the adequacy of his theories or usefulness of his definitions.

The word "command" was obviously not coined by Austin. It was current in ordinary language and in philosophical literature when he wrote. Austin reports and follows a usage which he specifies. He rarely, if ever, completely invents a meaning for a term. He is continually conscious in his work of the ordinary meaning of terms. He chooses the term "command" because with its connotations it best fits his purposes.

Sometimes, however, "command" can be ambiguous. It has been used to mean any imperative utterance (any utterance used to tell a person to do an act) and it has been used to mean a particular imperative use of language (e.g. commands differ from warnings). Austin makes it quite clear that he means by "command" *a type* of imperative. But once clear about this, we might still be unable to distinguish commands from threats or warnings. This, too, entails some clarifications of the boundaries of the term's meaning. But is is not an explicative definition which is at this point required, for the boundaries are for the most part there; we simply have to indicate clearly what they are.

The task becomes more complicated because the activity of defining is intimately related to a theoretical activity. Austin thinks he has good reasons for defining "command" in the way in which he does. He offers a theory of commands, much as Socrates and his companions offered theories of love and justice and courage. First, Austin does not attempt to narrow, by definition of the word "command," the sorts of situations which one might regard as "commanding situations," except in so far as he distinguishes commands from imperatives generally. Second, he is not defining a word in any of the senses of "defining" discussed in the first part of this study. Austin is concerned with understanding what is implied when a sentence of the form, "X commanded Y" is a true sentence. Like Socrates, then, he seeks the principle or principles in accordance with which a certain word is used. And the principle not only states what is the boundary between commands and other uses of language but also informs us of the general characteristics of a situation in which one commands another. Third, his theory is not the result of field-work. He did not interview people and inquire what their state of mind was when they commanded. Nor does the development of his theory require experimentation. Our knowing how to use the language makes this unnecessary. Nor does it result in prediction which can be verified and which will affect the theory. Fourth, if someone were to report some facts, agreed by everyone to constitute a case of commanding, and if Austin's theory did not take into account such facts, he would have to revise his theory; he could not simply say, "that is not a case of really commanding" or if he did say that, he would be deviating from his original purpose which was to indicate a principle of use. Fifth, the theory of commands is not offered as a description of any particular act of commanding nor is it an empirical generalization. The reasons presented in the discussion on theory of courage apply equally well here. Sixth, Austin, then, like Socrates is developing a "logical theory." It is a theory about the meaning or use of "commanding someone to do an act." The theory itself can be considered most appropriately as "adequate" or "inadequate"; one cannot speak of it as "simply a matter of convenience," or "a definition of words." It either does or does not properly specify the conditions of use.

When Austin defines "law" as "a species of command" he does not stipulate a definition for a *new* term. He is not simply saying, "let us take 'law' to mean . . ." where "law" has no meaning and we must, if we are to use the word, assign it one. There are current a number of different meanings of the word "law." Part of Austin's task is informative. But he does stipulate a definition. The proposal he makes is that we take as the meaning of this word a certain meaning already current. Of the numerous meanings current, one comes closet to meeting Austin's particular needs, and he expresses a preference for it, proceeds to distinguish it from other meanings which are current and then proposes it as the most desirable meaning for the science of jurisprudence. He does not invent a use, though he does, in an apparent legislative mood that has caused much misunderstanding, indicate that certain uses are "improper." What reasons he has for this, and he does have reasons, will occupy us later in this study. So we may say that his task is reporting uses of a certain word and then expressing a preference for one of the uses he does report and proposing that for his purposes this use be adopted.

Austin does more than define a word. He develops a theory of law, and the stipulative definition rests on a theoretical foundation. We are immediately confronted with difficulties. To develop a theory one must first stipulate a subject matter for study. We saw this with both courage and commands. There was no dispute over what acts were acts of courage or what types of expressions were commands. We could then proceed to examine an agreed upon subject matter. With law the situation seems immediately more complex, for there are various meanings of "law." To stipulate a subject matter for study, it appears, is to employ the very definition that depends on one's theory. And this seems an odd and circular procedure. Is law a command because we say that it is a command (by definition), or do we say, "law is a command" because it is one (theory and observation), or are these activities somehow combined? How do we solve this dilemma in Austin?

We can begin in the following way. First, Austin has an explicit preference for a subject matter which is to be the concern of the science of jurisprudence. This will include such matters as the penal laws of various complex political societies which are recognized as imposing obligations and providing for sanctions. It will exclude such things as laws set by fashion and laws of nature. Here there is a clear decision to disregard for purposes of the science of jurisprudence certain matters called "laws." This decision is not, however, an arbitrary one. We will go into its justification subsequently in some detail. Second, a theory is developed — rather taken over from thinkers such as Hobbes and Bentham and refined — which states that the laws which one includes within the scope of jurisprudence, and some other types of laws as well, are most adequately represented as imperatives and more particularly as commands. Third, we now possess a theory which accounts for the various distinctive characteristics of law and employing this theory we offer a definition of law —a definition to fit our purposes. The definition is such that "interpretatory" and "declaratory" and "repealing" laws are not laws for our purposes though they are to be included within the scope of the study of jurisprudence. The field of study, then, is limited by a certain preference, but a theory is also developed about that field of preference.

From this it appears that Austin's statement "law is a command" functions in at least three ways. It functions to exclude by definition such things as "laws set by fashion," "laws of nature," "customary law" and "international law." It is used as an expression setting the limits of the province of jurisprudence. And the Austinian may say to someone who claims that "international law is law" that "it is not what I mean by 'law.'" It is here that Professor Williams' point about "verbal disputes" has most relevance. But as we will shortly see Austin has reasons for applying the label "law" to certain phenomena and not other phenomena, and what he argues for his preference he moves away from standard types of verbal disputes. Just as Professor Williams by applying the phrase "verbal dispute" to some disputes draws our attention to features of these disputes which are distinctive, so Austin when he speaks of laws "properly and improperly so called" is drawing our attention to distinctive characteristics of various things. If we were to argue with Professor Williams over his label "verbal dispute" would he then say that *that* dispute was a verbal one? If so, his remark to begin with was "a merely verbal remark," and this would mislead us as to the contribution his remark has made. So too with Austin. His "playing with the word law," has a point and draws our attention to features of different laws. It is only when all the features are brought to our attention that something is gained by saying that the dispute should cease, for it is only "over words." Second, Austin's theory is a theory which accounts for the distinctiveness of a selected group of phenomena. It says something, in other words, about the "determined province." What it says is the result of an analysis; the conclusion of that analysis is that law is a command. Austin is saying, "this is what you must mean if you are to talk about law as a distinctive phenomena." It is clear that we can criticize the adequacy of Austin's analysis. It is, consequently, highly misleading for Professor Williams and for Felix Cohen to say that a legal theory is "a definition of words," for this will naturally lead us to think that it is a stipulative definition and is only appropriately criticized in terms of convenience and inconvenience. Third, it seems to assert that "whenever you find a law, you find someone commanding." We must now proceed to a more care-

ful analysis of the place of theory in Austin so that these points are sub-
stantiated.

What are the general characteristics of Austin's theory? First, the
term "law" like the term "courage" is one in ordinary use. But unlike
Socrates, Austin undertakes to make more exact the use of a term which
has been seriously affected by "analogy" and "metaphor." His purpose
requires more restricted application for the term.

Second, it is a theory and not simply a definition because it states
unique characteristics of a certain subject matter selected for study. The
subject matter can only be understood as distinctive if it is classified
within an imperative framework. The subject matter is a group of laws
which characterize political societies, laws which are regulations with
sanctions attached.

Third, in the case of courage we noted that "embarrassing cases,"
ones which our theory did not account for, could not be treated by a linguistic device like "that's not real courage." What does Austin do with
"embarrassing cases"? He seems to exclude them by definition. But this
notion of "embarrassing cases" is ambiguous. With courage they arise
from within the selected subject matter, that is, acts which are acts of
courage, without any dispute, and which are not accounted for. With law
they can arise, as we have noticed, from without the selected subject matter. A frequent argument against Austin is "but customary law is law!"
The theory in such cases is not in need of modification, for it may handle
the limited subject matter selected for consideration adequately. Customary law is not part of the selected subject matter. But the embarrassing case may arise from within the selected subject matter. To then dispose of such cases by appeal to definition is to defeat the purpose of the
theory which was to account for the facts chosen for study, to state the
essential characteristics of the selected subject matter. If, for example,
Austin's theory does not state a principle which would permit our calling
the penal law of England "law," he would be forced to modify or reject
his theory or so narrowly define its application as to make it virtually
empty and of no explanatory value.

Fourth, the theory does not describe the law of any particular community. It asserts something about "all" legal systems of the type selected
for study. It is general jurisprudence. And like a physical theory because
it expresses the "form" of something it may not say anything specifically
descriptive about any single legal system. Austin writes in confirmation
of this interpretation:

> The principles of General Jurisprudence will not coincide with any ac-
> tual system, but are intended to facilitate the acquisition of any, and to
> show their defects.

What type of assertion are we then confronted with when Austin says that "law is a command"? Is it about a characteristic shared by all laws the way all crows share the characteristic of being black? This it is not. Declaratory, interpretatory, repealing, and customary laws are not characterized in any way as commands. It is an assertion, then, about all laws of a particular kind. What kind? Those that are commands. What does it say about them? And here we may legitimately wonder what contribution had been made, for we seem to be saying that "those laws are commands which are commands." And how is one to criticize this? Have we after all but to return to the notion that in Austin theory and definition are the same thing? Our earlier observations indicate a way out. Austin viewed laws of certain legal systems—those evolved in refined communities—as only understandable within an imperative framework and more particularly as commands. This was their distinctive characteristic. What could it mean to talk about positive law as different from the laws of nature if this were not so? The Austinian might say, "don't you see that the statement 'law is a command' is not to be taken literally? It is to be regarded as an 'abstraction' or as a 'fiction' (not unlike the fiction of 'the economic man'), helpful because operating with it enables us to characterize facts which we observe within the legal sphere." This may be a fair characterization of the procedure, but it does not preclude criticism. When we criticize Austin, we will have to say something like, "law cannot adequately be represented within the framework you have selected." And by "cannot adequately" we may simply imply that the notion introduced—that of a "command"—though a helpful concept in elucidating certain aspects of a legal system is seriously misleading in other respects. It is as if thinking of an electron as a wave failed to account for what we observed continually to be the case. Thinking of the law as a command does not enable us to account for what we observe in the legal systems selected for study. Clearly, when we dispute with Austin on this point, our dispute is not just over words. Just why the command concept is inadequate is beyond the scope of this paper.

Fifth, there appears to be in Austin's theory something peculiarly "descriptive," something independent of questions of meaning. Austin argues, for example, that commanding characterizes the activity of democratic parliaments. This indicates that he regarded his theory as saying something about legal systems which one could verify if one looked at legal systems and knew what it was to command. But this sort of activity does not resemble an empirical generalization in at least one important particular. It does not extend beyond the observed facts to those that are unobserved and enable us to predict what will be the case for all things of a kind. The next democratic parliament may—it is irrelevant to Austin's theory—be able to get things done by simply making requests. If men became angels, Austin's theory would not be in the least affected.

Sixth, the theory is, as noted above, of no predictive value, however we interpret it. We cannot predict that a newly discovered system where people obey certain regulations will be analysable in terms of commands. It may resemble the systems we have selected for study and upon which we have based our theory in every particular except that one. And just this points to the danger of postulating "an essential element" for a legal system. It leads to terminological dogmatism.

Finally, the last point raises questions concerning the notion of "necessity" and its employment in Austin's theory. Here are several illustrative passages which will provide us with substance for discussion:

(1) "That *laws* emanate from *superiors*" is, therefore, an identical proposition. For the meaning it affects to import is contained in the subject.
(2) Of the principles, notions, and distinctions which are the subjects of general jurisprudence, some may be esteemed necessary. For we cannot imagine coherently a system of law (or a system of law as evolved in a refined community), without conceiving them as constituent parts of it.
(3) Jurisprudence is the science of what is essential to law. . . .
(4) General jurisprudence . . . is concerned with law as it necessarily is . . .

Austin's limitation of his subject matter to "systems of law evolved in refined communities" indicates his belief that other systems of social control are possible. He does not anywhere assert that it is a necessary condition of human existence that societies have systems of control which conform in essentials to the ones he has chosen to analyse. Second, there are some statements in Austin, illustrated by the first quotation, which are analytic and necessarily true. The notion of "superior" is embraced within the notion of "law" by a stipulative definition. Third, the necessity that a legal system in a refined community represent certain principles, notions, and distinctions is not a necessity that derives from a stipulative definition but one which is the consequence of an analysis of the concept "a legal system in a refined community." The necessity here, however, reduces on analysis to this: "if such principles, notions, distinctions are not represented in the legal system, then it is a legal system fundamentally different from the ones that now exist." All Austin appears to be saying is that we cannot imagine coherently a refined legal system unless we imagine it as it is. In fact, he mentions no principles that obtain necessarily and the distinctions which he cites as essential for a refined legal system appear to be challengeable. Finally, the remaining two quotations raise questions about the necessity of regarding the law as a command. In fact, most philosophers of law go some way with Austin in his belief that some notion, whether or not it is a command, is a necessary notion. If positive law is not in some sense imperative or does not in some sense "require" actions of people, it is difficult imagining it as a distinct phenomena. But there is no necessity in accepting the analytical tool of "a command." This notion may prove misleading while there are other notions available which are not misleading or at least are less so. But perhaps Austin meant that the notions of a superior, sanction, and obligation were essential and that the notion of a command was only a convenient class concept for "tying together" these essential notions. But to regard these elements as essential, it is worthwhile to repeat, is to make the assumption challenged in the earlier discussion on "definition by family resemblances" and to permit the "tiresome logomachy" which has characterized much discussion on the nature of law.

II

We concluded earlier that Austin both "determines the province of jurisprudence" and says something about the province so determined. We have also concluded that he is concerned primarily with problems of meaning within his subject matter. We have now to analyse more thoroughly what is involved when he determines the province of jurisprudence, for much dispute between Austinians and others arises over difficulties in this area. It is usually, perhaps, in connection with this aspect of Austin's theory that, after much dispute on "what is really law?", people are often predisposed to affirm, "well, it is really all a matter of how you define it" or "it's all a question of words."

Austin devotes much attention in the course of his *Province of Jurisprudence Determined* and his Lecture on *The Uses and Study of Jurisprudence* to justify several preferences. Let us refer to the implicit or explicit expression of such preferences as "decisions." There are, for Austin, several closely connected decisions which he must make. First, he decides that certain matters should be excluded from the scientific inquiry we refer to as "jurisprudence." The proper subject matter of jurisprudence is to be "laws strictly socalled." The field of inquiry in his study is quite explicitly narrowed so as to include only "mature and refined legal systems." These systems, he believes, are well represented by the Roman, French, German and English legal systems. Second, he decides that jurisprudence should be an empirical science, approaching the positive law as it is in fact, not as one, legitimately under some circumstances, might wish it to be. Evaluation of the law, for Austin, is necessary, but it is a proper concern of another "science." At the very least, these functions of comprehending and evaluating must be kept distinct or comprehension will be disadvantageously influenced. Jurisprudence, then, is to be concerned with law as it is, not law as it ought to be if we assume certain moral standards. Third, jurisprudence has a delimited field of inquiry—positive law—and its approach to this field is, in some sense, empirical. But Austin goes further and indicates, by the form which his theory takes, that the concern of jurisprudence is with "the meaning" of phenomena in the delimited field. While referring to this latter concern as one with "defining words" is misleading, it also may direct our attention to what is unique in such an inquiry, the respects in which it differs from empirical inquiries.

Our principal concern shall be with Austin's decision limiting the field of inquiry to what he calls "laws strictly socalled." Though much criticism has been directed at Austinians because of the other decisions noted just now above, we shall treat these only incidentally.

The limitation of the proper field of inquiry for jurisprudence is justified in several closely interrelated ways. First, Austin is prepared, as undoubtedly most of us would be, to say that there are certain matters which are simply different in kind—or substantially and significantly different—from matters with which jurisprudence should be concerned even though these matters are all labelled "law." To approach the subject without clarifying what is "law" for our purposes, when obviously so many different matters are called "law" is to risk great confusion. Thus, the laws of physics, though a proper concern of the physicist and philosopher of physics, are not a principal concern of the legal theoretician. Second, a theory of law, regarded as adequate, is used to justify the exclusion of certain matters not obviously different in kind from the matters with which we might expect jurisprudence to be concerned. Third, there are practical considerations which indicate both the desirability and necessity of limiting our investigations to certain specified legal systems.

The first sentence of the *Province of Jurisprudence Determined* informs us that "laws properly socalled are commands." Preceding the substance of his study, this is, as we have already at some length argued, misleading because it is a definition which reflects the analysis. There must, we have concluded, first have been a subject matter selected for analysis before the result of an analysis could be so formulated. This is confirmed when Austin writes:

> I determine the essence or nature which is common to all laws that are laws properly socalled.

One must have some idea of a proper subject matter before one can search for the essence ("the command") of that subject matter. The definition of law as a command, to be sure, is going to aid, through an employment of the implications of the command notion, in strictly limiting the field, but the definition offered is the result of analysis and presupposes a decision to limit the field of inquiry.

The preference, then, for a subject matter is best not expressed in terms of commands, for that is the result of analysis. It seems clear that Austin's fundamental decision is to consider as laws the laws of God and the laws operative in refined communities. These are the "standard cases" of laws. Other uses of the word "law" are derivative. These are the laws properly socalled and in Austin's view they are analysable in terms of commands. A group of positive moral rules are, as well, regarded as laws properly socalled, but these seem incorporated in the class through applying the command theory developed from the standard cases. These laws properly socalled are characterized by the imposition of obligations on persons by other persons through threats of sanctions. But what can "properly socalled" mean?

First, it does not mean the "proper" subject of jurisprudence. Divine laws and certain moral rules, though laws properly socalled, are not the proper subject matter of jurisprudence. And conversely, some laws, improperly socalled, are the subject matter of jurisprudence, namely, declaratory, interpretatory and repealing laws. Second, Austin's view is that jurisprudence must choose its "principal" subject matter from the class of laws properly socalled. It is to be concerned with a sub-class of laws properly socalled, and this sub-class is labelled "laws strictly socalled." It would be an incorrect interpretation of Austin's procedure to suppose that he simply labels just those laws, and no others, "laws properly socalled" with which he personally cares to have jurisprudence concerned. Jurisprudence is concerned with particular kinds of laws and what "law" means is independent of what Austin wishes it to mean. Third, for Austin, a word may have a "proper" meaning or application. In this respect his position does not differ from the lexicographer's. There is an "original" or "primitive" or "standard" application of a term ("the proper one") and an application which deviates from this is regarded by him as improper. Thus, the *Oxford English Dictionary* defines metaphor as:

> The figure of speech in which a name or descriptive term is transferred
> to some object different from but analogous to, that to which it is *properly*
> applicable. [emphasis added]

Fourth, the standard or primitive application of the word "law" for Austin, is represented in "divine laws" and "laws" of the state or community. Consequently, they are laws properly socalled and analysis shows that they are a class of commands. Fifth, the word "law," however, has been transferred so that it applies "improperly" to matters not analyzable in terms of commands. Sixth, underlying the transfer of the word, which has sometimes been made, not necessarily consciously, on the basis of close comparison, sometimes remote comparison, are the notions of "analogy" and "metaphor." Austin analyzes the "improper" applications of the word "law" in terms of analogy and metaphor and we shall now attempt to become clear about his views on these matters.

We must devote our attention to three important terms: "resemblance," "analogy," "metaphor." There are many types of rules called "laws"; some are related by resemblance, some by analogy only, some only by remote analogy or metaphor. Resemblance, in Austin's view, may be of two types: First, two objects which have any property in common may be said to resemble each other. Second, two objects possessing every "essential" property which belongs to all objects included within a specified class are said, by Austin, to resemble each other. In the first sense of "resemble" an apple resembles a tennis ball. In the second sense an apple resembles only other apples. Austin uses the word "resemblance" as a technical term in the second sense. All laws properly socalled resemble each other in this technical sense, that is, they all share the peculiarity of being analyzable in terms of commands, which is to say that they are wishes of a superior addressed to an inferior, supported by sanctions and consequently, for Austin, imposing obligations. Operating with this notion of a command, he is then prepared to exclude certain matters from laws properly socalled because that which is implied in the command notion, for example, a determinate superior, is not found in certain classes of rules called "laws." It should here be noted that Austin regards the class of laws properly socalled as having an "essential" characteristic. He writes:

> In the language of logic, objects which have all the qualities composing the essence of the class, and all the qualities which are the necessary consequences of those composing the essence, *resemble*.

In one sense "analogy" signifies "likeness or resemblance of any nature or degree." We could in this sense speak of an apple being analogous to another apple or of an apple being analogous to a tennis ball. Austin rejects this sense, for he wishes to distinguish from resemblance in the sense he employs the latter term. He proposes, then, the following definition: two objects are analogous to one another when one possesses all the properties common to a class and the other object possesses only

45

some of them. Thus, a potato is analogous to an apple. The apple possesses all the properties of the class of apples and the potato only some of them. Thus, too, customary law is analogous to positive law, for it possesses only some of the elements essential to the class of positive laws. Analogy is, then, the relation which obtains between laws properly socalled and laws improperly socalled.

It is just at this point that most fruitless disputes between Austinians and others arise. The issue is complicated, too, because Austin's theory of law is employed as a device for excluding certain matters from the sphere of laws properly socalled. Let us note here several common objections to Austin's procedure and language.

First, many have thought that Austin is legislating the use of a word. But we cannot be certain whether or not Austin intended the use of the words "proper" and "improper" to be so taken. His view is not that it is illegitimate to speak of "customary law" or "laws of physics." He seems to be saying that it is well to recognize the deviation from standard use in such applications. And further, it is his intention to limit the science of jurisprudence at least to this "proper use." Whether he is correct in his assessment of "standard" or "primitive" use, whether he regards it too narrowly, whether it should be a guide to the contents of jurisprudence are independent questions. Second, Austin operates with a narrow conception of definition, regarding certain elements as essential before the use of the word "law" is appropriate. As we have earlier noted, this procedure often leads to dogmatism in the use of a word. And Austin's procedure would have been better if he had recognized definition by way of family resemblances in the manner earlier discussed. Third, one may argue: "customary law" is just as "primitive" a use of the word "law," if not more so, as "law" when applied to state regulations. If Austin had regarded this type of law as law properly socalled, his theory would have been accordingly different. But this is not to say that the command theory is inadequate for the law he does discuss. Fourth, once the notion of "a command" is rejected, a notion the implications of which lead Austin to reject customary law and international law as laws properly socalled, such matters might be included within the scope of jurisprudence. In fact, Kelsen follows just this procedure and is consequently able to claim for his pure theory of law a wider applicability than Austin could claim for his theory.

There are laws which are laws by metaphor only. Such laws must be excluded, for Austin, from the scope of the science of jurisprudence. Few legal thinkers would challenge Austin at this point, though some may challenge his notion that an essential signification of the term "law" was "a regulation of human behavior." There are three notions which Austin regards as essential to metaphor.

There must be a ground of comparison. Metaphor springs from analogy. The ship that "ploughs" the waves is a situation which resembles in one or more particulars the activity of ploughing when the word "plough" is used in a primitive context, namely ploughing a field. Next, there is a transference. A term generally applied to a class of objects or a descriptive word is applied to an object or act falling within a different class. Thus, "out, out, brief candle!" is a use of the word "candle" for a job which it does not normally perform. Finally, the resemblance between the objects—let us suppose a human life and a candle—is remote. An apple and a potato are analogous because the analogy between them is not remote. But if someone were to say, "she is the apple of my eye," the comparison between the woman and the apple is metaphorical because of the remoteness of the comparison. Austin appears correct in asserting that these three notions are essential to metaphor. His actual definition of metaphor, however, is phrased in a way that causes misunderstanding.[60]

"Laws strictly socalled" are the proper province of jurisprudence. They are positive laws, laws imposed on human beings by a person or group of persons in a sovereign position. That they are laid down by a sovereign directly or indirectly is their distinctive characteristic. Austin, then, limits his field of inquiry to legal notions, principles and distinctions so as to put aside religious notions as well as moral ones. This is not done by use of analogy and metaphor, for divine law, positive law and some rules of positive morality are not analogous; they are, as we have noted, related by resemblance in Austin's technical sense. Austin's decision here enables jurisprudence to occupy itself with a distinctive empirical subject matter and to approach this subject matter in a scientific spirit and not in a legislative mood.

But Austin goes even further. In presenting his theory he limits his inquiry to several specified legal systems. All of these systems contain examples of laws, of course, strictly socalled. What justification does he give for such a limitation? He believes that the systems which are chosen for study are "pregnant with instruction" because of "their amplitude and

60. He defines metaphor as, "[T]he transference of a term from its primitive signification to subjects to which it is applied not in that, but in a secondary sense." *Lectures* at 168; *Province* at 121. Unfortunately, this definition of metaphor appears to destroy the subject it defines. This is so because in metaphor the meaning of terms must remain in some way constant. We do not, however, take the predication literally; if we did this, it would not be metaphor. But we abstract from the term's meaning those elements appropriate to the context. We grasp the metaphor when we see what the elements of the term's meaning are to be abstracted. When Macbeth says, "Out, out, brief candle!", "candle" is not being used in a secondary sense, though it is being used in a context which is not normal. It is a powerful metaphor just because it keeps its normal meaning in the abnormal context. Austin may have been mislead by the existence of "dead metaphors."

47

maturity." He especially concentrates on the Roman system, believing this has many advantages. He believes, too, that from the systems selected for study we can "presume" the characteristics of others. Finally, his plea is that there are only a few systems with which one can practically become acquainted.

What may we say of these justifications? First, let us consider Maine's classic presentation of the historical position in jurisprudence which on the face of it seems directly to conflict with the first justification listed above:

> The mistake which they committed is therefore analogous to the error of one who, in investigating the laws of the material universe, should commence by contemplating the existing physical world as a whole, instead of beginning with the particles which are its simple ingredients. One doesn't certainly see why such a scientific solecism should be more defensible in jurisprudence than in any other region of thought. It would seem antecedently that we ought to commence with the simplest social forms in a state as near as possible to their rudimentary condition. In other words, if we followed the course usual in such inquiries, we should penetrate as far up as we could in the history of primitive societies. The phenomena which early societies present us with are not easy at first to understand, but the difficulty of grappling with them bears no proportion to the perplexities which beset us in considering the baffling entanglement of modern social organization. It is a difficulty arising from their strangeness and uncouthness, not from their number and complexity. One does not readily get over the surprise which they occasion when looked at from a modern point of view; but when that is surmounted they are few enough and simple enough. But even if they gave more trouble than they do, no pains would be wasted in ascertaining the germs out of which has assuredly been unfolded every form of moral restraint which controls our actions and shapes our conduct at the present moment.

The principal question is this: will this study of "simplest social forms" enable us to better formulate a general theory of law about extant systems, systems which are "mature and refined"? First, interestingly enough, Maine nowhere indicates that the historical method can accomplish this task. Second, primitive systems might lack fundamental elements which characterized modern or mature systems. Maine does, in fact, imply that this may be so when he regards the "command theory" as satisfactory if limited to explaining mature systems. He writes of Austin's theory:

> The results of this separation of ingredients tally exactly with the facts of

mature jurisprudence; and by a little straining of language, they may be made to correspond in form with all laws, at all epochs.

And later in life he wrote:

> The laws with which the student of Jurisprudence is concerned in our own day are undoubtedly either the actual commands of sovereigns, understood as the portion of the community endowed with irresistible coercive force, or else they are practices of mankind brought under the formula, "a law is a command" by help of the formula "whatever the Sovereign permits, is his command."[64]

Maine merely criticized the historical pretensions which a positivist theory may have and indicates that one may have a legitimate scientific interest in the motives behind commands. Third, Maine is, more so than Austin, concerned with specific legal doctrines such as, for example, appear in the law of contracts and wills. He is interested in the development of the doctrines and the "fossils" that still remain. He is, to put it briefly, "an historian," one proposing a number of very general theories about the history of law as well as a general theory about how one can advantageously go about studying particular legal doctrines. Austin, on the other hand, is concerned with general notions such as right and duty which are largely, if not wholly, independent of development and appear in the same essential form in all mature systems. Austin implies that, in fact, these notions may not be present in systems less refined than the ones he has selected for study. Moreover, Austin and Maine do, in fact, choose the same subject matter for study, but their approach to it is different and consequently their views are not at all in conflict. Both are attracted to and recognize the importance of the Roman Law. Maine recognizes its importance because of "the germs" it contains and the aid it can give to us in our understanding of particular modern legal doctrines. Austin recognizes its importance because of the fact that several refined legal systems are derived from it and a fair inference will be that what fundamentally characterizes its concept will characterize the concepts of other systems as well. But he looks at the Roman system, not because of the role its elements play in more mature or modern systems, but because his problems of meaning can more profitably be discussed within the framework of that system. The logical arrangement and deductions of the Roman jurists create a great appeal for their system, not necessarily because of specific doctrines, but for the systematic treatment of the basic elements of concern to the philosopher of law.

64. *Lectures* at 1077; *Province* at 373.

Let us now address ourselves to the second justification which Austin offers. What is it that we may justifiably "presume" from those systems selected for study? And here a curious natural law element in Austin's thought appears. He writes:

> The proper subject of General or Universal Jurisprudence (as distinguished from Universal Legislation) is a description of such subjects and ends of Law as are common to all systems . . . which are bottomed in the common nature of man, or correspond to the resembling points in their several positions.

This would seem to imply that Austin's theory has universal scope because it is grounded in "resemblances" which "are bottomed in the common nature of man." But Austin's continual limitation of his theory to laws in a refined community seems to be an explicit disavowal of just this "common nature" theory. Unfortunately, Austin nowhere elaborates this notion.

Finally, little objection can be taken to Austin's third type of justification. Austin quite explicitly limits his theory to laws of mature and refined communities. He makes no claims, except perhaps in his general definition of law, to universal scope for his theory. When he speaks of "necessary notions, principles and distinctions," he is usually careful to limit the scope of his hypotheses.

We can now sum up the essentials of Austin's positivism in this way: It is a theory of law concerned with law as it is rather than law as it ought to be. It is not an ethical approach to law. This is what most people would understand by "positivism." Second, it is a theory concerned with the law laid down and enforced by the sovereign in a community. Thus, it is not addressed to international or customary law. Third, it is a general theory of the meaning of law and of legal concepts. And it concludes that law is a command. It does not address itself, as some schools of jurisprudence have, to an empirical study of the reasons motivating legislators or judges to create the law that they do create.

Gray, Nature and Sources of the Law*

Chapter IV. The Law

Sec. 191. The Law of the State or of any organized body of men is composed of the rules which the courts, that is, the judicial organs of

---

* [First ed. (Carpentier Lectures for 1908, Columbia University). New York: Columbia University Press, 1909. Reprinted by permission of Roland Gray.

that body, lay down for the determination of legal rights and duties. The difference in this matter between contending schools of Jurisprudence arises largely from not distinguishing between the Law and the Sources of the Law. On the one hand, to affirm the existence of *nicht positivisches Recht,* that is, of Law which the courts do not follow, is declared to be an absurdity; and on the other hand, it is declared to be an absurdity to say that the Law of a great nation means the opinions of half-a-dozen old gentlemen, some of them, conceivably, of very limited intelligence. The truth is, each party is looking at but one side of the shield. If those half-a-dozen old gentlemen form the highest judicial tribunal of a country, then no rule or principle which they refuse to follow is Law in that country. However desirable, for instance, it may be that a man should be obliged to make gifts which he has promised to make, yet if the courts of a country will not compel him to keep his promise, it is not the Law of that country that promises to make a gift are binding. On the other hand, those six men seek the rules which they follow not in their own whims, but they derive them from sources often of the most general and permanent character, to which they are directed, by the organized body to which they belong, to apply themselves. I believe the definition of Law that I have given to be correct; but let us consider some other definitions of the Law which have prevailed and which still prevail.

Sec. 192. Of the many definitions of the Law which have been given at various times and places, some are absolutely meaningless, and in others a spark of truth is distorted by a mist of rhetoric. But there are three theories which have commended themselves to accurate thinkers, which have had and which still have great acceptance, and which deserve examination. In all of them it is denied that the courts are the real authors of the Law, and it is contended that they are merely the mouthpieces which give it expression.

Sec. 193. The *first* of these theories is that Law is made up of the commands of the sovereign. This is Austin's view. "Every positive law," he says, "obtaining in any community, is a creature of the Sovereign or State; having been established immediately by the monarch or supreme body, as exercising legislative or judicial functions; or having been established immediately by a subject individual or body, as exercising rights

---

John Chipman Gray (1839-1915) was a fellow soldier with Holmes in the Union forces, a fellow student at Harvard Law School, and a fellow practitioner in Boston. Gray became a law professor at Harvard and served until 1913. A leading advocate of the "case method," Gray won wide repute in the field of real property, both his treatises (*Restraints on the Alienation of Property,* 1883, and *The Rule Against Perpetuities,* 1886) becoming the standard American works of their type.]

or powers of direct or judicial legislation, which the monarch or supreme body has expressly or tacitly conferred."[1]

Sec. 194. In a sense, this is true; the State can restrain its courts from following this or that rule, but it often leaves them free to follow what they think right; and it is certainly a forced expression to say that one commands things to be done, because he has power (which he does not exercise) to forbid their being done. . . .

Sec. 196. When an agent, servant, or official does acts as to which he has received no express orders from his principal, he may aim, or may be expected to aim, *directly* at the satisfaction of the principal, or he may not. Take an instance of the first,—a cook, in roasting meat or boiling eggs, has, or at any rate the ideal cook is expected to have, *directly* in view the wishes and tastes of her master. On the other hand, when a great painter is employed to cover a church wall with a picture, he is not expected to keep constantly in mind what will please the wardens and vestry; they are not to be in all his thoughts; if they are men of ordinary sense, they will not wish to be; he is to seek his inspiration elsewhere, and the picture when done is not the "creature" of the wardens and vestry; whereas, if the painter adopted an opposite course, and had bent his whole energies to divining what he thought would please them best, he would have been their "tool," and the picture might not unfairly be described as their creature.

Sec. 197. Now it is clear into which of these classes a judge falls. Where he has not received direct commands from the State, he does not consider, he is not expected to consider, *directly* what would please the State; his thoughts are directed to the question—What have other judges held? What does Ulpian or Lord Coke say about the matter? What decision does *elegantia juris* or sound morals require? . . .

Sec. 200. In this connection, the meaning of "Law," when preceded by the indefinite, is to be distinguished from that which it bears when preceded by the definite, article. Austin, indeed, defines the Law as being the aggregate of the rules established by political superiors,[2] and Bentham says, "*Law,* or *the Law,* taken indefinitely, is an abstract and collective term; which, when it means anything, can mean neither more nor less than the sum total of a number of individual laws taken together."[3] But this is not, I think, the ordinary meaning given to "the Law." A law ordinarily means a statute passed by the legislature of a state. "*The* Law" is the whole system of rules applied by the courts. The resemblance of

1. 2 *Jur.* (4th ed.) 550, 551.
2. 1 *Jur.* (4th ed.) 89.
3. 1 Benth. *Works,* 148.

the terms suggests the inference that the body of rules applied by the courts is composed wholly of the commands of the State, but to erect this suggestion into a demonstration, and say,—The system administered by the courts is "the Law," "the Law" consists of nothing but an aggregate of single laws, and all single laws are commands of the State—is not justifiable.* . . .

Sec. 202. Austin's theory was a natural reaction against the views which he found in possession of the field. Law had been defined as "the art of what is good and equitable"; "that which reason in such sort defines to be good that it must be done"; "the abstract expression of the general will existing in and for itself"; "the organic whole of the external conditions of the intellectual life." If Austin went too far in considering the Law as always proceeding from the State, he conferred a great benefit on Jurisprudence by bringing out clearly that the Law is at the mercy of the State.

Sec. 203. The *second* theory on the nature of Law is that the courts, in deciding cases, are, in truth, applying what has previously existed in the common consciousness of the people. Savigny is the ablest expounder of this theory. . . .

Sec. 204. Savigny is careful to discriminate between the common consciousness of the people and custom: "The foundation of the Law," he says, "has its existence, its reality, in the common consciousness of the people. This existence is invisible. How can we become acquainted with it? We become acquainted with it as it manifests itself in external acts, as it appears in practice, manners, and custom. By the uniformity of a continuous and continuing mode of action, we recognize that the belief of the people is its common root, and not mere chance. Thus, custom is the sign of positive law, not its foundation."[4]

Sec. 205. Savigny is confronted by a difficulty of the same kind as confronted Austin. The great bulk of the Law as it exists in any community is unknown to its rulers, and it is only by aid of the doctrine that what the sovereign permits he commands, that the Law can be considered as emanating from him; but equally, the great bulk of the Law is unknown to the people; how, then, can it be the product of their "common consciousness"? How can it be that of which they "feel the necessity as law"?

Sec. 206. Take a simple instance, one out of thousands. By the law of Massachusetts, a contract by letter is not complete until the answer of

---

*[Cf. Jethro Brown, *The Austinian Theory of Law* (1912), Excursus E: A Consideration of Some Objections to the Conception of Positive Law as State Command, pp. 331 et seq.]

4. 1 *Heut. roem. Recht,* §12, p. 35.

acceptance is received.[5] By the law of New York, it is complete when the answer is mailed. Is the common consciousness of the people of Massachusetts different on this point from that of the people of New York? Do the people of Massachusetts feel the necessity of one thing as law, and the people of New York feel the necessity of the precise opposite? In truth, not one in a hundred of the people of either State has the dimmest notion on the matter. If one of them has a notion, it is as likely as not to be contrary to the law of his State. . . .

Sec. 209. The jurists set forth the opinions of the people no more and no less than any other specially educated or trained class in a community sets forth the opinions of that community, each in its own sphere. They in no other way set forth the *Volksgeist* in the domain of Law than educated physicians set forth the *Volksgeist* in the matter of medicine. It might be very desirable that the conceptions of the *Volksgeist* should be those of the most skillful of the community, but however desirable this might be, it is not the case. The *Volksgeist* carries a piece of sulphur in its waistcoat pocket to keep off rheumatism, and thinks that butchers cannot sit on juries.

Sec. 210. Not only is popular opinion apart from professional opinion in Law as in other matters, but it has been at times positively hostile. Those who hold that jurists are the mouthpieces of the popular convictions in matters of law have never been able to deal satisfactorily with the reception of the Roman Law in Germany, for that Law was brought in not only without the wishes, but against the wishes, of the great mass of the people.

Sec. 211. A *third* theory of the Law remains to consider. That theory is to this effect: The rules followed by the courts in deciding questions are not the expression of the State's commands, nor are they the expression of the common consciousness of the people, but, although what the judges rule is the Law, it is putting the cart before the horse to say that the Law is what the judges rule. The Law, indeed, is identical with the rules laid down by the judges, but those rules are laid down by the judges because they are the Law, they are not the Law because they are laid down by the judges, or, as the late Mr. James C. Carter puts it, the judges are the discoverers, not the creators, of the Law. And this is the way that judges themselves are apt to speak of their functions.

Sec. 212. This theory concedes that the rules laid down by the judges correctly state the Law, but it denies that it is Law because they state it. . . .

Sec. 215. To come, then, to the question whether the judges discover

5. This used to be the Law in Massachusetts. I am not so sure that it is now.

preëxisting Law, or whether the body of rules that they lay down is not the expression of preëxisting Law, but the Law itself. Let us take a concrete instance: On many matters which have come in question in various jurisdictions, there is no doctrine received *semper, ubique, et ab omnibus.* For instance, Henry Pitt has built a reservoir on his land, and has filled it with water; and, without any negligence on his part, either in the care or construction of his reservoir, it bursts, and the water pouring forth, floods and damages the land of Pitt's neighbor, Thomas Underhill. Has Underhill a right to recover compensation from Pitt? In England, in the leading case of *Rylands v. Fletcher,* it was held that he could recover, and this decision has been followed in some of the United States—for instance, in Massachusetts; but in others, as, I believe, in New Jersey, the contrary is held.

Sec. 216. Now, suppose that Pitt's reservoir is in one of the newer States, say Utah, and suppose, further, that the question has never arisen there before; that there is no statute, no decision, no custom on the subject; the court has to decide the case somehow; suppose it should follow *Rylands v. Fletcher* and should rule that in such cases the party injured can recover. The State, then, through its judicial organ, backed by the executive power of the State, would be recognizing the rights of persons injured by such accidents, and, therefore, the doctrine of *Rylands v. Fletcher* would be undoubtedly the present Law in Utah.

Sec. 217. Suppose, again, that a similar state of facts arises in the adjoining State of Nevada, and that there also the question is presented for the first time, and that there is no statute, decision, or custom on the point; the Nevada court has to decide the case somehow; suppose it should decline to follow *Rylands v. Fletcher,* and should rule that in such cases the party injured is without remedy. Here the State of Nevada would refuse to recognize any right in the injured party and, therefore, it would unquestionably be the present Law in Nevada that a person injured by such an accident would have no right to compensation.

Sec. 218. Let us now assume that the conditions and habits of life are the same in these two adjoining States; that being so, these contradictory doctrines cannot both conform to an ideal rule of Law, and let us, therefore, assume that an all-wise and all-good intelligence, considering the question, would think that one of these doctrines was right and the other wrong, according to the true standard of morality, whatever that may be. It matters not, for the purpose of the discussion, which of the two doctrines it is, but let us suppose that the intelligence aforesaid would approve *Rylands v. Fletcher;* that is, it would think the Law as established in Nevada by the decision of its court did not conform to the eternal principles of right.

Sec. 219. The fact that the ideal theory of Law disapproved the Law as established in Nevada would not affect the present existence of that Law. However wrong intellectually or morally it might be, it would be the Law of that State to-day. But what was the Law in Nevada a week before a rule for decision of such questions was adopted by the courts of that State? Three views seem possible: *first,* that the Law was then ideally right, and contrary to the rule now declared and practiced on; *second,* that the Law was then the same as is now declared and practiced; *third,* that there was then no Law on the matter.

Sec. 220. The first theory seems untenable on any notion of discovery. A discoverer is a discoverer of that which is,—not of that which is not. The result of such a theory would be that when Underhill received the injury and brought his suit, he had in interest which would be protected by the State, and that it now turns out that he did not have it,—a contradiction in terms.

Sec. 221. We have thus to choose between the theory that the Law was at that time what it now is, and the theory that there was then no law at all on the subject. The latter is certainly the view of reason and of common sense alike. There was, at the time in question, *ex hypothesi,* no statute, no precedent, no custom on the subject; of the inhabitants of the State no one out of a hundred had an opinion on the matter or had ever thought of it; of the few, if any, to whom the question had ever occurred, the opinions were, as likely as not, conflicting. To say that on this subject there was really Law existing in Nevada, seems only to show how strong a root legal fictions can strike into our mental processes. . . .

Sec. 223. The difficulty of believing in preëxisting Law is still greater when there is a change in the decision of the courts. In Massachusetts it was held in 1849, by the Supreme Judicial Court, that if a man hired a horse in Boston on a Sunday to drive to Nahant, and drove instead to Nantasket, the keeper of the livery stable had no right to sue him in trover for the conversion of the horse. But in 1871 this decision was overruled and the right was given to the stable-keeper. Now, did stable-keepers have such rights, say, in 1845? If they did, then the court in 1849 did not discover the Law. If they did not, then the court in 1871 did not discover the Law. . . .

Chapter V. The Courts

. . . *Sec. 266. The Limits of Judicial Power.* Thus far we have seen that the Law is made up of the rules for decision which the courts lay down; that all such rules are Law; that rules for conduct which the courts do not apply are not Law; that the fact that the courts apply rules is what makes them Law; that there is no mysterious entity "The Law" apart from these rules; and that the judges are rather the creators than the discoverers of the Law.

Sec. 267. Is the power of the judges, then, absolute? Can the comparatively few individuals who fill judicial position in the State, for instance, lay down rules for the government of human intercourse at their bare pleasure or whim? Not so; the judges are but organs of the State; they have only such power as the organization of the State gives them; and what that organization is, is determined by the wills of the real rulers of the State.

Sec. 268. Who are the rulers of a State, is a question of fact and not of form. In a nominal autocracy, the real rulers may be a number of court favorites or the priests of a religion; and in a democracy, the real ruler may be a demagogue or political boss.

Sec. 269. It is conceivable that a body of judges may be the ruling wills of a community, and then they hold their powers by virtue of dominating other wills, but this, except in a very primitive community, can hardly ever be the case. The half-a-dozen elderly men sitting on a platform behind a green or red cloth, with very probably not commanding wills or powerful physique, can exercise their functions only within those limits which the real rulers of the State allow for the exercise; for the State and the court as an organ thereof are the product of the wills of those rulers.

Sec. 270. Who is to determine whether the judges are acting within those limits? In all the less important matters, the rulers intrust the determination of this question to the judges themselves; thus the judges are allowed to say what are the details of the organization of a State and the distribution of its powers among its organs; but, on the most vital matters, the rulers themselves determine what the organization of the body is and within what limits its organs shall work; and the acts and declarations of persons, being its organs, which are inconsistent with the very nature of the organization, are not acts and declarations of the State—are not its Law.

Sec. 271. How can it be told whether a rule laid down by a court is to be deemed not the Law, either because such a rule is inconsistent with the organization of the State as established by its rulers, or because it is beyond the limits of the power of the court as fixed by those rulers? The principal evidence that declarations of judges are inconsistent with the organization of the State, or beyond the limits fixed by it for their action, is the opinions of the members of the community to that effect. To determine whether such opinions are so strong and universal that they must be taken for the judgment of the rulers of the State, or whether the declarations, though much disregarded, are still to be deemed Law, there seems to be no general definite rule, applicable to all cases.

Sec. 272. It should be observed that the unexpressed, and, in formal shape, inexpressible, opinion of the rulers of society lies behind the Law none the less in those countries which possess written constitutions than in those which do not. The organization and powers of the ordinary legislative bodies may be indeed defined in a constitution, but whether there was power in any one to bring into effect the constitution, the constitution itself cannot determine, any more than a book can prove its own inspiration, or a man lift himself up by his boots. For instance, What are the geographical limits for which the constitution is to be in force? Who are to vote upon it,—men, women, or children? Can paupers, slaves, aliens, vote? By what collections of individuals, such as towns or boroughs, must representatives to frame a constitution be chosen? These are questions that the rulers of the State must determine; their decision is a prerequisite for the constitution coming into existence. The elephant may rest on the tortoise, but in the last result we have to go back to the wills of those who rule the society.

Sec. 273. The power of the rulers of the State or other community in reference to its judicial organs or courts is exercised in a twofold way,—first, by creating them, and secondly, in laying down limits for their action, or, in other words, indicating the sources from which they are to derive the rules which make up the Law. From what *sources* does the State or other community direct its judges to obtain the Law? These sources are defined for the most part in a very vague and general way, but one rule is clear and precise. The State requires that the acts of its legislative organ shall bind the courts, and so far as they go, shall be paramount to all other sources. This may be said to be a necessary consequence from the very conception of an organized community of men.

Sec. 274. The other sources from which courts may draw their general rules are fourfold,—judicial precedents, opinions of experts, customs, and principles of morality (using morality as including public policy). Whether there is any precedent, expert opinion, custom, or principle from which a rule can be drawn, and whether a rule shall be drawn accordingly, are questions which, in most communities, are left to the courts themselves, and yet there are probably in every community limits within or beyond which courts may, or, on the other hand, cannot, seek for rules from the sources mentioned, although the limits are not precisely defined. Take, for instance, a country where the English Common Law has prevailed. If a court in such a country should, in matters not governed by statute, absolutely refuse to follow any judicial precedents, it is not likely that the rulers of the country would recognize the doctrine of that court as Law; or, if a court should frame a rule based upon the principle that infanticide was not immoral, that rule would not be the Law.

Sec. 275. Though the commands by the rulers of a community as to the limits within which these last four classes of sources are to be sought by the courts are indefinite, while the command that legislative acts must be followed by the courts is precise and peremptory, the fact is that this latter rule, in its working, is almost as indefinite as those which are imposed on the courts with reference to the other sources; for, after all, it is only words that the legislature utters; it is for the courts to say what those words mean; that is, it is for them to interpret legislative acts; undoubtedly there are limits upon their power of interpretation, but these limits are almost as undefined as those which govern them in their dealing with the other sources.

Sec. 276. And this is the reason why legislative acts, statutes, are to be dealt with as sources of Law, and not as part of the Law itself, why they are to be coordinated with the other sources which I have mentioned. It has been sometimes said that the Law is composed of two parts, legislative law and judge-made law, but, in truth, all the Law is judge-made law. The shape in which a statute is imposed on the community as a guide for conduct is that statute as interpreted by the courts. The courts put life into the dead words of the statute. To quote again from Bishop Hoadly, a sentence which I have before given: "Nay, whoever hath an *absolute authority* to *interpret* any written or spoken law, it is *He* who is truly the Law Giver to all intents and purposes, and not the Person who first wrote and spoke them."[8] I will return to this later.*

Holmes, The Path of the Law†

When we study law we are not studying a mystery but a well-known profession. We are studying what we shall want in order to appear before judges, or to advise people in such a way as to keep them out of

---

8. Sermon preached before the King, 1717 (15 ed.), 12.

* [See M. R. Cohen, The Process of Judicial Legislation, 48 *Am. L. Rev.* 11, passim (1914).]

† [From Holmes, *Collected Legal Papers* 167-169, 171-175 (Harcourt, Brace and Company 1920). Also printed in 10 *Harv. L. Rev.* 457-462 (1897).

Oliver Wendell Holmes, Jr. (1841-1935) began his career practicing law in Boston. Intellectually dissatisfied with the more mundane aspects of private practice, he undertook the editorship of *The American Law Review* and taught at Harvard Law School. In 1881, Holmes' book, *The Common Law,* was published. The first great contribution to the history

court. The reason why it is a profession, why people will pay lawyers to argue for them or to advise them, is that in societies like ours the command of the public force is intrusted to the judges in certain cases, and the whole power of the state will be put forth, if necessary, to carry out their judgments and decrees. People want to know under what circumstances and how far they will run the risk of coming against what is so much stronger than themselves, and hence it becomes a business to find out when this danger is to be feared. The object of our study, then, is prediction, the prediction of the incidence of the public force through the instrumentality of the courts.

The means of the study are a body of reports, of treatises, and of statutes, in this country and in England, extending back for six hundred years, and now increasing annually by hundreds. In these sibylline leaves are gathered the scattered prophecies of the past upon the cases in which the axe will fall. These are what properly have been called the oracles of the law. Far the most important and pretty nearly the whole meaning of every new effort of legal thought is to make these prophecies more precise, and to generalize them into a thoroughly connected system. The process is one, from a lawyer's statement of a case, eliminating as it does all the dramatic elements with which his client's story has clothed it, and retaining only the facts of legal import, up to the final analyses and abstract universals of theoretic jurisprudence. The reason why a lawyer does not mention that his client wore a white hat when he made a contract, while Mrs. Quickly would be sure to dwell upon it along with the parcel gilt goblet and the sea-coal fire, is that he foresees that the public force will act in the same way whatever his client had upon his head. It is to make the prophecies easier to be remembered and to be understood that the teachings of the decisions of the past are put into general propositions and gathered into text-books, or that statutes are passed in a general form. The primary rights and duties with which jurisprudence busies itself again are nothing but prophecies. One of the

---

of the common law by an American author, *The Common Law* won instant international acclaim for Holmes. Less than a year later Holmes was appointed to the Supreme Court of Massachusetts, of which he became Chief Justice in 1889. In 1902, Holmes was appointed to the United States Supreme Court, on which he served until 1933. His *Collected Legal Papers*, edited by Harold J. Laski, were published in 1920. His correspondence with Sir Frederick Pollack, covering a period from 1874 to 1932, was published under the editorship of Mark DeWoolfe Howe in 1941. Some of Holmes' most important writing, including many of his judicial opinions, will be found in Max Lerner's *The Mind and Faith of Justice Holmes* (1943). For a more critical appraisal of Justice Holmes' thoughts, see M. R. Cohen, *Faith of a Liberal* 20-31 (1946).]

many evil effects of the confusion between legal and moral ideas, about which I shall have something to say in a moment, is that theory is apt to get the cart before the horse, and to consider the right or the duty as something existing apart from and independent of the consequences of its breach, to which certain sanctions are added afterward. But, as I shall try to show, a legal duty so called is nothing but a prediction that if a man does or omits certain things he will be made to suffer in this or that way by judgment of the court; and so of a legal right. . . .

. . . If you want to know the law and nothing else, you must look at it as a bad man, who cares only for the material consequences which such knowledge enables him to predict, not as a good one, who finds his reasons for conduct, whether inside the law or outside of it, in the vaguer sanctions of conscience. The theoretical importance of the distinction is no less, if you would reason on your subject aright. The law is full of phraseology drawn from morals, and by the mere force of language continually invites us to pass from one domain to the other without perceiving it, as we are sure to do unless we have the boundary constantly before our minds. The law talks about rights, and duties, and malice, and intent, and negligence, and so forth, and nothing is easier, or, I may say, more common in legal reasoning, than to take these words in their moral sense, at some stage of the argument, and so to drop into fallacy. For instance, when we speak of the rights of man in a moral sense, we mean to mark the limits of interference with individual freedom which we think are prescribed by conscience, or by our ideal, however reached. Yet it is certain that many laws have been enforced in the past, and it is likely that some are enforced now, which are condemned by the most enlightened opinion of the time, or which at all events pass the limit of interference as many consciences would draw it. Manifestly, therefore, nothing but confusion of thought can result from assuming that the rights of man in a moral sense are equally rights in the sense of the Constitution and the law. . . .

The confusion with which I am dealing besets confessedly legal conceptions. Take the fundamental question, What constitutes the law? You will find some text writers telling you that it is something different from what is decided by the courts of Massachusetts or England, that it is a system of reason, that it is a deduction from principles of ethics or admitted axioms or what not, which may or may not coincide with the decisions. But if we take the view of our friend the bad man we shall find that he does not care two straws for the axioms or deductions, but that he does want to know what the Massachusetts or English courts are likely to do in fact. I am much of his mind. The prophecies of what the court will do in fact, and nothing more pretentious, are what I mean by the law.

Take again a notion which as popularly understood is the widest conception which the law contains—the notion of legal duty, to which already I have referred. We fill the word with all the content which we draw from morals. But what does it mean to a bad man? Mainly, and in the first place, a prophecy that if he does certain things he will be subjected to disagreeable consequences by way of imprisonment or compulsory payment of money. But from his point of view, what is the difference between being fined and being taxed a certain sum for doing a certain thing? That his point of view is the test of legal principles is shown by the many discussions which have arisen in the courts on the very question whether a given statutory liability is a penalty or a tax. On the answer to this question depends the decision whether conduct is legally wrong or right, and also whether a man is under compulsion or free. Leaving the criminal law on one side, what is the difference between the liability under the mill acts or statutes authorizing a taking by eminent domain and the liability for what we call a wrongful conversion of property where restoration is out of the question. In both cases the party taking another man's property has to pay its fair value as assessed by a jury, and no more. What significance is there in calling one taking right and another wrong from the point of view of the law? It does not matter, so far as the given consequence, the compulsory payment, is concerned, whether the act to which it is attached is described in terms of praise or in terms of blame, or whether the law purports to prohibit it or to allow it. If it matters at all, still speaking from the bad man's point of view, it must be because in one case and not in the other some further disadvantages, or at least some further consequences, are attached to the act by the law. The only other disadvantages thus attached to it which I ever have been able to think of are to be found in two somewhat insignificant legal doctrines, both of which might be abolished without disturbance. One is, that a contract to do a prohibited act is unlawful, and the other, that, if one of two or more joint wrongdoers has to pay all the damages, he cannot recover contribution from his fellows. And that I believe is all. You see how the vague circumference of the notion of duty shrinks and at the same time grows more precise when we wash it with cynical acid and expel everything except the object of our study, the operations of the law.

Nowhere is the confusion between legal and moral ideas more manifest than in the law of contract. Among other things, here again the so called primary rights and duties are invested with a mystic significance beyond what can be assigned and explained. The duty to keep a contract at common law means a prediction that you must pay damages if you do not keep it—and nothing else. If you commit a tort, you are liable to pay a compensatory sum. If you commit a contract, you are liable to pay a compensatory sum unless the promised event comes to pass, and that is all the difference. But such a mode of looking at the matter stinks in the nostrils of those who think it advantageous to get as much ethics into the law as they can. It was good enough for Lord Coke, however, and here, as in many other cases, I am content to abide with him. In *Bromage v. Genning,*[1] a prohibition was sought in the King's Bench against a suit in the marches of Wales for the specific performance of a covenant to grant a lease, and Coke said that it would subvert the intention of the conven-antor, since he intends it to be at his election either to lose the damages or to make the lease. Sergeant Harris for the plaintiff confessed that he moved the matter against his conscience, and a prohibition was granted. This goes further than we should go now, but it shows what I venture to say has been the common law point of view from the beginning, although Mr. Harriman, in his very able little book upon Contracts has been misled, as I humbly think, to a different conclusion.

Pound, Law in Books and Law in Action*

When Tom Sawyer and Huck Finn had determined to rescue Jim by digging under the cabin where he was confined, it seemed to the unin-formed lay mind of Huck Finn that some old picks the boys had found were the proper implements to use. But Tom knew better. From reading he knew what was the right course in such cases, and he called for case-knives. "It don't make no difference," said Tom, "how foolish it is, it's the *right way*—and it's the regular way. And there ain't no other way that ever I heard of, and I've read all the books that gives any information about these things. They always dig out with a case-knife." So, in defer-ence to the books and the proprieties, the boys set to work with case-

1. Roll. Rep. 368.
* [44 *Am. L. Rev.* 12-13, 14, 15-16, 16-17, 19-20, 25, 31, 32-34 (1910).
Roscoe Pound (1870-1964) served in many public offices in addition to his long aca-demic career, during which he taught as Professor of Law at Northwestern and Chicago Universities, and as Professor and Dean at Nebraska and Harvard. He is considered the outstanding exponent of "sociological jurisprudence" in America.
In the field of general jurisprudence, Pound's most important studies were: The Scope and Purpose of Sociological Jurisprudence (1911-1912), 24 *Harv. L. Rev.* 591 (1911), 25 *Harv. L. Rev.* 140, 489 (1912); Justice According To Law, 13 *Colum. L. Rev.* 1, 103 (1914); The Limits of Effective Legal Action, 27 *Intl. J. Ethics* 150 (1917); *The Spirit of the Common Law* (1921); *Introduction to the Philosophy of Law* (1922); *Interpretations of Legal History* (1923); The Theory of Judicial Decision, 36 *Harv. L. Rev.* 641, 802, 940 (1923); *Law and Morals* (1924); The Call for a Realistic Jurisprudence, 44 *Harv. L. Rev.* 697 (1931).]

knives. But after they had dug till nearly midnight and they were tired and their hands were blistered, and they had made little progress, a light came to Tom's legal mind. He dropped his knife and, turning to Huck, said firmly, "Gimme a case-knife." Let Huck tell the rest:

> He had his own by him, but I handed him mine. He flung it down and says, "Gimme a *case-knife.*"
> I didn't know just what to do—but then I thought. I scratched around amongst the old tools and got a pickaxe and give it to him, and he took it and went to work and never said a word.
> He was always just that particular. *Full of principle.*

Tom had made over again one of the earliest discoveries of the law. When tradition prescribed case-knives for tasks for which pickaxes were better adapted, it seemed better to our forefathers, after a little vain struggle with case-knives, to adhere to principle—but use the pickaxe. They granted that law ought not to change. Changes in law were full of danger. But, on the other hand, it was highly inconvenient to use case-knives. And so the law has always managed to get a pickaxe in its hands, though it steadfastly demanded a case-knife, and to wield it in the virtuous belief that it was using the approved instrument.

It is worth while to recall some of the commonplaces of legal history by way of illustration. . . .

. . . When wager of law had made the action of debt a worthless remedy upon simple contracts, wager of law was not abolished, but the courts found a trespass and a breach of the king's peace in failure to perform a promise, if only something had been given presently in exchange for it, and thus imposed upon our law of contracts the formality of a consideration. When the delay and formalism of real actions and the incident of trial by battle made them inadequate remedies, a fictitious lease and fictitious ejectment were resorted to in order to make another remedy meet the situation. When the hard and fast form of writ and declaration failed to provide for new cases of conversion of a plaintiff's property, the form was not altered, but the loss and finding were assumed from the conversion; so that we are able to read in an American report of the nineteenth century that the plaintiff casually lost one hundred freight cars and the defendant casually found them and converted them to its own use, as if it were a watch or a pocket book that had been lost.

We are by no means so much wiser than our fathers as we sometimes assume. While we have few of the old fictions of procedure left, we can make new ones of our own upon occasion in the like spirit. . . .

Let us take a few examples. It is a settled dogma of the books that all doubts are to be resolved in favor of the constitutionality of a statute—that the courts will not declare it in conflict with the constitution unless clearly and indubitably driven to that conclusion. But it can not be maintained that such is the actual practice, especially with respect to social legislation claimed to be in conflict with constitutional guaranties of liberty and property. The mere fact that the Court of Appeals of New York and the Supreme Court of the United States differed on such questions as the power to regulate hours of labor on municipal and public contracts, and the power to regulate the hours of labor of bakers, the former holding adversely to the one[1] and upholding the other,[2] while the latter court had already ruled the opposite on the first question[3] and then reversed the ruling of the New York court on the second,[4] speaks for itself. Many more instances might be noted. But it is enough to say that any one who studies critically the course of decision upon constitutional questions in a majority of our state courts in recent years must agree with Professor Freund that the courts in practice tend to overturn all legislation which they deem unwise,[5] and must admit the truth of Professor Dodd's statement:

> The courts have now definitely invaded the field of public policy and are quick to declare unconstitutional almost any laws of which they disapprove, particularly in the fields of social and industrial legislation. The statement still repeated by the courts that laws will not be declared unconstitutional unless their repugnance to the constitution is clear beyond a reasonable doubt, seems now to have become "a mere courteous and smoothly transmitted platitude."[6]

. . . More striking still is the divergence between legal theory and current practice in the handling of persons suspected of crime. The "third degree" has become an every day feature of police investigation of crime. What is our law according to the books? "The prisoner," says Sir James Stephen, "is absolutely protected against all judicial questioning before or at the trial." "This," he adds, "contributes greatly to the dignity and apparent humanity of a criminal trial. It effectually avoids the appearance of harshness, not to say cruelty, which often shocks an English spectator in a French court of justice." Such is the legal rule. But prose-

1. *People v. Coler,* 116 N.Y. 1.
2. *People v. Lochner,* 177 N.Y. 145.
3. *U.S. v. Martin,* 94 U.S. 400.
4. *Lochner v. N.Y.,* 198 U.S. 45.
5. *Green Bag* XVII, 416.
6. The Growth of Judicial Power, *Pol. Sci. Quarterly,* XXIV, 193, 194.

cuting attorneys and police officers and police detectives do not hesitate to conduct the most searching, rigid and often brutal examinations of accused or suspected persons, with all the appearance of legality and of having the power of the state behind them. It is true, no rich man is ever subjected to this process to obtain proof of violation of anti-trust or rebate legislation and no powerful politician is thus dealt with in order to obtain proof of bribery and graft. The malefactor of means, the rogue who has an organization of rogues behind him to provide a lawyer and a writ of habeas corpus has the benefit of the law in the books. But the ordinary malefactor is bullied and even sometimes starved and tortured into confession by officers of the law. It is no doubt a sound instinct that makes us hesitate to give any such examinations the sanction of legality. We may agree with Sir James Stephen's informant that there is a deal of laziness behind it, that, to use his words, "it is far pleasanter to sit comfortably in the shade rubbing red pepper into a poor devil's eyes than to go about in the sun hunting up evidence." The fact remains, however, that the attempt of the books to compel prosecutors to use only a case-knife is failing. They will use the pick-axe in practice, and until the law has evolved some device by which they may use it in all cases the weak and friendless and lowly will be at a practical disadvantage, despite the legal theory. . . .

Another attempt at adjusting the letter of the law to the demands of administration in concrete cases, while apparently preserving the law unaltered, is to be seen in our American ritual, for in many jurisdictions it is little else, of written opinions, discussing and deducing from the precedents with great elaboration. As one reads the reports critically the conclusion is forced upon him that this ritual covers a deal of personal government by judges, a deal of "raw equity," or, as the Germans call it, of equitable application of law, and leaves many a soft spot in what is superficially a hard and fast rule, by means of which concrete causes are decided in practice as the good sense or feelings of fair play of the tribunal may dictate. One instance of this, in constitutional law, has been spoken of. Many others might be adduced from almost any department of private law. Let one suffice. In the law as to easements it is laid down that a right may be acquired by adverse user, although the known use was not objected to, if it was in fact, adverse. But the same courts say properly that a permissive user will give no right. When, however, one turns to the cases themselves and endeavors to fit each case in the scheme, not according to what the court said was the rule, but according to the facts of that case, he soon finds that the apparent rules to a great extent are no rules, and that where to allow the right would work a hardship the courts have discussed the decisions as to permissive user, and where, in the concrete cause, it seemed fair to grant the right they have insisted on the adverse character of the claimant's conduct. . . .

Settled habits of juristic thought are characteristic of American legal science. Our legal scholarship is historical and analytical. In either event it begins and ends substantially in Anglo-American case law. But the fundamental conceptions of that case law are by no means those of popular thought today. Nor is this condition in any way unique. "All sciences," wrote Ulrich Zäsius in 1520, "have put off their dirty clothes, only jurisprudence remains in her rags." . . .

Sometime in the future when a philosophical jurist writes upon the spirit of the common law, we may have a worthy account of the relation between Puritan theology and the common law. . . .

The fundamental proposition from which the Puritan proceeded was the doctrine that man was a free moral agent, with power to choose what he would do and a responsibility coincident with that power. He put individual conscience and individual judgment in the first place. No authority must be permitted to coerce them, but every one must assume and abide the consequences of the choice he was free to make. In its application this led to a regime of "consociation, but not subordination." "We are not over one another," said Robinson, "but with one another." Hence law was a device to secure liberty, its only justification was that it preserved individual liberty, and its sole basis was the free agreement of the individual to be bound by it. The early history of New England abounds in examples of attempts to make this a practical political doctrine. The good side of all this we know well. On the side of politics, the conception of the people—not as a mass, but as an aggregate of individuals—the precise ascription of rights to each of these individuals, the evolution of the legal rights of Englishmen into the natural rights of man, have their immediate origin in the religious phase of the Puritan revolution. But on the side of law it has given us the conception of liberty of contract, which is the bane of all labor legislation, the rooted objection to all power of application of rules to individual cases which has produced a decadence of equity in so many of our state courts, the insistence upon and faith in the mere machinery of justice which makes American legal procedure almost impossible of toleration in the business world of today, the notion of punishing the vicious will and of the necessary connection between wrongdoing and retribution which make it so difficult for our criminal law to deal with anti-social actions and to adjust itself in its application to the exigencies of concrete criminality.

Finally, our interpretation of jurisprudence and of legal history is either idealistic or political. Brooks Adams is the only American writer to insist upon the economic and social interpretation. But until we come to look at our legal history in this way, history on which our jurists rely chiefly is not unlikely to prove a blind guide. The history of juristic thought tells us nothing unless we know the social forces that lay behind it.

Demogue, Analysis of Fundamental Notions*

§200. *The Notion of Law Bound up with the Idea of a Continuous Protection of Varying Interests.* Whether a person has or has not a given right, is an idea which evidently has to do with a concern for the future. He who puts this question to himself, is interested in knowing what will happen, in case he does or does not do a certain act, and whether the consequences of his action or abstention will be advantageous to him. . . .

. . . If a given territory is usually devastated by storms or hail, if a certain business house is solidly established in a district in which it seems likely to hold its customers, if bands of evil-doers continually infest a particular region and are not molested, if public officials seek to injure one sort of enterprise and to aid another,—these are lasting facts of great importance. . . .

Among these probabilities which it is important to know should be classed the actions of strong, organized authorities. Composed of groups of men, they are stronger than isolated individuals, and more apt, also, to maintain their decisions, or those which have been made by their agents or representatives in their name. They have at once power and continuity. For the protection of interests, it is important to know the habits of these authorities, the result of which cannot be avoided. These habits may be expressed in different ways, as simple usages, as customs, or as rules which they have established for the future and which they observe.

When such a state of fact exists, when there is such a probably permanent situation, whether it is a result of the action of a powerful organized band, of a State, of force or of guile, of menace, ill-will, or the corruption of individuals, it produces a certain sequence in events which cannot be neglected.

In this zone of facts capable of arising because there are strong probabilities for them, lies the law,—that vague and fugitive notion which we are about to try to fix from the point of view of observation, then from that of the ideal. . . .

* [Vol. 6 of the Modern Legal Philosophy Series. Scott & Chamberlain, trans. New York: The Macmillan Company, 1916. Footnotes renumbered. Reprinted by permission.

René Demogue (1872-1938) gained international recognition after the publication in 1911 of his *Les Notions fondamentales du droit privé: Essai critique pour servir d'introduction à l'étude des obligations.*]

§201. *Realistically Defined, Law is that which is Imposed without Recourse by an Organized Force.* What must be understood by law from the point of view of observation alone? When does law exist? Law is that which is imposed by an organized force from which there is no appeal. Law is practically a synonym for social fact imposed if need be by coercion.[1] When a judgment regular in form and unappealable settles a point, it is law; so also when an administrative authority makes a decision which is unattackable or which has been fruitlessly attacked, or when a point is settled by a statute, which cannot be questioned according to our French notion, to the contrary of the American notion. This is the simple and most realistic idea of the law, that resulting from observation. . . .

§203. The ideas which we are here defending may be supported by the great authority of Jhering. "Law," says he, "exists for self-realization. Practical application is the life and the reality of law, it is law itself. That which does not find expression in real life, that which exists only in the statute books or on paper, is only a phantom of law—no more than words. On the contrary, that which takes effect as law is law, even if it is not on the statute book and the people and legal science have not yet recognized it as such."[2]

§204. *Law and Not-Law.* These statements, taken solely from observation, present to us the law in a somewhat different light from that in which it is usually shown. Obedient to the tendency of the human mind, which inclines toward simple categories, well marked frontiers, which unconsciously seeks security with a force of which we shall later have more to say, we are willing to believe that there are two distinct classes, one of illegal, one of legal, acts,[3] but we have a great deal of trouble in deciding in which class to put this or that act, and frequently end in doubt.

If we content ourselves with observing the facts, if we are interested less in simply following the tendencies of our minds than in presenting something more objective, our impressions are very different. Actual or possible facts appear as if ranged in an unbroken line between two extremes, legality and illegality. They are nearer to the limit of illegality in proportion to the interest taken by the organized forces in preventing or arresting them or in destroying the effect of their performance. They

1. Cf. Picard, *Le Droit Pur,* p. 40 and Alessandro Lévi, *La Société et l'Ordre Juridique* pp. 250 ff. Schatz very accurately says that where there is no force there is no law. *L'Individualisme Economique et Social,* p. 318. See in Mill the same idea, *Utilitarianism,* Chap. V.

2. *Geist des Römischen Rechts,* French ed., vol. iii. p. 15. (For this work see "Law as a Means to an End" in this Series, p. 455, Footnote.—Ed.) See in the same sense vol. i of this work, pp. 30 ff., where Jhering perhaps adds the embryo of a subjective idea by saying that law should be carried out as law.

3. In this sense see particularly Alessandro Lévi, *La Société et l'Ordre Juridique,* p. 100.

approach that of legality in proportion as the organized forces put in their way fewer obstacles, or afford more facilities for their accomplishment, consequently making individual resistance harder, and as these organized forces are directed by more stable wills, which are capable of more perseverance, of greater steadiness in conceptions, whose execution they are thus able to assure for a longer period.

The facts thus bring us to the conclusion that these two extremes, law and not-law, are of almost less importance from the point of view of the number of acts which can be directly classed under them, than are the intermediate situations.[4] If persons in authority change their minds, if written law or custom is modified, existing rights will be affected so far as they fall within the scope of the new order. Consequently, the law is a somewhat weak support for acts which are to continue over a long period such as are concerned in rights of property, companies, endowments, etc.; it can more be depended on for those which are to last but a short time, and which disappear almost as soon as they are done, for in such cases law is supported by the power force of inertia. Organized force is halted by the impossibility of reviewing all past acts, by the disorder which would ensue if it should be attempted by the difficulties which would be met with, and thus makes use of such expressions as limitations and the various other bars to actions. It thus accepts without question facts which have been accomplished in the past, though it would not tolerate the same thing at present, and this has always been so except for rare exceptions in periods frankly revolutionary. The force of circumstances, or better, the disproportion between effort and result, is, therefore, the strongest support of the principle of the non-retroactivity of laws.

We have thus explained that we have the law in our favor when our interest has received from an organized force, or, if it be preferred, a constituted authority, a guaranty on which it can depend as lasting.

Ehrlich, The Fundamental Principles of the Sociology of Law*

. . . Jurisprudence knows no scientific conception of law. Just as the structural engineer who deals with iron, if he speaks of iron, means not

---

4. Pascal certainly exaggerated when he said: "Force is easy to recognize and indisputable." This is not wholly, but very largely true; enough so for practical life, which must be contented with probabilities.

* [Chap. 1, pp. 6-8,15-16,17. Reprinted by permission of the publishers from Ehrlich: *Grundlegung der Soziologie des Rechts,* trans. by Walter L. Moll. Cambridge, Mass.: Harvard University Press, 1936.

the chemically pure substance that the chemist or mineralogist so characterizes, but rather the very impure iron that is used in building, so the jurist understands by law not that which lives and functions in human society as law but only (except for a few domains of public law) that which comes into view as law for the judge in his administration of justice.

From the judicial standpoint law is a rule according to which the judge has to decide the law-suits that are brought before him. . . . According to the definition which has prevailed in science especially in Germany, law would be a rule of human behavior. A rule of human behavior and a rule according to which a judge decides law-suits may be two very different things, for men certainly do not always behave in accordance with the same rules that are applied for the decision of their suits. The legal historian certainly conceives of law as a rule of human behavior; he portrays the rules according to which, in ancient times or in the middle ages, marriages were concluded, husband and wife, parent and child lived in the family, whether property was held individually or in common, whether the land of the owners was worked by rent-paying tenants or by serfs, and how bargains were concluded and goods inherited. One has the same experience if he requests a traveler who comes from a strange land to describe the law of the peoples that he has come to know. He will then relate how people there marry, live in the family, conclude transactions, but he will hardly come to tell how the rules sound according to which law-suits are decided.

This concept of law, which the jurist accepts quite automatically when he investigates the law of a strange people or a remote time with the interest of a pure scientist, he straightway renounces when he turns to the law in force in his own land and his own time. Quite unconsciously, underhandedly, so to say, the rule according to which men behave is turned into a rule according to which the behavior of men is judged by courts and magistrates. This is still a rule of behavior, but one only for a small section of the people, for the magistrates called upon to

---

Eugen Ehrlich (1862-1922), a distinguished Austrian jurist, taught at a number of Central European universities. He sought to establish a "sociology of law" based on the findings of the German historical jurists of the nineteenth century. Ehrlich envisioned a system in which the norms of "living law," rather than the codes, would furnish the primary material of judicial reference. The work from which the present excerpt is taken was originally published in 1913 as *Die Grundlegung der Soziologie des Rechts*. Other works of Ehrlich's include: *Freie Rechtsfindung und freie Rechtswissenschaft* (1903), which has been translated by E. Bruncken in part in *The Science of Legal Method* (Vol. 9, Modern Legal Philosophy Series, 1917); *Die Rechtsfähigkeit* (1909), (i.e., Legal Capacity); and *Die juristische Logik* (1918) (i.e., Juristic Logic).]

apply law, not, as formerly, for the broad general class. Instead of a scientific view there comes to the front simply the practical view fitted for those who hold judicial posts, and the official will still learn to know primarily the rules according to which he himself is to proceed. To be sure, the jurists still consider these rules to be rules of behavior, but there is manifestly a mental jump behind this. That is, they think that the rules according to which courts come to decisions are the rules according to which men *ought* to behave; and there is associated with this the dim thought that men will in time govern themselves by those rules according to which courts decide cases. Now a rule of behavior is self evidently a rule to which behavior not only conforms but also ought to conform, but the assumption that courts determine cases exclusively or even mainly upon the basis of this *Ought* is quite inadmissible; everyday experience teaches the contrary. That judicial decisions are of influence upon the actual behavior of men will certainly not be disputed, but one would still have to discover how far this is applicable and upon what circumstances it depends.

Every page of a juristic work, every juristic lecture affirms what has just been said. Almost every word shows that to the jurist, who deals with a jural relation, there is always but one question to be considered, namely how the conflicts which arise out of this jural relation are to be decided, and not the quite distinct question of how men conduct themselves and must conduct themselves in this relation. Even a man of the greatness of Maitland could say that to write the history of English actions was to write the history of English law. . . .

. . . For one, however, who sees in law primarily a rule of conduct, the coercion involved in punishment as well as that in the execution of judgments necessarily falls into the background. For him, human life is not enacted before courts. A moment's observation teaches him that every man stands in countless legal relationships and that with very few exceptions he does quite of his own accord what is obligatory upon him in these relationships; he fulfills his duties as father and son, as husband or wife, he refrains from disturbing his neighbor in the latter's enjoyment of his property, he pays his debts, delivers what he has sold, performs that for which he has bound himself to his employer. The jurist always has the reply ready that men do their duty only because they know that in any case they could be forced to do it by the courts. But if he would only take the unfamiliar trouble of observing men in their activities he would easily convince himself that for the most part they do not think at all of the coercion of courts. So far as they do not do what is naturally according to the rule of the situation, they give quite different reasons for their decisions: they might, if they acted differently, fall out with their dependents, lose their positions and trade, and get the reputation of a quarrelsome, dishonorable, unreliable man. But this fact, at least, even the jurist ought not to have ignored, namely that what men do as their legal duties in this sense of the word is often something quite different from, and sometimes something much more than, what they can be compelled by the authorities to do. Not infrequently the rule of conduct is entirely distinct from the enforceable rule. . . .

. . . Order in human society rests upon the fact that obligations in general are fulfilled, not on the fact that they are actionable.

F. S. Cohen, Transcendental Nonsense and the Functional Approach*

1. The Definition of Law

The starting point of functional analysis in American jurisprudence is found in Justice Holmes' definition of law as "prophecies of what the courts will do in fact." It is in "The Path of the Law,"[71] that this realistic conception of law is first clearly formulated:

> If you want to know the law and nothing else, you must look at it as a bad man, who cares only for the material consequences which such knowledge enables him to predict, not as a good one, who finds his reasons for conduct, whether inside the law or outside of it, in the vaguer sanctions of conscience. . . . Take the fundamental question, What constitutes the law? You will find some text writers telling you that it is

---

* [35 *Colum. L. Rev.* 809, 835-842 (1935). Reprinted by permission.

Felix S. Cohen (1907-1953) contributed to three broad areas of thought: law and philosophy, Indian problems, and democracy in action. His original interest and training in philosophy grew into a broad interest in ethics as applied to law and legal problems. During his fifteen years on the Solicitor's Staff of the Department of the Interior, he prepared numerous persuasive legal briefs. Felix Cohen was also a teacher of law and philosophy at Yale University Law School, the City College of New York, Rutgers Law School, and the New School for Social Research. His published books include *Ethical Systems and Legal Ideals* (1933), *Handbook of Federal Indian Law* (1941), and *Readings in Jurisprudence and Legal Philosophy* (1951). For a collection of Cohen's unpublished works, see *The Legal Conscience* (Lucy Kramer Cohen ed. 1960).]

71. Holmes, Path of the Law (1897) 10 *Harv. L. Rev.* 457, 459-461; *Collected Legal Papers* (1921) p. 167, 171-173. A more precise definition, following Holmes, is given in C. J. Keyser, On the Study of Legal Science (1929) 38 *Yale L.J.* 413.

something different from what is decided by the courts of Massachusetts or England, that it is a system of reason, that it is a deduction from principles of ethics or admitted axioms or what not, which may or may not coincide with the decisions. But if we take the view of our friend the bad man we shall find that he does not care two straws for the axioms or deductions, but that he does want to know what the Massachusetts or English courts are likely to do in fact. I am much of his mind. The prophecies of what the courts will do in fact, and nothing more pretentious, are what I mean by the law.

A good deal of fruitless controversy has arisen out of attempts to show that this definition of law as the way courts actually decide cases is either true or false.[72] A definition of law is *useful* or *useless*. It is not *true* or *false,* any more than a New Year's resolution or an insurance policy. A definition is in fact a type of insurance against certain risks of confusion. It cannot, any more than can a commercial insurance policy, eliminate all risks. Absolute certainty is as foreign to language as to life. There is no final insurance against an insurer's insolvency. And the words of a definition always carry their own aura of ambiguity. But a definition is useful if it insures against risks of confusion more serious than any that the definition itself contains.

"What courts do" is not entirely devoid of ambiguity. There is room for disagreement as to what a *court* is, whether, for instance, the Inter-

---

72. For examples of such argument see Dickinson, Legal Rules: Their Function in the Process of Decision (1931) 79 *U. of Pa. Law Rev.* 833; H. Kantorowicz, Some Rationalism about Realism (1934) 43 *Yale L.J.* 1240; Frank, *Law and The Modern Mind* (1930) 127-128. The vicious circle in Dickinson's attempted refutation of the realistic definition of law I have elsewhere analyzed. See F. S. Cohen, *Ethical Systems and Legal Ideals* (1933) 12, n. 16. Kantorowicz repeats the same argument, emphasizing the charge that a definition of law in terms of court decisions "puts the cart before the horse" and is as ridiculous as a definition of medicine in terms of the behavior of doctors. The parallel, though witty, is inapt: The correct analogy to a definition of the science of law as description of the behavior of judges would be a definition of the science of medicine as a description of the behavior of certain parasites, etc. Kantorowicz accepts uncritically the metaphysical assumption that definition is a one-way passage from the more general to the less general. But modern logic has demonstrated the hollowness of this assumption. It is useful for certain purposes to define points as functions of lines. For other purposes it is useful to define lines as functions of points. It is just as logical to define law in terms of courts as the other way about. The choice is a matter of convenience, not of logic or truth.

The same metaphysical fallacy vitiates the opposite argument of Frank, namely, that "primary" reality is particular and concrete, so that a definition of law must necessarily be in terms of actual decisions. To the eyes of modern logic, the world contains things *and* relations, neither of which can claim a superior grade of reality. One can start a fight or a scientific inquiry *either* with a concrete fact *or* with a general principle.

state Commerce Commission or the Hague Tribunal or the Council of Tesuque Pueblo is a court, and whether a judge acting in excess of those powers which the executive arm of the government will recognize acts as a court. There may even be disagreement as to the line of distinction between what courts *do* and what courts *say,* in view of the fact that most judicial behavior is verbal. But these sources of ambiguity in Holmes' definition of law are peripheral rather than central, and easily remedied. They are, therefore, far less dangerous sources of confusion than the basic ambiguity inherent in classical definitions of law which involve a confusion between what is and what ought to be.

The classical confusion against which realistic jurisprudence is a protest is exemplified in Blackstone's classical definition of law as "a rule of civil conduct, prescribed by the supreme power in a State, commanding what is right, and prohibiting what is wrong."[73]

In this definition we have an attempt to unite two incompatible ideas which, in the tradition of English jurisprudence, are most closely associated with the names of Hobbes and Coke, respectively.

Hobbes, the grandfather of realistic jurisprudence, saw in law the commands of a body to whom private individuals have surrendered their force. In a state of nature there is war of all against all. In order to achieve peace and security, each individual gives up something of his freedom, something of his power, and the commands of the collective power, that is the state, constitute law.

Hobbes' theory of law has been very unpopular with respectable citizens, but I venture to think that most of the criticism directed against it, in the last two and a half centuries, has been based upon a misconception of what Hobbes meant by a state of nature. So far as I know, Hobbes never refers to the state of nature as an actual historical era, at the end of which men came together and signed a social contract. The state of nature is a stage in analysis rather than a stage of history. It exists today and has always existed, to a greater or lesser degree, in various realms of human affairs. To the extent that any social relationship is exempt from governmental control it presents what Hobbes calls a state of nature.

In international relations today, at least to the extent that nations have not effectively surrendered their power through compacts establishing such rudimentary agencies of international government as the League of Nations or the Universal Postal Union, there is in fact a state of nature and a war of all against all. This war, as Hobbes insists, is present potentially before actual hostilities break out. Not only in international relations, but in industrial relations today do we find war of all

73. *Bl. Comm.* * 44.

against all, in regions to which governmental control has not been extended, or from which it has been withdrawn—if it existed.

Mutual concessions and delegations of power involved in an arbitration contract, an international treaty, an industrial "code," a corporate merger, or a collective labor agreement, are steps in the creation of government, and call into operation new rules of law and new agencies of law enforcement. Governments do not arise once and for all. Government is arising today in many regions of social existence, and it arises wherever individuals find the conflicts inherent in a state of nature unendurable. The process by which government is created and its commands formulated is a process of human bargaining, based upon actual consent but weighted by the relative power of conflicting individuals or groups.

In all this conception of law, there is no appeal to reason or goodness. Law commands obedience not because of its goodness, or its justice, or its rationality, but because of the power behind it. While this power does rest to a real extent upon popular beliefs about the value of certain legal ideals, it remains true today, as Hobbes says in his *Dialogue on the Common Law,* "In matter of government, when nothing else is turned up, clubs are trump."[74]

Quite different from this realistic conception of law is the theroy made famous by Coke that law is only the perfection of reason.[75] This is a notion which has had considerable force in American constitutional history, having served first as a basis for popular revolution against tyrannical violations of "natural law" and the "natural rights" of Englishmen, and serving more recently as a judicial ground for denying legality to statutes that judges consider "unreasonable." It would be absurd to deny the importance of this concept of natural law or justice as a standard by which to judge the acts of rulers, legislative, executive or judicial. It is clear, however, that the validity of this concept of law lies in a realm of values, which is not identical with the realm of social actualities.

The confusion and ambiguity which infest the classical conception of law, as formulated by Blackstone and implicitly accepted by most modern legal writers, arise from the attempt to throw together two inconsistent ideas. Blackstone attempts in effect to superimpose the picture of law drawn by the tender-minded hypocrite, Coke, upon the picture executed by the tough-minded cynic, Hobbes, and to give us a

74. Hobbes, *Dialogue Between a Philosopher and a Student of the Common Laws of England* (1681), Of Punishments.

75. *Co. Litt.* ★ 976.

composite photograph. Law, says Blackstone, is "a rule of civil conduct prescribed by the supreme power in a State (Hobbes speaking) commanding what is right and prohibiting what is wrong (Coke speaking)." [76] Putting these two ideas together, we have a fertile source of confusion, which many important legal scholars since Blackstone have found about as useful in legal polemics as the ink with which a cuttlefish befuddles his enemies.

Those theorists who adhere to the Blackstonian definition of law are able to spin legal theories to the heart's content without fear of refutation. If legislatures or courts disagree with a given theory, it is a simple matter to show that this disagreement is unjust, unreasonable, monstrous and, therefore, not "sound law." On the other hand, the intruding moralist who objects to a legal doctrine on the ground that it is unjust or undesirable can be told to go back to the realm of morality he came from, since the law is the command of the sovereign and not a matter of moral theory. Perhaps the chief usefulness of the Blackstonian theory is the gag it places upon legal criticism. Obviously, if the law is something that commands what is right and prohibits what is wrong, it is impossible to argue about the goodness or badness of any law, and any definition that deters people from criticism of the law is very useful to legal apologists for the existing order of society. As a modern authority on legal reason declares, "Thus all things made legal are at the same time legally ethical because it is law, and the law must be deemed ethical or the system itself must perish." [77]

2. The Nature of Legal Rules and Concepts

If the functionalists are correct, the meaning of a definition is found in its consequences. The definition of a general term like "law" is significant only because it affects all our definitions of specific legal concepts.

The consequence of defining law as a function of concrete judicial decisions is that we may proceed to define such concepts as "contract," "property," "title," "corporate personality," "right," and "duty," similarly as functions of concrete judicial decisions.

The consequence of defining law as a hodge-podge of political force and ethical value ambiguously amalgamated is that every legal concept, rule or question will present a similar ambiguity.

Consider the elementary legal question: "Is there a contract?"

---

76. That "right" and "wrong" are used in this definition as ethical, rather than strictly legal, terms is made clear in Blackstone's own exegesis upon his definition. *Comm.* ★ 54-55.
77. Brumbaugh, *Legal Reasoning and Briefing* (1917), 7.

When the realist asks this question, he is concerned with the actual behavior of courts. For the realist, the contractual relationship, like law in general, is a function of legal decisions. The question of what courts *ought* to do is irrelevant here. Where there is a promise that will be legally enforced there is a contract. So conceived, any answer to the question "Is there a contract" must be in the nature of a prophecy, based, like other prophecies, upon past and present facts. So conceived, the question "Is there a contract?" or for that matter any other legal question, may be broken up into a number of subordinate questions, each of which refers to the actual behavior of courts: (1) What courts are likely to pass upon a given transaction and its consequences? (2) What elements in this transaction will be viewed as relevant and important by these courts? (3) How have these courts dealt with transactions in the past which are *similar* to the given transaction, that is, *identical in those respects which the court will regard as important?* (4) What forces will tend to compel judicial conformity to the precedents that appear to be in point (e.g. inertia, conservatism, knowledge of the past, or intelligence sufficient to acquire such knowledge, respect for predecessors, superiors or brothers on the bench, a habit of deference to the established expectations of the bar or the public) and how strong are these forces? (5) What factors will tend to evoke new judicial treatment for the transaction in question (e.g. changing public opinion, judicial idiosyncrasies and prejudices, newly accepted theories of law, society or economics, or the changing social context of the case) and how powerful are these factors?

These are the questions which a successful practical lawyer faces and answers in any case. The law, as the realistic lawyer uses the term, is the body of answers to such questions. The task of prediction involves, in itself, no judgment of ethical value. Of course, even the most cynical practitioner will recognize that the positively existing ethical beliefs of judges are material facts in any case because they determine what facts the judge will view as important and what past rules he will regard as reasonable or unreasonable and worthy of being extended or restricted. But judicial beliefs about the values of life and the ideals of society are *facts,* just as the religious beliefs of the Andaman Islanders are facts, and the truth or falsity of such moral beliefs is a matter of complete unconcern to the practical lawyer, as to the scientific observer.

Washed in cynical acid, every legal problem can thus be interpreted as a question concerning the positive behavior of judges.

There is a second and radically different meaning which can be given to our type question, "Is there a contract?" When a judge puts this question, in the course of writing his opinion, he is not attempting to predict his own behavior. He is in effect raising the question, in an obscure way, of whether or not liability *should* be attached to certain acts. This is inescapably an ethical question. What a judge ought to do in a given case is quite as much a moral issue as any of the traditional problems of Sunday School morality.[78]

It is difficult for those who still conceive of morality in other-worldly terms to recognize that every case presents a moral question to the court. But this notion has no terrors for those who think of morality in earthly terms. Morality, so conceived, is vitally concerned with such facts as human expectations based upon past decisions, the stability of economic transactions, and even the maintenance of order and simplicity in our legal system. If ethical values are inherent in all realms of human conduct, the ethical appraisal of a legal situation is not to be found in the spontaneous outpourings of a sensitive conscience unfamiliar with the social context, the background of precedent, and the practices and expectations, legal and extra-legal, which have grown up around a given type of transaction.

It is the great disservice of the classical conception of law that it hides from judicial eyes the ethical character of every judicial question, and thus serves to perpetuate class prejudices and uncritical moral assumptions which could not survive the sunlight of free ethical controversy.

The Blackstonian conception of law as half-mortal and half-divine gives us a mythical conception of contract. When a master of classical jurisprudence like Williston asks the question "Is there a contract?", he has in mind neither the question of scientific prediction which the practical lawyer faces, nor the question of values which the conscientious judge faces. If he had in mind the former question, his studies would no doubt reveal the extent to which courts actually enforce various types of contractual obligation.[79] His conclusions would be in terms of probability and statistics. On the other hand, if Professor Williston were interested in the ethical aspects of contractual liability, he would undoubtedly offer a significant account of the human values and social costs involved in different types of agreements and in the means of their enforcement. In

---

78. Cf. F. S. Cohen, *Modern Ethics and the Law* (1934) 4 *Brooklyn L. Rev.* 33 on the conception of "Sunday School morality."

79. So hallowed is the juristic tradition of ignoring the actual facts of cases that a distinguished jurist, Professor Goodheart, can argue in all seriousness that the practice adopted by some American law libraries of putting the records of cases on file is very dangerous. Students might be distracted from the official ratio decidendi of the case, and might try to discover what the actual facts of the case were, which would be a death-blow to traditional jurisprudence. See Goodheart, Determining Ratio Decidendi of a Case (1930) 40 *Yale L.J.* 161, 172.

fact, however, the discussions of a Williston will oscillate between a theory of what courts actually do and a theory of what courts ought to do, without coming to rest either on the plane of social actualities or on the plane of values long enough to come to grips with significant problems. This confused wandering between the world of fact and the world of justice vitiates every argument and every analysis.

Intellectual clarity requires that we carefully distinguish between the two problems of (1) objective description, and (2) critical judgment, which classical jurisprudence lumps under the same phrase. Such a distinction realistic jurisprudence offers with the double-barreled thesis: (1) that every legal rule or concept is simply a function of judicial decisions to which all questions of value are irrelevant, and (2) that the problem of the judge is not whether a legal rule or concept actually exists but whether it *ought* to exist. Clarity on two fronts is the result. Description of legal facts becomes more objective, and legal criticism becomes more critical.

The realistic lawyer, when he attempts to discover how courts are actually dealing with certain situations, will seek to rise above his own moral bias and to discount the moral bias of the legal author whose treatise he consults.

The realistic author of textbooks will not muddy his descriptions of judicial behavior with wishful thinking; if he dislikes a decision or line of decisions, he will refrain from saying, "This cannot be the law because it is contrary to sound principle," and say instead, "This is the law, but I don't like it," or more usefully, "This rule leads to the following results, which are socially undesirable for the following reasons. . . ."

The realistic advocate, if he continues to use ritual language in addressing an unrealistic court, will at least not be fooled by his own words: he will use his "patter" to induce favorable judicial attitudes and at the same time to distract judicial attention from precedents and facts that look the wrong way (as the professional magician uses his "patter" to distract the attention of his audience from certain facts). Recognizing the circularity of conceptual argument, the realistic advocate will contrive to bring before the court the human values that favor his cause, and since the rules of evidence often stand in the way, he will perforce bring his materials to judicial attention by sleight-of-hand—through the appeal of a "sociological brief" to "judicial notice," through discussion of the background and consequences of past cases cited as precedents, through elaboration and exegesis upon admissible evidence, or even through a political speech or a lecture on economics in the summation of his case or argument.

The realistic judge, finally, will not fool himself or anyone else by basing decisions upon circular reasoning from the presence or absence of corporations, conspiracies, property rights, titles, contracts, proximate causes, or other legal derivatives of the judicial decision itself. Rather, he will frankly assess the conflicting human values that are opposed in every controversy, appraise the social importance of the precedents to which each claim appeals, open the courtroom to all evidence that will bring light to this delicate practical task of social adjustment, and consign to Von Jhering's heaven of legal concepts all attorneys whose only skill is that of the conceptual acrobat.

M. R. Cohen, On Absolutisms in
Legal Thought*

I. Logical Phase of Legal Absolutism

Absolutism in Definition

Let us begin by considering the vices of legal absolutism from the point of view of logic. The first manifestation of absolutism that suggests itself is the complacent assumption that there can be only one true or correct definition of any object. This assumption underlies the traditional controversies as to the nature of law and Kant's[1] famous reproach to jurists on this score. Yet on consulting any scholarly dictionary we can readily see that few words in common use have only one meaning. This should warn us that in controversies as to the proper definition of a term, the contestants, while using the same word (*definiendum*) may be really concerned with different things (*definiens*). Consider, for instance, Maine's[1a] criticism of Austin's[2] definition of law as an imperative or command of the sovereign. In substance Maine's objection is that there are

---

* [From *Reason and Law,* Chap. 3, pp. 65-67, 68 Glencoe, Ill.: The Free Press, 1950. The substance of this article appeared in 84 *U. Pa. L. Rev.* 681 (1936), under the title "On Absolutisms in Legal Thought." Reprinted by permission.

Morris Raphael Cohen (1880-1947), an American naturalistic philosopher, was born in Minsk, Russia. Cohen graduated from the City College of New York in 1900 and received his Ph.D. from Harvard University in 1906. Cohen was a pioneer in introducing legal philosophy as a significant study to universities and law schools. For Cohen, law is essentially a system for the orderly regulation of social action. Cohen's works include: *Reason and Nature: An Essay on the Meaning of the Scientific Method* (1931); *Law and the Social Order: Essays in Legal Philosophy* (1933); *An Introduction to Logic and the Scientific Method* (1934); *A Preface to Logic* (1945); *The Meaning of Human History* (1947); *A Dreamer's Journey* (1949); *Studies in Philosophy and Science* (1949); and *Reason and Law: Studies in Juristic Philosophy* (1950).]

1. *Kritik der reinen Vernunft* (5th ed. 1797) 759A note.

1a. Maine, *Lectures on Early History of Institutions* (1875), lectures 12 and 13.

2. 1 Austin, *Lectures on Jurisprudence* (2d ed. 1869) 15, 118, 120.

communities in which there is no one who habitually issues commands that are generally obeyed, and yet conduct in them is governed by some law. Now the word *law* is, doubtless, used to denote the customs according to which the members of certain primitive communities generally conduct their lives. But this is no objection at all to Austin's analysis of the law found in classical Rome and in modern civilized states. In the latter we certainly do find lawmaking bodies which abrogate certain customs, such as rebating or overcertification, and create new ones, such as those connected with income tax returns. It is not necessary for my present purpose to defend the complete adequacy of Austin's theory, but merely to note that Maine does not really refute the given definition when he shows that the word *law* is also used in another sense than that employed by Austin. Of course, the objects of these two senses are connected, and one may well contend that law in Austin's sense could not exist without law in Maine's sense, that is, that there could be no sovereign whose orders are generally obeyed unless there were certain more general customs actually prevailing, so that the phenomenon to which Austin refers is thus sociologically derivative and not primary. But while this statement may be true, those who make it are generally guilty of the genetic fallacy of the identification of a thing with its cause or condition. Law may be derived from custom but is obviously not identical with it. The law which is studied in our law schools, administered in our courts and about which men consult lawyers or agitate in the political forum for legislative changes is not the same as custom. The late Mr. Carter, who identified law and custom,[3] had the courage of his confusion and argued that judges are experts in the customs of the various subjects on which they have to rule. But no one else has taken that consequence of the theory seriously. Yet, the failure to distinguish clearly between law and custom underlies all the assumptions of Ehrlich's *Living Law*.[4] There are obviously many practices which actually prevail but are not recognized or enforced by the legal machinery, e.g., the practice of tipping waiters; and there are, on the other hand, laws regulating acts which are in no significant sense customary, e.g., the rules governing testamentary dispositions or equitable conversion. Indeed legal prescriptions through legislation are necessary precisely because custom proves inadequate to regulate our social relations satisfactorily.

Following Ehrlich, my friend Professor Llewellyn has argued with great force that court litigation represents only the pathology of law, the divergence from the normal practice. The converse of that proposition, however, cannot well be denied. Modern business practice is undoubt-

3. Carter, *Law: Its Origin, Growth and Function* (1907) 79.
4. Ehrlich, *Grundlegung der Soziologie des Rechts*, c. 21.

edly moulded by past and expected court litigation, by legislative enactments and by administrative orders. That is what gives point to political struggles to control the organs of government.

Law as custom and law through deliberate legislation are thus both realities and we cannot by an arbitrary definition disprove the existence of one or of the other. The important thing is rather to unravel their actual interrelations, and that cannot be done by a mere definition.

It may seem trite, but it is important to insist that while there is an arbitrary element in all definitions, the question of their truth or correctness cannot be altogether dismissed. If we ignore the facts of actual historic usage, a definition is a resolution to use a word as a sign or symbol for a certain object and involves no necessary assumption that the object exists in nature. If we do not like a word in common use we can always invent a new one to denote the particular object we have in mind. In organizing a theoretic system such as geometry we are also free to choose our indefinables and our definitions will then vary according to this choice. We cannot, however, safely ignore the question of consistency in our use of words and this involves (1) attention to the meanings which our words in fact actually convey to our public and to ourselves and (2) the fact that definitions must serve a definite function in any scientific system.

(1) There can be no doubt that departures from general usage do lead to inconsistencies and confusion. For common usage is a habit and the resolution to use a word in a new sense is, like any other resolution, more easily made than kept. In point of fact, therefore, whenever we define a word like law, crime, marriage, person, or the like, in a manner that departs from current customary usage, we sooner or later unwittingly fall back on the common use and thus confuse the meaning of our terms. Regard, therefore, for common usage is a counsel of prudence or practical wisdom. . . .

(2) Definitions, while not absolutely necessary in pure mathematics, are practically indispensable in all sciences or responsible discourse. They can help us to grasp more clearly the fundamental ideas or patterns in any field of study and thus serve to create a definite point of view or perspective for the organization of our subject matter. In this respect some definitions are certainly more helpful than others.

From this point of view we must condemn all definitions of law (or of parts of it, e.g., the criminal law) as that which is right, just, expresses the will of the majority, safeguards the social welfare or security, etc. For the historic complaints so bitterly and persistently made against the law raise issues of fact which cannot be properly disposed of by a mere definition. When any one says that an unjust law is not a law, that a legislative enactment is not a law unless it is the will of the majority, or that a provision of the criminal code is not a law if it does not in fact promote the safety of the community, he is resorting to a violent use of words to escape the problem of considering the factual elements in the case.

The law about which we shall be concerned in what follows is that with which judges, lawyers and law schools are concerned, i.e., with rules of conduct determinable by courts. That is what we commonly have in mind when we speak of the law of bankruptcy, divorce, etc., in any state; and our discussion of what is involved in a definition of law is thus only an illustration or paradigm of what is involved in the definition of any legal institution of property, contract, and the like, on which actual decisions depend.*

Hart, Definition and Theory in Jurisprudence†

I

In law as elsewhere, we can know and yet not understand. Shadows often obscure our knowledge which not only vary in intensity but are

---

* [To what extent do the various definitions of law given in the preceding pages represent mutually incompatible beliefs as to the characteristics of an agreed entity? To what extent are the authors listed simply talking about different things under the same term, "law," as Ehrlich suggests? Do such differences in the use of terms reflect any significant conflicts of valuation or interest?

Under which, if any, of the definitions of law given supra would the following provide a rule of law?

1. The provision in the federal constitution (Art. I, §3) requiring Congress to reapportion representatives every decade.

2. The provision in the Clayton Act (38 Stat. 730, C. 323, §8, 1914) forbidding interlocking directorates but providing no penalties for infraction.

3. A criminal statute the infringers of which are beyond the reach of the law (e.g., against successful suicide).

4. A criminal statute under which juries regularly refuse to convict, but according to which judicial instructions are framed.

5. A criminal statute under which no prosecutions are attempted.

6. A custom of juries to assess damages in negligence cases upon due consideration of the defendant's wealth.

7. A judicial custom of issuing injunction against defamation only when defendants are labor unions.

8. The rule that legal malice is a condition of liability for libel.

9. The rule that a man's real property extends to the center of the earth.

10. A practice in the lower courts of a state to enjoin peaceful picketing, regularly held lawful by the highest court.]

† [*Definition and Theory in Jurisprudence* (Inaugural Lecture at Oxford University, 1953) by H. L. A. Hart. Reprinted by permission of Oxford University Press.

cast by different obstacles to light. These cannot all be removed by the same methods and till the precise character of our perplexity is determined we cannot tell what tools we shall need.

The perplexities I propose to discuss are voiced in those questions of analytical jurisprudence which are usually characterised as requests for definitions: What is law? What is a State? What is a right? What is possession? I choose this topic because it seems to me that the common mode of definition is ill-adapted to the law and has complicated its exposition; its use has, I think, led at certain points to a divorce between jurisprudence and the study of the law at work, and has helped to create the impression that there are certain fundamental concepts that the lawyer cannot hope to elucidate without entering a forbidding jungle of philosophical argument. I wish to suggest that this is not so; that legal notions however fundamental can be elucidated by methods properly adapted to their special character. Such methods were glimpsed by our predecessors but have only been fully understood and developed in our own day.

Questions such as those I have mentioned "What is a State?" "What is law?" "What is a right?" have great ambiguity. The same form of words may be used to demand a definition or the cause or the purpose or the justification or the origin of a legal or political institution. But if, in the effort to free them from this risk of confusion with other questions, we rephrase these requests for definitions as "What is the meaning of the word 'State'?" "What is the meaning of the word 'right'?," those who ask are apt to feel uneasy as if this had trivialised their question. For what they want cannot be got out of a dictionary and this transformation of their question suggests it can. This uneasiness is the expression of an instinct which deserves respect: it emphasises the fact that those who ask these questions are not asking to be taught how to use these words in the correct way. This they know and yet are still puzzled. Hence it is no answer to this type of question merely to tender examples of what are cor-

---

Herbert Lionel Adolphus Hart (1907–   ) was educated at New College, Oxford. In 1932-1940 Hart was engaged in legal practice before the Chancery Bar. During World War II Hart served in the Ministry of War. Hart's academic career began after the war, in 1945, when he became a fellow and tutor at New College, Oxford. In 1952 he was elected Professor of Jurisprudence and became a fellow at University College. Hart resigned his professorship in 1968 to devote more time to his scholarly pursuits, among which was the preparation of a complete edition of the collected works of Jeremy Bentham. He is currently Principal of Brasenose College, Oxford. Among Hart's other significant works are *Causation in the Law* (with A. M. Honore, 1959), *The Concept of Law* (1961), and *Punishment and Responsibility* (1968). These works and others have established Hart as the foremost contemporary legal positivist. For further information on H. L. A. Hart and his works, see G. Christie, *Jurisprudence* 634-639 (1973).]

rectly called rights, laws, or corporate bodies, and to tell the questioner if he is still puzzled that he is free to abandon the public convention and use words as he pleases. For the puzzle arises from the fact that though the common use of these words is known it is not understood; and it is not understood because compared with most ordinary words these legal words are in different ways anomalous. Sometimes, as with the word "law" itself, one anomaly is that the range of cases to which it is applied has a diversity which baffles the initial attempt to extract any principle behind the application, yet we have the conviction that even here there is some principle and not an arbitrary convention underlying the surface differences; so that whereas it would be patently absurd to ask for elucidation of the principle in accordance with which different men are called Tom, it is not felt absurd to ask why, within municipal law the immense variety of different types of rules are called law, nor why municipal law and international law, in spite of striking differences, are so called.

But in this and other cases, we are puzzled by a different and more troubling anomaly. The first efforts to define words like "corporation" "right" or "duty" reveal that these do not have the straightforward connection with counterparts in the world of fact which most ordinary words have and to which we appeal in our definition of ordinary words. There is nothing which simply "corresponds" to these legal words and when we try to define them we find that the expressions we tender in our definition specifying kinds of persons, things, qualities, events, and processes, material or psychological, are never precisely the equivalent of these legal words though often connected with them in some way. This is most obvious in the case of expressions for corporate bodies and is commonly put by saying that a corporation is not a series or aggregate of persons. But it is true of other legal words. Though one who has a right usually has some expectation or power the expression "a right" is not synonymous with words like "expectation" or "power" even if we add "based on law" or "guaranteed by law." And so too, though we speak of men having duties to do or abstain from certain actions the word "duty" does not stand for or describe anything as ordinary words do. It has an altogether different function which makes the stock form of definition, "a duty is a . . . ," seem quite inappropriate.

These are genuine difficulties and in part account for something remarkable: that out of these innocent requests for definitions of fundamental legal notions there should have arisen vast and irreconcilable theories so that not merely whole books but whole schools of juristic thought may be characterised by the type of answer they give to questions like "What is a right?" or "What is a corporate body?" This alone, I think, suggests that something is wrong with the approach to definition; can we really not elucidate the meaning of words which every developed legal system handles smoothly and alike without assuming this incubus of theory? And the suspicion that something is amiss is confirmed by certain characteristics that many such theories have. In the first place they fall disquietingly often into a familiar triad.[2] Thus the American Realists striving to give us an answer in terms of plain fact tell us that a right is a term by which we describe the prophecies we make of the probable behaviour of courts or officials; the Scandinavian jurists after dealing the Realist theory blows that might well be thought fatal (if these matters were strictly judged) say that a right is nothing real at all but an ideal or fictitious or imaginary power, and then join with their opponents to denigrate the older type of theory that a right is an "objective reality"—an invisible entity existing apart from the behaviour of men. These theories are in form similar to the three great theories of corporate personality, each of which has dealt deadly blows to the other. There too we have been told by turn that the name of a corporate body like a limited company or an organisation like the State is really just a collective name or abbreviation for some complex but still plain facts about ordinary persons, or alternatively that it is the name of a fictitious person, or that on the contrary it is the name of a real person existing with a real will and life, but not a body of its own. And this same triad of theories has haunted the jurist even when concerned with relatively minor notions. Look for example at Austin's discussion of status and you will find that the choice lies for him between saying that it is a mere collective name for a set of special rights and duties, or that it is an "ideal" or "fictitious" basis for these rights and duties, or that it is an "occult quality" in the person who has the status, distinguishable both from the rights and duties and from the facts engendering them.

Secondly. Though these theories spring from the effort to define notions actually involved in the practice of a legal system they rarely throw light on the precise work they do there. They seem to the lawyer to stand apart with their head at least in the clouds; and hence it is that

2. The general form of this recurrent triad may be summarily described as follows. Theories of one type tell us that a word stands for some unexpected variant of the familiar —a complex fact where we expect something unified and simple, a future fact where we expect something present, a psychological fact where we expect something external; theories of the second type tell us that a word stands for what is in some sense a fiction; theories of a third (now unfashionable) type, tell us the word stands for something different from other things just in that we cannot touch it, hear it, see it, feel it.

very often the use of such terms in a legal system is neutral between competing theories. For that use "can be reconciled with any theory, but is authority for none."

Thirdly. In many of these theories there is often an amalgam of issues that should be distinguished. It is of course clear that the assertion that corporate bodies are real persons and the counterassertion that they are fictions of the law were often not the battle cries of analytical jurists. They were ways of asserting or denying the claims of organised groups to recognition by the State. But such claims have always been confused with the baffling analytical question "What is a corporate body?" so that the classification of such theories as Fiction or Realist or Concessionist is a criss-cross between logical and political criteria. So too the American Realist theories have much to tell us of value about the judicial process and how small a part deduction from predetermined premises may play in it, but the lesson is blurred when it is presented as a matter of definition of "law" or "a right"; not only analytical jurisprudence but every sort of jurisprudence suffers by this confusion of aim.

Hence though theory is to be welcomed, the growth of theory on the back of definition is not. Theories so grown, indeed represent valuable efforts to account for many puzzling things in law; and among these is the great anomaly of legal language—our inability to define its crucial words in terms of ordinary factual counterparts. But here I think they largely fail because their method of attack commits them all, in spite of their mutual hostility, to a form of answer that can only distort the distinctive characteristics of legal language.

II

Long ago Bentham issued a warning that legal words demanded a special method of elucidation and he enunciated a principle that is the beginning of wisdom in this matter though it is not the end. He said we must never take these words alone, but consider whole sentences in which they play their characteristic role. We must take not the *word* "right" but the sentence "You have a right" not the *word* "State" but the sentence "He is a member or an official of the State." His warning has largely been disregarded and jurists have continued to hammer away at single words. This may be because he hid the product of his logical insight behind technical terms of his own invention "Archetypation," "Phraseoplerosis," and the rest; it may also be because his further suggestions were not well adapted to the peculiarities of legal language which as part of the works of "Judge & Co." was perhaps distasteful to him. But in fact the language involved in the enunciation and application of rules constitutes a special segment of human discourse with special features which lead to confusion if neglected. Of this type of discourse the law is one very complex example and sometimes to see its features we need to look away from the law to simpler cases which in spite of many differences share these features. The economist or the scientist often uses a simple model with which to understand the complex; and this can be done for the law. So in what follows I shall use as a simple analogy the rules of a game which at many vital points have the same puzzling logical structure as rules of law. And I shall describe four distinctive features which show, I think, the method of elucidation we should apply to the law and why the common mode of definition fails.

1. First, let us take words like "right" or "duty" or the names of corporations not alone but in examples of typical contexts where these words are at work. Consider them when used in statements made on a particular occasion by a judge or an ordinary lawyer. They will be statements such as "*A* has a right to be paid £10 by *B*." "*A* is under a duty to fence off his machinery." "*A* & Company, Ltd. have a contract with *B*." It is obvious that the use of these sentences silently assumes a special and very complicated setting, namely the existence of a legal system with all that this implies by way of general obedience, the operation of the sanctions of the system, and the general likelihood that this will continue. But though this complex situation is assumed in the use of these statements of rights or duties they do not *state* that it exists. There is a parallel situation in a game. "He is out" said in the course of a game of cricket has as its proper context the playing of the game with all that *this* implies by way of general compliance by both the players and the officials of the game in the past, present, and future. Yet one who says "He is out" does not *state* that a game is being played or that the players and officials will comply with the rules. "He is out" is an expression used to appeal to rules, to make claims, or give decisions under them; it is not a statement *about* the rules to the effect that they will be enforced or acted on in a given case nor any other kind of statement *about* them. The analysis of statements of rights and duties as predictions ignores this distinction, yet it is just as erroneous to say that "*A* has a right" is a prediction that a court or official will treat *A* in a certain way as to say that "He is out" is a prediction that the umpire is likely to order the batsman off the field or the scorer to mark him out. No doubt, when someone has a legal right a corresponding prediction will normally be justified, but this should not lead us to identify two quite different forms of statement.

2. If we take "*A* has a right to be paid £10 by *B*" as an example, we can see what the distinctive function of this form of statement is. For it is

clear that as well as presupposing the existence of a legal system, the use of this statement has also a special connection with a particular rule of the system. This would be made explicit if we asked "Why has *A* this right?" For the appropriate answer could only consist of two things: first, the statement of some rule or rules of law (say those of Contract), under which given certain facts certain legal consequences follow; and secondly, a statement that these facts were here the case. But again it is important to see that one who says that "*A* has a right" does not *state* the relevant rule of law; and that though, given certain facts, it is correct to say "*A* has a right" one who says this does not state or describe those facts. He has done something different from either of these two things: he has drawn a conclusion from the relevant but unstated rule, and from the relevant but unstated facts of the case. "*A* has a right" like "He is out" is therefore the tail-end of a simple legal calculation: it records a result and may be well called a conclusion of law. It is not therefore used to predict the future as the American Realists say; it refers to the present as their opponents claim but unlike ordinary statements does not do this by describing present or continuing facts. This it is—this matter of principle—and not the existence of stray exceptions for lunatics or infants that frustrates the definition of a right in factual terms such as expectations or powers. A paralysed man watching the thief's hand close over his gold watch is properly said to have a right to retain it as against the thief, though he has neither expectation nor power in any ordinary sense of these words. This is possible just because the expression "a right" in this case does not describe or stand for any expectation, or power, or indeed anything else, but has meaning only as part of a sentence the function of which as a whole is to draw a conclusion of law from a specific kind of legal rule.

3.   A third peculiarity is this: the assertion "Smith has a right to be paid £10" said by a judge in deciding the case has a different status from the utterance of it out of court, where it may be used to make a claim, or an admission and in many other ways. The judge's utterance is official, authoritative and, let us assume, final; the other is none of these things, yet in spite of these differences the sentences are of the same sort: they are both conclusions of law. We can compare this difference in spite of similarity with "He is out" said by the umpire in giving his decision and said by a player to make a claim. Now of course the unofficial utterance may have to be withdrawn in the light of a later official utterance, but this is not a sufficient reason for treating the first as a prophecy of the last for plainly not all mistakes are mistaken predictions. Nor surely need the finality of a judge's decision either be confused with infallibility or tempt

us to *define* laws in terms of what courts do, even though there are many laws which the courts must first interpret before they can apply. We can acknowledge that what the scorer says is final; yet we can still abstain from defining the notion of a score as what the scorer says. And we can admit that the umpire may be wrong in his decision though the rules give us no remedy if he is and though there may be doubtful cases which he has to decide with but little help from the rules.

4. In any system, legal or not, rules may for excellent practical reasons attach identical consequences to any one of a set of very different facts. The rule of cricket attaches the same consequence to the batsman's being bowled, stumped, or caught. And the word "out" is used in giving decisions or making claims under the rule and in other verbal applications of it. It is easy to see here that no one of these different ways of being out is more essentially what the word means than the others, and that there need be nothing common to all these ways of being out other than their falling under the same rule, though there *may* be some similarity or analogy between them. But it is less easy to see this in those important cases where rules treat a *sequence* of different actions or states of affairs in a way which unifies them. In a game a rule may simply attach a single consequence to the successive actions of a set of different men—as when a team is said to have won a game. A more complex rule may prescribe that what is to be done at one point in a sequence shall depend on what was done or occurred earlier: and it may be indifferent to the identity of the persons concerned in the sequence so long as they fall under certain defining conditions. An example of this is when a team permitted by the rules of a tournament to have a varying membership is penalised only in the third round—when the membership has changed—for what was done in the first round. In all such cases a sequence of action or states of affairs is unified simply by falling under certain rules; they *may* be otherwise as different as you please. Here can be seen the essential elements of the language of legal corporations. For in law, the lives of ten men that overlap but do not coincide may fall under separate rules under which they have separate rights and duties and then they are a collection of individuals for the law; but their actions may fall under rules of a different kind which make what is to be done by any one or more of them depend in complex way on what was done or occurred earlier. And then we may speak in appropriately unified ways of the sequence so unified, using a terminology like that of corporation law which will show that it is *this* sort of rule we are applying to the facts. But here the unity of the rule may mislead us when we come to define this terminology. It may cast a shadow: we may look for an identical continuing

thing or person or quality *in* the sequence. We may find it—in "corporate spirit." This is real enough; but it is a secret of success not a criterion of identity.

III

These four general characteristics of legal language explain both why definition of words like "right," "duty," and "corporation" is baffled by the absence of some counterpart to "correspond" to these words, and also why the unobvious counterparts which have been so ingeniously contrived—the future facts, the complex facts or the psychological facts —turn out not to be something in terms of which we can define these words although to be connected with them in complex or indirect ways. The fundamental point is that the primary function of these[10] words is not to stand for or describe anything but a distinct function; this makes it vital to attend to Bentham's warning that we should not, as does the traditional method of definition, abstract words like "right" and "duty," "State," or "corporation" from the sentences in which alone their full function can be seen, and then demand of them so abstracted their genus and differentia.

Let us see what the use of this traditional method of definition presupposes and what the limits of its efficacy are, and why it may be misleading. It is of course the simplest form of definition, and also a peculiarly satisfying form because it gives us a set of words which can always be substituted for the word defined whenever it is used; it gives us a comprehensible synonym or translation for the word which puzzles us. It is peculiarly appropriate where the words have the straightforward function of standing for some kind of thing, or quality, person, process, or event, for here we are not mystified or puzzled about the general characteristics of our subject-matter, but we ask for a definition simply to locate within this familiar general kind or class some special subordinate kind or class. Thus since we are not puzzled about the general notions of furniture or animal we can take a word like "chair" or "cat" and give the principle of its use by first specifying the general class to which what it is

10. Lawyers might best understand the distinctive function of such expressions as "He has a right" and others which I discuss here, by comparing them to the *operative* words of a conveyance as distinct from the *descriptive* words of the recitals. The point of similarity is that "He has a right," like "X hereby conveys," is used to *operate with* legal rules and not to state or describe facts. Of course there are great differences: one who says "He has a right" operates with a rule by drawing a conclusion from it whereas one who uses operative words in a conveyance does something to which the rule attaches legal consequences.

used to describe belongs, and then going on to define the specific differences that mark it off from other species of the same general kind. And of course if we are *not* puzzled about the general notion of a corporate body but only wish to know how one species (say a college) differs from another (say a limited company) we can use this form of definition of single words perfectly well. But just because the method is appropriate at this level of inquiry, it cannot help us when our perplexities are deeper. For if our question arises, as it does with fundamental legal notions because we are puzzled about the general category to which something belongs and how some general type of expression relates to fact, and not merely about the place within that category, then until the puzzle is cleared up this form of definition is at the best unilluminating and at the worst profoundly misleading. It is unilluminating because a mode of definition designed to locate some subordinate species within some familiar category cannot elucidate the characteristics of some anomalous category; and it is misleading because it will suggest that what is in fact an anomalous category is after all some species of the familiar. Hence if applied to legal words like "right," "duty," "State," or "corporation" the common mode of definition suggests that these words like ordinary words stand for or describe some thing, person, quality, process, or event; when the difficulty of finding these becomes apparent, different contrivances varying with tastes are used to explain or explain away the anomaly. Some say the difference is that the things for which these legal words stand are real but not sensory, others that they are fictitious entities, others that these words stand for plain fact but of a complex, future, or psychological variety. So this standard mode of definition forces our familiar triad of theories into existence as a confused way of accounting for the anomalous character of legal words.

How then shall we define such words? If definition is the provision of a synonym which will not equally puzzle us these words cannot be defined. But I think there is a method of elucidation of quite general application and which we can call definition, if we wish. Bentham and others practised it, though they did not preach it. But before applying it to the highly complex legal cases, I shall illustrate it from the simple case of a game. Take the notion of a trick in a game of cards. Somebody says "What is a trick?" and you reply "I will explain: when you have a game and among its rules is one providing that when each of our players has played a card then the player who has put down the highest card scores a point, in these circumstances that player is said to have 'taken a trick.'" This natural explanation has not taken the form of a definition of the single word "trick": no synonym has been offered for it. Instead we have taken a sentence in which the word "trick" plays its characteristic role and explained it first by specifying the conditions under which the whole sentence is true, and secondly by showing how it is used in drawing a conclusion from the rules in a particular case. Suppose now that after such an explanation your questioner presses on: "That is all very well, that explains 'taking a trick'; but I still want to know what the word 'trick' means just by itself. I want a definition of 'trick'; I want something which can be substituted for it whenever it is used." If we yield to this demand for a single word definition we might reply: "The trick is just a collective name for the four cards." But someone may object: "The trick is not just a name for the four cards because these four cards will not always constitute a trick. It must therefore be some entity to which the four cards belong." A third might say: "No, the trick is a fictitious entity which the players pretend exists and to which by fiction which is part of the game they ascribe the cards." But in so simple a case we would not tolerate these theories, fraught as they are with mystery and empty of any guidance as to the use made of the word within the game: we would stand by the original two-fold explanation; for this surely gave us all we needed when it explained the conditions under which the statement "He has taken a trick" is true and showed us how it was used in drawing a conclusion from the rules in a particular case.

If we turn back to Bentham we shall find that when his explanation of legal notions is illuminating, as it very often is, it conforms to this method though only loosely. Yet curiously what he tells us to do is something different: it is to take a word like "right" or "duty" or "State": to embody it in a sentence such as "you have a right" where it plays a characteristic role and then to find a *translation* of it into what we should call factual terms. This he called the method of paraphrase—giving phrase for phrase not word for word. Now this method is applicable to many cases and has shed much light; but it distorts many legal words like "right" or "duty" whose characteristic role is not played in statements of fact but in conclusions of law. A paraphrase of these in factual terms is not possible and when Bentham proffers such a paraphrase it turns out not to be one at all.

But more often and much to our profit he does not claim to paraphrase: but he makes a different kind of remark, in order to elucidate these words—remarks such as these: "What you have a right to have me made do, is that which I am liable according to law upon a requisition made on your behalf to be punished for not doing" or "To know how to expound a right carry your eye to the act which in the circumstances in question would be a violation of that right; the law creates the right by forbidding that act." These, though defective, are on the right lines. They are not paraphrases but they specify some of the conditions necessary for the truth of a sentence of the form "You have a right." Bentham shows us how these conditions include the existence of a law imposing a duty on some other person; and moreover, that it must be a law which provides that the breach of the duty shall be visited with a sanction if you or someone on your behalf so choose. This has many virtues. By refusing to identify the meaning of the word "right" with any psychological or physical fact it correctly leaves open the question whether on any given occasion a person who has a right has in fact any expectation or power; and so it leaves us free to treat men's expectations or powers as what in general men will have if there is a system of rights, and as part of what a system of rights is generally intended to secure. Some of the improvements which should be made on Bentham's efforts are obvious. Instead of characterising a right in terms of punishment many would do so in terms of the remedy. But I would prefer to show the special position of one who has a right by mentioning not the remedy but the choice which is open to one who has a right as to whether the corresponding duty shall be performed or not. For it is, I think, characteristic of those laws that confer rights (as distinguished from those that only impose obligations) that the obligation to perform the corresponding duty is made by law to depend on the choice of the individual who is said to have the right or the choice of some person authorised to act on his behalf.

I would, therefore, tender the following as an elucidation of the expression "a legal right": (1) A statement of the form "X has a right" is true if the following conditions are satisfied:

(a) There is in existence a legal system.

(b) Under a rule or rules of the system some other person Y is, in the events which have happened, obliged to do or abstain from some action.

(c) This obligation is made by law dependent on the choice either of X or some other person authorised to act on his behalf so that either Y is bound to do or abstain from some action only if X (or some authorised person) so chooses or alternatively only until X (or such person) chooses otherwise. (2) A statement of the form "X has a right" is used to draw a conclusion of law in a particular case which falls under such rules.

IV

It is said by many that the juristic controversy over the nature of corporate personality is dead. If so we have a corpse and the opportunity to learn from its anatomy. Let us imagine an intelligent lawyer innocent of theories of corporate personality because he was educated in a legal Arcadia where rights and duties were ascribed only to individuals and all legal theory is banned. He is then introduced to our own and other systems and learns how in practice rights and duties are ascribed to bodies like the University of Oxford, to the State, to idols, to the *hereditas jacens* and also to the one-man tax-dodging company. He would learn with us that forms of statement were in daily use by which rights were ascribed to Smith & Co. Ltd. in circumstances and with consequences partly similar and partly different from those in which they were ascribed to Smith. He would see that the analogy was often thin, but that, given the circumstances specified in the Companies Acts and the general law, "Smith & Co. Ltd. owes White £10" applied as directly to the facts after its own fashion as "Smith owes White £10." Gradually he would discover that many ordinary words when used of a limited company were used in a special manner. For he would early learn that even if all the members and servants of the company are dead there are yet conditions under which it is true to say that the company still exists; if he was here in 1932 he would have learnt that it can be correctly said of a foreign corporation that though dissolved it still exists; and if he stayed till 1944 he would have learned that given certain circumstances it is true that a company has intended to deceive. On his return to Arcadia he would tell of the extension to corporate bodies of rules worked out for individuals and of the analogies followed and the adjustment of ordinary words involved in this extension. All this he would have to do and could do without mentioning fiction, collective names, abbreviations or brackets, or the *Gesammtperson* and the *Gesammtwille* of Realist theory. Would he not have said all there was to say about the legal personality of corporation? At what point then would the need be felt for a theory? Would it not be when someone asked, "When it is true that Smith owes Black £10, here is the name 'Smith' and there is the man Smith, but when Smith & Co. Ltd. owes £10 to Black what is there that corresponds to 'Smith & Co. Ltd.' as the man Smith corresponds to the name 'Smith'? What *is* Smith & Co. Ltd.? What is *it,* which has the right? Surely it can only be a collection of individuals or a real individual or a fictitious individual?" In other words we could make the simple Arcadian feel the theorists' agonies only by inducing him to ask "What is Smith & Co. Ltd.?" and not to admit in answer a description of how, and under what conditions, the names of corporate bodies are used in practice, but instead to start the search for what it is that the name taken alone describes, for what *it* stands, for what *it* means.

That the presentation of the question in this way has been crucial in the growth of theory could be proved from many famous passages in the literature. Let me take one example. Maitland in his greatness indeed sensed that the choice did not necessarily lie, as it seemed, between the traditional theories and that ultimately some mode of analysis might supply a different answer. I do not understand why he is called a Realist . . . for though he was certain that fiction and collective-name theories "denatured the facts," he left the matter with a final question to which he then saw no answer. But observe the significant form that question took: he imagined a sovereign State and inventing the Latin for Never-never land, called it Nusquamia. Of this he said:

> Like many other sovereign States, it owes money, and I will suppose that you are one of its creditors. . . .
> Now the question that I want to raise is this: Who is it that really owes you money? Nusquamia? Granted, but can you convert the proposition that Nusquamia owes you money into a series of propositions imposing duties on certain human beings that are now in existence? The task will not be easy. Clearly you do not think that every Nusquamian owes you some aliquot share of the debt. No one thinks in that way. The debt of Venezuela is not owed by Fulano y Zutano and the rest of them. Nor, I think, shall we get much good out of the word "collectively," which is the smudgiest word in the English language, for the largest "collection" of zeros is only zero. I do not wish to say that I have suggested an impossible task, and that the right-and-duty-bearing group must be for the philosopher an ultimate and unanalysable moral unit. . . Only if that task can be performed, I think that in the interests of jurisprudence and of moral philosophy it is eminently worthy of circumspect performance.[18]

Such was Maitland's question: When Nusquamia owes you money who owes you this? How should it be answered? Surely only by ceasing to batter our heads against the single word: Nusquamia. Pressing the question "Who or what when Nusquamia owes you £1,000 is it which owes you this?" is like demanding desperately: "When you lost that game what was it that you lost?" To the question so pressed the only answer is to repeat "a game," as to the other the only answer is to repeat "Nusquamia." This, of course, tells us precisely nothing but is at least neither mystifying nor false. To elucidate it we must obey Bentham's first injunction: we must take the whole statement "Nusquamia owes you £1,000" and describe its use perhaps as follows:

1. Here in the territory of Nusquamia there is a legal system in force; under the laws of this system certain persons on complying with certain conditions are authorised for certain purposes to receive sums of money and to do other actions analogous to those required to make a contract of loan between private individuals.

---

18. "Moral Personality and Legal Personality," *Collected Papers,* Vol. III, pp. 318-19.

2. When such persons do such acts certain consequences, analogous to those attached to the similar actions of private individuals, follow, including the liability of persons defined by law to repay the sums of money out of funds defined by law.

3. The expression "Nusquamia owes you £1,000" does not state the existence of these rules nor of these circumstances, but is true in a particular case when they exist, and is used in drawing a conclusion of law from these rules in a particular case.

How much detail should be given depends on the degree to which the questioner is puzzled. If all that he is puzzled by is his inability to say who or what Nusquamia is and the inadequacies of theories to explain this, he may be content with what has been done. But of course he may be puzzled by the notion of one and the same legal system existing throughout the lives of different men in terms of which this elucidation of "Nusquamia" has been offered. If so, this in its turn must be elucidated as it can be in the same manner.

There is of course nothing in this method to prevent its application to the ephemeral technical one-man company which Realists regarded as a difficulty for their theory. To explain what a limited company is we must refer to the relevant legal rules, which determine the conditions under which a characteristic sentence like "Smith & Co. owes White £10" is true. Then we must show how the name of a limited company functions as part of a conclusion of law which is used to apply both special company rules and also rules such as those of contract which were originally worked out for individuals. It will, of course, be necessary to stress that under the special conditions defined by the special rules, other rules are applied to the conduct of individuals in a manner radically different from though still analogous to that in which such rules apply to individuals apart from such special conditions. This we could express by restating the familiar principle of our company law "A company is a distinct entity from its members" as: "The name of a limited company is used in conclusions of law which apply legal rules in special circumstances in a manner distinct from though analogous to those in which such rules are applied to individuals apart from such circumstances." This restatement would show that we have to do not with anomalous or fictitious entities, but with a new and extended though analogous use of legal rules and of the expressions involved in them.

V

If we look now at the type of theory so attractive to common sense which asserts that statements referring to corporations are "abbreviations" and so can be reduced or translated into statements referring only to individuals, we can see now in precisely what way they failed. Their mistake was that of seeking a paraphrase or translation into other terms of statements referring to corporations instead of specifying the conditions under which such statements are true and the manner in which they are used. But in assessing these common-sense theories it is important to notice one very general feature of the language involved in the application of legal rules which the attempt to paraphrase always obscures. If we take a very simple legal statement like "Smith has made a contract with Y" we must distinguish the meaning of this conclusion of law, from two things: from (1) a statement of the facts required for its truth, e.g., that the parties have signed a written agreement, and also from (2) the statement of the legal consequences of it being true, e.g., that Y is bound to do certain things under the agreement. There is here at first sight something puzzling; it seems as if there is something intermediate between the facts, which make the conclusion of law true, and the legal consequences. But if we refer to the simple case of a game we can see what this is. When "He is out" is said of a batsman (whether by a player, or by the umpire) this neither makes the factual statement that the ball has struck the wicket nor states that he is bound to leave the wicket: it is an utterance the function of which is to draw a conclusion from a specific rule under which in circumstances such as these, consequences of this sort arise, and we should obviously neglect something vital in its meaning if, in the attempt to give a paraphrase, we said it meant the facts alone or the consequences alone or even the combination of these two. The combined statement "The ball has struck the wicket and he must leave the wicket" fails to give the whole meaning of "He is out" because it does not reproduce the distinctive manner in which the original statement is used to draw a conclusion from a specific but unstated rule under which such a consequence follows on such conditions. And no paraphrase can both elucidate the original and reproduce this feature.

I dwell on this point because it is here that the common-sense theories of corporate personality fail. The theory that statements referring to corporations are disguised abbreviations for statements about the rights and duties of individuals was usually expounded with such crudity as not to deserve consideration. It is easy to see that a statement about the rights of a limited company is not equivalent to the statement that its members have those same rights. A conveyance by Smith & Co. Ltd. to the sole shareholder Smith is of course not a conveyance by Smith to Smith. But a few theorists, among them Hohfeld, have stated this type of theory with a requisite degree of subtlety. Hohfeld saw that to say that Smith & Co. Ltd. has a contract with Y was, of course, not to say the same thing about the members of the company: he thought it was to say something different and very complicated about the way in which the capacities, rights, powers, privileges, and liabilities of the natural persons concerned in the company had been affected. Though more formidable in this guise, the theory fails because, although it gives us the legal consequences upon the individuals of the original statement, it does not give us the force and meaning of that statement itself. The alleged paraphrase is less than the original statement "Smith & Co. Ltd. has a contract with Y" because it gives no hint of what the original statement is used to do, namely, to draw a conclusion of law from special rules relating to companies and from rules extended by analogy from the case of individuals. So the paraphrase, complex and ingenious as it is, gives us too little; but it also gives us too much. It dissipates the unity of the simple statement "Smith & Co. has a contract with Y" and substitutes a statement of the myriad legal rights, duties, powers, etc., of numerous individuals of whom we never have thought nor could have thought in making the original statement. Hence it is that those who are attracted to this common-sense form of analysis feel cheated when they look at it more closely. And they *are* cheated; only they should not in despair clutch at the Realist or Fiction theories. For the elements which they miss in the translation, the analogy with individuals, the unity of the original statement, and its direct application to fact cannot be given them in these theories nor in any translation of the original; it can only be given in a detailed description of the conditions under which a statement of this form is true and of the distinctive manner in which it is used to draw a conclusion from specific rules in a particular case.

I have of course dealt only with the *legal* personality of corporations. I have argued that if we characterise adequately the distinctive manner in which expressions for corporate bodies are used in a legal system then there is no residual question of the form "What is a corporation?" There only *seems* to be one if we insist on a form of definition or elucidation which is inappropriate. Theories of the traditional form can only give a distorted account of the meaning of expressions for corporate bodies because they all, in spite of their mutual hostility, make the common assumption that these expressions must stand for or describe something, and then give separate and incompatible accounts of its peculiarity as a complex or recondite or a fictitious entity; whereas the peculiarity lies not here but in the distinctive characteristics of expressions used in the enunciation and application of rules. But of course it is not the legal personality but the "moral" personality of organised groups that perplexes most: these exist apart from legal rules (one confusing sense of "not fiction" is just to assert this fact) and no collective-name or abbreviation theory seems to be adequate; so we are tempted to ask, "What *is* a Church, a Nation, a School?" "What is any association or organised group?" But here too we should substitute for this ever-baffling form of question the following: "Under what conditions do we refer to numbers and sequences of men as aggregates of individuals and under what conditions do we adopt instead unifying phrases extended by analogy from individuals?" If we ask this and investigate the conditions of use of characteristic sentences ("The Nation suffered for 50 years," "The University expressed its gratitude," "The crowd was angry") we shall cease to talk about group-personality (and indeed individual personality) as if it were a single quality or set of qualities. For we shall find that there are many varieties of widely different conditions (psychological and others) under which we talk in this unifying personal way. Some of these conditions will be shown to be significant for legal or political purposes; others will not. It was surely one of the sentimentalities of *Genossenschafttheorie* that unity just as unity was made to appear significant or worthy of respect, as compared with the vulgar plurality of persons strolling in the street. After all mere unity is not very much, though it is far more various than it appears to be.

VI

If we put aside the question "What is a corporation?" and ask instead "Under what types of conditions does the law ascribe liabilities to corporations?" this is likely to clarify the actual working of a legal system and bring out the precise issues at stake when judges, who are supposed not to legislate, make some new extension to corporate bodies of rules worked out for individuals. Take for example the recent extension to corporations of liability for crimes involving knowledge and intention, or some other mental element which are such that a natural person would not be criminally responsible if his servant with the requisite knowledge and intention committed the *actus reus* in the course of his employment. There are two ways, one illuminating and the other misleading, of representing the issues at stake here: two ways, that is, of interpreting the word "can" in the question "can a limited company commit a crime involving knowledge and intention?" The illuminating way would be to exhibit the obstacle to such an extension as consisting in the type of analogy that has been followed in fitting corporate bodies into the general structure of our law. It is, of course, predominantly the analogy with the case of an individual held liable for what his servant does in the course of employment. It is by use of this analogy that the liabilities of corporations were extended from contract to ordinary torts and then to torts involving malice: and the whole vocabulary of the law of principle and agent has been adapted to the case of the limited companies. But for crimes of the type under consideration this analogy is useless and the fundamental question is: Is this the only analogy available to the courts? Is the law closed on this matter, or are there other criteria for the application to companies of rules originally applied to individuals? In fact the judges have felt that they were not restricted in this way and of course it has often been pointed out that it is possible in English law to find authority for imputing to a company the actions and mental states of those who are substantially carrying on its work. How far this alternative source of analogy can or should be utilised is of course a debatable legal issue, but the important thing is to see that this legal issue, and not some logical issue, is the character of the question. Here then is the force of the word "can" in "can a company be liable for a crime involving intention to deceive?" By contrast the confusing way of stating the issue is to bring in definitions of what a company is and to deduce from them answers to the question in hand. "A company is a mere abstraction, a fiction, a metaphysical entity." "A company has no mind and therefore cannot intend." These statements confuse the issue because they look like eternal truths about the nature of corporations given us by definitions: so it is made to appear that all legal statements about corporations *must* square with these if they are not to be logically inconsistent. It seems therefore that there is something over and above the analogies which are actually used in the legal system for the application to corporations of rules worked out for individuals and that this limits or controls that application. And of course a Fiction theory taken seriously can impose irrelevant barriers just as much as a Realist theory; for just as a Realist theory appears to tell us that a company "cannot" be bound by an agreement empowering another company to direct its business and appoint its personnel because this would be "to degrade to the position of a tool" a person with a real will, so a Fiction theory appears to say that a company "cannot" be guilty of certain crimes because it has no mind.

Indeed the *suggestio falsi* in the use of the notion of "fiction" in the exposition of this branch of the law merits our consideration. Its peculiar vice is to conceal that when words used normally of individuals are applied to companies as well as the analogy involved, there is also involved a radical difference in the mode in which such expressions are now used and so a shift in meaning. Even in the simplest case of all when we say "X is a servant of Y & Company" the facts which justify the use of the words "X is a servant" are not *just* the same as the facts which support "Smith is a servant of Brown." Hence any ordinary words or phrases when conjoined with the names of corporations take on a special legal use, for the words are now correlated with the facts, not solely by the rules of ordinary English but also by the rules of English law much as when we extend words like "take" or "lose" by using them of tricks in a game they become correlated with facts by the rules of that game. Now if we talk here of "fiction" we cannot do justice to this radical difference in use of ordinary expressions when conjoined with the names of corporations; we can only distort it. For when, for example, we say of a company that it resides in England even though its members and servants were killed last night by a bomb, the meaning of these words is to be found only by examining the legal rules which prescribe in what conditions such a statement is correct. But if we talk of "fiction" we suggest that we are using words in their ordinary sense and are merely pretending that something exists to which they apply. In novels—real fiction—we *do* preserve the ordinary meanings of words and pretend that there are persons of whom they are true in their ordinary sense. This is just what we do *not* do when we talk of corporations in law. Yet one of the most curious pieces of logic that ever threatened to obstruct the path of legal development owes, I think, its origin to the confusion of such a shift in meaning with fiction. It was once said that a corporation has no real will but a fictitious will imputed by law, and that since such a will so imputed could effect only lawful ends, we cannot, if we are logically consistent, say that it could commit a crime, or even perhaps a tort. Of course this use of the fiction theory does conjure up an allegorical picture: Law breathing into the nostrils of a Limited Company a Will Fictitious but like that of its Creator Good. But the picture is more misleading than even an allegory should be, because it conceals the fact that the word "will" shifts its meaning when we use it of a company: the sense in which a company has a will is not that it wants to do legal or illegal actions but that certain expressions used to describe the voluntary actions of individuals may be used of it under conditions prescribed by legal rules. And from the bare fact that the law does prescribe such conditions for a wide range of expressions (which is all that imputing a will to a company can mean) it cannot be deduced that these conditions do not include the commission of a criminal or tortious act. Analogy with a living person and shift of meaning are therefore of the essence of the mode of legal statement which refers to corporate bodies. But these are just what they are. Analogy is not identity, so though we can now (as lawyers) say that a company has intended to deceive this has no theoretical consequences; and shift in meaning is not fiction, so the need for logical consistency with an irrelevant notion of a law-created pure Will need not have been added to the difficulties of judges who, in a case law system, have to decide how far the analogies latent in the law permit them to extend to corporations rules worked out for individuals when justice seems to demand it.

This post-mortem has lasted long. I will add only this. It would of course be the merest provincialism to think of the history of jurisprudence in this matter of definition as a record of errors—even of illuminating errors. It is on the contrary full of invaluable hints as to what should be done to cater for the idiosyncrasies of legal language and the elucidation of its special concepts. Besides the precepts and practice of Bentham there is the practice of Austin at his best; there is Byrce's pregnant observation that fundamental legal notions could perhaps not be defined, only described, and much in Pollock and Maitland to show how the interplay of remedy with right has generated a special use of words. There is much, too, of value in Kocourek and Kelsen. Would it, I wonder, be folly to see in the Digest title *De acquirenda vel de amittenda possessione* with its evasion of the fruitless question: "What is possession?" an instinctive recognition of the cardinal principle that legal words can only be elucidated by considering the conditions under which statements in which they have their characteristic use are true? But though the subject of legal definition has this history, it is only since the beneficial turn of philosophical attention towards language that the general features have emerged of that whole style of human thought and discourse which is concerned with rules and their application to conduct. I at least could not see how much of this was visible in the works of our predecessors until I was taught how to look by my contemporaries.

Shuman, Jurisprudence and the Analysis of Fundamental Legal Terms*

Introduction

Despite increased need for greater understanding about the philosophical problems of jurisprudence, in recent times, there has been a steady diminution in the effort devoted to such matters. Instead, legal philosophy has come to be largely replaced by the effort to develop the relations which obtain between law and sociology, psychology, anthro-

* [8 *J. Legal Ed.* 437 (1956). Reprinted by permission.

Samuel I. Shuman (1925–) was educated at the University of Pennsylvania (A.B. 1947; A.M. 1948; Ph.D. 1951), the University of Michigan (J.D. 1954), and Harvard University (S.J.D. 1959). He has been on the law faculty at Wayne State University since 1957, and became Professor of Law and Psychiatry in 1965. He has been the American editor of *Archive* since 1961, and is the author of *Legal Positivism* (1963) and *Law and Disorder* (1971).]

pology, economics, or the other empirical, or hopefully empirical, social disciplines. The Second World War, with its preceding and attending circumstances, has somewhat revived interest in the relations between law and the morality of government. Especially has this been so as concerns the attempt to provide criteria for differentiating between acceptable and objectionable governmental behavior when both exhibit the usual characteristics required of positive law. This concern with morality of "legal" behavior has largely been responsible for the so-called revival of natural law thinking. The concern with such a jurisprudential approach has left almost no room, even in the shadows, for attention to efforts in legal philosophy which proceed from an approach other than that of natural law.

It is, consequently, of interest to note the rather thoroughly nonnatural law 1953 Oxford Inaugural Lecture of Professor H. L. A. Hart, entitled "Definition and Theory in Jurisprudence." The challenging and exceptionally provocative suggestions of that lecture are primarily responsible for prompting the remarks that follow. I say that Professor Hart's effort is challenging because his attempt is one of the very first in which the philosophic tools of the Oxford analysts are applied to the problems of law; suggestive because even where one may find difficulty in accepting the analysis, there are, nonetheless, provoked some interesting possibilities for further inquiry.

Attention will be devoted in what follows to some of the complexities involved in attempting to decide *how* there may be supplied suitable definitions for fundamental legal terms. The word "how" is emphasized because it is intended to reveal that the following comments are not to be concerned with actually supplying any definitions for legal terms—a task likely to be more difficult than that to which attention will here be devoted. Why the task of supplying definitions is considered so difficult may become clearer as concern is devoted to the particularly admirable effort of Professor Hart, who has supplied a kind of definition for so fundamental a legal term as "right."

Concerned as he was with the difficulties generated for jurisprudence by the classical approach to definition, Professor Hart touched upon some of the most ancient but still most troublesome problems which confront contemporary analytical jurisprudence. As the expression "analytical jurisprudence" is here employed, it designates not only the approach made familiar by Austin and more recently by Kelsen, but includes as well that attitude toward the doing of legal philosophy which recognizes the necessity for concern with the relationship between language and the special problems of the field.

It is probably a truism in the history of jurisprudence that the number of attempts to supply definitions for the fundamental legal terms is almost exactly equal to the number of failures. Of course, the critical word used here is "failure," and in what follows, it is hoped that there will appear some suggestions for judging the success of a legal definition. At the outset, and as a preliminary criterion, it is reasonable to demand that the definition at least not result in a greater confusion than that which results from the use of what is to be replaced. It is requisite that the systematic use of the term, that is, the substitution of the definiens, for the presystematic use of the term, the definiendum, result in a net increase in the efficiency with which the legal concept can be handled within the relevant framework. For our purposes, this framework is a legal system with its primitive and derived concepts and with the criteria for determining the efficiency of a definition little, if any, different from those employed in regard to any other framework.

Although by no means either precise or exhaustive, the comparative efficiency of various definienta for the same definiendum may be determined by the degree of simplicty effected, the degree of precision secured, and perhaps more generally the adequacy and the extent of the clarity achieved. Where definitions are introduced for explanatory purposes, as they are in a legal system, rather than for purposes of notational convenience, as in an uninterpreted symbolic system, the application of the above proposed criteria may present considerable difficulties were a truly systematic ordering of the competing definienta required. However, perhaps unfortunately, no such rigorous demand has yet been made for the proposed definitions offered for legal terms. Hence, the suggested criteria are intended to serve only as the basis for an heuristic principle to be utilized in evaluating the definitional work done in contemporary analytical jurisprudence.

Why are Legal Terms Particularly Difficult to Define

Despite the general recognition of the difficulty in defining fundamental legal terms, it is not always made clear why such terms suffer this infirmity to a greater extent than do other terms not necessarily indigenous to a legal system. One of the more obvious reasons for the difficulty in defining legal terms results from the inability to supply what have been called ostensive definitions. "Right," "duty," or "law" cannot be defined, their correct usage cannot be acquired, by having a talented attorney point to physically perceptible objects. Indeed, the proper usage of any fundamental legal term is not secured by any technique independent of the use of other words. Rather, in a constructional system, such as that which is the special province for jurisprudence, the introduction of a definition is required precisely in order to encourage the proper usage of the terms of the system, and such definitions are, or should be, constructed from other usually clearer terms than the definiendum.

In addition to the fact that we may learn how to use the concatenation of "c," "a," and "t" by someone pointing to certain types of furbearing quadripeds, while a similar educational process is ineffective for terms like "right,"[6] there are other difficulties in attempting to define fundamental legal terms. One of these difficulties, and one which to date has been most successfully dealt with by Hohfeld, is the inordinate degree of ambiguity seemingly inherent in terms like "right." Hohfeld distinguished four different classes of legal phenomena to which the term "right" was applied, often without any awareness of the the resulting diminution in the clarity which flowed from applying the same term to different kinds of legal phenomena. However, one of the difficulties has been in attempting to decide whether Hohfeld made available sufficient constructional apparatus with which to draw the lines among the four allegedly nonoverlapping classes to which the term "right" had been applied indiscriminately. The problem may be stated more tersely by indicating that although Hohfeld did suggest a systematic use of the term "right" which would avoid the undesirable consequences of ambiguously applying the term, his analysis may not have taken sufficient notice of the vagueness of the term. The recognition of the four different classes of legal phenomena to which "right" was previously applied, the new directions for applying "right" to only one of those classes and a different term to each of the others indeed went a long way toward removing some of the ambiguities involved in the use of "right." However, as suggested above, the vagueness of the term is yet to be avoided. Within each of the classes labeled "right," "privilege," "power," and "immunity," there still remained the problem of deciding where the line was to be

---

6. Although the point cannot be here developed, it may be worth noticing that there is some definitional process much like that of ostensive definition which may be utilized to define some fundamental legal terms. This ostensive-like process involves the use of *language* which "points" instead of the use of a finger. Thus, to define "chair," one might physically point to a certain object, or one might instead say, "If you go to the west side of the third floor of the Fair Value Department Store, what you will see are chairs." Now this utterance is not a chair, but is a verbal pointing. True, this may make more difficult the process of abstraction involved in successfully defining by physical pointing, but, nonetheless, it is like an ostensive definition.

Similarly, for legal phenomena, giving certain verbal directions may enable the hearer to observe certain phenomena (human behavior) which is typical for certain particular legal relations. Obviously, the process of abstraction will here be more complex and also more difficult because of the increased likelihood of improper "pointing."

drawn which separated the different phenomena which apparently fell within the same class.

To illustrate this problem by a term other than one which is fundamental for a legal system, consider the word "red." Since this word is ambiguous there could be indicated different classes of phenomena to which the term is applied. For example, certain color patches may be called red and certain persons may be called red, depending upon their political views. However, with that distinction drawn, there still remains the problem of drawing the line within each class. Thus, as regards the class of color patches, between what numbers of ängstrom units shall we include the color patch as properly within the class of red patches. Similarly, shall the term "red" be properly applied only to those persons who do actually carry a membership card in the Communist party? Absent the ability to impose some so easily ascertained criterion as the number of ängstrom units of the reflected light or the possession of a certain tangible object like a party card, there would be within each of the classes to which the term applied a certain area of coverage to which the application of the term was in doubt. It is this area that causes what has been called the vagueness of the term.[8] For fundamental legal terms the problem of vagueness is intensified by the fact that it is usually not even possible to separate, as we might wish, the different classes to which the same term is applied, let alone draw the line within each class. For this reason, and because there is no relatively precise test to decide between clear and doubtful cases, it is possible to have included within the class of privileges, for example, certain types of legal phenomena that are more properly within the class of rights or perhaps the class of powers.

The difficulties already mentioned may be sufficient to explain the long list of unsuccessful attempts at supplying efficient definitions for fundamental legal terms, but there need be mentioned further obstacles to success which probably account for more of the cases of disappointment than the ambiguity and vagueness of the terms. All too many of the definitional efforts in jurisprudence have generated more confusion than clarity precisely because the jurisprudent responsible for the definition has not specified that dimension of meaning upon which he was

8. See Black, Vagueness, in *Philosophy of Science* 427 (1937), reprinted in Max Black, *Language and Philosophy* 23 (1949). It is worth noticing that besides the ambiguity and the vagueness of terms, both of which circumstances can be cured or limited by effective rules, there is a further aspect of almost every term which, unlike the above two characteristics, is not curable by effective rules. It is the characteristic of terms which may be thought of as indefiniteness. See Waismann's discussion of this characteristic, which he refers to as "open texture," in Waismann, Verifiability, in Antony Flew [ed.], *Essays on Logic and Language* 117, 119 *et seq.* (1951), which originally appeared in 19 *Aristotelian Soc'y Supp. Vol.* 119 (1945).

operating and hence invited improper use of the definition or the application inappropriate criteria for ascertaining the efficiency of the definition. In addition, since the different senses of the same fundamental legal terms are so disparate as to bear to each other no more than what has been called "family resemblance," further confusion results from the typical failure to reveal with which sense the analysis is concerned. The most frequent disparity between that use which would be appropriate and that which is attempted probably occurs where the tendered definition is (consciously, or more usually unconsciously) intended to operate almost, if not exclusively, for persuasive purposes, but where the definition is said to be efficient for explanatory purposes.

Thus, to say that "X has a right to support from his father" means that "It is evil for a father to allow his own flesh and blood to suffer starvation," is rather obviously supplying an emotively packed definiens for a definiendum relatively lacking in that quality. A less persuasive approach to a definition for "X has a right to support from his father" may be "Fathers have a responsibility for the welfare of their children." But the utilization of either definition in a treatise on family law would only help to diminish the attention which should be devoted to the explanations of the law which are provided. On the other hand, if the definiens for "X has a right to support from his father" was "the financial contribution of the father is required by law," it is even more likely than with either of the prior two definienta, that attention to the legal explanation will not be subverted by emotive distractions.

Although any meaningful definition is capable of exercising an emotional impact which may alter one's attitude toward the subject under examination, this dimension may be minimized to the point where the attitude alteration is of neglectable significance in appraising the function of the definition. Relatively speaking, definitions of this type are emotively neutral but may be the most successful in encouraging the efficient handling of the defined term. This is not to suggest that such definitions do not affect any attitudes of importance. To the contrary, in revealing that certain matters merit special consideration, emotively neutral definitions indicate that at least certain evaluative judgments are involved. Nor should it be thought that such attitudes are unimportant as are involved in making a decision about subjects worthy of the kind of care required to secure emotively neutral definitions. Great intellectual struggles are constantly waged on just such questions.

The contrary might be expected, but examples of emotively neutral definitions are relatively rare in the literature of jurisprudence. Especially in recent natural law theories, it has been apparent that the desire to avoid definition of "law" or "right" as any form of behavior which might be morally objectionable has resulted in the identification of two rather separate problems. Instead of attempting first to provide emotively neutral explanatory definitions for fundamental legal terms with subsequent proposals for relating the definiens to ethical or moral criteria, there has been instead the increased confusion of issues which results almost necessarily when ethical considerations predetermine at least part of the direction for explanation or description. By no means is it here suggested that jurisprudence alone suffers from such a disability, for it is exceedingly common to find that what was intended to be a technical definition, nevertheless, does affect attitudes and is really a persuasive definition.

In order to avoid identifying as law those enactments of the Nazi regime which did comply with all the then prevailing procedural requirements for valid legislation, some have defined law as those promulgations which not only comply with the then effective and enforced requirements for legislation, but add that the legislation must also "be in accord with natural justice," or "satisfy the requirements of right reason," or "not do violence to fundamental rights," or "not be contrary to natural law." It is not difficult to see how such definitions for "law" detract from the explanatory function intended to be secured. The moral element of the definition diminishes the effectiveness with which an explanation is tendered because it requires appeal to criteria of a kind almost totally different from those required in deciding whether the nonmoral aspect of the definition is satisfied. Relatively simple empirical researches are sufficient to decide whether the official promulgation satisfies the then effective and enforced requirements of the legislative process. No such research will suffice to decide about the moral element of the definition because it has yet to be demonstrated that there is a research technique yielding intersubjectively verifiable results available for deciding when a law is in accord with the demands of natural law or natural justice. In addition, because of the emotive meaning generated by the moral element of the definition, even the other element may be so severely colored as to create problems which are otherwise avoidable.

Different Meanings for the Same Term

Cognizant of the inability to ostensively define fundamental legal terms, consideration needs then be devoted to the discovery of other approaches which may be attempted in the effort to define these elusive terms. Following Bentham, that for legal terms, sentences rather than words should be investigated, Professor Hart turns to the analysis of certain typical legal sentences in which are imbedded the terms for which definitions are desired. Hohfeld, nearly 40 years ago, also recognized that:

> The strictly fundamental legal relations are, after all, *sui generis;* and thus it is that attempts at formal definition are always unsatisfactory, if not altogether useless. Accordingly, the most promising line of procedure seems to consist in exhibiting all of the various relations in a scheme of "opposites" and "correlatives," and then proceeding to exemplify their individual scope and application in concrete cases.

In his discussion of powers and liabilities, Hohfeld further revealed his anticipation of some contemporary notions when he suggested that what was sometimes required instead of a definition was analysis or explication.

> But what is the intrinsic nature of a legal power as such? Is it possible to analyze the conception represented by this constantly employed and very important term of legal discourse? Too close an analysis might seem metaphysical rather than useful; so that what is here presented is intended only as an approximate explanation, sufficient for all practical purposes.

If it be agreed that sentences or concrete cases rather than words are the proper objects of examination, what is it that must be done to these objects of study so as to enhance our knowledge about the legal concepts involved? Because legal concepts take meaning against a background of a legal system, there is the preliminary matter of identifying what is meant by a legal system and with which particular system concern is to be had. Universalists may wish to have it be true that regardless of context, the different instances of "*A* has a right to vote" shall enjoy very similar meaning. However, even a relatively thin analysis reveals that the real life events which sentences describe or the consequences which flow from adopting the sentences as true, vary according to the context against which the sentence is uttered, that is, against the relevant legal system. Indeed, the meaning of the same group of words when uttered against the same legal system but by different persons may have substantially different meanings. Some words are uniquely egocentric; for example, "I," "now," "here," etc. But any word or group of words may take on some of the characteristics of the uniquely egocentric words. This circumstance is especially common in regard to fundamental legal terms because of what was previously indicated as their multi-dimensional function—that is, when legal terms, such as, "law" or "right" are used primarily for achieving certain alterations or strengthening of attitudes,

111

as in Cicero's definition of true law as right reason in agreement with nature. The meaning, or more properly, the meanings of the legal term used, may vary quite sharply with the user of the term. Thus, if true law were to be defined by Lenin in the same language as was used by Cicero, "law" as well as "true," "right," "reason," and "nature" would have a very different meaning from that intended by the author of De Republica.

When legal terms are utilized primarily for what are relative neutral emotive purposes, for example, as they are used by Hart or Hohfeld, the difficulty of meaning shifts because of user shifts may for some purposes be ignored. That is, if both Cicero and Lenin defined as true law those regulations enforced by effective sanctions applied by a specialized agency of government, it may be that each of the critical words of the definiens has the same meaning for each definer. True, Cicero and Lenin may satisfy each of the criteria of the definiens by describing a different phenomena; for example, Cicero may describe the *praefectura urbis* of Rome as the sanction applying agency, while Lenin details the operation of the N.K.V.D., but this only means that each definer refers to different designata of the same meaning (word), not that each means something different by the same word. In other words, there may not be any emotive overtones to the critical terms in the definiens which suggest that if not different descriptive meanings, at least different emotive meanings are intended.

Sometimes, there may be deception involved in thinking that shifts in descriptive meaning are not influenced by the emotive meaning of the terms used. This is especially dangerous where the definiendum is excessively charged with emotively meaningful terms, but the definiens appears to neutralize these effects on attitude alteration by replacement of the "objectionable" term with others that do not appear to substantially influence attitudes but, nevertheless, actually do so because there are implicit in the definiens terms with elaborate emotive meanings. Because different users now are able to ascribe their individual meanings (emotive and descriptive) to the implicit terms of the definiens, it may be utilized to achieve a uniformity in practice, a uniformity that is deceptive because there are covered by the same terms different ranges of emotive and even descriptive meaning. For legal as for ethical terms, such a definitional phenomenon is not to be unexpected.

What is here suggested may perhaps be better appreciated by consideration of a passage from the recently translated writings of Axel Hägerström. The passage is not actually an example of what has just been discussed, but it is close enough for present purposes and has the merit of revealing that even so competent a jurisprudent as Hägerström need be approached with caution when it is a matter of defining fundamental legal terms. Hägerström wrote in 1939:[14]

> What is meant by the word *illegality,* if one takes account only of *factual* reality and thus sets aside the moral quality with which that reality in certain cases is endowed? Nothing else than the behavior, whether it be omission or positive action, which calls forth a certain coercive reaction in accordance with the rules for coercion which are *in general* applied and irresistibly carried out as a matter of fact in a human community.

In the first sentence, Hägerström invites his reader to be prepared to agree with his definition by excluding from mind any of the moral qualities involved. (Parenthetically, is it obvious that moral qualities are any less factual than any other aspect of reality?) Because of this direction in the first sentence, readers of the second sentence may be tempted to accept the tendered definition of "illegality" despite the fact that there are actually implicit in the definiens terms with strong emotive meanings, which, if made explicit, might well diminish the agreement secured. In addition, the point made above is also illustrated by this definition because of these implicit terms. For example, it may be implicit to hearer *A* that "behavior" in the definiens means only intentional acts for which the actor could morally be held responsible; consequently, *A* accepts the definition. *B,* a different hearer, may either not think there is implicit any term modifying "behavior," or if he does think such a term to be present, his attitudinal response to its emotive meaning may be entirely different from that of *A;* and since at best the emotive term is only implicit, *B* may also accept the definiens. There are additional implicit adjectives in the definiens besides that mentioned which might modify the term "behavior."

Legal Realism and the Analysis of Fundamental Legal Terms

If the requisite conditions for the existence of a legal system have been established and the characteristics of a particular legal system have been identified, how then are we to proceed in order to acquire that degree of understanding about fundamental legal concepts which will enable us efficiently to handle them within the system. In the course of answering this question, Hart suggests that it is vital to distinguish between what sentences, such as, "*A* has a right to be paid ten pounds by *B,*" *state*

14. Alex Hägerström, *Inquiries into the Nature of Law and Morals* 349 (1953).

and what such sentences *assume*. Comparing the sentence "*A* has a right . . ." to the sentence "He is out," said in regard to a cricket player, Hart states:

> "He is out" is an expression used to appeal to rules, to make claims, or give decisions under them; it is not a statement *about* the rules to the effect that they will be enforced or acted on in a given case nor any other kind of statement *about* them. The analysis of statements of rights and duties as predictions ignores this distinction, yet it is just as erroneous to say that "*A* has a right" is a prediction that a court or official will treat *A* in a certain way as to say that "He is out" is a prediction that the umpire is likely to order the batsman off the field or the scorer to mark him out. No doubt, when someone has a legal right a corresponding prediction will normally be justified, but this should not lead us to identify two quite different forms of statement.

Several problems are generated by this passage—first, because it is by no means clear that a sentence such as "*A* has a right . . ." or "He is out" is in no way a statement about the system or rules. To the contrary, such sentences appear to give a good deal of information *about* the relevant rules, although it is probably accurate to say that the sentences do not *state* such information. However, it is surely confusing to conclude that it is "erroneous to say that 'A has a right' is a prediction that a court or official will treat A in a certain way . . ." None would argue that there was a translation equivalence between sentences about *A*'s rights and sentences about court behavior. That is, the realist argument is not that "*A* has a right" makes statements about court behavior, but rather that one way of avoiding the pitfall of attempting to specify what the sentence does state is to analyze the sentence into sentences which describe some of the possible consequences of behaving as though the sentence were true.

Instead of speaking of the realist error, it may be less misleading to indicate that there are alternative kinds of explications which are considered more efficient in securing the desired objective. To speak of error in regard to the prediction theory of legal phenomena suggests that criteria applicable to analysis in terms of definitional equivalents are applied to an inappropriate type of endeavor. An analysis of "*A* has a right" into other sentences which also refer to the present state of affairs may be judged in terms of whether the explication states the same thing as that which is analyzed, but the realists tender no such explication. The difference results from the fact that the realists have suggested an *interpretation* of "*X* has a right," whereas Hart wants to state at least some of the *descriptive* meaning for the expression. Hart treats "X has a right" as a descriptive sentence; the realists emphasize its metaphorical qualities. If the meaning of an expression is its disposition to affect cognition and emotion where the dispositional properties are rather tightly fixed by accepted linguistic patterns of behavior, then what Hart is attempting to supply is the specifications for determining just what are the relevant behavior patterns (rules) which result in affecting cognition. On the other hand, the realists recognize such a problem but are concerned rather with a very different one. For them, it is not the cognitive meaning of the expression that requires specification, but attention is rather focused upon the emotive meaning, and the form of exposition is largely behavioristic. The realists are constrained to characterize the emotive dispositions of the relevant expressions.

The emotive and cognitive dimensions of meaning are not different sides to a coin; rather they are different areas of the same side. For purposes of analysis and depending upon the objectives for which the analysis is undertaken, particular attention may be paid one or the other of the two overlapping areas. And in order to avoid a stultifying morass of detail, it may be desirable to pretend that the area of overlap is very narrow. The infirmity of the realist position is the assumption that there are not two areas, but one, and this area is the emotive dispositions of the expressions. It is, of course, an exaggeration to say that the realists pay no heed to descriptive meaning; but they do tend so far to that polar position as to suggest the exaggeration. Whether or not Hart overcompensates for the realists by adherence to the other polar position is not so clear. Perhaps the realists, too much impressed with Dewey, identified the descriptive judgment "X has a right" with its evaluative functions and then followed Dewey in developing a predictive theory to explain such functions. What Hart so thoroughly wishes to resist is any identification which will submerge the descriptive aspects of the terms or judgments involved.

Further complications are introduced when Hart writes:

> Nor surely need the finality of a judge's decision either be confused with infallibility or tempt us to *define* laws in terms of what courts do, even though there are many laws which the courts must interpret before they can apply. We can acknowledge that what the scorer says is final; yet we can still abstain from defining the notion of a score as what the scorer says. And we can admit that the umpire may be wrong in his decision though the rules give us no remedy if he is and though there may be doubtful cases which he has to decide with but little help from the rules.

It is important first to notice that what is now to be analyzed is a certain law, not a sentence such as "*A* has a right." With such the case, it becomes all the more obvious that the realist analysis is in no way an attempt at definition, except in a certain sense of explication. It is clear that no classical type of definition of "laws" is offered in terms of judicial behavior. Although high points may be reached while flaying straw men, it does seem unnecessary to so badly malign the realist position, which already suffers sufficient defects in its best formulation. Although the suggestion will only be roughly developed here, it may be worth noting that what both the realists and such contemporary analysts as Hart seek in regard to a definition may not be very far apart. Both recognize the inadequacy of attempts at correspondence definitions, and both are apparently striving toward an analysis which adequately accounts for the dispositional character of the terms involved. Although ancient philosophers, following Aristotle, spoke of the potential of things, it is now more common to discuss the dispositional properties of a phenomenon. And although upon cursory consideration it may appear that fundamental legal terms, no matter what they are, are not terms used to denote dispositional properties, further investigation may suggest that these legal terms do denote legal properties which have many of the indicia of dispositionals. It is because this may be so that both Hart and the realists find so much difficulty in attempting to explicate the terms involved. Even for the more precise dispositional predicates characteristic of the physical sciences, there are still unavailable suitable patterns of explication that might eventually be applied to the generally less precise predicates characteristic of law.

Perhaps the problem here hinted at may be made clearer by reference to what are believed to be the characteristics of a fundamental legal predicate such as "is a right" which merits treating the predicate as dispositional. Unlike what are typical dispositional properties such as "soluble," the allegedly dispositional properties within a legal system are not applicable to physical objects. This is what was meant before by saying that there is nothing to which one could point in attempting to illustrate what is a right. However, in the sense that "is a right" when predicated to certain kinds of relational phenomena does dispose certain individuals to certain kinds of action, the predicate does name dispositional properties. What the realists are saying is that these dispositions (both as to the judge and the other persons affected) are *psychological* dispositions. On the other hand, what Hart and others rightly search for is an explication of the nonpsychological dispositions. That is, Hart and others wish to offer an explication of the dispositional properties of the fundamental legal predicates in terms of the logic of the rules which compose legal systems. Instead of retorting that Y is or should be psychologically disposed to behaving in a certain way when X has a certain right, the analysts of Hart's persuasion would like to be able to retort that since X has a certain right, the logic of the rules imply that certain events may transpire. Or to put it slightly differently, when X has a certain right, then the logic of the rules requires that certain other sentences which involve other fundamental and derived terms of the legal system will then be true—e.g., Y has a certain duty, the sheriff has a certain power, etc.

As disturbing as the application of inappropriate criteria to the realist position is the unexplained suggestion that we may "admit" judges to be wrong,[19] although the rules provide for no relief from error. Acceptance of such a view implies either that some kind of higher law is to be included within the basic concepts of the legal system or that "admit" in the above contexts refers to some psychological game in which attorneys and others may indulge. Suffice it for the present to say that Professor Hart was probably not supporting any species of the natural law argument, and hence, it needs be decided what increase in understanding of basic legal concepts is effected by an analysis which concludes that judges are wrong because one may be unhappy about their decision. For is that not all that can be meant once it be admitted that there is no basis within the system for relief? To be sure, unhappiness about judicial behavior may lead to significant alterations of the rules which regulate that behavior, but again, this adds little to the analysis of fundamental legal concepts *except* precisely along the lines of the realists whose pragmatic theory was previously rejected.

There is a third possible explanation of what may be meant by saying that we may admit the judge to be wrong although there be no appeal from his decision. Instead of subscribing to a natural law theory or to a psychological game theory, there might be intended a fairly careful theory as to the relations between law and ethics. Under such a view, the words "admit" and "wrong" would refer to a nonlegal judgment and hence not detract from an emotively neutral definition or analysis of the fundamental legal terms involved. This is not to imply that, unlike law, sentences in ethics are incapable of what was referred to as emotively neutral analysis. Rather, what is implied is that a decision about the wrongness of a judicial judgment cannot be based upon the formal conditions or rules which obtain within a legal system, since the judgment is final and not appealable.

To use terminology developed elsewhere, Hart is saying either that we may have *attitudes* about the decision of the judge which are different

---

19. It is important to note Hart is not suggesting that a judicial decision is false.

117

from those of the judge or that there is a difference in *belief* about the correctness of the decision in regard to which we may or may not share the judge's attitude. However, if there is a difference in belief, that is a difference which is resolvable by empirical methods. And anyone, once shown the rules which reveal the incorrectness of the decision, will agree that it is wrong. However, this cannot be done within the legal system, since the rules themselves make the judgment final and unappealable. Consequently, the decision that the judgment is wrong must be based upon considerations outside the legal system—that is, it must be based either on a difference of attitude about the judge's decision or a difference in belief about something outside the legal system that affects our judgments that deal with judicial decisions. In either of the last two events, elaboration of the reasons for the difference may help to increase our understanding of the legal terms as they are utilized within the legal system, especially if the disagreement about the desired use of terms is attributable to disagreement in attitude, since a recognition of that basis for disagreement may reveal that there is no disagreement in belief. For example, it might develop that natural law adherents agree in belief with legal positivists that whenever organized sanctions can be applied, then there is a legal right. The reason the former type of jurisprudent rejects such a definition of right may be a result of a difference in the attitudes generated by the definition.

It is, in a sense, irrelevant whether or not the decision about the wrongness of the judgment is an emotive ejaculation or based upon a carefully elaborated set of ethical premises to be used in appraising judicial behavior—that is, a difference in ethical attitudes or beliefs. In either event, it requires stretching outside the legal system to conclude that the final decision is wrong, and hence the use of "wrong" in a context such as that above quoted from Hart is likely to be productive of avoidable difficulties. If there were other rules within the legal system to which appeal could be had when a judicial decision was final and unappealable and those rules permitted drawing conclusions about the judgment, then only would it be possible to say within the legal framework, "That judgment is wrong."

A question that remains to be considered is whether there may be a legal system within which rules permit a conclusion that a judgment final and unappealable by those rules is, nevertheless, recognized as wrong by the application of some of the system's rules. Depending upon how broadly the term "legal system" is conceived, it may be possible to find such a "system." For example, during the early stages in the evolution of a totalitarian legal structure, there may still be on the bench judges who have not yet learned to decide according to the "people's conscience," as has been proclaimed to be politically correct by the ruling powers. Consequently, after such a judge has rendered a judgment that by the rules still in force is not appealable, there is a judgment allegedly contrary to the people's conscience. The judge is then removed from office, and the executive branch of the government refuses to execute on the judgment he rendered. In such a case, where the term "legal system" is expanded to include among its rules those which provide for the political reactions to the final judicial pronouncements, it may be permissible to conclude that the rendered final judgment was wrong. However, if the term "legal system" is not so expanded, but instead is confined to a structure such as that prevailing in England or the United States; what rules within the legal system would permit concluding that a final judgment is wrong?

Consider this case. In an action for breach of contract, in order to establish the contract, the plaintiff attempts to show that there had been a sufficient agreement as to quantity and price. Plaintiff's correspondence file somehow does not contain a letter included in the defendant's file, which letter would clearly establish the plaintiff's contention that agreement had been reached on the disputed items. The defendant's counsel does not volunteer the letter, although aware of its existence. Consequently, the judgment is rendered in favor of his client because, as the court said, the plaintiff failed to prove the contract. If the defendant's counsel, over the evening cigar, confided his secret to us, could we then correctly admit that the judge's final decision was wrong? I believe the answer is quite clear. As regards the analysis of the legal concepts involved, the decision was in no way wrong. Surely a contrary conclusion would require that we demand not only wisdom, but omniscience of the judiciary. The rules of the system require judgments on the basis of the evidence presented. A more far-reaching rule would demand that the judge serve as investigator as well as judge. Even if the judge knew about the concealed fact, judgment rendered in favor of the defendant would still not be wrong in light of the legal rules which pertain to judicial notice.

If the rules for judicial notice permit the judge to base his decision upon any information he may have, whether or not proved in court, and judgment is still rendered in favor of the defendant, there would then be a case where it would seem that the relevant rules enable one to admit that the judgment is wrong. This extreme case, however, is made possible only for that legal system where a judgment secured by fraud or like conduct is, nevertheless, final and unappealable. However, even in this case, what is wrong is not the judgment, but the legal system, and here, "wrong" quite clearly means morally or socially wrong or perhaps politically objectionable. In the above hypothetical case, if the judicial notice rule were broadened to include any information possessed by the judge and the judge knew of the letter in the defendant's file, then a judgment

119

in favor of the defendant would appear to have been the result of the kind of judicial behavior which suggests fraud or collusion and from which the legal rules probably provide for relief. If the judicial notice rules included any knowledge had by the judge, and in the above case the judgment ran for the defendant when it was *suspected* that the judge knew about the letter in the defendant's file, then to say that we can admit the judgment was wrong, though final, would have a rather different meaning. Now, all that is meant is that certain facts are in dispute; and if the facts are as suspected, then the legal rules warranted a contrary judgment. However, this is a much less misleading formulation than to suggest that we can admit final and nonappealable judgments to be wrong.

Furthermore, the absence of any vigorous judicial logic makes the use of the term "wrong" questionable even as regards a final, but still appealable judgment. There are relatively few cases where the legal rules, as well as the operational and evidentiary facts, are so clear as to enable one to conclude prior to appeal that the rendered judgment at that time is wrong. True, subsequent appeal may result in reversal, but this does not necessarily mean that the earlier judgment was wrong. Rather, it means that if, while the rules remain unchanged, a case with the same operational and evidentiary facts is heard by a lower court within the same system after the reversal of the earlier judgment, and the lower court again decides as in the prior case, then the decision is wrong. Now "wrong" means that the legal rules themselves compel a reversal. This use of the term "wrong" is analogous to that where it is said that it would be wrong for a lead ball to fall upwards, away from the center of gravity. No examination of the records, statutes, or case law would be required where the question certified to the appeal court was, "Is a judgment on the same facts as those in the first case correct if that judgment is for the same party as it was in the earlier case, although judgment in the early case was reversed on appeal?" However, in any other case than the one where, as above, the rules for the mechanical operation of the legal machinery themselves require reversal, the application of the term "wrong" to a judgment is at best a prediction about subsequent judicial conduct and at worst a conclusion deduced from unstated, if indeed conscious, ethical or other nonlegal premises.

Problems Involved in Applying Professor Hart's Definitional Technique

Returning now to the basic problem of how elucidation shall be secured for fundamental legal terms, what is the special technique contributed by Professor Hart? His three-step method requires that one:

[1] take a sentence in which the term to be defined plays its characteristic role;

[2] explain the sentence "first by specifying the conditions under which the whole sentence is true",[23] and then,

[3] explain the sentence "by showing how it is used in drawing a conclusion from the rules in a particular case."

At the outset, it need be noticed that this approach to the definition of fundamental legal terms is not intended to introduce new terms into a system, but rather functions to explicate the use of old, familiar terms. A definition functions either to describe existing language habits or to predict future ones. Here, there apparently is a definition of the former type. Were this not true, the initial step in the proposed procedure would imply failure, since for a new term, the characteristic role is not yet known. Indeed, one may wonder whether a Hart-type definition is necessary if we already know the characteristic role the definiendum plays in sentences which may be true. For if a sentence in a natural language may be true, then it must be meaningful, and hence the words utilized in the construction of the sentence must have been combined in keeping with the rules which govern such constructions. It therefore appears that at least certain minimal demands for elucidation have been met if we are able to use the definiendum in constructing true sentences. Whether or not more is required depends upon the reasons for which the definition (or elucidation) was demanded, and this raises a veritable host of questions.

Why have jurisprudents for centuries sought to define terms like "law," "right," and "duty"? Is it because, like poets, they wish to paint beautiful word pictures that are pleasing? Although such an explanation may unfortunately come close to sufficing for some jurisprudential writings, there are more impressive explanations available for some of the work done. Law, as an enterprise, has the most ultimate test of its value in the way it regulates human behavior; or, to be more Jamesian, law is as good as it works. Consequently, a definition or elucidation of fundamental legal terms may be as delightful as an afternoon tea cake but equally useless in better facilitating the everyday dispatch of legal business. When definitions of legal terms are required, it must be because

---

23. Apparently this procedure must be distinguished from the seemingly similar technique of providing a statement of the conditions under which there are said to exist things of the sort "meant" by the term to be defined. Hart has written elsewhere that it is wrong "to succumb to the temptation, offered by modern theories of meaning, to identify the meaning of a legal concept, say 'contract,' with the statement of the conditions in which contracts are held to exist; since, owing to the defeasible character of the concept, such a statement, though it would express the necessary and sometimes sufficient conditions for the application of 'contract,' could not express conditions which were always sufficient."

121

there is some need felt in the workaday business of the law; it must be because there is avoidable confusion diminishing the efficiency of the legal machinery.

When these considerations are applied to the elucidation procedure outlined above, should it be concluded that more is required than knowing how to use legal terms in their characteristic way so as to make meaningful sentences? Although a user of legal terms may employ the term "right" in sentences which are meaningful, it would be more desirable if that user could also employ the term in sentences which are true, and even more desirable if the constructed sentences are also unambiguous and not vague. The problem, therefore, is whether step [1] in the above procedure is not only necessary, but, indeed, also sufficient for securing the requisite elucidation; or to state the matter differently, do we know all the elucidation is likely to supply if we know the characteristic way in which to use the definiendum? On the other hand, if the elucidation is required to explain the old and familiar, it may be that beginning with the characteristic way in which the term is used in a sentence is quite the reason why elucidiation is demanded—that is, it may be that definition is required in order to replace the old characteristic way the term is used.

If the reason for which elucidation is sought is to better enable the legal machinery to serve, and if the characteristic role played by the legal term is already known, what will steps [2] and [3] do to increase the efficiency of the machinery? Only if we assume that our knowledge of the characteristic role is accidental does [2] add to the efficiency with which the terms are used. Since [2] is only the *specifications* of the conditions under which the sentences of [1] are true, it is implied that [1] was true. Hence, it must be noticed that [2] is not the specification of conditions for distinguishing between true and false or between unambiguous and ambiguous or between not vague and vague instances of the terms used in the sentence. Rather, [2] merely meets the relatively weaker demand of making express what is already known. Indeed, as stated, [2] is satisfied if nothing more is done other than to make express the conditions for the ambiguous or vague use of the term to be elucidated.

It may be possible that [2] actually does much more than specify the conditions under which [1] is true. This is so for two reasons. First, because in defining or analyzing a vague term or expression and despite the intention to adhere to common usage, the analyst almost inevitably affects the meaning in the course of his analysis. Since [2] is really an analysis of [1], the specifications of the truth conditions may actually accomplish something in the way of redefinition. Second, and more important, it may have been the intention of Professor Hart to have [2] read as follows, instead of as it now reads:

[2′] Explain the characteristic sentence first by specifying the conditions under which the whole sentence *would be* true.

[2′] makes a considerably more powerful demand than does [2]. Now [2′] may not have the relatively trivial function of [2], which merely specified what was already required to be known. For example, if the characteristic sentence is "An employer has the privilege of firing employees because of their race, despite the existence of a contract which prohibits discharge except for improper performance of duty," the difference in the demands made by [2] and by [2′] becomes clearer. Where [2] is the rule, it may be necessary to state that the truth conditions cannot be specified because the sentence happens to be false for the particular legal system involved. Whereas where [2′] is the rule, there may then be developed the interesting legal doctrines which permit courts to refuse recovery for breach of the employment contract. For example, under [2′] it might be developed that recovery is denied because the employer had a duty to discharge the employee, and if persons are legally privileged to do their legal duty, then the sentence *would be* true.

As regards the first of the two above-mentioned functions of [2], it should not be thought that specification of "truth conditions" which do diminish the vagueness of a term are but accomplishing some relatively modest and unimportant linguistic reform. Especially where the critical terms involved are those characteristically fundamental for a legal system, it may be of decisive significance if the area of vagueness can be confined. Where a definition or analysis of a fundamental legal term does not resolve the vagueness of the term, exceptionally deceptive consequences may appear. Since one of the purposes of analysis or definition is to achieve clarity by achieving a certain degree of uniformity in the use of relevant terms, a definition which leaves the term vague may appear to achieve the desired result, whereas, in fact, the contrary is true. Perhaps an example will illustrate the point.

In the hope of replacing confusion and disagreement arising from contrary reactions to problems concerning an individual's rights in a certain area, *A* proposes a definition or analysis of the term. *A* suggests that "*X* has a right to privacy" means "it is not contrary to higher law for *X* to get a money damages judgment whenever anyone of a certain class in fringes that right." Now, to convince his audience that such an analysis removes disagreement, *A* asks *B* and *C* whether they believe it true to say "*X* has a right to privacy unless there is some public necessity for the contrary." If *B* and *C* both agree that the sentence is true, does this necessarily imply that they share an identical or substantially similar *belief* about whether *X* has the certain right? I think the answer is quite apparently in the negative since because of the vagueness of "not contrary to higher law," what *A* and *B* probably share is an agreement in attitude about *X*'s rights. When a term or expression continues vague after analysis, the various hearers of the term may each think of different qualities suggested by either the emotive or descriptive meanings of the term. For hearer *B* the assertion that "*X* has a right to privacy" results from the belief that certain qualities are present which qualities may not be considered present by *C*. Nevertheless, *C* considers other qualities to be present, and for him, these require the same conclusion as was reached by *B* because of totally different beliefs. It is also possible that *B* and *C* agree that *X* has the right not because they do share beliefs, but rather because they have no disagreement in attitude. When the vagueness of a term is reduced, the possibility of such seeming agreement in belief is also reduced because, at least in part, the process of eliminating vagueness is to reduce the number of different qualities suggested (or "meant") by the term. In addition, the vaguer a term, the weaker the distinction between what the term suggests and its descriptive meaning, and, consequently, there is greater likelihood for seeming agreement of belief.

If, as is suggested above, [2] is not intended to affect the vagueness of the expression, and if plurality of usage determines what is the characteristic role of the term to be defined, then [2] merely specifies what may be grossly careless legal linguistic habits. Nor is there much likelihood of escape from this difficulty by determining the characteristic role through something other than plurality of usage. Were some other test to be employed, it would imply that what was built into [1] was expected to be achieved by [2] and [3]. A test other than plurality of usage would imply that [1] required not merely a characteristic use, but a certain type of characteristic use—for example, the term as used by law professors or judges.[26] On the other hand, and treating the proposed technique for elucidation as something intended to benefit the actual user of fundamental legal terms, the empirical difficulties involved in satisfying [1] may be sufficient to drive some not too hearty souls back to essences.

If plurality of usage does determine the characteristic role, how then is plurality of usage decided? Shall every use of the term "right" by Hohfeld be accorded more weight, or perhaps less, than usage by the ordinary informed citizen? Just as plurality of popular suffrage may hardly be taken as the criterion of truth so, too, plurality of usage, without further limits, may hardly be the criterion to determine the charac-

26. Hohfeld so often refers to instances where legal specialists have improperly utilized fundamental legal terms as to suggest that perhaps law professors and judges are among the least desirable subjects to study in order to determine usage which is characteristic and acceptable.

teristic use for which elucidation would increase the efficiency of the legal machinery. But once this is admitted and it is recognized that some special characteristic usage is to be analyzed, there is then built into [1] what is supposed to be stated by [2].

There is one further manner in which [1] might be interpreted, but nothing written by Hart suggests or approves such an approach. What may be intended by the phrase "characteristic way" in [1] may be something very different from what is implicit in the above attempted analysis of what Hart intended [1] to be and to accomplish. Instead of searching for the *cognitive* characteristic way in which fundamental legal terms are used in sentences, perhaps attention should be paid instead to trying to discover what is the characteristic *emotive* way in which the terms are used. After such has been achieved, then an effort may be made to supply the other part of the story, that is, an analysis of the cognitive elements.

Obviously, there are many difficulties created by so interpreting [1]. Even more than before, the task of determining the characteristic emotive way in which the term is used may be more difficult than ascertaining the characteristic cognitive way in which the term is employed. Even more troublesome may be the fact that the characteristic emotive use of the term may be only remotely connected with the term when used in its characteristic cognitive role, and, consequently, [2] would require an even more elaborate formulation than otherwise. Despite such difficulties, there is something appealing about a pattern of analysis which attempts to reveal, if only by illustrations, insights into both the emotive and cognitive lines of legal terms. However, as is indicated above, there is nothing in Hart to intimate that he intends such an approach.

The third step in the above-suggested elucidation procedure is to show how the sentence is used in drawing a conclusion from the rules of the case. However, there may be some confusion here, for in one sense, whatever is used to draw a conclusion from the rules, it is not the sentence to be elucidated. Rather that sentence is the conclusion, and it can only be other sentences which are utilized in explicating how that conclusion is to be drawn. This will be true where the sentence to be analyzed is the end product of certain facts as examined in the light of legal rules. In a different sense, however, the sentence to be analyzed may be a premise to which certain legal rules are then applied. In either event, there may be serious difficulty, since the mechanics of drawing conclusions from certain legal rules is something about which there is considerable doubt. Some maintain that any effort to reveal any mechanization in drawing legal conclusions is doomed to failure because too many uncontrollable variables enter into the calculation. These variables, usually thought to be the judge and the jury, prevent any mechanical application of rules. If, on the other hand, conclusions are not deducible by the application of mechanical procedures, what is it that is to be shown by step [3]? The most that can be done in this stage of elucidation is to suggest that when certain operational facts are presented, some legal conclusions are more likely than others. What complicates [3] even further is the expression "the rules of the case." If the rules of the case refer to those rules of the relevant system which are possibly appropriate in any situation where certain operational facts are presented, [3] would convey rather little of value. If "the rules of the case" is intended to denote those rules of the system which are not only possibly appropriate, but most appropriate, then there should be some step between [2] and [3] which will suggest the criteria to be employed in making the determination which is pivotal in [3]—namely, which rules are most appropriate when certain operational facts are presented. However, even if the most appropriate rules are specified, that would show neither how the selected sentence was to be used in drawing a conclusion nor how the rules were used to draw the conclusions stated by the selected sentence. It would not be effecting any economy to have begun by requiring a definition for fundamental legal terms and to have discovered that in order to satisfy the demand, it necessitated an exposition about how legal conclusions are drawn. It would seem that before the latter task could be attempted, the satisfaction of the demand for adequate definitions would be a condition precedent.

Determining the Acceptability of a Definition

I believe that a considerable measure of the difficulty entailed by Professor Hart's method as well as that of many other methods results from the fact that too frequently a definition for some term is prematurely offered. Before a definition may be successful, there need be consideration devoted to certain preliminaries. One of these important preliminaries to a definition is the ascertainment of the purpose for which the definition has been requested. Failure to specify the purpose for which the definition is sought results from one of the most persistent misconceptions of analysis. It is the belief that a term or expression has at least one and at most one accurate meaning, and that since this is obviously so, there is no need to detail the basis of operation. In too many ways this is analogous to a bacteriologist peering through his microscope, hoping that some form of microscopic life will alight on his slide so that he may identify a new virus.

In addition to the above difficulty concerning purpose, before an attempt is made to supply a definition, it would be essential to know what equipment may be used. If the one demanding the definition agrees to rest content with a formula to which no test will be applied, it may then be sufficient to define "right" in terms of metaphysical elements, whether they be Platonic ideas, essences, or subjective intuitions. At the opposite extreme, if the only acceptable definition is one for which acceptance depends upon the ability to discover by experience or experiment the phenomena to which the definition applies, it is obvious that a very different formula will be required. It is important not to confuse tests for verifying a sentence with tests for deciding acceptability of a definition. The former tests are aimed at determining truth or something akin thereto, whereas the latter are designed to determine something quite different, something which is perhaps best called convenience. The reason the two are occasionally confused is probably attributable to the belief that acceptable definitions are those which increase the likelihood of securing a correspondence between certain words or groups of words and certain natural phenomena, and the not dissimilar belief that those sentences are true which somehow correspond to reality.

If consideration of definition in terms of essence is excluded, and if it is agreed that ostensive definition is in the main inapplicable to legal terms, then what alternatives are available for furthering the difficult tasks undertaken by Professor Hart? Perhaps the most that can be done, if all we wish is to correctly catalog rights, duties, etc., is to have some outstanding jurist or legal savant attach the label to all those legal events for which the term is thought to apply. Such would be a definition by specification of the extension, and for a thorough-going nominalist, no more suitable definition could be tendered. Thus, because of limits upon what is permissible material for constructing definitions, the nominalists may be required to accept definitions for fundamental legal terms which, for others, leaves much to be desired with regard to the usual conveniences for which a definition is sought. Primary among these lost conveniences is the fact that a definition by specification of the extension serves only to identify *past* cases. If new instances of the phenomena dealt with by the definition are to be included in the extension, then there needs be available some equipment (namely a technique for abstraction) which is more than the list identifying past cases.

In regard to a legal term, a definition by extension is all the more troublesome because what is needed is not so much a consistent usage for terms newly introduced into the system, but rather devices for making the old terms consistent. This is not to say that the *philosophic* task in regard to the definitions of fundamental legal terms may not be largely exhausted if there is indicated the extensions for the various ranges of meaning accompanied by a consideration of the emotive meaning problems. To the contrary, such an analysis would, for many practical purposes, terminate the clarificatory aspects of the problem, which is the task of philosophy. However, since jurisprudence is not merely philosophy, but rather philosophy applied to the problems of legal theory, the task of the jurisprudent may not be ended where the clarificatory objectives have been secured.

Were the legal term to be a new one, it might be possible to find a legal scholar of sufficient stature to specify the instances of the term. The introduction into American law of the conception of a right of privacy was largely the work of two men. Where, however, the term whose instances are to be specified is one with an hoary ancient history, such as "right" or "duty," an acceptable specifier may be hard to come by. Because no one is available whose decision is acceptable as to what is a right, a duty, or a law, there has been the persistent, frequently directionless effort to define, define, define! Of course, the effort need not be directionless. As was suggested earlier, the success of the definition may be judged in terms of the efficiency with which the defined term may be handled within the system as a result of a definition. However, if by chance or through experience one concerned with legal concepts so manipulates the terms required to work with those concepts as to achieve what for him is success, then he will recognize no need for definitions. It is only where some as yet unattained objective is desired that alteration of the linguistic habits and conceptual equipment is in order. For example, change in linguistic habits may be necessary where the available definitions for certain terms are inadequate in that the definition permits there to be included within the extension of the terms certain phenomena which, if excluded, might help increase the efficiency with which the term is utilized. For a legal system as a whole, the as yet unattained objectives are likely to be, at least for some systems, adequacy, certainty, simplicity, and economy, or perhaps more generally, though metaphorically, beauty.

The pernicious problem, then, is to decide when a definition does enhance at least one of the desired objectives. The more immediate problem discussed above has been whether or not the approach suggested by Professor Hart has contributed to reaching one of the desired objectives of a definition. In what has gone above, it has been suggested that rather than increasing the simplicity of the system, the contrary may be a consequence if the elucidation procedure of Hart is followed. In conclusion, it may be constructive to examine into what are the possible consequences of the application of Professor Hart's method to a particular fundamental legal term.

Acceptability of Professor Hart's Definition of "Right"

The exploration here is facilitated by the fact that there is tendered an elucidation of the expression "*A* has a legal right" by application of the above suggested method. Professor Hart writes:

> I would, therefore, tender the following as an elucidation of the ex-
> pression "a legal right": (1) A statement of the form "*X* has a right" is
> true if the following conditions are satisfied:
> (a) There is in existence a legal system.
> (b) Under a rule or rules of the system some other person *Y* is, in
> the events which have happened, obliged to do or abstain from some
> action.
> (c) This obligation is made by law dependent on the choice either
> of *X* or some other person authorized to act on his behalf so that either *Y*
> is bound to do or abstain from some action only if *X* (or some authorized
> person) so chooses or alternatively only until *X* (or such person) chooses
> otherwise. (2) A statement of the form "*X* has a right" is used to draw a
> conclusion of law in a particular case which falls under such rules.

As thorough-going analysis of the success of this elucidation as may be desired is not possible since the specific purposes for which the elucidation is offered are not specified. However, some conclusions may be suggested. Perhaps most important is the determination of whether the indicated truth conditions are both necessary and sufficient. One device for testing the elucidation is to consider cases of sentences of the form "*X* has a right" and see whether they do satisfy all the conditions of (1) but are yet contrary to what may be considered acceptable usage. If such a case could be discovered, it by no means implies that the above elucidation must be rejected. Rather, it does imply that we must either reject the elucidation or *else* reject as unacceptable what has hitherto been considered acceptable usage.

Consider the sentence [A]: "*X* has a right to be decapitated." It would seem that [A] is a strained, if not an utterly unacceptable, use of "*X* has a right." Yet, the sentence satisfies the truth conditions demanded by (1), (a), (b), and (c). There may be a legal system in which, by law, some official is authorized to decide when decapitation for *X* is desired, and his pronouncements on this topic may require action by *Y*. Sentence [A] satisfies this specified truth condition because (1)(c) demands only that the choice depend either on *X* or someone authorized to act on his behalf. If (1)(c) demanded instead that the choice depend on *X* or someone authorized by *X* to act on his behalf, the dilemma of rejecting either [A] or the proposed elucidation procedure might be avoided. However,

129

such an alternative to (1)(c) is then objectionable on other grounds, for there are many cases where the authority to act on X's behalf is created by operation of law and not dependent upon some act of approval by X. If the alternative (1)(c) includes the situation where X does authorize some other person to act on his behalf, even though the appointment and power of that person is by operation of law, because X approves such laws by virtue of his continued presence within the legal system, then such an argument does not solve any difficulties. However, the acceptance of the alternative (1)(c) implies that "X has a right," as used in [A], is an acceptable usage. This follows because if, by mere presence within the system, X is taken to approve the laws of the system, then X could be said to have authorized the official to decide about his decapitation.

It may be thought that [A] above is a mere oddity or that [A] is an erroneous usage of "right," because what is really meant is "liberty." Neither conclusion is warranted. Since [A] typifies a host of other examples, it is not a mere oddity. Also, since [A] does satisfy the specified truth conditions, and since those conditions are stated as applicable only to "right" as the correlative of duty, the use of "right" in [A] is not error if the truth conditions are sufficient as well as necessary.

Although [A] is typical of other counter-examples to the proposed analysis, it has been suggested that perhaps all that is necessary to eliminate such examples as [A] is to add one further condition. This condition, which may be referred to as (1)(d), requires that X generally welcome the occurrence of the events said to be dependent upon his choice or that of someone authorized to act on his behalf. This most challenging suggestion, of course, goes quite far beyond the kind of elucidation Professor Hart is attempting since (1)(d) introduces probabilistic conditions into an elucidation which is otherwise free of such empirical limitations. The suggestion is especially arresting because it reveals that almost universally accepted notion that rights are the sort of thing people wish for, a sort of ethically or socially desirable end. Such an element nowhere appears in the elucidation proposed by Professor Hart, and its inclusion would require an extensively elaborated analysis.

One aspect of the suggested (1)(d) merits a moment's attention. Should (1)(d) be, "X is generally likely to welcome the events . . . ," or should (1)(d) read, "X generally *ought* to welcome the events . . ."? Either formulation of (1)(d) would probably suffice to exclude [A] from being a counter-example, unless X has committed an act for which the legal rules permit decapitation. In that event, at best, only the second formulation of (1)(d), "X *ought* to welcome the events," would suffice. For if it is true that we have a right to do our duty, in the sense of "right" which is correlative to duty, there the second formulation of (1)(d) might be sufficient. The difficulty, of course, is the introduction of the most unwelcome word "ought" into what was before a fairly straightforward, empirical, nonemotive, nonethical approach to the elucidation of legal terms.

If the above discussion reveals, as I think it does, that (1) (a), (b), and (c) are not sufficient, the next problem is to decide if all three conditions are required. More specifically, is not (1)(a) stronger than necessary? What is it that is added to the suggested elucidation by requiring that there be a legal system? If (1)(a) merely specifies that effective sanctions are available to enforce the rules mentioned in (1)(b) and (1)(c), instead of requiring that there be a legal system, would it alter the effectiveness of the elucidation? A negative answer means that (1)(a) is stronger than necessary. An affirmative answer suggests that there is more built-in to the expression "legal system" than one of its dominant characteristics, and, hence, there needs be first an elucidation of that expression. If the existence of a legal system required, in addition to effective sanctions, a certain degree of efficiency, general compliance, etc., then in what way are these elements a part of the truth conditions for the test sentence? Does not X have the right involved if there are effective sanctions for the rules of (1)(b) and (1)(c) but there is not the requisite degree of general compliance to warrant the conclusion that there is in existence a legal system? If answer be in the affirmative, it is tantamount to admitting that the suggested elucidation is but a very clever way of saying "Might makes right," where right is the correlative of duty. If the answer is in the negative, then I think it apparent that there is much more required to elucidate so fundamental a legal term as "right."

There will be mentioned one further problem in regard to the above proposed elucidation procedure. Since (1) in the procedure is apparently all that is required to determine whether X does have a right, it would seem that any function of (2) is superfluous. If, on the other hand, (2) is also somehow a part of the conditions for determining whether X has a right, then as a grammatical matter, (1) and (2) should not be separate sentences; rather, (2) should be (1)(d). But more important than a question of grammar, is the problem of what is the function of (2), if we assume that by making (2) a separate sentence it was intended to have (2) do something other than help determine the truth of "X has a right."

It may be that (2) is intended to show something about the logic of the legal rules, since the rules plus the now known to be true sentence "X has a right" leads to other true sentences (conclusions of law). However, if this is the intended function of (2), then it does not give any particular elucidation about the term "right" but rather provides some insight into

131

the logic of the rules of the legal system. Although it is probably true that the greater one's knowledge of how the legal rules work, the greater will be one's ability to use the legal machinery, this need not imply that there is, therefore, any increased understanding of the meaning of the terms which occur in the rules of the system. One may know it to be true that a syzygetic phenomena will occur on June 1, 1956 and also know that this implies the conclusion that there will be an increase in the number of suicides on June 1st. However, does this knowledge of the logical connection between syzygies and suicides remove one's ignorance about syzygies? If in asking for a definition of "syzygy" it had been stated that the definition was requested in order to know what conclusions followed from the true sentence "A syzygetic phenomena will occur," then supplying the information about the logical connection to the sentence about suicides might be sufficient. However, Professor Hart, as is indicated above, has not stated his purpose in attempting to supply an elucidation for "X has a right," and, hence, it is difficult to decide whether or not (2) in his procedure is necessary, sufficient, or even useful.

Conclusion

In the preceding pages, an effort has been made to indicate some of the problems involved in defining fundamental legal terms. It was suggested that one of the primary difficulties results from the fact that all too often definitions are offered without knowing anything about either their intended function or how the definition is produced. Although such ignorance need not imply utter failure, it frequently impairs the effectiveness of the analysis and too often produces otherwise avoidable confusions. Consequently, it may be more than casually interesting to know in *advance* what are the philosophic commitments adhered to in attempting to frame the definition.

In addition to acquaintance with the philosophic basis of operation, it is also important to know what purpose is expected to be served by the definition or analysis. Just as in the conflict of laws, "procedure," "property," and other labels of qualification take on a different function when compared to the use of the same labels for internal law purposes, so, too, fundamental legal terms may operate to effect different legal purposes. It is, therefore, essential to know in advance which sense of the term is to be subjected to scrutiny. Further, it may be important in the analysis of fundamental legal terms to at least first surround the definiendum with sufficient safeguards to prevent the emotive meaning of the term from excessively affecting what is intended to be an analysis of the descriptive meaning. Where this is not done, and where no separate analysis of the emotive meaning is supplied, the analysis of the descriptive meaning is consequently less likely to accomplish the purpose for which the analysis has been undertaken. This may not be true where the purpose of analysis requires ignoring the emotive meaning problem in order to subsequently use the analyzed term for some (good or bad) propagandistic objective.

This aspect of the analysis problem, that is the question of emotive meaning, is particularly significant when dealing with problems in law because of the notorious political implications which can be and have been drawn from jurisprudential writings which purport to be dispassionate research not intended to be used on the political battlegrounds. Thus, even though Plato may have intended *The Republic* to be but a philosophical analysis of some problems in law and government, Karl Popper, among others, has found it to be anything but unbiased philosophical analysis. In more recent times, has not the work of Hans Kelsen evoked substantial antagonism because his jurisprudential position was thought to have politically objectionable implications? Although this is not the place to carefully defend or elaborate the thesis, I do believe that much of the politically objectionable consequences allegedly implied by the pure theory of law may vanish were sufficient attention devoted to the emotive meaning problems for some of the critical terms used by Kelsen. It is not here suggested that analysis of the emotive as well as descriptive meaning problems would make Hobbes or Austin useless for those anxious to support an unlimited sovereign. However, it is believed that attention to both dimensions of meaning is likely to be particularly rewarding where concern is had with fundamental legal terms.

Although much attention has been devoted above to indicating some of the problems involved in Hart's approach to definition, it is believed that his general technique is likely to be extremely rewarding. That is, it may be productive of much needed clarity if concern is had with the way legal language functions in the real life of attorneys, judges, and litigants instead of looking to some reified specimen of "Right" or "Law," where the first letter is always a capital. In addition, I believe Professor Hart's approach has what is almost an unique merit in jurisprudence. In most jurisprudential writing, even the willing reader is generally unable to examine the machinery used in the analysis but agrees (or disagrees) with the writer because some position taken agrees (or disagrees) with some previously held view of the reader. If this is not true in specific detail, it is likely to be the case as regards the broad outlines. In the work of Professor Hart, however, I believe it is possible to disagree with the conclusions but still admire the machinery for analysis, and this is much more important than agreement on conclusions, for it means that Professor Hart's method is, so to speak, "open for inspection."

II. POSITIVISM IN SEVERAL FORMS

Hubbard, "One Man's Theory . . .": A Metatheoretical Analysis of H. L. A. Hart's Model of Law*

2. The Model of Law—Law as Rules

Hart unequivocally states that law consists of rules. In reaching this conclusion he spends considerable time criticizing the shortcomings of other theories. This criticism will be referred to in some succeeding sections. At present the focus will be on Hart's discussion of the central role that rules play in all legal systems.

a. The Nature of Rules

Before developing a general definition of rules, it should be noted that Hart distinguishes between two basic types of rules—primary and secondary. The basis of this distinction is the assertion that a rule of the form:

"Thou shalt not do X (e.g., murder); if you do X then Y sanction (e.g., hanging) will be imposed."

is "fundamentally" different from a rule of the form:

"If you want to do A (e.g., make a will), then you must do B (e.g., have three witnesses)."

In the first case failure to comply usually results in intervention and affirmative action by the legal system. In the second case non-compliance

* [36 *Md. L. Rev.* 39, 54–69 (1976). Reprinted by permission.
F. Patrick Hubbard (1944–   ) is Associate Professor of Law at the University of South Carolina School of Law.]

results in nullity, nothing more. Given this distinction, Hart develops a two-fold typology of rules:[56]

> (R-1) Rules can be divided into two basic types:
>   (a) Primary rules which dictate certain behavior patterns and which usually, but *not necessarily,* provide that sanctions will be imposed for breach of the rule.
>   (b) Secondary rules which
>   (1) confer "power":
>   (A) to create primary rules or subordinate secondary rules;
>   (B) to interpret primary rules;
>   (C) to apply primary rules to facts; and
>   (D) to apply sanctions for breach of primary rules; and,
>   (2) nullify the attempted exercise of power if the rule is not followed.

It should be noted that in Hart's model a primary rule that prohibits murder is still a rule even though no penalty is provided; *by definition,* however, no such separation of nullity and a secondary rule is possible.

With these two basic types of rule in mind, it is possible to discuss Hart's general definition of a rule. Hart does not define a rule at any one place in *The Concept of Law.* However, when the book is read as a whole, it is apparent that a "rule" is viewed by Hart in terms of four elements: (1) a symbolic communication of a specified standard of conduct to someone who must conform to the standard; (2) an "internal attitude" toward the rule by those to whom it is directed, which is manifested as an awareness that the rule provides a "binding" standard, i.e., behavior "ought"

---

56. Hart, *Concept,* ch. 5. The basic thrust of Hart's distinction is reflected in the following quotation: "It is true that the idea of a rule is by no means a simple one: we have already seen in Chapter III the need, if we are to do justice to the complexity of a legal system, to discriminate between two different though related types. Under rules of the one type, which may well be considered the basic or primary type, human beings are required to do or abstain from certain actions, whether they wish to or not. Rules of the other type are in a sense parasitic upon or secondary to the first; for they provide that human beings may by doing or saying certain things introduce new rules of the primary type, extinguish or modify old ones, or in various ways determine their incidence or control their operations. Rules of the first type impose duties; rules of the second type confer powers, public or private. Rules of the first type concern actions involving physical movement or changes; rules of the second type provide for operations which lead not merely to physical movement or change, but to the creation or variation of duties or obligations."

to conform and the rule "justifies" the sanction for non-conformity;[60] (3) a pattern of behavior in conformity to the rule; and (4) the effect of non-compliance with the rule.

These four elements are all necessary in "studying" or understanding rules, but the first two aspects are very different from the last two. In Hart's scheme a rule is *defined* in terms of the first two elements—*there is no rule* unless there is both a communication and an internal sense of the binding nature of the communication. The third aspect of rules is not crucial to the *existence* of a rule because a rule is still a rule even if behavior does not conform: "broken" rules are still rules.

The final element in considering rules requires further discussion because the responses to or effects of non-compliance must be viewed not only in terms of the behavior which actually occurs when the rule is not followed, but also in terms of the "formal" theoretical requirements as to what the communication must declare concerning the effects of a

60. . . . This internal attitude is related to, but not the same as, "obligation." Since Hart regards an understanding of "obligation" as "crucial," some further development of this concept is in order:

"*A* orders *B* to hand over his money and threatens to shoot him if he does not comply. According to the theory of coercive orders this situation illustrates the notion of obligation or duty in general. . . . The plausibility of the claim that the gunman situation displays the meaning of obligation lies in the fact that it is certainly one in which we would say that *B,* if he obeyed, was 'obliged' to hand over his money. It is, however, equally certain that we should misdescribe the situation if we said, on these facts, that *B* 'had an obligation' or a 'duty' to hand over the money. . . .

". . . There is a difference . . . between the assertion that someone *was obliged* to do something and the assertion that he *had an obligation* to do it. The first is often a statement about the beliefs and motives with which an action is done: *B* was obliged to hand over his money may simply mean, as it does in the gunman case, that he believed that some harm or other unpleasant consequences would befall him if he did not hand it over and he handed it over to avoid those consequences. In such cases the prospect of what would happen to the agent if he disobeyed has rendered something he would otherwise have preferred to have done (keep the money) less eligible. . . .

". . . But the statement that someone *had an obligation* to do something is of a very different type and there are many signs of this difference. Thus not only is it the case that the facts about *B*'s action and his beliefs and motives in the gunman case, though sufficient to warrant the statement that *B* was obliged to hand over his purse, are *not sufficient* to warrant the statement that he had an obligation to do this; it is also the case that facts of this sort, i.e., facts about beliefs and motives, are *not necessary* for the truth of a statement that a person had an obligation to do something. Thus the statement that a person had an obligation, e.g., to tell the truth or report for military service, remains true even if he believed (reasonably or unreasonably) that he would never be found out and had nothing to fear from disobedience. Moreover, whereas the statement that he had this obligation is quite independent of the question whether or not he in fact reported for service, the statement that someone was obliged to do something, normally carries the implication that he actually did it."

breach. As indicated in the preceding discussion of the two types of rules, the "formal" theoretical requirements are as follows: (1) A primary rule is defined as still being a rule even if there is no provision for penalty in case of breach; and (2) A secondary rule is defined as a rule which provides that the effect of breach is nullity. The *behavioral* response to breach is measured by a less stringent standard: both types of rules are still rules even if breach does not in fact result in a penalty (primary rule) or nullity (secondary rule). In other words, an unenforced rule is still a rule so long as the two formal definitional requirements of the concept of a rule are satisfied.

Hart's use of these four elements in his model can be summarized in the following perspective on a rule:

(R-2) A rule:
    (a) *Requires:*
        (1) A "communication" of a prescribed standard of conduct (See Proposition R-3(a) below), and
        (2) An internal attitude manifested as an awareness of the "binding" nature of the standard.
    (b) Is *usually* (but not always) accompanied by a pattern of behavior in conformity with the rule. (However, see Proposition R-5 below).
    (c) Deals with breach of the rule as follows:
        (1) The formal declaration
            (A) of a primary rule will *usually* (but not always) provide a penalty for breach;
            (B) of a secondary rule will *always* provide that a breach results in nullity.
        (2) The actual enforcement for breach of rules will usually (but not always) conform with the declaration.

There is always a symbolic, informational aspect involved in dictating behavior (Proposition R-2(a)(1)), and certain characteristics of a rule are imposed by this aspect. For example, no information has been conveyed if the rule is unintelligible to the persons subject to the rule; thus, rules must be communicated in an intelligible fashion if they are to control. Similarly, the rules must be communicated prior to the actions involved if they are to be effective. However, given man's limited ability to foresee future developments, there may be situations where the symbolic communication occurs *after* the act.

As a result of man's limited ability to process information, other generalizations can be made about rules. First, rules cannot deal with every specific act. Instead, rules on the whole will have to be directed toward general classes of persons and/or classes of behavior. Moreover, even relatively specific commands are plagued by the inherent ambiguity of language. The net result of man's limited ability to foresee and consider all possible events and to communicate concerning those events is that rules cannot conclusively deal with all possible behavioral possibilities. There will always be a class of behavior which may or may not fall within the scope of the rule. This area of uncertain inclusion is referred to by Hart as the "open-textured" quality of rules.

Thus, based on the communication aspects of a rule the following proposition is included in Hart's model:

> (R-3) The symbolic component of a rule will
>   (a) *Usually* be communicated
>   (1) to those affected
>   (2) prior to the conduct involved, and
>   (3) in a form
>   (A) that is intelligible to those affected; and
>   (B) that refers to general classes of persons and conduct.
>   (b) *Always* be "open textured"—i.e., of the set of "possible behavior" there will be three subjects:
>   (1) a "closed" subset of behavior which is clearly included;
>   (2) a "closed" subset of behavior which is clearly excluded;
>   (3) an "open" subset of behavior which is not clearly included or excluded. . . .

b. Pattern or Formal Structure of Rules and Legal Systems in Society

Society requires a certain minimum of order. However, given a man's limitations, this co-ordination will not occur automatically. Therefore, constraints on behavior must be *imposed*. Obviously, these constraints cannot be imposed effectively unless they are communicated to the members of society. (Proposition R-3(a).) Because of man's limited ability to process information, these communications must be generalized. (Proposition R-3(a)(3)(B).) Moreover, given man's limited ability to impose his will on other men, those subject to the constraints must conform to them at least in part out of something more than "fear" of sanctions. This "something more" could be a number of things, but Hart asserts that it always includes an internal sense of obligation to some extent. (Compare Proposition R-11 below.) Therefore, Hart's model contains the following proposition:

(R-4) Societies *must* have rules.

Since a society must have a minimum of order, there must be not only rules but also some *consistency in rules*. Otherwise, different rule-prescribed patterns of behavior could conflict and the minimal order could not be achieved. Thus, societies must have "systems" of rules which form a coherent whole. This coherence is achieved by a "rule of recognition," which determines whether the other subordinate rules comply with the system—i.e., whether they are "valid."

The content of the rule of recognition—its definition of validity—is developed over time. This development has two dimensions:

> [O]ne is expressed in the external statement of fact that the rule exists in the actual practice of the system; the other is expressed in the internal statements of validity made by those who use it in identifying the law.

The first element is required because without a minimum level of obedience to the rule of recognition (which provides consistency),[79] the minimum-order requirement . . . is not satisfied. The second aspect is essential because the *rule* of recognition must satisfy the two requirements of the definition of a rule set out in Proposition R-2. The communication aspects of a rule (Proposition R-2(a)(1)) are satisfied by the *overt* reference to the rule by those who use it. Similarly, the internal aspects of a rule (Proposition R-2(a)(2)) are satisfied by these same people recognizing the binding nature of the rule of recognition.

It should be noted that there are two characteristics of the rule of

---

79. The "obedience" does not need to correlate with an internal perspective toward the rule: "[O]beying a rule (or an order) *need* involve no thought on the part of the person obeying that what he does is the right thing both for himself and for others to do: he need have no view of what he does as a fulfilment of a standard of behaviour for others of the social group. He need not think of his conforming behaviour as 'right,' 'correct,' or 'obligatory.' His attitude, in other words, need not have any of that critical character which is involved whenever social rules are accepted and types of conduct are treated as general standards. He need not, though he may, share the internal point of view accepting the rules as standards for all to whom they apply. Instead, he may think of the rule only as something demanding action from *him* under the threat of penalty; he may obey it out of fear of the consequences, or from inertia, without thinking of himself or others as having an obligation to do so and without being disposed to criticize either himself or others for deviations." Hart, *Concept* 112 (emphasis in original).

recognition, each of which makes it a unique type of rule. First, the internal acceptance need only be satisfied by the "officials" of the legal system.[80] Second, the minimum-obedience aspect of the rule of recognition makes it the only rule which requires that behavior conform to some degree of its prescriptions. A totally disregarded rule of recognition is logically impossible in Hart's system, while a totally disregarded lesser rule can logically still be termed a rule. (Proposition R-2(b)).

Given these two aspects—external observance and internal acceptance—the process of determining the existence and content of the "rule of recognition" in a society involves the following steps: (1) observe the society over time to determine whether its various rules are consistent; (2) if they are consistent, determine whether this consistency correlates with a supreme "rule" of validity which is "accepted" by the "officials" in the society; (3) if this acceptance exists, determine whether the behavior of citizens generally conforms to the supreme rule of validity, i.e., whether they generally obey the "rules" promulgated by the "officials." . . . In other words, the "rule of recognition" identifies a pattern persisting in the society over some period of time. Consequently, a particular statement of that society's rule of recognition at a given time cannot provide a prediction concerning the content of the rule in the *future*. Moreover, one cannot say that the content of the rule of recognition has changed until after a change has persisted for a period of time.

This concept of a rule of recognition is summarized in the following proposition:

> (R-5) Legal rules are unified into a system by a "rule of recognition" which is a type of secondary rule authorizing certain persons ("officials") to exercise various powers in a consistent, systematic manner. (Proposition R-1(b).)

---

80. Hart summarizes this distinction: "There are therefore two minimum conditions necessary and sufficient for the existence of a legal system. On the one hand those rules of behaviour which are valid according to the system's ultimate criteria of validity must be generally obeyed, and, on the other hand, its rules of recognition specifying the criteria of legal validity and its rules of change and adjudication must be effectively accepted as common public standards of official behaviour by its officials. The first condition is the only one which private citizens *need* satisfy: they may obey each 'for his part only' and from any motive whatever; though in a healthy society they will in fact often accept these rules as common standards of behaviour and acknowledge an obligation to obey them, or even trace this obligation to a more general obligation to respect the constitution. The second condition must also be satisfied by the officials of the system. They must regard these as common standards of official behaviour and appraise critically their own and each other's deviations as lapses."

(a) The rule of recognition has two dimensions:
    (1) A minimal level of obedience by citizens to the rules promulgated by the "officials" identified by the rule; and
    (2) A shared acceptance by the "officials" of the rule of recognition. Such "acceptance" is manifested by
        (A) a minimal level of obedience to the rule of recognition in exercising their power under the rule,
        (B) an internal awareness of the binding nature of the rule, and
        (C) external references to the rule.
(b) The rule of recognition is developed over time as the above pattern of obedience and acceptance manifests itself. Therefore,
    (1) it can only be identified retrospectively, and
    (2) changes over a short period of time do not affect it.

A society which has only primary rules is relatively static because it can change rules only gradually. (Proposition R-1 (b)(1)(A).) Similarly, without secondary rules to create "official powers," a society cannot use specialists in interpreting and applying rules and in imposing sanctions. (Proposition R-1(b)(1)(B), (C), (D).) Therefore, primitive societies with few or no secondary rules are less "efficient" than dynamic societies with a large proportion of complex secondary rules. Hart divides these secondary rules into four types,[88] but for present purposes it is sufficient to express the relationship between the society and secondary rules as follows:

> (R-6) Secondary rules make it possible for society to be dynamic and to have legal "officials." (Proposition R-1.) Therefore, societies with such rules are more "efficient" than societies without them.

[Figure 1] summarizes the development of Hart's model to this point. It should be noted that Hart is not merely asserting that *some* societies have this structure. The assertion is that *all* non-primitive societies have this pattern and that his model enables us to identify the pattern and "classify" its component parts.

---

88. The four types are: (1) "Rule of recognition." (2) "Rules of change." (3) "Rules of adjudication." (4) Secondary rules which "provide the centralized official 'sanctions' of the system."

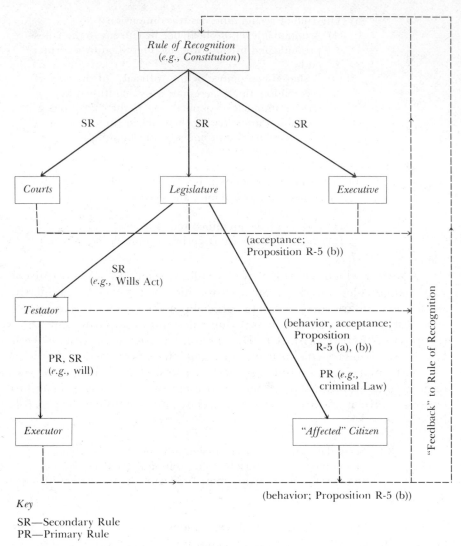

Key

SR—Secondary Rule
PR—Primary Rule

[Figure 1]

c. The Content of Law

Hart's model is not limited to the formal structure of rules in society. He also comments on the necessary substantive *content* of legal rules. The first such assertion is:

(R-7) The legal rules must limit the use of deadly force.

Given the central role of survival in Hart's model of man, the necessity of this requirement is obvious. The other substantive requirements demand more discussion.

Men have limited resources available to them. In order to provide minimal order, these resources must be divided in some reasonably stable, identifiable manner. Thus, a legal system must have some rules substantively concerned with material property:

(R-8) The legal rules must contain some substantive "property" rules governing material resources whereby:
    (a) at any particular time
    (b) a particular person(s) may exclude all others
    (c) from a particular material resource.

Hart has assumed that dynamic societies with a division of labor are more efficient. Thus the system of rules should include a way to achieve a society which is characterized by both change and a division of labor. Individuals, therefore, must be given some authority to engage in exchange and to determine the conditions of exchange. The following proposition results:

(R-9) The legal rules must contain some secondary rules which authorize individuals:
    (a) to *exchange* property and services, and
    (b) to "contract" for *future exchanges* of property and/or services.

Hart notes that the property rules (Proposition R-8) need not involve individual ownership, which is a broader concept than the power of exchange developed in Proposition R-9.

These exchange relationships will not be successful unless the communications between individuals are reliable. Therefore, individuals must be forbidden from dishonest, misleading communications, i.e., fraud and such dishonesty in exchange must be prohibited by the rules. More generally, a society where the members could not trust one another in vital matters would face difficulties in satisfying the minimal function of survival. Consequently, because societies must have rules which substantively limit dishonesty, the following proposition emerges:

(R-10) The legal rules must limit the use of dishonest or deliberately misleading communications.

143

Given limited resources and limited altruism, the preceding rules will not work unless there is some element of coercion. Moreover, these sanctions would not work unless men were all relatively equal, because if it were otherwise, "superstrong" rule violators could escape sanctions. Thus, all legal systems will have some substantive coercive elements:

> (R-11) The legal system must impose sanctions for some breaches in order to coerce behavior.

This proposition does not contradict the earlier statement that a rule does not necessarily require coercion. (Proposition R-1 (b) (2).) A rule is more likely to be *effective* if coercion is involved; consequently, Proposition R-11 asserts that societies must use sufficient coercion in support of (some) rules so that the requisite minimum order will be assured.

One aspect of the model of man is that no single person can impose his behavioral requirements on others for any period of time; therefore, an individual "ruler" needs the cooperation of a *significant part* of the society.

> [I]t is plain that neither the law nor the accepted morality of societies need extend their minimal protections and benefits to all within their scope. . . .
> . . . [But] if a system of rules is to be imposed by force on any, there must be a sufficient number who accept it voluntarily. Without their voluntary co-operation . . . the coercive power of law and government cannot be established.

Thus, Hart asserts that rules must be minimally beneficial to a substantial portion of a society by granting this portion mutual benefits in the content of law. The following proposition summarizes this mutuality in the content of law:

> (R-12) The rules must have some minimal mutuality of content for a significant part of society so that this segment of society will be given an incentive for co-operation with the rules.

The final requirement concerning the content of a system of rules is that the behavior must be possible. Rules which require the impossible will clearly fail as a method of social control. Thus the following proposition is part of the model:

> (R-13) Rules, particularly primary rules, must contain provisions that can in fact be obeyed.

144

R. M. Dworkin, The Model of Rules*

II. Positivism

Positivism has a few central and organizing propositions as its skeleton, and though not every philosopher who is called a positivist would subscribe to these in the way I present them, they do define the general position I want to examine. These key tenets may be stated as follows:

(a) The law of a community is a set of special rules used by the community directly or indirectly for the purpose of determining which behavior will be punished or coerced by the public power. These special rules can be identified and distinguished by specific criteria, by tests having to do not with their content but with their *pedigree* or the manner in which they were adopted or developed. These tests of pedigree can be used to distinguish valid legal rules from spurious legal rules (rules which lawyers and litigants wrongly argue are rules of law) and also from other sorts of social rules (generally lumped together as "moral rules") that the community follows but does not enforce through public power.

(b) The set of these valid legal rules is exhaustive of "the law," so that if someone's case is not clearly covered by such a rule (because there is none that seems appropriate, or those that seem appropriate are vague, or for some other reason) then that case cannot be decided by "applying the law." It must be decided by some official, like a judge, "exercising his discretion," which means reaching beyond the law for some other sort of standard to guide him in manufacturing a fresh legal rule or supplementing an old one.

(c) To say that someone has a "legal obligation" is to say that his case falls under a valid legal rule that requires him to do or to forbear from doing something. (To say he has a legal right, or has a legal power of some sort, or a legal privilege or immunity, is to assert, in a shorthand way, that others have actual or hypothetical legal obligations to act or not to act in certain ways touching him.) In the absence of such a valid legal rule there is no legal obligation; it follows that when the judge decides an issue by exercising his discretion, he is not enforcing a legal obligation as to that issue.

---

* [35 *U. Chi. L. Rev.* 14, 17–46) (1967). Copyright © 1967 by the University of Chicago. Reprinted by permission.

Ronald M. Dworkin (1931–) was educated at Harvard (A.B. 1953; LL.B. 1957) and Oxford (B.A. 1955) Universities. He practiced law from 1958 until 1962, when he became Associate Professor at Yale University. He was Professor of Law at Yale from 1965 until 1968. Since 1969, he has been Professor of Jurisprudence and Fellow, University College, Oxford.]

This is only the skeleton of positivism. The flesh is arranged differently by different positivists, and some even tinker with the bones. Different versions differ chiefly in their description of the fundamental test of pedigree a rule must meet to count as a rule of law.

Austin, for example, framed his version of the fundamental test as a series of interlocking definitions and distinctions.[2] He defined having an obligation as lying under a rule, a rule as a general command, and a command as an expression of desire that others behave in a particular way, backed by the power and will to enforce that expression in the event of disobedience. He distinguished classes of rules (legal, moral or religious) according to which person or group is the author of the general command the rule represents. In each political community, he thought, one will find a sovereign—a person or a determinate group whom the rest obey habitually, but who is not in the habit of obeying anyone else. The legal rules of a community are the general commands its sovereign has deployed. Austin's definition of legal obligation followed from this definition of law. One has a legal obligation, he thought, if one is among the addressees of some general order of the sovereign, and is in danger of suffering a sanction unless be obeys that order.

Of course, the sovereign cannot provide for all contingencies through any scheme of orders, and some of his orders will inevitably be vague or have furry edges. Therefore (according to Austin) the sovereign grants those who enforce the law (judges) discretion to make fresh orders when novel or troublesome cases are presented. The judges then make new rules or adapt old rules, and the sovereign either overturns their creations, or tacitly confirms them by failing to do so.

Austin's model is quite beautiful in its simplicity. It asserts the first tenet of positivism, that the law is a set of rules specially selected to govern public order, and offers a simple factual test—what has the sovereign commanded?—as the sole criterion for identifying those special rules. In time, however, those who studied and tried to apply Austin's model found it too simple. Many objections were raised, among which were two that seemed fundamental. First, Austin's key assumption that in each community a determinate group or institution can be found, which is in ultimate control of all other groups, seemed not to hold in a complex society. Political control in a modern nation is pluralistic and shifting, a matter of more or less, of compromise and cooperation and alliance, so that it is often impossible to say that any person or group has that dramatic control necessary to qualify as an Austinian sovereign. One wants to say, in the United States for example, that the "people" are

2. J. Austin, *The Province of Jurisprudence Determined* (1832).

sovereign. But this means almost nothing, and in itself provides no test for determining what the "people" have commanded, or distinguishing their legal from their social or moral commands.

Second, critics began to realize that Austin's analysis fails entirely to account for, even to recognize, certain striking facts about the attitudes we take toward "the law." We make an important distinction between law and even the general orders of a gangster. We feel that the law's strictures—and its sanctions—are different in that they are obligatory in a way that the outlaw's commands are not. Austin's analysis has no place for any such distinction, because it defines an obligation as subjection to the threat of force, and so founds the authority of law entirely on the sovereign's ability and will to harm those who disobey. Perhaps the distinction we make is illusory—perhaps our feelings of some special authority attaching to the law is based on religious hangover or another sort of mass self-deception. But Austin does not demonstrate this, and we are entitled to insist that an analysis of our concept of law either acknowledge and explain our attitudes, or show why they are mistaken.

H. L. A. Hart's version of positivism is more complex than Austin's, in two ways. First, he recognizes, as Austin did not, that rules are of different logical kinds (Hart distinguishes two kinds, which he calls "primary" and "secondary" rules). Second, he rejects Austin's theory that a rule is a kind of command, and substitutes a more elaborate general analysis of what rules are.

Hart's distinction between primary and secondary rules is of great importance.[3] Primary rules are those that grant rights or impose obligations upon members of the community. The rules of the criminal law that forbid us to rob, murder or drive too fast are good examples of primary rules. Secondary rules are those that stipulate how, and by whom, such primary rules may be formed, recognized, modified or extinguished. The rules that stipulate how Congress is composed, and how it enacts legislation, are examples of secondary rules. Rules about forming contracts and executing wills are also secondary rules because they stipulate how very particular rules governing particular legal obligations (i.e., the terms of a contract or the provisions of a will) come into existence and are changed.

His general analysis of rules is also of great importance. Austin had said that every rule is a general command, and that a person is obligated under a rule if he is liable to be hurt should he disobey it. Hart points out that this obliterates the distinction between being *obliged* to do something and being *obligated* to do it. If one is bound by a rule he is obligated, not

3. See H. L. A. Hart, *The Concept of Law* 89–96 (1961).

merely obliged, to do what it provides, and therefore being bound by a rule must be different from being subject to an injury if one disobeys an order. A rule differs from an order, among other ways, by being *norma-tive,* by setting a standard of behavior that has a call on its subject beyond the threat that may enforce it. A rule can never be binding just because some person with physical power wants it to be so. He must have *authority* to issue the rule or it is no rule, and such authority can only come from another rule which is already binding on those to whom he speaks. That is the difference between a valid law and the orders of a gunman.

So Hart offers a general theory of rules that does not make their authority depend upon the physical power of their authors. If we examine the way different rules come into being, he tells us, and attend to the distinction between primary and secondary rules, we see that there are two possible sources of a rule's authority.

(a) A rule may become binding upon a group of people because that group through its practices *accepts* the rule as a standard for its conduct. It is not enough that the group simply conforms to a pattern of behavior: even though most Englishmen may go to the movies on Saturday evening, they have not accepted a rule requiring that they do so. A practice constitutes the acceptance of a rule only when those who follow the practice regard the rule as binding, and recognize the rule as a reason or justification for their own behavior and as a reason for criticizing the behavior of others who do not obey it.

(b) A rule may also become binding in quite a different way, namely by being enacted in conformity with some *secondary* rule that stipulates that rules so enacted shall be binding. If the constitution of a club stipulates, for example, that by-laws may be adopted by a majority of the members, then particular by-laws so voted are binding upon all the members, not because of any practice of acceptance of these particular by-laws, but because the constitution says so. We use the concept of *valid-ity* in this connection: rules binding because they have been created in a manner stipulated by some secondary rule are called "valid" rules. Thus we can record Hart's fundamental distinction this way: a rule may be binding (a) because it is accepted or (b) because it is valid.

Hart's concept of law is a construction of these various distinctions. Primitive communities have only primary rules, and these are binding entirely because of practices of acceptance. Such communities cannot be said to have "law," because there is no way to distinguish a set of legal rules from amongst other social rules, as the first tenet of positivism requires. But when a particular community has developed a fundamental secondary rule that stipulates how legal rules are to be identified, the idea of a distinct set of legal rules, and thus of law, is born.

Hart calls such a fundamental secondary rule a "rule of recognition." The rule of recognition of a given community may be relatively simple ("What the king enacts is law") or it may be very complex (the United States Constitution, with all its difficulties of interpretation, may be considered a single rule of recognition). The demonstration that a particular rule is valid may therefore require tracing a complicated chain of validity back from that particular rule ultimately to the fundamental rule. Thus a parking ordinance of the city of New Haven is valid because it is adopted by a city council, pursuant to the procedures and within the competence specified by the municipal law adopted by the state of Connecticut, in conformity with the procedures and within the competence specified by the constitution of the state of Connecticut, which was in turn adopted consistently with the requirements of the United States Constitution.

Of course, a rule of recognition cannot itself be valid, because by hypothesis it is ultimate, and so cannot meet tests stipulated by a more fundamental rule. The rule of recognition is the sole rule in a legal system whose binding force depends upon its acceptance. If we wish to know what rule of recognition a particular community has adopted or follows, we must observe how its citizens, and particularly its officials, behave. We must observe what ultimate arguments they accept as showing the validity of a particular rule, and what ultimate arguments they use to criticize other officials or institutions. We can apply no mechanical test, but there is no danger of our confusing the rule of recognition of a community with its rules of morality. The rule of recognition is identified by the fact that its province is the operation of the governmental apparatus of legislatures, courts, agencies, policemen, and the rest.

In this way Hart rescues the fundamentals of positivism from Austin's mistakes. Hart agrees with Austin that valid rules of law may be created through the acts of officials and public institutions. But Austin thought that the authority of these institutions lay only in their monopoly of power. Hart finds their authority in the background of constitutional standards against which they act, constitutional standards that have been accepted, in the form of a fundmental rule of recognition, by the community which they govern. This background legitimates the decisions of government and gives them the cast and call of obligation that the naked commands of Austin's sovereign lacked. Hart's theory differs from Austin's also, in recognizing that different communities use different ultimate tests of law, and that some allow other means of creating law than the deliberate act of a legislative institution. Hart mentions "long customary practice" and "the relation [of a rule] to judicial decisions" as other criteria that are often used, though generally along with and subordinate to the test of legislation.

So Hart's version of positivism is more complex than Austin's, and

149

his test for valid rules of law is more sophisticated. In one respect, however, the two models are very similar. Hart, like Austin, recognizes that legal rules have furry edges (he speaks of them as having "open texture") and, again like Austin, he accounts for troublesome cases by saying that judges have and exercise discretion to decide these cases by fresh legislation. (I shall later try to show why one who thinks of law as a special set of rules is almost inevitably drawn to account for difficult cases in terms of someone's exercise of discretion.)

III. Rules, Principles, and Policies

I want to make a general attack on positivism, and I shall use H. L. A. Hart's version as a target, when a particular target is needed. My strategy will be organized around the fact that when lawyers reason or dispute about legal rights and obligations, particularly in those hard cases when our problems with these concepts seem most acute, they make use of standards that do not function as rules, but operate differently as principles, policies, and other sorts of standards. Positivism, I shall argue, is a model of and for a system of rules, and its central notion of a single fundamental test for law forces us to miss the important roles of these standards that are not rules.

I just spoke of "principles, policies, and other sorts of standards." Most often I shall use the term "principle" generically, to refer to the whole set of these standards other than rules; occasionally, however, I shall be more precise, and distinguish between principles and policies. Although nothing in the present argument will turn on the distinction, I should state how I draw it. I call a "policy" that kind of standard that sets out a goal to be reached, generally an improvement in some economic, political, or social feature of the community (though some goals are negative, in that they stipulate that some present feature is to be protected from adverse change). I call a "principle" a standard that is to be observed, not because it will advance or secure an economic, political, or social situation deemed desirable, but because it is a requirement of justice or fairness or some other dimension of morality. Thus the standard that automobile accidents are to be decreased is a policy, and the standard that no man may profit by his own wrong a principle. The distinction can be collapsed by construing a principle as stating a social goal (i.e., the goal of a society in which no man profits by his own wrong), or by construing a policy as stating a principle (i.e., the principle that the goal the policy embraces is a worthy one) or by adopting the utilitarian thesis that principles of justice are disguised statements of goals (securing the greatest happiness of the greatest number). In some contexts the distinction has uses which are lost if it is thus collapsed.[8]

My immediate purpose, however, is to distinguish principles in the generic sense from rules, and I shall start by collecting some examples of the former. The examples I offer are chosen haphazardly; almost any case in a law school casebook would provide examples that would serve as well. In 1889 a New York court, in the famous case of *Riggs v. Palmer*,[9] had to decide whether an heir named in the will of his grandfather could inherit under that will, even though he had murdered his grandfather to do so. The court began its reasoning with this admission: "It is quite true that statutes regulating the making, proof and effect of wills, and the devolution of property, if literally construed, and if their force and effect can in no way and under no circumstances be controlled or modified, give this property to the murderer." But the court continued to note that "all laws as well as all contracts may be controlled in their operation and effect by general, fundamental maxims of the common law. No one shall be permitted to profit by his own fraud, or to take advantage of his own wrong, or to found any claim upon his own inquity, or to acquire property by his own crime." The murderer did not receive his inheritance.

In 1960, a New Jersey court was faced, in *Henningsen v. Bloomfield Motors, Inc.*,[12] with the important question of whether (or how much) an automobile manufacturer may limit his liability in case the automobile is defective. Henningsen had bought a car, and signed a contract which said that the manufacturer's liability for defects was limited to "making good" defective parts—"this warranty being expressly in lieu of all other warranties, obligations or liabilities." Henningsen argued that, at least in the circumstances of his case, the manufacturer ought not to be protected by this limitation, and ought to be liable for the medical and other expenses of persons injured in a crash. He was not able to point to any statute, or to any established rule of law, that prevented the manufacturer from standing on the contract. The court nevertheless agreed with Henningsen. At various points in the court's argument the following appeals to standards are made: (a) "[W]e must keep in mind the general principle that, in the absence of fraud, one who does not choose to read a contract before signing it cannot later relieve himself of its burdens." (b) "In applying that principle, the basic tenet of freedom of competent

---

8. See Dworkin, Wasserstrom: The Judicial Decision, 75 *Ethics* 47 (1964), reprinted as Does Law Have a Function?, 74 *Yale L.J.* 640 (1965).
9. 115 N.Y. 506, 22 N.E. 188 (1889).
12. 32 N.J. 358, 161 A.2d 69 (1960).

parties to contract is a factor of importance." (c) "Freedom of contract is not such an immutable doctrine as to admit of no qualification in the area in which we are concerned." (d) "In a society such as ours, where the automobile is a common and necessary adjunct of daily life, and where its use is so fraught with danger to the driver, passengers and the public, the manufacturer is under a special obligation in connection with the construction, promotion and sale of his cars. Consequently, the courts must examine purchase agreements closely to see if consumer and public interests are treated fairly." (e) " '[I]s there any principle which is more familiar or more firmly embedded in the history of Anglo-American law than the basic doctrine that the courts will not permit themselves to be used as instruments of inequity and injustice?' " (f) " 'More specifically, the courts generally refuse to lend themselves to the enforcement of a "bargain" in which one party has unjustly taken advantage of the economic necessities of other. . . .' "

The standards set out in these quotations are not the sort we think of as legal rules. They seem very different from propositions like "The maximum legal speed on the turnpike is sixty miles an hour" or "A will is invalid unless signed by three witnesses." They are different because they are legal principles rather than legal rules.

The difference between legal principles and legal rules is a logical distinction. Both sets of standards point to particular decisions about legal obligation in particular circumstances, but they differ in the character of the direction they give. Rules are applicable in an all-or-nothing fashion. If the facts a rule stipulates are given, then either the rule is valid, in which case the answer it supplies must be accepted, or it is not, in which case it contributes nothing to the decision.

This all-or-nothing is seen most plainly if we look at the way rules operate, not in law, but in some enterprise they dominate—a game, for example. In baseball a rule provides that if the batter has had three strikes, he is out. An official cannot consistently acknowledge that this is an accurate statement of a baseball rule, and decide that a batter who has had three strikes is not out. Of course, a rule may have exceptions (the batter who has taken three strikes is not out if the catcher drops the third strike). However, an accurate statement of the rule would take this exception into account, and any that did not would be incomplete. If the list of exceptions is very large, it would be too clumsy to repeat them each time the rule is cited; there is, however, no reason in theory why they could not all be added on, and the more that are, the more accurate is the statement of the rule.

If we take baseball rules as a model, we find that rules of law, like the rule that a will is invalid unless signed by three witnesses, fit the model well. If the requirement of three witnesses is a valid legal rule, then it cannot be that a will has been signed by only two witnesses and is valid. The rule might have exceptions, but if it does then it is inaccurate and incomplete to state the rule so simply, without enumerating the exceptions. In theory, at least, the exceptions could all be listed, and the more of them that are, the more complete is the statement of the rule.

But this is not the way the sample principles in the quotations operate. Even those which look most like rules do not set out legal consequences that follow automatically when the conditions provided are met. We say that our law respects the principle that no man may profit from his own wrong, but we do not mean that the law never permits a man to profit from wrongs he commits. In fact, people often profit, perfectly legally, from their legal wrongs. The most notorious case is adverse possession—if I trespass on your land long enough, some day I will gain a right to cross your land whenever I please. There are many less dramatic examples. If a man leaves one job, breaking a contract, to take a much higher paying job, he may have to pay damages to his first employer, but he is usually entitled to keep his new salary. If a man jumps bail and crosses state lines to make a brilliant investment in another state, he may be sent back to jail, but he will keep his profits.

We do not treat these—and countless other counter-instances that can easily be imagined—as showing that the principle about profiting from one's wrongs is not a principle of our legal system, or that it is incomplete and needs qualifying exceptions. We do not treat counterinstances as exceptions (at least not exceptions in the way in which a catcher's dropping the third strike is an exception) because we could not hope to capture these counter-instances simply by a more extended statement of the principle. They are not, even in theory, subject to enumeration, because we would have to include not only these cases (like adverse possession) in which some institution has already provided that profit can be gained through a wrong, but also those numberless imaginary cases in which we know in advance that the principle would not hold. Listing some of these might sharpen our sense of the principle's weight (I shall mention that dimension in a moment), but it would not make for a more accurate or complete statement of the principle.

A principle like "No man may profit from his own wrong" does not even purport to set out conditions that make its application necessary. Rather, it states a reason that argues in one direction, but does not necessitate a particular decision. If a man has or is about to receive something, as a direct result of something illegal he did to get it, then that is a reason which the law will take into account in deciding whether he should keep it. There may be other principles or policies arguing in the other di-

153

rection—a policy of securing title, for example, or a principle limiting punishment to what the legislature has stipulated. If so, our principle may not prevail, but that does not mean that it is not a principle of our legal system, because in the next case, when these contravening considerations are absent or less weighty, the principle may be decisive. All that is meant, when we say that a particular principle is a principle of our law, is that the principle is one which officials must take into account, if it is relevant, as a consideration inclining in one direction or another.

The logical distinction between rules and principles appears more clearly when we consider principles that do not even look like rules. Consider the proposition, set out under "(d)" in the excerpts from the *Henningsen* opinion, that "the manufacturer is under a special obligation in connection with the construction, promotion and sale of his cars." This does not even purport to define the specific duties such a special obligation entails, or to tell us what rights automobile consumers acquire as a result. It merely states—and this is an essential link in the *Henningsen* argument—that automobile manufacturers must be held to higher standards than other manufacturers, and are less entitled to rely on the competing principle of freedom of contract. It does not mean that they may never rely on that principle, or that courts may rewrite automobile purchase contracts at will; it means only that if a particular clause seems unfair or burdensome, courts have less reason to enforce the clause than if it were for the purchase of neckties. The "special obligation" counts in favor, but does not in itself necessitate, a decision refusing to enforce the terms of an automobile purchase contract.

This first difference between rules and principles entails another. Principles have a dimension that rules do not—the dimension of weight or importance. When principles intersect (the policy of protecting automobile consumers intersecting with principles of freedom of contract, for example), one who must resolve the conflict has to take into account the relative weight of each. This cannot be, of course, an exact measurement, and the judgment that a particular principle or policy is more important than another will often be a controversial one. Nevertheless, it is an integral part of the concept of a principle that it has this dimension, that it makes sense to ask how important or how weighty it is.

Rules do not have this dimension. We can speak of rules as being *functionally* important or unimportant (the baseball rule that three strikes are out is more important than the rule that runners may advance on a balk, because the game would be much more changed with the first rule altered than the second). In this sense, one legal rule may be more important than another because it has a greater or more important role in regulating behavior. But we cannot say that one rule is more important than another within the system of rules, so that when two rules conflict one supercedes the other by virtue of its greater weight. If two rules conflict, one of them cannot be a valid rule. The decision as to which is valid, and which must be abandoned or recast, must be made by appealing to considerations beyond the rules themselves. A legal system might regulate such conflicts by other rules, which prefer the rule enacted by the higher authority, or the rule enacted later, or the more specific rule, or something of that sort. A legal system may also prefer the rule supported by the more important principles. (Our own legal system uses both of these techniques.)

It is not always clear from the form of a standard whether it is a rule or a principle. "A will is invalid unless signed by three witnesses" is not very different in form from "A man may not profit from his own wrong," but one who knows something of American law knows that he must take the first as stating a rule and the second as stating a principle. In many cases the distinction is difficult to make—it may not have been settled how the standard should operate, and this issue may itself be a focus of controversy. The first amendment to the United States Constitution contains the provision that Congress shall not abridge freedom of speech. Is this a rule, so that if a particular law does abridge freedom of speech, it follows that it is unconstitutional? Those who claim that the first amendment is "an absolute" say that it must be taken in this way, that is, as a rule. Or does it merely state a principle, so that when an abridgement of speech is discovered, it is unconstitutional unless the context presents some other policy or principle which in the circumstances is weighty enough to permit the abridgement? That is the position of those who argue for what is called the "clear and present danger" test or some other form of "balancing."

Sometimes a rule and a principle can play much the same role, and the difference between them is almost a matter of form alone. The first section of the Sherman Act states that every contract in restraint of trade shall be void. The Supreme Court had to make the decision whether this provision should be treated as a rule in its own terms (striking down every contract "which restrains trade," which almost any contract does) or as a principle, providing a reason for striking down a contract in the absence of effective contrary policies. The Court construed the provision as a rule, but treated that rule as containing the word "unreasonable," and as prohibiting only "unreasonable" restraints of trade.[19] This allowed the provision to function logically as a rule (whenever a court

---

19. Standard Oil v. United States, 221 U.S. 1, 60 (1911); United States v. American Tobacco Co., 221 U.S. 106, 180 (1911).

finds that the restraint is "unreasonable" it is bound to hold the contract invalid) and substantially as a principle (a court must take into account a variety of other principles and policies in determining whether a particular restraint in particular economic circumstances is "unreasonable").

Words like "reasonable," "negligent," "unjust," and "significant" often perform just this function. Each of these terms makes the application of the rule which contains it depend to some extent upon principles or policies lying beyond the rule, and in this way makes that rule itself more like a principle. But they do not quite turn the rule into a principle, because even the least confining of these terms restricts the *kind* of other principles and policies on which the rule depends. If we are bound by a rule that says that "unreasonable" contracts are void, or that grossly "unfair" contracts will not be enforced, much more judgment is required than if the quoted terms were omitted. But suppose a case in which some consideration of policy or principle suggests that a contract should be enforced even though its restraint is not reasonable, or even though it is grossly unfair. Enforcing these contracts would be forbidden by our rules, and thus permitted only if these rules were abandoned or modified. If we were dealing, however, not with a rule but with a policy against enforcing unreasonable contracts, or a principle that unfair contracts ought not to be enforced, the contracts could be enforced without alteration of the law.

IV. Principles and the Concept of Law

Once we identify legal principles as separate sorts of standards, different from legal rules, we are suddenly aware of them all around us. Law teachers teach them, lawbooks cite them, legal historians celebrate them. But they seem most energetically at work, carrying most weight, in difficult lawsuits like *Riggs* and *Henningsen.* In cases like these, principles play an essential part in arguments supporting judgments about particular legal rights and obligations. After the case is decided, we may say that the case stands for a particular rule (e.g., the rule that one who murders is not eligible to take under the will of his victim). But the rule does not exist before the case is decided; the court cites principles as its justification for adopting and applying a new rule. In *Riggs,* the court cited the principle that no man may profit from his own wrong as a background standard against which to read the statute of wills and in this way justified a new interpretation of that statute. In *Henningsen,* the court cited a variety of intersecting principles and policies as authority for a new rule respecting manufacturer's liability for automobile defects.

An analysis of the concept of legal obligation must therefore account for the important role of principles in reaching particular decisions of law. There are two very different tacks we might take.

(a) We might treat legal principles the way we treat legal rules and say that some principles are binding as law and must be taken into account by judges and lawyers who make decisions of legal obligation. If we took this tack, we should say that in the United States, at least, the "law" includes principles as well as rules.

(b) We might, on the other hand, deny that principles can be binding the way some rules are. We would say, instead, that in cases like *Riggs* or *Henningsen* the judge reaches beyond the rules that he is bound to apply (reaches, that is, beyond the "law") for extra-legal principles he is free to follow if he wishes.

One might think that there is not much difference between these two lines of attack, that it is only a verbal question of how one wants to use the word "law." But that is a mistake, because the choice between these two accounts has the greatest consequences for an analysis of legal obligation. It is a choice between two *concepts* of a legal principle, a choice we can clarify by comparing it to a choice we might make between two concepts of a legal rule. We sometimes say of someone that he "makes it a rule" to do something, when we mean that he has chosen to follow a certain practice. We might say that someone has made it a rule, for example, to run a mile before breakfast because he wants to be healthy and believes in a regimen. We do not mean, when we say this, that he is *bound* by the rule that he must run a mile before breakfast, or even that he regards it as binding upon him. Accepting a rule as binding is something different from making it a rule to do something. If we use Hart's example again, there is a difference between saying that Englishmen make it a rule to see a movie once a week, and saying that the English have a rule that one must see a movie once a week. The second implies that if an Englishman does not follow the rule, he is subject to criticism or censure, but the first does not. The first does not exclude the possibility of a *sort* of criticism—we can say that one who does not see movies is neglecting his education—but we do not suggest that he is doing something wrong *just* in not following the rule.

If we think of the judges of a community as a group, we could describe the rules of law they follow in these two different ways. We could say, for instance, that in a certain state the judges make it a rule not to enforce wills unless there are three witnesses. This would not imply that the rare judge who enforces such a rule is doing anything wrong just for that reason. On the other hand we can say that in that state a rule of law requires judges not to enforce such wills; this does imply that a judge who enforces them is doing something wrong. Hart, Austin and other

157

positivists, of course, would insist on this latter account of legal rules; they would not at all be satisfied with the "make it a rule" account. It is not a verbal question of which account is right. It is a question of which describes the social situation more accurately. Other important issues turn on which description we accept. If judges simply "make it a rule" not to enforce certain contracts, for example, then we cannot say, before the decision, that anyone is "entitled" to that result, and that proposition cannot enter into any justification we might offer for the decision.

The two lines of attack on principles parallel these two accounts of rules. The first tack treats principles as binding upon judges, so that they are wrong not to apply the principles when they are pertinent. The second tack treats principles as summaries of what most judges "make it a principle" to do when forced to go beyond the standards that bind them. The choice between these approaches will affect, perhaps even determine, the answer we can give to the question whether the judge in a hard case like *Riggs* or *Henningsen* is attempting to enforce pre-existing legal rights and obligations. If we take the first tack, we are still free to argue that because such judges are applying binding legal standards they are enforcing legal rights and obligations. But if we take the second, we are out of court on that issue, and we must acknowledge that the murderer's family in *Riggs* and the manufacturer in *Henningsen* were deprived of their property by an act of judicial discretion applied *ex post facto*. This may not shock many readers—the notion of judicial discretion has percolated through the legal community—but it does illustrate one of the most nettlesome of the puzzles that drive philosophers to worry about legal obligation. If taking property away in cases like these cannot be justified by appealing to an established obligation, another justification must be found, and nothing satisfactory has yet been supplied.

In my skeleton diagram of positivism, previously set out, I listed the doctrine of judicial discretion as the second tenet. Positivists hold that when a case is not covered by a clear rule, a judge must exercise his discretion to decide that case by what amounts to a fresh piece of legislation. There may be an important connection between this doctrine and the question of which of the two approaches to legal principles we must take. We shall therefore want to ask whether the doctrine is correct, and whether it implies the second approach, as it seems on its face to do. En route to these issues, however, we shall have to polish our understanding of the concept of discretion. I shall try to show how certain confusions about that concept, and in particular a failure to discriminate different senses in which it is used, account for the popularity of the doctrine of discretion. I shall argue that in the sense in which the doctrine does have a bearing on our treatment of principles, it is entirely unsupported by the arguments the positivists use to defend it.

V. Discretion

The concept of discretion was lifted by the positivists from ordinary language, and to understand it we must put it back *in habitat* for a moment. What does it mean, in ordinary life, to say that someone "has discretion"? The first thing to notice is that the concept is out of place in all but very special contexts. For example, you would not say that I either do or do not have discretion to choose a house for my family. It is not true that I have "no discretion" in making that choice, and yet it would be almost equally misleading to say that I do have discretion. The concept of discretion is at home in only one sort of context: when someone is in general charged with making decisions subject to standards set by a particular authority. It makes sense to speak of the discretion of a sergeant who is subject to orders of superiors, or the discretion of a sports official or contest judge who is governed by a rule book or the terms of the contest. Discretion, like the hole in a doughnut, does not exist except as an area left open by a surrounding belt of restriction. It is therefore a relative concept. It always makes sense to ask, "Discretion under which standards?" or "Discretion as to which authority?" Generally the context will make the answer to this plain, but in some cases the official may have discretion from one standpoint though not from another.

Like almost all terms, the precise meaning of "discretion" is affected by features of the context. The term is always colored by the background of understood information against which it is used. Although the shadings are many, it will be helpful for us to recognize some gross distinctions.

Sometimes we use "discretion" in a weak sense, simply to say that for some reason the standards an official must apply cannot be applied mechanically but demand the use of judgment. We use this weak sense when the context does not already make that clear, when the background our audience assumes does not contain that piece of information. Thus we might say, "The sergeant's orders left him a great deal of discretion," to those who do not know what the sergeant's orders were or who do not know something that made those orders vague or hard to carry out. It would make perfect sense to add, by way of amplification, that the lieutenant had ordered the sergeant to take his five most experienced men on patrol but that it was hard to determine which were the most experienced.

Sometimes we use the term in a different weak sense, to say only that some official has final authority to make a decision and cannot be reviewed and reversed by any other official. We speak this way when the official is part of a hierarchy of officials structured so that some have higher authority but in which the patterns of authority are different for different classes of decision. Thus we might say that in baseball certain decisions, like the decision whether the ball or the runner reached second base first, are left to the discretion of the second base umpire, if we mean that on this issue the head umpire has no power to substitute his own judgment if he disagrees.

I call both of these senses weak to distinguish them from a stronger sense. We use "discretion" sometimes not merely to say that an official must use judgment in applying the standards set him by authority, or that no one will review that exercise of judgment, but to say that on some issue he is simply not bound by standards set by the authority in question. In this sense we say that a sergeant has discretion who has been told to pick any five men for patrol he chooses or that a judge in a dog show has discretion to judge airedales before boxers if the rules do not stipulate an order of events. We use this sense not to comment on the vagueness or difficulty of the standards, or on who has the final word in applying them, but on their range and the decisions they purport to control. If the sergeant is told to take the five most experienced men, he does not have discretion in this strong sense because that order purports to govern his decision. The boxing referee who must decide which fighter has been more aggressive does not have discretion, in the strong sense, for the same reason.[21]

If anyone said that the sergeant or the referee had discretion in these cases, we should have to understand him, if the context permitted, as using the term in one of the weak senses. Suppose, for example, the lieutenant ordered the sergeant to select the five men he deemed most experienced, and then added that the sergeant had discretion to choose them. Or the rules provided that the referee should award the round to the more aggressive fighter, with discretion in selecting him. We should have to understand these statements in the second weak sense, as speaking to the question of review of the decision. The first weak sense—that

21. I have not spoken of that jurisprudential favorite, "limited" discretion, because that concept presents no special difficulties if we remember the relativity of discretion. Suppose the sergeant is told to choose from "amongst" experienced men, or to "take experience into account." We might say either that he has (limited) discretion in picking his patrol, or (full) discretion to either pick amongst experienced men or decide what else to take into account.

the decisions take judgment—would be otiose, and the third, strong sense is excluded by the statements themselves.

We must avoid one tempting confusion. The strong sense of discretion is not tantamount to license, and does not exclude criticism. Almost any situation in which a person acts (including those in which there is no question of decision under special authority, and so no question of discretion) makes relevant certain standards of rationality, fairness, and effectiveness. We criticize each other's acts in terms of these standards, and there is no reason not to do so when the acts are within the center rather than beyond the perimeter of the doughnut of special authority. So we can say that the sergeant who was given discretion (in the strong sense) to pick a patrol did so stupidly or maliciously or carelessly, or that the judge who had discretion in the order of viewing dogs made a mistake because he took boxers first although there were only three airedales and many more boxers. An official's discretion means not that he is free to decide without recourse to standards of sense and fairness, but only that his decision is not controlled by a standard furnished by the particular authority we have in mind when we raise the question of discretion. Of course this latter sort of freedom is important; that is why we have the strong sense of discretion. Someone who has discretion in this third sense can be criticized, but not for being disobedient, as in the case of the soldier. He can be said to have made a mistake, but not to have deprived a participant of a decision to which he was entitled, as in the case of a sports official or contest judge.

We may now return, with these observations in hand, to the positivists' doctrine of judicial discretion. That doctrine argues that if a case is not controlled by an established rule, the judge must decide it by exercising discretion. We want to examine this doctrine and to test its bearing on our treatment of principles; but first we must ask in which sense of discretion we are to understand it.

Some nominalists argue that judges always have discretion, even when a clear rule is in point, because judges are ultimately the final arbiters of the law. This doctrine of discretion uses the second weak sense of that term, because it makes the point that no higher authority reviews the decisions of the highest court. It therefore has no bearing on the issue of how we account for principles, any more than it bears on how we account for rules.

The positivists do not mean their doctrine this way, because they say that a judge has no discretion when a clear and established rule is available. If we attend to the positivists' arguments for the doctrine we may suspect that they use discretion in the first weak sense to mean only that judges must sometimes exercise judgment in applying legal standards.

Their arguments call attention to the fact that some rules of law are vague (Professor Hart, for example, says that all rules of law have "open texture"), and that some cases arise (like *Henningsen*) in which no established rule seems to be suitable. They emphasize that judges must sometimes agonize over points of law, and that two equally trained and intelligent judges will often disagree.

These points are easily made; they are commonplace to anyone who has any familiarity with law. Indeed, that is the difficulty with assuming that positivists mean to use "discretion" in this weak sense. The proposition that when no clear rule is available discretion in the sense of judgment must be used is a tautology. It has no bearing, moreover, on the problem of how to account for legal principles. It is perfectly consistent to say that the judge in *Riggs,* for example, had to use judgment, and that he was bound to follow the principle that no man may profit from his own wrong. The positivists speak as if their doctrine of judicial discretion is an insight rather than a tautology, and as if it does have a bearing on the treatment of principles. Hart, for example, says that when the judge's discretion is in play, we can no longer speak of his being bound by standards, but must speak rather of what standards he "characteristically uses." Hart thinks that when judges have discretion, the principles they cite must be treated on our second approach, as what courts "make it a principle" to do.

It therefore seems that positivists, at least sometimes, take their doctrine in the third, strong sense of discretion. In that sense it does bear on the treatment of principles; indeed, in that sense it is nothing less than a restatement of our second approach. It is the same thing to say that when a judge runs out of rules he has discretion, in the sense that he is not bound by any standards from the authority of law, as to say that the legal standards judges cite other than rules are not binding on them.

So we must examine the doctrine of judicial discretion in the strong sense. (I shall henceforth use the term "discretion" in that sense.) Do the principles judges cite in cases like *Riggs* or *Henningsen* control their decisions, as the sergeant's orders to take the most experienced men or the referee's duty to choose the more aggressive fighter control the decisions of these officials? What arguments could a positivist supply to show that they do not?

(1) A positivist might argue that principles cannot be binding or obligatory. That would be a mistake. It is always a question, of course, whether any particular principle is *in fact* binding upon some legal official. But there is nothing in the logical character of a principle that renders it incapable of binding him. Suppose that the judge in *Henningsen* had failed to take any account of the principle that automobile manufac-

turers have a special obligation to their consumers, or the principle that the courts seek to protect those whose bargaining position is weak, but had simply decided for the defendant by citing the principle of freedom of contract without more. His critics would not have been content to point out that he had not taken account of considerations that other judges have been attending to for some time. Most would have said that it was his duty to take the measure of these principles and that the plaintiff was entitled to have him do so. We mean no more, when we say that a *rule* is binding upon a judge, than that he must follow it if it applies, and that if he does not he will on that account have made a mistake.

It will not do to say that in a case like *Henningsen* the court is only "morally" obligated to take particular principles into account, or that it is "institutionally" obligated, or obligated as a matter of judicial "craft," or something of that sort. The question will still remain why this type of obligation (whatever we call it) is different from the obligation that rules impose upon judges, and why it entitles us to say that principles and policies are not part of the law but are merely extra-legal standards "courts characteristically use."

(2) A positivist might argue that even though some principles are binding, in the sense that the judge must take them into account, they cannot determine a particular result. This is a harder argument to assess because it is not clear what it means for a standard to "determine" a result. Perhaps it means that the standard *dictates* the result whenever it applies so that nothing else counts. If so, then it is certainly true that individual principles do not determine results, but that is only another way of saying that principles are not rules. Only rules dictate results, come what may. When a contrary result has been reached, the rule has been abandoned or changed. Principles do not work that way; they incline a decision one way, though not conclusively, and they survive intact when they do not prevail. This seems no reason for concluding that judges who must reckon with principles have discretion because a set of principles *can* dictate a result. If a judge believes that principles he is bound to recognize point in one direction and that principles pointing in the other direction, if any, are not of equal weight, then he must decide accordingly, just as he must follow what he believes to be a binding rule. He may, of course, be wrong in his assessment of the principles, but he may also be wrong in his judgment that the rule is binding. The sergeant and the referee, we might add, are often in the same boat. No one factor dictates which soldiers are the most experienced or which fighter the more aggressive. These officials must make judgments of the relative weights of these various factors; they do not on that account have discretion.

(3) A positivist might argue that principles cannot count as law be-

cause their authority, and even more so their weight, are congenitally *controversial*. It is true that generally we cannot *demonstrate* the authority or weight of a particular principle as we can sometimes demonstrate the validity of a rule by locating it in an act of Congress or in the opinion of an authoritative court. Instead, we make a case for a principle, and for its weight, by appealing to an amalgam of practice and other principles in which the implications of legislative and judicial history figure along with appeals to community practices and understandings. There is no litmus paper for testing the soundness of such a case—it is a matter of judgment, and reasonable men may disagree. But again this does not distinguish the judge from other officials who do not have discretion. The sergeant has no litmus paper for experience, the referee none for aggressiveness. Neither of these has discretion, because he is bound to reach an understanding, controversial or not, of what his orders or the rules require, and to act on that understanding. That is the judge's duty as well.

Of course, if the positivists are right in another of their doctrines— the theory that in each legal system there is an ultimate *test* for binding law like Professor Hart's rule of recognition—it follows that principles are not binding law. But the incompatibility of principles with the positivists' theory can hardly be taken as an argument that principles must be treated any particular way. That begs the question; we are interested in the status of principles because we want to evaluate the positivists' model. The positivist cannot defend his theory of a rule of recognition by fiat; if principles are not amenable to a test he must show some other reason why they cannot count as law. Since principles seem to play a role in arguments about legal obligation (witness, again, *Riggs* and *Henningsen*), a model that provides for that role has some initial advantage over one that excludes it, and the latter cannot properly be inveighed in its own support.

These are the most obvious of the arguments a positivist might use for the doctrine of discretion in the strong sense, and for the second approach to principles. I shall mention one strong counter-argument against that doctrine and in favor of the first approach. Unless at least some principles are acknowledged to be binding upon judges, requiring them as a set to reach particular decisions, then no rules, or very few rules, can be said to be binding upon them either.

In most American jurisdictions, and now in England also, the higher courts not infrequently reject established rules. Common law rules—those developed by earlier court decisions—are sometimes overruled directly, and sometimes radically altered by further development. Statutory rules are subjected to interpretation and reinterpretation, sometimes even when the result is not to carry out what is called the "legislative intent."[23] If courts had discretion to change established rules, then these rules would of course not be binding upon them, and so would not be law on the positivists' model. The positivist must therefore argue that there are standards, themselves binding upon judges, that determine when a judge may overrule or alter an established rule, and when he may not.

When, then, is a judge permitted to change an existing rule of law? Principles figure in the answer in two ways. First, it is necessary, though not sufficient, that the judge find that the change would advance some policy or serve some principle, which policy or principle thus justifies the change. In *Riggs* the change (a new interpretation of the statute of wills) was justified by the principle that no man should profit from his own wrong; in *Henningsen* certain rules about automobile manufacturer's liability were altered on the basis of the principles and policies I quoted from the opinion of the court.

But not any principle will do to justify a change, or no rule would ever be safe. There must be some principles that count and others that do not, and there must be some principles that count for more than others. It could not depend on the judge's own preferences amongst a sea of respectable extra-legal standards, any one in principle eligible, because if that were the case we could not say that any rules were binding. We could always imagine a judge whose preferences amongst extra-legal standards were such as would justify a shift or radical reinterpretation of even the most entrenched rule.

Second, any judge who proposes to change existing doctrine must take account of some important standards that argue against departures from established doctrine, and these standards are also for the most part principles. They include the doctrine of "legislative supremacy," a set of principles and policies that require the courts to pay a qualified deference to the acts of the legislature. They also include the doctrine of precedent, another set of principles and policies reflecting the equities and efficiencies of consistency. The doctrines of legislative supremacy and precedent incline toward the *status quo,* each within its sphere, but they do not command it. Judges are not free, however, to pick and choose amongst the principles and policies that make up these doctrines—if they were, again, no rule could be said to be binding.

Consider, therefore, what someone implies who says that a particular rule is binding. He may imply that the rule is affirmatively supported

---

23. See Wellington & Albert, Statutory Interpretation and the Political Process: A Comment on Sinclair v. Atkinson, 72 *Yale L.J.* 1547 (1963).

by principles the court is not free to disregard, and which are collectively more weighty than other principles that argue for a change. If not, he implies that any change would be condemned by a combination of conservative principles of legislative supremacy and precedent that the court is not free to ignore. Very often, he will imply both, for the conservative principles, being principles and not rules, are usually not powerful enough to save a common law rule or an aging statute that is entirely unsupported by substantive principles the court is bound to respect. Either of these implications, of course, treats a body of principles and policies as law in the sense that rules are; it treats them as standards binding upon the officials of a community, controlling their decisions of legal right and obligation.

We are left with this issue. If the positivists' theory of judicial discretion is either trivial because it uses "discretion" in a weak sense, or unsupported because the various arguments we can supply in its defense fall short, why have so many careful and intelligent lawyers embraced it? We can have no confidence in our treatment of that theory unless we can deal with that question. It is not enough to note (although perhaps it contributes to the explanation) that "discretion" has different senses that may be confused. We do not confuse these senses when we are not thinking about law.

Part of the explanation, at least, lies in a lawyer's natural tendency to associate laws and rules, and to think of "the law" as a collection or system of rules. Roscoe Pound, who diagnosed this tendency long ago, thought that English speaking lawyers were tricked into it by the fact that English uses the same word, changing only the article, for "a law" and "the law."[24] (Other languages, on the contrary, use two words: *"loi"* and *"droit,"* for example, and *"Gesetz"* and *"Recht."*) This may have had its effect, with the English speaking positivists, because the expression "a law" certainly does suggest a rule. But the principal reason for associating law with rules runs deeper, and lies, I think, in the fact that legal education has for a long time consisted of teaching and examining those established rules that form the cutting edge of law.

In any event, if a lawyer thinks of law as a system of rules, and yet recognizes, as he must, that judges change old rules and introduce new ones, he will come naturally to the theory of judicial discretion in the strong sense. In those other systems of rules with which he has experience (like games), the rules are the only special authority that govern official decisions, so that if an umpire could change a rule, he would have discretion as to the subject matter of that rule. Any principles umpires

24. R. Pound, *An Introduction to the Philosophy of Law* 56 (rev. ed. 1954).

might mention when changing the rules would represent only their "characteristic" preferences. Positivists treat law like baseball revised in this way.

There is another, more subtle consequence of this initial assumption that law is a system of rules. When the positivists do attend to principles and policies, they treat them as rules *manque*. They assume that *if* they are standards of law they must be rules, and so they read them as standards that are trying to be rules. When a positivist hears someone argue that legal principles are part of the law, he understands this to be an argument for what he calls the "higher law" theory, that these principles are the rules of a law above the law.[25] He refutes this theory by pointing out that these "rules" are sometimes followed and sometimes not, that for every "rule" like "no man shall profit from his own wrong" there is another competing "rule" like "the law favors security of title," and that there is no way to test the validity of "rules" like these. He concludes that these principles and policies are not valid rules of a law above the law, which is true, because they are not rules at all. He also concludes that they are extra-legal standards which each judge selects according to his own lights in the exercise of his discretion, which is false. It is as if a zoologist had proved that fish are not mammals, and then concluded that they are really only plants.

VI. The Rule of Recognition

This discussion was provoked by our two competing accounts of legal principles. We have been exploring the second account, which the positivists seem to adopt through their doctrine of judicial discretion, and we have discovered grave difficulties. It is time to return to the fork in the road. What if we adopt the first approach? What would the consequences of this be for the skeletal structure of positivism? Of course we should have to drop the second tenet, the doctrine of judicial discretion (or, in the alternative, to make plain that the doctrine is to be read merely to say that judges must often exercise judgment). Would we also have to abandon or modify the first tenet, the proposition that law is distinguished by tests of the sort that can be set out in a master rule like Professor Hart's rule of recognition? If principles of the *Riggs* and *Henningsen* sort are to count as law, and we are nevertheless to preserve the notion of a master rule for law, then we must be able to deploy some test that all (and only) the principles that do count as law meet. Let us begin

25. See e.g., Dickinson, The Law Behind Law (pts. 1 & 2), 29 *Colum. L. Rev.* 112, 254 (1929).

with the test Hart suggests for identifying valid *rules* of law, to see whether these can be made to work for principles as well.

Most rules of law, according to Hart, are valid because some competent institution enacted them. Some were created by a legislature, in the form of statutory enactments. Others were created by judges who formulated them to decide particular cases, and thus established them as precedents for the future. But this test of pedigree will not work for the *Riggs* and *Henningsen* principles. The origin of these as legal principles lies not in a particular decision of some legislature or court, but in a sense of appropriateness developed in the profession and the public over time. Their continued power depends upon this sense of appropriateness being sustained. If it no longer seemed unfair to allow people to profit by their wrongs, or fair to place special burdens upon oligopolies that manufacture potentially dangerous machines, these principles would no longer play much of a role in new cases, even if they had never been overruled or repealed. (Indeed, it hardly makes sense to speak of principles like these as being "overruled" or "repealed." When they decline they are eroded, not torpedoed.)

True, if we were challenged to back up our claim that some principle is a principle of law, we would mention any prior cases in which that principle was cited, or figured in the argument. We would also mention any statute that seemed to exemplify that principle (even better if the principle was cited in the preamble of the statute, or in the committee reports or other legislative documents that accompanied it). Unless we could find some such institutional support, we would probably fail to make out our case, and the more support we found, the more weight we could claim for the principle.

Yet we could not devise any formula for testing how much and what kind of institutional support is necessary to make a principle a legal principle, still less to fix its weight at a particular order of magnitude. We argue for a particular principle by grappling with a whole set of shifting, developing and interacting standards (themselves principles rather than rules) about institutional responsibility, statutory interpretation, the persuasive force of various sorts of precedent, the relation of all these to contemporary moral practices, and hosts of other such standards. We could not bolt all of these together into a single "rule," even a complex one, and if we could the result would bear little relation to Hart's picture of a rule of recognition, which is the picture of a fairly stable master rule specifying "some feature or features possession of which by a suggested rule is taken as a conclusive affirmative indication that it is a rule. . . ."

Moreover, the techniques we apply in arguing for another principle do not stand (as Hart's rule of recognition is designed to) on an entirely different level from the principles they support. Hart's sharp distinction between acceptance and validity does not hold. If we are arguing for the principle that a man should not profit from his own wrong, we could cite the acts of courts and legislatures that exemplify it, but this speaks as much to the principle's acceptance as its validity. (It seems odd to speak of a principle as being valid at all, perhaps because validity is an all-or-nothing concept, appropriate for rules, but inconsistent with a principle's dimension of weight.) If we are asked (as we might well be) to defend the particular doctrine of precedent, or the particular technique of statutory interpretation, that we used in this argument, we should certainly cite the practice of others in using that doctrine or technique. But we should also cite other general principles that we believe support that practice, and this introduces a note of validity into the chord of acceptance. We might argue, for example, that the use we make of earlier cases and statutes is supported by a particular analysis of the point of the practice of legislation or the doctrine of precedent, or by the principles of democratic theory, or by a particular position on the proper division of authority between national and local institutions, or something else of that sort. Nor is this path of support a one-way street leading to some ultimate principle resting on acceptance alone. Our principles of legislation, precedent, democracy, or federalism might be challenged too; and if they were we should argue for them, not only in terms of practice, but in terms of each other and in terms of the implications of trends of judicial and legislative decisions, even though this last would involve appealing to those same doctrines of interpretation we justified through the principles we are now trying to support. At this level of abstraction, in other words, principles rather hang together than link together.

So even though principles draw support from the official acts of legal institutions, they do not have a simple or direct enough connection with these acts to frame that connection in terms of criteria specified by some ultimate master rule of recognition. Is there any other route by which principles might be brought under such a rule?

Hart does say that a master rule might designate as law not only rules enacted by particular legal institutions, but rules established by *custom* as well. He has in mind a problem that bothered other positivists, including Austin. Many of our most ancient legal rules were never explicitly created by a legislature or a court. When they made their first appearance in legal opinions and texts, they were treated as already being part of the law because they represented the customary practice of the community, or some specialized part of it, like the business community.

169

(The examples ordinarily given are rules of mercantile practice, like the rules governing what rights arise under a standard form of commercial paper.)[27] Since Austin thought that all law was the command of a determinate sovereign, he held that these customary practices were not law until the courts (as agents of the sovereign) recognized them, and that the courts were indulging in a fiction in pretending otherwise. But that seemed arbitrary. If everyone thought custom might in itself be law, the fact that Austin's theory said otherwise was not persuasive.

Hart reversed Austin on this point. The master rule, he says, might stipulate that some custom counts as law even before the courts recognize it. But he does not face the difficulty this raises for his general theory because he does not attempt to set out the criteria a master rule might use for this purpose. It cannot use, as its only criterion, the provision that the community regard the practice as *morally* binding, for this would not distinguish legal customary rules from moral customary rules, and of course not all of the community's long-standing customary moral obligations are enforced at law. If, on the other hand, the test is whether the community regards the customary practice as *legally* binding, the whole point of the master rule is undercut, at least for this class of legal rules. The master rule, says Hart, marks the transformation from a primitive society to one with law, because it provides a test for determining social rules of law other than by measuring their acceptance. But if the master rule says merely that whatever other rules the community accepts as legally binding are legally binding, then it provides no such test at all, beyond the test we should use were there no master rule. The master rule becomes (for these cases) a non-rule of recognition; we might as well say that every primitive society has a secondary rule of recognition, namely the rule that whatever is accepted as binding is binding. Hart himself, in discussing international law, ridicules the idea that such a rule could be a rule of recognition, by describing the proposed rule as "an empty repetition of the mere fact that the society concerned . . . observes certain standards of conduct as obligatory rules."

Hart's treatment of custom amounts, indeed, to a confession that there are at least some rules of law that are not binding because they are valid under standards laid down by a master rule but are binding—like

---

27. See Note, Custom and Trade Usage: Its Application to Commercial Dealings and the Common Law, 55 *Colum. L. Rev.* 1192 (1955), and materials cited therein at 1193 n.1. As that note makes plain, the actual practices of courts in recognizing trade customs follow the pattern of applying a set of general principles and policies rather than a test that could be captured as part of a rule of recognition.

the master rule—because they are accepted as binding by the community. This chips at the neat pyramidal architecture we admired in Hart's theory: we can no longer say that only the master rule is binding because of its acceptance, all other rules being valid under its terms.

This is perhaps only a chip, because the customary rules Hart has in mind are no longer a very significant part of the law. But it does suggest that Hart would be reluctant to widen the damage by bringing under the head of "custom" all those crucial principles and policies we have been discussing. If he were to call these part of the law and yet admit that the only test of their force lies in the degree to which they are accepted as law by the community or some part thereof, he would very sharply reduce that area of the law over which his master rule held any dominion. It is not just that all the principles and policies would escape its sway, though that would be bad enough. Once these principles and policies are accepted as law, and thus as standards judges must follow in determining legal obligations, it would follow that *rules* like those announced for the first time in *Riggs* and *Henningsen* owe their force at least in part to the authority of principles and policies, and so not entirely to the master rule of recognition.

So we cannot adapt Hart's version of positivism by modifying his rule of recognition to embrace principles. No tests of pedigree, relating principles to acts of legislation, can be formulated, nor can his concept of customary law, itself an exception to the first tenet of positivism, be made to serve without abandoning that tenet altogether. One more possibility must be considered, however. If no rule of recognition can provide a test for identifying principles, why not say that principles are ultimate, and *form* the rule of recognition of our law? The answer to the general question "What is valid law in an American jurisdiction?" would then require us to state all the principles (as well as ultimate constitutional rules) in force in that jurisdiction at the time, together with appropriate assignments of weight. A positivist might then regard the complete set of these standards as the rule of recognition of the jurisdiction. This solution has the attraction of paradox, but of course it is an unconditional surrender. If we simply designate our rule of recognition by the phrase "the complete set of principles in force," we achieve only the tautology that law is law. If, instead, we tried actually to list all the principles in force we would fail. They are controversial, their weight is all important, they are numberless, and they shift and change so fast that the start of our list would be obsolete before we reached the middle. Even if we succeeded, we would not have a key for law because there would be nothing left for our key to unlock.

I conclude that if we treat principles as law we must reject the positivists' first tenet, that the law of a community is distinguished from other social standards by some test in the form of a master rule. We have already decided that we must then abandon the second tenet—the doctrine of judicial discretion—or clarify it into triviality. What of the third tenet, the positivists' theory of legal obligation?

This theory holds that a legal obligation exists when (and only when) an established rule of law imposes such an obligation. It follows from this that in a hard case—when no such established rule can be found—there is no legal obligation until the judge creates a new rule for the future. The judge may apply that new rule to the parties in the case, but this is *ex post facto* legislation, not the enforcement of an existing obligation.

The positivists' doctrine of discretion (in the strong sense) required this view of legal obligation, because if a judge has discretion there can be no legal right or obligation—no entitlement—that he must enforce. Once we abandon that doctrine, however, and treat principles as law, we raise the possibility that a legal obligation might be imposed by a constellation of principles as well as by an established rule. We might want to say that a legal obligation exists whenever the case supporting such an obligation, in terms of binding legal principles of different sorts, is stronger than the case against it.

Of course, many questions would have to be answered before we could accept that view of legal obligation. If there is no rule of recognition, no test for law in that sense, how do we decide which principles are to count, and how much, in making such a case? How do we decide whether one case is better than another? If legal obligation rests on an undemonstrable judgment of that sort, how can it provide a justification for a judicial decision that one party had a legal obligation? Does this view of obligation square with the way lawyers, judges and laymen speak, and is it consistent with our attitudes about moral obligation? Does this analysis help us to deal with the classical jurisprudential puzzles about the nature of law?

These questions must be faced, but even the questions promise more than positivism provides. Positivism, on its own thesis, stops short of just those puzzling, hard cases that send us to look for theories of law. When we reach these cases, the positivist remits us to a doctrine of discretion that leads nowhere and tells nothing. His picture of law as a system of rules has exercised a tenacious hold on our imagination, perhaps through its very simplicity. If we shake ourselves loose from this model of rules, we may be able to build a model truer to the complexity and sophistication of our own practices.

Kelsen, Pure Theory of Law*

1. The "Pure" Theory

The Pure Theory of Law is a theory of positive law. It is a theory of positive law in general, not of a specific legal order. It is a general theory of law, not an interpretation of specific national or international legal norms; but it offers a theory of interpretation.

As a theory, its exclusive purpose is to know and to describe its object. The theory attempts to answer the question what and how the law is, not how it ought to be. It is a science of law (jurisprudence), not legal politics.

It is called a "pure" theory of law, because it only describes the law and attempts to eliminate from the object of this description everything that is not strictly law: Its aim is to free the science of law from alien elements. This is the methodological basis of the theory.

Such an approach seems a matter of course. Yet, a glance upon the traditional science of law as it developed during the nineteenth and twentieth centuries clearly shows how far removed it is from the postulate of purity; uncritically the science of law has been mixed with elements of psychology, sociology, ethics, and political theory. This adulteration is understandable, because the latter disciplines deal with subject matters that are closely connected with law. The Pure Theory of Law undertakes to delimit the cognition of law against these disciplines, not because it ignores or denies the connection, but because it wishes to avoid the uncritical mixture of methodologically different disciplines (methodological syncretism) which obscures the essence of the science of law and obliterates the limits imposed upon it by the nature of its subject matter.

2. The Act and Its Legal Meaning

If we differentiate between natural and social sciences—and thereby between nature and society as two distinct objects of scientific

---

* [*The Pure Theory of Law* ch. 1, 1-54 (M. Knight transl. 1970). Copyright © 1967 by The Regents of the University of California; reprinted by permission of the University of California Press.

Hans Kelsen (1881-1973) was Professor of Law and Legal Philosophy at the universities in Vienna, Cologne, and Geneva. In 1940 he left Europe and moved to the United States. He became Professor of Political Science at the University of California at Berkeley in 1945, and taught there for the duration of his career. His principal works in English are *General Theory of Law and the State* (1943); *Society and Nature* (1943); *The Political Theory of Bolshevism* (1948); *The Common Theory of Law* (1955); and *What is Justice* (1957).]

cognition the question arises whether the science of law is a natural or a social science: whether law is a natural or a social phenomenon. But the clean delimitation between nature and society is not easy, because society, understood as the actual living together of human beings, may be thought of as part of life in general and hence of nature. Besides, law— or what is customarily so called—seems at least partly to be rooted in nature and to have a "natural" existence. For if you analyze any body of facts interpreted as "legal" or somehow tied up with law, such as a parliamentary decision, an administrative act, a judgment, a contract, or a crime, two elements are distinguishable: one, an act or series of acts—a happening occurring at a certain time and in a certain place, perceived by our senses: an external manifestation of human conduct; two, the legal meaning of this act, that is, the meaning conferred upon the act by the law. For example: People assemble in a large room, make speeches, some raise their hands, others do not—this is the external happening. Its meaning is that a statute is being passed, that law is created. We are faced here with the distinction (familiar to jurists) between the process of legislation and its product, the statute. To give other illustrations: A man in a robe and speaking from a dais says some words to a man standing before him; legally this external happening means: a judicial decision was passed. A merchant writes a letter of a certain content to another merchant, who, in turn answers with a letter; this means they have concluded a legally binding contract. Somebody causes the death of somebody else; legally, this means murder.

3. The Subjective and Objective Meanings of the Act; Its Self-Interpretation

The legal meaning of an act, as an external fact, is not immediately perceptible by the senses—such as, for instance, the color, hardness, weight, or other physical properties of an object can be perceived. To be sure, the man acting rationally, connects his act with a definite meaning that expresses itself in some way and is understood by others. This subjective meaning may, but need not necessarily, coincide with its objective meaning, that is, the meaning the act has according to the law. For example, somebody makes some dispositions, stating in writing what is to happen to his belongings when he dies. The subjective meaning of this act is a testament. Objectively, however, it is not, because some legal formalities were not observed. Suppose a secret organization intending to rid the nation of subversive elements, condemns to death a man thought to be a traitor, and has a member execute what it subjectively believes to be and calls "a death penalty"; objectively and legally, however, not a death

penalty but a Feme murder was carried out, although the external circumstances of a Feme murder are no different from the execution of a
legal death penalty.

A written or spoken act can even say something about its own legal
meaning. Therein lies a peculiarity of the objects of legal cognition. A
plant is unable to tell the classifying botanist anything about itself. It
makes no attempt to explain itself scientifically. But an act of human
conduct can indeed carry a legal self-interpretation: it can include a
statement indicating its legal meaning. The men assembled in parliament can expressly declare that they are enacting a statute; a man making a disposition about his property may call it "last will and testament";
two men can declare that they are making a contract. The scientist investigating the law, sometimes finds a legal self-interpretation which antici-
pates his own interpretation.

4. The Norm

(a) The Norm As a Scheme of Interpretation

The external fact whose objective meaning is a legal or illegal act is
always an event that can be perceived by the senses (because it occurs in
time and space) and therefore a natural phenomenon determined by
causality. However, this event as such, as an element of nature, is not an
object of legal cognition. What turns this event into a legal or illegal act is
not its physical existence, determined by the laws of causality prevailing
in nature, but the objective meaning resulting from its interpretation.
The specifically legal meaning of this act is derived from a "norm" whose
content refers to the act; this norm confers legal meaning to the act, so
that it may be interpreted according to this norm. The norm functions as
a scheme of interpretation. . . .

"Norm" is the meaning of an act by which a certain behavior is commanded, permitted, or authorized. The norm, as the specific meaning of
an act directed toward the behavior of someone else, is to be carefully
differentiated from the act of will whose meaning the norm is: the norm
is an *ought*, but the act of will is an *is*. Hence the situation constituted by
such an act must be described by the statement: The one individual wills
that the other individual ought to behave in a certain way. The first part
of this sentence refers to an *is*, the existing fact of the first individual's act
of volition; the second part to an *ought*, to a norm as the meaning of that
act. Therefore it is incorrect to assert—as is often done—that the statement: "An individual ought" merely means that another individual wills
something; that the *ought* can be reduced to an *is*. . . .

175

Acts whose meaning is a norm can be performed in various ways. For example, by a gesture: The traffic policeman, by a motion of his arms, orders the pedestrian to stop or to continue; or by a symbol: a red light constitutes a command for the driver to halt, a green light, to proceed; or by spoken or written words, either in the imperative form—be quiet!—or in the form of an indicative statement—I order you to be silent. In this way also permissions or authorizations may be formulated. They are statements about the act whose meaning is a command, a permission, an authorization. But their meaning is not that something is, but that something ought to be. They are not—as they linguistically seem to be—statements about a fact, but a norm, that is to say, a command, a permission, an authorization.

A criminal code might contain the sentence: Theft is punished by imprisonment. The meaning of this sentence is not, as the wording seems to indicate, a statement about an actual event; instead, the meaning is a norm: it is a command or an authorization, to punish theft by imprisonment. The legislative process consists of a series of acts which, in their totality, have the meaning of a norm. To say that acts, especially legislative acts, "create" or "posit" a norm, is merely a figure of speech for saying that the meaning or the significance of the act or acts that constitute the legislative process, is a norm. It is, however, necessary to distinguish the subjective and the objective meaning of the act. "Ought" is the subjective meaning of every act of will directed at the behavior of another. But not every such act has also objectively this meaning; and only if the act of will has also the objective meaning of an "ought," is this "ought" called a "norm." If the "ought" is also the objective meaning of the act, the behavior at which the act is directed is regarded as something that *ought* to be not only from the point of view of the individual who has performed the act, but also from the point of view of the individual at whose behavior the act is directed, and of a third individual not involved in the relation between the two. That the "ought" is the objective meaning of the act manifests itself in the fact that it is supposed to exist (that the "ought" is valid) even if the will ceases to exist whose subjective meaning it is—if we assume that an individual ought to behave in a certain way even if he does not know of the act whose meaning is that he ought to behave in this way. Then the "ought," as the objective meaning of an act, is a valid *norm* binding upon the addressee, that is, the individual at whom it is directed. The ought which is the subjective meaning of an act of will is also the objective meaning of this act, if this act has been invested with this meaning, if it has been authorized by a norm, which therefore has the character of a "higher" norm.

The command of a gangster to turn over to him a certain amount of money has the same subjective meaning as the command of an income-tax official, namely that the individual at whom the command is directed ought to pay something. But only the command of the official, not that of the gangster, has the meaning of a valid norm, binding upon the addressed individual. Only the one order, not the other, is a norm-positing act, because the official's act is authorized by a tax law, whereas the gangster's act is not based on such an authorizing norm. The legislative act, which subjectively has the meaning of *ought,* also has the objective meaning—that is, the meaning of a valid norm—because the constitution has conferred this objective meaning upon the legislative act. The act whose meaning is the constitution has not only the subjective but also the objective meaning of "ought," that is to say, the character of a binding norm, if—in case it is the historically first constitution—we presuppose in our juristic thinking that we ought to behave as the constitution prescribes.

If a man in need asks another man for help, the *subjective* meaning of this request is that the other ought to help him. But in an objective sense he ought to help (that is to say, he is morally obliged to help) only if a general norm—established, for instance, by the founder of a religion —is valid that commands, "Love your neighbor." And this latter norm is objectively valid only if it is presupposed that one ought to behave as the religious founder has commanded. Such a presupposition, establishing the objective validity of the norms of a moral or legal order, will here be called a *basic norm* (*Grundnorm*). Therefore, the objective validity of a norm which is the subjective meaning of an act of will that men ought to behave in a certain way, does not follow from the factual act, that is to say, from an *is,* but again from a norm authorizing this act, that is to say, from an *ought.*

Norms according to which men ought to behave in a certain way can also be created by custom. If men who socially live together behave for some time and under the same circumstances in the same way, then a tendency—that is, psychologically, a will—comes into an existence within the men to behave as the members of the group habitually do. At first the subjective meaning of the acts that constitute the custom is not an *ought.* But later, when these acts have existed for some time, the idea arises in the individual member that he ought to behave in the manner in which the other members customarily behave, and at the same time the will arises that the other members ought to behave in that same way. If one member of the group does not behave in the manner in which the other members customarily behave, then his behavior will be disapproved by the others, as contrary to their will. In this way the custom becomes the expression of a collective will whose subjective meaning is an *ought*. However, the subjective meaning of the acts that constitute the custom can be interpreted as an objectively valid norm only if the custom has been instituted by a higher norm as a norm-creating fact. Since custom is constituted by human acts, even norms created by custom are created by acts of human behavior, and are therefore—like the norms which are the subjective meaning of legislative acts—"posited" or "positive" norms. Custom may create moral or legal norms. Legal norms are created by custom, if the constitution of the social group institutes custom—a specially defined custom—as norm-creating fact. . . .

(c) Validity and Sphere of Validity of the Norm

By the word "validity" we designate the specific existence of a norm. When we describe the meaning or significance of a norm-creating act, we say: By this act some human behavior is ordered, commanded, prescribed, forbidden, or permitted, allowed, authorized. If we use the word *ought* to comprise all these meanings, as has been suggested, we can describe the validity of a norm by saying: Something ought to, or ought not to, be done. If we describe the specific existence of a norm as "validity," we express by this the special manner in which the norm—in contradistinction to a natural fact—is existent. The "existence" of a positive norm—that is to say, its "validity"—is not the same as the existence of the act of will, whose objective meaning the norm is. A norm can be valid, even if the act of will whose meaning the norm is, no longer exists. Indeed, the norm does not become valid until the act of will whose meaning the norm is has been accomplished and hence has ceased to exist. The individual who has created a legal norm by an act directed at the behavior of others, need not continue to will this conduct in order that the norm be valid. When the men who act as legislators have passed a statute regulating certain affairs and have put this statute into "force" (i.e., into validity), they turn in their decisions to the regulation of other affairs; and the statutes put into validity may be valid long after these men have died and therefore are unable to will anything. It is incorrect, therefore, to characterize norms in general, and legal norms in particular, as the "will" or the "command" of the legislator or state, if by "will" or "command" a psychological act of will is meant. The norm is the *meaning* of an act of will, not the act of will.

Since the validity of a norm is an *ought* and not an *is,* it is necessary to distinguish the validity of a norm from its effectiveness. Effectiveness is an "is-fact"—the fact that the norm is actually applied and obeyed, the fact that people actually behave according to the norm. To say that a norm is "valid," however, means something else than that it is actually applied and obeyed; it means that it *ought* to be obeyed and applied, although it is true that there may be some connection between validity and effectiveness. A general legal norm is regarded as valid only if the human behavior that is regulated by it actually conforms with it, at least to some degree. A norm that is not obeyed by anybody anywhere, in other words a norm that is not effective at least to some degree, is not regarded as a valid legal norm. A minimum of effectiveness is a condition of validity. "Validity" of a legal norm presupposes, however, that it is possible to behave in a way contrary to it: a norm that were to prescribe that something ought to be done of which everyone knows beforehand that it must happen necessarily according to the laws of nature always and everywhere would be as senseless as a norm which were to prescribe that something ought to be done of which one knows beforehand that it is impossible according to the laws of nature.

Nor do validity and effectiveness coincide in time. A legal norm becomes valid before it becomes effective, that is, before it is applied and obeyed; a law court that applies a statute immediately after promulgation—therefore before the statute had a chance to become "effective"—applies a valid legal norm. But a legal norm is no longer considered to be valid, if it remains permanently ineffective. Effectiveness is a condition of validity in the sense that effectiveness has to join the positing of a legal norm if the norm is not to lose its validity. . . .

(d) Positive and Negative Regulations: Commanding, Authorizing, Permitting

The behavior regulated by a normative order is either a definite action or the omission (nonperformance) of such an action. Human behavior, then, is either positively or negatively regulated by a normative order. Positively, when a definite action of a definite individual or when the omission of such an action is commanded. (When the omission of an action is commanded, the action is forbidden.) To say that the behavior of an individual is commanded by an objectively valid norm amounts to the same as saying the individual is obliged to behave in this way. If the individual behaves as the norm commands he fulfills his obligation—he obeys the norm; if he behaves in the opposite way, he "violates" the norm—he violates his obligation. Human behavior is positively regulated also, when an individual is authorized by the normative order to bring about, by a certain act, certain consequences determined by the order. Particularly an individual can be authorized (if the order regulates its own creation) to create norms or to participate in that creation;

or when, in case of a legal order providing for coercive acts as sanctions, an individual is authorized to perform these acts under the conditions stipulated by the legal order; or when a norm permits an individual to perform an act, otherwise forbidden—a norm which limits the sphere of validity of a general norm that forbids the act. An example for the last-mentioned alternative is self-defense: although a general norm forbids the use of force of one individual against another, a special norm permits such use of force in self-defense. When an individual acts as he is authorized by the norm or behaves as he is permitted by a norm, he "applies" the norm. The judge, authorized by a statute (that is, a general norm) to decide concrete cases, applies the statute to a concrete case by a decision which constitutes an *individual* norm. Again, authorized by a judicial decision to execute a certain punishment, the enforcement officer "applies" the individual norm of the judicial decision. In exercising self-defense, one applies the norm that permits the use of force. Further, a norm is also "applied" in rendering a judgment that an individual does, or does not, behave as he is commanded, authorized, or permitted by a norm.

In the broadest sense, any human behavior determined by a normative order as condition or consequence, can be considered as being authorized by this order and in this sense as being positively regulated. Human behavior is regulated negatively by a normative order if this behavior is not forbidden by the order without being positively permitted by a norm that limits the sphere of validity of a forbidding norm, and therefore is permitted only in a negative sense. This merely negative function of permitting has to be distinguished from the positive function of permitting—"positive," because it is the function of a positive norm, the meaning of an act of will. The positive character of a permission becomes particularly apparent when the limitation of the sphere of validity of a norm that forbids a certain conduct is brought about by a norm that permits the otherwise forbidden conduct under the condition that the permission has to be given by an organ of the community authorized thereto. The negative as well as positive function of permitting is therefore fundamentally connected with the function of commanding A definite human behavior can be *permitted* only within a normative order that *commands* different kinds of behavior.

5. The Social Order

(a) Social Orders Prescribing Sanctions

The behavior of an individual can be—but need not be—in relation to other individuals: a man can behave in a certain way toward another man, but he can do so also toward animals, plants, and inanimate objects. The relation of one individual to other individuals can be direct or indirect. Murder is the behavior of a murderer toward the murdered—a direct relation between one individual and another. He who destroys a valuable object acts directly in relation to a thing, but indirectly in relation to men who are interested in the object, particularly its owners. A normative order that regulates human behavior in its direct or indirect relations to other human beings, is a social order. Morals and law are such social orders.

On the other hand, logic has as its subject matter a normative order that does not have a social character. For the acts of human thought, which are regulated by the norms of this order, do not refer to other human beings; one does not think "toward" another man in the way that one acts toward another man.

The behavior of one individual toward others may be useful or detrimental for them. From a psychological-sociological point of view, the function of every social order is to bring about a certain behavior of the individuals subject to this order; to motivate them to refrain from certain acts deemed detrimental "socially," that is, to other individuals; and to perform certain acts deemed socially useful. This motivating function is rendered by the idea men have of norms, which command or forbid certain human acts.

Depending on the manner in which human acts are commanded or forbidden, different types may be distinguished—they are ideal types, not average types. The social order may command a certain human behavior without attaching any consequence to the obeying or disobeying of the command. Or the social order may command a definite human behavior and at the same time connect with that behavior the granting of an advantage, a reward; or with the opposite behavior a disadvantage, punishment in the broadest sense of the word. The principle, to react upon a certain human behavior with reward or punishment, is the principle of retribution. Reward and punishment may be called "sanctions," but usually only punishment, not reward, is so called.

Finally, a social order may—and a legal order does—command a certain behavior by just attaching a disadvantage to the opposite behavior, for example, deprivation of life, health, freedom, honor, material goods, that is, by punishment in the broadest sense of the word. Therefore, one may say that a certain behavior is "commanded" by a social order and—in case of a legal order—is legally commanded, only insofar as the contrary behavior is a condition of a sanction (in the narrower sense of the word). If a social order—like the legal order—commands a behavior by prescribing a sanction in case of the opposite behavior, this set of circumstances can be described by a sentence stating that in the

181

event of a certain behavior a certain sanction *ought* to be executed. By this is implied that the behavior conditioning the sanction is prohibited, the opposite behavior commanded: The behavior which is "commanded" is not the behavior which "ought" to be executed. That a behavior is "commanded" means that the contrary behavior is the condition of a sanction which "ought" to be executed. The execution of the sanction is *commanded* (i.e., it is the content of a legal obligation), if the nonexecution is the condition of a sanction. If this is not the case, the sanction is only authorized, not commanded. Since this regression cannot go on indefinitely, the last sanction in this chain can only be authorized, not commanded.

It follows that within such a normative order the same behavior may be—in this sense—commanded and forbidden at the same time, and that this situation may be described without logical contradiction. This is the case if a certain conduct is the condition of a sanction and at the same time the omission of this conduct is also the condition of a sanction. The two norms: "a ought to be" and "a ought not to be" exclude each other insofar as they cannot be obeyed or applied by the same individual at the same time; only one can be valid. But the two norms: "If a is, x ought to be" and "If non-a is, x ought to be" are not mutually exclusive. These two norms can be valid at the same time. Under a legal order a situation may exist in which a certain human behavior and at the same time the opposite behavior is the condition of a sanction which ought to be executed. The two norms can be valid side by side. They can be described without logical contradiction, but they express two conflicting political tendencies, a teleological conflict. The situation is possible, but politically unsatisfactory. Therefore legal orders usually contain rules according to which one of the two norms is invalid or may be invalidated.

Insofar as the evil that functions as a sanction—the punishment in the widest sense—has to be inflicted against the will of the affected individual; and insofar as, in case of resistance, the evil has to be inflicted by force, the sanction has the character of a coercive act. A normative order, which prescribes coercive acts as sanctions (that is, as reactions against a certain human behavior), is a coercive order. But coercive acts can be prescribed—and are so prescribed in a legal order, as we shall see—not only as sanctions, but as reactions against socially undesirable facts that do not have the character of human behavior and are therefore not to be regarded as prohibited.

From a sociological-psychological point of view, reward or punishment are ordered to make the desire for reward and the fear of punishment the motives for a socially desirable behavior. But actually this behavior may be brought about by other motives. According to its inherent meaning, the order may prescribe sanctions without regard to the motives that actually, in each single case, have brought about the behavior conditioning the sanctions. The meaning of the order is expressed in the statement that in the case of a certain behavior—brought about by whatever motives—a sanction (in the broader sense of the word, that is, reward or punishment) ought to be executed. Indeed, an order may attach a reward to a behavior only if it had not been motivated by the desire for reward. For example, a moral order may honor only the one who does good deeds for their own sake, not for honor's sake.

Since in the foregoing pages the validity of a social order has been distinguished from its effectiveness, it should be noted that a social order prescribing rewards or punishments is effective in the literal sense of the word insofar only as the behavior conditioning the reward is caused by the desire for the reward, and the behavior avoiding the punishment is caused by the fear of punishment. However, it is usual to speak of an effective order also if the behavior of the individuals subjected to the order by and large corresponds to the order, that is to say, if the individuals by and large by their behavior fulfill the conditions of the rewards and avoid the conditions of the punishments, without regard to the motive of their behavior. Used in this way the concept of effectiveness has a normative, not a causal, meaning.

(b) Are There Social Orders without Sanctions?

Distinctly different from a social order prescribing sanctions (in the wider sense of the word) is one that commands a certain behavior without attaching reward for it or punishment for its opposite—that is, an order in which the principle of retribution is not applied. Usually the moral order is considered to be such a social order, and is thereby distinguished from the legal order. . . .

It is remarkable that of the two sanctions, reward and punishment, the latter plays a much more important role in social reality than the former. This is shown not only by the fact that the most important social order, the legal order, essentially makes use only of punishment, but especially clearly under a social order which still has a purely religious character, that is, a social order guaranteed only by transcendental sanctions. The morally or legally correct behavior of primitive men, especially in the observance of the numerous prohibitions—the so-called tabus—is determined primarily by the fear of misfortunes imposed by a superhuman authority—the spirits of the dead—as a reaction against the violation of the traditional order. The hope of reward, if compared with the fear that dominates the life of the primitives, plays only a subordinate role. In the religious beliefs of civilized man, too, according to which divine retribution is not (or not only) imposed in this world but in the world beyond, fear of punishment after death takes first place. The image of hell as the place of punishment is much more vivid than the usually vague idea of a life in heaven which is the reward for piety. Even when no limits are imposed on man's wish-fulfilling phantasy, it produces a transcendental order which is not fundamentally different from that of the empirical society.

6. The Legal Order

(a) The Law: An Order of Human Behavior

A theory of law must begin by defining its object matter. To arrive at a definition of law, it is convenient to start from the usage of language, that is, to determine the meaning of the word "law" as equivalent to the German word *Recht,* French *droit,* Italian *diritto.** Our task will be to examine whether the social phenomena described by these words have common characteristics by which they may be distinguished from similar phenomena, and whether these characteristics are significant enough to serve as elements for a concept of social-scientific cognition. The result of such an investigation could conceivably be that the word "law" and its equivalents in other languages designates so many different objects that they cannot be comprehended in one concept. However, this is not so. Because, when we compare the objects that have been designated by the word "law" by different peoples at different times, we see that all these objects turn out to be *orders of human behavior.* An "order" is a system of norms whose unity is constituted by the fact that they all have the same reason for their validity; and the reason for the validity of a normative order is a basic norm—as we shall see—from which the validity of all norms of the order are derived. A single norm is a valid legal norm, if it corresponds to the concept of "law" and is part of a legal order; and it *is* part of a legal order, if its validity is based on the basic norm of that order.

The norms of a legal order regulate human behavior. At first sight it seems as if this sentence applied only to the social orders of civilized peoples, because in primitive societies the behavior of animals, plants, and even inanimate objects is also regulated by a legal order. For example,

---

* Translator's Note: This is the translation of the German text ". . . die Bedeutung festzustellen, die das Wort 'Recht' in der deutschen Sprache und seine Aequivalenten in anderen Sprachen (*law, droit, diritto* usw.) haben." The English word "law" is not confined to the legal sense but is also used for law of nature.

we read in the Bible that an ox that has killed a man ought to be killed—
evidently as a punishment. In ancient Athens, there was a special court,
in which a stone or spear or any other object could be tried by which a
man—presumably inadvertently—had been killed. In the Middle Ages
it was possible to sue an animal, for example a bull that had caused the
death of a man or grasshoppers that had destroyed a harvest. The accused animal was condemned and executed in formal legal procedure,
exactly like a human criminal. If the sanctions, provided by the legal
order, are directed not only against men but also against animals, this
means that not only human behavior, but also the behavior of animals is
legally commanded. This means further: if that which is legally commanded is to be regarded as the content of a legal duty, then not only
men, but also animals are regarded as being obliged to behave in a certain way. This, in our modern point of view, absurd legal content is the
result of animistic ideas, according to which not only men, but also animals, and inanimate objects have a "soul" and are therefore basically not
different from human beings. Consequently sanctions, and therefore
norms that establish legal duties, are applicable to men as well as animals
and things. Although modern legal orders regulate only the behavior of
men, not of animals, plants, and things, it is not excluded that these
orders prescribe the behavior of man toward animals, plants, and things.
For example, the killing of certain animals (in general or at specific
times), the damaging of rare plants or historically valuable buildings may
be prohibited. But these legal norms do not regulate the behavior of the
protected animals, plants, and things, but of the men against whom the
threat of punishment is directed.

This behavior may be a positive action or nonaction—a lack of action, an omission, a forbearance, a refrainment from action. The legal
order, as a social order, regulates positively the behavior of individuals
only so far as it refers, directly or indirectly, to other individuals. The
object of regulation by a legal order is the behavior of one individual in
relation to one, several, or all other individuals—the mutual behavior of
individuals. The relation of the behavior of one man to others may be an
individual one: for example, the norm that obliges every man to refrain
from killing other men; or the norm that obliges the debtor to pay the
creditor; or the norm that obliges everybody to respect the property of
others. But the relation may also have a collective character. For example, the behavior prescribed by the norm obliging a man to do military
service, is not the behavior of an individual versus another individual,
but versus the entire social community— versus all individuals subject to
the legal order. The same is true where suicide attempt is punishable.
And in the same way the mentioned norms protecting animals, plants,

and inanimate objects may be interpreted as social norms. The legal authority commands a certain human behavior, because the authority, rightly or wrongly, regards such behavior as necessary for the human legal community. In the last analysis, it is this relation to the legal community which is decisive for the legal regulation of the behavior of one individual to another. For the legal norm obliges the debtor not only and, perhaps, not so much in order to protect the creditor, but in order to maintain a certain economic system.

(b) The Law: A Coercive Order

The first characteristic, then, common to all social orders designated by the word "law" is that they are orders of human behavior. A second characteristic is that they are *coercive orders*. This means that they react against certain events, regarded as undesirable because detrimental to society, especially against human behavior of this kind, with a coercive act; that is to say, by inflicting on the responsible individual an evil—such as deprivation of life, health, liberty, or economic values—which, if necessary, is imposed upon the affected individual even against his will by the employment of physical force. By the coercive act an evil is inflicted in the sense that the affected individual ordinarily regards it as such, although it may occasionally happen that this is not so. For example, somebody who has committed a crime may regret his action so much that he actually wishes to suffer the punishment of the law and therefore does not regard it as an evil; or somebody commits a crime in order to go to jail where he can be sure of food and shelter. But these are, of course, exceptions. Since, ordinarily, the affected individual regards the coercive act as an evil, the social orders, designated as "law" are coercive orders of human behavior. They command a certain human behavior by attaching a coercive act to the opposite behavior. This coercive act is directed against the individual who behaves in this way (or against individuals who are in some social relation to him). That means: the coercive order authorizes a certain individual to direct a coercive act as a sanction against another individual. The sanctions prescribed by the legal order are socially immanent (as distinguished from transcendental) sanctions; besides, they are socially organized (as distinguished from mere approval or disapproval). . . .

As a coercive order, the law is distinguished from other social orders. The decisive criterion is the element of force—that means that the act prescribed by the order as a consequence of socially detrimental facts ought to be executed even against the will of the individual and, if he resists, by physical force. . . .

186

The Monopoly of Force of the Legal Community

Although the various legal orders largely agree about the coercive acts which may be attributed to the legal community—they always consist in the deprivation of the mentioned goods—these orders differ concerning the conditions to which the coercive acts are attached. They differ particularly concerning the human behavior whose opposite should be brought about by stipulating the sanctions, that is, concerning the socially desired status, which consists in the legal behavior prescribed by the legal order; in other words, concerning the *legal value* constituted by the legal norms. The development of the law from primitive beginnings to its present stage in the modern state displays, concerning the legal value to be realized, a tendency that is common to all legal orders. It is the tendency gradually and increasingly to prohibit the use of physical force from man to man. Use of force is prohibited by making it the condition for a sanction. But the sanction itself is a use of force. Therefore the prohibition of the use of force can only be a limited one; and one must distinguish between a permitted and a prohibited use of force. It is permitted as a reaction against a socially undesirable fact, especially against a socially detrimental human behavior, as a sanction, that is, as an authorized use of force attributable to the legal community. This distinction does not yet mean, however, that the use of force other than legally authorized as reaction against an undesirable fact, is prohibited and therefore illegal. Primitive legal orders do not prohibit all other kinds of use of force. Even the killing of men is prohibited to only a limited degree. Only the killing of free fellow countrymen is considered to be a crime in primitive societies, not the killing of aliens or slaves. The killing of the latter, insofar as it is not prohibited, is—in the negative sense— permitted. But it is not authorized as a sanction! Gradually, however, the principle is recognized that every use of physical force is prohibited unless—and this is a limitation of the principle—it is especially authorized as a reaction against a socially detrimental fact attributable to the legal community. In this case, the legal order determines exhaustively the conditions under which (and the men by whom) physical force may be used. Since the individual authorized to use force may be regarded as an organ of the legal order (or of the community constituted by the legal order), the execution of coercive acts by these individuals may be attributed to the community. Then we are confronted with a monopoly of force of the legal community. The monopoly is decentralized if the individuals authorized to use force do not have the character of special organs acting according to the principle of division of labor but if the legal order authorizes all individuals to use force who consider their interests violated by the illegal conduct of others; in other words if the principle of self-help still prevails.

Legal Order and Collective Security

When the legal order determines the conditions under which, and the individuals by whom, physical force is to be used, it protects the individuals who live under this order against the use of force by other individuals. When this protection has reached a certain minimum we speak of collective security, because the security is guaranteed by the legal order as a social order. This minimum of protection against the use of physical force can be regarded as existing even when monopoly of force is decentralized, that is, even when self-help still prevails. It is possible to consider such a state as the lowest degree of collective security. However, we may speak of collective security only in a narrower sense if the monopoly of force of the legal community has reached a minimum of centralization, so that self-help is excluded, at least in principle. Collective security, in this narrower sense, exists when at least the question of whether in a concrete situation the law was violated and of who is responsible for it, is not answered by the parties involved, but by a special organ, an independent court; when, therefore, the question of whether in a concrete case, the use of force is a delict or legal and an act that may be attributed to the community, particularly a sanction, can be objectively decided. . . .

The prohibition of all use of force reveals the tendency to enlarge the sphere of facts that are established by the legal order as condition of coercive acts; this tendency has developed far beyond this prohibition, by the attachment of coercive acts as consequences not only to the use of force, but also to other acts, and even to omissions of acts. If the coercive act established by the law is a reaction against socially detrimental behavior and if the function of such an establishment is to prevent such a behavior (individual or general prevention), then this act has the character of a sanction in the specific and narrower sense of the word; and the fact that a certain behavior is made the condition for a sanction in this sense means that this behavior is legally prohibited, a delict. There is a correlation between this concept of sanction and the concept of delict. The sanction is the consequence of the delict; the delict is the condition of the sanction. In primitive legal orders the reaction of the sanction against the delict is entirely decentralized. The reaction is left to the discretion of the individuals whose interests have been violated by the delict. They are authorized to identify *in concreto* as a delict what has been so identified by the legal order only *in abstracto;* and they are authorized to execute the sanction established by the legal order. The principle of self-help prevails. In the course of evolution this reaction against the delict is increasingly centralized, in that the identification of the delict and the execution of the sanction is reserved for special organs: the courts and executive authorities. Thereby the principle of self-help is limited, but it cannot be entirely eliminated. Even in the modern state, in which centralization has reached the highest degree, a minimum of self-help remains: self-defense. . . .

Coercive Acts other than Sanctions

. . . The concept of sanction may be extended to include all coercive acts established by the legal order, if the word is to express merely that the legal order reacts with this action against socially undesirable circumstances and qualifies in this way the circumstances as undesirable. This, indeed, is the common characteristic of all coercive actions commanded or authorized by legal orders. The concept of "sanction," understood in this broadest sense, then, the force monopoly of the legal community, may be formulated by the alternative: "The use of force of man against man is either a delict or a sanction."

(c) The Law As a Normative Coercive Order; Legal Community and Gang of Robbers

The law as a coercive order is sometimes characterized by the statement that the law commands a certain behavior "under threat" of coercive acts, that is, of certain evils. But this formulation ignores the normative meaning with which coercive acts in general and sanctions in particular are stipulated by the legal order. The meaning of a threat is that an evil *will be* inflicted under certain conditions; the meaning of a legal order is that certain evils *ought to be* inflicted under certain conditions or—expressed more generally—that certain coercive acts ought to be executed under certain conditions. This is not only the subjective meaning of the acts by which the law is established but also their objective meaning. Only because this normative meaning is the objective meaning of these acts, do they have the character of law-stipulating, norm-creating, or norm-executing acts. The action of a highwayman who under threat commands somebody to surrender his money also has the subjective meaning of an "ought." If the situation created by such a command is described by saying that one individual expresses a will directed toward the behavior of another individual, then one merely describes the action of the first as an actually happening event. The behavior of the other individual, however, which is intended by the will of the first, cannot be described as something that actually takes place, because he does not yet behave and may not behave at all in the way that the first one had intended. It can only be described as something that according to the subjective meaning of the command ought to take place.

In this way every situation must be described in which one individual expresses a will directed toward the behavior of another individual. In this respect (namely, so far as only the subjective meaning of the acts are considered), there is no difference between describing the command of a robber and the command of a legal organ. The difference appears only when the objective meaning of the command is described, the command directed from one individual toward another. Then we attribute only to the command of the legal organ, not to that of the robber, the objective meaning of a norm binding the addressed individual. In other words, we interpret the one command, but not the other, as an objectively valid norm; and then we interpret in the one case the connection of the nonfulfillment of the command with a coercive act merely as a "threat" (i.e., a statement that an evil *will be* inflicted), whereas in the other case, we interpret this connection to mean that an evil *ought to be* inflicted. Therefore we interpret the actual infliction of the evil in the second situation as the application or execution of an objectively valid norm, stipulating a coercive act as a sanction, but in the first situation—if we offer a normative interpretation—as a crime.

But why do we interpret the subjective meaning of the one act also as its objective meaning, but not so of the other act? Why do we suppose that of the two acts, which both have the subjective meaning of an "ought," only one established a valid, that is, binding, norm? In other words: What is the reason for the validity of the norm that we consider to be the objective meaning of this act? This is the decisive question.

By analyzing the judgments that interpret the acts as legal (that is, as acts whose objective meaning is norms) we get the answer to the question. Such an analysis reveals the *presupposition* that makes such an interpretation possible.

Let us start from the earlier-mentioned interpretation of the killing of one individual by another as the execution of a death sentence and not as murder. Our interpretation is based on the recognition that the act of killing constitutes the execution of a court decision that has commanded the killing as a punishment. This means: We attribute to the act of the court the objective meaning of an individual norm and in this way interpret the individuals who perform the act, as a court. We do this, because we recognize the act of the court as the execution of a statute (that is, of general norms stipulating coercive acts) in which we see not only the subjective but also the objective meaning of an act that had been established by certain individuals whom we consider, for this reason, as legislators. For we regard the act of legislation as the execution of the constitution, that is, of general norms that, according to their subjective meaning, authorize these individuals to establish general norms prescribing coercive acts. In this way we interpret these individuals as legislative organs. By regarding the norms authorizing the legislative organ not only as the subjective but also as the objective meaning of an act performed by definite individuals, we interpret these norms as "constitution." For the historically first constitution such an interpretation is possible only, if we *presuppose* that one ought to behave according to the subjective meaning of the act, that one ought to perform coercive acts only under the conditions and in the manner the constitution stipulates; if, in other words, we presuppose a norm according to which (a) the act whose meaning is to be interpreted as "constitution" is to be regarded as establishing objectively valid norms, and (b) the individuals who establish this act as the constitutional authorities. As will be developed later, this norm is the basic norm, of the national legal order. It is not established by a positive legal act, but is presupposed, *if* the act mentioned under (a) is interpreted as establishing a constitution and the acts based on the constitutions are interpreted as legal acts. To make manifest this presupposition is an essential function of legal science. This presupposition is the ultimate (but in its character conditional and therefore hypothetical) reason for the validity of the legal order.

By making these statements we are considering, at this point, only a national legal order, that is, a legal order whose territorial sphere of validity is limited to the territory of a state. The reason for the validity of international law, whose territorial sphere of validity is not so limited, and the relationship of the international legal order to the national legal orders, are, for the present, outside our discussion.

It was observed earlier that the validity of a norm (which means that one ought to behave as the norm stipulates) should not be confounded with the effectiveness of the norm (which means that one, in fact, does so behave); but that an essential relation may exist between the two concepts, namely, that a coercive order, presenting itself as the law, is regarded as valid only if it is by and large effective. That means: The basic norm which is the reason for the validity of a legal order, refers only to a constitution which is the basis of an effective coercive order. Only if the actual behavior of the individuals conforms, by and large, with the subjective meaning of the acts directed toward this behavior—if, in other words, the subjective meaning is recognized as the objective meaning— only then are the acts interpreted as legal acts.

191

Now we are ready to answer the question why we do not attribute to the command of a robber, issued under threat of death, the objective meaning of a valid norm binding on the addressed victim; why we do not interpret this act as a legal act; why we regard the realization of the threat as a crime, and not as the execution of a sanction.

An isolated act of one individual cannot be regarded as a legal act, its meaning cannot be regarded as a legal norm, because law, as mentioned, is not a single norm, but a system of norms; and a particular norm may be regarded as a legal norm only as a part of such a system. How about a situation, however, in which an organized gang systematically jeopardizes a certain territory by forcing the people living there, under threat, to surrender their money? In this situation we will have to distinguish between the order that regulates the mutual behavior of the members of this robber gang and the external order, that is, the commands that the members of the gang direct at outsiders under the threat of inflicting evils. For it is only in relation to outsiders that the group behaves as a *robber* gang. If robbery and murder were not forbidden in the relations between the robbers, no community, no robber *gang* would exist. Nevertheless, even the internal order of the gang may be in conflict with the coercive order, considered to be a legal order, valid for the territory in which the gang is active. Why is the coercive order that constitutes the community of the robber gang and comprises the internal and external order not interpreted as a legal order? Why is the subjective meaning of this coercive order (that one ought to behave in conformity with it) not interpreted as its objective meaning? Because no basic norm is presupposed according to which one ought to behave in conformity with this order. But why is no such basic norm presupposed? Because this order does not have the lasting effectiveness without which no basic norm is presupposed. The robbers' coercive order does not have this effectiveness, if the norms of the legal order in whose territorial sphere of validity the gang operates are actually applied to the robbers' activity as being illegal behavior; if the members of the gang are deprived of their liberty or their lives by coercive acts that are interpreted as imprisonment and death sentences; and if thus the activity of the gang is terminated—in short, if the coercive order regarded as the legal order is more effective than the coercive order constituting the gang. . . .

(d) Legal Obligations without Sanctions?

If the law is conceived of as a coercive order, then the formula by which the basic norm of a national legal order is expressed runs as follows: "Coercion of man against man ought to be exercised in the manner and under the conditions determined by the historically first constitu-

192

tion." The basic norm delegates the first constitution to prescribe the procedure by which the norms stipulating coercive acts are to be created. To be interpreted objectively as a legal norm, a norm must be the subjective meaning of an act performed in this procedure, hence in accordance with the basic norm; besides, the norm must stipulate a coercive act or must be in essential relation to such a norm. Together with the basic norm the definition of law as a coercive order is presupposed. From the definition of law as a coercive order follows that a behavior may be regarded as legally commanded (i.e., as the content of a legal obligation) only if the contrary behavior is made the condition of a coercive act directed against the individual thus behaving. It is to be noted, however, that the coercive act itself need not be commanded in this sense: its ordering and executing may be merely authorized.

Against the definition of law as a coercive order, that is, against the inclusion of the element of coercion into the concept of law, the objections have been raised (1) that legal orders actually contain norms that do not stipulate coercive acts: norms that permit or authorize a behavior, and also norms that command a behavior without attaching to the opposite behavior a coercive act; and (2) that the nonapplication of the norms that stipulate coercive acts are frequently not made the condition for coercive acts functioning as sanctions.

The second objection is not valid, because the definition of law as a coercive order can be maintained even if the norm that stipulates a coercive act is not itself essentially connected with a norm that attaches, in a concrete case, a sanction to the nonordering or nonexecuting of the coercive act—if, therefore, the coercive act stipulated in the general norm is to be interpreted objectively not as commanded but only as authorized or positively permitted (although the subjective meaning of the act by which the general norm stipulates the coercive act is a commanding). As for the first objection, the definition of law as a coercive order can be maintained even with respect to norms that authorize a behavior not having the character of a coercive act; or norms that positively permit such a behavior insofar as they are *dependent* norms, because they are essentially connected with norms that stipulate the coercive acts. A typical example for norms cited as arguments against the inclusion of coercion into the definition of law are the norms of constitutional law. It is argued that the norms of the constitution that regulate the procedure of legislation do not stipulate sanctions as a reaction against nonobservance. Closer analysis shows, however, that these are dependent norms establishing only one of the conditions under which coercive acts stipulated by other norms are to be ordered and executed. Constitutional norms authorize the legislator to create norms—they do not command the creation of norms; and therefore the stipulation of sanctions do not come into question at all. If the provisions of the constitution are not observed, valid legal norms do not come into existence, the norms created in this way are void or voidable. This means: the subjective meaning of the acts established unconstitutionally and therefore not according to the basic norm, is not interpreted as their objective meaning or such a temporary interpretation is annulled.

The most important case of norms which according to traditional science of law constitute legal obligations without stipulating sanctions, is the so-called natural obligation. Natural obligations are obligations whose fulfillment cannot be asserted in a court, and whose nonfulfillment is not the condition of a civil execution. Still, one speaks of a legal obligation, because that which, in fulfillment of a so-called natural obligation, has been given by one individual to another cannot be recovered as an unjustified enrichment. If this is so, however, it merely means: A general norm is valid stipulating that: (1) if the beneficiary of a performance to which the performer was legally not obligated refuses restitution, civil execution ought to be directed into the property of the beneficiary; and (2) the validity of this coercion-stipulating norm is restricted with respect to cases determined by the legal order. This situation, therefore, can be described as a restriction of the validity of a sanction-stipulating norm; it is not necessary to assume the existence of a sanctionless norm.

It is possible, of course, for a legislator to establish, in a procedure conforming with the basic norm, an act whose subjective meaning is a behavior-commanding norm, without (1) establishing an act whose subjective meaning is a norm prescribing a sanction as a reaction against the opposite behavior; and without (2) the possibility of describing the situation as "restriction of the validity of a sanction-stipulating norm." In this case the subjective meaning of the act in question cannot be interpreted as its objective meaning; the norm, which is the act's subjective meaning cannot be interpreted as a legal norm, but must be regarded as legally irrelevant. . . .

Since the law regulates the procedure by which it is itself created, one might distinguish this legally regulated procedure as *legal form* from the *legal content* established by the procedure, and speak of a legally irrelevant legal content. In traditional science of law this thought is expressed to some extent by the distinction between law in the formal sense and law in the material sense. This distinction acknowledges the fact that not only general behavior-regulating norms are issued in the form of laws, but also administrative decisions, such as the naturalization of a person, the approval of the state budget, or judicial decisions (when, in certain cases, the legislator acts as a judge). But it would be more correct to speak of form of law and content of law rather than of law in the formal and in the material sense. However, the words "legal form" and "legal content" are unprecise and even misleading in this respect; in order to be interpreted as a legal act it is not only required that the act be established by a certain procedure, but also that the act have a certain subjective meaning. The meaning depends on the definition of law, presupposed together with the basic norm. If the law is not defined as a coercive order, but only as an order established according to the basic norm (and if, therefore, the basic norm is formulated as: one ought to behave as the historically first constitution prescribes), then sanctionless legal norms could exist, that is, legal norms that under certain conditions command a human behavior without another norm stipulating a sanction as a reaction against nonobservance. In this case the subjective meaning of an act, established in accordance with the basic norm—if this meaning is not a norm and in no relation to a norm—would be legally irrelevant. Then, a norm established by the constitutional legislator and commanding a certain behavior without attaching a coercive act to its nonobservance, could be distinguished from a moral norm only by its origin; and a legal norm established by custom could not be distinguished from a customarily established moral norm at all.

If the constitution has established custom as a law-creating fact, then all moral norms created by custom constitute a part of the legal order.

Therefore, then, a definition of law, which does not determine law as a coercive order, must be rejected (1) because only by including the element of coercion into the definition of law is the law clearly distinguished from any other social order; (2) because coercion is a factor of great importance for the cognition of social relationships and highly characteristic of the social orders called "law"; and, (3) particularly, because by defining law as a coercive order, a connection is accounted for that exists in the case most important for the cognition of the law, the law of the modern state: the connection between law and state. The modern state is essentially a coercive order—a centralized coercive order, limited in its territorial validity. . . .

Simpson, The Common Law and Legal Theory*

I. Introduction

In England and in those parts of the world where the English legal tradition has been received the characteristic type of law is common law,

* [From *Oxford Essays in Jurisprudence* edited by A. W. B. Simpson, © Oxford University Press 1973, pp. 77-79. Reprinted by permission of Oxford University Press.

as contrasted with statute law. Common law in this sense has of course been modified by equity, but then equity is just another form of common law. The common law has in its time been given a variety of classifying titles which reflect different views as to its distinguishing or characteristic feature—for example "case law," "judiciary law," "judge-made law," "customary law," and "unwritten law." Names such as these reflect theories as to the nature of the common law, and it would be easy enough to cull from legal writings the expression of very divergent views of the institution. It seems to me however that to date no very satisfactory analysis of the nature of the common law has been provided by legal theory; indeed the matter has received remarkably little sustained attention by theoretical writers. What has been the subject of much writing is the doctrine of precedent or *stare decisis;* indeed a search of the literature for discussions of the nature of the common law tends to locate only accounts of the working of this doctrine, which is itself I suppose "part of" the common law. To a historian at least any identification between the common law system and the doctrine of precedent, any attempt to explain the nature of the common law in terms of *stare decisis,* is bound to seem unsatisfactory, for the elaboration of rules and principles governing the use of precedents and their status as authorities is relatively modern, and the idea that there could be binding precedents more recent still. The common law had been in existence for centuries before anybody was very excited about these matters, and yet it functioned as a system of law without such props as the concept of the *ratio decidendi,* and functioned well enough. Nor does the common law appear to have wholly altered its character over the years, and a theory of the common law, if it is to seem satisfactory, must cater for this continuity. It must accommodate the common law of the seventeenth century as well as the common law of the twentieth, or at least provide a view of the common law which will serve to explain whatever changes have occurred in the general character of the institution. One such change is indeed the increased importance attached to authority, in particular quoted judicial opinions, in the working of the system.

In the sense used here a theory or general view of the common law represents an attempt to provide an answer to the question whether the common law can be said to exist at all—and this has been seriously doubted—and if so in what sense. Put rather differently, such a theory

---

Alfred William Brian Simpson (1931–) is a distinguished British legal historian and philosopher. He is the author of *A History of the Common Law of Contract: The Rise of the Action of Assumpsit* (1975), *An Introduction to the History of the Land Law* (1961), and editor of *Oxford Essays in Jurisprudence* (1973).]

will seek to explain how, if at all, statements in the form "It is the law that . . . ," such as "It is the law that contracts require consideration," can meaningfully be made, when such statements are conceived to be statements of the common law. Such an explanation is essential to the understanding of the workings of the judicial process, which is conducted upon the assumption that the common law (we are not concerned with statute) always provides an answer to the matter in issue, and one which is independent of the will of the court. What may be called general theoretical propositions of the common law, which are the stuff of legal argument and justification, take a variety of forms. Sometimes they are said to state *doctrines* of the common law (the doctrine of offer and acceptance), sometimes *principles* or *general principles* (the principle of "volenti non fit iniuria") sometimes *rules* (the rule in *Rylands v. Fletcher*), sometimes *definitions* (the definition of conversion), and this is by no means an exclusive list of a diversity which is recognized more generously in the language of lawyers than in the writings of legal philosophers. Some attempts have been made to differentiate these concepts; thus Bingham,[1] and more recently Dworkin,[2] have sought to distinguish *rules* from *principles*. For present purposes these distinctions are not important, and all legal propositions may be considered together, and merely distinguished from propositions which purport only to be *about* the common law. An example would be such a statement as "The common law does not favour self-help." Put forward in a different form, for example like this, "It is a principle of the common law that self help is to be discouraged," this would in my scheme rank as a general theoretical proposition of the common law; it would then purport to state the law rather than pass an observation about the law. It is primarily with propositions of law that I am here concerned.

In passing it is however important to notice that in legal reasoning propositions which are neither propositions *of* law nor propositions *about* law feature prominently. For example, when Lord Devlin said in the course of his judgment in *Behrens v. Bertram Mills,*[3] "If a person wakes up in the middle of the night and finds an escaping tiger on top of his bed and suffers a heart attack, it would be nothing to the point that the intentions of the tiger were quite amiable," he was not making a legal observation, but justifying a decision on the law governing liability for dangerous animals by an appeal to common sense. No doubt these non-legal justificatory propositions could be further divided—some for example

1. J. W. Bingham. What is the Law? (1912), 11 *Mich. L.R.* 1 and 109 at p. 22.
2. R. M. Dworkin. Is Law a System of Rules? *Essays in Legal Philosophy* (1968), ed. Summers, p. 25 at p. 34 ff.
3. [1957] 2 Q.B. 1 at p. 17.

refer to moral considerations, others to expediency—and they are used to claim for a decision a rationality which is not based upon the artificial reason of the law; though not themselves legal propositions they may be used to support the contention that this or that is the law. In the common law system no very clear distinction exists between saying that a particular solution to a problem is in accordance with the law, and saying that it is the rational, or fair, or just solution.

If, however, we confine attention to specifically legal propositions, how are they to be explained? The type of answer given to this question will depend upon the particular theoretical viewpoint adopted, for there appear to me to be a number of different possible conceptions of the nature of the common law. The predominant conception today is that the common law consists of a system of rules; in terms of this legal propositions (if correct) state what is contained in these rules. I wish to consider the utility of this conception, and to contrast it with an alternative idea—the idea that the common law is best understood as a system of customary law, that is, as a body of traditional ideas received within a caste of experts.

II. Positivism and the Common Law As a System of Rules

The idea that the common law is a set of rules, in some unusual sense forming a system, is intimately associated with the movement known as legal positivism. Though purporting to be an observation, it is best viewed as a dogma, which derives basically from viewing all law in terms of a model of statute law. In its purest form legal positivism involves two basic assumptions, which will be found, variously elaborated, or sometimes merely covertly adopted, in very many theoretical writings. The first is that all law is positive law, and what this means at its simplest is that all laws owe their status as such to the fact that they have been laid down. In the curious and archaic language of Austin, laws properly so called are laws *by position;*[4] they are set, or prescribed, and human law at least is laid down by humans to humans. Blackstone, though inconsistent in his positivism, thought that municipal law was prescribed by what he called the supreme power in the State,[5] whilst Gray thought that laws were rules of conduct laid down by the courts.[6] Both assumed that laws must have been laid down by somebody or other to rank as laws, and to

4. J. Austin, *The Province of Jurisprudence Determined,* ed. Hart (1954), xliii.
5. W. Blackstone, *Commentaries on the Laws of England* (1809 ed.), p. 44.
6. J. C. Gray, *The Nature and Sources of the Law,* 2nd ed. (1948), p. 84.

this extent were positivists. When in a modern book on the doctrine of precedent Professor Cross[7] writes, "Such a rule (one derived from a precedent or series of precedents) is law 'properly so called' and law *because it was made by the judges,* [my italics] and not because it originated in common usage, or the judges' idea of justice and public convenience," he is expressing the first basic assumption of positivism. In an uneasily modified form the same assumption is writ large in Kelsen:[8] "Law is always positive law, and its positivity lies in the fact that it is created and annulled by acts of human beings, thus being independent of morality and other norm systems." The insistence that all law is positive law originally stood in opposition to the claim that some laws, or all laws, owed their status as such to the fact that they were in accordance with or sanctioned by nature. Pure positivism thus involves the notion that there is only one possible alternative basis for law to that provided by natural law theories. The most obvious point at which difficulty is encountered in maintaining the thesis that all law is posited is when dealing with custom, which common sense would suggest is not laid down; customs, we know, grow up. Kelsen runs into difficulty over this; though admitting custom as a possible type of law (to be contrasted with statute law) he is at pains to insist that even the norms of customary law, in a system which admits custom as "a law-creating act," are *positive.* To preserve the dogma the notion of laying down or prescribing law has to be emasculated until it means only that the norms of customary law are the products of acts of will, even though these acts of will are not directed to the making of law at all. "Since custom is constituted by human acts, even norms created by custom are created by acts of human behaviour, and are therefore like the norms which are the subjective meaning of legislative acts—'posted' or 'positive' norms"[9] This is hardly convincing, but my point is only to illustrate the basic *credo.*

The second basic assumption is less easy to state with precision. It involves conceiving of law as a sort of code. The law, including the common law, is identified with a notional set of propositions which embody the corpus of rules, principles, commands, norms, maxims, or whatever, which have, at any given time, been laid down. For present purposes nothing turns upon distinctions between rules, principles, maxims, et cetera, so this second assumption can be put thus: the law exists as a set of rules, the rules being identical with and constituting the law. Combining

7. Rupert Cross, *Precedent in English Law,* 1st ed., p. 23.
8. H. Kelsen, *General Theory of Law and the State* (1961), p. 114.
9. H. Kelsen, *The Pure Theory of Law* (1967), p. 9.

these two assumptions of positivism the common law must be conceived of as existing as a set or code of rules which have been laid down by somebody or other, and which owe their status as law to the fact that they have been so laid down. We are to conceive of the common law, somewhat perversely, as if it had already been codified, when we all know it has not. And if communication by words is the manner in which the action of laying down the law takes place, then the words used will constitute the law. In terms of such a model the general theoretical propositions of the common law can be thought of as stating rules of the common law, if "correct", or as putative statements which may or may not be correct.

Around these two basic assumptions cluster various ideas either derived from them or at least intimately associated with them. Thus if all laws are laid down, all laws must have an author, for someone must have performed the act of positing the law. Secondly, there must be some test or criterion for identifying the lawmaker or lawmakers who have authority to lay down the law, or entitlement to do so, for it would be absurd if anyone who cared to do so could lay down law; the primary ground for saying that this or that is the law will be the fact that the right person or group laid it down. Thirdly, if law is by definition laid down, all law must originate in legislation, or in some law-creating act. Fourthly, law so conceived will appear as the product of acts of will, and the law which results as the will of the lawmaker. Fifthly, if laws owe their status to their having been laid down by the right author, it cannot be a necessary characteristic of law that it should have a particular content, for its content will depend upon the will of the lawmaker, who may be devil or angel or something in between—hence the separation of law and morals. And sixthly, if law consists of what has been laid down, then what has been laid down, conceived as a code, is exhaustive of the law at any given moment, so that where nothing has been laid down, there is no law; the law is conceived of as in principle a finite system. And unless one admits the possibility of the existence of a number of co-existing common laws, which seems absurd, there must at one moment be one unique set of rules constituting the common law.

This may be called the "school-rules concept" of law, and it more or less assimilates all law to statute law. In recent times there have been advanced what may be called weaker versions of positivism, which have gone some way towards abandoning the first assumption whilst retaining the second: law continues to be conceived of as a set of rules, but their status as law does not necessarily depend upon their having been laid down. Examples are to be found in the legal theories of Kelsen (who, as we have seen, still maintains that all law is positive in a peculiar sense) and Hart.[10] Such theories are committed to giving some explanation of how one is to tell whether a putative rule belongs to the club or not. The answer given is that membership depends upon the satisfaction of tests provided by some other higher or basic rule or rules, sometimes called power-conferring rules or rules of competence, in absent-minded conformity to the idea that all law originates in legislation. Those which qualify are characterized as valid—valid meaning "binding" or "existing as a rule of the system"—and the corpus of rules possessing the quality of validity, together with the basic rule or rules (*grundnorm,* constitution, rule of recognition) constitute the legal system. A legal system is conceived not as an institution, but as a code of rules, systematic only in the peculiar sense that the contents of the code satisfies the tests. Although it might seem consistent with such an approach to admit the possibility that some rules might qualify because of their content (the rule possessing some supposed quality, such as being in accordance with the will of God or the principle of utility) both Kelsen and, less clearly, Hart seem to have in mind criteria dealing with the mode of origin of the rule, or, as Dworkin has put it, with the "pedigree" of the rule, rather than content. All law is like statute law in that its authority is independent of its content.

As applied to the common law such weak versions of positivism could in principle no doubt cater for the possibility that it consists of rules which are not necessarily of legislative origin, nobody having ever laid them down. Kelsen does not really develop the application of his theory to the common law. In his *General Theory of Law and the State* he conceives of law, in the form of general norms, as originating either in custom or legislation, statutory law and customary law being the two fundamental types of law. In so far as the common law derives from judicial precedents he apparently conceives of it as statutory; in so far as it is based upon the long practice of the courts it is customary law. Hart too does not devote more than a small part of *The Concept of Law* to the detailed application of his theory to the common law. But he envisages the possibility that in a complex legal system the criteria for the validity of rules may include reference to "customary practice," "general declarations of specified persons," and "past judicial decisions" in addition to reference to an "authoritative text" or "legislative enactment"; such criteria no doubt are included to cater for the common law. Elsewhere he seems to regard the activities of courts as sometimes legislative in character; like Kelsen, Hart perhaps conceives of the common law as a medley of rules of different character. But in the absence of a rather more full

10. H. L. A. Hart, *The Concept of Law* (1961).

treatment of the subject it is not at all easy to see quite how the common law fits into the scheme of things.

III. Defects of Positivism

But both in its strong and weak forms positivism seems to me to present a defective scheme for understanding the nature of the common law. In its strong form, as presented by Austin, it claims that the common law consists of rules which owe their status as law to the fact that they have been laid down. Now the plausibility of claiming that the common law has been posited—presumably by judges. . . . Austin presented his hearers with the alternative of either agreeing that the common law was laid down by the judges, or believing in the childish fiction (as he called it) that the common law was "a miraculous something made by nobody, existing, I suppose, from eternity and merely declared from time to time by the judges."[15] Confronted with this crude choice it is natural to prefer the former view. But difficulties arise if an attempt is made to apply Austin's view to a specific instance. Consider, for example, the rule that parole contracts require consideration (I choose this example because nobody would, I think, deny that this is a rule of the common law). Austin tells us "there can be no law without a legislative act"[16] and the legislative act here must be a judicial decision, if one is to be found. Now it is well known that this rule has been on the common law scene since the sixteenth century, and some hundreds of reported cases would seem to a historian to be relevant to the understanding of the history and evolution of the rule. There would be no difficulty whatever in citing *authority* for the existence of the rule—that is to say acceptable warrants for the contention that there is such a rule. . . . No doubt the best possible authority would be a recent case. . . . It would seem to me to be absurd to identify . . . a case with an act of legislation, conferring the status of law on the rule. For we know that in some meaningful sense the rule has been law for centuries before this. The point is that the production of authority that this or that is the law is not the same as the identification of acts of legislation. Conversely what might plausibly rank as an act of judicial legislation will not necessarily rank as good authority. Suppose that one was able to find a case, decided say in 1540, where the assembled judges ruled that consideration was necessary in parole contracts, and there was every reason to suppose that this was the first case in which this ruling was given. Not only would it seem wrong to say that the rule

15. Austin, *Lectures,* 5th ed. (1855), ii, 655.
16. Austin, *Lectures,* ii, 216.

derived its status as law today from this antique decision, but the decision would not even rank as particularly good authority for the rule. We may contrast the case of a rule which is of legislative origin—by way of example take that jurisprudential old chestnut, the rule that a will requires two witnesses. Here we can identify the act of legislation which conferred the status of law on the rule as the Wills Act of 1837, and this enactment (granted certain presuppositions) is the reason why today wills do require two witnesses for effective attestation. The statute is both the only reason and a conclusive reason for saying that this is the law. The notion that the common law consists of rules which are the product of a series of acts of legislation (mostly untraceable) by judges (most of whose names are forgotten) cannot be made to work, if taken seriously, because common law rules enjoy whatever status they possess not because of the circumstances of their origin, but because of their continued reception. Of course, it is true that judges are voluntary agents, and the way in which they decide cases and the views they express in their opinions are what they choose to express. Their actions create precedents, but creating a precedent is not the same thing as laying down the law. The opinions they express possess in varying and uncertain degree authority, as do opinions expressed by learned writers, but to express an authoritative opinion is not the same thing as to legislate. There exists no context in which a judicial statement to the effect that this or that is the law confers the status of law on the words uttered, and it is merely misleading to speak of judicial legislation.

Weaker versions of positivism escape the difficulty involved in the claim that all the rules of the common law are the product of judicial legislative acts. They share however with pure positivism the claim that the law—and this includes the common law—consists of a set of rules, a sort of code, which satisfies tests of validity prescribed by other rules. Such theories suffer from defects which have their source in the confusion of ideals with reality. Put simply, life might be much simpler if the common law consisted of a code of rules, identifiable by reference to source rules, but the reality of the matter is that it is all much more chaotic than that, and the only way to make the common law conform to the ideal would be to codify the system, which would then cease to be common law at all.

It is firstly central to such theories that there exist rules setting out the criteria which must be satisfied by other rules for them to belong to the system. These rules exist either in the sense that they are used and accepted by those concerned—roughly by the caste of lawyers—as the proper way of identifying other rules, or in the sense that they are the necessary presuppositions which make the identification of other rules possible. Either way it seems we must locate these supposed rules by considering the way in which legal propositions are justified, and legal argument conducted. Now it is quite true that in relatively recent times in the long history of the common law growing attention has been devoted, both by the judiciary and by legal commentators, to the formulation of rules governing the use of authorities in legal argument. Such rules constitute attempts to state the proper practice over such questions as what courts are bound by what decisions, how one is to distinguish authoritative statements of law from statements of no authority, what law reports should be used and what difference, if any, it makes if a writer is dead or alive. It is all a very theological world, with mysteries similar to those which surround the doctrine of papal infallibility. These rules governing the proper use of authority and the reverence due to it are notoriously controversial, and we all know both that the practice of the courts is not at all consistent in these matters, and that judicial views as to the proper thing to do both differ and change. . . . Furthermore arguments to the effect that this or that is the law are commonly supported by reference to ideas which are not specifically legal—expediency, commonsense, morality, and so forth—as in the example of Lord Devlin and the errant tiger; they are supported by reference to reason and not authority. And nobody, I think, would claim that rationality in the common law can be reduced to rules. These familiar facts form the background to the notion of tests of validity, which involves a claim that legal reasoning and justification is governed by rules to an extent which it is not; legal life is far too untidy. Only if it were the case both that the use of authority in the law was wholly rule-governed, and all legal argument based upon authority, would such a theory correspond with reality.

A second objection to the notion of the common law as a system of rules turns upon the contrast between the essentially shadowy character of the common law and the crisp picture of a set of identifiable rules. Consider for example contexts in which a common lawyer might well talk of rules—the rule in *Rylands v. Fletcher,*[19] the rule in *Shelley's Case,*[20] or the rule in *Hadley v. Baxendale.*[21] These I take to be paradigm cases of rules of the common law, and to say that the common law consists of rules suggests a system of law in which such rules are the norm rather than the exception. Now one obvious characteristic of these rules is that their text is fairly well settled, though even in the cases where this is so the text is not utterly sacrosanct; the rule in *Rylands v. Fletcher* might for

19. 1866 L.R. 1 Ex. 265, L.R. 3 H.L. 330.
20. (1581) 1 Co. Rep. 936.
21. (1854) 9 Exch. 341.

example be reformulated or more elegantly stated without the heavens falling; furthermore there may exist exceptions to these rules which are not included in a statement of the rule. But the general position in the common law is that it lacks an authoritative authentic text; as Pollock put it, the common law ". . . professes . . . to develop and apply principles that have never been committed to any authentic form of words."[22] It consequently distorts the nature of the system to conceive of the common law as a set of rules, an essentially precise and finite notion, as if one could in principle both state the rules of the common law and count them like so many sheep, or engrave them on tablets of stone.

IV. Is the Common Law a Fiction?

Indeed in an important sense it is in general the case that one cannot say what the common law is, if its existence is conceived of as consisting of a set of rules, and if saying what the law is means reporting what rules are to be found in the catalogue. The realization that this was so led Jeremy Bentham into the most powerful attack ever made upon the idea that the common law could be meaningfully said to exist at all, and it is no accident that this attack was made by a positivist. Although his view of the matter wavered, his extreme and characteristic opinion was that the existence of the common law was "a fiction from beginning to end," and belief in its existence no more than "a mischievous delusion."[23] Of the expression "common law" he wrote: "In these two words you have a name pretended to be the name of a really existent object:—look for any such existing object—look for it till doomsday, no such object will you find."[24] The common law was "mock law," "sham law," "quasi-law," and in consequence the exercise of the judicial function an example of "power everywhere arbitrary." It is instructive to see what drove Bentham into this scepticism. What he perceived very clearly was the existence of an incompatibility between the "school-rules concept" of law and the thesis that the common law could be regarded as existing in any real sense. His thesis is perhaps most clearly stated in the *Comment on the Commentaries:* "*As a system of general rules,* the common law is a thing merely imaginary."[26] The italics are mine, the point being that Bentham's scepticism leaves open the possibility that in some other sense the predication of existence to the common law might be meaningful.

22. F. Pollock, *A First Book of Jurisprudence,* 3rd ed. (1911), p. 249.
23. J. Bentham, *Collected Works,* IV, 483.
24. [And See Ryle on "category" mistakes in Chapter 7.]
26. J. Bentham, *A Comment on the Commentaries,* ed. Everett (1928), p. 125.

Bentham's scepticism depends mainly upon the fact that rules can only be stated in a language—if somebody asks me to tell him one of the rules of chess I have to *say* something or *write* something in reply. But it is a feature of the common law system that there is no way of settling the correct text or formulation of the rules, so that it is inherently impossible to state so much as a single rule in what Pollock called "any authentic form of words." How can it be said that the common law exists as a system of general rules, when it is impossible to say what they are?

Bentham's point depends upon the familiar fact that if six pundits of the profession, however sound and distinguished, are asked to write down what they conceive to be the rule or rules governing the doctrine of *res ipsa loquitur,* the definition of murder or manslaughter, the principles governing frustration of contract or mistake as to the person, it is in the highest degree unlikely that they will fail to write down six different rules or sets of rules. And if by some happy chance they all write down (for example) "killing with malice aforethought" an invitation to explain what *that* means will inevitably produce *tot jurisprudentes quot leges.* Again we all know that no two legal treatises state the law in the same terms, there being a law of torts according to Street, and Heuston, and Jolowich and James and the contributors to Clerk and Lindsell, and we buy them all because they are all different. And what is true of the academics is true perhaps even more dramatically of the judges, who are forever disagreeing, often at inordinate length. When, after long and expensive argument the Law Lords deliver themselves *ex cathedra* of their opinions— and this is the best we can do—they either confine themselves to laconic agreement or *all say different things, and this even when they claim to be in complete agreement.* It would hardly be worth their while to deliver separate opinions if this were not so. Nor does the common law system admit the possibility of a court, however elevated, reaching a final, authoritative statement of what the law is in a general abstract sense. It is as if the system placed particular value upon dissension, obscurity, and the tentative character of judicial utterances. As a system of legal thought the common law then is inherently vague; it is a feature of the system that uniquely authentic statements of the rules which, so positivists tell us, comprise the common law, cannot be made.

Such extreme scepticism as Bentham's seems to me to carry us too far, for at any given moment in time there appear to me to be many propositions of law which would secure general agreement amongst expert lawyers as being correct, and if there are wide differences in the way in which propositions of law are formulated there is at the same time a very considerable measure of agreement as to the practical application of the law in actual cases. If the common law is a fiction from beginning to end, and the exercise of judicial power everywhere arbitrary, it is difficult to see what explanation can be given of this. Now one way of explaining this cohesion of thought is to say that in spite of a certain degree of vagueness and uncertainty the source rules of the common law do not work at all badly. Hart, for example, says: "The result of the English system of precedent has been to produce, by its use, a body of rules of which a vast number of both major and minor importance, are as determinate as any statutory rule. They can only be altered by statute."[27] I doubt this explanation. If we look back into the history of the common law before there were doctrines of precedent and articles on the *ratio decidendi* of a case the same phenomenon—a cohesion of ideas—is to be found; indeed I suspect (though this is not capable of strict proof) that there was a much greater degree of cohesion in say the fifteenth century than there is today. The explanation for this cannot be the use of tests of valid law. Furthermore it seems to me that the contemporary rules for the use of authority in the common law are as we have seen vague, uncertain, changing, and in any event incapable of settling the correct formulation of legal rules. Nor does it seem to me to be true, as positivists must have us believe, that once a rule satisfies the tests it can only be altered by legislation. The reality of the matter is that well settled propositions of law—propositions with which very few would disagree—do suffer rejection. The point about the common law is not that everything is always in the melting-pot, but that you never quite know what will go in next. Few in 1920 would have doubted that manufacturers of products were immune from the liability soon to be imposed upon them. . . .

V. The Common Law As Customary Law

If however we abandon the positivist conception of the common law, in terms of what other conception can the institution be more realistically depicted and its peculiar characteristic explained? Positivists take as their basic model of law an enacted code, but a better starting-point, if we are concerned with the common law, is the traditional notion of the common law as custom, which was standard form in the older writers. . . . This view of the common law has today fallen almost wholly out of favour, and the reason for this, or at least one predominant reason, is not far to seek. By a custom we commonly mean some practice, such as drinking the health of the Queen after dinner, which is regularly observed and has been regularly observed for some time in a group, and which is regarded within the group as the normal and proper practice. It

---

27. Hart, *The Concept of Law* 132 (1961).

is also integral to the idea of a custom that the past practice of conformity is conceived of as providing at least part of the reason why the practice is thought to be proper and the right thing to do. Clearly the common law as an institution is in part customary in this sense. If however one considers general theoretical propositions of the common law—for example the rule against perpetuities, or the doctrine of anticipatory breach, it is perfectly absurd to regard propositions stating such rules and doctrines as putative descriptions of the customary practices of Englishmen. It may be true that such parts of the common law reflect, or are based upon, or consistent with, ideas and values which either are or once were current in the upper ranks of English society, or in society generally, but this does not make them into customs.

. . . [Now] custom seems an inappropriate term for abstract propositions of law; laws are not customs simply. We need rather to conceive of the common law as a system of customary law, and recognize that such systems may embrace complex theoretical notions which both serve to explain and justify past practice in the settlement of disputes and the punishment of offences, and provide a guide to future conduct in these matters. In the second place we are rather more conscious of change in the law—we know for example that although the doctrine of consideration is old, it is not of immemorial antiquity, and that there are recently evolved doctrines too; some come and go, like the deserted wife's equity, and others survive. With these modifications however it seems to me that the common law system is properly located as a customary system of law in this sense, that it consists of a body of practices observed and ideas received by a caste of lawyers, these ideas being used by them as providing guidance in what is conceived to be the rational determination of disputes litigated before them, or by them on behalf of clients, and in other contexts. These ideas and practices exist only in the sense that they are accepted and acted upon within the legal profession, just as customary practices may be said to exist within a group in the sense that they are observed, accepted as appropriate forms of behaviour, and transmitted both by example and precept as membership of the group changes. The ideas and practices which comprise the common law are customary in that their status is thought to be dependent upon conformity with the past, and they are traditional in the sense that they are transmitted through time as a received body of knowledge and learning. Now such a view of the common law does not require us to *identify* theoretical propositions of the common law—putative formulations of these ideas and practices—with the common law, any more than we would identify statements of the customs observed within a group with the practices which constitute the customs. And this, as it seems to me, disposes of

Bentham's main difficulty in admitting the existence of the common law. Formulations of the common law are to be conceived of as similar to grammarians' rules, which both describe linguistic practices and attempt to systematize and order them; such rules serve as guides to proper practice since the proper practice is in part the normal practice; such formulations are inherently corrigible, for it is always possible that they may be improved upon, or require modification as what they describe changes.

VI. The Achievement of Cohesion in a Customary System

It is no doubt impossible in principle to attach precision to such notions as acceptance and reception within the caste of lawyers, and the definition of membership of this group is essentially imprecise. Nevertheless it seems to me that . . . the relative value of formulated propositions of the common law depends upon the degree to which such propositions are accepted as accurate statements of received ideas or practice, and one must add the degree to which practice is consistent with them. Now a customary system of law can function only if it can preserve a considerable measure of continuity and cohesion, and it can do this only if mechanisms exist for the transmission of traditional ideas and the encouragement of orthodoxy. There must exist within the group—particularly amongst its most powerful members—strong pressures against innovation; young members of the group must be thoroughly indoctrinated before they achieve any position of influence, and anything more than the most modest originality of thought treated as heresy. In past centuries in the common law these conditions were almost ideally satisfied. The law was the peculiar possession of a small, tightly organized group comprising those who were concerned in the operation of the Royal courts, and within this group the serjeants and judges were dominant. Orthodox ideas were transmitted largely orally, and even the available literary sources were written in a private language as late as the seventeenth century. A wide variety of institutional arrangements tended to produce cohesion of thought. The organization of the profession was gerontocratic, as indeed it still is, and promotion depended upon approval by the senior members of the profession. The system of education and apprenticeship, the residential arrangements, the organization of dispute and argument—for example the sitting of judges *in banc* and the existence of institutions such as the old informal Exchequer Chamber—all assisted in producing cohesion in orthodoxy and continuity. So too did such beliefs as the belief that the common law was of immemorial antiquity, and the belief that if only the matter was considered long enough and with sufficient care a uniquely correct answer could be distilled for every problem. The combination between institutional arrangements and conservative dogma is well illustrated in Blackstone's description of "the chief cornerstone" of the laws of England: ". . . which is general immemorial custom or common law, from time to time declared in the decisions of the courts of justice; which decisions are preserved amongst our public records, explained in our reports, and digested for general use in the authoritative writings of the venerable sages of the law." . . .

In such a system of law as the common law the explanation for the degree of consensus which exists at any one time will be very complex, and no *general* explanation will be possible, and this remains true today. . . . Settled doctrines, principles, and rules of the common law are settled because, for complex reasons, they happen to be matters upon which agreement exists, not, I suspect, because they satisfy tests. The tests are attempts to explain the consensus, not the reason for it.

To study such a system, whether one is concerned with it at present, or in the past, involves, amongst other things, an attempt to identify what ideas are or were current at any particular period, and what ideas received or acted upon. What is involved is basically an oral tradition, still only imperfectly reduced to published writing. . . . A historian is confined to the use of written sources—records, note books, legal writings, and indeed any document which throws light on the matter; his interest is not limited to a search for authorities. From such sources it is within limits possible to show that the doctrine of offer and acceptance was not a going idea in 1800, though by 1879 when Anson published his book on contract law it had come to be orthodoxy. Opinions as to what ideas were current, and what ideas generally accepted, are necessarily imprecise; there cannot in principle be a catalogue of such ideas, and in any event different and incompatible doctrines and views can co-exist. This seems to me to be just as true today as it was in the past. To argue that this or that is the correct view, as academics, judges, and counsel do, is to *participate* in the system, not simply to study it scientifically. For the purposes of action the judge or legal adviser must of course choose between incompatible views, selecting one or other as the law, and the fiction that the common law provides a unique solution is only a way of expressing this necessity.

When there is disagreement within a customary system there must, if the system is to function, be some way of settling at a practical level which view should be acted upon—for example for the purpose of directing a jury or determining an appeal. This problem is solved by procedures, and these may take a wide variety of forms, though all will involve vesting a power of decision in some person or persons. In a system which lays claim to rationality—and the common law did—it will be supposed that differences can be resolved by argument and discussion, and that the method adopted to solve disputes at a practical level is in principle capable of producing in general a correct solution to the general question—What is the law? In a tightly cohesive group there will exist a wide measure of consensus upon basic ideas and values as well as upon what views are tenable. Argument and discussion will commonly produce agreement in the end, and so long as this is the case there will be little interest in how or why this consensus is achieved. There is no *a priori* reason for supposing that just because agreement is commonly reached this is because there in fact is a rational way of deciding disputes. When however cohesion has begun to break down, and a failure to achieve consensus becomes a commoner phenomenon, interest will begin to develop in the formulation of tests as to how the correctness of legal propositions can be demonstrated, and in the formulation of rules as to the use of authorities—that is to say warrants or proofs that this or that is the law. This is the phenomenon of laws of citation, and it has really struck the common law only in the last century. It seems to me to be a symptom of the breakdown of a system of customary or traditional law. For the only function served by rules telling lawyers how to identify correct propositions of law is to secure acceptance of a corpus of ideas as constituting the law. If agreement and consensus actually exist, no such rules are needed, and if it is lacking to any marked degree it seems highly unlikely that such rules, which are basically anti-rational, will be capable of producing it. It is therefore not surprising to find that today, when there is great interest in the formulation of source rules in the common law world, the law is less settled and predictable than it was in the past when nobody troubled about such matters. In a sense this is obvious. There is only a felt need for authority for a legal proposition when there is some doubt as to whether it is correct or not; in a world in which all propositions require support from authority, there must be widespread doubt. The explanation for the breakdown in the cohesion of the common law is complex, but it is easy to see that the institutional changes of the nineteenth century, and the progressive increase in the scale of operations, had much to do with the process. . . .*

How then are we to view the positivists' notion of the common law as a body of rules, forming a system in that the rules satisfy tests of validity? We must start by recognizing what common sense suggests, which is that the common law is more like a muddle than a system, and that it would

* [Simpson points out that there are both more appellate judges and more dissenting opinions.]

be difficult to conceive of a less systematic body of law. The systematization of the common law—its reduction to a code of rules which satisfy accepted tests provided by other rules—is surely a programme, or an ideal, and not a description of the status quo. (Indeed even in the case of law of statutory origin common law judges shrink from identifying the law with the text of the statute, which they rapidly encrust with interpretation—consider the fate of the definition of diminished responsibility, no longer to be simply read out to the jury as "the law.") It is the ideal of an expositor of the law, grappling with the untidy shambles of the law reports, the product of the common law mind which is repelled by brevity, lucidity and system, and it is no accident that its attraction as a model grows as the reality departs further and further from it. It is, I suspect, a rather futile ideal; the only effective technique for reducing the common law to a set of rules is codification, coupled of course with a deliberate reduction in the status of the judiciary and some sort of ban on law reporting. But to portray the common law as actually conforming to this ideal is to confuse the aspirations of those who are attempting to arrest the collapse of a degenerate system of customary law with the reality.

III. AMERICAN LEGAL REALISM

Llewellyn, Some Realism About Realism*

. . . One thing is clear. There is no school of realists. There is no likelihood that there will be such a school. There is no group with an official or accepted, or even with an emerging creed. There is no abnegation of independent striking out. We hope that there may never be. New recruits acquire tools and stimulus, not masters, nor over-mastering ideas. Old recruits diverge in interests from each other. They are related, says Frank, only in their negations, and in their skepticisms, and in their curiosity.

* [44 *Harv. L. Rev.* 1222 (1931). Copyright 1931 by The Harvard Law Review Association. Reprinted by permission.

Karl Nickerson Llewellyn (1893-1962) was a leading figure in the American legal realist movement. Educated at the University of Lausanne, the University of Paris, and Yale University, Llewellyn taught at Yale, Columbia University, and the University of Chicago. His published works include *The Bramble Bush* (1930), *Jurisprudence: Realism in Theory and in Practice* (1968), *The Common Law Tradition: Deciding Appeals* (1960), and *The Cheyenne Way: Conflict and Case Law in Primitive Jurisprudence* (with E. A. Hoebel, 1941).]

What one does find as he observes them is twofold. First (and to be expected) certain points of departure are common to them all. Second (and this, when one can find neither school nor striking likenesses among individuals, is startling) a cross-relevance, a complementing, an interlocking of their varied results "as if they were guided by an invisible hand." A third thing may be mentioned in passing: a fighting faith in their methods of attack on legal problems; but in these last years the battle with the facts has proved so much more exciting than any battle with traditionalism. . . .

Maps of the United States prepared respectively by a political geographer and a student of climate would show some resemblance; each would show a coherent picture; but neither's map would give much satisfaction to the other. So here. I speak for myself of that movement which in its sum is realism; I do not speak of "the realists"; still less do I speak *for* the participants or any of them. And I shall endeavor to keep in mind as I go that the justification for grouping these men together lies not in that they are *alike* in belief or work, but in that from certain common points of departure they have branched into lines of work which seem to be building themselves into a whole, a whole planned by none, foreseen by none, and (it may well be) not yet adequately grasped by any.

The common points of departure are several.

(1) The conception of law in flux, of moving law, and of judicial creation of law.

(2) The conception of law as a means to social ends and not as an end in itself; so that any part needs constantly to be examined for its purpose, and for its effect, and to be judged in the light of both and of their relation to each other.

(3) The conception of society in flux, and in flux typically faster than the law, so that the probability is always given that any portion of law needs reëxamination to determine how far it fits the society it purports to serve.

(4) The *temporary* divorce of Is and Ought for purposes of study. By this I mean that whereas value judgments must always be appealed to in order to set objectives for inquiry, yet during the inquiry itself into what Is, the observation, the description, and the establishment of relations between the things described are to remain *as largely as possible* uncontaminated by the desires of the observer or by what he wishes might be or thinks ought (ethically) to be. More particularly, this involves during the study of what courts are doing the effort to disregard the question what they ought to do. Such divorce of Is and Ought is, of course, not conceived as permanent. To men who begin with a suspicion that change is needed, a permanent divorce would be impossible. The argument is sim-

ply that no judgment of what Ought to be done in the future with respect to any part of law can be intelligently made without knowing objectively, as far as possible, what that part of law is now doing. And realists believe that experience shows the intrusion of Ought-spectacles *during the investigation of the facts* to make it very difficult to see what is being done. On the Ought side this means an insistence on informed evaluations instead of armchair speculations. Its full implications on the side of Is-investigation can be appreciated only when one follows the contributions to objective description in business law and practice made by realists whose social philosophy rejects many of the accepted foundations of the existing economic order.

(5) Distrust of traditional legal rules and concepts insofar as they purport to *describe* what either courts or people are actually doing. Hence the constant emphasis on rules as "generalized predictions of what courts will do." This is much more widespread as yet than its counterpart: the careful severance of rules *for* doing (precepts) from rules *of* doing (practices).

(6) Hand in hand with this distrust of traditional rules (on the descriptive side) goes a distrust of the theory that traditional prescriptive rule-formulations are *the* heavily operative factor in producing court decisions. This involves the tentative adoption [better: exploration] of the theory of rationalization for [what light it can give in] the study of opinions. It will be noted that "distrust" in this and the preceding point is not at all equivalent to "negation in any given instance."

(7) The belief in the worthwhileness of grouping cases and legal situations into narrower categories than has been the practice in the past.[c] This is connected with the distrust of verbally simple rules—which so often cover dissimilar and non-simple fact situations (dissimilarity being tested partly by the way cases come out, and partly by the observer's judgment as to how they ought to come out; but a realist tries to indicate explicitly which criterion he is applying in any particular instance).

(8) An insistence on evaluation of any part of law in terms of its effects, and an insistence on the worthwhileness of trying to find these effects.

(9) Insistence on *sustained and programmatic attack* on the problems of law along any of these lines. *None of the ideas set forth in this list is new.* Each can be matched from somewhere; each can be matched from recent or-

---

c. The quest for narrower, more significant, categories is always a sound *first* approach to wide categories which are not giving satisfaction-in-use. But of course, once satisfactory narrower categories have been found and tested, the eternal quest recurs, for wider synthesis—but one which will really stand up in use.

thodox work in law. New twists and combinations do appear here and there. What is as novel as it is vital is for a goodly number of men to pick up ideas which have been expressed and dropped, used for an hour and dropped, played with from time to time and dropped—to pick up such ideas and set about *consistently, persistently, insistently to carry them through.* Grant that the idea or point of view is familiar—the results of steady, sustained, systematic work with it are not familiar. Not hit-or-miss stuff, not the insight which flashes and is forgotten, but sustained effort to force an old insight into its full bearing, to exploit it to the point where it laps over upon an apparently inconsistent insight, to explore their bearing on each other by the test of fact. This urge, in law, is quite new enough over the last decades to excuse a touch of frenzy among the locust-eaters.

The first, second, third and fifth of the above items, while common to the workers of the newer movement, are not peculiar to them. But the other items (4, 6, 7, 8, and 9) are to me the characteristic marks of the movement. Men or work fitting those specifications are to me "realistic" whatever label they may wear. Such, and none other, are the perfect fauna of this new land. Not all the work cited below fits my peculiar definition in all points. All such work fits most of the points.

Bound, as all "innovators" are, by prior thinking, these innovating "realists" brought their batteries to bear in first instance on the work of appellate courts. Still wholly within the tradition of our law, they strove to improve on that tradition.

(a) An early and fruitful line of attack borrowed from psychology the concept of *rationalization* already mentioned. To recanvass the opinions, viewing them no longer as mirroring the process of deciding cases, but rather as trained lawyers' arguments made by the judges (after the decision has been reached), intended to make the decision seem plausible, legally decent, legally right, to make it seem, indeed, legally inevitable—this was to open up new vision. It was assumed that the deductive logic of opinions need by no means be either a *description* of the process of decision, or an *explanation* of how the decision had been reached. Indeed over-enthusiasm has at times assumed that the logic of the opinion *could* be neither; and similar over-enthusiasm, perceiving case after case in which the opinion is clearly almost valueless as an indication of how that case came to decision, has worked at times almost as if the opinion were equally valueless in predicting what a later court will do.

But the line of inquiry via rationalization has come close to demonstrating that in any case doubtful enough to make litigation respectable the available authoritative premises—i.e., premises legitimate and impeccable under the traditional legal techniques—are at least two, and that the two are mutually contradictory as applied to the case in hand. Which opens the question of what made the court select the one available premise rather than the other. And which raises the greatest of doubts as to *how far* any supposed certainty in decision which may derive merely [or even chiefly] from the presence of accepted rules really goes.

(b) A second line of attack has been to discriminate among rules with reference to their relative significance. Too much is written and thought about "law" and "rules," lump-wise. Which part of law? Which rule? Iron rules of policy, and rules "in the absence of agreement"; rules which keep a case from the jury, and rules as to the etiquette of instructions necessary to make a verdict stick—if one can get it; rules "of pure decision" for hospital cases, and rules which counsellors rely on in their counselling; rules which affect many (and which many, and how?) and rules which affect few. Such discriminations affect the traditional law curriculum, the traditional organization of law books and, above all, the orientation of study: to drive into *the most important* fields of ignorance.

(c) A further line of attack on the apparent conflict and uncertainty among the decisions in appellate courts has been to seek more understandable statement of them by grouping the facts in new—and typically but not always narrower—categories. The search is for correlations of fact-situation and outcome which (aided by common sense) may reveal *when* courts seize on one rather than another of the available competing premises. One may even stumble on the trail of *why* they do.

. . . Perhaps, indeed, contracts in what we may broadly call family relations do not work out in general as they do in business.[43] If so, the rules—viewed as statements of the course of judicial behavior—as *predictions* of what will happen—need to be restated. Sometimes it is a question of carving out hitherto unnoticed exceptions. But sometimes the results force the worker to reclassify an area altogether. Typically, as stated, the classes of situations which result are narrower, much narrower than the traditional classes. The process is in essence the orthodox technique of making distinctions, and reformulating—but undertaken systematically; exploited consciously, instead of being reserved until facts which refuse to be twisted by "interpretation" force action. The departure from orthodox procedure lies chiefly in distrust of, instead of search for, the widest sweep of generalization words permit. Not that such sweeping generalizations are not desired—*if they can be made so as to state what judges do* [or ought to do.]

43. Perhaps they should not—but that is an Ought question. One will be forced to raise it, if he finds courts in their results persistently evading the consequences of what accepted doctrine declares to be the general rule.

All of these three earliest lines of attack converge to a single conclusion: *there is less possibility of accurate prediction of what courts will do than the traditional rules would lead us to suppose*[47] (and what possibility there is must be found in good measure outside these same traditional rules). The particular kind of certainty that men have thus far thought to find in law is in good measure an illusion. Realistic workers have sometimes insisted on this truth so hard that they have been thought pleased with it. (The danger lies close, for one thinking indiscriminately of Is and Ought, to suspect announcements of fact to reflect preferences, ethically normative judgments, on the part of those who do the announcing.)

But announcements of fact are not appraisals of worth. The contrary holds. The immediate results of the preliminary work thus far described has been a further, varied series of endeavors; *the focussing of conscious attack on discovering the factors thus far unpredictable, in good part with a view to their control.*[d] Not wholly with a view to such elimination; part of the conscious attack is directed to finding where and when and how far *un*certainty has value. Much of what has been taken as insistence on the exclusive significance of the particular (with supposed implicit denial of the existence of valid or apposite generalizations) represents in fact a clearing of the ground for such attack. Close study of particular unpredictables may lessen unpredictability. It may increase the value of what remains. It certainly makes clearer what the present situation is. . . .

(i) There is the question of the personality of the judge. (Little has as yet been attempted in study of the jury; Frank, *Law and the Modern Mind,* makes a beginning.) Within this field, again, attempts diverge. Some have attempted study of the particular judge—a line that will certainly lead to inquiry into his social conditioning. Some have attempted to bring various psychological hypotheses to bear. All that has become clear is that our government is not a government of laws, but one of law through men.

47. Partly, as I have tried to develop elsewhere (Llewellyn, *Legal Illusion,* 31 *Colum. L. Rev.* 82, 87 (1931); . . . because the "certainty" sought is conceived verbally, and in terms of lawyers, not factually and in terms of laymen. Neither can commonly be had save at the cost of the other. We get enough of each to upset the other. One effect of the realist approach is to center on certainty for laymen and improve the machinery for attaining it. The present dilemma is quickly stated: if there is *no* certainty in law (rules and concepts *plus* intuition *plus* laymen's practices) why is not any layman qualified to practice or to judge? But if the certainty is what the rule-believers claim, how can two good lawyers disagree about an appealed case?

d. It is interesting, thirty years later, to meet this formulation out of the days when anything other than rules, principles, etc., was suspect as being, if not illegitimate, at least subject to unforeseeable arbitrary abuse. Yet the problems of regularization and control remain. See my *Common Law Tradition* (1960), and esp. 323-332.

(ii) There has been some attempt to work out the varieties of inter-action between the traditional concepts (the judge's "legal" equipment for thinking, seeing, judging) and the fact-pressures of the cases. This is a question not—as above—of getting at results on particular facts, but of studying the effect, e.g., of a series of cases in which the facts either press successively in the one direction, or alternate in their pressures and counteract each other. Closely related in substance, but wholly diverse in both method and aim, is study of the machinery by which fact-pressures can under our procedure be brought to bear upon the court.[52]

(iii) First efforts have been made to capitalize the wealth of our re-ported cases to make large-scale quantitative studies of facts and out-come; the hope has been that these might develop lines of prediction more sure, or at least capable of adding further certainty to the predic-tions based as hitherto on intensive study of smaller bodies of cases. This represents a more ambitious development of the procedure described above, under (c); I know of no published results. [Here the recent Uni-versity of Chicago studies need attention.]

(iv) Repeated effort has been made to work with the cases of single states, to see how far additional predictability might thus be gained.

(v) Study has been attempted of "substantive rules" in the particular light of the available remedial procedure; the hope·being to discover in the court's unmentioned knowledge of the immediate consequences of this rule or that, in the case at hand, a motivation for decision which cuts deeper than any shown by the opinion. Related, but distinct, is the reas-sertion of the fundamental quality of remedy, and the general approach to restating "what the law is" (on the side of prediction) in terms not of rights, but of what can be done: Not only "no remedy, no right," but "precisely as much right as remedy."

(vi) The set-up of men's ways and practices and ideas on the subject matter of the controversy has been studied, in the hope that this might yield a further or even final basis for prediction. The work here ranges from more or less indefinite reference to custom (the historical school), or mores (Corbin), through rough or more careful canvasses of business practice and ideology . . . to painstaking and detailed studies in which practice is much more considered than is any prevailing set of ideas about what the practices are (Klaus) or—even—to studies in which the concept of "practice" is itself broken up into behavior-sequences pre-

52. The famous Brandeis brief and its successors mark the beginning. In commercial cases both Germany and England have evolved effective machinery. [The importance of type-fact-situation pressures is more fully discussed in my *Common Law Tradition—Deciding Appeals* (1960).]

sented with careful note of the degree of their frequency and recurrence, and in which all reference to actor's own ideas is deprecated or excluded (Moore and Sussman). While grouped here together, under one formula, these workers show differences in degree and manner of interest in the backgroundways which range from one pole to the other. Corbin's main interest is the appellate case; most of the second group mentioned rely on semi-special information and readily available material from economics, sociology, etc., with occasional careful studies of their own, and carry a strong interest into drafting or counselling work; Klaus insists on full canvass of all relevant literature, buttressed by and viewed in the light of intensive personal investigation; Moore's canvass and study is so original and thorough in technique as to offer as vital and important a contribution to ethnology and sociology as to banking practice. This is not one "school"; here alone are the germs of many "schools."

(vii) Another line of attack, hardly begun, is that on the effect of the lawyer on the outcome of cases, as an element in prediction. The lawyer *in litigation* has been the subject thus far only of desultory comment. Groping approach has been made to the counsellor as field general, in the business field: in drafting, and in counselling (and so in the building of practices and professional understandings which influence court action later), and in the strategy of presenting cases in favorable series, settling the unfavorable cases, etc.

All of the above has focussed on how to tell what appellate courts will do, however far afield any new scent may have led the individual hunter. But the interest in *effects* on laymen of what the courts will do leads rapidly from this still respectably traditional sphere of legal discussion into a series of further inquiries whose legal decorum is more dubious. They soon extend far beyond what has in recent years been conceived (in regard to the developed state) as law at all. I can not stop to consider these inquiries in detail. Space presses. Each of the following phases could be, and should be, elaborated at least into such a rough sketch as the foregoing. Through each would continue to run interest in what actually eventuates; interest in accurate description of what eventuates; interest in attempting, where prediction becomes uncertain, some conscious attack on hidden factors whose study might lessen the uncertainty; and interest in effects—on laymen. Finally, insistence that Ought-judgement should be bottomed on knowledge. And that action should be bottomed on all the knowledge that can be got in time to act.

I. *There is first the question of what lower courts and especially trial courts are doing, and what relation their doing has to the sayings and doings of upper courts and legislatures.*

Here the question has been to begin to find out, to find some way, some ways, of getting the hitherto unavailable facts, to find some significant way or ways of classifying what business is done, how long it takes, how various parts of the procedural machinery work. Another attack begins by inquiry not into records, but into the processes of trial and their effects on the outcome of cases. This, on the civil side, where we have (save for memoirs) been wholly in the dark. On the criminal side, beginnings lie further back.

. . . All that is really clear to date is that until we know more here our "rules" give us no remote suggestion of *what law means* to persons in the lower income brackets, and give us misleading suggestions as to the whole body of cases unappealed. Meantime, the techniques of the social sciences are being drawn upon and modified to make the work possible.

II. *There is the question of administrative bodies*—not merely on the side of administrative law (itself a novel concept recently enough)—but including all the action which state officials take "under the law" so far as it proves to affect people. And with this we begin departing from the orthodox. To be sure, the practicing lawyer today knows his commission as he knows his court. But the trail thus broken leads into the wilds of government, and politics, and queer events in both.

III. *There is the question of legislative regulation*—in terms of what it *means in action, and to whom,* not merely in terms of what it says. And with that, the question of what goes into producing legislative change—or blocking it—especially so far as the profession participates therein; legislative history on the official record; but as well the background of fact and interest and need. And, no less vital, there is the fact-inquiry into areas of life where maladjustment capable of legal remedy exists.

IV. Finally, and cutting now completely beyond the tradition-bounded area of law, there is the matter not of describing or predicting the action of officials—be they appellate courts, trial courts, legislators, administrators—but of describing and predicting *the effects of their action on the laymen of the community.* "Law" without effect approaches zero in its meaning. To be ignorant of its effect is to be ignorant of its meaning. To know its effect without study of the persons whom it affects is impossible. Here the antecedents of court action touch its results. To know law, then, to know *anything* of what is necessary to judge or evaluate law, we must proceed into these areas which have traditionally been conceived (save by the historical school) as not-law. Not only what courts do instead of what courts say, but also what difference it makes to anybody that they do it. And no sooner does one begin such a study than it becomes clear that there can be no broad talk of "law" nor of "the community"; but that it is a question of reaching the particular part of the community relevant to some particular part of law. There are persons sought to be affected, and persons not sought to be affected. Of the former, some are not in fact materially affected (the gangster-feud); of the latter, some are (depositors in a failing bank which the bank laws have *not* controlled). There is the range of questions as to those legal "helpful devices" (corporation, contract, lease) designed to make it easier for men to get where they want and what they want. There is all the information social scientists have gathered to be explored, in its bearings on the law. There is all the information they have not been interested in gathering, likewise to be explored—but, first, to be gathered.

Here are the matters one or another of the new fermenters is ploughing into. Even the sketchy citations here are enough to make clear that their lines of work organize curiously into a whole.

But again rises the query: are the matters *new?* What realist knows so little of law or the ways of human thought as to make such a claim? Which of the inquiries has not been made, or started, or adumbrated, in the past? Which of the techniques does not rest on our prior culture? New, I repeat, is one thing only: the *systematic* effort to carry one· problem through, to carry a succession of problems through, to *consistently,* not occasionally, choose the best available technique, to *consistently* keep description on the descriptive level, to *consistently distinguish* the fact basis which will feed evaluation from the evaluation which it will later feed, to *consistently* seek *all* the relevant data one can find to *add* to the haphazard single-life experience, to *add* to general common sense. . . .

Is it not obvious that—if this be realism—realism is a mass of trends in legal work and thinking? (1) They have their common core, present to some extent wherever realistic work is done: recognition of law as means; recognition of change in society that may call for change in law; interest in what happens; interest in effects; recognition of the need for effort toward keeping perception of the facts uncolored by one's views on Ought; a distrust of the received set of rules and concepts as adequate indications of what is happening in the courts; a drive toward narrowing the categories of description. (2) They have grown out of the study of the action of appellate courts, and that study still remains their potent stimulus. Uncertainty in the action of such courts is one main problem: to find the why of it; to find means to reduce it, where it needs reduction; to find where it needs reduction, where expansion.[e] (3) But into the work of lower courts, of administrative bodies, of legislatures, of the life which lies before and behind "law," the ferment of investigation spreads.

e. On the value and vitality of the concept of "reasonable regularity" in contrast to that of certainty—a major contribution of John R. Commons—see my *Common Law Tradition,* esp. at 215ff.

Some one or other of these realistic trends takes up the whole time of many; a hundred more participate in them to various degrees who yet would scorn the appellation "realist." The trends are centered in no man, in no coherent group. There is no leader. Spokesmen are self-appointed. They speak not for the whole but for the work each is himself concerned with—at times with little or no thought of the whole, at times with the exaggeration of controversy or innovation. Yet who should know better than lawyers the exaggeration of controversy; who should have more skill than they to limit argument and dictum to the particular issue, to read it in the light thereof. One will find, reading thus, little said by realistic spokesmen that does not warrant careful pondering. Indeed, on *careful* pondering, one will find little of exaggeration in their writing. Meantime, the proof of the pudding: are there results?

There are. They are results, primarily, on the side of the descriptive sociology of law discussed thus far. They are big with meaning for attack on the field of Ought—either on what courts ought to do with existing rules, or on what changes in rules are called for.

Already we have a series, lengthening impressively, of *more accurate* reformulations of what appellate courts are doing and may be expected to do. We are making headway in *seeing* (not just "knowing" without inquiry) what effects their doing has on some of the persons interested. We are accumulating some *knowledge* (i.e., more than guesses) on phases of our life as to which our law seems out of joint.

We have, moreover, a first attack upon the realm of the unpredictable in the actions of [appellate] courts. That attack suggests strongly that one large element in the now incalculable consists in the traditional pretense or belief (sometimes the one, sometimes the other) that there is no such area of uncertainty, or that it is much smaller than it is. To *recognize* that there are limits to the certainty sought by words and deduction, to seek to define those limits, is to open the door to that other and far more useful judicial procedure: *conscious seeking, within the limits laid down by precedent and statute,* for the wise decision. Decisions thus reached, *within those limits,* may fairly be hoped to be more certainly predictable than decisions are now—for today no man can tell when the court will, and when it will not, thus seek the wise decision, but hide the seeking under words. And not only more certain, but what is no whit less important: more just and wise (or more frequently just and wise).

Indeed, the most fascinating result of the realistic effort appears as one returns from trial court or the ways of laymen to the tradition-hallowed problem of appellate case-law. Criticized by those who refuse to disentangle Is and Ought because of their supposed deliberate neglect of the normative aspect of law, the realists prove the value, for the normative, of temporarily putting the normative aside. They return from their excursion into the purest description they can manage with a demonstration that the field of free play for Ought in appellate courts is vastly wider than traditional Ought-bound thinking ever had made clear. This, *within* the confines of precedent as we have it, *within* the limits and on the basis of our present order. Let me summarize the points of the brief:

(a) If deduction does not solve cases, but only shows the effect of a given premise; and if there is available a competing but equally authoritative premise that leads to a different conclusion—then there is a choice in the case; a choice to be justified; a choice which *can* be justified only as a question of policy—for the authoritative tradition speaks with a forked tongue.

(b) If (i) the possible inductions from one case or a series of cases— even if those cases really had each a single fixed meaning—are nonetheless not single, but many; and if (ii) the standard authoritative techniques[71] of dealing with precedent range for limiting the case to its narrowest issue on facts and procedure, and even searching the record for a hidden distinguishing fact, all the way to giving it the widest meaning the rule expressed will allow, or even thrusting under it a principle which was not announced in the opinion at all—then the available leeway in *interpretation of precedent* is (relatively to what the older tradition has *consciously* conceived) nothing less than huge. And only policy considerations and the facing of policy considerations can justify "interpreting" (making, shaping, drawing conclusions from) the relevant body of precedent in one way or in another. And—the essence of all—*stare decisis* has in the past been, now is, and must continue to be, a norm of change, and a means of change, as well as a norm of staying put, and a means of staying put. *The growth of the past has been achieved by "standing on" the decided cases;* rarely by overturning them. Let this be recognized, and precedent is clearly seen to be a way of change as well as a way of refusing to change. Let that, in turn, be recognized, and that peculiar one of the ways of working with precedent which consists in blinding the eyes to policy loses the fictitious sanctity with which it is now enveloped *some of the time:* to wit, whenever judges for any reason do not wish to look at policy.

71. I mean not those approved by the schoolmen, but those *used* by authoritative courts in dealing with "authority." On this as on other matters, the rules of the schoolmen are to be subjected to the check of fact—here, of what courts do, and do both openly and with clean conscience. See Llewellyn, *Bramble Bush* (1930) c. IV. Contrast Goodhart, *Determining the Ratio Decidendi of a Case,* 40 Yale L.J. 161 (1930). [And see the demonstration in my *Common Law Tradition—Deciding Appeals* (1960).]

(c) If the classification of raw facts is largely an arbitrary [better: *creative*] process, raw facts having in most doubtful cases the possibility of ready classification along various lines, then "certainty," even under pure deductive thinking, has not the meaning that people who have wanted certainty in law are looking for. The quest of this unreal certainty, this certainty unattained in result, is the major reason for one self-denying ordinance of judges: their refusal to look beyond words to things. Let them once see that the "certainty" thus achieved is *un*certainty for the non-law-tutored layman in his living and dealing, and the way is open to reach for *layman's* certainty-through-law, by seeking for the fair or wise outcome, so far as precedent and statute make such outcome *possible*. To see the problem thus is also to open the way to conscious discrimination, e.g., between current commercial dealings on the one hand and real estate conveyancing or corporate indenture drafting on the other. In the latter the *lawyer's* peculiar reliance on formulae may be assumed as of course; whereas in the former cause needs to be shown for making such an assumption.

Thus, as various of the self-designated realistic spokesmen have been shouting: the temporary divorce of Is and Ought brings to the re-union a sharper eye, a fuller equipment, a sounder judgment—even a wider opportunity as to that case-law which tradition has painted as peculiarly ridden by the past. That on the fact side, as to the particular questions studied, the temporary divorce yields no less gratifying results is demonstrated by the literature.

When the matter of *program in the normative aspect* is raised, the answer is: *there is none.* A likeness of method in approaching Ought-questions is apparent. If there be, beyond that, general lines of fairly wide agreement, they are hardly specific enough to mean anything on any given issue. Partly, this derives from differences in temperament and outlook. Partly, it derives from the total lack of organization or desire to schoolify among the men concerned. But partly, it is due to the range of work involved. Business lawyers have some pet Oughts, each in the material he has become familiar with; torts lawyers have the like in torts; public lawyers in public law. And so it goes. Partly also, the lack of programmatic agreement derives from the time and effort consumed in getting at facts, either the facts strictly legal or the "foreign" facts bearing on the law. Specialized interest must alone spell absence of group-program. Yet some general points of view may be hazarded.

(1) There is fairly general agreement on the importance of personnel, and of court organization, as essential to making laws have meaning. This both as to triers of fact and as to triers of law. There is some tendency, too, to urge specialization of tribunals.

(2) There is very general agreement on the need for courts to face

squarely the policy questions in their cases, and use the full freedom precedent affords in working toward conclusions that seem indicated. There is fairly general agreement that effects of rules, so far as known, should be taken account of in making or remaking the rules. There is fairly general agreement that we need improved machinery for making the facts about such effects—or about needs and conditions to be affected by a decision—available to courts.

(3) There is a strong tendency to think it wiser [for purposes of initial inquiry] to narrow rather than to widen the categories in which concepts and rules *either about judging or for judging* are made.

(4) There is a strong tendency to approach most legal problems as problems in allocation of risks, and so far as possible, as problems of their reduction, and so to insist on the effects of rules on parties who not only are not in court, but are not fairly represented by the parties who are in court. To approach not only tort but business matters, in a word, as matters of *general* policy.

And so I close as I began. What is there novel here? In the ideas, nothing. In the sustained attempt to make one or another of them fruitful, much. In the narrowness of fact-category together with the wide range of fact-inquiry, much. In the techniques availed of, much—for lawyers. But let this be noted—for the summary above runs so largely to the purely descriptive side: When writers of realistic inclination are writing in general, they are bound to stress the need of some accurate description, of Is and not of Ought. There lies the *common* ground of their thinking; there lies the area of new and puzzling development. There lies the point of discrimination which they must drive home. To get perspective on their stand about ethically normative matters one must pick up the work of each man in his special field of work. There one will find no lack of interest or effort toward improvement in the law. As to whether change is called for, or any *given* point of law, and if so, how much change, and in what direction, there is no agreement. Why should there be? A *group* philosophy or program, a *group* credo of social welfare, these realists have not. They are not a group.

Llewellyn, The Common Law Tradition*

. . . I want to write a word about a movement in thought which was vibrant and vocal when the study began, was violently misunderstood and misrepresented, and today, even where partly understood and rec-

* [Pp. 508-518 (Little, Brown and Company 1960). Reprinted by permission. For biographical information, see page 212 supra.]

ognized, is tending in modern American jurisprudential writing to be treated as an episode to be relegated to history. I refer to what has come to be known as American Legal Realism. . . . There is no lack of current need for realism. There is indeed no lack of need to stop painting goblins. All that has shifted is the field of operation: after the need to do combat comes the need to do work. And I put this book forward both in its plan and on its descriptive side as a solid and unmistakable product and embodiment of American Legal Realism. I should indeed like to use the book to shame either old critics of the movement or later ones.

The situation is astoundingly simple, and the amount of print wasted on it is equally astounding.

Realism was never a philosophy,[2] nor did any group of realists as such ever attempt to present any rounded view, or *whole* approach. One or two—perhaps for instance Underhill Moore—may (though without companion or adherent) have conceived and even put forward his thinking as sufficiently complete to deserve description as a philosophy, as expressing views on those phases of the institution of law which reach beyond description and the techniques of operation. I know of no other such, however, unless Jerome Frank's faith in the unreachability of fact be deemed of this nature. No. What realism was, and is, is a method, nothing more, and the only tenet involved is that the method is a good one. "See it fresh," "See it as it works"—that was to be the foundation of any solid work, to *any* end. From there, one goes on into inquiry about e.g. What-it-is-for (function or goal), or e.g. to build a judgment on how far the measure fits the purpose, or e.g. on how far the particular purpose harmonizes with the Good Life, or e.g. on whether we do not then have to reexamine the original data about "How it has been working"—a matter which often answers very differently to different questions.

Of all of these things, only "see it fresh," "see it clean" and "come back to make sure" are of the essence. They go to method. *That method is eternal.* That is point 1. The method may have come into first discussion among lawyers in relation to rules and judicial decision, but it is no more limited to that area than it is to matters legal. It applies to anything. That is point 2. But *the method* includes nothing at all about whither to go. That is point 3. *Realism* is *not* a philosophy, but a *technology.* That is why it is eternal. The fresh look is always the fresh hope. The fresh inquiry into results is always the needed check-up.

2. It is persistently treated as such. But realism is a method which can serve any goal at all. A main trouble with treating either the descriptive or the technological branch of a discipline as a philosophy is that any preliminary or partial work is likely to be viewed as if it were trying to be a whole, with negative implications read in, indeed read in even though they be denied.

If any person caught up in the enthusiasms of the moment paraded a banner that suggested more than this, he was a parader, not a thinker, no *real* realist, certainly not one who had status to speak for any "movement," much less for any "school." It is true that there were a few misguided souls who, having observed with accuracy that often neither the established and accepted generalizations ("rules" of law) nor the ones a court in trouble was swinging around at the moment would fit into any comfortable simple pattern of prediction or of guidance, arrived at the strange conclusion that no generalizations in the law got anywhere or meant anything. . . . [A] single sentence from page 3 of the original *Bramble Bush:* "What these officials do about disputes is, to my mind, the law itself"—became, without anybody's reading either the context or the rest of *Bramble Bush,* and in august disregard of 1081 pages published the same year which centered on the rules of Sales law and the proper construction of the governing statute—this lone lorn sentence became, internationally, *the* cited goblin-painting of realism.[4a] . . . The manner of such general neglect of what is not on the immediate page reminds me of the general treatment of Jerome Michael. His work in *course books* in the fields of crime and procedure establish his standing as perhaps the most powerful and original American thinker of his time in *jurisprudence.* Books on jurisprudence do not even mention him. Truly jurisprudence-in-English is still bound by the labels put not only on "schools" but on book covers.

In any event, I claim to have introduced the term "Realistic Jurisprudence" into the modern literature;[5] I claim to have made moderately clear, as soon as the wilder type of controversy started, what was really up[6] as well as to have followed the matter up, after a decade of controversy and of pudding-proof by many hands, with a rather careful survey.[7] I therefore claim to know what it was about, and what it is about. I now put forward, explicitly as a proper product and exhibit of *real* realism, this book.

Here you can meet not the goblin, but the horse. . . .

The whole job became possible when an invitation to lecture in

---

4a. "It is easy to paint a goblin. It is hard to paint a horse." The book was my *Cases and Materials on Sales* (1930). I had then already been serving for four years as Commissioner on Uniform State Laws for the Conference, and had been the draftsman for them of the Uniform Chattel Mortgage Act. But the passage "shows" me to deny both the existence and the function of rules of law. The goblin passage is quoted by A. W. Hummel from Yen Yüan, 28 *Bull. Am. U. Prof.* 358, 366 (1942).

5. A Realistic Jurisprudence—The Next Step, 30 *Columb. L. Rev.* 431 (1930).

6. Some Realism About Realism, 44 *Harv. L. Rev.* 1222 (1931).

7. On Reading and Using the Newer Jurisprudence, 40 *Columb. L. Rev.* 581 (1940).

Leipzig about American case law happened to coincide with labor over an unusually extensive and intensive book of cases and materials on Sales.[8] The need for explaining to lawyers of completely different background and training not *what* our case results were, but *how* we got them, threw the judicial opinions into a completely different lighting; and the cases being handled in and for the Sales book suddenly came in for detailed examination of *exactly what they had been doing to the materials* which they had used to work with and from, and of how far their new version of what the earlier authorities had stood for amounted to a reshaping of those prior authorities. This gave me new eyes. It opened up not only a new way of reading opinions but a new world of thought and light.

Then, a few years later, the law of the Cheyenne Indians made clear to me what I had never before dreamed: to wit, that law and justice had no need at all to be in conflict or even in too much tension, but could instead represent a daily working harmony.[10] For in common with most lawyers, and indeed with most jurisprudes, I had mostly taken for granted a sort of perpetual struggle between the needs of regularity and form and of the precedent-phase of justice on the one side and, on the other, any dynamic readjustment of a going system to what just needed to be done. Pound had rightly stressed shifting tides in the struggle, and that I had seen. But I had to get to the Cheyennes in order to wake up to the fact that tension between form, or precedent, or other tradition and perceived need requires, in nature, to be a tension *only for the single crisis*. It does not have to be a continuing tension in the legal system as a whole, because an adequately resilient legal system can on occasion, or even almost regularly, absorb the particular trouble and resolve it each time into a new, usefully guiding, forward-looking felt standard-for-action or even rule-of-law.[11] To think of such steady readjustment—what Mentschikoff calls the legal artist's job of producing a new technical guiding form which can supply both needs at once—this was to get a further new pair of eyes. And it was on this foundation of experience with Cheyenne law that I became able to spot and understand the Grand Style as I met it in the early work of our own courts.[12] These, along with a deep interest in Gothic, were so far as I can reach back, the two big intellectual jolts

8. *How Appellate Courts Decide Cases* (Brandeis Lawyers Society Series).
10. See Llewellyn and Hoebel, *The Cheyenne Way* (1941), especially c. 12.
11. In a developed system, this is the singing rule.
12. This is the kind of contribution by anthropology to Jurisprudence for which I have always hoped. You suddenly hit upon beauty and vision in a strange culture, and you may be the person in whom a seed takes root, so that light is shed at home. The values of comparative law and comparative politics are not different, except that the chances of deep illumination may be less.

which opened up for me the material of this book. But I see no reason why any other person should be in need of similar disruptive or volcanic jolts. The door is open; anybody can go through. The obvious is obvious: the judicial opinion is a human document and a fascinating record, there, for anybody's use. From the standpoint of behavioral study these are data in which so many factors are held equal as to outrun the results of an ordinary ten- or even hundred-thousand-dollar grant. All there. All waiting. Already gathered. Merely neglected.

There is little use in preaching, and less in indignation. But when I find an economic historian leaping like a tomcat in May upon some colonial court record of 1758, while neither he nor his sociological confrere nor his colleagues in psychology nor even his brothers in government are willing to save foundation money and their own time by exploring from the behavioral side the amazing *gathered* treasure of the law reports —then I feel I ought at least to point the fact that these ready records, *with all kinds of factors "held equal,"* are there waiting for exploitation. And they are rich. On "small-group behavior"—in decision or otherwise, three or five hundred of the opinions from a single court, in sequence, and really studied, will make the results available from any normal *large* research grant look sick. The number of factors "held equal," I repeat, is unbelievable, if measured in terms of any known experimental techniques. Furthermore, in the same series of reports, one can simply move five or six years, and then commonly find a "control group" in which again oodles of identifiable factors are held more equal than they are on any large scale in today's normal (and expensive) testing methods.

This goes obviously to decision-making, and, as the text above makes clear, it goes to much nicer lines of discrimination in this area than current socio-psychological "design" has as yet preached: certainly to nicer lines than have been open to any but those gifted—gifted both by God and by Foundations. But that is not all. For instance, the lines of interacting person-and-personality within a working group not only have not been but are not soon likely to be recorded with the fullness and clarity which the law reports reveal. *And the Supreme Court is not the*

I am fortunate in having persuasive record of the process. The warranty material in the Sales book was historically dealt with and took me into a good deal of the judging of the Grand Style, especially in New York and Massachusetts. What I found was law and the theory of case law; and both were exciting. *Courts, Quality of Goods, and a Credit Economy* (1937) (corrected reprints from 36 *Columb. L. Rev.* 699 and 37 ibid. 341) contains another and deeper historical study in the same field. But it was done after Cheyenne results had been cooking for two years, and were jelling. So there turned up not only law, theory of case law, and enriched understanding of judging generally, but clear recognition of the Grand Style and its meaning. . . .

best focus of such study. It is too much in the public eye. Its documents are too much consciously built for public view. Its issues are too likely to distract the student of human behavior by their general importance and by his own desires, and indeed to obscure, among the judges themselves, the normal interactions of a less intense environment. But the reports from New York, or Ohio, or North Carolina, or Pennsylvania, or California, studied in this light: these are gifts to behavioral research as valuable, let me repeat, as tens of thousands from foundations. The type of thing I have in mind is quick to suggest; in this one study various probable effects of Cardozo on his court are suggested:

(1) By repeated discussions of one small series of cases on indefiniteness in business agreements; this is a qualitative examination, in sequence, on a single theme, with particular personnel particularly regarded. What is wanted is the spotting and tracing of a dozen more of such sequences, with their similarities and dissimilarities. Things unmentioned in the present text (such as arrival of new judges, the exact line-ups of votes, case by case, individual studies of the individual judges concerned) would be of the essence. If such studies were then pursued until three or five of them were in hand for comparison, I submit the results would be as striking and informative as anything in print.

(2) By the rough but exciting purely quantitative checks on the growth and nature of dissent in the Court of Appeals. (Here, indeed, I think the whole relation of shift in style of decision to dissent to be a further valuable and feasible project.)

(3) By the detailed case studies, one of which suggests the power of a great judge's persuasiveness by way of substance, the other his power, in spite of absence of substance, to mislead by prestige and manner.

Such lines of approach, and more, would be needed in combination, and suggest that a behavioral science man would do well to team up with a law man, to throw variant techniques and combined insights into the needed smelter. And they will find that they talk at cross-purposes for longer than they will enjoy. But what a product they can bring out!

Note that I am talking thus far of the law reports almost pure. If one can add to them the type of letters which enrich Taft's biography,[13] or Stone's,[14] or the working papers which Cardozo bequeathed to Columbia University, or any other material with similar supplementary value, the volume and range of the law report evidence still stands ready as the base material, waiting to be deepened, widened, and intensified. . . .

There are three remaining things I feel need to say. I do not like, in

13. Pringle, *The Life and Times of William Howard Taft* (1939).
14. Mason, *Harlan Fiske Stone, Pillar of the Law* (1956).

case analysis, to leave out the person and the variation. But in dealing with a multitude of courts upon a multitude of themes, as in our cross-section samples, individuals are not met with sufficient contact to justify risking judgments, and time is lacking to extend the acquaintance by study outside the samples. Moreover, the study is directed at courts *and not* at individuals, and the "average" appellate judge displays himself better in the blurred but real corporate person of the court and in the corporate behavior than he can by any analysis of individuals and averaging of their attributes. I therefore make no apology for adding my own piece of depersonizing to the depersonizing sought and somewhat accomplished by our general institutional machinery.

The second matter I like even less. I do not like coarse analysis and coarse results when more refined analysis and results are available. To come out of a study merely with a picture of a process dominated by the authorities on the one hand, the judge's best judgment about sense and justice on the other, the interaction being played upon by counsel, by the craft tradition, and by one's colleagues, but in differential fashion case by case, and the whole—both intake perception, organization for meditation, and standards against which to set the case for judgment—being conditioned by what are for law-governmental purposes accidents, the accidents somewhat of temperament and endowment, but more of individual experience—this is in itself an almost disgustingly crude and loose result in terms of crude and loose factors in what sounds almost like free association. And better, very much better, can be done, as, e.g., the forthcoming results of Mentschikoff and Haggard make quite clear. Each of the factors mentioned can be broken down, the statement of interactions can be materially clarified and tightened and (I am convinced) shown to differ in perceptible fashion in reasonably identifiable type-situations. Being fully persuaded of such things, it irks me to leave the analytical results in the shape they are. Yet once again I have no intention of making any apology:

A job is the job it is, and it is not any other. The tools to use and the results to get are those which fit that job. My task here has not been to push social or behavioral science techniques and results as far along as I was able. My task has been to wrestle with an unjustified crisis of lawyers' confidence in appellate courts, and with worries among the courts themselves which slow and hamper their work. To do that I must come up with tools of analysis which any thinking man of law can understand both in their nature and in their use, and I must come out with results in words which he can not only understand but put to work. Refinement, therefore, must go not into analysis for professional students of behavior, but into communicable knowhow for practical application by the men of law. That, if I may recur to the opening of this Appendix, is what realism calls for. That, to the best of my ability, is what I have done.

The third matter which needs mention is the difference in treatment of the same material as between such a study as the present and one directed to the growth-processes and growth-results of case law, whether in our own system, or generally. This latter field is an old sweetheart of mine. It also uses cases as the primary raw materials; it also involves the reading of the opinion as a human document. Not only that, but it also requires attention to the process of deciding and to the nature of facts, situation, and general background in their impact on the court. It may have some value for general method, therefore, to indicate briefly some of the ways in which the two lines of inquiry diverge.

The first and most striking difference is of course that for case law study *every* decision requires to be placed in its own time sequence of doctrine, and requires to have its own doctrinal background fully explored, so that the state of relevant doctrine as it came to bear becomes concrete, clear, and close to complete. That is the body of doctrine about to be affected, and must be so known in order to determine either what its effect ought, doctrinally, to be, or what effect the actual decision has upon it. . . .

The next difference, which hardly needs mention, is that whereas for us the way of use or reshaping or discard or neglect of each prior pressing authority has been a question merely of what *kind of treatment* it got, for the case law student the question is also: what happened to it in *substance?* What did the change or nonchange result in? (set in the whole time-sequence of the particular line of doctrine, past and prospective).

But common to the two lines of inquiry is the question of *why* any of this occurred; there I see little difference in the lines of interest or of work. Save in this: that the intense concern of the student of case law with the impact of the particular judge or combination of judges (the kind of thing we have touched on in the indefiniteness cases) belongs, for a study of appellate deciding, not on the elementary level of the present job, but to more advanced and refined inquiry. Common again is the interest in style and manner of the court, its sensitivity to or knowledge of the situation, and the like, and in whether the court does a craftsman-like job either on the facts, or on situation-sense, or on the framing of the measure, or on tidying up behind, or all of these. But the minute the particular decision has been handed down, interest forks again: the effects we have sought to follow, if we could, are the effects on bar, on public, and inside the court itself, of the manner and general cumulation of the work; the effects which interest our case law inquirer are the effects of each single case and of the particular succession of cases on his pet body of doctrine and on *its* effects outside. Deciding is, for him, the moving chisel of doctrine. Doctrine has been for us, on the other hand, one major force in the shaping of decision.

In similar fashion, the use of case materials for the study of case law opens out into the whole doctrinal structure and the *system's* methods for readjustment thereof, whereas the use of those materials for the study of deciding heads rather into the particular craft of the appellate judge and into the system's organization of courts and appellate procedure. Like us, the student of case law finds himself welcoming the earthiness of the case law approach to rule-making and rule-revision, but he is forced to canvass also prices which are no part of our problem in the present study: What does it cost a polity in delay and uncertainty and in legal discomfort or injustice to have the making or review of a rule wait upon the chance raising and appeal of issues one by one by dragging one? Consider, in contrast, what a Uniform Commercial Act or a Uniform Commercial Code does in making available in a jurisdiction where rulings are sparse the experience and wisdom of the whole country—all at a single stroke. Or consider the problem of accessibility of doctrine, as it bears on the man-hours of talented labor (if there is to be accuracy based on knowledge), and so on the expense, needed for advice. Such things are not our worry here. We note rather that one contributing factor, perhaps a major one, to that rigidification we call the Formal Style may well have been the relative inaccessibility of authorities and stimulus from the other States; and that the all-State finding-apparatus which began to be available in 1896 may well have been one important factor in that re-entry of overt sense and reason which has come to mark the modern style.

Thus it is much as if the study of deciding were the study of the point in flux, and that of case law rather the study of the resulting curve: though they both use and focus on the same basic stuff.

Chapter 2

The Nature of the Judicial Process

I. GENERAL AND APPELLATE

Ehrlich, Judicial Freedom of Decision: Its Principles and Objects*

I. Bureaucratic Law as Contrasted with People's Law

§1. *Relations of Legislator and Judge.* Modern systematic legal science inclines to explain each rule of law principally by seeking to discover the intention of the legislator; but sufficient stress has never been laid on the fact that the significance of law in the daily life of a people depends far more on the persons charged with its administration than on the principles according to which it is administered. The same rule is likely to have an essentially different meaning in different countries or at different periods, for no other reason than that the persons sitting on the bench are differently trained, have a different temperament, hold a different official or social position. This is apt to be more vividly realized by the trained historian of law than by the analytical student. To the historian, the *"praetor"* and the *"prudentes"* still speak in the Pandects, the *"Schöffen"* in the old German law, and the judges of the Superior Courts with the Chancellor, in English common law and equity grown out of the same

---

* [Translated from *"Freie Rechtsfindung und freie Rechtswissenchaft"* in volume 9, pp. 48-51, 53-54, 61-63, 65-66, 71-72, 74, 76, 77-78 of Modern Legal Philosophy Series, *Science of Legal Method.* Bruncken, trans. New York: The Macmillan Company, 1903 Reprinted by permission.

For biographical information, see page 70 supra.]

235

Germanic root. Similarly, the law prevailing to-day on the European continent must be viewed as a system of law peculiar to a judiciary composed of learned bureaucratic judges. . . .

We are all children of the bureaucratic State which has now dominated our political and social life for several centuries. Hardly one of us is likely, without great difficulty, to free himself from the conceptions and lines of thought generated and fostered thereby. In the eyes of a bureaucracy law is properly nothing but a body of directions given by the Government to its officials. . . .

§2. *Increased Importance of Statutory Law.* . . . The essential nature of the bureaucratic State is expressed by the fact that for us the statute is the predominant form of law. Similarly, the content of the law of the bureaucratic State depends on the essential character of that form of government. In essence, such a system of law is simply a rule of decision. Its exclusive or almost exclusive purpose is to direct officials how to deal with the matters intrusted to them, and particularly how to decide legal controversies. That is, of course, a very one-sided conception; for law as a rule of decision may indeed be the side of law most interesting to the lawyer, but it is by no means the only and not even the most important side. Law exists for other very different purposes in addition to the settlement of controversies. It is the very foundation of the social organism, or (to use an expression of Schäffle, already growing antiquated), law is the skeleton of the social body. . . .

§4. *The Importance of Unwritten Law.* But, even of rules of decision, the smallest part is the result of State action. Every sort of protection of rights by the State begins with enforcing the payment of compensatory damages, which in primitive times the injured party sought to recover on his own authority and by his own power. At the moment when the judgment of a court is substituted for this primitive self-help, there are no rules of decision in existence except those flowing from the very nature of the social organization. In other words, they are derived from such sources as the nature of property in the form it assumed directly under the conditions of primitive ownership; also from the nature of those associations, which are of so much importance in primitive society, like the clan, the family, the community, the guild; from the customary subject-matters and forms of the most ancient contracts, and the primitive forms of intercourse, which are mostly older than any sort of legal protection. Decisions are first preserved by oral tradition, then written down, collected, commented upon, generalized, and at last codified. Thus arise those peculiar systems of law in the special keeping of lawyers, which are, in many different forms, characteristic of the early times of all the nations of the world. They are legal science and legal rule all in one, like the old *"jus civile"* of the Romans which still lives, unchanged in essentials, in the writings of the classical Roman jurists and the great compilation of Justinian.

The decisions, therefore, are not based on the rules of law, but the rules of law are deduced from the decisions. The law on which the decisions are based is the *"jus quod est."* Paulus, who could still observe the actual working of a living law of this kind, puts what he has learned in actual experience tersely into the famous maxim: *"Non ex regula jus sumatur, sed ex jure quod est regula fit."* The decisions are older than the rules,— the law of the lawyers older and incomparably richer than the law of legislatures. . . .

§11. *Inadequacy of Mere Statutory Law.* . . . No theory of the application of law can get around the difficulty that every body of formulated rules is in its very nature incomplete; that it is really antiquated the very moment it has been formulated. . . .

II. Statutory Law and Its Obstructions to Free Judicial Decision

. . . §13. *Legal Technicalism.* . . . Generally speaking, it is undoubtedly much easier to decide a definite case correctly than to establish an abstract rule universally applicable for all imaginable cases; and surely it can hardly be maintained seriously that such a rule will invariably result in the fairest decision, even in those cases which nobody had thought of when the rule was made. As a matter of fact no such thing is attempted by the technical judicial method of decision; its goal is quite different. A rule is to be framed, not necessarily always just, but at least certain, that can be ascertained in advance and will afford protection against arbitrary and biased judgments. In order to attain this end, the judge is to be subjected, bound hand and foot, to a rule that determines all things in advance. . . .

§14. *Further Objections to the Technical Method.* But how about the possibility of foreseeing what the decision of the court will be? In what cases is such foresight actually attained under the technical method? Apparently in those few cases only in which the law is so clear and definite that there is really no need of searching for it. In cases of this sort, however, the method of free decision would make no change, for it would come into play merely when there is no clear provision in the formulated law. There is good reason to claim that a better guaranty for certainty of the law than by the technical method may be found in a method of free decision—bound only by judicial precedents, but not beyond that. Even to-day, a judge feels greater assurance when he can refer to a series of adjudications than when he has nothing but a construction of the statute which may at any time be upset by some other artist in construction.

On still another ground, however, one may venture to call the

237

method of legal technicalism nothing less than the sin against the Holy Spirit. For this method has obscured our eyes to the only true principle at the foundation not merely of a certain and unbiased administration of justice, but also of a justice dominated by great ideals: . . . By making legislation the center of our system of law, and by nothing else, has it been possible to hide for so long a period the recognition of the simple truth that the greatest task that can be given a man to discharge, Justice, requires a standard of mental and moral greatness far above the common average. Thus, and thus only, can people fail to see that for such a task a man is not fit merely because by examination and a little practice he has proved that he can, after a fashion, find his way through the sections of a code. . . .

III. Characteristics of the Principle of Free Judicial Decision

§17. *Free Decision Not Arbitrary.* A modern judge who assumes it to be his duty always to base his decisions on an express statute naturally will ask what is to serve as foundation for the administration of justice if that of a statute is to be withdrawn.

One might be tempted to reply simply that in every period of time there has existed a justice not hedged about by code sections. Such justice, however, is by no means arbitrary. As already emphasized at the opening of this essay, it grows out of the principles of juridical tradition. Every kind of freedom of decision starts with juridical tradition and tends toward what Stammler has called "correct law" (*"richtiges Recht"*). The very peculiarity of the judicial office is the assumption that the judge's utterance represents, not his personal opinion, but the law. And this law is found primarily in the legal records of the past, in statutes, in decisions of courts, in legal literature. No Roman jurist ever deviated farther from the traditional rules than he was compelled to do by necessity. Blackstone, in a famous passage of his *Commentaries,* speaking of the English common law, represents the English judge as only declaring, not as making, the rules of law.[10] Free decision is conservative, as every kind of freedom is; for freedom means responsibility, while restraint shifts responsibility upon other shoulders. . . .

§20. *The Personality of the Judge.* Thus the administration of justice has always contained a personal element. In all ages, social, political and cultural movements have necessarily exerted an influence upon it; but whether an individual jurist yields more or less to such influences whether he is more inclined in his *"quae traditae sunt perseverare"* or rather

10. *Blackstone's Commentaries* (Cooley, 3d ed.), p. 69.

"ingenii qualitate et fiducia doctrinae plurima innovare constituit," depends of course less on any theory of legal method than on his own personal temperament. The point is that this fact should not be tolerated as something unavoidable, but should be gladly welcomed. For the one important desideratum is that his personality must be great enough to be properly intrusted with such functions. The principle of free decision is really not concerned with the substance of the law, but with the proper selection of judges; in other words, it is the problem of how to organize the judiciary so as to give plenty of scope to strong personalities. Everything depends upon that. . . .

It would be unfair if we failed to recognize that there are further and perhaps better-founded reasons for the existing antipathy to free legal decision. One such reason may be found especially in traditional conceptions regarding the proper limits of the functions of Government and the separation of powers. In the tendency to make the bureaucratic judge base his judicial opinion invariably on the letter of the statute we may find a good portion of the old-fashioned Liberal distrust of the Government; and on the other hand it will take a long time before the idea will be thoroughly familiar that the function of legislation does not extend to every form of lawmaking but is confined to the passing of express statutes. Those ways of thinking, however, really belong to a theory of the State which is already antiquated, although like every political theory it was the scientific expression of conditions historically developed.

IV. The Tasks Awaiting Freedom of Judicial Decision

§21. *The Work of Legal Science.* We may now cast a glance at the science of law, and consider what tasks will remain for it after technicalism has been supplanted by free decision.

First of all, it becomes plain that after this change there can be no further place for the traditional essay on rules of construction. The moment it is recognized that a statute provides only for what it provides, and that what is not so provided simply remains unprovided, there can be no further excuse for using a hairsplitting machine,—or as it were, for squeezing decisions out of a statute with a hydraulic press. . . .

§22. *The Practical Operation of the Law.* . . . It is the business of legal science to teach the law as it actually works. Whoever knows but the "intent of the legislator" is still far from knowing the law that is really in effect.

In this sense the traditional, dogmatic conception of law may be contrasted with a dynamic conception. For the latter, the problem is not simply to know what a rule means, but how it lives and works, how it adapts itself to the different relations of life, how it is being circumvented and how it succeeds in frustrating circumvention. . . .

Here we must turn first to the decisions of the courts. From these principally we may learn the *"jus quod est,"* from them alone we can gather what rules of decision have actually entered into daily life, and how they have done so. But it is not enough to cite decisions in a text, or in notes, and to approve or condemn them according as they are deemed correct or otherwise. A legal decision is always the result of a number of factors influencing the judge; meaning and text of a rule is one of these factors, but not the only one. Every decision expresses some actually existing social movement; even the most abstruse scholastical reason, the most manifest misinterpretations or conscious perversions of law, at least help to show these facts as coefficients of social tendencies. One of the duties of legal science is to examine the origin, nature, effect, and value of the tendencies that become apparent in legal decisions, and thus to furnish a picture of what is going on in the administration of justice and what the causes thereof may be.[15]

M. R. Cohen, The Process of Judicial Legislation*

Whether because of the general overturning of ordinary interests brought about by the World War, or for some other reason, the controversy over the recall of judges and judicial decisions that raged some years ago seems to have disappeared. The leaders of the American bar claim to have settled the matter by a campaign of education. The keynote of this campaign was sounded by Elihu Root when he urged that the public be educated to an appreciation of the true function of the judge, which he expressed as follows: "It is not his function or within his power to enlarge or improve or change the law."[2] In Sharswood's "Essay on Professional Ethics," republished by the American Bar Association,

15. In my paper on *"Die stillschweigende Willenserklärung,"* I have tried to make use of the decisions in this manner.

* [From *Law and the Social Order,* 112-113, 121-124, by M. R. Cohen, copyright, 1933, by Harcourt, Brace and Company, Inc. The major part of this essay was read at the first meeting of the Conference on Legal and Social Philosophy, April 26, 1913, and published under this title in 48 *Am. L. Rev.,* 161 (1914). Portions of the present essay are taken from a paper represented at the thirty-eighth annual meeting of the New York State Bar Association, January 22–23, 1915, and published under the title "Legal Theories and Social Science" in *Internatl. J. Ethics,* Vol. XXV (1915), p. 469. Reprinted by permission.

For biographical information, see page 81 supra.]

2. "The Importance of an Independent Judiciary," *Independent,* Vol. LXXII (1912), p. 704.

judicial legislation is the one cardinal sin of which jurists must beware.[3]

In spite, however, of the apparent authority back of this theory, a philosopher need not hesitate to declare it demonstrably false, i.e., contrary to fact. If judges never make law, how could the body of rules known as the common law ever have arisen or have undergone the changes which it has?

Moreover, not only is the common law changed from time to time by judicial decisions, but we may with Professor Gray[4] go on to assert that in the last analysis the courts also make our statute law; for it is the court's interpretation of the meaning of a statute that constitutes the law. If anyone needed to be convinced of this, a mere reference to the history of the Sherman Anti-Trust Act would be sufficient. The situation, however, becomes quite transparent in the realm of constitutional law. Who has made the body of law dealing with the police power of the states if not judges within the last forty years? Indeed the same men who insist that judges never make the law also tell us, as Mr. Hornblower does, how much better judge-made law is than that which we get from our legislators.[5] What respectable lawyer is not ready, at a moment's notice, to extol the work of John Marshall in shaping the national Constitution? If the judges are in no way to change or make the law, what business had Marshall to shape the Constitution?[6] . . .

The theory, then, that law pre-exists judicial decision, and that judges, therefore, can and should do their work without at the same time making new law, can be defended only on the assumption of the eternal self-sufficiency of the existing law. If, however, life is continually developing new and unforeseeable situations not covered by precedent, and judges are obliged to decide every case before them (these decisions serving as binding precedents), it follows that they must in the course of their work develop new rules.[25]

3. American Bar Association, *Reports,* Vol. III (1907), pp. 45 et seq.

4. Gray, *Nature and Sources of the Law,* 1909, sec. 275-76.

5. Hornblower, "A Century of 'Judge-Made' Law," *Columbia Law Review,* Vol. VII (1907), pp. 453-57. In historical and biographical estimates of various judges it is quite usual to find them praised for developing or creating certain branches of law, e.g., nearly all accounts of Story praise him for having created our admiralty law, which, in truth, he did.

6. "He (Marshall) was not the commentator upon American Constitutional Law; he was not the expounder of it; he was the author, the creator of it." Phelps, "Annual Address," *Annual Report* American Bar Association, 1879, pp. 173, 176.

25. The flimsy fiction that judicial decisions do not make the law, but are only the evidence of it, is really inconsistent with the doctrine of *stare decisis.* If decisions were only evidence of the law, why could not courts of coordinate or even inferior jurisdiction entertain evidence that any previous decision or judgment was wrong? Obviously, to the extent that such evidence is excluded, the past decision has made law.

There is no space here to indicate fully the logical confusion in the classical theory that

The process according to which this law-making takes place may be viewed under the three headings of finding, interpreting, and applying the law.

I. Finding or Making the Law

In the physical world no antithesis seems more justified than that between making and finding. Inventing and finding a continent are surely incompatible. When, however, we come to human affairs, the antithesis becomes less sharp. Making and finding an opportunity, making or finding time, making or finding a theory, are not so clearly antagonistic. Hence we need not be surprised that under the pressure of a prevailing theory, embodied in a current terminology, the process of law-making should be called finding the law. Some simple-hearted people believe that the names we give to things do not matter. But though the rose by any other name might smell as sweet, the history of civilization bears ample testimony to the momentous influence of names. At any rate, whether the process of judicial legislation should be called finding or making the law is undoubtedly of great practical moment.

To speak of finding the law seems to connote that the law exists before the decision, and thus tends to minimize the importance of the judicial contribution to the law or of the *arbitrium judicium* and the factors that determine it.

How is the law found? Consider, to begin with, cases of first impression that have no clear precedent. They are decided, we are told, on principle.[26] But what principle, and where does it come from? If we examine the decisions of the great creative minds in our legal history, of

---

each particular decision embodies a general rule as its *ratio decidendi*. A particular proposition can never uniquely determine a general one, and as a matter of fact any case, no matter how simple, can be cited in our system as an authority for various propositions of law of different degrees of generality. The true relation between decisions or judgments and rules of law is analogous to that between given points and the curves that can be drawn through them.

Professor Geldart and others seem to think it absurd to suppose that when a new case is decided "the facts of the case were previously governed by no law" (*Elements of English Law*, 1911, p. 23). This objection is based on a confusion between potential and actual existence, but we may here meet it by simply calling attention to the undoubted fact that vast regions of human relations, such as informal agreements, formerly not governed by the common law have by judicial decision been brought within its sway.

26. See Sneddeker v. Waring, 12 N.Y. 170, 174 (1854).

judges like Mansfield, Gibson, or Shaw, we find the prevailing ideas of justice, public convenience, and what is "reasonable" are always appealed to as decisive. (It has been noted that Marshall seldom cited precedents.) Moral rules or considerations of public convenience do not, of course, of themselves have the force of law. It is only when courts, balancing considerations of justice and policy, decide to enforce a moral or political rule that they transform it into a legal rule.[27] At any rate, there can be no doubt that by direct judicial legislation based on supposed principles of justice have been developed the bodies of law known as quasi contract, the common counts, the law of boycott, etc. Principles of public policy can be seen in the law of trade and other fixtures, in the doctrine of contracts void against public policy, the law of agency, the distinction between libel and slander, the law of privileged communications, the law of corporations, etc.[28] A great deal of judicial legislation also takes place under cover of finding what is "reasonable" under given circumstances. Thus our whole law of negligence consists essentially of various standards of conduct set up by courts to which people must conform at their peril. The same process can be observed in the law as to what are the reasonable necessities of an infant, what is a reasonable time for notice of dishonour of a bill, what is reasonable cause in an action for malicious prosecution or false arrest, and what is the reasonable income to which a public service corporation is entitled.[29]

It may be urged that these cases of first impression which constitute the leading cases of any branch of law are rare and must continue to become rarer as the number of precedents increases. To this we may reply that the cases of first impression are rare only because, in consequence of the prevailing theory, we tend to lose sight of them. Every case differs in some respect from previous ones. But the felt necessity of finding precedents produces the tendency to ignore or minimize these differences. Nor is it true that as the number of decided cases increases, the number

27. For modern instances or illustrations see Lefroy, "The Basis of Case Law," *Law Quarterly Review,* Vol. XXII (1906), p. 293 *et seq.* From the Continental and the comparative point of view this has been significantly treated by Kohler, *"Die Menschenhülfe in Privatrecht," Jherings Jahrbücher für die Dogmatik,* Vol. XXV (1887), pp. 1-141.

28. For the classical common-law conception of public policy see Co. Litt. 66a (1st Amer. ed., 1853) and Sheppard's *Touchstone,* Chap. 6. The attempt of Baron Parke to narrow the meaning of the term "public policy" to mean simply the policy already established in the law was, as Lefroy has pointed out, rejected by the House of Lords in Egerton v. Earl of Brownlow, 4 H.L.C. 1 (1853).

29. See Willcox v. The Consolidated Gas Co., 212 U.S. 19, 29 Sup. Ct. 192 (1919). "Reasonableness in these cases belongeth to the knowledge of the law, and therefore to be decided by the justices." (Co. Litt. 56, b.)

of cases of first impression must necessarily diminish. The possibility of these latter cases depends not so much on the mass of adjudicated cases as on the rapidity with which conditions of life are changing. Moreover, as the number of precedents increases, skilful counsel can and do all the more readily find precedents on both sides, so that the process of judicial decision is, as a matter of fact, determined consciously or unconsciously by the judges' views of fair play, public policy, and the general nature and fitness of things. It is true that judges of a certain temperament, the so-called strong-minded judges, frequently stop short at most tempting equities with the plea that authoritative precedent or well-settled law will not permit them to mete out the justice that they would like to enforce.[30] This, however, does not mean that justice is not a ground of decision with such judges; for we find them in other cases reasoning that that which leads to unjust or monstrous consequences cannot be the law.

The same judges who could not, because of the Fourteenth Amendment or its equivalent, approve the constitutionality of an admittedly just workmen's compensation law, had no difficulty in declaring unconstitutional a primary law that for all its iniquity did not seem to run afoul of any specific constitutional provision.[31] The simple fact is that the desire to do justice is a constant motive, but the sense for juristic consistency or symmetry is another that sometimes outweighs it. The relative weight of these two, as a matter of fact, varies with the psychology or temperament of the judge. Whatever may be the constitution of the ideal judge, it is not unreasonable to suppose that the minds of most judges work like those of other mortals, that is, having in various ways been unconsciously determined to decide one way or another, they look for and find reasons or precedents for such decisions. It was not a layman but a president of the American Bar Association who said that "a judge may decide almost any question any way, and still be supported by an array of cases."[32]

30. E. R. Thayer, "Judicial Legislation," *Harvard Law Review,* Vol. V (1891), pp. 170, 180.

31. People ex rel. Hotchkiss v. Smith, 206 N. Y. 231, 99 N. E. 568 (1912). The court condemns certain things because "unnecessary" and others pass as "not sufficiently onerous." But "requirements which shock the sense of justice" (p. 242) are not always unconstitutional.

32. Wigmore, *Evidence,* 2d ed., 1923, Vol. 1, p. xv. Judge Baldwin cites with approval the statement of an English judge that "nine-tenths of the cases which had ever gone to judgment in the highest court of England might have been decided the other way without any violence to the principles of the common law." Baldwin, *The American Judiciary,* 1905, p. 54.

Cardozo, The Nature of the Judicial Process*

Lecture I. Introduction. The Method of Philosophy

The work of deciding cases goes on every day in hundreds of courts throughout the land. Any judge, one might suppose, would find it easy to describe the process which he had followed a thousand times and more. Nothing could be farther from the truth. Let some intelligent layman ask him to explain: he will not go very far before taking refuge in the excuse that the language of craftsmen is unintelligible to those untutored in the craft. Such an excuse may cover with a semblance of respectability an otherwise ignominious retreat. It will hardly serve to still the pricks of curiosity and conscience. In moments of introspection, when there is no longer a necessity of putting off with a show of wisdom the uninitiated interlocutor, the troublesome problem will recur, and press for a solution. What is it that I do when I decide a case? To what sources of information do I appeal for guidance? In what proportions do I permit them to contribute to the result? In what proportions ought they to contribute? If a precedent is applicable, when do I refuse to follow it? If no precedent is applicable, how do I reach the rule that will make a precedent for the future? If I am seeking logical consistency, the symmetry of the legal structure, how far shall I seek it? At what point shall the quest be halted by some discrepant custom, by some consideration of the social welfare, by my own or the common standards of justice and morals? Into that strange compound which is brewed daily in the caldron of the courts, all these ingredients enter in varying proportions. I am not concerned to inquire whether judges ought to be allowed to brew such a compound at all. I take judge-made law as one of the existing realities of life. There, before us, is the brew. Not a judge on the bench but

---

* [Pp. 9-11, 14-23, 28-31 (New Haven: Yale University Press, 1921). Reprinted by permission.

Benjamin Nathan Cardozo (1870-1938), after practicing in New York from 1891 until 1914, was elected a Justice of the New York Supreme Court, and was almost immediately elevated to the Court of Appeals of that state, to which he was twice reelected. In 1932 President Hoover appointed Cardozo an Associate Justice of the United States Supreme Court, a position which he occupied until his death. His bestknown works are: *The Nature of the Judicial Process* (1921); *The Growth of the Law* (1924); *The Paradoxes of Legal Science* (1928); and *Law and Literature and Other Essays* (1931). The best account of Cardozo's significance in American law and jurisprudence will be found in the first chapter of B. L. Shientag, *Moulders of Legal Thought* (1943).]

has had a hand in the making. The elements have not come together by chance. *Some* principle, however unavowed and inarticulate and subconscious, has regulated the infusion. It may not have been the same principle for all judges at any time, nor the same principle for any judge at all times. But a choice there has been, not a submission to the decree of Fate; and the considerations and motives determining the choice, even if often obscure, do not utterly resist analysis. . . .

Before we can determine the proportions of a blend, we must know the ingredients to be blended. Our first inquiry should therefore be: Where does the judge find the law which he embodies in his judgment? There are times when the source is obvious. The rule that fits the case may be supplied by the constitution or by statute. If that is so, the judge looks no farther. The correspondence ascertained, his duty is to obey. The constitution overrides a statute, but a statute, if consistent with the constitution, overrides the law of judges. In this sense, judge-made law is secondary and subordinate to the law that is made by legislators. It is true that codes and statutes do not render the judge superfluous, nor his work perfunctory and mechanical. There are gaps to be filled. There are doubts and ambiguities to be cleared. There are hardships and wrongs to be mitigated if not avoided. Interpretation is often spoken of as if it were nothing but the search and the discovery of a meaning which, however obscure and latent, had none the less a real and ascertainable preexistence in the legislator's mind. The process is, indeed, that at times, but it is often something more. The ascertainment of intention may be the least of a judge's troubles in ascribing meaning to a statute. "The fact is," says Gray in his lectures on the "Nature and Sources of the Law,"[3] "that the difficulties of so-called interpretation arise when the legislature has had no meaning at all; when the question which is raised on the statute never occurred to it; when what the judges have to do is, not to determine what the legislature did mean on a point which was present to its mind, but to guess what it would have intended on a point not present to its mind, if the point has been present."[4] So Brutt:[5] "One weighty task of the system of the application of law consists then in this, to make more profound the discovery of the latent meaning of positive law. Much more important, however, is the second task which the system serves, namely the filling of the gaps which are found in every positive law in greater or less measure." You may call this process legislation, if you will. In any event, no system of *jus scriptum* has been able to escape the need of

3. Sec. 370, p. 165.
4. Cf. Pound, "Courts and Legislation," 9 Modern Legal Philosophy Series, p. 226.
5. *"Die Kunst der Rechtsanwendung,"* p. 72.

it. Today a great school of continental jurists is pleading for a still wider freedom of adaptation and construction. The statute, they say, is often fragmentary and ill-considered and unjust. The judge as the interpreter for the community of its sense of law and order must supply omissions, correct uncertainties, and harmonize results with justice through a method of free decision—*"libre recherche scientifique."* That is the view of Gény and Ehrlich and Gmelin and others.[6] Courts are to "search for light among the social elements of every kind that are the living force behind the facts they deal with."[7] The power thus put in their hands is great, and subject, like all power, to abuse; but we are not to flinch from granting it. In the long run "there is no guaranty of justice," says Ehrlich,[8] "except the personality of the judge."[9]. . . .

. . . Sometimes the rule of constitution or of statute is clear, and then the difficulties vanish. Even when they are present, they lack at times some of that element of mystery which accompanies creative energy. We reach the land of mystery when constitution and statute are silent, and the judge must look to the common law for the rule that fits the case. He is the "living oracle of the law" in Blackstone's vivid phrase. Looking at Sir Oracle in action, viewing his work in the dry light of realism, how does he set about his task?

The first thing he does is to compare the case before him with the precedents, whether stored in his mind or hidden in the books. I do not mean that precedents are ultimate sources of the law, supplying the sole equipment that is needed for the legal armory, the sole tools, to borrow Maitland's phrase,[11] "in the legal smithy." Back of precedents are the basic juridical conceptions which are the postulates of judicial reasoning, and farther back are the habits of life, the institutions of society, in which those conceptions had their origin, and which, by a process of interaction, they have modified in turn.[12] None the less, in a system so highly developed as our own, precedents have so covered the ground that they fix the point of departure from which the labor of the judge begins. Al-

6. "Science of Legal Method," 9 Modern Legal Philosophy Series, pp. 4, 45, 65, 72, 124, 130, 159.

7. Gény, *"Méthode d'Interprétation et Sources en droit privé positif,"* vol. II, p. 180, sec. 176, ed. 1919; transl. 9 Modern Legal Philosophy Series, p. 45.

8. P. 65, supra; *"Freie Rechtsfindung und freie Rechtswissenchaft,"* 9 Modern Legal Philosophy Series.

9. Cf. Gnaeus Flavius (Kantorowicz), *"Der Kampf um Rechtswissenschaft,"* p. 48: *"Von der Kultur des Richters hängt im letzten Grunde aller Fortschritt der Rechtsentwicklung ab."*

11. Introduction to Gierke's "Political Theories of the Middle Age," p. viii.

12. Saleilles, *"De la Personnalité Juridique,"* p. 45; Ehrlich, *"Grundlegung der Soziologie des Rechts,"* pp. 34, 35; Pound, "Proceedings of American Bar Assn.1919," p. 455.

most invariably, his first step is to examine and compare them. If they are plain and to the point, there may be need of nothing more. *Stare decisis* is at least the everyday working rule of our law. I shall have something to say later about the propriety of relaxing the rule in exceptional conditions. But unless those conditions are present, the work of deciding cases in accordance with precedents that plainly fit them is a process similar in its nature to that of deciding cases in accordance with a statute. It is a process of search, comparison, and little more. Some judges seldom get beyond that process in any case. Their notion of their duty is to match the colors of the case at hand against the colors of many sample cases spread out upon their desk. The sample nearest in shade supplies the applicable rule. But, of course, no system of living law can be evolved by such a process, and no judge of a high court, worthy of his office, views the function of his place so narrowly. If that were all there was to our calling, there would be little of intellectual interest about it. The man who had the best card index of the cases would also be the wisest judge. It is when the colors do not match, when the references in the index fail, when there is no decisive precedent, that the serious business of the judge begins. . . .

In the life of the mind as in life elsewhere, there is a tendency toward the reproduction of kind. Every judgment has a generative power. It begets in its own image. Every precedent, in the words of Redlich, has a "directive force for future cases of the same or similar nature."[14]. . . The common law does not work from pre-established truths of universal and inflexible validity to conclusions derived from them deductively. Its method is inductive, and it draws its generalizations from particulars. The process has been admirably stated by Munroe Smith: . . .*

In this perpetual flux, the problem which confronts the judge is in reality a twofold one: he must first extract from the precedents the underlying principle, the *ratio decidendi;* he must then determine the path

14. Redlich, "The Case Method in American Law Schools," Bulletin No. 8, Carnegie Foundation, p. 37.

* [Cardozo here refers to Munroe Smith's comment: "In their effort to give to the social sense of justice articulate expression in rules and in principles, the method of the lawfinding experts has always been experimental. The rules and principles of case law have never been treated as final truths, but as working hypotheses, continually retested in those great laboratories of the law, the courts of justice. Every new case is an experiment; and if the accepted rule which seems applicable yields a result which is felt to be unjust, the rule is reconsidered. It may not be modified at once, for the attempt to do absolute justice in every single case would make the development and maintenance of general rules impossible; but if a rule continues to work injustice, it will eventually be reformulated. The principles themselves are continually retested; for if the rules derived from a principle do not work well, the principle itself must ultimately be re-examined."]

or direction along which the principle is to move and develop, if it is not to wither and die.

The first branch of the problem is the one to which we are accustomed to address ourselves more consciously than to the other. Cases do not unfold their principles for the asking. They yield up their kernel slowly and painfully. The instance cannot lead to a generalization till we know it as it is. That in itself is no easy task. For the thing adjudged comes to us oftentimes swathed in obscuring dicta, which must be stripped off and cast aside. Judges differ greatly in their reverence for the illustrations and comments and side-remarks of their predecessors, to make no mention of their own. All agree that there may be dissent when the opinion is filed. Some would seem to hold that there must be none a moment thereafter. Plenary inspiration has then descended upon the work of the majority. No one, of course, avows such a belief, and yet sometimes there is an approach to it in conduct. I own that it is a good deal of a mystery to me how judges, of all persons in the world, should put their faith in dicta. A brief experience on the bench was enough to reveal to me all sorts of cracks and crevices and loopholes in my own opinions when picked up a few months after delivery, and re-read with due contrition. The persuasion that one's own infallibility is a myth leads by easy stages and with somewhat greater satisfaction to a refusal to ascribe infallibility to others. But dicta are not always ticketed as such, and one does not recognize them always at a glance. There is the constant need, as every law student knows, to separate the accidental and the nonessential from the essential and inherent. Let us assume, however, that this task has been achieved, and that the precedent is known as it really is. Let us assume however, that this task has been achieved, and that the precedent is known as it really is. Let us assume too that the principle, latent within it, has been skillfully extracted and accurately stated. Only half or less than half of the work has yet been done. The problem remains to fix the bounds and the tendencies of development and growth, to set the directive force in motion along the right path at the parting of the ways.

The directive force of a principle may be exerted along the line of logical progression; this I will call the rule of analogy or the method of philosophy; along the line of historical development; this I will call the method of evolution; along the line of the customs of the community; this I will call the method of tradition; along the lines of justice, morals and social welfare, the *mores* of the day; and this I will call the method of sociology.

I have put first among the principles of selection to guide our choice of paths, the rule of analogy or the method of philosophy. In putting it first, I do not mean to rate it as most important. On the contrary, it is often sacrificed to others. I have put it first because it has, I think, a certain presumption in its favor. Given a mass of particulars, a congeries of judgments on related topics, the principle that unifies and rationalizes them has a tendency, and a legitimate one, to project and extend itself to new cases within the limits of its capacity to unify and rationalize. It has the primacy that comes from natural and orderly and logical succession.

Haines, General Observations on the Effects of Personal, Political, and Economic Influences in the Decisions of Judges*

The mechanical theory which postulates absolute legal principles, existing prior to and independent of all judicial decisions, and merely discovered and applied by courts,[4] has been characterized as a theory of a "judicial slot machine."[5] According to this theory, it is assumed that provisions have been made in advance for legal principles, so that it is merely necessary to put the facts into the machine and draw therefrom an appropriate decision.[6] This view of the function of a judge has been subjected to constant criticisms,[7] and yet it continues to hold sway in Anglo-American law as one of the strong determining forces guiding lawyers and judges. In fact, despite all influences to the contrary, American courts have clung to the belief that justice must be administered in accordance with fixed rules, which can be applied by a rather mechanical process of logical reasoning to a given state of facts and can be made to

* [17 *Ill. L. Rev.* 96, 97-98, 103-106, 107, 110, 113-114, 115-116 (1922). Reprinted by permission of the Illinois Law Review (Northwestern University School of Law).

Charles Grove Haines was professor of history, political science, and law at Ursinus College, Whitman College, University of Chicago, U.C.L.A., and Harvard, and author of many books and articles on the judiciary, among them *The Supreme Court in United States History* (1935) and *Revival of Natural Law Concepts* (1930).]

4. Pound, in "The Science of Legal Method" 205-206.

5. Kantorowicz *"Rechtswissenschaft und Soziologie"* 5.

6. Cf. Pound in "The Science of Legal Method" 206; see also Cohen "Legal Theories and Social Science" N.Y. Bar Assn. Reports (1915) at p. 184, in which this theory is styled the "phonograph theory of the judicial function."

7. For example Austin referred with contempt to "The childish fiction employed by our judges that judiciary or common law is not made by them, but is a miraculous something made by nobody, existing, I suppose, from eternity and merely declared from time to time by the judges": *Jurisprudence* (4 ed.) 655. See also Pound "Mechanical Jurisprudence" *Col. L. Rev.* (1908) VIII 605.

produce an inevitable result.[7a] And it is assumed that the very nature of law requires such a mechanical application of its rules and principles. Due to the general acceptance of this view by the legal fraternity, it has become a habit of those trained in law to bestow little attention upon their individual views of prejudices and to turn attention instead to precedents which are regarded as forming the authoritative basis of the law. . . .

Among the foremost of those who have challenged prevailing traditions as to the judge's function are Holmes and Ehrlich. Justice Holmes expressed his views many years ago in his well known work, "The Common Law":

> The very considerations which judges most rarely mention and always with an apology are the secret root from which the law draws all the juices of life. I mean, of course, considerations of what is expedient to the community concerned. Every important principle which is developed by litigation is in fact and at bottom the result of more or less definitely understood views of public policy; most generally, to be sure, under our practice and traditions, the unconscious result of instinctive preferences and inarticulate convictions, but none the less traceable to views of public policy in the last analysis.[26]

In law review articles and numerous opinions he has reiterated this view. A few noteworthy comments deserve repetition here:

> I think that the judges themselves have failed adequately to recognize their duty of weighing considerations of social advantage. The duty is inevitable, and the result of the often proclaimed judicial aversion to deal with such considerations is simply to leave the very ground and foundation of judgments inarticulate and often unconscious.[27]

> Perhaps one of the reasons why judges do not like to discuss questions of policy, or to put a decision in terms upon their views as lawmakers, is that the moment you leave the path of merely logical deduction you lose the illusion of certainty which makes legal reasoning seem like mathematics. But the certainty is only an illusion, nevertheless. Views of public policy are taught by experience of the interests of life.

7a. Note on "Rule and Discretion in the Administration of Justice" *Har. L. Rev.* (1919-20) XXXIII 972.

26. "The Common Law" 35, 6 and 106.

27. "The Path of the Law" *Har. L. Rev.* (1896-1897) X 456, 467; "Collected Legal Papers" 184.

Those interests are fields of battle. Whatever decisions are made must be against the wishes and opinions of one party, and the distinctions on which they go will be distinctions of degree.[28]

The true grounds of decisions are consideration of policy and of social advantage, and it is vain to suppose that solutions can be attained merely by logic and the general propositions of law which nobody disputes.[29]

Approval is here given to the type of judge who looks at the equities of a cause and then searches for precedents to sustain the desired results.[30] Where no rule has been definitely formulated, it is conceded that judicial decisions must be based on judicial conceptions of public policy.[31] The whole body of the common law is, in fact, made up of "compromises of conflicting individual interests in which we turn to some social interest frequently under the name of public policy, to determine the limits of a reasonable adjustment."[32]

To Ehrlich, likewise, the significance of law in the daily life of a people depends far more on the persons charged with its administration than on the principles according to which it is administered.[33] To continue in his suggestive words—

The administration of justice has always contained a personal element. In all ages, social, political, and cultural movements have necessarily exerted an influence upon it; but whether an individual jurist

28. "Privilege, Malice, and Intent" *Har. L. Rev.* (1894) VIII 7; "Collected Legal Papers" 126. With regard to the doctrine of *stare decisis* and its main object to secure certainty, Dean Wigmore observes "but the sufficient answer is that it has not in fact secured it. Our judicial law is as uncertain as any law could well be. We possess all the detriment of uncertainty which *stare decisis* was supposed to avoid, and also all the detriment of law-lumber which *stare decisis* concededly involves—the government of the living by the dead as Herbert Spencer has called it": "Problems of Law" 79, 80.

29. Dissenting opinion in Vegelahn v. Guntner (1896) 167 Mass. 92, 105, 106.

30. "No man has seen more plainly that the court was measuring the legislature's reasons by its own intellectual yardstick than has Justice Holmes; none more keenly perceived that the notation thereupon marked those results of environment and education which many men seem to regard": C. M. Hough "Due Process of Law—Today" *Harv. L. Rev.* (1918-1919) XXXII 232; for comments of Justice Holmes see Lochner v. New York (1905) 198 U.S. 45, 75, and Grant Timber Co. v. Gray (1915) 236 U.S. 133.

31. See Waite "Public Policy and Personal Opinion" *Mich. L. Rev.* (1920-21) XIX 265, where it is observed "There can be no question but that where no rule at all has been definitely precipitated, judicial decisions are time and again founded on nothing but the judicial apprehension, or conception, of public policy."

32. Pound "A Theory of Social Interests" *Pub. Am. Soc. Society* XV 17.

33. Ehrlich in "The Science of Legal Method" p. 48.

yields more or less to such influences, whether he is more inclined to follow tradition or is rather disposed to introduce changes and innovations, depends, of course, less on any theory of legal method than on his own personal temperament.[34]

Psychological motives and influences have been subjected to analysis in their effects upon political conduct to some extent, and it is conceded that these motives and influences are not alerted when one assumes the role of judge. Just as is the case with other opinions of individuals, judicial opinions necessarily represent in a measure the personal impulses of the judge, in relation to the situation before him, and these impulses are determined by the judge's lifelong series of previous experiences.[35] The psychologists recently have emphasized the fact that all of us have predispositions which unconsciously attach themselves to the conscious consideration of any question. Every conclusion is expressive of a dominant personal motive and is a resultant of the evolutionary status of the individual's mind.[36] Apparent as these facts are, they have received scant consideration in the discussion of problems in the administration of justice.[37] A noteworthy exception to the usual attitude of indifference toward psychic or personal influences in judicial administration is found in the reports of the statistician of the City Magistrates' Courts of New York City.

In a survey of the records of the 41 magistrates of the city courts, the percentage of cases discharged or dismissed for the year 1915 varied from 6.7 per cent to 73.7 per cent. The opportunity for a discharge or dismissal therefore depended to a considerable degree upon the magistrate before which the prisoner was arraigned. In 1916, 17,075 persons were charged before the magistrates with intoxication. Of these, 92 per cent were convicted. But the examination of the record of individual judges showed that one judge discharged 79 per cent of this class of cases. In cases for disorderly conduct one judge heard 566 cases and discharged one person, whereas another judge discharged 18 per cent; another 54 per cent. Numerous instances of similar variations in the results of the consideration of cases by different magistrates were presented in the reports of the City Magistrates' Courts for 1914 and 1915. The tabu-

34. Ibid. p. 74.

35. T. Schroeder "The Psychologic Study of Judicial Opinions" *Cal. L. Rev.* (1917-18) VI 93.

36. Schroeder op. cit. 94.

37. For a discriminating analysis of the relation of psychology to political science and to jurisprudence see J. M. Williams, "The Foundations of Social Science," especially Books I and II (N.Y. 1920).

lations of the statistician were prepared in part to discover the personal equation in the administration of justice and they showed that the magistrates differed to an amazing degree in their treatment of similar classes of cases. The conclusion was inescapable that justice is a personal thing, reflecting the temperament, the personality, the education, environment, and personal traits of the magistrates.[38] The results showing to what extent justice is affected by the personality of the judge were so startling and so disconcerting that it seemed advisable to discontinue the comparative tables of the records of the justices. Some time, no doubt, more facts regarding the personal element in the administration of justice will be rendered available, and, perhaps, a better educated public will be prepared to know the truth—namely, that the process of judicial decision is determined to a considerable extent by the judges' views of fair play, public policy, and their general consensus as to what is right and just.[39] Law and politics are indeed inseparable and politics is the very stuff of life. Its motives are interlaced with the whole fibre of experience, private and public. Its relations are intensely human, and generally intimately personal.[40]

"In approaching the problem, then, of the administration of justice," says Dean Pound, "It is becoming clear that men count for more than machinery and that there are many subtle forces at work of which we are but partially conscious. Tradition, education, physical surroundings, race, class and professional solidarity, and economic, political and social influences of all sorts and degrees make up a complex environment in which men endeavor to reach certain results by means of legal machinery. No discussion simply in terms of men or of legal and political machinery, or both, ignoring this complex environment, will serve. At whatever cost in the loss of dramatic interest or satisfying simplicity of plan, we must insist on plurality of causes and plurality and relativity of remedies."[41]

The role of discretion in the administration of justice, in which the effects of personality are always evident, is a phase of judicial activity as yet largely unexplored.[42]. . . .

38. G. Everson "Human Element in Justice" *Jour. Crim. L.* [Vol.] X 98.
39. Cf. Cohen [supra n.6] at p. 171.
40. Woodrow Wilson "Law and the Facts" *Am. Pol. Sc. Rev.* V 3.
41. "Criminal Justice in the American City" *The Survey* Oct. 29, 1921.
42. "Investigation of the essential nature of legal rules develops the conclusion that discretion instead of being a casual defect of legal systems, a vice to be wholly eradicated by the aid of legal science and legislative skill, is a standing and permanent characteristic of law, and one of the great levers of legal evolution": Kocourek "Formal Relation Between Law and Discretion" *Ill. L. Rev.* (1914-1915) IX 225.

If considerations of public policy form a vital part in the development of the common law, does it not follow that even greater weight should be given to these considerations in the growth of constitutional law? Justice Holmes frequently warns his associates against "the subtle danger of the unconscious identification of personal views with constitutional sanction" and brings to the fore the fact that our public law is truly one of the living forces in which we have, as in other avenues, the operation of instincts and interests. . . .

Judicial legislation, whether it operates in public or in private law, is imbued with certain characteristics which have been suggestively analyzed by Professor Dicey:

> The courts or the judges, when acting as legislators, are, of course, influenced by the beliefs and feelings of their time, and are guided to a considerable extent by the dominant current of public opinion; Eldon and Kenyon belonged to the era of old Toryism as distinctly as Denman, Campbell, Erle and Bramwell belonged to the age of Benthamite liberalism. But whilst our tribunals, or the judges of whom they are composed, are swayed by the prevailing beliefs of a particular time, they are also guided by professional opinions and ways of thinking which are to a certain extent independent of and possibly opposed to the general tone of public opinion. The judges are the heads of the legal professions. They are advanced in life. They are for the most part persons of a conservative disposition. They are in no way dependent for their emoluments, dignity, or reputation upon the favor of the electors, or even of ministers who represent in the long run the wishes of the electorate. They are most likely to be biased by professional habits and feeling than by the popular sentiment of the hour. Hence, judicial legislation will often be marked by certain characteristics rarely found in acts of Parliament.[51]

Judicial legislation thus aims at the maintenance of the logic or the symmetry of the law and great care is exercised to secure consistency. It aims at securing certainty rather than the development of the law and tends toward the maintenance of a fixed legal system. It frequently results also that ideas of expediency or policy accepted by the courts may differ considerably from the ideas which at a given time have acquired predominant influence among the general public.[52] The morality of courts may be higher than the morality of traders or of politicians, but it has, of course, often happened that the ideas entertained by the judges have fallen below the highest and most enlightened public opinion of a

51. Dicey op. cit. [*Law and Opinion in England*] 361, 362.
52. Dicey op. cit. 365.

particular time.[53] As a general rule, judge-made law represents the conviction of an earlier age and is characterized by conservatism.[54]. . .

While in theory, then, we have often been led to believe that constitutional law has been developed solely through the application of the rules of formal logic in accordance with well established principles, in reality we have found it has been to a considerable extent the result of human forces in which the personality of the judges, their education, associations, and individual views are of prime importance. The former of these two elements, legal logic, tradition and precedent, has received extended and adequate treatment at the hands of lawyers and political scientists; the latter, the element of free conception, in which individual views and personal notions have influenced and have frequently predetermined judicial decisions, has received scant attention.[68] To be sure, the subject is a difficult one. It carries the diligent seeker for truth into wide and varied fields wherein the personal and political doctrines of public men are formed. But difficult as is the search, the important bearings of the decisions of our highest courts renders it desirable that more attention be given than heretofore to the personal and political doctrines of those favored few who are elevated to the bench and whose decisions affect profoundly public and private interests. . . .

. . . As an individual's views in political and legal matters are likely to be in part, at least, determined by his interests, training, environment and long-continued associations, it is suggestive to analyze these personal factors with a view of determining some of the influences which affect federal constitutional law. The factors likely to influence judicial decisions are:

    A. Remote and Indirect—
        1. Education—
            (a) General.
            (b) Legal.
        2. Family and personal associations; wealth and social position.

53. Dicey op. cit. 365.
54. Ibid. 367.
68. In a discussion of the "Spirit of Our Judges," Mr. E. V. Abbott claims "we are overawed by the authority of their position; we let them do many things which they have no business to do; we do not sufficiently examine their decisions to note what they are doing; we are too lenient when we do criticise and we are content to leave them at all times in a position of practically irresponsible power": *Am. L. Rev.* (1920) LIV 240. "If the judges continue," says Dean Lewis, "to act as elder statesmen and to veto acts which shock their sense of justice and fairness, it becomes imperative that public criticism and control be more actively exercised": See *Pro. of Acad. of Pol. Sc.* (Jan. 1913) III 45.

B. Direct—
1. Legal and political experience.
2. Political affiliations and opinions.
3. Intellectual and temperamental traits.

A consideration of all of these factors has been made for only a few of the justices, and in numerous instances the records and biographical accounts are far from adequate for anything like a complete analysis. But the evidence available reveals instances of personal and political influences in decisions on federal constitutional law which deserve careful consideration.

Hutcheson, The Judgment Intuitive: The Function of the "Hunch"[1] in Judicial Decision*

Many years ago, at the conclusion of a particularly difficult case both in point of law and fact, tried to a court without a jury, the judge, a man of great learning and ability, announced from the Bench that since the narrow and prejudiced modern view of the obligations of a judge in the decision of causes prevented his resort to the judgment aleatory by the use of his "little, small dice" he would take the case under advisement, and, brooding over it, wait for his hunch.

To me, a young, indeed a very young lawyer, picked, while yet the dew was on me and I had just begun to sprout, from the classic gardens of a University, where I had been trained to regard the law as a system of

---

1. "A strong, intuitive impression that something is about to happen." *Webster, International Dictionary*.

* [14 *Cornell L.Q.* 274, 275, 276, 277-278, 280-281, 282, 284-285, 287-288 (1929). © Copyright 1929 by Cornell University. Reprinted by permission of the Cornell Law Review and Fred B. Rothman & Company.

Joseph C. Hutcheson, Jr. (1879-1973) received his LL.B. from the University of Texas in 1900. After graduating from law school, Hutcheson was a practicing attorney in Houston, Texas. He was Chief Legal Advisor to the city of Houston from 1913 to 1917, and Mayor of Houston trom 1917 to 1918. In 1918 he was appointed Judge of the United States District Court for the Southern District of Texas, where he served until 1930, when he was appointed to the United States Circuit Court of Appeals for the Fifth Circuit. He was Chief Judge of the Fifth Circuit from 1948 until his retirement in 1959. Since 1959, he has been a senior circuit judge. In addition to his many opinions, which are noted for the clarity of their reasoning, Hutcheson's written works include *Law as Liberator* (1937) and *Judgment Intuitive* (1938).]

rules and precedents, of categories and concepts, and the judge had been spoken of as an administrator, austere, remote, "his intellect a cold logic engine," who, in that rarified atmosphere in which he lived coldly and logically determined the relation of the facts of a particular case to some of these established precedents, it appeared that the judge was making a jest, and a very poor one, at that. . . .

I knew that judges "are the depositories of the laws like the oracles, who must decide in all cases of doubt and are bound by an oath to decide according to the law of the land,"[2] but I believed that creation and evolution were at an end, that in modern law only deduction had place, and that the judges must decide "through being long personally accustomed to and acquainted with the judicial decisions of their predecessors."[3]. . . .

As I grew older, however, and knew and understood better the judge to whom I have in this opening referred; as I associated more with real lawyers, whose intuitive faculties were developed and made acute by the use of a trained and cultivated imagination; as I read more after and came more under the spell of those great lawyers and judges whose thesis is that "modification is the life of the law,"[4] I came to see that "as long as the matter to be considered is debated in artificial terms, there is danger of being led by a technical definition to apply a certain name and then to deduce consequences which have no relation to the grounds on which the name was applied";[5] that "the process of inclusion and exclusion so often applied in developing a rule, cannot end with its first enunciation. The rule announced must be deemed tentative. For the many and varying facts to which it will be applied cannot be foreseen."[6]

I came to see that "every opinion tends to become a law."[7] That "regulations, the wisdom, necessity and validity of which as applied to, existing conditions, are so apparent that they are now uniformly sustained, a century ago, or even half a century ago, would probably have been rejected as arbitrary and oppressive, . . . and that in a changing world it is impossible that it should be otherwise."[8]

I came to see that "resort to first principles is, in the last analysis, the only safe way to a solution of litigated matters."[9]. . .

2. *Bl. Comm.* 169.
3. Ibid.
4. Carter, *Law, Its Origin, Growth and Function* (1907). "Modification implies growth. It is the life of the Law." Washington v. Dawson, 264 U.S. 219, 236, 44 Sup. Ct. 302 (1924), Brandeis, J., dissenting.
5. Guy v. Donald, 203 U.S., 399, 406, 27 Sup. Ct. 63 (1926).
6. Washington v. Dawson, supra note 4.
7. Lochner v. New York, 198 U.S. 45, 76, 25 Sup. Ct. 539 (1905).
8. Euclid Valley v. Ambler, 272 U.S. 365, 47 Sup. Ct. 114 (1926).
9. Old Colony Trust Co. v. Sugarland Industries. 296 Fed. 129, 138 (S.D. Tex. 1924).

And so, after eleven years on the Bench following eighteen at the Bar, I, being well advised by observation and experience of what I am about to set down, have thought it both wise and decorous to now boldly affirm that "having well and exactly seen, surveyed, overlooked, reviewed, recognized, read and read over again, turned and tossed about, seriously perused and examined the preparatories, productions, evidences, proofs, allegations, depositions, cross speeches, contradictions . . . and other such like confects and spiceries, both at the one and the other side, as a good judge ought to do, I posit on the end of the table in my closet all the pokes and bags of the defendants—that being done I thereafter lay down upon the other end of the same table the bags and satchels of the plaintiff."[12]

Thereafter I proceed "to understand and revolve the obscurities of these various and seeming contrary passages in the law, which are laid claim to by the suitors and pleading parties," even just as Judge Bridlegoose did, with one difference only. "That when the matter is more plain, clear and liquid, that is to say, when there are fewer bags," and he would have used his "other large, great dice, fair and goodly ones," I decide the case more or less offhand and by the rule of thumb. While when the case is difficult or involved, and turns upon a hairsbreadth of law or of fact, that is to say, "when there are many bags on the one side and on the other" and Judge Bridlegoose would have used his "little small dice," I, after canvassing all the available material at my command, and duly cogitating upon it, give my imagination play, and brooding over the cause, wait for the feeling, the hunch—that intuitive flash of understanding which makes the jump-spark connection between question and decision, and at the point where the path is darkest for the judicial feet, sheds its light along the way. . . .

Now, what is this faculty? What are its springs, what its uses? Many men have spoken of it most beautifully. Some call it "intuition"—some "imagination" this sensitiveness to new ideas, this power to range when the track is cold, this power to cast in ever widening circles to find a fresh scent, instead of standing baying where the track was lost.

> Imagination, that wondrous faculty, which properly controlled by experience and reflection, becomes the noblest attribute of man, the source of poetic genius, the instrument of discovery in science.[17]

With accurate experiment and observation to work upon, imagination becomes the architect of physical theory. Newton's passage from a

12. Rabelais, Book III, c. 39.
17. Address to the Royal Society of England, November 3, 1859, Sir Benjamin Brodie, quoted from *Fragments of Science,* 109.

falling apple to a falling moon was an act of the prepared imagination without which the laws of Keppler could never have been traced to their foundations.

Out of the facts of chemistry the constructive imagination of Dalton formed the atomic theory. Scientific men fight shy of the word because of its ultrascientific connotations, but the fact is that without the exercise of this power our knowledge of nature would be a mere tabulation of co-existences and sequences.[18]

"When I once asked the best administrator whom I knew," writes Mr. Wallas, "how he formed his decisions, he laughed, and with the air of letting out for the first time a guilty secret, said: 'Oh, I always decide by feeling. So and so always decides by calculation, and that is no good.' When again I asked an American judge, who is widely admired both for his skill and for his impartiality, how he and his fellows formed their conclusions, he also laughed, and said that he would be stoned in the street if it were known that, after listening with full consciousness to all the evidence, and following as carefully as he could all the arguments, he waited until he 'felt' one way or the other. He had elided the preparation and the brooding, or at least had come to think of them as processes of faint kinship with the state of mind that followed." "When the conclusion is there," says William James, "we have already forgotten most of the steps preceding its attainment."[21]

Time was when judges, lawyers, law writers and teachers of the law refused to recognize in the judge this right and power of intuitive decision. It is true that the trial judge was always supposed to have superior facilities for decision, but these were objectivized in formulas, such as— the trial judge has the best opportunity of observing the witnesses, their demeanor,—the trial judge can see the play and interplay of forces as they operate in the actual class of the trial.

Under the influence of this kind of logomachy, this sticking in the "skin" of thought, the trial judge's superior opportunity was granted, but the real reason for that superior position, that the trial creates an atmosphere springing from but more than the facts themselves, in which and out of which the judge may get the feeling which takes him to the desired end, was deliberately suppressed.

Later writers, however, not only recognize but emphasize this faculty, nowhere more attractively than in Judge Cardozo's lectures before the law schools of Yale University, in 1921[27] and Columbia University in

18. "Scientific Use of the Imagination" Address delivered before the British Association at Liverpool, Sept. 16, 1860 by Tyndall, quoted from *Fragments of Science,* III.

21. Cardozo, *Paradoxes of Legal Science* (1928) 59, 60.

27. Cardozo, *The Nature of the Judicial Process* (1921).

1927,[28] while Max Radin, in 1925, in a most sympathetic and charming way, takes the judge's works apart, and shows us how his wheels go round.[29]

He tells us, first, that the judge is a human being; that therefore he does not decide causes by the abstract application of rules of justice or of right, but having heard the cause and determined that the decision ought to go this way or that way, he then takes up his search for some category of the law into which the case will fit.

He tells us that the judge really feels or thinks that a certain result seems desirable, and he then tries to make his decision accomplish that result. "What makes certain results seem desirable to a judge?" he asks, and answers his question that that seems desirable to the judge which, according to his training, his experience, and his general point of view, strikes him as the jural consequence that ought to flow from the facts, and he advises us that what gives the judge the struggle in the case is the effort so to state the reasons for his judgment that they will pass muster.

Now what is he saying except that the judge really decides by feeling, and not by judgment; by "hunching" and not by ratiocination, and that the ratiocination appears only in the opinion?

Now what is he saying but that the vital, motivating impulse for the decision is an intuitive sense of what is right and wrong for that cause, and that the astute judge, having so decided, enlists his every faculty and belabors his laggard mind, not only to justify that intuition to himself, but to make it pass muster with his critics?

There is nothing unreal or untrue about this picture of the judge, nor is there anything in it from which a just judge should turn away. It is true, and right that it is true, that judges really do try to select categories or concepts into which to place a particular case so as to produce what the judge regards as a righteous result, or, to avoid any confusion in the matter of morals, I will say a "proper result."

This is true. I think we should go further, and say it ought to be true. No reasoning applied to practical matters is ever really effective unless motivated by some impulse. . . .

There is not one among us but knows that while too often cases must be decided without that "feeling" which is the triumphant precursor of the just judgment, that just as "sometimes a light surprises the Christian while he sings," so sometimes, after long travail and struggle of the mind, there does come to the dullest of us, flooding the brain with the vigorous blood of decision, the hunch that there is, or is not inven-

28. Supra note 21.
29. Radin, Theory of Judicial Decision (1925) 2 *Am. B.A.J.* 359.

tion; that there is, or is not, anticipation; that the plaintiff should be protected by a decree, or should be denied protection. This hunch, sweeping aside hesitancy and doubt, takes the judge vigorously on to his decision; and yet, the cause decided, the way thither, which was for the blinding moment a blazing trail, becomes wholly lost to view.

Sometimes again that same intuition or hunch, which warming his brain and lighting his feet produced the decision, abides with the decider "while working his judgment backward" as he blazes his trail "from a desirable conclusion back to one or another of a stock of logical premises."[33]

It is such judicial intuitions, and the opinions lighted and warmed by the feeling which produced them, that not only give justice in the cause, but like a great white way, make plain in the wilderness the way of the Lord for judicial feet to follow.

Levi, The Nature of Judicial Reasoning*

I

The topic of judicial reasoning evokes the memory of countless after dinner talks given by members of the judiciary and a kind of entourage of lawyers and law professors. This is not all it evokes, of course. In any case many of the talks are good, and it would be churlish to mention this except to suggest one point and to ask a first question. The point is

33. Supra note 29.

* [32 *U. Chi. L. Rev.* 397, 397-411 (1965). First presented by the author at the sixth annual New York University Institute of Philosophy in May 1963, and published in *Law and Philosophy* (S. Hook ed. 1964), New York University Press. Reprinted by permission.

Edward H. Levi (1911–) was educated at the University of Chicago (Ph.B. 1932; J.D. 1935) and at Yale University (S.J.D. 1938). Levi began his academic career in 1936 as Associate Professor of Law at the University of Chicago. In 1940, Levi temporarily set aside his professorial duties to become a special assistant to the then Attorney General Robert Jackson, and also served under Jackson's successor, Francis Biddle, when the former was appointed to the United States Supreme Court. He returned to the University of Chicago in 1945 as Professor of Law. Subsequently he became Dean of the Law School (1950), Provost of the University (1962), Acting Dean of the Undergraduate College (1965), and President of the University (1967). He was appointed Attorney General of the United States by Gerald Ford in 1975. Upon accepting the appointment, he was made President Emeritus of the University of Chicago. Levi is best known for his short book, *An Introduction to Legal Reasoning* (1948), regarded by many as the unofficial model of American legal reasoning. He was also the co-author of *Elements of the Law* (with R. T. Steffen, 1950) and author of many articles in law reviews and journals.]

somewhat difficult to make. It involves questions of emphasis and degree and qualification to such an extent that I cannot help but have doubts about it. Yet to put it in the large it would be this: it would be difficult to think of another scholarly profession which speaks as little of the consequences of its acts or the discoveries it has made and as much about the circumstances of its own behavior. Surely these public expressions of wonderment at the difficulties and niceties of the judge's behavior are not to be dismissed simply as orgies of narcissism or flattery. I am not of course speaking of the judicial opinion, although there is a relationship between the opinion and talks about how opinions get to be written. A fact to the point is that, as I believe, the literature about judging is an American, possibly an Anglo-American, phenomenon.

I have put the point which I am suggesting in terms of a concern with judging and a lack of inquiry into the effects of judging. This must be qualified. Inquiries into judicial behavior are related to inquiries into effect. A shift in constitutional interpretation can have obvious consequences, suggesting questions as to the relationship between judging and the justification for the shift. Perhaps it should be said that the effect of the shift so far as the judge or lawyer is concerned is primarily on the fabric of the law. The lawyer's or the judge's function may be sufficiently self-delimited so as to exclude from the realm of their professional competence the larger social consequences, for example, of the school desegregation decision or the recent reapportionment cases, even though the lawyer or judge will know or believe what others in that kind of segment of society will know or believe. For the judge or lawyer the relevant effects are upon the web of the law, the administration of law and respect for it. These are large items, and the priest who only keeps his temple in good repair is not to be condemned on that account. Yet with all these qualifications, and even with the difficulties which analogous illustrations suggest, the point though battered seems to me to persist. Is the analogy to be the man of medicine who describes not what the virus does and how it is to be counteracted but rather emphasizes the difficulties and virtues of his diagnostic art? Is it to be to the scientist who cares less about his discovery and more about how he made it? Again it is to be recognized that perhaps the discovery is more the way and less the result. Perhaps the analogy should be to the novelist who thinks his reactions and growth are matters of importance to an understanding of the craft. I think the analogies on balance emphasize the point that there is indeed unusual concern with the decision-making processes of judges, and the question to be put is whether this unusual concern, if it does exist, points to a uniqueness in the judicial process itself.

The uniqueness does not appear to arise in any simple way from the

263

importance of the items ruled upon by the judge. Much of what a judge decides, if you look at the situations with which he deals, is no more or less important than what a plumber does, to speak of the plumber as the symbol of the worker on every day items without whose skill matters could be uncomfortable, annoying, and at times catastrophic. Of course there is a difference, since the judge, even though the case before him may involve price-fixing on plumbing items, is dealing with rights and duties imposed or acknowledged by the state, and he is an instrument of government. But this is true also of the legislator, the policeman, and the prosecutor. Behavioral scientists do attempt to study the decision-making processes of these occupations. We know these groups do make important decisions, yet the literature of the wonderment and agony of the road to determination does not really pertain to them. A comparison between the judge and the legislator seems particularly suggestive, because even though we were traditionally told that the judge only applies old rules through specific determinations to cases brought before him, while the legislator changes the law, we know that to a considerable extent the judge and the legislator perform the same function. By this I mean that the legislator also must have points of reference to basic doctrines which justify the determinations of changes he makes. Yet the differences in the American practice between judge and legislator are there to be seen. First, there are many legislators, and while appellate judges are more than one, the comparison is not so much between individual judges and individual legislators as it is between a judge and the legislative body. The legislator is champion of a point of view. If all points of view are to be represented it is because the debate, if that is what it can be called, has brought them out and the legislator is but a participant, although a later voter, in that debate. On the contrary, the judge who writes an opinion has the task of reflecting the outlines of the debate, to show that he is aware of the different voices and that his thought processes have traveled through an inner debate prior to determination. In short, while this is honored in varying degrees, the judge, although he may feel strongly, does not appear as an advocate. Second, while we know that both judges and legislators change the law and both refer to immutable principles, the emphasis in the court in the American system is not only on the prior or stated rule but on its application in other cases, creating for the judge the problem of showing how an old equity can be preserved and better and new justice be done. Third, the assumption for the judge is that the process of determination is one of reason. There is almost a claim to infallibility if the system works properly. The result is not one of indifference or bias but follows from inner thought processes which bring the right result implicit in the rule. Judicial reasoning no doubt is like any other kind of reasoning which involves the use of a moving classification system. But here a moral judgment is frequently involved in the conclusions reached by the judge. Moreover, as I will indicate later, the integrity of the process in which the judge is engaged depends not only on distinctions which he may make reasonably, but also on his own belief in the legitimacy and decisiveness of these distinctions. Thus, there is an astonishing combination of compulsions on the Anglo-American judge: the duty of representing many voices, of justifying the new application in terms of a prior rule and the equality of other cases, the assumption that reason is a sufficient and necessary guide, the responsibility for moral judgment and the importance of sincerity—all these do tend to give uniqueness to the institution of judicial reasoning in our system and in our society.

II

I come now to the second point which is that the technique of judicial reasoning is admirably adapted to a moving classification system and has a built-in device for the exploration and creation of ambiguities. At the same time the process tends to obscure the problem of the relationship between equality and change. Equality seems to be the moving principle which justifies, indeed compels, reference to the handling of similar cases once this material is readily available. I realize the reference to a similar specific instance could be considered solely as a means of supplying or clarifying a definition of a key concept in a rule. I do not mean to suggest either that the sole style of legal reasoning is from case to case to the creation of a rule. Styles change and the structure of the opinion at any given time and with a particular judge may appear to be from the general proposition downward. The problem of the determination of the application of the general proposition to the cluster of facts still remains, however. The adversary system, which is closely related to the idea of a fair hearing, creates a forum in which competing versions of the factual situation can be explored, and this is another way of saying that competing propositions are being advanced. And it is a little difficult even under the most static and simple view of law to see how competing versions of the same fact situation can be avoided. The briefs of counsel further the idea of the comparison of situations by their citation of cases. Yet it is true that the cases may be cited more for the statement of general propositions and less or not at all for any close scrutiny of similarity of factual situations. A judge with strong convictions and an authoritarian view as to good and bad cases and a well formed, logically held structure of the law in mind may cite only those good cases which reflect his view as to the appropriate and correct application of the right terms—much as it appears the early casebooks tended to do. One could then conceive of the process as laying down an understood logical structure of terms illustrated through cases which in their functions with respect to the system are quite passive. Thus I would not want to say here that what is usually called reasoning by analogy is the sole judicial technique in opinion writing, nor even that it is the concealed starting point for the judge's own working out of the problem. But I do think that a closer look at how reasoning by analogy or example works in the judicial process reveals some interesting problems.

The Anglo-American legal system has as one of its comfort points the idea of dictum. The system is not very precise as to what dictum is. In some sense the idea undoubtedly is a necessary one since otherwise the judge could write a treatise as an opinion and accomplish an unacceptable codification of the law. So we say loosely that the judge's observations on matters not before him for decision, or which are perhaps not necessary for the conclusion which he reaches, are only dicta and not binding on future judges. At one extreme the doctrine suggests that the particular views of a given judge on propositions of law can be decisive on future cases, and indeed must be, if these views are given with cogent reference to the precise issues he had to decide. At the other extreme the doctrine contends that we need not permit the prior judge to overreach and establish law by his own exaggerated view of the issues or the relevance of what he feels called upon to say. At the same time, as we all know, in the web of the law one can find the compelling influence of repeated doctrine even though close scrutiny would show that for all the appellate cases which have discussed it the doctrine could be called only dictum. But the phrase "close scrutiny," while it may indicate diligence and the bringing to bear of an expert mind, does not disclose the rules of the game. I suggest as a starting point for inquiry the question of how pivotal the position taken by a prior judge is made to be by the inner discipline of the system. I believe a view of the system through the structure of reasoning by example is helpful in this connection.

From the standpoint of reasoning by example, the circumstances before the court are compared with a number of somewhat similar circumstances which have been classified in terms of opposing categories. These categories would result in opposite or at least different legal conclusions and different although presumably compatible rules of law. The fact cluster before the court could be included within either category. After enough successive fact clusters have been added, the probability is that it will be apparent that the original rule of law has changed its meaning and this may be reflected in a change in the name of the determining concept and therefore in the language of the rule. If it is correct that the fact cluster could be classified equally well under the categories of opposing concepts and rules, this must be because no authoritative definition has removed ambiguity. If reliance is to be on the authority of a prior case for the scope and effectiveness of an announced rule of law now to be applied, then the similarity and difference between the present fact cluster now up for decision and the fact cluster of the prior case are decisive. What power does the judge in the prior case have to establish for all time the compelling and, in the future, decisive aspects of the case before him, including (1) a determination of what is irrelevant and therefore would make no difference if present or absent, and (2) a determination of what cannot be done without? Thus, what is to be the result if the first judge forecasts similarity when the second and later judge finds a reasonable difference?

I think the answer in Anglo-American law, although some English writers have suggested this is only true of American and not English practice, is that the second judge, where only case law is involved, is free to make his own determination of decisive similarity or difference. This of course gives the law a great deal of flexibility and capacity for growth. I am not suggesting that the inner discipline of the system permits the later judge to create distinctions which he regards as irrelevant. If the judge reworks the system and has a new classification, he is under compulsion to supply reasons for reworked old cases in order to project a pattern which can guide later cases. The distinctions which he makes must appear reasonable to him. Under one view of the judge's restricted power the amount of change is limited by the judge's ability to encompass it within a logical structure which explains all prior cases, albeit the judges of the prior cases would have rejected the explanation. Under this view there is a sense in which the system is engaged not in change but in explication. At best this view of the constraint upon the judge is somewhat idealized. It is recognized that cases are discarded and are explained in terms of the now inoperative ideas of their time rather than in terms of any present pattern. Particularly in those areas of the law where reported cases are so numerous, the present judge is really not compelled to organize them all. Yet the compulsion upon him is real and effective even though it does not require him to make sense out of every case which has ever occurred and even though now and then he may recognize a shift in the law so that he is not required to take account of an older view. If the views of the prior judge and the distinctions he made were decisive, the system would be much more rigid and change more frequently would have to come about through legislation.

When English commentators describe their system as one in which the second and later judge is bound by the determinations of the first judge, they appear to have reference to cases in which the question is one of statutory interpretation. They thus do not distinguish between common law cases and cases where the issue is the meaning of legislation. I believe that to a considerable degree it can be shown that in this country also the second and later judge finds himself much more bound by the prior court's views when the prior court is construing a statute. In such situations the prior court's views even when broadly stated as dictum frequently determine the direction of future statutory construction. I state the matter too simply of course, but I think there is this basic difference in the freedom of the judge in case law areas as contrasted with the case law-statutory interpretation fields. The explanation may be that dictum places a gloss upon the statute; it is a kind of communication to the legislature as to how its words will be interpreted, and since the legislature has manifested an interest in the area anyway, if the gloss is not to its liking it can change the statute. This line of argument is not fully satisfying since it can be said that court and legislature should be considered in a partnership even in the absence of legislation. It may be that subsequent court interpretations of legislation reveal less leeway for the second court for the very reason that interpretation must focus on specific language and its meaning, and there may be a natural inclination to assume that the document takes on and keeps the meaning assigned to it. One way the restriction of the second court in statutory matters manifests itself in our country is in the plea of a judge that he is free of the restraints of the previous case because this is a case involving basic or constitutional issues. The written constitution and the insistence that it and not its interpretations must prevail, in marked contrast to the situation when legislation is involved, make it possible in constitutional matters to change from the even flow of common law case law accretions or from the more rigid following down the path in statutory interpretation to an abrupt, although usually foreshadowed, change in direction.

I do not deny that there are difficulties in the way of the application of this analysis. For example, the United States Supreme Court in 1922 held that the antitrust laws did not apply to baseball since the exhibition, although made for money, was not to be called trade or commerce.[1] In subsequent years as a matter of constitutional interpretation the scope of the commerce power of the United States was greatly increased. In 1953 the Court was again asked to rule on the application of the Sherman Act to baseball.[2] Quite apart from the point that the Sherman Act is so vague

1. Federal Baseball Club v. National League, 259 U.S. 200 (1922).
2. Toolson v. New York Yankees, Inc., 346 U.S. 356 (1953).

it may be regarded less as legislation and more as common law, one can argue that if this is a matter of statutory interpretation, then the 1922 opinion, assuming the basic facts of baseball are the same, must be adhered to; if it is a matter of constitutional interpretation, then presumably the wider impact of federal power would be acknowledged to exist. As we know, the way the matter was handled compels us to distinguish between baseball on the one side and theatres and boxing on the other, leading to the interesting argument, which failed when football was considered, that football was a team sport like baseball and unlike boxing and therefore should be exempt also. The point is that the jurisprudential question of the leeway in the law for particular categories really decided these cases.

This analysis of judicial reasoning is rudimentary and could be made more elaborate, paying more attention to those cases where there is a mixture of legislation and case law interpretation, or cases where legislation is persuasive as indicating a shift in policy or perhaps is to be treated much as an analogous case for reasoning by example to work upon. It is surprising, however, that a judicial reasoning system which places such great store on the correct analysis of cases should have as little doctrine as ours does upon the crucial question of whether the judge's own explanation of the decisive features of the case, a successor judge's rationale or perhaps the underlying structure as seen by some commentator are all equally available methods for finding or justifying the law. To the extent that there is any general assumption about this I would suppose that it is that the first judge's language, when not dictum, is decisive—a view which is not only unclear but wrong. This in itself suggests that for the effective operations of the system it is not necessary to be either clear or correct about such matters.

The compatibility of judicial reasoning, which relies heavily on reasoning by example, with a moving classification system is, I think, clear. The movement in the system frequently will not be apparent. When it is apparent, it is often justified obliquely on the basis that this policy step was taken some time ago and is reflected in prior decisions. The system permits a foreshadowing of results and therefore has built into it the likelihood of a period of preparation so that future decisions appear as a belated finding and not a making of law. The joint exploration through competing examples to fill the ambiguities of one or many propositions has the advantage of permitting the use in the system of propositions or concepts saved from being contradictory because they are ambiguous, and on this account more acceptable as ideals or common-place truths; the advantage, also, of postponing difficult problems until they arise, and of providing an inner discipline for the system by forcing an analysis of general propositions in terms of concrete situations. The avoidance of explicit policy determinations by referring to prior and selected examples appears as a substitution of the idea of equality for a head-on examination of issues of policy. Undoubtedly some of the magic of the judicial process stems from this fact, and also some of the doubt which has given rise to the literature of self-examination.

III

Against this background it seems to me that a third point is at least tenable and it is this: the caliber of a court's opinion even in a constitutional case is not to be made dependent on its announcement of a principle which is fully satisfying in reason and which will indicate for us how future cases are to be decided. I put the matter this way in reaction to Professor Wechsler's observations on neutral or articulated principles[3] and upon the basis that the caliber of an opinion is to be seen in terms of the governmental function it performs. What Professor Wechsler said was that the courts in exercising their duty to review the actions of the other branches of the government in the light of constitutional provisions, must act as courts of law and not as naked power organs. The determinations of the courts, then, to have legal quality must be "entirely principled," and a "principled decision . . . is one that rests on reasons with respect to all the issues in the case, reasons that in their generality and their neutrality transcend any immediate result that is involved."[4] The emphasis throughout his superb essay is on "standards that transcend the case at hand" and upon "principled articulation." I have heard it suggested that the use of the "neutrality" concept is unfortunate since it seems to give the impression that the values about which the judge feels deeply may not be the appropriately articulated reasons for decision. And this has thrown the essay into a kind of maelstrom of discussion as to whether judges should be neutralists or umpires or social reformers. I would suppose that all would agree with the answer I think is suggested by Professor Wechsler's essay: namely, that a judge who makes changes in the law must take seriously the duty of reworking the pattern of the law. The distinctions which he makes must be genuine, articulated, and sufficiently acceptable. But granted the description of judicial reasoning as the working or reworking of a moving classification system, to what extent must the judge have worked out the full impact

3. Wechsler, Toward Neutral Principles of Constitutional Law, 73 *Harv. L. Rev.* 1 (1959).
4. Id. at 19.

upon future cases of conflicting values and legal concepts? And to what extent is it appropriate or necessary for a judge to plot out in the written opinion, as contrasted with the inner process of decision, the future course of the law as to those instances and future distinctions which seem foreseeable to him?

Surely there are several meaningful ways in which the Constitution is something more than what a court says it is. In our country in any event the Constitution is a written document embracing basic and sometimes contradictory values and using both very broad and sometimes rather specific concepts. The freedom which the Court has to abandon its prior reading of the Constitution is a recognition of primacy of the document. Granted the right and duty of the Court to interpret the document, it has not been given the duty or the opportunity to rewrite the words. It can decide cases on the basis of its interpretation of the words, but if the analysis of reasoning by example means anything, it means that a later court can accept the results in those cases but justify them on a different theory. And the value of court action as opposed to action by a constitutional convention or a legislature is that the matter can be taken one step at a time. This does not mean that the steps can be taken without justification—the discipline requires a justification which will explain the way prior cases and this case have been handled, and may even be a justification which latches onto a shift in constitutional interpretation. But I do not think this is equivalent to demanding a fully satisfying theory which projects a line to the future and steers a safe course for future conflicts. Particularly where a constitution is involved, with its conflicting values, such a demand seems unobtainable. In addition to the point that it is one of the values of court action that it can deal with the case at hand and avoid the broad reach, there is the more central complexity that with conflicting values a political system has to decide some things on the basis of specific decisions approaching a dividing line which in fact may be a moving line and not one which can be grandly fixed through articulation. Because the Supreme Court has ventured into an enlarged circle where primaries are protected from racial discrimination does not, I think, require it or make it desirable for it to attempt to leap to a determination of whether under any and all circumstances political parties should be prevented from being organized on racial or religious grounds in the United States. An attempt to make a judicial pronouncement on this subject might be more fraught with mischief than a wrong decision crossing a line which it should not cross and resulting from the misapplication of a more standard principle that a governmental function must be carried on without that kind of clear discrimination. And so for the opinion of the Supreme Court in the segregated schools case,[5] I would not suppose it would be desirable for the Court to have attempted to articulate its adjudication upon the basis of a resolution of the conflict between the right of freedom of association and the right to not associate—a conflict which Professor Wechsler has suggested he would like to see come out on the side of association, but where he indicates there are certain difficulties, and, as he said, he has "not yet written the opinion."[6] It is because Professor Wechsler has not yet written the opinion that I am dubious that others can. But it does not follow that segregation in schools should be allowed to persist. It is possible that the *Brown* case should have been decided with the same result but with less of an immediate jump and on the partial basis of an old and accepted theory.

The recognition and preservation of future leeways in the law until the time for decision has been reached is of course not a new thought or a new value. The doctrine that constitutional matters should not be decided until their resolution is necessary to the case at hand is in part a reflection of that thought. Of course it is virtuous in terms of the legal process to be willing to deny the legitimacy of desired results which cannot be reached through appropriate reasoning. But the process of judicial reasoning is frequently, perhaps basically, retrospective, taking advantage of situations which have been met. This in itself involves some projection into the future as well, going beyond the case at hand, but it can also involve care not to foreclose the consideration of future distinctions and further relevance. This is in recognition that time has its advantages, that the constitutional or legal posture of later cases may be doctrinely different, that situations which seem the same now under a new light may appear otherwise, and that situations and doctrine may be more interrelated than is earlier realized.

Having said this much I hasten to add that I realized that a call for responsible articulated reasons does not mean that a judge must shoulder the responsibility for deciding all future cases. And probably the articulation of reasons in the opinion is of greater or at least different importance in constitutional cases to the extent that the Court's overriding authority has to be justified. The course of common law cases in which one can find inchoate theories, incomplete expressions of new views, and then finally the better expression of the theory is well known and includes the best judges as the writers of opinions. Shocking as it may be, even the case which has no articulated theory to support it but seems right and is treated as a kind of unique incident has a place in our juris-

5. Brown v. Board of Education, 347 U.S. 483 (1954).
6. Wechsler, supra note 3, at 34.

prudence. Perhaps one's point of view on the importance of the completed theory depends upon whether one sees the theory in some sense as prior to the determination of result or rather as arising out of the same process of seeing similarity and difference. If it is the latter, then the completed theory is less important than the description of the process of comparison (which of course includes a statement of what are the crucial points of comparison) for after all it is that process upon which we must rely. I trust that the category of articulated neutral principles is broad enough to permit this approach.

IV

I have tried to describe some of the strains inherent in judicial reasoning which perhaps have contributed to the literature of self-examination, and to describe also the process of this reasoning which is adapted to a moving classification system. I have urged that the articulation of neutral principles be regarded in the light of a process of judging in which the direction of perceived standards and the comparison of situations both play a part but one in which it is not always possible or wise to anticipate the inevitable collision of important values too far beyond the case at hand. But of course the choice of the preferred way of judicial reasoning depends upon a judgment as to the functions which judicial reasoning is to perform. Clearly these functions are not always the same. They depend in part upon the needs of a society at a given time and the availability of other and possibly better ways of fulfilling these needs. The classic function for judging is to redress a wrong caused by a violation of a sufficiently understood legally authorized standard. The clearer the standard, and the more acceptable that standard is to elements within the community, the greater the moral judgment carried by the decision. Because rewards and punishment are involved and the relationship to moral judgment very close, judging is an important educational and changing factor. The interpreter of the standard becomes the creator of the standard. And the standard or law which is applied may become in varying degrees no more than, but as much as, the changing customs or value systems of the community as seen through a particular mechanism. As we know, there need not be an institutional separation of judging from executive or legislative authority. The functional lines between them can become exceedingly blurred in part because even naked power hardly ever is that simple. We can begin with a skeletonized view of the judicial process: the received standard, the adversary proceeding, the focusing on a single situation and the exemplification of the standard

273

in similar actual or hypothetical cases. But these are the broad outlines and the working of the process will change as needs are felt differently.

It is perhaps relevant to remind outselves that law as regulated by the judicial opinion operates within a literary tradition. One function of the opinion has been to map out the contours of the law, much as a text writer would do, and in this sense the reasoning of the judge as dictum has been quite important. But the view of the judge on the effects of laws or on the quantity and types of cases and issues which may arise within the legal system itself may be quite limited. I do not know whether it is worthwhile, but modern methods of research could tell us a great deal more about the operations of the legal system itself—that is, the frequency with which particular types of cases arise, the relationships among issues, the likelihood of recovery and similar questions, than can be handled appropriately in legal opinions. This limitation of judicial reasoning to an examination of the facts which arise in the particular case, an acceptance of enlightened or sound social views and an intense scrutiny of the intellectual issues thought to be involved in the case is no doubt regarded as a positive value by members of our craft. Judges are not behavioral scientists. The point is, however, that there was a time when no one else was, and the sphere of the judge as social philosopher was less limited or threatened. Today the organization by the bar of various instruments for mapping out the law and also for such collaborative research as can be done both on the operations within the legal system and the effect of laws on social problems—all these suggest a certain limitation on the need for formal judicial reasoning as words on high to fill these gaps. We still want to know what the judge thought was relevant in deciding the case but the thought that he might do some research on his own in matters economic or sociological fills us, no doubt correctly, with dread.

But we still think of the judge as appropriately law reformer and also as wise man or political scientist for the community. The meaning of the image of the judge as law reformer is clouded because in part it refers only to the restating and remaking of the case law as the pattern of the law. But the fact is that in our society the law court is a powerful instrument for effecting changes which the legislature will not enact or for preventing for some time at least the changes which legislatures do enact. And the defense of judicial action against the charge that its behavior is simply legislative, and therefore the assumption of naked power, is frequently but not always that where action is prevented, the matter is so great as to go to the essential spirit of institutions, and where change is effected, that the amount of change is so small that a comparison of other situations will show it has already occurred. It would be comforting to think that an analysis of proper judicial reasoning would show which actions were appropriate. I do not think an articulation of powerful reasons and serious concern is sufficient to separate proper judicial from improper judicial or essentially legislative behavior or wise from imprudent judicial behavior. It seems to be a question partly of time and place, the acceptability of what is done and the need for it. It can be plausibly argued that all great judges have recognized this, and that it is one of the tragedies of judging that, with this recognition and perhaps because of it, misconceptions of felt needs can make for unwise decisions. Of course a court which operates in areas where there are strong differences of views runs great risks, but in our system it is supposed to do so somewhat. The analysis of jurisprudence which makes much of the difference between the *is* and the *ought* does not seem to me to be helpful at this point. A judicial system which makes this distinction and eschews the *ought* will have lost both the spirit and symbol of justice. In effect it will have made the *was* the *is*.

Yet it can be asked whether at a particular time and place it is valuable for a court to become the main forum for basic political debate. It is somewhat anomalous in a highly developed political society that lawyers in court and lawyers in robes should have to discuss matters of political power which certainly as appropriately come within the province of lawyers in the legislature, but which presumably are inadequately treated there. The fact of the anomaly is not necessarily a criticism of the Court's behavior. The fact is that in our society, although some may disapprove, the Court has advantages as a forum for the discussion of political-moral issues. In a broadly based, vocal and literate society, susceptible to the persuasion of many tongues and pens, and with inadequate structuring of relevant debate, the Court has a useful function not only in staying time for sober second thought but in focusing issues. It is sometimes the only forum in which issues can be sharply focused or appear to be so. It has the drama of views which are more opposing and less scattered because its procedures require a certain amount of relevance. It operates more within a structure of logical ideas, and yet one into which current views may be infused through new words which must find a relationship to the old and through new meanings. It has the drama of a limited number of personalities who are called upon to explain their views. It has the advantage of beginning with certain agreed upon premises to which all participants profess loyalty and thus can force concentration upon the partial clarification of ambiguities. It must reach a conclusion for the particular situation which has the force of a moral judgment. The Court operates from a base in which the identification of its members is explicitly to the higher ideals of the entire community. This freedom and responsibility minimizes that kind of double standard between public and private convictions which cannot so clearly be said to be inappropriate in other areas. This does not mean that the price for such participation by a court does not come high nor that there are not substantial weaknesses in its fulfillment of these functions. A basic insecurity in the foundation of a court's approach to such issues is that it must proceed with a standard of constitutionality, including problems of distribution of powers, or a rule of minimum fairness distorts the lesson. It makes for poor public education even though it may be the best available. Finally, without regard for the technical propriety of what the Court does, there is no doubt that the Court's influence as an acceptable objective force is diminished the greater the controversy. This easy and customary point, however, must be corrected by an awareness that it is the Court's appeal to our better selves, connoting some controversy, which is the source of its moral power and persuasion.

In this setting the function of articulated judicial reasoning is to help protect the Court's moral power by giving some assurance that private views are not masquerading behind public views. This might lead to the conclusion that the more controversial the issues the more the Court should endeavor to spell out the future rules of the road. But I doubt if this conclusion follows. I do not ignore the obligation of higher courts to give directions to trial and intermediate courts, the need greater in some areas than in others to guide private transactions, the special duty to enforce rules of fairness when court procedures are involved, and the requirement that law not be segmented but be a continuing pattern. But the existence of controversy on public issues may speak for a less decisive and far-reaching determination by a court which can have the advantage of taking the law a step at a time. The commentators' happy and useful lament that the reasoning is unclear and that ambiguities and uncertainties remain in itself is no cause for alarm; future courts can and will take advantage of such learning and hindsight as they take advantage of their own. What is needed in the judicial opinion is an indication of the points at issue, a narrowing of the determinative factors, and to some extent care not to take unnecessary steps until they can be taken in a sense retrospectively. This is not an argument for the thoughtless decision. It is rather an argument that the decision must bear witness that it was reached through the discipline of the pattern of the law, which provides both restrictions and leeway. It is indeed the recognition of the present and future leeway, as much as of the prior restrictions, which compels the thoughtful decision and makes of judicial reasoning something more than arrangements to be projected on a computer or predicted from the bias of a judge.

Craven, Paean to Pragmatism*

In Perkins House at the Harvard Law School in the fall of 1939, it was possible to get up a serious discussion about whether judges decided cases and then figured out the reasons for the decisions or whether they were inevitably led to a decision by the reasons. I thought then and think now that the chicken generally comes first and lays down its reason to justify its existence. The opposite conclusion seems to me a bit naive, but some scholars of distinction apparently hold to the contrary and insist that there are neutral controlling principles[1] brooding more or less omnipresently in the sky.

I believe that there are only two kinds of judges at all levels of courts: those who are admittedly (maybe not to the public) result-oriented, and those who are also result-oriented but either do not know it or decline for various purposes to admit it. Those who are unaware of their result-orientation have an advantage; they get where they want to go without the inhibition of a conscious awareness of how they got there. Those who know themselves well enough to recognize their result-orientation are inhibited by the knowledge that they may put into judicial decisions value judgments that may not have enduring validity and may even turn out to be wrong. A judge who is that introspective tends to be more flexible than his less perceptive brother who knows not what he does—if only because he is aware that he is constantly choosing, usually not between right and wrong but between two goods or two evils embraced within conflicting principles.

All judges in America are subject to the supreme authority of the United States Supreme Court. There are some things judges of inferior courts cannot do. If the United States Supreme Court has spoken clearly, it cannot be ignored, however horrible the result that may ensue in application of the principle to a given fact situation. If state law is settled, however wrongly, it may not be ignored. Whatever I may think of capital punishment, and I think poorly of it, I cannot presently vote to afford relief to one fairly convicted of first-degree murder and sentenced to death. However absurd I may think some applications of the

---

* [50 *N.C.L. Rev.* 977 (1972). Reprinted by permission.

J. Braxton Craven, Jr. (1918-1977), a distinguished jurist, was Judge of the United States Court of Appeals for the Fourth Circuit. Intensely interested in legal education, Judge Craven occasionally taught in various American law schools.]

1. Wechsler, Toward Neutral Principles of Constitutional Law, 73 *Harv. L. Rev.* 1 (1959). Cf. Clark, A Plea for the Unprincipled Decision, 49 *Va. L. Rev.* 660 (1963), and Birmingham, The Neutrality of Adherence to Precedent, 1971 *Duke L.J.* 541.

exclusionary rules of evidence in criminal cases to be, and I am not alone. . . .

. . . I must sometimes vote to let the criminal go free because the constable blundered. Whatever my sense of outrage that the statute of limitations in North Carolina used to run from the day the doctor left the sponge in the intestinal cavity and not from the day it is discovered, I was bound by *Erie Railroad v. Tompkins* to apply this unjust rule in a diversity case arising in North Carolina. However fair and reasonable would be an interpretation of the conscientious objector statute that would allow selective opposition to the Vietnam War, and however well supported such an idea may be by Christian doctrines of the unjust war, I cannot vote to relieve one who is willing to defend America but whose conscience will not permit him to serve in Vietnam. There are, as I say, some things judges cannot do.

These are examples of that group of cases, perhaps thirty to forty percent of the total volume,[9] that can be decided but one way. Whether result-oriented in terms of justice or in terms of sterile intellectualism, a judge need not ponder long such questions. In these situations and others like them, he must "plunge the knife with averted gaze."

Marshal Foch, when jumped over the heads of senior officers, is supposed to have said to Lloyd George that the higher one goes the easier it gets. He was speaking in practical terms, saying that as commander-in-chief of the allied armies he would have a bigger staff and more expert assistance, but what he said is also true with regard to the exercise of judicial power. A judge of the United States Court of Appeals is bound only by the decisions of the United States Supreme Court, and as to state law in diversity cases by decisions of the highest court (that has spoken) of the particular state. He is free to ignore the most well reasoned decision of the Second Circuit, the Fifth and the Ninth and all the others, not to mention the most persuasive opinions of the district judges. If he can get another judge to vote with him, he may lawfully "overrule" or ignore a panel decision of his own circuit, although he will likely hesitate to do it and may, instead, suggest en banc consideration. There are more limitations on trial courts, and above the courts of appeals, in the rarefied atmosphere of the United States Supreme Court, there is almost but not quite complete freedom. The limitations there are more political than legalistic, although often they are expressed technically.

I have never had the misfortune to be closely associated with a truly conservative judge. I do not mean "conservative" in its ordinary sense. A more apt word is, perhaps, "sterile." I have in mind sterile intellectual-

9. Cardozo estimated over 50% in this category. See B. Cardozo, *The Nature of the Judicial Process* 164 (1921).

ism that is not in the least offended but, instead, is delighted that there may be no reason for decision other than that the rule "was laid down in the time of Henry IV." I have known very few such judges, and them only at a distance, but I have read others. This is the kind of judge who, if he is a trial judge, likes to say from the bench, "This is not a court of justice; it is a court of law." When I was a young judge (under age forty) I said it once or twice myself and am sorry for it. This is cold intellectualism that finds no room at the inn for people. This type of legal mind is concerned with "legal problems"—entirely unaware that the term is a misnomer, that there are only peoples' problems for which the law sometimes may afford answers. The life principle of such a judge is stare decisis. He fervently believes that it is far, far better that rule be certain and unjust than that he tinker with it. It is a delight to him to construct painstakingly, with adequate display of erudition, an edifice of logic and precedent upon which justice may be sacrificed. That the result in terms of the people involved would make an Apache cry is to him simply proof in full measure of his dedication to law. When one reads such an opinion, complete with pious disavowal of judicial power to usurp the legislative prerogative, the feeling comes through that the author is not sorry that he cannot and may even be glad that the legislature will not. Such a judge categorically rejects Holmes' aphorism that the life of the law is not logic but experience, and such a judge, of course, has never entertained the following thought of Yeats: "God guard me from those thoughts men think In the mind alone; He that sings a lasting song thinks in (the) marrow-bone."[12]

It may be thought that I have refuted my own thesis that all judges are result-oriented. I think not. The result-orientation of a sterile judge is toward continuity, certainty, and intellectual symmetry and against change. He loves law instead of people and may indeed have a deep hostility towards people. He is as much predisposed to the vindication of precedent for its own sake as his brother may be predisposed to achieving within the framework of the law a just result. Such a sterile judge may hold justice in contempt. Because it cannot be defined, he is likely to believe it does not exist. But he probably would not say the same thing about love and certainly not about obscenity.

Compared with other judges, the lot of the sterile judge is an easy one. He can pretty well accomplish his objective by doing nothing, and when he does nothing he can wear the robe of humility—an appealing garment. There is something for everyone when a judge points toward justice and wrings his hands that he cannot attain it.

Nor can I define justice, but I am quite certain that it exists, both

12. W. B. Yeats, "A Prayer for Old Age."

abstractly and in the context of every adversary proceeding. In five years of sitting on the Fourth Circuit with six other judges of diverse backgrounds and predilections, I do not believe there have been more than half a dozen instances of disagreement as to the "desirable" or "just" result. More often there has been disagreement as to whether the desirable or just result is attainable within the framework of the law.

There is not as much sterile intellectualism in the law schools today as there used to be, but there is still too much. There are probably yet some law professors who think the word "justice" belongs in Sociology I rather than in Property II. Perhaps the greatest contribution of Chief Justice Warren was to make respectable a very simple question: "Is it fair?" The legal mind that will not talk about injustice because it cannot be defined is like a surgeon who will not treat cancer because it is not yet fully understood. It might well be remembered that the United States Constitution was ordained to establish "justice"—not law.

If I have exaggerated the result-orientation of judges, and perhaps I have, I think it difficult to exaggerate the overriding importance of the result in the most important cases—all of which are, of course, constitutional law cases. In the truly "big" case I should think the mind of a sterile judge would boggle, and even he must think in terms of the "desirable" result in view of the interests of the people and the Nation. I believe the truly important constitutional decisions are exercises in pragmatics often clothed in legalistic syllogisms and that the controlling principle, seldom expressed, is expediency: What is best for the nation? Sometimes the true rationale of decision is never mentioned. Worse, it may be covered up and buried beneath page after page of legalese.

Of the three branches of government, the judicial branch alone must assign and articulate reasons for its decisions. Conclusions are not enough. No American appellate court has ever simply announced that the result below is unjust and unwise and therefore ought to be and is reversed. The assigned reasons must be precedent-related and plausibly interpretive of prior decisions, and in addition our judicial tradition demands that the contrary reasons advanced by the losing litigant be examined, discussed, and plausibly rejected, again in harmony with, even though a departure from, prior decisions and interpretations. Manifestly this tradition, to which I think every lawyer and judge would adhere, strictly limits the range of choice available and sometimes dictates to the most free-wheeling and "unprincipled" judge how he must vote and decide the matter. . . .

Somewhere along the line, beginning with the first classroom command to state what a case *holds,* every good lawyer-judge learns to distrust what an appellate court *says.* Doubt goes far beyond mere dictum, whether admitted or otherwise obvious. What is held may not be even what the court *says* it holds. The discerning lawyer-judge doubts the rationale of decision except in its own factual context, and sometimes even there. This is not because appellate judges are less intellectually honest than their counterparts in other walks of life. Indeed, I think there is less dissembling on the bench than off it. But the very nature of the judicial process, hallowed in tradition, is to explicate decision interpretatively, whether of legislative intent or prior judicial decision. It is accepted judicial craftsmanship to show that the new result rests solidly upon an old foundation. The technique runs something like this: Case *A* is very old and is very bad. Cases *B*, *C*, *D*, *E*, *F*, and *G*, although adhering to *A*, have gradually eroded it so that it will come as no surprise to discerning members of the bar that we now reject it. In so doing we make no sharp break with the past; instead, we merely follow the established precedent of *B* and especially *F* and *G*. If this is done expertly enough, and not too often, the shock wave of change will scarcely register on the law review seismograph. Indeed, if enough time has been allowed to elapse from *A* to *G*, or if *G* can obviously win a popularity contest over *A*, the appellate court may even dare to praise *G* in terms not of law but of fairness and decency and excoriate *A* as a mere hobgoblin of an unenlightened era.

But because fairness and decency are seldom demonstrable, although they do exist, the rationale of decision does not always contain the reason for it. It would be a brave judge indeed who would ever admit in an opinion that his intuitive thought in an insurance coverage case is that if the fellow has paid his premiums he ought to have his coverage. But I strongly suspect that fleeting thoughts—such as, "No matter how good a tax lawyer one has, he still ought to pay *some* taxes"—have as much to do with the decision-making process, consciously or subconsciously, as do the articulated reasons.

Maybe the distinction is between the reason for a decision and its motivation. I leave to psychologists whether the two can be kept apart.

I am entirely convinced that the most compelling principle of decision in the area of constitutional law is pragmatism. I believe it entirely possible for a bright but "dumb" law student to memorize and fully grasp every constitutional maxim and be wholly unable to project future constitutional decisions. Logic, reason, and awareness of subordinate constitutional principles will not, I think, take one very far in this field. . . .

In no other area of the law is there more room for healthy skepticism of the articulated rationale of decision. The real question in these cases always seems to me to be whether the result will work in the national interest. I agreed to write this article in praise of pragmatism on the assumption that it would be demonstrable as the one great overriding principle in constitutional law.

II. THE TRIAL PROCESS

Llewellyn, A Realistic Jurisprudence— The Next Step*

The Place and Treatment of Paper Rules

Are "rules of law" in the accepted sense eliminated in such a course of thought? Somewhat obviously not. Whether they be pure paper rules, or are the accepted patter of the law officials, they remain present, and their presence remains an actuality—an actuality of importance—but an actuality whose *precise* importance, whose bearing and influence become clear. First of all they appear as what they are: rules of authoritative ought, addressed *to* officials, telling *officials* what the *officials* ought to do.[14] To which telling the officials either pay no heed at all (the pure paper rule; the dead-letter statute; the obsolete case) or listen partly (the rule "construed" out of recognition; the rule to which lip-service only is paid, while practice runs another course) or listen with all care (the rule with which the official practice pretty accurately coincides). I think that every such official precept-on-the-books (statute, doctrine laid down in the decision of a court, administrative regulation) tacitly contains an element of pseudo-description along with its statement of what officials ought to do; a tacit statement that officials do act according to the tenor of the rule; a tacit prediction that officials will act according to its tenor. Neither statement nor prediction is often true *in toto*. And the first point of the approach here made is skepticism as to the truth of either in the case in hand. Yet it is accepted convention to act and talk as if this statement and prediction were most solemn truth: a tradition marked peculiarly among the legal profession when engaged officially. It is indeed of

* [30 *Colum. L. Rev.* 431, 449-451 (1930). Reprinted by permission.
For biographical information, see page 212 supra.]
14. This I think holds true of *all* official ought-rules, irrespective of their form. I speak of their effects, not of their purposes. And the rights of laymen result through the screen of the official's practice, by a kind of social reflex. Ehrlich described the phenomenon cogently, so far as concerned the rules governing the set-up of the state governmental machine. A legal philosopher or a normatizer, with his mind fixed on the purpose of rules to ultimately affect the conduct of the "governed," will quarrel with this. A sociologist is content to see and describe what happens—and *compare* that with what is proposed.

first importance to remember that such a tradition contains a tendency to verify itself.[15] But no more so than to remember that such a tendency is no more powerful than its opposite: that other tendency to move quietly into falsifying the prediction in fact, while laying on an ointment of conventional words to soothe such as wish to believe the prediction has worked out.

Thus the problem of official formulations of rules and rights becomes complex. First, as to formulation already present, already existent; the accepted doctrine. There, I repeat, one lifts an eye canny and skeptical as to whether judicial behavior is in fact what the paper rule purports (implicitly) to state. One seeks the real practice on the subject, by study of how the cases do in fact eventuate. One seeks to determine how far the paper rule is real, how far *merely* paper.[16] One seeks an understanding of *actual* judicial behavior, in that comparison of rule with practice; one follows also the use made of the paper rule in agrument by judges and by counsel, and the apparent influence of its official presence on decisions. One seeks to determine when it is stated, but ignored; when it is stated and followed; when and why it is *expressly* narrowed or extended or modified, so that a new paper rule is created. One observes the level of *silent* application or modification or escape, in the "interpretation" of the facts of a case, in contrast to that other and quite distinct level of express wrestling with the language of the paper rule. One observes how strongly ingrained is the tradition of requiring a good paper justification, in terms of officially accepted paper rules, before any decision, however appealing on the facts, can be regarded as likely of acceptance. And by the same token, one observes the importance of the official formulae as tools of argument and persuasion; one observes both the stimuli to be derived from, and the limitations set by, their language. Very rapidly, too, one perceives that neither are all official formulae alike in these regards, nor are all courts, nor are all times and circumstances for the same formula in the same court. The *handling* of the official formulae to influence court behavior then comes to appear as an art, capable only to a limited extent of routinization or (to date) of accurate

15. Ehrlich, again, brings this out beautifully.

16. And on moving into the further fields of contact between judicial or official behavior and lay behavior, one gets into much deeper water: how does the paper rule work out (i.e., have a reflection or a counterpart in behavior) in lower court cases, unappealed? How often does it have any influence? What influence on administrative officials? On transactions between laymen which never reach any officials? All signs point to this being vastly more important than the set-up of doctrine, or even than the actual practices of higher courts. What is documented takes on a specious appearance of value, as against the unexplored.

and satisfying description. And the discrepancy, great or small, between the official formula and what actually results, obtains the limelight attention it deserves.

Frank, What Courts Do in Fact*

It is plain where all this leaves lawyers and clients. Jones and Smith enter into a transaction. Later a lawsuit arises concerning that transaction. If it is "contested," the court's decision (judgment) will turn on what the court will guess what that transaction was. That guess, made by the court, as to what happened, is by no means sure to be identical with what actually happened. Ergo, *the decision (judgment) was not knowable when Jones and Smith acted. It was not knowable when Jones consulted his lawyer, or Smith his lawyer.* (To lapse for the moment into verbiage I have promised to forego, the "law" and/or the legal "rights" and "duties" of Jones and Smith were unknown and unknowable when Jones and Smith acted or when they consulted their respective lawyers, because at that time no one could know whether there would be a lawsuit; or whether, if there was a lawsuit, it would be "contested"; or if it was "contested," what the court's guess would be as a result of hearing the conflicting testimony, or what would be the court's reaction to that guess.) . . .

But talks with candid judges have begun to disclose that, whatever is said in opinions, the judge often arrives at his decision before he tries to explain it. With little or no preliminary attention to legal rules or a definite statement of facts, he often makes up his mind that Jones should win the lawsuit, not Smith; that Mrs. White should have the custody of the children; that McCarthy should be reinstated as keeper of the dog pound. After the judge has so decided, then the judge writes his "opinion.". . .

The judge's opinion makes it *appear* as if the decision were a result solely of playing the game of law-in-discourse. But this explanation is often truncated, incomplete. Worse, it is frequently unreal, artificial, dis-

---

* [26 *Ill. L. Rev.* 645, 651, 653-655, 657, 662-663 (1932). Reprinted by permission of the Illinois Law Review (Northwestern University School of Law).

Jerome Frank (1889-1957) was educated at the University of Chicago (B.A. 1909; LL.B. 1912). Frank joined a Chicago law firm after graduation from law school, and then moved to a New York firm in 1927. He was appointed a Sterling Fellow at the Yale Law School in 1932. He served in various government positions in the New Deal era, and was appointed Chairman of the Securities and Exchange Commission in 1939. In 1941 he was appointed to the United States Court of Appeals for the Second Circuit, where he served until his death. His principal works are *Law and the Modern Mind* (1930), *If Men Were Angels* (1942), *Courts on Trial* (1949), and *Not Guilty* (with Barbara Frank Kristein, 1957).]

torted. It is in large measure an after-thought. It omits all mention of many of the factors which induced the judge to decide the case.[17] Those factors (even to the extent that the judge is aware of them) are excluded from the opinion. So far as opinions are concerned, those factors are tabu, unmentionables.

Opinions, then, disclose but little of how judges come to their conclusions. The opinions are often *ex post facto;* they are *censored expositions.* To study those eviscerated expositions as the principal bases of forecasts of future judicial action is to delude oneself.[18] It is far more unwise than it would be for a botanist to assume that plants are merely what appears above the ground, or for an anatomist to content himself with scrutinizing the outside of the body.

It is helpful for the lawyer to borrow the point of view of the political scientist and look at the judge as one kind of governmental official. When William Howard Taft, as President, gave his reasons for recommending or vetoing a bill, urging the adoption of a treaty, espousing a higher tariff, or finding that charges against his Secretary of the Interior were groundless, many wise students of government recognized that his explanations were sometimes artificial or incomplete and that sometimes he formulated them long after he had reached the decisions which he formally explained.[19] If William Howard Taft, when on the bench, followed a not unlike course, he was adopting the admitted practice of some of the ablest of those governmental officials we call judges. One recalls the story about Marshall (recently quoted by Llewellyn): "Judgment for the plaintiff; Mr. Justice Story will furnish the authorities."[20] Chancellor Kent, when off the bench, explained that in arriving at a ju-

---

17. The artificial character of opinions is usually not due to hypocrisy or intellectual or moral dishonesty. As I have devoted a considerable portion of a book to pointing out the unconscious self-deception involved in many judicial opinions, I shall not redevelop that thesis here. See Frank, loc. cit. [*Law and the Modern Mind*] 37, 120, 144-147, 152-153, 362, and the next instalment of this paper.

18. See Appendix to the next instalment of this article.

19. Cf. Senate Document No. 719, 61st Congress, 3d Session, Vol. I, 60-62.

20. Put that story in formal-law speech and it reads: "The general rule of law to be applied to a particular case must be conceived as existing before the particular concrete case to which it is applied occurred." Cf. Zane "German Legal Philosophy" (1918) 16 *Mich. Law Rev.* 287 at 311. Zane also says (338): "The rule of law and its application may be reached in a thousand different ways, but a judgment of a court is always this pure deduction. Now it must be apparent to any one who is willing to admit the rules governing rational mental action that unless the rule of the major premise exists as antecedent to the ascertainment of the fact or facts put into the minor premise, there is no judicial act in stating the judgment."

Of course, the mere fact that the reason given for an act or a judgment is *ex post facto*

dicial decision he first made himself "master of the facts." That done, he wrote,

> I saw where justice lay, and the moral sense decided the court half the time. I then sat down to search the authorities . . . I might once in a while be embarrassed by a technical rule, but I almost always found principles suited to my view of the case.

A member of an upper court once told me that the chief justice said to him after the oral argument of a case, "We'll have to lick that plaintiff somehow and it's up to you to find some theory and authorities that will help us to it." The chief justice of another important upper court recently wrote to a friend of mine that in his court it was the usual practice for the judges first to determine the "abstract justice" of a case and then to examine the "law."

How then does a judge arrive at his decision? In terse terms, he does so by a "hunch" as to what is fair and just or wise or expedient. So we have recently been advised by one of our ablest federal judges, Hutcheson.[21] The lawyer's task, then, becomes this: The determination of what produces the judge's hunches. What, then, does produce the judicial hunch? The answer must be vague: The effect of innumerable stimuli on what is loosely termed "the personality of the judge." If you have a liking for mathematical formulas you can let S be the stimuli, P be the judge's personality; D be the decision; you can then say "$S \times P = D$."

"The personality of the judge" is a phrase which too glibly describes an exquisitely complicated mass of phenomena.[22] The phrase "judicial hunch" is likewise beautifully vague. But those phrases will do for pres-

---

does not invalidate that reason. Jones may hit Smith, or vote for Hoover, or make love to a girl, or explore the arctic without reflecting on his conduct. When asked to explain or justify his acts he may give excellent reasons which are entirely satisfactory. But sometimes it is impossible to ascertain the soundness of those reasons because it is impossible to ascertain the truth of the facts asserted in his fact premise. This is peculiarly true of judicial opinions because the facts stated in the judge's fact premise are often "subjective." This point is discussed further in the next installment of this paper.

21. Hutcheson "The Judgment Intuitive: The Function of the 'Hunch' in Judicial Decisions" (1929) 14 *Cornell Law Quar.* 274. Cf. Douglas and Shanks in (1929) *Yale Law Jour.* 193. It should be said that Judge Hutcheson values the jury highly and, generally speaking, considers somewhat excessive such views on the judicial process as those expressed in this paper.

22. See Frank, loc. cit. 104-106, 114, 147, 338, note 7.

ent purposes. Be it noted then that "the personality of the judge" and the "judicial hunch" are not and cannot be described in terms of legal rules and principles.[23] They are therefore not recognized or referred to by formal law—except in jocular asides or allegedly humorous foot-notes. . . .

For the practicing lawyer and his client the specific decisions of actual specific cases are ultimates. Decisions, not opinions. What the lawyer and his client want are judgments and decrees—regardless of the presence or absence of concomitant opinions, irrespective of the contents of the opinions, if there are any.[27] . . .

8. Let us here take stock. (1) Specific enforceable decisions (i.e., judgments, orders, and decrees) in concrete cases are of the essence of the lawyer's work. All else is subsidiary. (2) Specific decisions are the result of the judge's hunches.[34] (3) To predict or bring about decisions, one should know something about what produces judicial hunches. (4) The so-called legal rules and principles are some of the many hunch producers. (5) Whatever may be the stimuli to the making of those hunches, those stimuli must operate through their effects of what may loosely be described as the judge's personality. (6) Neither the background stimuli nor the congeries labelled "judge's personality" are stated or statable in terms of the conventional legal rules and principles. (7) The failure to recognize the composite nature of this hunch and the artificial breaking up of the decisional process into "rules" and "facts" accounts in part for the delusion of the formalist as to the exclusive value of the "rules." (8) The formalist errs also in overlooking the circumstance that it is impossible to predict what cases will be "contested" and the subjective nature of the "facts" of a "contested" case and the resulting unchallengeability of the judge's statement of those "facts."[35] (9) The formalist conveniently neglects the jury.

23. The same is true of the innumerable external stimuli which activate the judge's personality and yield the hunch. In the equation $S \times P = D$, both S and P are the loosest of loose symbols. See further in the next instalment of this paper.

27. Of course, to the extent that the opinion in one case will be one of the stimuli producing decisions in future cases, the lawyer is interested in the opinion. See Frank, loc. cit. 104, 126-127, 130-131. This point will be further discussed in the next instalment of this paper. Nothing said in the text of this instalment is to be taken as indicating a belief that there are no such things as "legal rules, principles and precepts" or that they are without any effect on decisions.

34. As to the jury's, see Frank, loc. cit. 170-185.

35. See further discussion of this point in the Appendix to the next instalment of this paper.

F. S. Cohen, Transcendental Nonsense and the Functional Approach*

3. The Theory of Legal Decisions

The uses of the functional approach are not exhausted by "realistic jurisprudence." "Realistic jurisprudence," as that term is currently used,[80] is a theory of the nature of law, and therefore a theory of the nature of legal rules, legal concepts, and legal questions. Its essence is the definition of law as a function of judicial decisions. This definition is of tremendous value in the development of legal science, since it enables us to dispel the supernatural mists that envelop the legal order and to deal with the elements of the legal order in objective, scientific terms. But this process of definition and clarification is only a preliminary stage in the life of legal science. When we have analyzed legal rules and concepts as patterns of decisions, it becomes relevant to ask, "What are judicial decisions made of?"

If we conceive of legal rules and concepts as functions of judicial decisions, it is convenient, for purposes of this analysis, to think of these decisions as hard and simple facts. Just as every physical object may be analyzed as a complex of positive and negative electrons, so every legal institution, every legal rule or concept may be analyzed as a complex of plaintiff decisions and defendant decisions. But simplicity is relative to the level of analysis. For the chemist, the atom is the lowest term of analysis. But the physicist cannot stop the process of analysis with the atom or even the electron. It would be heresy to the faith of science to endow either with final simplicity and perpetual immunity from further analysis. Unfortunately, certain advocates of realistic jurisprudence, after using the functional method to break down rules and concepts into atomic decisions, refuse to go any further with the analytic process. They are willing to look upon decisions as simple unanalyzable products of judicial hunches or indigestion.

The "hunch" theory of law,[81] by magnifying the personal and acci-

* [35 *Colum. L. Rev.* 809, 842-847 (1935). Reprinted by permission.
For biographical information, see page 73 supra.]

80. See K. N. Llewellyn, A Realistic Jurisprudence—The Next Step (1930) 30 *Columbia Law Rev.* 431; Pound, The Call for a Realist Jurisprudence (1931) 44 *Harv. L. Rev.* 697; Llewellyn, Some Realism about Realism: Responding to Dean Pound (1931) 44 *Harv. L. Rev.* 1222.

81. See Hutcheson, The Judgment Intuitive: The Function of the "Hunch" in Judicial Decisions (1929) 14 *Corn. L.Q.* 274; Hutcheson, Lawyer's Law and the Little, Small Dice (1932) 7 *Tulane L. Rev.* 1; Frank, *Law and the Modern Mind* (1930) c. 12-13; T. Schroeder, The Psychologic Study of Judicial Opinions (1918) 6 *Calif. L. Rev.* 89.

dental factors in judicial behavior, implicitly denies the relevance of significant, predictable, social determinants that govern the course of judicial decision. Those who have advanced this viewpoint have performed a
real service in indicating the large realm of uncertainty in the actual law.
But actual experience does reveal a significant body of predictable uniformity in the behavior of courts. Law is not a mass of unrelated decisions nor a product of judicial bellyaches. Judges are human, but they
are a peculiar breed of humans, selected to a type and held to service
under a potent system of governmental controls. Their acts are "judicial" only within a system which provides for appeals, re-hearings, im-
peachments, and legislation. The decision that is "peculiar" suffers erosion—unless it represents the first salient manifestation of a new social
force, in which case it soon ceases to be peculiar. It is more useful to analyze a judicial "hunch" in terms of the continued impact of a judge's
study of precedents, his conversations with associates, his reading of
newspapers, and his recollections of college courses, than in strictly
physiological terms.

A truly realistic theory of judicial decisions must conceive every decision as something more than an expression of individual personality,
as concomitantly and even more importantly a function of social forces,
that is to say, as a product of social determinants and an index of social
consequences. A judicial decision is a social event. Like the enactment of
a Federal statute, or the equipping of police cars with radios, a judicial
decision is an intersection of social forces: Behind the decision are social
forces that play upon it to give it a resultant momentum and direction;
beyond the decision are human activities affected by it. The decision is
without significant social dimensions when it is viewed simply at the moment in which it is rendered. Only by probing behind the decision to the
forces which it reflects, or projecting beyond the decision the lines of its
force upon the future, do we come to an understanding of the meaning
of the decision itself. The distinction between "holding" and "dictum" in
any decision is not to be discovered by the logical inspection of the opinion or by historical inquiry into the actual facts of the case.[82] That distinction involves us in a prediction, a prophecy of the weight that courts will
give to future citations of the decision rendered. This is a question not of
pure logic but of human psychology, economics and politics.

82. Compare the orthodox wild goose chase of Goodhart after a formula which will
determine the "real" *ratio decidendi* of a case (Goodhart, Determining the Ratio Decidendi
of a Case (1930) 40 *Yale L.J.* 161) with the sane description by Llewellyn of the way in which
cases come to stand for propositions of narrow or wide scope. *The Bramble Bush* (1930) 47,
61-66. Cf. also Oliphant, A Return to Stare Decisis (1928) 6 *Am. L. School Rev.* 215, 217-
218; F. S. Cohen, *Ethical Systems and Legal Ideals* (1933) 33-37.

What is the meaning of a judicial decision, summed up in the words, "Judgment for the plaintiff"? Obviously, the significance of the decision, even for the parties directly involved in the case, depends upon certain predictable uniformities of official behavior, e.g., that a sheriff or marshall will enforce the decision, in one way or another, over a period of time, that the given decision will be respected or followed in the same court or other courts if the question at issue is relitigated, and that certain procedures will be followed in the event of an appeal, etc. When we go beyond the merely private significance of an actual decision, we are involved in a new set of predictions concerning the extent to which other cases, similiar in certain respects, are likely to receive the same treatment in the same courts or in other courts within a given jurisdiction. Except in the context of such predictions the announcement of a judicial decision is only a noise. If reasonably certain predictions of this sort could never be made, as Jerome Frank at times seems to say,[83] then all legal decisions would be simply noises, and no better grist for science than the magical phrases of transcendental jurisprudence.

If the understanding of any decision involves us necessarily in prophecy (and thus in history), then the notion of law as something that exists completely and systematically at any given moment in time is false.[84] Law is a social process, a complex of human activities, and an adequate legal science must deal with human activity, with cause and effect, with the past and the future. Legal science, as traditionally conceived, attempts to give an instantaneous snapshot of an existing and completed system of rights and duties. Within that system there are no temporal processes, no cause and no effect, no past and no future. A legal decision is thus conceived as a logical deduction from fixed principles. Its meaning is expressed only in terms of its logical consequences. A legal system, thus viewed, is as far removed from temporal activity as a system of pure geometry. In fact, jurisprudence is as much a part of pure mathematics as is algebra, unless it be conceived as a study of human behavior,— human behavior as it molds and is molded by judicial decisions. Legal systems, principles, rules, institutions, concepts, and decisions can be understood only as functions of human behavior.[85]

83. See Frank, *Law and the Modern Mind* (1930), 7, 53, 104-111, 132-134.
84. In this, law is no different from other social institutions or physical objects. Cf. C. I. Lewis, op. cit. supra note 48 [*Mind and the World-Order* (1929)], c. 5.
85. "To say that a legal institution—private property, the federal government of the United States, Columbia University,—exists is to say that a group of persons is doing something, is acting in some way. It is to point to a particular aspect of human behavior. . . . But a legal institution is something more than the way men act on a single occasion. . . . A legal institution is the happening over and over again of the same kind of behavior." U. Moore, loc. cit supra note 32. ["Rational Basis of Legal Institutions" 23 *Col. L. Rev.* 609 (1923).]

Such a view of legal science reveals gaps in our legal knowledge to which, I think, legal research will give increasing attention.

We are still in the stage of guesswork and accidentally collected information, when it comes to formulating the social forces which mold the course of judicial decision. We know, in a general way, that dominant economic forces play a part in judicial decision, that judges usually reflect the attitudes of their own income class on social questions, that their views on law are molded to a certain extent by their past legal experience as counsel for special interests, and that the impact of counsel's skill and eloquence is a cumulative force which slowly hammers the law into forms desired by those who can best afford to hire legal skill and eloquence; but nobody has ever charted, in scientific fashion, the extent of such economic influences.[86] We know, too, that judges are craftsmen, with aesthetic ideals,[87] concerned with the aesthetic judgments that the bar and the law schools will pass upon their awkward or skillful, harmonious or unharmonious, anomalous or satisfying, actions and theories; but again we have no specific information on the extent of this aesthetic bias in the various branches of the law. We know that courts are, at least in this country, a generally conservative social force, and more like a brake than a motor in the social mechanism, but we have no scientific factual comparison of judicial, legislative, and executive organs of government, from the standpoint of social engineering. Concretely and specifically, we know that Judge So-and-so, a former attorney for a non-union shop, has very definite ideas about labor injunctions, that another judge, who has had an unfortunate sex life, is parsimonious in the fixing of alimony; that another judge can be "fixed" by a certain political "boss"; that a series of notorious kidnappings will bring about a wave of maximum sentences in kidnapping cases. All this knowledge is useful to the practicing lawyer, to the public official, to the social reformer, and to the disinterested student of society. But it is most meager, and what little of it we have, individually, is not collectively available. There is at present

86. Promising first steps towards such a study have been taken in: Brooks Adams, op. cit. supra note 32 [Law and Inequality; Monopoly, in *Centralization and the Law* (1906) Lecture 2]; Gustavus Myers, *History of the Supreme Court* (1912); Boudin, op. cit. supra note 27 [*Government by Judiciary*] (1932); Walter Nelles, Commonwealth v. Hunt (1932) 32 *Columbia Law Rev.* 1128; Nelles, The First American Labor Case (1931) 41 *Yale L.J.* 165; Max Lerner, The Supreme Court and American Capitalism (1933) 42 *Yale L.J.* 668; W. Hamilton, Judicial Tolerance of Farmers' Cooperatives (1929) 38 *Yale L.J.* 936; articles of Haines [General Observations on the Effects of Personal, Political and Economic Influences in the Decisions of Judges (1922) 17 *Ill. L. Rev.* 96], Brown [Police Power—Legislation for Health and Personal Safety (1929) 42 *Harv. L. Rev.* 545], and Cushman [The Social and Economic Interpretation of the Fourteenth Amendment (1922) 20 *Mich. L. Rev.* 737] cited supra note 38.

87. Cf. F. S. Cohen, *Ethical Systems and Legal Ideals* (1933) 56-61; Modern Ethics and the Law (1934) 4 *Brooklyn L. Rev.* 33, 48-50.

no publication showing the political, economic, and professional background and activities of our various judges. Such a reference work would be exceedingly valuable, not only to the practical lawyer who wants to bring a motion or try a case before a sympathetic court, but also to the disinterested student of the law. Such a Judicial Index is not published, however, because it would be disrespectable.[88] According to the classical theory, these things have nothing to do with the way courts decide cases. A witty critic of the functional approach regards it as a *reductio ad absurdum* of this approach that law schools of the future may investigate judicial psychology, teach the art of bribery, and produce graduate detectives.[89] This is far from a *reductio ad absurdum.* Our understanding of the law will be greatly enriched when we learn more about how judges think, about the exact extent of judicial corruption, and about the techniques for investigating legally relevant facts. Of course, this knowledge may be used for improper purposes, but cannot the same be said of the knowledge which traditional legal education distributes?

If we know little today of the motivating forces which mold legal decisions, we know even less of the human consequences of these decisions. We do not even know how far the appellate cases, with which legal treatises are almost exclusively concerned, are actually followed in the trial courts.[90] Here, again, the experienced practitioner is likely to have accumulated a good deal of empirical information, but the young law clerk, just out of a first-rate law school, is not even aware that such a problem exists. Likewise, the problem of the actual enforcement of judgments has received almost no critical study. Discussion of the extent to which various statutes are actually enforced regularly moves in the thin air of polemic theory. It is usually practically impossible to find out whether a given statute has ever been enforced unless its enforcement has raised a legal tangle for appellate courts.

When we advance beyond the realm of official conduct and seek to discover the social consequences of particular statutes or decisions, we

88. Frank reports (*Law and the Modern Mind,* 112-115) the discontinuance of a statistical study of the decisions of various New York magistrates which revealed startling differences in the treatment of certain offenses.

89. Kantorowicz, Some Rationalism about Realism (1934) 43 *Yale L.J.* 1240.

90. The Institute of Law of Johns Hopkins broke the ice in the modern study of trial court decisions. See *Study of Civil Justice in New York* (1931). See also Marshall, *Study of Judicial System of Maryland* (1932); C. E. Clark, Fact Research in Law Administration (1928) 2 *Conn. Bar J.* 211; B. L. Shientag and F. S. Cohen, Summary Judgments in the Supreme Court of New York (1932) 32 *Columbia Law Rev.* 825, and works cited therein, notes 6 and 7; Saxe, Summary Judgments in New York—A Statistical Study (1934) 19 *Corn. L. Q.* 237; B. L. Shientag, Summary Judgment (1935) 4 *Fordham L. Rev.* 186.

find a few promising programs of research[91] but almost no factual studies.[92] Today the inclusion of factual annotations in a code, showing the extent and effects of law enforcement, would strike most lawyers as almost obscene. But notions of obscenity change, and every significant intellectual revolution raises to prominence facts once obscure and disrespectable. It is reasonable to expect that some day even the impudencies of Holmes and Llewellyn will appear sage and respectable.

Chayes, The Role of the Judge in Public Law Litigation*

I. The Received Tradition

The traditional conception of adjudication reflected the late nineteenth century vision of society, which assumed that the major social and economic arrangements would result from the activities of autonomous individuals. In such a setting, the courts could be seen as an adjunct to private ordering, whose primary function was the resolution of disputes about the fair implications of individual interactions. The basic concep-

91. See for example, Pound, The Scope and Purpose of Sociological Jurisprudence (1911-1912) 24 *Harv. L. Rev.* 591, 25 id. 140, 489; F. K. Beutel, Some Implications of Experimental Jurisprudence (1934) 48 *Harv. L. Rev.* 169, 191-194.

92. Notable exceptions are: McCracken, *Strike Injunctions in the New South* (1931); Brissenden and Swayzee, The Use of the Labor Injunction in the New York Needle Trades (1929) 44 *Pol. Sci. Q.* 548, (1930) 45 id. 87. In addition to these direct studies of the effects of legal rules or decisions, there is a growing literature on the social materials with which law is concerned. Examples of such work are: Pound and Frankfurter, *Criminal Justice in Cleveland* (1922); R. R. Powell and Looker, Decedents' Estates: Illumination from Probate and Tax Records (1930) 30 *Columbia Law Rev.* 919; Smith, Lilly and Dowling, Compensation for Automobile Accidents: A Symposium (1932) 32 *Columbia Law Rev.* 785; S. and E. T. Glueck, Predictability in the Administration of Criminal Justice (1929) 42 *Harv. L. Rev.* 297.

* [89 *Harv. L. Rev.* 1281, 1285-1304 (1976). Reprinted by permission.

Abram Chayes (1922–) was educated at Harvard University (A.B. 1943; LL.B. 1949). He was President and Note Editor of the Harvard Law Review. Chayes held various legal posts for the State of Connecticut and for the federal government. He was Law Clerk (1951-1952) to Justice Felix Frankfurter of the United States Supreme Court. After three years in private practice, he joined the faculty of Harvard University School of Law in 1955 and became Professor of Law three years later. Chayes left Harvard in 1961, but returned in 1965, having spent the intervening years as Legal Advisor, U.S. Department of State (1961-1964) and in private practice (1964-1965). He is currently Felix Frankfurter Professor of Law, Harvard University. His published works include *The International Legal Process* (with Ehrlich & Lowenfeld, 1968), *Satellite Broadcasting* (with Fawcett, Ito & Kiss, 1968), and *ABM: An Evaluation of the Decision to Deploy an Anti-Missile System* (with Weisner, 1969).]

tions governing legal liability were "intention" and "fault." Intentional arrangements, not in conflict with more or less universal attitudes like opposition to force or fraud, were entitled to be respected, and other private activities to be protected unless culpable. Government regulatory action was presumptively suspect, and was tested by what was in form a common law action against the offending official in his private person. The predominating influence of the private law model can be seen even in constitutional litigation, which, from its first appearance in *Marbury v. Madison,* was understood as an outgrowth of the judicial duty to decide otherwise-existing private disputes.

Litigation also performed another important function—clarification of the law to guide future private actions. This understanding of the legal system, together with the common law doctrine of stare decisis, focussed professional and scholarly concern on adjudication at the appellate level, for only there did the process reach beyond the immediate parties to achieve a wider import through the elaboration of generally applicable legal rules. So, in the academic debate about the judicial function, the protagonist was the appellate judge (not, interestingly enough, the appellate *court*), and the spotlight of teaching, writing, and analysis was almost exclusively on appellate decisions. In practice, the circle was even more narrowly confined to the decisions of the United States Supreme Court, the English high courts (though decreasingly so in recent years), and a few "influential" federal and state appellate judges. As to this tiny handful of decisions subjected to critical scrutiny, the criterion for evaluation was primarily the technical skill of the opinion in disposing of the case adequately within the framework of precedent and other doctrinal materials, so as to achieve an increasingly more systematic and refined articulation of the governing legal rules.

In contrast to the appellate court, to which the motive power in the system was allocated, the functions of the trial judge were curiously neglected in the traditional model. Presumably, the trial judge, like the multitude of private persons who were supposed to order their affairs with reference to appellate pronouncements, would be governed by those decisions in disposing smoothly and expeditiously of the mine-run of cases. But if only by negative implication, the traditional conception of adjudication carried with it a set of strong notions about the role of the trial judge. In general he was passive. He was to decide only those issues identified by the parties, in accordance with the rules established by the appellate courts, or, infrequently, the legislature.

Passivity was not limited to the law aspects of the case. It was strikingly manifested in the limited involvement of the judge in factfinding. Indeed, the sharp distinction that Anglo-American law draws between factfinding and law declaration is itself remarkable. In the developed common law system, these were not only regarded as analytically distinct processes, but each was assigned to a different tribunal for performance. The jury found the facts. The judge was a neutral umpire, charged with little or no responsibility for the factual aspects of the case or for shaping and organizing the litigation for trial.

Because the immediate impact of the judgment was confined to the parties, the traditional model was relatively relaxed about the accuracy of its factfinding. If the facts were not assumed as stated in the pleadings or on the view most favorable to one of the parties or determined on the basis of burdens or presumptions, they were remitted to a kind of black box, the jury. True, some of the law of evidence reflects an active suspicion of the jury. And if the evidence adduced would not "rationally" support a finding for one party or the other, the case could be taken from the jury. But the limits of rationality are inevitably commodious. Even law application, unless there was a special verdict (never much favored in this country), was left to the jury's relatively untrammeled discretion. Indeed, one of the virtues of the jury was thought to be its exercise of a rough-hewn equity, deviating from the dictates of the law where justice or changing community mores required.

The emphasis on systematic statement of liability rules involved a corresponding disregard of the problems of relief. There was, to be sure, a good deal of discussion of measure of damages, as a corollary to the analysis of substantive rights and duties. Similarly, the question of the availability of specific performance and other equitable remedies came in for a share of attention. But the discussion was carried forward within the accepted framework that compensatory money damages was the usual form of relief. Prospective relief was highly exceptional in the traditional model and was largely remitted to the discretion of the trial judge.

So in theory. But from another perspective, it seems remarkable that the system—and for the most part its critics as well—could attach so much importance to uniformity and consistency of doctrinal statement in appellate opinions, while at the same time displaying an almost complete lack of curiosity about actual uniformity of decision in the vast bulk of cases heard. The realist analysis, which demonstrated the painful inevitability of choice for appellate judges on questions of law, was equally applicable at the trial level. The uncertainties introduced by remitting factfinding and fact characterization to the jury were also ignored. Such factors as differences among potential litigants in practical access to the system or in the availability of litigating resources were not even perceived as problems. Although it was well that particular disputes should be fairly settled, there was comfort in the thought that the consequences of the settlement would be confined to the individuals involved. And

295

since the parties controlled the litigating process, it was not unfair to cast the burden of any malfunction upon them.

Besides its inherent plausibility in the nineteenth century American setting, the traditional model of adjudication answered a number of important political and intellectual needs. The conception of litigation as a private contest between private parties with only minimal judicial intrusion confirmed the general view of government powers as stringently limited. The emphasis on the appellate function, conceived as an exercise in deduction from a few embracing principles themselves induced from the data of the cases, supplied the demand of the new legal academics for an intellectual discipline comparable to that of their faculty colleagues in the sciences, and for a body of teachable materials. For practitioners and judges, the same conception provided a professional methodology that could be self-consciously employed. Most importantly, the formulation operated to legitimate the increasingly visible political consequences of the actions of a judiciary that was not politically accountable in the usual sense.

II. The Public Law Litigation Model

Sometime after 1875, the private law theory of civil adjudication became increasingly precarious in the face of a growing body of legislation designed explicitly to modify and regulate basic social and economic arrangements. At the same time, the scientific and deductive character of judicial lawmaking came under attack, as the political consequences of judicial review of that legislation became urgent.

These developments are well known and have become an accepted part of our political and intellectual history. I want to address in somewhat greater detail the correlative changes that have occurred in the procedural structure of the lawsuit. Most discussion of these procedural developments, while recognizing that change has been far-reaching, proceeds on the assumption that the new devices are no more than piecemeal "reforms" aimed at improving the functional characteristics or the efficiency of litigation conducted essentially in the traditional mode. I suggest, however, that these developments are interrelated as members of a recognizable, if changing, system and that taken together they display a new model of judicial action and the judicial role, both of which depart sharply from received conceptions.

A. The Demise of the Bipolar Structure

Joinder of parties, which was strictly limited at common law, was verbally liberalized under the codes to conform with the approach of equity calling for joinder of all parties having an "interest" in the controversy. The codes, however, did not at first produce much freedom of joinder. Instead, the courts defined the concept of "interest" narrowly to exclude those without an independent legal right to the remedy to be given in the main dispute. The definition itself illustrates the continuing power of the traditional model. The limited interpretation of the joinder provisions ultimately fell before the banners of "rationality" and "efficiency." But the important point is that the narrow joinder rule could be perceived as irrational or inefficient only because of a growing sense that the effects of the litigation were not really confined to the persons at either end of the right-remedy axis.

The familiar story of the attempted liberalization of pleadings under the codes is not dissimilar. Sweeping away the convolutions of the forms of action did not lead to the hoped-for elimination of technicality and formality in pleading. The immediate response was the construction of cause-of-action rules that turned out to be almost as intricate as the forms themselves. The power of the right-remedy connection was at work here too, but so also was the late nineteenth century impulse toward systemization, which tended to focus attention on accurate statement of legal theory. The proponents of "efficiency" argued for a more informal and flexible approach, to the end that the courts should not have to rehear the same complex of events. This argument ultimately shifted the focus of the lawsuit from legal theory to factual context—the "transaction or occurrence" from which the action arose. This in turn made it easier to view the set of events in dispute as giving rise to a range of legal consequences all of which ought to be considered together.

This more open-ended view of the subject matter of the litigation fed back upon party questions and especially intervention. Here, too, the sharp constraints dictated by the right-remedy nexus give way. And if the right to participate in litigation is no longer determined by one's claim to relief at the hands of another party or one's potential liability to satisfy the claim, it becomes hard to draw the line determining those who may participate so as to eliminate anyone who is or might be significantly (a weasel word) affected by the outcome—and the latest revision of the Federal Rules of Civil Procedure has more or less abandoned the attempt.

The question of the right to intervene is inevitably linked to the question of standing to initiate litigation in the first place. The standing issue could hardly arise at common law or under early code pleading rules, that is, under the traditional model. There the question of plaintiff's standing merged with the legal merits: On the facts pleaded, does this particular plaintiff have a right to the particular relief sought from the particular defendant from whom he is seeking it? With the erosion

297

of the tight structural integration of the lawsuit, the pressure to expand the circle of potential plaintiffs has been inexorable. Today, the Supreme Court is struggling manfully, but with questionable success, to establish a formula for delimiting who may sue that stops short of "anybody who might be significantly affected by the situation he seeks to litigate."

"Anybody"— even "almost anybody"— can be a lot of people, particularly where the matters in issue are not relatively individualized private transactions or encounters. Thus, the stage is set for the class action, which is discussed at length in the remainder of this issue. Whatever the resolution of the current controversies surrounding class actions, I think it unlikely that the class action will ever be taught to behave in accordance with the precepts of the traditional model of adjudication. The class suit is a reflection of our growing awareness that a host of important public and private interactions—perhaps the most important in defining the conditions and opportunities of life for most people—are conducted on a routine or bureaucratized basis and can no longer be visualized as bilateral transactions between private individuals. From another angle, the class action responds to the proliferation of more or less well-organized groups in our society and the tendency to perceive interests as group interests, at least in very important aspects.

The emergence of the group as the real subject or object of the litigation not only transforms the party problem, but raises far-reaching new questions. How far can the group be extended and homogenized? To what extent and by what methods will we permit the presentation of views diverging from that of the group representative? When the judgment treads on numerous—perhaps innumerable—absentees, can the traditional doctrines of finality and preclusion hold? And in the absence of a particular client, capable of concretely defining his own interest, can we rely on the assumptions of the adversary system as a guide to the conduct and duty of the lawyer?

These questions are brought into sharp focus by the class action device. But it would be a mistake to think that they are confined to that procedural setting. The class action is only one mechanism for presenting group interests for adjudication, and the same basic questions will arise in a number of more familiar litigating contexts. Indeed, it may not be too much to say that they are pervasive in the new model.

B. The Triumph of Equity

One of the most striking procedural developments of this century is the increasing importance of equitable relief. It is perhaps too soon to reverse the traditional maxim to read that money damages will be awarded only when no suitable form of specific relief can be devised. But surely, the old sense of equitable remedies as "extraordinary" has faded.

I am not concerned here with specific performance—the compelled transfer of a piece of land or a unique thing. This remedy is structurally little different from traditional money-damages. It is a one-time, one-way transfer requiring for its enforcement no continuing involvement of the court. Injunctive relief, however, is different in kind, even when it takes the form of a simple negative order. Such an order is a presently operative prohibition, enforceable by contempt, and it is a much greater constraint on activity than the risk of future liability implicit in the damage remedy. Moreover, the injunction is continuing. Over time, the parties may resort to the court for enforcement or modification of the original order in light of changing circumstances. Finally, by issuing the injunction, the court takes public responsibility for any consequences of its decree that may adversely affect strangers to the action.

Beyond these differences, the prospective character of the relief introduces large elements of contingency and prediction into the proceedings. Instead of a dispute retrospectively oriented toward the consequences of a closed set of events, the court has a controversy about future probabilities. Equitable doctrine, naturally enough, given the intrusiveness of the injunction and the contingent nature of the harm, calls for a balancing of the interests of the parties. And if the immediate parties' interests were to be weighed and evaluated, it was not too difficult to proceed to a consideration of other interests that might be affected by the order.

The comparative evaluation of the competing interests of plaintiff and defendant required by the remedial approach of equity often discloses alternatives to a winner-takes-all decision. An arrangement might be fashioned that could safeguard at least partially the interests of both parties, and perhaps even of others as well. And to the extent such an arrangement is possible, equity seems to require it. Negative orders directed to one of the parties—even though pregnant with affirmative implications—are often not adequate to this end. And so the historic power of equity to order affirmative action gradually freed itself from the encrustation of nineteenth century restraints. The result has often been a decree embodying an affirmative regime to govern the range of activities in litigation and having the force of law for those represented before the court.

At this point, right and remedy are pretty thoroughly disconnected. The form of relief does not flow ineluctably from the liability determination, but is fashioned ad hoc. In the process, moreover, right and remedy have been to some extent transmuted. The liability determination is not simply a pronouncement of the legal consequences of past events, but to some extent a prediction of what is likely to be in the future. And relief is not a terminal, compensatory transfer, but an effort to devise a program to contain future consequences in a way that accommodates the range of interests involved.

The interests of absentees, recognized to some extent by equity's balancing of the public interest in individual suits for injunction, become more pressing as social and economic activity is increasingly organized through large aggregates of people. An order nominally addressed to an individual litigant—the labor injunction is an early example—has obvious and visible impact on persons not individually before the court. Nor must the form of the action be equitable: A suit against an individual to collect a tax, if it results in a determination of the constitutional invalidity of the taxing statute, has the same result for absentees as a grant or denial of an injunction. Statutory construction, for example of welfare or housing legislation, may have a similar extended impact, again even if the relief is not equitable in form. Officials will almost inevitably act in accordance with the judicial interpretation in the countless similar situations cast up by a sprawling bureaucratic program. We may call this a *stare decisis* effect, but it is quite different from the traditional image of autonomous adjustment of individual private transactions in response to judicial decisions. In cases of this kind, the fundamental conception of litigation as a mechanism for private dispute settlement is no longer viable. The argument is about whether or how a government policy or program shall be carried out.

Recognition of the policy functions of litigation feeds the already intense pressure against limitations on standing, as well as against the other traditional limitations on justiciability—political question, ripeness, mootness and the like. At the same time, the breadth of interests that may be affected by public law litigation raises questions about the adequacy of the representation afforded by a plaintiff whose interest is narrowly traditional.

Again, as in private litigation, the screw gets another turn when simple prohibitory orders are inadequate to provide relief. If a mental patient complains that he has been denied a right to treatment, it will not do to order the superintendent to "cease to deny" it. So with segregation in education, discrimination in hiring, apportionment of legislative districts, environmental management. And the list could be extended. If judicial intervention is invoked on the basis of congressional enactment, the going assumption is that the statute embodies an affirmative regulatory objective. Even when the suit is premised on constitutional provisions, traditionally regarded as constraining government power, there is an increasing tendency to treat them as embodying affirmative values, to be fostered and encouraged by judicial action. In either case, if litigation discloses that the relevant purposes or values have been frustrated, the relief that seems to be called for is often an affirmative program to implement them. And courts, recognizing the undeniable presence of competing interests, many of them unrepresented by the litigants, are increasingly faced with the difficult problem of shaping relief to give due weight to the concerns of the unrepresented.

C. The Changing Character of Factfinding

The traditional model of adjudication was primarily concerned with assessing the consequences for the parties of specific past instances of conduct. This retrospective orientation is often inapposite in public law litigation, where the lawsuit generally seeks to enjoin future or threatened action, or to modify a course of conduct presently in train or a condition presently existing. In the former situation, the question whether threatened action will materialize, in what circumstances, and with what consequences can, in the nature of things, be answered only by an educated guess. In the latter case, the inquiry is only secondarily concerned with how the condition came about, and even less with the subjective attitudes of the actors, since positive regulatory goals are ordinarily defined without reference to such matters. Indeed, in dealing with the actions of large political or corporate aggregates, notions of will, intention, or fault increasingly become only metaphors.

In the remedial phases of public law litigation, factfinding is even more clearly prospective. As emphasized above, the contours of relief are not derived logically from the substantive wrong adjudged, as in the traditional model. The elaboration of a decree is largely a discretionary process within which the trial judge is called upon to assess and appraise the consequences of alternative programs that might correct the substantive fault. In both the liability and remedial phases, the relevant inquiry is largely the same: How can the policies of a public law best be served in a concrete case?

In public law litigation, then, factfinding is principally concerned with "legislative" rather than "adjudicative" fact. And "fact evaluation" is perhaps a more accurate term than "factfinding." The whole process begins to look like the traditional description of legislation: Attention is drawn to a "mischief," existing or threatened, and the activity of the parties and court is directed to the development of on-going measures designed to cure that mischief. Indeed, if, as is often the case, the decree sets up an affirmative regime governing the activities in controversy for the indefinite future and having binding force for persons within its ambit, then it is not very much of a stretch to see it as, *pro tanto*, a legislative act.

Given these consequences, the casual attitude of the traditional model toward factfinding is no longer tolerable. The extended impact of the judgment demands a more visibly reliable and credible procedure for establishing and evaluating the fact elements in the litigation, and one that more explicitly recognizes the complex and continuous interplay between fact evaluation and legal consequence. The major response to the new requirements has been to place the responsibility for factfinding increasingly on the trial judge. The shift was in large part accomplished as a function of the growth of equitable business in the federal courts, for historically the chancellor was trier of fact in suits in equity. But on the "law side" also, despite the Supreme Court's expansion of the federal right to jury trial, there has been a pronounced decline in the exercise of the right, apart, perhaps, from personal injury cases.

The courts, it seems, continue to rely primarily on the litigants to produce and develop factual materials, but a number of factors make it impossible to leave the organization of the trial exclusively in their hands. With the diffusion of the party structure, fact issues are no longer sharply drawn in a confrontation between two adversaries, one asserting the affirmative and the other the negative. The litigation is often extraordinarily complex and extended in time, with a continuous and intricate interplay between factual and legal elements. It is hardly feasible and, absent a jury, unnecessary to set aside a contiguous block of time for a "trial stage" at which all significant factual issues will be presented. The scope of the fact investigation and the sheer volume of factual material that can be exhumed by the discovery process pose enormous problems of organization and assimilation. All these factors thrust the trial judge into an active role in shaping, organizing and facilitating the litigation. We may not yet have reached the investigative judge of the continental systems, but we have left the passive arbiter of the traditional model a long way behind.

D. The Decree

The centerpiece of the emerging public law model is the decree. It differs in almost every relevant characteristic from relief in the traditional model of adjudication, not the least in that it *is* the centerpiece. The decree seeks to adjust future behavior, not to compensate for past wrong. It is deliberately fashioned rather than logically deduced from the nature of the legal harm suffered. It provides for a complex, on-going regime of performance rather than a simple, one-shot, one-way transfer. Finally, it prolongs and deepens, rather than terminates, the court's involvement with the dispute.

The decree is also an order of the court, signed by the judge and issued under his responsibility (itself a shift from the classical money judgment). But it cannot be supposed that the judge, at least in a case of any complexity, composes it out of his own head. How then is the relief formulated?

The reports provide little guidance on this question. Let me none-theless suggest a prototype that I think finds some support in the available materials. The court will ask the parties to agree on an order or it will ask one party to prepare a draft. In the first case, a negotiation is stipulated. In the second, the dynamic leads almost inevitably in that direction. The draftsman understands that his proposed decree will be subject to comment and objection by the other side and that it must be approved by the court. He is therefore likely to submit it to his opponents in advance to see whether differences cannot be resolved. Even if the court itself should prepare the initial draft of the order, some form of negotiation will almost inevitably ensue upon submission of the draft to the parties for comment.

The negotiating process ought to minimize the need for judicial resolution of remedial issues. Each party recognizes that it must make some response to the demands of the other party, for issues left unresolved will be submitted to the court, a recourse that is always chancy and may result in a solution less acceptable than might be reached by horse-trading. Moreover, it will generally be advantageous to the demanding party to reach a solution through accommodation rather than through a judicial fiat that may be performed "in a literally compliant but substantively grudging and unsatisfactory way." Thus, the formulation of the decree in public law litigation introduces a good deal of party control over the practical outcome. Indeed, relief by way of order after a determination on the merits tends to converge with relief through a consent decree or voluntary settlement. And this in turn mitigates a major theoretical objection to affirmative relief—the danger of intruding on an elaborate and organic network of interparty relationships.

Nevertheless it cannot be supposed that this process will relieve the court entirely of responsibility for fashioning the remedy. The parties may fail to agree. Or the agreement reached may fail to comport with the requirements of substantive law as the judge sees them. Or the interests of absentees may be inadequately accommodated. In these situations, the judge will not, as in the traditional model, be able to derive his responses directly from the liability determination, since, as we have seen, the substantive law will point out only the general direction to be pursued and a few salient landmarks to be sought out or avoided. How then is the judge to prescribe an appropriate remedy?

If the parties are simply in disagreement, it seems plausible to suppose that the judge's choice among proposals advanced by the *quondam* negotiators will be governed by his appraisal of their good faith in seeking a way to implement the constitutional or statutory command as he has construed it. The interest in a decree that will be voluntarily obeyed can be promoted by enforcing a regime of good faith bargaining among the parties. Without detailed knowledge of the negotiations, however, any attempt to enforce such a regime can rest on little more than an uneasy base of intuition and impression. Where a proposed decree is agreed among the parties, but is inadequate because the interests shared by the litigants do not span the range that the court thinks must be taken into account, resubmission for further negotiation may not cure this fundamental defect. Here too, the judge will be unable to fill the gap without a detailed understanding of the issues at stake in the bargaining among the parties.

For these reasons, the judge will often find himself a personal participant in the negotiations on relief. But this course has obvious disadvantages, not least in its inroads on the judge's time and his pretentions to disinterestedness. To avoid these problems, judges have increasingly resorted to outside help—masters, amici, experts, panels, advisory committees—for information and evaluation of proposals for relief. These outside sources commonly find themselves exercising mediating and even adjudicatory functions among the parties. They may put forward their own remedial suggestions, whether at the request of the judge or otherwise.

Once an ongoing remedial regime is established, the same procedure may be repeated in connection with the implementation and enforcement of the decree. Compliance problems may be brought to the court for resolution and, if necessary, further remediation. Again, the court will often have no alternative but to resort to its own sources of information and evaluation.

I suggested above that a judicial decree establishing an ongoing affirmative regime of conduct is *pro tanto* a legislative act. But in actively shaping and monitoring the decree, mediating between the parties, developing his own sources of expertise and information, the trial judge has passed beyond even the role of legislator and has become a policy planner and manager.

E. A Morphology of Public Law Litigation

The public law litigation model portrayed in this paper reverses many of the crucial characteristics and assumptions of the traditional concept of adjudication:

(1) The scope of the lawsuit is not exogenously given but is shaped primarily by the court and parties.

(2) The party structure is not rigidly bilateral but sprawling and amorphous.

(3) The fact inquiry is not historical and adjudicative but predictive and legislative.

(4) Relief is not conceived as compensation for past wrong in a form logically derived from the substantive liability and confined in its impact to the immediate parties; instead, it is forward looking, fashioned ad hoc on flexible and broadly remedial lines, often having important consequences for many persons including absentees.

(5) The remedy is not imposed but negotiated.

(6) The decree does not terminate judicial involvement in the affair: its administration requires the continuing participation of the court.

(7) The judge is not passive, his function limited to analysis and statement of governing legal rules; he is active, with responsibility not only for credible fact evaluation but for organizing and shaping the litigation to ensure a just and viable outcome.

(8) The subject matter of the lawsuit is not a dispute between private individuals about private rights, but a grievance about the operation of public policy.

In fact, one might say that, from the perspective of the traditional model, the proceeding is recognizable as a lawsuit only because it takes place in a courtroom before an official called a judge. But that is surely too sensational in tone. All of the procedural mechanisms outlined above were historically familiar in equity practice. It is not surprising that they should be adopted and strengthened as the importance of equity has grown in modern times.

We have yet to ask how pervasive is the new model. Is it, as was traditional equity, a supplementary weapon in the judicial armory, destined at best for a subordinate role? Is it a temporary, add-on phenomenon, more extensive perhaps, but not more significant than the railroad reorganization functions that the courts assumed (or were given) in other times? Or can we say that the new form has already or is likely to become the dominant form of litigation in the federal courts, either in terms of judicial resources applied to such cases, or in its impact on society and on attitudes toward the judicial role and function?

The question is not wholly quantitative, but certainly it has a quantitative dimension. A crude index for the new model in federal civil litigation is the well-known shift from diversity to federal question cases in the federal courts. Since most of the features I have discussed derive from the fact that public law provides the basis of the action, it seems plausible that litigation in the new model would increase concomitantly with the predominance of federal question jurisdiction. But the quantitative analysis is in patent need of much further development.

On the other hand, qualitatively—that is, in terms of the importance and interest of the cases and their impact on the public perception of the legal system—it seems abundantly clear that public law litigation is of massive and growing significance. The cases that are the focus of professional debate, law review and academic comment, and journalistic attention are overwhelmingly, I think, new model cases. It could hardly be otherwise, since, by hypothesis, these cases involve currently agitated questions of public policy, and their immediate consequences are to a considerable extent generalized.

I would, I think, go further and argue that just as the traditional concept reflected and related to a system in which social and economic arrangements were remitted to autonomous private action, so the new model reflects and relates to a regulatory system where these arrangements are the product of positive enactment. In such a system, enforcement and application of law is necessarily implementation of regulatory policy. Litigation inevitably becomes an explicitly political forum and the court a visible arm of the political process.

Rosenberg, Contemporary Litigation in the United States*

If colonial Americans ever were shy about suing one another, their descendants have shed every vestige of the trait. In the nation's bicentennial year there is abroad in the land an abandoned eagerness to hail into court all and sundry. The dubious joys of litigating fall literally upon millions each year. For reasons to be explored, the society seems bent on waging total law and the courts have been made the main battlegrounds.

* [From *Legal Institutions Today: English and American Approaches Compared,* Harry Jones, ed., 152-161 (1977). This paper was commissioned and published as part of Bicentennial observation by the American Bar Association. Reprinted by permission.

In them are deployed an army of upwards of 20,000 judges. Supporting these are hundreds of thousands of lawyers, heavily armed with fearsome engines capable of firing barrages at 500 copies a minute, supported by batteries of self-correcting typewriters, and using supplies of paper in quantities large enough to fill craters or empty forests. . . .

In this century in the United States the fever to sue has been a dominant trait; for more than a generation it has been at an uncomfortably elevated pitch. Yet we seem not only to survive, but even to thrive. Can it actually be good for a society to be quick to quarrel in courts? As to that, reasonable minds differ; but whether hairtrigger suing is good or bad, we ought to know all we can discover about the factors that stimulate it. . . .

In heading for court, potential plaintiffs find themselves aided by institutional arrangements that tend to make lawsuits in this country easy to maintain and tolerable to lose. First of these is the contingent fee. A few preliminary observations are offered here regarding this strange phenomenon; later it receives closer inspection. When someone wants advice about a claim in which a sizeable recovery beckons and the chances are not far-fetched, lawyers respond zestfully. They are ready to take the case without the client's agreeing to part with any money at the outset or obliging himself to pay a fee if the suit fails at the end. Lawyers in America are generally content to risk their services on the contingency that if a recovery is realized by settlement or judgment, a slice will be lopped off as the lawyer's share—usually one-third, give or take.[1] There is no doubt that many clients who would not advance a single dollar of their own to pay the lawyer's services are more than willing to promise the lawyer a fractional share of any recovery in return for representation. Thus, the contingent fee lubricates the machinery of the private bar. This is particularly true in personal injury cases, which are high in volume and high in economic significance, contributing as they do no less than $1 billion a year to lawyers' income.

Maurice Rosenberg (1919–) received an A.B. from Syracuse University (1940) and an LL.B. from Columbia University (1947). From 1947 to 1949 he was secretary to Judge Stanley H. Field, New York Court of Appeals. He practiced law in New York City for the next seven years, until joining the faculty of Columbia University as Associate Professor of Law in 1956. Since 1958, he has been Professor of Law at Columbia. He has served as Chairman of the Advisory Council for Appellate Justice (1971-1976) and President of the Association of American Law Schools (1973). He is author of *The Pre-Trial Conference and Effective Justice* (1964), and a co-author of *Civil Procedure* (with Weinstein, Smit, & Korn, 1976) and *Justice on Appeal* (with Carrington and Meador, 1976).]

1. Rosenberg & Sovern, Delay and the Dynamics of Personal Injury Litigation, 59 *Colum. L. Rev.* 1115 (1959); Franklin, Chanin & Mark, Accidents, Money and the Law: A Study of the Economics of Personal Injury Litigation, 61 *Colum. L. Rev.* 1 (1961).

A second institutional arrangement that eases and even promotes litigating is the emergence of new forms of advocacy enterprises. Some are governmental; others are non-official but public in their resource base; still others are adjuncts to organizations formed for purposes apart from litigating; and yet others are agents of group legal insurance ventures. Many of them are merely high-energy mutations of legal aid societies and ethnically- or racially-oriented advocacy facilities attached to parent organizations. Some have sprung up in only the past dozen years in reflection of the society's growing concern for legally defenseless indigent persons, inmates of mental or penal institutions, and the large, amorphous "consumer" groupings that at one time or another include nearly everyone. For the most part these organizations carry on the advocate's classic function of serving clients—although sometimes on a wholesale basis rather than singly. In contrast are some other recently developed advocacy enterprises that concentrate on serving causes rather than clients as such. The causes are the ones those who run the firms identify with the public interest. Public interest law firms have an affinity for large social issues: threats to the ecological balance, concentration of economic power, business practices hurtful to consumers, and the like.

Whether the institutional advocates are at work on lawsuits to redress massive social failures or to remedy a perceived legal injury to an individual client, they have a common attribute of immense significance for most civil litigation in the United States. They have set aside the well-known process of comparing dollar costs with dollar benefits, the calculation that traditionally influenced the client's decision to go to law or not, and that ordinarily impelled adversaries to settle at less than the best figure they hoped for, in order to avoid the risk and expense of persisting to judgment. A decade ago a person of severely limited means who bought an allegedly defective washing machine for $250 or who became embroiled in a quarrel with the landlord over replacing a $100 sink would not have thought of retaining a lawyer for several times the sum involved to press the claims in court. Today, wherever access to public-funded legal services for have-not persons is available, cost is no longer a strong restraint on the urge to sue. Dramatic evidence of this is the fact that the United States Congress has shown, by creating the Legal Services Corporation with funding over the $100,000,000-a-year level,[2] it is prepared to pay from the general treasury to vindicate the legal interests of indigents. This is a highly visible embodiment of the perceptible shift to cost-free legal assistance for persons with dollar-measured claims who

2. 25 *Higher Education and National Affairs,* No. 21, at 2 (May 28, 1976).

not only lack the money to go to law, but who if they did have the funds to cover their legal expenses, would rarely if ever spend them to litigate over the lesser stakes in controversy.

There is nothing new about society's providing courts that absorb more tax money to try a particular case than the case itself involves. What is new is a full-scale commitment to support and encourage claimants regularly to invoke public resources exceeding the amounts they seek to recover or protect without investing any of their own resources. To point this out is not to say that poor persons of modest economic means are less than fully deserving of society's concern and help in their skirmishes with merchants, manufacturers, bureaucrats and landlords. In the annals of the poor, petty torments are more likely events than colossal injustices; and from being neglected minor grievances can swell to full-blown outrage. They most certainly deserve melioration. The serious question is whether they do not deserve relief more promptly, less agonizingly and with more sensitivity to cost-benefit relations than launching all-out litigation entails.[3]

In cause-oriented suits, money costs are by definition no object. They are conducted by advocacy enterprises that are expected and paid to litigate. Among these entities are public interest law firms, agencies for environmental protection, and defense funds for inmates, consumers and demographically identifiable groups of many kinds. While institutional advocates for causes welcome recapturing at least their expenses if their suit prevails, and keep pressing for laws that will award counsel fees and slices of damage judgments recovered for *en masse* wrongs, they have so far shown the capacity to conduct significant litigations with resources provided by combinations of tax-raised grants and charitable subsidies. The cases they bring tend to be large-scale, complex and explicitly designed to make law. The advocate groups ask courts to recognize new rights, impose new duties and enunciate new legal doctrines of kinds that would until recent years have been thought entirely appropriate for the legislature. Obviously, the increased use of efforts to bring about social change through courts instead of legislatures is a fact of much importance that must be kept in view in a survey of litigation in America today.

3. A model of an easier, quicker, less costly and potentially more effective mechanism is the suggestion for a "Department of Economic Justice" that would pay public funds in small amounts on the basis of consumer-claimants' affidavits. Random audits like those conducted by the Internal Revenue Service would be announced to discourage fraudulent claims. The Department's enforcement could pursue civil and penal remedies against persistent wrongdoers. See Rosenberg, Devising Procedures that are Civil to Promote Justice that is Civilized, 69 *Mich. L. Rev.* 797, 814-16 (1971).

Doubtless the reasons are apparent for the steady surge of lawsuits designed for law-declaring purposes. Courts have clear advantages in settling controversies over large and widely-contested alleged interests or entitlements. For one thing, they draw the spotlight to an immediate and concrete case. This assures that the dispute will have the concentrated attention of officials in visible positions of authority. The judges who sit in the case have no choice but to decide: It is quite unusual for a court to send the litigants on their way with an avowal that it is unable to resolve their legal problem. Finally, courts are not only authoritative and responsive, but conclusive. If they do not always tuck in every loose end of the controversy, they usually come to grips with central issues and speak definitively upon them. . . .

Along with the enlarged law-declaring function is a step-up in the complexity of the matters submitted for resolution. More and more they require knowledge and data outside the ordinary experience of judges and lawyers. Often law-trained professionals cannot even tell whether the evidence presented is nonsensical or respectable. Several factors aggravate the seriousness of this deficiency: the pervasiveness of technology; the tighter interdependence of people in society; the greater likelihood that a decision will radiate direct consequences for masses of people not before the court; and a heightened awareness on the part of many judges that it is important to try to gauge the social impact of a legal declaration before making it. The information-getting and evaluating capacities of courts need to be improved if they are to function wisely in the new breeds of cases, whether in adjudicating facts that are particular to the litigants or in deciding "legislative facts" that are critical to decision. . . .

Our busy courts are like completely saturated sponges. If we force them to absorb new types of cases, we must inevitably squeeze out some old types. Much of the discussion about courts in this country centers on what trade-offs we should make and how we should settle the controversies we deflect from the courts. Diverse choices present themselves. Some disputes can be settled by other types of tribunals—arbitration boards, administrative agencies, etc. Others can be stilled at birth by rewriting substantive rules to make clear that there is to be no contest. Various "no-fault" systems that are spreading in the law and programs for awarding compensation without litigation are examples.

Many thoughtful observers resist steps that remit classes of disputes to non-court tribunals because they fear restricting access to courts. However, they fail to take account of the heavy costs of constantly expanding judicial forums. Legal conflict cannot all be managed in the courts. If the only costs were for new courthouses, judges and staffs, there would be an arguable case for indefinitely expanding the courts. However, there are more serious costs that cannot be defrayed by money alone. Serious dysfunctions quickly appear as a court system grows from jumbo to elephantine size. One of the gravest of these is the difficulty of handling the pressure on appellate courts as the intake of cases at the trial level steadily increases.

Another reason for seeking alternatives to court litigation is the sheer expense of a lawsuit. Just as caseloads tend to outgrow the capacity of courts to handle all of them with dignity and dispatch, so the costs of litigating outrun the capacity of disputes to bear them—at least, if we preserve the usual paraphernalia and procedures of the judicial process. Thus, one of the large questions in improving court justice is how to find alternative procedures to resolve the small scale disputes that remain in the courts. Is it tolerable to provide full processes for large claims and mini-procedures for small ones, or will it be charged that the differentiated treatment of small cases is invidious: that little claims get little justice?

The dilemma posed is real and urgent. Non-lawyers have charged that the legal profession shares blame for much of the violence, bitterness and dissatisfaction in society precisely because it has failed to provide the kind of substantive relief for grievances that other societies supply as a matter of course. Among the new forums proposed to deal with these grievances, a preference is given to structures and processes in which laymen are the prime actors, rather than exclusively lawyers and judges.*

Vestal, Publishing District Court Opinions in the 1970's†

It is fairly well agreed that the reported decisions of courts are extremely important. They indicate how legal problems have been decided in the past and so, under the doctrine of stare decisis, suggest how cases should be decided in the future. All lawyers and judges know about the

* In the rest of this paper the emphasis will be upon four problems in improving court justice in civil cases: costs, delay, the place of the jury, and adversarialism.

† [17 *Loyola L. Rev.* 673 (1963). Reprinted by permission.

Alan D. Vestal (1920–) is Carver Professor, University of Iowa College of Law, where he has taught since 1949. He was educated at De Pauw (A.B. 1943) and Yale (LL.B. 1949) Universities. He is the author of *Res Judicata / Preclusion* (1969), *Iowa Practice* (with Wilson, 1974), and *Civil Procedure* (with others, 1975). He is an Advisor for the *Restatement of Judgments (Second)*.]

reports of the decisions of the Supreme Court of the United States, and the courts of appeal, and the highest courts of the various states, and even other state courts, as well as about the reported decisions of the federal district courts. Not all opinions of the courts of appeal are found in the Federal Second; not all of the decisions of the state courts are found in the state reports; and certainly not all opinions handed down by the federal district courts are found in the Federal Supplement. However, not everyone is conscious of the fact that the reported district court opinions represent only a portion of the decisions rendered or the opinions written. . . .

At the outset, some preliminary statements should be made.

First, very little is known about the reporting of opinions by federal district court judges. The author examined the matter about five years ago and reported his findings at that time in three law review articles.[1] No other published studies of the matter appear to be available. The Administrative Office of the United States Courts is unable to be of any assistance in this area. The opinions of federal district court judges are reported in a number of reports other than the Federal Supplement and the Federal Rules Decision. About one quarter of the reported opinions in fiscal 1962 were found in reports other than the West series. This article concerns only the opinions appearing in the West reports. . . .

There are opinions written by district court judges which are not published in any series of reports. In the Supreme Court decision in *Donovan v. City of Dallas,* the writer of that opinion mentions two district court opinions which were unreported. In the federal court in Iowa recently an excellent opinion in a pendent jurisdiction case was never reported. Recently, the Court of Appeals for the Fifth Circuit in *Olympic Insurance Company v. H.D. Harrison, Inc.,* stated, per curiam, "We disagree largely for the reasons advanced in the unpublished memorandum of the district court," which had been written by Judge Cassibry. It, of course, is impossible to determine the number of opinions written in a year which have not been published, but the number must be large.

With those preliminary statements it is appropriate to look to the past to get some idea of what has happened in the writing and reporting of district court opinions.

The bulk of opinions reported is growing. This should not be surprising in view of the increase in litigation. There was a possibility that

1. A Survey of Federal District Court Opinions: West Publishing Company Reports, 20 *S.W.L.J.* 63 (1966); Reported Federal District Court Opinions: Fiscal 1962, 4 *Hous. L. Rev.* 185 (1966); Reported Opinions of the Federal District Courts: Analysis and Suggestions, 52 *Iowa L. Rev.* 379 (1966). See also Note, 50 *Iowa L. Rev.* 1114 (1965) which explains the research techniques used.

the additional work of the judges might keep them so busy that they would not have time to write publishable opinions or opinions which would be published, but this has not happened. The library at the University of Iowa, for example, reports that it received:

for the calendar year	
1964	12 volumes of F. Supp.
1965	12 volumes
1966	12 volumes
1967	14 volumes
1968	16 volumes
1969	15 volumes
thus far in 1970	8 volumes

. . . [T]he number of published opinions rose from 259 (1962) to 293 (1963) to 377 (1968). Pages increased from 1105 to 1514. The increase, 1968 over 1962, for all practical purposes, occurred in Louisiana (73), Texas (22), and Florida (20).

. . . The ratio of opinions reported to cases terminated [in fiscal 1968] is rather interesting. In Louisiana the district judges published one opinion for every 29 cases terminated. (In 1962 this was 1 for every 39.) On the other hand, the ratio was 1 to 79 cases terminated in Texas and 1 for every 92 cases terminated in Florida (1 to 113 in 1962).

The available statistics also show the ratio of final opinions per terminations by court action. Mississippi has a ratio of 1 to 16. Louisiana has a ratio of 1 to 26. Florida has a ratio of 1 to 56. The Mississippi figure is explained in some measure by the fact that a relatively low percentage of the cases terminated are terminated by court action. The total figures on termination and opinion writing and reporting should be noted. More than 22 thousand cases were terminated in the circuit with only 377 number opinions reported by West Publishing Company.

. . . It should be noted that the opinion writing and reporting practices of the various judges vary considerably. One judge from Texas had no opinion published; seven judges had a single opinion reported; nine judges had two opinions reported; six had three; seven had four. Thus, thirty judges had four or fewer opinions published.

At the other end of the scale the top was 36 by one judge, followed by 22, 20, 17, 16, 15, and two at 14. These eight judges had 154 of the 377 opinions. It also should be noted that six of these eight prolific judges are from Louisiana.

It seems obvious that these statistics do not reveal the entire picture concerning the opinion reporting practices of the various judges. It would be desirable to examine the background and circumstances surrounding specific cases to ascertain why the writing judges chose to have the opinions in those cases published. Moving from gross figures to individual cases may be difficult, but it should be attempted, and it is probable that the district court judges would be willing to cooperate in this research. The statistics do not suggest that there is a need for investigation and for a clearer understanding of what is being done in the reporting of opinions. This is where the choice for the future lies. Either past practices may be followed or attempts to understand the process and act in a rational manner may be made.

Simply stated, the reporting of district court opinions is justified in terms of the creation of a body of law—decided cases—by a group of judges of acknowledged capabilities. But not all rulings and judgments are reported; there is a selection process; and this is where the rub comes. Some judges obviously are reluctant to have opinions reported; others seem to be taken with the idea.

This selection process is the point at which a real contribution can be made to make sure that the proper cases are reported and that the unimportant or insignificant cases are not reported. . . .

First, judges might decide to withhold from publication any final opinion in a case which is being appealed. The opinion would be available to the court of appeals but it would not be published. According to the information now available this would include 85 of the final opinions reported in 1968. This is about 32% of these final opinions. Incidentally, it can be reported that the court of appeals affirmed the action of the trial court in about three quarters of the cases wherein an opinion was reported in fiscal 1968. . . .

Second, judges might consider withholding final opinions in diversity cases. . . . There may be some justification for not reporting diversity cases if it is true, as one court of appeals stated, "Federal court decisions in diversity cases have no percedential value as state law and only determine the issues between the parties."[8]. . .

Third, district judges might adopt a policy of careful publication of opinions dealing with matters uniquely within their competence. There are a number of occasions when the opinion handed down by the district court will be unappealable as a matter of law or not subject to review for all practical purposes. . . .

An example of an order practically unappealable is an order in discovery matters. Perhaps it can be reviewed on review of the final judgment, or under 1292(b) or in a contempt proceeding, but these are un-

---

8. Peterson v. U-Haul Co., 409 F.2d 1174, 1177 (8th Cir. 1969).

usual. In the ordinary case there is no review of discovery matters. Perhaps these should be reported, so that the written, available law is the same as the law actually being applied.[11] With the new discovery rules, there is an even greater need for clear exposition of the law, and reported opinions can be of great assistance.

The motion practice of the district courts—judgment on the pleadings, summary judgment, motions to strike and for a more definite statement—all these are areas where the voices of the district courts should be clearly heard through reported opinions.

Fourth, district judges might attempt to make sure that the reported opinions accurately reflect the law which is being applied by the district courts. On well-settled points of law, a representative sampling of cases would suffice. On the edge of the law, even when the judge is uncertain about the decision, the opinion should be reported so that the legal profession is aware of the developing law. Here, too, the greatest assistance can be given to other members of the judiciary. At the cutting edge there is the greatest need for exposition of positions taken.

One sitting in the towers of academe occasionally has the feeling that the reported cases simply do not reflect what is actually happening in the courts. Or at least they do not reflect what is actually happening in some sections of the country. One law school graduate in a large city reported that a federal judge in a removal case told the attorney for the defendant, a large corporation, that he would have to stipulate that the loss suffered, if there were a judgment against the defendant, would be more than $10,000. If this were not stipulated, then the case would be remanded. This is not found in the written opinions; this may not be the law in that district, but at least this has been related by a practicing attorney. If this is the practice, then the reported opinions should indicate it.

Fifth, the judges should make the decision about the publication of the opinions. There is a danger that, left to litigants to request publication, the opinions will represent a skewed view of the law. Government departments will request publication of the opinions in their favor; the departments will not request publication of the opinions in cases where they lose. It would appear that each judge should feel some obligation to contribute to the creation of a corpus juris through the reporting of district court opinions. This means that he should not wait for a request before sending in an opinion.

There is a need for the full participation of the district court judges in the promulgation of federal law. To illustrate the problem which may

11. See Shuchman, Discovering the Law of Discovery by Low Level Investigation, 38 *Geo. Wash. L. Rev.* 32 (1969).

exist, consider fiscal 1963 and the reported opinions dealing with social security. During that year 151 opinions dealing with the subject can be found. Fifty-seven of these came from West Virginia and thirty-three of these were written by a single judge. This one judge wrote more than 20% of the social security opinions reported that year. Perhaps his statement of the law was entirely accurate, but an outsider might well question law so created. The reported law should come from a broad cross-section of the courts.

Perhaps, at some time in the future, it may be necessary to consider the use of a body specially designated to decide the question of publication. New York has taken this away from the writing judge and has vested it in a separate body. The success of this plan has not been overwhelming, but at least a body of information is being collected about the success of the plan. California also has tried selective reporting.[13] Perhaps the federal district courts will wish to look to these experiences at some time in the future.

Before leaving this matter of reporting, consideration should be given to the possibility of doing away with opinion reporting for federal district courts.[14] . . . Before the decision is made to do away with the publishing of district court opinions, one should balance very carefully the benefits derived against the disadvantages. The publishing of selected opinions in specific areas, such as discovery, remanding to state courts, pre-trial procedures, is eminently desirable. In other words selective publication is appropriate. Establishing the standards to be applied is a difficult problem, but this is not insurmountable.

13. Rule 976 of the California Rules of Court provides that opinions of the courts of appeal are to be published unless a majority of the rendering court certifies that the opinion does not meet the standard for publication. "It is estimated that from January 1964 to July 1, 1969, . . . there has been a reduction of 45 volumes of California Appellate Reports which would otherwise have been published." The courts have been averaging between 50 and 55% nonpublication for five years. Judicial Council of California, *Annual Report of the Administrative Office,* 87-88 (1970).

14. Since the Federal Supplement and the Federal Rules Decisions are unofficial reports, there may be some question about the control which the courts have over the series. Publishing companies, including the West Publishing Company, have exhibited an ability to collect and publish opinions regardless of the wishes of the courts concerned. For example, it is occurring in California following the adoption of Rule 976. See, e.g., People v. Allenthorp, 47 Cal. 47 (3d Dist. Ct. App. 1965); People v. Arnold, 47 Cal. 525 (3d Dist. Ct. App. 1965); People v. Butler, 47 Cal. 512 (2d Dist. Ct. App. 1965), which apparently are not reported in the official reporters because hearings were granted. See *Cal. R. Civ.* p. 976. See also *Shepard's California Citations—Case Edition Supplement 1946-1966,* at 8, where reference is made to "California cases which are reported in the California Reporter [West Publishing Company] but are not also reported in the California reports. . . ."

In conclusion, it seems that enough questions have been raised about the opinion writing and publishing practices of the federal district court judges that it is desirable to have a comprehensive study made. Only by knowing all the facts will a rational move in the next decade be possible. The law cannot afford to be skewed by the incomplete reporting of district court opinions, nor created by only a handful of judges who may, or may not, present the law as it is being applied in the district courts. It might be desirable to investigate in depth why judges decide to publish or not publish opinions which they have written. Information along these lines might help other judges in the decisions they make about publication. If the opinions of the district courts are to be reported, the reported opinions should be accurate, comprehensive cross-sections of the law being applied.

Kalven & Zeisel, The American Jury*

The Anglo-American jury is a remarkable political institution. We have had it with us for so long that any sense of surprise over its main characteristics has perhaps somewhat dulled. It recruits a group of twelve laymen, chosen at random from the widest population; it convenes them for the purpose of the particular trial; it entrusts them with great official powers of decision; it permits them to carry on deliberations in secret and to report out their final judgment without giving reasons for it; and, after their momentary service to the state has been completed, it orders them to disband and return to private life. The jury thus represents a deep commitment to the use of laymen in the administration of justice, a commitment that finds its analogue in the widespread

* [Pp. 3-11, 492-499 (Little, Brown and Company 1966). Reprinted by permission.

Harry Kalven, Jr. (1914-1976) was educated at the University of Chicago (A.B. 1935; J.D. 1938) and later returned there to teach after spending three years (1939-1942) in private practice and two more years in the army. He became Professor of Law in 1953. He is author of *Cases and Materials in Torts* (with C. Gregory, 1959 and 1969), *Public Law Perspectives on a Private Law Problem* (with W. J. Blum, 1965), *The Negro and the First Amendment* (1965), and *Uneasy Cure for Progressive Taxation* (with W. J. Blum, 1953).

Hans Zeisel (1905–) is Professor Emeritus of the University of Chicago School of Law. He received Dr. Jur. and Dr. Pol. Sci. degrees from the University of Vienna. His published works include *Say It With Figures* (1947 and 1968), *Manenthal* (co-author 1932 and 1971), and "Statistics as Legal Evidence" (*New Encyclopedia of Social Science* 1968).

The partnership of Kalven and Zeisel has been a fruitful one. In addition to writing *The American Jury,* they collaborated with Bernard Bucholz to produce *Delay in the Court* (1959), and they have co-authored numerous articles for law reviews and journals.]

use of lay judges in the criminal courts of other countries.[1] It opposes the cadre of professional, experienced judges with this transient, everchanging, ever-inexperienced group of amateurs. The jury is thus by definition an exciting experiment in the conduct of serious human affairs, and it is not surprising that, virtually from its inception, it has been the subject of deep controversy, attracting at once the most extravagant praise and the most harsh criticism.

The jury controversy has recruited some of the great names of political philosophy and the law: Alexander Hamilton, de Tocqueville, Blackstone, Montesquieu, Bentham, Spencer, Livingston, Holmes, Stephen, Corbin, Wigmore, Pound, Sunderland; and, more recently, Frank, Curtis, Green, Wyzanski, Bok, Glanville Williams, Denning, Devlin, and Griswold.[2]

1. Lay judges have been a persistent part of the administration of criminal justice since antiquity. During the Middle Ages Europe developed two forms of lay participation in the criminal process, independently both of each other and of the Greco-Roman tradition: on the European continent, the scabini or Schöffen, and in England the jury. See Dawson, *A History of Lay Judges* (1960).

The Schöffen courts have survived in the mixed tribunals which today are the principal triers of criminal cases in Central, Eastern and Northern Europe. The jury migrated from its English home in two directions. The expanding orbit of the English law took it through what was then the British Empire. The French revolution and its aftermath brought it to Europe, where since Montesquieu's *Esprit des Lois* the jury had been looked at as democracy's way of administering criminal justice. From France the jury spread across Europe and further, first under the direct impact of the revolution and the Napoleonic conquest and, after 1848, more permanently when the second revolutionary wave carried democratic institutions eastward across the continent as far as Czarist Russia, which instituted jury trial in 1864.

On the whole, the European graft did not take well. See Ch. 2, note 3. But while the jury in recent decades has lost some ground, the principle of lay participation in the criminal process is more firmly established than ever. In the large, only the Near East and Japan and some of the Latin American countries have left the criminal trial exclusively to the learned judiciary.

2. A complete bibliography on praise and blame of the jury would be formidable; we list a sampling: Livingston, *A System of Penal Law for the State of Louisiana,* pp. 10 et seq. (1833); Pound, Law in Books and Law in Action, *Am. L. Rev.,* v. 44, p. 12 (1910); Sunderland, Verdicts, General and Special, *Yale L.J.,* v. 29, p. 253 (1920); Wigmore, A Program for the Trial of a Jury Trial, *J. Am. Jud. Soc.,* v. 12, p. 166 (1929); Green, *Judge and Jury* (1930); Frank, *Law and the Modern Mind,* Ch. XVI (1930); Frank, *Courts on Trial* (1949); Curtis, The Trial Judge and the Jury, *Vand. L. Rev.,* v. 5, p. 150 (1952); Wyzanski, A Trial Judge's Freedom and Responsibility, *Harv. L. Rev.,* v. 65, p. 1281 (1952); Devlin, *Trial by Jury* (1956); Williams, *The Proof of Guilt* (3d ed. 1963). See also, Broeder, The Functions of the Jury: Facts or Fictions, *U. Chi. L. Rev.,* v. 21, p. 386 (1954). A reasonably complete bibliography on the jury debate was prepared by Professor Dale Broeder for the University of Chicago Jury Project as a staff memorandum; ironically it owes its publication to the Congressional hearings on jury tapping. See Hearing Before the Subcommittee to Investigate the Administration of the Internal Security Act of the Senate Committee on the Judiciary, 84th Cong., 1st Sess., pp. 63-81 (1955).

Yet this long tradition of controversy over the jury system has produced unsatisfactory debate. Much of the criticism has stemmed from not more than the a priori guess that, since the jury was employing laymen amateurs in what must be a technical and serious business, it could not be a good idea. In comparable fashion, the enthusiasts of the jury have tended to lapse into sentimentality and to equate literally the jury with democracy. Not surprisingly, therefore, the very characteristics which the critics point to as defects, the jury's champions herald as assets.

The wide range of opinions about the jury is easily documented. We begin with a very recent statement by one of the critics. The Dean of the Harvard Law School, in the course of his annual report for 1962-1963, made certain recommendations for improving the administration of justice, among them the abolition of the jury in civil cases. Dean Griswold argued:

> The jury trial at best is the apotheosis of the amateur. Why should anyone think that 12 persons brought in from the street, selected in various ways, for their lack of general ability, should have any special capacity for deciding controversies between persons?[4]

The more exasperated form of criticism is illustrated by the following excerpt from an article in the *American Bar Association Journal* in 1924:

> Too long has the effete and sterile jury system been permitted to tug at the throat of the nation's judiciary as it sinks under the smothering deluge of the obloquy of those it was designed to serve. Too long has ignorance been permitted to sit ensconced in the places of judicial administration where knowledge is so sorely needed. Too long has the lament of the Shakespearean character been echoed, "Justice has fled to brutish beasts and men have lost their reason."[5]

And to add still another unfriendly voice, the distinguished English scholar Glanville Williams, in the Seventh Series of Hamlyn Lectures in 1955 had, among other things, this to say of the jury:

> If one proceeds by the light of reason, there seems to be a formidable weight of argument against the jury system. To begin with, the twelve men and women are chosen haphazard. There is a slight property qualification—too slight to be used as an index of ability, if indeed the mere possession of property can ever be so used; on the other hand,

4. *1962-1963 Harvard Law School Dean's Report,* pp. 5-6.
5. Sebille, Trial by Jury: An Ineffective Survival, *A.B.A.J.,* v. 10, pp. 53, 55 (1924).

exemption is given to some professional people who would seem to be among the best qualified to serve—clergymen, ministers of religion, lawyers, doctors, dentists, chemists, justices of the peace (as well as all ranks of the armed forces). The subtraction of relatively intelligent classes means that it is an understatement to describe a jury, with Herbert Spencer, as a group of twelve people of average ignorance. There is no guarantee that members of a particular jury may not be quite unusually ignorant, credulous, slow-witted, narrow-minded, biased or temperamental. The danger of this happening is not one that can be removed by some minor procedural adjustment; it is inherent in the English notion of a jury as a body chosen from the general population at random.[6]

The defenders of the jury are equally emphatic. Lord Justice Devlin, an experienced and greatly admired English judge, may speak here for them. In 1956, in the Eighth Hamlyn Lecture Series, he said of the jury:

> Each jury is a little parliament. The jury sense is the parliamentary sense. I cannot see the one dying and the other surviving. The first object of any tyrant in Whitehall would be to make Parliament utterly subservient to his will; and the next to overthrow or diminish trial by jury, for no tyrant could afford to leave a subject's freedom in the hands of twelve of his countrymen. So that trial by jury is more than an instrument of justice and more than one wheel of the constitution: it is the lamp that shows that freedom lives.[7]

Justice Devlin found it appropriate to conclude his lectures on the jury by quoting the famous passage from Blackstone, the words of which, he said, are still "after two centuries as fresh and meaningful as when they were written":

> So that the liberties of England cannot but subsist, so long as this *palladium* remains sacred and inviolate; not only from all open attacks, (which none will be so hardy as to make), but also from all secret machinations, which may sap and undermine it; by introducing new and arbitrary methods of trial, by justices of the peace, commissioners of the revenue, and courts of conscience. And however *convenient* these may appear at first, (as doubtless all arbitrary powers, well executed, are the most *convenient*) yet let it be again remembered, that delays, and little inconveniences in the forms of justice, are the price that all free nations

6. Williams, *The Proof of Guilt,* pp. 271-272 (3d ed. 1963).
7. Devlin, *Trial by Jury,* p. 164 (1956).

must pay for their liberty in more substantial matters; that these inroads upon this sacred bulwark of the nation are fundamentally opposite to the spirit of our constitution; and that, though begun in trifles, the precedent may gradually increase and spread, to the utter disuse of juries in questions of the most momentous concern.[8]

Thus, after two hundred years, the debate over the jury system, with distinguished participants on both sides, is still going on apace.

This is not the occasion to review the debate systematically. It may be useful, however, to suggest its broad outline. The controversy centers around three large issues. First, there is a series of collateral advantages and disadvantages that are often charged against, or pointed to on behalf of, the jury as an institution. In this realm fall such positive points as that the jury provides an important civic experience for the citizen; that, because of popular participation, the jury makes tolerable the stringency of certain decisions; that, because of its transient personnel, the jury acts as a sort of lightning rod for animosity and suspicion which otherwise might center on the more permanent judge; and that the jury is a guarantor of integrity, since it is said to be more difficult to reach twelve men than one. Against such affirmative claims, serious collateral disadvantages have been urged, chiefly that the jury is expensive; that it contributes to delay in civil litigation; that jury service imposes an unfair tax and social cost on those forced to serve; and that, in general, exposure to jury duty disenchants the citizen and causes him to lose confidence in the administration of justice.

Second, there is a group of issues that touch directly on the competence of the jury. Here the debate has been fascinating but bitter. On the one hand, it is urged that the judge, as a result of training, discipline, recurrent experience, and superior intelligence, will be better able to understand the law and analyze the facts than laymen, selected from a wide range of intelligence levels, who have no particular experience with matters of this sort, and who have no durable official responsibility. On the other hand, it is argued that twelve heads are inevitably better than one; that the jury as a group has wisdom and strength which need not characterize any of its individual members; that it makes up in common sense and common experience what it may lack in professional training, and that its very inexperience is an asset because it secures a fresh perception of each trial, avoiding the stereotypes said to infect the judicial eye.

The third group of issues about the jury goes to what is perhaps the most interesting point. The critics complain that the jury will not follow

8. *Commentaries,* v. IV, p. 350 (11th ed. 1791).

the law, either because it does not understand it or because it does not like it, and that thus only a very uneven and unequal administration of justice can result from reliance on the jury; indeed, it is said that the jury is likely to produce that government by man, and not by rule of law, against which Anglo-American political tradition is so steadfastly set.

This same flexibility of the jury is offered by its champions as its most endearing and most important characteristic. The jury, it is said, is a remarkable device for insuring that we are governed by the spirit of the law and not by its letter; for insuring that rigidity of any general rule of law can be shaped to justice in the particular case. One is tempted to say that what is one man's equity is another man's anarchy.

From even so brief a summary, it is apparent that there is little chance that the debate over the jury will soon be resolved; it is too threaded with difficult value judgments. For the special purposes of this book, however, three characteristics emerge as salient. First, most praise or blame of the jury can come only by way of the comparison of trial by jury with trial by a judge, the one serious and significant alternative to it.

Thus, throughout the jury controversy there is at least the implicit assumption on both sides that the decisions of the jury will sometimes and to some degree be different from those that would be given by the judge in the same case. Its critics point to these differences as evidence of the jury's fallibility and incompetence; its champions point to these differences as proof of the jury's distinctive function and its strength.

Second, most of the unrest over the jury today is limited to its use in civil trials.[9] It is agreed that the case for the jury in criminal trials is different and much stronger.

Third, while in no small part the jury controversy is clearly in the realm of value judgments and is but a variation on the age-old theme of rule versus equity, nevertheless much of the argument appears to rest on assumptions as to what the facts are—the facts, that is, as to how the jury actually performs. . . .

While this book then is essentially an empirical study of the jury in operation, we would pause to note its broader implications. It is a contribution to what has often been called realist jurisprudence; it is an effort to find out how the law in operation, as contrasted to the law on the books, is working. There are innumerable other instances of unwritten law in action besides those afforded by the jury, and the study may,

9. See generally, Kalven, The Dignity of the Civil Jury, *Va. L. Rev.*, v. 50, p. 1055 (1964). See also Green, Juries and Justice—The Jury's Role in Personal Injury Cases, 1962 *U. Ill. L.F.*, p. 152; Joiner, *Civil Justice and the Jury* (1962). The argument about the jury in civil cases has become much involved with the problem of court congestion.

therefore, be taken as some indication of what empirical efforts to map out the law in action can yield.

. . . Trial by judge and trial by jury will emerge not simply as two different modes of adjudication, but as different systems of law. In that sense this is a comparative study of two legal cultures, that of the jury and that of the judge.

[The authors conclude:]

A Last Word

There are so many difficulties in providing a systematic chapter of conclusions for a study of this sort that we have decided not to attempt it. The architecture of the book is, we hope, sufficiently and accessibly explicit to make tedious and unnecessary a summary of specific points and findings. We have completed what we set out to do, to pass before the reader the total business of the contemporary American jury in criminal cases and to permit him to be a spectator at close range of its decisions. The companion report on the jury in civil cases is to follow. It will be time enough, if then, to confront the larger significances of our lengthy inquiry into the jury.

In this brief epilogue we aspire to nothing more than a few final reflections on the venture and its results.

As to method, just two comments. It has been characteristic of the study both carefully to count cases as units and to experience them intimately as individual instances. We trust we have shown that quantification of behavior can be powerful and sustained and at the same time blend in partnership with qualitative emphasis. Indeed, we would argue that this partnership is needed for successful study of social institutions. We see no war here between two cultures.

And it is a special advantage of empirical studies of legal institutions that the law supplies a pre-existing framework of significance and expectation to which the quantitative dimension can be added; it permits, that is, measurement with meaning.

At the technical level, it is appropriate to emphasize once more the wide use of the technique of reason assessment in individual cases, the method which provided the key to much of the study. And it is noteworthy that on several occasions we were able to confront the results of the reason assessment with the corresponding cross-tabulations, thus corroborating the one method by the other.

As to matters of substance, it is hard not to bring to mind here particular ideas or reactions of the jury that struck us as especially flavorsome, as though we were sketching the profile of a colorful personality we had come to know. We note especially its perception that Providence may have punished the defendant enough, its sympathy for the sexual difficulties of the cripple, its recognition of intoxication only when it appears to have altered the character of the defendant, its feeling that young men old enough to fight for their country are old enough to drink in it, its sense of humor, and its new concept of petty robbery. But to go down this road would involve us in simply restating a substantial portion of the text and so we come at the matter in a more general way.

In the large, the mind of the jury in criminal cases might perhaps be said to exhibit four dominant traits. First, there is the niceness of its calculus of equities; it will treat provocation as justifying defensive moves by the victim but only to the extent of the one-punch battery; it may even treat injury to the victim as punishment for the actor, but only where the relationship is close and the conduct is inadvertent. Second, there is the jury's broad tendency to see little difference between tort and crime and thus to see the victim rather than the state as the other party to the case, with the consequence that the public controversy is appraised largely as though it were a private quarrel. Third, there is a comparably broad tendency to merge at several points considerations of penalty with those of guilt. Finally, and this is a point on which we will say more in a moment, there is a quality of formal symmetry about the jury's responses. In what we have called the simple rape cases the jury seems to say, whatever kind of offense the defendant had committed, it just was not rape; conversely, in the cases of sexual approach to children, it says that whatever the defendant did, even though far short of rape, it was some kind of offense. Thus while the jury is often moved to leniency by adding a distinction the law does not make, it is at times moved to be more severe than the judge because it wishes to override a distinction the law does make.

It is true, of course, that our study has its provincial aspects. It is the study of only one decision-making institution in a particular country and at a particular time. Nevertheless, it has been possible at various points to generalize about how the American jury performs today, and these generalizations constitute a kind of theory of the jury. Since these points have been scattered throughout the text, there may be some value in collecting them here.

Although a substantial part of the jury's work is the finding of facts, this, as has long been suspected, is not its total function in the real world. As a fact-finder it is not in any interesting way different from the judge, although it will not always reach the same conclusion. When only pure fact-finding is involved the jury tends to give more weight than the judge to the norm that there should be no conviction without proof beyond a reasonable doubt. And there is every indication that the jury follows the evidence and understands the case.

324

The more interesting and controversial aspects of the jury's performance emerge in cases in which it does more than find facts; where, depending on how one looks at it, the jury can be said to do equity, to legislate interstitially, to implement its own norms, or to exhibit bias.

All this is fairly familiar. The distinctive bite of this study resides in the following supplementary propositions about the jury as legislator.

First, we can estimate with some precision how frequently the jury engages in more than fact-finding. It will be recalled that about three quarters of the time it agrees with the judge; and that most, but not all of the time it agrees with him, it is not importing values of its own into the case. But roughly two thirds of the disagreements with the judge are marked by some jury response to values.

Second, the jury imports its values into the law not so much by open revolt in the teeth of the law and the facts, although in a minority of cases it does do this, as by what we termed the liberation hypothesis. The jury, in the guise of resolving doubts about the issues of fact, gives reign to its sense of values. It will not often be doing this consciously; as the equities of the case press, the jury may, as one judge put it, "hunt for doubts." Its war with the law is thus both modest and subtle. The upshot is that when the jury reaches a different conclusion from the judge on the same evidence, it does so not because it is a sloppy or inaccurate finder of facts, but because it gives recognition to values which fall outside the official rules.

Third, we suspect there is little or no intrinsic directionality in the jury's response. It is not fundamentally defendant-prone, rather it is non-rule minded; it will move where the equities are. And where the equities are at any given time will depend on both the state of the law and the climate of public opinion.

Fourth, the extent to which the jury will disagree with the judge will depend on the selection of cases that come before the jury. Since, under current waiver rules and practice, the defendant in effect has the final say on whether there is to be a jury trial or a bench trial, the cases coming before the jury will be skewed and include a disproportionate number in which there are factors that appeal to the jury. The selection will be affected also by pleas of guilty and, to a lesser degree, by decisions of the prosecutor not to prosecute, and even in some instances by decisions of the police not to arrest. Thus the commonplace impression that the criminal jury is defendant-prone may be largely an artifact of the dynamics by which the cases are sorted out for jury trial.

Fifth, we have said, the jury's reaction will in part depend on the lay of public sentiment on any given point. The extensive agreement between judge and jury indicates that there is in our society at this time widespread consensus on the values embodied in the law. As a result, a jury drawn at random from the public, does not often have representatives of a dissenting view.

On some points there is sufficient dissent so that the random drawing will at times place on the jury representatives of a view contrary to the existing law. Indeed on some matters the public will even be ambivalent, with factions that deviate from the law in opposite directions.

Thus, it makes a good deal of difference in this decision-making who the personnel are. The consequence of the fact that no two juries are alike is that statements about trends in jury decision-making are probabilistic at best. We cannot assert that all juries will always feel that a man who has suffered personal disasters since committing the crime has been punished enough. We can only say that this idea is prevalent enough so that it has some chance of moving the jury away from the judge in any given instance in which it is present.

Sixth, the explanation of how a disagreement is generated requires one more fundamental point. The thesis is that to a substantial degree the jury verdict is determined by the posture of the vote at the start of the deliberation process and not by the impact of this process as rational persuasion. The jury tends to decide in the end whichever way the initial majority lies. The result is that a sentiment need be spread only so widely among the public as to produce enough representatives on the jury to yield the initial majority. On this view the study can be thought of as a study of the sentiments that will lead to initial majorities.

Seventh, and as a corollary, the deliberation process although rich in human interest and color appears not to be at the heart of jury decision-making. Rather, deliberation is the route by which small group pressures produce consensus out of the initial majority.

More than once in the course of the book we have had occasion to note parallels with the concerns of the legal realists who so shook up American jurisprudence in the twenties and thirties. They emphasized the translation of rules of law into patterns of official behavior and took a skeptical view of the public reasons offered by courts for their decisions. Their quest was for a law in action as contrasted to a law on the books, and for latent or hidden reasons. A fair description of our study is that it is an effort to trace the law in action, to see how juries, the final arbiters of so much criminal law, really decide cases.

What emerges perhaps as something of a surprise is that this reality has so legal a texture. When the jury deviates from the official rules and writes its own law, the categories of thought are familiar. For the largest part the hidden reasons of the jury are reasons which can stand public scrutiny; not infrequently the jury's rule turns out to be the law in another jurisdiction. The realist emphasis seemed often to lend itself to a kind of inside dopester jurisprudence in which the real reasons for decisions would be very different from the surface reasons, and probably rather nasty. Insofar as this study can be said to be a venture in realism, it suggests that the ideas embodied in the formal rules and doctrines of law are close to the policies that actually motivate decision-makers in the real world.

As we attempt to step back and gain some distance from the detail of the study, it may be useful to put two quite general and interrelated questions: Why do judge and jury ever disagree, and why do they not disagree more often?

Judge and jury have experienced the same case and received the same rules of law to apply to it; why do these two deciders ever disagree? We seek for the moment an explanation more general than that offered throughout the book in terms of specific factors of evidence, sentiment, and defendant. Why do they not react the same way to the stimuli? Why does the judge not move over to the jury view, or the jury stay with the judge?

The answer must turn on the intrinsic differences between the two institutions. The judge very often perceives the stimulus that moves the jury, but does not yield to it. Indeed it is interesting how often the judge describes with sensitivity a factor which he then excludes from his own considerations. Somehow the combination of official role, tradition, discipline, and repeated experience with the task make of the judge one kind of decider. The perennial amateur, layman jury cannot be so quickly domesticated to official role and tradition; it remains accessible to stimuli which the judge will exclude.

The better question is the second. Since the jury does at times recognize and use its de facto freedom, why does it not deviate from the judge more often? Why is it not more of a wildcat operation? In many ways our single most basic finding is that the jury, despite its autonomy, spins so close to the legal baseline.

The study does not answer directly, but it does lay the ground for three plausible suggestions. As just noted, the official law has done pretty well in adjusting to the equities, and there is therefore no great gap between the official values and the popular. Again, the group nature of the jury decision will moderate and brake eccentric views. Lastly, the jury is not simply a corner gang picked from the street; it has been invested with a public task, brought under the influence of a judge, and put to work in solemn surroundings. Perhaps one reason why the jury exercises its very real power so sparingly is because it is officially told it has none.

The jury thus represents a uniquely subtle distribution of official power, an unusual arrangement of checks and balances. It represents also an impressive way of building discretion, equity, and flexibility into

327

a legal system. Not the least of the advantages is that the jury, relieved of the burdens of creating precedent, can bend the law without breaking it.

For the very last word it is appropriate to return to the tradition of controversy over the jury system. Can we now at long last answer whether the jury is a worthy institution or whether it would be more sensible to have all cases tried to judges alone? As foreshadowed in Chapter 1, we cannot answer, and there is no embarrassment that so lengthy and systematic a study does not end more conclusively for this issue.

Our purpose was not to evaluate but only to find out as carefully as we could how the jury actually performs. And in the detailed inventory we have provided of its behavior, assuredly both friends and critics will find new ammunition for their case.

Whether the jury is a desirable institution depends in no small measure on what we think about the judge. We have given a candid and rounded picture of the jury, but we treated the judge as abstract, a baseline representing the law. We know, of course, that on the side of the judge too, discretion, freedom, and sentiment will be at work, and that the judge too is human. Until an equally full and candid story of the judge is available, we have only half the knowledge needed.

And there is another point which goes to the time limitations of our study. We have noted that at this moment in history the jury's quarrel with the law is a slight one. But there have been times when the difference was larger and such times may come again.

But no additional facts can decide the policy issue; they can only make it more precise. In the end, evaluation must turn on one's jurisprudence, on how, given the limitations of human foresight, experience, and character one hopes to achieve the ideal of the rule of law. Whether or not one comes to admire the jury system as much as we have, it must rank as a daring effort in human arrangement to work out a solution to the tensions between law and equity and anarchy.

Wright, Beyond Discretionary Justice*

In his little book *The Morality of Law,* Lon Fuller relates an allegory about a King Rex who sets out to reform the legal system of his kingdom.

* [Book Review (K. Davis, *Discretionary Justice–A Preliminary Inquiry* (1969) (paper ed. 1971)), 81 *Yale L.J.* 575-596 (1972). Reprinted by permission of The Yale Law Journal Company and Fred B. Rothman & Company from The Yale Law Journal, Vol. 81, pp. 575-596.

The Honorable J. Skelly Wright (1911–   ) is United States Circuit Court Judge for the District of Columbia Circuit.]

Upon assuming the throne, King Rex repeals all existing law and, lacking the confidence to write a new code, begins the process of developing new rules on a case-by-case basis.

> In this way under the stimulus of a variety of cases he hoped that his latent powers of generalization might develop and, proceeding case by case, he would gradually work out a system of rules that could be incorporated in a code. Unfortunately the defects in his education were more deep-seated than he had supposed. The venture failed completely. After he had handed down literally hundreds of decisions neither he nor his subjects could detect in those decisions any pattern whatsoever. Such tentatives toward generalization as were to be found in his opinions only compounded the confusion, for they gave false leads to his subjects and threw his own meager powers of judgment off balance in the decision of later cases.

In the allegory, King Rex eventually dies, "old before his time and deeply disillusioned with his subjects." In the real world, the King is still with us, enthroned in the legal department of a federal regulatory agency.

I

. . . Professor Davis, in his powerful manifesto *Discretionary Justice,* has proposed that we modify King Rex's powers, turning him into a constitutional monarch. Davis argues that the administrative system in this country is shot through with unnecessary discretion. The police, prosecutors, and petty bureaucrats in our local and national governments are free to run loose in an Alice-in-Wonderland of unchannelled, unreviewable, untrammelled discretion. The result, unsurprisingly, is a crazy quilt of secret, ad hoc decisions which are essentially lawless, because they are presently beyond the power of law to control. Professor Davis has the temerity to suggest that this is an intolerable situation in a country theoretically dedicated to equal justice under law. He then proceeds to provide a series of specific suggestions for how administrative discretion can be checked or channelled and made subject to binding, prospective rules. This is not to say that he argues for complete elimination of discretionary decision-making. He would not exchange Lewis Carroll's fantasy for Franz Kafka's nightmare. A tyranny of petty bureaucrats who lack power to change the rules even an iota in order to do justice is at least as bad as a tyranny of petty bureaucrats who make up the rules as they go along.

But the need for some discretion in no way justifies the vast scope of unnecessary discretionary authority which is harbored in our present administrative apparatus. While an agency is new and unfamiliar with the subject matter with which it is dealing, it may have to feel its way around for a while on a case-by-case basis. But from the very beginning, the agency should concentrate considerable attention on the problem of developing coherent general principles to guide its decisions. As soon as such principles can be formulated, they should be publicly discussed and, if found satisfactory, set down in the form of binding rules. If the agency is still too uncertain to issue a complete set of rules, it should promulgate them for areas which have become well settled. If general rules to cover all cases are impossible, specific rules to cover identifiable sub-categories of cases should be issued. If the agency feels unable to do even this much, then it should be compelled to explain publicly the reasons for its inability to formulate prospective rules in a specific class of cases, and it should utilize other devices such as fair informal procedures, effective review by superior officers, and nonbinding policy statements to ensure that individual decisions are not arbitrary and capricious. The underlying tone of *Discretionary Justice* is optimistic: although there may be a hard core of decisionmaking which must remain discretionary, there is nothing intractable about most of the problem. If we have the will to create an effective system of law to guide and channel administrative decisionmaking, then the monster can be tamed.

II

The real question, of course, is whether we have the will. Professor Davis subtitles his book "A Preliminary Inquiry," and that caveat should be taken seriously. Davis has brilliantly and systematically laid bare the soft underbelly of the American legal system. Moreover, he has tentatively outlined means by which the most important abuses of discretionary power can be curbed. He is at his most convincing when he argues that "the procedure of administrative rule-making is . . . one of the greatest inventions of modern government," and his solution follows plainly: "the chief hope for confining discretionary power . . . [lies] . . . in much more extensive administrative rulemaking." An interlocking network of rules, laid out in advance, can serve as a bulwark which strengthens the agency and prevents cooptation by the forces which it is attempting to regulate. The absence of rules has too often meant that the agency is at the mercy of the pressures brought to bear on it, its decisions little more than the resulting vector produced by conflicting political and economic forces.[6]

But while Professor Davis' perception of the problem is clear, when it comes to outlining methods by which agencies can be forced to make rules and to obey the rules they do make, he barely scratches the surface. This is a shortcoming which leaves Davis' work seriously flawed. He seems to suppose that many agencies will suddenly see the error of their ways. In his view, "the chief hope for confining discretionary power" lies in voluntary agency rule-making. If that is true, there may be no hope at all. For the sad fact is that powerful forces are at work which incline agencies toward an ad hoc, case-by-case mode of operation. The first of these is simply the bureaucratic imperative of keeping the wheels turning. As Professor Jaffe has written,

> [t]ime has corrected one dearly held illusion. It was thought in the heyday of the New Deal that an operating administrative agency, because of its continuous exposure to the problems of an area, was ideally fitted for progressive planning and programming. We have found that such is not the case. The agency is so deeply, so anxiously involved in solving the problems of the moment that most of its effort goes out in keeping astride of its operating agenda. Furthermore, buffeted by strong, opposing forces, it looks for compromise, expediency, and short-term solutions. After its first strenuous years of conflict with those whom it must regulate, it may arrive at a modus vivendi which it looks upon and pronounces to be good.[7]

Once this accommodation is reached, the agency is sheltered from the scrutiny of Congress, the courts, and the public. It seems clear that the amorphous, ad hoc mode in which most agencies operate has made them resistant to congressional control. Of course, some agencies are notoriously vulnerable to a well-timed telephone call from a congressman or a threat from a powerful committee chairman. But these are essentially ad hoc devices to deal with ad hoc decisions. Most of the time they reflect the sort of constituent pressure from private interest groups which has too much effect on agency decisions already.[8] In the aggre-

6. See Shapiro, The Choice of Rulemaking or Adjudication in the Development of Administrative Policy, 78 *Harv. L. Rev.* 921, 952 (1965).

7. L. Jaffe, *Judicial Control of Administrative Action* 51 (1965).

8. The late Senator Dirksen's intervention in administrative affairs for the benefit of individual constituents, and his vociferous defense of this practice, are notorious. He once remarked, "I have been calling agencies for 25 years. . . . Are we to be put on the carpet because we represent our constituents, make inquiries, and find out what the status of matters is, and so serve our constituents?" 105 *Cong. Rec.* 14057 (1959).

gate, all of the individual calls from congressmen and threats at appropriations time do not add up to systematic congressional control at the policy level. The ineluctable fact is that all too often there can be no congressional supervision of agency policy because the agency has no policy to supervise. Congress will never be able to influence the directions in which agencies are heading until the agencies begin to head in *some* direction and stop floundering in the morass of case-by-case litigation.

Moreover, ad hoc decisions tend to leave the agency freer to change direction at will and allow it to avoid the risks inherent in advance commitments.[9] As Professor Shapiro has pointed out, a reviewing court which might declare invalid a clearly promulgated regulation may well affirm the application in a particular case of a principle of adjudication based on past agency decisions.[10] In addition, an agency will be more readily permitted to ignore its past principles of adjudication than to depart from its regulations.[11]

Given this historical and legal context, it is unrealistic to suppose that many agencies will dramatically move to confine their own discretion. Fortunately, however, there are other strategies available to implement Professor Davis' plans for administrative reform of executive agencies. The publication of *Discretionary Justice* coincides with the culmination of a number of trends in American thought—trends which can be utilized to make the Davis solution something more than an unrealizable ideal. On the one hand, there has been a growing sense of disillusion with the role which regulatory agencies play in the political and economic processes of the country. Credit for the genesis of these critiques must go to conservative economic theoreticians who yearn for a return to a free market economy and view administrative intervention as officious intermeddling.[12] But the sense of disillusion has spread throughout the political spectrum, and critics from the right and left now generally agree that many regulatory agencies are inept, inefficient, and overly protective of the interests which they are supposed to regulate.[13]

9. There may also be something to Professor Jaffe's observations: "The question may be asked whether there is not an essential conflict of attitude between the task of adjudication and long-range planning. The former may be thought to intensify the sense of the particular to a degree which makes planning appear inexact, insensitive, Utopian, and futile." Jaffe, supra note 7, at 20.

10. Shapiro, supra note 6, at 944-47.

11. Id. at 947-52.

12. See, e.g., M. Friedman, *Capitalism and Freedom* 119-60 (1962).

13. See, e.g., *Moss v. CAB*, 430 F.2d 891, 893 (D.C. Cir. 1970); F. Cox, R. Fellmeth, & J. Schultz, *"The Nader Report" on the Federal Trade Commission* (1969); Meyers, The Root of the FTC's Confusion, in *Public Policies and Their Politics* 104-09 (R. Ripley ed. 1966).

On the other hand, we have seen in the last few years a dramatic, if still incipient, reassertion of congressional power which poses the first serious challenge to the practical supremacy of the executive branch since the early days of the New Deal. This movement began with congressional frustration over the inability of the legislature to affect the conduct of the Vietnam war. It has quickly spilled over, however, into numerous other areas. The right of the executive to impound appropriated funds and to impose sweeping wage-price controls without congressional guidance has recently come under challenge. More and more legislators have come to realize that the so-called "expertise" of the executive branch is in reality no more than a cloak which hides the raw exercise of untrammelled power. Whereas once it was believed that administrative "experts" could magically provide a "scientific" solution to public policy problems,[14] many congressmen now realize that most questions of policy are questions of values, and that the people must determine for themselves the values which they favor. In time, the movement for greater balance between the legislature and the executive promises to bring about the first substantial reallocation of power in almost two generations. . . .

. . . [A]dministrative agencies . . . have to be given substantial power to resolve individual controversies. The problem, as Professor Davis correctly perceives it, is to force the agencies to exercise that power through purposeful and coherent prospective rules rather than in the random, ad hoc, and secret manner in which they all too frequently operate at present. Once again, it seems to me the legal tools which could be utilized to reach this goal have already been fashioned. All we need do is bring those tools to bear on the problem in a forceful and determined manner.

Chief among these tools is the due process clause of the Constitution. It should be obvious that to have due process of law it is necessary for the decision involved to be subject to law. Yet when we say a decision is ad hoc, random, or unreviewable we mean in effect the decision is lawless. As Professor Fuller has stated with admirable directness: "The first desideratum of a system for subjecting human conduct to the governance of rules is an obvious one: there must be rules."

It is time, then, we came to recognize that in at least some circumstances there is a due process right to have one's conduct governed by rules which are stated in advance. Moreover, these rules must be clearly formulated and publicly promulgated. These requirements have been recognized for centuries in the area of criminal law. No one would con-

14. See J. Landis, *The Administrative Process* 9-12 (1938).

tend that a man could be arrested, tried, and convicted of a "crime" for acts which were perfectly legal at the time they were committed. Moreover, it has long been recognized that a criminal statute must be publicly promulgated and written precisely enough to give fair warning. Similarly, when noncriminal regulation borders on constitutionally protected conduct, the courts have repeatedly held that the statutes involved must be precisely drawn so as to make clear what is lawful and what is not *before the conduct in question takes place.*

As an abstract proposition, few would argue that these requirements are limited to the areas of criminal law and constitutional rights. Imagine, for example, a system where individual social workers are given the unfettered right to grant and deny welfare benefits to whomever they please on whatever basis they please. Or imagine a system under which a man's right to pursue his chosen occupation depends upon his ability to get approval from a board which gives no hint of when it will give such approval and when it will withhold it. Is it really open to question that such schemes would be unconstitutional? Regulatory systems which operate without rules are inherently irrational and arbitrary. The purpose of such a system is presumably to bring primary conduct into conformance with agreed upon societal norms. Yet a system operating without rules cannot possibly achieve this goal, since the people being regulated are not informed of what the societal norms are. Unless they are prescient, they cannot possibly be expected to mold their conduct in accordance with rules which, if they can be said to exist at all, are created after the conduct occurs.

Moreover, it should be apparent that *any* system which operates without rules chills the exercise of constitutional rights. When a court strikes down a vaguely worded statute providing for licensing of public demonstrations, it presumably does so because the statute permits those charged with administering it to make decisions on the basis of criteria which are forbidden by the First Amendment. Yet precisely the same flaw is inherent in the statutory schemes described above. A social worker administering a standardless public assistance program might deny benefits because the applicant is a Black Panther. The medical board described above might withhold a license to an otherwise qualified physician because he belongs to the Republican Party. It might be argued that these possibilities do not in themselves make the schemes unconstitutional but rather only demonstrate that they are subject to abuse. When the individual abuses come to light, the argument goes, they will be corrected. But the trouble with a standardless regime is that the abuses may never come to light. In a system under which governmental officials do not have to act in accordance with publicly stated rules, it is very difficult to know when they are acting in accordance with secret, illicit rules.

When these propositions are baldly stated, they seem obvious to the point of triteness. Yet the sad fact is that we have barely begun to apply these fundamental due process precepts to the millions of discretionary decisions made by government officials every day. Welfare workers *do* exist who possess the de facto power to grant or deny benefits as they choose. Government boards *do* control access to various professions without reference to any discernible criteria. Indeed, even in the area of criminal law, where the necessity for prospective rules is most widely recognized, police, prosecutors, judges, and parole officers continue to arrest and incarcerate people on the basis of standards which are apparent only to themselves. Under a criminal justice system which makes such conduct as petty gambling, possession of marijuana, statutory rape, and abortion criminal offenses, a large proportion of the population becomes criminal. When the law enforcement establishment picks and chooses on an ad hoc basis which of these "criminals" are to be arrested and prosecuted, they are in effect making up the criminal law as they go along, in a manner which suits the whims and prejudices of individual policemen and prosecutors. Similarly, when a judge decides to impose a maximum sentence or a parole board denies release without a statement of reasons, they make the degree of punishment subject to considerations which were not publicly explicated at the time the offense was committed. . . .

. . . [W]hen agencies refuse to make use of their rule-making powers, the courts need not take "no" for an answer. Under well established principles of law, the courts have the authority to demand that agency action be subject to rules. This is true because it is what the Constitution requires, because it is what Congress often intends, and because it is what the courts must do if they are to preserve their reviewing function. But, whatever theoretical pigeonhole is chosen, it is ultimately true because fair procedures are impossible without rules which guide agency action. We cannot have a society under law without first having laws. The judiciary fulfills its highest obligation when it insists not only that the laws be obeyed but also that there *be* laws to be obeyed.

C. The Judicial Role: Review Without Rules

Having said all this, I should hasten to add a caveat. I do not intend to adopt what Professor Davis has called the extravagant version of the rule of law. Advocates of discretionary decisionmaking can argue with some force that there is a value in flexible, empirical growth of the law and that the rules for resolving some problems are for one reason or another simply not susceptible to neat codifications.

My view is that these arguments are correct as far as they go, but that they are essentially incomplete. While I do not wish to dispute the proposition that in some situations comprehensive prospective rule-making is impossible or undesirable, I share Professor Davis' view that a great deal more can be done. The criminal justice system provides an excellent example. It is doubtless true that the decision to prosecute or not to prosecute a suspected offender is a complex one and it would be a mistake to require the determination to be made in accordance with totally inflexible rules. But this is not to say that prosecutorial discretion cannot be significantly narrowed without interfering with the sort of individualized justice that empirical decisionmaking is designed to protect. Studies of prosecutorial decisionmaking reveal that the decision to prosecute is based at least in part on a number of factors which are quite readily generalizable, such as the amount of evidence available and the likelihood of conviction. I see no reason why these relatively straightforward considerations cannot be stated in the form of prospective rules so that they can be judicially enforced and fairly applied.

Of course it is true that even after this has been done there will remain aspects of prosecutorial decisions which cannot be put in the form of binding, prospective rules. Some of these considerations will be too individual in nature to be generalized beyond the one case to which they apply. Others are more general in nature, but involve decisions as to allocation of prosecutorial resources which, if publicly announced, might encourage criminal conduct. But the important point to be made is that, although in some situations it may be impossible to formulate prospective rules governing official conduct, it does not follow that unbridled discretion should reign supreme. Although publicly announced prospective rules should be the preferred method of limiting agency discretion, there are other methods as well.

These alternative methods once again derive from basic notions about what courts are supposed to do in a constitutional democracy. One of their underlying functions is to ensure that official action is not irrational or invidious. The Administrative Procedure Act clearly empowers courts to set aside agency action which is "arbitrary, capricious, an abuse of discretion, or otherwise not in accordance with law," or which is "contrary to constitutional right, power, privilege, or immunity." Thus even in situations where the agency cannot articulate a rule in advance, the courts should still oversee agency action to ensure that the agency is following *some* rational and permissible rule of decision. While it is sometimes inevitable that the rule of decision be developed on a case-by-case basis, this development should not be confused with a system under which decisions are made without rules. When the prosecutor chooses to press charges in one case but not in another, for example, he should be able to point to some distinction between the two cases which it is permissible for him to consider. While he may not be able to articulate in advance what all the distinguishing factors in all cases will be, he must at least be able to show later that cases treated differently were in fact different in some relevant respect—that is, that he is following some sort of rational, non-discriminatory rule. If he cannot make such a showing, his different treatment of the two cases is irrational or invidious, and hence violative of equal protection.

. . . [M]ethods are available to control agency discretion even in cases where prospective rule-making is impossible. Nor need these methods always involve constitutional adjudication. Even in stiuations where the agency is able to offer plausible reasons for distinguishing between different cases, it is still possible for the courts to limit the scope of agency choice. The administrative agencies, after all, derive all of their delegated power from statutes passed by the legislative body, and it is the task of the courts to interpret those statutes in cases which are properly brought before them.

Once again, the Administrative Procedure Act is quite explicit: "To the extent necessary to decision and when presented, the reviewing court shall decide all relevant questions of law, interpret constitutional and statutory provisions, and determine the meaning or applicability of the terms of an agency action." If the agency acts beyond its statutory authority as the relevant statute is interpreted by the courts, the agency action must be reversed.

Of course many congressional delegations are phrased in extremely broad terms and, literally read, they permit an exceedingly wide range of agency choice. But the very breadth of such statutes provides an argument for a narrowing judicial construction in accordance with congressional intent. Advocates of administrative discretion seem to forget that the courts construe broad statutory mandates all the time—that indeed, the courts have no choice but to do so when faced with the problem of applying a vaguely worded statute to a specific set of facts. As Professor Jaffe has said,

> [t]he scope of judicial review is ultimately conditioned and determined by the major proposition that the constitutional courts of this country are the acknowledged architects and guarantors of the integrity of the legal system. . . . An agency is not an island entire of itself. It is one of the many rooms in the magnificent mansion of the law. The very subor-

dination of the agency to judicial jurisdiction is intended to proclaim the premise that each agency is to be brought into harmony with the totality of the law; the law as it is found in the statute at hand, the statute book at large, the principles and conceptions of the "common law" and the ultimate guarantees associated with the Constitution.

It may nonetheless be true that in situations where the agency sets out to limit and define its own mandate by adopting prospective rules to guide it in consideration of individual cases, the courts have some obligation to respect agency expertise. But when the agency has defaulted— when it purports to do no more than follow the vague statutory mandate without additional prospective rules of its own—the courts have no obligation to respect undemonstrated or hypothetical expertise. Instead, the reviewing court should look at the statute on its own and determine for itself whether the agency decision is within the congressional purpose. In this way, judges can narrow the scope of agency discretion even if the administrators are unwilling to narrow its scope themselves.

Chapter 3

Legislation

I. NATURE AND SCOPE OF LEGISLATION

Maine, Early History of Institutions*

The capital fact in the mechanism of modern States is the energy of legislatures. Until the fact existed, I do not, as I have said, believe that the [analytical] system of Hobbes, Bentham and Austin could have been conceived; wherever it exhibits itself imperfectly, I think that the system is never properly appreciated. The comparative neglect with which German writers have treated it seems to me to be explained by the comparative recency of legislative activity in Germany. It is however impossible to observe on the connection between legislation and the analytical theory of law without having the mind carried to the famous addition which Bentham and Austin engrafted on the speculations of Hobbes. This addition consisted in coupling them with the doctrine or theory of utility— of the greatest happiness of the greatest number considered as the basis of law and morals. What, then, is the connection essential or historical, between the utilitarian theory and the analytical theory of law? I certainly do not affect to be able, especially at the close of a lecture, to exhaust a subject of such extent and difficulty, but I have a few words to say of it. To myself the most interesting thing about the theory of Utility

---

* [Pp. 398-400 (9d ed. 1880). The first edition of this work appeared in 1874.

Sir Henry Maine (1822-1888) was Whewell Professor of International Law at Cambridge University. His earlier years were spent as a tutor, scholar, and journalist. Maine also spent seven years in India as a legislative adviser to the colonial government in Calcutta. Maine's chief claim to recognition is based upon his works, *Ancient Law: Its Connection with the Early History of Society and Its Relation to Modern Ideas* (1861), *Early History of Institutions* (1875), and *Village Communities* (1871).]

is that it presupposes the theory of Equality. The greatest number is the greatest number of men taken as units; "one shall only count for one," said Bentham emphatically and over and over again. In fact, the most conclusive objection to the doctrine would consist in denying this equality; and I have myself heard an Indian Brahmin dispute it on the ground that, according to the clear teaching of his religion, a Brahmin was entitled to twenty times as much happiness as anybody else. Now how did this fundamental assumption of equality which (I may observe) broadly distinguishes Bentham's theories from some systems with which it is supposed to share the reproach of having pure selfishness for its base—how did it suggest itself to Bentham's mind? He saw plainly—nobody more clearly—that men are not as a fact equal; the proposition that men are by nature equal he expressly denounced as an anarchical sophism. Whence then came the equality which is a postulate of his famous doctrine about the greatest happiness of the greatest number? I venture to think that this doctrine is nothing more than a working rule of legislation, and that in this form it was originally conceived by Bentham. Assume a numerous and tolerably homogeneous community—assume a Sovereign whose commands take a legislative shape—assume great energy, actual or potential, in this legislature—the only possible, the only conceivable, principle which can guide legislation on a great scale is the greatest happiness of the greatest number. It is in fact a condition of legislation which, like certain characteristics of laws, has grown out of the distance from which sovereign power acts upon subjects in modern political societies, and of the necessity under which it is thereby placed of neglecting differences, even real differences, between the units of which they are composed. Bentham was in truth neither a jurist nor a moralist in the proper sense of the word. He theorises not on law but on legislation; when carefully examined, he may be seen to be a legislator even in morals. No doubt his language seems sometimes to imply that he is explaining moral phenomena; in reality he wishes to alter or rearrange them according to a working rule gathered from his reflections on legislation. This transfer of his working rule from legislation to morality seems to me the true ground of the criticisms to which Bentham is justly open as an analyst of moral facts.

Bishin, The Law Finders: An Essay in Statutory Interpretation*

. . . The busiest area of judicial activity is a place where people still view adjudication as divorced from legislation and where courts must

* [38 *S. Cal. L. Rev.* 1, 2-3, 13-17 (1965). Reprinted by permission. Deletions made by

take up their traveling gear in search of the relevant "is." In the administration of the statutory law it is still fashionable to view the courts as "interpreters," not lawgivers.[5] No one will deny that even here the task of creation is often thrust upon the judges, but, it will be said, only when the sources of preexisting doctrine fail to yield their fruit.[6] These cases, of which the number is not insubstantial, might be termed the I-can't-help-it-but-I've-got-to-legislate decisions: invariably they contain overtones of the apologetic refrain.[7]

The model to which we repair, then, when we wish to evaluate the work of a judge construing statutes, is the Law Finder. Although that prototype has been largely discredited in other areas, one can see how it might seem controlling in this one. Here the lawgiver is no "brooding omnipresence in the sky"[8] but an earthly legislature, empowered to enact laws and dependent upon the courts to see that those laws govern the everyday affairs of the people. It is a cooperative enterprise of institutions which, it might seem, are very different from individual human beings. Yet the means for reaching the common goals cooperatively are the same ones that individuals use: symbols. A law is viewed as an act of communication by the lawmakers to the courts[9]— and the energies of the interpreters must be directed toward effectuating the goal which prompted the communication.[10] The process is often pictured as a search for the "legislative intent,"[11] but sophisticated commentators consider this a misleading description.[12] "Intent" connotes a concern with the subjective state of mind of the lawmakers; the courts should not attempt to determine what the legislators thought they were doing.[13] In-

---

the editor.

William R. Bishin (1939–   ) was educated at Columbia and Harvard Universities. He is Professor at the University of Southern California Law Center, where he has taught since 1963. In addition to teaching, he has been a Juvenile Court referee since 1971. He is co-author of *Law, Language and Ethics* (with C. D. Stone, 1972).]

5. See, e.g., Sinclair Ref. Co. v. Atkinson, 370 U.S. 195, 214–15 (1962).

6. See Landis, A Note on "Statutory Interpretation," 43 *Harv. L. Rev.* 886, 893 (1930).

7. Cf. Hand, J., in United States v. Klinger, 199 F.2d 645, 648 (2d Cir. 1952): " . . . Flinch as we may, what we do, and must do, is to project ourselves, as best we can, into the position of those who uttered the words, and to impute to them how they would have dealt with the concrete occasion."

8. Holmes, J., dissenting in Southern Pacific Co. v. Jensen, 244 U.S. 205, 222 (1917), and see Guaranty Trust Co. v. York, 326 U.S. 99, 102 (1945).

9. See Landis, op. cit. supra note 6, at 886.

10. See Frankfurter, Some Reflections on the Reading of Statutes, 47 *Colum. L. Rev.* 527, 538-39 (1947).

11. See, e.g., Jones, Statutory Doubts and Legislative Intention, 40 *Colum. L. Rev.* 957, 968 (1940).

12. See Frankfurter, supra note 10, at 538.

13. See Cardozo, J., dissenting in United States v. Constantine, 296 U.S. 287, 298, 299

stead, they must judge the product of their activity by external criteria, i.e., how, one supposes, it would appear to a "reasonable" interpreter.[14] The standard must be objective, said Justice Holmes, who did not "care what their intention was," only wishing "to know what the words mean."[15]

Yet whether one searches for a "legislative intent" or analyzes legislative symbols the goal remains an "is." Our commentators on construction will concede that the problems of interpretation arise when the legislature has not in terms directed itself toward the court's difficulty;[16] but they will insist nonetheless that an exhaustive search be made for a legislative solution. Sometimes the search turns up little—and the courts are forced to confront the freedom of their common law alter egos—but more often there is a wealth of evidence with which to establish the fact of law. The text of the statute is subjected to analysis into its minutest parts and the nicest inferences are drawn from what was said to determine legislative thinking on what was not said. Committee reports and hearings, legislative debates, discarded bills, chronologies of amendment are picked clean. In this treasure trove what judge could not find the answer to his statutory problem? Perhaps only the least imaginative.[17] . . .

The basic work on a statute[59] is done in committee without the participation of most of the legislators. Their knowledge of the bill comes from reading the text and the committee reports, listening to debate,

_____

(1936); see generally Frankfurter, supra note 10.

14. Cf. Hand, J., in Hotchkiss v. National City Bank, 200 Fed. 287, 293 (S.D.N.Y., 1911): "A contract has, strictly speaking, nothing to do with the personal, or individual, intent of the parties. A contract is an obligation attached by the mere force of law to certain acts of the parties, usually words which ordinarily accompany and represent a known intent. If, however, it were proved by twenty bishops that either party, when he used the words, intended something else than the usual meaning which the law imposes upon them, he would still be held, unless there were some mutual mistake, or something else of the sort. Of course, if it appear by other words, or acts, of the parties, that they attribute a peculiar meaning to such words as they use in the contract, that meaning will prevail, but only by virtue of the other words, and not because of their unexpressed intent."

15. Letter from Justice Holmes to unidentified correspondent, quoted in Frankfurter, supra note 10.

16. See, e.g., Frankfurter, supra note 10, at 528-29.

17. For a minority view contrary to the approach discussed above, see Hart & Sacks, *The Legal Process: Basic Problems in the Making and Application of Law* (tent. ed. 1958). The influence of this work is so pervasive in this paper that it is hard to find any idea herein which was not affected by it. For a similar approach see also Witherspoon, The Essential Focus of Statutory Interpretation, 36 *Ind. L.J.* 423, 433-34 (1961), and Morris & Mishkin, *On Law in Courts* 189-344 (1964).

59. For studies of the federal legislative process, see Gross, *The Legislative Struggle*

perhaps actually speaking to a committee member. All of these modes of communication are intrinsically defective. Nonparticipating legislators who have no particular interest in the details of the legislation may fail to read the reports with care, or, what is not unlikely, may fail to read them at all. Nonparticipating legislators will be busy with their own legislation, with their constituents, with politics. They will often not be present during debates; if they are, they may not be listening. They may be in and out of the chamber, in the cloakroom or elsewhere, responding only to quorum calls when the party whip arrives. Even personal contact with a draftsman or committeeman—which of course will not be known to the judge perusing the history—may be unsatisfactory if the draftsman decides his interrogator would like a particular answer. Legislation may be railroaded through one House, leaving the members no opportunity to discover anything about its particular provisions except perhaps what is revealed by the statutory text. And this is not unlikely when the majority is already aware of the bill's general import and urgency is the order of the day.

Take a case involving committee reports, traditionally regarded as the most reliable of legislative evidence. A fifty page report is printed and distributed. It contains explanations of the 25 sections of a newly reported bill. On one of these pages—let us say in the middle of the report—it is noted that a certain provision is expected to have a certain effect. The statement is not prominent, it is not hidden. It is just another of perhaps hundreds of declarative statements, not all of which can or will be read by the nonparticipating legislators. Even if it is read, it may be read carelessly, or it may be forgotten before the vote is taken. A court unable to resolve an ambiguity in the statute finds the statement; it now becomes a conclusive expression of the legislative intent.

In rare instances the evidence may seem compelling. For example, where a debate on the meaning of a particular provision is immediately followed by a vote, it would seem acceptable to say that the legislators in that chamber adopted the construction developed by debate. Yet even in that case it is possible that a large number of those voting for the bill were outside the chamber during debate, and the Congressional Record will not tell us how many rushed in just before the ayes and nays responded.[65]

(1953); Galloway, *The Legislative Process in Congress* (1953); Bailey & Samuel, *Congress at Work* (1952); Bailey, *Congress Makes a Law* (1950); Wilson, *Congressional Government* (13th ed. 1898).

65. And, of course, this evidence tells us nothing about the majority's position in the other house—or the President's understanding when he signs the bill.

These are merely problems of communication; legislators are also capable of connivance—e.g., in the manufacture of legislative history. They are responsive to political pressures and so may try to camouflage their legislative activity in a manner which could have one meaning for the judge and another for the political columnist. Then there are problems of motive. The chairman says the statute means one thing. One legislator thinks he is wrong, but votes for the bill because he thinks it will be taken by the courts to mean something else. Another thinks the statute is not that broad. Another that it is not that restrictive. All vote for the provision assuming the validity of their own construction.

Given the complexity of the legislative process and its total dependence on an intricate, super-ramified system of delegation, it seems certain that data gleaned from legislative history will represent the position of only a very small portion of the lawmaking body. Though a duly constituted committee, should their will control? Under one theory, the answer would be "yes."[66] This notion would view, for example, the vote accepting a committee draft as an act of acquiescence in the meaning expressed outside the statute by committeemen—whether or not known to the enacting majority. Yet this is at best a legal conclusion, not a factual description. No evidence has been adduced to show that nonparticipating legislators really believe they are tacitly adopting interpretive statements made in committee reports and debates when they approve a statute. If invalid as description, this fiction must be discarded because it has not been shown to serve any other legitimate (e.g., analytical) function.

It has also been intimated that it is somehow *necessary* to look to the committee, if the partnership between legislature and courts is to fulfill its constitutional function.[67] Learned Hand seems to have been of this persuasion.

> It is, of course, true that members who vote upon a bill do not all know, probably very few of them know, what has taken place in committee. On the most rigid theory possibly we ought to assume that they accept the words just as the words read, without any background of amendment or other evidence as to their meaning. But courts have come to treat the facts more really; they recognize that while members deliberately express their position upon the general purposes of the legislation, as to the details of its articulation they accept the work of the committees; so much they delegate because legislation could not go on in any other way.[68]

66. See Landis, A Note on "Statutory Interpretation," 43 *Harv. L. Rev.* 886 (1930).
67. See Jones, Statutory Doubts and Legislative Intention, 40 *Colum. L. Rev.* 957, 969 (1940).
68. SEC v. Robert Collier & Co., 76 F.2d 939, 941 (2d Cir. 1935).

Conceding that Congress has the power to delegate to a small group the primary responsibility for particular legislation, is this anything more than a very good reason why the courts cannot refuse to administer the resulting enactment? The commission of the courts is to enforce the law so long as it is passed according to certain institutional rules. Indeed, the courts may not even look to see if these rules have been respected by the legislative organ so long as there has been a colorable enactment. But a useful distinction can be drawn between a court's duty to enforce statutes and its duty to interpret them. The former duty is stern and unbending. It cannot admit of a judicial reevaluation of the procedures by which legislation has been passed. A court which proceeded to examine the likelihood that a statute was actually considered and understood by those who enacted it would be arrogating to itself a dangerous power. It would in effect have devised a method for undermining the separation of powers in its most meaningful aspect. The duty of interpretation, on the other hand, has always been within the domain of judges. And so they must decide to which aids they will repair in determining the legal effect an enactment's words should be given. The courts have no institutional obligation to enforce the words of committeemen, if the words are not found in the statutory text. They may, of course, give such words controlling weight if their theory of statutory construction requires it. They may completely ignore such statements if their approach to statutory construction requires that.

In the absence of legislative history, the court would be obliged to undertake a sophisticated analysis of the structure and explicit purposes of the statute. With the results of this scrutiny it would consider other generally accepted social policies. Its task would then be one of synthesis —the creation of a new policy fashioned to accommodate and further the theses and antitheses which it has initially uncovered. Faced by a committee report which suggests a contrary resolution, should not a decision to acquiesce be based on an honest belief that the committee's is the *best* resolution? After all, the committee is not given constitutional authority to enact legislative directions. Indeed, the absence from the statutory text of the committee's dictum makes suspect the general legislative acceptability of that resolution. If it commanded majority approval why was there not conformity to the rules by which our society determines whether the sovereign has commanded?[70] Of course, the committeemen are elected representatives and their actions may have a special claim to legitimacy in a democracy. But there is no proof that they are representative of a legislative majority and that is the only pertinent test of legitimacy in this context. Finally, it should be realized that the failure

---

70. Cf. H. L. A. Hart, *The Concept of Law* 97-107 (1961).

of a legislature to embody a policy choice in the statutory text may yield an unwonted opportunity. Where the statute has grown stale with age, the existence of gaps which are yet to be filled may make it possible to effectuate a policy which is closer to the recognized needs of the present.

Legislative history can have important functions. It may suggest lines of analysis for the judges; it may serve as a check on the analysis reached, giving the judicial analyst reason to retrace his steps. Thus, the foregoing attack is really no more than a criticism of the approach taken by the Court toward legislative history. When it views the history as repository of "the answer" to its statutory problem the Court is likely to find an answer whether or not it is there to be found.[71] The inherent defects of legislative history are hard to appreciate when the Court is confronted with a legislator's statement; the humble judge will prefer to shift the burden of decision to the man who was there. And the lazy judge is likely to take the legislative history as an excuse for foregoing the difficult problems of statutory analysis which it is his responsibility to meet.

J. Cohen, Towards Realism in Legisprudence*

On paper, at least, the pragmatic revolt against arid conceptualism in the law is perhaps one of the most significant developments of modern jurisprudence. Pragmatists, functionalists, experimentalists—"realists" of all shades: Holmes, Pound, Cook, Llewellyn, Radin, Arnold, and Frank, to mention but a few—though flying different banners, and employing different weapons of warfare, stormed the citadel of the formal-

71. Cf. Corry, The Use of Legislative History in the Interpretation of Statutes, 32 *Can. B. Rev.* 624 (1954): "But not the least of the dangers of reference to legislative history is its tendency to draw interpreters away from hard thinking about the context and the general scheme embodied in the act in search of an easy road to learning in the legislative history. The frequent reliance of the federal courts in the United States on legislative history has prompted the jibe that the court will not look at the act unless the legislative history is obscure!" Id. at 636.

* [59 *Yale L.J.* 886-897 (1950). Reprinted by permission of The Yale Law Journal Company and Fred B. Rothman & Company from The Yale Law Journal, Vol. 59, pp. 886-897.

Julius Cohen (1910–) was educated at the University of West Virginia (A.B. 1931; M.A. 1932; J.D. 1937) and Harvard (LL.M. 1938). He has held numerous positions in state and federal government and has taught political science and law. Since 1957, he has been Professor of Law at Rutgers, Newark. His published works include *Parental Authority: The Community and the Law* (with Robson & Bates, 1958), *The Law School of Tomorrow* (with Haber, 1968), and *Materials and Problems on Legislation* (2d ed. 1967).]

ists, united in the belief that the meaning of legal concepts is to be found in the consequences that they produce, that is, in terms of human gains and deprivations. Actually, the "storming" was more on paper than on the battlefield, with victory claimed only by those optimistic generals who take the long range view of the future and blithely write off the present as having passed. The foot-soldiers in the court-room and in the law schools are still engaged in heavy combat; to them, the present is still very real, and the outcome of the struggle by no means certain.

What is to be deplored, however, is less the lag between plan and execution than the fact that the attack upon the formalists of the law has been planned for only one front—the judicial. . . . Assuming much of judicial law to be nothing more than policy-making, is there anything inherently unique in its make-up or in its impact upon human relations to justify the realists in singling out this area of policy-making as the major target of their attacks? Is one to assume that policy-making on the legislative level is not in need of a good dose of the same kind of "realism"? How explain so bold an attack on so narrow a front?

Perhaps the basic reason is the ingrained habit of regarding law as genuine only if it is labelled "judge-made." Thus, for example, the view of Holmes that: "The prophecies of what the *courts* will do in fact, and nothing more pretentious, are what I mean by the law";[11] and the position of John Chipman Gray that statutes are merely one of many "sources of law."[12] To such realists, law is simply a forecast of the manner in which the force of government will act upon an individual; and inasmuch as the impact of government is felt primarily through the courts (so they assumed), they reasoned that law and the decisions of courts are synonymous. This thought pattern is understandable when considered in the light of an ingrained tradition that considered legislation as nothing more than a meddlesome intrusion upon the mighty fortress of the common law.[13] It becomes even more understandable in view of the fact that the law schools, from whence many of the paper attacks of the realists have been launched, have for so long been geared almost exclusively to the Langdellian case system of teaching. Legislative law is dealt with not as one of the prime sources of policy-making, but merely as a factor which a court must consider in reaching a decision in a litigated issue.

But the fiction that courts are the only conduits through which the force of government is carried to the individual ignores what should now be obvious to any realist—that, in human experience, obedience to

11. Holmes, The Path of the Law, 10 *Harv. L. Rev.* 457, 461 (1897).
12. J. C. Gray, *The Nature and Sources of Law* §191 (1909).
13. Pound, Common Law and Legislation, 21 *Harv. L. Rev.* 383 (1908).

legislative policy does not necessarily await the judicial green light. Legislation calling for a "blackout" during an air-raid does not have to be litigated before it is obeyed. And, needless to say, where there is obedience there is impact. . . .

For the realist, then, policy-making is the common denominator of both the judicial and legislative processes. But the similarity does not stop here. If arid conceptualism is descriptive of policy-making on the judicial level, the conceptualism is no less arid on the legislative; and, if there is a crying need for "realism" in the one area, there is more than sufficient evidence of such need in the other.

As early as 1921, Cardozo publicly voiced concern over the fact that "courts are not helped as they could and ought to be in the adaptation of law to justice."[17] "The duty must," he said, "be cast on some man or group of men to watch the law in action, observe the manner of its functioning, and report the changes needed when function is deranged." His plea for the creation of a Ministry of Justice was prompted by the belief that, unless the effects of judge-made law are constantly measured and evaluated, that is, in terms of its impact upon those who are affected, it becomes sterile and defeats the ends of justice. The need is for the *facts* —the most accurately ascertainable facts available—concerning the effects of such law in operation. Without such facts constantly available to the judges, there is danger that socially undesirable policies will be perpetuated by the application of a relentless logic, which places consistency above the demands of justice. That other distinguished members of the profession have continued to urge the establishment of a Ministry of Justice[19] is evidence that the plea has gone unheeded. At best, however, it has been taken as one of confession and avoidance—confession of the need, but avoidance of a whole-hearted effort to cope with it.

On the judicial level, the need, then, is still with us; and the efforts to cope with it recognize that judicial policy-making is blind unless it is bottomed on reliable information concerning what the policy has done, and reliable estimates of what it will do—in terms of human gains and deprivations. It impliedly admits that this information cannot with complete reliance be obtained from the briefs or arguments of counsel representing the adversary interests involved; that this body of knowledge must come from some reliable *independent* source. It recognizes the need

17. Cardozo, A Ministry of Justice, 35 *Harv. L. Rev.* 113 (1921).
19. See Frank, *Courts on Trial* 291 (1949); S. Glueck, The Ministry of Justice and the Problem of Crime, 4 *American Review* 139 (1926); Lobinger, Precedent in Legal Systems, 44 *Mich L. Rev.* 955 (1946); Yntema, Legal Science and Reform, 34 *Col. L. Rev.* 207, 215-29 (1934).

for accurate measuring rods of human behavior—measuring rods the creation and application of which would tax the ingenuity and skills of our best social scientists.

The blindness of policy-making and the need for scientific measuring rods are no less evident on the legislative level.[20] On this level, the chief instrument for ascertaining the facts concerning the effects of past social policy and the estimates of what a future policy will probably do is the "hearing" before a legislative committee. It is before the committees —standing and special—that the "facts" concerning a pending policy issue before Congress are paraded. Presumably, it is from a careful weighing of these "facts" that a policy is born—at least so the fiction goes. But what facts? Facts so reliable as to foreclose disputation? And who presents the facts? Impartial, independent students, who are not only competent to gather them but also not afraid of letting the "chips fall where they may"? Or is it by representatives of adversary interests who slant the facts to support the policy sought to be enacted? In brief, what is the nature of the fact-finding process which supposedly underlies legislative policy-making? Perhaps a clue to the workings of this process—at least on the federal level—can be found by examining its operation in connection with three of the most controversial policy issues which faced the first session of the 81st Congress—(1) the Taft-Hartley Act, (2) basing points, and (3) displaced persons.

The Taft-Hartley issue involved, among other things, heated controversies over what the Taft-Hartley Act actually accomplished in practice. The proponents of repeal claimed that the Act produced certain results; those who advocated the retention of the Act denied that it produced these results. There were large areas of agreement as to the ultimate ends an appropriate Labor-Management Relations Act should achieve; but much of the controversy was concerned with whether the Taft-Hartley Act, as a means to these ends, did accomplish them during its period of operation. For example, both sides publicly avowed that legislation regulating labor-management relations should (1) not discourage membership in labor unions; (2) improve the processes of collective bargaining; (3) insure the greatest effectiveness of the conciliation service; (4) lessen the amount of labor-management strife; (5) eliminate Communists from positions of control in labor unions; (6) increase the efficiency of the National Labor Relations Board; (7) be impartially ad-

---

20. This was recognized as early as 1823 by Bentham, who urged the creation of a Ministry of Justice as a method for better preparing legislators for their tasks as policy-makers. On this, see Pound, A Ministry of Justice as a Means of Making Progress in Medicine Available to Courts and Legislatures, 10 *U. of Chi. L. Rev.* 323, 331 et seq. (1943).

ministered; and (8) provide an effective method for settling national emergency disputes. But both sides were in heated disagreement over whether the machinery of the Taft-Hartley Act advanced or retarded these ends. The facts with respect to the accomplishments of the Act were in dispute.

How were these facts resolved—if at all? The chief forums made available for this purpose were the Committees of the House and Senate, to which bills calling for repeal of the Taft-Hartley Act were referred for a "hearing"—a normal procedure for airing considerations which underlie legislative policy decisions. Those familiar generally with the workings of the hearing process agree that the hearings on these bills followed rather conventional lines. Spokesmen for the pros and cons— carefully screened and selected by the majority and minority leadership on the Committee—were permitted to appear as "witnesses" to "testify." In the main, these consisted of key governmental officials charged with administering the Act, representatives of powerful management and labor groups, and independent "experts" in labor-management relations. Though considerably more informal than a judicial proceeding involving the trial of an issue of fact, it is evident that a certain flavor of the judicial prevailed at the hearings. The "witnesses" were adversaries— parties in interest. Even the "experts" appear to have been chosen for their particular slant on the issues at hand. The chief method of "proof" was by testimonial—testimonials not only as to what the law *ought to be*, but what the Taft-Hartley Act *actually did*. Additional major types of evidence included sporadic "case studies" of experiences under the Act, opinions from newspaper editorials and magazine articles, assumed facts, a few scattered statistics from which conflicting inferences could be drawn, letters and telegrams from constituents, the results of questionable questionnaires aimed at recording group attitudes on labor policy, etc. But throughout the 1700 printed pages upon which the House hearings were recorded, and throughout the 3500-odd pages which were consumed on the Senate side, one looks in vain for a reliable resolution of the conflicting versions of many of the major "facts" upon which a great number of the conflicting policies presumably were bottomed. Facts which should and could have been resolved remained in the realm of disputation—each side presenting competing hypotheses as to what they were, and then drawing logical, but competing, policy conclusions with respect to them.

The use of testimonials is understandable, of course, in instances in which opinion is sought on the probable course of *future* conduct. But what of the above-mentioned facts in dispute that related to the *past*? Many of them were, admittedly, difficult to establish. But this does not mean that better methods than those used at the hearings were not available for tracking many of them down—for reducing the area of disputation to the barest minimum. As clumsy and as crude as many of the present tools of the social sciences are, no one can seriously doubt that they could have yielded findings considerably more reliable than those obtained at the hearings. Given the opportunity, experiments for obtaining the answers to such fact controversies could have been designed by competent social scientists. The methods used and the findings that resulted could have been subjected to as rigorous a critical scrutiny as one can apply to experiments in the physical sciences.

This assumes that the basic purpose of a legislative hearing is to get at the facts, to make the policy decisions as rational as possible. It is doubtful, however, whether such an assumption is justified. Not infrequently, the hearing is used merely as a political sounding board for legislative policy-makers. It provides them with an opportunity to ascertain what power groups support or oppose a certain legislative proposal; it gives them an opportunity to assess not only their strength of conviction, but their relative power; it serves as an instrument for calculating the political advantages and disadvantages of casting a "yea" or "nay" vote if and when the measure reaches the floor. Not infrequently, too, one finds the hearing used as a device to be manipulated by those who, through party government and a system of seniority, control the machinery and the personnel of the committee. The manipulation may take many forms. The hearing might, for example, be used as a method by which those already committed to a legislative policy give that policy an aura of well-reasoned respectability by making it appear that the decision was arrived at on rational grounds. This method is familiar to policy-makers on the judicial level who often endeavor to buttress a decision with judicial logic long after that decision was reached on other than logical grounds. One will find all of these purposes—and more—operative in the hearings on the Taft-Hartley issue.

Those who control the committee machinery may also use the hearings as a device to *suppress* facts salient to a policy issue because of the fear that an exposure of the facts might lend support to a policy which they do not wish to be enacted into law. . . .* One should add that when those who by control of the hearing process not only suppress the facts, but by doing so draw from it and propagate the false inference that "silence means acquiescence," then the manipulation yields double dividends.

If these examples of the legislative hearing process were the excep-

---

* [Two examples of this point have been omitted.]

tion rather than the rule, there would not be too great a cause for concern, even though the three legislative policy issues were of widespread importance. One suspects, however, that accurate, objective fact-finding to illuminate the pathways of proposed policy decisions is, by and large, not the chief function of the hearing process as it is used today. Exceptions there are, of course, but their existence as exceptions would seem merely to strengthen the suspicion of the general rule. . . .

It should be evident from all of this that, not only on the judicial level, but on the legislative level as well, there is great need for better fact-finding methods if policy-making is to become more rational. If something akin to a Ministry of Justice is needed to assist the courts in gauging the efficacy of past and proposed judicial policy-making, something similar but of considerably greater scope is needed for legislative policy-making. In its ideal form, it would require a vast army of our very best scientists—social and physical—who would be authorized to undertake an untold number of studies: diagnostic, to determine whether action is required; prognostic, to forecast trends and plan future needs; evaluative, to assess the efficacy of existing programs; fact studies, to illuminate the pathways of alternative policy choices.[29] In brief we must use all phases of applied research which would permit a transplantation of our best scientific knowledge to the field of policy-making.

Of course this is asking for the moon, but it is a target towards which to shoot. Its realization in its ideal form would obviously be hampered by many conditions, the most serious of them being: (1) the unwillingness of some policy-makers to assume the "rational" as an ethical postulate; (2) the undeveloped state of the social sciences; and (3) the fear that science will dictate what people *should* want. But the first should not deter one from the pursuit of the "rational" as a basic value in a democratic society. Nor need the second factor cause one to shy away from whatever contributions, however few, the social sciences have to make. And there *have* been a few, despite the attacks of those who refuse to recognize the worth of any advance that does not measure up in magnitude to the accomplishments of the physical sciences. Even in its primitive state, social science today can go far beyond the capacity of our average legislative policy-makers and their coteries of advisers in presenting a fairly accurate picture of the salient factors, e.g., conditions, resources and possible alternatives, which are germane to the making of rational policy judgments.[30] . . .

29. This follows, somewhat, the classificatory scheme developed by the Columbia University Bureau of Applied Research. See Merton, The Role of Applied Social Science in the Formation of Policy: A Research Memorandum, 16 *Philosophy of Science* 161, 174 (1949).

30. On this point, see Shils, Social Science and Social Policy, 16 *Philosophy of Science* 219, 236-7 (1949).

Realism in jurisprudence calls for a working arrangement between science and judicial law. Realism in legisprudence calls for a similar arrangement with legislative law. Both are but facets of a single purpose—the illumination of the pathways of policy-making with the best light that human knowledge and experience can possibly provide. Both assume that "law" can properly be understood only by a constant examination of the nature of its impact upon those whom it affects. But neither necessarily minimizes the tremendous difficulties in the way of arranging a rendezvous between science and policy-making. Some policy-makers may resent the intrusion of science out of fear that it will expose their hand, or invade an area which they regard as their exclusive domain; others may try to exploit it only when it will bolster or adorn a decision reached on other grounds; still others, impressed only with the immaturity of the social sciences, are frightened at the risk of having a rendezvous with a minor. Difficulties there are, to be sure, but the approach seems to hold the only hope for those who still cling to the pursuit of reason as the *sine qua non* of the democratic way of life.

II. STATUTORY INTERPRETATION

Heydon's Case
Exchequer, 1584
3 Co. 7a, 76 Eng. Rep. 637

. . . And it was resolved by them, that for the sure and true interpretation of all statutes in general (be they penal or beneficial, restrictive or enlarging of the common law,) four things are to be discerned and considered:—

1st. What was the common law before the making of the Act.

2nd. What was the mischief and defect for which the common law did not provide.

3rd. What remedy the Parliament hath resolved and appointed to cure the disease of the commonwealth.

And, 4th. The true reason of the remedy; and then the office of all the Judges is always to make sure construction as shall suppress the mischief, and advance the remedy, and to suppress subtle inventions and evasions for continuance of the mischief, and *pro privato commodo,* and to add force and life to the cure and remedy, according to the true intent of the makers of the Act, *pro bono publico.* . . .

Pound, Common Law and Legislation*

Not the least notable characteristics of American law today are the excessive output of legislation in all our jurisdictions and the indifference, if not contempt, with which that output is regarded by courts and lawyers. Text-writers who scrupulously gather up from every remote corner the most obsolete decisions and cite all of them, seldom cite any statutes except those landmarks which have become a part of our American common law, or, if they do refer to legislation, do so through the judicial decisions which apply it. The courts, likewise, incline to ignore important legislation; not merely deciding it to be declaratory, but sometimes assuming silently that it is declaratory without adducing any reasons, citing prior judicial decisions and making no mention of the statute.[1] In the same way, lawyers in the legislature often conceive it more expedient to make of a statute the barest outline, leaving details of the most vital importance to be filled in by judicial law-making.[2] It is fashionable to point out the deficiencies of legislation and to declare that there are things that legislators cannot do try how they will.[3] It is fashionable to preach the superiority of judge-made law.[4] It may be well, however, for judges and lawyers to remember that there is coming to be a science of legislation and that modern statutes are not to be disposed of lightly as off-hand products of a crude desire to do something, but represent long and patient study by experts, careful consideration by conferences or congresses or associations, press discussions in which public opinion is focussed upon all important details, and hearings before legislative committees. It may be well to remember also that while bench and bar are never weary of pointing out the deficiencies of legislation, to others the deficiencies of judge-made law are no less apparent. To economists and sociologists, judicial attempts to force Benthamite conceptions of free-

---

* [21 *Harv. L. Rev.* 383-388, 390, 403-404, 406-407 (1908). Footnotes have been renumbered; some footnotes omitted. Copyright 1908 by The Harvard Law Review Association. Reprinted by permission.

For biographical information, see page 63 supra.]

1. See address of Amasa M. Eaton, Proceedings of Seventeenth Annual Conference of Commissioners on Uniform State Laws, 45.

2. E.g., the Sherman Anti-Trust Act, also Senator Knox's plan for an Employers' Liability Act.

3. For examples from the juristic literature of the past two years, see Carter, *Law, Its Origin, Growth and Function,* 3; Parker, The Congestion of Law, 29 *Rep. Am. Bar Ass'n,* 383; Parker, Address as President of the Am. Bar Ass'n 1907, 19 *Green Bag* 581; Dos Passos, *The American Lawyer,* 169; Hughes, *Datum Posts of Jurisp.,* 106; 2 Andrews, *Am. Law,* 2 ed., 1190.

4. An excellent example may be seen in the Introduction (by Judge Baldwin) to *Two Centuries' Growth of American Law.*

dom of contract and common law conceptions of individualism upon the public of today are no less amusing—or even irritating—than legislative attempts to do away with or get away from these conceptions are to bench and bar. The nullifying of these legislative attempts is not regarded by lay scholars with the complacent satisfaction[5] with which lawyers are wont to speak of it. They do not hesitate to say that "the judicial mind has not kept pace with the strides of industrial development."[6] They express the opinion that "belated and anti-social" decisions have been a fruitful cause of strikes, industrial discord, and consequent lawlessness.[7] They charge that "the attitude of the courts has been responsible for much of our political immorality."[8]

There are two ways in which the courts impede or thwart social legislation demanded by the industrial conditions of today. The first is narrow and illiberal construction of constitutional provisions, state and federal. "Petty judicial interpretations," says Professor Thayer, "have always been, are now, and will always be, a very serious danger to the country."[9] The second is a narrow and illiberal attitude toward legislation conceded to be constitutional, regarding it as out of place in the legal system, as an alien element to be held down to the strictest limits and not to be applied beyond the requirements of its express language. The second is by no means so conspicuous as the first, but is not on that account the less unfortunate or the less dangerous. Let us see what this attitude is, how it arose, and why it exists in an industrial community and an age of legislation.

5. E.g., a recent writer, assuming that certain common law doctrines as to procedure inhere in nature, points out that despite legislative attempts to get away from them, courts have preserved them. This is assumed to show that the legislature had attempted the impossible. 2 Andrews, *Am. Law,* §§646, 684. Of course, one might answer that there are jurisdictions where such legislation has been given effect by the courts. Gartner v. Corwine, 57 Oh. St. 246; Rogers v. Duhart, 97 Cal. 200. One might also say that if courts had been as zealous to enforce the spirit of the New York Code of 1848 as they were to graft common law upon it and to show that its leading ideas could not be carried out, the cases might tell another story.

6. Kelley, *Some Ethical Gains through Legislation,* 142. See also Seager, *Introduction to Economics,* §236.

7. Ibid. 144, 156 [sic].

8. Smith, *Spirit of Am. Gov.,* c. xii. Professor Smith says: "By protecting the capitalist in the possession and enjoyment of privileges unwisely and even corruptly granted, they have greatly strengthened the motive for employing bribery and other corrupt means in securing the grant of special privileges. If the courts had all along held that any proof of fraud or corruption in obtaining a franchise or other legislative grant was sufficient to justify its revocation, the lobbyist, the bribe-giver and the 'innocent purchaser' of rights and privileges stolen from the people, would have found the traffic in legislative favors a precarious and much less profitable mode of acquiring wealth." 329-330.

9. Thayer, *Legal Essays,* 159.

Four ways may be conceived of in which courts in such a legal system as ours might deal with a legislative innovation. (1) They might receive it fully into the body of the law as affording not only a rule to be applied but a principle from which to reason, and hold it, as a later and more direct expression of the general will, of superior authority to judge-made rules on the same general subject; and so reason from it by analogy in preference to them. (2) They might receive it fully into the body of the law to be reasoned from by analogy the same as any other rule of law, regarding it, however, as of equal or co-ordinate authority in this respect with judge-made rules upon the same general subject. (3) They might refuse to receive it fully into the body of the law and give effect to it directly only; refusing to reason from it by analogy but giving it, nevertheless, a liberal interpretation to cover the whole field it was intended to cover. (4) They might not only refuse to reason from it by analogy and apply it directly only, but also give to it a strict and narrow interpretation, holding it down rigidly to those cases which it covers expressly. The fourth hypothesis represents the orthodox common law attitude toward legislative innovations. Probably the third hypothesis, however, represents more nearly the attitude toward which we are tending. The second and first hypotheses doubtless appeal to the common law lawyer as absurd. He can hardly conceive that a rule of statutory origin may be treated as a permanent part of the general body of the law. But it is submitted that the course of legal development upon which we have entered already must lead us to adopt the method of the second and eventually the method of the first hypothesis. . . .

. . . The proposition that statutes in derogation of the common law are to be construed strictly has no such justification. It assumes that legislation is something to be deprecated. As no statute of any consequence dealing with any relation of private law can be anything but in derogation of the common law, the social reformer and the legal reformer, under this doctrine, must always face the situation that the legislative act which represents the fruit of their labors will find no sympathy in those who apply it, will be construed strictly, and will be made to interfere with the status quo as little as possible. The New York Code of Civil Procedure of 1848 affords a conspicuous example of how completely this attitude on the part of courts may nullify legislative action.[10] Some regard

---

10. "You have the State of New York before you as a terrible example. I believe our practice today is infinitely more technical than that in New Jersey. Even the attempt to abolish forms of action and especially the attempt to abolish the distinction between law and equity practice have been dismal failures. The distinction between trover and assumpsit is today even more rigidly observed than under the common law practice. It is impossi-

this attitude toward legislation as a basic principle of jurisprudence.[11] Others are content to make of it an ancient and fundamental principle of the common law.[12] In either event they agree in praising it as a wise and useful institution.[13] It is not difficult to show, however, that it is not necessary to and inherent in a legal system; that it is not an ancient and fundamental doctrine of the common law; that it had its origin in archaic notions of interpretation generally, now obsolete, and survived in its present form because of judicial jealousy of the reform movement; and that it is wholly inapplicable to and out of place in American law of today.

That the attitude of our courts toward legislation is not necessary to and inherent in a legal system is apparent when we turn to a great legal system in which it is wholly unknown. Not only is this view of legislation unknown to Roman law, but quite an opposite doctrine was established in Roman law countries even before they enacted codes. "Where a gap has been left by any statutory rule, it is filled up, according to this method, by reference to another rule, contained in the same statute, in connection with which a point left open in the first mentioned rule is expressly provided for, and the *ratio juris* of the last mentioned expression is taken to be a general rule of law applicable to all cases." . . .

. . . As legislation was in point of fact a relatively unimportant element throughout the growing period of our legal system, it was natural that statutes should come to be regarded as furnishing rules for particular, definite situations, but not principles for cases not within their tenor, or from which to reason by analogy.[17] And the tendency to conceive of a statute as something exceptional and more or less foreign to the body of legal rules in which legislation had endeavored to insert it, which such a doctrine fostered, was furthered by the growth of an idea of limitations

---

ble to amend upon a trial from trover to assumpsit or vice versa." W. B. Hornblower, quoted in 2 Andrews, *Am. Law,* 2 ed., §635, n. 29. But the impossibility of amendment spoken of and the rigid distinction were introduced into code practice by the judges in the teeth of express code provisions upon common law considerations. De Graw v. Elmore, 50 N.Y. 1. See N.Y. Code Civ. Proc. 1848, §§69, 173, 176.

11. Robinson, *Am. Jurisp.,* §301.

12. E.g., Carter, *Law, Its Origin, Growth and Function,* 308.

13. Dr. Robinson says of the proposition that statutes in derogation of the common law are to be construed strictly that it is "a positive but reasonable rule." *Am. Jurisp.,* §301. Mr. Carter says that judges "displayed their wisdom by adopting it."

17. The phrase "common law" was borrowed from the canonists in the thirteenth century, meaning, both in its lay and in its ecclesiastical use, general, as opposed to local, law and custom. The use of "common law" in contrast to "statute law" is later, arising from the circumstance that statutes were rare. Maitland, *Canon Law in the Church of England,* 4.

upon legislation which, through our doctrine of judicial power over unconstitutional legislation, has become very strong in America. . . .

If, however, we should concede that an attitude of antipathy toward legislative innovation is a fundamental common law principle, we should have to inquire whether that principle is applicable to American conditions and is a part of our American common law. . . . For one thing, the political occasions for judicial interference with legislation have come to an end. In the sixteenth and seventeenth centuries the judiciary stood between the public and the crown. It protected the individual from the state when he required that protection. Today, when it assumes to stand between the legislature and the public and thus again to protect the individual from the state, it really stands between the public and what the public needs and desires, and protects individuals who need no protection against society which does need it. Hence the side of the courts is no longer the popular side. Moreover, courts are less and less competent to formulate rules for new relations which require legislation. They have the experience of the past. But they do not have the facts of the present. They have but one case before them, to be decided upon the principles of the past, the equities of the one situation, and the prejudices which the individualism of common law institutional writers, the dogmas learned in a college course in economics, and habitual association with the business and professional class, must inevitably produce.[18] It is a sound instinct in the community that objects to the settlement of questions of the highest social import in private litigations between John Doe and Richard Roe. It is a sound instinct that objects to an agricultural view of industrial legislation.[19] Judicial law-making for sheer lack of means to get at the real situation, operates unjustly and inequitably in a complex social organization. One might find more than one illustration in the conflict between judicial decision and labor legislation. . . .

Formerly it was argued that common law was superior to legislation because it was customary and rested upon the consent of the governed.[20] Today we recognize that the so-called custom is a custom of judicial decision, not a custom of popular action. We recognize that legislation is the more truly democratic form of law-making. We see in legislation the more direct and accurate expression of the general will.[21] We are told

---

18. "It is not to be expected from human nature that the *few* should be always attentive to the interests of the *many*." 4 *Bl. Comm.* 379. One must not forget that counsel on both sides belong to the same class and have had the same training as the judges.

19. Kelley, *Some Ethical Gains through Legislation,* 142.

20. 1 *Wilson's Works,* Andrews' ed., 183 (written 1790).

21. Bosanquet, *Philosophical Theory of the State,* 120-123.

that law-making of the future will consist in putting the sanction of society on what has been worked out in the sociological laboratory.[22] That courts cannot conduct such laboratories is self evident. Courts are fond of saying that they apply old principles to new situations.[23] But at times they must apply new principles to situations both old and new. The new principles are in legislation. The old principles are in common law. The former are as much to be respected and made effective as the latter — probably more so as our legislation improves. The public cannot be relied upon permanently to tolerate judicial obstruction or nullification of the social policies to which more and more it is compelled to be committed.

M. R. Cohen, The Process of Judicial Legislation*

II. Interpretation as a Mode of Judicial Legislation

There are few branches of the law of which the theory is so confused and disorganized as in the case of the interpretation and construction of written instruments. For this condition the theory of judicial passivity is in no slight degree responsible. This theory finds expression in the assertion that legal interpretation consists solely in finding the intention of the writer. But can any one maintain that the accepted rules of legal interpretation are simply scientific rules for the discovery of actual intention? Doubtless judges, like others, do sometimes seek and find the actual intention of parties as revealed in writings before them; but when they do so, they make use of the ordinary knowledge of language and affairs and they do not use any special rules or organon any more than they do in interpreting the oral communications of witnesses. Perhaps the day is not far distant when a scientific psychology of written language will be in a position to offer definite data to the jurist, but the prevailing technical rules of construction are not of this character. They come down to us largely from the Roman law, and their main function, so far as they partake of the nature of the rules, is first, to introduce certainty by fixing a meaning in cases where conflicting meanings are otherwise

22. Ward, *Applied Sociology*, 338.
23. E.g., Rensselaer Glass Factory v. Reed, 5 Cow. (N.Y.) 587, which has been quoted repeatedly.
* [From *Law and the Social Order*. New York: Harcourt, Brace and Company, 1933. Reprinted by permission.
For biographical information, see page 81 supra.]

possible (all questions of meaning for the court arise, of course, through the fact that two different meanings are claimed by the contending parties),[44] and, secondly, to subordinate the intention of the parties to considerations of public policy and the convenience of judicial administration. Just as the rules of evidence are, in the main, fashioned to exclude what is logically probative, so our rules of interpretation and construction of written instruments are, for the most part, rules for the exclusion of inquiry into the actual psychological intention. Considerations of public policy and of the convenient administration of justice require us to attach certain consequences to words, irrespective of the actual intention of the writer.[45] It is because of such considerations, and not in the interest of scientific truth, that the rules for the interpretation of wills differ from the rules for the interpretation of contracts or deeds, and the rule of executory from those of executed trusts.[46] Again, a blind fear of paternalism makes us say that the proper duty of the court is to interpret people's contracts, to give effect to their actual intention, and not to make contracts or impose obligations that the parties did not intend when they contracted. But as a matter of fact most of the disputes about contracts arise because of the emerging of unexpected conditions that were not in the contemplation of the parties when they made their agreement. In all such cases the courts do not enforce the real intentions of the parties, for there were none, but decide on the rights of the contestants in accordance with their sense of the equities of the case or the suggestion of analogous rules of legal obligation.

These considerations are suggestive in enabling us to avoid some confusing fiction in the theory of statutory interpretation.

Austin, Lieber, and most eminent writers after them define interpretation as the discovery of the true meaning of a statute or law. In harmony with the phonograph theory of the judicial function, this true meaning is lodged in the mind of the legislature, and the upright judge simply finds it and in no way modifies it. In actual judicial interpretation, however, this is certainly not always true. If I have any difficulty in interpreting a passage in a book, I consider myself fortunate if I can interrogate the author himself. But for the courts to ask those who actually

44. A distinction between interpretation and construction is sometimes drawn, the latter being necessary only when the meaning is doubtful. But when parties are interested in finding different meanings, "constructions will be found." (This phrase was used by such a pillar of the orthodox theory as Elihu Root.)

45. Thayer, *Preliminary Treatise on Evidence,* 1898, p. 204.

46. Maitland, *Equity,* 1910, p. 66.

drew up a statute what they meant would be absurd,[47] nay, even an expressed declaration by a legislature as to what was meant in a previous statute is effective not from the time of the original, but only from the time of the declaratory act.[48] In defence of this rule we are told that the rights acquired under the original act must not be presumed to be divested by a subsequent declaratory act. But if the actual intention of the legislator makes law, how could any rights be acquired contrary to the intention of the law?[49] We can get rid of this and other difficulties by recognizing that the legislative intent is an eliminable fiction. Experience amply shows that the drafters or framers of a law, the committee that reports it, the majority of the members of the two houses that, for various reasons, pass it, and the executive that signs it are by no means always agreed as to its meaning.[50] Hence the rule that parliamentary debates are of no direct value in the interpretation of statutes.[51]

Back, however, of the motives and ideas of the various individuals who constitute the legislature are the various interests concerned in the passing of a measure into law. We do not, of course, avoid fiction altogether by calling the triumph of one of these interests or the final compromise between conflicting claims "the will of the people." But such language brings us nearer to the actual procedure of courts in interpreting statutes, and helps us to understand the real significance of the state-

47. Thus Lord Halsbury distinctly asserts that the worst person to construe a statute is the person who drafted it, because he tends to confuse what he intended to say with what he actually said. (Hilder v. Dexter (1902) A.C. 474, 477.) A judge who drafted a bill must thus divest his mind of all past impressions of it. In re Mew and Thorne, 31 L.J. Bcy. (1862) 87.

48. Odgen, Administrator v. Blackedge, Executor, 2 Cranch 272 (1804); Dash v. Van Kleeck, 7 Johns. R. 477, Kent, J., at p. 512 (1811); Smith v. Syracuse Ins. Co., 161 N.Y. 484, 55 N.E. 1077 (1900). This rule, however, is not followed in England (Attorney General v. Theobald, 24 Q.B.D. 557 (1890) and cases therein cited). This has been carried to the extent of collecting duties, even though property has meanwhile passed to others.

49. Wahl, Les successions, 1902, Vol. I, p. 513. For criticism of the classical theory of retroactivity and vested or acquired rights, see Vareilles-Sommieres in Nouvelle revue de l'histoire du droit, 1893, pp. 241 et seq. Cf. Aubry et Rau, Cours de droit, 3d ed., 1856, Vol I, p. 30; and Planiol, op. cit. (note 40) [Traité élémentaire du droit civil (1908)], Vol. I, pp. 250 et seq.

50. A striking instance of this is to be found in Art. 757, French Civil Code. It was voted by the Assembly on the assurance by Treilhard, the reporter of the commission that edited it, that it provided for the wife a high rank among the heirs of the husband. As a matter of fact it puts the wife after all relatives, and even after natural children. See Mallieux, L'exégèse des codes, 1908, p. 16.

51. Regina v. Hartford College, 3 Q.B.D. 693, 707.

ment that courts interpret not the actual intention of the legislator but the meaning of the statute before them.

What is the meaning of a statute? The rule that courts must interpret the meaning of the statute rather than the intention of the legislature is frequently conceived as if it implied that the words of a statute are sufficient to determine every question that arises under it. This would lead to a revival of the stage of strict law in which the strictly literal meaning of words is followed no matter how unjust or absurd the consequences. Doubtless there are many who still believe juristic interpretation to be a kind of magic whereby a whole body of law is made to spring out of a few words or phrases. But most modern jurists are outgrowing the superstitious awe of the printed word and its magic potency. The meaning of a statue consists in the system of social consequences to which it leads or of the solutions to all the possible social questions that can arise under it.[52] These solutions or systems of consequences cannot be determined solely from the words used, but require a knowledge of the social conditions to which the law is to be applied as well as of the circumstances which led to its enactment. Legal rules relate to human life, and grammar or formal logic alone will not enable us to deduce their juridical consequences. The proof of the fact that the interpretation of legal rules is impossible without an intimate knowledge of the factual world to which they are to be applied, is seen in the many rules of Roman law that are today unintelligible because we do not know sufficiently under what conditions they were intended to work. The meaning of a statute, then, is a juridical creation in the light of social demands. It decides not so much what the legislature actually intended, nor what the words of a statute ordinarily mean, but *what the public, taking all the circumstances of the case into account, should act on.*[53]

Consider the rules of statutory interpretation laid down in any text-

---

52. *Scire leges non hoc est verba earum tenere sed vim ac potestatem* (Celsus, Dig. I, 3, 17). On the Continent the movement for "free" creative or sociological interpretation has now met with general acceptance. It was elaborated with unusual keenness by Kohler in articles in *Grünhuts Zeitschrift,* Vol. XIII (1886), pp. 1-61, and *Jherings Jahrbücher,* Vol. XXV (1887), pp. 262-97, but received little attention until the adoption of the German and Swiss civil codes made the topic a pressing one. Since the publication of Geny's *Méthode d'interprétation,* 1899, a whole literature on the subject has grown up, references to which will be found in Sternberg, *Einführung in die Rechtswissenschaft,* 1912, Vol. I, pp. 141-42; Cosentine, *La réforme de la législation civile,* 1913, pp. 268-78; and On Continental Legal Philosophy, pp. 286-318 of this volume [M. R. Cohen, *Law and the Social Order*]. The logical and historical parallel between the rules and methods of legal interpretation and those of Biblical exegesis offers a theme that has not been developed.

53. It also decides, incidentally, what the public should have understood or have taken the statute to mean.

book, for example, that penal statutes, or statutes in derogation of the common law, should be strictly construed, that remedial statutes should be liberally construed, and that there is an almost conclusive presumption against an unreasonable or inconvenient intention on the part of the legislator. These are not scientific rules for the discovery of actual intentions or the meanings of words, but *maxims of public policy to guide judges in the process of making law out of statutes.* It is notorious that the assumption of legislative reasonableness and regard for public welfare is one that judges privately do not hold, but public policy requires it in the administration of law. It is certainly only from this latter point of view that we can find any rationale in the rules against retroactivity. Why, for instance, can rules against retroactivity be invoked against new rights but not against new remedies, against penal legislation but not against remedial provisions? It is only by the recognition of the fact that judicial interpretation makes law that we can justify the position that decisions, like statutes, are not to be interpreted retroactively;[54] that the judicial construction of a statute is "as much a part of the statute as the text itself, and a change of decision is to all intents and purposes the same in its effects on contracts as an amendment of the law by means of a legislative act or amendment."[55] The whole Gordian knot of controversy over *Gelpoke v. Dubuque,* together with the seeming force of Justice Miller's dissenting opinion, is certainly removed by the recognition that courts do and must make law.[56]

It is generally stated that the reason why questions of interpretation arise at all is because of the necessary obscurity of language; and doubtless it is impossible to formulate regulations that shall be so unequivocal in all situations as to render unnecessary judicial selection from possible meanings. Reference, however, to the rules of interpretation applied by English courts, dealing with statutes very carefully drawn, shows that most of the questions of interpretation arise not so much because of the obscurities of language, but rather because the *courts have to apply a general law to a situation that could not have been foreseen by the legislature.* Take as an instance the Workmen's Compensation Act of 1906. This act was practically an extension of the act of 1897, as amended in 1900. The original act was most carefully drawn, and its workings carefully studied by the Digby Commission, whose report the framers of the act of 1906 had before them. Yet in spite of a mass of supplementary legislation, in the form of orders by the Home Secretary, volumes of court decisions

54. Rowan v. Runnels, 5 How. 134, 139 (1847).
55. Douglass v. County of Pike, 101 U.S. 677, 687 (1879).
56. Thayer, *Legal Essays,* 1908, p. 150.

have been necessary to determine whether certain situations shall be brought within the scope of the bill or not. In our own country, where statutes are not so carefully drawn (because of perennially green legislators), where we do not have anything to compare in thoroughness with the English statutory interpretation act of 1889, and where, because of the mischievous dogma that legislative powers cannot be delegated, we do not allow administrative officers ample power of supplementary legislation, all this mass of supplementary legislation has to be enacted by the courts, in the form of judicial interpretations, and no one really knows a law thoroughly unless he knows what the courts have made of it.[57]

Not only must courts supplement legislative enactments by supplying the detailed rules and regulations, but the interests of any workable justice demand that courts should also in effect exercise a limited power of amending the law. Legislatures are the commissioners of warring social interests. They can draw up general treaties of peace, but the details have at all times been and must be inserted by the courts, else we should have a constant recurrence to a state of lawlessness. Courts must necessarily attach a somewhat different meaning to statutes than do the legislators, owing to the necessarily different point of view. The conditions of legislation make legislators view even the most general statutes exclusively as measures of relief to certain social demands. Courts, however, must construe them as integral parts of the legal system that controls the whole of life. Legislators can never have in mind all the possible consequences of their enactments, and many of them would be shocked and would refuse to pass the bills they do if they could realize these consequences. Hence, every system of legal administration that is not impossibly rigorous allows the judge, who has had the chance of seeing the actual working of the statute in concrete situations, some power of amendment—hard and fast legal and political theories to the contrary notwithstanding.[58]

The process by which the terms of laws are widened or narrowed has been called spurious interpretation. Such interpretation is spurious only so far as it pretends to discover the actual intention of the legislator, but the process of extending or restricting the meaning of a statute is inevitable. Unless we are wilfully to blind ourselves by some dogma of

57. One of the most usual ways in which courts supplement a statute is by supplying definitions, for instance, defining "person" in the Fourteenth Amendment to include corporations. Again, if the legislature in an income-tax law defines "income" to include the unearned increment of land value, there is no doubt that this is substantial legislation. Would it be less so if, in the absence of legislative expression, the courts would so define it?

58. For example, see Thayer, op. cit. (note 45) pp. 195-96.

legislative omniscience, we must recognize that supplementary legislation by judges or other administrative officials is absolutely necessary to make statutes workable.[59] Statutes must be expressed in general and more or less abstract terms. *To make a detailed description of specific human actions forbidden or allowed and their consequences would be an endless and impossible task.* The judge, however, must apply the general rule to specific cases. To prevent an impossible uniformity or rigour, and to give statutes a form and content that will adapt them to the complicated needs of life, judges must classify the cases under the rule and use what is called equitable interpretation as a corrective or supplement to the abstract generality of the law before them. That equitable interpretation is not foreign to the essence of the common law can be seen in such writers as Littleton, Coke, and Sheppard. Some of our courts and textbook writers have said that the doctrine of equitable interpretaion has been abandoned in modern times. But does not the well established rule and practice that an inconvenient and inequitable interpretation is to be avoided, that the spirit rather than the letter of the statute is to be given effect, amount to the same thing? The extent to which this latter rule is carried can be shown by the fact that courts will, in the interests of equitable interpretation, change the tense of a statute,[60] interpret the phrase "single man" to include widows,[61] or the term "woman" to exclude married women,[62] and the like. Nothing is more usual in the interpretation of statutes than to find them construed as operating between certain persons only, or for certain purposes only, though the language expresses no such limitation;[63] or cases where the language is extended to include things that were not known and could not have been contemplated by the legislators when the statute was passed—for example, when the word "telegraph" is held to cover the telephone invented subsequent to the law in question.[64]

59. It is interesting to note that, in spite of the wide power of supplementary legislation given to administrative officers on the Continent, modern Continental codes recognize the need of judicial legislation, the German Civil Code implicitly (e.g., sec. 626) and the Swiss Code explicitly (Civil Code, Art. 1, 2). Cf. the Italian Civil Code, Art. 3, and the Austrian Civil Code, Art 7. Even the framers of the Napoleonic Code recognized this. "A host of things are necessarily left to the rule of usage, to the discipline of learned men, and to the decision of judges." Portalis, *"Discours préliminaire"* (1836), Fenet, *Recueil complet des travaux préparatoires du Code Civil,* p. 476.

60. Malloy v. Chicago & N.W.R. Co., 109 Wis. 29, 85 N.W. 130 (1901).

61. Silver v. Ladd, 7 Wall. 219 (1868).

62. R. v. Harrald, L.R. 7 Q.B. 361 (1872).

63. See cases quoted by Maxwell, *Statutory Interpretation,* 1884, pp. 115, 118, 163-68; and W. H. Loyd, "The Equity of a Statute," *University of Pennsylvania Law Review,* Vol. LVIII (1909), p. 76.

64. Attorney General v. Edison Tel. Co., 6 Q.B.D. 244 (1880).

Llewellyn, The Common Law Tradition*

[A great deal can be learned about the process of statutory interpretation by comparing it to the doctrine of precedent. Many of the vagaries and inconsistencies of precedent† are] paralleled, in regard to statutes, because of (1) the power of the legislature both to choose policy and to select measures; and (2) the necessity that the legislature shall, in so doing, use language—language fixed in particular words; and (3) the continuing duty of the courts to make sense, but to make sense under, with, and within the law.

For just as prior courts can have been skillful or unskillful, clear or unclear, wise or unwise, so can legislatures. And just as prior courts have commonly been looking at only a single piece of our whole law at a time, so have legislatures.

But a court must strive to make sense *as a whole* out of our law *as a whole*. It must, to use Frank's figure,‡ take the music of any statute as written by the legislature; it must take the text of the play as written by the legislature. But there are many ways to play that music, to play that play, and a court's duty is to play it well, and to play it in harmony with the other music of the legal system.

Hence, in the field of statutory construction also, there are "correct," unchallengeable rules of "how to read" which lead in happily variant directions.

* [Pp. 373-374, 521-527 (Little, Brown and Company 1960). Reprinted by permission. For biographical information, see page 212 supra.]

† [Llewellyn discussed the role of precedent in appellate decisions. He stressed the divergent ways in which courts apply prior cases to present disputes. "Impeccable and correct doctrine" indicates that a case holds only so much as is required to sustain its decision. Everything else is dicta, and need not be consulted in future cases. According to this view, any distinction between the facts of prior and instant cases would be ample cause to distinguish the earlier case and discard its alleged holding. However, doctrine "equally impeccable and correct" dictates that a case always holds the rule upon which the court chose to base its judgment, and that that rule properly controls all future cases to which the reason of the rule applies, including even cases with clearly distinguishable facts. Similarly contradictory approaches are commonly used when courts analyze series or bodies of cases and trends in the law.

Llewellyn emphasized the fact that such apparent inconsistency is not a departure from or an evasion of precedent. The appearance of inconsistency is actually the product of the popular fallacy that prior cases, in and of themselves, provide a single, correct answer to current disputes of law when the court properly applies existing rules on how to handle cases. In appellate decisions, there are almost always several—or even many—correct answers to a legal problem. Therefore, the court's job is to *select* and *apply* one of these several possible correct answers.]

‡ [Frank, Words and Music: Some Remarks on Statutory Interpretation, 47 *Col. L. Rev.* 1259 (1947).]

This must be so until courts recognize that here, as in case law, the real guide is Sense-for-All-of-Us. It must be so, so long as we and the courts pretend that there has been only one single correct answer possible. Until we give up that foolish pretense there must be a set of mutually contradictory or conflicting *correct* rules on How to Construe Statutes: either or any available as duty and sense may require.

Until then, also, the problem will recur in statutory construction as in the handling of case law: *Which* of the technically correct answers (1) *should* be given; (2) *will* be given—and Why?

And everything said above about the temper of the court, the temper of the court's tradition, the sense of the type-situation, and the sense of the particular case applies here as well.

Thus in the period of the Grand Style of case law statutes were construed "freely" to implement their purpose, the court commonly accepting the legislature's choice of policy and setting to work to implement it. (Criminal statutes and, to some extent, statutes on procedure were exceptions.) Whereas in the Formal period statutes tended to be limited or even eviscerated by wooden and literal reading, in a sort of long-drawn battle between a balky, stiff necked, wrongheaded court and a legislature which had only words with which to drive that court. Today the courts have regained, in the main, a cheerful acceptance of legislative choice of policy, but in carrying such policies forward they are still hampered to some extent by the Formal period's insistence on precise language.

One last thing is to be noted:

If a statute is to make sense, it must be read in the light of some assumed purpose. A statute merely declaring a rule, with no purpose or objective, is nonsense.

If a statute is to be merged into a going system of law, moreover, the court must do the merging, and must in so doing take account of the policy of the statute—or else substitute its own version of such policy. Creative reshaping of the net result is thus inevitable.

But the policy of a statute is of two wholly different kinds—each kind somewhat limited in effect by the statute's choice of measures, and by the statute's choice of fixed language. On the one hand there are the ideas consciously before the draftsmen, the committee, the legislature: a known goal to be attained, a deliberate choice of one line of approach rather than another. Here talk of "intent" is reasonably realistic; committee reports, legislative debate, historical knowledge of contemporary thinking or campaigning which points up the evil or the goal can have significance.

But on the other hand—and increasingly as any statute gains in age

—its language is called upon to deal with circumstances utterly uncontemplated at the time of its passage. Here the quest is not properly for the sense originally intended by the statute, for the sense sought originally to be *put into it,* but rather for the sense which *can be quarried out of it* in the light of the new situation. Broad purposes can indeed reach far beyond details known or knowable at the time of drafting. A "dangerous weapon" statute of 1840 can include Tommy guns, tear gas, or atomic bombs. "Vehicle," in a statute of 1840, can properly be read, when sense so suggests, to include an automobile, or a hydroplane that lacks wheels. But for all that, the sound quest does not run primarily in terms of historical intent. It runs in terms of what the words can be made to bear, in making sense in the new light of what was originally unforeseen. . . .

When it comes to presenting a proposed statutory construction in court, there is an accepted conventional vocabulary. As in argument over points of case-law, the accepted convention still, unhappily, requires discussion as if only one single correct meaning could exist. Hence there are two opposing canons on almost every point. An arranged selection is appended. Every lawyer must be familiar with them all: they are still needed tools of argument.

Plainly, to make any canon take hold in a particular instance, the construction contended for must be sold, essentially, by means other than the use of the canon: The good sense of the situation and a *simple* construction of the available language to achieve that sense, *by tenable means, out of the statutory language.*

Canons of Construction

Thrust	But	Parry
1. A statute cannot go beyond its text.[3]		1. To effect its purpose a statute may be implemented beyond its text.[4]
2. Statutes in derogation of the common law will not be extended by construction.[5]		2. Such acts will be liberally construed if their nature is remedial.[6]
3. Statutes are to be read in the light of the common law and a statute		3. The common law gives way to a statute which is inconsistent with it and

3. First National Bank v. DeBerriz, 87 W. Va. 477, 105 S.E. 900 (1921): Sutherland, *Statutory Construction* §388 (2d ed. 1904); 59 C.J., *Statutes* §575 (1932).

4. Dooley v. Penn. R.R., 250 Fed. 142 (D. Minn. 1918); 59 C.J., *Statutes* §575 (1932).

5. Devers v. City of Scranton, 308 Pa. 13, 161 Atl. 540 (1932); Black, *Construction and Interpretation of Laws* §113 (2d ed. 1911); Sutherland, *Statutory Construction* §573 (2d ed. 1904); 25 R.C.L., *Statutes* §281 (1919).

6. Becker v. Brown, 65 Neb. 264, 91 N.W. 178 (1902); Black, *Construction and Interpretation of Laws* §113 (2d ed. 1911); Sutherland, *Statutory Construction* §§573-75 (2d ed. 1904); 59, C.J., *Statutes* §657 (1932).

Thrust	*But*	*Parry*

Thrust   *But*   *Parry*

affirming a common law rule is to be construed in accordance with the common law.[7]

7. A statute imposing a new penalty or forfeiture, or a new liability or disability, or creating a new right of action will not be construed as having a retroactive effect.[15]

8. Where design has been distinctly stated no place is left for construction.[17]

9. Definitions and rules of construction contained in an interpretation clause are part of the law and binding.[19]

11. Titles do not control meaning; preambles do not expand scope; section headings do not change language.[23]

when a statute is designed as a revision of a whole body of law applicable to a given subject it supersedes the common law.[8]

7. Remedial statutes are to be liberally construed and if a retroactive interpretation will promote the end of justice, they should receive such construction.[16]

8. Courts have the power to inquire into real—as distinct from ostensible—purpose.[18]

9. Definitions and rules of construction in a statute will not be extended beyond their necessary import nor allowed to defeat intention otherwise manifested.[20]

11. The title may be consulted as a guide when there is doubt or obscurity in the body; preambles may be consulted to determine rationale, and thus the true construction of terms; section headings may be looked upon as part of the statute itself.[24]

7. Bandfield v. Bandfield, 117 Mich. 80, 75 N.W. 287 (1898); 25 R.C.L., *Statutes* §280 (1919).

8. Hamilton v. Rathbone, 175 U.S. 414, 20 Sup. Ct. 155, 44 L. Ed. 219 (1899); State v. Lewis, 142 N.C. 626, 55 S.E. 600 (1906); 25 R.C.L., *Statutes* §§280, 289 (1919).

15. Keeley v. Great Northern Ry., 139 Wis. 448, 121 N.W. 167 (1909); Black *Construction and Interpretation of Laws* §119 (2d ed. 1911).

16. Falls v. Key, 278 S.W. 893 (Tex. Civ. App. 1925); Black, *Construction and Interpretation of Laws* §120 (2d ed. 1911).

17. Federoff v. Birks Bros., 75 Cal. App. 345, 242 Pac. 885 (1925); Sutherland, *Statutory Construction* §358 (2d ed. 1904); 59 C.J., *Statutes* §570 (1932).

18. Coulter v. Pool, 187 Cal. 181, 201 Pac. 120 (1921); 59 C.J., *Statutes* §570 (1932).

19. Smith v. State, 28 Ind. 321 (1867); Black, *Construction and Interpretation of Laws* §89 (2d ed. 1911); 59 C.J., *Statutes* §567 (1932).

20. In re Bissell, 245 App. Div. 395, 282 N.Y. Supp. 983 (4th Dep't 1935); Black, *Construction and Interpretation of Laws* §89 (2d ed. 1911); 59 C.J., *Statutes* §566 (1932).

23. Westbrook v. McDonald, 184 Ark. 740, 44 S.W.2d 331 (1931); Huntworth v. Tanner, 87 Wash. 670, 152 Pac. 523 (1915); Black, *Construction and Interpretation of Laws* §§83-85 (2d ed. 1911); Sutherland, *Statutory Construction* §§339-42 (2d ed. 1904); 59 C.J., *Statutes* §599 (1932); 25 R.C.L., *Statutes* §§266-267 (1919).

24. Brown v. Robinson, 275 Mass. 55, 175 N.E. 269 (1931); Gulley v. Jackson, 165 Miss. 103, 145 So. 905 (1933); Black, *Construction and Interpretation of Laws* §§83-85 (2d ed. 1911); Sutherland, *Statutory Construction* §§339-42 (2d ed. 1904); 59 C.J., *Statutes* §§598-99 (1932); 25 R.C.L., *Statutes* §§266, 267 (1919).

Thrust	*But*	*Parry*
12. If language is plain and unambiguous it must be given effect.[25]		12. Not when literal interpretation would lead to absurd or mischievous consequences or thwart manifest purpose.[26]
15. Words are to be taken in their ordinary meaning unless they are technical terms or words of art.[31]		15. Popular words may bear a technical meaning and technical words may have a popular signification and they should be so construed as to agree with evident intention or to make the statute operative.[32]
17. The same language used repeatedly in the same connection is presumed to bear the same meaning throughout the statute.[35]		17. This presumption will be disregarded where it is necessary to assign different meanings to make the statute consistent.[36]
18. Words are to be interpreted according to the proper grammatical effect of their arrangement within the statute.[37]		18. Rules of grammar will be disregarded where strict adherence would defeat purpose.[38]
21. General terms are to receive a general construction.[43]		21. They may be limited by specific terms with which they are associated or by the scope and purpose of the statute.[44]

25. Newhall v. Sanger, 92 U.S. 761, 23 L. Ed. 769 (1875); Black, *Construction and Interpretation of Laws* §51 (2d ed. 1911); 59 C.J., *Statutes* §569 (1932); 25 R.C.L., *Statutes* §§213, 225 (1919).

26. Clark v. Murray, 141 Kan. 533, 41 P.2d 1042 (1935); Sutherland, *Statutory Construction* §363 (2d ed. 1904); 59 C.J., *Statutes* §573 (1932); 25 R.C.L., *Statutes* §§214, 257 (1919).

31. Hawley Coal Co. v. Bruce, 252 Ky. 455, 67 S.W.2d 703 (1934); Black, *Construction and Interpretation of Laws* §63 (2d ed. 1911); Sutherland, *Statutory Construction* §§390, 393 (2d ed. 1904); 59 C.J., *Statutes* §§577, 578 (1932).

32. Robinson v. Varnell, 16 Tex. 382 (1856); Black, *Construction and Interpretation of Laws* §63 (2d ed. 1911); Sutherland, *Statutory Construction* §395 (2d ed. 1904); 59 C.J., *Statutes* §§577, 578 (1932).

35. Spring Canyon Coal Co. v. Industrial Comm'n, 74 Utah 103, 277 Pac. 206 (1929); Black, *Construction and Interpretation of Laws* §53 (2d ed. 1911).

36. State v. Knowles, 90 Md. 646, 45 Atl. 877 (1900); Black, *Construction and Interpretation of Laws* §53 (2d ed. 1911).

37. Harris v. Commonwealth, 142 Va. 620, 128 S.E. 578 (1925); Black, *Construction and Interpretation of Laws* §55 (2d ed. 1911); Sutherland, *Statutory Construction* §408 (2d ed. 1904).

38. Fisher v. Connard, 100 Pa. 63 (1882); Black, *Construction and Interpretation of Laws* §55 (2d ed. 1911); Sutherland, *Statutory Construction* §408 (2d ed. 1904).

43. De Witt v. San Francisco, 2 Cal. 289 (1852); Black, *Construction and Interpretation of Laws* §68 (2d ed. 1911); 59 C.J., *Statutes* §580 (1932).

44. People ex rel. Krause v. Harrison, 191 Ill. 257, 61 N.E. 99 (1901); Black, *Construction and Interpretation of Laws* §69 (1911); Sutherland, *Statutory Construction* §347 (2d ed. 1904).

Thrust	*But*	*Parry*

22. It is a general rule of construction that where general words follow an enumeration they are to be held as applying only to persons and things of the same general kind or class specifically mentioned (*ejusdem generis*).[45]

24. Punctuation will govern when a statute is open to two constructions.[49]

26. There is a distinction between words of permission and mandatory words.[53]

22. General words must operate on something. Further, *ejusdem generis* is only an aid in getting the meaning and does not warrant confining the operations of a statute within narrower limits than were intended.[46]

24. Punctuation marks will not control the plain and evident meaning of language.[50]

26. Words imparting permission may be read as mandatory and words imparting command may be read as permissive when such construction is made necessary by evident intention or by the rights of the public.[54]

MacCallum, Legislative Intent*

Introduction

Appeals to legislative intent are a commonplace part of our judicial process. Nevertheless there are many unresolved disputes about the ex-

45. Hull Hospital v. Wheeler, 216 Iowa 1394, 250 N.W. 637 (1933); Black, *Construction and Interpretation of Laws* §71 (2d ed. 1911); Sutherland, *Statutory Construction* §§422-34 (2d ed. 1904); 59 C.J., *Statutes* §581 (1932); 25 R.C.L., *Statutes* §240 (1919).

46. Texas v. United States, 292 U.S. 522, 54 Sup. Ct. 819, 78 L. Ed. 1402 (1934); Grosjean v. American Paint Works, 160 So. 449 (La. App. 1935); Black, *Construction and Interpretation of Laws* §71 (2d ed. 1911); Sutherland, *Statutory Construction* §§437-41 (2d ed. 1904); 59 C.J., *Statutes* §581 (1932); 25 R.C.L., *Statutes* §240 (1919).

49. United States v. Marshall Field & Co., 18 C.C.P.A. 228 (1930); Black, *Construction and Interpretation of Laws* §87 (2d ed. 1911); Sutherland, *Statutory Construction* §361 (2d ed. 1904); 59 C.J., *Statutes* §590 (1932).

50. State v. Baird, 36 Ariz. 531, 288 Pac. 1 (1930); Black, *Construction and Interpretation of Laws,* §87 (2d ed. 1911); Sutherland, *Statutory Construction* §361 (2d ed. 1904); 59 C.J., *Statutes* §590 (1932).

53. Koch & Dryfus v. Bridges, 45 Miss. 247 (1871); Black, *Construction and Interpretation of Laws* §150 (2d ed. 1911).

54. Jennings v. Suggs, 180 Ga. 141, 178 S.E. 282 (1935); Ewing v. Union Central Bank, 254 Ky. 623, 72 S.W.2d 4 (1934); *Black, Construction and Interpretation of Laws* §151 (2d ed. 1911); 59 C.J., *Statutes* §631 (1932).

* [75 *Yale L.J.* 754-787 (1966). Reprinted by permission of The Yale Law Journal Company and Fred B. Rothman & Company from The Yale Law Journal, Vol. 75, pp. 754-787. The writing of this paper was supported in part by the Research Committee of the Graduate School of the University of Wisconsin from funds supplied by the Wisconsin Alumni Research Foundation.

Gerald C. MacCallum, Jr. (1925–) is Professor of Philosophy at the University of

istence and discoverability of legislative intent. In 1930, Max Radin argued that the presence of genuine legislative intent in connection with a statute is at best a rare circumstance and that, in any event, the legislative intent could not be discovered from the records of the legislative proceedings.[1] This argument drew an immediate response from James Landis. Landis distinguished between two senses of "intent"—"intent" as "intended meaning" and "intent" as "purpose." He maintained that legislative intent in the first sense (and apparently in the second also) is an ordinary although not invariable feature of legislative processes. Furthermore, he contended that this feature, when present, is clearly discoverable in the records of the legislative proceedings.[2]

The Radin-Landis dispute has had a curious history. Since 1930, treatises and articles on statutory interpretation have often mentioned the dispute and have sometimes taken sides. But commentators siding with Radin, although abandoning talk about legislative intent, proceed to talk freely about the "legislative purposes," "policies," and "objectives" of statutes. Because it is not obvious that these expressions refer to anything different from legislative intent, one would expect careful discussion of where the differences lie. In particular, one would expect to find a showing that arguments leading to the rejection of talk about legislative intent have no force against these new expressions. But no such showing is to be found in the leading discussions of the matter—including those by Willis,[4] Frankfurter,[5] Corry[6] and Radin himself[7]. . . .

Again, we find unsupported assumptions that statutes would be wholly meaningless in the absence of anything identifiable as legislative

Wisconsin. He was educated at the University of California, Berkeley, and was a Fulbright Scholar at Oxford University and a Fellow of the American Council of Learned Societies.]

1. Radin, Statutory Interpretation, 43 *Harv. L. Rev.* 863 (1930). Radin also denied the relevance of appeals to legislative intent. This article, however, is only concerned with the prior questions of the existence and discoverability of legislative intent. For earlier criticisms of the notion of legislative intent, see Sedgwick, *The Interpretation and Construction of Statutory and Constitutional Law* 327-28 (2d ed. 1874); Bruncken, Interpretation of Written Law, 25 *Yale L.J.* 129 (1915); Kocourek, *An Introduction to the Science of Law* 201 (1930).

2. Landis, A Note on "Statutory Interpretation," 43 *Harv. L. Rev.* 886 (1930).

4. Willis, Statute Interpretation in a Nutshell, 16 *Can. Bar Rev.* 1 (1938).

5. Frankfurter, Some Reflections on the Reading of Statutes, 47 *Colum. L. Rev.* 527 (1947).

6. Corry, Administrative Law and the Interpretation of Statutes, 1 *U. Toronto L.J.* 286 (1936). See also Corry, The Use of Legislative History in the Interpretation of Statutes, 32 *Can. Bar Rev.* 624 (1954).

7. Radin, A Short Way With Statutes, 56 *Harv. L. Rev.* 388 (1942).

intent,[10] and that the meaning assigned to them "must be one intended by the law-makers or the law-makers do not legislate."[11] Such remarks raise interesting issues, but, as will be seen below, the arguments supporting them cannot stand. . . .

I

The most obvious difficulty with the notion of legislative intent concerns the relationship between the intent of a collegiate legislature and the intentions of the several legislators. Many difficulties would remain, however, if a legislature had only one authoritative member. We would profit, therefore, by asking what it could mean to speak of the legislative intent of a single legislator.

The fundamental question "what was the legislator's intent" subsumes a number of more specific questions:

1. Was his intent to enact a statute—i.e., was the "enacting" performance not, perchance, done accidentally, inadvertently or by mistake?
2. Was his intent to enact *this* statute—i.e., was this the *document* (the draft) he thought he was endorsing?
3. Was his intent to enact *this* statute—i.e., are the *words* in this document precisely those he supposed to be there when he enacted it as a statute?
4. Was his intent to enact *this* statute—i.e., do these words *mean* precisely what he supposed them to mean when he endorsed their use in the statute?
5. How did *he* intend these words to be understood?
6. What was his intent in enacting the statute—i.e., what did he intend the enactment of the statute to achieve?
7. What was his intent in enacting the statute—i.e., what did he intend the enactment of the statute to achieve *in terms of his own career?*[12]

Failure to distinguish between these more specific questions is responsible for much of the confusion in debates about the existence, dis-

---

10. Cf. Crawford, *The Construction of Statutes* 255 (1940).
11. Id. at 256.
12. Witherspoon, Administrative Discretion to Determine Statutory Meaning: "The Middle Road": I, 40 *Texas L. Rev.* 751, 796-800 (1962), distinguishes twenty-two "forms or configurations of legislative purpose that may be discovered at work in any particular legislative process productive of a statute."

coverability and relevance of legislative intent. It is therefore important to examine closely the relationships between the more troublesome of these questions.

A. *The Aims of the Legislator:* the distinction between
   6. What did he intend enactment of the statute to achieve? and
   7. What did he intend enactment to achieve in terms of his own career?

These questions distinguish between two kinds of reasons the legislator may have for enacting a statute—reasons looking to the effects of enactment upon the legal system, and reasons looking to the effects of enactment on his own career.[13] This distinction is crucial to any discussion of the relevance of legislative intent, since judges and administrators are unlikely to regard as significant the legislator's concern with his own career. The distinction is also important when one is discussing the existence and discoverability of legislative intent. To say there was no intent at all, for example, might mean that the enactment was motiveless, e.g., inadvertent or accidental. On the other hand, it might mean that no intent of the relevant sort was present, that the legislator had only his personal career in mind when enacting the statute. Furthermore, depending on the records available, one kind of intent might be discoverable while the other is not. Thus the two must be kept distinct.

B. *Intent as Intended Meaning and Intent as Purpose:* the distinction between
   6. What did he intend the enactment of the statute to achieve? and
   5. How did *he* intend these words to be understood?

Landis notes the way the distinction between intent as (intended) meaning and intent as purpose becomes obscured when he says:

> Purpose and meaning commonly react upon each other. Their exact differentiation would require an extended philosophical essay. . . . [T]he Distinction . . . is a nice one.[14]

Even though the distinction may be a "nice one," no lengthy essay is needed to underscore the importance of distinguishing questions about

13. See de Sloovère, Preliminary Questions in Statutory Interpretation, 9 *N.Y.U.L. Rev.* 407, 415 (1932), where his remark about "individual and combined motives" encourages, if it does not actually constitute, a conflation of the questions.
14. See Note, A Note on "Statutory Interpretation," 43 *Harv. L. Rev.* 886, 888 (1930).

the purposes of specific legislators from general questions about the meanings of statutory words. The major source of confusion has been the belief that we must always guide our understanding of statutory words by an understanding of legislative purposes, as though we could not understand the words without prior knowledge of the purposes. This belief is most readily countered with the reminder that our primary source of "evidence" of specific legislative purposes in connection with a statute generally lies in the words of the statute itself, and that these words could not provide such evidence if their meanings were not determined independently of consideration of the purposes in question.[16]

Confusion about the interplay between purpose and meaning has become so embedded in discussions of statutory interpretation that a more extended argument may be desirable. In particular, it may be helpful to show that the distinction between purpose and meaning exists even when the considerable concessions suggested by question 5 are made in the direction of establishing a connection between the purpose of a legislator and the meaning of what he says in a statute. Suppose we stipulate (i) that a legislator's words always mean precisely what he thinks they mean, and (ii) that the purposes in question concern the career of the statute rather than the career of the legislator. The first stipulation seems to go as far as possible in the direction of a tight connection between statutory meaning and the intentions or purposes of the legislator. The second stipulation restricts the purposes in question to those most generally thought to enter legitimately into issues of statutory interpretation. Even with these stipulations, however, one may show that persons normally need not be aware of legislative purposes in order to understand legislative words.

Although the problem is an "interpreter's" problem, it will be helpful to consider the matter first from the point of view of the legislator, and on the simplifying assumption that he is the author of the statutes he enacts. He is typically interested in enacting a piece of legislation because he wants to effect certain changes in the society. The words he uses are the instruments by means of which he expects or hopes to effect these changes. What gives him this expectation or this hope is his belief that he can anticipate how others (e.g., judges and administrators) will understand these words. The words would be useless to him if he could not anticipate how they would be understood by these other persons. Insofar as this concern for how his words will be understood is a concern

16. Cf. E. A. Dreidger, *The Composition of Legislation* 159 (1957). It is true that we sometimes allow our understanding of legislative purposes to shed light on puzzling passages in a statute. But we could not even attempt this if we did not believe we already understood most of the words in the statute.

about the "meaning" of his words, this "meaning" must thus generally be determinable independently of consideration of his purposes; for, until he forms opinions about the "meaning" of the words, he cannot consider whether they will serve his purpose.

The legislator can attempt to assure that his words will be correctly understood in various ways, e.g., by stipulation. But if he stipulates he must use other words about which he will have the same general concern. Ultimately, he must recognize that with the bulk of his words he cannot create but only can utilize the conventions in the light of which his words will be understood.[18] The legislator will be interested primarily in the conventions of statutory interpretation—that is, in the current conventional approaches by judges, administrators, lawyers and citizens to the understanding of statutes. Although these conventions will not guarantee specific results, they are all that he has to work with.

Consider the matter now from the point of view of the interpreters of statutes. Maintaining a perspective favorable to the association of legislative purpose with statutory meaning, suppose that the interpreters declare themselves bound by what the legislator wanted at the time the statute was enacted. Suppose, in particular, that, rather than raising any questions about how the legislator *ought* to have expected his words to be understood, the interpreters assume that their only legitimate task is the discovery of the legislator's actual expectations.

Difficulties arise immediately. There may be a lack of fit between how the legislator expected the words of the statute to be understood, and what he hoped to achieve by means of the statute. That is, the statute itself, or some constituent parts of it, may have been poorly chosen instruments for the achievement of his goals—not in the sense that the words were not understood as he expected them to be, but rather in the

18. Of course, one convention of statutory interpretation might permit or require that one's understanding of statutory language be guided by consideration of the legislator's purpose. Such a convention would invite the legislator to attempt to lay down a trail of his "purposes" for others to follow; hence the use, in jurisdictions where legislators believe that interpreters of statutes will seek and heed such "evidence," of statutory preambles, carefully manufactured "legislative histories," etc. The only feature of note about this convention is that it offers the legislator an opportunity to influence rather than merely to anticipate how his statutory words will be understood. In this respect, it is analogous to conventions for stipulation and for formal definition. Nevertheless, the "trail" he is able to lay down, both within and outside of the statute, will be primarily if not exclusively a verbal one. As with stipulations, if the legislator believes he can influence the understanding of his statutory words, it is only because he has certain expectations about how certain other words will be understood. These expectations also must be formed independently of consideration of his purposes, because until he has the expectations he can have no notion of whether these other words will serve his purposes.

sense that, even when the words *were* understood as he expected, behavior in accordance with this understanding did not produce the results he thought it would produce. There are, in short, at least *two* distinct ways in which things could go wrong from the legislator's point of view: (1) people might not understand the words of the statute in the way he thought they would, or (2) the behavior of people who understand the words as he thought they would and who act truly in accordance with this understanding, might not produce the results that the legislator anticipated. In the first case, the legislator would have made a mistake in predicting how his words would be understood; in the second case, he would have made a mistake in predicting what would happen if people behaved in certain ways.[19] The difference between the two kinds of mistakes is obscured for the "interpreter," and his view of statutory interpretation is consequently muddied, if he supposes that an understanding of the legislator's "purposes" is either a sufficient or normally necessary guide to how the legislator expected the words of the statute to be understood.

As the legislator may simply have misjudged the effectiveness of the statutory scheme in achieving the purported purpose, a resolve to interpret the words of the statute so that the statute *will be* an effective instrument for the achievement of the purpose would be simply a refusal to consider the possibility of this kind of legislative misjudgment. The importance of this observation lies in the fact that, where such legislative misjudgment has actually occurred, the method of interpretation under consideration may not produce an understanding of the words of the statute corresponding to that which the legislator expected—the very understanding that figured in his deliberate choice of those words. In the end, there may be nothing *wrong* with this; the legislator may be delighted with a method of interpretation which hides his own misjudgment. But are the interpreters really being faithful to to the "intentions" of the legislator when they interpret his words differently from what he had expected? At the very least, this problem should be brought into the open and faced squarely—something that has not been done and is not likely to be done so long as intent as "meaning" and intent as purpose are conflated.

One may wonder how intended legislative meaning could possibly

---

19. The distinction between the two is clear enough even though there may be a large shadowy area between them where the legislator's expectations were not well-formed, and where even he might not be able to say whether, on the one hand, his words had not been understood as he expected, or rather, on the other hand, that he had proposed in the statute an ineffective way of achieving what he wished to achieve. See Hagerstrom, *Inquiries into the Nature of Law and Morals* 79-81 (Broad trans. 1953).

be discovered *without* appeal to knowledge of legislative purpose. The answer is that discovery depends primarily upon our awareness of the linguistic conventions the legislator looked to in forming his expectations about how his words would be understood. Awareness of these conventions will provide us with good (although not infallible) grounds for believing we know what his expectations were. Moreover, there is no great problem in attaining this awareness. We know perfectly well how to tell whether a man speaks the same language we do, and how to tell whether we can speak his language. Our capacity to do this provides us with a generally adequate basis for determining when the legislator and we are both familiar with the linguistic conventions in the light of which various understandings of his words will be formed, and for determining whether we can understand these conventions in the same ways. Further, if we are the specific audience to whom his remarks are directed, we are merely asking ourselves what our own linguistic conventions are, and how well he might have understood them. The fact that statutory language ordinarily serves us quite well in this respect indicates that we are able to use the same linguistic conventions as the legislator and to know that we are doing so.

In sum, for us as well as for the legislator, practical understanding of his language is ordinarily founded on a grasp of the linguistic conventions utilized, rather than a grasp of his specific purposes in enacting the statute. This explains both how his words can serve us as evidence of his purposes, and why there is ordinarily no need to search for his purposes in order to understand what he meant.

C. Can the Legislator Misunderstand His Own Words? the distinction between

4. Do these words *mean* precisely what he supposed them to mean when he endorsed their use in the statute? and
5. How did *he* intend these words to be understood?

Question (4) pinpoints, as question (5) does not, the possibility that the *legislator* has misunderstood the words he used in a statutory document. Reading some discussions on statutory interpretation, one would think it impossible for a legislator to misunderstand what he has written or endorsed. In these discussions, the entire burden of understanding or misunderstanding the statute seemingly is placed upon others—the judge, the lawyer, the citizen. The effective slogan of these discussions might well be that the words of the statute mean what their author-endorser (the legislator) intended them to mean. But, as we have seen, words in statutes are of use both to legislators and to others because they have acquired significance through the growth or stipulation of conventions regarding their use. Indeed, we could not recognize something *as* a word, rather than as merely a contour (or range of contours) of sounds or a certain form (or range of forms) of scribblings if we were not aware that sounds and scribblings with such contours and forms have a significance, function, or value resulting from the growth or stipulation of such conventions. *Our* belief that we can understand what a man says, and *his* belief that he will be understood, mutually depend upon the recognition, acceptance, and utilization of such conventions. Furthermore, as we have also noted, even when such conventions are stipulated by a speaker, the stipulations ultimately rely upon words whose meanings are not stipulated but are assumed to be already understood in the light of existing conventions. It follows that if a speaker is not understood as he expected to be, this may be because *he* misunderstood or because some member of his audience misunderstood linguistic conventions of which they should have been aware.

Of course, having recognized that a legislator might possibly misunderstand the conventions determining the commonly accepted significance of the words he uses, we might for some reason wish to give more importance to his (mistaken) beliefs about the significance of his words than to their actual significance—that is, we might feel bound more by what he *meant* to say than by what, on any ordinary view, he *did* say. We could remind ourselves of this with the slogan that the words in statutory documents mean what the legislators intended them to mean, and could regard as always authoritative, even when mistaken, the beliefs of legislators as to how their words would be understood, and, in particular, their beliefs as to the commonly accepted significance of their words.

The adoption of such a policy, however, would lead to practical and conceptual problems. The legislator's audience (judges, lawyers, administrators, citizens) would have to ignore what the legislator said (the commonly accepted significance of his words) and take upon itself the responsibility of seeking out what the legislator meant (what he expected them to understand). A serious attempt to fulfill this responsibility would, to say the least, require complex and tedious investigation. Furthermore, if we insist that the audience is responsible for what the legislator meant rather than for what he said, we must concede that either (a) the statute consists of the string of words actually on the rolls, in which case that statute (i.e., that string of words) [may not be] binding, or (b) the statute is binding but [may] consist of a different string of words from that on the rolls.

Perhaps this analysis merely reveals that we are in a quandary when it comes to interpreting statutes. With statutes, some peculiar authority attaches to what the legislator *says* (for that is virtually all that most persons may have to go by), and some authority may attach also to what the legislator is *trying* to say (after all, under the separation-of-powers doctrine we have in some way obligated ourselves to submit to his wishes on certain matters). But at least we need a formulation of the issues that allows us to see the quandary for what it is. Wholehearted acceptance of the slogan that statutory words mean what the legislator intended them to mean would make this insight impossible.

We have seen that appeals to the legislative intent of even a single legislator are attended by numerous difficulties and sources of confusion. But we have not yet approached the major problem about legislative intent. Judges and administrators appeal to the intent of entire *collegiate* legislatures. Many commentators believe that such appeals are futile—that it is senseless to speak of the intent of a collegiate legislature. Our examination of the intent of the single legislator is a prologue to this central controversy.

II

A. Introduction to the Skeptical Arguments

Does it make any sense at all to talk about the intentions of a collegiate legislature? Radin says:

> A legislature certainly has no intention whatever in connection with words which some two or three men drafted, which a considerable number rejected, and in regard to which many of the approving majority might have had, and often demonstrably did have, different ideas and beliefs.[24]

Stronger views have been taken. Kocourek's argument to the effect that such intentions "never existed" is based upon an unsupported assertion that: "Legislation is a group activity and it is impossible to conceive a group mind or cerebration." Willis says flatly and without argument: "A composite body can hardly have a single intent."[26] More recently D. J. Payne also appears to dismiss the possibility when he says:" [T]he legislature, being a composite body, cannot have a single state of mind and so cannot have a single intention."[27]

24. Radin, supra note 1, at 870.
26. Willis, supra note 4, at 3.
27. Payne, The Intention of the Legislature in the Interpretation of Statutes, 9 *Current Legal Problems* 96, 97-8 (1956).

Concerning at least the latter three views, there are two issues to be sorted out: (a) the extent to which they are based on the notion that two or more men cannot have the same intention, and (b) the extent to which they are based on the notion that a group of men is incapable of having an intention. Kocourek's remark appears to raise the second of these issues; Payne's, despite appearances, raises the first.

Although we shall deal with Payne's arguments more fully below, consider for a moment the supposition in (a). *Is* it possible for two or more men to "have a single intention"? Anyone wishing to deny the possibility must tell us why we cannot truthfully say in the simple case of two men rolling a log toward the river bank with the purpose of floating it down the river that there is at least one intention both these men have— viz., to get the log to the river so that they can float it down the river. It would be unhelpful to reply that one man's intention cannot be identical with another man's because each is his own and not the other's. There is no reason to confine ourselves to counting intentions *only* in this way. Further, if we did so confine ourselves, the central claim that two men cannot have the same intention would turn out to be merely a disguised tautology.

B. The Deeper Roots of Skepticism

The claim in (b) raises much more difficult issues. Should we agree that legislatures, being *groups* of men, cannot have intentions? One possible argument here might be: legislatures are not men; only men can have intentions; therefore, legislatures cannot have intentions.[28]

Kocourek makes a more specific claim that there are necessary conditions for having intentions—conditions absent in the case of legislatures. His candidates are mind and "cerebration." But it is clear that the temptation to name these as necessary conditions lies only in thinking of them as preconditions for purposive behavior and for deliberation—two more immediate preconditions for having intentions. When one moves directly to a consideration of whether legislatures are capable of purposive behavior and deliberation, the reply that they are seems neither false nor (without further argument) only figurative. We do, after all, speak quite freely and precisely about legislatures deliberating, and this, aside from our talk about their debating, investigating, etc., implies a capacity for purposive behavior. Of course, if someone tried to elucidate such talk without any reference whatever to the deliberating, investigat-

---

28. But of course this argument will founder on the shoals of debate about whether things other than men, e.g., animals, have intentions.

ing, debating, etc. of officers, members, agents, or employees of the legislature, we might find this mysterious or unacceptable. But no one has proposed eliminating these references, and the point remains that we have clear notions of what it means to say that a *legislature* is doing these things and we know that legislatures sometimes do them. Thus, a protest that legislatures do not ever do them, or, perhaps, do not "literally" do them, is not prima facie intelligible.

But the skeptic may argue that when he claims that a capacity to deliberate is a necessary condition for having intentions, he is not thinking of the deliberating in which legislatures are conventionally said to engage; rather, his is thinking of the deliberating engaged in by individual men. Though the former normally requires at least some cases of the latter, the two are not sufficiently alike for him.

The skeptic may feel that the notion of intention and the allied notions of deliberation, etc. are stretched "too far" when applied to legislatures. Although no one can say precisely how far is "too far," the line of reply to the skeptic is clear. Legislatures are not men, and if only men clearly have intentions, then one's arguments must cultivate analogies between legislatures and men—the point being to argue that legislatures are enough like men in important respects to be counted as having intentions. Such arguments cannot lead to a *discovery* that legislatures might, after all, have intentions. Rather, the arguments can at most persuade us that it would not, under certain circumstances, be unreasonable to attribute intentions to legislatures—because the expression "intention of the legislature" could still have practicable and reasonable applications without moving from what many people now understand it to mean, and *also* without moving too far from what they understand such an expression as "intention of Jones" to mean. . . .

D. The Futility of the Common Skeptical Arguments

Payne accepts without question the common view that the intentions of a legislature relative to a statute must be identified with the intentions of those legislators who voted for the bill, and further that the intentions of the legislature are the intentions those legislators share. But he claims that the legislature cannot have a single state of mind.

Context does much to fix the extension of a general word, but even the fullest consideration of context generally leaves an uncertain fringe of meaning, and it is this uncertain fringe of meaning which gives rise to so many problems of statutory interpretation. For example, is linoleum "furniture"? . . . It is impossible to decide such questions by reference to the intention of the legislature since the mental images of the various members of the legislature who vote for a bill containing such a general word will exhibit the same imprecision and lack of agreement as found in the common usage of the word. This would be true even if every member of the legislature voting for the bill reflected at length on the extension of the particular general word, *for reflection would not necessarily entail agreement.*[38]

What Payne says here seems quite sensible, but the italicized portion shows his error. He has tried to move from saying that reflection does not entail agreement to saying that, even with reflection, agreement is impossible. This move is illegitimate, and consequently he has not shown that there *cannot* be a single state of mind (agreement).

Notice next that his claim about the unlikelihood or impossibility of a single state of mind is indeterminate. This is revealed by his concentration in the above passage upon borderline or "fringe areas" of the extensions of general words. The question which should be asked about his claim is—a single state of mind pertaining to what? The whole extension of the word? Or only some part of that extension? It is surely not necessary for persons to agree in *all* cases in order for them to agree in *some* cases. What Payne has done here . . . is to claim that there cannot *ever* be agreement, although he demonstrates only that there cannot *always* be agreement. But surely, if agreement among the legislators is a prerequisite of legislative intent, a person who wishes to claim that there is legislative intent in this or that specific case is not bound to claim that there is always intent in every case. It is true that some persons may have committed themselves to the view that there is *always* intent of the sort Payne is discussing; his argument might shake them. But he is very far from having shown that there cannot sometimes be such intent, or even that there cannot often be such intent.

Consider next his supposition, shared without argument by Radin, Jones, de Sloovère, and perhaps Landis, that in order for several legislators to have the same intention relative to the understanding of a general word in a statute, it is necessary for them to have had the same "mental images," at least relative to the instant case.[41] Payne argues:

38. Payne, supra note 27, at 98 (emphasis added).
41. See Radin, supra note 1, at 869-70. Landis is chary of this kind of talk, but his discussion of "determinates" implies a similar view. Landis, A Note on "Statutory Interpretation," 43 *Harv. L. Rev.* 886, 889 (1930). For other examples of the view in question, see Jones, Statutory Doubts and Legislative Intention, 40 *Colum. L. Rev.* 957, 967 (1940); and de Sloovère, Extrinsic Aids in the Intrepretation of Statutes, 88 *U. Pa. L. Rev.* 527, 533–38 (1940). Perhaps Frankfurter would also be sympathetic to this view; see Frankfurter, supra note 5.

> How can it be said that [the legislator] has any intention in respect of a particular covered by the general word which did not occur to his mind. . . ? [I]t would, I suggest, be a strange use of language to say that the user of such a general word "intends" it to apply to a particular that never occurred to his mind.[42]

Payne has only the vestige of a good point here. The behavior of a man who took Payne seriously could be extraordinary. Suppose that, needing a large number of ashtrays for an impending meeting in a building unfamiliar to me, I ask my assistant to scout around and bring back all the ashtrays he can find in the building. He comes back empty-handed, saying the following: "I found a good many ashtrays, but naturally wanted to bring back only those you intended me to bring back. So, as I picked up each one, I asked myself—did he intend me to bring this ashtray back? Upon doing this, I realized in each case that it would certainly be a strange use of language to say that you 'intended' me to bring back that ashtray, as it was virtually certain that the thought of that ashtray had never occurred to you—after all, you had never even been in this building before. In the end, therefore, I found it most sensible to return without any."

Clearly, such behavior would be idiotic. But it is also true that my assistant could have erred at the opposite extreme. Suppose he had ripped built-in ashtrays off the walls of the building, snatched ashtrays from persons using them and removed a hundred thousand ashtrays from a storage room. In each of these situations I might protest that I had not intended him to do that, and that he should have known better than to think I did. The ground for the latter claim, however, would not be that he should have realized that the thought of those particular ashtrays had never occurred to me; after all, he was already virtually certain of this. Rather, the ground would be that, given the circumstances, he should have understood that I did not need a hundred thousand ashtrays and that my interest in having ashtrays was not so pressing as to require him to rip them off walls, etc. It is true that I might say that the thought never occurred to me that there were any built-in ashtrays in the building; or, the thought never occurred to me that he would snatch ashtrays out of people's hands. Thus, I might react against the claim that I

---

42. Payne, supra note 27, at 101. But he also says later: "A statute is a formal document intended to warrant the conduct of judges and officials, and if any intention can fairly be ascribed to the legislature, it is that the statute should be applied to situations not present to the mind of its members." Id. at 105. The whole challenge lies, if one is to make sense of Payne's arguments, in understanding how the claims in these two sets of remarks are related to each other; but he does not enlighten us here. Perhaps he is moving toward the agency theory discussed below.

had intended *x* by making statements roughly in the form: "the thought of such a thing as *x* never occurred to me." But the point of this remark is not merely that the thought of such a thing as *x* had not occurred to me; there is also a clear suggestion that *if* such a thought had occurred to me I would have *excepted* such things as *x*.[43] Without this further suggestion, my remark would surely seem pointless.

The mere fact that the thought of such a thing as *x* hadn't occurred to me does not imply anything about what I did or did not intend. It follows that in our ashtray case the thought of this or that kind of ashtray, or the thought of getting ashtrays in this or that kind of circumstance, need not have occurred to me in order for me to have intended that my assistant get such ashtrays or get ashtrays under such circumstances. Payne, Radin and any others who have discussed legislative intent in terms of "mental images," "mental pictures," and "the contents of the mind of the legislator" have been fundamentally wrong in certain important respects. If, as the above discussion shows, a legislator voting for a bill need not actually have thought of each and every particular that he can reasonably be said to have intended the words of the bill to cover, nor thought of each and every *type* of particular, then the mere fact that two legislators have not thought of the same particulars or of particulars of the same types in connection with some general word in a bill shows neither that they disagreed nor that they agreed in their intention to have those particulars or particulars of those types covered by the bill. Of course, what a legislator did think of does make a difference. But what he did not think of does not make a difference *unless* he would have excepted it had he thought of it.

But how are we to *know* whether he would have excepted it? Supposing that we cannot interview him (or that, if we did, he and we might find it difficult to distinguish between his intention *then* and his decision *now*), would not we always be uncertain? Hagerstrom, in the course of arguing against certain appeals to the intention of the legislator, thinks so.[44] In an interesting discussion of the "unprovided-for case," he concludes that in reality the decisive factor is only the degree to which the

43. Note also that the key phrase is not that which Payne's remarks suggest: for, "such a thing as *X*" refers to a *type* of particular rather than to a particular. (Furthermore, some of the types referred to were types of circumstances, rather than types of ashtrays.)

Radin, and by implication Landis, may have had this in mind when discussing the "determinate" as the issue in litigation. They may, that is, have been referring to issuetypes. More likely, they may have been counting issues in such a way that one and the same issue could appear in many cases. But if they were doing either, then Radin's talk about "mental images" and "pictures" becomes inappropriate, as Payne rightly recognizes and argues. See Payne, supra note 27, at 99; see also Radin, supra note 1, at 869; Landis, supra note 2, at 887.

44. Hagerstrom, op. cit. supra note 19, at 82-83.

interpreter's feelings of value are shocked. If, for example, my assistant, while out gathering ashtrays for me, were to be shocked by the idea of snatching ashtrays from people currently using them, he will impute to me an intention not to have him do that, even though I had made no mention of such a case but had merely said "bring back all the ashtrays you can find."

But such results are not inevitable. My assistant may react differently. He may be a very crude fellow, or one who places a much greater importance on having ashtrays for the meeting than I do. In either case, *he* might not be disturbed at all by the thought of snatching ashtrays from people; but, knowing me, he might think: "That silly old fool *would* be shocked by this, so I'd better not do it." We can also imagine the reverse—that is, a case where the assistant *is* shocked, but realizing that I would not be, steels himself to the task.

Imputed intentions may require a fair degree of intimacy with the person whose intentions are being considered. Even then, there may be circumstances in which the imputations would be highly uncertain. These two considerations are important—especially in dealing with the intentions of legislators vis-à-vis circumstances that, so far as we can tell, they did not contemplate or foresee. The interpreter of a statute may be remote in time, place, social stratum or background from many or all of the legislators who had a hand in enacting the statute. There may only be a small range of cases in which he can reasonably impute to them approval or disapproval of various outcomes. But there will surely be such a range, provided that the interpreter is not completely ignorant of the beliefs and attitudes of these men. The *frequency* with which such imputations may be made depends upon the cases that arise; there may be many or few cases within the range of reasonable imputation.

What, however, of cases where the uncontemplated and unforeseen things, circumstances, or types thereof are such that the legislator would not unhesitatingly have designated them by the general words he used? To return to the ashtray example, suppose that when I asked my assistant to bring back all the ashtrays he could find, it never occurred to me that he might run across some items that were for me not clearly ashtrays, but were enough like ashtrays to have made me hesitate over them. If he ran across such items, neither he nor I might be clear about whether I had intended him to bring them back. Insofar as I was not certain whether they *were* ashtrays, I could not be certain that I had intended him to bring them back; insofar as I was not certain they *were not* ashtrays, I could not be certain that I had not intended him to bring them back. Thus, the question of whether I would have excepted them if I had thought of them may have no decisive answer.

A common move at this point is to claim that I had no intentions whatever in connection with such cases. This is misleading. The occurrence of such a case may be an occasion for abandoning reliance upon what was intended; but the abandonment should not be justified by denying that one had any intentions at all in connection with the case; it should be justified simply by pointing out that the applicability of one's intentions to the case is not clear, and that appeal to intentions therefore does not afford guidance in the case. The undecidability is not due to limitations on our tools of investigation (e.g., that we do not have total recall); rather it is due both to the fact that there are limitations on the preciseness of the intentions a person can have, and to the fact that there are limitations on the preciseness of the intentions a person can have, and to the fact that new experience can challenge the rationale of old classifications. But it is misleading in such circumstances to claim that we had no intentions whatsoever. This claim suggests something quite false —that there is no connection between the circumstances and our intentions—whereas, the whole problem lies in the fact that there is a connection but one which is not clear enough to afford us guidance when we appeal to the intentions.

It is now timely to reconsider the crucial assumption on which all the arguments and counterarguments were based—the agreeement that an intention vis-à-vis a bill shared by all the legislators in the majority voting for the bill would count as an intention of the legislature. As previously noted, one might argue that this agreement has only been provisional. One might claim that Radin, Payne and other skeptics stop here only because they believe they can, even on this assumption, show the impossibility of such a thing as an intention of a legislature. But the examination of Payne's arguments shows the skeptical arguments to be insufficient. Thus, we are forced to confront the agreement in question, and consider its status. Is it only provisional? *Would* most or all of the skeptics retreat to some position behind it? What would this position be? . . .

F. Models of Legislative Intent

The following discussion of models of legislative intent attempts to discover what support each can muster against the above arguments.

1. *The Majority Model.* Consider initially the following straightforward argument for the sufficiency of the majority model of legislative intent. On the supposition that judges and administrators believe themselves to have a legitimate interest in the intentions of the legislature, if there were any such intentions, they might argue as follows:

"The idea of a legislature intending x without *any* of its members, officers or agents intending *x* would hardly give us even a beginning for an acceptable account of the intentions of the legislature. But, if at least some member(s), officer(s) or agent(s) of the legislature must intend *x*, then which and how many? Given that our interest is in the intentions of the legislature concerning a statute enacted by it, we may start by considering the conditions under which the statement 'The legislature enacted the statute' is true. What, in short, counts as a legislature's enacting a statute?

"The important thing is to see what, in accordance with constitutional and legislative rules, results in and amounts to the enactment of a statute. Ordinarily this has to do with majorities of affirmative votes by the legislators, taken and tallied under specified conditions.[50] But, if such a coincidence in behavior (voting affirmatively) by a majority of the legislators is sufficient for and equivalent to saying that the *legislature* has acted (i.e., has enacted a piece of legislation), then a coincidence in the intentions of those very same legislators vis-à-vis the bill and their affirmative votes for it should be sufficient in determining what the *legislature* intended (if anything) by the act or relative to the act.

"The main principle behind our argument is as follows: When there is a group, organization or association recognized by a legal system as a unit for the assignment of rights, powers, duties, etc. (e.g., the *legislature* has the legal capacity to legislate, and the legislators do not, either separately or collectively, *except* when acting in such a way that they constitute a legislature), certain activities on the part of officers, agents or employees of the organization will in certain circumstances be recognized at law as resulting in and amounting to acts of the organization. In such cases, it is reasonable to identify as the intention of the organization in so acting at least whatever intentions are shared by those of its officers, agents, etc., who have discretionary powers in determining or contributing to the determination of what the group does. This is a conventional approach to the intentions of corporations. It should apply to legislatures as well."

From the viewpoint of judges and administrators, this hypothesized argument might seem reasonable. But do the actual practices of these officials support the majority model argued for? Anyone taking a close look at current judicial and administrative practices must conclude that

---

50. Excluding executive endorsement or acquiescence (the expression "intention of the legislature" does not require use to consider them), and leaving open whether we would allow something to count as a statute if it were not subsequently enrolled or promulgated. Accounting for bicameral legislatures would, of course, complicate but not vitiate the argument.

these practices have only the slightest relationship to that model. While judges and administrators obviously utilize evidence of the intentions of various individual legislators, they make no serious attempts to discover the actual intentions of the voting majorities; further, our records of legislative proceedings are still not sufficient to support such an enterprise. There are presumptions galore about what, in the light of our records, the legislators must have been aware of and agreed with, but the realities of legislative processes are such that few of these presumptions are thought to be reliable *enough*.

This may persuade some commentators that courts and administrators generally have not been genuinely interested in the intentions of legislatures. But the behavior of judges and administrators vis-à-vis legislative intent would clearly be capricious and irresponsible only if they believed that the majority model set out necessary as well as sufficient conditions for the existence of legislative intent. There is no reason to suppose the judges and administrators believe this, nor did "their" argument above suppose it. Thus there is no good reason to believe that their behavior is either capricious or irresponsible until it is seen to be so in the light of a model plausibly supposed to be their model of the *minimal* conditions for the existence of legislative intent.

Of course, it may not be necessary to move immediately to searching for such a weaker model. Instead we may attempt to uphold the majority model, but restrict the scope of its legitimate application. The conventional move by commentators is to reject appeals to legislative intentions in favor of appeals to legislative purposes. For these commentators, appeals to the former are appeals to the aims of the *details* of statutes, whereas appeals to the latter are appeals to the much more highly generalized purposes behind the statutes, taken as wholes.[53]

The motive behind such a move is obvious. It is an attempt to show that judicial and administrative practices do support the majority model of legislative intent if the applicability of the model is restricted to the

---

53. See, e.g., Corry, Administrative Law and the Interpretation of Statutes, 1 *U. Toronto L.J.* 286, 290-92 (1936): "Even the majority who vote for complex legislation do not have any common intention *as to its detailed provisions.* Though the intention of the legislature is a fiction, the purpose or object of the legislation is very real. *No enactment is ever passed for the sake of its details; it is passed in an attempt to realize a social purpose.* It is what is variously called the aim and object of the enactment, the spirit of the legislation, the mischief and the remedy." (Emphasis added).

It is not always clear when a commentator is in fact making this move. Talk about the (general) purposes of the statute sometimes seems to refer to what the statute was designed to achieve and sometimes to the purposes interpreters can find for the statute. See Radin, supra note 7, at 422-23, and 406, 408, 411, and 419.

more highly general intentions of the legislators.[54] The argument is that, in view of modern legislative processes, coincident purposes among the legislators regarding the highly general aims of a statute are more likely than coincident purposes regarding the specific aims of portions of the statute. Thus, special investigations of each legislator in the majority relative to such more "general" purposes are not needed.[55]

Is it a valid presumption that consensus among the legislators on various purposes of a statute is more likely in proportion to the generality of the purposes? A distinction must be drawn between a purpose that a legislator actually has, and a purpose that he is aware of as one he is supposed to have or is presumed to have. For, as one considers purposes of greater and greater generality, it becomes more and more likely—not so much that the legislators share those purposes—but rather that they are aware of them as purposes that others have, or as purposes that they themselves are presumed to have. Witherspoon's example of such a general "purpose" is:

> To have the statutory formula so administered as to avoid specific procedural or substantive evils collateral to the main purposes of the statute: e.g., undue federal intrusion into matters normally committed to resolution by state authority.[56]

It is easy to imagine a legislator knowing that he is supposed or presumed to have this purpose or that others have it, but it is also easy to imagine him not having it—even though he votes for the legislation in question. Some commentators, realizing that more legislators are likely to be *aware* of such purposes than are aware of the specific purposes of the details of the legislation in question, have either (i) too facilely assumed that being aware of the purpose is equivalent to having it, or (ii) too facilely assumed that silence in the face of knowledge that one may possibly be presumed to share a certain purpose is a good sign that one actually does share the purpose. In fact, there seems little reason to believe that the generality of the purpose alone much increases the confidence with which we can say that the voting majority has it.

---

54. Witherspoon in fact extends this generality to consideration, not merely of specific aims vis-à-vis a particular statute, but also to whole programs of statute-making, and even to the aims of the legislative process itself, as seen in the light of the traditional functions of legislatures. See Witherspoon, supra note 12, at 758, 795-805, 831-32.

55. Another argument sometimes made in support of the restriction is that highly general aims are more important to the legislators themselves than specific aims. Cf. Witherspoon, supra note 12, at 790, 812, 827.

56. Witherspoon, supra note 12, at 799-800.

It is not much easier to learn about the general purposes of legislators than to learn about the specific intentions of legislators. Thus, even if we look only at general purposes, current judicial and administrative practices are insufficient to support the majority model. We must search for another model of legislative intent which comports more closely with judicial and administrative behavior.

2. *The Agency Model.* It is possible that judges and administrators use an agency model of legislative intent. This model recognizes that legislatures delegate certain responsibilities (such as filling in the statutory details) to various persons (legislative draftsmen, committee chairmen, judges, administrators), and that this may justify appealing to the intentions of these persons as the intentions of the legislature regarding the aims of statutes or the details thereof.

Few commentators have explicitly appealed to the agency model, but several have touched on it. Driedger appears to identify the intention of the legislature with the intentions of the draftsmen. The competent draftsman

> has in his mind a complete legislative scheme and he attempts to give expression to that scheme in a logical and orderly manner; every provision in the statute must fit into that scheme, and the scheme is as complete as he can conceive it.
>
> It is this legislative scheme that should be regarded as the purpose, object, intent, spirit, of the Act.[57]

The following remark by Judge Learned Hand suggests identifying the intentions of the legislature with the intentions of legislative committees. He says:

> [Courts] recognize that while members deliberately express their personal position upon the general purposes of the legislation, as to the details of its articulation they accept the work of the committees; so much they delegate because legislation could not go on in any other way.[58]

A remark by de Sloovère, taken in isolation, suggests turning in quite a different direction—viz., to the interpreter, or a least to a class of interpreters. He says:

> The only legislative intention, whenever the statute is not plain and explicit, is to authorize the courts to attribute a meaning to a statute within

57. Driedger, op. cit. supra note 16, at 161. See also Bruncken, supra note 1, at 130.
58. SEC v. Collier, 76 F.2d 939, 941 (2d Cir. 1935). At least one commentator agrees that Judge Hand's statement here implies agency.

the limitations prescribed by the text and by the context. . . . In other words, a single meaning which the text will reasonably bear must, if genuine, be considered not as the conclusion which the legislature would have arrived at, *but one which the legislature by the text has authorized the courts to find.*[59]

These remarks suggest that the legislature delegates certain responsibilities to other persons in connection with statutes, and in doing so, the legislature exhibits its intention to rely on the judgment and discretion of these persons concerning how to achieve what the legislature wants the statute to achieve. Consequently, the judgment of these persons, having been authorized by the legislature, may stand for the judgment of the legislature. These persons now have somewhat, if not actually, the status of agents of the legislature.[60] Thus, our discovery of what these persons intended in attempting to carry out the assignment of the legislature (e.g., to draft a bill that would, in their judgment, achieve what the legislature wanted to achieve; to interpret the language of the bill so as, in their judgment, to achieve what the legislature wanted to achieve) is a discovery of intentions that the legislature stood behind, wished us to attend to, wished us to regard as authoritative as their own—indeed, wished us to regard *as* their own. These intentions may therefore be taken as, and in fact are, the intentions of the legislature.

The agency model *would* render rational the present "investigations" of judges and administrators into legislative intent, and it would do this without reliance on so many presumptions about the significance of the silence of individual legislators. Investigations of the intentions of "agents" would be sufficient to establish (because they would be equivalent to) the intentions of the legislature. However, the agency model is extremely perilous. It not only requires us to consider whether any of its variations are persuasively similar to typical agency situations, but it confronts us with difficult problems concerning agency itself and in particular concerning the reasonableness of identifying the will of the agent with the will of his principal. Consider the following:

(a) If the legislature is to be thought of as the principal, we presumably would need to know how to identify the actions and intentions of this principal. But, what model of the *latter* are we to use? We would

59. de Sloovère, Preliminary Questions in Statutory Interpretation, 9 *N.Y.U.L.Q. Rev.* 407, 415 (1932). (Emphasis added.)

60. "An agent . . . is one who acts as a conduit pipe through which legal relations flow from his principal to another. Agency is created by a juristic act by which one person (the principal) gives to another (the agent) the power to do something for *and in the name of* the principal so as to bind the latter directly." Paton, *A Textbook of Jurisprudence* 285 (1964).

need to feel at home with some *other* model of legislative intention and purpose before we could get on with establishing the plausibility of this new model. Presumably, this earlier model would be the majority model. But the adequacy of this model has not yet been decisively established.

(b) Even with the traditions of agency the proposal that the actions and judgment of an agent be taken for the actions and judgment of his principal is open to charges of fictionalizing every bit as severe as the initial charges concerning the intentions of legislatures (and by way of them, concerning the nature of corporate personalities). For example, as with the initial controversy, there would be difficulties about whether analogies sufficiently strong to support a claim of identity could be found between the relationship of a principal to his own acts and his relationship to the acts of his agent. Also there will be a worry similar to our earlier worry about the *explicitness* of the legal rules supporting the claims made—that is, a worry about the character of the "juristic act" by which a person designates someone as his agent, and about the degree of explicitness needed in such a "bestowal" of power.

(c) Finally, and closely connected with this last point, each variation of the agency-model—delegation to committee, to courts, etc.—would have to be examined separately in order to discover the justifiability of saying that such a specific "bestowal" of power had actually been made by the legislature.

The strongest case for the bestowal of such power could surely be made in the case of legislative reliance upon draftsmen and committee chairmen. In view of the realities of legislative proceedings, it is certainly plausible to say that legislatures go very far in relying on the judgment and discretion of such persons.[64] When it comes to the interpreters of statutes such as judges and administrators, the claim that legislatures have bestowed such power seems highly dubious. Hagerstrom, for example, gives such a claim short shrift. He says:

> Such a general authorization cannot usually be shown to exist. It is a mere fiction motivated by desire to defend the will-theory, and it may be compared with similarly motivated fictions concerning customary law as the general will.[65]

It should be noted, too, that Hagerstrom is here talking about a well-hedged and limited authorization.

64. Cf. Witherspoon, Administrative Discretion to Determine Statutory Meaning: "The Low Road," 38 *Texas L. Rev.* 392, 430, (1959). It should be noted however, that the work of draftsmen and committee chairmen has no legal effect until endorsed by the legislative. This is a striking *dis*analogy with the customary situation in agency.

65. Hagerstrom, op, cit, supra note 19, at 93.

One might counter, however, by claiming that the authorization need not be explicit. In the law of agency, after all, the authorization is not always explicit either—as in instances of so-called "agency of necessity."[66] It would surely be a matter of "necessity" that the best judgment of judges and administrators be relied upon by legislatures. But this argument appears to go too far. We would not want in any wholesale way to hold legislatures responsible for what judges and administrators make out of statutes.

So much, then, for various models of legislative intent and for the justifiability of *de novo* introduction of the use of such models. We have seen that one strongly justified model of such intentions (the majority model) finds little serious support in current judicial and administrative investigations of the intentions of legislatures. We have also seen that the model fitting these investigations best (the agency model) is also the most difficult to justify. But, while the arguments on behalf of either model cannot be decisive, neither are they negligible. In the end our use of either or both of the models may depend simply upon how many ragged edges we are willing to tolerate in the conceptual framework we use to approach legal problems; or, alternatively, our use may depend, as will be suggested below, on how far we are willing to go in developing our legal institutions in such a way as to eliminate these ragged edges.

G. *The Significance of Model-Entrenchment*

Our exploration of the justifiability of talk about legislative intentions cannot stop here. The "realism" of such talk must be examined not only from the standpoint of the reasonableness of *introducing* such talk in light of our present institutions and practices; it must also be examined from the standpoint of how the reasonableness of such talk is supported by the fact that it is already a well-established part of the legal environment. That is, one should consider whether the established use of *references* to legislative intent does not itself produce conditions under which the references become more reasonable as the practice of making them becomes entrenched.

Quite apart from any consideration of whether starting the practice was a good idea in the first place, once it *has* been started it provides part of the institutional background against which legislators recognize themselves to be acting when proposing, investigating, discussing, and voting for bills. For example, all legislators now understand that views of the intentions of the legislature may well be formed in the light of certain

66. See Paton, op. cit. supra note 60, at 287.

standard presumptions (e.g., that there is no intent to interfere with the common law unless explicitly stated) and "investigations" (e.g., of debates and committee reports on the bill). If the legislators have a capacity to contribute to the materials and to rebut the presumptions they know will be used by judges and administrators as indicia of the intentions of the legislature, their behavior will influence what the intentions of the legislature can reasonably be said to be.

At present, judicial and administrative uses of materials and presumptions are not always clear or predictable enough to provide a guide for the legislators. But one *can* describe circumstances in which the picture would be much clearer. Courts and administrators could establish much greater regularity in their use of preparatory materials and of "presumptions" concerning legislative intent—a regularity sufficient to enable trained persons to predict with reasonable accuracy what the outcomes of these uses would be in specific cases. Furthermore, legislatures could control the issuing of preparatory materials with a view to their use in just such ways by judges and administrators. In such circumstances, judicial and administrative investigations of the "intentions of the legislature" would surely look more realistic and reasonable than they do today. Even today, however, circumstances provide *some* reason, although perhaps not *enough* reason, to say that realistic references to legislative intent can be made. Even now these references are made in an institutional environment which to some extent sustains their reasonableness.[68]

Conclusions

We have proposed several models of legislative intent and have examined (1) whether judges and administrators actually could be regarded as taking any of them seriously, and (2) whether they would be

---

68. Notice in particular how present practices strengthen the temptation of all participants to treat legislatures as persons. When attempting to discover the intentions of a person *vis-à-vis* an action of his, we would think it helpful to be privy to his deliberations (if any) on whether to engage in that action. On analogy, when attempting to discover the intentions of a legislature *vis-à-vis* a statute, we obviously think it helpful to be privy to *its* deliberations on whether to enact the statute. Clearly, insofar as judges and administrators appeal to proceedings on the floor of the house, they are appealing to the deliberations of the legislature (as well as to the deliberations of the legislators). This is just what one would do, if he could, when attempting to learn more about the intentions of any creature. Furthermore, insofar as the investigator thinks that being privy to such deliberations would be helpful, it is not because he supposes that the picture gained will be clear, unequivocal and decisive. Deliberations of individuals on important acts may well be rehearsals of pros and cons quite as indefinite in character as the proceedings of many legislative deliberations.

justified in taking any of them seriously. As predicted, the results of this examination are not conclusive. No one model of legislative intent is either so strongly or so weakly supported as to make its use either unproblematic or absurd. This is not surprising, given that the controversy about the intentions of legislatures has gone on for so long. But it is an important result to reach and to substantiate. We too often continue to demand clear-cut and decisive answers in the face of facts that simply will not support such answers, thus perpetuating controversy (because there always *is* something to be said for the other side) and rendering ourselves ineffective in dealing with the matters at hand. Our detailed discussion of the controversy over the existence and discoverability of legislative intent enables us to understand, for example, the inappropriateness of treating it only as a straight-forward controversy over facts. Instead of continuing to ask only—*Are* legislatures capable of intent?— we should also shift to such question as the following:

(a) Are there any policy considerations sufficient to justify continuance of references to legislative intent in view of the difficulties exposed? What, after all, *hangs* on whether the references are continued? This is essentially an inquiry into the *relevance* of appeals to legislative intent—an inquiry that has not been embarked upon here. But it is an inquiry given a new twist by what we have shown. The question is no longer simply: (i) Supposing that there is a legislative intent, what hangs on appealing to it? It is rather: (ii) Does enough hang on such appeals to make their continuance worthwhile even in the face of the difficulties exposed?

But, we may also ask: (b) Is it worth our while in terms of the ideological and practical importance of such appeals, to seek institutional changes strengthening the analogies between these appeals and appeals to intentions elsewhere in law and in life generally (this being the same for us as increasing the rationality of the appeals)? It is important to notice that the difficulties exposed above are not unavoidable facts of life; legislatures and the institutional environments in which they operate are, in a sense, our creatures and can be altered. Depending upon the model of legislative intent one has in mind (and I should emphasize that only the most obvious ones have been examined here), one may seek to bring the appeals closer to the conditions under which we attribute intentions to corporations, to principals via the intentions of their agents, or, above all, to individual men. The institutional changes accomplishing this could amount to such diverse measures as the fixing of formal limits on what may count as good evidence of legislative intent on the one hand, and alterations in the operating procedures of legislatures on the other.

Chapter 4
Law and Logic

I. LOGIC, EXPERIENCE, AND SCIENTIFIC METHOD

Holmes, The Common Law*

Lecture I. Early Forms of Liability

The object of this book is to present a general view of the Common Law. To accomplish the task, other tools are needed besides logic. It is something to show that the consistency of a system requires a particular result, but it is not all. The life of the law has not been logic: it has been experience.The felt necessities of the time, the prevalent moral and political theories, intuitions of public policy, avowed or unconscious, even the prejudices which judges share with their fellow-men, have had a good deal more to do than the syllogism in determining the rules by which men should be governed. The law embodies the story of a nation's development through many centuries, and it cannot be dealt with as if it contained only the axioms and corollaries of a book of mathematics. In order to know what it is, we must know what it has been, and what it tends to become. We must alternately consult history and existing theories of legislation. But the most difficult labor will be to understand the combination of the two into new products at every stage. The substance of the law at any given time pretty nearly corresponds, so far as it goes, with what is then understood to be convenient; but its form and

* [Pp. 1-2, 35-37 (1881).
For biographical information, see page 59 supra.]

397

machinery, and the degree to which it is able to work out desired results, depend very much upon its past. . . .

The foregoing history, apart from the purposes for which it has been given, well illustrates the paradox of form and substance in the development of law. In form its growth is logical. The official theory is that each new decision follows syllogistically from existing precedents. But just as the clavicle in the cat only tells of the existence of some earlier creature to which a collar-bone was useful, precedents survive in the law long after the use they once served is at an end and the reason for them has been forgotten. The result of following them must often be failure and confusion from the merely logical point of view.

On the other hand, in substance the growth of the law is legislative. And this in a deeper sense than that what the courts declare to have always been the law is in fact new. It is legislative in its grounds. The very considerations which judges most rarely mention, and always with an apology, are the secret root from which the law draws all the juices of life. I mean, of course, considerations of what is expedient for the community concerned. Every important principle which is developed by litigation is in fact and at bottom the result of more or less definitely understood views of public policy; most generally, to be sure, under our practice and traditions, the unconscious result of instinctive preferences and inarticulate convictions, but none the less traceable to views of public policy in the last analysis. And as the law is administered by able and experienced men, who know too much to sacrifice good sense to a syllogism, it will be found that, when ancient rules maintain themselves in the way that has been and will be shown in this book, new reasons more fitted to the time have been found for them, and that they gradually receive a new content, and at last a new form, from the grounds to which they have been transplanted.

But hitherto this process has been largely unconscious. It is important, on that account, to bring to mind what the actual course of events has been. If it were only to insist on a more conscious recognition of the legislative function of the courts, as just explained, it would be useful, as we shall see more clearly further on.

What has been said will explain the failure of all theories which consider the law only from its formal side, whether they attempt to deduce the *corpus* from *a priori* postulates, or fall into the humbler error of supposing the science of the law to reside in the *elegantia juris,* or *logical* cohesion of part with part. The truth is, that the law is always approaching, and never reaching, consistency. It is forever adopting new principles from life at one end, and it always retains old ones from history at the other, which have not yet been absorbed or sloughed off. It will become entirely consistent only when it ceases to grow.

398

The study upon which we have been engaged is necessary both for the knowledge and for the revision of the law.

However much we may codify the law into a series of seemingly self-sufficient propositions, those propositions will be but a phase in a continuous growth. To understand their scope fully, to know how they will be dealt with by judges trained in the past which the law embodies, we must ourselves know something of that past. The history of what the law has been is necessary to the knowledge of what the law is.

Cardozo, Paradoxes of Legal Science*

Introduction—Rest and Motion—Stability and Progress

"They do things better with logarithms." The wail escapes me now and again after putting forth the best that is in me, I look upon the finished product, and cannot say that it is good. In these moments of disquietude, I figure to myself the peace of mind that must come, let us say, to the designer of a mighty bridge. The finished product of his work is there before his eyes with all the beauty and simplicity and inevitableness of truth. He is not harrowed by misgivings whether the towers and piers and cables will stand the stress and strain. His business is to know. If his bridge were to fall, he would go down with it in disgrace and ruin. Yet withal, he has never a fear. No mere experiment has he wrought, but a highway to carry men and women from shore to shore, to carry them secure and unafraid, though the floods rage and boil below.

So I cry out at times in rebellion, "why cannot I do as much, or at least something measurably as much, to bridge with my rules of law the torrents of life?" I have given my years to the task, and behind me are untold generations, the judges and lawgivers of old, who strove with a passion as burning. Code and commentary, manor-roll and year-book, treatise and law-report, reveal the processes of trial and error by which they struggled to attain the truth, enshrine their blunders and their triumphs for warning and example. All these memorials are mine; yet unwritten is my table of logarithms, the index of the power to which a precedent must be raised to produce the formula of justice. My bridges are experiments. I cannot span the tiniest stream in a region unexplored by judges or lawgivers before me, and go to rest in the secure belief that the span is wisely laid.

* [Pp. 1-3, Carpentier Lectures, Columbia University, for 1927. Reprinted from B. N. Cardozo: *The Paradoxes of Legal Science,* New York: Columbia University Press, 1928, by permission of the publisher.

For biographical information, see page 245 supra.]

Let me not seem to cavil at the difficulties that learning can subdue. They are trying enough in all conscience, yet what industry can master, it would be weakness to lament. I am not thinking of the multitude of precedents and the labor of making them our own. The pangs that convulse are born of other trials. Diligence and memory and normal powers of reasoning may suffice to guide us truly in those fields where the judicial function is imitative or static, where known rules are to be applied to combinations of facts identical with present patterns, or, at worst, but slightly different. The travail comes when the judicial function is dynamic or creative. The rule must be announced for a novel situation where competitive analogies supply a hint or clew, but where precedents are lacking with authoritative commands.

I know the common answer to these and like laments. The law is not an exact science, we are told, and there the matter ends, if we are willing there to end it. One does not appease the rebellion of the intellect by the reaffirmance of the evil against which intellect rebels. Exactness may be impossible, but this is not enough to cause the mind to acquiesce in a predestined incoherence. Jurisprudence will be the gainer in the long run by fanning the fires of mental insurrection instead of smothering them with platitudes. "If science," says Whitehead,[1] "is not to degenerate into a medley of *ad hoc* hypotheses, it must become philosophical and must enter upon a thorough criticism of its own foundations." We may say the like of law.

Pound, Mechanical Jurisprudence*

. . . *Scientific law is a reasoned body of principles for the administration of justice,* and its antithesis is a system of enforcing magisterial caprice, however honest, and however much disguised under the name of justice or equity or natural law. But this scientific character of law is a means—a means toward the end of law, which is the administration of justice. Law is forced to take on this character in order to accomplish its end fully, equally, and exactly; and in so far as it fails to perform its function fully, equally, and exactly, it fails in the end for which it exists. *Law is scientific in order to eliminate so far as may be the personal equation in judicial administration,* to preclude corruption and to limit the dangerous possibilities of magisterial ignorance. Law is not scientific for the sake of science. Being

1. *Science and the Modern World,* p. 24.
* [8 *Colum. L. Rev.* 605-610 (1908). Reprinted by permission.
For biographical information, see page 63 supra.]

scientific as a means toward an end, it must be judged by the results it achieves, not by the niceties of its internal structure; it must be valued by the extent to which it meets its end, not by the beauty of its logical processes or the strictness with which its rules proceed from the dogmas it takes for its foundation.

Two dangers have to be guarded against in a scientific legal system, one of them in the direction of the effect of its scientific and artificial character upon the public, the other in the direction of its effect upon the courts and the legal profession. With respect to the first danger, it is well to remember that law must not become too scientific for the people to appreciate its workings.[4] Law has the practical function of adjusting every-day relations so as to meet current ideas of fair play. It must not become so completely artificial that the public is led to regard it as wholly arbitrary. No institution can stand upon such a basis to-day. Reverence for institutions of the past will not preserve, of itself, an institution that touches every-day life as profoundly as does the law. Legal theory can no more stand as a sacred tradition in the modern world than can political theory. It has been one of the great merits of English law that its votaries have always borne this in mind. When Lord Esher said, "the law of England is not a science," he meant to protest against a pseudo-science of technical rules existing for their own sake and subserving supposed ends of science, while defeating justice.[5] And it is the importance of the role of jurors in tempering the administration of justice with common-sense and preserving a due connection of the rules governing every-day relations with every-day needs of ordinary men that has atoned for the manifold and conspicuous defects of trial by jury and is keeping it alive. In Germany to-day one of the problems of law reform is how to achieve a similar tempering of the justice administered by highly trained specialists.[6]

In the other direction, the effect of a scientific legal system upon the courts and upon the legal profession is more subtle and far-reaching. The effect of all system is apt to be petrification of the subject systematized. Perfection of scientific system and exposition tends to cut off individual initiative in the future, to stifle independent consideration of new problems and of new phases of old problems, and to impose the ideas of one generation upon another. This is so in all departments of learning. One of the obstacles to advance in every science is the domination of the

4. Cf. Lord Herschell's remark to Sir George Jessel: "Important as it was that people should get justice, it was even more important that they should be made to feel and see that they were getting it." Atlay, *Victorian Chancellors*, II, 460.

5. See Manson, *The Builders of our Law*, 398.

6. Sternberg, *Kirchmann und seine Kritik der Rechtswissenschaft*, xi.

ghosts of departed masters. Their sound methods are forgotten, while their unsound conclusions are held for gospel.[7] Legal science is not exempt from this tendency. Legal systems have their periods in which science degenerates, in which system decays into technicality, in which a scientific jurisprudence becomes a mechanical jurisprudence.

Roman law in its decadence furnishes a striking example. The Valentinian "law of citations" made a selection of jurisconsults of the past and allowed their writings only to be cited. It declared them, with the exception of Papinian, equal in authority. It confined the judge, when questions of law were in issue, to the purely mechanical task of counting and of determining the numerical preponderance of authority.[8] Principles were no longer resorted to in order to make rules to fit cases. The rules were at hand in a fixed and final form, and cases were to be fitted to the rule.[9] The classical jurisprudence of principles had developed, by the very weight of its authority, a jurisprudence of rules; and it is in the nature of rules to operate mechanically.

Undoubtedly one cause of the tendency of scientific law to become mechanical is to be found in the average man's admiration for the ingenious in any direction, his love of technicality as a manifestation of cleverness, his feeling that law, as a developed institution, ought to have a certain ballast of mysterious technicality. "Philosophy's queerest arguments," says James, "tickle agreeably our sense of subtlety and ingenuity."[10] Every practitioner has encountered the lay obsession as to invalidity of a signing with a lead pencil. Every law-teacher has had to combat the student obsession that notice, however cogent, may be disregarded unless it is official. Lay hair-splitting over rules and regulations goes far beyond anything of which lawyers are capable. Experienced advocates have insisted that in argument to a jury, along with a just, common-sense theory of the merits, one ought to have a specious technicality for good measure. But apart from this general human tendency, there is the special tendency of the lawyer to regard artificiality in law as an end, to hold science something to be pursued for its own sake, to forget in this pursuit the purpose of law and hence of scientific law, and to judge rules and doctrines by their conformity to a supposed science and not by the

7. The reasons for this and the laws by which the process takes place are well set forth in Ross, *Social Psychology*, chaps. 12, 13, 14.

8. Cod. Theod. I, 4, 3. Karlowa, *Römische Rechtsgeschichte*, I, 933.

9. This is said to be the period at which the notion that application of law is a purely mechanical process arose. Gnaeus Flavius (Kantorowicz), *Der Kampf um die Rechtswissenschaft*, 7.

10. *Pragmatism*, 5. Dernburg refers to this as an "innate sense for formalism." *Pandekten*, I, 97.

results to which they lead. In periods of growth and expansion, this tendency is repressed. In periods of maturity and stability, when the opportunity for constructive work is largely eliminated, it becomes very marked.

"I have known judges," said Chief Justice Erle, "bred in the world of legal studies, who delighted in nothing so much as in a strong decision. Now a strong decision is a decision opposed to common-sense and to common convenience. . . . A great part of the law made by judges consists of strong decisions, and as one strong decision is a precedent for another a little stronger, the law at last, on some matters, becomes such a nuisance that equity intervenes, or an Act of Parliament must be passed to sweep the whole away."[11]

The instance suggested in the conversation from which the foregoing extract is taken illustrates very well the development of a mechanical legal doctrine. Successive decisions upon the construction of wills had passed upon the meaning of particular words and phrases in particular wills. These decisions were used as guides in the construction of other wills. Presently rules grew up whereby it was settled that particular words and phrases had prescribed hard and fast meanings, and the construction of wills became so artificial, so scientific, that it defeated the very end of construction and compelled a series of sections in the Wills Act of 1886.

I have referred to mechanical jurisprudence as scientific because those who administer it believe it such. But in truth it is not science at all. We no longer hold anything scientific merely because it exhibits a rigid scheme of deductions from *a priori* conceptions. In the philosophy of today, theories are "instruments, not answers to enigmas, in which we can rest."[12] The idea of science as a system of deductions has become obsolete, and the revolution which has taken place in other sciences in this regard must take place and is taking place in jurisprudence also. This revolution in science at large was achieved in the middle of the nineteenth century. In the first half of that century, scientific method in every department of learning was dominated by the classical German philosophy. Men conceived that by dialectics and deduction from controlling conceptions they could construe the whole content of knowledge. Even in the natural sciences this belief prevailed and had long dictated theories of nature and of natural phenomena. Linnaeus, for instance, lays down a proposition, *omne vivum ex ovo,* and from this fundamental conception deduces a theory of homologies between animal

11. Senior, *Conversations with Distinguished Persons* (ed. of 1880) 314.
12. James, *Pragmatism,* 53.

and vegetable organs.[13] He deemed no study of the organisms and the organs themselves necessary to reach or to sustain these conclusions. Yet, to-day, study of the organisms themselves has overthrown his fundamental proposition. The substitution of efficient for final causes as explanations of natural phenomena has been paralleled by a revolution in political thought. We do not base institutions upon deduction from assumed principles of human nature; we require them to exhibit practical utility, and we rest them upon a foundation of policy and established adaptation to human needs. It has been asserted that to no small extent the old mode of procedure was borrowed from the law. We are told that it involved a "fundamentally juristic conception of the world in which all kinds of action and every sort of judgment was expressed in legal phraseology."[14] We are told that "in the Middle Ages human welfare and even religion was conceived under the form of legality, and in the modern world this has given place to utility."[15] We have, then, the same task in jurisprudence that has been achieved in philosophy, in the natural sciences and in politics. We have to rid ourselves of this sort of legality and to attain a pragmatic, a sociological legal science.

"What is needed nowadays," it has been said, "is that as against an abstract and unreal theory of State omnipotence on the one hand, and an atomistic and artificial view of individual independence on the other, the facts of the world with its innumerable bonds of association and the naturalness of social authority should be generally recognized, and become the basis of our laws, as it is of our life."[16]

Herein is the task of the sociological jurist. Professor Small defines the sociological movement as a "frank endeavor to secure for the human factor in experience the central place which belongs to it in our whole scheme of thought and action."[17] The sociological movement in jurisprudence is a movement for pragmatism as a philosophy of law; for the adjustment of principles and doctrines to the human conditions they are to govern rather than to assumed first principles; for putting the human factor in the central place and relegating logic to its true position as an instrument.

Jurisprudence is last in the march of the sciences away from the method of deduction from predetermined conceptions. On the continent of Europe, both the historical school of jurists and the philosophical

13. *Philosophia Botanica,* aphorisms 134, et seq.
14. Figgis, *From Gerson to Grotius,* 152.
15. Ibid., 14.
16. Ibid., 206.
17. The Meaning of Sociology, 14 *Am. Journ. Sociol.* 13.

school, which were dominant until at least the last quarter of the nineteenth century, proceeded in this way. The difference between them lay in the manner in which they arrived at their fundamental conceptions. The former derived them from the history of juristic speculation and the historical development of the Roman sources. The latter, through metaphysical inquiries, arrived at certain propositions as to human nature, and deduced a system from them. This was the philosophical theory behind the eighteenth-century movement for codification.[18] Ihering[19] was the pioneer in the work of superseding this jurisprudence of conceptions (*Begriffsjurisprudenz*) by a jurisprudence of results (*Wirklichkeitsjurisprudenz*).[20] He insisted that we should begin at the other end; that the first question should be, how will a rule or a decision operate in practice?

M. R. Cohen, The Place of Logic in the Law*

It is a curious fact that while critics and reformers of the law formerly used to take their stand of self-evident truths, and eternal principles of justice and reason, their appeal now is predominantly to vital needs, social welfare, the real or practical need of the times, etc. Those who believe law to be not an isolated island *in vacuo* but a province of the life we call civilization, occupying similar soil and subject to the same change of intellectual season as the other provinces, will see in the fact noted above nothing but an indication of the general passing out of fashion of the old rationalism or intellectualism.

The seed of the protest against the over-emphasis of the logical element in the law was planted by Von Jhering and Justice Holmes over a generation ago.[2] But legal science in this country was then so far behind that of Germany that the logical elaboration and systematization of the law embodied in the work of Langdell and Ames proved the more press-

18. See *Code of Frederick the Great,* part I, Book I, tit. 2, §3, 4.

19. *Der Zweck im Recht* (1878); *Scherz und Ernst in der Jurisprudenz* (1884) especially the two essays *"Im juristischen Begriffshimmel"* and *"Wieder auf Erden."*

20. Sternberg, *Allgemeine Rechtslehre,* I, 188. See Brutt, Die Kunst der Rechtsanwendung, §5.

* [From *Law and the Social Order* 165-176, 177-178, 180-183, by Morris R. Cohen, copyright, 1933, by Harcourt, Brace and Company, Inc. Reprinted, with minor modifications, from 29 *Harv. L. Rev.* 622 (1915). Reprinted by permission.

For biographical information, see page 81 supra.]

2. Jhering, *Geist des römischen Rechts,* 1865-69, Vol. III, sec. 69; *Scherz und Ernst in der Jurisprudenz,* 1884, Chap. I, pts. 3-4; Holmes, *The Common Law,* 1881, Chap. I.

ing need and obtained the right of way. There are many indications that the forces of anti-intellectualism are now rising in American legal thought, and they are sure to find powerful support in the public impatience with legal technicalities.

Imitators or followers seldom possess the many-sided catholicity of the pioneer or master. Thus Jhering and Justice Holmes, while emphasizing other factors, by no means deny all importance to legal logic. A large part of Jhering's *Geist* is devoted to a logical analysis of the method and general ideas of the law;[3] Justice Holmes is careful to emphasize the function of general ideas in the development of the law (e.g., the idea of identity in succession after death and *inter vivos*), and his book abounds in illustrations of how difficult legal problems can be cleared up by just logical analyses.[4] But the new, more zealous crusaders against legal ideology are less cautious, and are inclined to deny all value to logic and general principles.[5] Now it is a rather simple task to show the inadequacies of the proposed substitutes for the traditional principles of legal science. Sound common sense, the lessons of experience, the unspoiled sense of justice, the teachings of the as-yet-to-be-established science of sociology, or the somewhat elusive and perhaps altogether mythical will of the dominant class, cannot, without the aid of a logical legal technique, help us elaborate the laws of gifts, sales, mortgages, or determine the precise liability of a railroad company to those who use its sleeping-car service. It is also easy enough to refute these new crusaders out of their own mouths and show that they themselves attach great value to a clear and logically consistent elaboration of the law.[6] But such easy refutations, while they may be just, are seldom illuminating, unless we examine the situation with some thoroughness. This may lead us into the supposedly foreign fields of logic and metaphysics. But at the time when the foundations of our legal system are questioned both inside and outside of the legal fraternity, it would be only the wisdom of the ostrich which would counsel us to refrain from entering into these fields because, forsooth, the old tradition says that law is law, and has nothing to do with any other field of human inquiry. It may be reassuring to orthodox legal

3. Jhering, op. cit. (note 2), secs. 44-46, 59-68, and especially 45, 64, 65.

4. Holmes, op. cit. (note 2). Note the quotation at the end of the preface, and the important place of "reasons" in the development of the law, pp. 5, 36; see also pp. 214, 219, 220, 239, 289.

5. Wüstendörfer, *"Die deutsche Rechtsprechung," Archiv für die civilistische Praxis,* Vol. CX (1910), p. 223; Fuchs, *Die Gemeinschädlichkeit der konstruktiven Jurisprudenz,* 1909, Chaps. 1-2; Bentley, *The Process of Government,* 1908, Chap. I; Brooks Adams, *Centralization and the Law,* 1908, Lectures 1-2.

6. Adams, op. cit. (note 5), pp. 39, 41, 43; Wüstendörfer, op. cit. (note 5), 219-22.

scholarship to note that the foremost representatives of the exact and natural sciences have now outgrown the childish fear of metaphysics as the intellectual bogey—witness the writings of Russell, Poincaré, Duhem, Ostwald, and Driesch.

I

A suggestive parallel can be drawn between the functions of the law and of natural science. Both facilitate transactions by increasing our reliance on the future. We build our modern houses, bridges, and machinery because science makes us more certain that these structures will withstand the variations of pressure, etc. We enter into business because we expect that people will continue to desire certain commodities, and we count on the state to continue to protect us against robbery. We sell on credit not only because we expect that most people will be moved (by habit or conscience) to pay, but also because the law provides us with a machinery for collecting what is due. If our debtors also know that this machinery exists, they will pay more readily and the expense of using this legal machinery will be accordingly reduced. That the law should be readily knowable is, thus, essential to its usefulness. So far is this true that there are many inconveniences or injustices in the law that men would rather suffer than be paralyzed in their action by uncertainty. Primitive law, i.e., all legal systems uninfluenced by Greek science, try to achieve this certainty by fixed rules or dooms enumerating specific actions and their consequences, just as they store up wisdom in isolated saws or proverbs. Clearly the multitudinous and complicated relations of modern life could not possibly be regulated by such a method. Like the classical Romans, we utilize instead that most wonderful discovery, or invention, of the Greeks—the rational deductive system. We try to reduce the law to the smallest number of general principles from which all possible cases can be reached, just as we try to reduce our knowledge of nature to a deductive mathematical system. This rational form also gives the law the appearance of complete freedom from arbitrary will and thus satisfies the modern demand for equality in the enforcement of law.[7]

The law, of course, never succeeds in becoming a completely deductive system. It does not even succeed in becoming completely consistent.

---

7. "Arbitrary discretion is excluded by the certainty resulting from a strict scientific method" (Savigny, *Of the Vocation of Our Age for Legislation and Jurisprudence,* trans. by Hayward, 1831, p. 151).

But the effort to assume the form of a deductive system underlies all constructive legal scholarship. In our own day, for instance, Thayer's general views on evidence and Wigmore's classical treatise on the subject have transformed a conglomeration of disconnected rules into something like a system. Ames' doctrine of unjust enrichment has brought together a number of artificially tacked-on appendages to the law of contract into the somewhat coherent body of law known as quasi-contract. Forty years ago we had so little of a general theory of torts that if anyone had thought of writing a treatise on the subject he might simply have treated of a number of torts in alphabetic order. Today we have not only a general theory of liability, but also there is a marked tendency to make the law of torts and the law of contracts branches of the law of obligations. This effort at generalization and system has always been the task of the jurist. We use the notions of property, contract, or obligation so often now that we are apt to think that they are "as old as the law itself." But legal history shows clearly enough that the notion of property came as a result of a long process of unification of diverse laws against robbery. A great deal of material had to be eliminated before the abstract idea of property could be extracted. The idea of contract is so late that even as developed a legal system as the Roman had no general law of contract, but merely laws of *stipulatio, depositum, pignus, locatio conductio,* etc. The notion of possession seems to the classical jurists simply one of fact. But the possessory remedies did not originate in the principle of possession but rather in a number of diverse situations.[8]

In thus endeavoring to make the law systematic, jurists are not merely pursuing their own purely theoretic or scientific interest. They are performing a duty to the community by thus transforming the law. A legal system that works with general principles has powerful instruments. Just as the generalized arithmetic which we call advanced mathematics has increased manifold our power of solving physical problems, so a generalized jurisprudence enlarges the law's control over the diversity of legal situations. It is like fishing with large nets instead of with single lines.

As nature has other cares besides letting us paint her deductive charm, she constantly reveals aspects that hamper or complicate our beautiful analytic equations. So, also, the affairs of practical life generate situations which mock our well-intentioned efforts to reduce the law to a rational system. In the presence of these, as of other seemingly insurmountable obstacles, human frailty is tempted to blink at the difficulties. So urgent is the need for assured first principles that most people resent

8. Dernburg, *System des römischen Rechts,* 1912, sec. 220.

the service that the skeptical-minded—the stray dogs of the intellectual world—render by showing the uninhabitableness of our hastily constructed legal or philosophic kennels. In the legal field, the blinking at the practical difficulties is facilitated by the ready assurance that if our principles are just it is none of our fault if any inconvenience results. *Fiat justitia pereat mundus,* is a very edifying excuse for refusing to reexamine our principles in the light of the harsh results to which they lead.

According to the prevailing popular theory, facts are "out there" in nature and absolutely rigid, while principles are somewhere "in the mind" under our scalps and changeable at will. According to this view scientific theories are made to fit preexisting facts somewhat as clothes are made to fit people. A single inconsistent fact, and the whole theory is abandoned. Actually, however, what we call facts are not so rigid and theories not so flexible; and when the two do not fit, the process of adaptation is a bilateral one. When new facts come up inconsistent with previous theories, we do not give up the latter, but modify both the theory and our view of the facts by the introduction of new distinctions or hypothetical elements. If the facts of radiation do not fit in with the theory of the conservation of energy, an ether is invented and endowed with just as many properties as are necessary to effect a reconciliation, though in the end this results in inordinate complexity. Similarly legal theories, attempting to assimilate new facts by stretching old rules and introducing distinctions and fictions, become so complex and full of arbitrary elements that the very end of legal system is thereby defeated. It is this artificial complexity that caused the abandonment of the Ptolemaic astronomy and is causing the abandonment of the physics of the ether today. The classical system of common-law pleading, based on a few self-evident principles, was just such a system. It fell precisely because, as the forms of actions expanded to comprehend the new industrial order, the system became so choked with artificial distinctions and fictions that a conservative and long-suffering people had to sweep it all away. Similarly has the law of employers' liability, based on a simple principle—no responsibility without fault—grown to such monstrous complexity (witness Labatt's voluminous book)[9] that legislation is sweeping it away.

The foregoing parallel between natural science and legal system should, of course, be corrected by noting the important differences between the two. Legal principles are not so simple or so readily applicable to single cases as are the principles of physics; nor are the facts of the legal order so definite and so rigid as those of the physical order. Crucial experiments are possible in science. Single experiments have sometimes

9. Labatt, *Commentaries on the Law of Master and Servant,* 1913, 8 vols.

caused such difficulties to reigning theories as to lead to their ultimate abandonment. The facts of physics admit of highly exact description in terms of number and can be indefinitely repeated, whereas the "facts" of the legal order, "practices," or decisions, can almost always be disputed and disregarded as entirely wrong in principle. Nevertheless, enough has been said above to indicate that the rule of deduction is not an accidental incident in law and natural science but is rather an essential part of their life.

II

In modern times the widespread opinion has grown up that deduction is incapable of genuinely extending our knowledge and can serve at best only as an ornament of exposition. It is sometimes thought that the introduction of the "case method" in law teaching marks the entrance of inductive scientific methods in law. The latter view is, however, obviously a misapprehension. Both Langdell and Ames regarded the case method as a sound pedagogical device, but in no way doubted the existence of legal principles according to which cases should be decided. Langdell even asserted that the number of such principles is very small.[10] It is from an entirely different quarter that the whole of traditional legal science has, because of this very belief in principles, been attacked as scholastic and out of harmony with the methods of modern science.[11] Whatever may be these critics' knowledge of modern science, they certainly have a very vague idea of scholasticism, and use the term as a locus for all that is intellectually undesirable, a sort of inferno for all ideas to which they are opposed. Now there is one virtue which no one who has ever read Aquinas or Duns Scotus denies them, and that is clarity and consistency—a virtue which, if not sufficient for admission into the modern juristic heaven, is at least not to be altogether despised. Moreover, every student of the history of thought knows that the contrast between modern science and medieval philosophy is not to be dismissed by the mere shibboleth of induction or deduction. The founders of modern science —Copernicus, Kepler, Galileo, Huygens, Descartes, and Newton—certainly did not despise deduction. The history of science completely belies the dogma as to the fruitlessness of deduction, and shows many important physical discoveries, such as Maxwell's discovery of the electro-mag-

10. Langdell, *Cases on Contracts*, 1871, p. vi.
11. Bozi, *Die Weltanschauung der Jurisprudenz*, 1907; Brooks Adams and Bentley, op. cit. (note 5). See also note in Jung, *Das Problem des natürlichen Rechts*, 1912, p. 172.

netic character of light, brought about by deductive or mathematical procedure. The great apostle of induction was Bacon—a good lawyer, trained in the handling of cases in the Inns of Court, but one who made no contribution at all to any natural science.[12] The present apotheosis of induction arose in the middle of the nineteenth century as a result of a violent reaction against the frenzied excesses brought about by the classical German philosophies of Fichte, Hegel, and Schelling. It became a dogma of popular philosophy through the popularity of Mill's *Logic*. Now Mill was not himself a scientist. He was an administrator—an official of the East India Company—and his acquaintance with natural science was gathered from such secondhand sources as Whewell's *History of the Inductive Sciences*. But so strong has become the hold of Mill's simple formulae on popular thought that even men of science have accepted his account of scientific method—which is not surprising if we remember that healthy men or athletes are not necessarily good physiologists or trainers. The actual procedure, however, of natural as well as of legal science involves constant reliance on principles, and is incompatible with Mill's nominalism, i.e., the assumption that only particulars exist in nature.

It may seem a bold and reckless statement to assert that an adequate discussion of cases like *Berry v. Donovan,*[13] *Adair v. United States*[14] or *Commonwealth v. Boston and Maine R.,*[15] involves the whole medieval controversy over the reality of universals. And yet, the confident assertion of "fundamental principles of justice inhere in the very idea of free government"[16] made by the writers of these decisions, and the equally confident assertion of their critics that there are no such principles,[17] show how impossible it is to keep out of metaphysics. Can we dodge the question by saying that while legal principles are unchanging the law is a practical or progressive science?[18] How can a principle or undisputed formula remain the same if all the cases to which it is to be applied are constantly changing? You may decide to enter the realm of metaphysics or not, just as you may decide to go to church or not; but you cannot deny that an intelligent decision in either case demands considerable thought.

12. Harvey, the discoverer of the circulation of the blood, said of Bacon: "He writes science like a Lord Chancellor."

13. 188 Mass. 353, 74 N.E. 603 (1905).

14. 208 U.S. 161, 28 Sup. Ct. 277 (1908).

15. 222 Mass. 206, 110 N.E. 264 (1915).

16. Twining v. New Jersey, 211 U.S. 78, 106, 29 Sup. Ct. 14 (1908).

17. Adams, op. cit. (note 5), pp. 20 et seq. And see Lewis, "The Social Sciences as the Basis of Legal Education," *University of Pennsylvania Law Review*, Vol. LXI (1913), pp. 531, 533.

18. National Protective Association v. Cumming, 170 N.Y. 315, 63 N.E. 369 (1902).

The matter is not very difficult if we refuse to be browbeaten by a word like "reality," which often represents nothing definite except a certain emotional afflatus. It ought to be quite clear that abstractions and universals exist in every situation in which individual things can be said to exist, and by the same evidence. If any statement like, "Smith is white and an honest man" is true, whiteness, honesty, and manhood must exist as truly as Smith. Similarly, if it is true that one body is equal to, greater than, or less than another, then the relations of equality, greater than, or less than, exist just as truly as the bodies between which they hold. If the results of logical and mathematical reasoning are observed to hold true of nature, it seems more proper to say that nature is logical and mathematical than to suppose that logical and mathematical principles are just words having no meaning in nature, or that they have a dubious existence "in the mind only" (the "mind" being conceived as outside of nature). The difficulty that most people have in conceiving of the existence of universals is due to the tendency to *reify* all relations, i.e., to think of these relations or universals as if they were themselves additional *things,* instead of what they are defined to be, viz., qualities or relations of things. This shows itself in the naïve question, *"Where* do these universals exist?" as if universals were particular entities occupying space. In brief, it seems that the actual procedure of natural and legal science demands the doctrine that universals do exist, but that they exist as universals, not as additional individual things. Surely a barren if somewhat truistic doctrine, you may say. But the following may show that it offers us a clew whereby to distinguish the use from the abuse of logic in the law.

III

Every science must use logic to test whether certain conclusions do follow from given premises. But that which distinguishes one science from another, e.g., law from physical chemistry, is the subject-matter, the axioms and postulates from which conclusions are drawn. The subject-matter of the law is the regulation of the conduct of individuals living in those more or less permanent relations which we call society. Now, from the point of view of logic the existence of men in society or their desire to regulate their mutual relations is just as brute an empirical fact as that water expands when cooled just above the freezing point. All metaphysical philosophies of law (like Stammler's) which pretend to have no empirical elements at their basis, thus really attempt the logically impossible. You cannot construct a building merely out of the rules of architecture. As a matter of fact, all metaphysical philosophies of law do smuggle in, in more or less disguised form, the main material facts of the social order. In this they are assisted by a fact that empiricists—especially those intoxicated with the doctrine of evolution—do not fully realize, viz., the large fund of common humanity possessed by all peoples whose history we can study. Private law especially deals with those traits of human nature that have changed least in the comparatively short period that is covered by the whole of legal history. Our history "starts with man full grown. It may be assumed that the earliest barbarian whose practices are to be considered had a good many of the same feelings and passions as ourselves."[19] Thus is explained the paradoxical fact that metaphysical philosophers of law, who try to ignore or rise high above the factual order, are frequently more productive of genuine social insight than those who are lost in the multitudinous but unimportant details of historic or ethnologic jurisprudence.

The law, at any given time, is administered and expounded by men who cannot help taking for granted the prevalent ideas and attitudes of the community in which they live. Even if it were logically, it would certainly not be psychically, possible for any man to think out an absolutely new system of jural relations. The law reformer who urges the most radical change, can justify his proposal only by appealing to some actually prevailing idea as to what is desirable; and the history of the law shows how comparatively small is the addition or subtraction to the system of jural concepts and ideas that the most creative judges and jurists have been able to bring about. There are, therefore, first or fundamental principles of the law that may be regarded as practically or *quasi a priori*. But though we cannot avoid relying on principles, the complex and constantly changing subject-matter requires continuous caution and a mind humbly open to the dangers of the eternal tendency of all intellectual effort in the direction of oversimplification.

Among the first principles of the law there are at least two kinds: (1) axioms or fundamental assumptions (*a*) as to fact, e.g., that men desire their economic advantage, and are deterred from actions to which penalties are attached, and (*b*) as to the aim of the law, e.g., that property should be protected, that men should be equal before the law, etc.; and (2) postulates which are really ways of procedure or methods of analysis and construction, e.g., the distinction between rights and duties, or between law and equity, the principle that no man can be his own agent, or that no man can convey more or a greater estate than that which in law he has. The abuse of first principles of the first class consists in setting up economic or political maxims of public policy that are at best applicable

19. Holmes, op. cit. (note 3), p. 2. Cf. Boas, *Mind of Primitive Man*, 1911.

only to a given period or historical economic system, as eternal principles for all times. Examples of this may be found in the use of the principle that the public interest always demands competition, a free market, and an open shop, and the maxim that only by the separation of powers, checks and balances, and judicial control over legislation can liberty be maintained. The fallacy of regarding these as eternal first principles is readily detected and has been frequently pointed out in recent times. The fallacy, however, of setting up what I have called above postulates, as eternal necessities of all legal system, is less easily detected. These postulates have the appearance of self-evident truths. But physics has learned to regret accepting such seemingly self-evident propositions as that a thing cannot act where it is not, and modern mathematics has learned that such seemingly self-evident assertions as that the whole is greater than a part, or Euclid's parallel postulate, are not necessarily true. The theoretical sciences now select their fundamental propositions not because of their immediate self-evidence, but because of the system of consequences that follows from them. A practical science like the law ought not to despise that procedure.

The abuse of self-evident principles is at the basis of what the Germans call *Begriffsjurisprudenz,* which Professor Pound calls mechanical jurisprudence,[20] and also of that which is unsatisfactory in the old natural law. The analysis of a few additional examples may perhaps make my point clearer.

In discussing creditors' bills in equity, Langdell says:[21] "Indeed, when a debtor dies, his debts would all die with him, did not positive law *interpose* to keep them alive; for every debt is created by means of an obligation imposed upon the debtor, and it is *impossible* that an obligation should continue to exist after the obligor had ceased to exist." I have italicized the words "interpose" and "impossible" because these and the later expression that the question is "as old as the law itself" bring into relief the underlying view that the law itself is a logical system in which it is forever impossible for a debt to survive the debtor. But if that were so, how could positive law bring about the impossible? Could positive law change the rules of arithmetic, or make the diagonal and the side of a square commensurate? In point of fact the principle in question is not logically necessary at all. It arose at a time when the creditor could dispose of the actual body and life of the defaulting debtor, hence the rela-

20. Pound, "Mechanical Jurisprudence" (1908), *Columbia Law Review,* Vol. VIII (1908), p. 605; Korkunov, *The General Theory of Law,* 1909, p. 15; Bekker, *Ernst und Scherz über unsere Wissenschaft,* 1892, Chap. VII.

21. *Brief Survey of Equity Jurisprudence,* 1905, p. 126.

tion between debtor and creditor could have been entered only by people who personally trusted each other. If the law of the Twelve Tables had allowed an assignment of a debt, it would have been socially as serious as if our law allowed an assignment of marital rights. Later on, when the rigour of the old law was softened, the practical reason why the creditor might not be replaced by another person disappeared, and the debtor-creditor relation became depersonalized at one end. The difficulties in the way of depersonalization at the other end were not the logical ones but the practical ones of harmonizing the security of credit and the maintenance of family continuity on the basis of inheritance. But habits of legal thought in regard to the personal character of the debtor-creditor relation still produce the familiar difficulties of subrogation, etc. . . .

Closely connected with the use and abuse of first principles is the use of artificial concepts or abstractions in the law. Jhering has long ago pointed out[25] that juristic technique is able to reconstruct and simplify the law by a process of analysis similar to the process whereby, in the course of history, language becomes represented by a more or less phonetic alphabet. The natural unit of language is the sentence or the word, represented in primitive form by a picture. By a process of abstraction we pass from that stage in which thousands of signs are needed to the stage where a few simple phonetic elements suffice to reproduce all the possible combinations of language. Just so, scientific jurisprudence endeavors to analyze all laws as combinations of a few recurrent simple elements. From this point of view, the artificiality of legal concepts is not an objection to their employment. Indeed, there is an advantage in purely artificial symbols. They carry with them only the amount of meaning contained in their definition, without the intellectual and emotional penumbra that more familiar terms always drag with them. The most dangerous concepts of the law are those like direct tax, republican form of government, interstate commerce, restraint of trade, and the like. They seem to be definite in themselves, but when we come to apply them, they prove most illusive. The law, for instance, says, "no taxation except for public purposes." What are public purposes? The courts have ruled that municipalities may give bounties to grist mills and railroads, but not to factories. Communities may sell gas and electricity, but not coal; may abate a dam for the relief of privately owned meadows, but may not lend money for rebuilding a burnt district.[26] This seems quite arbitrary. And

25. Jhering, *Geist des römischen Rechts*, sec. 44.

26. Rogers v. Burlington, 3 Wall. (U.S.) 654 (1865); Opinion of the Justices, 150 Mass. 592, 24 N.E. 1084 (1890); Lowell v. Boston, 111 Mass. 454 (1873). And cf. Parkersbury v. Brown, 106 U.S. 487 (1882).

when judges try to rationalize their position by introducing such distinctions as that between direct and incidental benefits to the community, a logician cannot help feeling that while the decisions may be good, the reasons are certainly bad. It is the pernicious fiction that judges never make the law but only declare "the will of the legislator" that makes people blink at the essential indefiniteness of concepts like "due process of law" or "interstate commerce," and pretend to believe that all the constitutional law on these subjects is deduced from the few words of the constitutional enactments. The real work of judicial interpretation is precisely that of *making* these concepts definite by fixing their limits as questions about them come up. . . .

The various instances of the abuse of legal logic adduced by writers like Jhering, Korkunov, Demogue, and Pound are all cases of an overhasty application of logic to a complex material and do not, of course, show the break-down of logic itself. Nevertheless, it is fair to add that a great many of the difficulties are due to the inadequacies of the popular accounts of logic. The Aristotelian logic, with its subject-predicate doctrine, is primarily a logic of subsumption and applies best to a system like the biology of which Aristotle was a master, viz., a system of fixed classes. Modern logic can deal more adequately with a changing system, since modern logic, like modern mathematics, operates with the invariant rules governing possible transformations.

The limitation that underlies the traditional logic shows itself in the familiar difficulty as to the presence of discretion in the law. The law is primarily directed toward certainty, which, according to the classical view, can be produced only by definite rules that leave no room for individual discretion. Individual discretion, whether of judge or of legislator acting under constitutionally limited powers, appears to this view synonymous with the absence of law. Thus in the criminal law the old maxim is, Fix the offense definitely and the definite penalty. To individualize punishment seems to the old view to abandon legal security and to open the flood-gates of judicial arbitrariness. This view, however, is based on an inadequate logic, which fails to appreciate the necessarily provisional character of all legal classification and the consequent necessity of discretion to make definite that which would otherwise be really indefinite. Logically the task of the law is similar to that of the wholesale manufacturer of shoes or any similar commodity. Human feet vary in size, and perhaps there is truth in the saying that no two are exactly alike. On the assumption that the shoe should fit the foot, the theoretical consequence would be that no two shoes should be made exactly alike. Experience, however, without contradicting these postulates of the perfect art of shoe-making, finds that a limited number of classes of "sizes" will satisfy all normal demands. How is the number of these "sizes" determined?

416

Obviously by striking a balance between the (very slight) inconvenience of having a shoe that may be one sixteenth of an inch too long and the inconvenience of doubling or tripling the number of sizes. The same method is at the basis of the criminal law. The number of ways and circumstances, for instance, in which the life of one person can be destroyed by another is endless. What the law does is to group them into a small number of classes, viz., murder, manslaughter, etc., attempting to define the characteristics of each type in such a way that no one can take the life of a fellow-being in a way that society disapproves without falling in one or other of these groups. There is, of course, no logical reason why the division into groups should be so rough, and it is abstractly possible to carry the classification to any degree of fineness and discrimination,—except that the difficulty of making juries understand the difference between murder in the first degree, murder in the second degree and manslaughter is already sufficiently great. It is foolish to attempt results more delicate than the instruments at your disposal will permit. Would we attempt to carve a delicately featured wooden statue with an ax? Judicial discretion in the individualization of punishment is simply an attempt to bring into the penal machinery a greater degree of discrimination than is practically possible by the prescription of hard and fast general rules.

The same argument applies to legislative discretion. "If the legislature has power to fix the maximum number of hours in an industry to ten, then why not nine, etc.? Where are you going to draw the line?" The answer is that no such line can be drawn *a priori,* since we are dealing with a line that must necessarily vary in different industries and at different times.

Jurists, like other men, are in their attitude to the employment of logic either intellectualists or mystics. The intellectualist not only trusts implicitly all the results of reasoning, but believes that no safe result can be obtained in any other way. Hence in law he emphasizes the rule rather than the decision. This, however, leads to an ignoring of the absurd consequences to which the logical application of rules frequently leads. *Summum jus, summa injuria.* The mystics distrust reasoning. They have faith in intuition, sense, or feeling. "Men are wiser than they know," says Emerson, and the Autocrat of the Breakfast Table, who was not a stranger to the study of the law, adds, "You can hire logic, in the shape of a lawyer, to prove anything that you want to prove." But shall we subscribe to the primitive superstition that only the frenzied and the mentally beclouded are divinely inspired? Like other useful instruments, logic is very dangerous, and it requires great wisdom to use it properly. A logical science of law can help us digest our legal material, but we must get our food before we can digest it. The law draws its sap from feelings

417

of justice and social need. It has grown and been improved by sensitively minded judges attending to the conflicting claims of the various interests before them, and leaving it to subsequent developments to demonstrate the full wisdom or unwisdom of the decision. The intellectualist would have the judge certain of everything before deciding, but this is impossible. Like other human efforts, the law must experiment, which always involves a leap into the dark future. But for that very reason the judge's *feelings* as to right and wrong must be logically and scientifically trained. The trained mind sees in a flash of intuition that which the untrained mind can succeed in seeing only after painfully treading many steps. They who scorn the idea of the judge as a logical automaton are apt to fall into the opposite error of exaggerating as irresistible the force of bias or prejudice. But the judge who realizes before listening to a case that all men are biased is more likely to make a conscientious effort at impartiality than one who believes that elevation to the bench makes him at once an organ of infallible logical truth.

A good deal of the wisdom of life is apt to appear foolishness to a narrow logic. We urge our horse down hill and yet put the brake on the wheel—clearly a contradictory process to a logic too proud to learn from experience. But a genuinely scientific logic would see in this humble illustration a symbol of that measured straining in opposite directions which is the essence of the homely wisdom which makes life livable.

Dewey, Logical Method and Law*

. . . Justice Holmes says, "The language of judicial decision is mainly the language of logic. And the logical method and form flatter that longing for certainty and for repose which is in every human mind.

---

* [10 *Cornell L.Q.* 17, 20-21, 22, 22-23, 24-27 (1924). © Copyright 1924 by Cornell University. Reprinted by permission of the Cornell Law Review and Fred B. Rothman & Company.

John Dewey (1859-1952) was educated at the University of Vermont (B.A. 1878) and Johns Hopkins University (Ph.D. 1884). During his long career, he taught at the University of Michigan (1884-1888, 1889-1894), the University of Minnesota (1888-1889), the University of Chicago (1894-1904), and Columbia University (1904-1930). After retiring, Dewey continued to publish works clarifying his philosophy. His principle writings are *Outlines of a Critical Theory of Ethics* (1891), *The Study of Ethics* (1894), *Studies in Logical Theory* (1903), *How We Think* (1910), *Reconstruction in Philosophy (1920), Human Nature and Conduct* (1922), *Experience and Nature* (1925), *The Public and Its Problems* (1927), *The Quest for Certainty* (1929), *Individualism Old and New* (1930), *Philosophy and Civilization* (1931), *Liberalism and Social Action* (1935), *Logic: The Theory of Inquiry* (1938), *Freedom and Culture* (1939), *Problems of Men* (1946), and *Knowing and the Known* (1949).]

But certainty generally is an illusion." From the view of logical methods here set forth, however, the undoubted facts which Justice Holmes has in mind do not concern logic but rather certain tendencies of the human creatures who use logic; tendencies which a sound logic will guard against. For they spring from the momentum of habit once forced, and express the effect of habit upon our feelings of ease and stability—feelings which have little to do with the actual facts of the case.

However this is only part of the story. The rest of the story is brought to light in some other passages of Justice Holmes. "The actual life of the law has not been logic: it has been experience. The felt necessities of the times, the prevalent moral and political theories, intuitions of public policy, avowed or unconscious, even the prejudices which judges share with their fellow-men, have had a good deal more to do than the syllogism in determining the rules by which men should be governed." In other words, Justice Holmes is thinking of logic as equivalent with the syllogism, as he is quite entitled to do in accord with the orthodox tradition. From the standpoint of the syllogism as the logical model which was made current by scholasticism there *is* an antithesis between experience and logic, between logic and good sense. For the philosophy embodied in the formal theory of the syllogism asserted that thought or reason has fixed forms of its own, anterior to and independent of concrete subject-matters, and to which the latter have to be adapted whether or no. This defines the negative aspect of this discussion; and it shows by contrast the need of another kind of logic which shall reduce the influence of habit, and shall facilitate the use of good sense regarding matters of social consequence.

In other words, there are different logics in use. One of these, the one which has had greatest historic currency and exercised greatest influence on legal decisions, is that of the syllogism. To this logic the strictures of Justice Holmes apply in full force. For it purports to be a logic of rigid demonstration, not of search and discovery. . . .

It thus implies that for every possible case which may arise, there is a fixed antecedent rule already at hand; that the case in question is either simple and unambiguous, or is resolvable by direct inspection into a collection of simple and indubitable facts, such as Socrates is a man. It thus tends, when it is accepted, to produce and confirm what Professor Pound has called mechanical jurisprudence; it flatters that longing for certainty of which Justice Holmes speaks; it reinforces those inert factors in human nature which make me hug as long as possible any idea which has once gained lodgment in the mind. . . .

If we trust to an experimental logic, we find that general principles emerge as statements of generic ways in which it has been found helpful to treat concrete cases. The real force of the proposition that all men are mortal is found in the expectancy tables of insurance companies, which with their accompanying rates show how it is prudent and socially useful to deal with human mortality. The universal stated in the major premise is not outside of and antecedent to particular cases; neither is it a selection of something found in a variety of cases. It is an indication of a single way of treating cases for certain purposes or consequences in spite of their diversity. Hence its meaning and worth are subject to inquiry and revision in view of what happens, what the consequences are, when it is used as a method of treatment.

As a matter of fact, men do not begin thinking with premises. They begin with some complicated and confused case, apparently admitting of alternative modes of treatment and solution. Premises only gradually emerge from analysis of the total situation. The problem is not to draw a conclusion from given premises; that can best be done by a piece of inanimate machinery by fingering a keyboard. The problem is to *find* statements, of general principle and of particular fact, which are worthy to serve as premises. As matter of actual fact, we generally begin with some vague anticipation of a conclusion (or at least of alternative conclusions), and then we look around for principles and data which will substantiate it or which will enable us to choose intelligently between rival conclusions. No lawyer ever thought out the case of a client in terms of the syllogism. He begins with a conclusion which he intends to reach, favorable to his client of course, and then analyzes the facts of the situation to find material out of which to construct a favorable statement of facts, to *form* a minor premise. At the same time he goes over recorded cases to find rules of law employed in cases which can be presented as similar, rules which will substantiate a certain way of looking at and interpreting the facts. And as his acquaintance with rules of law judged applicable widens, he probably alters perspective and emphasis in selection of the facts which are to form his evidential data. And as he learns more of the facts of the case he may modify his selection of rules of law upon which he bases his case.

I do not for a moment set up this procedure as a model of scientific method; it is too precommitted to the establishment of a particular and partisan conclusion to serve as such as model. But it does illustrate, in spite of this deficiency, the particular point which is being made here: namely, that thinking actually sets out from a more or less confused situation, which is vague and ambiguous with respect to the conclusion it indicates, and that the formation of both major premise and minor proceed tentatively and correlatively in the course of analysis of this situation and of prior rules. As soon as acceptable premises are given and of course the judge and jury have eventually to do with their becoming accepted—and the conclusion is also given. In strict logic, the conclusion does not follow from premises; conclusions and premises are two ways of stating the same thing. Thinking may be defined either as a development of premises or development of a conclusion, as far as it is one operation it is the other. . . .

It is at this point that the chief stimulus and temptation to mechanical logic and abstract use of formal concepts come in. Just because the personal element cannot be wholly excluded, while at the same time the decision must assume as nearly as possible an impersonal, objective, rational form, the temptation is to surrender the vital logic which has actually yielded the conclusion and to substitute for it forms of speech which are rigorous in appearance and which give an illusion of certitude.

Another moving force is the undoubted need for the maximum possible of stability and regularity of expectation in determining course of conduct. Men need to know the legal consequences which society through the courts will attach to their specific transactions, the liabilities they are assuming, the fruits they may count upon in entering upon a given course of action.

This is a legitimate requirement from the standpoint of the interests of the community and of particular individuals. Enormous confusion has resulted, however, from confusion of *theoretical* certainty and practical certainty. There is a wide gap separating the reasonable proposition that judicial decisions should possess the maximum possible regularity in order to enable persons in planning their conduct to foresee the legal import of their acts, and the absurd because impossible proposition that every decision should flow with formal logical necessity from antecedently known premises. To attain the former result there are required general principles of interpreting cases—rules of law—and procedures of pleading and trying cases which do not alter arbitrarily. But principles of interpretation do not signify rules so rigid that they can be stated once for all and then be literally and mechanically adhered to. For the situations to which they are to be applied do not literally repeat one another in all details, and questions of degree of this factor or that have the chief weight in determining which general rule will be employed to judge the situation in question. A large part of what has been asserted concerning the necessity of absolutely uniform and immutable antecedent rules of law is in effect an attempt to evade the really important issue of finding and employing rules of law, substantive and procedural, which will actually secure to the members of the community a reasonable measure of practical certainty of expectation in framing their courses of conduct. The mechanical ease of the court in disposing of cases and not the actual security of agents is the real cause, for example, of making rules of pleading hard and fast. The result introduces an unnecessary element of gamble into the behavior of those seeking settlement of disputes, while it affords to the judges only that factitious ease and simplicity which is supplied by any routine habit of action. It substitutes a mechanical procedure for the need of analytic thought.

There is of course every reason why rules of law should be as regular and as definite as possible. But the amount and kind of antecedent assurance which is actually attainable is a matter of fact, not of form. It is large wherever social conditions are pretty uniform, and when industry, commerce, transportation, etc., move in the channels of old customs. It is much less wherever invention is active and when new devices in business and communication bring about new forms of human relationship. Thus the use of power machinery radically modifies the old terms of association of master and servant and fellow servants; rapid transportation brings into general use commercial bills of lading; mass production engenders organization of laborers and collective bargaining; industrial conditions favor concentration of capital. In part legislation endeavors to reshape old rules of law to make them applicable to new conditions. But statutes have never kept up with the variety and subtlety of social change. . . .

The facts involved in this discussion are commonplace and they are not offered as presenting anything original or novel. What we are concerned with is their bearing upon the logic of judicial decisions. For the implications are more revolutionary than they might at first seem to be. They indicate either that logic must be abandoned or that it must be a logic *relative to consequences rather than to antecedents,* a logic of prediction of probabilities rather than one of deduction of certainties. For the purposes of a logic of inquiry into probable consequences, general principles can only be tools justified by the work they do. They are means of intellectual survey, analysis, and insight into the factors of the situation to be dealt with. Like other tools they must be modified when they are applied to new conditions and new results have to be achieved. Here is where the great practical evil of the doctrine of immutable and necessary antecedent rules comes in. It sanctifies the old; adherence to it in practice constantly widens the gap between current social conditions and the principles used by the courts. The effect is to breed irritation, disrespect for law, together with virtual alliance between the judiciary and entrenched interests that correspond most nearly to the conditions under which the rules of law were previously laid down.

Failure to recognize that general legal rules and principles are working hypotheses, needing to be constantly tested by the way in which they work out in application to concrete situations, explains the otherwise paradoxical fact that the slogans of the liberalism of one period often become the bulwarks of reaction in a subsequent era. There was a time in the eighteenth century when the great social need was emancipation of industry and trade from a multitude of restrictions which held over from the feudal estate of Europe. Adapted well enough to the localized and fixed conditions of that earlier age, they become hindrances and annoyances as the effects of methods, use of coal and steam, showed themselves. The movement of emancipation expressed itself in principles of liberty in use of property, and freedom of contract, which were embodied in a mass of legal decisions. But the absolutistic logic of rigid syllogistic forms infected these ideas. It was soon forgotten that they were relative to analysis of existing situations in order to secure orderly methods in behalf of economic social welfare. Thus these principles became in turn so rigid as to be almost as socially obstructive as "immutable" feudal laws had been in their day.

That the remarks which have been made, commonplace as they are in themselves, have a profound practical import may also be seen in the present reaction against the individualistic formulae of an older liberalism. The last thirty years has seen an intermittent tendency in the direction of legislation, and to a less extent of judicial decision, towards what is vaguely known as "social justice," toward formulae of a collectivistic character. Now it is quite possible that the newer rules may be needed and useful at a certain juncture, and yet that they may also become harmful and socially obstructive if they are hardened into absolute and fixed antecedent premises. But if they are conceived as tools to be adapted to the conditions in which they are employed rather than as absolute and intrinsic "principles," attention will go to the facts of social life, and the rules will not be allowed to engross attention and become absolute truths to be maintained intact at all costs. Otherwise we shall in the end merely have substituted one set of formally absolute and immutable syllogistic premises for another set.

If we recur then to our introductory conception that logic is really a theory about empirical phenomena, subject to growth and improvement like any other empirical discipline, we recur to it with an added conviction: namely, that the issue is not a purely speculative one, but implies consequences vastly significant for practise. I should indeed not hesitate to assert that the sanctification of ready-made antecedent universal principles as methods of thinking is the chief obstacle to the kind of thinking which is the indispensable prerequisite of steady, secure and intelligent social reforms in general and social advance by means of law in particular. If this be so infiltration into law of a more experimental and flexible logic is a social as well as an intellectual need.

Loevinger, An Introduction to Legal Logic*

II

. . . With particular reference to law, analysis will show that there are at least six distinct stages in reaching a conclusion on a doubtful case or legal problem, whether it is presented in a court trial, administrative proceeding, law office conference or elsewhere.

(1) The judge (lawyer or administrator, as the case may be) must determine the point of conflict and the problem or issues involved. Usually this is relatively easy for a judge who has pleadings presented to him by lawyers presumably skilled in sifting facts and presenting legal issues. It is even easier for an appellate court which has the assistance not only of the lawyers but also of the lower court. However, as every practising lawyer knows, this is often a vexing problem in dealing with clients. Many a man is certain he has been grievously wronged without having the slightest idea what, if any, the nature of his legal injury may be. That this matter is not always simple even for appellate courts is shown by the occasional disagreements on the upper benches as to what issues the appellate courts should decide on appeal.

(2) Having discovered the issues or points of conflict, the judge must decide on the area of relevance. This does not mean that a decision must be made in advance on all points of evidence, such as the possibility of collateral impeachment of witnesses. It does mean that the lawyers and court must know what the elements involved in the legal concept at issue are, and what the nature of the facts to prove such elements will be. Without such a mental outline a lawyer could not tell whether his client had a case worth suing on and a judge could not tell whether pleadings stated a case appropriate for relief or a cause of action, or whether a plaintiff had made a *prima facie* case. Further, this outline must be exclusive as well as inclusive. A lawyer cannot list all of his client's grudges

* [27 *Ind. L.J.* 471, 485-492 (1952). Reprinted by permission.

Lee Loevinger (1913–   ) was educated at the University of Minnesota (B.A. 1933; J.D. 1936). Currently a member of the Washington, D.C. law firm of Hogan and Hartson, Loevinger is a former commissioner of the Federal Communications Commission (1963-1968) and was Assistant Attorney General in charge of the Antitrust Division, U.S. Department of Justice (1961-1963).]

against an adversary in the complaint, but only such as relate to the issues. Likewise, a judge will not permit the reception of evidence that does not bear upon what he has decided to be an issue in the case.

(3) Having defined the issues and the areas of relevance as to each, the judge and lawyers must then select the evidence tending to establish the facts relevant to each issue, and the judge must select from among conflicting bits of evidence those to which he will give probative value and must determine the relative probative values to be assigned to the various items of evidence.

(4) Having thus postulated the relevant facts, the judge must then select some standard of decision. Some issues may be easily determined by reference to a statute, once the facts are decided. In other cases, the judge may rely upon the precedent of former decisions. Other standards that may be used are the custom and tradition of the community, generally accepted ideas of social welfare, justice and community mores, and even the judge's own private ideas of morals, ethics or justice. It was essentially this problem that Cardozo was discussing in his analysis of the judicial process.

(5) Having selected a standard of decision, the judge must still analyze the controlling considerations implicit in the standard selected. With rare exceptions, self-evident principles are not to be gleaned from statutes, cases, traditions, ideas of social welfare, or even personal codes of justice. Statutes must be construed, cases must be gathered and analyzed, traditions and mores must be interpreted. Conceivably this might be done in terms so narrow as to fit only the case in hand. But the law strives to generalize. Thus the controlling principle distilled from whatever standard is resorted to will ordinarily be stated in terms at least slightly broader than the immediate case.

(6) Finally, the judge will reach the actual decision of the case by applying the principle thus arrived at to the facts thus determined. Where a single individual has taken each of the preceding steps, the final step of applying the principle selected for the case to the facts may be nearly automatic. But here again the dissents and reversals from our appellate courts warn that even where there is substantial agreement on issues, facts and applicable principles, there is still room for occasional disagreement on the final result. If the amount of damages or the provisions of a remedial decree are involved, this may even be the most difficult and doubtful step in the entire process.

Since these steps are merely stages in a single inquiry, they are, of course, not discrete or mutually exclusive. Even before determining the issues, it is obviously necessary to learn some of the facts. However, it will avoid much confusion to remember that what is true of legal reasoning at one stage of the legal process is not necessarily true at another. Thus it becomes useful to have a division into stages. The analysis suggested seems to be a convenient and useful one, but it is assuredly not intimated that it is the only possible one, or even the best or most useful one.

Before attempting to examine the patterns of legal reasoning at the several stages of the legal process, the semantic principles of modern logic require that the frame of reference to be used should be specified. There are at least four distinguishable viewpoints or levels of analysis which may be employed in examining the operation of the legal process at any one of its stages.

(A) The most common is what we may call the *ostensible*. Decisions of courts and opinions of lawyers are almost always accompanied by or based upon some kind of ostensible reasoning. They assume certain facts and employ some legal rules or principles to relate these facts to the conclusion reached. An examination of the opinions of courts and the attempt to relate and systematize the principles stated is an example of analysis at the ostensible level. What lawyers call "research" is nearly always conducted within this frame of reference. The questions which can be asked within this frame of reference are: What facts are assumed in reaching the decision? and What reasoning or rationale is employed to relate these facts to the conclusion reached?

(B) The *logical* viewpoint or frame of reference implies quite a different approach. Whereas the ostensible level of analysis accepts the language of legal opinions at substantially its face value, the logical analysis inquires into the implications and significance of the terms and the context used. In the modern view, logic itself constitutes a different frame of reference than ordinary language. Logic, in the modern lexicon is a meta-language. To put it simply, language is a system of terms that refer to objects or things, whereas logic is a system of terms that refer to language; or, as Carnap puts it, logic is the syntax of language. The necessity for so regarding it arises from the fact that an inquiry into the validity of reasoning demands the use of some tools other than the reasoning itself. Reasoning, of whatever order, cannot validate itself. It was the failure to recognize this that led to the concern over the classical logical paradoxes that have puzzled and amused so many generations of college students. A simple example is this:

> **EVERY STATEMENT WITHIN THESE LINES IS FALSE.**

If that proposition is true, then, since the proposition is itself a statement within the lines, it is false. But, if the proposition is false, then, since it refers to itself it must be true. No matter how regarded, the proposition implies its own contradictory. The solution of the paradox is in the principle that a class cannot be a member of itself. Statements about things represent a class of propositions of one order (the linguistic level); statements about statements represent a class of propositions of another order (the logical level). Thus a logical proposition about statements may refer to other statements but not to the one containing that proposition. It is important to remember that any attempt to analyze legal reasoning on the logical level means an inquiry into the validity of the reasoning, and therefore implies something more than examination of the reasoning itself on its own terms. A comparison of the ostensible reasoning of other cases is not a logical analysis of the reasoning of one case. So long as the inquiry is confined to the reasoning employed in the opinions of any number of precedents and legal principles, the examination remains on the ostensible or linguistic level. However, when the inquiry extends beyond the language used to its necessary meaning and implications or to the form of reasoning used, then it is adopting the logical frame of reference. The questions that can be asked within this frame of reference are: What are the meanings of the terms and contexts used? What are the implications of the principles and conclusions adopted? What is the form of the reasoning employed? In the circumstances, is this valid reasoning?

(C) To be clearly distinguished from the ostensible and the logical viewpoints is the *psychological* inquiry. Neither the ostensible nor the logical foundations of a decision are necessarily the reason for its adoption. This is most obvious in law office practice, where the lawyer frequently is called upon either to justify some action already taken or to invent a rationale that will permit his client to take some desired action. Although it is seldom the avowed judicial procedure, it is the contention of the "realists" that judicial conclusions are usually arrived at for psychological reasons unrelated to the ostensible or logical process of justification which subsequently appears in the opinion. To take an extreme instance (which happily may be assumed to be rare), when a judge is bribed, his actual motives for reaching the decision announced will clearly have little to do with whatever reasons he may give publicly. Although less dramatic, a judge's prejudices, attitudes, experience and temperament all will influence him, perhaps decisively, in his judicial conduct. These influences may or may not be expressed in the ostensible reasoning given by the judge. They may or may not be revealed by logical analysis. Ultimately the determination of the psychological basis for judicial action can be established only by empirical investigation. An examination of cases can be, at best, only suggestive of psychological conclusions. The questions which are within the psychological frame of reference are:

What are the motives that have impelled a judge to reach the conclusion, adopt the reasoning and assume the facts that he has accepted in any given situation? Such an inquiry can be generalized to seek to discover the influences which usually move a particular judge, or even, what influences are predominate in the action of a group of judges. However, no inquiry confined to the usual legal sources can be more than suggestive of an answer. The psychological level of inquiry is concerned not with apparent or formal reasons or the implications of decisions, but with actual influences that are operative upon specific real individuals. These constitute objective facts the nature of which can be known with assurance only on the basis of scientific investigation.

(D) Related to each of the foregoing viewpoints, but constituting an independent frame of reference for the investigation of the legal process is the *empirical* inquiry. As has been stated, the questions arising within the psychological frame of reference can be definitely answered only by empirical inquiry. However, the empirical frame of reference is not confined to investigating the psychological foundations of legal and judicial opinions. It is legitimate to ask whether or not the facts assumed by a court in its decision are consistent with the facts to be ascertained by an objective scientific investigation, and whether the implications to be logically derived from a decision are compatible with observable facts relating to the subject matter of the propositions thus derived. Such questions as these are not to be answered by a formal analysis of legal material, but require scientific investigation by the techniques independently established in the natural and social sciences.

By distinguishing the various aspects of the legal process and the viewpoints from which they may be regarded, we can reconcile many of the apparent conflicts in the earlier writings on this topic. Holmes and those following his lead are quite right in asserting that the logical form does not compel any particular decision in a specific legal controversy. They are probably correct in asserting that the determinants of judicial action are attitudes, preconceived ideas regarding social advantage, prejudices and similar influences, although this does not necessarily follow from a demonstration of the fallacy of logical form. On the other hand, the traditionalists are justified in demanding that regardless of motivation legal decisions should be capable of logical formulation, justification and analysis. However, they err in assuming that the ability to put the ostensible justification for legal action in a logically valid form supports any inference as to the psychological foundation for the action.

With the exception of Jerome Frank, who has attempted to emphasize the influence of the selection of facts in determining the legal result, most of the writers on this subject have tended to consider only the factors involved in selecting, analyzing and applying a standard of decision to a disputed case. Some, like Cardozo, have emphasized the factors involved in the selection of an appropriate standard of decision. Others, like Stone, have emphasized the stages of application of the controlling principles to the case in hand. Levi handles his material almost wholly within the framework of ostensible or conventional legal reasoning. Stone and Patterson adopt and maintain the logical viewpoint rather consistently. Jerome Frank and Felix Cohen base much of their analysis upon material derived from the psychological frame of reference. Morris Cohen, Roscoe Pound and Julius Cohen tend to emphasize the empirical viewpoint as the foundation for their views.

Some legal thinkers have fallen into fallacies by seeking to base conclusions within one frame of reference upon premises drawn from another. Logical validity requires that conclusions be based only upon premises arising within the same frame of reference. This does not preclude the exchange of data between viewpoints, but it does require that data be cast in concepts of the frame of reference within which they are to be used.

Nearly all legal writers to the present time, apparently misled either by the limited outlook of traditional scholastic logic or by remarks such as the epigrammatic comment of Holmes,* have mistakenly assumed a false alternative between the use of logic and experience or empirical data in the legal process.

Stone, The Lords at the Crossroads— When to "Depart" and How!†

I

The famous "Practice Statement" of 1966 has now been interestingly redubbed in *Jones v. Secretary of State for Social Services* a "unanimous resolution of the Lords of Appeal in Ordinary." Its provisions may be recalled:[2]

---

* ["The life of the law has not been logic; it has been experience." Holmes, *The Common Law* Lecture I (1881), page 397 supra.]

† [46 *Australian L.J.* 483-488 (1972). Reprinted by permission. The author reserves all rights as to further reproduction, in whole or in part, of the above article.

Julius Stone (1907–   ) is Professor of Law at the University of New South Wales, Australia. His publications include *Aggression and World Order, Human Law and Human Justice, Legal Controls of International Conflict,* and *Social Dimensions of Law and Justice.*]

2. See Practice Statement [1966] 1 W.L.R. 1234; Note [1966] 3 All E.R. 77.

Their lordships regard the use of precedent as an indispensable foundation upon which to decide what is the law and its application to individual cases. It provides at least some degree of certainty upon which individuals can rely in the conduct of their affairs, as well as a basis for orderly development of legal rules.

Their lordships nevertheless recognise that too rigid adherence to precedent may lead to injustice in a particular case and also unduly restrict the proper development of the law. They propose, therefore, to modify their present practice and, while treating former decisions of this House as normally binding, to depart from a previous decision when it appears right to do so.

In this connexion they will bear in mind the danger of disturbing retrospectively the basis on which contracts, settlements of property and fiscal arrangements have been entered into and also the especial need for certainty as to the criminal law.

This announcement is not intended to affect the use of precedent elsewhere than in this House.

Jones' case involved conjoined appeals under identical provisions for disablement benefit of the National Insurance (Industrial Injuries) Acts, 1946 and 1965. The act, inter alia, provides for injury benefit and (after injury benefit ceases) for disablement benefit, when an accident has occurred. The appellant Jones suffered back and chest pains after lifting heavy iron scrap, and the injuries appeal tribunal in due course awarded injury benefit in respect of a myocardial infarction. On Jones' later application for disablement benefit, the medical board and medical appeal tribunal, while acknowledging that there was an infarction as well as a strained back, only allowed disablement benefit in respect of the strained back, denying that the accident played any part in producing the myocardial infarction.

The central question in *Jones'* case was whether the earlier finding of the above statutory injuries authority for the purpose of injury benefit, was binding on the statutory (medical) disablement authority in its consideration of disablement benefit. On this a decision of the House of only four years before became a bone of bitter contention. In *Minister of Social Security v. Amalgamated Engineering Union (Re Dowling)*[3] a majority (Lords Reid, Morris, Hodson and Guest) had held that the finding of the statutory injuries authority that an accident, in the course of lifting a heavy flagstone, contributed to the injury (hiatus hernia) for which benefit was awarded, was binding on the medical authorities in considering entitlement to disablement benefit.

3. [1967] 1 A.C. 725.

The majority who held the medical authorities to be so bound, did so on diverse grounds. Lord Morris's opinion turned on the exceptional features that there was only one single identifiable injury in the course of doing the claimant's ordinary work and that occurrence of the injury constituted also the relevant "accident" within the Act. So that, since the accident and the injury were thus inseparable, "the medical authorities would be destroying the basis of their own jurisdiction" if they failed to accept the prior decision of the statutory authorities that there had been an injury resulting from the accident. For by their terms of reference their task was merely to pass on certain results of "a relevant accident," not to determine whether the accident was relevant or whether there had been an accident at all. Lord Hodson, on the other hand, speaking also for the majority other than Lord Morris, though he noted these special features of the case, proceeded on the following legal propositions. Under the provisions of the relevant National Insurance (Industrial Injuries) Act, 1946 (s. 36(3) and s. 50(1) of the 1965 Act) the first decision of the statutory authorities on any "claim or question" within their jurisdiction is "final." "Final" here meant conclusive for all purposes under the Act, and not merely for the purposes of the particular claim or particular kind of claim on which the first decision was made. It followed that the decision of the medical authorities on disablement benefit inconsistent with such a "final" prior decision of the statutory authorities on injury benefit was a nullity.

The final outcome of their Lordships' consideration of *Dowling's* case in the later *Jones* case can be briefly stated by saying that four out of the specially assembled full committee of seven thought that *Dowling's* case was wrong[4] and three thought it was right. However, while three of the four who thought it wrong thought it should be departed from, one of them, Lord Simon, held that it should nevertheless not be overruled. So that his vote against departure, combined with the votes of the three Lords who thought *Dowling's* case to be right, meant that that case, held by a majority of four to be wrong, was still deliberately maintained as representing binding authority by a different majority of four. This paradoxical situation may introduce us to an era in which, when we read in a headnote that a precedent has been "disapproved" by the highest authority, we may still have to ask whether or not it is still a binding authority.

---

4. Diplock at 189; Dilhorne at 164, 168, 171; Wilberforce at 173; Simon at 197-198. There were refined and sometimes dubious differences of fact between the two conjoined cases of *Jones* and *Hudson;* on which see especially Lord Morris at 155-160, Viscount Dilhorne at 163, 168-169, Lord Pearson at 178-180, and Lord Simon at 193-196.

II

This paradox is, however, the beginning rather than the end of the dramatic legal interest of *Jones'* case. The Divisional Court and Court of Appeal below had, naturally enough, taken *Dowling's* case as binding on them, but they had held that the instant facts in *Jones'* case were to be distinguished. They adopted Lord Morris's version of the *Dowling* ratio, namely, that with a *single* identifiable injury which was also the accident (as found by the injury authorities) the disablement board could not deny that the accident contributed to the injury, since this would be to deny both accident and related injury, and with these its own competence to deal with the case at all. On this narrow version of the ratio of *Dowling*, they distinguished the facts of *Jones'* case, where there were ostensibly two injuries found by the authorities as proceeding from the same accident, and the disablement board allowed one and disallowed the other. Where there were thus two injuries, they in effect said, and the disablement board allowed one, the board was not denying that there was an accident resulting in an injury, and its competence was unimpaired.

But, of course, as was sharply observed by the majority in *Jones'* case who thought that *Dowling* was wrong, no one could ensure that the ratio of *Dowling's* case would continue to be found in this narrow ground of Lord Morris, all the less since the three Lords for whom Lord Hodson spoke took a much wider ground. This, they recalled, was that under s. 36(3) and s. 50(1) of the Acts the injury authority's determination that an industrial accident had contributed to the injury is "final," and therefore binding for all purposes under the Acts. In so far as it was thus binding on the disablement board, that board's contrary decision would be a nullity: and it did not matter for this purpose to how many injuries the accident may have been found to contribute.

Dowling's case, on this interpretation of its ratio, would in the view of the majority Lords who disapproved it, undermine the whole statutory scheme for injury and disablement benefit. Under that scheme claims for injury benefits were necessarily to be dealt with in a comparatively summary manner, to alleviate immediate hardship; whereas disablement claims, involving possibly long-term and large-scale benefits, are to be dealt with by more expert medical authorities, at a more deliberate pace. But the effect of *Dowling* was to annul any finding of the more expert and deliberative authorities, on the more substantial questions, which contradicted the less expert, more summary determinations of the injury authorities.

Not only the four Lords who, on this reading of its ratio, held *Dow-*

ling to be wrong, but also Lords Reid, Morris and Pearson, who were prepared to accept it as right, addressed themselves in view of the close division on substance to the question whether *if it were wrong* it should be departed from. As already observed, Lord Simon finally defected to the minority on this issue, establishing a different majority against departure.

III

The concern of this article is to examine their Lordships' arguments for or against departure. And it is obvious that in so far as other tiers in the hierarchy of courts, like the Court of Appeal in England or the High Court of Australia, may come to exercise an analogous power to "depart" from their own or co-ordinate decisions, the scope and nature of these arguments may become of wider importance. It will be shown that the arguments thus far offered stop drastically short of clear guidance. Lord Reid, indeed, disowned any present intention of categorizing cases where the House should or should not depart. He thought that "as time passes experience will supply some guide." The present modest objective is merely to begin the analysis of this experience.

All the Lords in *Jones'* case seemed agreed on the cardinal point, apparent perhaps from the 1966 Statement itself, that the mere finding that an earlier decision is wrong, even by a presently unanimous House, would not in itself warrant departing from it. In Lord Reid's view, the 1966 Statement was intended to promote certainty, even in its concern with "a comparatively small number" of decisions thought to be impeding the proper development of the law or causing injustice or violating public policy. The old practice of *evading* such decisions by over-fine distinctions promoted still further uncertainty as to the standing of the disapproved precedent. Yet the House should also (he thought) be slow to increase uncertainty by too much overruling. How to decide which disapproved cases to depart from would have to be gathered from experience. But Lord Reid thought that *Jones'* case illustrated one category where departures should be rare. This was in questions of construction of statutes or instruments, especially complex ones like the National Insurance (Industrial Injuries) Acts, 1946 and 1965, where no broad issue of policy or justice or legal policy is involved. In such matters, judicial opinions tend to differ according to approach; and as to this particular Act, it was open to the departmental litigant (he thought) to move for legislative correction of whatever construction was adopted.

Lord Morris, as the writer of a main speech in *Dowling's* case, naturally agreed with Lord Reid that *Dowling's* case was correctly decided, and he also thought they should rarely overrule decisions on mere construction. Lord Pearson also agreed on both points, even (he stressed as to the latter) when the impugned construction was reached by only a bare majority of judges through all the instances. Even Lord Simon, who emphatically thought *Dowling's* case to be wrong, also offered closely similar reasons why he opposed overruling it. He added that the rule in *Dowling's* case did not involve the kind of "injustice in a particular case" envisaged in the 1966 Statement, and that prophecies that this construction of the Act would bring dire administrative problems, had not eventuated. In such cases (he thought) overruling would encourage repeated litigation of the same point by routine litigants like government departments concerned, on the chance of finding "a favourably constituted Committee."

The other three judges thought both that *Dowling's* case was wrongly decided *and that it should be overruled.* Viscount Dilhorne recognized, as did others (including Lord Simon—who would not overrule), that the question whether a disapproved precedent should be overruled depends, in part, on *whether it can be distinguished* from the instant case. Once he had answered this negatively, Viscount Dilhorne saw "no valid reason" for not overruling cases on statutory construction. Lord Simon said that the very aspiration of the 1966 Statement "to obviate . . . refinement in distinction and . . . capriciousness in result" would make it absurd for him to take a distinction which was neither supported by the majority in *Dowling's* case nor accorded with his own view, despite the fact that the courts below had been willing to take it. For Viscount Dilhorne, as for Lord Diplock, the fact that *Dowling's* case was as recent as 1967 made it easier to depart from rather than otherwise, there having been that much less reliance on it.

Lord Wilberforce's position is of particular interest, since he was among those who both disapproved the *Dowling* decision and wished to overrule it. For he did so despite his agreement with Lord Reid and the others about the special objections against overruling in cases on the construction of a statute, a matter on which the House (subject to Parliament) "has the last word." His final decision to overrule turned on the main controversy as to what was the ratio of *Dowling's* case. The ratio which Lord Morris gave for concurring with the majority holding in that case hinged on the supposed *exceptional nature of the facts* in *Dowling's* case, which had the effect of barring the medical authorities, whose decision was impugned, from deciding certain issues differently from the statutory authorities. The ratio of the majority in *Dowling's* case, however, as expressed by Lord Hodson and concurred in by Lords Reid and

Guest, was of much greater potential ambit, touching the meaning of "final" in the National Insurance (Industrial Injuries) Act, 1946, s. 36(3) (1965 Act, s. 50(1)). Lord Wilberforce was clear that if the ratio could have been held down to the narrow ground, he would not agree to overrule. But since, in his view, the ratio was the wider one, he was of opinion, despite his "loyalty to *stare decisis,*" that *Dowling's* case should be overruled. Lord Diplock identified himself with this important consideration for overruling *Dowling's* case. He added (as already noted) the converse point that since the wider potential ratio had only just come to recognition, an early overruling would defeat comparatively few expectations.

Perhaps the most novel guideline offered in *Jones'* case about overruling under the 1966 Statement was Lord Simon's frank avowal that instead of deciding against overruling as he had done, he would have preferred (if it were only possible) to overrule *prospectively,* so as not to prejudice cases arising between *Dowling's* case in 1967 and *Jones'* case in 1972. Referring to a relevant United States Supreme Court decision,[16] he recognized that for this to be possible in England would require change in the prevailing theory that judges only declare law and "that every case was governed by a relevant rule of law, existing somewhere and discoverable somehow." The theory, so far as it required judicial rulings to be retrospective, served (he recognized) to check lightness in judicial innovation and to protect the legislative sphere. Yet (Lord Simon thought) judicial lawmaking was inescapable and increasingly acknowledged, as the 1966 Statement itself witnessed. Prospective overruling would be consistent with all this, though professional opinion, the suspicion of usurpation of legislative power, and the need to be clear which courts of final resort could use prospective overruling, indicated that its introduction should be by legislation.

IV

The gist of these varied positions could be summarized briefly, though not always with internal consistency, in the following propositions.

1. According to the 1966 Statement itself, "too rigid adherence to precedent" should yield where it leads to "injustice in a particular case" or threatens the "proper development of the law." This injunction is plainly too vague to be often helpful.

2. Also according to the Statement, care should be taken in the

---

16. Linkletter v. Walker (1965) 381 U.S. 618.

course of the above relaxation not to disturb retrospectively contracts, settlements of property and fiscal arrangements, and the certainty of the criminal law.

3. Most of the Lords in *Jones'* case seemed to agree with Lord Reid in extending this shelter to "questions of construction of statutes and other documents." This was sometimes on the ground that a precedent construction often "cannot be said positively" to be either "right or wrong" (Lord Reid at 149), that to depart would lead to undesirable "changes of course" in cases where "this House has the last word," or to overzealous institutional litigants repeatedly trying out differently constituted courts (Lord Wilberforce at 173).

4. Lord Reid (at 149, and perhaps also Lord Wilberforce at 172) suggested, rather inconsistently with his reasons for sheltering questions of construction, that departure *should* be considered preeminently where the old decision, now thought wrong, involves "some broad issue." This guide, with which at least three Lords did *not* go, cuts across his reason for sheltering questions of construction, namely that there may usually be conflicting views on them. Have not some of the most striking cases of recent times involved "broad issues" on which nevertheless conflicting views are very usual—*Conway v. Rimmer,* the *Dorset Yacht* case, *Boys v. Chaplin* and *Cassell v. Broome,* to mention no others?

5. Lord Simon's proposal that the judges should be readier to "depart" if they could do so with only "prospective" effect on the law, though Lord Diplock showed some interest in it, seems, even in the terms in which Lord Simon offered it, rather distant from any early practical adoption in British courts. The approach through merely "prospective" overruling involves, in any case, a welter of additional considerations for which a separate study would be required.

6. In general, their Lordships seemed to assume that the fact that *Dowling's* case was decided as recently as 1967 was a reason against overruling. Lord Diplock, however, saw "no greater reason for perpetuating recent error than for leaving ancient error uncorrected" (at 189).

These, it must be admitted, are rather inadequate guideposts for the creative overseeing functions of the highest courts in determining when earlier precedents of the highest courts should be departed from. If we now seek to probe beyond particular expressions of their Lordships to their overall handling of the impugned *Dowling* case, the results are perhaps more illuminating, though still far from final clarity.

The House's task in deciding whether to depart from the precedent seems to have been taken in two main phases. A first phase concerned the determination whether the rule established by the challenged precedent did fall short of justice, or hampered the "proper development of the law," in the sense of the 1966 Statement. And this, of course, presupposed that the House attributed some rule (ratio) to that precedent, and determined that what the law *ought to be* on the point differed from the rule so attributed.

A second phase, which can be described with perhaps some confidence, was the determination whether such shortfall was substantial enough (again in terms of the 1966 Statement) to outweigh the considerations of "certainty" and "orderly development of legal rules" which support adherence to precedent. As Lord Simon's position showed particularly clearly, the mere fact that the rule established by a precedent falls somewhat short of what the law ought to be, does not in itself require departure.

When we examine more closely this latter phase of deciding whether *the degree* of shortfall requires departure, it is seen to involve two sub-phases.

In the first sub-phase the degree of evil constituted by the shortfall from justice and "proper" legal development has to be weighed against the evil effects of departing from the precedent. For both the former and the latter are variable from case to case. For instance, as against the degree of evil arising from shortfall of the *Dowling* case rule which they detected, one or other of their Lordships detected the following countervailing evils which would arise from departing: first, judicial chopping and changing on notoriously debatable matters like statutory construction (Lords Reid, Morris and Pearson); second, encouragement of litigants' repeated adventurism (Lord Simon); third, disturbance of expectations in pending cases; fourth, disturbance of decisions already in course between the date of the case departed from and the instant case. The degree of each of these countervailing evils itself, moreover, might be variable from case to case. Lords Wilberforce and Diplock, for example, while agreed generally on the first evil above, thought that when the ratio of the impugned precedent was (as they found) of wide ambit, the reasons for sheltering it should give way.

Such calculations are of course complex, and they are quantitative, though necessarily *in only rather a gross sense.* Moreover, the complexity may be increased, as indeed it was in the *Jones* case, by a second subphase in the weighing of the evils of the rule set by the ratio of the precedent against the evils of departure. This sub-phase arises from some central puzzles of the ratio notion itself. As already noted, what is the rule set by the ratio of the impugned case must in some sense be determined before the judges can say, under the first phase above, that the precedent is "right" or "wrong," "approved" or "disapproved." It is only after they have taken positions on this that the question in the second phase arises whether the shortfall in that rule is great enough to outweigh the evils arising from departure from it. But at the present sub-phase of this second phase, when the court is weighing the competing evils, the *Jones'* case shows that what is taken as the ratio of the impugned precedent may also powerfully affect the calculus of evils.

Thus, if the rule set by the ratio of *Dowling's* case was the narrow one there laid down by Lord Morris, and in the *Jones'* case adopted by the Divisional Court and the Court of Appeal and Lords Reid, Morris and Pearson, the evils flowing from the shortfall of that rule, in the view of the four Lords who disapproved it, would be correspondingly less. Lord Wilberforce, for example, who finally held that *Dowling* should be departed from, made explicit that if he thought its future influence on the law could be held down to this narrower ratio, he would have declined to depart from it. In so far, however, as the ratio was now said to be a wider rule, namely, that s. 36(3) of the 1945 Act made determinations by a competent statutory authority final for all purposes under the Act, he thought his "loyalty to *stare decisis*" must yield and they must overrule. So Lord Diplock thought that to overrule *Dowling* on the assumption that its ratio was the narrow one would disturb the expectation of only a few claimants, while to leave it standing, despite the fact that a far wider ratio was "attributable" to it, would result in unacceptable evils of fortuitous and arbitrary consequences. It was "unrealistic" to think that amending legislation could remedy these evils quickly (at 189).

Lord Simon made the same point in other words when he concluded that to narrow the *Dowling* ratio would produce the kind of "refinement in distinction" and "capriciousness in result" to avoid which the 1966 power to "depart" was taken. (It adds spice to this mixture that, as already seen, Lord Simon finally voted that *Dowling's* case, though clearly wrong, should *not* be departed from. But this was on the ground that the evils on the other side of the balance (that is, of the shortfall of the rule in *Dowling's* case) were less great than his other three colleagues who thought it wrong assumed them to be.)

In other words, at this second sub-phase, after the ratio attributed to the precedent has been disapproved and when the evils of maintaining it or departing from it are being weighed, there may intervene a *reconsideration* of the ratio as a part of this weighing process. In part, this is an effort to see whether, in face of the evils of departure, it might be better *even at that stage* to distinguish the precedent from the instant case (and thus avoid altogether the issue of departing). The Lords have to bear in mind that the 1966 Statement itself also declared refinement and capriciousness of distinctions to be evils. The consideration of what distinctions are available is involved in determining what weight to give to the competing evils which would flow, on the one hand, from "departure" and on the other from avoiding "departure" by distinguishing. Whether a narrower or a wider issue is attributed to the precedent must necessarily affect the weight to be allotted to some of the relevant evils.

We may perhaps sum up this sketch of their Lordships' overall approach to the question of departing. At one end of this deliberation, for which the House's new Direction 12(a) now specially provides, is the search for the rule for which the impugned precedent (its ratio) is to be deemed to stand. Until this is fixed, the question whether the precedent is to be approved or disapproved can scarcely arise; the case remains still in a kind of *upper* purgatory to the region in which the matter of "departure" actually arises. At the other end of this process, after a ratio has thus been attributed and the rule it affords disapproved as falling short of the requirements of justice or proper development of the law, the evils of departing from the precedent must be compared with the evils thought to arise from maintaining that rule as law. Here, however, the respective degrees of evil also depend, inter alia, on the width of the rule (or ratio) of the precedent. An embracing rule catching more cases will obviously tend to give rise to more evils than a narrow one catching few cases.

In strict logic, perhaps, one would have to say that once one rule (or ratio) has been attributed in the upper purgatorial process, the weighing of evils should proceed exclusively on that basis. *Jones'* case seems to show, however, that it is not so simple. For the choice between the competing rules (or ratios) of the precedent case is often (and for cases of the present kind which reach the House, usually) most problematical. This, of course, is the more so when, as in *Jones'* case, the House itself splits as to the correct choice. In this situation the course taken in *Jones'* case by the majority of four who disapproved of *Dowling* suggests that another stage must be added to the deliberations about "departure." This is a *reconsideration* (now in a lower purgatory, as it were) of the ratio for which the impugned precedent *might be held in the future* to stand, if it is not now stripped of its authority. For the evils flowing from that problematical ratio have to be put into the balance, along with the evils of using, in order to salvage it, the over-refined and capricious distinctions at which the 1966 Statement was aimed, before it can be decided whether or not to depart.

Levi, The Nature of Judicial Reasoning

See page 262 supra.

M. R. Cohen, Law and Scientific Method*

It was an English judge who once thanked God that the law of England was not a science. The sense of gratitude to God is often somewhat capricious; but there can be no doubt that the English bar has not only neglected the science of law but has felt a positive aversion for it. This was not overstated by one who said that the very word "jurisprudence" was offensive to the nostrils of the English lawyer. Nor is this merely the English preference for muddling through. We must take into account the historic facts as to the relation between the English universities and the Inns of Court. As the universities would not teach English law, the business of preparing men for the well-organized profession of law fell into the hands of strictly professional corporations, whose traditions had little in common with the clerical and other-worldly traditions that prevailed in Oxford and Cambridge up to very recent days. And yet some part of the scientific spirit—something of the scholar's interest in history and respect for fact, and something of the spirit of detachment—did penetrate the English bar, partly through the separation of the barrister from the business of the solicitor and partly at least through the philologic studies that leaders of the bar pursued in the classical courses at the public schools and at Oxford and Cambridge. Certainly the old rules of pleading showed a highly refined logical technique.

Much more unfavorable for the development of any science of law have been the conditions in this country. Up to the last quarter of the nineteenth century, we had no real universities; and the practical demands on the service of lawyers was so great that any attempt to regulate their educational qualifications was resented by the public as an undue interference with the natural right of every enterprising citizen to choose and pursue his own calling. It is therefore not surprising that until very recently our law schools functioned practically as trade schools, and their connection with the colleges or universities was rather nominal. For men to make the teaching of law their major occupation is for us a new phenomenon, and I cannot help recalling the contemptuous references to the teachers of law that I heard at a meeting of a great state bar association not so long ago. To one who was neither a lawyer nor a teacher of law the vehemence of the contempt was rather amusing.

I venture to submit these trite observations in order to call your at-

* [From *Law and the Social Order*, 184-187, 192-197, by Morris R. Cohen, copyright, 1933, by Harcourt, Brace and Company, Inc. Substance of this essay given as address at 25th Annual Meeting of Association of American Law Schools, December 29, 1927, and first published in *6 Am. L. School Rev.* 231 (1928). Reprinted by permission.

For biographical information, see page 81 supra.]

tention to the fact that despite the rapid expansion of our law schools in the last decade, and despite the increase of scientific interest in the law as shown in our law reviews, we are still under tremendous pressure to prepare our students for practical success at the bar rather than to advance the science of the law. We may, when we view the situation abstractly, admit that ultimately the most practical thing that our law school can do for the community is to promote the science of law; but under pressure of immediate practicality we are loth to change the strictly professional curriculum. We fear to introduce theoretic studies as remote from immediately practical legal issues as are pathology in the school of medicine, physiological psychology in the school of education, or rational mechanics in the school of engineering. Men were undoubtedly successful physicians, teachers, and engineers, before the introduction of such studies, but no one doubts today their necessity to give men a liberal insight into their work. So men have been and will continue to be successful at the bar without direct attention to the science of the law. Indeed, if we were to judge by purely and immediately practical results, our present law school curriculum might be viewed as already too theoretical. A knowledge of the existing law, let us courageously admit, is not the sole, nor perhaps even the most important, condition for practical success at the bar. The art of properly manipulating judges, juries, and clients is at least as important, and yet does not, and rightly should not, receive the attention of the law school. The public interest that the university ought to serve is no more intimately connected with the personal success of the lawyer than with that of the modiste, the shoe-maker, or the plumber. The primary object of the university as a public institution can only be the advancement of our legal institutions through the development of a liberal understanding or science of the law.

I

If scientific method be a way of avoiding certain human pitfalls in the search for truth, then the law surely compares favourably in this respect with other human occupations. Court procedure to determine whether A and B did make a contract, or whether C did commit a criminal act, shows a regard for orderly attainment of truth that compares very favourably with the procedure of a vestry board in determining the fitness of a minister, or of a college in selecting a professor.

When we come, however, to the appellate work of higher courts, in which new public policies are decided under the guise of their legality or constitutionality, we find courts making all sorts of factual generalizations without adequate information. The facilities of our courts for acquiring information as to actual conditions are very limited. Courts have to decide all sorts of complicated issues after a few hours of oral argument and briefs by lawyers. Are ten hours per day in the old-type bakery a strain on the baker's health? Will a workmen's compensation act or a minimum wage law, take away the property of the employer, or of the worker that receives less than the minimum of subsistence? It is not to the credit of any system that its chief exponents can put their amateurish opinions against those of physicians or economists who have given these questions careful scientific study. Yet the law cannot simply and uncritically accept all the opinions of economists or sociologists. After all, on many important points social scientists are not agreed among themselves; and certainly the social sciences do not demonstrate their results as rigorously as do the natural sciences. Much of what passes as social science is just exercise in technical vocabulary, or mere plausible impressionism, without any critical methods for testing data or accurately determining whether certain assumed results are really true. A good deal of psychology, normal and abnormal, is still in that condition. This, of course, is no argument for the law's ignoring what experts in these fields have to say. But it should impress upon us the necessity for the law itself —in the persons of jurists, judges and advocates—to have a trained sense of scientific method.

It was the great Poincaré who once said that, while physical scientists were busy solving their problems, social scientists were busy discussing their methods. Making due allowance for Gallic wit, there is in this statement much to sober a too sanguine generation that expects heaven on earth as a result of a universal conversion to scientific method. A little critical reflection shows that the term "scientific method" is seldom used with a very definite meaning. If it denotes the art of teaching men how to make discoveries in the sciences, we may well say that such an art is as unknown as the art of training great poets. Certainly we should expect little in this respect from books of logic, the authors of which have seldom made any contributions to science, and indeed often write from mere hearsay about it. . . .

III

If at this point I am accused of still believing in the old classical deductive methods—so discredited in the minds of modernistic illuminati —I must enter a plea of confession and avoidance. I admit faith in the hypothetico-deductive method, but I deny that it has ever been justly discredited. On the contrary, the method of beginning with hypotheses and deducing conclusions, and then comparing these conclusions with the factual world, seems to me still the essence of sound scientific method. The prejudice against deduction is inspired by the abuse of that method on the part of those deficient in knowledge. Such abuse, however, is inherent in all human methods.

Stated positively, deduction has three functions in scientific method that ought to be rather obvious in the field of law:

First, it enables us to develop the implications of propositions and thus find out their true meaning. Knowledge grows most rapidly when we can properly utilize previous knowledge. Those who know make the most discoveries.

In the second place, deduction helps to make our assumptions explicit and this makes possible a critical attitude towards them.

In the third place, deduction enables us to deal not only with the actual, but also with the possible. It thus liberates us to explore the field of possibility, where there are to be found many things better than the actual.

Let me say a word about the second of these services. I say we begin always with hypotheses or assumptions. For the most part, however, it never occurs to us that we are making assumptions. We think we are starting with obvious truths. But propositions seem to us self-evident simply because it has never occurred to us to doubt them. It is, however, the business of scientific method to doubt all that pretends to be self-evident—e.g., that all property must have an owner, that no one can acquire rights by committing wrongs, that the maxim *Caveat emptor* is necessary to encourage commerce, etc. Modern geometry has discovered new regions of investigation by learning to look at Euclid's axioms as assumptions. The same is true of the axioms of Newtonian mechanics. Recently a distinguished economist has shown that a rational economic science can be built up on assumption contrary to those prevailing among orthodox economists.[4] It would not be difficult to show that most of the principles appealed to as self-evident in legal discussion might easily be denied and their contrary shown to be just as plausible.

This does not mean universal skepticism, but only the recognition of the fact that as human beings we start not with absolute certainties, but with hypotheses or guesses suggested generally by tradition and previous knowledge, but not on that account necessarily free from error. Scientific methodology has no objection to traditional views as such except

4. See J. M. Clark, "Non-Euclidean Economics" in *The Trend of Economics*, ed. by Tugwell, pp. 86 et. seq.

to warn us that, as traditional views are fallible, the only way of getting at the truth is to treat them as among a number of possible views and compare them with others. This process may lead us in the end to maintain the established views as the best. We may even contend that that which has stood the test of long experience has much to commend it. But even when the traditional view is accepted, a critical, logical examination of it refines it and thus enables us to eliminate irrelevant and unfortunate excrescences on it.

A deductive system that enables us to derive many legal rules from a few principles makes the law more certain, so that people can better know their rights. You cannot pass from past decisions to future ones without making assumptions. From the statement that a court has ruled so and so in certain cases nothing follows except in so far as the new cases are assumed to be like the old ones. But this likeness depends upon our logical analysis of classes of cases.

The fact that, like other human institutions, the law does not always succeed in being consistent, is no argument against its trying to be so. The fact that we do not always succeed in attaining health is not an argument for being satisfied with disease. The admission that death will overtake us is no reason against seeking to prolong life.

The law cannot abandon the effort at consistency. We must remember that the law always defeats the expectation of at least one party in every lawsuit. To maintain its prestige, in spite of that, requires such persistent and conspicuous effort at impartiality that even the defeated party will be impressed. This is most effectively promoted by genuine devotion to scientific method.

Those who distrust logic commonly appeal to experience. But the fact is that experience without logical vision is stupid and brutish and supplies no guide for the good or civilized life.

What is experience? In its original sense, and the one which it still has to those uncorrupted by subjectivistic philosophy, experience denotes something personal that happens to us. Thus, we say we are fortunate in never having experienced the effects of ether or of certain diseases. In this sense, personal experience is obviously not an adequate basis on which to decide the policies of the law. But, if we generalize the term "experience" to include all that which has happened to human beings in general, and is likely to happen in the future, experience is certainly not something that is given in itself, but the very thing to be discovered by logical methods. Certainly the experience of the past, or the future, is not given to us, and it is by scientific study relying on the canons of logic that we reconstruct the past and predict the future.

Trust life rather than theory, say our modernists. But is it true that by mere living our problems are solved? Is not life full of illusions and frustrations? Life is the seat of all that is ugly as well as beautiful; of disease as well as health; of all that is vile and loathsome as well as of all that is inspiring. At all times it carries the seeds of death. The law, like other institutions of civilization is organized to advance the good life, and what distinguishes that is not to be attained by abandoning our intelligence.

Law without concepts or rational ideas, law that is not logical, is like pre-scientific medicine—a hodge-podge of sense and superstition, as has indeed been most of the world's common sense as distinguished from science.

To urge that judges, for instance, should rely on their experience or intuition in disregard of logically formulated principles is to urge sentimental anarchy. Men will generalize in spite of themselves. If they do it consciously in accordance with logical principles, they will do it more carefully and will be liberally tolerant to other possible generalizations. But those who distrust all logic think that they deal with facts when they are occupied with the product of their own grotesque theories.

Science, to be sure, is abstract. It tends to emphasize abstract considerations and deals with the definable classes rather than with the particular cases. But in doing so it forces us to see things from a wider point of view, and this tends to make us more just to the diversity of human interests. The air of unreality that science presents to the uninitiated is like the unreality which modern machinery presents to the old-fashioned artisan or those who cultivate the soil by hand.

Nor can we respect the metaphysical objection that life is changing but concepts are fixed. It is precisely because concepts are fixed in meaning that we can measure or determine the rate of change. Should the rules of arithmetic be changed whenever the volume of our business transactions is changed? Will even the change of our system of weights and measures require us to discard the multiplication table?

The real objection to conceptually mechanical jurisprudence is one against all human activity that is unintelligent. So-called strong judges, who decide to follow principles regardless of consequences, are simply too lazy to examine countervailing considerations and special circumstances which are relevant to the application of these principles. At best they are guilty of the fallacy of simplism, of supposing that the law always consists of theoretically simple cases, whereas the concrete cases actually before us are more complex because they generally involve many principles. This is the root of what is sound in the distinction between "law in books" and "law in action," and in the warning that the needs of life should not be sacrificed to the needs of the study.

From this point of view we can see reason for rejecting the extreme formalism of Stammler and of the school of Kelsen, which seems to dominate contemporary European legal thought. There is a downright logical absurdity in Stammler's efforts to derive substantive rules of law from purely formal or logical principles. Nor can Kelsen establish by quasi-mathematical methods positive rules of law that can be the rules of any actual jurisdiction. The force of the analogy of mathematical physics which he, Felix Kaufmann, and his other followers invoke is really against them, since mathematical physics differs from pure mathematics precisely by making assumptions as to what exists—something which can never be derived from formal or pure mathematics.

In general, law is a specific type of existence and its specific nature cannot be deduced from something else. Kelsen's argument for a pure or unitary method would be sound if the law were the object of a pure and unitary science. But this cannot be, so long as the jurist has to deal with different kinds of problems, historical, psychological, logical, and ethical, as well as mixed questions such as when we ask: What is it that courts do when they interpret a statute?

The law, and especially present American law, is desperately in need of a scientific elaboration. The old way of dealing with the law as a body of empirical rules has definitely broken down. *Stare decisis* means little in a changing society when for every new case the number of possible precedents is practically unwieldy. Without principles as guides, the body of precedents becomes an uncharted sea; and reliance on principles is worse than useless unless these principles receive critical scientific attention.

Ross, Tu-Tu*

On the Noîsulli Islands in the South Pacific lives the Noît-cif tribe, generally regarded as one of the more primitive peoples to be found in the world today. Their civilization has recently been described by the Illyrian anthropologist Ydobon, from whose account the following is taken.

* [70 *Harv. L. Rev.* 812-825 (1957). Copyright 1957 by the Harvard Law Review Association. Reprinted by permission.

Alf Ross (1899–) received his law degree from the University of Copenhagen in 1922. He received his Ph.D. from the University of Uppsala in Sweden in 1929 and earned his doctorate in law from the University of Copenhagen in 1933. Ross was Professor of Law at the University of Copenhagen from 1938 until his retirement in 1969. Since 1956, he has been a member of the European Court of Human Rights. His publications include *Textbook of International Law* (1947), *Why Democracy?* (1952), *The United Nations: Peace and Progress* (1966), and *Towards a Realistic Jurisprudence* (1946).]

This tribe, according to Mr. Ydobon, holds the belief that in the case of an infringement of certain taboos—for example, if a man encounters his mother-in-law, or if a totem animal is killed, or if someone has eaten of the food prepared for the chief—there arises what is called *tû-tû*. The members of the tribe also say that the person who committed the infringement has become *tû-tû*. It is very difficult to explain what is meant by this. Perhaps the nearest one can get to an explanation is to say that *tû-tû* is conceived of as a kind of dangerous force or infection which attaches to the guilty person and threatens the whole community with disaster. For this reason a person who has become *tû-tû* must be subjected to a special ceremony of purification.

It is obvious that the Noît-cif tribe dwells in a state of darkest superstition. "Tû-tû" is of course nothing at all, a word devoid of any meaning whatever. To be sure, the above situations of infringement of taboo give rise to various natural effects, such as a feeling of dread and terror, but obviously it is not these, any more than any other demonstrable phenomena, which are designated as *tû-tû*. The talk about *tû-tû* is pure nonsense.

Nevertheless, and this is what is remarkable, from the accounts given by Mr. Ydobon it appears that this word, in spite of its lack of meaning, has a function to perform in the daily language of the people. The *tû-tû* pronouncements seem able to fulfill the two main functions of all language: to prescribe and to describe; or, to be more explicit, to express commands or rules, and to make assertions about facts.[2]

If I say, in three different languages, "My father is dead," "Mein Vater ist gestorben," and "Mon père est mort," we have three different sentences, but only one assertion. Despite their differing linguistic forms, all three sentences refer to one and the same state of affairs (my father's being dead), and this state of affairs is asserted as existing in reality, as distinct from being merely imagined. The state of affairs to which a sentence refers is called its semantic reference. It can more precisely be defined as that state of affairs which is related to the assertion in such a way that if the state of affairs is assumed actually to exist then the assertion is assumed to be true. The semantic reference of a sentence will depend upon the linguistic usages prevailing in the community. According to these usages a certain definite state of affairs is the stimulus to saying "My father is dead." This state of affairs constitutes the semantic reference of the pronouncement and can be established quite independently of any ideas the speaker may possibly have concerning death—for example, that the soul at death departs from the body.

2. On the distinction between prescriptive and descriptive language, see Hare, *The Language of Morals* (1952).

On the other hand, if I say to my son "Shut the door," this sentence is clearly not the expression of any assertion. True, it has reference to a state of affairs, but in a quite different way. This state of affairs (the door's being shut) is not indicated as actually existing, but is presented as a guide for my son's behavior. Such pronouncements are said to be the expression of a prescription.

According to Mr. Ydobon's account, within the community of the Noît-cif tribe there are in use, among others, the following two pronouncements:

(1) If a person has eaten of the chief's food he is *tû-tû*.
(2) If a person is *tû-tû* he shall be subjected to a ceremony of purification.

Now it is plain that quite apart from what "*tû-tû*" stands for, or even whether it stands for anything at all, these two pronouncements, when combined in accordance with the usual rules of logic, will amount to the same thing as the following pronouncement:

(3) If a person has eaten of the chief's food he shall be subjected to a ceremony of purification.

This statement obviously is a completely meaningful prescriptive pronouncement, without the slightest trace of mysticism. This result is not really surprising, for it is simply due to the fact that we are here using a technique of expression of the same kind as this: "When x = y and y = z, then x = z," a proposition which holds good whatever "y" stands for, or even if it stands for nothing at all.

Although the word "*tû-tû*" in itself has no meaning whatever, yet the pronouncements in which this word occurs are not made in a haphazard fashion. Like other pronouncements of assertion they are stimulated in conformity with the prevailing linguistic customs by quite definite states of affairs. This explains why the *tû-tû* pronouncements have semantic reference although the word is meaningless. The pronouncement of the assertion "N. N. is *tû-tû*" clearly occurs in definite semantic connection with a complex situation of which two parts can be distinguished:

(1) The state of affairs in which N. N. has either eaten of the chief's food or has killed a totem animal or has encountered his mother-in-law, etc. This state of affairs will hereinafter be referred to as affairs$_1$.

(2) The state of affairs in which the valid norm which requires ceremonial purification is applicable to N. N., more precisely stated as the state of affairs in which if N. N. does not submit himself to the ceremony

he will in all probability be exposed to a given reaction on the part of the community. This state of affairs will hereinafter be referred to as affairs₂.

Given the existence of these two states of affairs, the pronouncement that N. N. is *tû-tû* is assumed to be true. Thus, the combination of the two states, in consequence of the definition, is the semantic reference of the pronouncement. It is quite another matter that the members of the Noît-cif tribe are not themselves aware of this, but rather, in their superstitious imaginings, ascribe to the pronouncement the occurrence of a dangerous force, a different reference from that which it has in reality. This, however, does not prevent one from discussing quite reasonably whether or not a person in given circumstances really is *tû-tû*. The reasoning, then, sets out to show whether the person in question has committed one of the relevant infringements of taboo and whether the purification norm is applicable to him in consequence.

An assertion to the effect that N. N. is *tû-tû* can thus be verified by proving the existence of either the first or the second state of affairs. It makes no difference which, because according to the ideology prevailing in the tribe these two states of affairs are always bound up with one another. It is therefore equally correct to say "N. N. is *tû-tû*, because he has eaten of the chief's food (and therefore must be subjected to a ceremonial purification)" or "N. N. is *tû-tû*, because the purification norm is applicable to him (because he has eaten of the chief's food)." The latter does not preclude the possibility of also saying at the same time "The purification norm is applicable to N. N. because he is *tû-tû* (because he has eaten of the chief's food)." The vicious circle which apparently results here is in reality nonexistent, since the word "*tû-tû*" stands for nothing whatever, and there thus exists no relation, either causal or logical, between the presumed *tû-tû* phenomenon and the application of the purification norm. In reality all three statements—as indicated in the added parentheses—express, each in its own way, nothing more than that the person who has eaten of the chief's food shall undergo a ceremonial purification.

What has been said here in no way upsets the assertion that "*tû-tû*" is a meaningless word. It is only the statement "N. N. is *tû-tû*" to which, taken in its entirety, semantic reference can be ascribed. But there cannot be distinguished in this reference a certain reality or quality which can be ascribed to N. N. and which corresponds to the word "*tû-tû*." The form of the statement is inadequate in relation to what is referred to, and this inadequacy is of course a consequence of the superstitious beliefs held by the tribe.

Thus any attempt to ascribe to the word "*tû-tû*" an independent semantic reference in propositions like the following is doomed to failure:

(1) If a person has eaten of the chief's food he is *tû-tû*.
(2) If a person is *tû-tû* he shall be subjected to a ceremony of purification.

The attempt might be made in the following possible ways:

(*a*) In proposition (1), for "*tû-tû*" substitute affairs$_2$; and in proposition (2), for "*tû-tû*" substitute affairs$_1$. Each will then acquire a meaning on its own.[3] But this solution is inadmissable, because the two propositions constitute the major and minor premises for the conclusion that a person who has eaten of the chief's food shall be subjected to a ceremony of purification. The word "*tû-tû*," therefore, if it means anything at all, must mean the same thing in both of them.

(*b*) In both propositions, for "*tû-tû*"substitute affairs$_1$. This will not do, for in that case proposition (1) becomes analytically void and without any semantic reference whatever. For the sense of it will be: "When a person has eaten of the chief's food, the state of affairs exists where he has either eaten of the chief's food or killed a totem animal or. . . ."

(*c*) In both propositions, for "*tû-tû*" substitute affairs$_2$. This will not do either, for in that case proposition (2) becomes analytically void, as can be demonstrated by exact analogy with the above paragraph.

Mr. Ydobon tells of a Swedish missionary who had worked for a number of years among the Noît-cif tribe, ardently endeavoring to make the natives understand that "*tû-tû*" signified nothing whatever and that it was an abominable heathen superstition to maintain that something mystical and indeterminable comes into being because a man encounters his mother-in-law. In this, of course, the good man was quite right. However, it was an excess of zeal which led him to denounce anyone who continued to use the word "*tû-tû*" as a sinful heathen. In so doing he overlooked what has been demonstrated, that quite apart from the fact that the word in itself has no semantic reference whatever and quite apart from the ideas of mystical forces attaching to it, pronouncements in which the word occurs can nevertheless function effectively as the expression of prescriptions and assertions.

Of course it would be possible to omit this meaningless word altogether, and instead of the circumlocution:

(1) He who kills a totem animal becomes *tû-tû*;
(2) He who is *tû-tû* shall undergo a ceremony of purification,

3. Proposition (1) would mean, "If a person has eaten of the chief's food, he shall be subjected to a ceremony of purification"; and proposition (2), "If a person has either eaten of the chief's food or . . . , he shall be subjected to a ceremony of purification."

to use the straightforward statement:

(3) He who has killed a totem animal shall undergo a ceremony of purification.

One might therefore ask whether—when people have realized that *tû-tû* is nothing but an illusion—it would not be advantageous to follow this line. As I shall proceed to show later, however, this is not the case. On the contrary, sound reasons based on the technique of formulation may be adduced for continuing to make use of the *"tû-tû"* construction. But although the *"tû-tû"* formulation may have certain advantages from the point of view of technique, it must be admitted that it could in certain cases lead to irrational results if against all better judgment the idea that *tû-tû* is a reality is allowed to exert its influence. If this should be the case, it must be the task of criticism to demonstrate the error and to cleanse one's thinking of the dross of such imaginary ideas. But even so, there would be no grounds for giving up the *tû-tû* terminology.

But perhaps it is now time to drop all pretense and openly admit what the reader must by now have discovered, that the allegory concerns ourselves. It is the argument concerning the use of terms such as "right" and "duty" approached from a new angle.[4] For our legal rules are in a wide measure couched in a *"tû-tû"* terminology. We find the following phrases, for example, in legal language:

(1) If a loan is granted, there comes into being a claim;
(2) If a claim exists, then payment shall be made on the day it falls due.

This is only a roundabout way of saying:

(3) If a loan is granted, then payment shall be made on the day it falls due.

4. The "Swedish missionary" of the fable refers to the late Professor A. V. Lundstedt. Throughout his writings, e.g., 1 Lundstedt, *Die Unwissenschaftlichkeit der Rechtswissenschaft* (1932), he has emphasized that the only demonstrable reality in the so-called situations of rights consists in the function of the machinery of the law. Under given conditions a person can, according to the law in force, institute proceedings and thereby set the machinery of the law in motion, with the result that the public power is exercised for his benefit. He can achieve judgment and execution by force, creating for himself an advantageous position, a possibility of action, an economic benefit. And that is all. One can readily agree with the author up to this point. But then, instead of proceeding to ask what is characteristic of the situations designated as rights and how the concept of rights may be analyzed and used as a tool for the description of these situations, Lundstedt gives a peculiar twist to his critical account by saying that rights do not exist and that anybody using this term is talking rubbish about something that does not exist. Similar views have been defended by Léon Duguit, 1 Duguit, *Traité de Droit Constitutionnel* (3d ed. 1927), and earlier by Jeremy Bentham, e.g., Bentham, *The Limits of Jurisprudence Defined* 57-88 (1945).

The claim mentioned in (1) and (2), but not in (3), is obviously, like *tû-tû,* not a real thing; it is nothing at all, merely a word, an empty word devoid of all semantic reference. Similarly, our assertion to the effect that the borrower becomes pledged corresponds to the allegorical tribe's assertion that the person who kills a totem animal becomes *tû-tû.*

We too, then, express ourselves as though something had come into being between the conditioning fact (juristic fact) and the conditioned legal consequence, namely, a claim, a right, which like an intervening vehicle or causal connecting link promotes an effect or provides the basis for a legal consequence. Nor, really, can we wholly deny that this terminology is associated for us with more or less indefinite ideas that a right is a power of an incorporeal nature, a kind of inner, invisible dominion over the object of the right, a power manifested in, but nevertheless different from, the exercise of force (judgment and execution) by which the factual and apparent use and enjoyment of the right is effectuated.

In this way, it must be admitted, our terminology and our ideas bear a considerable structural resemblance to primitive magic thought concerning the invocation of supernatural powers which in turn are converted into factual effects. Nor can we deny the possibility that this resemblance is rooted in a tradition which, bound up with language and its power over thought, is an age-old legacy from the infancy of our civilization. But after these admissions have been made, there still remains the important question—whether sound, rational grounds may be adduced in favor of the retention of a *"tû-tû"* presentation of legal rules, a form of circumlocution in which between the juristic fact and the legal consequence there are inserted imaginary rights. If this question is to be answered in the affirmative, the ban on the mention of rights must be lifted. I believe that this question must be answered in the affirmative and shall take the concept of ownership as my point of departure.

The legal rules concerning ownership could, without doubt, be expressed without the use of this term. In that case a large number of rules would have to be formulated, directly linking the individual legal consequences to the individual legal facts. For example:

> If a person has lawfully acquired a thing by purchase, judgment for recovery shall be given in favor of the purchaser against other persons retaining the thing in their possession.
>
> If a person has inherited a thing, judgment for damages shall be given in favor of the heir against other persons who culpably damage the thing.
>
> If a person by prescription has acquired a thing and raised a loan that is not repaid at the proper time, the creditor shall be given judgment for satisfaction out of the thing.

If a person has occupied a *res nullius* and by legacy bequeathed it to another person, judgment shall be given in favor of the legatee against the testator's estate for the surrender of the thing.

If a person has acquired a thing by means of execution as a creditor and the object is subsequently appropriated by another person, the latter shall be punished for theft.

An account along these lines would, however, be so unwieldy as to be practically worthless. It is the task of legal thinking to conceptualize the legal rules in such a way that they are reduced to systematic order and by this means to give an account of the law in force which is as plain and convenient as possible. This can be achieved with the aid of the following technique of presentation.

On looking at a large number of legal rules on the lines indicated, one will find that it is possible to select from among them a certain group that can be arranged in the following way:

$$
\begin{array}{llllll}
F_1 - C_1 & F_2 - C_1 & F_3 - C_1 & \ldots\ldots & F_p - C_1 \\
F_1 - C_2 & F_2 - C_2 & F_3 - C_2 & \ldots\ldots & F_p - C_2 \\
F_1 - C_3 & F_2 - C_3 & F_3 - C_3 & \ldots\ldots & F_p - C_3 \\
\quad\cdot & \quad\cdot & \quad\cdot & & \quad\cdot \\
\quad\cdot & \quad\cdot & \quad\cdot & & \quad\cdot \\
\quad\cdot & \quad\cdot & \quad\cdot & & \quad\cdot \\
F_1 - C_n & F_2 - C_n & F_3 - C_n & \ldots\ldots & F_p - C_n
\end{array}
$$

The conditioning fact F_1 is connected with the legal consequence C_1, etc. This means that each single one of a certain totality of conditioning facts ($F_1 - F_p$) is connected with each single one of a certain group of legal consequences ($C_1 - C_n$); or, that it is true of each single F that it is connected with the same group of legal consequences ($C_1 + C_2 \ldots + C_n$); or, that a cumulative plurality of legal consequences is connected to a disjunctive plurality of conditioning facts.

These n × p individual legal rules can be stated more simply and more manageably [as in Figure 2]. "O" (ownership) merely stands for the systematic connection that F_1 as well as F_2, F_3 . . . F^p entail the totality of legal consequences C_1, C_2, C_3 . . . C_n. As a technique of presentation this is expressed then by stating in one series of rules the facts that "create ownership" and in another series the legal consequences that "ownership" entails.

It will be clear from this that the "ownership" inserted between the conditioning facts and the conditioned consequences is in reality a meaningless word, a word without any semantic reference whatever, serving

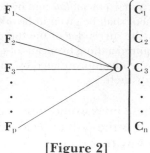

[Figure 2]

solely as a tool of presentation. We talk as if ownership were a causal link between F and C, an effect occasioned or created by every F, and which in turn is the cause of a totality of legal consequences. We say, for example, that:

(1) If A has lawfully purchased an object (F_2), ownership of the object is thereby created for him.
(2) If A is the owner of an object, he has (among other things) the right of recovery (C_1).

It is clear, however, that (1) + (2) is only a rephrasing of one of the presupposed norms ($F_2 - C_1$), that purchase as a conditioning fact entails the possibility of recovery as a legal consequence. The notion that between purchase and access to recovery something was created that can be designated as ownership is nonsense. Nothing is created as the result of A and B exchanging a few sentences legally interpreted as a contract of purchase. All that has occurred is that the judge will now take this fact into consideration and give judgment for the purchaser in an action for recovery.

What has been described here is a simple example of reduction by reason to systematic order. In the final instance it is, to be sure, the task of legal science to undertake this process of simplification, but this task has largely been anticipated by prescientific thought. The idea of certain rights took shape at an early stage in history. A systematic simplification can be carried out, of course, in more ways than one, and this explains why the categories of rights vary somewhat from one legal system to another, though this circumstance does not necessarily reflect a corresponding difference in the law in force.

The same technique of presentation can frequently be employed without the idea of an intervening right. In international law, for example, one series of rules may state which area belongs to a specific state as its territory. That this area has the character of "territory" is per se meaningless. This characterization has meaning only when taken together with another set of rules expressing the legal consequences that are attached to an area's character as territory. In this example it would also be possible to state the legal relations without using the interpolated concept "territory," although such a statement would undeniably be complicated.

Sometimes the intermediate link is not a single right, but a complex legal condition of rights and duties. This is the case, for example, when in family law a distinction is made between the conditions for contracting marriage and the legal effects of marriage, when in constitutional law a distinction is made between the acquisition of nationality and the legal effects of nationality, or in administrative law between the creation of civil-servant status and its legal effects. In these and similar situations it is usual to speak of the creation of a status. Whatever the construction, the reality behind it is in each case the same: a technique which is highly important if we are to achieve clarity and order in a complicated series of legal rules.

"Ownership," "claim," and other words, when used in legal language, have the same function as the word "*tû-tû*"; they are words without meaning, without any semantic reference, and serve a purpose only as a technique of presentation. Nevertheless, it is possible to talk with meaning about rights, both in the form of prescriptions and assertions.

With regard to prescriptions, this emerges from the foregoing. The two propositions "A person who has purchased a thing has the ownership of it" and "A person who has the ownership of a thing can obtain recovery of it" together produce the meaningful prescriptive rule that a person who has purchased a thing can obtain recovery of it.

With regard to assertions, the following holds good by exact analogy with the exposition given above in respect to "*tû-tû*" assertions: the assertion that *A* possesses the ownership of a thing, when taken in its entirety, has semantic reference to the complex situation that there exists one of those facts which are said to establish ownership, and that *A* can obtain recovery, claim damages, etc. It is thus possible with equal correctness to say:

> *A* has the ownership of the thing because he has purchased it (and can therefore obtain recovery, claim damages, etc.)

and

> *A* has the ownership of the thing because he can obtain recovery, claim damages, etc. (because he has purchased it).

The latter does not preclude its being possible also to say:

> *A* can obtain recovery of the thing and claim damages, etc., because he has the ownership of the thing (because he has purchased it).

Just as in the case of the corresponding *"tû-tû"* formulations, there is here no vicious circle, since "ownership" does not stand for anything at all, and there thus exists no relation, either causal or logical, between the suposed phenomenon of ownership and the legal consequences mentioned. All three pronouncements—as indicated by the added parentheses—express, each in its own way, nothing more than that the person who has purchased a thing can obtain recovery of the same, claim damages, etc.

On the other hand it is impossible to ascribe to the word "ownership" an independent semantic reference in the arguments operating with the word.[6] Any attempt to take it as a designation of either legal facts or of legal consequences, of both together, or of anything else whatever, is foredoomed to failure. Let us, for example, consider the following syllogisms:

> (*A*) If there is a purchase, there exists also ownership for the purchaser. Here there is a purchase. Therefore there exists also ownership for the purchaser.
> (*B*) If ownership exists, the owner can obtain recovery. Here there is ownership. Therefore recovery can be obtained.

Together (*A*) and (*B*) express the meaningful rule that a person who has purchased a thing can obtain recovery of it. This conclusion holds

---

6. In an article published shortly after the original publication of the present Comment, but evidently without knowledge of it, Anders Wedberg arrived at conclusions similar to mine:

"It may be shocking to unsophisticated common sense to admit such 'meaningless' expressions in the serious discourse of legal scientists. But, as a matter of fact, there is no reason why all expressions employed in a discourse, which as a whole is highly 'meaningful,' should themselves have a 'meaning.' It appears likely that many expressions employed by other sciences, especially the so-called exact sciences, lack interpretation and solely function as vehicles of systematization and deduction. Why should not the situation be the same within legal science?" Wedberg, Some Problems in the Logical Analysis of Legal Science, 17 *Theoria* 246, 273 (Sweden 1951).

A similar view has since been expressed by H. L. A. Hart. It is possible, that author maintains, to define a term such as "right" not by substituting for it other words describing some quality, process, or event, but only by indicating the conditions necessary for the truth of a sentence of the form "You have a right." Hart, Definition and Theory in Jurisprudence, 70 *L.Q. Rev.* 37, 41-42, 45-49 (1954).

good whatever "ownership" may stand for, or even if it stands for nothing at all. For "ownership" there could be substituted "old cheese" or "*tû-tû*" and the conclusion would be just as valid.

On the other hand, it is impossible in this conclusion to ascribe to the word "ownership" a semantic reference such that each of the conclusions (*A*) and (*B*) considered in isolation can acquire meaning or legal function. The conceivable possibilities of such an attempt are the same as those given above in the analysis of the corresponding "*tû-tû*" propositions, and the results also correspond:

(*a*) If we substitute for "ownership" in (*A*) the cumulative totality of legal consequences, and in (*B*) the disjunctive totality of conditions, (*A*) and (*B*) each acquire meaning, but cannot be combined in a syllogism since the middle term is not the same.

(*b*) If in both cases we substitute for "ownership" the disjunctive totality of conditioning facts, the major premise in (*A*) becomes analytically void and thus without any semantic reference.

(*c*) If in both cases we substitute for "ownership" the cumulative totality of legal consequences, then the major premise in (*B*) becomes analytically void.

I will leave it to the reader to work out for himself the correctness of these assertions by exact analogy with the analysis of the corresponding "*tû-tû*" pronouncements.

The observations I have made here are well fitted to throw light on a most interesting controversy conducted in recent years in Scandinavian literature between Per Olof Ekelöf and Ivar Strahl concerning the meaning in which the concept of rights is taken when used in legal reasoning.[7] Ekelöf started the discussion in an attempt to find out what states of affairs could be substituted in such reasoning for an expression couched in terms of rights. This attempt is the same thing as a quest for the semantic reference of the term. It is interesting to follow the course of the controversy, as it amusingly illustrates the correctness of what has been maintained here.

In broad outline, the course of the controversy was as follows. Ekelöf began by assuming that the term "claim" (this is the term he operated with in his examples, which in other respects were completely analogous to the (*A*) and (*B*) formulations adduced above) does not stand for the same thing in both (*A*) and (*B*), but respectively for the legal consequence and the legal fact. This corresponds exactly with the possibility marked by (*a*) in the experiment set out above. Strahl countered with the

7. The discussion was conducted in the Scandinavian legal reviews *Tidsskrift for Rettsvitenskap* and *Svensk Juristtidning* in the years 1945 to 1950.

powerful argument that such an interpretation was inadmissible because the term must of necessity be used with one and the same meaning in both the (A) and (B) propositions because these constitute the premises of a conclusion. Strahl made himself the spokesman for the position that the concept of rights in both propositions stands for the juridical fact, the disjunctive totality of conditioning facts. This position corresponds to the possibility set out above under (b). To this Ekelöf replied with the argument that if that is so the major premise in case (A) becomes analytically void. Subsequently Ekelöf adopted Strahl's theory that the word must stand for the same state of affairs in both (A) and (B), but maintained that it did not follow as a matter of course that this state of affairs common to both was necessarily the juridical fact. He discovered that the conclusion comprising (A) and (B) held good whatever was substituted for the "rights" concept—whether juridical fact, legal consequence, or both of them together. But he got no further. He did not realize that the conclusion would hold good even if for the concept of rights there were substituted "old cheese" or "tû-tû."

In this controversy it was Strahl who came closer to the truth, when he asserted that the concept of right in case (A) is used to designate the circumstance which in case (B) serves as juridical fact and went on to characterize this as a device serving the technique of presentation. But what Strahl did not see was that the concept of a right does not designate any "circumstance" at all, and that the right as "fact" is not a fact at all, and that it is hopeless to attempt to ascribe a meaning to the major premises in the (A) and (B) syllogisms when each of them is considered in isolation. For "the device serving the technique of presentation" means that the two propositions have meaning only as fragments of a larger whole in which they both occur, causing the concept of rights as the common middle term in a syllogism to vanish as completely meaningless.

In making these critical observations I have not in any way intended to belittle the value of the research undertaken by Ekelöf and Strahl. On the contrary, I think that Ekelöf's substitution method was a fortunate line to take and that it sharpened the issues; and I must add that it was along these lines that I was led to the view which I believe to be the true one, that the concept of rights is a tool for the technique of presentation serving exclusively systematic ends, and that in itself it means no more and no less than does "tû-tû."[8]

8. I have tried elsewhere to show how the concept of rights can lead to errors and dogmatic postulates if it is wrongly taken, not merely as being the systematic unit in a set of legal rules, but as being an independent "substance." Ross, op. cit. supra note 5, at 189-202.

Simpson, The Analysis of Legal Concepts*

I

. . . Ross' claim that "*tû-tû*" is a meaningless word is connected by him with a general theory of meaning; according to this theory the two main functions of language are to describe and prescribe. A modification of Ross' argument would be to say only that the word "*tû-tû*," when used in a sentence whose function it is to describe a state of affairs, is meaningless; in such a sentence the word is meaningless because it lacks any "semantic reference."[14] This, which I think would be a softened form of the thesis, would leave open the question whether the word is meaningless in sentences whose function was different; thus it would leave open the question whether the word is meaningless (or the sentences nonsense) when it occurs in Ross' article in the *Harvard Law Review*, for Ross is not there concerned to describe a state of affairs which has ever existed. But it does not seem that the thesis is tenable, even in this softened form, for to say that the word "*tû-tû*" in the sentence "a person who encounters his mother-in-law is '*tû-tû*'" is meaningless because there is no such thing as "*tû-tû*" is no different from saying that the proposition which the sentence asserts is not true. This may very well be the case, though Ross gives us no reason for scepticism about "*tû-tû*," and having invented an island and islanders, he could if he wished invent an

---

* [80 *L.Q. Rev.* 535, 538-544, 548-549, 551-553 (1964). Reprinted by permission.
For biographical information, see page 195 supra.]

14. I find some difficulty in following the argument here, for Ross maintains that although the word "*tû-tû*" is meaningless, since it lacks semantic reference, yet nevertheless sentences containing the word "*tû-tû*" which assert the existence of states of affairs are not meaningless since such sentences do have semantic reference, semantic reference here meaning the state of affairs to which a sentence refers. But if it is a feature of the word "*tû-tû*" that it is meaningless because it refers to something which does not exist (which Ross equates with not referring at all) how can the sentence "He is '*tû-tû*'" be in better case? To what state of affairs which does exist can it refer? Ross tries to explain that such sentences have semantic reference because they are not "made in a haphazard fashion. Like other pronouncements of assertion they are stimulated in conformity with the prevailing linguistic customs by quite definite states of affairs," but here he simply changes the meaning of "meaningless," for the same could be said of the word "*tû-tû*." There is a sense in which substantives on their own never refer—if I simply squawk "cat," or "*tû-tû*," will my utterance lack meaning? But this will depend on the context—consider the word DOG on a dog bowl—and I do not think that this is Ross' point. What is surely required is a more elaborate analysis of "referring," a term which Ross is here using in a special philosophical sense but which he does not explain fully.

infection too. But the logical status of the word "*tû-tû*," and the status of descriptive sentences containing the word, cannot depend upon hypothetical contingent facts about the existence of "*tû-tû*"; all that can be said, given the allegory, is that the proposition that a person who encounters his mother-in-law is "*tû-tû*" is (logically) *capable* of being true or false (this supposing it to fall into the category of propositions which describe states of affairs). We may compare the position of the gorilla. It is a purely contingent fact that gorillas exist, and it is a melancholy fact that these attractive and agreeable creatures are currently in danger of extinction. But if it happens that the last gorilla expires, and goes the way of the passenger pigeon, nothing of logical importance will have occurred, nor will the meaning of the word "gorilla" change in an instant of time, much less disappear.

A consequence of Ross' argument, and one which he stresses, is that since the word "*tû-tû*" has no semantic reference, the meaning of the two propositions:

(A) If a person has eaten of the chief's food he is "*tû-tû*."
(B) If a person is "*tû-tû*" he shall be subjected to a ceremony of purification.

amounts to no more than the meaning of the proposition:

(C) If a person has eaten of the chief's food he shall be subjected to a ceremony of purification.

Propositions A and B do no more than state, in a roundabout way, proposition C, which he admits to be a meaningful prescription. Now proposition A is presumably conceived of by the islanders, if they give their attention to these matters, as a statement of what is the case; at any rate this is how Ross conceived it, for he thinks that it is not true. This being so, it seems clear that a person who was acquainted with proposition C, but was ignorant of A and B, would be less well informed about the islanders than a person who did know about their acceptance of both A and B. Unlike Ross, he would be unable to say that the islanders were superstitious. He would also not know *why* a person who had eaten of the chief's food was thought to be suitable purification fodder.

Further to this, if a person knew propositions A and B, and in addition knew proposition AA, "If a person kills a totem animal he is '*tû-tû*,'" he would be in a position to draw the conclusion that such a person should be subjected to a ceremony of purification. But a person who knew only proposition C and proposition AA would be unable to draw this conclusion. It seems obvious therefore that the "cash value" of the two propositions A and B is greater than the "cash value" of the single proposition C.

Here it might be objected that one who knew all the A-type propositions, and in addition knew proposition B, would be no better informed than one who knew all the possible C-type propositions, particularly since he could *deduce* the systematic connection, which, Ross claims, is the only reality expressed by the word *"tû-tû."* But this is not so, for he would not be able to tell that all persons who were to be subjected to purification under rules C, CC, etc., were thought by the islanders to need purification for the same reason—because they had become *"tû-tû."* It is perfectly possible, indeed, that there may be other reasons why islanders require purification, which are quite distinct from *"tû-tû"*; the presentation of island custom in C-type rules will conceal from us whether this is the case or not.

Notwithstanding his claim that *"tû-tû"* is a meaningless word, Ross nevertheless claims that the word has a perfectly useful job to do in the language of the tribe, in that it can be used as a tool of presentation, and it is this same function which he allows to legal words, and to the legal concepts which lie behind the use of legal words. The examples he gives of such words are these: "right," "duty," "claim," "ownership," "territory," "marriage," "nationality," "civil servant status"; I think that there is no doubt that his analysis is supposed to apply to all legal words (or if one prefers it, legal concepts). Other examples would be "contract," "possessions," "tort," "crime." (In passing, and I shall later return to this point, it is worth noticing that Ross gives no indication of any independent criteria by which it is to be decided whether a particular word is a *"tû-tû"* word or, as we might say a *legal* word.) The function which such words have is that they enable us to express the law in a neat and systematic way, and no more. Thus, Ross argues, it would be *possible* to express all the rules about "ownership" without actually using the word by compiling a list of rules in the following form:

(i) *If a person has lawfully acquired a thing by purchase,* judgment for recovery shall be given in favour of the purchaser against other persons retaining the thing in their possession.

(ii) *If a person has inherited a thing,* judgment for damages shall be given in favour of the heir against other persons who culpably damage the thing.

etc., etc.

But this procedure would be excessively inconvenient and long-winded; instead it is simpler to interpose a concept, the concept of ownership,

461

between the conditioning fact or facts (indicated by the italics) and the legal consequence, and to state the law in the form of a list of the circumstances which give rise to "ownership," and a separate list of the consequences of "ownership." This technique, the "*tû-tû*" technique, can be represented schematically [as in Figure 3], where F represents a conditioning fact, and C a legal consequence. In such a scheme " 'O' (ownership) merely stands for the systematic connection that F_1 as well as F_2, F_3 . . . F_p entail the totality of legal consequences C_1, C_2, C_3 . . . C_n."

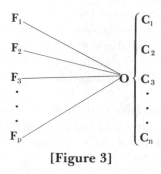

[Figure 3]

II

An initial difficulty about the analysis is this: it is not clear that Ross is correct in supposing that the function of the word "*tû-tû*" in the allegory is the same as the function of such words as "ownership"; and if this is not the case then even if Ross' analysis of "*tû-tû*" is correct, it would not follow that "ownership" (and other "legal" words) were susceptible of the same analysis. This is not a matter which is free from difficulty, and, to anticipate a conclusion, I do not think that the question is soluble, *because of our ignorance of the linguistic habits of the islanders.* However, I think that an attempt to answer it, and an explanation of why it is unanswerable, may throw some light upon a matter which is of some general importance in analytical jurisprudence—the concept of a legal concept, or, what makes a concept a legal concept.

Now Ross tells us that:

"within the community of the Noît-cîf tribe there are in use, among others, the following two pronouncements:
    (1) If a person has eaten of the chief's food he is '*tû-tû*.'
    (2) If a person is '*tû-tû*' he shall be subjected to a ceremony of purification."

This being so, it would seem that the first proposition, and such further propositions as:

"Urk is 'tû-tû' this morning, poor fellow";
" 'Tû-tû' is rotting the fibres of our society,"

are all propositions which assert that something is the case, and are (logically) capable of being true or false. It would be natural to call them statements of fact. If we contrast such statements with these:

"John Doe has just acquired ownership of Blackacre";
"Richard Roe has transferred ownership of Blackacre to John Style,"

there appears to be a difference, because, it has been suggested, the propriety of making statements of this second class *seems* to turn *both* upon the existence of certain states of affairs or the occurrence of certain events *and* upon the existence of certain rules, and for this reason the label "statement of fact" seems rather inappropriate. An equally inappropriate label would be "statement of law," for these statements do not simply (or indeed at all) tell us what the rule in question is; rather they apply the rule. Professor Hart, in "Definition and Theory in Jurisprudence," has both made this point and urges the importance of placing such statements in a separate conceptual compartment; such statements are *statements of legal conclusions*.

Hart's argument would suggest that "Urk is 'tû-tû' " is a statement of fact, whilst "John Doe has acquired ownership of Blackacre" is a conclusion of law, and from this it would seem to follow that the function of the word "tû-tû" is different from the function of the word "ownership"; *ergo* Ross's use of the allegory is likely to mislead us. But this is not so obvious as it seems, for a difficulty centres upon the implications of saying, in this context, that a statement is a statement of fact. Now it may well be the case that both the significance of saying that a statement is a statement of fact, and the criteria by which it is decided that a statement is a statement of fact, vary according to the context in which the concept is used; for example, sometimes say that a statement is a statement of fact means only that the statement is in fact true, whilst on other occasions the implication may be that the statement is capable (logically) of truth or falsity. In "Definition and Theory" "statements of fact" are contrasted with conclusions of law, and it is upon this contrast that we need to concentrate.

If I have followed Hart's reasoning correctly, the characteristic feature of a conclusion of law, as opposed to a statement of fact, is that it is a statement which applies a legal rule. As a simple model of such a statement Hart uses the statement "He is out," uttered in the context of a game of cricket. If the word "out" is to be used correctly in such a statement, not only must certain events have happened (the ball must have hit the wicket, or been caught without bouncing after having been struck whilst in play by the batsman's bat, or, I understand, wrist, etc.), but also whatever it is that has happened must count as being out according to the rules of cricket. With the conclusion "He is out" Hart contrasts the statement of fact "The ball has hit the wicket" (or whatever it is). But this contrast is not easy to see, for just as "being out," cricket-wise, is *rule-defined,* so are "ball" and "wicket" *rule defined* by the laws of the game; not *any* object which could with linguistic propriety be called a ball counts as a cricket ball, but only certain balls made of certain materials of a certain size and weight. And the same is true of the wicket. Now it is curious to find that Hart, when he applies his own theory to the simple model of cricket, classifies what surely ought to be a conclusion of law as a statement of fact. And perhaps the explanation is that the contrast which Hart is trying to identify has in reality nothing to do with a difference between the functions of sentences; instead the difference is that the word "possession" (or "ball") when used on certain occasions and for certain purposes is (legally) rule-defined, quite irrespective of the type or function of the sentence in which the word is used.

We can push the argument from cricket further. "He is out," viewed as a conclusion, depends upon "The ball has hit the wicket," which itself, according to the same criteria, is another conclusion. We could say that we have reached a statement of fact only when we reach a statement couched in words which currently are not rule-defined by the rules of cricket; something like this would serve: "a spherical object of such and such a weight, size and composition has hit ("hit" is not defined in the laws of cricket, or is it?) three cylindrical pieces of wood arranged in such a place in such a way." This technique of "pushing it back," which Hart's argument would require of us if we are to find a statement of fact, would be required also if, having accepted Ross's argument, we wanted to find a statement which did not employ a "*tû-tû*" (and therefore meaningless and dispensable) concept. This can be illustrated by examining one of the propositions in which Ross reformulates the rules about "ownership" without using the "*tû-tû*" concept of ownership:

> "*If a person has lawfully acquired a thing by purchase,* judgment for recovery shall be given in favour of the purchaser against other persons retaining the thing in his possession."

If we take the clause italicised (though the same argument would apply to the rest), we find that this is said to be a statement of conditioning

464

facts—"individual legal facts." But surely "person," "lawfully," "acquired," "thing" and "purchase" are all *"tû-tû"* words themselves, let alone "possession," which is as *"tû-tû"* as could well be. We should have to go much further if we wish to reach a statement which avoids *"tû-tû"* like the plague. . . .

IV

This discussion of the nature of legal concepts should make it clear why it is impossible to determine whether the islander's concept of *"tû-tû"* is analogous to the legal concept of ownership; for we do not possess enough information about the linguistic habits of the islanders to enable us to tell whether there is a divergence between the meaning of *"tû-tû"* in law and its meaning outside the law; we cannot tell whether the pronouncement "He who kills a totem animal is *'tû-tû'*" defines a legal concept or not. Further to this, theorists who attempt to explain the use of legal concepts and legal terms by supposing either that legal terms or the sentences in which they occur possess a peculiar logical function, are mistaken; the error is to suppose that a technical vocabulary must be linked to a logical function. To a motor-mechanic, *qua* mechanic, "sump" means a particular part of a car engine; to a speleologist "sump" means a passage filled with water for part of its length. But when a speleologist uses the word "sump" he does not necessarily or typically use the word in a *logically* different way from a motor mechanic; he simply uses the word with a different though related meaning. Of course the word "sump" might feature in the rules of a speleological society ("Nobody is to go through two sumps in one day, upon pain of expulsion") or for that matter in an Act of Parliament, and there would be a difference in function between these *formulations of rules* and a statement made by a speleologist in the course of a caving expedition—"There is a sump ahead." But the difference in logical function has nothing to do with the existence of speleological, motor-mechanics and (let us suppose that there are legal decisions about sumps) legal meanings of the word sump, for the logical differences between prescriptions and descriptions would still exist even if everybody for all purposes made use of precisely the same conception of a sump. And in the same way, even if there were no legal concepts, and no divergence ever between the meaning which lawyers attached to words and the meanings which other folk attached to them, the logical difference between prescriptions and descriptions would remain.

. . . A theory of this kind again neglects to attach any importance to the fact that legal rules and legal talk is not conducted in a private set of squiggles, but in words which are part of a language—be it English,

French or Tamil—and further that the use of words by lawyers is related to the extra-legal use, although it may diverge from it. To substitute "old cheese" for "ownership" would sever this relationship, and the operation would only leave the position as it was, if it was understood that for "old cheese" one must read "ownership." Consider how else would one translate an English law book into French. Ross's argument further suggests that a knowledge of all the legal rules about "ownership" (notice his inability to identify these rules without using the concept!), these rules being expressed without using the term, would be equivalent to a knowledge of these rules expressed in terms of ownership. An argument which claims that a concept is redundant but which can only be advanced by using the same concept has gone wrong somewhere; the only terms upon which we can discard a classifying concept are that we abandon the classification, for we cannot at one and the same time maintain that the concept of an elephant is unnecessary whilst we continue to talk about elephants. Again it can be seen to what lengths Ross is driven through his initial attempt to identify legal concepts by reference to a theory about the logical function of legal words.

Ross's attempt to explain the humble function of legal concepts as organising concepts forms the positive part of his argument; words which function in this way are contrasted with words which describe facts. The word "ownership" ("O" in the scheme reproduced) "merely stands for the systematic connection that F_1 as well as F_2, F_3, . . . F_p entail the totality of legal consequences C_1, C_2, C_3, . . . C_n." To this analysis a number of objections can be made.

(a) This analysis fails to explain why the word "ownership" is used —why not "old cheese"? Indeed why not "*tû-tû*"?

(b) It is not clear that to say that a person is owner does entail all the legal consequences of "ownership." Or take the concept of a contract. We may list the circumstances which give rise to a contract—offer, acceptance, consideration and perhaps intent to create legal relations—but when we list the consequences we have to hedge our list with words like "usually," "unless," "sometimes." Indeed we may find it necessary to do the same with the circumstances which give rise to a contract. The function of the word "contract" and of the word "ownership" cannot therefore be explained so simply as Ross suggests. And the reason for this is that legal rules commonly have exceptions to them, and in turn the reason for this is that legal rules are expressed in general words which classify, but unfortunately overlap. This overlapping of categories would produce contradictions between different legal rules, which cannot be tolerated, and we avoid this by exceptions. An example may make this clear. Suppose we think it convenient or just (or whatever it is) that agreements should in general, but not always be actionable, and that one

466

sort of agreement which we think should not be actionable is one entered into under duress. We have two categories—*agreements,* and *agreements entered into by duress.* Clearly the first category includes the second, and there happen to be no two words in the language which precisely fit the two categories we wish to demarcate; we solve the problem by expressing our rule ("agreements are actionable") and adding an exception ("but not when entered into by duress"). An alternative technique is to express the rule, and define "agreement" in a special way—"an agreement in the eyes of the law does not include an agreement entered into under duress"; the substance remains the same.

(c) Sometimes a decision that a certain result ought to follow turns upon the question, "Is X owner?" How can this be explained if the application of the word "owner" depends upon the consequences?

It seems therefore that Ross's attempt to show that legal words have a peculiar logical function both fails and leads him into an untenable position.

II. The Logical Nature of Legal Propositions and Questions

F. S. Cohen, Transcendental Nonsense and the Functional Approach*

1. The Eradication of Meaningless Concepts

On its negative side (naturally of special prominence in a protestant movement), functionalism represents an assault upon all dogmas and devices that cannot be translated into terms of actual experience.

In physics, the functional or operational method is an assault upon such supernatural concepts as absolute space and absolute time; in mathematics, upon supernatural concepts of real and imaginary, rational and irrational, positive and negative numbers. In psychology, William James inaugurates the functional method (of which behaviorism is an extreme form) by asking the naive question: "Does consciousness exist?"[33] Mod-

---

* [35 *Colum. L. Rev.* 809, 822-829 (1935). Reprinted by permission.

For biographical information, see page 73 supra.]

33. *Essays in Radical Empiricism* (1912) 1. Answering this question, James asserts, "There is . . . no aboriginal stuff or quality of being, contrasted with that of which material objects are made, out of which our thoughts of them are made; but there is a function in experience which thoughts perform . . ." (pp. 3-4).

ern "functional grammar" is an assault upon grammatical theories and distinctions which, as applied to the English language, simply have no verifiable significance—such empty concepts, for instance, as that of noun, syntax, with its unverifiable distinction between a nominative, an objective, and a possessive case.[34] And passing to the field of art, we find that functional architecture is likewise a repudiation of outworn symbols and functionless forms that have no meaning,—hollow marble pillars that do not support, fake buttresses, and false fronts.[35]

So, too, in law. Our legal system is filled with supernatural concepts, that is to say, concepts which cannot be defined in terms of experience, and from which all sorts of empirical decisions are supposed to flow. Against these unverifiable concepts modern jurisprudence presents an ultimatum. Any word that cannot pay up in the currency of fact, upon demand, is to be declared bankrupt, and we are to have no further dealings with it. Llewellyn has filed an involuntary petition in bankruptcy against the concept Title,[36] Oliphant against the concept Contract,[37] Haines, Brown, T. R. Powell, Finkelstein, and Cushman against Due Process, Police Power, and similar word-charms of constitutional law,[38] Hale, Richberg, Bonbright, and others against the concept of Fair Value in rate regulation, Cook and Yntema against the concept of Vested Rights in the conflict of laws.[40] Each of these men has tried to expose the confusions of current legal thinking engendered by these concepts and to reformulate the problems in his field in terms which show the concrete relevance of legal decisions to social facts.

2. The Abatement of Meaningless Questions

It is a consequence of the functional attack upon unverifiable concepts that many of the traditional problems of science, law, and philoso-

---

34. See H. N. Rivlin, *Functional Grammar* (1930); and cf. L. Bloomfield, *Language* (1933), p. 266 et passim.

35. See F. L. Wright, *Modern Architecture* (1931).

36. Llewellyn, *Cases and Materials on the Law of Sales* (1930).

37. Oliphant, Mutuality of Obligation in Bilateral Contracts at Law (1925) 25 *Columbia Law Rev.* 705; (1928) 28 *Columbia Law Rev.* 997.

38. C. G. Haines, General Observations on the Effects of Personal, Political and Economic Influences in the Decisions of Judges (1922) 17 *Ill. L. Rev.* 96; R. A. Brown, Police Power—Legislation for Health and Personal Safety (1929) 42 *Harv. L. Rev.* 866; T. R. Powell, The Judiciality of Minimum Wage Legislation (1924) 37 *Harv. L. Rev.* 545; M. Finkelstein, Judicial Self-Limitation (1924) 37 *Harv. L. Rev.* 338; R. E. Cushman, The Social and Economic Interpretation of the Fourteenth Amendment (1922) 20 *Mich. L. Rev.* 737.

40. Cook, Logical and Legal Bases of the Conflict of Laws (1924) 33 *Yale L.J.* 457; Yntema, The Hornbook Method and the Conflict of Laws (1928) 37 *Yale L.J.* 468.

phy are revealed as pseudo-problems devoid of meaning. As the protagonist of logical positivism, Wittgenstein, says of the traditional problems of philosophy:

> Most propositions and questions, that have been written about philosophical matters, are not false, but senseless. We cannot, therefore, answer questions of this kind at all, but only state their senselessness. Most questions and propositions of the philosophers result from the fact that we do not understand the logic of our language. (They are of the same kind as the question whether the Good is more or less identical than the Beautiful.) And so it is not to be wondered at that the deepest problems are really no problems.[41]

The same thing may be said of the problems of traditional jurisprudence. As commonly formulated, such "problems" as, "What is the holding or *ratio decidendi* of a case?"[42] or "Which came first,—the law or the state?"[43] or "What is the essential distinction between a crime and a tort?"[44] or "Where is a corporation?" are in fact meaningless, and can serve only as invitations to equally meaningless displays of conceptual acrobatics.

Fundamentally there are only two significant questions in the field of law. One is, "How do courts actually decide cases of a given kind?" The other is, "How ought they to decide cases of a given kind?" Unless a legal "problem" can be subsumed under one of these forms, it is not a meaningful question and any answer to it must be nonsense.[45]

3. The Redefinition of Concepts

Although the negative aspect of the functional method is apt to assume peculiar prominence in polemic controversy, the value of the

41. Wittgenstein, *Tractatus Logico-Philosophicus* (1922), prop. 4.003. And cf. James, *Pragmatism* (1908): "The pragmatic method is primarily a method of settling metaphysical disputes that otherwise might be interminable. . . . The pragmatic method in such cases is to try to interpret each notion by tracing its respective practical consequences. . . . If no practical differences whatever can be traced, then the alternatives mean practically the same thing, and all dispute is idle. . . . It is astonishing to see how many philosophical disputes collapse into insignificance the moment you subject them to this simple test of tracing a practical consequence." (Pp. 45-49.)

42. See Goodhart, Determining the *Ratio Decidendi* of a Case (1930) 40 *Yale L.J.* 161; and cf. Llewellyn, *Bramble Bush* (1930) 47.

43. Fortunately there is very little literature in the English language on this problem. German jurists, however, are inordinately fond of it.

44. See C. K. Allen, *Legal Duties and Other Essays in Jurisprudence* (1931) 226. And cf. W. W. Cook, Book Review (1932) 42 *Yale L.J.* 299.

45. Cf. F. S. Cohen, What Is a Question? (1929) 39 *Monist* 350 [infra, page 480].

method depends, in the last analysis, upon its positive contributions to the advancement of knowledge. Judged from this standpoint, I think it is fair to say that the functional method has justified itself in every scientific field to which it has been actually applied, and that functional redefinition of scientific concepts has been the keynote of most significant theoretical advances in the sciences during the last half century.

The tremendous advance made in our understanding of the foundations of pure mathematics, achieved through the work of such men as Frege, Peano, Whitehead, and Russell,[46] offers an illuminating example of the functional method in action. . . .

Similarly, modern advances in mathematics have made it clear that rational and irrational, real and imaginary, numbers are not numbers at all, in the original sense of the term, but are functions of such numbers.[47] The so-called arithmetization of mathematics, and the definition of the concepts of mathematics by Whitehead and Russell, as constructs of certain simple logical terms, have stripped mathematical terms of their supernatural significations, illumined and eliminated hidden inconsistencies, and clarified the relationships of mathematical concepts not only to each other but to the material world.

A similar use of the functional method has characterized the most significant advances of modern philosophy. The attack upon transcendental conceptions of God, matter, the Absolute, essence and accident, substance and attribute, has been vigorously pressed by C. S. Peirce, James, Dewey, Russell, Whitehead, C. I. Lewis, C. D. Broad, and most recently by the Viennese School, primarily by Wittgenstein and Carnap.[48] These men fall into various schools,—pragmatism, pragmaticism (which is the word Peirce shifted to when he saw what his followers were doing to the word "pragmatism"), neo-realism, critical realism, functional realism, and logical positivism. It would be unfair to minimize the real differences between some of these schools, but in one fundamental

46. See Russell, *Principles of Mathematics* (1903); *Introduction to Mathematical Philosophy* (1919); Russell and Whitehead, *Principia Mathematica* (1910); Frege, *Die Grundlagen der Arithmetik* (1884).

47. See Russell, *Introduction to Mathematical Philosophy* (1919) c. 7.

48. See C. S. Peirce, *Chance, Love and Logic* (1923); *Collected Papers* (1931-1934), especially vol. 5; James, *Pragmatism* (1908); *Essays in Radical Empiricism* (1912); Dewey, Appearing and Appearance, in *Philosophy and Civilization* (1931) 51; Russell, *Our Knowledge of the External World as a Field for Scientific Method in Philosophy* (1914); *Mysticism and Logic* (1918); Whitehead, *The Principles of Natural Knowledge* (1919); *The Concept of Nature* (1920); C. I. Lewis, *Mind and the World-Order* (1929); C. D. Broad, *Scientific Thought* (1923); Wittgenstein, *Tractatus Logico-Philosophicus* (1922); Carnap, *Ueberwindung der Metaphysik durch logische Analyse der Sprache* (1932) 2 *Erkenntnis* no. 4; J. E. Boodin, Functional Realism (1934) 43 *Philosophical Review* 147.

470

respect they assume an identical position. This is currently expressed in the sentence, "A thing is what it does." More precise is the language of Peirce: "In order to ascertain the meaning of an intellectual conception one should consider what practical consequences might conceivably result by necessity from the truth of that conception; and the sum of these consequences will constitute the entire meaning of the conception."[49] The methodological implications of this maxim are summed up by Russell in these words:

"The supreme maxim in scientific philosophising is this: *Wherever possible, logical constructions are to be substituted for inferred entities.*"[50]

In other words, instead of assuming hidden causes or transcendental principles behind everything we see or do, we are to redefine the concepts of abstract thought as constructs, or functions, or complexes, or patterns, or arrangements, of the things that we do actually see or do. All concepts that cannot be defined in terms of the elements of actual experience are meaningless.

The task of modern philosophy is the salvaging of whatever significance attaches to the traditional concepts of metaphysics, through the redefinition of these concepts as functions of actual experience. Whatever differences may exist among modern philosophers in the choice of experiential terms which are to serve as the basic terms of functional analysis —"events," "sensa," and "atomic facts" are but a few of these basic terms —few would disagree with the point of view expressed by William James when he says that in our investigation of any abstract concept the central question must be: "What is its cash value in terms of particular experience? and what special differences would come into the world if it were true or false?"[51]

A similar use of the functional method characterizes recent advances in physics. Instead of conceiving of space as something into which physical things fit, but which somehow exists, unverifiably, apart from the things that fill it (as the Common Law is supposed to exist apart from and prior to actual decisions), and then assuming that there is an ether that fills space when it is empty, modern physicists conceive space as a manifold of relations between physical objects or events. The theory of relativity begins with the recognition that relations between physical objects or events involve a temporal as well as a spatial aspect. Thus it becomes convenient for certain purposes to substitute the notion of space-time for that of space, or even to substitute a notion which includes mass as well as space and time.

49. 5 C. S. Peirce, *Collected Papers* 6.
50. Russell, *Mysticism and Logic* (1918) 155.
51. James, The Pragmatic Method (1904) 1 *Jour. of Philosophy* 673.

The parallel between the functional method of modern physics and the program of realistic jurisprudence is so well sketched by a distinguished Chinese jurist that I can only offer a quotation without comment:[52]

> Professor Eddington, in a recent book on "The Nature of the Physical World," observes: "A thing must be defined according to the way in which it is in practice recognized and not according to some ulterior significance that we suppose it to possess." So Professor Bridgman, in "The Logic of Modern Physics":
>
> "Hitherto many of the concepts of physics have been defined in terms of their properties." But now, "in general, we mean by any concept nothing more than a set of operations; *the concept is synonymous with the corresponding set of operations.* If the concept is physical, as of length, the operations are actual physical operations, namely, those by which length is measured; or if the concept is mental, as of mathematical continuity, the operations are mental operations, namely those by which we determine whether a given aggregate of magnitudes is continuous."
>
> Now, this way of dealing with concepts was precisely what Holmes introduced into the science of law early in the '80's. . . .
>
> It may be conceded at the outset that all these definitions are capable of being further developed or improved upon: The important point to note is the complete departure from the way the old Classical Jurisprudence defined things. Hostile as he was to the traditional logic, Holmes touched the springs of the neo-realistic logic in his analysis of legal concepts. He departed entirely from the subject-predicate form of logic, and employed a logic of relations. He did not try to show how a legal entity possesses certain inherent properties. What he was trying everywhere to bring out is: If a certain group of facts is true of a person, then the person will receive a certain group of consequences attached by the law to that group of facts. Instead of treating a legal concept as a substance which in its nature necessarily contains certain inherent properties, we have here a logic which regards it as a mere signpost of a real relation subsisting between an antecedent and a consequent, and, as one of the New Realists so aptly puts it, all signposts must be kept up to date, with their inscriptions legible and their pointing true. In short, by turning the juristic logic from a subject-predicate form to an antecedent-consequent form, Holmes virtually created an inductive science of law. For both the antecedent and the consequent are to be proved and ascertained empirically.

52. John C. H. Wu, Realistic Analysis of Legal Concepts: A Study in the Legal Method of Mr. Justice Holmes (1932) 5 *China L. Rev.* 1, 2.

In brief, Holmes and, one should add, Hohfeld[53] have offered a logical basis for the redefinition of every legal concept in empirical terms, *i.e.* in terms of judicial decisions. The ghost-world of supernatural legal entities to whom courts delegate the moral responsibility of deciding cases vanishes; in its place we see legal concepts as patterns of judicial behavior: behavior which affects human lives for better or worse and is therefore subject to moral criticism. Of the functional method in legal science, one may say, as Russell has said of the method in contemporary philosophy, "Our procedure here is precisely analogous to that which has swept away from the philosophy of mathematics the useless menagerie of metaphysical monsters with which it used to be infested."[54]

F. S. Cohen, Field Theory and Judicial Logic*

A new concept appears in physics, the most important invention since Newton's time: the field. It needed great scientific imagination to realize that it is not the charges nor the particles but the field in the space between the charges and the particles which is essential for the description of physical phenomena.†

I. The Paradoxes of Judicial Logic

Are Lawyers Liars? Anyone who has read the statement of facts in a large number of briefs of appellants and appellees is likely to conclude that any resemblances between opposing accounts of the same facts are purely fortuitous and unintentional. The impression that opposing lawyers seldom agree on the facts is strengthened if one listens to opposing counsel in almost any trial. Now, as a matter of simple logic, two inconsistent statements cannot both be true. At least *one* must be false. And it is always possible that *both* are false, as, for example, when the plaintiff's attorney says the defendent speeded into the zone of the accident at sixty miles an hour and the defendant's counsel insists his client was jogging along at twenty miles an hour, while, in fact, he was moving at forty miles an hour. Thus, a logician may conclude that either (1) at least half of our

---

53. See Hohfeld, *Fundamental Legal Conceptions* (1919).

54. Russell, loc. cit. supra note 50.

* [59 *Yale L.J.* 238-244 (1950). Reprinted by permission of The Yale Law Journal Company and Fred B. Rothman & Company from The Yale Law Journal, Vol. 59, pp. 238-244.

For biographical information, see page 73 supra.]

† Einstein and Infeld, *The Evolution of Physics* 259 (1938).

practicing lawyers utter falsehoods whenever they open their mouths or fountain pens, or (2) that a substantial majority of practicing lawyers utter falsehoods on a substantial number of such occasions. If we define a liar as a person who frequently utters such falsehoods,[1] it would seem to follow logically that most lawyers are liars.

How the edifice of justice can be supported by the efforts of liars at the bar and ex-liars on the bench is one of the paradoxes of legal logic which the man in the street has never solved. The bitter sketch of "Two Lawyers" by Daumier still expresses the accepted public view of the legal profession. So, too, does the oft-told story of Satan's refusal to mend the party wall between Heaven and Hell when it was his turn to do so, of St. Peter's fruitless protests and threats to bring suit, and of Satan's crushing comeback: "Where do you think you will find a lawyer?"

Of course, lawyers know that the popular opinion on these subjects is inaccurate. Lawyers have ample opportunity to know how earnestly two litigants will swear to inconsistent accounts of a single event. Lawyers thus have special opportunities to learn what many logicians have not yet recognized: that truth on earth is a matter of degree, and that, whatever may be the case in Heaven, a terrestrial major league batting average above .300 is nothing to be sneezed at.

The difference between the lawyer's and the logician's view of truth is worth more attention than it has had from either lawyers or logicians.

From the standpoint of rigorous logic, a proposition is either true or false. There is no middle ground. A statement such as "It is raining," which is true at one time and place and not at another, is ambiguous, and an ambiguous sentence is not a proposition, though each of its possible meanings may constitute a proposition. Indeed, the characteristic of being either true or false is commonly utilized in modern logic as the defining characteristic of propositions.

Life, unfortunately, is not so simple. Logicians may define propositions, but whether they can find or create propositions is another matter. Even if we convince ourselves that there *are* propositions, it does not necessarily follow that we can actually create them or find them; we may convince ourselves that there is, somewhere, an oldest man on earth, without ever being sure who he is.

One of the greatest modern logicians, Alfred North Whitehead, used to say: "We shall meet propositions in Heaven." By this he meant that the symbolism of terrestrial life is too fuzzy ever to reach absolute

---

1. To define a liar as a person who *always* lies would be to set standards practically incapable of human attainment. Even the most confirmed liar is likely to tell the truth sometimes. Otherwise, the people he talks to will not believe him and the purpose of his lying will not be accomplished.

precision, so that unambiguousness is an ideal rather than an attainable fact. Every actual humanly constructed sentence has different shades of meaning to different readers. This is most likely to be the case in fields of controversy where different readers bring different examples, contexts, and values to bear on any given word. In any such situation a sentence will embody not a single proposition but several propositions which are ideally distinguishable. Some of these propositions may be true. Some may be false. The relation of true meanings to false meanings that flow from a single sentence generally involves a complicated quantitative distribution pattern. The simple, traditional true-false dichotomy is often quite useless.

Take, for instance, a typical humanly constructed sentence, one which has been uttered, down through some 3000 years, by hundreds of millions of human beings of many races, many tongues, and many religions:

The Lord is my shepherd; I shall not want.

What sense does it make to ask whether this sentence is true or false? Of course, there may be literal-minded readers of the Bible who will insist that the sentence has only one "correct" meaning, which is true, and that any variant interpretation is simply erroneous.

There are, no doubt, equally dogmatic individuals who will insist that the sentence is simply false. If they are dogmatic atheists, they will tell us: "There is no Lord, and therefore He cannot possibly be a shepherd." If they are Montana cattlemen, they may add that nobody in the sheep business could possibly deserve to bear the name of the Lord. Others there are who have outgrown the effort to make God in man's image, but still recite these words with full sincerity. To some such, the words of the Psalmist mean that the forces of evil are somehow self-defeating, that ultimate victory rests with the forces of righteousness, that none of us is self-sufficient, that none of us is capable of protecting himself against all the dangers that surround us from cradle to grave, and that sanity requires a faith in an unseen power that will protect us and guide us as a faithful shepherd guides his sheep, seeing that their wants are fulfilled. But one who thus translates the words of an ancient poet into the context of his own beliefs has no right to assume that this is the only context in which those words have significance. He will be content to say that they have truth for him.

This dependence of meaning upon a personal frame of reference is something that many of us take for granted when we refuse to argue over affirmations of religious faith. May not the same dependence of

475

meaning and truth upon varying contexts be found in non-religious fields as well, even in the mundane fields which concern lawyers and their clients? May we not say, even, that law as, *par excellence,* the field of controversies, is the field in which the imposition of different meanings upon the same verbal formula is most characteristic and most significant?

If anybody asks us whether the first sentence of the Twenty-third Psalm is true or false, we may properly conclude that the interrogator is lacking in imagination and guilty of the fallacy of misplaced concreteness. That is because we realize that a sentence of this sort (and perhaps every other humanly constructed sentence, in greater or lesser degree) means many things to many minds. Perhaps, if we look closely enough, a sentence never means exactly the same thing to any two different people. For no two minds bring the same apperceptive mass of understanding and background to bear on the external fact of a sound or a series of marks. Indeed, I doubt whether any sentence means exactly the same thing to me the first time I hear it that it means the tenth time or the hundredth time. Of course, for many practical purposes, we are disposed to overlook such variations of meaning. Each of us is likely to try to fix on a particular segment of our thinking, at a particular time, as "the real meaning" of any sentence. We may then consider all other interpretations as more or less serious aberrations. Perhaps we may be justified in holding that our own specific understanding of the sentence at a particular time is a proposition, and either false or true. But what, then, shall we say of the sentence as a social fact, a source of many interpretations, a matrix of many propositions? Must we not say that the truth of any assertion is a matter of degree, that from certain angles the sentence may give light and that at other angles it may obscure more light than it gives? The angle or perspective and the context are part of the meaning of any proposition, and therefore a part of whatever it is that is true or false.

The location of words in a context is essential to their meaning and truth. The fallacy of simple location in physical space-time has finally been superseded in physics. We now realize that the Copernican view that the earth moves around the sun and the older Ptolemaic view that the sun moves around the earth can both be true, and that for practical though not aesthetic or religious purposes the Ptolemaic and Copernican astronomics may be used interchangeably. We realize that Euclidean and non-Euclidean geometries can both be true. What is a straight line in one system may be an ellipse in another system, just as a penny may be round in one perspective, oval in a second, and rectangular in a third.

A prosecuting attorney who assumes that policemen are accurate and impartial observers of traffic speeds will arrive at one estimate of the speed of a defendant charged with reckless driving. The defendant's attorney, if he assumes that his client is an honest man and that policemen on the witness stand generally exaggerate in order to build up an impressive record of convictions, will arrive at another estimate. If each honestly gives his views the court will have the benefit of synoptic vision. Appreciation of the importance of such synoptic vision is a distinguishing mark of liberal civilization. To the anthropologist, the tolerance that is institutionalized in a judicial system agreed to hear two sides in every case represents a major step in man's liberation from the tyranny of word-magic. If we do not feel that we have to annihilate those who say things we do not believe or, what is generally more irritating, say things we do believe but say them in strange ways or in unfamiliar accents, we are able to conserve our energy for more useful purposes. Energy so conserved may produce science, art, baseball, and various other substitutes for indiscriminate individualistic slaughter.

The disagreements of opposing lawyers on statements of simple fact, and the even wider disagreements that characterize their views on more complicated facts ("opinion" and "law"), call for a more humane and social view of truth and meaning than appears in most of the traditional logic books. This is not to say that the traditional logic books are wrong. It is only to say that so far the logicians, having concentrated their vision on the logical heavens where words continue at rest and mean the same thing forever, have not fully explored the imperfect efforts of human beings to communicate with each other. But there are welcome indications today that logicians are beginning to pay more attention to the real world where people seldom say exactly what they mean or mean all they say, where no two people ever quite understand each other, where the accumulation of different views of the same event is the only remedy we have found for fanaticism, and where the logic of fiction has a more direct bearing upon every-day discourse than the logic of science.[3]

In a certain sense, it is true that lawyers are liars. In the same sense, poets, historians, and map-makers are also liars. For it is the function of lawyers, poets, historians, and map-makers not to reproduce reality but to illumine some aspect of reality, and it always makes for deceit to pretend that what is thus illumined is the whole of reality. None of us can ever possibly tell the whole truth, though we may conscientiously will to do so and ask divine help towards that end. The ancient wisdom of our

3. See M. R. Cohen, *A Preface to Logic*, cc. 4, 5 (1944); Thouless, *How to Think Straight* (1948).

common law recognizes that men are bound to differ in their views of fact and law, not because some are honest and others dishonest, but because each of us operates in a value-charged field which gives shape and color to whatever we see. The proposition that no man should be a judge of his own cause embodies the ancient wisdom that only a many-perspectived view of the world can relieve us of the endless anarchy of one-eyed vision.

Thus, it happens that there are implicit in our judicial process certain attitudes towards truth and reality which have recently become explicit in physical science. The importance of Einstein's special and general theories of relativity is not that they make us see that motion is relative to an observation post. This was recognized long ago. The real importance of Einstein is his development of formulae by which many different accounts of the same physical event may be correlated with each other, so that from the position and direction of an event in any physical system we can calculate its position and direction in any other system.[4] Einstein has made it possible for us to say that what is reported as a straight line in one system will be reported in another system as a curve of a defined form.

What is needed in law, if law is to become more scientific in the future than it has been in the past, is a body of learning from which we can predict that what looks like a straight story or a straight sale from one standpoint will look like a crooked story or a crooked sale from another, and from which we can predict the successive "distortions" that any observed social fact will undergo as it passes through different value-charged fields in the "world-line"[5] of its history.

Concretely, if we see either of the following headlines, we should be able to predict the other one:

Wall Street Journal	*Pravda (Truth)*
SOVIET ARMIES INVADE YUGOSLAVIA	**YUGOSLAV PEOPLE LIQUIDATE PUPPETS OF CAPITALIST POWERS**

4. "Indeed, it is quite enough to know the results obtained by an observer in one CS [Coordinate System] to know those obtained by an observer in the other." Einstein and Infeld, *The Evolution of Physics* 166 (1938).

"The general theory of relativity attempts to formulate physical laws for all CS." Id. at 249.

5. The "world-line" of a body, in modern physics, is the series of all its locations in space-time. That the earth was between the sun and the moon on a certain day would be a point in the series that constitutes the world-line of the earth.

Similarly, we should be able to predict that what Justice X will view as "judicial protection of fundamental constitutional liberties" will be viewed by Justice Y as "federal interference with the constitutional freedom of the states to experiment in the solution of their own social problems." We should be able to understand how the simple physical fact of a man's skull colliding with a policeman's club will be reported by the *New York Times,* the *Daily Worker,* the attorney for the club, the attorney for the skull, and the various judges who will view the event at second hand. Given the report of the event recorded by any of these observation posts, and knowing the value field of the observation post, we should be able to predict the report that will be recorded by any other observation post whose value field we can identify.

That such a form of knowledge is attainable is no empty dream. Roughly, crudely, and implicitly, we all have some basis in experience for predicting and discounting the ways in which value fields affect the reporting of facts.

One of the simplest shifts of perspective is that which is formalized in grammar by the distinction between first, second, and third person. Bertrand Russell, in a radio broadcast, under the heading of "conjugation of irregular adjectives," offered this illuminating example:

1. I am firm.
2. You are obstinate.
3. He is a pig-headed fool.

The *New Statesman and Nation* recently secured from its readers large quantities of similar conjugations, of which the following are typical:

1. I am righteously indignant.
2. You are annoyed.
3. He is making a fuss about nothing.

1. I have about me something of the subtle, haunting, mysterious fragrance of the Orient.
2. You rather overdo it, dear.
3. She stinks.

It is unnecessary to multiply examples. The question that confronts jurisprudence is whether the practical know-how that enables an experienced judge to discount bias can be formulated and rendered more systematic and less haphazard. Can we do in law what the mathematicians and the physicists have done in their more precise domains?

F. S. Cohen, What is a Question?*

. . . [I]t is obvious that many apparent questions lack significance, that for want of recognizable criteria of interrogatory significance much philosophical discussion consists of a useless attempt to answer meaningless questions, that a good deal of superficial and unjustified support is given to the skeptical or inquiring attitude as opposed to the dogmatic because of a failure to realize the intellectual responsibilities determined by the logical presuppositions of significant questions, and that a cloud is thrown across many philosophical problems by a failure to analyze the general relation of a question to an answer.

I

. . . Those who have formulated the world's problems have more often deserved the name "philosopher" than those who have settled them. . . .

II

A question, it is submitted, is simply a propositional function (or propositional form). "What is the sum of 3 and 5?" seems to be identical in logical content with "$x = 3 + 5$." Whatever difference appears between the two phrases seems to reside merely in the psychological connotations commonly adhering to the different styles of expression. That is to say, we generally want an answer when we ask a question, although we frequently put a propositional function without any demand that its values be supplied. But this matter of compulsive flavor, in which our two expressions may find a shadowy distinction, does not go to the logical content of either.

As a logical entity the question is the clear embodiment of the characters by which the propositional function has been defined. It is neither true nor false, while its values (answers) are true or false. It is of the form of the proposition, yet differing from the latter by the substitution of a variable for some constant. *Who, which, what, when, where, why,* etc. are the variables of every-day speech. . . .

* [39 *Monist* 350-351, 353-354, 359-363 (1929). Reprinted from The Monist, Vol. 39, No. 3, with the permission of the publisher.
  For biographical information, see page 73 supra.]

IV

The foregoing considerations may be viewed as defining question and answer in the widest sense of the terms. Thus every propositional function is a question, although it may be indeterminate or insignificant, and every value of such a function is an answer, although it may be false. This terminology does not constitute an untoward strain of language, since we do commonly apply these adjectives to certain questions and answers. And in any case, it offers a clear verbal framework for the essential problem that remains to be considered. What questions are significant, and what answers are correct?

By a significant question, I mean a question to which some proposition is *the* true answer. Two things are thus demanded for interrogatory significance. In the first place, there must be at least one true proposition that is a value of the given propositional function, and in the second place, there must be not more than one such proposition. Questions which violate the former condition may be appropriately called *invalid*. Thus "What cat has eight lives?",[9] "Who discovered America in 1491?", and "$x \cdot 0 = 1$" are typical examples of invalid questions. We may, without committing any logical fallacy, ask such questions as: "When did you stop beating your wife?", "What is the highest good?", "Where is the mind?", and "What are the ultimate simples of sense-experience?" But we do fall into error when we assume, (as we usually do when we ask questions), that such questions must have true answers, and ignore the fact that to justify the validity of these questions it is necessary to show that the person addressed has stopped beating his wife, that there is a highest good, that the mind exists in space, that there are elements of sense-experience which are ultimately simple, etc.

Every propositional function lays down a range of significance determined by the possible values of the variable term, and an inner range of truth further determined by the constant terms of the expression. Thus the presumption of validity in a question is an assumption that this latter range (and therefore the former range as well) contains at least one member. Such an assumption will be true or false. When false, any answer to the question must be incorrect. The chief usefulness of questions (apart from riddles) arises from the fact that we can sometimes know that such a value exists without knowing what it is.

9. It might be supposed that "No cat has eight lives" is a correct answer to this question. But although this may be a very appropriate retort to an invalid question, it is entirely different in form from a real answer, being a negative universal, while the values of the propositional function advanced are all particulars. An oversight at this point tempts the inference that since one cat has one more life than no cat, one cat has nine lives.

The second condition of what we have called a significant question is that it have not more than one true answer. Questions which violate this requirement may be called indeterminate. Thus, "Who did what when?" and "$1^x = 1$," are indeterminate and therefore non-significant (in our defined sense of that word,—we do not mean to imply that invalid or indeterminate questions have no meaning). To such questions we may indeed give true answers, but we can never give *the* true answer to any of them. Thus in claiming significance or simply determinateness for a given question,—and we do this whenever we attempt to show that one answer is incorrect by demonstrating that a materially different answer is correct,—we are under the responsibility of showing that not more than one true proposition is a value of our propositional function. The relevance of this principle to philosophical discussion is obvious. "What is the first mover?" in a world where rest and motion are relative to variable coordinates, is the type of a great class of questions which lead inevitably to error when they are regarded as determinate. The fundamental question of ethics, "What is the good?" has regularly been treated as if it were (abstractly) determinate. Thus the more basic question of whether *good* is a constant or a variable (similar to *mine*) is never clearly faced and always unconsciously answered.

At this point a distinction of crucial importance must be made between questions that are indeterminate and those that are ambiguous, applying the latter predicate to questions which have no uniquely determined meaning. An indeterminate question we have seen to be a definitely denoted propositional function which has more than one true value. But an ambiguous question is not, in the logical sense, a question at all. It is rather a group of questions, or, more accurately, an ambiguous symbol, a verbal matrix from which various questions may be derived. In asking whether certain things are real or practical or right, I may have in mind something quite different from what another person understands by the words. What would constitute a correct answer to the question in my mind may be a false answer or no answer at all to the question in my neighbor's. But both of these questions may be determinate and significant. Ambiguity, then, is something which attaches not to the idea which a set of words suggests (and it is with the analysis of such ideas that we are concerned), but to the set of words itself in so far as it suggests various meanings.

That words and sentences, declarative or interrogative, do convey different meanings to different people and even to the same person in varying circumstances is too obvious a fact to be labored, yet the ignoring of this fact is perhaps the most fertile source of philosophical and non-philosophical argument. Bertrand Russell somewhere says that no two philosophers ever understand each other. If one may confess to an understanding of that remark, it appears to be very near the truth. Certainly we shall never bridge the chasms about a human soul with our primitive marks and noises, but if there is to be any rational intercourse between man and man, we must somehow approach the ideal of unambiguous speech. And to do this we must remember that the ideal is beyond the language that pursues it.

Ambiguity is as prevalent and as dangerous in our interrogations as in our statements, but the problems which it raises in this connection are problems of thought and human intercourse in general, and as such are irrelevant to a study of the logical nature of a question, except in so far as they help to explain what we are not talking about.[10] If, as Professor Whitehead hopes, we shall find real propositions in the kingdom of heaven, there too shall we find real questions. But it is the divine task of the logician to examine these ideal entities that we may better discern meaning and direction in the world of human thought. The significant question is, like every object of reason, an abstraction from actual experience.

III. LOGIC AND ETHICS

F. S. Cohen, The Ethical Basis of Legal Criticism*

The ethical responsibilities of the judge have so often been obscured by the supposed duty to be logically consistent in the decision of different cases that it may be pertinent to ask whether any legal decision can ever be logically inconsistent with any other decision. In order to find such an inconsistency we must have two judgments, one for the plaintiff and one for the defendant. But this means that we must have two cases,

10. The distinction between indeterminateness and ambiguity is paralleled by the more obvious distinction between invalidity and meaningless. A symbol which has no meaning,—e.g., Wittgenstein's creation, "Is the Good more or less identical than the Beautiful?"—is not, in the logical sense, a question. But a question may have no true answer. In other words, the predicates meaningful, meaningless, ambiguous, and unambiguous refer to interrogations and interrogative sentences, but not to questions. Meanings do not *have* meaning.

* [41 *Yale L.J.* 201 (1931), reprinted, substantially, in *Ethical Systems and Legal Ideals* (1933), pp. 30-40. Reprinted here by permission of The Yale Law Journal Company and Fred B. Rothman & Company from The Yale Law Journal, Vol. 41, pp. 201 et seq.

For biographical information, see page 73 supra.]

since a second judgment in the same case would supercede the first judgment. And between the facts of any two cases there must be some difference, so that it will always be logically possible to frame a single legal rule requiring both decisions, given the facts of the two cases. Of course such a rule will seem absurd if the difference between the two cases in unimportant (e.g., in the names or heights of the two defendants). But whether the difference is important or unimportant is a problem not of logic but of ethics, and one to which the opposing counsel in the later case may propose opposite answers without becoming involved in self-contradiction.

The confusion arises when we think of a judicial decision as implying a rule from which, given the facts of the case, the decision may be derived (the logical fallacy of affirming the consequent).[39] That logically startling deduction of the "law of precedents" from judicial precedents, Black's *Handbook of the Law of Judicial Precedents,* thus sums up the matter:

> Even if the opinion of the court should be concerned with unnecessary considerations, or should state the proposition of law imperfectly or incorrectly, yet there is a proposition necessarily involved in the decision and without which the judgment in the case could not have been given;

39. The periodic attempts of students of the common law to put forward logical formulae for discovering "the rule of a case" all betray an elementary ignorance of the logical fact that no particular proposition can imply a general proposition. Wambaugh, Salmond, Gray, Black, Morgan, and Goodhart agree that the rule of a case (the *ratio decidendi,* the proposition for which a case is a precedent) is a general proposition necessary to the particular decision. See Wambaugh, *Study of Cases* (2d ed. 1894) c. 2; Salmond, Theory of Judicial Precedents (1900) 16 *L.Q. Rev.* 376; Gray, op. cit. supra [*Nature and Sources of the Law*] note 11, at §555; Black, *Judicial Precedents* (1912) 40; Morgan, op. cit. supra [*Introduction to the Study of Law*] note 29, at 109-10; Goodhart, Determining the *Ratio Decidendi* of a Case (1930) 40 *Yale L.J.* 161. Logical objections to this conception are dismissed by Professor Morgan as "hypercritical" and "too refined for practical purposes." But Professor Oliphant, who refuses to be deterred by such warnings (see his reply in Mutuality of Obligation in Bilateral Contracts at Law (1928) 28 *Col. L. Rev.* 997, n. 2 to Professor Williston's charges of scholasticism, The Effect of One Void Promise in a Bilateral Agreement (1925) 25 *Col. L. Rev.* 857, 869) has suggested an alternative conception that is logically sound and practically far more useful. Rules of increasing generality, each of them linking the given result to the given facts, spread pyramid-wise from a decision. The possibility of alternative modes of analysis makes a decision the apex not of one but many such pyramids. No one of these rules has any logical priority; courts and lawyers choose among competing propositions on extra-logical grounds. Oliphant, A Return to *Stare Decisis* (1928) 6 *Am. Law School Rev.* 215, 217-218; and cf. Llewellyn, *Bramble Bush* (1930) 61-66; Bingham, What Is the Law? (1912) 11 *Mich. L. Rev.* 1, 109, 111 n. 31. The picture clearly suggests that the decision bears to the rules the same relation that Professor Whitehead has traced between a point and the surfaces that would ordinarily be said to include the point. See *The Principles of Natural Knowledge* (1919) c. 8; *The Concept of Nature* (1919) c. 4.

and it is this proposition which is established by the decision (so far as it goes) and for which alone the case may be cited as an authority.[40]

But elementary logic teaches us that every legal decision and every finite set of decisions can be subsumed under an infinite number of different general rules, just as an infinite number of different curves may be traced through any point or finite collection of points. Every decision is a choice between different rules which logically fit all past decisions but logically dictate conflicting results in the instant case. Logic provides the spring-board but it does not guarantee the success of any particular dive.

If the doctrine of *stare decisis* means anything, and one can hardly maintain the contrary despite the infelicitous formulations which have been given to the doctrine, the consistency which it demands cannot be a logical consistency. The consistency in question is more akin to that quality of dough which is necessary for the fixing of a durable shape. Decisions are fluid until they are given "morals." It is often important to conserve with new obeisance the morals which lawyers and laymen have read into past decisions and in reliance upon which they have acted. We do not deny that importance when we recognize that with equal logical justification lawyers and laymen might have attached other morals to the old cases had their habits of legal classification or their general social premises been different. But we do shift the focus of our vision from a stage where social and professional prejudices wear the terrible armor of Pure Reason to an arena where human hopes and expectations wrestle naked for supremacy.

No doubt the doctrine of *stare decisis* and the argument for consistency have a significance which is not exhausted by the social usefulness of predictable law. Even in fields where past court decisions play a negligible role in molding expectations, courts may be justified in looking to former rulings for guidance. The time of judges is more limited than the boundaries of injustice. At some risk the results of past deliberation in a case similar to the case at bar must be accepted. But again we invite fatal confusion if we think of this similarity as a logical rather than an ethical relation. To the cold eyes of logic the difference between the names of the parties in the two decisions bulks as large as the difference between care and negligence. The question before the judge is, "Granted that there are differences between the cited precedent and the case at bar, and assuming that the decision in the earlier case was a desirable one, is it desirable to attach legal weight to any of the factual differences between the instant case and the earlier case?" Obviously this is an ethical question. Should a rich woman accused of larceny receive the same treatment as a poor woman? Should a rich man who has accidentally injured

40. Loc. cit. supra note 39.

another come under the same obligations as a poor man? Should a group of persons, e.g., an unincorporated labor union, be privileged to make all statements that an individual may lawfully make? Neither the ringing hexameters of *Barbara Celarent* nor the logic machine of Jevons nor the true-false patterns of Wittgenstein will produce answers to these questions.

What then shall we think of attempts to frame practical legal issues as conflicts between morality, common sense, history or sociology, and logic (logic playing regularly the Satanic role)? One hesitates to convict the foremost jurists on the American bench of elementary logical error. It is more likely that they have simply used the word "logic" in peculiar ways, as to which they may find many precedents in the current logic textbooks.[41]

Bertrand Russell has warned us:

> When it is said, for example, that the French are "logical," what is meant is that, when they accept a premise, they also accept everything that a person totally devoid of logical subtlety would erroneously suppose to follow from that premise. . . . Logic was, formerly, the art of drawing inferences; it has now become the art of abstaining from inferences, since it has appeared that the inferences we feel naturally inclined to make are hardly ever valid.[42]

If we construe the word "logic" in the light of this warning, we may readily agree with Mr. Justice Holmes when he asserts that "the whole outline of the law is the resultant of a conflict at every point between logic [viz., hasty generalization] and good sense"[43] and find some meaning in the statement of Judge Cardozo that "the logic of one principle" prevails over the logic of another[44] or in his pride that "We in the United States have been readier to subordinate logic to utility."[45]

We may have to interpret the word "logical" as synonymous with "aesthetically satisfying" in order to understand the statement of Mr. Justice Brandeis and Mr. Warren that a distinction between cases where "substantial mental suffering would be the natural and probable result" of an act and cases "where no mental suffering would ordinarily result"

41. See M. R. Cohen, The Subject Matter of Formal Logic (1918) 15 *Jour. of Phil.* 673.
42. Russell, *Sceptical Essays* (1928) c. 7 (Behaviorism and Values) 99.
43. Holmes, *Collected Legal Papers* (1920) (Agency) 49, 50.
44. Cardozo, *Nature of the Judicial Process,* (1921) c. 1 (Introduction. The Method of Philosophy) 41. Judge Cardozo illustrates (op. cit. 38-39) the method of logic or philosophy, which is distinguished from the methods of history or evolution, of custom or tradition, and of sociology, with the rule that one who contracts to purchase real property must pay for it even though, before the sale is actually completed, the property is substantially destroyed. This, he maintains, is the projection to its logical outcome of the principle that "equity treats that as done which ought to be done," a principle which does not apply to the

is not logical though very practical.[46] Such an identification of the rules of logic with those of intellectual aesthetics seems to be assumed at times by Judge Cardozo as well.[47]

No verbal definition is intrinsically objectionable. But it seems fair to suggest that the use of the word "logic" in the senses exemplified in these typical passages seriously lowers the probability of clear thinking on the relation between law and ethics. Most of us think of logic as the most general and formal of the sciences.[48] Upon that basis we may say, paraphrasing a remark of Mr. Justice Holmes, that conformity with logic is only a necessity and not a duty. The bad judge is no more able to violate the laws of logic than he is to violate the laws of gravitation. He may, of course, ignore both. It is not our purpose to deny that there would be less judicial stumbling were courts more constantly aware of the logical relations between particular and universal, between premise and conclusion, between form and content.

---

sale of chattels which did not come under the jurisdiction of Chancery. But what sort of principle is this? It is certainly not a logical principle, i.e., a proposition certifiable on logical grounds alone, since it is obviously false. If it were true no plaintiff in equity could ever obtain a judgment since he could never in the face of such a rule show that the defendant had *not* done what he ought to have done. Would it not be quite as logical for a court to say "equity does not treat that as done which has not been done"? If a rule is undesirable we do not make it less undesirable by deducing it from another rule too vague to be liked or disliked and then concentrating our attention on the process of inference rather than the premise. What is in question in the case proposed is not a logical problem or a choice of judicial methods but a conflict of social interests, and there is much that may be said in favor of throwing upon the party who contemplates future enjoyment of a definite piece of real property the risk of its destruction and the necessity of insurance. But what may thus be said bears no peculiar *imprimatur* of logic. See also Cardozo, *The Growth of the Law* (1924) 79-80.

45. Cardozo, *The Growth of the Law* (1924) 77. This is said with regard to the tendency in recent decisions (of which Judge Cardozo's opinion in MacPherson v. Buick Mfg. Co., 217 N.Y. 382, 111 N.E. 1050 (1916) is a noteworthy landmark) to extend the scope of a manufacturer's obligations to the ultimate consumer with regard to the quality of the product. Again the rejected "privity" analysis of the situation seems to be peculiarly "logical" because it permits the deduction of an undesirable rule from another undesirable rule which is too vague to arouse the resentment which the deduced rule arouses.

See also ibid. 83, where "adherence to logic and advancement of utility" are balanced in terms of "the social interest which each is capable of promoting."

46. Warren and Brandeis, The Right of Privacy (1890) 4 *Harv. L. Rev.* 193, reprinted in *Selected Essays in the Law of Torts* (1924) 122, 126.

47. "If I am seeking logical consistency, the symmetry of the legal structure, how far shall I seek it?" Cardozo, *Nature of the Judicial Process* 10, and cf. ibid. 33-34.

48. "If it was so, it might be; and if it were so, it would be, but as it isn't, it ain't. That's logic." Carroll, *Through the Looking Glass* c. 4. And see Wittgenstein, *Tractatus Logico-Philosophicus* (1922) §§6.1, 6.1262; M. R. Cohen op. cit. supra note 41 p. 465; Hoernle, Review of *Science of Legal Method* (1918) 31 *Harv. L. Rev.* 807; Russell, *Principles of Mathematics,* (1903) c. 1; Adler, *Law and the Modern Mind: A* Symposium (1931) 31 *Col. L. Rev.* 99-101; Keyser, On the Study of Legal Science (1929) 38 *Yale L.J.* 413.

Chapter 5

Law and Ethics

I. SEMINAL CONCEPTS

Kant, The Philosophy of Law*

PROLEGOMENA

General Introduction to the Metaphysic of Morals

II. The Idea and Necessity of a Metaphysic of Morals

. . . [Moral laws] in contradistinction to Natural Laws, are only valid *as* Laws, in so far as they can be rationally established *à priori* and comprehended as *necessary*. In fact, conceptions and judgments regarding ourselves and our conduct have no *moral* significance, if they contain only what may be learned from experience; and when any one is, so to speak, misled into making a Moral Principle out of anything derived from this latter source, he is already in danger of falling into the coarsest and most fatal errors.

If the Philosophy of Morals were nothing more than a Theory of Happiness (*Eudoemonism*), it would be absurd to search after Principles *à priori* as a foundation for it. For however plausible it may sound to say that Reason, even prior to experience, can comprehend by what means

---

*[(1796.) Pp. 15-17, 33-34, 43-47, 55-57 (Hastie transl. 1887).

Immanuel Kant (1724-1804) believed that the methods of natural science, and particularly of Newtonian physics, could also be applied to law, ethics, and philosophy. His chief efforts in this direction are *The Critique of Pure Reason* (1781), *The Metaphysics of Morals* (1785), and *The Critique of Practical Reason* (1786).]

we may attain to a lasting enjoyment of the real pleasures of life, yet all that is taught on this subject *à priori* is either tautological, or is assumed wholly without foundation. It is only Experience that can show what will bring us enjoyment. The natural impulses directed towards nourishment, the sexual instinct, or the tendency to rest and motion, as well as the higher desires of honour, the acquisition of knowledge, and such like, as developed with our natural capacities, are alone capable of showing in what those enjoyments are to be *found*. And, further, the knowledge thus acquired, is available for each individual merely in his own way; and it is only thus he can learn the means by which he has to *seek* those enjoyments. All specious rationalizing *à priori*, in this connection, is nothing at bottom but carrying facts of Experience up to generalizations by induction (*secundum principia generalia non universalia*); and the generality thus attained is still so limited that numberless exceptions must be allowed to every individual in order that he may adapt the choice of his mode of life to his own particular inclinations and his capacity for pleasure. And, after all, the individual has really to acquire his Prudence at the cost of his own suffering or that of his neighbours.

But it is quite otherwise with the Principles of Morality. They lay down Commands for every one without regard to his particular inclinations, and merely because and so far as he is free, and has a practical Reason. Instruction in the Laws of Morality is not drawn from observation of oneself or of our animal nature, nor from perception of the course of the world in regard to what happens, or how men act.[1] But Reason commands how we *ought* to act, even although no example of such action were to be found; nor does Reason give any regard to the Advantage which may accrue to us by so acting, and which Experience could alone actually show. . . .

General Divisions of the Metaphysic of Morals

IV. General Preliminary Conceptions Defined and Explained

. . . *Natural and Positive Laws.*—Obligatory Laws for which an external Legislation is possible, are called generally *External Laws*. Those External Laws, the obligatoriness of which can be recognised by Reason *à priori* even without an external Legislation, are called Natural Laws. Those Laws, again, which are not obligatory without actual External Legislation, are called Positive Laws. An External Legislation, contain-

---

1. This holds notwithstanding the fact that the term "Morals," in Latin *Mores,* and in German *Sitten,* signifies originally only *Manners* or *Mode of Life*.

ing pure Natural Laws, is therefore conceivable; but in that case a previous Natural Law must be presupposed to establish the authority of the Lawgiver by the Right to subject others to Obligation through his own act of Will.

Maxims. — The Principle which makes a certain action a Duty, is a Practical Law. The Rule of the Agent or Actor, which he forms as a Principle for himself on subjective grounds, is called his Maxim. Hence, even when the Law is one and invariable, the Maxims of the Agent may yet be very different.

The Categorical Imperative. — The Categorical Imperative only expresses generally what constitutes Obligation. It may be rendered by the following Formula: "Act according to a Maxim which can be adopted at the same time as a Universal Law." Actions must therefore be considered, in the first place, according to their subjective Principle; but whether this principle is also valid objectively, can only be known by the criterion of the Categorical Imperative. For Reason brings the principle or maxim of any action to the test, by calling upon the Agent to think of himself in connection with it as at the same time laying down a Universal Law, and to consider whether his action is so qualified as to be fit for entering into such a Universal Legislation. . . .

INTRODUCTION TO THE SCIENCE OF RIGHT

General Definitions and Divisions

A. What the Science of Right Is

The Science of Right has for its object the Principles of all the Laws which it is possible to promulgate by external legislation. . . .

B. What Is Right ?

This question may be said to be about as embarrassing to the Jurist as the well-known question, "What is Truth?" is to the Logician. It is all the more so, if, on reflection, he strives to avoid tautology in his reply, and recognise the fact that a reference to what holds true merely of the laws of some one country at a particular time, is not a solution of the general problem thus proposed. It is quite easy to state what may be right in particular cases (*quid sit juris*), as being what the laws of a certain place and of a certain time say or may have said; but it is much more difficult to determine whether what they have enacted is right in itself, and to lay down a universal Criterion by which Right and Wrong in general, and what is just and unjust, may be recognised. All this may remain entirely hidden even from the practical Jurist until he abandon his empirical principles for a time, and search in the pure Reason for the sources of such judgments, in order to lay a real foundation for actual positive Legislation. In this search his empirical Laws may, indeed, furnish him with excellent guidance; but a merely empirical system that is void of rational principles is, like the wooden head in the fable of Phaedrus, fine enough in appearance, but unfortunately it wants brain.

1. The conception of Right,—as referring to a corresponding Obligation which is the moral aspect of it,—in the *first* place, has regard only to the external and practical relation of one Person to another, in so far as they can have influence upon each other, immediately or mediately, by their *Actions* as facts. 2. In the *second* place, the conception of Right does not indicate the relation of the action of an individual to the *wish* or the mere desire of another, as in acts of benevolence or of unkindness, but only the relation of his free action to the freedom of *action* of the other. 3. And, in the *third* place, in this reciprocal relation of voluntary actions, the conception of Right does not take into consideration the *matter* of the act of Will in so far as the end which any one may have in view in willing it, is concerned. In other words, it is not asked in a question of Right whether any one on buying goods for his own business realizes a profit by the transaction or not; but only the *form* of the transaction is taken into account, in considering the relation of the mutual acts of Will. Acts of Will or voluntary Choice are thus regarded only in so far as they are *free,* and as to whether the action of one can harmonize with the Freedom of another, according to a universal Law.

Right, therefore, comprehends the whole of the conditions under which the voluntary actions of any one Person can be harmonized in reality with the voluntary actions of every other Person, according to a universal Law of Freedom.

C. Universal Principle of Right

"Every Action is *right* which in itself, or in the maxim on which it proceeds, is such that it can co-exist along with the Freedom of the Will of each and all in action, according to a universal Law."

If, then, my action or my condition generally can co-exist with the freedom of every other, according to a universal Law, any one does me a wrong who hinders me in the performance of this action, or in the maintenance of this condition. For such a hindrance or obstruction cannot co-exist with Freedom according to universal Laws.

It follows also that it cannot be demanded as a matter of Right, that this universal Principle of all maxims shall itself be adopted as my maxim, that is, that I shall make it the *maxim* of my actions. For any one may be free, although his Freedom is entirely indifferent to me, or even if I wished in my heart to infringe it, so long as I do not actually violate that freedom by *my external action.* Ethics, however, as distinguished from Jurisprudence, imposes upon me the obligation to make the fulfilment of Right a *maxim* of my conduct.

The universal Law of Right may then be expressed, thus: "Act externally in such a manner that the free exercise of thy Will may be able to co-exist with the Freedom of all others, according to a universal Law." This is undoubtedly a Law which imposes obligation upon me; but it does not at all imply and still less command that I *ought,* merely on account of this obligation, to limit my freedom to these very conditions. Reason in this connection says only that it *is* restricted thus far by its Idea, and may be likewise thus limited in fact by others; and it lays this down as a Postulate which is not capable of further proof. As the object in view is not to teach Virtue, but to explain what Right *is,* thus far the Law of Right, as thus laid down, may not and should not be represented as a motive-principle of action.

D. Right Is Conjoined with the Title or Authority to Compel

The resistance which is opposed to any hindrance of an effect, is in reality a furtherance of this effect, and is in accordance with its accomplishment. Now, everything that is wrong is a hindrance of freedom, according to universal Laws; and Compulsion or Constraint of any kind is a hindrance or resistance made to Freedom. Consequently, if a certain exercise of Freedom is itself a hindrance of the Freedom that is according to universal Laws, it is wrong; and the compulsion or constraint which is opposed to it is right, as being *a hindering of a hindrance of Freedom,* and as being in accord with the Freedom which exists in accordance with universal Laws. Hence, according to the logical principle of Contradiction, all Right is accompanied with an implied Title or warrant to bring compulsion to bear on any one who may violate it in fact. . . .

Division of the Science of Right

B. Universal Division of Rights

I. Natural Right and Positive Right

The System of Rights, viewed as a scientific System of Doctrines, is divided into Natural Right and Positive Right. Natural Right rests upon pure rational Principles *à priori;* Positive or Statutory Right is what proceeds from the Will of a Legislator.

II. Innate Right and Acquired Right

The System of Rights may again be regarded in reference to the implied Powers of dealing morally with others as bound by Obligations, that is, as furnishing a legal Title of action in relation to them. Thus viewed, the System is divided into Innate Right and Acquired Right. Innate Right is that Right which belongs to every one by Nature, independent of all juridical acts of experience. Acquired Right is that Right which is founded upon such juridical acts.

Innate Right may also be called the "Internal Mine and Thine" (*Meum vel Tuum internum*); for External Right must always be acquired.

There is only one Innate Right,
the Birthright of Freedom.

Freedom is Independence of the compulsory Will of another; and in so far as it can co-exist with the Freedom of all according to a universal Law, it is the one sole original, inborn Right belonging to every man in virtue of his Humanity. There is, indeed, an innate Equality belonging to every man which consists in his Right to be independent of being bound by others to anything more than that to which he may also reciprocally bind them. It is, consequently, the inborn quality of every man in virtue of which he ought to be *his own master by Right* (*sui juris*). There is, also, the natural quality of Justness attributable to a man as naturally of *unimpeachable Right* (*justi*), because he has done no Wrong to any one prior to his own juridical actions. And, further, there is also the innate Right of Common Action on the part of every man so that he may do towards others what does not infringe their Rights or take away anything that is theirs unless they are willing to appropriate it. . . . But all these Rights or Titles are already included in the Principle of Innate Freedom, and are not really distinguished from it, even as dividing members under a higher species of Right. . . .

Bentham, An Introduction to the Principles of Morals and Legislation*

Chapter I. Of the Principle of Utility

1. Nature has placed mankind under the governance of two sovereign masters, *pain* and *pleasure*. It is for them alone to point out what we

*[Ch. 1, sections 1-14; Ch. 2, sections 1, 3, 9-11, 13-14; Ch. 4, sections 1-8; Ch. 7, sec-

ought to do, as well as to determine what we shall do. On the one hand the standard of right and wrong, on the other the chain of causes and effects, are fastened to their throne. They govern us in all we do, in all we say, in all we think: every effort we can make to throw off our subjection, will serve but to demonstrate and confirm it. In words a man may pretend to abjure their empire: but in reality he will remain subject to it all the while. The *principle of utility* recognises this subjection, and assumes it for the foundation of that system, the object of which is to rear the fabric of felicity by the hands of reason and of law. Systems which attempt to question it, deal in sounds instead of sense, in caprice instead of reason, in darkness instead of light.

But enough of metaphor and declamation: it is not by such means that moral science is to be improved.

2. The principle of utility is the foundation of the present work: it will be proper therefore at the outset to give an explicit and determinate account of what is meant by it. By the principle of utility is meant that principle which approves or disapproves of every action whatsoever, according to the tendency which it appears to have to augment or diminish the happiness of the party whose interest is in question: or, what is the same thing in other words, to promote or to oppose that happiness. I say of every action whatsoever; and therefore not only of every action of a private individual, but of every measure of government.

3. By utility is meant that property in any object, whereby it tends to produce benefit, advantage, pleasure, good, or happiness, (all this in the present case comes to the same thing) or (what comes again to the same thing) to prevent the happening of mischief, pain, evil, or unhappiness to the party whose interest is considered: if that party be the community in general, then the happiness of the community: if a particular individual, then the happiness of that individual.

4. The interest of the community is one of the most general expres-

---

tions 1-6; Ch. 8, sections 1-3; Ch. 17, sections 8-9 (1789).

Jeremy Bentham (1748-1832), a philosopher, political theorist, and jurist, is best known as the founder of modern utilitarianism. Defining the "community" as "the sum of the interests of its members," Bentham's philosophy aimed at that which produced the greatest happiness for the greatest number. His work led to many political, legal, and penal reforms in England and the United States.

Bentham was an eccentric individual with a taste for irony. In his late work, *Auto Icon,* he suggested that every man could, with proper embalming, become his own monument, and that notables might be interspersed with trees in public parks. In his will, he stipulated that his skeleton be preserved . . . clothed.

Bentham's jurisprudential works include *Fragment on Government* (1776), *Introductory View of the Rationale of Evidence* (1812), and *Rationale of Judicial Evidence* (1827).]

sions that can occur in the phraseology of morals: no wonder that the meaning of it is often lost. When it has a meaning, it is this. The community is a fictitious *body,* composed of the individual persons who are considered as constituting as it were its *members*. The interest of the community then is, what?—the sum of the interests of the several members who compose it.

5. It is in vain to talk of the interest of the community, without understanding what is the interest of the individual. A thing is said to promote the interest, or to be *for* the interest, of an individual, when it tends to add to the sum total of his pleasures: or, what comes to the same thing, to diminish the sum total of his pains.

6. An action then may be said to be conformable to the principle of utility, or, for shortness sake, to utility, (meaning with respect to the community at large) when the tendency it has to augment the happiness of the community is greater than any it has to diminish it.

7. A measure of government (which is but a particular kind of action, performed by a particular person or persons) may be said to be conformable to or dictated by the principle of utility, when in like manner the tendency which it has to augment the happiness of the community is greater than any which it has to diminish it.

8. When an action, or in particular a measure of government, is supposed by a man to be conformable to the principle of utility, it may be convenient, for the purposes of discourse, to imagine a kind of law or dictate, called a law or dictate of utility: and to speak of the action in question, as being conformable to such law or dictate.

9. A man may be said to be a partisan of the principle of utility, when the approbation or disapprobation he annexes to any action, or to any measure, is determined by, and proportioned to the tendency which he conceives it to have to augment or to diminish the happiness of the community: or in other words, to its conformity or unconformity to the laws or dictates of utility.

10. Of an action that is conformable to the principle of utility, one may always say either that it is one that ought to be done, or at least that it is not one that ought not to be done. One may say also, that it is right it should be done; at least that it is not wrong it should be done: that it is a right action; at least that it is not a wrong action. When thus interpreted, the words *ought,* and *right* and *wrong,* and others of that stamp, have a meaning: when otherwise, they have none.

11. Has the rectitude of this principle been ever formally contested? It should seem that it had, by those who have not known what they have been meaning. Is it susceptible of any direct proof? it should seem not: for that which is used to prove every thing else, cannot itself be

proved: a chain of proofs must have their commencement somewhere. To give such proof is as impossible as it is needless.

12. Not that there is or ever has been that human creature breathing, however stupid or perverse, who has not on many, perhaps on most occasions of his life, deferred to it. By the natural constitution of the human frame, on most occasions of their lives men in general embrace this principle, without thinking of it: if not for the ordering of their own actions, yet for the trying of their own actions, as well as of those of other men. There have been, at the same time, not many, perhaps, even of the most intelligent, who have been disposed to embrace it purely and without reserve. There are even few who have not taken some occasion or other to quarrel with it, either on account of their not understanding always how to apply it, or on account of some prejudice or other which they were afraid to examine into, or could not bear to part with. For such is the stuff that man is made of: in principle and in practice, in a right track and in a wrong one, the rarest of all human qualities is consistency.

13. When a man attempts to combat the principle of utility, it is with reasons drawn, without his being aware of it, from that very principle itself. His arguments, if they prove any thing, prove not that the principle is *wrong*, but that, according to the applications he supposes to be made of it, it is *misapplied*. Is it possible for a man to move the earth? Yes; but he must first find out another earth to stand upon.

14. To disprove the propriety of it by arguments is impossible; but, from the causes that have been mentioned, or from some confused or partial view of it, a man may happen to be disposed not to relish it. Where this is the case, if he thinks the settling of his opinions on such a subject worth the trouble, let him take the following steps, and at length, perhaps, he may come to reconcile himself to it.

(1) Let him settle with himself, whether he would wish to discard this principle altogether; if so, let him consider what it is that all his reasonings (in matters of politics especially) can amount to?

(2) If he would, let him settle with himself, whether he would judge and act without any principle, or whether there is any other he would judge and act by?

(3) If there be, let him examine and satisfy himself whether the principle he thinks he has found is really any separate intelligible principle; or whether it be not a mere principle in words, a kind of phrase, which at bottom expresses neither more nor less than the mere averment of his own unfounded sentiments; that is, what in another person he might be apt to call *caprice?*

(4) If he is inclined to think that his own approbation or disapprobation, annexed to the idea of an act, without any regard to its conse-

quences, is a sufficient foundation for him to judge and act upon, let him ask himself whether his sentiment is to be a standard of right and wrong, with respect to every other man, or whether every man's sentiment has the same privilege of being a standard to itself?

(5) In the first case, let him ask himself whether his principle is not despotical, and hostile to all the rest of human race?

(6) In the second case, whether it is not anarchical, and whether at this rate there are not as many different standards of right and wrong as there are men? and whether even to the same man, the same thing, which is right today, may not (without the least change in its nature) be wrong to-morrow? and whether the same thing is not right and wrong in the same place at the same time? and in either case, whether all argument is not at an end? and whether, when two men have said, "I like this," and "I don't like it," they can (upon such a principle) have any thing more to say?

(7) If he should have said to himself, No: for that the sentiment which he proposes as a standard must be grounded on reflection, let him say on what particulars the reflection is to turn? if on particulars having relation to the utility of the act, then let him say whether this is not deserting his own principle, and borrowing assistance from that very one in opposition to which he sets it up: or if not on those particulars, on what other particulars?

(8) If he should be for compounding the matter, and adopting his own principle in part, and the principle of utility in part, let him say how far he will adopt it?

(9) When he has settled with himself where he will stop, then let him ask himself how he justifies to himself the adopting it so far? and why he will not adopt it any farther?

(10) Admitting any other principle than the principle of utility to be a right principle, a principle that it is right for a man to pursue; admitting (what is not true) that the word *right* can have a meaning without reference to utility, let him say whether there is any such thing as a *motive* that a man can have to pursue the dictates of it: if there is, let him say what that motive is, and how it is to be distinguished from those which enforce the dictates of utility: if not, then lastly let him say what it is this other principle can be good for?

Chapter II. Of Principles Adverse to that of Utility

1. If the principle of utility be a right principle to be governed by, and that in all cases, it follows from what has been just observed, that whatever principle differs from it in any case must necessarily be a

wrong one. To prove any other principle, therefore, to be a wrong one, there needs no more than just to show it to be what it is, a principle of which the dictates are in some point or other different from those of the principle of utility: to state it is to confute it. . . .

3. By the principle of asceticism I mean that principle, which, like the principle of utility, approves or disapproves of any action, according to the tendency which it appears to have to augment or diminish the happiness of the party whose interest is in question; but in an inverse manner: approving of actions in as far as they tend to diminish his happiness; disapproving of them in as far as they tend to augment it. . . .

9. The principle of asceticism seems originally to have been the reverie of certain hasty speculators, who having perceived, or fancied, that certain pleasures, when reaped in certain circumstances, have, at the long run, been attended with pains more than equivalent to them, took occasion to quarrel with every thing that offered itself under the name of pleasure. Having then got thus far, and having forgot the point which they set out from, they pushed on, and went so much further as to think it meritorious to fall in love with pain. Even this, we see, is at bottom but the principle of utility misapplied.

10. The principle of utility is capable of being consistently pursued; and it is but tautology to say, that the more consistently it is pursued, the better it must ever be for human-kind. The principle of asceticism never was, nor ever can be, consistently pursued by any living creature. Let but one tenth part of the inhabitants of this earth pursue it consistently, and in a day's time they will have turned it into a hell.

11. Among principles adverse to that of utility, that which at this day seems to have most influence in matters of government, is what may be called the principle of sympathy and antipathy. By the principle of sympathy and antipathy, I mean that principle which approves or disapproves of certain actions, not on account of their tending to augment the happiness, nor yet on account of their tending to diminish the happiness of the party whose interest is in question, but merely because a man finds himself disposed to approve or disapprove of them: holding up that approbation or disapprobation as a sufficient reason for itself, and disclaiming the necessity of looking out for any extrinsic ground. Thus far in the general department of morals: and in the particular department of politics, measuring out the quantum (as well as determining the ground) of punishment, by the degree of the disapprobation. . . .

13. In looking over the catalogue of human actions (says a partisan of this principle) in order to determine which of them are to be marked with the seal of disapprobation, you need but to take counsel of your own feelings: whatever you find in yourself a propensity to condemn, is

wrong for that very reason. For the same reason it is also meet for punishment: in what proportion it is adverse to utility, or whether it be adverse to utility at all, is a matter that makes no difference. In that same *proportion* also is it meet for punishment: if you hate much, punish much: if you hate little, punish little: punish as you hate. If you hate not at all, punish not at all: the fine feelings of the soul are not to be overborne and tyrannized by the harsh and rugged dictates of political utility.

14. The various systems that have been formed concerning the standard of right and wrong, may all be reduced to the principle of sympathy and antipathy. One account may serve for all of them. They consist all of them in so many contrivances for avoiding the obligation of appealing to any external standard, and for prevailing upon the reader to accept of the author's sentiment or opinion as a reason and that a sufficient one for itself. The phrases different, but the principle the same. . . .

Chapter IV. Value of a Lot of Pleasure or Pain, How to be Measured

1. Pleasures then, and the avoidance of pains, are the *ends* which the legislator has in view: it behoves him therefore to understand their *value.* Pleasures and pains are the *instruments* he has to work with: it behoves him therefore to understand their force, which is again, in another point of view, their value.

2. To a person considered *by himself,* the value of a pleasure or pain considered *by itself,* will be greater or less, according to the four following circumstances.

(1) Its *intensity.*

(2) Its *duration.*

(3) Its *certainty* or *uncertainty.*

(4) Its *propinquity* or *remoteness.*

3. These are the circumstances which are to be considered in estimating a pleasure or a pain considered each of them by itself. But when the value of any pleasure or pain is considered for the purpose of estimating the tendency of any *act* by which it is produced, there are two other circumstances to be taken into the account; these are,

(5) Its *fecundity,* or the chance it has of being followed by sensations of the *same* kind: that is, pleasures, if it be a pleasure: pains, if it be a pain.

(6) Its *purity,* or the chance it has of *not* being followed by sensations of the *opposite* kind: that is, pains, if it be a pleasure: pleasures, if it be a pain.

These two last, however, are in strictness scarcely to be deemed properties of the pleasure or the pain itself; they are not, therefore, in strictness to be taken into the account of the value of that pleasure or that pain. They are in strictness to be deemed properties only of the act, or other event, by which such pleasure or pain has been produced; and accordingly are only to be taken into the account of the tendency of such act or such event.

4. To a *number* of persons, with reference to each of whom the value of a pleasure or a pain is considered, it will be greater or less, according to seven circumstances: to wit, the six preceding ones; viz.

(1) Its *intensity*.

(2) Its *duration*.

(3) Its *certainty* or *uncertainty*.

(4) Its *propinquity* or *remoteness*.

(5) Its *fecundity*.

(6) Its *purity*.

And one other; to wit:

(7) Its *extent;* that is, the number of persons to whom it *extends;* or (in other words) who are affected by it.

5. To take an exact account then of the general tendency of any act, by which the interests of a community are affected, proceed as follows. Begin with any one person of those whose interests seem most immediately to be affected by it: and take an account,

(1) Of the value of each distinguishable *pleasure* which appears to be produced by it in the *first* instance.

(2) Of the value of each *pain* which appears to be produced by it in the *first* instance.

(3) Of the value of each pleasure which appears to be produced by it *after* the first. This constitutes the *fecundity* of the first *pleasure* and the *impurity* of the first *pain*.

(4) Of the value of each *pain* which appears to be produced by it after the first. This constitutes the *fecundity* of the first *pain*, and the *impurity* of the first pleasure.

(5) Sum up all the values of all the *pleasures* on the one side, and those of all the *pains* on the other. The balance, if it be on the side of pleasure, will give the *good* tendency of the act upon the whole, with respect to the interests of that *individual* person; if on the side of pain, the *bad* tendency of it upon the whole.

(6) Take an account of the *number* of persons whose interests appear to be concerned; and repeat the above process with respect to each. *Sum up* the numbers expressive of the degrees of *good* tendency, which the act has, with respect to each individual, in regard to whom the tend-

ency of it is *good* upon the whole: do this again with respect to each individual, in regard to whom the tendency of it is *good* upon the whole: do this again with respect to each individual, in regard to whom the tendency of it is *bad* upon the whole. Take the *balance;* which, if on the side of *pleasure,* will give the general *good tendency* of the act, with respect to the total number or community of individuals concerned; if on the side of pain, the general *evil tendency,* with respect to the same community.

6. It is not to be expected that this process should be strictly pursued previously to every moral judgment, or to every legislative or judicial operation. It may, however, be always kept in view: and as near as the process actually pursued on these occasions approaches to it, so near will such process approach to the character of an exact one.

7. The same process is alike applicable to pleasure and pain, in whatever shape they appear: and by whatever denomination they are distinguished: to pleasure, whether it be called *good* (which is properly the cause or instrument of pleasure) or *profit* (which is distant pleasure, or the cause or instrument of distant pleasure,) or *convenience,* or *advantage, benefit, emolument, happiness,* and so forth: to pain, whether it be called *evil,* (which corresponds to *good*) or *mischief,* or *inconvenience,* or *disadvantage,* or *loss,* or *unhappiness,* and so forth.

8. Nor is this a novel and unwarranted, any more than it is a useless theory. In all this there is nothing but what the practice of mankind, wheresoever they have a clear view of their own interest, is perfectly conformable to. An article of property, an estate in land, for instance, is valuable, on what account? On account of the pleasures of all kinds which it enables a man to produce, and what comes to the same thing the pains of all kinds which it enables him to avert. But the value of such an article of property is universally understood to rise or fall according to the length or shortness of the time which a man has in it: the certainty or uncertainty of its coming into possession: and the nearness or remoteness of the time at which, if at all, it is to come into possession. As to the *intensity* of the pleasures which a man may derive from it, this is never thought of, because it depends upon the use which each particular person may come to make of it; which cannot be estimated till the particular pleasures he may come to derive from it, or the particular pains he may come to exclude by means of it, are brought to view. For the same reason, neither does he think of the *fecundity* or *purity* of those pleasures. . . .

Chapter VII. Of Human Actions in General

1. The business of government is to promote the happiness of the society, by punishing and rewarding. That part of its business which con-

sists in punishing, is more particularly the subject of penal law. In proportion as an act tends to disturb that happiness, in proportion as the tendency of it is pernicious, will be the demand it creates for punishment. What happiness consists of we have already seen: enjoyment of pleasures, security from pains.

2. The general tendency of an act is more or less pernicious, according to the sum total of its consequences: that is, according to the difference between the sum of such as are good, and the sum of such as are evil.

3. It is to be observed, that here, as well as henceforward, whereever consequences are spoken of, such only are meant as are *material.* Of the consequences of any act, the multitude and variety must needs be infinite: but such of them only as are material are worth regarding. Now among the consequences of an act, be they what they may, such only, by one who views them in the capacity of a legislator, can be said to be material, as either consist of pain or pleasure, or have an influence in the production of pain or pleasure.

4. It is also to be observed, that into the account of the consequences of the act, are to be taken not such only as might have ensued, were intention out of the question, but such also as depend upon the connexion there may be between these first-mentioned consequences and the intention. The connexion there is between the intention and certain consequences is, as we shall see hereafter, a means of producing other consequences. In this lies the difference between rational agency and irrational.

5. Now the intention, with regard to the consequences of an act, will depend upon two things: 1. The state of the will or intention, with respect to the act itself. And, 2. The state of the understanding, or perceptive faculties, with regard to the circumstances which it is, or may appear to be, accompanied with. Now with respect to these circumstances, the perceptive faculty is susceptible of three states: consciousness, unconsciousness, and false consciousness. Consciousness, when the party believes precisely those circumstances, and no others, to subsist, which really do subsist: unconsciousness, when he fails of perceiving certain circumstances to subsist, which, however, do subsist: false consciousness, when he believes or imagines certain circumstances to subsist, which in truth do not subsist.

6. In every transaction, therefore, which is examined with a view to punishment, there are four articles to be considered: 1. The *act* itself, which is done. 2. The *circumstances* in which it is done. 3. The *intentionality* that may have accompanied it. 4. The *consciousness,* unconsciousness, or false consciousness, that may have accompanied it. . . .

Chapter VIII. Of Intentionality

1. So much with regard to the two first of the articles upon which the evil tendency of an action may depend: viz. the act itself, and the general assemblage of the circumstances with which it may have been accompanied. We come now to consider the ways in which the particular circumstance of *intention* may be concerned in it.

2. First, then, the intention or will may regard either of two objects: 1. The act itself: or, 2. Its consequences. Of these objects, that which the intention regards may be styled *intentional.* If it regards the act, then the act may be said to be intentional: if the consequences, so also then may the consequences. If it regards both the act and consequences, the whole *action* may be said to be intentional. Whichever of those articles is not the object of the intention, may of course be said to be *unintentional.*

3. The act may very easily be intentional without the consequences; and often is so. Thus, you may intend to touch a man, without intending to hurt him: and yet, as the consequences turn out, you may chance to hurt him. . . .

Chapter XVII. Of the Limits of the Penal Branch of Jurisprudence

8. Now private ethics has happiness for its end: and legislation can have no other. Private ethics concerns every member, that is, the happiness and the actions of every member of any community that can be proposed; and legislation can concern no more. Thus far, then, private ethics and the art of legislation go hand in hand. The end they have, or ought to have, in view, is of the same nature. The persons whose happiness they ought to have in view, as also the persons whose conduct they ought to be occupied in directing, are precisely the same. The very acts they ought to be conversant about, are even in a *great measure* the same. Where then lies the difference? In that the acts which they ought to be conversant about, though in a great measure, are not *perfectly and throughout* the same. There is no case in which a private man ought not to direct his own conduct to the production of his own happiness, and of that of his fellow-creatures: but there are cases in which the legislator ought not (in a direct way at least, and by means of punishment applied immediately to particular *individual* acts) to attempt to direct the conduct of the several other members of the community. Every act which promises to be beneficial upon the whole to the community (himself included) each individual ought to perform of himself: but it is not every such act that the legislator ought to compel him to perform. Every act which promises to be pernicious upon the whole to the community (himself in-

cluded) each individual ought to abstain from of himself: but it is not every such act that the legislator ought to compel him to abstain from.

9. Where then is the line to be drawn?—We shall not have far to seek for it. The business is to give an idea of the cases in which ethics ought, and in which legislation ought not (in a direct manner at least) to interfere. If legislation interferes in a direct manner, it must be by punishment. Now the cases in which punishment, meaning the punishment of the political sanction, ought not to be inflicted, have been already stated. If then there be any of these cases in which, although legislation ought not, private ethics does or ought to interfere, these cases will serve to point out the limits between the two arts or branches of science. These cases, it may be remembered, are of four sorts: 1. Where punishment would be groundless. 2. Where it would be inefficacious. 3. Where it would be unprofitable. 4. Where it would be needless. Let us look over all these cases, and see whether in any of them there is room for the interference of private ethics, at the same time that there is none for the direct interference of legislation. . . .

II. THE RELATIONSHIP BETWEEN ETHICS AND LAW

F. S. Cohen, Ethical Systems and Legal Ideals*

Chapter 1. The Ethical Basis of Legal Criticism

1. The Problems of Legal Criticism

. . . An ethics, like a metaphysics, is no more certain and no less dangerous because it is unconsciously held. There are few judges, psychoanalysts, or economists today who do not begin a consideration of their typical problems with some formula designed to cause all moral ideals to disappear and to produce an issue purified for the procedure of positive empirical science. But the ideals have generally retired to hats from which later wonders will magically arise. A historical school of law disclaims concern with ethics[1] and repeatedly invokes a *Zeitgeist* or a

*[Pp. 3-7, 16-17, 18-21, 21-28 (Falcon Press 1933). Reprinted by permission. For biographical information, see page 73 supra.]

1. See Savigny, *"Ueber den Zweck dieser Zeitschrift "* (1815) 1 *Zeitschrift für geschicht. Rechtswissenschaft* pp. 4-5; Maine, *Early History of Institutions* (7th ed. 1914) p. 370 and Lectures 12 and 13 passim.

Volksgeist to decide what the law ought to be.[2] An analytical school of jurisprudence again dismisses questions of morality,[3] and again decides what the law ought to be by reference to a so-called logical ideal, which is not an ideal of logic at all, but an aesthetic ideal of symmetrical analogical development.[4] Those who derive the law from the will of the sovereign usually introduce without further justification the premise that it is good to obey that will.[5] And those who define law in terms of actually prevailing social demands or interests make frequent use of the undisclosed principle that these demands *ought* to be satisfied.[6]

The objection, then, is not that jurists have renounced ethical judgment but that they have renounced ethical science. Ethical science involves an analysis of ethical judgments, a clarification of ethical premises. Among the current legal crypto-idealisms there can be no edifying con-

2. See J. C. Carter, *The Proposed Codification of our Common Law* (A Paper Prepared at the Request of the Committee of the Bar Association of the City of New York, Appointed to Oppose the Measure) (1884) pp. 86 et seq. This pamphlet is largely based upon Savigny's essay, *The Vocation of Our Age for Legislation and Jurisprudence* (1814, trans. by Hayward 1831), which was written under somewhat similar circumstances in answer to the demand for codification of German law (See Thibaut, *Ueber die Nothwendigkeit eines allgemeinen bürgerlichen Rechts für Deutschland,* reprinted in Thibaut, *Civilistische Abhandlungen* [1814] p. 404).

It was characteristic that Maine's famous generalization "the movement of the progressive societies has hitherto been a movement *from Status to Contract*" (*Ancient Law* [1861] ch. 5), was proposed and generally received as an indication of the *desirability* of free contract.

3. See Amos, *Science of Jurisprudence* (1872) p. 18; Pollock, *Essays in Jurisprudence and Ethics* (1882) ch. 1. (The Nature of Jurisprudence), pp. 18-32.

4. A good example of this ethical use of analysis is found in the development of the *prima facie* theory of torts (See Pollock, *Law of Torts,* 1st ed. [1887] ch. 1), which purports to be merely an analysis of what has always been the law but actually gives the old doctrine of conspiracy a new impetus (see Note [1930] 30 *Columbia Law Rev.* 510), and threatens to extend the vagaries of that doctrine over individual conduct.

5. "Legislatures and courts formulate or seek to formulate the will of all of us as to the conduct of each of us in our relations with each other and with all. That will ought to be wholly effective. That it fails of effect in any degree is a misfortune." Pound, "Enforcement of Law" (1908) 20 *Green Bag* 401.

6. "In the actual practice of courts and jurists, after stating claims or demands in general terms as social interests, attempt is made, more or less consciously, to secure as much as possible of the whole scheme of social interests with the least sacrifice. This is the pragmatist ethical principle stated by William James. How far it is a sound ethical criterion we need not inquire. . . . The task of the jurist is to make us conscious of the method that actually obtains and to give it more precision. He should aim at all times, and in all the compromises and adjustments and reconcilings involved in the legal order, to give effect to as much of the whole body of social interests as possible." Pound, "Jurisprudence" in *History and Prospects of the Social Sciences* (1925) p. 472. See also Pound, *Introduction to the Philosophy of Law* (1922) pp. 95-99.

troversy, since there is no recognition of the moral issues to which their differences reduce. One looks in vain in legal treatises and law-review articles for legal criticism conscious of its moral presuppositions. The vocabularies of logic and aesthetics are freely drawn upon in the attempt to avoid the disagreeable assertion that something or other is intrinsically better than something else. Particular decisions or legal rules are "anomalous" or "illogical," "incorrect" or "impractical," "reactionary" or "liberal," and unarguable ethical innuendo takes the place of critical analysis.[7] Little wonder then that on a more abstract plane of thought the classification of ideas has taken the place of legal philosophy,[8] while Hegelian pictures of inevitable trends are offered as substitutes for the delineation of the desirable.[9]

But the relevance of ethics to the philosophy of law would be clear

7. One might expect to find in the American Law Institute's attempted "Restatements" of various branches of the common law some attempt to work out the meaning of controversial rules of law in terms of social consequences and some indication of the moral standards which make the rule laid down in Mississippi (say) preferable to the rule laid down in Ohio. Instead, one meets the pious fiction, implicit in the very title of the enterprise, that the common law is a system within which intellectual inspection reveals a definite answer for every legal question. Decisions are hailed as "correct" or "incorrect" rather than "good" or "bad," and truth is obtained either in accordance with the mathematical precepts of the Valentinian Law of Citations (426 A.D.), or by projecting evolutionary "tendencies" found in the past decisions of courts, or by reacting aesthetically to the harmony or discord between a questioned rule and the rest of the legal "system." Cf. the strictures of Professor Kantorowicz upon the German Civil Code, in *Rechtswissenschaft und Soziologie* (1911) p. 8.

8. All who appreciate Dean Pound's unparalleled equipment in legal philosophy must hope that such taxonomic studies as *Law and Morals* (1924); "The Scope and Purpose of Sociological Jurisprudence" (1911) 24 *Harvard Law Rev.* 591, (1911-12) 25 *Harvard Law Rev.* 140, 489; "The End of Law as Developed in Legal Rules and Doctrines" (1914) 27 *Harvard Law Rev.* 195; "The End of Law as Developed in Juristic Thought" (1914) 27 *Harvard Law Rev.* 605, (1917) 30 *Harvard Law Rev.* 201, are preludes to some affirmative statement of valid legal standards or ideals.

9. Courts frequently rely not on actual decisions but on tendencies in series of past decisions. The fact that two earlier cases have each stretched a rule a little further than existing precedents in each case warranted is taken to indicate the desirability of stretching the rule still further in a third case. The assumption seems to be that all change is for the better and is infinitely capable of extension. The philosophical generalization of this type of argument is, of course, evolutionism. Dean Pound has frequently followed Hegel, Marx, and Spencer in putting forward evolutionary schemes of legal history in answer to strictly ethical questions. See *Introduction to the Philosophy of Law* (1922) pp. 95-99; "Justice According to Law" (1913) 13 *Columbia Law Rev.* 696 (1914); 14 *Columbia Law Rev.* 1, 103, esp. at 117-121; "The Theory of Judicial Decision" (1923) 36 *Harvard Law Rev.* 641, 802, 940, esp. at 954-958. But this identification of the inevitable and the desirable under the banner of Progress is, as Huxley, Sidgwick, G. E. Moore, and M. R. Cohen have demonstrated, intellectually indefensible, however gratifying emotionally it may be to feel that cheering for the winning side is the substance of morality.

even if it were not unconsciously assumed by those who appear to deny or to ignore the connection. For ethics is the study of the meaning and application of judgments of *good, bad, right, wrong*, etc., and every valuation of law involves an ethical judgment. When we say, for instance, that a given law is bad, that one judicial decision is better than another, that the American constitution ought to be revised, or that laws ought to be obeyed, we are passing judgments whose truth or falsity cannot be established without a consideration of ethics. That portion of jurisprudence which is not concerned merely with the positive nature of law or with its technical relation to assumed ends is, accordingly, a part of the domain of ethics.

There is no way of avoiding this ultimate responsibility of law to ethics. Every final determination of the general end of law, the standard of legal criticism, (whether this be labeled "justice," "natural law," "the protection of natural rights," or "the organization of social interests"), must reduce to the general form, "The law ought to bring about as much good as it can."

Our problem is to give content to this formal principle by defining the nature of the good and indicating the extent of the law's actual powers over the realm. . . .

4. Law and the Good Life

On the basis of the foregoing definitions the indispensability of ethics in legal criticism is immediately obvious. Ethics involves all final applications of the terms *good, bad,* etc. We may decide whether law is good for strengthening social bonds or bad for the peace of mind of criminals, without any appeal to ethics, but when we come to the question of whether the strengthening of social bonds or the peace of mind of criminals is good, and whether law which has the described effects is good, we are in the realm of ethics. Thus every valuation of law, every formulation of the ideal object or end of law, must be either categorical and ethical, or conditional, in terms of some ulterior aim which can itself be valued ethically. In either case, there is no way of escaping the final responsibility of law to ethics, and, since the field of law lies within the field of human conduct, to morality.[20] It is the task of legal philosophy to demonstrate the precise scope and character of those ethical judgments which form the base or the content of valuations of law. . . .

20. Cf. Laird, *Study in Moral Theory* (1926) pp. 26-29; Demogue, *Analysis of Fundamental Notions* (1911, trans. by Scott and Chamberlain 1916), in *Modern French Legal Philosophy*, Modern Legal Philosophy Series, vol. 7 §§206-221; Pound, "Jurisprudence," in *History and Prospects of the Social Sciences* (1925) p. 472.

. . . It is certainly true that we cannot calculate all the effects of law or of anything else. And it is equally obvious that our knowledge of ethics and of human nature is not great enough to permit us to describe completely and in detail what constitutes the good life for each person or even for man in the abstract. But if there is any such thing as human knowledge, we certainly have enough of it upon both these subjects to formulate definite problems and to reject unsatisfactory solutions. And, as a great French jurist, M. Pierre Tourtoulon, has said, "There is no need to throw to the dogs everything that is not fit for the altars of the gods." A recognition of the inadequacy of our knowledge in these fields can bring a sweet scepticism into our political beliefs, but it cannot deny them. To quote again from Tourtoulon, "The greatest jurist has only very vague ideas concerning the services that the laws which he expounds and explains render to society. . . . The first step toward wisdom is the knowledge that we are ignorant of nearly all the functions of our laws, or of the evil or the good which they may bring us."[24] And one more quotation: "A little scepticism will render him [the judge] more scrupulous, more indulgent to every one and consequently more just."[25]

The inadequacy of human knowledge, we may fairly assume, does not destroy the usefulness of our fundamental principle of legal criticism. In fact, a judgment of ethical values the truth of which is recognized to be partially dependent upon the accuracy of human scientific knowledge, seems to be far more useful than the sort of judgment which assumes that, however uncertain the physical results of an act may be, we can know clearly in advance whether they will be good or bad.[26]

. . . In this field of the valuation of law, as in most other domains of thought, confusion is a more potent source of evil than is error. A formal principle of this sort cannot insure against error, but it can bring light to the foundations of our thinking. It can bring our traditional legal controversies into the fertilizing context of ethical science. It can free legal criticism from blind deduction from obsolete moral postulates. It can illumine "social engineering" by inducing a critical attitude towards the

24. Tourtoulon, *Philosophy in the Development of Law* (1919, trans. by Read 1922), Modern Legal Philosophy Series, vol. 13, p. 24.

25. Ibid. p. 487.

26. Cf. Bentham, "The Influence of Time and Place in Matters of Legislation" ch. 3, 1 *Works* (ed. by Bowring, 1843) 183: "In all such matters, the cautious statesman will avoid the tone of peremptoriness and decision: his conclusions will always, in the first instance, be hypothetical. If such and such events are the likeliest to take place: But are they? This is a matter which ought to be stated as accompanied with the degree of uncertainty that belongs to it. Beware of those who by the vehemence of their assertions, by the confidence of their predictions, make up for the weakness of their reasons."

social interests that the law is asked to protect.[27] It can bring legal scholarship into a more intimate contact with practical legal problems by reminding jurists that logical, historical, and sociological analyses of law are merely necessary introductions to the argument: This decision or statute is desirable because in some way it promotes the good life. . . .

5. Crypto-Idealism

No less significant and important, then, must be the consequences of a denial of this basic principle. For although it is, indeed a truism, it is not a commonplace. The ignoring or tacit repudiation of this principle is extremely general in juristic literature, although few legal writers have made their disavowal explicit. To M. Leon Duguit we may profitably appeal for a statement of the typical position that the field of law is independent of ethics and morality. To show the inadequacy of his doctrine is to point to the fallacy upon which a vast amount of legal philosophizing is squarely based.

Law, according to Duguit, has for its sole purpose social solidarity. Solidarity, he insists, is a fact, not a rule of conduct. "It is not an imperative."[28] Duguit shows inductively that law makes for social solidarity and that such solidarity is a feature of all societies. But, as with so many other jurists, this inductive generalization suffers a gradual metamorphosis[29]

27. The current notion that the function of the jurist is simply to secure adequate enforcement for the expressed demands of society (see L. K. Frank, "Institutional Analysis of the Law" (1924) 24 *Columbia Law Rev.* 480, 497-498 for an interesting *reductio ad absurdum* of this view) derives from a dangerous metaphor. Society is not vocal. The expressed demands of society are the demands of vocally organized groups, and a discreet deference to the power of such groups should not lead us to confuse their demands with "social welfare." Cf. Judge Hough's criticism of this confusion in his review of Dean Pound's *Spirit of the Common Law,* in (1922) 22 *Columbia Law Rev.* 385: "The present lecturer can and does sum up the judicial duty of decision by saying that the jurists of today (and judges are presumably jurists) are content to seek the jural postulates of the civilization of the time,—a phrase extremely easy of translation into keeping one's ear to the ground to hear the tramp of insistent crowds."

28. Duguit, *Theory of Objective Law Anterior to the State* (1901, trans. by Scott and Chamberlain 1916), in *Modern French Legal Philosophy,* Modern Legal Philosophy Series, vol. 7, p. 259.

29. Professor Husik, in a review of Tourtoulon's *Philosophy in the Development of Law* (71 *U. of Pa. Law Rev.* (1923) 416, 418-419) thus summarizes the procedure: " . . . one starts with the proposition, 'Men live in society,' which is perfectly true, and ends up with the statement, 'The aim of the life of the individual is to contribute to the development of the social body,' which is far from being a scientific statement and may easily be denied. Moreover if the last proposition is intended as imposing an obligation, it can never be logically derived from the statement of a fact. Most if not all the books dealing with natural law by advocates of that doctrine, such as Thomas Aquinas, Grotius, Lorimer, are guilty of this fallacy."

and is finally used as the sole basis for such commands or ethical judgments as the following: "Respect every act of individual will determined by an end of social solidarity";[30] "Every individual ought to abstain from any act that would be determined by an end contrary to social solidarity";[31] "It is a crime to preach the struggle of classes."[32] Since it is impossible to derive the goodness of an act from its frequency or universality, Duguit's judgments can be true only if the doctrine of solidarity is, in contradiction to his own claims, an ethical imperative. It seems fair to characterize such a position as crypto-idealism. Duguit has not gotten rid of ethics at all, as he proposes to do, but he has agreed not to use the word "ethics" lest his extremely shaky ethical system be challenged.[33]

Although Duguit's aversion to the concepts of ethics may seem to be the product of philosophical *naïveté,* he can claim the support of many philosophers for the faulty method by which he actually builds up his ethical system. Bertrand Russell thus analyzes the method:

> It may be laid down that every ethical system is based upon a certain *non sequitur.* The philosopher first invents a false theory as to the nature of things, and then deduces that wicked actions are those which show that his theory is false. To begin with the traditional Christian: he argues that, since everything always obeys the will of God, wickedness consists in disobedience to the will of God. We then come on to the Hegelian, who argues that the universe consists of parts which harmonize in a perfect organism, and therefore wickedness consists of behavior which diminishes the harmony—though it is difficult to see how such behavior is possible, since complete harmony is metaphysically necessary. Bergson . . . shows that human beings never behave mechanically, and then, in his book on *Laughter,* he argues that what makes us laugh is to see a person behaving mechanically—i.e. you are ridiculous when you do something that shows Bergson's philosophy to be false, and only then. These examples have, I hope, made it plain that metaphysic can never have ethical consequences except in virtue of its falsehood: if it were true, the acts which it defines as sin would be impossible.[34]

30. Duguit, op. cit. p. 290.

31. Ibid. p. 292.

32. Duguit, *Changes of Principle in the Field of Liberty, Contract, Liability, and Property* (1912, trans. by Register 1918), in *The Progress of Continental Law in the Nineteenth Century,* Continental Legal History Series, vol. 11, p. 135.

33. M. Duguit naïvely confesses to having experienced some disquietude with his ultimate appeal to social fact when German armies vanquished Belgium. But the final punishment of Germany apparently convinced him that social force is its own justification. "Objective Law" (1920-1921) 20 *Columbia Law Rev.* 817, 21 *Columbia Law Rev.* 17, 126, 242, esp. 254-256.

34. *Sceptical Essays* (1928), ch. 7 (Behaviorism and Values), p. 91.

The application of this analysis has been modestly underestimated by Mr. Russell. For all ethical theories which are extracted from positive thought, scientific as well as metaphysical, show a similar weakness. Everything obeys the law of evolution. Therefore those societies that do not obey the law of evolution are inferior. All commercial transactions take place in accordance with the laws of supply and demand. Therefore every interference with the laws of supply and demand is undesirable. All law springs from the national spirit. Therefore law which does not spring from this spirit (code law, etc.) is bad.[35] It is unnecessary to multiply examples.

The abduction of law from the domain of morality is defended by Professor Morgan in a slightly different manner. "It must be remembered," he writes, "that the law does not have the same purpose as religion or ethics or morals. It is not concerned with developing the spiritual or moral character of the individual but with regulating his objective conduct toward his fellows. Consequently courts will have to formulate and apply some rules which have no relation at all to morals, some which have to place a loss upon one of two equally blameless persons, some which impose liability regardless of fault and some which refuse to penalize conduct denounced by even the morally blind. It must be apparent that the moral law has no mandate upon the content of the rules of the road."[36]

This position is so representative of the class of theories we are considering, and so generally accepted, at least in our American law schools, that it may be worth while to point out in detail some of the ambiguities and fallacies it involves. In the first sentence we are told that law does not have the same *purpose* as religion or ethics or morals. It is upon the ambiguity of this word that the specious force of the rest of the argument depends. If the word refers to the state of mind of judges or legislators, the assertion that this differs from the state of mind of moralists, ethical philosophers and religious leaders is perhaps true, but it is completely

---

35. It is only with the aid of this fallacy that the historical, analytical, metaphysical, and sociological schools of jurisprudence are able to wage civil war. Were the interests of these schools properly confined to the history, the internal analysis, the metaphysical status, and the sociological functioning of law, respectively, conflict would be impossible and we should see, instead, simply a salutary division of labor. But each school has smuggled an ethics into its positive studies. To the argument of the historicists that since law is a product of national custom, the *Rechtsgefühl,* or the *Volksgeist,* it *ought* to follow these lines, the analytical school replies that since law is the command of the sovereign or the ruling of the courts, it *ought* to obey these latter masters. Jurists of metaphysical and sociological persuasion add to the heat of the fray with equally invalid brands of crypto-idealism.

36. E. M. Morgan, *Introduction to the Study of Law* (1926) pp. 32-33.

irrelevant to Professor Morgan's ethical conclusions as to what the law ought to do. If by the *purpose* of law is meant that at which law *ought* to aim, the statement is relevant, indeed basic, to his further conclusions, but obviously false. For the law ought to secure the good life, which is the *ideal* purpose of moral and religious rule as well.

In the second sentence of this excerpt we are told that law is *not concerned* with certain noble ends. Again, the same basic ambiguity. If the law is not actually concerned with man's spiritual or moral character, that is an unfortunate fact which we ought to remedy. But if this assertion means that the law ought not to be determined by such factors, it is simply false. Man's moral life is fundamentally moulded by rules of property law, family law, etc., and the refusal to follow the meaning of such legal rules into their ultimate moral or spiritual implications is the essence of legalistic obscurantism.

In the next sentence, we are told that *consequently* courts *have to* formulate rules which have no relation at all to morals, and here the confusion between the *is* and the *ought* bears its first fruits. Thus far Morgan's statements can be justified on a positive interpretation, but if that interpretation be given, the inference of *have to* (apparently ethical) from *does* and *is* is clearly fallacious. Here an ethical interpretation of the foregoing premises is required, and that, we have seen, results in patent error.

Thus the resolution of the foregoing ambiguities leads us to a dilemma. Professor Morgan's inferences are, if valid, based upon false premises, and if based upon true premises, invalid. Their truth, as distinguished from the validity of their inference, can be defended, but only upon the assumption that the word *morality* is severed from reference to objective conduct and even to such problems of "inner belief" as are involved in the distribution of liability apart from fault, etc. Of course, if any one wishes to use the words *morality* and *ethics* in this milk-and-watery significance, no logical objection can be raised. But when such a use of terms results in, or springs from, the belief that judgments of good and bad can legitimately be applied only to man's secret intentions, we are called upon to point out that this is an indefensible theory of morality.

A great many other jurists attempt in one way or another to discover an end of law independent of ethics or morality. Korkunov writes, "Morality furnishes the criterion for the proper evaluation of our interests; law marks out the limits within which they ought to be confined."[37]But obviously law does not actually do this, and if the reply is made that at

---

37. Korkunov, *General Theory of Law* (1894, trans. by Hastings 1909), Modern Legal Philosophy Series, vol. 4, p. 52.

least law ought to do this, then we must turn to morality for the basis and significance of this *ought*. Vinogradoff writes, ". . . law is clearly distinguishable from morality. The object of law is the submission of the individual to the will of organized society, while the tendency of morality is to subject the individual to the dictates of his own conscience."[38] Berolzheimer supplies the following argument, based, it seems, upon the unpleasant connotations of the idea of *expediency:* "If all law has in view the welfare of society, then law abdicates in favor of administration; the ideal of political expediency displaces the idea of right."[39] It is unnecessary to multiply instances of this juristic attempt to abduct law from the domain of ethics and morality. For the writers who make the ideal end of law independent of morality never refrain from passing ethical or moral judgments upon law. They have simply rejected particular moral theories, such as that of the infallibility of conscience (Vinogradoff), believing, correctly, for the most part, that these doctrines are useless for jurisprudence, and incorrectly assuming that they are the whole of morality. A more or less unconscious moral standard is made the basis of their valuations of law, and while such a morality has frequently been more nearly correct than the current ethical theory which was rejected, the resulting confusions of thought have been atrocious.

The attempt to free legal criticism from an ethical and moral basis is logically doomed to failure and results practically only in the confusions of crypto-idealism. Law cannot be abducted from the domain and sovereignty of ethics simply because every abductor, in his own person, is bound by that sovereignty, and with his every step, enlarges that domain.

F. S. Cohen, Transcendental Nonsense and the Functional Approach*

4. Legal Criticism

It is perhaps the chief service of the functional approach that in cleansing legal rules, concepts, and institutions of the compulsive flavors of legal logic or metaphysics, room is made for conscious ethical criticism of law. In traditional jurisprudence, criticism, where it exists, is found masked in the protective camouflage of transcendental nonsense: "The law *must* (or *cannot*) be thus and so, because the *nature* of contracts, cor-

---

38. Vinogradoff, *Common Sense in Law* (1914) p. 58.
39. Berolzheimer, *Rechtsphilosophische Studien* (1903), ch.6, § 22.
*[35 *Colum. L. Rev.* 809, 847–849 (1935). Reprinted by permission. For biographical information, see page 73 supra.]

porations, or contingent remainders so requires." The functional approach permits ethics to come out of hiding. When we recognize that legal rules are simply formulae describing uniformities of judicial decision, that legal concepts likewise are patterns or functions of judicial decisions, that decisions themselves are not products of logical parthenogenesis born of pre-existing legal principles but are social events with social causes and consequences, then we are ready for the serious business of appraising law and legal institutions in terms of some standard of human values.

The importance for legal criticism of clear, objective description of judicial behavior, its causes and its consequences, is coming to be generally recognized. What is not so easily recognized is the importance for objective legal science of legal criticism.

Since the brilliant achievements of Bentham, descriptive legal science has made almost no progress in determining the consequences of legal rules.[93] This failure of scholarship, in the light of the encouraging progress of modern research into the antecedents and social context of judicial decision, calls for explanation.

Possibly this gap is to be explained in terms of an inherited assumption that statutes and decisions are self-executing, that the consequences of a law or a judgment are, therefore, clearly indicated by the language of the statute or decision itself, and that factual research is therefore a work of supererogation. Possibly this failure of research is to be explained in terms of the dominance of the private lawyer in our legal education. The private attorney is interested in the *causes* of judicial decisions, but his interest in consequences is likely to stop with the payment of a fee. I am inclined to think, however, that the failure of our legal scholarship in this direction may be attributed to a more fundamental difficulty. The prospect of determining the consequences of a given rule of law appears to be an infinite task, and is indeed an infinite task unless we approach it with some discriminating criterion of what consequences are *important*. Now a criterion of *importance* presupposes a criterion of values, which is precisely what modern thinkers of the "sociological" and "realistic" schools of jurisprudence have never had. Dean Pound has

---

93. The following spiritual exercise is recommended by Professor Kantorowicz. Let the unconverted lawyer or law student read a code of laws in the following way: "Let him ask himself with respect to each statement . . . what harms would social life undergo if instead of this statement the opposite were enacted. And then let him turn to all textbooks, commentaries, monographs and reports of decisions and see how many questions of this sort he will find answered and how many he will find even put." *Rechtswissenschaft und Soziologie* (1911) 8, quoted in Pound, supra note 91 [*The Scope and Purpose of Sociological Jurisprudence,* (1911-1912)], 25 *Harv. L. Rev.* 489, 513.

talked for many years of the "balancing" of interests, but without ever indicating which interests are more important than ŏthers or how a standard of weight or fineness can be constructed for the appraisal of "interests."[94] Contemporary "realists" have, in general, either denied absolutely that absolute standards of importance can exist,[95]or else insisted that we must thoroughly understand the facts as they are before we begin to evaluate them. Such a postponement of the problem of values is equivalent to its repudiation. We never shall thoroughly understand the facts as they are, and we are not likely to make much progress towards such understanding unless we at the same time bring into play a critical theory of values. In terms of such a theory, particular human desires and habits are important, and the task of research into legal consequences passes from the realm of vague curiosity to the problem form: How do these rules of law strengthen or change these important habits and satisfy or impede these important desires?

. . . The relation between positive legal science and legal criticism is not a relation of temporal priority, but of mutual dependence. [97] Legal criticism is empty without objective description of the causes and consequences of legal decisions. Legal description is blind without the guiding light of a theory of values. It is through the union of objective legal science and a critical theory of social values that our understanding of the human significance of law will be enriched. It is loyalty to this union of distinct disciplines that will mark whatever is of lasting importance in contemporary legal science and legal philosophy.

Kelsen, Pure Theory of Law*

I. Law and Nature

10. Law as a Part of Morals

Once law and morals are recognized as different kinds of normative systems, the question of the relationship of law and morals arises. This question has two meanings: One, What *is* the relationship between the

94. Cf. W. L. Grossman, *The Legal Philosophy of Roscoe Pound* (1935) 44 *Yale L. J.*605, 608-611; John C. H. Wu, *The Juristic Philosophy of Roscoe Pound* (1924) 18 *Ill. Law Rev.* 285, 294-304.

95. See U. Moore, *Rational Basis of Legal Institutions* (1923) 23 *Columbia Law Rev.* 609, 612; W. Nelles, Book Review (1933) 33 *Columbia Law Rev.* 763, 765-768.

97. I have attempted to trace these relations in some detail in *Ethical Systems and Legal Ideals* (1933) and again, more briefly and in words of one and two syllables, in *Modern Ethics and the Law* (1934) 4 *Brooklyn L. Rev. 33.*

*[Pp. 62-69 (1967). Published in 1967 by The Regents of the University of California; reprinted by permission of the University of California Press.

For biographical information, see page 173 supra.]

two? The other, What *ought* it be? If both questions are intermingled, misunderstandings result. The first question is sometimes answered by saying that law by its very nature is moral, which means that the behavior commanded or prohibited by legal norms is also commanded or prohibited by the moral norms. Furthermore, that if a social order commands a behavior prohibited by morals or prohibits a behavior commanded by morals, this order is not law, because it is not just. The question is also answered, however, by stating that the law may, but need not, be moral —in the mentioned sense, that is, "just"; that a social order that is not moral (which means: just) may nevertheless be law, although the postulate is admitted that the law ought to be moral, which means: just.

If the question of the relationship between law and morals is understood as a question concerning the content of law and not as a question concerning its form; if it is said that law according to its nature has a moral content or constitutes a moral value; then one asserts by these statements that law is valid within the sphere of morals, that the legal order is a part of the moral order, that law is moral and therefore by its nature just. So far as such an assertion aims at a justification of law—and this is its true meaning—it must presuppose that only one moral order is valid constituting an absolute moral value; and that only norms that conform with this moral order and therefore constitute an absolute moral value, can be regarded as "law." This means: one proceeds from a definition of law, which determines law as a part of morals, which identifies law and justice.

11. Relativity of Moral Value

But if an absolute value in general and an absolute moral value in particular is rejected from the point of view of scientific cognition, because an absolute value can be assumed only on the basis of religious faith in the absolute and transcendent authority of a deity; if one must admit that, from this viewpoint, an absolute moral order excluding the possibility of the validity of another moral order does not exist; if one denies that what is good or just according to that moral order is good under all circumstances, and what is evil according to that order is evil under all circumstances; if, further, one admits that at different times and with different nations and even within the same nation, depending on various classes and professions, very different and contradictory moral systems are valid; if one grants that under different circumstances different behavior may be considered good or evil, just or unjust, and nothing has to be considered good or evil, just or unjust, under all possible circumstances; if, in short, one acknowledges that moral values are only relative: then, the assertion that social norms must have a moral

517

content, must be just in order to qualify as law, can only mean that these norms must contain something common to all possible moral systems, as systems of justice. In view of the extraordinary heterogeneity, however, of what men in fact have considered as good or evil, just or unjust, at different times and in different places, no element common to the contents of the various moral orders is detectable. . . . But even if one could detect an element common to all moral systems valid so far, there would not be sufficient reason to regard as not "moral" or not "just" and therefore not as "law" a coercive order that does not contain this element, that commands a behavior that so far in no community has been considered to be good or just and that prohibits a behavior that so far in no community has been considered to be evil or unjust. For if one does not presuppose an a-priori, that is, absolute, moral value, one is unable to determine what must be considered good and evil, just and unjust, under all circumstances. And then, undeniably, also that which the mentioned coercive order commands may be considered as good and just, and that which it prohibits as evil and unjust; so that this order too is—relatively—moral or just. All moral orders have only one thing in common: namely, that they are social norms, that is, norms that order a certain behavior of men—directly or indirectly—toward other men. All possible moral systems have in common their form, the "ought": they prescribe something, they have normative character. Morally good is that which conforms with the social norm that prescribes a certain human behavior; morally evil that which is opposed to such a norm. The relative moral value is established by a social norm that men ought to behave in a certain way. Norm and value are correlative concepts.

Under these presuppositions the statement "law is moral by nature" does not mean that law has a certain content, but that it is norm—namely a social norm that men ought to behave in a certain way. Then, in this relative sense, every law is moral; every law constitutes a —relative—moral value. And this means: The question about the relationship between law and morals is not a question about the content of the law, but one about its form. Then one cannot say, as is sometimes said, that the law is not only norm (or command) but also constitutes or realizes a value—such an assertion is meaningful only if an absolute, divine value is presupposed. For the law constitutes a value precisely by the fact that it is a norm: it constitutes the *legal value* which, at the same time, is a (relative) moral value; which merely means that the law is norm.

The theory, however, that the law in its essence represents a moral minimum—that a coercive order, to be regarded as law, must fulfill a minimum moral postulate—is not thereby accepted. For to assume the existence of this postulate presupposes an absolute morality, determined by its content, or at least a content common to all positive moral systems —usually the ideal of peace. From what has been said it follows that the legal value, as used here, does not represent a moral minimum in this sense—that, specifically, the peace value is not an element essential for the concept of law.

12. Separation of Legal and Moral Orders

If it is assumed that law *is* moral by nature, then, presupposing an absolute moral value, it is meaningless to demand that the law *ought* to be moral. Such a postulate is meaningful only (and the presupposed morality represents a yardstick for the law only), if the possibility of the existence of an immoral law is admitted—if, in other words, the definition of law does not include the element of moral content. If a theory of positive law demands a distinction between law and morals in general, and between law and justice in particular, then this theory is directed against the traditional view, regarded as obvious by most jurists, which presupposes that only *one* absolutely valid moral order and therefore only one absolute justice exists. The demand for a separation between law and morals, law and justice, means that the validity of a positive legal order is independent of the validity of this one, solely valid, absolute moral order, "the" moral order, the moral order *par excellence*. If only relative moral values are presupposed, then the postulate that the law *ought* to be moral, that is, just, can only mean that the formation of positive law ought to conform to one specific moral system among the many possible systems. This, however, does not exclude the possibility of the postulate that the formation of positive law ought to conform with another moral system—and actually perhaps conforms with it—while it does not conform with a moral system that is different from it. If, presupposing only relative values, the demand is made to separate law and morals in general, and law and justice in particular, then this demand does not mean that law and morals, law and justice, are unrelated; it does not mean that the concept of law is outside the concept of the Good. For the concept of the "good" cannot be defined otherwise than as that which ought to be: that which conforms to a social norm; and if law is defined as norm, then this implies that what is lawful is "good." The postulate, made under the supposition of a relativistic theory of value, to separate law and morals and therefore law and justice, merely means this: (1) If a legal order is judged to be moral or immoral, just or unjust, these evaluations express the relation of the legal order to one of many possible moral systems but not to "the" moral system and therefore constitute only a relative, not an absolute, value judgment; and (2) the validity of a positive legal order does not depend on its conformity with some moral system.

A relativistic theory of value is often misunderstood to mean that there are no values and, particularly, that there is no justice. It means rather that values are relative, not absolute, that justice is relative not absolute; that the values as established by our norm-creating acts cannot claim to exclude the possibility of opposite values.

It is obvious that merely relative morals cannot render the function —consciously or unconsciously demanded—to provide an absolute standard for the evaluation of a positive legal order. Such a standard of evaluation simply cannot be found by scientific cognition. But this does not mean that there is no such standard—every moral system can serve as such. But one must be aware, in judging a positive legal order from a moral point of view (as good or bad, as just or unjust) that the standard of evaluation is relative and that an evaluation based on a different moral system is not excluded; further, that a legal order evaluated on the basis of one moral system as unjust may well be evaluated as just on the basis of another moral system.

13. Justification of Law through Morals

A justification of positive law through morals is possible only if a contrast can exist between the moral and the legal norms—if there can be a morally good and a morally bad law. If a moral order, like the one proclaimed by Paul in his Letter to the Romans prescribes to observe under all circumstances the norms enacted by the legal authority and thereby excludes any discrepancy between it and positive law, then it is not possible to legitimize the positive law by the moral order. For if all positive law, as willed by God, is just (like everything else that exists is good insofar as it is willed by God); and if no positive law is unjust, because nothing that exists can be evil; if law is identified with justice; and if that which *is* is identified with that which *ought* to be, then the concept of justice as well as the concept of the Good have lost their meanings. If nothing bad (unjust) exists, then nothing good (just) can exist. The postulate to differentiate law and morals, jurisprudence and ethics, means this: from the standpoint of scientific cognition of positive law, its justification by a moral order different from the legal order, is irrelevant, because the task of the science of law is not to approve or disapprove its subject, but to know and describe it. True, legal norms, as prescriptions of what ought to be, constitute values; yet the function of the science of law is not the evaluation of its subject but its free description. The legal scientist does not identify himself with any value, not even with the legal value he describes.

If the moral order does not prescribe to obey the positive legal order under all circumstances, if, in other words, a discrepancy between a moral and a legal order is possible, then the postulate to separate law and morals, science of law and ethics means that the validity of positive legal norms does not depend on their conformity with the moral order; it means, that from the standpoint of a cognition directed toward positive law a legal norm may be considered valid, even if it is at variance with the moral order.

It is paramount and cannot be emphasized enough to understand that not only one moral order exists, but many different and even conflicting ones; that a positive legal order may on the whole conform with the moral views of a certain group of the population (especially the ruling one), yet may conflict with the moral views of another group; and that above all, the judgment of what is morally good or evil, morally justifiable or unjustifiable, is subject to continuous change, as is the law, and that a legal order (or some of its norms) that at the time of its validity may have conformed with the postulates of the moral order then prevalent, may still be judged to be immoral today. The thesis, widely accepted by traditional science of law but rejected by the Pure Theory of Law, that the law by its nature must be moral and that an immoral social order is not a legal order, presupposes an absolute moral order, that is, one valid at all times and places. Otherwise it would not be possible to evaluate a positive social order by a fixed standard of right and wrong, independent of time and place.

The thesis that law is moral by nature—in the sense that only a moral social order is law—is rejected by the Pure Theory of Law not only because this thesis presupposes an absolute moral order, but also because in its actual application by the science of law prevailing in a certain legal community, this thesis amounts to an uncritical justification of the national coercive order that constitutes this community. For it is taken for granted that one's own national coercive order is a legal order. The dubious standard of an absolute morality is applied only to the coercive order of other nations. Only they are disqualified as immoral and therefore as nonlaw, when they do not conform with certain postulates with which one's own coercive order conforms—for example, when they recognize or do not recognize private property, or when they are democratic or not democratic. But since one's own coercive order is law, then, according to the above-mentioned thesis, it must also be moral. Such justification of the positive law may politically be convenient, even though logically inadmissible. From the point of view of a science of law it must be rejected, because it is not the task of this science to justify the law by absolute or relative morals; but to know and to describe it.

521

Fuller, Positivism and Fidelity to Law:
A Reply to Professor Hart *

. . . Without any inquiry into the actual workings of whatever remained of a legal system under the Nazis, Professor Hart assumes that
something must have persisted that still deserved the name of law in a
sense that would make meaningful the ideal of fidelity to law. Not that
Professor Hart believes the Nazis' laws should have been obeyed. Rather
he considers that a decision to disobey them presented not a mere question of prudence or courage, but a genuine moral dilemma in which the
ideal of fidelity to law had to be sacrificed in favor of more fundamental
goals. I should have thought it unwise to pass such a judgment without
first inquiring with more particularity what "law" itself meant under the
Nazi regime.
. . . It is his neglect to analyze the demands of a morality of order
that leads him throughout his essay to treat law as a datum projecting
itself into human experience and not as an object of human striving.
When we realize that order itself is something that must be worked for, it
becomes apparent that the existence of a legal system, even a bad or evil
legal system, is always a matter of degree. When we recognize this simple
fact of everyday legal experience, it becomes impossible to dismiss the
problems presented by the Nazi regime with a simple assertion: "Under
the Nazis there was law, even if it was bad law." We have instead to inquire how much of a legal system survived the general debasement and
perversion of all forms of social order that occurred under the Nazi rule,

---

* [71 *Harv. L. Rev.* 630, 633, 646, 655, 660 (1958). Copyright 1958 by The Harvard
Law Review Association. Reprinted by permission.

Lon L. Fuller (1902–) is retired Carter Professor of Jurisprudence at Harvard University. His publications include *Anatomy of the Law* (1968), *The Law in Quest of Itself* (1940),
and *Legal Fictions* (1967).

In this article, Fuller is replying to H. L. A. Hart's Positivism and the Separation of
Law and Morals, 71 *Harv. L. Rev.* 593 (1958). In his article, Hart argues for the positivist
distinction between what is legal and what is moral. The discussion between Hart and
Fuller often centers upon the example of Nazi Germany.

One German philosopher, Gustav Radbruch, noted the ease with which the Nazis had
exploited the concept of obedience to the law and the unwillingness of the German legal
profession to protest the perversions of law which they were required to perpetrate in the
name of law. Radbruch thus concluded that the positivists' wedge between law and morality had contributed to the rise of the Nazi regime. Consequently, Radbruch renounced his
positivist views and adopted the position that no statute was properly considered a statute
or law unless it met basic principles of morality. In reply to Radbruch, Hart suggests that
Radbruch's contention will obscure the true nature of the problem and will encourage the
view that "all the values we cherish will fit into a single system." Hart concludes that law
does not lose its legal character simply because it is immoral.]

and what moral implications this mutilated system had for the conscientious citizen forced to live under it . . .

Professor Hart castigates the German courts and Radbruch, not so much for what they believed had to be done, but because they failed to see that they were confronted by a moral dilemma of a sort that would have been immediately apparent to Bentham and Austin. By the simple dodge of saying, "When a statute is sufficiently evil it ceases to be law," they ran away from the problem they should have faced.

This criticism is, I believe, without justification. So far as the courts are concerned, matters certainly would not have been helped if, instead of saying, "This is not law," they had said, "This is law but it is so evil we will refuse to apply it." Surely moral confusion reaches its height when a court refuses to apply something it admits to be law, and Professor Hart does not recommend any such "facing of the true issue" by the courts themselves. . . .

To me there is nothing shocking in saying that a dictatorship which clothes itself with a tinsel of legal form can so far depart from the morality of order, from the inner morality of law itself, that it ceases to be a legal system. When a system calling itself law is predicated upon a general disregard by judges of the terms of the laws they purport to enforce, when this system habitually cures its legal irregularities, even the grossest, by retroactive statutes, when it has only to resort to forays of terror in the streets, which no one dares challenge, in order to escape even those scant restraints imposed by the pretence of legality—when all these things have become true of a dictatorship, it is not hard for me, at least, to deny to it the name of law.

Devlin, The Enforcement of Morals*

I. Morals and the Criminal Law†

The Report of the Committee on Homosexual Offences and Prostitution, generally known as the Wolfenden Report, is recognized to be an excellent study of two very difficult legal and social problems. But

*[Pp. 1-3, 7-18, 21-25 (1965). Footnotes renumbered; some omitted. From *The Enforcement of Morals* by Patrick Devlin, © Oxford University Press 1965. Reprinted by permission of Oxford University Press.

Lord Patrick Devlin (1905-   ), a British judge, was educated at Christ's College, Cambridge. He served as Prosecuting Counsel to the Mint (1931-1939) and as Justice of the High Court, Queen's Bench Division (1948-1960). He was Lord Justice of Appeal (1960-1961) and Lord of Appeal in Ordinary (1961-1964). He has also served as judge of the Administrative Tribunal of the ILO from 1964 to the present and has been High Steward of Cambridge University since 1966.]

†Maccabaean Lecture in Jurisprudence read at the British Academy on 18 March

it has also a particular claim to the respect of those interested in jurisprudence; it does what law reformers so rarely do; it sets out clearly and
carefully what in relation to its subjects it considers the function of the
law to be.[1] Statutory additions to the criminal law are too often made on
the simple principle that "there ought to be a law against it." The greater
part of the law relating to sexual offences is the creation of statute and it
is difficult to ascertain any logical relationship between it and the moral
ideas which most of us uphold.

. . . Early in the Report the Committee put forward:

> Our own formulation of the function of the criminal law so far as it con-
> cerns the subjects of this enquiry. In this field, its function, as we see it, is
> to preserve public order and decency, to protect the citizen from what is
> offensive or injurious, and to provide sufficient safeguards against ex-
> ploitation and corruption of others, particularly those who are specially
> vulnerable because they are young, weak in body or mind, inex-
> perienced, or in a state of special physical, official or economic depen-
> dence.
>
> It is not, in our view, the function of the law to intervene in the pri-
> vate lives of citizens, or to seek to enforce any particular pattern of beha-
> viour, further than is necessary to carry out the purposes we have out-
> lined.

The Committee preface their most important recommendation

that homosexual behaviour between consenting adults in private should
no longer be a criminal offence, [by stating the argument] which we believe to be decisive, namely, the importance which society and the law
ought to give to individual freedom of choice and action in matters of
private morality. Unless a deliberate attempt is to be made by society,
acting through the agency of the law, to equate the sphere of crime with
that of sin, there must remain a realm of private morality and immorality which is, in brief and crude terms, not the law's business. To say this
is not to condone or encourage private immorality . . .

[I]f the criminal law were to be reformed so as to eliminate from it

---

1959 and printed in the *Proceedings of the British Academy,* vol. xlv, under the title "The Enforcement of Morals."

1. The Committee's "statement of juristic philosophy" (to quote Lord Pakenham) was
considered by him in a debate in the House of Lords on 4 December 1957, reported in
Hansard Lords Debates, vol. ccvi at 738; and also in the same debate by the Archbishop of
Canterbury at 753 and Lord Denning at 806. The subject has also been considered by Mr.
J. E. Hall Williams in the *Law Quarterly Review,* January 1958, vol. lxxiv, p. 76.

everything that was not designed to preserve order and decency or to protect citizens (including the protection of youth from corruption), it would overturn a fundamental principle. It would also end a number of specific crimes. Euthanasia or the killing of another at his own request, suicide, attempted suicide and suicide pacts, duelling, abortion, incest between brother and sister, are all acts which can be done in private and without offence to others and need not involve the corruption or exploitation of others. Many people think that the law on some of these subjects is in need of reform, but no one hitherto has gone so far as to suggest that they should all be left outside the criminal law as matters of private morality. They can be brought within it only as a matter of moral principle. It must be remembered also that although there is much immorality that is not punished by the law, there is none that is condoned by the law. The law will not allow its processes to be used by those engaged in immorality of any sort. For example, a house may not be let for immoral purposes; the lease is invalid and would not be enforced. But if what goes on inside there is a matter of private morality and not the law's business, why does the law inquire into it at all?

I think it is clear that the criminal law as we know it is based upon moral principle. In a number of crimes its function is simply to enforce a moral principle and nothing else. The law, both criminal and civil, claims to be able to speak about morality and immorality generally. Where does it get its authority to do this and how does it settle the moral principles which it enforces? Undoubtedly, as a matter of history, it derived both from Christian teaching. But I think that the strict logician is right when he says that the law can no longer rely on doctrines in which citizens are entitled to disbelieve. It is necessary therefore to look for some other source.

In jurisprudence, as I have said, everything is thrown open to discussion and, in the belief that they cover the whole field, I have framed three interrogatories addressed to myself to answer:

1. Has society the right to pass judgement at all on matters of morals? Ought there, in other words, to be a public morality, or are morals always a matter for private judgement?
2. If society has the right to pass judgement, has it also the right to use the weapon of the law to enforce it?
3. If so, ought it to use that weapon in all cases or only in some; and if only in some, on what principles should it distinguish?

I shall begin with the first interrogatory and consider what is meant by the right of society to pass a moral judgement, that is, a judgement about what is good and what is evil. The fact that a majority of people may disapprove of a practice does not of itself make it a matter for society as a whole. Nine men out of ten may disapprove of what the tenth man is doing and still say that it is not their business. There is a case for a collective judgement (as distinct from a large number of individual opinions which sensible people may even refrain from pronouncing at all if it is upon somebody else's private affairs) only if society is affected. Without a collective judgement there can be no case at all for intervention. Let me take as an illustration the Englishman's attitude to religion as it is now and as it has been in the past. His attitude now is that a man's religion is his private affair; he may think of another man's religion that it is right or wrong, true or untrue, but not that it is good or bad. In earlier times that was not so; a man was denied the right to practise what was thought of as heresy, and heresy was thought of as destructive of society.

The language used in the passages I have quoted from the Wolfenden Report suggests the view that there ought not to be a collective judgement about immorality *per se*. Is this what is meant by "private morality" and "individual freedom of choice and action"? Some people sincerely believe that homosexuality is neither immoral nor unnatural. Is the "freedom of choice and action" that is offered to the individual, freedom to decide for himself what is moral or immoral, society remaining neutral; or is it freedom to be immoral if he wants to be? The language of the Report may be open to question, but the conclusions at which the Committee arrive answer this question unambiguously. If society is not prepared to say that homosexuality is morally wrong, there would be no basis for a law protecting youth from "corruption" or punishing a man for living on the "immoral" earnings of a homosexual prostitute, as the Report recommends. This attitude the Committee make even clearer when they come to deal with prostitution. In truth, the Report takes it for granted that there is in existence a public morality which condemns homosexuality and prostitution. What the Report seems to mean by private morality might perhaps be better described as private behaviour in matters of morals. . . .

The institution of marriage is a good example for my purpose because it bridges the division, if there is one, between politics and morals. Marriage is part of the structure of our society and it is also the basis of a moral code which condemns fornication and adultery. The institution of marriage would be gravely threatened if individual judgements were permitted about the morality of adultery; on these points there must be a public morality. But public morality is not to be confined to those moral principles which support institutions such as marriage. People do not think of monogamy as something which has to be supported because our society has chosen to organize itself upon it; they think of it as something that is good in itself and offering a good way of life and that it is for that reason that our society has adopted it. I return to the statement that I have already made, that society means a community of ideas; without shared ideas on politics, morals, and ethics no society can exist. Each one of us has ideas about what is good and what is evil; they cannot be kept private from the society in which we live. If men and women try to create a society in which there is no fundamental agreement about good and evil they will fail; if, having based it on common agreement, the agreement goes, the society will disintegrate. For society is not something that is kept together physically; it is held by the invisible bonds of common thought. If the bonds were too far relaxed the members would drift apart. A common morality is part of the bondage. The bondage is part of the price of society; and mankind, which needs society, must pay its price. . . .

You may think that I have taken far too long in contending that there is such a thing as public morality, a proposition which most people would readily accept, and may have left myself too little time to discuss the next question which to many minds may cause greater difficulty: to what extent should society use the law to enforce its moral judgements? But I believe that the answer to the first question determines the way in which the second should be approached and may indeed very nearly dictate the answer to the second question. If society has no right to make judgements on morals, the law must find some special justification for entering the field of morality: if homosexuality and prostitution are not in themselves wrong, then the onus is very clearly on the lawgiver who wants to frame a law against certain aspects of them to justify the exceptional treatment. But if society has the right to make a judgement and has it on the basis that a recognized morality is as necessary to society as, say, a recognized government, then society may use the law to preserve morality in the same way as it uses it to safeguard anything else that is essential to its existence. If therefore the first proposition is securely established with all its implications, society has a prima facie right to legislate against immorality as such. . . .

I think, therefore, that it is not possible to set theoretical limits to the power of the State to legislate against immorality. It is not possible to settle in advance exceptions to the general rule or to define inflexibly areas of morality into which the law is in no circumstances to be allowed to enter. Society is entitled by means of its laws to protect itself from dangers, whether from within or without. Here again I think that the political parallel is legitimate. The law of treason is directed against aiding the king's enemies and against sedition from within. The justification for this is that established government is necessary for the existence of society and therefore its safety against violent overthrow must be secured. But an established morality is as necessary as good government to the welfare of society. Societies disintegrate from within more frequently than they are broken up by external pressures. There is disintegration when no common morality is observed and history shows that the loosening of moral bonds is often the first stage of disintegration, so that society is justified in taking the same steps to preserve its moral code as it does to preserve its government and other essential institutions. The suppression of vice is as much the law's business as the suppression of subversive activities; it is no more possible to define a sphere of private morality than it is to define one of private subversive activity. It is wrong to talk of private morality or of the law not being concerned with immorality as such or to try to set rigid bounds to the part which the law may play in the suppression of vice. There are no theoretical limits to the power of the State to legislate against treason and sedition, and likewise I think there can be no theoretical limits to legislation against immorality. You may argue that if a man's sins affect only himself it cannot be the concern of society. If he chooses to get drunk every night in the privacy of his own home, is any one except himself the worse for it? But suppose a quarter or a half of the population got drunk every night, what sort of society would it be? You cannot set a theoretical limit to the number of people who can get drunk before society is entitled to legislate against drunkenness. The same may be said of gambling. The Royal Commission on Betting, Lotteries, and Gaming took as their test the character of the citizen as a member of society. They said: "Our concern with the ethical significance of gambling is confined to the effect which it may have on the character of the gambler as a member of society. If we were convinced that whatever the degree of gambling this effect must be harmful we should be inclined to think that it was the duty of the state to restrict gambling to the greatest extent practicable."

In what circumstances the State should exercise its power is the third of the interrogatories I have framed. But before I get to it I must raise a point which might have been brought up in any one of the three. How are the moral judgements of society to be ascertained? By leaving it until now, I can ask it in the more limited form that is now suffcient for my purpose. How is the law-maker to ascertain the moral judgements of society? It is surely not enough that they should be reached by the opinion of the majority; it would be too much to require the individual assent of every citizen. English law has evolved and regularly uses a standard which does not depend on the counting of heads. It is that of the reasonable man. He is not to be confused with the rational man. He is not expected to reason about anything and his judgement may be largely a matter of feeling. It is the viewpoint of the man in the street—or to use an archaism familiar to all lawyers—the man in the Clapham omnibus. He might also be called the right-minded man. For my purpose I should like to call him the man in the jury box, for the moral judgement of society must be something about which any twelve men or women drawn at random might after discussion be expected to be unanimous. This was the standard the judges applied in the days before Parliament was as active as it is now and when they laid down rules of public policy. They did not think of themselves as making law but simply as stating principles which every right-minded person would accept as valid. It is what Pollock called "practical morality," which is based not on theological or philosophical foundations but "in the mass of continuous experience half-consciously or unconsciously accumulated and embodied in the morality of common sense." He called it also "a certain way of thinking on questions of morality which we expect to find in a reasonable civilized man or a reasonable Englishman, taken at random."[2]

Immorality then, for the purpose of the law, is what every right-minded person is presumed to consider to be immoral. Any immorality is capable of affecting society injuriously and in effect to a greater or lesser extent it usually does; this is what gives the law its *locus standi*. It cannot be shut out. But—and this brings me to the third question—the individual has a *locus standi* too; he cannot be expected to surrender to the judgement of society the whole conduct of his life. It is the old and familiar question of striking a balance between the rights and interests of society and those of the individual. This is something which the law is constantly doing in matters large and small. To take a very down-to-earth example, let me consider the right of the individual whose house adjoins the highway to have access to it; that means in these days the right to have vehicles stationary in the highway, sometimes for a considerable time if there is a lot of loading or unloading. There are many cases in which the courts have had to balance the private right of access against the public right to use the highway without obstruction. It cannot be done by carving up the highway into public and private areas. It is done by recognizing that each have rights over the whole; that if each were to exercise their rights to the full, they would come into conflict; and therefore that the rights of each must be curtailed so as to ensure as

2. *Essays in Jurisprudence and Ethics* (1882), Macmillan, pp. 278 and 353.

far as possible that the essential needs of each are safeguarded.

I do not think that one can talk sensibly of a public and private morality any more than one can of a public or private highway. Morality is a sphere in which there is a public interest and a private interest, often in conflict, and the problem is to reconcile the two. This does not mean that it is impossible to put forward any general statements about how in our society the balance ought to be struck. Such statements cannot of their nature be rigid or precise; they would not be designed to circumscribe the operation of the lawmaking power but to guide those who have to apply it. While every decision which a court of law makes when it balances the public against the private interest is an *ad hoc* decision, the cases contain statements of principle to which the court should have regard when it reaches its decision. In the same way it is possible to make general statements of principle which it may be thought the legislature should bear in mind when it is considering the enactment of laws enforcing morals.

I believe that most people would agree upon the chief of these elastic principles. There must be toleration of the maximum individual freedom that is consistent with the integrity of society. It cannot be said that this is a principle that runs all through the criminal law. Much of the criminal law that is regulatory in character—the part of it that deals with *malum prohibitum* rather than *malum in se*—is based upon the opposite principle, that is, that the choice of the individual must give way to the convenience of the many. But in all matters of conscience the principle I have stated is generally held to prevail. It is not confined to thought and speech; it extends to action, as is shown by the recognition of the right to conscientious objection in war-time; this example shows also that conscience will be respected even in times of national danger. The principle appears to me to be peculiarly appropriate to all questions of morals. Nothing should be punished by the law that does not lie beyond the limits of tolerance. It is not nearly enough to say that a majority dislike a practice; there must be a real feeling of reprobation. Those who are dissatisfied with the present law on homosexuality often say that the opponents of reform are swayed simply by disgust. If that were so it would be wrong, but I do not think one can ignore disgust if it is deeply felt and not manufactured. Its presence is a good indication that the bounds of toleration are being reached. Not everything is to be tolerated. No society can do without intolerance, indignation, and disgust; they are the forces behind the moral law, and indeed it can be argued that if they or something like them are not present, the feelings of society cannot be weighty enough to deprive the individual of freedom of choice. I suppose that there is hardly anyone nowadays who would not be disgusted by the thought of deliberate cruelty to animals. No one proposes to relegate that or any other form of sadism to the realm of private morality or to allow it to be practised in public or in private. It would be possible no doubt to point out that until a comparatively short while ago nobody thought very much of cruelty to animals and also that pity and kindliness and the unwillingness to inflict pain are virtues more generally esteemed now than they have ever been in the past. But matters of this sort are not determined by rational argument. Every moral judgement, unless it claims a divine source, is simply a feeling that no right-minded man could behave in any other way without admitting that he was doing wrong. It is the power of a common sense and not the power of reason that is behind the judgements of society. But before a society can put a practice beyond the limits of tolerance there must be a deliberate judgement that the practice is injurious to society. There is, for example, a general abhorrence of homosexuality. We should ask ourselves in the first instance whether, looking at it calmly and dispassionately, we regard it as a vice so abominable that its mere presence is an offence. If that is the genuine feeling of the society in which we live, I do not see how society can be denied the right to eradicate it. Our feeling may not be so intense as that. We may feel about it that, if confined, it is tolerable, but that if it spread it might be gravely injurious; it is in this way that most societies look upon fornication, seeing it as a natural weakness which must be kept within bounds but which cannot be rooted out. It becomes then a question of balance, the danger to society in one scale and the extent of the restriction in the other. On this sort of point the value of an investigation by such a body as the Wolfenden Committee and of its conclusions is manifest. . . .

This then is how I believe my third interrogatory should be answered—not by the formulation of hard and fast rules, but by a judgement in each case taking into account the sort of factors I have been mentioning. The line that divides the criminal law from the moral is not determinable by the application of any clear-cut principle. It is like a line that divides land and sea, a coastline of irregularities and indentations. There are gaps and promontories, such as adultery and fornication, which the law has for centuries left substantially untouched. Adultery of the sort that breaks up marriage seems to me to be just as harmful to the social fabric as homosexuality or bigamy. The only ground for putting it outside the criminal law is that a law which made it a crime would be too difficult to enforce; it is too generally regarded as a human weakness not suitably punished by imprisonment. All that the law can do with fornication is to act against its worst manifestations; there is a general abhorrence of the commercialization of vice, and that sentiment gives strength to the law against brothels and immoral earnings. There is no logic to be found in this. The boundary between the criminal law and the moral law is fixed by balancing in the case of each particular crime the pros and cons of legal enforcement in accordance with the sort of considerations I have been outlining. The fact that adultery, fornication, and lesbianism are untouched by the criminal law does not prove that homosexuality ought not to be touched. The error of jurisprudence in the Wolfenden Report is caused by the search for some single principle to explain the division between crime and sin. The Report finds it in the principle that the criminal law exists for the protection of individuals; on this principle fornication in private between consenting adults is outside the law and thus it becomes logically indefensible to bring homosexuality between consenting adults in private within it. But the true principle is that the law exists for the protection of society. It does not discharge its function by protecting the individual from injury, annoyance, corruption, and exploitation; the law must protect also the institutions and the community of ideas, political and moral, without which people cannot live together. Society cannot ignore the morality of the individual any more than it can his loyalty; it flourishes on both and without either it dies.

I have said that the morals which underly the law must be derived from the sense of right and wrong which resides in the community as a whole; it does not matter whence the community of thought comes, whether from one body of doctrine or another or from the knowledge of good and evil which no man is without. If the reasonable man believes that a practice is immoral and believes also—no matter whether the belief is right or wrong, so be it that it is honest and dispassionate—that no right-minded member of his society could think otherwise, then for the purpose of the law it is immoral. This, you may say, makes immorality a question of fact—what the law would consider as self-evident fact no doubt, but still with no higher authority than any other doctrine of public policy. I think that that is so, and indeed the law does not distinguish between an act that is immoral and one that is contrary to public policy. But the law has never yet had occasion to inquire into the differences between Christian morals and those which every right-minded member of society is expected to hold. The inquiry would, I believe, be academic. Moralists would find differences; indeed they would find them between different branches of the Christian faith on subjects such as divorce and birth-control. But for the purpose of the limited entry which the law makes into the field of morals, there is no practical difference. It seems to me therefore that the free-thinker and the non-Christian can accept, without offence to his convictions, the fact that Christian morals are the basis of the criminal law and that he can recognize, also without taking offence, that without the support of the churches the moral order, which has its origin in and takes its strength from Christian beliefs, would collapse.

. . . Society cannot live without morals. Its morals are those standards of conduct which the reasonable man approves. A rational man, who is also a good man, may have other standards. If he has no standards at all he is not a good man and need not be further considered. If he has standards, they may be very different; he may, for example, not disapprove of homosexuality or abortion. In that case he will not share in the common morality; but that should not make him deny that it is a social necessity. A rebel may be rational in thinking that he is right but he is irrational if he thinks that society can leave him free to rebel.

A man who concedes that morality is necessary to society must support the use of those instruments without which morality cannot be maintained. The two instruments are those of teaching, which is doctrine, and of enforcement, which is the law. If morals could be taught simply on the basis that they are necessary to society, there would be no social need for religion; it could be left as a purely personal affair. But morality cannot be taught in that way. Loyalty is not taught in that way either. No society has yet solved the problem of how to teach morality without religion. So the law must base itself on Christian morals and to the limit of its ability enforce them; not simply because they are the morals of most of us, nor simply because they are the morals which are taught by the established Church—on these points the law recognizes the right to dissent—but for the compelling reason that without the help of Christian teaching the law will fail.

R. M. Dworkin, The Enforcement of Morals*

The First Argument: Society's Right to Protect Itself

The first argument—and the argument which has received by far the major part of the critics' attention—is this:[9]

(1) In a modern society there are a variety of moral principles which

---

*[75 *Yale L. J.* 986, 989-992, 1000-1002 (1966). Reprinted by permission of The Yale Law Journal Company and Fred B. Rothman & Company from The Yale Law Journal, Vol. 75, pp. 986, 1000-1002.

For biographical information, see page 145 supra.]

9. It is developed chiefly in Devlin [*The Enforcement of Morals*] 7-25 [(Oxford University Press 1965), hereinafter cited as Devlin].

some men adopt for their own guidance and do not attempt to impose upon others. There are also moral standards which the majority places beyond toleration and imposes upon those who dissent. For us, the dictates of particular religion are an example of the former class, and the practice of monogamy an example of the latter. A society cannot survive unless some standards are of the second class, because some moral conformity is essential to its life. Every society has a right to preserve its own existence, and therefore the right to insist on some such conformity.

(2) If society has such a right, then it has the right to use the institutions and sanctions of its criminal law to enforce the right—"[S]ociety may use the law to preserve morality in the same way it uses it to safeguard anything else if it is essential to its existence."[10] Just as society may use its law to prevent treason, it may use it to prevent a corruption of that conformity which ties it together.

(3) But society's right to punish immorality by law should not necessarily be exercised against every sort and on every occasion of immorality—we must recognize the impact and the importance of some restraining principles. There are several of these, but the most important is that there "must be toleration of the maximum individual freedom that is consistent with the integrity of society."[11] These restraining principles, taken together, require that we exercise caution in concluding that a practice is considered profoundly immoral. The law should stay its hand if it detects any uneasiness or half-heartedness or latent toleration in society's condemnation of the practice. But none of these restraining principles apply, and hence society is free to enforce its rights, when public feeling is high, enduring and relentless, when, in Lord Devlin's phrase, it rises to "intolerance, indignation and disgust."[12] Hence the summary conclusion about homosexuality: if it is genuinely regarded as an abominable vice, society's right to eradicate it cannot be denied.

We must guard against a possible, indeed tempting, misconception of this argument. It does not depend upon any assumption that when the vast bulk of a community thinks a practice is immoral they are likely right. What Lord Devlin thinks is at stake, when our public morality is challenged, is the very survival of society, and he believes that society is entitled to preserve itself without vouching for the morality that holds it together.

Is this argument sound? Professor H. L. A. Hart, responding to its appearance at the heart of the Maccabaean lecture,[13] thought that it

10. Id. at 11.
11. Id. at 16.
12. Id. at 17.
13. H. L. A. Hart, *Law, Liberty and Morality* 51 (1963).

rested upon a confused conception of what a society is. If one holds any-thing like a conventional notion of a society, he said, it is absurd to sug-gest that every practice the society views as profoundly immoral and dis-gusting threatens its survival. This is as silly as arguing that society's existence is threatened by the death of one of its members or the birth of another, and Lord Devlin, he reminds us, offers nothing by way of evi-dence to support any such claim. But if one adopts an artificial definition of a society, such that a society consists of that particular complex of moral ideas and attitudes which its members happen to hold at a particu-lar moment in time, it is intolerable that each such moral status quo should have the right to preserve its precarious existence by force. So, Professor Hart argued, Lord Devlin's argument fails whether a conven-tional or an artificial sense of "society" is taken.

Lord Devlin replies to Professor Hart in a new and lengthy foot-note. After summarizing Hart's criticism he comments, "I do not assert that *any* deviation from a society's shared morality threatens its existence any more than I assert that *any* subversive activity threatens its existence. I assert that they are both activities which are capable in their nature of threatening the existence of society so that neither can be put beyond the law."[14] This reply exposes a serious flaw in the architecture of the argu-ment.

It tells us that we must understand the second step of the argument —the crucial claim that society has a right to enforce its public morality by law—as limited to a denial of the proposition that society never has such a right. Lord Devlin apparently understood the Wolfenden Re-port's statement of a "realm of private morality . . . not the law's busi-ness" to assert a fixed jurisdictional barrier placing private sexual prac-tices forever beyond the law's scrutiny. His arguments, the new footnote tells us, are designed to show merely that no such constitutional barrier should be raised, because it is possible that the challenge to established morality might be so profound that the very existence of a conformity in morals, and hence of the society itself, would be threatened.[15]

14. Devlin 13.
15. This reading had great support in the text even without the new footnote: "I think, therefore, that it is not possible to set theoretical limits to the power of the State to legislate against immorality. It is not possible to settle in advance exceptions to the general rule or to define inflexibly areas of morality into which the law is in no circumstances to be allowed to enter." Devlin 12-13.

The arguments presented bear out this construction. They are of the *reductio ad absur-dum* variety, exploiting the possibility that what is immoral can in theory become subversive of society. "But suppose a quarter or a half of the population got drunk every night, what sort of society would it be? You cannot set a theoretical limit to the number of people who

We might well remain unconvinced, even of this limited point. We might believe that the danger which any unpopular practice can present to the existence of society is so small that it would be wise policy, a prudent protection of individual liberty from transient hysteria, to raise just this sort of constitutional barrier and forbid periodic reassessments of the risk.

But if we were persuaded to forego this constitutional barrier we would expect the third step in the argument to answer the inevitable next question: Granted that a challenge to deep-seated and genuine public morality may conceivably threaten society's existence, and so must be placed above the threshold of the law's concern, how shall we know when the danger is sufficiently clear and present to justify not merely scrutiny but action? What more is needed beyond the fact of passionate public disapproval to show that we are in the presence of an actual threat?

The rhetoric of the third step makes it seem responsive to this question—there is much talk of "freedom" and "toleration" and even "balancing." But the argument is not responsive, for freedom, toleration and balancing turn out to be appropriate only when the public outrage diagnosed at the second step is shown to be overstated, when the fever, that is, turns out to be feigned. When the fever is confirmed, when the intolerance, indignation and disgust are genuine, the principle that calls for "the maximum individual freedom consistent with the integrity of society" no longer applies. But this means that nothing more than passionate public disapproval is necessary after all.

In short, the argument involves an intellectual sleight of hand. At the second step, public outrage is presented as a threshold criterion, merely placing the practice in a category which the law is not forbidden to regulate. But offstage, somewhere in the transition to the third step,

------

can get drunk before society is entitled to legislate against drunkenness. The same may be said of gambling." Id. at 14.

Each example argues that no jurisdictional limit may be drawn, not that every drunk or every act of gambling threatens society. There is no suggestion that society is entitled actually to make drunkenness or gambling crimes if the practice in fact falls below the level of danger. Indeed Lord Devlin quotes the Royal Commission on Betting, Lotteries, and Gaming to support his example on gambling: "If we were convinced that whatever the degree of gambling this effect [on the character of the gambler as a member of society] must be harmful we should be inclined to think that it was the duty of the state to restrict gambling to the greatest extent practicable." (Cmd. No. 8190 at para. 159 (1951), quoted in Devlin 14).

The implication is that society may scrutinize and be ready to regulate, but should not actually do so until the threat of harm in fact exists.

this threshold criterion becomes itself a dispositive affirmative reason for action, so that when it is clearly met the law may proceed without more. The power of this manoeuvre is proved by the passage on homosexuality. Lord Devlin concludes that if our society hates homosexuality enough it is justified in outlawing it, and forcing human beings to choose between the miseries of frustration and persecution, because of the danger the practice presents to society's existence. He manages this conclusion without offering evidence that homosexuality presents any danger at all to society's existence, beyond the naked claim that all "deviations from a society's shared morality . . . are capable in their nature of threatening the existence of society" and so "cannot be put beyond the law."[16] . . .

Lord Devlin's Morality

We may now return to Lord Devlin's second argument. He argues that when legislators must decide a moral issue (as by his hypothesis they must when a practice threatens a valued social arrangement), they must follow any consensus of moral position which the community at large has reached, because this is required by the democratic principle, and because a community is entitled to follow its own lights. The argument would have some plausibility if Lord Devlin meant, in speaking of the moral consensus of the community, those positions which are moral positions in the discriminatory sense we have been exploring.

But he means nothing of the sort. His definition of a moral position shows he is using it in what I called the anthropological sense. The ordinary man whose opinions we must enforce he says, ". . . is not expected to reason about anything and his judgment may be largely a matter of feeling."[18] "If the reasonable man believes," he adds, "that a practice is immoral and believes also—no matter whether the belief is right or wrong, so be it that it is honest and dispassionate—that no right-minded member of his society could think otherwise, then for the purpose of the law it is immoral."[19] Elsewhere he quotes with approval Dean Rostow's attribution to him of the view that "the common morality of a society at any time is a blend of custom and conviction, of reason and feeling, of experience and prejudice."[20] His sense of what a moral conviction is

16. Devlin 13, n.1.
18. Devlin 15.
19. Id. at 22-23.
20. Rostow, The Enforcement of Morals, 1960 *Camb. L. J.* 174, 197; reprinted in E. V. Rostow, *The Sovereign Prerogative* 45, 78 (1962). Quoted in Devlin 95.

emerges most clearly of all from the famous remark about homosexuals. If the ordinary man regards homosexuality "as a vice so abominable that its mere presence is an offence,"[21] this demonstrates for him that the ordinary man's feelings about homosexuals are a matter of moral conviction.[22]

His conclusions fail because they depend upon using "moral position" in this anthropological sense. Even if it is true that most men think homosexuality an abominable vice and cannot tolerate its presence, it remains possible that this common opinion is a compound of prejudice (resting on the assumption that homosexuals are morally inferior creatures because they are effeminate), rationalization (based on assumptions of fact so unsupported that they challenge the community's own standards of rationality), and personal aversion (representing no conviction but merely blind hate rising from unacknowledged self-suspicion). It remains possible that the ordinary man could produce no reason for his view, but would simply parrot his neighbor who in turn parrots him, or that he would produce a reason which presupposes a general moral position he could not sincerely or consistently claim to hold. If so, the principles of democracy we follow do not call for the enforcement of the consensus, for the belief that prejudices, personal aversions and rationalizations do not justify restricting another's freedom itself occupies a critical and fundamental position in our popular morality. Nor would the bulk of the community then be entitled to follow its own lights, for the community does not extend that privilege to one who acts on the basis of prejudice, rationalization, or personal aversion. Indeed, the distinction between these and moral convictions, in the discriminatory sense, exists largely to mark off the former as the sort of positions one is not entitled to pursue.

A conscientious legislator who is told a moral consensus exists must

21. Id. at 17.

22. In the preface (Id. at viii) Lord Devlin acknowledges that the language of the original lecture might have placed "too much emphasis on feeling and too little on reason," and he states that the legislator is entitled to disregard "irrational" beliefs. He gives as an example of the latter the belief that homosexuality causes earthquakes, and asserts that the exclusion of irrationality "is usually an easy and comparatively unimportant process." I think it fair to conclude that this is all Lord Devlin would allow him to exclude. If I am wrong, and Lord Devlin would ask him to exclude prejudices, personal aversions, arbitrary stands and the rest as well, he should have said so, and attempted to work some of these distinctions out. If he had, his conclusions would have been different and would no doubt have met with a different reaction.

test the credentials of that consensus. He cannot, of course, examine the beliefs or behavior of individual citizens; he cannot hold hearings on the Clapham omnibus. That is not the point.

The claim that a moral consensus exists is not itself based on a poll. It is based on an appeal to the legislator's sense of how his community reacts to some disfavored practice. But this same sense includes an awareness of the grounds on which that reaction is generally supported. If there has been a public debate involving the editiorial columns, speeches of his colleagues, the testimony of interested groups, and his own correspondence, these will sharpen his awareness of what arguments and positions are in the field. He must sift these arguments and positions, trying to determine which are prejudices or rationalizations, which presuppose general principles or theories vast parts of the population could not be supposed to accept, and so on. It may be that when he has finished this process of reflection he will find that the claim of a moral consensus has not been made out. In the case of homosexuality, I expect, it would not be, and that is what makes Lord Devlin's undiscriminating hypothetical so serious a misstatement. What is shocking and wrong is not his idea that the community's morality counts, but his idea of what counts as the community's morality.

Of course the legislator must apply these tests for himself. If he shares the popular views he is less likely to find them wanting, though if he is self-critical the exercise may convert him. His answer, in any event, will depend upon his own understanding of what our shared morality requires. That is inevitable, for whatever criteria we urge him to apply, he can apply them only as he understands them.

A legislator who proceeds in this way, who refuses to take popular indignation, intolerance and disgust as the moral conviction of his community, is not guilty of moral elitism. He is not simply setting his own educated views against those of a vast public which rejects them. He is doing his best to enforce a distinct, and fundamentally important, part of his community's morality, a consensus more essential to society's existence in the form we know it than the opinion Lord Devlin bids him follow.

No legislator can afford to ignore the public's outrage. It is a fact he must reckon with. It will set the boundries of what is politically feasible, and it will determine his strategies of persuasion and enforcement within these boundries. But we must not confuse strategy with justice, nor facts of political life with principles of political morality. Lord Devlin understands these distinctions, but his arguments will appeal most, I am afraid, to those who do not. . . .

Devlin, Law, Democracy, and Morality*†

II. The Basis of Morals Legislation

The state may claim on two grounds to legislate on matters of morals. The Platonic ideal is that the state exists to promote virtue among its citizens. If that is its function, then whatever power is sovereign in the state—an autocrat, if there be one, or in a democracy the majority—must have the right and duty to declare what standards of morality are to be observed as virtuous and must ascertain them as it thinks best. This is not acceptable to Anglo-American thought. It invests the state with power of determination between good and evil, destroys freedom of conscience, and is the paved road to tyranny. It is against this concept of the state's power that Mill's words are chiefly directed.

The alternative ground is that society may legislate to preserve itself. This is the ground, I think, taken by Lord Simonds when he says that the purpose of the law is to conserve the moral welfare of the state; and all the speeches in the House show, especially when they are laying down the part to be played by the jury, that the work of the courts is to be the guarding of a heritage and not the creation of a system. "The ultimate foundation of a free society is the binding tie of cohesive sentiment."[10] What makes a society is a community of ideas, not political ideas alone but also ideas about the way its members should behave and govern their lives. . . .

A law that enforces moral standards must like any other law be enacted by the appropriate constitutional organ, the monarch or the legislative majority as the case may be. The essential difference between the two theories is that under the first the lawmaker must determine for himself what is good for his subjects. He may be expected to do so not arbitrarily but to the best of his understanding; but it is his decision, based on his judgment of what is best, from which alone the law derives authority. The demcratic system of government goes some way—not all the way, for no representative can be the mirror of the voters' thoughts —to insure that the decision of the lawmaker will be acceptable to the majority, but the majority is not the whole. A written constitution may

---

*[110 *U. Pa. L. Rev.* 635, 638-649 (1962). Reprinted by permission of the University of Pennsylvania Law Review and Fred B. Rothman & Company.

For biographical information, see page 523 supra.

†This paper is taken from the Owen J. Roberts Memorial Lecture, delivered Sept. 28, 1961, under the auspices of the Pennsylvania Chapter of the Order of the Coif and the University of Pennsylvania Law School.

10. Minersville School Dist. v. Gobitis, 310 U.S. 586, 596 (1940) (Frankfurter, J.).

safeguard to a great extent and for a long time the conscience of a minority, but not entirely and forever; for a written constitution is only a fundamental enactment that is difficult to alter.

But under the second theory the lawmaker is not required to make any judgment about what is good and what is bad. The morals which he enforces are those ideas about right and wrong which are already accepted by the society for which he is legislating and which are necessary to preserve its integrity. He has not to argue with himself about the merits of monogamy and polygamy; he has merely to observe that monogamy is an essential part of the structure of the society to which he belongs. Naturally he will assume that the morals of his society are good and true; if he does not, he should not be playing an active part in government. But he has not to vouch for their goodness and truth. His mandate is to preserve the essentials of his society, not to reconstruct them according to his own ideas.

How does the lawmaker ascertain the moral principles that are accepted by the society to which he belongs? He is concerned only with the fundament that is surely accepted, for legal sanctions are inappropriate for the enforcement of moral standards that are in dispute. He does not therefore need the assistance of moral philosophers, nor does he have to study the arguments upon peripheral questions. He is concerned with what is acceptable to the ordinary man, the man in the jury box, who might also be called the reasonable man or the right-minded man. When I call him the man in the jury box, I do not mean to imply that the ordinary citizen when he enters the jury box is invested with some peculiar quality that enables him to pronounce *ex cathedra* on morals. I still think of him simply as the ordinary reasonable man, but by placing him in the jury box I call attention to three points. First, the verdict of a jury must be unanimous; so a moral principle, if it is to be given the force of law, should be one which twelve men and women drawn at random from the community can be expected not only to approve but to take so seriously that they regard a breach of it as fit for punishment. Second, the man in the jury box does not give a snap judgment but returns his verdict after argument, instruction, and deliberation. Third, the jury box is a place in which the ordinary man's views on morals become directly effective. The lawmaker who makes the mistake of thinking that what he has to preserve is not the health of society but a particular regimen, will find that particular laws wither away. An important part of the machinery for hastening obsolescence is the lay element in the administration of English justice, the man in the jury box and the lay magistrate. The magistrates can act by the imposition of nominal penalties; the juryman acts by acquittal. If he gravely dislikes a law or thinks its application too harsh, he has the power, which from time immemorial he has exercised, to return a verdict of acquittal that is unassailable; and of its unassailability in English law William Penn and Bushell the juror stand as immortal witnesses.[12]

III. The View of the Philosophers

What I want to discuss immediately is the reaction that many philosophers and academic lawyers have to the doctrine I have just outlined. They dislike it very much. It reduces morality, they feel, to the level of a question of fact. What Professor H.L.A. Hart calls rationalist morality,[13] which I take to be morality embodied in the rational judgment of men who have studied moral questions and pondered long on what the answers ought to be, will be blown aside by a gust of popular morality compounded of all the irrational prejudices and emotions of the man-in-the-street. Societies in the past have tolerated witch-hunting and burnt heretics: was that done in the name of morality? There are societies today whose moral standards permit them to discriminate against men because of their color: have we to accept that? Is reason to play no part in the separation of right from wrong?

The most significant thing about questions of this type is that none of the questioners would think them worth asking if the point at issue had nothing in it of the spiritual. It is a commonplace that in our sort of society questions of great moment are settled in accordance with the opinion of the ordinary citizen who acts no more and no less rationally in matters of policy than in matters of morals. Such is the consequence of democracy and universal suffrage. Those who have had the benefit of a higher education and feel themselves better equipped to solve the nation's problems than the average may find it distasteful to submit to herd opinion. History tells them that democracies are far from perfect and have in the past done many foolish and even wicked things. But they do not dispute that in the end the will of the people must prevail, nor do they seek to appeal from it to the throne of reason. . . .

12. See Bushell's Case, Jones 1, at 13, 84 Eng. Rep. 1123 (K. B. 1670). This gives the common man, when sitting in the jury box, a sort of veto upon the enforcement of morals. One of the most interesting features of *Shaw's* case is that (in respect to uncategorized immorality contrary to common law as distinct from offenses defined by statute) it confers on the jury a right and duty more potent than an unofficial veto; it makes the jury a constitutional organ for determining what amounts to immorality and when the law should be enforced.

13. Hart, Immorality and Treason, 62 *The Listener* 162, 163 (1959). Professor Hart's views on this point have been considered by Dean Rostow in The Enforcement of Morals, 1960 *Camb. L.J.* 174, 184-92. I cannot improve on what the Dean has said; I merely elaborate it in my own words.

It is said or implied that [a collective conscience may be found] by accepting the sovereignty of reason which will direct the conscience of every man to the same conclusion. The humbler way of using the power of reason is to hold, as Aquinas did, that through it it is possible to ascertain the law as God ordered it, the natural law, the law as it ought to be; the prouder is to assert that the reason of man unaided can construct the law as it ought to be. If the latter view is right, then one must ask: As men of reason are all men equal? If they are, if every man has equivalent power of reasoning and strength of mind to subdue the baser faculties of feeling and emotion, there can be no objection to morality being a matter for the popular vote. The objection is sustainable only upon the view that the opinion of the trained and educated mind, reached as its owner believes by an unimpassioned rational process, is as a source of morals superior to the opinion of ordinary men.[15]

To the whole of this thesis, however it be put and whether or not it is valid for the individual mind that is governed by philosophy or faith, the lawmaker in a democratic society must advance insuperable objections, both practical and theoretical. The practical objection is that after centuries of debate men of undoubted reasoning power and honesty of purpose have shown themselves unable to agree on what the moral law should be, differing sometimes upon the answer to the simplest moral problem. To say this is not to deny the value of discussion among moral philosophers or to overlook the possibility that sometime between now and the end of the world universal agreement may be reached, but it is to say that as a guide to the degree of definition required by the lawmaker the method is valueless. Theoretically the method is inadmissible. If what the reason has to discover is the law of God, it is inadmissible because it assumes, as of course Aquinas did, belief in God as a lawgiver. If it is the law of man and if a common opinion on any point is held by the educated elite, what is obtained except to substitute for the voice of God the voice of the Superior Person? A free society is as much offended by the dictates of an intellectual oligarchy as by those of an autocrat.

IV. The Task of the Lawmaker

For myself I have found no satisfactory alternative to the thesis I have proposed. The opposition to it, I cannot help thinking, has not rid itself of the idea, natural to a philosopher, that a man who is seeking a moral law ought also to be in pursuit of absolute truth. If he were, they

15. In a letter published in The Times (London), March 22, 1961, p. 13 col. 5, a distinguished historian wrote that what clinched the issue in the relationship between morality and the law was "simply that it is impossible to administer justice on a law as to which there is a fundamental disagreement among *educated* opinion." (Emphasis added.)

would think it surprising if he found truth at the bottom of the popular vote. I do not think it as far from this as some learned people suppose, and I have known them to search for it in what seem to me to be odder places. But that is a subject outside the scope of this paper, which is not concerned with absolute truth. I have said that a sense of right and wrong is necessary for the life of a community. It is not necessary that their appreciation of right and wrong, tested in the light of one set or another of those abstract propositions about which men forever dispute, should be correct. If it were, only one society at most could survive. What the lawmaker has to ascertain is not the true belief but the common belief.

When I talk of the lawmaker I mean a man whose business it is to make the law whether it takes the form of a legislative enactment or of a judicial decision, as contrasted with the lawyer whose business is to interpret and apply the law as it is. Of course the two functions often overlap; judges especially are thought of as performing both. No one now is shocked by the idea that the lawyer is concerned simply with the law as it is and not as he thinks it ought to be. No one need be shocked by the idea that the lawmaker is concerned with morality as it is. There are, have been, and will be bad laws, bad morals, and bad societies. Probably no lawmaker believes that the morality he is enacting is false, but that does not make it true. Unfortunately bad societies can live on bad morals just as well as good societies on good ones.

In a democracy educated men cannot be put into a separate category for the decision of moral questions. But that does not mean that in a free society they cannot enjoy and exploit the advantage of the superior mind. The lawmaker's task, even in a democracy, is not the drab one of counting heads or of synthesizing answers to moral questions set up in a Gallup poll. In theory a sharp line can be drawn between law and morality as they are—positive law and positive morality—and as they ought to be; but in practice no such line can be drawn, because positive morality, like every other basis for the law, is subject to change, and consequently the law has to be developed. A judge is tethered to the positive law but not tied to it. So long as he does not break away from the positive law, that is, from the precedents which are set for him or the clear language of the statute which he is applying, he can determine for himself the distance and direction of his advance. Naturally he will move towards the law as he thinks it ought to be. If he has moved in the right direction, along the way his society would wish to go, there will come a time when the tetheringpoint is uprooted and moved nearer to the position he has taken; if he has moved in the wrong direction, he or his successors will be pulled back.

The legislator as an enforcer of morals has far greater latitude than the modern judge. Legislation of that sort is not usually made an election issue but is left to the initiative of those who are returned to power. In deciding whether or not to take the initiative the relevant question nearly always is not what popular morality is but whether it should be enforced by the criminal law. If there is a reasonable doubt on the first point, that doubt of itself answers the whole question in the negative. The legislator must gauge the intensity with which a popular moral conviction is held, because it is only when the obverse is generally thought to be intolerable that the criminal law can safely and properly be used. But if he decides that point in favor of the proposed legislation, there are many other factors, some of principle and some of expediency, to be weighed, and these give the legislator a very wide discretion in determining how far he will go in the direction of the law as he thinks it ought to be. The restraint upon him is that if he moves too far from the common sense of his society, he will forfeit the popular goodwill and risk seeing his work undone by his successor. . . .

VII. Morality as a Question of Fact

. . . *Shaw's* case* settles for the purposes of the law that morality in England means what twelve men and women think it means—in other words, it is to be ascertained as a question of fact. I am not repelled by that phrase, nor do I resent in such a matter submission to the mentality of the common man. . . .[Those who are opposed] must ask themselves what they *mean* when they say that they believe in democracy. Not that all men are born with equal brains—we cannot believe that; but that they have at their command—and that in this they are all born in the same degree—the faculty of telling right from wrong: this is the whole meaning of democracy, for if in this endowment men were not equal, it would be pernicious that in the government of any society they should have equal rights.

To hold that morality is a question of fact is not to deify the *status quo* or to deny the perfectibility of man. The unending search for truth goes

* Shaw v. Director of Pub. Prosecutions, [1961] 2 Weekly L.R. 897, 918, 932 (H.L.).

[Mr. Shaw had published a magazine entitled "The Ladies' Directory," which contained the names and phone numbers of prostitutes in his area. In addition to two statutory offenses, he was charged in the first count with common-law conspiracy to corrupt the public morals. The defense argued that there was no such criminal offense and that "conspiracy to corrupt the public morals" was too vague to support a criminal indictment. The House of Lords determined that the state retained the residual power to preserve the moral welfare of the public and that defining "corrupting the public morals" was within the province of the jury rather than the judge.]

on and so does the struggle towards the perfect society. It is our common creed that no society can be perfect unless it is a free society; and a free society is one that is created not as an end in itself but as a means of securing and advancing the bounds of freedom for the individuals who live within it. This is not the creed of all mankind. In this world as it is no man can be free unless he lives within the protection of a free society; if a free man needed society for no other reason, he would need it for this, that if he stood alone his freedom would be in peril. In the free society there are men, fighters for freedom, who strain at the bonds of their society, having a vision of life as they feel it ought to be. They live gloriously, and many of them die gloriously, and in life and death they magnify freedom. What they gain and as they gain it becomes the property of their society and is to be kept: the law is its keeper. So there are others, defenders and not attackers, but also fighters for freedom, for those who defend a free society defend freedom. These others are those who serve the law. They do not look up too often to the heights of what ought to be lest they lose sight of the ground on which they stand and which it is their duty to defend—the law as it is, morality as it is, freedom as it is—none of them perfect but the things that their society has got and must not let go. It is the faith of the English lawyer, as it is of all those other lawyers who took and enriched the law that Englishmen first made, that most of what their societies have got is good. With that faith they serve the law, saying as Cicero said, *"Legum denique . . . omnes servi sumus ut liberi esse possimus."* In the end we are all of us slaves to the law, for that is the condition of our freedom.

III. THE RELATIONSHIP BETWEEN SOCIAL FACT AND MORAL JUDGMENT

F. S. Cohen, Transcendental Nonsense and the Functional Approach*

I. The Heaven of Legal Concepts

Some fifty years ago a great German jurist had a curious dream. He dreamed that he died and was taken to a special heaven reserved for the theoreticians of the law. In this heaven one met, face to face, the many

* [35 *Colum. L. Rev.* 809 (1935). Footnote omitted. Reprinted by permission. For biographical information, see page 73 supra.]

concepts of jurisprudence in their absolute purity, freed from all entangling alliances with human life. Here were the disembodied spirits of good faith and bad faith, property, possession, *laches,* and rights *in rem.* Here were all the logical instruments needed to manipulate and transform these legal concepts and thus to create and to solve the most beautiful of legal problems. Here one found a dialectic-hydraulic-interpretation press, which could press an indefinite number of meanings out of any text or statute, an apparatus for constructing fictions, and a hair-splitting machine that could divide a single hair into 999,999 equal parts and, when operated by the most expert jurists, could split each of these parts again into 999,999 equal parts. The boundless opportunities of this heaven of legal concepts were open to all properly qualified jurists, provided only they drank the Lethean draught which induced forgetfulness of terrestrial human affairs. But for the most accomplished jurists the Lethean draught was entirely superfluous. They had nothing to forget.

Scientific Research and Moral Judgment*

A Philosophic Perspective

In his philosophical perspective on scientific research and moral judgment, Professor Abraham Edel of the City University of New York explored the relationship between science and ethics. The isolation of morality from the fruitful currents of scientific inquiry has given moral judgment the character of being merely expressive or emotive, Dr. Edel said. There has been a sharp conceptual dualism in both science and philosophy between *fact* and *value,* the *is* and the *ought.* This allegedly unbridgeable gap has been used to bar attempts to study the specific relationship between science and ethics. It has been assumed that science can do no more than furnish facts and means; that it is closed out of the reckoning of ends. Yet science contains values as well as facts, and ethics contains facts are well as values.

There is no reason why sophisticated philosophers or scientists should be bound by the image of a father figure who lays down stern laws and tells people what is right and proper and good for them. There is a sharp difference between integrity of moral judgment, or what we may call moral autonomy, and ethical isolationism which puts the sciences at arm's length and says that they have nothing to say which will alter the proposition that such-and-such is good, or such-and-such is

* [*The Acquisition and Development of Values,* Report of a Conference, National Institute of Child Health and Human Development, Washington, D.C. (1968).]

right. We must not become enslaved by categories of our own making which we have developed to serve specific purposes.

The distinction of fact and value can, however, serve useful purposes. It can prevent the smuggling of values through apparently factual concepts. For example, to declare something a "need" is an apparently factual statement—yet it contains a value element in its implication that if it is not satisfied, certain *undesirable* consequences will ensue. There is actually nothing that is put before us that we cannot ask value questions about. Nothing is closed. Everything contains the permanent possibility of evaluation.

Thus the issue which faces us is not really whether we can get philosophical values from scientific facts, but whether we can clarify values through the mediation of scientific knowledge. To the degree that one permits the insights of the biological, psychological, social and historical sciences to be used, moral judgments become more definite but less arbitrary. This should not be misconstrued as saying that science can solve all moral problems. There may not be complete answers to most of our moral problems, but at least science can help us to make better rather than worse stabs in the dark.

There is no single key, no single way that science enters into moral judgment. Many tasks are involved in moral judgment, from structuring the problems and determining which moral principles are relevant, to interpreting these underlying ideas so that an effective ordering of alternative choices can be developed for achievement of the path that is chosen. There is no touchstone of rationality by which one can say this is the correct and rational judgment. An accumulation of knowledge, methods, techniques and criteria developed over the whole long history of ethics and human knowledge is involved, and the type of answer you get depends on which of these are selected and how they are combined. For example, when Mussolini invaded Ethiopia he justified his conquest by saying that all the other great powers had colonies but Italy had none, and that this was unjust. Obviously, some moral structurings are better than others for determining what should happen in a given situation; and the question is, how can we decide which principles are relevant.

[T]o decide what is at issue is not merely to evolve a bare description of the situation but to analyze it in terms of the best available psychological, social and historical understanding. This initial structuring of the problem plays the same role in ethics as does the way a question is formulated in science, yet it is often overlooked how influential in moral judgment this structuring is. The correctness of the structure chosen hangs on the extent and scope and systematic character of the scientific knowledge applied rather than on arbitrary preference. . . .

A second task in developing criteria for the correctness of moral judgment centers around the interpretation of moral ideas. This must go deeper than interpretation merely of central ethical concepts like right and wrong, good and bad, virtue and vice. The notion of justice, for example, cannot be analyzed purely in terms of a generalized common sense idea of fairness. To analyze justice adequately as a basis for moral judgment requires analysis of the principles operative in a given society. Questions of justice have to be judged on the basis of a full understanding of the notions of property, distribution, risk, reward, punishment, and so on in a society.

Similarly, in relation to honesty we have to understand the psychological, cultural and even historical depth of the conduct that is being assessed. Hartshorne and May's *Studies in Deceit* showed the situational character of honesty. To assess what is honest, we have to know the difference in attitude in the society toward such questions as taking from an impersonal corporation and from an individual, or toward juveniles who steal a car for a joyride and an organized group that appropriates cars for resale. Failure to distinguish specific content leaves us with the paradox of the same act now right, now wrong.

Gratitude is another example. In medieval times, the concept of gratitude was tied in with a complex social matrix of feudal attitudes and their class-residue, so that ingratitude toward those upon whom one depended for safety and support was almost equivalent to treason. It is no accident that Dante placed treason as a form of ingratitude at the very bottom of the bottomless pit.

If we stay only on the surface level, interpreting moral ideas without relation to specific content, we make moral judgments without depth and with restricted relevance. To unpack the psychological, social and cultural content in the case of concepts we employ is to sharpen our criteria for more adequate judgments.

The way that concepts are ordered also affects the validity of moral judgment. We have many status notions surrounding the concepts of natural, universal, absolute, normal, and their opposites. A pervasive or universal value is thought superior to a merely local one, a moral rule that is absolute to one that allows many exceptions. A value that expresses man's nature is assumed to have a large measure of justification.

In ancient tradition, the idea that something was natural tied together a bundle of three different ideas—universality, inherence and goodness. It was felt that species had directions in which they were moving, that these directions were inherent in the nature of the species, and that the good was constituted by the direction of their action. This bundle of disparate ideas was not broken by the passage of time but by evolutionary theory; and when it was broken, it was no longer possible to say this is the way men behave universally; therefore it is right. The ethical question becomes greater when these ideas are separated. The good is left to stand on its own without the reinforcement of universality and inherence, and must find its basis and relations in much more complex ways.

The concept of normal versus abnormal also has a built-in implication of status or order. If you say that a certain kind of behavior is abnormal, but have no scientific theory or data to support this statement, abnormal becomes an emotive or expressive term of vituperation. You are, in a sense, recommending conformity to a statistical norm just because a certain percentage of people do it; you are making conformity an ethical criterion. Kinsey, for example, found that a certain percentage of American males have a least one homosexual experience. He therefore regarded this as normal, with the implication that it is therefore all right. This remains a controversial question, with many psychiatrists regarding homosexuality as abnormal, and articulate homosexuals defending their way of life as a viable alternative value-set only made to seem distorted by cultural prejudice. It is, of course, possible that there are different types of homosexuality, some of which are abnormal and some of which are not. The point is, without deeper scientific knowledge, the judgment of such issues remains merely an emotional expression of attitudes and not an adequate basis for moral judgment. It may have sincerity and commitment, but without a base of scientific knowledge, it carries only the weight of liking or disliking, not the weight of correctness or incorrectness. . . .

The ways in which morality has been defined have built-in factual assumptions about the world and built-in human purposes and aims. There is no reason why the grand category of the moral should not submit to the same kind of intellectual, philosophical and scientific analysis as many other categories of human affairs. . . .

[S]ome of the characteristic functions of morality change over time. To understand the moral at any one period of human thought in history, it is necessary to see what has been built into it of human aims and purposes and presuppositions about the world. As we refine and stabilize our concept of morality by seeing how the values that were put into it originally have combined with added knowledge, the concept itself will be reconstructed—as is any concept which is appraised in the light of experience.

F. S. Cohen, Ethical Systems and Legal Ideals*

Chapter II. Legal Ideals and the Good Life

1. The Positive and the Normative in the Construction of Legal Ideals

The standard of the *good life* as applied to legal criticism points in two directions. It points to *life* as the material in which the symbolism of statute and court decision must be seen and judged,—to life, that is, rather than to such limited aspects of life as we commonly subsume under the ideas of justice or liberty or peace. It points as well to the *good* as the ultimate idea of legal activity,—again to something distinguished by its inclusiveness from the limited goods and the still more limited "oughts" which have from time to time been set up as sufficient ideals for the fashioning of the legal order. Are we justified in maintaining that there is no more simple or certain source of knowledge in legal criticism than a jurisprudence which is responsible not only to pure ethics but to all the natural and social sciences that explain the life of man?

We have seen that the attempt of legal criticism to evade the idea of the good is suicidal. What of the converse attempt to eliminate the positive sciences from the apparatus of legal criticism?

A complete science of ethics would afford the answer to every problem of legal criticism. To suppose, however, that nonethical science is therefore irrelevant in the valuation of law is to mistake the essential nature of ethical science. It is logically conceivable that men should be blessed with infallible intuitions concerning the value of all things. Without knowing what the effects of a particular lie or a particular legal decision were to be, one might be aware that those effects would be bad. In such a world positive science, while useful in many practical affairs of life, would be irrelevant to our judgments of good and bad in the field of law or in any other field. In such a world ethical science would be independent of economics, psychology, physiology, and every other positive discipline. We should not have to know, for instance, what effect a given medicine might have on the human system. It would be enough to know that under the circumstances the medicine ought to be administered. Many moral philosophers and jurists have believed that we do live in this sort of world. If, however, the ethical intuitions that we do have are limited to the objects of our direct experience, we will have to learn how

---

*[Pp. 43-46, 48 (Falcon Press 1933). Reprinted by permission.
For biographical information, see page 73 supra.]

these scattered and usually trivial objects are related to the larger wholes that we seek to value. And these relations will be disclosed not by ethical intuition but by positive science. We do not in fact have ethical reactions to the real character of a man or the real consequences of a law until we know what that character or those consequences are, and it is to psychology, economics, or some other positive science that we must turn in the endeavor to relate the complex thing that we judge to things of which we do have immediate moral knowledge.

Thus positive science plays in ethics a role similar to that which mathematical science plays in physics. Every proposition about masses and velocities is an empirical proposition which might conceivably be directly verified; and since all the propositions of physics are of that type, mathematics might seem irrelevant to physical science. But we cannot actually verify every empirical proposition of physics, and mathematics supplies the relations between propositions that we can verify and those that we cannot. Thus our direct knowledge of physical events, in itself fragmentary and trivial, is rendered fruitful and capable of systematic scientific development. So the fructifying of our ethical insights through positive science is integral to the development of a science of ethics. The knowledge that happiness is good will not lead us to the conclusion that the abolition of poverty is good without the additional assumption, upon the truth of which ethics throws no light, that poverty is a cause of unhappiness. That the abolition of poverty is desirable will not show that usury laws are good unless the effect of such laws is to reduce poverty, again a purely positive assumption. That portion of ethical science which we have called legal criticism is thus intimately dependent upon non-ethical propositions which it is the function of positive science to verify and organize.

It is important to recognize that the truth of these propositions is in no way guaranteed or illumined by ethics. The type of legal thinking we have called crypto-idealism springs naturally from something that may be called crypto-positivism. Legal philosophers like Kant, Hegel, Stammler, and Kohler, who have insisted upon the basic dependence of legal criticism upon ethics, have often minimized or ignored the equally basic dependence of legal criticism upon positive science.[1] In deducing practical rules as to marriage, slavery, property, and contract from abstract and formal moral postulates, they have regularly failed to make explicit the positive premise involved in every step of the descent from the heaven of ethical axioms to the terrestrial fields of law administra-

1. Cf. M. R. Cohen, *Reason and Nature* (1931) pp. 416-419.

tion. The result has been that their positive premises are as unenlightened as are the ethical premises of positivistic jurists. . . .

But what shall be the terms of analysis in our positive legal science? We cannot hope to trace in every aspect the consequences of legal activity. It is notorious that social science freed from ethical thought produces horrid wildernesses of useless statistics.[4] Ethics will not help us to decide whether social statistics of any given sort are true. It will help us, however, to decide whether they are useful. A conception of the good is essential to the distinction between important and unimportant studies. Sociological jurisprudence, we may venture to predict, will remain a pious hope and a program until its advocates adopt some ethical system which indicates, as does hedonism, a definite variable to look for in tracking down the significance of any legal element.

Llewellyn, Some Realism About Realism

See page 212 supra.

Fuller, American Legal Realism*

It is well to remember that the difference between the realist and the "conceptualist" is not so much a matter of specific beliefs as it is of mental constitutions. The conceptualist is not naïve enough to suppose that his principles always realize themselves in practice. Indeed, since he is usually a practical man, he is apt to be more familiar with the specific ways in which life fails to conform to the rules imposed on it than the more philosophic realist. It is not, then, that the conceptualist is ignorant of the discrepancy between Is and Ought. He is simply undisturbed by it.

On the other hand, the cleft between Is and Ought causes acute distress to the realist. He sets about resolutely to eliminate it. There are two ways in which this may be done. The Is may be compelled to conform to the Ought, or the Ought may be permitted to acquiesce in the Is. There

4. "Very little experience of using current official statistics is required to convince that statistics gathered for no purpose beyond filling a report with impressive tabulations are seldom valuable for anything else." Pound, The Call for a Realistic Jurisprudence (1931) 44 *Harvard Law Rev.* 697, 701.

*[82 *U. Pa. L. Rev.* 429, 461-462 (1934). Reprinted by permission of the University of Pennsylvania Law Review and Fred B. Rothman & Company.

For biographical information, see page 522 supra.]

are enormous difficulties in the first course. Life resists our attempts to subject it to rules; the muddy flow of Being sweeps contemptuously over the barriers of our Ought. There is something even more disheartening. We find it impossible to say exactly what it is we wish life to conform to, what our Ought is. Life laughs at our rules, and even our rules betray us by refusing to reveal their nature to us. The easier course beckons temptingly, to let the Ought acquiesce in the Is, to let law surrender to life.

The realist ends in ambiguity. About one thing he is clear. The disgraceful discrepancy between life and rules must be eliminated. But he is not sure whether his prescription is to force life into conformity with a new, more carefully drawn set of rules, or to permit rules to give way to life. This ambiguity is found in what is perhaps the most ancient formulation of legal realism: *Regula est, quae rem quae est breviter enarrat. Non ex regula ius sumatur, sed ex jure quod est regula fiat.*[76] *Don't get your law from rules, but get your rules from the law that is.* Is this merely a methodological caution, warning us that paper rules often fail to express adequately the principles actually in force? Or does it mean that principles really have no force, and we must get our rules from the "law" of life itself? The clarity of the realist position has not increased perceptibly since the time of Paulus. The modern realist is still not clear in his own mind whether he objects to "conceptualism" because it fails to achieve an accurate formulation of its principles, or because it pretends to proceed according to principle at all.

F. S. Cohen, The Problems of a Functional Jurisprudence*

Function and Value

. . . It is one of the serious dangers of the functional approach that those who invoke it for the purpose of description may without further thought utilise it as a criterion of value. It is important for the jurist to remember that when he has described the human significance of a rule he has not thereby justified its existence. The task of valuation remains to be faced.

Caution against normative use of a functional definition of law is particularly pertinent because of the ambiguity of the word "function."

76. Paulus in Dig. 50, 17, *De diversis regulis,* 1.
* [1 *Mod. L. Rev.* 5, 24-26 (1937). Reprinted by permission.
For biographical information, see page 73 supra.]

When one says, for instance, that it is the function of the judge to apply pre-existing law to the facts of a case, one may mean that this is what a judge *ought* to do or simply that this is what judges *actually* do. A statement of the latter type is purely descriptive. A statement of the former type assumes a standard of values, and is, in effect, an ethical judgment.

It is to be emphasised that functional analysis of a legal rule or decision is purely a descriptive process. On the other hand, an intelligent value judgment upon any legal rule or decision presupposes such descriptive functional analysis, but also involves an ethical premise.

It was Bentham's great and enduring contribution to legal criticism to insist that the value of a legal rule depends upon its human consequences. In the field of legal criticism, or normative jurisprudence, functionalism is simply a development of utilitarianism. It is a development, however, which seeks to overcome certain weaknesses in the philosophy and method of Bentham and his immediate successors.

In the first place, Bentham failed to distinguish between his general theory of value, i.e. that the value of any act depends upon its consequences, and his theory of the good, i.e. that pleasure or happiness is the only good. The latter theory is one that many reasonable people reject, and although I happen to believe that all the objections thus far levelled against Bentham's hedonism are inconclusive,[45] I should agree that one may adopt alternative standards of ultimate value without getting into logical self-contradiction.

But no matter what other standards of value one may adopt, the essential basis of utilitarianism remains.[46]

Bentham's doctrine that the value of any legal rule depends upon its consequences was met with the philosophical challenge: Why should we assume that the value of anything depends upon its consequences? Functionalism exposes the emptiness of this challenge, by showing that the distinction between law and its consequences is purely arbitrary. The meaning of a legal rule is not action commanded but action caused. One cannot evaluate a legal rule or institution intelligently without knowing the action caused which constitutes the human meaning of the rule or institution. The challenge to Bentham's general theory of value turns out to be only a verbal confusion.

A further weakness in Bentham's utilitarianism springs from the general state of the social sciences at the time Bentham wrote. While insisting that the value of law depends upon the effect of law on human

45. F. S. Cohen, *Ethical Systems and Legal Ideals* (1933), pp. 185-220
46. This is recognised by so vigorous a critic of hedonism as G. E. Moore. *Ethics* (1912), chaps. 1-3; *Principia Ethica* (1903), chaps. 1-2.

conduct, Bentham himself was unable to utilise any scientific study of such effects, for the simple reason that no scientific study of such effects had ever been made. The bare materials for such a study—judicial statistics, general social statistics, and social case studies—were lacking. Bentham therefore had to rely entirely upon common observation in making his own calculations of the effects of various legal rules and institutions. To-day jurisprudence can draw upon a wealth of material, scientifically collected and organised, in tracing the effects of law in human society.

In the field of legal criticism the functional method may thus be conceived as essentially a reorientation of utilitarianism to a wider philosophical perspective and to a broader horizon of relevant knowledge in the fields of psychology, economics, criminology, and general sociology.

Chapter 6

Law and Metaphysics: Of Natural Law

Holmes, Natural Law*

It is not enough for the knight of romance that you agree that his lady is a very nice girl—if you do not admit that she is the best that God ever made or will make, you must fight. There is in all men a demand for the superlative, so much so that the poor devil who has no other way of reaching it attains it by getting drunk. It seems to me that this demand is at the bottom of the philosopher's effort to prove that truth is absolute and of the jurist's search for criteria of universal validity which he collects under the head of natural law. . . .

. . . If, as I have suggested elsewhere, the truth may be defined as the system of my (intellectual) limitations,[1] what gives it objectivity is the fact that I find my fellow man to greater or less extent (never wholly) subject to the same *Can't Helps*. If I think that I am sitting at a table I find that the other persons present agree with me; so if I say that the sum of the angles of a triangle is equal to two right angles. If I am in a minority of one they send for a doctor or lock me up; and I am so far able to transcend the to me convincing testimony of my senses or my reason as to recognize that if I am alone probably something is wrong with my works.

* [From *Collected Legal Papers* 310, 311-316 by Oliver Wendell Holmes, copyright, 1920, by Harcourt, Brace and Company, Inc. Originally published in 32 *Harv. L. Rev.* 40, (1918). Suggested by reading François Gény, *Science et technique en droit positif privé*, Paris, 1915. Reprinted by permission.

For biographical information, see page 59 supra.]
1. *Ideals and Doubts,* in *Collected Legal Papers.*

557

Certitude is not the test of certainty. We have been cocksure of
many things that were not so. If I may quote myself again, property,
friendship, and truth have a common root in time. One cannot be
wrenched from the rocky crevices into which one has grown for many
years without feeling that one is attacked in one's life. What we most love
and revere generally is determined by early associations. I love granite
rocks and barberry bushes, no doubt because with them were my earliest
joys that reach back through the past eternity of my life. But while one's
experience thus makes certain preferences dogmatic for oneself, recognition of how they came to be so leaves one able to see that others, poor
souls, may be equally dogmatic about something else. And this again
means scepticism. Not that one's belief or love does not remain. Not that
we would not fight and die for it if important—we all, whether we know
it or not, are fighting to make the kind of a world that we should like—
but that we have learned to recognize that others will fight and die to
make a different world, with equal sincerity or belief. Deep-seated preferences cannot be argued about—you can not argue a man into liking a
glass of beer—and therefore, when differences are sufficiently far
reaching, we try to kill the other man rather than let him have his way.
But that is perfectly consistent with admitting that, so far as appears, his
grounds are just as good as ours.

The jurists who believe in natural law seem to me to be in that naive
state of mind that accepts what has been familiar and accepted by them
and their neighbors as something that must be accepted by all men everywhere. No doubt it is true that, so far as we can see ahead, some arrangements and the rudiments of familiar institutions seem to be necessary
elements in any society that may spring from our own and that would
seem to us to be civilized—some form of permanent association between
the sexes—some residue of property individually owned—some mode
of binding oneself to specified future conduct—at the bottom of all,
some protection for the person. But without speculating whether a
group is imaginable in which all but the last of these might disappear
and the last be subject to qualifications that most of us would abhor, the
question remains as to the *Ought* of natural law.

It is true that beliefs and wishes have a transcendental basis in the
sense that their foundation is arbitrary. You can not help entertaining
and feeling them, and there is an end of it. As an arbitrary fact people
wish to live, and we say with various degrees of certainty that they can do
so only on certain conditions. To do it they must eat and drink. That
necessity is absolute. It is a necessity of less degree but practically general
that they should live in society. If they live in society, so far as we can see,
there are further conditions. Reason working on experience does tell us,

no doubt, that if our wish to live continues, we can do it only on those terms. But that seems to me the whole of the matter. I see no *a priori* duty to live with others and in that way, but simply a statement of what I must do if I wish to remain alive. If I do live with others they tell me that I must do and abstain from doing various things or they will put the screws on to me. I believe that they will, and being of the same mind as to their conduct I not only accept the rules but come in time to accept them with sympathy and emotional affirmation and begin to talk about duties and rights. But for legal purposes a right is only the hypostasis of a prophecy—the imagination of a substance supporting the fact that the public force will be brought to bear upon those who do things said to contravene it—just as we talk of the force of gravitation accounting for the conduct of bodies in space. One phrase adds no more than the other to what we know without it. No doubt behind these legal rights is the fighting will of the subject to maintain them, and the spread of his emotions to the general rules by which they are maintained; but that does not seem to me the same thing as the supposed *a priori* discernment of a duty or the assertion of a preëxisting right. A dog will fight for his bone.

The most fundamental of the supposed preëxisting rights the right to life—is sacrificed without a scruple not only in war, but whenever the interest of society, that is, of the predominant power in the community, is thought to demand it. Whether that interest is the interest of mankind in the long run no one can tell, and as, in any event, to those who do not think with Kant and Hegel it is only an interest, the sanctity disappears. I remember a very tender-hearted judge being of opinion that closing a hatch to stop a fire and the destruction of a cargo was justified even if it was known that doing so would stifle a man below. It is idle to illustrate further, because to those who agree with me I am uttering commonplaces and to those who disagree I am ignoring the necessary foundations of thought. The *a priori* men generally call the dissentients superficial. But I do agree with them in believing that one's attitude on these matters is closely connected with one's general attitude toward the universe. Proximately, as has been suggested, it is determined largely by early associations and temperament, coupled with the desire to have an absolute guide. Men to a great extent believe what they want to—although I see in that no basis for a philosophy that tells us what we should want to want.

Now when we come to our attitude toward the universe I do not see any rational ground for demanding the superlative—for being dissatisfied unless we are assured that our truth is cosmic truth, if there is such a thing—that the ultimates of a little creature on this little earth are the last word of the unimaginable whole. If a man sees no reason for believing that significance, consciousness and ideals are more than marks of the finite, that does not justify what has been familiar in French sceptics; getting upon a pedestal and professing to look with haughty scorn upon a world in ruins. . . .

That the universe has in it more than we understand, that the private soldiers have not been told the plan of campaign, or even that there is one, rather than some vaster unthinkable to which every predicate is an impertinence, has no bearing upon our conduct. We still shall fight— all of us because we want to live, some, at least, because we want to realize our spontaneity and prove our powers, for the joy of it, and we may leave to the unknown the supposed final valuation of that which in any event has value to us. It is enough for us that the universe has produced us and has within it, as less than it, all that we believe and love.

M. R. Cohen,
Justice Holmes and
the Nature of Law*

Nominalism and the Reality of Rules

The decisive role of judicial decisions in modern law leads some behaviourists to substitute the behaviour of the judge for that of the people, as the substance of the law. The most direct expression of this is the view of Professor Bingham that the law consists of the actual individual decisions and that rules are no part of the law, but are mere subjective ideas in the minds of those who think about the law.[18]

If we are to have a rational science of law, we must realize the untenability of this position, which is not at all involved in Holmes's dictum that "the prophecies of what the courts will do in fact and nothing more pretentious are what I mean by law."

Bingham's position is explicitly based on a dualistic metaphysics that assumes a mind and a world external to it. Judges, cases, and decisions presumably exist in the external world. But "Principles and rules cannot exist outside the mind. . . . The external expression of them does . . . the meaning then exists only in the mind of the speaker or

---

* [From *Law and the Social Order* 208-214, by Morris R. Cohen, copyright, 1933, by Harcourt, Brace and Company, Inc. Reprinted, with slight modifications, from 31 *Col. L. Rev.* 360 (1931). Reprinted by permission.

For biographical information, see page 81 supra.]

18. Bingham, "What is the Law?" (1912) *Mich. L. Rev.* Vol. XI, (1912), pp. 109 et seq; Bingham, "Legal Philosophy and the Law" *Ill. L. Rev.,* Vol. IX (1914), p. 96 et seq.

writer as he makes it." This is an old popular metaphysics going back to medieval times, and still regnant, but quite untenable on reflection.

Let us in the first place distinguish between the meaning of things, and what exists in our minds when we apprehend this meaning. The former belongs to or follows from the nature of the things considered, while the latter depends not only on there being such objective meaning but also on our willingness and ability to apprehend. Consider, for instance, the meaning of entropy or of the chemical law of multiple proportion. It consists, as Peirce has shown, of all the possible consequences that follow from it. We may, by study, learn more or less of this meaning, and it may then in a metaphorical sense be said to have entered into, and to be in, our mind. But the condition of this happening is that there should be such things in the nature of the things studied. If the law of entropy or that of multiple proportion is true, its objective meaning or set of consequences held true before they entered the mind of any speaker or writer—indeed before our planetary system was formed. The meanings of things do not, then, depend on the mind of the individual thinker, speaker, or writer. Rather does the fate of the individual depend on his seeing what there is to be seen of the principles or rules which enter into these meanings.

Far from its being absurd, as Bingham asserts, to suppose that principles and rules can exist independently of the comprehension of the individual observer, that is exactly what we all assume whenever we undertake to teach any science or systematic truth. And the law is no exception. Certainly when the lawyer argues any case or tries to expound any legal doctrine, he tries to make his hearer or reader comprehend the meaning of certain rules or general principles previously not in the mind of the hearer or reader. And it is a sheer fallacy to suppose that because meanings may in a sense be said to enter into or exist in our minds when we apprehend them, they cannot therefore be genuine parts or features of the objective world apprehended.

Back, however, of the subjectivist's failure to realize the objectivity of meaning is the nominalist's difficulty in seeing the reality of the universals that enter into all meaning. This difficulty, as has been intimated before, arises from the fallacy of reification, that is, of regarding universals as if they were additional particular things, so that it seems reasonable to ask, Where are they? But the question shows a confusion, since everything localized in time and space is by definition particular. As all, however, that we can ever say about anything involves abstract traits, relations, or universals, no one can well dismiss them as mere meaningless sounds or words on paper, and the nominalist tries to meet the difficulty by locating all universals or abstractions in the mind. But if there is any difficulty about conceiving them in objective nature, that difficulty is not cured by putting them in the mind. For if the nominalistic logic is good it should lead us, as it led Berkeley, to deny that there can be any universal ideas in the mind. My idea of a triangle (in the sense of an image existing in the mind) must be of a particular size, scalene or isosceles, etc. Indeed, Professor Bingham does argue that there is no real identity between a rule in the mind of A and a rule in the mind of B that in common speech would be called the same rule.[19]

But why stop here? If the same rule cannot exist in two different minds, can it exist in the same mind at different times? Indeed, how can any existing mind or anything whatsoever be the same if there is no identity in nature? And if there is no identity in nature, all references to any object as the same are false or meaningless. If, *per contra,* abstract identity and diversity are real traits of things in nature, there is no difficulty in recognizing them as universal principles that are part of the objective meaning of things. Things and their meanings do not exist in absolutely separate worlds "external" to each other, if these meanings follow from or express the nature of things. Rules, we are told, help us to analyze the facts. They could not do so if the facts were unrelated to them and had nothing in common with them.

The root difficulty of the nominalist is that he confuses the existence of particular images in individual minds with the objective meaning of principles or rules in our common world. In considering a rule, such as the rule in Shelley's case, different thinkers may look at it from different points of view and see different phases of it. They will have different images in their minds and will express themselves in different words, perhaps in different languages. Yet it is possible for them to mean or refer to the same object. Otherwise, there could be no possibility of argument or communication. Communication presupposes a common world.

If the reader finds the foregoing paragraphs too abstruse, he may consider the reality of rules and principles independently of the metaphysical quagmire on which Bingham chooses to rest it. The gist of the question is, Do or do not legal decisions that form the law necessarily involve rules and principles? The issue may perhaps be made somewhat clearer if we ask whether a given judge is acting in an official or a purely personal capacity. Obviously, if we make any such distinction it is because there are rules that give legal effect to the judge's decision only when he acts in conformity with them. Moreover, within the scope of the judge's legal power we may distinguish between the rulings that are taken as precedents in similar cases and the exercise of discretionary

19. Bingham, "Legal Philosophy and the Law," as cited, pp. 96, 114.

power that issues binding orders which do not serve as rules for the future. Thus a judge may legally deny the plea of counsel for an adjournment; but so long as it does not serve as a precedent the denial cannot be said to make law, though it is within the law. The same is true of any discretionary administrative act, e.g., when a postmaster refuses to listen to my suggestions as to the improvement of the service.

The *mediatore* in the Spanish market who terminates the haggling by making the two parties close the bargain can hardly be called a judge. Neither is an arbitrator a judge, unless his decisions are supposed to follow or embody some rule or principle of social authority. Consider on the other hand a court of appeal deciding that the trial judge erred in admitting certain evidence, that replacement value rather than original cost is the proper basis on which to compute railway rates, or that the law of the domicile should govern the validity of a divorce. In these cases, the decisions are clearly meaningless apart from the rule which they explicitly embody. But every decision of a court is taken nowadays by the community as a norm or rule for all similar cases because of the community's faith that the courts will consistently enforce that rule. Mr. X sues Bank Y for a specific amount of money computed on the basis of the value of the Russian ruble at a specific time. We can say that the court decides only the case before it. But in fact all who deal in foreign exchange are affected and adjust their practices accordingly. For they expect that the courts will rule similarly in all similar cases. The element of identity which makes different cases similar is what we formulate as the rule of the case.

Bingham admits that courts are and should be governed by constitutional provisions and statutes enacted by legislatures. Are not these formulated in general rules? And are not parts of the common law as definite as that?

The present wave of nominalism in juristic science is a reaction by younger men against the *abuse* of abstract principles by an older generation that neglected the adequate factual analysis necessary to make principles properly applicable. It is natural, therefore, for the rebels to claim as their own one who for more than the time of one generation has valiently stood for the need of more factual knowledge in the law. But no group can claim Justice Holmes as its own unless it shares his respect for the complexity of the legal situation and exercises the same caution against hastily jumping from one extreme error to the opposite. Holmes's position is, I judge, in perfect agreement with that of a logical pragmatist like Peirce: Legal principles have no meaning apart from the judicial decisions in concrete cases that can be deduced from them, and principles alone (i.e. without knowledge or assumption as to the facts) cannot logically decide cases. But Holmes has always insisted that the man of science in the law must not only possess an eye for detail but also "insight which tells him what details are significant."[20] And significance involves general principles that determine which facts are relevant and which may be neglected as irrelevant. The law consists of prophecies as to how the public force (as directed by courts) will act. But the judge whom Holmes[21] most respects is the one who, like Shaw, not only has technical knowledge, but also understands "the ground of public policy to which all laws must ultimately be referred." Indeed, no modern state appoints judges at random or backs up their arbitrary whims. Judges are generally required to have some legal knowledge, so that their decisions, despite the element of discretion,[22] should conform to the general pattern of the legal system. Such conformity would be impossible if the judicial decisions were entirely capricious. If the decision of each case were independent of any principle explicitly stated by some authority or implicitly contained in previous cases, there could be no point in judge, counsel, or any one else studying or knowing any law. No case can serve as a clue to any other except to the extent that they both contain some common elements to which a common principle is applicable.

The fact that the judge has a large element of discretion need not prevent us from expecting of him, as of any other official—perhaps even more than of others—conformity to the law. "Sittest thou to judge me after the law and commandest me to be smitten contrary to the law?" Justice involves conformity to some rule, not anarchy.

The difficulty of seeing what rule a given case involves is partly due to the traditional way of talking about the *ratio decidendi* as if a single case by itself could logically determine a rule. Since every individual case can be subsumed under any number of rules of varying generality, it clearly cannot establish any of them. It is only because every case is related more or less to previous cases—no human situation can be altogether unrelated to all previous situations—that a decision on it tends to fix the immediate direction of the stream of legal decision. The relation between

20. *Collected Legal Papers,* p. 224.

21. *The Common Law,* p. 106; cf. *Collected Legal Papers,* p. 198.

22. The regimental commander or the classroom teacher also has a large element of discretion. But if there is any difference between wise and unwise, loyal or disloyal use of discretion, it must ultimately be expressible in some formula or rule that gives the rational ground of the distinction. The rule need not be always explicitly formulated. But the gift of acting in accordance with it goes more often with trained than with untrained intuition. And training must consist in seeking to grasp a rule so that we may recognize old elements in new situations. Cf. the essay "Rule vs. Discretion," pp. 259-267 of this volume.

decisions and rules may thus be viewed as analogous to that between points and a line. No single point nor, in strict accuracy, any finite number of points can by themselves completely determine the nature of the line or curve that passes through them.

M. R. Cohen, Reason and Nature*

Natural Rights and Positive Law[1]

§1. A Priori *Objections to the Doctrine of Natural Law*

To defend a doctrine of natural rights today, requires either insensibility to the world's progress or else considerable courage in the face of it. Whether all doctrines of natural rights of man died with the French Revolution or were killed by the historical learning of the nineteenth century, every one who enjoys the consciousness of being enlightened knows that they are, and by right ought to be, dead.[2] The attempt to defend a doctrine of natural rights before historians and political scientists would be treated very much like an attempt to defend the belief in witchcraft. It would be regarded as emanating only from the intellectual underworld. And yet, while in this country only old judges and hopelessly antiquated text-book writers still cling to this supposedly eighteenth-century doctrine, on the Continent the doctrine of natural law has been revived by advanced jurists of diverse schools, in France, Germany, Belgium, and Italy, and stands forth unabashed and in militant attire.

There are, of course, important differences between the new and the old brands of natural law, which show that the attack on the old natural law was not without some justification. Yet the name "natural law" is not inappropriately applied to the new doctrines, which are, in essence, a reassertion of the old in a form more in harmony with modern thought.

---

* [Harcourt, Brace and Company, Inc. 1931), Book III, Chap. 4, pp. 401-417, 417-423, 424-426. Reprinted by permission.

For biographical information, see page 81 supra.]

1. The greater part of this chapter has been printed in two separate articles, "*Jus Naturale Redivivum*," *Philosophical Review*, Vol. XXV (1916), p. 761, and "Positivism and the Limits of Idealism in the Law," *Columbia Law Review*, Vol. XXVII (1927), p. 238.

2. Thus in an address before the American Historical Association, Dr. James Sullivan referred to popular discussion of inalienable rights as only serving to "illustrate the wide gulf which separates the scholarly world from the general public. The world of learning has long abandoned the state of nature theory." (Report of the American Historical Association for 1902, pp. 67-68.) The assumption, however, that with the fall of the "state of nature" theory all questions of inalienable rights are eliminated is quite gratuitous and in no way borne out by Dr. Sullivan's own evidence.

That this reassertion is scientifically possible I shall try to show by a critical examination of the four usual arguments against the theory of natural law, namely, the historical, the psychologic, the legal, and the metaphysical.

(A) Historical Argument

The first and most popular argument is the historical one. This argument assumes that the old doctrine of natural law rested on a belief in the actual existence of human beings in a state of nature prior to organized society; and as history has not shown that such a state ever existed, natural law falls to the ground. To this very simple argument the reply is that the old doctrines of natural law rested on no such foundation. Even Rousseau disclaims it in his maturer work, as is well known to those who take the unusual course of actually reading his *Contrat Social.* When Grotius, Hobbes, and their followers speak of a state of nature they do not as a rule mean to refer to a past event. The "state of nature" is a term of logical or psychologic analysis, denoting that which would or does exist apart from civil authority. It is logically, not chronologically, prior to the "civil state." Similarly the "social contract" is not a past event, but a concept of a continuous social transformation.[4]

There is, doubtless, a good deal of *a priori* history to be found in seventeenth and eighteenth century thought. But consider the general and now almost classical belief that human progress passes through certain necessary stages, and that by the proper handling of our scant and crude information about certain savage or primitive races, we can reconstruct the universal history of mankind. Is not this likewise *a priori* history? Yet, would it be fair to reject entirely a legal philosophy such as Kohler's for no other reason than that it assumes a necessary succession of matriarchal and patriarchal stages which, from the point of view of scientific history, are entirely mythical? The essence of the old natural law was an appeal from the actual or merely existing to an ideal of what is desirable, or ought to be, and historical considerations alone will not settle the matter.

It would be absurd, of course, to deny all value to historical study as an aid in the correction of the aberrations of the old natural law theories.

4. This comes out most clearly in Kant, who discusses the whole matter on purely ethical postulates. That Hobbes, also, kept free from historical assumptions is clearly brought out by Dunning, *Political Theories,* Vol. 2. There are two or three passages in Locke and one, at least, in Kant—not to mention Rousseau's immature discourse—in which the "state of nature" is spoken of in the past tense. But these lapses into the common way of speaking cannot be shown to have had any influence on the general ideas of Locke or Kant.

Historical study has helped to break down what might be called either the absolutism or the provincialism of the old natural law, under the aegis of which people assumed their own local ideals to be valid for all times, places, and conditions. But historical study has been only one of the elements which have brought about our cosmopolitan thought. The widening of human geography by purely physical means, the increased ease of communication between different peoples, the more intimate acquaintance with oriental and other types of social life, are other and in some respects even more important elements. In the writings of Hegel, Karl Marx, and the German historical school of jurisprudence, the real nature of historicism as an inverted or romantic form of rationalism becomes apparent. The absolute, the system of production, and the *Volksgeist* simply take the place of ordinary human reason. They function in an entirely *a priori* rationalistic way. Instead of refuting the normative standpoint of the old natural law, these writers substitute an unconscious natural law of their own. Instead of the revolutionary dogma of the complete plasticity of social institutions, they substitute the equally absurd conservative dogma of the futility of human effort. Even the English historical school of jurisprudence has been shown by Professor Pound to be guilty of the same offence of setting up its own idealization of the prevailing system as necessarily valid for all times.[5] The great enemy in our field is not rationalism, but the identification of the definitive universal goal with something merely historical, as the supposed condition of the Hebrews before the monarchy, the system of equity in Lord Eldon's day, or the Prussian state of the time of Hegel. Even more vicious and extravagant is the dogma that every state is the best for its time.

(B) Psychological Argument

The second type of argument, the psychologic, is based on the assumption that all theories of natural law must be intellectualistic and individualistic. The eighteenth century was undoubtedly intellectualistic, in the sense that it attributed entirely too much to conscious experience, deliberate invention, or consensual contract,[6] and too little to slow unconscious growth; and we can but smile at the astounding naïveté of such

---

5. "The Scope and Purpose of Sociological Jurisprudence," *Harvard Law Review,* Vol. XXIV (1911), pp. 600-604.

6. The classical theory of natural law embodied in the Canon Law or in the writings of St. Thomas is entirely free from this tendency to reduce all obligations to contractual ones. Anglo-American historical jurisprudence, however, influenced by Maine's maxim, "Legal progress is from status to contract," has gone far in reading fictional consent or contract into the law.

views as that religion is an invention of the priests. But while a shallow mechanical intellectualism did colour all the speculation of the Enlightenment, there is no necessary connection between it and the theories of natural law. Certainly the jural views of Grotius, Hobbes, and Spinoza, or even those of Locke and Rousseau cannot be so easily condemned. Moreover, a great deal may be said for the view that would prefer the shallow intellectualism of the Enlightenment to the romantic distrust of human reason, which denies (as do Hegel, Karl Marx, and, in part, Savigny) that reflective thought can aid in the transformation of jural and political institutions.[7]

Similar considerations hold in regard to the supposed individualism of all natural law theories. Eighteenth and even seventeenth century speculation did undoubtedly err in attributing a self-sufficiency to the abstract or isolated individual which modern psychology holds he could not have in the absence of organized society. Government and laws, we now see, are not mere external checks over affairs which might prosper without them, but necessary conditions of organized social life. There might be physical objects, but there can be no property, industry, or family continuity without property and family law adequately enforced.[7a] But while laws and government protection create legal rights, the effectiveness of this process depends on the recognition of previously existing fundamental psychic or social interests. To the extent that these interests exist and demand protection even prior to the specific law which meets their demand, they are the raw material of natural rights. There is no property in ideas or published works before the existence of patent and copyright laws; but interests and claims do exist prior to and not as creatures of these laws which they call into being. The latter must justify themselves by the services they render to these and other interests.

(C) Legalistic Argument

The third or purely legal argument has received its definitive form in Bergbohm's *Jurisprudenz und Rechtsphilosophie*. It is not unfair to represent his attitude to natural law as parallel to that of the pious Mohammedan to learning outside that of the Koran: Natural law either repeats the rules of positive law, and is futile, or it contradicts them and is illegal and

---

7. It may seem strange that a panlogist like Hegel should be such a contemner of reflective reason. But that he was so influenced by the Romantic reaction against the Enlightenment and the Revolution, his *Rechtsphilosophie* proves beyond doubt.

7a. See "Property and Sovereignty," *Cornell Law Quarterly,* Vol. XIII (1927) p. 8.

not law at all. Conditioning this is, of course, the belief in the all-sufficiency of positive law as a closed legal system to regulate all possible cases. Unfortunately, however, the distinction between positive and natural law is not as well defined as that between the Koran and all other books. If positive law means law actually enacted by some human agency devoid of supernatural omniscience, it is clear that it cannot foresee and regulate all possible contingencies. The domains of life thus not provided for in the positive law are regulated by the customary rules of what people think fair, which thus constitute a natural or non-positive law. Where such rules, though non-legal, are fairly well established, judges will be bound by them (except in cases where their own sense of fairness asserts itself). Those who believe in the closed or all-comprehensive character of the positive law have tried to save their theory from these facts by saying that the positive law is only formally, not materially, closed. But this, like the fiction that whatever the sovereign has not prohibited happens by his command, gives us very little insight into the life of the law. It certainly ought not to hide the fact that ethical views as to what is fair and just are, and always have been, streaming into the law through all the human agencies that are connected with it, judges and jurists as well as legislature and public opinion. Indeed, the body of the law could not long maintain itself if it did not conform in large measure to the prevailing sense of justice.

Reviewing Lorimer's *Institutes of Law,* Pollock says of natural law that it "either does not exist or does not concern lawyers more than any one else," and "I do not see that a jurist is bound to be a moral philosopher more than other men." But twenty years later he says:[8] "Some English writers half a century behind their time still maintain the absolute Benthamite aversion to its name (natural law). Meanwhile, our courts have to go on making a great deal of law, which is really natural law, whether they know it or not, for they must find a solution for every question that comes before them, and general considerations of justice and convenience must be relied on in default of positive authority."

But if the sense of justice must necessarily exercise an influence in any growing law,[9] it becomes of utmost importance to the jurist that the

8. Pollock, *Essays in Ethics and Jurisprudence,* pp. 19, 23, and the *Expansion of the Common Law,* Ch. IV.

9. I have developed this point at length in "The Process of Judicial Legislation," *American Law Review,* Vol. XLVIII (1914), p. 161, and need not repeat the arguments there made. I may, however, mention two arguments that have been advanced against the position there indicated. (1) Judges, we are told, have no license to legislate at will in the interests of justice and morality. Certainly not. But neither have they authority to decide any cases that are not presented to them. When, however, cases *are* presented, they must de-

principles of justice or natural law should receive the careful and critical treatment which we call scientific method. Hence, the Continental jurists who are giving up the view that legal interpretation is a mechanical process of extracting from the words of a statute a peculiar and magical essence called the will of the legislator, and who recognize that jurisprudence must necessarily be growing and creative, are also beginning to recognize the need of a systematic science of justice or natural law.

As foreign ideas, however, may seem undesirable immigrants in the field of American jurisprudence, we can press the last point in the field that is peculiarly native to us, that is, our constitutional law. The bills of rights of our Federal and State Constitutions embody certain popular principles of justice, and in spite of over a century of judicature, such phrases as "due process of law," "equal protection of rights," etc., are still essentially more or less vague moral maxims—the effort to transform them into legal principles of fixed meaning being thwarted by the imperative need of making an eighteenth century document fit the needs of twentieth century life. Hence, the problem of justice remains an inescapable one in the field of constitutional law.

Those who would denude the phrases of our bills of rights of their moral connotation urge that it is not well for courts of law to become courts of morals. Without wishing at this point to discuss the advisability of a system of government whereby a very small number of non-elective judges must, on the basis of a few hours' argument, say the deciding word on grave public questions, such as railroad rates, industrial combinations, etc., and without wishing to pass judgment on the actual results of our courts' efforts to enforce the body of moral principles (some at least of which they hold to be independent or anterior to all written constitutions), we may still urge that the fear of our courts becoming censors of morals is not well taken. The objection is not well taken because it fails to distinguish between individual morals, which must take into account personal motives, and questions of right and wrong in external and enforcible relations. The moral principles of our bills of rights are entirely of the latter kind. It is for that reason that I think it advisable to keep the old distinction between the science of natural rights or justice and the science of personal morals or ethics. The principles of justice applicable

---

cide; and when issues come up, as they certainly do nowadays, which require the weighing of considerations of public policy, social welfare or justice, judges must legislate. (2) It is also urged that in new cases, judges must depend on the analogy of established principles. But it is a poor lawyer who cannot meet an analogy against him with another one in his favour, and upright judges, in choosing or weighing the force of different or competing analogies, must inevitably rely on their sense of justice.

and enforcible in public relations may be regarded as part of social ethics, but they form a distinct group of problems relatively as independent of the other problems as the questions of economics are of the other questions of sociology. If the work of our courts in applying maxims of natural law has proved unsatisfactory, it does not follow that principles of justice cannot or ought not be worked into the law. Legal history shows that they always have been the life of the law.[10] So far as the use of the moral maxims of our bills of rights has actually proved unsatisfactory, the causes are to be sought in the specific conditions under which our courts have done their work. Of these conditions not the least harmful is the belief that jurists need no special training in the science of justice (either because law has nothing to do with justice, or else because what constitutes justice under any given condition is something which any one can readily determine by asking a magical arbiter called conscience). It may well be that such phrases as "due process of law," "cruel and unusual punishment," "republican form of government," and "direct tax," are too hopelessly vague to serve as definite legal rules. But these phrases will not prevent courts giving the stamp of constitutionality to legislation the justice of which can be shown to them.

The essence of all doctrines of natural law is the appeal from positive law to justice, from the law that is to the law which ought to be; and unless we are ready to assert that the concept of a law that ought to be is for some reason an inadmissible one, the roots of natural law remain untouched. Now, it is true that the issue has seldom been so sharply put, for to do so is to espouse an amount of dualism between the *is* and the *ought* which is shocking to the philosophically respectable. The respectable dread to admit the existence of real conflicts in our intellectual household; they would rather conceal them by ambiguous terms such as *natural* or *normal*. This is most apparent in the most philistine of all philosophic schools, the Stoics, whose tremendous influence in jurisprudence has brought about much intellectual confusion. There have not, of course, been wanting intellectual radicals who, in the interests of a strident monism have clearly and conscientiously attempted to eliminate the chasm between the *ought* and the *is,* either by denying the former, or by trying to reduce it to a species of the latter. Thrasymachus's definition of justice as the interest of the stronger, finds its modern form in the definition of right as the will of the sovereign, of the people, or of the dominant group. But few of these radical positivists have had the courage of

10. There is no adequate direct history of the interaction between positive and natural law; but material will be found in the writings of M. Voigt, in Landsberg's *Geschichte,* F. von Liszt's *Das deutsche Strafrecht,* and Gierke's *Genossenschaftsrecht,* Vol. IV.

their convictions; they smuggle in some normative principle, such as harmony with the tendency of evolution, social solidarity, etc., as *the* valid ideal. Marx may have boasted that he never made use of the word *justice* in his writings; but his followers would dwindle into insignificance if they could not appeal against the crying injustices of the present "system." The most courageous of all such positivists, Hobbes and Nietzsche, have not escaped the necessity of admitting, in a more or less thinly disguised form, a moral imperative contrary to the actually established forces. Our analytical school of jurisprudence, pretending to study only the law that is, has been repeatedly shown to be permeated with an anonymous natural law.

The boldest attempt in history to do away with the antithesis between what is and what ought to be is, of course, the Hegelian philosophy, with its violent assertion of the complete identity of the real and the rational. And it is one of the instructive ironies of fate that this most monistic utterance of man should have led to the widest rift that ever separated the adherents of a philosophic school. To the orthodox or conservative right this meant the glorification or deification of the actual Prussian state. To the revolutionary left, of the type of Karl Marx, it meant the denial of the right of existence to the irrational actual state. Nor need this surprise us, as the Hegelian philosophy is at least as fluid as its object, of which, indeed, it professes to be the outcome. By its own dialectic it sets up its own opposite, so that its assertion of the identity of the real and the rational gives way to the insight that in the necessary opposition between these two we have the clue to the process or life of civilization. If the jurist objects that this is indeed fishing in muddy rather than deep waters, and that the science of law has, fortunately, nothing to do with all this, our answer is that this is precisely the muddy condition in which the legal theory of this country finds itself today. In the prevalent legal theory we find the conflicting assertions that the law is (and ought to be) the will of the people, and that it is (and ought to be) the expression of immutable justice; and an unwillingness to recognize the inconsistency which this involves. Professional philosophers, it seems, are not the only ones to take refuge in a twilight zone when their eyes are not strong enough to face sun-clear distinctions. The intellectual motives which lead to this disinclination to admit a sharp distinction between what is and what ought to be, come out perhaps clearest in the noble efforts of physicians engaged in teaching sex hygiene and furthering sex morality. They are afraid to characterize certain practices as immoral. They think it is more scientific to use such terms as unnatural or abnormal, knowing full well that these practices are natural in the sense that they are due to what are called natural causes, and normal in the sense that they are, alas, quite usual and widespread.

572

One of the roots of this error, which is also the basis of all empiricism, is the assumption that science necessarily deals only with the actual. It would take us far afield to point out that this is based on the inadequate analysis of scientific procedure which is embodied in the Aristotelian or scholastic logic with its underlying assumption that all propositions are of the substance-attribute type. If instead of the classificatory zoology, which is the science that Aristotle had in mind, we look at the sciences which use the hypothetic-deductive method, we get a different perspective. The objects of two contrary hypotheses cannot both exist; yet in every branch of any developed science progress depends upon such rival hypotheses receiving equally careful scientific elaboration before either can be rejected. Indeed, every branch of science aims to assume the form of rational mechanics or geometry, in which we do not directly deal with the realm of existence, but rather with the realm of validity or the valid consequences of given hypotheses or axioms. And not only scientific progress, but all practical activities, such as those of statesmanship, depend upon reasoning of the form, "What *would happen* if this engine were perfect or frictionless?" even though we know such perfection to be impossible. Intelligent action demands that we know what will happen if we turn to the right and what will happen if we turn to the left, though it is certain we cannot do both.

(D) Metaphysical Argument

The metaphysical objection to the possibility of a theory of natural law or justice runs thus[12a]—"Questions of justice are relative to time, place, and the changing conditions of life. Hence there cannot be such a thing as a definite science of these matters." The widespread prevalence of this view, even in high places, shows how woefully unfamiliar is the logic of science. The objection ignores the difference between a substantive code and a science of principles, a distinction which ought to be as clear as that between the directions of the engineer to the builder and the science of mechanics. The temperature or the time of sunrise of different places undoubtedly varies, yet that does not prove the absence of a rule or formula for computing it. Similarly substantive rules such as those of property cannot be well drawn without taking into account specific agricultural or industrial conditions. But this does not deny—on the contrary, it presupposes—the existence of a general rule or method for the determination of how far any property rule justly meets the demands of its time.

Moreover, there are indications that the variability of social judg-

12a. See Lévy-Bruhl, *La Morale et la Science des Moeurs*, pp. 257–260, 279.

ments, such as those with regard to justice, has as a matter of fact been greatly misunderstood. The first impression of savage life as gathered from the reports of scientifically untrained travellers and others interested in noting striking differences, together with the intellectual intoxication produced by the frenzied acceptance of the principle of universal evolution, have combined to produce an over-emphasis on the diversities of human culture. As soon, however, as we get over the disposition to run wild with the concept of evolution, and examine the matter somewhat soberly, the fundamental resemblances of all human races and modes of life will be seen not to have lost significance. Historians as radical and free from metaphysical preferences as Robinson find it necessary to emphasize the fundamental unity of human history, as opposed to the differences which separate us from the Greeks or Assyrians, and critical ethnologists like Boas are pointing out that the unscientific, uncritical reports of untrained observers as to so-called primitive life have produced false impressions of radical moral differences, and that the actual variations of moral opinion are largely explicable by the variation of social conditions.[13] In ordinary affairs and in public discussion we all do undoubtedly assume a large amount of agreement as to what constitutes justice. And while such agreement is not conclusive, it offers a sufficiently definite starting point for a critical science, which, according to the Platonic method, consists in positing ideals (or hypotheses) and criticizing or testing them in the light of ascertained social fact.

Militating against this programme are the prevalent views (1) that questions of justice are all matters of opinion, and (2) that all things are in a flux but that there is no *logos* (reason or formula) to determine the fact that things are changing, and no definite measure according to which they do so. Against the first, or Sophistic position, it is sufficient to point out that no one in practice disbelieves that one opinion may be better founded than another. Against the blind worship of the dogma of universal and absolute change, it ought to be sufficient to point out that chance and constancy are strictly co-relative terms. The world of experience certainly does not show us anything constant except in reference to that which is changing, nor any change except by reference to something constant. We may generalize change as much as we like, saying that even the most general laws of nature that we now know, such as the laws of mechanics, are slowly changing, but this change can be established and have meaning only by means of or in reference to some logical constant. The belief that the world consists of all change and no constancy is no better than the belief that all vessels have insides but no outsides.

13. Robinson, "The Unity of History," in *International Congress of Art and Sciences* (1904), Vol. II; Boas, *The Mind of Primitive Man.*

§2. Difficulties in the Path of Natural Law

Approaching the subject from the point of view of the requirements of a scientific theory, let us ask what is the character of the principles of legal justice or natural law, and how are they to be established? The traditional answer from the Stoics down to our own day is that they are axioms whose self-evidence is revealed to us by the light of natural reason. This belief is implied in the way in which these principles are appealed to in popular discussion of natural rights. In a Catholic manual of socialism, we have a long list of such eternal first principles, which are put in the same class with such axioms as "The whole is greater than any part," "The cause must be equal to the effect," and the like. As the model for this view is presented by the Euclidean geometry it is suggestive to apply to these self-evident axioms the criticism which modern mathematics has applied to the Euclidean systems. The discovery of non-Euclidean geometry and the whole trend of modern mathematical thought has led us to discard as unreliable the self-evident character of axioms or principles. Such principles as that two magnitudes equal to the same are equal to each other, or that a straight line is the shortest distance between two points, are seen to be simply definitions, while others are either hypotheses or assumptions or else rules of procedure or postulates, whose contraries may not only be just as conceivable but even preferable in certain systems of mechanics. If now we apply the same criticism to our assumed principles of natural law, such as "All men are equal before the law," or "All men have the right to life, to the product of their labour, etc.," it becomes evident that it will not do to rely on their apparent self-evidence, and that the only way to defend them against those who would deny them is to show that like other scientific principles, e.g., the Copernican hypothesis in astronomy, they yield a body or system of propositions which is preferable to that which can possibly be established on the basis of their denial.

Like other scientific hypotheses they are to be tested by their certainty, accuracy, universality, and coherency. No science of justice can be built up by an intellectual *coup de main;* patient analysis of the multitudes of fact as well as the proper use of principles is required. No mere postulating of principles nor unimaginative abandonment to the infinity of details will enable us to make the necessary progress. We must control the work of philosophy with the wealth of the facts revealed by legal science, and analyze these facts in the light of the best available philosophy.

In particular, we must observe the limitations which are imposed upon the ideal of justice, as upon any ethical norm, by the positive factors in our problem, factors which, by varying in different environments, justify the diversity and reveal the unity of natural or ideal law. This much, indeed, we may grant to the critics of the classical natural law theories: that the proponents of such doctrines, either because of limited historical and anthropological learning or because of a cosmopolitan emphasis upon the similarity of all races and all ages, have generally minimized the role played by contingent, empirical facts in the materialization of our formal principles of justice.

To a certain extent the problem is common to all normative science. If our ultimate standards be formulated in terms of desire, we must ask what, as a matter of brute fact, the people of a given time and place do desire, if in terms of happiness, what will actually make present-day Americans (say) happy, and so on. Even the narrowest ethical commandments, e.g., "Respect private property," or "Cure the sick," demand non-ethical investigation of extreme complexity and difficulty if they are to achieve a practical concreteness. In part, however, the problem of interpreting natural law for a given social milieu is specifically one of legal science. What, we must ask, are the limitations which law, as an instrument of social control, imposes upon the ideal that it serves? And finally we must frankly recognize the dependence of natural law upon ultimate ethical principles. No doctrine of natural law can claim a greater degree of certainty and completeness than attaches to the basic ethical principles which it presupposes.

Our rejection, therefore, of the various *a priori* arguments against the possibility of natural law leaves us with a problem in which three difficulties must be faced, namely (a) the indeterminateness of our jural ideals, (b) the intractability of the human materials with which law works, and (c) the inherent limitations of general rules.

(A) The Indeterminateness of our Jural Ideals

It is a common illusion to suppose that for all questions that can possibly arise our ideal of justice determines a specific answer. Our ideals are in fact much hazier than we ever care to admit.

We all begin by accepting the judgments prevailing in our community. Popular judgments and proverbial wisdom, however, though they may contain a kernel of enduring truth, seldom express it with a high degree of accuracy or consistency. It is because of this vagueness and inconsistency in popular judgment that science is needed as a corrective. The greater simplicity of their subject-matter, the more definitely elaborated technique, and a certain amount of ethical neutrality as to their result, enable the natural sciences to depart from popular opinion to a far greater extent than is possible in the social sciences.

This, together with the natural difficulty of seeing any justice in doctrines or sectaries abhorrent to us, makes the elaboration of a consistent ideal of justice a task of the utmost difficulty. That this difficulty has not been fully overcome in treatises on ethics, natural law, or legal philosophy, becomes obvious when we ask: What precisely is the content of justice and on what evidence are its disputed claims based?

The classical legal definition of justice makes it consist in rendering every one his own: *suum cuique tribuere*.[14] But what is rightly anybody's own is precisely the problem which the law must determine according to some principle of justice. Otherwise the just becomes simply the legal and there is no possibility of unjust law.

If we go to books on ethics we are told that justice accords to every one that which he has earned, or that a just law protects every one in the enjoyment of the product of his labour. But what in a co-operative social state is the product of any one man's labour? In practice this is settled somewhat arbitrarily, by appeal to the law which happens to exist. Moreover even if we could determine on principle what is the product of any one's labour it would be very doubtful morality if one could keep it all when others, the sick, the infant, or the very aged, were to perish because of the exercise of this right.

That legal justice in some way demands the principle of equality seems certain. But what exactly do we mean by equality before the law? In the end nothing more than fidelity to the classification that the law has already laid down. If all creditors are to share alike in a bankrupt's estate, equality before the law means that the judge must not favour any one party. Obviously, this does not enlighten us as to whether the classification that the law has created is itself just. Should not the law give certain creditors precedence, for example, those who are creditors of a railroad by virtue of having suffered bodily injury? Legal justice is formal. It is important that the law, once created, should be justly, i.e. faithfully, administered. But it is also important that the law should be just in content to begin with and purely formal considerations are insufficient to determine this.

The Kantian and neo-Kantian efforts to derive conclusions as to specific questions of justice from purely formal principles ignore the logical fact, made clear by modern logic, that from pure universals no particular existential propositions can properly be deduced. Pure universals are hypotheses and you cannot prove a fact by piling up nothing but suppositions. This can be seen in Kant's own efforts to derive the rules of perfect and imperfect obligations from purely formal considerations.

14. *Dig.* I. i. 10.

These rules follow only if we accept certain empirical ends of life and assume certain conditions of life to remain permanent. For our present purpose we can see this best in Stammler's legal philosophy.[15] Stammler's ideal of a community of free-willing men appeals to us for various historic reasons, chiefly because of linguistic associations of the word *freedom*. Critical reflection, however, shows that his ideal itself is essentially vague and indeterminate, if not completely empty. It does not in fact logically support any of the conclusions which Stammler tries to derive from it, since quite different conclusions can be derived from his ideal with equal logical propriety. Let us take a concrete example. Two people mutually agree to live together in free love or being married voluntarily agree to separate and live with other parties. Stammler supports the view of most civilized countries in refusing to sanction a contract of this sort. Yet he does not *prove* that there is anything here contrary to the ideal of a community of free wills. Nor does this ideal enable us to determine whether a contract of employment, dictated by economic necessity, should be enforced. Something more empirical and specific than abstract free will is necessary to arrive at a rational account as to what kinds of agreements should and what kinds should not be legally enforced. Again, in time of war we conscript men against their will to be killed or maimed for life. Can the right to do this be derived in strict logic from the ideal of a community of free-willing men? Stammler evades all real problems of this sort by circularly defining the free will as the rational will that is bent on rendering to each what is objectively just. This circular dependence of justice on free will and free will on justice makes the whole enterprise fruitless. Had Stammler used free will in its ordinary sense, as the freedom of the empirical wills of ordinary human beings, Stammler's theory might have been more a condemnation than a derivation of most of our criminal and public law, especially of our laws of taxation, tariff duties, etc. It is noteworthy that despite Stammler's pretensions to establish absolute principles, the only law he condemns as unjust is that of slavery. But what is slavery? Do not many labour contracts differ from slavery only in arbitrary legal form, rather than in the substance of things? His rule that "the contents of a given volition must not be arbitrarily made subject to another volition" is devoid of definite meaning, since the word "arbitrarily" is just a blank term that can be filled with question-begging interpretations, so that by means of it you can condemn or justify anything you please. . . .

15. See his *Theory of Justice* (1925) in the Legal Philosophy Series. For criticism see E. Kaufmann, *Kritik der neukantischen Rechtsphilosophie* (1921), and Wielikowski, *Die Neukantianer in der Rechtsphilosophie* (1914).

The fundamental indeterminism of Stammler's ideal has compelled some of his disciples[16] to speak of the ideal of "the place and the epoch" instead of the ideal valid for all time and place. Doubtless, the ideal prevailing in any given country at any time is much more definite. But that this always coincides with justice it is difficult to admit when we remember that some opposing countries feel and think quite differently. The Austrians felt quite justified in regarding the Trentino as a region to be saved for German culture. Italy is certain that "sacred egoism" demands that the south Tyrolese be compelled to become Italians. Surely both cannot be right. Is it any different between peoples of different grades of culture? European nations professing Christian love feel themselves thereby justified in bombarding with air-bombs Mohammedan villages that refuse to be ruled by them; but the Mohammedans are not thereby convinced.

Nor do we get much farther if with the neo-Hegelians we set up the ideal of "the epoch of civilization." The term civilization is at best a vague one, and the division of the continuous stream of human history into epochs varies with the purpose of the historian. In any case, we get little help here in deciding the nature of justice. To assert that the ideal of justice varies with time does not help us to know what is and what is not just at any given time, for example, at the present. Indeed, no answer is possible at all on an Hegelian or on any other monistic determinism, which allows no real chasm between what is and what ought to be—a chasm which gives meaning to the human struggle and its tragic, though noble, defeat through the ages. The actual efforts of neo-Hegelians, like Kohler and Berolzheimer, to determine what is right by reference to the ideal of our own epoch are certainly not always and altogether fortunate —witness Kohler's remark on the retributive theory of punishment, or Berolzheimer's remark, in 1908, on the effect of strengthening the German fleet.[17] I am the last man in the world to maintain that the neo-Hegelians are the only ones to talk nonsense when they are certain that they have caught the idea of the epoch of our civilization. Kohler was undoubtedly a man of genius though erratic and uncritically opinionated. But his occasional insights have little support in the vague neo-Hegelian philosophy which he professes.

On a subject teeming with human significance rigorous logic is of the utmost importance. Such logic shows us a radical and incurable difficulty in all idealistic philosophies of law: either their ideal is, like the

16. See Brütt, *Die Kunst der Rechtsanwendung* (1907).
17. Kohler, *Moderne Rechtsprobleme* (1913), and Berolzheimer, *System der Rechtsund Wirtschaftsphilosophie* (1907), end of Vol. IV.

Kantian, purely formal and incapable of solving material issues, or, like the older theories of natural law and the post-Kantian idealism, they uncritically assume certain material principles as self-evident. Critical reflection generally shows these self-evident ethical and jural propositions to be either question-begging, purely verbal plausibilities, or rhetorical justifications for preferences that are too spasmodic to serve as the basis of developed legal systems.

Can we abandon the effort to formulate a rational ideal that is to govern the facts of the law? Can the ideal of justice be derived from history or the empirical study of the facts themselves? Obviously not, if history or empirical study is restricted to the realm of existential facts, since our conclusion cannot contain an *ought* if all our premises are restricted to what *is*. But even if we begin with empirical judgments of what ought to be in concrete cases, we need some comprehensive ideal to organize our conflicting judgments into something like a coherent body. It is doubtless true that our ideal grows more definite as our experience expands and we get more opportunity to develop as well as to test our ideal by applying it. Still, any ideal that is to govern facts of conduct must be more simple, uniform and constant than these facts themselves. Otherwise it could not serve as a guide.

Dean Pound has used the postulates of civilization as a justification for the laws that secure the interests of personality, possession and transactions.[18] Certainly without such security our type of civilization is impossible. But these postulates do not undertake to settle questions of justice as to which of two heterogeneous and conflicting interests should prevail. An injunction is asked against striking employes. If the injunction is not granted, irreparable property injury will result. If it is granted, the workingmen will not be able to keep up the organization which protects their standard of living. Which of the two conflicting interests should justly prevail? The law has to balance interests but it has no scientific scale to measure the weight of conflicting interests nor has it even any means of reducing them to some common denominator.

I conclude, therefore, that no ideal so far suggested is both formally necessary and materially adequate to determine definitely which of our actually conflicting interests should justly prevail. So long as this is the case, law must be, as it is, in large part a special technique for determining what would otherwise be uncertain and subject to conflict. It is socially necessary to have a rule of the road but it is morally indifferent whether it requires us to turn to the right or to the left.

This need for certainty and the inconvenience involved in changing

18. See his *Introduction to the Philosophy of Law* (1922).

580

men's rights enforce the human inertia which generally makes the law lag behind the best moral insight. As obedience to law rests on habit, a philosopher like Aristotle can plausibly argue that it is better that an unjust law should prevail than that law should become uncertain by change.

In the absence of an adequately determinate moral ideal many questions must be left to the discretion of judges and administrators. If the judge is both intelligent and well disposed, his exercise of the discretion is one of the ways whereby concrete justice is found. Yet the need for discretion indicates a limitation of legal justice. To be ruled by a judge is, to the extent that he is not bound by law, tyranny or despotism. It may often be intelligent and benevolent, but it is tyranny just the same. For political reasons it may be well to cultivate respect for judges; but from a philosophic point of view it is a crude superstition to suppose that any one can escape the limits of his intelligence and the bias of his limited experience by being elevated to an office. History does not show that the partisan bias of limited group experience can always be removed by legal training or by the criticism of the legal profession. Professional opinion is itself class opinion. This is not to disparage the judge or the legal profession. On the contrary! He surely is no friend of any profession who encourages its members to think that they are free from human limitations—ὕβειζ invites the wrath of the gods.

(B) The Intractability of Human Materials

The inevitable imperfections in the human beings that have to make, to enforce, and to obey the law constitute a second serious obstacle in the elaboration of legal ideals.

We may view the limitations of imperfect human nature (1) from the point of view of the legislator, (2) from the point of view of those who have to obey the law, and (3) from the point of view of those who have to enforce it or operate the legal machinery.

(1) *Inherent limits of legislative power.* The obvious fact which no glorification of law can obscure is that it is made by human beings subject to the limitations of human ignorance and of inadequate sympathy or good will.

(i) The ignorance of the legislator may relate to the end of the law which he helps to bring about. Moved by the demand for the redress of some grievance, the legislature enacts a statute. But changing the law is like making a change in the intricate plot of a highly organized drama. You cannot change one part without other parts being affected in unexpected ways. Legislatures thus seldom have an adequate idea of what they intend to bring about. The Napoleonic Code intended to guarantee that all the children shall have some part of the patrimony. Did its authors have any idea that they were erecting a check to the growth of population?

(ii) Assuming that the legislator knows what effect he wants to produce, he may be ignorant of the natural circumstances involved. Our southern legislatures feel competent to pass on the truths of biologic evolution and one of our western states came near decreeing some absurd value for π. All our state legislatures feel competent to pass on the truths of history to be taught in the public schools. Modern states all contain heterogenous elements. Hence laws applicable to a vast majority may be absurd for some groups or regions—e.g. trial by jury in those United States possessions inhabited by Negritos. Rural legislators do not know or sympathize with urban industrial life and city legislators do not always understand the conditions of farm life.

(iii) Of special importance is the imperfect power of the legislature to control the subsequent interpretation of its enactments. The legislature can express its intention only in general terms. It cannot foresee all actual cases. It cannot therefore completely control the interpretation and application of its statutes by courts and administrators bent on making the law serve other and wide purposes. The legislature generally looks to the removal of a specific abuse while the judge and the jurist must look upon any statute as a part of the whole legal system. Thus the first legislatures that wished to change the common law as to the property rights of married women were repeatedly defeated by courts that persisted in thinking of these statutes in terms of the traditional common law.

(2) *Inherent difficulties in forcing obedience to the law.* That in a democracy the law is the will of the people is a statement not of a fact but of an aspiration. A great deal of the law is and necessarily must be the work of legislatures, courts, and jurists, whose work is seldom fully known to the majority of the people. Indeed, as to rules of conduct on which people are fairly unanimous there is no need for the enactment of any law. Enacted law represents the will of some part of the community and the rest obey either out of respect or by force of habitual obedience to regular authority. Yet neither legislatures, courts, jurists, nor all combined are omnipotent. There is no way of securing perfect obedience where there are strong human motives for disobedience or evasion.

The failure of the law to secure obedience has been historically shown in at least four fields of human life, viz. religion, personal morals, economics, and politics.

In the field of religion, the persistence despite persecution of the

Christian Churches in the early Roman Empire, of the Jews and Christian dissenters in Russia, England, and elsewhere, shows how persistently small minorities may defy and defeat the law.

The field of personal morals has always been a favourite interest of the law, but legal failures in this field are proverbial. It is true that sumptuary laws have often been generally obeyed, e.g., in the Middle Ages. But this happened only so long as they conformed to the general moral feeling of mediaeval society. When they cease to express a strong moral consensus they cease to be effective. Take for instance the case of the New York law which makes adultery a crime. Though many thousands of divorces have been granted for that offence there seem to have been hardly any convictions for the crime. As a criminal law it is a dead letter. Yet any proposal to repeal it would meet with widespread resentment. The majority of the people of New York State emphatically wish the statute book to express their disapproval of adultery. Why, then, has there been no enforcement of it? The answer is to be found in the inherent difficulty of enforcement. It is an unpleasant and unedifying thing to bring into court. Moreover it is extremely doubtful whether convictions would greatly reduce the number of actual offences, or result in more good than harm.

The experience of our national prohibition law and the many evils which its enforcement involves, especially the violation of the law by the very agents of the government, are too flagrant to need anything but bare mention here.

It is interesting, however, to reflect that these evils are not merely contemporary. Long ago a most detached philosopher, Spinoza, wrote, "He who tries to fix and determine everything by law will inflame rather than correct the vices of the world."[19] He also observed:

"Many attempts have been made to frame sumptuary laws. But these attempts have never succeeded in their end. For all laws that can be violated without doing any one an injury are laughed at. Nay, so far are they from doing anything to control the desires and passions of men, that, on the contrary, they direct and incite men's thoughts the more towards those very objects; for we always strive for what is forbidden, and desire the things we are not allowed to have. And men of leisure are never deficient in the ingenuity needed to enable them to outwit laws framed to regulate things which cannot be entirely forbidden. . . . My conclusion, then, is that those vices which are commonly bred in a state of peace . . . can never be directly prevented but only indirectly. That is to say, we can only prevent them by constituting the state in such a way

19. *Tractatus Theol. Polit.*, Ch. 20.

583

that most men will not indeed live with wisdom (for that cannot be secured simply by law), but will be led by those emotions from which the state will derive most advantage."[20]. . .

(3) *The limits of legal machinery.* Dean Pound has treated this topic with his usual thoroughness in an essay on "The Limits of Effective Legal Action"[22] and I may add only a few remarks. Legal machinery, we must remember, never operates apart from human beings, judges, juries, police officials, etc. The imperfect knowledge or intelligence of these human beings is bound to assert itself. It is therefore vain to expect that the legal machinery will work with a perfection that no other human institution does. We cannot expect results too fine for the discrimination of the ordinary juryman. A great deal of injustice cannot be prevented by law because the attempt to do so is bound to produce greater evil than it can cure. I think that the action for breach of promise to marry well illustrates this. Apart from the injury to public decency from the fact that this action is so often used purely for blackmail, it is a bad policy for the law to put a monetary value on the marriage promise and to seem in any way to force people into the marriage relation when the churches so strenuously insist that no matter what promises have passed between the two parties there shall be no marriage performed unless both parties are perfectly willing at the time of the ceremony.

It would be foolishness to contend that in the various fields mentioned, law has never been effective. Few injustices are absolutely beyond all human effort, if we are willing to make sufficient sacrifice to remove them. But it is folly to centre our attention on some result desirable in itself and ignore the fearful cost of incidental consequences required to attain it.

We conclude then that in view of the necessary limitations of any legal system and the many insuperable difficulties in the way of enforcing all sorts of moral considerations, it is a wicked stupidity that insists on "justice regardless of consequences." *Fiat justitia pereat mundus* is the device of the fanatic, too lazy to think out the consequences of his position. The more wisdom is summed up in saying, *summum ius, summa injuria.*

(C) The Abstractness of Legal Rules[23]

The third limitation of legal idealism is due to the fact that legal justice must operate with abstract general rules. To guarantee equality be-

20. *Tractatus Polit.*, Ch. 10, 5–6.
22. *International Journal of Ethics*, Vol. XXVII (1917), p. 150.
23. I have treated this topic at greater length in "Rule vs. Discretion," *Journal of Philosophy*, Vol. XI (1914), p. 208.

fore the law and eliminate favouritism or partiality, the law must operate with rules that are to apply to every one. No one is allowed to beg in the street whether he be poor or rich, strong or sick, young or old. Any one under twenty-one years has certain privileges in connection with contracts, no matter how developed intellectually or in the way of business experience. The injustice which this abstract uniformity works in particular cases has generally been recognized and many efforts are made within the legal system to correct it by some form of individualization, *equity,* or *epieikeia.*[24] This individualization itself, however, becomes subject to rule or else it remains lawless. The demand for abstract uniformity of legal rules is intensified by the fact that a developed legal system must assume a scientific form and that it can do so only as other sciences do, namely by the discovery of principles in terms of concepts so that multitudes of rules can be deduced from a few such principles. This abstract universality of legal rule is necessary to secure certainty. It ministers to a certain sense of justice which may be viewed as the rationalization of jealousy. But all rigid rules applied to life tend to suppress favourable as well as unfavourable variation. At times it becomes obvious that it is only the better element of a community that suffers from certain laws, while the worse elements evade or successfully defy them. Thus, while the law cannot admit the sovereignty of individual conscience without opening the door to anarchy, it must also recognize that individual conscience may be a much more delicate instrument for moral apprehension, so that to suppress it is to bar the way for more enlightened justice. This inherent difficulty of legal justice, like other difficulties of social life, is not overcome by the Hegelian trick of making *Sittlichkeit* or social ethics supersede the morality of conscience.

An uncritical reliance on the abstract universality of legal justice is the crowning ethical defect of the so-called critical philosophy. It legalizes ethics without moralizing the law. It formulates its imperative in the abstract legalistic manner to the neglect of individual differences. Thus Kant's argument that it is always wrong to tell a lie is a striking example of legalistic ethics. In the end it is based on bad logic as well as on moral insensitiveness, as is Kant's horrible view of marriage as a mutual lease of the sexual organs.

Universality and individuality, justice, and the law, the ideal and the actual, are inseparable, yet never completely identifiable. Like being and becoming, unity and plurality, rest and motion, they are polar categories. Deny one and the other becomes meaningless. Yet the two must always remain opposed. Theoretically, the legal system may be viewed

24. Aristotle, *Nichomachean Ethics,* V.

completely from either pole. You may even insist that there is little difference if any between a positivism like Gray's which allows for moral judgments upon the law, and an idealism that admits the inherent limitation of any ideal of justice that can be applied to human affairs. There is a sense in which the same system of legal rights and duties might be expressed in positivistic or in idealistic language. But not only is language itself a most important factor in human affairs—since all sorts of emotional differences arise from differences of expression—but so long as our knowledge remains incomplete it makes a difference from which end we view the legal system. The positivistic and the idealistic perspective cannot be identical on the level of human knowledge. Positivists fail in trying to separate law from all ideals, and Hegelians fail in trying to identify the ideal with some form of the actual, whether the Prussian or any other state.

The deeper and more ancient wisdom is to recognize that divine perfection is denied to human beings in legal as in other practical affairs. It is romantic foolishness to expect that man can by his own puny efforts make a heaven of earth. But to wear out our lives in the pursuit of worthy though imperfectly attainable ideals is the essence of human dignity.

M. R. Cohen, Reason and Nature*

§V. The Principle of Polarity

The foregoing considerations are all applications of a wider principle, viz. the principle of polarity. By this I mean that opposites such as immediacy and mediation, unity and plurality, the fixed and the flux, substance and function, ideal and real, actual and possible, etc., like the north (positive) and south (negative) poles of a magnet, all involve each other when applied to any significant entity. Familiar illustrations of this are: that physical action is not possible without resistance or reaction and that protoplasm, in the language of Huxley, cannot live except by continually dying. The idea is as old as philosophy. Anaximander expressed it in saying that determinate form arises out of the indefinite (*to apeiron*) with the emergence of opposites like hot and cold, dry and moist, etc. And Heraclitus insisted that strife was the father of all things and that the balancing of opposite forces, as in the string of the bow or lyre, gave form to things. The essential Hellenic wisdom of Socrates and Plato

* [Harcourt, Brace and Company, Inc. 1931), Book I, Chap. 4, pp. 165-168. Reprinted by permission.

For biographical information, see page 81 supra.]

which viewed justice and the other virtues as conduct according to measure (Aristotle's mean) involves the idea of adjustment of opposite considerations. The relativity of form and matter, according to Aristotle, is determinative of all existence (save the divine essence).[1]

This principle of polarity seems to me to represent what is sound in the Hegelian dialectic without the indecent confusion at which we arrive if we violate the principle of contradiction and try to wipe out the distinctions of the understanding. The being and non-being of anything are always opposed and never identical, though all determination involves both affirmation and negation. Far from overriding the distinctions of the understanding the principle of polarity shows their necessity and proper use. Thus physical science employs this principle when it eliminates the vagueness and indetermination of popular categories like *high* and *low, hot* and *cold, large* and *small, far* and *near,* etc. It does so by substituting a definite determination such as a determinate number of yards or degrees of temperature. The indetermination and consequent inconclusiveness of metaphysical and of a good deal of sociologic discussion results from uncritically adhering to simple alternatives instead of resorting to the laborious process of integrating opposite assertions by finding the proper distinctions and qualifications.

Under the head of polarities we may distinguish between contradictions, antinomies, and aporias or difficulties. Strictly, speaking, contradictions are always dialectical, i.e., they hold only in a logical universe. Thus if I say a house is thirty years old, and some one else says it is thirty-one years old, the two statements are contradictory in the sense that both cannot possibly be true at the same time and in the same respect. Both statements, however, can certainly be true if we draw a distinction, e.g. thirty-one years since the beginning and thirty years since the completion of its building.

Thus two statements which, taken abstractly, are contradictory, may both be true of concrete existence provided they can be assigned to sepa-

1. The reading of Plato's *Parmenides* first impressed upon me the lesson taught to the young Socrates, viz. that it is impossible to arrive at sound philosophy without experience in tracing the diverse and opposed dialectic implications of such propositions as "unity exists" and thus learning to guard oneself against their pitfalls. Propositions are not bare tautologies but significant predications because non-being has being of a sort and *the one* is inseparable from, though not identical with, *the other*.

I am indebted to Professor Felix Adler for the figure of the scissors to denote the fact that the mind never operates effectively except by using both unity and plurality like the two blades which move in opposite directions. Professor Marshall, in his *Principles of Economics,* has used the same figure to express the mutual dependence of the two factors of supply and demand. We may, if we like, also use the figure of the pestle and mortar, of our jaws in mastication, or of applying brakes when going down a hill.

rate domains or aspects. A plurality of aspects is an essential trait of things in existence. Determinate existence thus continues free from self-contradiction because there is a distinction between the domains in which these opposing statements are each separately true. When opposing statements are completed by reference to the domains wherein they are true, there is no logical difficulty in combining them. In the purely logical or mathematical field, however, we deal not with complexes of existence, but with abstract determinations as such. Here two contradictory assertions always produce a resultant which is zero, i.e. the entity of which they are asserted is absolutely impossible.

Of incompletely determined existence—as in the case of the total universe—contradictory propositions do not annihilate each other (since they refer to a complex of existences); and yet they cannot always (because of the indefiniteness of the subject) be reconciled with each other. This gives rise to the antinomies of metaphysics.

In general, the opposite statements that are true in regard to existing things give rise to difficulties when we cannot see how to draw the proper distinction which will enable us to reconcile and combine these seeming contradictions. Thus we frequently find certain facts in a scientific realm calling for one theory, e.g., the corpuscular theory of light, and other facts calling for a diametrically opposite one, viz. the wave theory. Such difficulties are solved either by discovering new facts which give one of these theories a preponderance or else by discovering a way of combining the two theories. Sometimes an intellectual dilemma is avoided by rejecting both alternatives. This is illustrated by the old difficulty as to whether language was a human invention or a special revelation. The difficulty was avoided by introducing the concept of natural growth.

Nature also presents us with seeming impossibilities in the form of practical difficulties, e.g., how to live long without getting old, how to eat our cake and yet have it too, etc. Such contingent or physical impossibilities may baffle us forever. Yet some of them may be solved by finding the proper distinction. Thus the invention of boats enabled us to eliminate a former impossibility—namely, how to cross a river without getting wet.

This analysis puts us on guard against two opposite evil intellectual habits: on the one hand to regard real difficulties as absolute impossibilities, and on the other to belittle such difficulties by calling them false alternatives. Thus it is not sufficient to say that the old controversy between the claims of the active and those of the contemplative life represents a false alternative, and that we need both. It is in fact most frequently impossible to follow both and the actual problem of how much of one we need to sacrifice to the other often requires more knowledge than is at our disposal.

If it be urged that this after all is the essence of the Hegelian logic I should not object—provided it does not include Hegel's explicit identification of the historical and the logical, the real and the rational. The heart of Hegel's philosophy is, after all, the attempt at a synthesis calculated to do justice both to the classic rationalism of the Enlightenment and to the inspiring sweep of the romanticism of Fichte, Schelling, and their associates. Such a synthesis seems to me to be the great desideratum of our age. We cannot today accept Hegel's methods and results precisely because they are not—despite all their pretentions—sufficiently rational or logically rigorous. But his tremendous influence in law, art, and religion, as in the development of all the social sciences, shows that he grappled with a vital problem. If, as I think we should all admit, he was guilty of indecent haste due to intellectual *hubris,* it is for us to face a similar task with greater patience and honest resoluteness not to minimize the obstacles to rational inquiry.

F. S. Cohen, Field Theory and Judicial Logic*

III. Through The Blind Alleys of Jurisprudence

The Elephant and the Judicial Problem

The six blind men of Hindustan who went to see the elephant and, in the manner of the House of Lords, delivered six separate opinions on the beast, reported respectively (according to the poetic fable) that the elephant was something like a wall, a spear, a snake, a tree, a fan, and a rope. In much the same fashion, a careful historian of legal philosophy, having completed his researches into the juridical reflections of thirteen philosophers, and having "put aside immediately the attractive thought that the fundamental truths of the various philosophies of law should be sifted out and then combined into one harmonious whole," gives us the dreary and orthodox picture of thirteen great legal philosophers who could not agree even on what it was they were all talking about:

> We have been told by Plato that law is a form of social control, an instrument of the good life, the way to the discovery of reality, the true reality of the social structure; by Aristotle that it is a rule of conduct, a contract, an ideal of reason, a rule of decision, a form of order; by Cicero that it is the agreement of reason and nature, the distinction between the just and the unjust, a command or prohibition; by Aquinas

* [59 *Yale L.J.* 238, 266-272 (1950). Reprinted by permission of The Yale Law Journal and Fred B. Rothman & Company from The Yale Law Journal, Vol. 59, pp. 238, 266-272. For biographical information, see page 73 supra.]

that it is an ordinance of reason for the common good, made by him who has care of the community, and promulgated; by Bacon that certainty is the prime necessity of law; by Hobbes that law is the command of the sovereign; by Spinoza that it is a plan of life; by Leibniz that its character is determined by the structure of society; by Locke that it is a norm established by the commonwealth; by Hume that it is a body of precepts; by Kant that it is a harmonizing of wills by means of universal rules in the interests of freedom; by Fichte that it is a relation between human beings; by Hegel that it is an unfolding or realizing of the idea of right.[47]

Accepting the rough validity of Mr. Cairns' summaries of philosophical insights, is there any reason to suppose that these insights are incompatible, one with the other? Cannot the legal order be at one and the same time a "form of social control" (Plato), a "rule of conduct" and a "form of order" (Aristotle), a "command or prohibition" (Cicero) of the "sovereign" (Hobbes) or the "commonwealth" (Locke); a "plan of life" (Spinoza), "determined by the structure of society" (Leibniz); a "body of precepts" (Hume); and a "relation between human beings" (Fichte)? Even if we all meant exactly the same thing by the word "law," could we not subsume law under many broader categories, including those of "contract" (Aristotle), "rule of decision" (Aristotle), and a "way to the discovery of . . . the true reality of the social structure" (Plato)? And even if it be true that Plato, Aristotle, Cicero and Aquinas formulated their ideals of law in terms of reason and the good life, while Bacon stressed the need for certainty, and Kant and Hegel expressed an historical ideal of legal evolution towards universal justice and freedom, cannot all these views illuminate the possible goods achievable through the law? Why should we fall prey to the monolithic fallacy that only those who use a prescribed set of words can attain salvation?

If we view philosophy, including jurisprudence, not as a set of propositions but as a way of understanding, we may say that one philosophy is superior to another if it achieves a greater degree of generality so that it can include other philosophies as special cases within a larger framework of convergent perspectives. Recognition of the relativity of definitions permits the establishment of a family of perspectives (e.g., Euclidean, Riemannian, and Lobachewskian geometries).[48] A comprehensive legal philosophy can find room for the insights of many different thinkers.

47. Cairns, *Legal Philosophy from Plato to Hegel* 556 (1949).
48. The most comprehensive statement of the relativity of systems that I know of is to be found in the brief paper of Henry M. Sheffer on Notational Relativity in *Proceedings of the Sixth International Congress of Philosophy* 348-51 (1927).

Legal philosophy is not a bad play in which each actor clears the stage by killing off his predecessors. Rather is legal philosophy, like philosophy generally, a great cooperative exploration of possible perspectives (*Weltanschuungen*) through which life's many-faceted problems can be viewed.[49] Progress in legal philosophy does not depend upon rejection of the insights that came to Plato and Aristotle, any more than progress in poetry depends upon rejection of Homer, or progress in music upon contempt for Bach and Beethoven. Nor is it necessary to assume, in the fashion popularized by Hegel and Pound, that every "school" (perish the word!) of jurisprudence supersedes its predecessors. The history of legal philosophy is not, as some of Pound's writings have suggested, a sad history of successive errors, each thesis producing, in Hegelian-Marxian fashion, its own antithesis and destruction, until, by a series of stages, we come to the ultimate product of the juristic mind, sociological jurisprudence, after which anything different must be considered as one of time's typographical errors.

More tolerance may give us more truth. The house of jurisprudence has many mansions. Of law and the legal order many questions may be asked. The seekers after "natural law," who have tried to formulate in legal patterns the most general needs of human society, are not contradicted or displaced when men turn to inquire into the historical forces that produce diverse legal systems in different lands and epochs. Those who have given us the logical analysis of legal terms that goes by the name of analytical jurisprudence never denied the role of legal sociology in exploring the social sources of legal orders and disorders. Indeed, the great exponents of analytical jurisprudence, Austin, Bentham, and Holmes, were precisely the men who called most cogently for scientific inquiry into the social context and consequences of law. Those who have earned the name of "realists" by drawing clear distinctions between the *law that is* and the *law that ought to be* do not obstruct efforts at social reform by their distinction.[50] Rather, each line of exploration is likely to disclose landmarks which will prove of value to other explorers moving in different directions and starting from different approaches.

Wilmon Sheldon has acutely observed that philosophers are generally right in what they affirm of their own vision and generally wrong in what they deny of the vision of others. Now it may be true that denying the vision of others adds controversy to the spice of life and thus

49. The conception of philosophy here stated I have attempted to develop more fully in The Relativity of Philosophical Systems and the Method of Systematic Relativism, 36 *J. of Philosophy* 57 (1939).

50. See the incisive study of Garlan, *Legal Realism and Justice* (1941).

draws attention to important views that would otherwise fail to attract serious consideration. And certainly it is only natural for proponents of new thoughts, and even more natural for the camp-followers of original thinkers, to claim for these thoughts dominion over the universe of ideas. But a saner perspective shows that no philosophical or jurisprudential doctrine has ever filled the space of our intellectual universe, and that the products of human thinking across a hundred centuries, all together, illuminate only a few of the darker corners of the world we seek to understand. It is the part of wisdom, in jurisprudence, as in science and philosophy generally, to avoid extravagant claims and to give those on whose thinking we build as much respect as we hope to deserve from those who come after us.

A synoptic vision which can find value in many perspectives is not to be confused with mushy-minded scissors-and-paste eclecticism. Stringing together the views of many men who followed divergent paths is a fruitless enterprise, productive only of a sense of complete futility and confusion. If the six blind men of Hindustan who reported on the elephant had each noted the direction of his approach and the point at which he made contact with the beast, the six reports might have been systematically coordinated and a correct, though incomplete, account of the animal might have emerged. So, too, if we took account of the different perspectives from which legal philosophers have approached the problem of the nature of law, we should not only be in a better position to appraise each of their contributions but we should be able to systematize their various insights and perhaps emerge with a more comprehensive, synoptic vision of the legal order than any past generation has enjoyed.

The judge who understands how two lawyers can disagree on the elementary facts of a simple case, why each lawyer thinks the other's precedents are not in point, and how they can differ even in their causal judgments, may achieve a higher level of understanding than the most brilliant of advocates. Similarly, the vision of legal philosophy as a family of possible perspectives upon the legal order may help us to achieve a broader and deeper understanding than is attained by even the most brilliant of jurisprudential advocates.

The systematization of possible logical systems outlined by Sheffer[51] points to the possibility of a systematization of jurisprudential systems. The difficulties in such a task are serious. But if we face the difficulties resolutely, none of them appears insuperable.

51. See note 48 supra.

The Inarticulate Value Judgments of Legal Philosophers

The first difficulty in systematizing juristic perspectives lies in the fact that legal philosophers, like judges and human beings generally, do not ordinarily make explicit their own purposes or the value patterns out of which their purposes emerge. It therefore becomes necessary for those of us who seek to locate the perspective of Hobbes, Spinoza, Locke or Kant, for example, within a more comprehensive family of perspectives to understand what these men were driving at when they put forward their very different conceptions of law. If we appreciate the evils of civil warfare and anarchy which Hobbes experienced and portrayed so vividly, and if we consider his analysis of law and sovereignty as a persistent inquiry into the ways of avoiding these evils, we can hardly be satisfied with the fashionable practice of dumping Hobbes into a dustbin marked "defenders of despotism." For the evils that Hobbes saw are still before us, and though his analysis, as developed by Bentham, Austin, and Holmes, does not answer all juridical problems, it must be a part of any comprehensive view of law and the world order.

That Spinoza and his follower Locke were more concerned than Hobbes with the evils of tyranny and anxious to establish realms of civil liberty which demand respect even from governments, gives us, who are the heirs of Spinoza and Locke, as well as of Hobbes, the wherewithal to balance the needs of order and the needs of freedom in the difficult social problems that face us today.

Even the forbidding formalism of Kant comes to make practical sense if we appreciate Kant's concern with a problem which he saw more clearly a century and a half ago than many of our contemporary statesmen do today: the problem of how men pursuing radically different social goals and capable of destroying each other with the weapons of modern science can possibly evolve a pattern of living together in mutual respect, a pattern more fundamental than any of the things that mark off nation from nation, class from class, and man from man.[52]

The Relativity of Definitions

Among the difficulties that stand in the way of a comprehensive view of the legal order is the naive view of definitions as propositions which are true or false. All of the endless arguments as to whether inter-

---

52. I think the human objectives of Kant's juridical quest become clearest in his *Idea of a Universal History from a Cosmopolitical Point of View* (1784) and his *Essay on Perpetual Peace* (1795). See *Kant's Principles of Politics* (Hastie ed. 1891).

national law is really law, whether an unenforced statute is really law, etc., depend for their continuance upon the notion that only one definition of law can be correct. Once we recognize that a definition is, strictly speaking, neither true nor false but rather a resolution to use language in a certain way,[53] we are able to pass the only judgment that ever needs to be passed on a definition, a judgment of utility or inutility. We can then recognize that Holmes' definition of law as the way courts decide cases is an instrument of tremendous value for the practicing lawyer or for any critical observer of the role played by courts in modern civilization. On the other hand, we may frankly admit that the definition has very slight utility to an anthropologist investigating the ways in which Eskimos deal with murder or divorce. Clarity requires not that all of us forever adhere to a single definition but that we make clear what definition of law we are using in any given context, so that what we say can be fairly translated into other people's universes of discourse.

The Theory of Translation, and the Relativity of Nonsense

The true significance of Einstein's general theory of relativity, as we have noted,[54] is not that it calls attention to the long-recognized diversity of physical perspectives, but that it makes possible a translation from any perspective into any other perspective.

Can we translate a thought from one social perspective to another?

Certainly we try to do this whenever we translate from one language to another. Sometimes we succeed. When we fail, it is often because we forget that a language embodies the history of a people's thinking and that different people have partitioned the world in different ways.

Mark Twain, when he saw what French translators had done to his Jumping Frog story, was moved to words of despair:

> When I say, "Well, I don't see no p'ints about that frog that's any better'n any other frog," is it kind, is it just, for this Frenchman to try to make it appear that I said, "Eh bien! I no saw not that that frog had nothing of better than each frog"? I have no heart to write more. I never felt so about anything before.[55]

53. See F. S. Cohen, Transcendental Nonsense and the Functional Approach, 35 *Col. L., Rev.* 809, 835-6 (1935); M. R. Cohen, On Absolutisms in Legal Thought, 84 *U. of Pa. L. Rev.* 681 (1936).

54. See Note 4 supra. [P. 478.]

55. Mark Twain, *The Family Mark Twain* 1080 (1935) ("The Jumping Frog: In English. Then in French. Then clawed back into a civilized language once more by patient, unremunerated toil.")

Every lawyer who has seen his views of the law or the facts of a case restated or summarized by a judge who does not agree with them knows how Mark Twain felt.

Of course, some translators do better than others. A particularly fine performance was given a few years ago at a labor convention in El Paso attended by labor delegates from both sides of the Rio Grande. Those from the north side of the river made matter-of-fact speeches in English about wage increases and the reduction of working hours. Those from across the stream made impassioned speeches in Spanish about the role of labor unions in the social revolution. The translator was equal to the occasion. All the English speeches, when translated into Spanish, were about the social revolution, and all the Spanish speeches, when translated into English were about hours and wages. Mutual appreciation and understanding grew. Bonds of harmony were established that would certainly have been smashed if Mark Twain's Jumping Frog translator had sneaked into the El Paso convention.

Only in mathematics do we find perfect translations—the sort of thing that enables us to translate any proposition about a straight line in Euclidean geometry into an equivalent proposition about a curve in Riemannian geometry. But outside of mathematics, though we live in a world of imperfections, some imperfections are worse than others. Those of us who take our law in realistic doses are less likely to misunderstand writers on natural law if we translate their propositions about "law" into equivalent propositions about "legal ideals." Operating with such formulae of translation law students who have been prone to distrust all discourse written in unfamiliar terms are sometimes amazed to learn how much good sense was devoted centuries ago to some of the problems that still trouble us.

As yet this sort of translation among the different tongues of jurisprudence is mostly in the inarticulate stage of "hunch" and "intuition." The achievements of modern mathematics and physics, however, give ground for hoping that we shall some day achieve a powerful new organon for mutual understanding,—a theory of translation. Until that day comes, we may do well to remember that no two philosophers and no two jurists can ever contradict each other unless they are talking about the same thing, and that there is no reason to believe that those who use the same words necessarily mean the same things. In fact, I find it to be a fair working assumption that when a legal philosopher says something that I recognize to be absurd, the statement probably meant something different to him than it means to me. As an appendix to a theory of translation we need a doctrine of the relativity of nonsense.

Until mathematicians become lawyers or lawyers become mathematicians, we may at least cultivate the spirit of tolerance which begins by recognizing that what is worth saying can be said in any language.

Fuller, Human Purpose and Natural Law*

It is difficult to achieve effective communication in any discussion of a term that bears as many meanings as does "natural law." An adequate semantic analysis of this term would not only have to discriminate among such distinct meanings as can be discerned, but would also have to undertake something much more diffcult, that is, to trace the complicated overlappings among these meanings that make them appear to have some sort of family resemblance. Such an analysis would not advance the purposes of this paper, for the problem I wish to present relates to a fundamental insight of onotology of the sort that may indeed be presupposed in the process of definition, but can scarcely be advanced by it.

It may help to avoid misunderstanding if I state briefly what I am not attempting to do in this paper. I am not, in any usual sense, advancing a "theory of natural law." I do not bring with me any code of nature. I do not hold myself open to deal with problems of casuistry, to say how "my concept of natural law" would solve this or that case. My concern is primarily to present a problem, and only incidentally and imperfectly to suggest a solution for it. The problem to which I address myself is one with which most theories of natural law attempt to deal, however clumsily. It is a problem that positivism commonly treats as simply nonexistent.

The problem I have in mind is that which arises when we attempt to reconcile the now generally accepted dichotomy of fact and value with a purposive interpretation of human behavior. For it is my thesis that when we accept the full consequences that flow from a view which treats human action as goal-directed, the relation between fact and value assumes an aspect entirely different from that implied in the alleged "truism" that from *what is* nothing whatever follows as to *what ought to be*. Let me illustrate.

I see at a distance a boy who holds in his hand a small, gray, roundish object. He seems to be contemplating this object intently. After a period of hesitation, he places the object carefully between his palms and repeatedly presses on it. He then relaxes his grip, holds the object loosely

* [3 *Nat. L. Forum* 68-76 (1958). Reprinted by permission.
For biographical information, see page 522 supra.]

in his left hand, and begins to look about him on the ground. He apparently finds what he wants, for he bends over and picks up a stick. This he uses for a while to prod or push against the object. He then throws the stick away and bends to strike the object several times against a rock. Shortly he gives up this activity and walks about as if undecided what to do next. Suddenly he begins to gather sticks together, arranges them on the ground in a pile, lights a match to them, places the object in the fire, and then stands off in an attitude of expectancy.

Now it is obvious that something happens to this account, a sudden accretion of meaning occurs, when we learn that the boy was throughout trying to open a clam. Without this clue I could not interpret what I observed, retain accurately in memory the shape of the events that occurred, or give to another a really coherent account of what happened.

A former age would have said quite simply that this clue of purpose was necessary to "understand" what was happening. Let us, however, define "understanding" in terms consonant with modern conceptions of scientific method; that is, let us consider that we have "understanding" when we are able to *control* and *predict* events. It is obvious that any chance I might have of redirecting the boy's actions, by diverting him into a new line of activity, would depend in large measure on my knowing what he was trying to do. In a similar manner, if at any stage I was able to predict what he would do next—for example, if I had guessed correctly what he would do after he had gathered the sticks together—it would be because I had discerned, in general terms at least, the purpose he was pursuing.

Now it can be demonstrated, I believe, that in any interpretation of events which treats what is observed as purposive, fact and value merge. In such a case the view that value is something foreign to a purely factual account—something projected by the observer on the thing observed— simply will not stand scrutiny. If I can predict that the boy's attempt to open the clam by pressing it between his hands will soon be given up, it is because I know that this is not a "good" way to open clams; judged in the light of the boy's purpose it lacks "value." Here the structure of the events as they unroll—the reality of what happens through time—contains an element of value, so that we can say: "This is bad, it will not last," or "This is good, we may expect it to continue."

It will be objected at this point, I am sure, that this whole demonstration rests on the most transparent of fallacies. It will be said that a "value" element is no more intrinsic to the facts I have recounted than it would be, let us say, if I were to observe a five-foot ladder leaning against a fifteen-foot wall. Certainly this state of affairs, as related, suggests nothing like a value judgment, yet I can say of it, "This is bad," *if* I assume that someone of normal stature plans to use the ladder to scale the wall, and *if* I provisionally accept his purpose as a valid one. The only difference between this case and my previous illustration, it will be said, is that as we watch the boy with the clam, the observation of the physical events, the perception of the boy's purpose, and our provisional acceptance of that purpose as a standard for valuing what occurs, all proceed contemporaneously, so that what is in principle distinct is here blended, thus creating an illusion that fact and value have somehow merged. That they remain distinct even when we are observing the results of purposive action is made clear by the illustration of the ladder and the wall.

This argument ignores the fact that when we are dealing with purposive action projected through time, the structure that we observe, recall, and report lies, not in any instantaneous state of affairs, but in a course of happening, which can be understood only if we participate in a process of evaluation by which the bad is rejected and the good retained. If I look over the shoulder of a mathematician working on a problem beyond my comprehension, I cannot predict or control what he will do, nor will I be able to give more than a trivial account of what I have observed. In such a case, as in that of the boy and the clam, the "fact" of the event can be understood only by one sufficiently capable of evaluation to know what is happening when a good thing is embraced or a bad one rejected. If any of my illustrations produces an "illusion" it is that of the ladder leaning against the wall, where an interruption in purposive action leaves a deposit in the form of a temporary collocation of physical objects we can talk about without importing into it any greater purposive element than is intrinsic to all language.

At this point it will be argued, I am sure, that my observations confuse the question of ultimate value with that of selecting the most effective means for realizing an immediate purpose. It may be true, it will be said, that to understand and describe purposive action we have to participate vicariously in an act of valuation, but any such valuation is necessarily relative to what Dewey called the "end-in-view." That there are good and bad ways of opening clams leaves untouched the question whether opening clams is itself an activity entitled to be called good.

But is it true that a course of purposive action can be understood simply by perceiving at any given moment of time whatever immediate purpose is then being pursued? Shall we treat the shift from one purpose to another as a kind of miracle, neither requiring nor permitting any participation by the observer in the evaluation that produced the shift?

In my now sadly overworked molluscoidal illustration I described a case where a series of apparently discrete acts were directed toward what

I called a single purpose. Actually it would have been better, even in that simple case, to speak, not of a purpose, but of a congeries of related purposes. "Opening a clam" by pressing on it is obviously something different from the "opening" that might result from prying. But suppose a still greater shift in the direction of the boy's activities. He is told, for example, that there is an aquarium nearby where he can observe clams feeding and digging in the sand as they would in their native habitat. He drops his clam and runs to look at the aquarium. Shall we say that there has now been a complete break in the continuity of his actions, or shall we say that he has merely hit on a better means of satisfying what was his true purpose through out? Other shifts in the boy's activities might be imagined, such as putting down the clam and turning to an encyclopedia, where before reaching the C's he becomes entranced with an article on astronomy. The essential point I am trying to convey is that to understand a course of action of any complexity a single "purpose" does not suffice. If I understand what the boy is doing it is because of our shared human nature, a nature that in both of us is at all times incomplete and in process of development.

Any single human purpose—whether expressed in actions or words—is an incomplete thing when severed from the total system of which it forms a part. The meaning of any given purpose is always controlled by latent purposes in interaction with it. This is beautifully illustrated in an example of Wittgenstein's:

> Someone says to me: "Show the children a game." I teach them gaming with dice, and the other says, "I didn't mean that sort of game." Must the exclusion of the game with dice have come before his mind when he gave me the order?[1]

Those who claim large powers to ascribe to words or human actions a meaning innocent of evaluation will do well to ponder this example.

The dilemma we confront when we attempt to apply the fact-value dichotomy to human purpose may be restated in terms of the means-end relation. To anyone who reflects on moral issues two lines of thought will open up with respect to means and ends, each carrying with it the quality of self-evidence. On the one hand, it seems clear that the selection of an apt means for the realization of a given end is an activity engaging man's reasoning faculties and his capacity for accurate analysis and observation. The other line of thought leads, with equal persuasiveness, to the conclusion that this activity must have a terminal point and that the end

---

1. *Philosophical Investigations* 33 (1953).

ultimately pursued cannot be determined by analysis or observation, but must in some manner or other be projected upon events. These two lines of thought can coexist peacefully so long as they are not applied to any process of decision. When that happens the distinction that holds them apart disappears and their latent conflict becomes manifest. For when we are confronted with the necessity of making an actual decision about a course of action, means and ends no longer arrange themselves in tandem fashion, but move in circles of interaction.

One answer to this predicament is by now thoroughly familiar. In its most extreme form it runs somewhat as follows: The validity of human ends and "values" is not a matter for reasoned demonstration. While the selection of an apt means has the quality of an intellectual undertaking, a means without an end is a monstrosity. Until we have selected an end by some fiat of the will, any discussion of means is therefore futile. Every means-end problem is unique. If it were not, this would imply that the formation of ends is itself a lawful process, subject to rational cognition, which, it is assumed, cannot be the case.

From the same human predicament, an opposing school of thought extracts the opposite conclusion. Since in the process of decision means and ends interact, it is impossible to assign in advance precise limits to the role of reason. Let us therefore push our understanding as far as it will take us into the obscure area where means and ends interact; let us seek collectively to discover as much agreement in this area as the nature of the case permits.

This view asserts the reality of a process that may be called the collaborative articulation of shared purposes. Through the centuries it has been—in spite of all of its extravagances and dogmatisms—the school of natural law that has kept alive faith in that process. Is the faith justified?

I believe we have much evidence that it is. In the affairs of daily life, we all know from personal experience that in moments of crisis consultation with a friend will often help us to understand what we really want. It does not make much difference whether our adviser tells us, in effect, "Look carefully to your means," or "Consider carefully your end." The effect of the advice is in either case to initiate a process of reflection and consultation that may change our whole understanding of ourselves. The rapport needed to make such a consultation profitable is obviously difficult to achieve, and it may seem, therefore, that collaboration on such a personal level is without relevance to the larger issues of law and ethics.

Yet I think that in the history of the common law we have an example which teaches how a social institution may derive its integrity and vitality from the same spirit of consultation as that which animates the discussion of two friends sharing a problem together. The common law is not the work of any one judge, but of many, collaborating through time. In the course of its history the implementation of its rules has been improved and refined. At the same time, the rules themselves have often been revised to make possible an effective implementation of them. Though the common law is said to be built on precedent, there is no controlling verbal formulation of the meaning of any particular precedent. What the court said in a former case is always subject to reinterpretation as new situations arise. The scope of the precedent is determined not only in the light of the end-in-view pursued by the court that decided it, but in the light of ends then out of view because not stirred into active consciousness by the facts of the case being decided. The problem posed by Wittgenstein's example of the children's game is so familiar to the common law as hardly to seem novel at all. And, except for occasional lapses into literalism, its response has always been, "No, he did not mean that kind of game."

What I have called the collaborative articulation of shared purposes is also illustrated, I believe, on a much homelier plane, familiar to everyone. I refer to the problem of giving an adequate definition for everyday words. In modern discussions of semantics it is a commonplace to assert that the lexicographer is merely an observer and recorder of usage. This is nonsense. We all know that developing a good definition for a familiar word is hard intellectual labor. If one will take a common word like "stove" or "money" and compare his own offhand definition with that given in a good dictionary, he may learn, to be sure, that usages exist which he overlooked or which were unfamiliar to him. But what he will chiefly discover is how miserably his own definition failed to articulate clearly the purposive core of the word, which he "knew" as well as anyone, but was unable on short notice to bring to adequate formulation. A good lexicographer not only knows more about usage than you and I, but his skill in analysis may enable him to predict, more successfully than we could, how we ourselves use the word in contexts we have not yet confronted.

The modern rejection of any notion that men may be pooling their intellectual resources come to understand better what their true purposes are is revealed in the scorn that generally greets essays carrying such titles as "What is Art?" Of course much that is pretentious and empty appears under such titles, but the modern rejection does not rest on the quality of the offerings, being grounded rather on principle. It is said that any such title invites a confusion of fact and value and serves generally as a cover for a fraudulent intent to pass off the subjective opinion of the author about what art ought to be for a description of what it is in fact—as if it were possible to describe a major area of human striving without participation in that striving and as if that participation could be otherwise than creative! If the objection is more radically phrased so that it could not be removed by changing the title to read, "What I Think Art Ought to Be," then what is really being rejected is the reality of what I have called the collaborative articulation of shared purposes.

That rejection makes itself most tragically felt today, I believe, in our failure to carry on the work of former generations in analyzing and discussing what may be called the forms of social order. I use that term broadly to include rules, procedures, and institutions—all the ways, in short, in which the relations of human beings to one another are subjected to a formal ordering, whether by consent, habit, or command. As I use the term it cuts across law, politics, economics, sociology and ethics, and even includes systems of play. Thus, contract, adjudication, the majority principle, and the three-strike, four-ball rule are all forms of social order.

These forms are generally viewed only in their most obvious aspect, that is, as means to the realization of human ends. But they are also themselves ends, in two closely related senses. They are ends in the sense that, although we make them, they help to make us what we are, man's dependence on society being what it is. Any particular economic system not only serves to satisfy antecedent wants, but also generates its own peculiar pattern of human wants. Secondly, any form of social order contains, as it were, its own internal morality. Thus, we may judge football by an external standard and say, "Football is a good game," but we may also judge it by standards drawn from its own internal requirements and say, "Football will become impossible if this sort of thing is allowed to go on." We may appraise adjudication as a means of settling disputes and compare it with alternative methods of accomplishing the same object. We may also analyze its intrinsic demands and recognize that any attempt to combine the functions of judge and mediator represents a dangerous undertaking. . . .

These remarks may be taken to indicate an interest in practical problems of economics, law, and politics, rather than any concern for ethical theory. I believe, however, that the forms of social order cast their shadows across ethical discussions which contain no explicit reference to them. Thus we find the ideal of voluntary settlement (contract), or the informed judgment of a disinterested third party (adjudication), or the majority principle serving as tacit premises in discussions that seem remote from anything like the technical problems of social organization.

The issues I have tried to suggest in these concluding remarks range from the most trivial to the most crucial that human beings can face. These issues were once in active discussion and dispute. We are still living with the resolutions former generations found for them. It is difficult to see how the interrupted work of these generations can be resumed until we have reacquired some measure of sympathy for the essential aims of the school of natural law.

E. Nagel, On the Fusion of Fact and Value: A Reply to Professor Fuller*

Although the doctrine of natural law is obviously not uncongenial to himself, Professor Fuller explicitly disclaims that in his contribution to this symposium he is arguing for any version of natural law theory. But unless I completely misunderstand him, his paper does make a vigorous plea for developing standards for evaluating the practices and the rules of the law, with the view to determining and clarifying the import of the legal order for human life. On the question of the paramount importance of such a double task, nothing divides me from him. No social institution, and certainly not the law, is exempt from moral criticism. And in my opinion it is one of the major, though not exclusive, tasks of an adequate philosophy of law to analyze proposed principles for assessing legal rules; to develop, in the light of such analysis, responsibly grounded criteria for evaluating the law; and to construct thereby the intellectual tools with the help of which we may form objective estimates of the worth of existing as well as of projected bodies of law.

It is a notorious fact, however, that on the basic issue as to the source and nature of standards of evaluation, philosophies of law are widely at variance, the variety of proposed standards and of their attempted validation being at least as great as the variety of moral theories in the history of thought. It is well to note, therefore, that the doctrine of natural law, either in its ancient or in its medieval formulations, is just *one* of many theories that have been advanced concerning the nature of the standards to be used. I must emphasize this obvious point, because in much recent literature the label "natural law doctrine" is often attached to almost any view which proposes objective standards for the moral

* [3 *Nat. L. Forum* 76-82 (1958). Reprinted by permission.

Ernest Nagel was born in Novomesto, Czechoslovakia in 1901. He was educated at the City College of New York (B.S. 1923) and Columbia University (A.M. 1925; Ph.D. 1931), and is the recipient of numerous honorary degrees. He has taught philosophy at Columbia since 1931. His published works include *Sovereign Reason* (1954), *Logic Without Metaphysics* (1957), and *The Structure of Science* (1961).]

evaluation of the law. In my opinion, this rather indiscriminate extension of the label debases the intellectual coinage, and produces little but confusion. But in any event, though I agree that the law is subject to moral criticism, and though I believe that the formal standards involved in such criticism may have an indefinitely large (if not universal) range of application, I wish explicitly to disavow any commitment, as a consequence of this belief, to what I take to be the distinctive tenets of natural law theory. And since my function in this symposium is simply that of a commentator, I can only register my conviction that natural law doctrine supplies neither a tenable nor a useful basis for evaluating existing law.

But despite my agreement with what I understand to be the aim of Professor Fuller's paper, I am frankly puzzled by the considerations he introduces to support his views; and I am not at all confident that I have grasped either his intent or his argument. I shall nevertheless try to show that (1) insofar as I do understand it, the contention upon which he places greatest weight is thoroughly unsound; (2) his implicit conception of purposive behavior and of human history is at least dubious; and (3) his premises are not obviously relevant for grounding his conclusions.

(1) Professor Fuller begins his discussion by challenging what he calls the "truism" that "from *what is* nothing follows as to *what ought to be*." He bases his dissent on the claim that "in any interpretation of events which treats what is observed as purposive, fact and value merge," so that value judgments cannot be regarded as "something foreign to a purely factual account." Is this challenge of the dictum that what ought to be does not follow from what exists well taken?

(a) The dictum may be, and indeed has been, interpreted to assert that statements of what is the case are always irrelevant to the determination of what ought to be. And if Professor Fuller finds the dictum so construed to be dubious, I must again admit my agreement with him. If, however, he is merely challenging the dictum when read this way, he has misunderstood many writers whom he has criticized for subscribing to the dictum, since they espouse the dictum with a different interpretation of it. There certainly have been thinkers in recent years, even among the group of so-called legal "realists" and "positivists," who, though they profess the truism Professor Fuller is questioning, also maintain that responsible claims as to what ought to be must be supported by empirical study of the physical, biological, and social requirements of human life, and of the import of various institutions and regulations. Within the framework of such a moral theory, judgments as to what ought to be done do not follow logically from judgments as to what is actual; nevertheless, judgments asserting what ought to be are conceived as hypotheses about ways of resolving conflicting needs and interests. Accordingly, though on this view there is a sharp distinction between what is and what ought to be, value judgments are not thereby regarded as foreign intrusions into the study of human behavior.

(b) It seems unlikely, however, that Professor Fuller is claiming no more than that judgments of fact are *relevant* to the determination of the adequacy of judgments of value. For as he explicitly says, he believes that in the examination of purposive behavior the notions of fact and value merge, so that a sharp distinction between judgments of fact and judgments of value cannot be made. But I do not find this contention plausible. On the contrary, Professor Fuller's own example seems to me to reinforce the distinction he thinks he is undermining; and his discussion, insofar as I understand it, appears to me to establish what is at best a tautology.

(i) I shall first try to show that Professor Fuller's illustration presupposes the distinction between fact and value. According to him, when we once grasp the purpose which actuates a boy's manipulation of a clam, we discover in the structure of events as they unroll "an element of value"; and we can anticipate whether a certain action will be continued or not, because the action is recognized as good or as bad as a means for achieving the boy's objective. But just how does the example show that fact and value *merge?* In characterizing one of the boy's actions as "bad," it is surely pertinent to ask *what* it is we are so characterizing; and the answer must inevitably be descriptive of a fact. Indeed, unless a careful factual account can be given, one which is not colored by a surreptitious value imputation, we cannot judge competently whether the act does have the value attributed to it. . . . [W]hen in a court of law an individual is on trial for a crime, it is imperative to establish with utmost care just what the person did do, before a judgment is rendered on the goodness or badness of his acts in relation to the crime with which he is charged. It is undoubtedly true that many people do not distinguish their value imputations from the facts they are judging; but this is surely regrettable, and does not mean that the distinction cannot be made. In short, I do not find that Professor Fuller has given us any reasons for holding that in discussing purposive behavior the distinction between judgments of fact and of value breaks down, or that in such contexts fact and value merge.

(ii) I next want to argue that in claiming an element of "intrinsic" value to be present in situations involving purposive behavior, Professor Fuller is asserting what is at best a tautology. . . . [W]henever we are analyzing the operations of a system which is assumed to be a teleological or "goal-directed" one, *whether the system is a purely physical one or involves the presence of human agents,* value judgments necessarily occur with re-

605

spect to the roles played by the component "parts" of the system in maintaining or progressively realizing specified "goals." All this, however, seems to me logically truistic, for it simply explicates what it is we are doing when we are studying purposive or other forms of teleological behavior. But although Professor Fuller maintains that in such inquiries the merging of fact and value can be demonstrated, I hope to have said enough to show that on this point he is mistaken. Moreover, while he explicitly notes the objection to his view that the actions he is considering are not "intrinsically" valuable, but possess a value only insofar as they are functional or dysfunctional in relation to specified ends, I have unfortunately not succeeded in ascertaining how he thinks he has turned the force of this objection.

(2) There is, however, another thesis for which Professor Fuller also breaks a lance, but which is far from being a truistic one. He reminds us that the structure of purposive action is not constituted by a set of discrete happenings. He notes that even in the case of the working out of what is ostensibly an "immediate" or "single" purpose (as in the example of the boy manipulating a clam), a "congeries of related purposes" is in general operative, and that in consequence we cannot hope to understand the course of purposive action "simply by perceiving at any given moment whatever immediate purpose is then being pursued." So far these observations seem to me sound. But is the only alternative to an atomistic conception of human purposes and goals one which assumes that all immediate purposes, whether individual or social, are elements in a temporally developing but organically integrated system of ends? While I am not confident that I have understood the positive import of Professor Fuller's rejection of the atomistic conception, it is some such view as this which is suggested by much that he says.

> [He declares, for example, that "any single human purpose . . . is an incomplete thing when severed from the total system of which it forms a part," and he also says that the meaning of any single purpose is always controlled by the "latent" purposes in interaction with it. Again, he asserts that in what he regards as the somewhat "mysterious" process wherein we determine "what we really want," we frequently consult with friends and so engage in a process of the "collaborative articulation of shared purposes"; and he cites the history of the common law as an example which teaches "how a social institution may derive its integrity and vitality from the same spirit of consultation as that which animates the discussion of two friends sharing a problem together."

Such a view, in any case, I find incredible, for it is incompatible with the identifiable facts of contemporary human experience, as well as with the known character of human history. There is much evidence to show that individuals and groups sometimes engage in a collaborative process in which common goals are established and articulated. There is no evidence that the total life of a human individual or of the human race is a process in which a shared common purpose is gradually though imperfectly created and unfolded. (Indeed, I cannot make clear sense of the supposition that what is loosely called "human history" *is* a single *process.*) I cannot even see in the history of the common law the operation of such a process; and I find it gratuitous to assume that the manner in which legal precedents were used in courts of common law in the nineteenth century for settling historically novel issues, would have been regarded by seventeenth century common law judges as implementations of a common end-in-view, where that end-in-view was "then out of view because not stirred into active consciousness by the facts of the case being decided." An end-in-view that is nevertheless not explicitly present in active consciousness seems to me just a myth, the product of the same type of dubious reasoning which assumes that the outcome of a complex series of changes can be explained only by postulating the outcome as already "implicitly present" in the initial terms of the series.

I can on this occasion only assert dogmatically what seems to me obvious—that in actuality there are competing and even incompatible human objectives, both individual and social, and that the task of moral theory is to provide standards with the help of which such conflicts may in some measure be adjusted. Accordingly, the mere existence of purposes and goals does not settle the question as to what ought to be done when a moral problem arises. It is chiefly for this reason that the distinction between what is actual fact and what ought to be is both unavoidable and useful when moral deliberation is initiated. . . .

(3) This brings me to my final difficulty with Professor Fuller's essay. I am entirely unclear how his claim concerning the fusion of fact and value, even if the claim were sound, is relevant to his belief in the possibility of an objective moral evaluation of the law, or what light that alleged fusion throws on the nature and authority of the principles to be employed in such evaluation. The norms for a responsible assessment of legal rules, so I am supposing, must codify the more enduring and general objectives of the institution of the law, on the basis of available though corrigible knowledge about individual and social needs. Such norms therefore provide a measure for judging the adequacy of existing legal arrangements and practices, and they supply general directives for estimating the worth of particular legal rules as well as for introducing needed changes in the law. These norms may not be invariant for all societies and for all times without thereby losing their authority for a given

social order; and a philosophy of law sensitive to innovations in that order and to fresh knowledge about human needs and capacities will suitably modify its principles of evaluation. But implicit in this conception of the office of standards of criticism is the distinction between fact and value; and I do not see how, by denying that distinction, one can hope either to establish the need for such standards or to clarify their nature and function. A *fully embodied* ideal ceases to be an *ideal;* and an action is purposive only as long as the ends sought by that action have not already been achieved. It is only by a prolepsis that the qualities which may characterize the possible outcome of purposive behavior can be predicated as intrinsic features of that behavior. Accordingly, I find little but confusion in fuzzing the distinction between fact and value. By refusing to make that distinction we not only contribute nothing to the problem concerning the nature and role of principles of moral criticism. My fear is that by refusing to make it, or even by softening its edges, we are well on our way to ignoring that there is such a problem at all.

Fuller, A Rejoinder to Professor Nagel*

. . . Professor Nagel begins on a tentative note and with an expression of apologetic doubt whether he has truly understood my meaning. But as he proceeds, these uncertainties disappear; and before he is through, I am presented as someone intent on "fuzzing" the most obvious truths, presumably in the interest of some unclean social doctrine. Indeed, I am made to "break a lance" for the most extraordinary views: that the whole of human history is a single process which may be described as the unfolding of one purpose shared by all mankind; that if the judges of former centuries could revisit the earth they would recognize that our courts are merely bringing to more successful articulation what they had been trying to say centuries before, etc. When one is confronted by misinterpretations of this magnitude, it is hard to know where to begin in trying to re-establish effective communication. I shall, however, do my best.

The Meaning of "Natural Law"

In the first paragraph of my essay I recognized the difficulties which arise from the fact that the term "natural law" has many meanings. My object was to concentrate on one crucial issue which seems generally to

---

* [3 *Nat. L. Forum* 83-99, 101-104 (1958). Reprinted by permission. For biographical information, see page 596 supra.]

be implicated whenever men speak of the opposition of the schools of "natural law" and "positivism." I considered it unwise to complicate that issue by attempting to pass judgment en route on the views of the differing schools of thought which may be brought under the common rubric of "natural law."

. . . I discern, and share, one central aim common to all the schools of natural law, that of discovering those principles of social order which will enable men to attain a satisfactory life in common. It is an acceptance of the possibility of "discovery" in the moral realm that seems to me to distinguish all the theories of natural law from opposing views. In varying measure, it is assumed in all theories of natural law that the process of moral discovery is a social one, and that there is something akin to a "collaborative articulation of shared purposes" by which men come to understand better their own ends and to discern more clearly the means for achieving them.

Apparently this notion of a "collaborative articulation of shared purposes" is to Professor Nagel the sheerest nonsense, with the qualification that "individuals and groups" do at times "engage in a collaborative process by which common goals are established and articulated." The meaning of this concession, and the reason it is restricted as it is, are unclear to me. The explanation nearest at hand is that Professor Nagel believes that collaboration of the type I have envisaged is possible only within a group where some uniformity of moral values has already been impressed on its members by a common social environment. If this is the meaning intended, it remains puzzling why collaborative discussion could clarify or improve a culturally conditioned uniformity; a man scarcely turns to his fellows for assistance in discerning what the forces of his environment compel him to do; one hardly needs help in responding to inevitability. I am inclined to believe that even with respect to the small group Professor Nagel means something different by his articulation of common goals than I do when I speak of an articulation of shared purposes. He apparently believes that even within the small group it is absurd to think that a pooling of insight and experience could assist the members of the group to understand more truly their own ends. This interpretation seems to be supported by the fact that Professor Nagel couples the "articulation" of common goals with their "establishment." Apparently he has in mind that "common goals," that is, goals already understood and shared, may be "articulated" by being brought unchanged to adequate verbal expression, and may then be "established," that is, given some formal sanction as a part of the rules governing the activities of the group. Beyond this he seems unwilling to concede any function to collective intellectual effort.

609

At this point I encounter what is to me the most puzzling aspect of the philosophy implied in Professor Nagel's comments. On the one hand, he seems to reject as intellectual folly any collaborative quest for a better understanding of the proper ends of a society. At the same time, he castigates "the doctrine of natural law" for pretending to be the only theory that attempts to formulate "objective standards for the moral evaluation of the law." This claim he counters by asserting that the natural law doctrine is only one of many ethical theories professing to offer "objective standards" of moral evaluation. One wishes at this point he had identified at least one of these rival theories and had explained how it is that a standard can be "objective" and yet not be capable of improvement by common intellectual effort. . . .

Toward a Delimitation of the Issues

One argument made by Professor Nagel seems to me to be quite unresponsive to any issue raised by my article. This is his declaration that what I am asserting "is at best a tautology," and amounts to saying that there is an element of evaluation in any inquiry which seeks to determine how effectively a purposive system (such as a machine or a human being) is accomplishing its objective. I must say that however groping and unsatisfactory my discussion may be, I do not think I was foolish enough to advance as an important truth the proposition that evaluation equals evaluation.

I have never denied that there are two postures of the mind toward reality that can be called "descriptive" and "evaluative." The question I proposed for discussion was whether an attempt at description can succeed in eliminating evaluative elements when it is addressed toward the functioning of a purposive system. It was precisely because I wished to raise this question without running the risk of falling into a tautology that I chose my illustration of the boy with the clam, where descriptive and evaluative efforts cannot at the outset be considered as being carried on simultaneously because we do not at first know what the boy is trying to do.

Another false issue seems to me to be raised by those passages in Professor Nagel's article in which he appears to say that I am, in effect, counselling snap judgments, that if my views were taken seriously . . . the judge [would feel free] to sentence the accused without hearing the evidence, etc. I see nothing in my position suggesting any disparagement of careful observation, painstaking analysis, patient reflection, or the fair treatment of defendants. Professor Nagel's assumption to the contrary simply reflects his belief that none of these desiderata will be achieved unless we are prepared to accept his views concerning the nature of the evaluative process. This simply brings us back to the central issue of the whole debate.

Still another general point is made which, it seems to me, in no way advances our discussion. This consists in asserting that my "premises are not obviously relevant for grounding my conclusions." By this I take it Professor Nagel means to suggest that even if I were correct in what I have to say about the relation of "is" and "ought," I would still have established nothing "obviously relevant" to the assertions made, and the questions raised, in the latter part of my article. Certainly I can understand why Professor Nagel is unable to discern any clear line of thought connecting the various portions of my article. Essentially he seems to regard the questions I raise concerning the relation of "is" and "ought" as nonsensical. If I myself were to encounter an ethical theory which took as its starting point the question whether all garks are savigrous I, like Professor Nagel, would have difficulty in seeing what either an affirmative or negative answer to that question would entail.

It is Professor Nagel's deep conviction that the question I am raising is nonsensical which is responsible, I believe, for the truly colossal failure of communication which has taken place between us. The fact that he approaches my whole article with that conviction has made it impossible for him to approach sympathetically the notions I was trying to expound in the last part of my article, though I regret to say it has not prevented him from passing some sweeping negative judgments about views which he seems obviously not to have understood. If there is any hope for understanding, it must lie in a clarification of the basic issue raised by my article.

A Restatement of the Issues Raised in My Article

As I see it, two closely related issues are raised by the exchange between Professor Nagel and myself:

(1) Is it always possible to give an adequate non-evaluative account of any object that is itself the subject of an evaluation?

(2) If so, does evaluation become legitimate (or "competent") only when its object is first identified by such a non-evaluative account?

If I understand him correctly Professor Nagel gives an affirmative answer to both of these questions. . . .

The insistence that there must always be something that can be described in non-evaluative terms before evaluation itself can be justified reminds one of the controversy about empirical verification that arose out of the movement called logical positivism. Logical positivism started with the proposition that it is only those sentences which can be "empirically verified" that are meaningful, that is, proper subjects for intelligent discussion and argument. As it gradually became clear what complexities inhere in the notion of empirical verification, particularly as applied to "a sentence," the adherents of logical positivism found it necessary to retreat from their original position. A convenient cover for this retreat was found in the notion of verification "in principle." It having been discovered that it was impossible in practice to give a meaningful account of what would be involved in actually verifying a sentence empirically, the original proposition was modified to read: "Only those sentences are meaningful that are *in principle* subject to empirical verification." So in a similar manner we now find it being asserted that "in principle" evaluation never becomes justified until we have described accurately in nonevaluative terms the thing we are evaluating. . . .

How far this insistence can be carried is illustrated in the comments of another critic. In a book discussed by this writer I had remarked that if we were confronted by a dubious assemblage of mechanical parts and were to ask of it, "Is it a steam engine?" and, "Is it a good steam engine?" these two questions would "overlap mightily."[3] My critic responded that this is not necessarily so at all and indicated that the whole difficulty could be removed by a little definitional ingenuity. He suggested that by stipulation we might define a steam engine in non-evaluative terms, as requiring certain parts, arranged in a certain relationship to one another. Of course, an attempt at such a definition might be made, but what earthly purpose could it serve unless it be to support "in principle" a philosophic position taken in advance and now confronted by an embarrassing example? Parenthetically, it can be confidently predicted that the attempt at a "non-evaluative" definition of a steam engine would inevitably miss its mark; ambiguities would always be latent in the definition which would have to be resolved in favor of that meaning most apt in describing a machine fit to serve the general purpose of a steam engine. Professor Nagel's position seems to be essentially that of the critic just discussed. He too supports the rigid separation "in principle" of "is" and "ought," though he cautiously refrains from informing us how he himself would describe in non-evaluative terms those physical actions which he would categorize as "good" or "bad" attempts to open a clam. . . .

If we move the discussion to the realm of legal and moral ideas, the whole controversy assumes a different aspect. Here the picture of a kind of evaluative finger pointing itself toward "things" loses even the specious appeal it has in more elementary contexts. During the oral discus-

3. *The Law in Quest of Itself* 11-12 (1940).

sion of my paper I attempted unsuccessfully to induce Professor Nagel to state how he would deal with problems of the following sort: Let us suppose a rule of the common law. Though this rule is treated by lawyers, judges, and legal scholars as if it were a single, existent thing, it never receives quite the same verbal formulation in any two statements of it. In such a situation evaluation may be comparatively easy. To those who have given serious thought to the problems involved, it may be possible to range the various formulations of "the rule" roughly on a scale of adequacy; in any event it is easy to recognize gross ineptitudes. But what shall we say of "existence"? What "is" the thing, or what "are" the things, lawyers have in mind when they agree in saying, "*This* is a poor formulation of *the* rule"? In neither case can the "thing" be mere words on paper, for the same words will provoke different responses in different readers. A perceptive reader may pass over almost unnoticed an inadequacy in formulation, since his mind seizes at once the thought toward which the author was groping unsuccessfully. The mind of a less perceptive reader may waver in indecision among various obscure and unsatisfactory meanings. The same uncertainty of response even more obviously makes impossible a definition of "the rule" in terms of patterns of human behavior. I have asked, and I ask again: In this sort of context how do we apply the dogma that before we can evaluate we must first define clearly in non-evaluative terms the thing it is we are evaluating?

The fundamental article of the positivist faith is that "law" either exists or does not and that no evaluation is involved in reaching a judgment about its existence. I have tried to show the difficulty in maintaining this belief when we apply it to "law" in the sense of a "rule of law." But suppose the question to be, not that of the existence of a particular rule of law, but of a legal order. Here again the view of positivism is that a legal system can be thoroughly "bad" from top to bottom by any number of standards and yet be a regime of law. But by what process of judgment do we decide whether something "is" a legal order?

I suppose that no one would discern a "legal order" in any of the following imaginary situations: (1) verbal directives called laws are issued by something that calls itself a government, but there is no discernible correspondence whatever between the acts of those who purport to enforce the law and the rules they purport to enforce; (2) verbal directives called laws are issued, but they are all kept secret or are published in a cipher known only to the legislator; (3) verbal directives called laws are issued, but they are all retrospective in effect and no prospective laws are ever enacted. In all of these situations there is so gross a departure from the ideal of a legal order, even of an order devoted to evil ends, that nothing exists in any of them we would be tempted to call "law." Yet the ideal of a legal order is never attained perfectly. In all legal systems there

613

is some discrepancy between formal rules and governmental actions taken pursuant to them. Everywhere we encounter the problem of poorly drafted rules and rules that are conveyed inadequately to those who are affected by them. Probably all governments have from time to time undertaken to cure past irregularities by retroactive statutes.

If what I have just said is correct, it follows that the "existence" of a legal order is always a matter of degree and cannot be measured in "non-evaluative" terms. How, then, in determining whether a legal order "exists" do we distinguish between the "existent thing" and its "value"? Or is the doctrine of a strict separation of "is" and "ought" to be rescued once more "in principle"? Will the answer be that there must always exist in a given society some particular complex of words, attitudes, and actions before I can say of it, "This falls short of the ideal of a legal order"? What utility is there in this insistence if in fact the only significant thing I can say about this social complex is that it *does* fall short of the ideal of a legal order? Surely it would be absurd to assert that I must colligate in "neutral" terms every existent thing embraced by such a judgment before the judgment itself can be "competent." To do so would be like saying that unless we can trace the precise trajectory of a marksman's bullet we have no right to assert that it missed the target. Surely we can say that a legal system is missing its target without having to report the precise angle of divergence of every human action that contributes to that missing. We can also say of something that calls itself a legal order that it is missing that target so woefully that it cannot in any meaningful sense be termed a system of law. It has, if you will, so little "value" that it has ceased to "exist." . . .

Fact and Value in the Administration of the Law

In his brief reference to courts of law, Professor Nagel appears to assume that the administration of the law presents no special difficulties for his view. Indeed he seems to believe that it is especially obvious in the law that evaluation cannot be competent unless it is directed toward an object first identified in non-evaluative terms. I believe, on the contrary, that an open-minded examination of legal problems will reveal how impossible it is to maintain in any actual process of human decision a rigid separation of fact and value of the kind recommended by Professor Nagel.

The great advantage of the study of legal materials lies in the fact that the law cannot be content to maintain a distinction "in principle"; if it accepts a distinction as sound, it is compelled to find some way of giving effective expression to it in the actual decision of controversies. If it is believed that a witness must report what he saw in completely non-evaluative terms, then the judge must decide what questions may properly be addressed to him and what forms his responses may take. Let me illustrate the difference between problems as they arise in the administration of the law and as they are likely to be conceived in philosophic discourse.

Two philosophers are debating about "value" and "fact." One of them says, "It is not true that evaluation only becomes possible if its object can be identified in non-evaluative terms. For example, I can say of a dancer, 'He is trying to tango, but is not succeeding.' I can say this even though it would be impossible for me to describe what he is in fact doing." His opponent, quite undisturbed by this example, may reply, "Ah, but there must always exist some pattern of motions to which your value judgment that his attempt to tango is unsuccessful can apply; otherwise it would be meaningless. The more accurately this pattern is described, the more competent will be the value judgment passed on it." There the matter has to rest.

Suppose, however, that a dancing couple is employed by a night club on the basis of an assurance that they can do all the standard ballroom steps. On their first appearance a tango is played, and they are discharged for being unable to tango. They bring suit for improper discharge. In support of its case the company operating the night club wishes to put on the stand various patrons who were present during the disputed dance. The judge must now decide what form their testimony may take. Will they be required to describe the dance performed in terms of physical motions, leaving it to the jury to determine whether the dance so described is an adequate tango? Or will they be permitted (subject to cross examination on their competence) to say something like, "Whatever they were doing, it was not a tango"?

The philosopher may be inclined to distrust the alleged lessons of legal experience. He may consider that the judicial process is surrounded by an air of exigence not conducive to clarity of analysis, or that the law to get its job done has to make compromises that would not be tolerated in philosophic discussion. I do not think the possible contribution of the law to philosophic theory can be dismissed so casually. After all, the most relevant peculiarity of the law lies in its responsibility to reach and explain decisions. It seems to me that modern epistemology is coming more and more to recognize that there is an element of responsible decision in all intellectual activities, including those of science.[5] One philosopher suggests that the present "age of analysis" is giving way to an "age of decision."[6] Surely if this is true the decisional science called law should offer something of interest to the epistemologist.

5. Michael Polanyi, *The Logic of Liberty* (1951).
6. Morton Gabriel White, *Toward Reunion in Philosophy* (1956).

I have already tried to show that in legal reasoning generally no such distinction as that insisted on by Professor Nagel is or can be made. Consider, for example, the rules which state under what circumstances the various forms of legal responsibility arise. Most of these rules will turn on fault or negligence. *A* enters into an oral agreement with *B*: he thinks he said one thing; *B* interpreted him to mean something else. In general the principle is that there is no contract if both were at fault in the misunderstanding or if both were without blame. If, however, one was negligent while the other was not, the court will enforce the contract in accordance with the understanding of the prudent party. The term "negligence" is plainly a term of evaluation, but there is generally in the law no "non-evaluative" colligation of the things or instances to which this term should be applied. The ways of missing the target are countless and unpredictable; they can only be given a meaningful classification under the rubric "misses."

Again, though it is said to be the function of a jury to determine "facts," when a jury is asked to bring in a special verdict, the question addressed to it will almost invariably be one soliciting what in philosophic discussions would be regarded as an evaluation: "Was the defendant proceeding with due care?" "Was the apartment in suitable condition for occupancy?"

Generally speaking it is only with respect to the testimony of witnesses that it becomes possible even to consider maintaining a distinction between evaluating and identifying the object of the evaluation in "neutral" or "factual" terms. There is in this field an interesting experiment directed toward giving effective legal sanction to the desideratum urged so strongly by Professor Nagel. This is the Opinion Rule as developed in this country, though not followed in England or on the Continent. In general terms this rule states that an ordinary witness who has observed some event may testify only to what he heard and saw; he may not give "opinions."

Under this rule a witness who observed an accident when an automobile skidded on glare ice may not tell the jury that the defendant was going "too fast"; he must instead attempt to estimate the speed of the car in miles per hour and leave it to the jury to say whether operating a car at that speed under the conditions then obtaining was an act of negligence. Again, a witness may not describe a fence along a railroad right of way as being "not in a fit condition to turn cattle," but must attempt some more "factual" account of its condition, from which the jury may decide whether a fence so described was "fit" to turn cattle.

There have always been exceptions to this rule. Curiously, one of the most firmly established is that relating to testimony concerning economic value. Under this exception a plaintiff is permitted to testify, for example, to the value of services rendered as a part-time housekeeper or to the value of a used desk lost in shipment. Other exceptions permit the witness to say that a person "looked angry," or "acted insane," or "seemed to be sick." Perhaps statements of the last-mentioned variety might be dismissed from the present discussion on the ground that, although they may be called "opinions," they are not evaluative. I suggest, however, that the difficulty in knowing just what kinds of testimony should be regarded as "evaluative" is something that should be pondered before Professor Nagel's view is accepted as a general guide in the actual solution of legal problems of proof.

With all its exceptions and qualifications, the Opinion Rule has been condemned, I believe, by every careful student of the law of evidence.[7] The reason for this condemnation does not lie in the notion that the jury ought to have the benefit of the witness's opinion or "value judgment." It is rather that in many situations it is simply impossible for the witness to communicate to the jury the fact of what he saw in non-evaluative terms; he can feel more assured of his own honesty if he says "the car was going too fast when it skidded," than if he is compelled to give an estimate of its speed in miles per hour. Of course, the conclusion that a statement of value, "too fast," may be the most effective way of communicating a situation of fact to the jury presupposes some community of purpose and some common human nature shared by the witness and the jury. Some may regard this as a fatal objection to it. But those concerned with the actual administration of the law have to accept this supposition of it seems to have reality in the discourse of man with man.

Ends Out of View and the Collaborative
Articulation of Shared Purposes

We now reach that portion of my article where, in Professor Nagel's opinion, absurdity reaches its acme and where he confesses he finds my views "incredible."

With respect to the "end out of view," Professor Nagel's demonstration of the absurdity of my remarks is somewhat facilitated by a misquo-

---

7. 7 *Wigmore on Evidence* §§1917-1929 (3d ed., 1940). McCormick, *Evidence* 19-28 (1954); American Law Institute, *Model Code of Evidence,* Rule 401 (1942). The virtual abolition of the rule as it existed in the American common law in Rule 401 of the Code is thus explained, p. 201: "Where a witness is attempting to communicate the impressions made upon his senses by what he has perceived, any attempt to distinguish between so-called fact and opinion is likely to result in profitless quibbling. Analytically no such distinction is possible."

tation in which I am made to speak of the "end-in-view" being "out of view." While I certainly said nothing like that, the idea I attempted to convey was that in disposing of controversies and issuing directives we may operate within a framework of purposes which conditions our decisions even though only certain of these purposes are called into consciousness by the facts of the case at hand. Although I had thought of this as being an almost obvious truth of psychology, it is for Professor Nagel a "myth."

All I can assert in response is that I am unable to attribute any clear meaning to Professor Nagel's discussion of this point. What he *seems* to say—which I in turn find "incredible"—is that our actions and words can never be directed or conditioned by any end or assumption not actively present in consciousness. If this were so, I could not go into the library and come back absorbed in reading a book unless I had formed the conscious purpose of returning to my office. I am puzzled by Professor Nagel's failure to touch even tangentially on the illustration I borrowed from Wittgenstein. I say to another person, "Show these children a game." The possibility that this might be taken to mean they should be taught to throw dice does not enter my mind. Had the addressee of my remarks been a notorious gambler, I might well have added, "but not your kind of game." In the actual context of my remark, however, there was as little reason to give conscious attention to that possibility as there is for me to ask myself as I get out of bed in the morning whether the floor will be still there to receive me. In his illustration Wittgenstein asks whether I can truthfully say, "I did not mean that kind of game," only if I had consciously considered the throwing of dice and had consciously excluded it. I can see no justification for Professor Nagel's casual dismissal of this problem with such epithets as "myth" and "product of dubious reasoning."

Closely associated with the notion of "the end out of view" was my discussion of the "collaborative articulation of shared purposes." Here again Professor Nagel seems to me to say nothing to which I can respond except by trying to convey more adequately the point I attempted to make in the first place.

Let me this time give an illustration in the form of a series of imaginary judicial decisions. Of necessity, my presentation will be schematic, and I shall have to leave it to the reader familiar with the growth of the common law to say whether I have truthfully portrayed any aspect of the judicial process. The cases that follow are given in the order of their assumed chronology. The parties in each case are different persons, but to facilitate comparisons the symbols used to designate the parties will be the same throughout and will indicate the role played by the particular party; thus in all five cases *O* will designate the original owner of the horse which came by theft or fraud into the hands of *T*.

Case No. 1. T steals *O's* horse and sells it to *G*, who pays full value for it and had no reason to know it had been stolen from *O*. *O* brings suit against *G* to recover the horse. *Held,* for *O*. One of the deterrents to thievery is the difficulty of disposing of stolen goods. If a purchaser like *G* were able to take free of the claim of the true owner, a market for stolen goods would be created and, thus, an incentive to theft. In any event, it was impossible for *T*, a thief who had no rightful title to the horse, to pass any title to *G;* he who has nothing can give nothing.

Case No. 2. T buys a horse from *O* giving as payment a forged note purporting to be that of *X*. *T* knew that the note was forged. After delivering the horse to *T*, *O* discovers that he has been defrauded. He brings suit against *T* to recover the horse. It is argued on behalf of *T* that *O* delivered the horse to him with the intent to confer title; the horse is now *T's*, and *O's* only remedy is to sue for the price. *Held,* for *O*. The passage of title was vitiated by the fraud of *T;* title throughout remained in *O*.

Case No. 3. The case is similar to *Case No. 2,* except that after receiving possession of the horse, *T* sold it to *G*, who knew that *T* had bought it from *O*, but had no reason to know that *T* had worked any fraud on *O*. *O* brings suit against *G* to recover the horse. It is argued on behalf of *O* that title remained in him in accordance with the principle laid down in *Case No. 2*. Since *T* had no title, he could pass none to *G*. *Held,* for *G*. It would be an intolerable burden on commerce if purchasers of property were compelled to scrutinize the details of a transaction by which the former owner voluntarily delivered it into the hands of the person now offering it for sale. Fraud takes many and subtle forms; if the victim could not recognize it, it is unreasonable to ask of a stranger to the transaction that he ascertain whether it was present. With respect to *Case No. 2,* all that was said there was with reference to the legal relations between the owner and the defrauder; the court's mind was not directed toward the possibility that a subsequent purchaser, like *G*, might intervene. The principle we are here applying is that if the horse is in the hands of *T*, or of someone who knew of his fraud, it may be recovered by *O*. In the hands of an innocent purchaser like *G*, the horse may not be recovered by *O*, for reasons we have already indicated.

Case No. 4. The case is like *Case No. 3,* except that after buying the horse from *T*, *G* sold it to *K*, who, before he bought the horse from *G*, had been informed of the fraud worked by *T* on *O*. *O* sues *K* to recover the horse. It is argued on behalf of *O* that *K* was not an innocent purchaser, since he knew of *T's* fraud when he bought the horse. In accordance with the principle laid down in *Case No. 3*, *O* became entitled to the horse when it came into the hands of *K*. *Held*, for *K*. If the argument made by *O* were accepted, it would be possible for a person in the position of *O* to destroy the value of the title acquired by *G* simply by giving general publicity to the fact that *T* had induced the sale by fraud. Thus the objective of protecting the bona fide purchaser *G* would be defeated, for his property would become unsaleable. When the court in *Case No. 3* said that *O* could recover the horse from anyone who knew of the fraud of *T*, it did not have in mind the possibility that the horse might have passed previously through the hands of a bona fide purchaser like *G*. When the horse was bought from *T* by *G*, title to it was perfected and was no longer vulnerable to attack by *O*. *G* was then free to sell it to anyone he saw fit.

At this point I urge the reader to stop and consider whether we are now at the end of this development, and whether there is any new situation likely to arise which will require a reformulation of the principles laid down in *Case No. 4*. When he has assured himself on that point, he may proceed to *Case No. 5*. This case is like *Case No. 4*, except that *K* not only knew of *T's* fraud, but had participated in it by forging *X's* name on the note used by *T* to pay *O* for the horse. *O* sues *K* to recover the horse. *K* rests his defense on the reasoning of *Case No. 4*; *G* had title to the horse and was free to sell it to anyone he saw fit. If *K* was guilty of any misconduct, that is a question for the criminal law; it ought not to affect his property rights. *Held*? . . . Perhaps the point of my illustration will be most effectively conveyed if at this point I leave to the reader, not only the burden of decision, but the more onerous burden of explanation.

To me it does not seem absurd to claim that the series of cases I have reported reveals something that might be called "the collaborative articulation of shared purposes." If this expression seems too pretentious, I would be content to say that these cases show that communication among men, and a consideration by them of different situations of fact, can enable them to see more truly what they were all trying to do from the beginning. In answer to Professor Nagel's contention that nothing like this can happen except in a tightly knit group, I suggest that, without losing their point at all, the five cases I have reported might each be separated by a half century from its predecessor, and that the courts which decided them might be those of five different nations. To be sure, the legal development I have suggested would be unintelligible to a human being who knew nothing of property, or of sale or of contract. But what is the use of a search through time and space for this creature, unless it be to discredit any attempt to discover and articulate those principles which will promote a satisfactory life in common for the human beings we know and understand, and by whom we can in turn be understood?

I hope it will be clear to the reader, as apparently it was not to Professor Nagel, that I am not foolish enough to suppose that the whole essence of legal history is compacted in the phrase, "the collaborative articulation of shared purposes." The history of the common law reveals many things, including instances of wooden literalness and even of corruption. All I am asserting is that the development indicated in my series of imaginary cases is one important aspect of legal history. How important it will be in the future depends upon whether it is Professor Nagel's philosophy of adjudication that is accepted or that which I have attempted to express here. . . .

What Is at Stake?

. . . The poverty of the results produced by so many empirical studies of human attitudes and preferences seems also to be traceable to a methodology deriving essentially from the position taken by Professor Nagel. No one would deny, I suppose, that human attitudes and preferences characteristically change with time. It is also clear, I believe, that if the organization and proper orientation of the attitudes and preferences under study is a problem, not only for the individuals being studied, but also for the observer, the observer will be unable to predict the future course of these attitudes and preferences. One who knows the answer to a puzzle can often predict roughly the steps another will follow in solving it; if the observer is ignorant of the answer, he can only participate vicariously in the process of solution. In this participation the "clear" distinction between what is observed and its appraisal disappears. Where human attitudes and preferences are of real interest they generally relate to problems of life that are problems equally for the observer and for the observed. The consequence is that if the social scientist studying attitudes and preferences is to secure anything that can be called a reportable "datum," he must take toward his subject a point of view that effects a cross section through time, producing a kind of instantaneous snapshot arresting all motion and development. This operation does violence to the nature of the thing under observation, so that its essential reality is lost. When an attempt is made to restore at least a part of that reality, it consists in taking a series of snapshots, spaced through time and revealing a "trend." If this "trend" conveys any significant meaning, it is generally because in interpreting it we surreptitiously reintroduce the process of vicarious evaluation that was ruled out by Professor Nagel's maxim at the outset. The result is that after a study conducted by the method I have described, our understanding of the subject matter often seems to have been impoverished rather than enriched.

No one would dream of following any such self-defeating procedure if the inquiry fell within the area, say, of technology. Suppose, for example, we wanted to ascertain the "preferences" of construction engineers in solving some problems of their specialty. It would be apparent at once that we would have to take into account knowledge, experience, and insight. Plainly a statement of preference coming from a wise and experienced engineer is not only more valuable than, but something different in fact from, that of a younger and less experienced one. The older man might very well state more accurately than the younger what the latter's preference would actually be if he were forced to deal with the problem in question. The younger man may report his own preference inaccurately because he is unable to discern the demands of the situation until it becomes something he must face in real life; the older man's insight and understanding can dispense with this crutch of direct confrontation.

So soon, however, as we touch on anything that seems to smack of "values," all of this common sense falls into the discard, and the quest for the elusive "neutral" datum is resumed with almost religious fervor. Yet is it not plain that insight and understanding can play a role in ethical judgments as well as in those of engineering? When we encounter differences of opinion among lawyers about what are in fact the ethical standards of their profession, do not these differences often reflect variations in insight and experience, rather than different opinions as to what actually "exists"? It is true of course that before we can weigh insight and experience into the balance we must ourselves participate in the process of judgment going on in the minds of our respondents. When this happens some fuzz may develop around the distinction between fact and value, but I do not think this too high a price to pay for recovering meaningful contact with reality.

These are brief and inadequate observations about what seem to me to be the things at stake in the debate between Professor Nagel and myself. I should like to make it clear that my fundamental objection to his position is that it is intellectually untenable. I do believe that a general and literal acceptance of the theory would entail disastrous consequences for law and morality. But these consequences would result from the falsity of the theory, not from the fact that it was consciously aimed at producing them.

Is the Purpose of Law and Morality the Resolution of Social Conflict?

As one studies his remarks it is not easy to discern clearly Professor Nagel's own legal and moral philosophy; the negations of his article so outweigh the affirmations, both in number and explicitness, that it takes some searching to find any of the latter at all. I believe, however, that there are two passages which reveal a positive theory of morality, and presumably also of law. Essentially this is the theory that the basic and perhaps exclusive object of morality is to resolve human conflicts. . . . "[J]udgments asserting what ought to be are conceived [by Professor Nagel] as hypotheses about ways of resolving conflicting needs and interests." Again, . . . he asserts that "there are competing and even incompatible human objectives, both individual and social, and that the task of moral theory is to provide standards with the help of which such conflicts may in some measure be adjusted."

As applied to the law this is a conception closely associated with the position of legal positivism. There are traces of it in most writers belonging to that school, though as usual it is Kelsen who brings the view to most explicit statement:

> Justice is an irrational ideal. . . . Regarded from the point of view of rational cognition, there are only interests, and hence conflicts of interests. They can be solved by an order that either satisfies one interest at the expense of the other, or seeks to establish a compromise between the two.[9]

The notion that the purpose of law is simply to settle disputes is almost a cliché of legal thinking, though I think a dangerous one. When one extends the same view to morality, as Professor Nagel apparently does, it certainly loses any platitudinous quality it might previously have had, and becomes a novel and even startling conception of the role played by moral rules in human life.

It is not difficult, I think, to show the inadequacy of any theory which treats law and morals as being exclusively concerned with the resolution of conflict. In the first place, any such theory must default before the question, What conflicts *require* resolution? Some conflicts between individuals and groups are beneficial, some are harmful. How shall we discriminate between the two? The second major default of the suggested theory is in answering the question, *How* shall we resolve particu-

9. The Pure Theory of Law and Analytical Jurisprudence, 55 *Harvard Law Review* 44, 48-49 (1941).

lar conflicts? If the resolution of conflicts is to be a rational process it must in time develop principles, and those principles will inevitably enter into and shape the lives of men for good or ill. How then are we to articulate those principles by which conflicts and disputes are to be decided? If the answer is that we should choose those principles which give the greatest assurance that conflict will not recur, we are simply brought back full circle to the theory's first default.

If the theory is as unacceptable as I have just indicated, why is it even suggested that the purpose of law and morality is exhausted in the resolution of conflict? An easy answer would be to say that this view is required if the principle of a sharp distinction between fact and value is to preserve even a minimum plausibility; the recognition that law and morality have more affirmative tasks would make it clear as daylight that the "existence" of both of them consists in a striving which we can understand only in terms of ends that are never fully attained.

I believe, however, it would be unfair to suggest that Professor Nagel adopts the theory of law and morality he does only because this theory enables him to maintain his principal position. Rather I think the explanation lies in a moral conviction of the value of diversity and variety in human life and in the directions of human striving. This is a view I ardently share. I have attempted elsewhere to show, however, that though the moral goals of legal positivism are worthy, it serves these goals badly and indeed endangers the very ideals it so properly holds to be previous.[11] I refer the reader to that discussion as a supplement to what I have been able to say here. I believe it will be found to offer a sympathetic account of the essential aims of positivism—or at least as sympathetic an account as is possible when it is assumed that one's opponents in argument do not truly understand their own motivation. But in conclusion I want to repeat that my objection to Professor Nagel's view does not rest on any conjectural motivation that may lie behind it, but on the ground that it seems to me to falsify the relation between human beings and the reality by which they are compelled to orient their lives.

E. Nagel, Fact, Value and Human Purpose*

I

Professor Fuller's central thesis, as formulated in his first paper, is that "in any interpretation of events which treats what is observed as

11. Positivism and Fidelity to Law—A Reply to Professor Hart's Essay, 71 *Harvard Law Review* 630, 669-672 (1958).

* [4 *Nat. L. Forum* 27-40 (1959). Reprinted by permission.

purposive, fact and value merge." Although he rejects as "quite unresponsive" my argument that in making this claim he is at best asserting a tautology, to my regret he does not come to grips with my difficulty, and I have found nothing in his *Rejoinder* which requires me to retract my criticism as pointless. I have nevertheless profited from the restatement of his major thesis, and in consequence I believe I am able to present more clearly my continuing difficulties with his central claim. There are in fact three sorts of defects I find in his arguments for it: a confounding of several disparate senses of the word "evaluation" (and, correspondingly, of the word "value"); a failure to distinguish between a term as *evaluative* and a term as *vague;* and a confusion of the question whether or not men actually use a term without explicitly recognizing the distinction between fact and value, with the quite different question whether or not it is possible and important in such cases to make that distinction. It will not be convenient, however, to discuss each of these defects separately.

1. Professor Fuller fully agrees that the mind may have a "descriptive" as distinct from an "evaluative posture" toward reality, although in his view these postures merge when we are dealing with purposive events. He reformulates the issue as stated in his original essay in two related questions: "(1) Is it always possible to give an adequate non-evaluative account of any object that is itself the subject of an evaluation? (2) If so, does evaluation become legitimate (or 'competent') only when its object is first identified in such a non-evaluative account?" He maintains that the answer in each case is negative, basing his conclusion on a number of illustrative examples. However, the first question seems to me unclear as it stands, and requires some discussion of what is to be understood by "adequate" and "evaluation."

(a) Professor Fuller nowhere explains what is the force of the adjective "adequate." It is manifestly a value term, and involves at least tacit reference to some purpose or objective for the sake of which an account is undertaken. Thus, when a physicist offers a non-evaluative account of a given system of pulleys (i.e., when he assumes a "descriptive posture" toward his subject matter), if his aim is simply to discover what is the mechanical advantage of the system, his account is *not* inadequate because he fails to note the weight of the pulleys, the length and tensile strength of the cord, or the purchase price of the machine. On the other hand, a builder assessing the physical and economic suitability of the pulley system for lifting construction materials used in his business, *would* be giving an inadequate account were he to ignore these items. In brief, *every*

For biographical information, see page 603 supra.]

account of things and processes, whether it is descriptive or evaluative, is instituted for the sake of some objective; and the adequacy of an account can be judged only by reference to the purpose for which it has been instituted. But although this point is obvious, it is also important. For it calls attention to the circumstance that an account may be entirely adequate (relative to a given purpose), even when the account is an admittedly non-evaluative one, despite the fact that it does not provide an "exhaustively" detailed and "absolutely" precise description of the subjects under discussion.

Nevertheless, Professor Fuller appears to ignore this obvious point when, in reverting to his original molluscoidal example, he claims that even if our concern is giving an account of the boy's behavior with the clam were "in the 'pure fact' of the occurrences there related—say, in the directions and dimensions of the boy's physical movements—we could envisage that 'pure fact' more accurately if we knew what the boy was trying to do." If our intent is to characterize the boy's behavior with a view to relating his activities to his purpose (assuming that he has one), we will undoubtedly attend to different things in his total behavior than if our intent were something else; and even if our interest is to evaluate the boy's behavior as a means for achieving his aims, we will doubtless note varyingly different features in his actions should we modify our conceptions (or hypotheses) concerning the boy's objective. Professor Fuller is very perceptive when he calls attention to "the effect of a disclosure of the boy's purpose in bringing about a sudden enlargement of perspective." But I can find no warrant for his assertion that when we realize what the boy is trying to do, we are able to give a more accurate account of the boy's physical movements. For the accuracy of an account, like its adequacy, can be judged only in reference to the purpose for which the account is instituted. However, since an account undertaken for assessing the boy's behavior as a means for realizing his ostensible objective has a different purpose than an account undertaken for describing the directions and the dimensions of his physical movements (perhaps for the sake of determining whether the boy has recovered from a crippling illness), the adequacy or the accuracy of the latter account follows from the former one neither in strict logic nor in normal fact. This is not the only example in which Professor Fuller has apparently forgotten that the adequacy of an account is relative to the purpose controlling that account. I shall try to show that his claim concerning the merging of fact and value is in part the consequence of his not remembering this point.

(b) The primary, though I think not exclusive, sense in which Professor Fuller employs the term "evaluation" is for judgments in which the worth of some action, process, or object is assessed as a means for achieving some end, however tacitly or vaguely the end may be entertained, and whether or not the judgment is explicitly formulated. At any rate, this seems to be the sense required in his discussion of the original molluscoidal example, as well as of several others he advances in his *Rejoinder* in support of his central thesis. Some of these latter examples are especially helpful to me in stating my difficulties; and since I would be repeating myself were I to comment on each of Professor Fuller's illustrations, I will examine only two of them in the present context.

(i) Professor Fuller raises the question whether the "existence" of a "legal order" in some society can be decided without evaluations being involved in the process. However, he declares that "the *ideal* of a legal order is never attained perfectly," so that "the 'existence' of a legal order is always a matter of degree and cannot be measured in 'non-evaluative' terms." How, then, he asks, "in determining whether a legal order 'exists' do we distinguish between the 'existent thing' and its 'value'?" Moreover, he suggests it would be absurd to maintain that we must first describe in neutral, non-evaluative terms "every existent thing embraced by such a judgment [i.e., a judgment as to whether a legal order exists] before the judgment itself can be 'competent.'"

I have several comments to make on this example of an alleged merging of fact and value. Professor Fuller is perhaps calling our attention to the familiar difficulty of formulating a "suitable" general definition of "legal order" (although I am sure he intends more than this) precise enough to enable us to decide in a uniform manner whether a given social system (e.g., Hitler's Germany) is an instance belonging to the extension of that term. But in any event the term "legal order," like many other terms in common use, has no precise definition, certainly not one that is acceptable to all who employ it. Although there may be a considerable measure of uniformity in the way men apply it in many instances, it is also clear that many individuals differ in the criteria they associate with the term for its correct application. Accordingly, two individuals who disagree on whether a given society possesses a legal order, may disagree not because they base their predications on different descriptive (or non-evaluative) accounts of the society, but simply because they operate with different standards for the correct application of the label. In an analogous way, a bat may be characterized as a bird by one person and denied that characterization by another, because the connotations of the term "bird" are for them not the same, even though they agree in all other respects in their accounts of the object both have observed.

Now although Professor Fuller is not proposing a fully developed definition of "legal order," he does suggest what for him must be a component in any acceptable definition of the term. If I do not misread him, he is saying that no system of politically enforced regulations can properly be called a "legal order," unless the system approximates to an "ideal" order, and so embodies patterns of human behavior which both conforms to certain minimal moral standards and contributes to the realization of a progressively unfolding series of moral ends. Accordingly, so I understand him to maintain, it is not possible to decide whether, for example, a legal order did exist in Nazi Germany without characterizing the operations of Hitler's society in evaluative terms. I will not dispute here the suitability of a definition of "legal order" along the lines Professor Fuller suggests (despite my doubts about the desirability of a definition of the term which would require us to refuse this title to a "thoroughly bad" system of politically instituted and enforced regulations), since the precise form which a definition of the term ought to take is not pertinent to the issue under discussion. I gladly admit that if the term is to have any connotation, there must be *some* minimal conditions for its correct application; and I also freely grant that a definition such as the one Professor Fuller appears to have in mind is entirely possible. Nor do I deny that on his and similar conceptions of what is a legal order, any decision as to whether or not a legal order exists in a given society involves the use of evaluative terms. For if such conceptions are adopted, it is trivially or tautologically true that evaluative terms must be employed. What does puzzle me, however, and leads me to wonder whether I do understand him, is why Professor Fuller thinks he is not asserting the tautology to which I tried to call his attention in my *Reply*.

It is barely possible that Professor Fuller finds my criticism "unresponsive," because I have not made sufficiently clear that when anything is characterized in what I propose to call "functional" terms, the use of such terms *necessarily* requires evaluative judgments. Let me therefore try to make my point with a biological example. A certain organ in the human body can be identified as a kidney by way of its gross anatomy, so that in the anatomical sense of the word we can give an account of some particular kidney (or of kidneys in general) in what are commonly regarded as non-evaluative terms. However, we have discovered that one of the normal functions of kidneys so identified is to maintain the blood in a certain chemical state. We may in consequence (and indeed frequently do) include this capacity of the organ in our conception of what it is to be a kidney. We may in fact make it part of our notion that to be a kidney an organ must maintain the blood in an "ideal" chemical balance, even if we should discover that actual organs vary in their capacity to do so; and we may in consequence come to regard it "a matter of degree" whether a given organ is really a kidney. On either of these two suppositions, however, the term "kidney" in its functional sense is an evaluative term, since we can determine whether a given organ is a kidney only by assessing its performance as a means for achieving a certain end.[3]

Similarly, in the sense associated with it by Professor Fuller, the functional term "legal order" is *necessarily* an evaluative one, because in that sense no system of human activities is a legal order if it is not conducive to the maintenance and the realization of certain moral objectives. Accordingly, though we may all agree in all our non-evaluative accounts of the Hitler regime, if there is room for doubt whether the decrees and enactments issued under the Nazis, together with the mechanisms of enforcement, were means for attaining those objectives, there is ground for doubt whether a legal order existed under Hitler. But if my statement of Professor Fuller's view is reasonably accurate, is he not after all asserting a tautology when he claims that this example illustrates a merging of fact and value?

But in any event, he heaps scorn on the notion that for an evaluative account to be legitimate, its object must first be identified in non-evaluative terms. He declares that to urge this notion is

> like saying that unless we can trace the precise trajectory of a marksman's bullet we have no right to assert that it missed the target. Surely we can say that a legal system is missing its target without having to report the precise angle of divergence of every human action that contributes to that missing. We can also say of something that calls itself a legal order that it is missing that target so woefully that it cannot in any meaningful sense be termed a system of law. It has, if you will, so little "value" that it has ceased to "exist."

Ridicule and exaggeration, however, though they doubtless have their use, do not really turn the point of an argument. Professor Fuller is battling with straw men if he supposes those whom he calls "positivists" to maintain that a necessary condition for a competent evaluation is an absurdly minute and photographically precise non-evaluative description of the object evaluated. It has apparently not occurred to him that the sole alternative to an evaluative account is not an impossibly detailed non-evaluative one. And he seems to have forgotten in this instance, as

3. To avoid misunderstanding, I want to emphasize that on my view it is a *discovery* that kidneys identified by way of anatomical features do in general have this capacity, and not the result of any decision concerning the connotation to be assigned to the word "kidney." However, if in the light of that discovery we decide to modify the initial sense of the word, it is a consequence of this *decision* that to be a kidney (in the new, functional connotation of the word) necessarily implies the possession of the indicated capacity.

he did in the example I discussed earlier, that every account is unavoidably selective, and that the adequacy of a non-evaluative account has to be measured, not against an ideal of "absolute" precision, but in relation to the particular purpose that instituted it. Accordingly, since a non-evaluative account that is not exhaustive of its subject may nevertheless be adequate to the purpose of the account, and since the judgment that an account is adequate involves an evaluation, I can explain Professor Fuller's tacit assumption that a non-exhaustive but adequate account of its subject must somehow be evaluative, only on the hypothesis that he mistakenly thinks the evaluative character of a *judgment of adequacy* of an account entails that the account is itself evaluative.

However this may be, I do not understand how anyone is able to evaluate anything responsibly, unless he can identify that thing in non-evaluative terms. If he is unable to do so, even though in a relatively sketchy and imprecise way only, I find it a puzzle to know *what* is being evaluated. I am, of course, *not* maintaining that such non-evaluative descriptions are in all instances explicitly formulated, and are invariably distinguished from evaluative judgments. Thus, the builder in my example above may not formally assert such statements as "The cord in this pulley is 200 feet long" and "This pulley is capable of doing the kind of jobs I need done in my business more effectively and economically than any other machine now on the market." Nor may the builder be aware in making such judgments (whether or not he states them explicitly) that one of them is descriptive while the other is evaluative. I *am* maintaining that the builder can be evaluating something only if he identifies that thing (perhaps only by way of unformulated perceptions) in non-evaluative terms. Moreover, I believe that when some evaluation of ours (such as my builder's) is challenged, we can meet the challenge responsibly only if we first articulate our descriptive characterizations, distinguish as carefully as we can our tacit evaluations from our factual claims, and perhaps (in order to make our evaluations more reliable) increase the detail and the precision of our descriptive accounts. Professor Fuller questions the utility of such descriptive accounts, at any rate in his discussion of the "existence" of a legal order, on the ground that "the only significant thing [we] can say about [a] social complex is that it *does* fall short of the ideal of a legal order." But their utility seems to me obvious, if we are at all concerned with diagnosing a social complex, with the objective of changing what is actual in the direction of a better approximation to some ideal. Does Professor Fuller have a better alternative to the general policy of determining what is the actual state of affairs (with a degree of precision depending on the problem), as a condition for competent prognosis and therapy?

(ii) Consider next Professor Fuller's example of the dancing couple who bring suit for improper discharge from employment, where the point at issue is whether or not the couple really did perform a tango. He notes that in such cases the judge must decide what form the testimony of witnesses may take; and he suggests that witnesses might not be required to describe the dance they saw performed "in terms of physical motions," and would be permitted to testify somewhat in the fashion: "Whatever they were doing, it was not a tango." Professor Fuller therefore concludes that an adequate account of the action in dispute in this case would not be presented in non-evaluative terms, so that in this instance, at any rate, ostensibly factual description and evaluation coalesce.

My comments on this example will be brief. I have already argued that it is a blunder to suppose that the sole way of characterizing anything in non-evaluative terms (in this instance a dance) is to describe it "in terms of physical motions"—where such a description will count as an adequate one only if it states every detail in the pattern of motions embodied in the performance. Moreover, were this standard for a non-evaluative description adopted, most, if not all, of the accounts of things we are accustomed to regard as non-evaluative would then have to be rebaptized as evaluative ones. Accordingly, by doing violence to the accepted distinction between judgments of fact and judgments of value (i.e., to the sense of the distinction in terms of which the issue raised by Professor Fuller is formulated), the question under discussion would be settled in Professor Fuller's favor—but only by redefining the terms used in stating the issue, and so reducing the latter to triviality. Thus, when we characterize a certain occurrence as the flight of a barn swallow, few of us are capable of rendering in explicit language the detailed patterns of the bird's shape, coloring, or motion. Nevertheless, most of us would probably deny that in describing that occurrence in the stated manner we are engaged in an evaluation. Whatever it is that we are doing when we declare that a certain occurrence is the flight of a swallow (or that a certain performance is not a tango), we are *not* making an evaluation in the sense of assessing the worth of a thing as a means for realizing some objective.

But what is it that we are doing in such cases? It will be helpful to note that the terms ordinarily employed in identifying and describing things connote more or less extensive (and more or less precisely delimited) classes of attributes. Accordingly, no term is correctly predicated of a given object, unless the latter does in fact possess all the connoted attributes. On the other hand, we rarely make sure (sometimes because we are not in the position to do so) when we predicate some term of an object that the latter actually possesses each of the connoted attributes; and in consequence, the available observational evidence on the basis of which a term is applied to an object is usually (if not invariably) logically insufficient to guarantee with demonstrable certainty the correctness of the predication. For example, the connotation of the term "oak tree" includes the attributes of having leaves with a characteristic shape, a bark with a distinctive texture and color, a trunk and limbs with a certain grain and degree of hardness, a capacity for producing acorns, and so on. But when judging a tree to be an oak we do not normally first establish that the object really does have all these traits, and we base our judgment on noting the presence of a relatively small number of them.

Nevertheless, though in cases of this sort the observational evidence for a predicative judgment may be logically incomplete, the incompleteness may vary. In some instances the evidence may be so extensive that the judgment is accepted as beyond reasonable doubt. In other cases the evidence is far less compelling, and the judgment is felt to be only probable in some degree. In short, predicative judgments are commonly asserted on the basis of incomplete evidence, which must be "estimated." This estimation is sometimes a conscious and deliberate weighing of the evidence. At other times, especially in routine situations of life, there may be no explicit consideration of the observational data; in such cases a deliberative estimation is replaced by habit, so that predicative judgments are asserted—with varying degrees of confidence on the basis of the observed data—almost automatically. But to estimate the weight of evidence, in whatever way such an estimate may be made, is to engage in an activity that is not improperly characterized as an "evaluation"— though in a sense of the word distinct from the senses thus far discussed. Certainly the witnesses in the dancing couple example, who testify whether or not the couple were performing a tango, are *not* offering an evaluative account of the performance, in the sense that they are assessing an action as a means for realizing some purpose. They *are* offering an evaluative account, in the sense that their predicative judgments are ostensibly based on estimates of the evidential weight of their observed data. Accordingly, I concur entirely in Professor Fuller's view that "there is an element of responsible decision in all intellectual activities," if this means that the decision in question involves an evaluation in the sense just indicated. However, unless different meanings of "evaluation" are confounded, the occurrence in the dancing couple example of evaluations in the present sense does not support his claim that the example illustrates the merging of fact and value.

2. Professor Fuller thinks that the administration of the law presents special difficulties for the view that "in any actual process of human

decision [there is] a rigid separation of fact and value." I have already discussed the case of the dancing couple, one of the several examples he employs in this connection to support his thesis. I want to examine another example in this group, in order to exhibit another facet in my difficulties.

Professor Fuller cites the rule that if one party to an oral contract was negligent in interpreting the terms of the agreement while the other party was not, the court will enforce the contract in accordance with the understanding of the prudent party. He appends the comment that "the term 'negligence' is plainly a term of evaluation, but there is generally in the law no 'non-evaluative' colligation of the things or instances to which this term should be applied." I need hardly say that on questions of law I am happy to be Professor Fuller's pupil. However, when he declares that "negligence" is "plainly a term of evaluation," he does not seem to me to be making a judgment simply in his capacity as a distinguished legal scholar. To be sure, the term "negligence" contains an evaluative component, as does the biological term "kidney"; for an action is characterized as negligent with reference to the likely consequences to which, in the light of our general experience, actions of that type are believed to lead. It is also undoubtedly the case that there is in general no descriptively characterized and precisely demarcated set of things to which the term is applied in the law. Nevertheless, as innumerable writers on legal subjects have noted (and I hope I do not appear to be presumptuous in venturing to remind Professor Fuller of this), the law of torts recognizes standards of nonnegligent action—even if those standards are determined in part by uncodified custom, are elastic, and are subject to alteration as society itself changes. Accordingly, the term "negligence" is not *merely* evaluative (any more than is the term "kidney"), so that in a large number of instances its application is controlled by rules referring to paradigmatic situations that are identifiable in non-evaluative language.

On the other hand, the term "negligence" is notoriously a highly vague one. It is vague in the sense that the term "bald" is also quite vague, while for all practical purposes the term "kidney" is not—in the sense, namely, that there is a large class of actions for which habits of usage are indeterminate as to whether or not the term applies to them. In consequence, when borderline cases become subjects of litigation, a decision must be made whether or not to include them in the extension of the term. Such decisions are frequently made in the light of evaluations of the conjectured consequences of those acts, and under the influence of the purposes (whether explicit or tacit) of those making the decisions. Nevertheless, the fact that evaluations and purposes enter into the formation of such decisions does not blur the distinction between "is" and "ought." On the contrary, that fact does not make nonsense of the question whether, prior to a decision to count a given action as an instance of negligence, the action *ought* to be included in the scope of some law dealing with behavior deemed to be negligent, or whether, subsequent to that decision, the action *ought* to have been so included. Unless an action, even though a borderline case for the application of the law, is presented to a court by way of an account which is at least partly non-evaluative, I confess my inability to understand what there is for the court to decide.

Accordingly, when individuals disagree in their judgments on whether or not a given action is marked by negligence, their disagreement may have various reasons: The individuals may agree in their conceptions or criteria of negligence, but may differ in their evaluations of the likely consequences of actions similar to the one under consideration; they may agree in their criteria, but they may be basing their judgments in this particular case on different non-evaluative accounts of the action being discussed; or they may disagree (just as men often disagree in classifying some person as bald) primarily because of the vagueness of the term "negligence" and because the given action is a borderline case. Professor Fuller's claim that the term "negligence" is "plainly a term of evaluation," and that its use illustrates the merging of fact and value, thus seems to me to be a consequence of his lumping together under the ambiguous rubric "evaluation" such quite distinct factors that may control men's judgments.

Professor Fuller's examples show beyond doubt how difficult it frequently is to make descriptive judgments not colored by tacit assumptions concerning human purposes and by implicit moral evaluations. But he is flaying an imaginary whipping boy when he castigates those who believe a distinction must be made between "is" and "ought," if he supposes them to maintain that the distinction is one that men invariably make or can make easily and without effort. He is not arguing to the point when he notes, in support of his major thesis, that the Opinion Rule is condemned by careful students of the law of evidence. For the issue, as I understand it, is not whether most witnesses are able to disentangle fact from opinion, or fact from value, especially when they are testifying on matters in which they may have received no serious training. The issue is whether the distinction between "is" and "ought" is not implicit in all moral deliberation, and whether, in the interest of making our evaluations more responsible, a persistent effort to make that distinction explicit in practice is not of highest moment.

II

I now turn to Professor Fuller's view that there is "a process that may be called the collaborative articulation of shared purposes," exhibited not only "in the affairs of daily life" but also in the history of the common law. In my *Reply* I stated my agreement with his rejection of an atomistic conception of human purposes and goals. But I also expressed my disagreement with what seemed to me to be a "holistic" interpretation of individual and social purposive action which he adopted, an interpretation according to which, as I understood it, there is an implicit collaborative pursuit of valid "forms of social order" by men, even when this end-in-view is not explicitly entertained by them. . . . [I]n his *Rejoinder* he repeats the substance (though not the phrase "out of view") of the position I had criticized, for he declares that "in disposing of controversies and issuing directives we may operate within a framework of purposes which conditions our decisions even though only certain of these purposes are called into consciousness by the facts of the case at hand." Since in my *Reply* I did say that "an end-in-view that is nevertheless not explicitly present in active consciousness seems to me just a myth," I am bound to explain why in my opinion Professor Fuller *is* accepting a myth as "an almost obvious truth of psychology."

Let me say at once that like Professor Fuller I accept as an obvious truth the familiar fact that many of our purposive actions, directed toward realizing some objective lying in the future which had been consciously envisaged by us as an end-in-view at some time or other, are performed by us through force of habit, so that the objective is not continuously in consciousness during the action. For example, it would never have occurred to me to question such facts as that I often leave a friend's home with the intent of returning to my own residence, and then walk, board a train, converse with companions, and do much else besides, without the thought of my objective crossing my mind during most of the process. Nor do I question that I may gather with neighbors with the aim of developing plans for getting better schools in our community, but that this objective does not remain in the foreground of anyone's attention at every moment of the discussion, and that none of us had any clear ideas at the start of the meeting as to what such plans involve. I do deny, however, that if, as a consequence of a set of actions which have been deliberately instituted for realizing a certain goal, a quite different outcome is obtained that was neither intended by anyone nor ever consciously entertained even as a possible end-result, this actual outcome is the "end-in-view" that controls and determines the various decisions which may have been made during the process. I readily admit that the ends-in-view we consciously pursue are often only vaguely conceived by us when we begin to deliberate about ways to realize them or when we initiate some action in order to realize those ends; and I also admit with equal alacrity that when such initially vague objectives become more definite, and are perhaps even realized in some precise but surprising form, we may judge the outcome of our deliberation or action as something that we had "really wanted" from the beginning. But I regard it as a myth to suppose, and at best as a perversion of language to say, that the *unintended* product of our actions is the "end-in-view" toward which those actions had been *directed* all along. Such a supposition seems to me no less a myth because it is professed by some contemporary schools of psychology, which maintain that unconscious *purposes,* though never actually entertained by an individual, are nevertheless the "objectives" and determinants of his behavior.

In point of fact, Professor Fuller does not make it easy for his readers to grasp what he understands by the "collaborative articulation of shared purposes." In his original essay he rejected the claim that it is futile in human affairs to debate means until ends are proposed; and he construed the history of the common law in particular as a process in which rules of law are improved, not only to achieve the explicit ends-in-view courts entertain in interpreting precedents when applying them to the concrete cases under litigation, but also "in the light of ends then out of view because not stirred into active consciousness by the facts of the case being decided." In my *Reply* I agreed that there is indeed a collaborative articulation of shared purposes, in the sense that at various times and among various groups of men there are collaborative attempts at establishing and articulating common goals.[4] But I took issue with what seemed to me the possible import of Professor Fuller's words that however much men may be separated in space and time, and however

4. Professor Fuller takes me to task for admitting the existence of a collaborative articulation of shared purposes only with the qualification stated in the text. He construes the qualification to mean that according to me such processes take place "only within a group where some uniformity of social values has already been impressed on its members by a common social environment." He therefore asks with obvious irony "why collaborative discussion could clarify or improve a culturally conditioned uniformity." However, Professor Fuller has read my qualification in a sense I had not intended; and I certainly did not maintain, as he suggests I did, that it is absurd to suppose "a pooling of insight and experience could assist the members of the group to understand more truly their own ends." As I explain in the text above, my qualification was intended to express my rejection of the notion that a single "purpose," at best only occasionally at the focus of explicit attention of a relatively small number of men, underlies the development of such institutions as the common law.

little they may be explicitly aware of any common objectives, mankind is a single community engaged in a collaborative search for "forms of social order," and that the history of the common law illustrates this collaborative articulation of shared purposes. And I rejected this view, though I expressed doubt whether Professor Fuller subscribed to it, on the ground that it is mythical (in the sense of the preceding paragraph) and that it is incredible history.

In his *Rejoinder* Professor Fuller dismisses my criticisms of this view as beside the point and as not pertinent to anything he said in his original essay. He now reformulates his thesis, and helpfully offers a temporally ordered series of five (imaginary but allegedly typical) judicial decisions to illustrate the collaborative articulation of shared purposes in the common law. Nevertheless, I still fail to understand what his thesis is, if it is not the one I found untenable in my *Reply*. He declares his examples "show that communication among men, and a consideration by them of different situations of fact, can enable them to see more truly what they were all trying to do from the beginning"—as if I had denied that communication between men often clarifies common purposes. The difficulty I find in the examples is that though they supposedly illustrate a collaborative articulation of shared purposes, Professor Fuller himself suggests that each judicial decision in the series can be assumed to be separated from its predecessor by half century, and that courts deciding the five cases might well be those of five different nations. But what reason is there for supposing that the problem confronting the court in the fifth decision was envisaged by the first court, or that the actual purposes and ends-in-view of the first court were shared by the last one in the series? If there is no compelling evidence for such supposals, how does Professor Fuller differentiate his view from the one I criticized in my *Reply,* and why does he think he is not subscribing to the mythical notion of purposive human action which I had attributed to him?

Let me therefore cite some actual examples of judicial decisions rather than contrived ones. To the best of my knowledge, no one has shown that a common, shared purpose underlies the series of judicial decisions concerning the liability of manufacturers of "things by their nature dangerous," beginning with *Thomas v. Winchester* in 1852 and terminating in *MacPherson v. Buick Motor Co.* in 1916. I do not find it obvious that there is such a purpose; a reading of some of the leading decisions in this bit of legal history does not seem to me to support the claim that there is one; and in any event the hypothesis that there is one does not, as far as I can make out, help to explain why the notion of inherently dangerous things has undergone the transformations that it did. . . .

Perhaps because I have failed to understand Professor Fuller's thesis concerning the collaborative articulation of shared purposes, I have also failed to find in his *Rejoinder* a resolution of my difficulty in seeing any connection between that thesis and his central thesis on the merging of fact and value. To be sure, he may believe that the truth of his views on the moral purposes underlying the development of the common law entails the truth of some form of natural law doctrine, so that the principles which promote a satisfactory human life are eternally valid and are gradually discovered through the collaborative articulation of common purposes. In consequence, if there were such an entailment, that doctrine would be a necessary presupposition of the interpretation of the development of the common law which Professor Fuller appears to hold. However, the conception of the nature of moral principles and moral values implicit in that doctrine has been historically associated with a firm *distinction* between the "is" and the "ought," and certainly does not imply the denial of this distinction. Accordingly, even if this doctrine as well as Professor Fuller's perspective on the history of the common law were accepted as sound, his views on that history would nevertheless not constitute relevant evidence for his central claim that fact and value merge. I am therefore compelled to render the Scotch verdict that a connection between these views and this central claim has not been proven.

III

. . . 2. Professor Fuller comments adversely on the notion, stated briefly and only in passing in my *Reply,* that judgments of value are hypotheses about ways of resolving conflicting needs and interests. For he maintains that no theory of law is acceptable which holds the purpose of the law and of morality to be exhausted in the resolution of conflicts.

I would be seriously lacking in appreciation of the complex problems any ethical theory must solve, were I to attempt at the tail end of what is essentially a polemical article an adequate statement and defense of the conception of value judgments which I professed in my *Reply*. I can do no more on this occasion than indicate briefly why Professor Fuller's strictures on that conception seem to me without force. In the first place, he observes quite rightly that not all conflicts are harmful, and not all require legal intervention. He therefore rejects as inadequate the conception that value judgments are hypotheses for resolving conflicts, on the ground that this conception does not state how beneficial conflicts are to be distinguished from harmful ones. However, my brief formulation of that conception was not advanced as a full-scale analysis, but only as an indication of a necessary condition for the institution of value judgments, not the sufficient conditions for their introduction. The formulation was intended to suggest why value judgments cannot rightly be regarded as self-certifying, and why questions concerning their validity can be settled only by reference both to the actual ends-in-view men entertain in given situations as well as to non-evaluatively described matters of fact (including the satisfactions and dissatisfactions men obtain, or are likely to obtain, from pursuing those ends). But in any event, I agree with Professor Fuller (if that is indeed the point of his criticism) that the distinction between beneficial and harmful conflicts cannot be made exclusively in terms of the notion of conflict. For without reference to the kinds and varieties of satisfactions and dissatisfactions men obtain from their activities, the distinction makes no sense to me. However, no proponent of the conception of value judgments under discussion has to my knowledge ever assumed anything to the contrary. The first part of his criticism therefore seems to me to be directed against a nonexistent target.

But Professor Fuller also maintains, in the second place, that if the resolution of conflicts is to be effected through a rational process, principles must in time be developed that enter into and shape the lives of men for good and evil. He therefore rejects the view of value judgments under consideration, because it allegedly fails to state how those principles are to be articulated by which conflicts and disputes are to be decided. However, though to be sure my *Reply* did not discuss these questions, the standard and readily available literature on the subject certainly does, so that the allegation seems to me baseless. In brief, the answer to Professor Fuller's censure is as follows. Certain types of conflict generate consequences that are discovered to be injurious to the well-being not only of those who may engage in them, but in various ways and degrees of other members of a community. These conflicts are also discovered to be capable of regulation, where some forms of regulation turn out to acerbate the undesirable consequences of conflicts, while other forms are found either to diminish the harm those conflicts produce or to divert the springs of human action into channels so as to generate consequences which augment human satisfactions. Accordingly, the principles by which conflicts are to be decided are principles whose use has been discovered to yield greater human satisfactions or lesser dissatisfactions or both, and in general to increase the happiness and well-being of the communities of men in which those principles are employed. This answer certainly offers no solution to any concrete problems in which conflicts require to be adjudicated. It suffices to show, however, that Professor Fuller's criticism is far from fatal.

639

Professor Fuller's animus against those he calls "positivists"—a category which appears to include everyone who maintains a firm distinction between "is" and "ought"—seems to me to have its source in the curious belief that anyone who accepts this distinction is barred in principle from evaluating the law in terms of objective moral standards. But such a belief is not only incompatible with the historical record concerning the role of "positivistic" philosophy as a critique of social institutions. The belief is also based on a false conception of how the study of fact can be related to the study of value. I find it difficult to escape the impression that those who hold the belief accept it on grounds of a fallacious argument—an argument entirely analogous to one which would conclude that a biologist, seeking to ascertain the various characteristics of microorganisms, whatever may be the import of such organisms for human life, is thereby precluded from distinguishing bacteria harmful to the human body from bacteria beneficial to man.

Selznick, Sociology and Natural Law*

. . . First I shall consider two obstacles to natural law thinking in sociology—the separation of fact and value and the doctrine of moral relativism. Then I shall analyze the meaning of legality and of positive law, finally turning to some attributes of natural law as they bear on sociological inquiry.

The main drift of contemporary sociology has been toward positivism, especially toward an ever-greater emphasis on empirical observation and techniques of measurement. A striving for objectivity, for clarity of thought, and for scientific respectability has produced a strong feeling against speculative inquiry and especially against moral philosophy. At least, these ancient preoccupations are thought to have no place in modern sociology, whatever other value they might have as literature. This movement of thought has much to commend it. At the same time, just because it is a "movement," it harbors many illusions and often serves to close minds rather than to open them. It is a procedural canon of inquiry that the study of fact must be assiduously protected from contamination by the value preferences of the observer. From this method-

* [6 *Nat. L. Forum* 84-108 (1961). Reprinted by permission.

Philip Selznick (1919–) is Professor of Sociology and Chairman, Center for the Study of Law and Society, University of California at Berkeley. His writings include *TVA and the Grass Roots* (1949), *The Organizational Weapon* (1952), *Leadership in Administration* (1958), and *Law, Society, and Industrial Justice* (1969).]

ological requirement has been derived a quasi-metaphysical dogma, namely, that fact and value belong to alien spheres.

It is easy to understand why this separation of fact and value should arise. Surely one of the first necessities of education is to impress upon unsophisticated minds the necessity of distinguishing what the world is really like from what they would like it to be. As educators, we certainly have the obligation to lead the student toward realistic understandings. This very often requires that harsh truths be faced and that old habits of thought, so largely influenced by private needs and wishes, be set aside. Furthermore, the advance of science seems to require that we respect the autonomy of nature and recognize that there are structures in being and forces at work whose existence depends not at all on human awareness or contrivance. For these and similar reasons it makes good sense to segregate preference from observation and to stress the logical distinction between normative statements and fact statements. . . .

Social scientists are not troubled by the idea of a "norm" or standard of behavior. A great deal of anthropological and sociological writing is devoted to the description and analysis of norms and systems of norms. That a cultural prescription exists, that it changes, that it is related to other prescriptions in determinate ways—these matters of fact can be handled by the social scientist quite blandly, without an uneasy conscience. From the standpoint of the observer, norms are factual data and that is that.

But suppose we are interested in the following: friendship, scholarship, statesmanship, love, fatherhood, citizenship, consensus, reason, public opinion, culture (in its common-sense and value-laden meaning), democracy. These and a great many other similar phenomena are "normative systems," in a special and "strong" sense of that term. I have in mind more than a set of related norms. A democracy is a normative system in that much complex behavior, as well as many specific norms, is governed by a master ideal. Behavior, feeling, thought, and organization are all bound together by a commitment to the realization of democratic values. It is impossible to understand any of these phenomena without also understanding what ideal states are to be approximated. In addition we must understand what forces are produced within the system, and what pressures exerted on it which inhibit or facilitate fulfilling the ideal.

In a normative system, the relation between the master ideal and discrete norms may be quite complex. For example, it might be concluded that under certain circumstances maximizing the number of people who vote, irrespective of competence or interest, would undermine rather than further the democratic ideal. This is one reason for stressing the difference between a normative system and a set of related norms. A

641

normative system is a living reality, a cluster of problem-solving individuals and groups, and its elements are subject to change as new circumstances and new opportunities alter the relation between the system and its master ideal. Put another way, the norms applicable to friendship or democracy are derived, not directly from the master ideal, but also from knowledge of what men and institutions are like. Only thus can we know what specific norms are required to fulfill the ideal.

The study of friendship cannot long avoid an evaluation of the extent to which particular social bonds approximate the ideal. Nor can it properly escape specifying the elements of friendship—what modes of response and obligation are called for by the ideal. None of this is inconsistent with detachment on the part of the observer. The observer need not have any personal commitment to the value in question, at least at the time and in the circumstances at hand. He may assess, quite objectively and impersonally, such connections and discrepancies as may exist between the ideal and its fulfillment.

Though this may be true, there is an odd reluctance on the part of social scientists to deal with normative systems. The disposition is to reduce such phenomena to arrangements that can be studied without assessment by the investigator, even when that assessment would entail nothing more than applying a culturally defined standard as to how far an implicit ideal has been realized. Thus, in the name of objectivity and rigor, the idea of friendship is left largely unanalyzed, and sociometric studies of reciprocal choice or differential association become the major line of inquiry. These measures, of course, say little about the quality of the relationship, not so much because they are incapable of doing so as because the studies do not begin with the normative perspective that would be appropriate. Similarly, the study of public opinion, where it is not mere polling, looks for stable patterns of response and for underlying attitudes and values, without much concern for public opinion as a normative idea. Again, social scientists have been much happier with the word "culture" since they have been able to strip it of normative significance and to bar the view that the idea of culture has something to do with excellence.

There is another side to this story, however. In theory, as opposed to the main trend of empirical research, some recognition of normative systems does exist. There is not much of a theory of friendship, or of love, in social science, but we do have the concept of the "primary relation," of which love and friendship are characteristic illustrations. What is a primary relation? It is a social bond marked by the free and spontaneous interaction of whole persons, as distinguished from the constrained and guarded arms-length contact of individuals who commit only a part of themselves to the social situation. In the primary relation, there is deep and extensive communication; individuals enter this experience as a way of directly attaining personal security and well-being, not as a means to other ends. This rough and elliptical statement is very close to what most sociologists would accept. Yet clearly it states an ideal only incompletely realized in the actual experience of living persons.

This illustration permits us to clarify the role of assessment in the observation and analysis of normative systems. The normative concept or model tells us what are the attributes of a primary relation. Only with this in mind can we properly classify our observations or identify the significant forces at work. To formulate the ideal primary relation is part of what theory is about in social psychology. This formulation, to be sure, will avoid the language of morality. It will specify social and psychological states, such as the quality of communication. Still, the intellectual function of the model is to provide a framework for diagnosis, including standards against which to assess the experience being studied. The small nuclear family is largely based on primary relations, but where communication between generations is weakened, and where authority requires impersonal judgment and discipline, the fulfillment of the primary-relations ideal is limited.

Whatever the assessment, it is always *from the standpoint of the normative system being studied.* The student of a normative system need not have any personal commitment to the desirability of that system. We may all agree that primary relations are a good thing, and the values they realize "genuine" values, but it is precisely the role of the social scientists to avoid the moralistic fallacy that primary relations are always a good thing. Where impersonality and objectivity are needed, the intimacy and commitment associated with primary relations may well be inappropriate. A different ideal, that of "official" behavior, may be called for. This ideal, too, is a demanding one and it is likely to be fulfilled in practice only partially. The investigator, in making his assessments from the standpoint of some purportedly operating normative system, can be quite detached about whether that system's ideals should be striven for in the circumstances. Indeed, the social scientist should be able to say whether the context is appropriate for the institution and support of a particular normative system. It might well be concluded that in the circumstances the attempt to create a friendship, to sustain a university, or to establish a democracy could only result in a distortion of the ideals these phenomena embody.

These remarks about detachment are made without prejudice to the view that certain ideals may be elements of an objective moral order. Whatever we may think of the appropriateness of friendship or love in a *given* context, we may still conclude that the values inherent in primary relations are of vital importance to man's well-being, and sometimes to his survival. This is only to say that he must find them somewhere, not that they are always appropriate. It may also be argued that no normative system is possible, or at least viable, unless it contains some ideals that all men can recognize as having a general moral validity. This position has much merit, but it is not necessary to the argument I am developing here.

Another illustration of support in sociological theory for the relevance of normative systems is the concept of "public opinion." Again, the trend of empirical research is to neutralize the term, to reduce it to the mere distribution of attitudes in a population. But conceptually a "public" is usually distinguished from a "crowd" or "mass" in that the behavior of a public, including the formation of public opinion, has a greater rational component and a greater self-consciousness. The member of a public acts rationally usually in his own immediate self-interest, but also potentially in the light of a larger sense of public interest. The formation of public opinion involves rational debate and is not merely the result of suggestibility or emotional rapport.

Clearly this view of public opinion presumes a normatively oriented system of organization and interaction. Given such a concept, which specifies standards, we can critically analyze opinion-making, not out of our own subjective preferences, but on the basis of a theory stating the conditions under which public opinion as a distinctive phenomenon is created. It follows that the state of opinion we actually observe will only approximate the theoretical ideal.

Concepts that specify ideal states are familiar enough in social science, and elsewhere as well. Any typology must designate, at least implicitly, a "pure" or "ideal" state with which purported instances of the type may be compared. The term "model" suggests a similar logic. However, not all types or models are normative; they do not necessarily have to do with the realization of values. When the realization of values is involved, social scientists seem to lose their zest for model-building. This probably has much to do with anxieties provoked by the epistemological dogma that values are "subjective."

The study of normative systems is one way of bridging the gap between fact and value. At the same time, the objectivity and detachment of the investigator can remain unsullied. The great gain is that we can more readily perceive latent values in the world of fact. This we do when we recognize, for example, that fatherhood, sexuality, leadership, and many other phenomena have a natural potential for "envaluation." Biological parenthood is readily transferred into a relationship guided by ideals. This occurs, not because of arbitrary social convention, but because the satisfactions associated with parenthood—satisfactions which are biologically functional—are not fully realized unless a guiding ideal emerges. The same holds true for the dialectic of sex and satisfaction. On a different plane, but according to the same logic, if leadership is to be effective and satisfying, it must go beyond simple domination to encompass a sense of responsibility.

This perception of latent values in behavior and organization is no mere sop to the moralizer. It enriches the thought and refines the observations of the student of society. Taken seriously, it may also serve to clear up some difficulties in contemporary sociological theory. Thus much attention is devoted these days to "functionalism." This is the view that items of behavior and of social structure should be examined for the work they do in sustaining or undermining some going concern or system. What is apparently or manifestly propaganda may be interpreted as latently a way of contributing to group cohesion by keeping members busy; a mode of punishment sustains the common conscience; selective recruitment of administrative personnel undermines an established policy or bolsters a shaky elite. Functional analysis is most familiar in the study of personality where a great many items of perception and behavior become meaningful only when their contribution to the maintenance of personal adjustment, including neurotic adjustment, is understood.

In all such interpretations, a system must be posited, whether it be at the level of personality or of group structure. The system is known insofar as a theory can be elaborated stating what the system "needs" to sustain itself. These needs are sometimes called "functional requisites." But here a persistent difficulty arises. There is a strong and understandable tendency to identify what is required for the maintenance of a system with what is required for the *bare survival* of a group or individual. The very term "survival" suggests that what is at stake is the biological extinction of the individual or the complete dissolution of the group. In fact, however, systems may decay despite the continuity of individual or group life. If a man extricates himself from neurotic dependence on another person, then a system has changed. If an organization maintains its personnel and budget, and even its formal identity, but transforms its effective goals, capabilities, commitments, and role in the community, then too a system has changed. To be sure, *some* systems are indispensable if life is to exist at all; but other systems are required if a certain *kind* of life is to survive. And it is fair to say that in social science the most important analyses have to do not with the bare continuity of life but with certain kinds and levels of organization.

A great many such systems are normative in the sense that their organization and development are governed by certain master ideals. A familiar and widespread illustration is the governing ideal of rationality in economic and administrative systems. In normative systems, it should be noted, terms like "maintenance" and "survival" are relevant but not adequate. They do not prepare us for observing, when it occurs, the evolutionary development of the system toward increased realization of its implicit ideals. . . .

A second barrier to the acceptance of natural law among social scientists is the widespread commitment to moral relativism. But whatever else it may or may not be, the natural law philosophy is not relativist. At least, it is committed to the view that universal characteristics of man, and concomitant principles of justice, are discoverable. It does not necessarily hold that such generalizations are *known*, only that they are *knowable*.

What should a reading of modern sociology, and related subjects, tell us on this issue? Here we must remember the polemical context within which sociology developed. We must also keep in mind the moral impulses, and the high-minded educational aspirations, that have guided writing and teaching in this field. Sociology was nurtured by the revolt against an atomist, individualist image of man and the corollary view of society as the product of human will, albeit an imperfect will. Society was the dependent variable, created by beings endowed *ab initio* with mind and self. Sociological theory countered by stressing the *creative* role of society, especially in making possible just those attributes of self-awareness, reason, and symbolic imagination that are distinctively human. This approach proved seminal indeed, and a great deal of very valuable work, in many special areas, has resulted from it. At the same time, it lent powerful support to the notion that there really is no such thing as "human nature," that, in familiar accents, man may have a history, but not a nature. . . .

That there is unity in this diversity—what some anthropologists have called the "psychic unity of mankind"—is often acknowledged. This acknowledgment comes easily if we are speaking of drives, such as hunger or sex, and potentialities, such as the capacity to learn and use language. But there are other features of man's psychic unity (not much studied, to be sure) more directly relevant to what is universal in social organization and pervasive in human values. I have in mind such motivating forces as the search for respect, including self-respect, for affection, and for surcease of anxiety; such potentialities as the union of sex and love, the enlargement of social insight and understanding, reason, and esthetic creativity. That man has morally relevant needs, weaknesses, and potentialities is supported, not contradicted, by the anthro-

646

pological evidence. Moreover, if there are many different ways in which self-respect can be won, it does not follow that a study of those ways would not reveal certain common attributes. Human dignity, and the conditions for sustaining it, would be a proper subject for sustained inquiry. But there has been little interest in it.

There is an odd paradox in the teachings of cultural relativism. The very impulse which moves these teachings presumes that there is a morally relevant common humanity. *The whole point of the doctrine has been to encourage respect for others as human.* The underlying assumption is that all men need and deserve respect despite their diverse ways of life. What is this if not a theory of human nature? Moreover, the doctrine assumes that there are general principles for showing respect effectively, despite the fact that for each culture there may be variations in detail. The paradox is that a moral impulse, a bid for humility and sympathetic understanding, has become an obstacle to moral judgment. But that need not be so. A more careful consideration of the conclusions regarding man's nature implicit in the doctrine of cultural relativism, and derivable from comparative studies, can remove the paradox and free inquiry from some formidable roadblocks.

I conclude that the findings of modern social science do not refute the view that generalizations about human nature are possible, despite the effects of social environment and the diversity of cultures. Nothing we know today precludes an effort to define "ends proper to man's nature" and to discover objective standards of moral judgment. This does not mean that proper ends and objective standards are knowable apart from scientific inquiry. It does mean that psychic health and well-being are, in principle, amenable to definition; and that the conditions weakening or supporting psychic health can be discovered scientifically. It also means that all such conclusions are subject to revision as our work proceeds.

Whether we are able now to say what human nature consists of, is not important. We are not completely at a loss, but any current formulations would still be very crude. The essential point is that *we must avoid any dogma that blocks inquiry.* Relativism is pernicious when it insists, on woefully inadequate theoretical and empirical grounds, that the study of human nature is a chimera, a foolish fancy. To say we "know" there is no such thing, and that there is no use looking for it, is to abandon the self-corrective method of science. It is also to ignore much evidence regarding the psychic unity of mankind.

Most definitions of law—and they are not really so various as is sometimes suggested—remind us that we are dealing with a normative system and a master ideal, in the sense discussed above. Aquinas is perhaps most explicit, calling law "an ordinance of reason for the common good, made and promulgated by him who has care of the community." But even the efforts of Gray and Holmes to avoid a normative definition surely falter when they emphasize "the rules which the courts, that is, the judicial organs of that body, lay down for the determination of legal rights and duties" or, in the Holmesian formula, "the prophecies of what the courts will do in fact, and nothing more pretentious, are what I mean by the law." For the meaning of "court" or "judicial organ" is plentifully supplied with normative connotations, such as the idea of being duly constituted, independent rather than servile, and offering grounded decisions.

In framing a general concept of law it is indeed difficult to avoid terms that suggest normative standards. This is so because the phenomenon itself is defined by—it does not exist apart from—values to be realized.[1] The name for these values is "legality." Sometimes this is spoken of as "the rule of law" or, simply, "the legal order." Legality is a complex ideal embracing standards for assessing and criticizing decisions that purport to be legal, whether made by a legislature or a court, whether elaborating a rule or applying it to specific cases.

The essential element in legality, or the rule of law, is the governance of official power by rational principles of civic order. Official action, even at the highest levels of authority, is enmeshed in and restrained by a web of accepted general rules. Where this ideal exists, no power is immune from criticism nor completely free to follow its own bent, however well-intentioned it may be. Legality imposes an objective environment of constraint, of tests to be met, of standards to be observed, and, not less important, of ideals to be fulfilled.

This concept of legality is broad enough, but it is not so broad as the idea of justice. Justice extends beyond the legal order as such. It may have to do with the distribution of wealth, the allocation of responsibility for private harms, the definition of crimes or parental rights. Such issues may be decided politically, and law may be used to implement whatever decision is made. But the decision is not a peculiarly legal one, and many alternative arrangements are possible within the framework of the rule of law. How far government should intervene to direct social and economic life is a question of political prudence, in the light of justice, but how the government behaves if it does exercise broader controls or enter new spheres of life quickly raises questions of legality.

---

1. Author's note: For a revised formulation, distinguishing the *concept* of law, which embraces legal ideals, from a weaker *definition* of law, see Selznick, Law, Society, and Moral Evolution (Ch. 1, pp. 4-11, from Selznick, *Law, Society, and Industrial Justice* (1969)), reprinted below in Chapter 11.

The ideal of legality has to do with the way rules are made and with how they are applied, but for the most part it does not prescribe the content of legal rules and doctrines. The vast majority of rules, including judge-made rules, spell out policy choices, choices not uniquely determined by the requirements of legality. Whether contracts must be supported by consideration; whether a defendant in an accident case should be spared liability because of plaintiff's contributory negligence; whether minors should be relieved of legal consequences that might otherwise apply to their actions—these and a host of other issues treated in the common law are basically matters of general public policy. For practical purposes, and especially because they arise in the course of controversies to be adjudicated, a great many of these policy matters are decided by the courts in the absence of, or as a supplement to, legislative determination. In making these decisions, and in devising substantive rules, the courts are concerned with dimensions of justice that go beyond the ideal of legality. Legality is a part of justice, but only a part. It is indeed the special province of jurists, but it is not their only concern. On the other hand, when they act outside the province where the ideal of legality is at issue, the courts share with other agencies of government the responsibility for doing justice. It is not legality alone which determines what the rule should be or how the case should be decided. That depends also on the nature of the subject matter and on the claims and interests at stake. Whether the outcome is just or unjust depends on more than legality.

However, there are times when the ideal of legality does determine the content of a legal rule or doctrine. This occurs when the purpose of the rules is precisely to implement that ideal, the most obvious illustration being the elaboration of procedural rules of pleading and evidence. In addition, principles of statutory interpretation, including much of constitutional law, directly serve the aim of creating and sustaining the "legal state." Some of these rules are "merely" procedural in the sense that they are arbitrary conveniences, chosen because some device was necessary, for which some other procedure might readily be substituted. Others are vital to just those substantial rights which the ideal of legality is meant to protect. These include all that we term civil rights, the rights of members of a polity to act as full citizens and to be free of oppressive and arbitrary official power. Again, it is not the aim of this ideal to protect the individual against all power, but only against the misuse of power by those whose actions have the color of authority. Of course, in our society we may have to extend our notions of who it is that acts "officially."

Perhaps the most difficult area governed by the ideal of legality is the process of judicial reasoning itself. Fundamentally, of course, this is part of the law of procedure, but it has a special obscurity as well as a special significance. The crucial problem here is to justify *as legal* the exercise of judicial creativity. That there is and must be creativity, whatever the name we give to it, is no longer seriously disputed. The question remains, however, whether there is something beyond the bare authority of the court, or reliance on a vague "sense of justice," to support the idea that judge-made policy has the stamp of legality.

One approach to this problem gives special weight to the legal tradition, to the received body of concepts, principles, doctrines, and rules. By working with these pre-existent legal materials, the law is in some weak sense "discovered," at the same time that creativity is permitted. Using familiar concepts establishes a link with the past and tends to create (though it does not guarantee) a smooth, gradual transition from one accepted policy to another. In this way legal craftsmanship, defined by its familiarity with the limits and potentialities of a certain body of materials and certain modes of decision, can ease social change by extending the mantle of legitimacy. A new policy, if it can be blanketed into contract doctrine or fitted into the law of torts, can have a peculiarly "legal" quality simply because of the ideas with which it is associated. It seems fair to say that this peculiar function of the law is weakening because it has become less attractive to the legal profession. This is so in part because of the modern interest in avoiding arcane language, in making policy objectives explicit, and in criticizing conventional legal categories. One may wonder, however, whether enough attention has been given to the role of legal concepts in defining an implicit delegation of power to the courts. This might be thought of as a working arrangement by which society allows the courts to make policy within areas marked out by the received body of legal ideas. It is assumed that these ideas are bounded, not limitless; that legal reasoning and judicial behavior contain some built-in restraints; and there is no contrary action by a legislature.

Another approach is to emphasize, not the "artificial reason" of the law, but the role of natural reason in the ideal of legality. Among the attributes of legality is a commitment to the search for truth, to consistency of thought, and to logical analysis of evidence as relevant, of classifications as inclusive, of analogies as persuasive. In this sense, there is no special legal reasoning; there is only the universal logic of rational assessment and scientific inquiry. The ideals of science and of legality are not the same, but they do overlap. Judicial conclusions gain in *legal* authority as they are based on good reasoning, including sound knowledge of human personality, human groups, human institutions.

The *meaning* of law includes the ideal of legality. That ideal, even though not yet completely clarified or specified, is the source of critical judgment concerning constituent parts of the legal order, especially particular rules and decisions. When a part of the law fails to meet the standards set by that ideal, it is to that extent wanting in legality. It does not necessarily cease to be law, however. It may be inferior law and yet properly command the respect and obligation of all who are committed to the legal order as a whole. At the same time, a mature legal system will develop ways of spreading the ideals of legality and of expunging offending elements.

The subtlety and scope of legal ideas, and the variety of legal materials, should give pause to any effort to define law within some simple formula. The attempt to find such a formula often leads to a disregard for more elusive parts of the law and excessive attention to specific rules. But even a cursory look at the law will remind us that a great deal more is included than rules. Legal ideas, variously and unclearly labeled "concepts," "doctrines," and "principles," have a vital place in authoritative decision. "Detrimental reliance," "attractive nuisance," "reasonable doubt," "exhaustion of remedies," "agency," and "interstate commerce" are among the many familiar concepts which purport to grasp some truth and provide a foundation for the elaboration of specific rules. In addition, of course, there are even more general ideas or principles stating, e.g., the necessary conditions of "ordered liberty" or that guilt is individual rather than collective. It would be pointless to speak of these as merely a "source" of law; they are too closely woven into the fabric of legal thought and have too direct a role in decision-making.

Variety in law is manifest in other ways, too. We may speak, for example, of variety in function: Law is called upon to organize public enterprises; to establish enforceable moral standards; to mediate differences while maintaining going concerns; to arrange contractual or marital divorces; to make public grants; to investigate; to regulate some private associations, to destroy others. These and other functions have yet to be adequately classified or systematically studied. It seems obvious that such study is a precondition for formulating a valid theory of law.

There are also well-known qualitative differences in the authority of legal pronouncements. If opinions are divided; if there is manifest confusion of concepts, monitored by legal scholarship; if rules or concepts are based on received tradition alone; if a particular rule is inconsistent with the general principles of a particular branch of law—then the authority of opinion or judgment is weakened. If all laws are authoritative, some are more authoritative than others.

These considerations support Lon Fuller's view that the legal order has an implicit or internal morality, a morality defined by distinctive ideals and purposes. To say this, of course, is not to end inquiry but virtually to begin it. We must learn to distinguish more sharply between "bad law" that is merely bad public policy and law that is bad because it violates or incompletely realizes the ideals of legality. And we must attain a better understanding of how public purpose affects legal principle, as when we recognize that society binds itself especially tightly in the administration of criminal justice, generally requiring evidence of intent and barring retroactive legislation.

If the legal order includes a set of standards, an internal basis for criticism and reconstruction, then an essential foundation is laid for a viable theory of justice. In his sympathetic treatment of the natural law position, Morris Cohen was almost right in arguing that we must be able to appeal from the law that is to the law that ought to be, from positive law to principles of justice. But he did not quite see that at least some principles of justice are ingredients of the ideal of legality and are therefore part of "the law that is." In many cases, we appeal from specific rules or concepts in the law to other concepts and to more general principles that are also part of the law. This is sometimes put as an appeal from "laws" to "the law," and there is merit in that approach. But it has the disadvantage of suggesting that "the law" is something disembodied and unspecifiable, when in fact all we mean is that general principles of legality are counterposed to more specific legal materials. Both belong to a normative system whose "existence" embraces principles of criticism and potentialities for evolution.

With this approach in mind, we can give to positive law its proper place and meaning. "Positive law" refers to those public obligations *that have been defined* by duly constituted authorities. This is not the whole of law, and it may be bad law. Law is "positive" when a particular conclusion has been reached by some authorized body—a conclusion expressed as an unambiguous rule or as a judgment duly rendered. This definition differs from the suggestion made by Holmes that law is what the courts *will* do, assuming that he meant to define positive law. I am emphasizing what the courts *have done,* because what they will do may depend on the whole body of legal materials.

Positive law is the product of legal problem solving. The legal order has the job of producing positive law as society's best effort to regulate conduct and settle disputes. What is done may be only imperfectly guided by legal principles, perhaps because those principles themselves are inadequate, but it remains law for the time being. As such, it has a claim on obedience. Positive law invokes a suspension of personal preference and judgment with regard to the *specific issue.* To suspend judgment, of course, is not necessarily to fail to have a judgment, but someone else's judgment is taken as an authoritative guide to behavior. Suspension in this sense is rightfully invoked because obedience to positive law is essential to the survival and integrity of the system as a whole. For the system to function, it is necessary that only specially appointed individuals may disregard a positive law, by changing or reinterpreting it, or by modifying its effect in a particular case when other rules can be brought to bear.

Obedience to positive law, irrespective of private judgment, is not an abandonment of reason. On the contrary, as has been well understood for a long time, it is a natural outcome of reasoned assent to the system as a whole. It in no way precludes criticism or testing of positive law, including the assertion that it is void and without effect. But criticism, testing, and change proceed within the broader framework of the legal order, appealing to its own ideals and purposes when they are relevant. Of special importance is the duty of legal officers, including private counsel, to respond critically to the positive law.

Plainly, positive law includes an arbitrary element. For him who must obey it, it is to some extent brute fact and brute command. But this arbitrary element, while necessary and inevitable, is repugnant to the ideal of legality. Therefore the proper aim of the legal order, and the special contribution of legal scholarship, is *progressively to reduce the degree of arbitrariness in the positive law.* This rule is comparable to that in science where the aim is to reduce the degree of empiricism, that is, the number of theoretically ungrounded factual generalizations within the corpus of scientific knowledge.

If reducing the degree of arbitrariness is accepted as the central task of jurisprudence, a long step is taken toward natural law philosophy. For whatever its variations, or its special errors, the concept of natural law has survived, and flourished periodically, precisely because of the need to minimize the role of arbitrary will in the legal order. The basic aim of this philosophy is to ground law in reason. The question then is, What shall we understand as the meaning of "reason"? I shall take it to mean what John Dewey meant by "intelligence" and, following his basic teachings, suggest that scientific inquiry, including inquiry about proper ends and values, is the road to a science of justice or natural law. . . .

By its very name, "natural law" connotes a concern for drawing conclusions about nature. In other words, natural law *presumes inquiry.* And this entails a commitment to the ideals and canons of responsible thought. This does not mean, of course, that legal rules or doctrines are the same as scientific generalizations. The latter are "laws" in a quite different sense. Legal norms or principles are "natural law" to the extent that they are *based upon* scientific generalizations, *grounded in* warranted assertions about men, about groups, about the effects of law itself.

To put the matter this way may seem all too innocent. Among those who seek to improve legal doctrine and the administration of justice, few would question the importance of having more knowledge about how people behave in legal settings. Studies of deterrence and criminal law, of jury behavior, of arbitration, and of legally relevant changes in industrial organization, would all be welcome. Such studies are safe enough when they do not address themselves to the basic ideals of legality and therefore to the constitution of the legal order. In principle, however, there is no reason why the most general concepts of law—equality, reasonableness, fairness, and the like—should not be as subject to criticism, on the basis of scientific' investigation, as are narrower legal concerns. When that occurs all innocence is lost and the quest for law is uneasily resumed.

Whatever the scope of our concern, natural law inquiry *presumes a set of ideals or values.* Most broadly, this is the welfare of man in society; law is examined for its potential contribution to that welfare. A more specific objective of natural law inquiry is to study the structure of the legal order as a normative system and to discover how the system can be brought closer to its own inherent ideals. Thus law is tested in two ways: first, against conclusions regarding the needs of man, including his need for a functioning society; second, against tested generalizations as to the requirements of a legal order. To some extent, the latter really includes the former, because among the requirements of a legal order is the capacity to serve human well-being by protecting and facilitating at least some vital aspects of social life.

On one vital point it seems wise to limit our intellectual commitments. It is not necessary for natural law supporters to prove or maintain that man *qua* man has any inherent duties, including the duty to live at all or to choose the good and avoid evil. This may be so on other grounds, but it is not essential to the natural law perspective. To be sure, the duties of man as father or as citizen are subject to social and legal definition, but that is a more limited assertion. Moreover, I should like to shift the emphasis. From the standpoint of natural law, *the duty lies in the legal order.* If there is to be a legal order, it must serve the proper ends of man. It must not debase him or corrupt him. It must not deprive him of what is essential to the dignity and status of a human being. Whether or not any particular human being accepts a commitment to life, or to the good life, the law has no such freedom. It exists, on any theory, precisely to insure that at least the minimum conditions for the protection of life are established. The master ideals of justice and legality broaden that commitment considerably. But broad or narrow, it is the *system* that has the commitment.

. . . Functionalism, in stating "the requirements of a going concern," must identify what is essential to the system it is studying and then work out what is needed to sustain it at some specified level of activity or achievement. The level specified is not necessarily an arbitrary preference; it is at least partly set by the theory of what "is" a nuclear family or a trade union or an industrial society. To study a type of society is to learn what its distinctive structure is, and what it is capable of, as well as what forces are generated within it tending to break it down or transform it. At no point in that analysis is it necessary to show that all participants desire the system or have a duty to uphold it. But if the system is to be maintained, then certain requirements, taking account of natural processes, must be met.

Thus far I have argued:

(a) Natural law presumes scientific inquiry;

(b) Natural law presumes an end-in-view, a master ideal which guides inquiry;

(c) Natural law searches for and incorporates enduring truths regarding the morally relevant nature of man, e.g., his need for self-respect;

(d) Natural law searches for and incorporates enduring truths regarding the morally relevant nature of society, e.g., the distribution and use of social power;

(e) Natural law searches for and incorporates enduring truths regarding the nature and requirements of a legal order.

It is obvious that the authority of natural law, and its development, must depend on progress in the social sciences. Where social knowledge is weak, as in the formulation of theoretically well-grounded and empirically tested generalizations about universal psychic or political phenomena, natural law must also be limited in its authority. Just because this is so, the natural law school has the right and the obligation to criticize social science and help make it more fruitful and more sophisticated.

One response to the difficulty of discovering general truths about man and society is to emphasize the "flexibility" or "variable content" of natural law. (This may also be a defensive reaction to the criticism of natural law philosophy as absolutist and dogmatic.) There is an important insight here, but it must be placed in proper perspective. It is true that natural law *presumes changing legal norms,* but this does not require abandoning the quest for universals or the assertion of them when they are warranted. A grasp of this point is essential if the relation between sociology and natural law is to be rightly understood.

Why does natural law presume changing norms? The reason is that its basic commitment is to a governing ideal, not to a specific set of injunctions. This ideal is to be realized in history and not outside of it. But history makes its own demands. Even when we know the meaning of legality we must still work out the relation between general principles and the changing structure of society. New circumstances do not necessarily alter principles, but they may and do require that new rules of law be formulated and old ones changed.

In a system governed by a master ideal, many specific norms, for a time part of that system, may be expendable. The test is whether they contribute to the realization of the ideal. Many norms evolve or are devised to take account of quite specific circumstances; and when those circumstances change, the norm may lose its value for the system. Thus the governing ideal of the system may be administrative rationality, but specific norms will vary depending on the purpose of the enterprise and upon its stage of development. For example, the norm of decentralization does not always serve the end of administrative rationality. Yet that end continues to have a vital influence on the selection of appropriate norms.

There are two valid interpretations of the idea that natural law has a changing content. (1) As inquiry proceeds, it is always possible that basic premises about legality, including underlying assumptions regarding human nature and social life, will be revised. (2) As society changes, new rules and doctrines are needed in order to give effect to natural law principles by adapting them to new demands, new circumstances, new opportunities. These perspectives demand that we detach natural law from illusions of eternal stability. They also require us to reject the notion that natural law must be a directly applicable code or it is nothing. A set of principles is not a code, any more than the principle of the conservation of energy is a specific physical theory. Natural law provides the authoritative materials for devising codes and for criticizing them, in precisely the same way as constitutional principles affect legislation and judge-made rules.

. . . [M]embers or owners of large enterprises, abdicating effective control, are in need of outside support for the protection of their interests. Such support can come by invoking the principle of fiduciary responsibility. This will not necessarily be effective in the courts, or in legislation, depending on whether the application of it in these circumstances can meet other demands, including consistency with related legal rules and with the effective administration of justice. But the natural law principle can be a starting point for legal craftsmanship.

The application of such a principle often depends on what may be called "institutional assessment." I have in mind the study of a complex enterprise, or type of enterprise, such as a school, church, political party, business firm, or government agency. The aim of institutional assessment is to determine what goals or objectives can be attributed to the enterprise, the capabilities it has, the strategies it lives by, its characteristic weaknesses, the distinctive significance it has for the life of the member, and what its probable line of evolution may be. Institutional assessment is one of the great practical and theoretical aims of social science, to which the sociology of large-scale organizations can make very important contributions. The development of this line of inquiry is still very primitive, but the needs of the legal order may require us to do the best we can with the intellectual tools now available. This is just what is being done in current discussions of the responsibilities of corporation directors and trade union leaders. . . .

A general theory of responsibility and authority would be part of natural law. The theory rests on both and experience, on the clarification of meanings as well as on propositions about anxiety, aspiration, and group structure. Insofar as its elements withstand the test of inquiry, the theory remains a permanent part of the legal order. But how and where principles of responsible authority are applied depends on social needs and opportunities, as well as on circumstances that determine whether a particular rule will have the desired effect.

The significance of historical opportunity may merit a special word. When we consider the problems of large organization, it is tempting to take the view that the growth of private power has created vast new possibilities of oppression, and to make this the ground for seeking the extension of legal protection. I doubt that this accords with reality, and I think it reflects a mistaken view of legal development. Our problem is not so much the resistance of oppression as it is the fulfillment of opportunities. This is not to say that oppression is absent, or that new forms of it have not developed. But far more important is the fact that we now have opportunities not available before to build the ethic of legality into large segments of the economic order. Extending the ideals of due process to private associations might at any time have been a worthy objective. But the development of an inner order within bureaucratic enterprises brings that objective into close accord with a naturally evolving social reality. Legal ideals cannot always be completely realized, principles of justice cannot always be effectively applied, but they remain as living potentialities, awaiting the appearance of historical developments that will permit their application.

A legal principle, including a principle of natural law, belongs to an intricate, interdependent whole. It is not applied mechanically, in isolation from other legal materials. For this reason, among others, *natural law is applied with caution.* This is not an unfamiliar idea, as students of judicial review well know. Natural law, like constitutional interpretation, presumes a conservative posture. Excesses of logical extrapolation, over-confidence in the power and authority of an abstract idea, will thereby be minimized. This means also that the effects of a change in rule or doctrine on the legal system as a whole, or on some especially integrated parts of it, will be weighed.

The principle of caution recognizes a rebuttable presumption in favor of positive law. This is so for two reasons. First, it helps sustain the authority of the machinery for making positive law, and this is necessary to the integrity and effectiveness of the entire legal order. Second, the presumption recognizes that the funded experience of the political community has a special merit, although not absolute merit. Positive law is always partly a reflection of arbitrary will and naked power politics, but it also registers the problem-solving experience of the community. Above all, it can be a vehicle for the emergence of rational consensus. Therefore positive law makes its own vital contribution to the development of natural law. As a road to natural law, the evolution of positive law has a special claim to respect, because it is a kind of funded experience and because it can bring with it an added dimension of legal authority. This is a corollary of the statement made earlier about "reducing the degree of arbitrariness" in positive law. As that is done, the competence of positive law to aid the development of general legal principles will be enhanced.

Cahn, The Sense of Injustice*

. . . Why do we speak of the "sense of injustice" rather than the "sense of justice"? Because "justice" has been so beclouded by natural-law writings that it almost inevitably brings to mind some ideal relation or static condition or set of preceptual standards, while we are concerned, on the contrary, with what is active, vital, and experiential in the reactions of human beings. Where justice is thought of in the customary manner as an ideal mode or condition, the human response will be merely contemplative, and contemplation bakes no loaves. But the re-

* [Pp. 13-27 (Indiana University Press 1949). Reprinted by permission.

Edmond N. Cahn (1906-1964) was educated at Tulane University (B.A. 1925; J.D. 1927). After a lengthy career in private practice, Cahn became Professor of Law at the New York University School of Law in 1948. He is the author of *The Sense of Injustice* (1949), *The Moral Decision* (1955), and *The Predicament of Man* (1961).]

sponse to a real or imagined instance of injustice is something quite different; it is alive with movement and warmth in the human organism. For this reason, the name "sense of injustice" seems much to be preferred. What then would be meant by "justice" in the context of the approach adopted in this book? The answer would appear to be: not a state, but a process; not a condition, but an action. "Justice," as we shall use the term, means the *active process* of remedying or preventing what would arouse the sense of injustice.

And now for some instances:

Instance A. Five men who had met to dine together are brought before a judge, on the complaint of the same police officer that each of them parked his automobile one hour overtime in the same block. All plead "not guilty" but offer no evidence or explanation. The testimony of the policeman is uniform regarding each alleged offense. The judge acquits three, imposes a five-dollar fine on one, and sends the fifth defendant to jail for ninety days. This evokes the sense of injustice.

Obviously, in a given ethos all five might have been acquitted; alternately, all might have been convicted and punished in some appropriate manner. Regardless of the individual dispositions, the inequalities arbitrarily created arouse the sense of injustice, because equal treatment of those similarly situated with respect to the issue before the court is a deep implicit expectation of the legal order.

Now equality is in general the creature of positive law.[6] Courts and legislatures establish classes of humanity, categorizing for one or another purpose the duties and rights they desire to effect, to destroy, or to qualify. Thus, before a court, those only are equal whom the law has elected to equalize. The point is that the inequalities resulting from the law must make sense. If decisions differ, some discernible distinction must be found bearing an intelligible relation to the difference in result. The sense of injustice revolts against whatever is unequal by caprice. The arbitrary, though indispensable to many of law's daily operations, is always suspect; it becomes unjust when it discriminates between indistinguishables.

As human integers, men are indistinguishables. This natural fact imposes a limit on the classificatory discretion of positive law. The sense of injustice does not tolerate juridic classes by which the integral status of man is violated. Legal slavery, for example, was doomed to disappear everywhere, for no other reason than that a slave is a man. Here we rec-

---

6. The instance given is advisedly extreme, but so extensive is the operation of positive law on this issue of equality that we should have to add that all five men were duly licensed to drive and that none of them had a previous unfavorable record.

ognize one of the fixed stars of an anthropocentric jurisprudence: nature has made man a prime which positive law cannot justly differentiate.

Why does the sense of injustice call actively for equality? One explanation is that equal treatment of all within a recognized class is a necessary attribute of any legal order; the very concept of law requires this minimal regularity. In terms of pure intellection, such an analysis appears quite persuasive, but it can hardly account for the sense of injustice. One does not become outraged and furious merely because some decision has violated a dialectic pattern. The true reason must go considerably deeper, below the threshold of feeling. It must make clear why the humble and illiterate, the drawers of water and hewers of wood can hate injustice with a burning hatred. . . .

Instance B. Two shoe-factory employees, carrying a large amount of money, are waylaid, robbed, and fatally injured. The incident occurs during a period of intense public feeling against radicals of every kind. Subsequently, a shoemaker and a fish peddler are charged with the crime and, though entirely innocent, are convicted on flimsy circumstantial evidence. The fact that the fish peddler is an avowed anarchist influences the decisions of the trial judge, the jury, the appellate court, and an advisory commission appointed by the governor. After languishing in jail for seven years, the accused are executed. This is felt to be unjust.

Here the sense of injustice attaches itself to the notion of desert. The law is regarded as an implement for giving men what they deserve, balancing awards and punishments in the scale of merit. As *general* merit is so difficult of admeasurement, legal action is usually expected to relate to *particular* merit; that is, to the right, duty, or guilt acquired in a specific circumstance. Sometimes, because of its own clumsiness, the law cannot fulfill this function. Then it may convict a murderer for a murder he has not committed, or a gangster for failure to report his income. In such case, the legal subterfuge does not evoke a keen sense of injustice, for desert has been somehow accorded. Thus, not merely the truth or falsity of a verdict but its relation to desert is a criterion of approval.

Nothing can so heartily satisfy this sense as an incident of "poetic" justice. That he who lives by the sword shall die by the sword, who digs a pit for his neighbor shall fall therein, who builds a high gallows for the innocent shall hang thereon—all these denouements seem peculiarly fitting. But the law cannot so variously adapt the punishment to the crime; it has a limited stock of beneficences and sanctions, limited by the need of legislative control over the inventive imagination of judges. Poetic justice, rare enough as it is, is also imperfect, for the wholesale malefactor can die only once. The sense of injustice does not call for highly dramatic or individualized awards. It adjusts to familiar imperfections. What it cannot stomach is the use of law to raise up the guilty or to punish the innocent.

Instance C. The defendant is convicted of treasonable utterances by which he successfully sought to impair the morale and obedience of combat soldiers in time of war. The sentence of the court is that he be compelled to submit to a surgical operation on his vocal chords, so that thereafter he may only bark like a dog. This affronts the sense of injustice.

Here the main concern is with human dignity. From early times, cruel and unusual punishments have been relegated to the discretion of deity or destiny; law has pulled away from vengeance and humiliation. Vicious and debasing punishments are felt to dishonor the court and the humanity whose authority it wields. Forty stripes were the ancient limit, not so much in the interest of the criminal as of the general respect for man. On the same theory, an alien visitor was considered to be entitled to legal safeguards. In Athens, it was an execrable crime . . . because the stranger who had lost his way had a residual status as a man.

Human dignity is one of the tacit assumptions of the law. It expresses itself generally in the deep distinctions among accidental, innocent intentional, and guilty intentional conduct. Motives count because man is assumed to be primarily rational, free of will, and capable of choice. When he acts accidentally, he is regarded as the mere instrument of external forces; when he acts intentionally but in good faith, guilt may attach within circumscribed areas: only evil purpose will invoke mortal guilt. No one judges Oedipus as he does Nero, though each intentionally killed a person who was his parent.[10]

Positive law, building upon this dignity, may make it expensive. Thus the ancient Pharisees held that it precluded vicarious responsibility in law, e.g., liability for the wrongful acts of one's slave. And, in our own times, dignity has been held incompatible with requiring collective action in employee relations or prohibiting child labor. The sense of injustice is not so easily taken in: it can penetrate the masquerade.

Instance D. An important patent litigation is pending before an appellate court of three judges. One of them, having received a bribe from the appellant's attorney, succeeds in persuading his honorable colleagues to join with him in deciding for the appellant.

Here we have an example of injustice involved in the operation of the judicial process. The nature of that process requires certain familiar

---

10. This reference was lifted baldly from David Hume's *An Enquiry Concerning the Principles of Morals* (1740), where I thought it originated until, as usual, I found the archetype in Aristotle (*Nicomachean Ethics,* 1135a).

attributes and procedures, such as impartiality, notice, fair hearing, and judgment of defined issues predicated upon identifiable evidence. Of course, the judicial process, even when ideally applied, does not lead to ascertainment of all the truth, for there are subliminal values in most disputes which not even the most thorough hearing will disclose. Nor does it lead to judgments of perfect wisdom: the law cannot so individualize its operations as to meet the idiosyncrasy, the irreducible uniqueness of each case. Patterns are developed in the light of the repetitive aspects of litigation, and much that protrudes beyond the pattern must be ignored. But, whatever its pragmatic limitations, the judicial process is required to exhibit a fair effort at finding truth and exercising wisdom. Without that effort—involving notice, hearing, and deliberation—it loses its rank as process; it becomes gross will. Informed by this view, the sense of injustice protests all the more angrily against abuse of legal procedures to serve oppressive or vindictive ends.

Instance E. Some workmen engaged in excavation dig up certain ancient Pythagorean manuscripts and turn them over to the owner of the land. Their contents, hitherto unknown, excite much discussion, which reaches the ears of the city magistrate. He borrows the manuscripts, reads only the table of contents, and determines that the text will have a tendency to undermine established religion. Thereupon the legislature is consulted and, after hearing the magistrate take oath that the books ought not to be read or preserved, decrees that they be publicly burned.[12] This is felt to be unjust.

The concern in this instance is with the authorized functions of government, its right of censorship and relation to freedom of inquiry. There is hardly a conceivable function that government has not arrogated to itself at one time or another, under pretext of divine authority, public welfare, or bald caprice; and judgments of propriety on this score are almost completely relative.[13] Yet censorship of thought somehow remains the most obnoxious of all such interferences, perhaps because it eventually prevents all intelligent amelioration of government itself, perhaps because it insults and degrades the rational claims of the citizen.

What powers men delegate to their governments depend upon what they think of themselves and of their needs. Recognized needs may call for severe abnegation, especially in times of great public emergency. But

12. This instance was taken almost literally from Livy XL. 29 (Bohn's trans. 1915), 1885-86.

13. A negative instance would also have been appropriate; that is, one of the failure of government to fulfill functions that custom or circumstances rendered obligatory. Failure to provide opportunity for productive employment of those able to work might illustrate the case.

if the citizenry thinks well of its own intelligence and wisdom, it will bridle at censorship; it will struggle for access to facts and to ideas. Men who do not respect human capacity will raise no such objections. They will feel no loss in being closed out from what they cannot use. Thus, here again the view of law parallels closely the view of human capacities.

Instance F. Relying on a series of formal charters, colonists set out from their homeland and, despite fearful perils and hardships, succeed in building the beginnings of a new pioneer society. They organize local governments and militia, open courts and schools, construct highways, harbors, and trading centers. Fighting back the savage aborigines, they hew down forests, plough and plant the land, and establish their councils of self-rule. Just at the dawn of their success, the home legislature, thousands of miles away from their new problems and free mores, passes a decree that it has the right to bind the colonies in all cases whatsoever. The sense of injustice is outraged.

In this instance, normal expectations have been disappointed—a species of injustice that embraces many varied actions of legislatures and courts. Any retroactive change in substantive law would, of course, furnish a conspicuous example of such disappointment, for the law itself creates expectation of the consistency and continuity of its own operations. But expectations may arise from other sources, such as the moral views and practices of the community and its economic fabric. The positive law may be unjust in breaking not only its promise of regularity but likewise its promise of adequacy and utility. What is the law good for, if it is deaf to patent needs?

One of these is the need for evolutionary change in the law itself. There is a legitimate expectation that courts and legislatures will discern what is useful and good in new occasions. The sense of injustice may find as much offense in a regularity that is slavish as in an inconsiderate change. In the former case, the provocation generally seems lighter, for the expectation has not been weighted with reliance and the direction of legal progress remains debatable. A prestige of legitimacy attaches to the known law, rebuttable only by showing that it is substantially wrong. At times, there arise revolutionary needs that demand a clean sweep of the established order and will not permit vested rights to stand in the way; but in the usual situation the law can fulfill its function best by seeing that contracts are performed, existing social standards are enforced, and relations which it invited men to create are sustained. Thus it is that judges in moving the law forward, case by case, are always impeded; attitudes and reliances intervene between the precedent and the attempt to improve it. Positive law as it progresses must weigh the utility of the new rule against that of confidence and certainty. The sense of injustice warns against either standing still or leaping forward; it calls for movement in an intelligible design.

What the Instances Show. These instances prick the contours of our topic. The sense of injustice may now be described as a general phenomenon operative in the law. Among its facets are the demands for equality, desert, human dignity, conscientious adjudication, confinement of government to its proper functions, and fulfillment of common expectations. These are facets, not categories. They tend to overlap one another and do not together exhaust the sense of injustice. . . .

Are these aspects ethical in their nature? They are, for they posit certain explicit values in the realm of human conduct. But they are not merely ethical: as they enter into the shaping of positive law, they acquire a special direction and form qualified by the past history and present felt needs of the juridic system, and modified again by the factor of sanction. An ethical impulse to which legal sanctions have been attached is not quite the same as it was; its content and intensity must shrink to the size of its new responsibility.

Are these aspects of justice universal? Hardly. The claim might be made that they are limits which the variables of positive law tend to approach, and as we presently consider the sources of the sense of injustice that claim may gain some support. It must be remembered, however, that most of these aspects pertain to the operation of law rather than to its substance, and that positive rules contribute a great deal to the body and meaning of equality, legitimacy of expectations, and so forth. The universal element would thus appear exceedingly narrow, and may be restricted to inescapable natural dimensions such as the integral status of individual man.

Concepts may be real without being universal. In any sound pragmatic sense, principles are real so far as they have meaningful consequences. Of course, their rank may be made to vary with their universality, but loftiness of rank is all too often achieved by means of dilution and excessive thinning. Our interest here is rather in the real qua efficacious. Utterly universal operation of one cause would crowd out all others; it would destroy the dynamism of nature and level human life to monotony. Insistence on perfect universality would lead only to an ultimate colorless abstraction "sans everything." In the finite world of which we speak, the genuinely efficient causes are finite and plural; finite effects suggest and indicate finite causes. The justice that we can learn to know is neither completely universal nor categorically right; by that token, it is real in human affairs. It makes a practical difference.

Nor need we view the sense of injustice as dangling beneath some hypostatic framework of natural law, itself suspended from divine law in a chain of infinite regress. The law of nature may exist, may not exist, or may linger in the limbo of doubt for purposes of this inquiry, whose movement is forward to consequences, not backward to origins. We are concerned with studying the sense of injustice, not as a product or effect, but as an operative cause in the law. Thus it is that Ockham's razor excises natural law from our present interest; it does not excise the sense of injustice unless all the phenomena of positive law could be explained without it.

Finally, the sense of injustice is no mere generic label for the concepts already reviewed. It denotes that sympathetic reaction of outrage, horror, shock, resentment, and anger, those affections of the viscera and abnormal secretions of the adrenals that prepare the human animal to resist attack. Nature has thus equipped all men to regard injustice to another as personal aggression. Through a mysterious and magical *empathy* or imaginative interchange, each projects himself into the shoes of the other, not in pity or compassion merely, but in the vigor of self-defense. Injustice is transmuted into assault; the sense of injustice is the implement by which assault is discerned and defense is prepared.

Justice thus acquires its public meaning, as those in a given ethos perceive the same threat and experience the same organic reactions. It is possible to speak of justice without utter relativism or solipsism, just because of this astonishing interchangeability within man's imagination. If a man did not have the capacity to recognize oppression of another as a species of attack upon himself, he would be unready—in the glandular sense—to face the requirements of juridic survival. In fine, the human animal is predisposed to fight injustice. . . .

The experience of the sense of injustice is of a social nature, enlarging the calculus of individual chances. What may or may not affect the particular human being in his own small ambit will inevitably, in the course of sufficient time, touch someone somewhere. That is why the jural status of each is felt to depend upon a just order of increasingly wide extension.

The sense of injustice now appears as an indissociable blend of reason and empathy. It is evolutionary in its manifestations. Without reason, it could not serve the ends of social utility, which only observation, analysis, and science can discern. Without empathy, it would lose its warm sensibility and its cogent natural drive. It is compounded, indissolubly, of both and can subsist on neither alone. For sheer rationality without an empathic fundament would usually degenerate to extreme skepticism and doubt; while empathy, uninformed by reason, would serve up only the illiterate gropings of animal faith. Together reason and empathy support our juridic world. Through them men may learn to identify their own interests with those of an unlimited community, no longer doubting in philosophy what they do not doubt in their hearts.

Is the sense of injustice right? Certainly not, if rightness means conformity to some absolute and inflexible standard. There is nothing so easy or mechanical about it. Blended as it is of empathy and reason, its correctness in particular cases will vary greatly, for how can we know that the intellect has understood and that projection has comprehended every last relevant factor? Who will measure the limits of inquiry or affix the seal of completeness?

Fortunately we appear able to dispense with such a seal, accepting in its stead the assurances that come from inner conviction and from juridic experience. The sense of injustice is right in so far as its claims are recognized in action. Its logical justification must be found in its efficacy, for it succeeds in fact precisely to the extent that relevant circumstances have been understood, felt, and appreciated. Like other biological equipment it endures because it serves, and serves better through progressive adaptation. So, despite all blunders and insensibilities, the sense of injustice is on the right side, the side of fallible men. Offering a common language for communication and mutual defense, it reduces the perils of isolation. It affords some warrant of a progressively better legal order, and thus makes law a vehicle of persuasion.

Chapter 7

Problems of Knowledge
in the Law

Ryle, The Concept of Mind*

I must first indicate what is meant by the phrase "Category-mistake." This I do in a series of illustrations.

A foreigner visiting Oxford or Cambridge for the first time is shown a number of colleges, libraries, playing fields, museums, scientific departments and administrative offices. He then asks "But where is the University? I have seen where the members of the Colleges live, where the Registrar works, where the scientists experiment and the rest. But I have not yet seen the University in which reside and work the members of your University." It has then to be explained to him that the University is not another collateral institution, some ulterior counterpart to the colleges, laboratories and offices which he has seen. The University is just the way in which all that he has already seen is organized. When they are seen and when their co-ordination is understood, the University has

---

* [From pp. 16-17 of *The Concept of Mind* by Gilbert Ryle, copyright 1949 by Gilbert Ryle. Reprinted by permission of Barnes & Noble Books (Div. of Harper & Row, Publishers, Inc.).

Gilbert Ryle (1900-1976) was a Fellow of Magdalen College, Oxford, and a Tutor in Philosophy at Christ Church College from 1924 to 1945. From 1954 until his retirement in 1968, he was Wayneflete Professor of Metaphysical Philosophy at Oxford. Ryle based his philosophy on the notion that mind and body are a single entity. In his seminal work, *The Concept of Mind* (1949), he rejected Descartes' dualistic view of personality, characterizing it as "the ghost in the machine." Ryle's other works include *Systematically Misleading Expressions* (1931), *Dilemmas* (1954), and *Plato's Progress* (1966). Ryle was the editor of the philosophical journal *Mind* from 1948 to 1971.]

been seen. His mistake lay in his innocent assumption that it was correct to speak of Christ Church, the Bodleian Library, the Ashmolean Museum *and* the University, to speak, that is, as if "the University" stood for an extra member of the class of which these other units are members. He was mistakenly allocating the University to the same category as that to which the other institutions belong.

The same mistake would be made by a child witnessing the march-past of a division, who, having had pointed out to him such and such battalions, batteries, squadrons, etc., asked when the division was going to appear. He would be supposing that a division was a counterpart to the units already seen, partly similar to them and partly unlike them. He would be shown his mistake by being told that in watching the battalions, batteries and squadrons marching past he had been watching the division marching past. The march-past was not a parade of battalions, batteries and squadrons *and* a division; it was a parade of the battalions, batteries and squadrons *of* a division.

One more illustration. A foreigner watching his first game of cricket learns what are the functions of the bowlers, the batsmen, the fielders, the umpires and the scorers. He then says "But there is no one left on the field to contribute the famous element of team-spirit. I see who does the bowling, the batting and the wicket-keeping; but I do not see whose role it is to exercise *esprit de corps*." Once more, it would have to be explained that he was looking for the wrong type of thing. Team-spirit is not another cricketing-operation supplementary to all of the other special tasks. It is, roughly, the keenness with which each of the special tasks is performed, and performing a task keenly is not performing two tasks. Certainly exhibiting team-spirit is not the same thing as bowling or catching, but nor is it a third thing such that we can say that the bowler first bowls *and* then exhibits team-spirit or that a fielder is at a given moment *either* catching *or* displaying *esprit de corps*.

These illustrations of category-mistakes have a common feature which must be noticed. The mistakes were made by people who did not know how to wield the concepts *University, division* and *team-spirit*. Their puzzles arose from inability to use certain items in the English vocabulary.

Eddington, The Nature of the Physical World*

An aged college Bursar once dwelt secluded in his rooms devoting himself entirely to accounts. He realised the intellectual and other activities of the college only as they presented themselves in the bills. He

---

* [Pp. 231-233 (Cambridge University Press 1928). Reprinted by permission.

vaguely conjectured an objective reality at the back of it all—some sort of parallel to the real college—though he could only picture it in terms of the pounds, shillings and pence which made up what he would call "the commonsense college of everyday experience." The method of account-keeping had become inveterate habit handed down from generations of hermit-like bursars; he accepted the form of accounts as being part of the nature of things. But he was of a scientific turn and he wanted to learn more about the college. One day in looking over his books he discovered a remarkable law. For every item on the credit side an equal item appeared somewhere else on the debit side. "Ha!" said the Bursar, "I have discovered one of the great laws controlling the college. It is a perfect and exact law of the real world. Credit must be called plus and debit minus; and so we have the law of conservation of £s.d. This is the true way to find out things, and there is no limit to what may ultimately be discovered by this scientific method. I will pay no more heed to the superstitions held by some of the Fellows as to a beneficent spirit called the King or evil spirits called the University Commissioners. I have only to go on in this way and I shall succeed in understanding why prices are always going up."

I have no quarrel with the Bursar for believing that scientific investigation of the accounts is a road to exact (though necessarily partial) knowledge of the reality behind them. Things may be discovered by this method which go deeper than the mere truism revealed by his first effort. In any case his life is especially concerned with accounts and it is proper that he should discover the laws of accounts whatever their nature. But I would point out to him that a discovery of the overlapping of the different aspects in which the realities of the college present themselves in the world of accounts, is not a discovery of the laws controlling the college; that he has not even begun to find the controlling laws. The college may totter but the Bursar's accounts still balance.

Loevinger, Facts, Evidence and Legal Proof*

Law, in the traditional view, is a set of rules for the guidance of conduct and the determination of controversies. While the philosophers have debated whether the rules spring from divine pronouncements, the discoveries of man's reason, the lessons of experience, social com-

Sir Arthur Eddington (1882-1944) was appointed Director of the Observatory in 1914 and was knighted in 1930.]

* [9 *Case W. Res. L. Rev.* 154, 155-156, 158-174 (1958). Reprinted by permission. For biographical information, see page 424 supra.]

pacts, the dominance of force, or other sources, they have not doubted that law is a means of governing social conduct and settling personal disputes by the application of recognized or established principles to the "facts" of specific situations. The difficulty in the administration of law, which keeps so many lawyers and judges employed, is assumed, in this view, to be the problem of finding or formulating the proper rule to govern a given set of "facts."

Taking issue with the traditional view during the last quarter of a century is a group of legal thinkers that has usually, but roughly, been classified together as "legal realists." These have tended to minimize the importance of general principles as determinants of legal action and to emphasize the importance of the "facts" of the individual case. Although few lawyers or judges are either interested or informed enough to be aware of any doctrinal affiliation in legal philosophy, a very large part of the profession has been influenced, it not wholly persuaded, by the arguments of legal realism. It is commonly assumed by most practicing lawyers and trial judges that lawsuits are decided more often on their "facts" than on the "law." It is now widely recognized that all general legal rules are bounded on one side by numerous special exceptions, and on the other side by corollary rules compelling a contrary result. Whether a particular case shall be governed by Rule A, by the exceptions to Rule A, or by Rule Contra-A depends entirely upon what the court or jury believes the "facts" to be; and a very slight difference in the "facts" found by the tribunal may make a vast difference in the result of a case. Indeed, it is the observation of most experienced lawyers that at least 9 out of 10 cases are determined in their result by the opinion of the court or jury as to the "facts" of the case. Further, what is true in this respect of lawsuits is equally true of matters that are disposed of in lawyers' offices without reaching court, except that these are determined by the opinion of lawyers as to the "facts" rather than that of judges or juries.

In these circumstances it would seem that the law—which in this context must mean the body of the profession—should be much concerned with the methods by which "facts" are legally determined. Actually it is not. In all the overwhelmingly vast literature of the law, including reports of decisions, digests and encyclopedias, there is relatively little direct consideration of this problem. Although the problem of "fact" determination is involved in virtually all decided cases, it is explicitly considered in any of its aspects in no more than a minor fraction of one percent of the decisions. A few legal writers and thinkers, and the ubiquitous "reformers," have urged the importance of this part of the legal process, but most lawyers and judges do not seem to be much interested. Meantime the inevitable accommodation of general legal principles to the "facts" of specific cases continues to be accomplished by a proliferation of ostensible legal rules, refinements of rules, distinctions in the refinements, exceptions to the distinctions in the refinements, refinements and distinctions in the exceptions, and so forth ad infinitum.

When we look beyond the symbolic labels currently used to describe the legal process to see what the participants are actually doing, one thing stands out clearly; lawsuits are never decided on "facts." Neither judges nor juries, nor even lawyers in the usual situation, ever come in contact with the "facts" of any case, taking "facts" to mean the transactions or occurrences which gave rise to the controversy. Lawsuits are social post-mortems; they do not deal with the diagnosis of living situations, but with judgments as to dead and past events. All that is available by way of data for the task is the report that individuals can give of the present state of their recollection of past observation and whatever record may be contained in existing documents and, occasionally, other things. Recollections, documents and things relating to past events constitute the "evidence" on which courts and lawyers act and are the stuff out of which the "facts" are constructed. At best, lawsuits are decided on such evidence; at worst, they are decided on a refusal to consider this evidence and on a hunch, rule or prejudice as to which party should be favored in the absence of evidence.

The determination of lawsuits on the basis of evidence rather than of "facts" is obviously not the result of some arbitrary principle of law, but is the inevitable consequence of the character of problems with which the law deals. In this the law is not so very different from many of the natural sciences. In all of the sciences from astronomy to zoology many of the questions to be answered concern phenomena that cannot be directly observed and that can be studied only on the basis of circumstantial and more or less remote evidence. Even in chemistry and physics today much of the frontier research deals with things and events, or perhaps more accurately concepts, that are so minute as to be incapable of direct observation and that can be studied only by their indirect effects.

Much the same thing is also true of everyday life. Relatively little of our knowledge is derived directly from personal observation of the "facts"; and everyone is constantly reaching and acting on conclusions and opinions based on various kinds of evidence relating to matters that cannot be personally observed. Information is acquired in ways too numerous to catalogue: through the mass media of newspapers, radio, television, magazines; through personal reports and letters, by word of mouth; from books; and from an infinite variety of other sources. . . .

What is true of such a relatively simple matter as naming a color, is equally true of more complicated matters. Ordinarily the more complex the phenomena involved, the greater will be the variation in the perception and description of different observers. In matters complicated enough to be the subject of lawsuits, the variation in the versions of different observers will often be so great as to make the versions irreconcilable with each other, as well as with what we may regard as the "facts." This is not a new observation. Experienced trial judges and lawyers must necessarily learn this, although they have various rationalizations of it. Scientific demonstrations and reports have been made by numerous investigators. As long ago as half a century, Munsterberg reported some of these with the remark that "we never know from the material itself whether we remember, perceive, or imagine, and in the borderland regions there must result plenty of confusion which cannot always remain without dangerous consequences in the courtroom."[7]

Among the other consequences of these considerations, some of which will be mentioned later, is the conclusion that the differentiation between "fact," "opinion" and "evidence" is a much more vague and subtle one than the common use of these terms would suggest. It seems to be the common assumption of courts and lawyers that there are objective ascertainable things which we call "facts," that these can be somehow ascertained by weighing the "evidence" and that this "evidence" must consist of reports of immediate perceptions of the facts and not of subjective impressions, which are called "opinions." One of our best courts has recently stated:

> The difference between a "fact" (such as an act, transaction, occurrence or event) and an "opinion" is one of the fundamental differences in the law of evidence. A fact can be testified to by any witness, but, with a few exceptions, an opinion can be given in evidence only by an expert. . . .

If it is true that the law of evidence rests upon such a fundamental assumption—and it probably is—then its foundation is very unsound indeed. The difference between what a witness will report as his observation of a "fact" and what may be reported as an "opinion" may rest entirely on the degree of intelligence, education and sophistication of the witness; or it may rest upon the court's reaction to the testimony offered. In the case quoted above the court excluded medical records containing the opinion of psychiatrists as to the mental condition of the defendant on the grounds that such records were admissible only with respect to "facts" and not with respect to "opinions." (Three judges dissented.)

7. Munsterberg, *On the Witness Stand* 61 (1908).

However, in an earlier case the same court admitted similar records containing a doctor's diagnosis of a physical condition. There are several decisions of other courts to the same effect, and numerous other kinds of records have been held admissible for the purpose of showing the conclusions, or "opinions," of other experts. Some of these decisions expressly hold that the business records statutes do permit the reception in evidence of records containing the opinions of experts. However, it is purely arbitrary to characterize as either "fact" or "opinion" a statement as to a patient's condition, as to the cause of death, as to the cause of an explosion or accident, or as to any similar matter. The difference may lie in the degree of assurance felt or stated by the witness; and this, in turn, may depend upon his intelligence and education. The more intelligent and better educated the witness is, the more likely he will be to realize the limitations of his own observations and to state them with reservations. Thus it may well be that the "opinions" stated by one witness may be more reliable than the "facts" testified to by another because the source of the former is better qualified.

The basic difficulty here is that the distinction between "facts" and "opinions" implies a kind of differentiation that is misleading. There is no hard and clear distinction between "subjective" and "objective," or between "perceptions" and "conclusions" observable in the phenomena with which we are dealing. We tend to think in these terms because the traditional patterns of both our vocabulary and language structure contain such dualisms. No doubt these dichotomies did suggest important distinctions and serve important functions in the development of thought. However, they are no longer accurate, adequate or appropriate to contemporary thought. We have learned that what we regard as the simplest perceptions are the product both of the immediate external stimuli and of our own concepts. This is true not only in social, psychological and biological fields, but also in the physical sciences. Heisenberg, father of the "indeterminacy principle" in modern physics, says of physical science:

> Nature thus escapes accurate determination, in terms of our commonsense ideas, by an unavoidable disturbance which is part of every observation. . . . We decide, by our selection of the type of observation employed, which aspects of nature are to be determined and which are to be blurred in the course of the observation. . . .
>
> When we talk about reality, we never start at the beginning and we use concepts which become more accurately defined only by their application. Even the most concise systems of concepts satisfying all demands of logical and mathematical precision can only be tentative efforts of finding our way in limited fields of reality.

673

To import the Heisenberg principle by a somewhat free paraphrase into the field of law, it is no longer valid to regard the "facts" and the "evidence" as wholly independent elements in the legal process or an individual case. The "evidence" does not simply disclose the "facts." The "evidence" is an indistinguishable part of the "facts," and the "evidence" determines the "facts" as much as the "facts" control the "evidence." When the law establishes principles for securing or receiving evidence, it thereby also determines or establishes the "facts" of cases in which those principles are applied, just as the methods of observation employed in physical science determine the character of the "facts" that will be discovered.

Apart from the peculiarities of the legal rules of evidence there is nothing in the process of legal proof that is unique, or even very unusual. The problem of legal "proof" is the task of reasoning from presently available data to a logical inference as to something that has occurred in the past. The law does have various standards of "proof," requiring more, for example, to sustain a conviction of a crime than a recovery of damages in a civil action. The significance of these varying standards of "proof" is too broad a topic for discussion here. It is sufficient to observe here that in the legal process "proof" means simply a sufficient quantum of evidence to move the tribunal to act in a manner consistent with the existence of the proposition thus "proved." For most cases the degree of "proof" required is that expressed by the common phrase "a preponderance of the evidence," or the "greater weight" of the evidence. This means simply a "preponderance of probability," or a conclusion that it is more probable that the proposition is true than untrue.

These same standards are used by normally rational people in other fields, including everyday living, business and industry, and scientific research. One does not act upon a proposition unless it is believed more likely to be true than untrue unless there is, for some reason, an inducement or desire to gamble on a "long shot." In important matters one may desire a greater assurance than the "preponderance of probability" and so may withhold action until there is a greater quantum of evidence supporting the proposition on which action must depend. In science, conclusions are always stated in terms of degrees of probability, and scientific "proof" means establishing a degree of probability for a proposition, usually one that can be expressed in a quantitative form.

Thus the problem of legal proof is nothing more than a particular aspect of the universal problem of drawing valid inferences from data. The only aspect of legal proof that is unique is the relationship to the rules of evidence which determine the data that can be used in the process of proof in a legal case. These are without counterpart in any other field or discipline.

The rules of evidence, in all their full glory, constitute a body of law that takes at the least a volume and at the most several volumes to state fully and accurately. However they can be epitomized by a relatively few principles. Basically the rules of evidence in our system of law state that:

(A) Evidence not relevant to the legal issues before the court cannot be received.

(B) Hearsay evidence cannot be received, except for numerous special cases in which such evidence is received. (Hearsay is essentially assertions, whether written or oral, made outside the courtroom.)

(C) Testimony in the form of opinions or conclusions cannot be received, except from experts.

(D) Secondary evidence as to the content or intent of writings cannot be received.

(E) Privileged communications cannot be received. These include involuntary responses from one accused of crime; communications between spouses; communications to a lawyer, doctor or priest and other classes of communication established by statutes in various states.

(F) Evidence must be offered in accordance with specified formal and procedural rules. Thus leading, argumentative and hypothetical questions are generally forbidden; interrogation at each stage of examination of a witness must be within the "scope" of the preceding stage; and so forth.

Of course the full statement of each of the rules of evidence contains numerous complex qualifications and even more numerous exceptions. Nevertheless, it remains true that the rules are basically principles of *exclusion,* the purpose and effect of which is to put various classes of evidence beyond the consideration of the fact-finding tribunal. Ostensibly the law has no criteria for weighing or evaluating evidence; and it is a cliché in the trial courts that the admissibility or inadmissibility of proffered evidence must be determined by reference to the rules but the weight of the evidence is wholly for the court or jury. Although it is not hard to find many expressions by lawyers and judges in panegyric praise of the legal system and its operation, scholars who have studied the rules of evidence are nearly unanimous in finding them unsatisfactory and ill-suited to their function. . . .

At the outset we are met by the fact that legal discussions of problems of evidence all ostensibly relate to the issue of "competence" or "admissibility," and not of the "weight" of the evidence which is said to be another matter not included within the field of consideration. Actually, however, the rationalization for most of the exclusionary rules rests on assumptions as to the unreliability of the excluded category of evidence as compared with other categories not excluded. Since the discussion is conducted with highly abstract, and frequently pejorative, terms it is difficult to come to grips with the underlying assumptions.

Examination of the specific rules or principles of evidence discloses that the important and troublesome ones are grounded on very little more than tradition in the form of judicial precedent, generalization on a level of high abstraction, and prejudice against change. For example, the principle that only "relevant" evidence shall be admitted seems, superficially, to be the very spirit of rationality. Certainly it cannot reasonably be argued that the result of an inquiry should be influenced by irrelevant evidence. But this is just the point of difficulty. Assuming a fact-finder capable of dealing with an inquiry at all on a level of rationality, it is obvious that irrelevant evidence will not influence the decision. Evidence which is truly irrelevant need not be feared; the only objection to its admission is the waste of time involved, and every experienced trial lawyer and judge knows that usually far more time is spent in haggling over relevance than would be wasted in admitting all proffered evidence. What then is the real problem?

The true objection to most evidence which is excluded on the grounds of "irrelevance" is not that it is logically irrelevant, or unrelated to the subject matter, but that it is of a kind very likely to be influential with the fact-finder but which should not be considered because of some legal principle or policy. Sometimes an argument as to the "relevance" of evidence is a convenient method of securing an early determination as to the applicable principle of substantive law in a trial. More often, it is a method of expressing a legal policy based on considerations other than the logical relationship between the evidence and subject matter in controversy. For example, ordinarily a court would exclude as "irrelevant" evidence as to the character of a party who has not put his character in issue, habit as showing action on a particular occasion, specific incidents as indicative of character or reputation, other similar accidents or claims in the past, prior consistent statements of a witness, and many other similar matters difficult to state without undue detail or reference to the facts of specific cases. In most cases evidence of this character will be of a kind which a trained investigator, an agency such as the F.B.I., or even the average intelligent person would regard as sufficiently significant to be worthy of note and consideration in relation to the controversy. Indeed, most lawyers will seek to ascertain information of this kind for their own guidance in appraising a case even though they know that the evidence will not be admitted at the trial. Thus it is not the lack of logical "relevance" that causes the courts to exclude such kinds of evidence. Rather it is a policy judgment that the introduction of such evidence will consume undue time in relation to the importance of the issues, the other work of the court and the other demands for expedition, that the evidence may cause unfair surprise to the adverse party, or that the evidence will be given more importance than it deserves by the jury, thus causing prejudice to the other party. Such a judgment clearly involves weighing the evidence and comparing its probative weight with other factors.

The hearsay rule even more patently involves concealed assumptions as to probative weight. Like the rule as to relevance, the hearsay rule has a superficial rationality that is appealing. In general it sounds quite sensible to refuse to consider testimonial evidence which is not given before the tribunal and subject to examination, and cross-examination, in the trial. Probably there was a period in the development of legal procedure when this was an appropriate approach. What happened then was that all evidence consisting of assertions offered for their truth which were not given before the tribunal were given a name —"hearsay." Thereafter lawyers and judges began to think of all such evidence as being "hearsay," having some quality in common which differentiated it from other kinds of evidence. The sheer necessity of getting the work of the courts done required the creation of an increasing number of exceptions to the rule of exclusion of "hearsay," but the professionals continued to use the term and to think of it as designating some legitimate class of evidence. Even the perceptive experts who refused to attempt a restatement of the law of evidence and instead formulated a "model code" continued to think and speak in terms of "hearsay," although much liberalizing the rule of exclusion. . . .

The courts are able to function at all only by ignoring their own rules in this respect a good deal of the time. Slight reflection will show that remarkably little of the testimony that passes unchallenged in ordinary proceedings is actually wholly free from the taint of recognizable "hearsay." No one could possibly know from anything but a hearsay source the answer to such questions as: "Who is your father?," "How old are you?" and "Where were you born?" (Incidentally, while such information might be secured under the "pedigree exception" to the hearsay rule, the answers are very seldom given in a form which would qualify under the technical requirements of that exception.) Although not necessarily so, there is usually no more than a hearsay basis for the answers to such common questions as: "How much money do you have in the bank?," "Who is the president of your company?," "What is the current price of that security?" and many similar questions relating to commercial activity. Even such simple questions as "What is (or was) the date?" and "What time is (or was) it?" require that we rely upon the assurance of a newspaper, a calendar or clock that we assume has been correctly written, constructed or calibrated by someone else. Similarly a strict insistence upon a first-hand knowledge basis for all testimony would preclude the utilization of an adding or calculating machine, a speedometer or ruler, or any other instrument of measurement that had not been constructed or calibrated by the witness. When the courts are unfamiliar with an instrument they do require such first-hand verification of its construction and operation, as, for instance, with the relatively new radar speed measuring devices. However, with familiar culture products of the time-binding process, such as clocks, calendars and measuring sticks, the courts conveniently forget the rules which they apply to more novel devices.

Of course, the point is not that the courts should reject such evidence because it is technically based on a second-hand foundation; but that the rule which purports to require a first-hand foundation for evidence is an invalid, unrealistic and ultimately unworkable one. There may well be a sound reason for differentiating between evidence based on clocks, calendars and calculating machines on the one hand, and on radar, drunkometers and other more recently developed devices on the other hand. The reason, however, cannot be that the latter evidence is "hearsay" or second-hand, whereas the former is not, because that reason is simply false. The reason, if it is to be valid, must be based upon a judgment as to the reliability of the respective devices. There is no purely formal ground for differentiating between such classes of evidence. A sound determination of such issues requires consideration of the substantive "weight" of the evidence.

Part of the confusion in this field arises from the tendency engendered by our language structure and the prevalence of teaching in terms of Aristotelian logical forms to make judgments in terms of either-or, and A or Non-A, rather than in terms of degree or position on a scale. We tend to think in terms of mutually exclusive alternatives: evidence is said to be first-hand knowledge or hearsay; fact or opinion. Yet the dichotomy between "hearsay" and "first-hand knowledge" is as invalid as that between "fact" and "opinion." Both dichotomies point to valid differences. In the sense in which the terms are used in the field of evidence, "fact" and "opinion" point to the differentiations between levels of abstraction, "opinion" being a higher order of abstraction than "fact." Similarly, "hearsay" and "non-hearsay" point to the degree of verification in personal experience underlying an assertion. Both of these things are important matters for the consideration of a fact-finding tribunal in weighing evidence. However, we confuse and mislead ourselves by speaking and thinking of these things in terms of categorical differences rather than differences of degree on a continuum. The language and concepts presently employed by the law of evidence to deal with these points is as inadequate as would be an attempt to describe human stature by classifying everyone as either "tall" or "short" without using any modifying or quantifying terms. The absurdity and inadequacy of such an arbitrary attempt at categorization is self-evident, but it is self-evident only because we are familiar with the description of physical stature in quantitative terms that permit relatively precise description of the infinite variation that exists in this quality. The absurdity of forcing the infinite variety of the kinds of evidence into the Procrustean beds of "hearsay" and "non-hearsay," and "fact" and "opinion" is less obvious only because these are familiar terms.

Fortunately, there is beginning to be a wider recognition of the basic assumptions as to policy underlying the other rules of evidence. The "parol evidence rule" which excludes testimonial evidence as to intent in the drafting of written instruments is generally recognized now as a rule of substantive law. This means that the courts are excluding this class of evidence not because of some supposed vice in the quality of the evidence, but on the ground that as a matter of legal policy parties who assent to a written agreement should be bound by its terms without the privilege of seeking to alter them by oral evidence. Whether or not this policy is justified; this is the kind of judgment that should be made with respect to such an issue. Without undertaking a detailed examination of the other principles of the law of evidence, it may be remarked that there is at least a beginning of a similar consciousness of their basis. Thus Louisell, writing of the general field of privilege, says:

> I believe that the historic privileges of confidential communication protect significant human values in the interest of the holders of the privileges, and that the fact that the existence of these guarantees sometimes results in the exclusion from a trial of probative evidence is merely a secondary and incidental feature of the privileges' vitality.

Taking the law of evidence as a whole, it can be said that all of the exclusionary rules comprising this body of law are based either on a judgment as to the supposed weight, or reliability, of a certain kind of evidence, or on a judgment as to the social desirability as a matter of policy of permitting an inquiry into certain matters. Both kinds of judgment are proper ones for the law to make. The difficulty with the law of evidence in its present form is that as to the most influential and commonly invoked rules the judgment is concealed and therefore not consciously or intelligently made, and the rules operate in terms of arbitrary and artificial categories with respect to data which cannot validly be categorized. The effect is that large quantities of important evidence are excluded on the basis of quite adventitious characteristics without any examination of the specific evidence offered in a particular case or rational consideration of its significance or reliability. This is not an attitude or procedure which should commend itself to those who purport to be reasonable.

Another difficulty with the present law of evidence is that it tends to interfere seriously with the process of securing testimony from witnesses. The process of securing testimonial evidence is, after all, nothing more than a specific problem in human communication. It involves, at the minimum, four distinguishable problems: (1) the observations or abstractions, made by the witness initially from the environment; (2) the retention in memory of these impressions by the witness; (3) the expression by the witness of his recollection; (4) the reaction, or comprehension, by the fact finder to the witness' expression. The relationship between the first element—observation or abstraction by the witness—and the hearsay and opinion rules has already been discussed. The law of evidence has almost nothing to say about the second element; so long as the witness is willing to state a recollection the tribunal will receive his statement, other conditions of the rules being satisfied. The third and fourth elements—the witness' expression and the fact-finder's reaction to it—constitute the problem of communication in the trial process itself. The insistence by the courts upon the eliciting of testimony in the artificial manner of courtroom interrogation, rather than by normal narration, at its best necessarily imposes a severe handicap on successful communication. To a large extent the purpose of this insistence is to permit another even more serious interference with communication. The normal and effective expression of any witness, lay or expert, is impeded by the excision of all that the law has come to regard as "irrelevant" or "hearsay," and by the limitations on the expressions of "opinion," not to mention the atrocities of the current practice with respect to the hypothetical question. . . . For the lawyers to attempt to insist that the rest of the world must learn to speak in the artificial vocabulary and syntax of the law in order to express itself in the courtroom is to betray such a lack of understanding of humanity as to cast doubt on the ability of the lawyers to communicate successfully with others on any level. The burden is obviously on the legal profession to modify its principles and procedures so far as necessary to permit adequate communication with the rest of society or else to lose to others the task of finding facts and determining individual controversies.

The task of adapting legal principles of evidence to a more modern and rational system may not be as difficult as it seems at first impression. A good deal of scientific research and analysis has been done in recent years in the overlapping fields of communications, semantics and logic. One of the basic conclusions of this work has been that the reasoning required in dealing adequately with social data and human problems must be probabilistic, or many-valued, rather than syllogistic, or two-valued.

A syllogistic, or two-valued, logic requires that the data which is employed be cast in the form of categories and that all phenomena be classified as either included or excluded with respect to each category. It has no means of dealing with differences in degree or differentiations on a continuum. A probabilistic logic, on the other hand, specifically takes account of the differences of degree in its data. It does not require categorization into *A* and Non-*A,* and therefore is many-valued in its ability to deal with an infinite variety of phenomena that are differentiated only in degree or position on a continuum. Such an approach is now being used in scientific studies of communications, and similar problems. Thus the report of a recent study of communication and social systems states, "Our model is probabilistic, our measures are distributive, and our test of fit is correlational."

Although the law may not yet be able to achieve quite such a scientific standard in its investigations, it does have precedent for considerably more liberal and rational principles in the fact-finding field than the present rules of evidence. For nearly a quarter of a century the classical statement of the principle that should guide administrative tribunals has been: "Evidence or testimony . . . of the kind that usually affects fair-minded men in the conduct of their daily and more important affairs, should be received and considered; but it should be fairly done."[35]

This rule, which is far from revolutionary, is a many-valued rule which permits the differentiation between important and reliable "hearsay" and inconsequential and unreliable "hearsay," and which permits the reception of the reports of able observation or inquiry regardless of whether the report is offered as a cautious "opinion" or as a dogmatic "fact." Certainly the use of such a rule does not impair the validity of the conclusions reached by tribunals using it. As one court has observed:

> It is a mistake to suppose a conclusion cannot be reached safely by administrative bodies unless they proceed in accordance with jury trial rules of evidence. Most of the world's work is done without that.[36]

35. John Bene & Sons v. Federal Trade Commission, 299 Fed. 468 (2d Cir. 1924).
36. State ex rel. Hardstone Brick Co. v. Dept. of Commerce, 174 Minn. 200, 219 N.W. 81 (1928).

The conventional objection to the use of this liberal principle in the trial of lawsuits in court is that the exclusionary rules are necessary in order to prevent the jury from being misled. This excuse does not explain the fact that courts generally follow the same rules of evidence whether the trial is before a jury or a judge (although the rules are usually interpreted somewhat more liberally in the latter case). This objection also fails to suggest any basis for the assumption that fair-minded men are able to conduct their daily and more important affairs on the basis of reliable evidence outside the courtroom, but not when they are called to act as jurymen. The legal profession must face the fact that the problem of deciding what evidence is sufficient to support belief and induce action is not a problem for judges and lawyers alone, but is the daily concern of every man of affairs. Even so far as the government itself is concerned, in a democratic society every competent adult citizen is permitted to reach a decision as to who should control the legislative and executive branches of government, and, in many states, also the judiciary. The ability to reach such a decision presumably involves some ability to cope with the problem of weighing conflicting claims, arguments and evidence. In terms of the rules of evidence themselves, the objection that the exclusionary rules are required because of the incapacity of juries to act reasonably in their absence is an assumption based on an opinion derived from a surmise, and altogether lacking in evidence, competent or incompetent, to support it.

Nevertheless it must be recognized that the exclusionary rules do have certain practical consequences that are usually not taken into account in discussions of them. Being rules of exclusion that restrict the evidence that can be offered and received, they tend to handicap the party who has the burden of proof and to assist the party who does not have the burden of proof on any issue. Ordinarily the plaintiff has the burden of proof on most issues; and usually plaintiffs tend to be individuals, small businesses and economically less privileged, whereas defendants tend to be corporations, large businesses and the economically more favored. Thus, in addition to the usual division between those who favor and those who oppose almost any change, the fight for reform of the rules of evidence tends to enlist political "liberals" on one side in favor and political "conservatives" on the other side opposed. While there are numerous exceptions, and while all of the rules of evidence "cut both ways," as is often pointed out, there can be little doubt that much of the opposition to the badly needed reforms in the law of evidence stems from a realistic appraisal of the effects of the rules in their present form upon the economic interests of those who are most frequently involved in litigation as defendants.

A corollary of this is that in the continuing contest between government power and individual liberty the government itself is usually the plaintiff and the individual is usually the defendant. This is true of all criminal cases and of many civil proceedings between the government and the citizen. In such cases, the rules throw their weight on the side of the individual by imposing their handicaps on the government as plaintiff. To this extent the exclusionary rules may serve, on occasion, to strengthen the position of personal liberty. However, the principal instrument for the enforcement of governmental authority over the life and activity of the citizen in recent decades has been the administrative agency. These agencies have never been bound by the rules of evidence, and although they have sometimes been charged with arbitrary action, their freedom from the artificial restrictions of the exclusionary rules has usually been counted as in their favor. It is responsibly contended that the administrative agencies should be emulated by the courts in this respect.

A second practical consequence of the rules of evidence that is seldom noted is their effect in forcing the production of evidence that might otherwise not be secured. The rules themselves are cast almost wholly in terms of the exclusion of evidence, but as every experienced trial lawyer and judge knows, the practical effect of the rules often is simply to require that certain "foundation" material be made available to the court or opposing counsel. For example, secondary and even tertiary evidence of the contents of business records is often received by the court provided that the underlying books themselves are made available for inspection and auditing by opposing counsel. Ordinarily a court will prefer not to have the record cluttered up with voluminous records that are difficult to inspect and analyze and will rely upon the vigilance of the adverse party to assure that the summary offered is a correct one so long as the records are available to both parties. This is a sensible procedure. However, it should not require the inflexible and technical complications of the exclusionary rules in order to secure the production of records or witnesses that it is within the power of a party to produce. The simple and straightforward approach to this aid in the investigation of facts is to have the court exercise the power to require the production of witnesses or records whenever such production is appropriate and useful in the investigation of any issue before the court. Perhaps the courts have such a power now; but most courts are very reluctant to exercise it, and usually do so only indirectly by rulings that exclude proffered evidence unless certain "foundation" evidence is also produced.

The rule of general admissibility of evidence, suggested above, does not, of course, purport to deal with considerations of privilege which are based on judgments as to the social values served by forbidding certain inquiries. So long as such judgments are reached by a clear recognition of the interests that are being served and the interests that are being sacrificed and by making an explicit choice between them, the principles of rational discourse are satisfied.

The general body of the rules of evidence do not satisfy the principles of rational discourse as they are recognized in other areas of contemporary thought and action for reasons which have been suggested. More than this, they are patently inadequate to the needs of society which law is supposed to meet, and are in large part responsible for the dissatisfaction with the legal process which is expressed directly in widespread criticism and indirectly in the establishment of non-judicial agencies of all kinds to supplant or substitute for the courts that still adhere to the exclusionary rules. So long as the legal profession continues to think and talk in terms of "hearsay," "legal relevance," "opinions and conclusions" and of "competent" or "incompetent," "admissible" or "inadmissible," it will not be able to struggle out of the morass in which the present law of evidence has mired it. The profession will not progress so long as it employs as its principal intellectual tools these arbitrary categories and the syllogistic thinking in which such categories are an indispensable part. The profession will begin to meet the needs of modern society and to make sense to its contemporary peers only when it recognizes that the problems with which it must deal are those of arriving at reasonable conclusions on the basis of the weight of *all* the evidence available for rational consideration of any issue; and that such problems can be handled only by a language that speaks of variations of degree, rather than discrete and exclusive categories, and by a logic of probabilities rather than syllogisms.

Loevinger, Law and Science as Rival Systems*

The rise of what we now call modern civilization is largely the result of two great systems of gathering and organizing data—the dialectic and the empiric. The two systems developed at about the same time, during the period ranging roughly through the 17th, 18th and 19th centuries, as a reaction against primitive superstition and medieval scholasticism. The dialectic system is embodied in modern legal procedure and the empiric system has become contemporary scientific discipline.

* [19 *U. Fla. L. Rev.* 530 (1967). Reprinted by permission.
For biographical information, see page 424 supra.]

It is sometimes suggested or assumed that law and science have differing methods because the law is more ancient whereas science is a relatively modern innovation. This view is not supported by historical analysis. The origins and the roots of both science and law are equally ancient, and, indeed, are substantially the same; and the principal characteristics of each as data systems developed during the same period and in the same culture. The origins of both law and science lie buried deep in primitive religion and superstition, and both were dominated by the priesthood until the emancipation of the intellectual revolution which was the real foundation of the scientific revolution, the industrial revolution, and the period of enlightenment and political emancipation that began in the 16th century. The great legal historian, Maine, says:

> It is now clearly seen by all trustworthy observers of the primitive condition of mankind that, in the infancy of the race, men could only account for sustained or periodically recurring action by supposing a personal agent. Thus, the wind blowing was a person and of course a divine person; the earth yielding her increase was a person and divine. As, then, in the physical world, so in the moral. When a king decided a dispute by a sentence, the judgment was assumed to be the result of direct inspiration. . . . The only authoritative statement of right and wrong is a judicial sentence after the facts, not one presupposing a law which has been violated, but one which is breathed for the first time by a higher power into the judge's mind at the moment of adjudication."[1]

Throughout most of the history of mankind such factual issues as the law undertook to determine were settled by submission to the wager of law (or compurgation), the wager of battle, ordeal, or torture.[2] These barbaric practices were not the result of sadistic impulse but rather were methods of appealing to some supernatural or divine power for a decision because of the "natural tendency in the human mind to cast the burden of its doubts upon a higher power, and to relieve itself from the effort of decision by seeking in the unknown the solution of its difficulties." The ordeal as a mode of trial began to decline in 1215 when Pope Innocent III forbade the participation of priests in ordeals thus depriving them of their divine sanction. However, the ordeal persisted in one form or another into the 19th century, and appeared in its most vulgar and abhorrent form in the episode of sorcery and witchcraft trials in the

1. Henry S. Maine, *Ancient Law* (1861; 3rd American Edition 1888), pp. 4, 7.
2. Henry C. Lee, *Superstition and Force* (1878). This is one of the great works of scholarship in legal history and traces the history of early legal practices that are not commonly studied in law schools or known to lawyers although they prevailed over a much longer period than the more modern and refined practices with which we are familiar.

16th and 17th centuries. Trial by compurgation and accusatorial conjurators was maintained until the 16th century, the use of torture persisted in England into the 17th century, and in Scotland until the 18th century, and trial by battle survived until finally abolished by law in England in the early 19th century.

In English law there were no rules of evidence at least until the 13th century, since under the primitive practices of trial by compurgation, battle, and ordeal, proof was accomplished by appeal to God. During the period from the 13th to the 16th centuries there was a gradual change to trial by jury with a differentiation of the process of pleading and procedure from that of proof; and the foundation for the rules of evidence was not laid until the 16th century when this process had taken place. The principle that a verdict must be reached solely on evidence presented in court was not established until the end of the 17th century; and it was not until Bushell's Case in 1670 that English courts accepted the principle that jurors may not be punished for acquitting a defendant. Right of cross-examination by counsel was established at the beginning of the 18th century. The rules of evidence were fully developed during the 18th century and the first treatise on the law of evidence was published in 1726. The rules of evidence were fully developed into a system by the early 19th century.

In the early 19th century the primitive modes of trial or truth-seeking were formally abolished, and the two basic evidentiary principles of modern legal procedure were established: first, none but facts having rational probative value are admissible; and, second, all facts having rational probative value are admissible unless some specific rule excludes them.

Ancient science, like ancient law, was taught by priests and was not a distinct or separate subject of its own. While primitive man sought to study and to control nature, he employed magic based on superstitious belief in rite and spell and a faith that superhuman powers would intervene directly in response to such rituals, as in the case of legal battle and ordeal. Science as an organized discipline with recognized tactics and strategy involving rigorous modes of observation and experiment has been developed only since the early 17th century. . . .

It is probably more than coincidence that Francis Bacon (1561-1626), who is mentioned as an important figure in the early development of modern law, is better known as the author of an essay on a new method ("Novum Organum") in the early history of modern science. It was Bacon who perceived the vices of the scholastic method and set forth clearly the widening breach which separated the men of his day from the Middle Ages. The writings of Bacon were an impetus to the foundation of the Royal Society, and he is thought by some to be one of the founders of the empiric method in science.

Even a casual survey of the pioneering work in the major fields of science will show the concomitance in the development of modern science and modern law.

. . . [S]cience and law both had their origins in the superstitions of primitive religion and both developed their modern intellectual outlooks during the 17th, 18th and 19th centuries as a reaction against and rejection of medieval scholasticism and superstition. The common elements in both have been an effort to be wholly rational, to organize and institutionalize the search for truthful data, and, above all, to seek truthful data as the basis for judgments. Science can equally well accept the basic principles of the legal system of evidence: to accept only rationally probative evidence, and to examine all relevant evidence unless there is some overriding reason for disregarding it.

Nevertheless it is clear that the legal and the scientific methods of inquiry are, despite those similarities, quite different. The legal method of inquiry relies primarily on the testimony of human observers, tested by examination and cross-examination, and subjectively weighed by a judge or jury. Essentially this is the method of inquiry by interrogation which may appropriately be called "dialectic." The dialectic method is most organized and formalized in the evidentiary and procedural rules for the conduct of legal trials. However, essentially the same method is employed throughout the ramifications of government in all but the most undeveloped countries. In the legislative process, as in litigation, information is sought in hearings which employ the dialectic method, although the more formal and rigorous rules of the evidentiary system are not commonly employed. It is fair to say that, taking law in its largest sense as encompassing all aspects of government, the predominant mode of securing legal data is the dialectic method.

The scientific method is clearly a different and distinguishable approach to data gathering, although it is not nearly so clear as was once thought that there is any specific and unique technique that is entitled to be known as "the scientific method." Science is like law in that it is a mode of securing agreement among different individuals with respect to certain kinds of questions and problems. The strength of science derives from its objective and demonstrative, and therefore highly persuasive, techniques. The limitation of science is that it is not applicable to all kinds of questions and problems. Essentially the scientific method is applicable only to questions of the kind commonly characterized as those involving issues of "fact."

The basic methods of science are experimental, statistical and clinical. The experimental method is to control the variation of one or a few elements in a series of phenomena while observing the concomitant variation of other elements. The statistical method involves observation of a relatively large number of cases, either directly or by a representative sample of the universe, to ascertain the concomitant variation of specific elements within the universe. The clinical method involves the observation and analysis of individual cases to determine causal, necessary, or influential, relationships among the elements of a given class of phenomena. Although scientific inquiry may thus be experimental, statistical inquiry may thus be experimental, statistical, clinical, or possibly taxonomic or something else, it is always empiric. Science recognizes no meaning that is not empirically definable and accepts no significance that is not empirically demonstrable.

The difference in the legal and scientific modes of securing data is, as has often been observed, at least partially a function of the different tasks performed by law and science. While science seeks to analyze and predict phenomena, law seeks to classify and control conduct. In the most simple and elementary terms it may be said that the function of science is descriptive and that of law is prescriptive. The essential legal function of prescribing norms is not and cannot be scientific in any sense which the contemporary scientific community would recognize as scientific.

But this is only one aspect of the matter. Much of the activity of government, including that of law-makers, judges, administrators and other lawyers consists of investigating and ascertaining facts. The facts sometimes concern a single instance, as in investigating the circumstances of a particular lawsuit, and other times involve ascertaining data concerning a class or universe, as in a legislative investigation to determine the need for a new law and the abuses to be cured by it. However, "facts" never exist in isolation; even when an inquiry appears to be directed at a single set of circumstances it necessarily involves either data or assumptions regarding the universe in which those circumstances occurred. Implicit in the whole legal system of seeking and accepting evidence in particular cases are a host of assumptions concerning the reliability of observation, retention and recall by human witnesses and the effectiveness of examination and cross-examination as a means of soliciting and testing recollection. These assumptions are themselves not subject either to falsification or corroboration by the dialectic method and are precisely the kind which can be investigated and tested by the empiric method. Nevertheless the law has, to date, made no systematic effort either to investigate the validity and reliability of testimonial evidence or to utilize the scientific data on this subject that are available. This raises the issue as to what the relation between law and science is and should be.

It requires no great effort to ascertain that up to the present time law has made little use of science, or of the empiric method, and that lawyers generally have little understanding of science or its concepts and methods. The literature of law, like the literature of every other field, necessarily reflects its current knowledge and wisdom. A catalogue search of the law library serving the largest and possibly best-group of practicing lawyers in this country, the Federal Department of Justice, discloses almost no books that can be regarded as truly scientific and only a few periodicals that carry any but the most infrequent scientific reports. In this, as in other law libraries, there are journals which report on the use of scientific techniques in crime detection and on medico-legal matters of significance in personal injury and related fields. Beyond this, only the political science journals will reflect any of the vast amount of work being done in the behavioral sciences that may be of significance to law.

The same picture will be found by observation of the law reviews. I have systematically surveyed the articles carried by American law reviews as reflected in the index of the Law Review Digest and over a period of years there are not enough articles reporting truly scientific work to be of numerical significance. . . .

The limited efforts by lawmen to adopt and use the empiric methods of science suggest the question whether these methods are appropriate and useful in the field of law, or whether the dialectic method of law is a complete alternative that leaves no need or place for the empiric method. A simple inspection of other fields would seem to create at least a prima facie presumption that science can usefully be employed on legal problems. Clearly science has been among the most potent of those forces that have created modern society, both in its social aspects and in the material health and well-being that characterize the industrialist countries. The study of science, its methods and its subject matter, . . . regardless of its employment for strictly legal purposes, science appears to be such a major aspect of modern culture that a discipline which purports to establish normative principles for that culture would seem required at least to understand it.

Thus, the question arises as to why there has been so little study or use of science in American law schools. A variety of answers can be and have been given. It is sometimes suggested that the case method of study is the legal equivalent of scientific empiricism. But this answer will not stand critical analysis. There is almost nothing in common between the case method as employed in American law schools and the scientific method of inquiry. To begin with, the "cases" which are studied are almost exclusively the opinions of appellate courts rather than the raw data of clients' complaints, the testimony of witnesses or even the records

689

of trials. The case method does not involve starting with data and working through to conclusions, but rather the contrary, starting with conclusions and working back to the most generalized and abstract statement of the fewest data that will support the conclusions. Cases are studied in law school within a normative and not a descriptive framework. Indeed, the case method is little more than a pedagogical variant of text-book study.[36] Whatever its vices or virtues as a pedagogical method, the case method is clearly not science.

Perhaps the most common answer to the question why science is not employed in law is that the problems of law are different from those of science, and, therefore, are not subject to empiric study. There is a kernel of truth in this response, since there are certainly problems within the field of law that are not appropriately subject to scientific investigation or analysis. However, it is also the case, as will be noted below, that even within the field of science there are problems which cannot be resolved by the empiric method. The significant point is that there are many problems within the field of law that clearly are subject to empiric study and analysis, and that even as to these there has been little or no effort made to engage in such research. . . .

The traditional hostility of the legal profession, including its teachers, to a study of either the methods or subject matter of science is too pervasive, persistent and impractical to be explicable on either historical or practical grounds. Rather it seems that lawyers view science as a rival system which would displace the dialectic methods of law with techniques alien to the law and uncongenial to lawyers. . . .

The dialectic method of law is highly formalized in both procedure and substance. Despite the seeming simplicity of its two basic principles, legal dialectic is today institutionalized in an elaborate set of rules that has no counterpart in science. The dialectic method of law is essentially clinical in the sense that it is best adapted to investigation and determination of the "facts" of individual cases, and it is not well adapted to the investigation of mass or social problems. Legal procedures tend to stall or break down under the influx of large numbers of cases (as in the recent flood of anti-trust cases in the electrical industry), and simply have no means of coping with large populations or broad social investigations. Legal dialectic, for all its formality and strict procedure, has only the most vague criteria of inference or proof. The "presumptions" of law are essentially rules dispensing with the need for evidence. The stan-

---

36. David Reisman characterizes the case method as an "impious treatment of cases." David Reisman, Toward an Anthropological Science of Law and the Legal Profession in *Individualism Reconsidered* and other essays (1954) p. 440 et seq.

dards of inference are couched in such terms as "a preponderance of evidence" and "beyond a reasonable doubt." There is no way of quantifying or specifying these criteria and the law generally rejects any attempt to do so. Thus the dialectic method of law stands as a formal, flexible, clinical approach to data gathering which is suitable to the investigation of individual cases but not to group or mass phenomena.

The empiric method of science, in contrast, is informal in the sense that it involves no specified procedures and has no rules respecting the kind of evidence that is acceptable or unacceptable. Science is, however, rigorous in the sense that it has standards of inference that are quantitative and specific and that have no counterpart in law. There are, for example, statistical measures of correlation that are regarded as criteria of significance in that correlations of a given order will support an inference of a relationship whereas correlations of a lower order do not justify any inference of a relationship. Furthermore, virtually all observations in science are reported with either an explicit or an implicit range of error or uncertainty. There are well-recognized conventions in science for specifying such uncertainty. While science does, on occasion, employ the clinical method, it does not recognize clinical reports except insofar as these are based upon some specified framework drawn from statistical, experimental or sampling data. In general, science is statistical, and based upon measurements of central tendency and dispersion among ranges of quantifiable observations. Such an approach is well adapted to dealing with problems involving groups and masses, but ill adapted to dealing with single or unique instances.

Thus the dialectic system of law and the empiric system of science are differing systems for securing data in differing circumstances, each with its own appropriate function and proper field. Much of the difficulty in the relationship between law and science has arisen from the failure of both lawyers and behavioral scientists to recognize the limitations of their respective methods and the kinds of problems to which they are appropriate.

Probably the main reason science has produced so little of significance in the field of law to date is that so far the effort has been mainly to produce theories rather than data. Among those most familiar with legal problems there has been very little understanding of the need for data, the technique of gathering or mode of interpreting data in a scientific manner. Many seem to have labored under the mistaken assumption that formulating a hypothesis in scientific language was enough to make it scientific. It has been overlooked that the function of a hypothesis in science is to suggest an area of observation and the means of testing for data, and that a scientific hypothesis is merely a step in securing data which, in turn, may lead to the formulation of theory. Unfortunately many who have worked in the field of law are so accustomed to dealing in theory that they elevate each hypothesis to a theory, omit the arduous task of gathering corroborative data, and then regard each theory as an established "fact." Thus many of the attempts to invoke science in the field of law have been devoted to constructing large theories as to the prediction of judicial decisions, particularly on collegiate courts, rather than to attempt to answer the more modest and limited questions that science is presently able to handle competently. Whether this misdirection of effort is due to the scientists or the lawyers is not of much importance. It seems unlikely that science will be invoked by lawyers to answer the myriad practical and significant questions it is capable of investigating within the field of law until there has been a much closer integration between legal and scientific education, which means until lawyers and law professors learn a good deal more about science. It seems clear that the need in law today is not for more theories but for more data. What science has to offer law in this generation, and probably in several succeeding ones, is knowledge of how to gather, analyze and test data. The theories will come—perhaps too soon, too fast and too profusely. Most men much prefer the grand generalization and the stirring conclusion to the limited observation and the partial correlation.[44] For the present and the foreseeable future science will serve law better by encouraging a fact-skepticism than by promoting a theory-dogmatism.[45]

What then are the kinds of questions which can usefully be asked by lawyers with a reasonable expectation that valid and reliable data in response can be provided by the empiric methods of science? Certainly no comprehensive or complete answer can be given at any one time, for it is of the essence of the empiric method that questions lead to data which

44. Long ago Maine observed that: "The inquiries of the jurist are in truth prosecuted much as inquiry in physics and physiology was prosecuted before observation had taken the place of assumption. Theories, plausible and comprehensive, but absolutely unverified, such as the Law of Nature or the Social Compact, enjoy a universal preference over sober research into the primitive history of society and law; and they obscure the truth not only by diverting attention from the only quarter in which it can be found, but by that most real and important influence which, when once entertained and believed in, they are enabled to exercise on the later stages of jurisprudence." Henry S. Maine, *Ancient Law* (1861; 5th ed. 1873) 3.

45. David Reisman observes that social science today operates within a range the ends of which are "theory" and "data." He says that there are really extraordinary difficulties in linking important social science generalizations to measurable data. David Reisman, Some Observations on Social Science Research, in *Individualism Reconsidered* and other essays (1954) p. 467 et seq.

lead to more questions that lead to more data, and so on, in an infinite progression. However from a cursory survey of the field a number of possibilities are apparent.

To begin with, the pioneering work of the Chicago jury project should be the beginning, not the end, of a systematic attempt to gather scientific evidence as to the behavior of juries.[46]

An obvious rich mine of data, that lies virtually untouched, is the records of judgments in the hundreds of trial courts throughout the country in various categories of cases. Any competent surgeon is prepared to advise a patient of the general statistics as to success in a given type of operation. Such statistics reflect only the experience of the general population and, as both surgeon and patient recognize, do not necessarily indicate the prognosis for an individual, the professional judgment of the surgeon is necessarily involved in advising whether a given individual has an average, better than average, or worse than average chance of surviving an operation and enjoying a successful result. Strangely enough, there are no comparable data available to lawyers. Individual experienced trial lawyers have their own observations to report. But the kind of data that are routinely gathered in other fields have, up to the present time, been ignored in the law. . . .

. . . The statistics as to judgments in various categories of both criminal and civil cases should be routinely gathered and reported by disinterested agencies, and should be readily available to litigants or other interested parties without any suspicion that the interest of the parties may have influenced the data.

Similarly, statistics as to criminal sentences imposed, sufficiently detailed to permit the correlation of severity with both crimes and criminals, should be routinely gathered and available, as well as statistics showing the subsequent criminal or non-criminal records of defendants who have been subject to such sentences.[49]

An ubiquitous problem which should be, but seldom is, studied in law schools is that of the reliability of observation and recall by wit-

46. See Harry Kalven, Jr. and Hans Zeisel, *The American Jury* (1966); Charles W. Joiner, *Civil Justice and the Jury* (1962).

49. It has recently been reported that a special committee has been appointed in Great Britain to study the use of computers to achieve more consistent sentences by the courts. It is proposed that sentences for all types of crimes based on records for the last ten years of all magistrate's courts would be stored in a central computer and thus be available for retrieval and study. *World Peace Through Law Center Bulletin*, Vol. 3, No. 4 (April 1966). The lack of such data has occasioned the criticism of criminal sentencing as a "guess in a vacuum."

nesses.[50] A related problem, of equal importance, that receives even less attention is as to the effect of cross-examination in eliciting reliable recall.[51]

The award of damages as compensation for various categories of torts involves a host of specific quantifiable questions for investigation. There are questions as to whether damage awards are in fact compensatory and adequate to restore injured parties to normalcy, questions as to what the effects of actual and potential liability and liability insurance have as deterrents to tortious conduct, and questions as to the social cost of accidents, compensation, and the maintenance of the system of determining and awarding compensation.[52]

. . . Perhaps the largest, most important—and most fallow—field for investigation in the area of law is that involving the meaning of terms used. There is an ineluctable relationship between science and semantics, and the first requirement of scientific procedure is a clear specification in concrete or operational terms of the symbols used.[54] This has led, in turn, to a recognition of the influence of language upon observations and ideas.[55] As a beginning, some effort should be made to ascertain whether or not lawyers and judges have similar or different ideas when they use such vague and abstract terms as "justice," "obscenity," "reasonable," and "public interest." There is reason to think that such terms do not have any commonly understood or agreed meaning, and merely mask disagreement and misunderstanding. A simple objective survey of such a commonly used term as "public interest" indicates that it has no common core of meaning which is capable of being made operational either as a guide to public officials in making decisions or to scholars in investigating government actions.[56] There are techniques which permit experimental and quantitative investigation of such semantic questions.

One simple experimental design so readily suggests itself, it is remarkable it has not yet been utilized. A statement of the major facts in-

50. Hugo Munsterberg, *On the Witness Stand* (1908); James Marshall, *Law and Psychology in Conflict* (1966); James L. McGaugh, Time-Dependent Processes in Memory Storage, 153 *Science* 1351 (Sept. 15, 1966). James Marshall, supra, suggests a number of questions for future research in the field although without proposing any experimental design.

51. William Stern, The Psychology of Testimony, 34 *Journal of Abnormal and Social Psychology* 3 (1939).

52. *Studies in the Economics of Injury Reparation,* University of Michigan Press (1964); A. F. Conard and J. E. Jacobs, New Hope for Consensus in the Automobile Injury Impasse, 52 *A.B.A.J.* 533 (1966).

54. P. W. Bridgman, *The Logic of Modern Physics* (1927).

55. Benjamin Lee Whorf, *Language, Thought and Reality* (1956: MIT Paperback Edition 1964), especially the Essay on Science and Linguistics, p. 207 et seq.

56. Glendon Schubert, *The Public Interest* (1960).

volved in a series of either actual or hypothetical cases might be validated by submission to an appropriate panel of judges and lawyers to insure that issues involving questions of justice (or some other specified concept) were involved. Such statements could then be submitted to representative samples of judges, lawyers, members of other professions, college graduates, and the general population in various communities for judgment as to the results dictated by their individual sense of justice. If the results from all groups were sufficiently congruent, an inference might be drawn that it makes some sense to talk about a "sense of justice" or of injustice, or whatever. However, if there are significant differences between or within such groups as to the dictates of their "sense of justice," or their understanding of the term being investigated, then it would seem that we should stop using such verbalization as though it represented an identifiable phenomenon, at least until we can discover or formulate some operational correlate.

Scientific work on any of these questions, or similar ones, will not only produce data of value in law, but, perhaps of even more importance, will help to educate lawyers in understanding the empiric method of science, and the concepts and thought habits to which it has given rise. A fallacy popular among lawyers is that you have solved a problem when you have applied a label to it. . . .

Nevertheless, it is apparent that many of the questions which science is best equipped to investigate in the field of law are questions concerning mass or group behavior, and lie in the field that has traditionally been known as "public law," as contrasted with private law. Conceivably our system of private law can struggle along for many years employing only the dialectic method and taking little or no account of science and its data. However, we cannot survive and prosper as a society without the study and cultivation of public law. The decline of public law as a subject of study and concern in our law schools, may well be due to the fact that its effective pursuit now requires knowledge and use of the empiric method of science and that this is not yet either accepted or understood in American law schools.

. . . Unfortunately the teaching and the practice of law are still largely based upon an earlier period when statutes were few and relatively simple statements of policy, and when practical law was made in court. As a result, we have separated the study of law-making, which we call politicial science, from law interpreting and applying, which we call the practice of law. This makes about as much sense as separating the study of anatomy and physiology from the practice of medicine. The difficulty with incorporating the scientific study of law into law school curricula is that it offers most to the branch of law called public law, or political science, and the profit and interest is in the branch called the practice of law. The great hiatus in law today is of an institutional means of conducting empiric research and of collecting, reporting, and collating the results for consideration by decision makers.

Frankel, The Search for Truth— An Umpireal View*

My theme, to be elaborated at some length, is that our adversary system rates truth too low among the values that institutions of justice are meant to serve. Having worked for nine years at judging, and having evolved in that job the doubts and questions to be shared with you, I find it convenient to move into the subject with some initial reminders about our judges, who they are, how they come to be, and how their arena looks to them.

Except when we rely upon credentials even more questionable, we tend to select our trial judges from among people with substantial experience as trial lawyers. Most of us have had occasion to think of the analogy to the selection of former athletes as umpires for athletic contests. It may not press the comparison too hard to say it serves as a reminder that the "sporting theory" continues to infuse much of the business of our trial courts. Reflective people have suggested from time to time that qualities of detachment and calm neutrality are not necessarily cultivated by long years of partisan combat. Merely in passing, because it is not central for this occasion, I question whether we are wise to have rejected totally the widespread practice in civil-law countries of having career magistrates, selected as relative youths to function in the role of impartial adjudicators. Reserving a fuller effort for another time, I wonder now whether we might benefit from some admixture of such magistrates to leaven or test our trial benches of elderly lawyers.

In any event, our more or less typical lawyer selected as a trial judge experiences a dramatic change in perspective as he moves to the other side of the bench. It is said, commonly by judges, that "[t]he basic purpose of a trial is the determination of truth. . . ." Judge David W. Peck, lecturing from this platform, identified "truth and . . . the right result" as not merely "basic" but as "the sole objective of the judge. . . ."

*[123 *U. Pa. L. Rev.* 1031, 1032-1041 (1975). Reprinted by permission. Originally published in 30 *The Record of the Bar of the City of New York* 14 (1975).

Marvin E. Frankel (1920–) is United States District Judge for the Southern District of New York. He was educated at Queens College (A.B. 1942) and Columbia University (LL.B. 1948). Judge Frankel is a member of the faculty at Columbia University School of Law, and is the author of numerous publications on the subject of criminal sentencing.]

These are not questionable propositions as a matter of doctrine or logic. Trials occur because there are questions of fact. The paramount objective in principle is the truth. Nevertheless, for the advocate turned judge, this objective marks a sharp break with settled habits of partisanship. The novelty is quickly accepted because it has been seen for so long from the other side. But the novelty is palpable, and the change of role may be unsettling. Many judges, withdrawn from the fray, watch it with benign and detached affection, chuckling nostalgically now and then as the truth suffers injury or death in the process. The shop talk in judges' lunchrooms includes tales, told often with pleasure, of wily advocates who bested the facts and prevailed. For many other judges, however, probably a majority at one time or another, the habit of adversariness tends to be re-channeled in at least some measure and to become a combative yearning for truth. With perhaps a touch of the convert's zeal, they may suffer righteously when the truth is being blocked or mutilated, turn against former comrades in the arena, feel (and sometimes yield to) the urge to spring into the contest with brilliant questions that light the way.

However the trial judge reacts, in general or from time to time, the bench affords a changed and broadened view of the adversary process. "Many things look different from the bench. Being a judge is a different profession from being a lawyer." In the strictest sense I can speak only for myself, but I believe many other trial judges would affirm that the different perspective helps to arouse doubts about a process there had been neither time nor impetus to question in the years at the bar. It becomes evident that the search for truth fails too much of the time. The rules and devices accounting for the failures come to seem less agreeable and less clearly worthy than they once did. The skills of the advocate seem less noble, and the place of the judge, which once looked so high, is lowered in consequence. There is, despite the years of professional weathering that went before the judicial office, a measure of disillusionment.

The disillusionment is, as I indicated at the outset, only a modest element of the judicial experience. It is relevant here, however. It accounts for recurrent expressions from judges that seem critical of the bar when they probably stem from more basic dissatisfactions. In any event, it is undoubtedly part of the genesis of this essay.

II

The preceding comments on the transition from bar to bench have touched explicitly upon the role of the advocate. That role is not, however, a matter of sharp and universally agreed definition. The conception from which this paper proceeds should be outlined, as will be done now.

In a passage partially quoted above, Presiding Justice David W. Peck said:

> The object of a lawsuit is to get at the truth and arrive at the right result. That is the sole objective of the judge, and counsel should never lose sight of that objective in thinking that the end purpose is to win for his side. Counsel exclusively bent on winning may find that he and the umpire are not in the same game.

Earlier, stating his theme that court and counsel "complement" each other, Justice Peck said:

> Unfortunately, true understanding of the judicial process is not shared by all lawyers or judges. Instead of regarding themselves as occupying a reciprocal relationship in a common purpose, they are apt to think of themselves as representing opposite poles and exercising divergent functions. The lawyer is active, the judge passive. The lawyer partisan, the judge neutral. The lawyer imaginative, the judge reflective.

Perhaps unfortunately, and certainly with deference, I find myself leaning toward the camp the Justice criticized. The plainest thing about the advocate is that he is indeed partisan, and thus exercises a function sharply divergent from that of the judge. Whether or not the judge generally achieves or maintains neutrality, it is his assigned task to be nonpartisan and to promote through the trial an objective search for the truth. The advocate in the trial courtroom is not engaged much more than half the time—and then only coincidentally—in the search for truth. The advocate's prime loyalty is to his client, not to truth as such. All of us remember some stirring and defiant declarations by advocates of their heroic, selfless devotion to The Client—leaving the nation, all other men, and truth to fend for themselves. Recall Lord Brougham's familiar words:

> An advocate, in the discharge of his duty, knows but one person in all the world, and that person is his client. To save that client by all means and expedients, and at all hazards and costs to other persons, and, amongst them, to himself, is his first and only duty; and in performing this duty he must not regard the alarm, the torments, the destruction which he may bring upon others. Separating the duty of a patriot from that of an advocate, he must go on reckless of the consequences, though it should be his unhappy fate to involve his country in confusion.

Neither the sentiment nor even the words sound archaic after a century and a half. They were invoked not longer than a few months ago by a thoughtful and humane scholar answering criticisms that efforts of counsel for President Nixon might "involve his country in confusion" There are, I think, no comparable lyrics by lawyers to The Truth.

This is a topic on which our profession has practiced some self-deception. We proclaim to each other and to the world that the clash of adversaries is a powerful means for hammering out the truth. Sometimes, less guardedly, we say it is "best calculated to getting out all the facts. . . ." That the adversary technique is useful within limits none will doubt. That it is "best" we should all doubt if we were able to be objective about the question. Despite our untested statements of self-congratulation, we know that others searching after facts—in history, geography, medicine, whatever—do not emulate our adversary system. We know that most countries of the world seek justice by different routes. What is much more to the point, we know that many of the rules and devices of adversary litigation as we conduct it are not geared for, but are often suited to defeat, development of the truth.

We are unlikely ever to know how effectively the adversary technique would work toward truth if that were the objective of the contestants. Employed by interested parties, the process often achieves truth only as a convenience, a by-product, or an accidental approximation. The business of the advocate, simply stated, is to win if possible without violating the law. (The phrase "if possible" is meant to modify what precedes it, but the danger of slippage is well known.) His is not the search for truth as such. To put that thought more exactly, the truth and victory are mutually incompatible for some considerable percentage of the attorneys trying cases at any given time.

Certainly, if one may speak the unspeakable, most defendants who go to trial in criminal cases are not desirous that the whole truth about the matters in controversy be exposed to scrutiny. This is not to question the presumption of innocence or the prosecution's burden of proof beyond a reasonable doubt. In any particular case, because we are unwilling to risk more than minimally conviction of the innocent, these bedrock principles must prevail. The statistical fact remains that the preponderant majority of those brought to trial did substantially what they are charged with. While we undoubtedly convict some innocent people, a truth horrifying to confront, we also acquit a far larger number who are guilty, a fact we bear with much more equanimity.

One reason we bear it so well is our awareness in the last analysis that truth is not the goal. An exceedingly able criminal defense lawyer who regularly serves in our court makes a special point of this. I have heard him at once defy and cajole juries with the reminder that the question is not at all "guilt or innocence," but only whether guilt has been shown beyond a reasonable doubt. Whether that is always an astute tactic may be debated. Its doctrinal soundness is clear.

Whatever doctrine teaches, it is a fact of interest here that most criminal defense counsel are not bent at all upon full disclosure of the truth. To a lesser degree, from the same ethos, we know how fiercely prosecutors have resisted disclosure, how often they have winked at police lapses, how mixed has been their enthusiasm for the principle that they must seek justice, not merely convictions. While the patterns of civil cases are different, and variable, we may say that it is the rare case in which either side yearns to have the witnesses, or anyone, give *the whole truth*. And our techniques for developing evidence feature devices for blocking and limiting such unqualified revelations.

The devices are too familiar to warrant more than a fleeting reminder for this audience. To begin with, we leave most of the investigatory work to paid partisans, which is scarcely a guarantee of thorough and detached exploration. Our courts wait passively for what the parties will present, almost never knowing—often not suspecting—what the parties have chosen not to present. The ethical standards governing counsel command loyalty and zeal for the client, but no positive obligation at all to the truth. Counsel must not knowingly break the law or commit or countenance fraud. Within these unconfining limits, advocates freely employ time-honored tricks and stratagems to block or distort the truth.

As a matter of strict logic, in the run of cases where there are flatly contradictory assertions about matters of fact, one side must be correct, the other wrong. Where the question is

> Did the defendant pass a red light?
>   or
> Does the plaintiff have a scarred retina?
>   or
> Was the accused warned of the reasons why anyone of sound mind would keep quiet and did he then proceed nevertheless like a suicidal idiot to destroy himself by talking?

the "facts" are, or were, one way or the other. To be sure, honest people may honestly differ, and we mere lawyers cannot—actually, must not— set ourselves up as judges of the facts. That is the great release from effective ethical inhibitions. We are not to pass judgment, but only to marshal our skills to present and test the witnesses and other evidence—the skills being to make the most of these for our side and the least for the opposition. What will out, we sometimes tell ourselves and often tell others, is the truth. And, if the worst comes to the worst, who really knows in the end what is truth?

There is much in this of cant, hyprocrisy, and convenient overlooking. As people, we know or powerfully suspect a good deal more than we are prepared as lawyers to admit or explore further. The clearest cases are those in which the advocate has been informed directly by a competent client, or has learned from evidence too clear to admit of genuine doubt, that the client's position rests upon falsehood. It is not possible to be certain, but I believe from recollection and conversation such cases are far from rare. Much more numerous are the cases in which we manage as counsel to avoid too much knowledge. The sharp eye of the cynical lawyer becomes at strategic moments a demurely averted and filmy gaze. It may be agreeable not to listen to the client's tape recordings of vital conversations that may contain embarrassments for the ultimate goal of vindicating the client. Unfettered by the clear prohibitions actual "knowledge" of the truth might impose, lawyers may be effective and exuberant in employing the familiar skills: techniques that make a witness look unreliable when the look stems only from counsel's artifice, cunning questions that stop short of discomfiting revelations, complaisant experts for whom some shopping may have been necessary. The credo that frees counsel for such arts is not a doctrine of truth-seeking.

The litigator's devices, let us be clear, have utility in testing dishonest witnesses, and thus ferreting out falsehoods, and thus exposing the truth. But the devices are to a considerable degree like other potent weapons—equally lethal for heroes and villains. It is worth stressing, therefore, that the gladiator using the weapons in the courtroom is not primarily crusading after truth, but seeking to win. If this is banal, it is also overlooked too much and, in any event, basic to my thesis of this evening.

Reverting to the time before trial, our unlovely practice of plea bargaining—substantially unique to the United States—reflects as one of its incidents the solemn duty of defense counsel to seek the acquittal of guilty people. Plea negotiations must begin, in principles governing all but some exotic cases, with the understanding that the defendant is guilty. Plea negotiations should not otherwise be happening. But the negotiations break down in many cases—most often because there is no mutually acceptable deal on the sentence, the key concern. When that occurs, the defendant goes to trial, and the usual measures to prevent conviction are to be taken by his advocate. The general, seemingly principled view would hold his tendered plea and attendant discussions inadmissible at trial. Does all this make sense? Is it comfortable? All of us in the law have explained patiently to laymen that "guilty" means not simply that "he did it"; it means nothing less than that he has been "found-guilty-beyond-a-reasonable-doubt-by-a-unanimous-jury-in-accordance-with-law-after-a-fair-trial." Despite the sarcastic hyphens, all of us mean that and live by it. But when a fair trial entails a trial so tortured and obstacle-strewn as our adversary process, we make the system barely tolerable, if not widely admired, by contriving that most of those theoretically eligible get no trial at all. The result suggests we might inquire how things work on the European continent, where the guilty plea, at least in technical strictness, is scarcely known and the plea bargain seems to be truly nonexistent.

Our relatively low regard for truth-seeking is perhaps the chief reason for the dubious esteem in which the legal profession is held. The temptation to quote poetical diatribes is great. Before fighting it off altogether, let us recall only Macaulay on Francis Bacon, purporting not to

> inquire . . . whether it be right that a man should, with a wig on his head, and a band around his neck, do for a guinea what, without those appendages, he would think it wicked and infamous to do for an empire; whether it be right that, not merely believing but knowing a statement to be true, he should do all that can be done by sophistry, by rhetoric, by solemn asseveration, by indignant exclamation, by gesture, by play of features, by terrifying one honest witness, by perplexing another, to cause a jury to think that statement false.

Less elegant then Macaulay but also numbered among the laymen that do not honor us for our dealings with the truth are many beneficiaries of such stratagems. One of the least edifying, but not uncommon, of trial happenings is the litigant exhibiting a special blend of triumph, scorn, complicity, and moral superiority when his false position has scored a point in artful cross-examination or some other feat of advocacy. This is a kind of fugitive scene difficult to document in standard ways, but described here in the belief that courtroom habitués will confirm it from their own observations.

Jones, Legal Inquiry and the Methods of Science*

To the mind of the Middle Ages, the world of science and the world of law were not as far apart as they seem to the modern mind. In the world view of the thirteenth and fourteenth centuries, the eternal law, God's ordained and promulgated reason, provided both the govern-

---

* [*Law and the Social Role of Science* 120-M (H. Jones ed., Rockefeller University Press

ment of inanimate nature and the constitution for control of human behavior and interpersonal relations. The man of science and the man of law were both interpreters: the scientist striving to discern and formulate the eternal laws of nature that explain physical phenomena, the lawyer striving to apprehend and make effective the moral structures of God's natural law for man. It would not have occurred to Thomas Aquinas that there would be any great intellectual or cultural difficulty about interdisciplinary understanding between scientists and lawyers—he would have said that the scientist and the jurist are, at farthest remove, workers in neighboring vineyards.

This felt affinity of science and law has disappeared with the theocentric world view that gave it birth. No explicit postulate of divine ordinance supports the logical structure of contemporary science, and law, for its part, is studied and appraised as a product of human will, judgment, and artifice. The old affinity of law and science seems remote and even quaint to us; the best we can do to relate the scientist's vocation to the lawyer's is to say that there is a certain unity in the creative process, that science and law—however manifest their differences in method, effect, and product are both forms of man's culture, efforts by human intelligence to understand, explicate, and universalize the varieties of experience.

Beyond this, we are properly suspicious of claims that the work of the scientist and the work of the lawyer can be reduced to anything like a common denominator. The scientist's field of action has become increasingly inaccessible to the lawyer, as to other outsiders, as science becomes ever more abstract and deductive in character. The "hard" sciences are, indeed, hard going for the legally trained mind. A lawyer of scientific interests can still, if he works hard at it, achieve an amateur's beginning of an understanding of the essentials of contemporary physiology, where observation and laws proceeding directly from observation are still relatively central, but he is lost in the abstract world of contemporary physics, where the scientist speaks the Pythagorean language and seems

1966) (footnotes omitted). Reprinted by permission.

Harry Jones (1911-   ) is Cardozo Professor of Jurisprudence at Columbia University School of Law. He was educated at Washington University, St. Louis (LL.B. 1934), and Columbia University (LL.M. 1939), and is the recipient of several honorary degrees. He has served in various academic and governmental positions in the course of his distinguished career. His publications include *The Efficacy of Law* (1969), *Law and the Social Role of Science* (1967), and *The Courts, the Public and the Law Explosion* (1965). Professor Jones has been an Advisor for the *Restatement of the Law of Contracts,* American Law Institute, since 1958.]

to roam in a world far removed from the world of ordinary sense-experience. And, since Lord Snow has been cited more than once during our discussions, let me proclaim that the admission fee to these mysterious precincts of science is far more than the mastery of the second law of thermodynamics. I know, because I have done my own homework on-Lord Kelvin, with the hope that this might give me a Rosetta stone, but the literature of contemporary physics remains as opaque to me as it was when I thought that a Carnot cycle was some kind of velocipede.

Limitations on the Scientific Analogy for Law

My first point then—and here I anticipate one central and pessimistic conclusion of this paper—is that I am highly skeptical as to whether the methods of contemporary science provide any pat analogy that can be taken over bodily from one or more of the natural sciences for the modernization and enrichment of legal inquiry.

The scientist, for his part, must be warned that legal scholarship, at times, uses an Aesopian language. When law is spoken of as itself a "science," as it was eighty years ago by Dean Langdell, the founder of the law school case method and, more recently, by Mortimer Adler and Hans Kelsen, the speaker's manifest analogy is not to methodology in the physical and life sciences but to the "sciences"—if they can be properly so characterized—of formal logic and mathematics. The idea reflected in this analogy is that law can be approached as if it were, like formal logic, an abstract deductive system without basis in, or point of contact with, particular empirical data. Said Langdell: "Law is a science, and all the available materials of that science are contained in printed books." Similarly, Adler's "science of law in discourse" is, in his own words, "a purely formal science, like mathematics; its subject matter is entirely propositional; its only instrumentality is formal logic." The purity of Kelsen's "Pure Science of Law" is achieved only by excluding from the province of jurisprudence all questions concerning the desirable content of legal rules, all issues about the efficacy or inefficacy of particular legal norms as influences on individual and social behavior, and all speculation or investigation as to the extent to which decision-making officials of the legal order conform their rulings to formal legal prescriptions. In short, legal discourse is made "scientific," in this formal logical sense, by excluding precisely the questions—the nature of the social reality to which law is addressed—on which scientific knowledge is most needed and for which the scientific spirit of disciplined empirical investigation and verification seems best designed. It is as if empirical investigation in physics were to have stopped after Newton, and the whole genius of contemporary physics been given to the sharper definition and formal elaboration of the concepts of Newton and his predecessors, without continuing enrichment from challenging new postulates and their experimental verification and ultimate inclusion in the deductive structure of scientific knowledge.

The promise of the scientific analogy for the improvement of legal or law-related inquiry is further reduced by the unhappy but inevitable intercultural circumstance that is often an outmoded, unduly literary or otherwise oversimplified version of scientific method that is used as a model by the enthusiast for a more "scientific" approach to the problems of the legal order. The literature of legal and social philosophy furnishes many instances of this kind of reasoning from a false or misleading scientific analogy. Charles Darwin's theory of the origin of species, seized upon and spectacularly oversimplified by Herbert Spencer, was transmuted into the social and legal theory of cultural evolution; law and government should not intervene to mitigate the sufferings of the indigent because that would interfere with the workings of the all pervasive process of "the survival of the fittest," the "beneficent but severe discipline" by which the unfit and their dependents are eliminated from society. The late Judge Jerome Frank, a man of great good sense and intellectual resourcefulness, once built an imposing edifice of legal theory on a popularized version of psychoanalytic theory that would have horrified Sigmund Freud fully as much as Spencer's "philosophy of evolution" must have horrified Charles Darwin. Legal scholars of my generation were substantially misled, I think, by an oversimplified account of scientific method in the writings of John Dewey, particularly in an article entitled "Logical Method in Law," in which he said—or seemed to us scientifically unsophisticated law professors to be saying—that scientific method was, above all, the method of experiment, and that the postulational structure of the sciences was of only secondary importance. Whether the fault was Dewey's or our own, many legal scholars, for at least a decade, tended to equate scientific method with simple trial-and-error procedures and proclaimed that law could be made more "scientific" at once if legal scholars and practitioners would only become more experimental in temper and pay less attention to general ideas.

Certainly there are characteristics of scientific procedure that can be borrowed for the disciplining of legal inquiry. We must give more thought than we have so far in law to quantitative measurements of the measurable and to the design of procedures to measure the presently unmeasurable. We have a great deal to learn from science about the importance of casting the results of legal inquiry into a form permitting verification by others and about the central significance, for social inquiry, of rules of correspondence that will relate theoretical notions to observable societal data. But it is wildly uncritical to suggest that the methods of science can be taken over lock, stock, and barrel for investigation of the problems of law in society. Dr. Bronk and I may be workers in neighboring vineyards, but I cannot easily copy his methods of cultivation for my very different soil and vines. Nor can he too easily copy mine, assuming for the moment that he would ever want to.

Law is not a science, and references, however casual, to "legal science" or to "the science of law" are deceptive and misleading. However law is to be characterized—as a discipline, an art, a control system, or a technology—law exhibits none of the essential attributes of a science. Legal propositions have their origin not in empirical observation but in authoritative pronouncement by a court or legislature. Neither do these propositions constitute a unified system; the propositions of law, even in a code country like France or Germany, are at most an aggregate, not a deductive hierarchy. And propositions of law are not verifiable by experiment or investigation; the ultimate test of legal truth is not verifiability of results by other members of the legal community but an authoritative adjudication, often arrived at, in the frontier areas of legal dialectic, by a vote of five judges to four or six to three. A fact in science is not important in itself but has its significance as an instance of a general law. A *case* in law is wholly misunderstood if approached as merely an instance of some general rule; indeed, law's general rules are means of diagnosis, instruments for the just and consistent decision of particular cases.

Even the sociology of legal scholarship differs dramatically from the sociology of scientific scholarship. The scientist chooses as his subjects for investigation those within his competence that can contribute most to the advancement of knowledge. If he thinks at all of the practical applications his postulate will have, once it is verified, this thought is at most secondary. By contrast, the legal scholar is incurably—and I think rightly—reformist and application-oriented in his choice of subjects for investigation. The best "scientific" work—or most nearly approaching scientific work—now in progress in legal scholarship is in areas like judicial administration and criminal law enforcement, where the applications are clear whenever trustworthy knowledge is arrived at and made accessible.

The scientist who would understand law and legal inquiry must be mindful that law has its own unique purposes and values, even its own logic. Law's great purpose is not the advancement of knowledge—although we lawyers like to think that law provides and maintains the conditions without which effective pursuit of knowledge would be impossible—but the maintenance of social stability, that is, preservation of the public peace and of certainty in human affairs, the settlement of disputes, and the engineering of social change. Law is imperative in its essential tenor. It prescribes the norms to which members of society are to conform their conduct, and coercion, sanction, and obligation are the forces by which law's imperatives are made effective. Science, by contrast, is descriptive and explanatory; the scientist may manipulate natural forces, as in his controlled experiments, but only to verify his hypotheses and so to extend the frontiers of knowledge. Law's controls are imposed not as means of experimental investigation but because it has already been decided, and more than provisionally, that the behavior ordered is in the public interest.

Perhaps the most striking difference of all is that law, as a discipline and cultural form, is far less *autonomous* than science. Scientific truth is objectively verifiable. The community of scientists is the ultimate tribunal in which asserted new contributions to knowledge are appraised and judged. Law lacks this autonomy and is inseparably linked to political processes and to public understanding and acceptance. Every legal scholar in the United States might agree that a certain projected ordering of affairs would be just and socially preferable to that provided by the existing law, but that new proposal would not be law—"legal truth," if you will—until some high court or, in farther-reaching matters, some legislative body has authoritatively declared that it is to be the law. Scientists might be kinder to their legal brethren, and more patient than they are about the glacial rate of change and improvement in legal institutions as compared to the explosion of knowledge in the natural sciences during the past fifty years, if they kept in mind the fact that fundamental changes in the legal order, even those aspects of the legal order that bear most directly on science, can be accomplished only at the sufferance of popularly elected lawmakers. It is as if natural scientists in the United States had been unable to proceed along the directions pointed to by Bohr's theory of the atom or Heisenberg's indeterminacy principle unless and until two congressional committees and a majority of the members of both houses of the Congress of the United States were satisfied that Bohr and Heisenberg were quite right in their theoretical conclusions.

It should be evident from what I have said so far that the better characterization of law is that it is not a science but a complex and crucially important social technology. This is not to say that social phenomena—individual and group behavior—are not proper subjects for truly scientific study. It is to say that the societal equivalents of physics, chemistry, biology, and the other natural sciences are not *legal* disciplines but

are rather sociology, anthropology, social psychology, and the other social or "behavioral" sciences. Even in the universe of intellect and high
theory, law is not an autonomous discipline; fundamental improvements
in the technology of law and government will come, over the long pull,
only as we begin to acquire genuinely scientific knowledge concerning
human nature and conduct. I am wary of the dangers involved in drawing hard and fast lines between "basic" and "applied" sciences, as if these
were clear and mutually exclusive categories, but it is instructive, I think,
to suggest that law as an applied science relates to sociology, economics,
and the other social sciences in much the same way as engineering relates to physics, industrial technology to chemistry, and the applied science of medicine to biology and physiology.

The analogy to medicine as an applied science—and art—is particularly appropriate because in law, as in medicine, a technology applied by
the working profession was fully grown before its corresponding "pure"
sciences began even to emerge from postulational and methodological
infancy. Medicine as a profession and technology was prescientific,
roughly and often hazily empirical, until at most fifty years ago. The miraculous advances of medicine are, in a sense, by-products of revolutionary theoretical advances in fundamental scientific knowledge. Similarly, until the tardy emergence of the behavioral sciences, law was an
applied science in search of a basic science. Nothing is further from my
mind than to belittle the social function of law or to suggest in any way
that legal propositions and practical legal decisions were arrived at arbitrarily and a priori, in disregard of understood causes and consequences. Law, in a real sense, was the custodian of such behavioral science as there was in the universities and elsewhere, and many of the
great men of the law—Ulpian, Bentham, John Marshall, Geny, Holmes,
and, in our own day, Pound and Llewellyn—had piercing insights about
social values and forces and about the norms of individual and social behavior. But these legal insights were and are speculative and prescientific, that is, intuitive, largely unverifiable, and commonsensical. Some
great guesswork went into the construction of the great institutions of
Roman law, and into the great institutions of our common law, but in
any truly scientific sense guesswork it was.

Does punishment deter? What is the relative force of coercion and
internal obligation as influences on law-observing behavior? To what extent do rules control decisions? These are among the great themes of
jurisprudence, themes to which profound legal thinkers have devoted
their best efforts for two thousand years, but we have no really verifiable
scientific knowledge on any of them, and the social sciences, as yet, have
little help to offer us. Lawyers, I make bold to assert, are by natural ca-

pacity, training, and experience the most resourceful technicians in our society but, as yet, they have little scientific knowledge to draw on. The social sciences, despite the great advances they have made since World War II, are still relatively primitive in their methodology and conceptual structure, not only as compared to the perfect deductive edifice of contemporary physics but also as compared to the state of knowledge in what the physicist or the chemist considers the "soft" sciences.

Serious consideration of the question, "Can law be scientific?" thus leads directly and inevitably to the question of whether the newer sciences of society—sociology, social psychology, economics, political science, and the like—can ever achieve anything remotely comparable to the conceptual structure of verifiable postulates characteristic of present-day scientific knowledge. By and large, the contemporary social sciences are fully "scientific" only in their aspiration—and perhaps in the unintelligibility of much of their rhetoric to the interested outsider— and vast methodological problems loom ahead as these infant sciences move towards maturity. These methodological problems—the very limited availability of controlled experimentation as an instrument of inquiry and verification in the investigation of social phenomena; the restrictions on social inquiry imposed by the social values embodied in the right of privacy; the difficulties involved in distinguishing spurious from genuinely causal correlations in controlled empirical inquiry; the elusiveness of any effort to establish comprehensively transcultural laws of social behavior—are analyzed brilliantly in Chapters 13 and 14 of Ernest Nagel's great book, *The Structure of Science.* I will not try to add anything to Nagel's appraisal of the methodological problems ahead for the social sciences, except to say that I am convinced and heartened, as a legal scholar, by Professor Nagel's ultimate conclusion that genuinely scientific knowledge is not unachievable in the social sciences, if social scientists are truly scientific and not in too much of a hurry to assert final conclusions. We lawyers and legal scholars have a great stake in the development of the social sciences because they alone can give us, over the long pull of many years, the scientific knowledge we need to enrich our historic technology.

For more than twenty-five years, scholarly lawyers, judges, and law professors have been aware of the promise of social science method and social science knowledge for the understanding and improvement of legal institutions. At least a few of the best of our company have worked out effective patterns of "colleagueship"—to borrow Donald Young's term—for investigation of law-related social phenomena by social scientists and lawyers jointly. The results of this collaborative scholarship have been wonderfully encouraging; my only concern is that we lawyers tend to be unduly attentive to immediate applications of social science methodology—for example, what sociology can tell us today about today's problem of law administration—and to be insufficiently aware that fundamental knowledge comes, in the social sciences as in the natural sciences, only when truth is sought as an end in itself, without too much concern, at the stages of basic inquiry, with possible practical applications. This tendency to be in too much of a hurry about immediate applications is, I fear, as characteristic of social scientists generally as it is of lawyers.

It is harder to keep inquiry value-free in the social sciences than in the natural sciences because the data under investigation are always value-impregnated. Undue concern with immediate applications creates additional danger that evaluative preferences may color or distort the results of social science inquiry. The great lesson I read in the history of science and technology is that if basic scientific inquiry is imaginative, intellectually autonomous, and free, the applications will take care of themselves in due time. The most important of all science's possible analogies for law is that law, as a great social technology and control system, has even more to gain, in a long-run view of things, from the perfection of the social sciences as "basic" sciences than from such immediate applications of social science methods and insights as may be helpful to law from time to time as the social disciplines move towards scientific maturity.

The Importance of Interdisciplinary Understanding

The second part of this volume is entitled "Towards Interdisciplinary Understanding," and I wonder whether I have made much of a case for the importance of that understanding, either for law or for the advancement of science. Fortunately, the preceding contributors have made that case, particularly as they have examined the points of confrontation and mutual misunderstanding at which law and science meet. These are points at which the scientist must take account of legal restrictions and policies and at which the lawyer, in his decision-making roles, must be able to grasp, if only from the outside, the seriousness of the scientific issues that may be at stake in what seems at first to be a "legal" decision. These confrontations of law and science increase with greater public and political awareness of what we have called here the "social role" of science.

When science is viewed in its social role, there is a reappearance of something like the old affinity of science and law. The world we live in is being remade by modern science and its applications in contemporary technology, and it is the task of law to see to it that this remade world be one of order, justice, and the common good.

Change and progress are not synonyms. Two hundred years ago, scientists and enthusiasts for science were inspired and sustained by the optimistic assumption—held by Franklin and Jefferson and their opposite numbers in every European country—that the advancement of scientific knowledge would inevitably be accompanied by a higher quality of civilization and material and spiritual well-being for everyone. The formula, they thought, was simple and infallible: if truth is advanced, progress follows. The philosophical orientation of contemporary science is no longer utilitarian. Today's creative scientist is more inclined to say, rather defensively, that the quest for truth is the single and sufficient purpose of science and that the scientist is not concerned with, or responsible for, the technological applications that may be made of his discoveries.

This he says, but I wonder whether he means it. I have known a good many scientists, even a few great ones, and it is my distinct impression from their less guarded conversations that the scientist, disavow it as he may, clings to the old conviction, whatever may be the contemporary evidence against it, that the advancement of truth will, in the long run of things, contribute to the greater fulfillment and happiness of mankind. "Ye shall know the truth, and the truth shall make you free" is still, I think, a postulate of the scientist's vocation, if not of his conceptual system.

The lawyer, similarly, is not centrally concerned with progress. Law and lawyers are not for or against social and technological change as such. It is rather the purpose of law in society to see to it that inevitable change be accomplished without friction, disruption, and social conflict. Yet the lawyer, too, however self-consciously hard-boiled his protestations in the matter, has a profoundly optimistic conception about the social utility of the rule of law: if social order and security are maintained, truth will be advanced and progress achieved.

Neither science nor law assures genuine social progress. Each provides one of the indispensable conditions without which progress is impossible. If, as I believe, men of science and men of law are the most important molders of contemporary and future society, it is of the highest urgency that they understand each other, that is, that men of law be less distrustful of scientists and their mysterious works and men of science less condescending towards lawyers and their imperfect legal institutions. There are no easy methodological analogies; law's processes cannot really be appraised in scientific terms, nor the methods of science understood by analogy with the workings of law. Scientists and lawyers are likely to be quite different people in temperament and inclination. But our vocations have their inevitable point of confrontation at the idea of social progress, the social role that is inevitable for science and central for law. Scientists and lawyers must understand each other and know the values to which each is dedicated, if we are both to be fully equipped to go about our, and Our Father's, business.

Chapter 8

Law and History

Gordon, Introduction: J. Willard Hurst and the Common Law Tradition in American Legal Historiography*

In 1963 the Italian historiographer Arnaldo Momigliano told an assembly of legal historians that they were gathered to celebrate "a historical event of some importance, the end of history of law as an autonomous branch of historical research." At least in the historiography of ancient law, he said, "the elimination of history of law as independent history now seems to me to be settled."

Nor is it important to debate whether it was Max Weber or the French school of sociology or the teaching of Marx and Engels or, finally, the influence of Marc Bloch that precipitated this solution. It is inherent in the general recognition that law, as a systematization of social relations at a given level, cannot be understood without an analysis of the sexual orientations, the moral and religious beliefs, the economic production and the military forces that characterize a given society at a given moment, and are expressed in associations of individuals and in conflicts. It is conceivable today that history of literature, history of art, history of

* [10 *Law & Soc. Rev.* 9–11 (1975). The Law & Society Review is the official publication of the Law and Society Association, which holds the copyright to the article. Reprinted by permission.

Robert W. Gordon (1941–) is Associate Professor at the New York State University School of Law at Buffalo. Gordon was educated at Harvard University, receiving his A.B. in 1967 and his J.D. in 1971. His subjects include legal history, contracts, consumer law, and evidence. Gordon is a member of the Law & Society Association and the American Society for Legal History.]

science, and history of religion can each retain some sort of autonomy, inasmuch as each is concerned with a specific activity of man. But what is no longer conceivable is that history of law should be autonomous; for by its very nature it is a formulation of human relations rooted in manifold human activities. And if, in some civilizations, there is a class of jurisconsults with special rules of conduct and of reasoning, this too is a social phenomenon to be interpreted.[1]

. . . American legal historians have usually worked on the assumption that, at least for the purpose of dividing academic labor, it makes sense to identify a sphere of "legal" phenomena in society, and to write about how these have changed over time. It has never, of course, been possible to mark off the precise boundaries of such a field, but as a practical matter it almost inevitably turns out that they are drawn around the institutions, the occupations, the ideas and the procedures that have the appearance at any one time of being *distinctively legal*.[2] One might crudely represent this way of looking at law in society [as in Figure 4].

Inside the box is "the law," whatever appears autonomous about the legal order—courts, equitable maxims, motions for summary judgment; outside lies "society," the wide realm of the nonlegal, the political, economic, religious, social; the "inputs" are social influences upon the shape of the mass of things inside the law-box, the "outputs" the effects, or impact, of the mass upon society. Within the structure of this crude model there is, of course, a great range of possible theories of law, from a theory asserting that law derives its shape almost wholly from sources within

1. A.D. Momigliano, "The Consequences of New Trends in the History of Ancient Law," in Momigliano, *Studies in Historiography* 239, 240-241 (1966).

2. This would seem to imply that no one could write the legal history of a society that had no notion of "law" as a bundle of specialized activities distinct from, and to some extent autonomous of, other social phenomena—e.g., a society that did not distinguish between legal and religious norms. Legal historians usually solve this problem by treating of the aspects of such societies that appear to serve counterpart social functions to those of the relatively autonomous legal systems. For example, courts perform certain dispute settlement functions in modern Western societies which might, in other societies of the past, have been performed by councils of warriors or village elders. The warriors or elders will therefore be treated in the legal history of the other society. Yet though dispute settlement may be done by warriors or elders in modern Western societies also, that is not "law" and is therefore usually of no interest to legal historians. This somewhat curious manner of defining the field of specialization is partly responsible for the fact that focus abruptly shifts (and narrows) whenever a society exhibits traces of an autonomous legal order. On this point, see text at notes 29-31, 40-44, infra. On the emergence of "autonomous" legal orders in modern societies, see *Max Weber on Law and Economy in Society* (Rheinstein ed. 1954), especially chs. 7-9, 11; for a brilliant recent reinterpretation, Roberto Mangabeira Unger, *Law in Modern Society* (forthcoming, 1976), especially at 52ff.

714

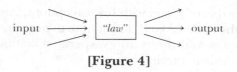

[Figure 4]

the box (i.e. that it is really autonomous as well as seeming so), to one claiming that the box is really empty, the apparent distinctiveness of its contents illusory, since they are all the product of external social forces. Yet even those who incline to the latter view[3] take the contents of the box, epiphenomenal though they may be, as the main subject-matter of concern to the legal historian. Not that this is the only way of treating law historically . . . but it probably *is* the only way for someone who defines himself as a "legal" historian; he has no choice.

Where he does have a choice, and an important one, is between writing internal and external legal history.[5] The internal legal historian stays as much as possible within the box of distinctive-appearing legal things; his sources are legal, and so are the basic matters he wants to describe or explain, such as changes in pleading rules, in the jurisdiction of a court, the texts assigned to beginning law students, or the doctrine of contributory negligence. The external historian writes about the interaction between the boxful of legal things and the wider society of which they are a part, in particular to explore the social context of law and its social effects, and he is usually looking for conclusions about those effects.

3. Lawrence M. Friedman probably inclines as far as anyone. See e.g., his *History of American Law* (1973): "This book treats American law . . . not as a kingdom unto itself, not as a set of rules and concepts, not as the province of lawyers alone, but as a mirror of society. It takes nothing as historical accident, nothing as autonomous, everything as relative and molded by economy and society. . . . The [legal] system works like a blind, insensate machine. It does the bidding of those whose hands are on the controls. . . . [T]he strongest ingredient in American law, at any given time, is the present: current emotions, real economic interests, concrete political groups." Id. at 10, 14.

Professor Friedman acknowledges the existence of legal phenomena that are purely "internal" or "formal"—technical aspects of the system that can be altered or adjusted without affecting much (if at all) the outside society. See his "Law Reform in Historical Perspective," 13 *St. Louis U.L.J.* 351 (1969). He also recognizes that people living in some societies may perceive their legal order to be autonomous and to associate autonomy with legitimacy; he would classify such beliefs as part of a society's "legal culture"—"values and attitudes which . . . determine the place of the legal system in the culture of the society as a whole." See his "Legal Culture and Social Development," 4 *L. & Soc'y. Rev.* 29, 34 (1969).

5. These terms are borrowed from T. S. Kuhn's treatments of (remarkably similar!) problems in the historiography of science. See especially his "Relations between History and History of Science," 100 *Daedalus* 271, 279 (1971). "External history" seems to me a better label than "social" history because it is more inclusive; specifically, it includes intellectual and cultural history.

Up until very recently, and with few exceptions, American legal history has been of the internal kind. From time to time the few proponents of external history would direct an exasperated complaint against this situation, without much altering it.[6]

Hurst, Legal Elements in United States History*

1. Work in legal history has tended to focus too much on courts, and with unfortunate limitations even within that range. The United States Supreme Court has captured too much attention, at the expense of the state courts (which, for example, have had at least as important roles in developing public policy on corporations, franchises, taxation, and social capital investment). Students have identified the law too much with the work of appellate courts, state and federal, at the expense of properly weighting the impress of trial courts on public policy. Emphasis on judge-made law does not necessarily mean, but in practice has meant, want of due attention to the legislative process, to rule-making and prec-

6. The best of these are, I think, Daniel J. Boorstin, "Tradition and Method in Legal History," 54 *Harv. L. Rev.* 424 (1951); George L. Haskins, "Law and Colonial Society," 9 *Am. Q.* 354 (1957); Stanley N. Katz, "Looking Backward: The Early History of American Law," 33 *U. Chi. L. Rev.* 867 (1966); Lawrence M. Friedman, "Some Problems and Possibilities of American Legal History," in *The State of American History* 3 (Bass ed. 1970); Morton J. Horwitz, "The Conservative Tradition in the Writing of American Legal History," 17 *Am. J. Leg. Hist.* 275 (1973); Herbert Alan Johnson, "American Colonial Legal History: A Historiographical Interpretation," in *Perspectives on Early American History* 250 (Vaughan & Billias eds. 1973), hereinafter Johnson, "Colonial Legal History"; and the many historiographical contributions of Willard Hurst, of which the most comprehensive, as well as the most recent, is "Legal Elements in United States History," in *Law in American History* 3 (Fleming & Bailyn eds. 1971), hereinafter Hurst, "Legal Elements." Much acerbic and astute criticism of the state of the art has appeared over the years in the *Annual Survey of American Law*'s "Legal History" sections written by John Phillip Reid (1962-66); Reid and William E. Nelson (1969-70); and Nelson (1967-69; 1973-present). I am very indebted to all the articles cited here. One of the many ironies connected with American legal history is that its shortcomings have called forth so useful a historiographical literature.

* [From *Law in American History* 6-13 (D. Fleming & B. Bailyn eds., Little, Brown and Company 1971). Previously published in Volume V (1971) of *Perspectives in American History*. Reprinted by permission.

James Willard Hurst (1910–) is Vilas Professor, University of Wisconsin Law School, where he has taught since 1937. He was educated at Williams College (B.A. 1932), Harvard University (LL.B. 1935) and Cambridge University (M.A., 1967). He is the author of *The Growth of American Law: The Law Makers* (1950), *Law and the Conditions of Freedom in the Nineteenth Century United States* (1956), and *Law and Economic Growth* (1964).]

edent-building by executive and administrative offices, and to the great body of operating public policy created by the ways in which lawyers and their clients, and laymen working without benefit of counsel shape affairs with more or less use, avoidance, or evasion of the law emanating from official agencies. Thus, the legal history of contract should not become fascinated with the evolution of judges' formulae on consideration and ignore the growth of statutory and administrative prescriptions for the practical content of agreements in one specialized field of transactions after another, as in insurance, labor relations, public utility service, corporate securities, negotiable instruments, and urban residential leases. Nor can a realistic history of contract look simply at the breakdown of relationships which produces lawsuits, and ignore the creative contributions made by inventions and adjustments of businessmen and their lawyers in negotiating, drafting, and administering the great bodies of transactions which do not break down.[12]

2. Research in legal history has tended to exaggerate attention to judge-made constitutional law, as the prime type of legal contribution to social structure. Great parts of constitutional law itself consist in lines of authority marked out mainly by legislative and executive debate, practice, and decision. Most of the purse power has been so defined, with most of the law of legislative and executive privilege, and most demarcations of roles of central and local government within the states. Moreover, measured by continuity and impact upon distribution of functions basic to social life, much law has been constitutive which does not fit the conventional historical preoccupation with formal constitutional law. Given the constitutive roles in this society of the market, the business corporation, public utilities, the church, trade associations, trade unions, public and private educational organizations, and welfare and research foundations, aspects of law related to the legitimation and distribution of practical power within and among such institutions must be taken to be parts of the functional history of the law. To be specific: with the emergence of the large-scale business corporation, the course of public policy on the relations of investors and corporate management should be reckoned a relevant part of the history of law bearing on the basic structure of power. Again: given the growth in social impact of developments in scientific and technical knowledge, the effects of the law on evolving roles of government-determined and government-supported research

12. Lawrence M. Friedman, *Contract Law in America: A Social and Economic Case Study* (Madison, 1965), chap. iv; Stewart Macaulay, *Law and the Balance of Power* (New York, 1966), pp. 202-207.

compared with research directed or aided by private foundations belong to a realistically broad concept of the "constitutional" roles of law.[13]

3. Legal history studied within a legal tradition which puts as much stress as ours does on separation of powers among formal legal agencies and on the procedures of such agencies tends to give inadequate attention to the substantive content of public policy. In giving form and content to wants and needs and means of pursuing them, the law entered into a wide range of men's concerns extending beyond the law's own operations. Thus legal processes affected conditions of mutual trust (in standardizing agreements, or in attacking fraud or duress), security of expectations (in protecting against breach of contract or loss from personal injury), biological integrity (in public health and sanitation laws, or in laws regarding the natural environment), and the range of options open to will (through the law affecting education, research, communication, and association). The beginning of wisdom is to recognize that the law typically operated only in marginal areas or with marginal effects upon such broad human concerns. Yet even a quick inventory of statute books teaches that these marginal operations grew to affect large sectors of life.

4. So far as it ventured outside the study of separation-of-powers and agency-procedure issues, legal history tended to identify the history of public policy too much with regulation (setting and enforcing legal standards or rules of behavior, in the relations of individuals and groups with the government, or with each other). This emphasis ignored or underplayed the impress which law made by allocating scarce economic resources. Law allocated resources directly by taxing and spending and transferring public property (selling public lands, granting radio or TV franchises to use public air waves). It allocated resources indirectly through tax exemptions (as to churches), or tax deductions (as to promote private investment by depreciation allowances), or indeed by regulatory laws which worked to shift economic burdens (as when workmen's compensation acts transfer some of the cost of industrial accidents from the injured workers to the consumers of the product). Emphasis on regulation likewise tended to ignore or underplay the law's effects in legitimating forms of conduct to implement private choices—as in offering the privilege of incorporation under terms which left large discretion to

13. Adolph A. Berle, Jr., *The 20th Century Capitalist Revolution* (New York, 1954), chaps. i, iii; Harold M. Kelle, "Note on Congressional Investigations," *American Bar Association Journal*, 40 (1954), 154; Marion R. Fremont-Smith, *Foundations and Government: State and Federal Law and Supervision* (New York, 1965), passim; Warren Weaver, *U.S. Philanthropic Foundations* (New York, 1967), chaps. ix, xiv.

private draftsmen in fixing the corporate structure, or providing stand-ardized but optional terms for certain kinds of contracts or property titles. To point up such uses of the law is to note that legal history must be broad enough to include the considerable effects law had by indirect as well as direct compulsion (as when we seek results by taxing and spending instead of invoking the policeman), by structuring general sit-uations as well as acting on specific relationships (as when we build and operate public recreational facilities as well as providing juvenile courts to contain the exploring energies of youth), and by channeling conduct for ends of utility or justice by providing convenient legal services or in-struments as well as by providing penalties (as when we provided a reli-able coinage by creating a public mint, without formally outlawing pri-vately made metal tokens, while we used the criminal law to protect public coins against counterfeiters). The prevailing attitudes which in-sisted that the law help in making social organization useful and just—that is, constitutional—embodied demands inherently too far-reaching to be met simply by legal Thou Shalts or Thou Shalt Nots. Legal history should match the range of uses of the law.[15]

5. Related to exaggeration of direct legal regulation as compared with uses of the law for indirect compulsion or situation structuring was a tendency to exaggerate areas of combat in examining substantive pub-lic policy. Emphasis on overt clashes of interests comes naturally in study-ing an institution which prominently creates forums for resolving or-dered conflict, whether in legislative halls, administrative hearing rooms, or courthouses. But legal history should recognize that law was involved also in the continuities of such social institutions as the market, that the content of public policy was made in large part by flows of uncontested legal administration (for example, in the day-in, day-out regular opera-tion of tax laws or laws providing social security payments), and that a great part (indeed probably the greater part) of men's social experience in which the law was involved entailed neither combat nor consent, but merely the mindless cumulation of unperceived, unplanned, unchosen events. Precisely because the constitutional ideal made heavy demands for directed use of law, a realistic legal history must take due account of the full pervasiveness of law as it operated consciously in other-than-combat situations, and its involvement in the undirected drift which

---

15. James M. Buchanan, *Public Finance in Democratic Process* (Chapel Hill, 1967), chaps. iii, iv; Cornelius P. Cotter, *Government and Private Enterprise* (New York, 1960), chaps. i, ii, xv; K. William Kapp, *The Social Costs of Private Enterprise* (Cambridge, 1950), chap. xvi; Walz v. Tax Commission of the City of New York, 90 S. Ct. 1409 (1970).

challenged constitutionalism in ways more potent and subtle than those presented by conflict of interests.[16]

There are substantial scholarly contributions to legal history which do not so style themselves. We learn about the roles of law from historians of politics and politicians who, like Dumas Malone in his biography of Jefferson, describe not only the internal life of parties but also the interplay of partisan maneuvers with formal public policy and the structure and traditions of legal agencies. Historical studies in public administration, such as Leonard White's volumes on the federal executive branch or those of George Galloway on Congress, tell parts of legal history. So do monographs on economic history which emphasize the uses of law in structuring economic activity (for example, the Handlins' examination of law and economic growth in Massachusetts, the similiar Hartz inquiry into Pennsylvania policy before the Civil War, and Scheiber's history of Ohio's venture in building and operating a canal system in the early-nineteenth century).[17] Even within this broader bibliography, however, familiar limitations appear. Political historians and political scientists have given more attention to processes than to the content of public policy. Disproportionate attention is given to contested situations, at the expense of due attention either to institutional continuities or to institutional drift. With honorable exceptions, too much emphasis has been placed on federal lawmaking without a balancing study of the history of state and local government, especially in the nineteenth century. The disappointing character of the literature lies not so much in what has been published—for that includes much helpful work —as in what has not been. Thus we lack sufficient studies of the law's roles concerning race and social class in United States society, the functional structure and changing resource-allocations roles of markets, the use of the natural environment, and the course of scientific and technical knowledge. These deficiencies are specially marked for the nineteenth century, in decades which set the terms of important twentieth-century problems.[18]

16. Robert A. Dahl and Charles E. Lindblom, *Politics, Economics and Welfare* (New York, 1953), chaps. iii, iv; note 10, above.

17. George B. Galloway, *History of the House of Representatives* (New York, 1961); Oscar and Mary Flug Handlin, *Commonwealth: A Study of the Role of Government in the American Economy: Massachusetts, 1774-1861* (Cambridge, 1969); Louis Hartz, *Economic Policy and Democratic Thought: Pennsylvania, 1776-1860* (Cambridge, 1948); Dumas Malone, *Jefferson: The President* (Boston, 1970); Harry N. Scheiber, *Ohio Canal Era* (Athens, Ohio, 1969); Leonard D. White, *The Federalists: A Study in Administrative History* (New York, 1948).

18. Cf. Willard Hurst, "Perspectives upon Research into Legal Order," *Wisconsin Law Review* (1961), 356.

Apart from such limitations of subject matter, researchers without some specialized training often fail to realize the possibilities in legal source materials. They tend to take judges' words too much at face value —readily accept the invocation of "police power" as an explanation rather than merely a statement of a result. They tend to watch only the star acts under the spotlights of political controversy, and to neglect substantial issues implicit in what seem colorless, routine affairs. For example, scholars have been slow to see that the technical details of property rights have often served to affect the incidence of economic benefits and costs among economic interests, and not merely to regularize titles or relations between parties to particular transactions.[19] Students not specially trained to handle legal sources have largely neglected the evidence afforded by such sources of what people have believed, or how they have perceived or experienced life. Thus, for historians of ideas there is evidence of applied theories of human nature in the law of negligence and contributory negligence, as in the law of master and servant, or the rules of evidence, or in the law demarcating private and public morality.[20] Finally, the student who has not become specially adept in squeezing out of legal sources all the juice he can will probably fall short of realizing their possibilities for helping to identify and to weigh growth, change, stability, and inertia in wants, needs, functions, gains, and costs in men's social experience. Because of the sobering costs of using legal processes, and because compared with other modes of social adjustment law yields an uncommon amount of formally defined choices and decisions, legal sources present to a knowledgeable reader a specially reliable means to identify continuities and discontinuities or changes of direction in social relations. Trends in the statute books, for example, can help to identify, to place in time, and to measure the substantial shift from an almost wholly producer orientation of public policy to more and more of a consumer orientation in the hundred years since 1870. To use the statute books so, however, means using them in more detail, with more attention to their technical content over substantial periods of time, than general historians have been accustomed to do.[21]

19. Edwin W. Patterson, *Jurisprudence: Men and Ideas of the Law* (Brooklyn, 1953), pp. 95, 103, 520-522, 524.

20. Edmond N. Cahn, *The Sense of Injustice* (New York, 1949), pp. 56-92, 124-132, 148-150; Julius Cohen, Reginald A. H. Robson and Alan Bates, *Parental Authority: The Community and the Law* (New Brunswick, 1958), passim.

21. Frank E. Horack, Jr., "The Common Law of Legislation," *Iowa Law Review*, 23 (1937), 41.

Horwitz, The Conservative Tradition in the Writing of American Legal History*

One of the most important characteristics of the writing of American legal—as opposed to constitutional—history is that it has almost exclusively been written by lawyers. There are several rather obvious reasons for this situation. The study of the history of American law inevitably involves the mastery of technical legal doctrine, which, barring such distinguished but extraordinarily rare exceptions as Leonard Levy's study of Chief Justice Shaw, seems to have left historians paralyzed with fear. Even Perry Miller's provocative study of the ante-bellum legal mind focuses on legal rhetoric spun out by lawyers on celebratory or self-congratulatory occasions. It almost never seriously comes to terms with substantive legal doctrine or with forms of legal reasoning. Indeed, studies of the legal profession as well as of legal education tend to emphasize patterns of recruitment and training for the bar, while ignoring the relationship between what lawyers do and their political function.

The contrast between orthodox legal history on one hand and constitutional history on the other is also instructive. Constitutional history has always been a major subject of the historian. And whether historians have been drawn to constitutional history because of its obvious political content or whether its political focus is a consequence of interest by historians, the writing of constitutional history has always been involved in controversy over fundamental political questions concerning the nature of American society and the meaning of the American past.

Legal historiography, by contrast, has rarely been explicitly or self-consciously involved in political debate. Written largely by lawyers, it has been stamped by lawyer-like concerns. Its most characteristic mark has been an emphasis on continuity and a corresponding deemphasis of change. In the study of legal doctrine, lawyer's legal history has been devoted to finding the origin of doctrines, most dramatically illustrated by Holmes' effort to find the fault principle in the earliest history of English law. The work of Langdell and Ames is also of this genre.

The single most influential representative of orthodox lawyer's legal history is the writing of Roscoe Pound. Wherever one looks in the writing of legal history one finds unexamined traces of Pound's assumptions

* [17 *Am. J. Legal Hist.* 275 (1973). Reprinted by permission.

Morton J. Horwitz (1938–) is Professor of Law at Harvard University. He was educated at C.C.N.Y. (A.B. 1959) and Harvard University (Ph.D. 1964; LL.B. 1967). He served as Law Clerk to Judge Spottswood Robinson III, United States Court of Appeals, District of Columbia Circuit (1967-1968).]

about the role of law and of the legal profession in American society. Until just recently most of these assumptions had seemed to me to be the result of an expert's neutral view of American legal history. Only after my reading of James McClellan's recent book, *Joseph Story and the American Constitution,* did Pound's ideological influence begin to seem clear. Suffice it to say for now that McClellan invokes a whole tradition of lawyer's legal history to advance a profoundly conservative interpretation of the role of law in American society. Yet, I believe that McClellan is correct in finding sustenance in that tradition, for its basic categories contain fundamentally conservative political preferences dressed up in the neutral garb of expert and objective legal history.

There are many important ideological elements in lawyer's legal history. I have already mentioned two—the emphasis on continuity and the search for origins. My aim now is to identify several others and then to show why they are part of a politically conservative ideology of legalism that has prevailed in America from at least the post-revolutionary period and in England from the beginning of the seventeenth century. In attempting to suggest causal connections, however, I can offer only the barest sketch of a theory. Thus, I will primarily emphasize the political function of professionalization and its ideological manifestation in legal history. I will have little to say about the social structure of the profession, or the particular functions of law in society during these periods. Finally, I will have nothing to say about some of the clearly beneficial effects of the ideology of legalism on the course of Anglo-American history for 350 years.

I have chosen first to discuss some of Roscoe Pound's work in legal history in order to provide illustrations of these conservative themes in American legal historiography. There are three fundamental themes that amount to articles of faith in Pound's writings on nineteenth century American law. First, the happy and glorious triumph of the common law over the postrevolutionary Francophiles and Anglophobes and then, in a repeat performance, over their successors, the codifiers of the 1830's and 1840's. Second, measurement of periods of rise or decline of the legal profession in terms of narrow criteria of craftsmanship or of technical training in law. Thus, according to conventional wisdom, the rabble controlled courts before the happy nineteenth century appearance of the professional lawyer on the bench. Similarly, an orthodox identification of periods of decline of the bar by how open it was. Thus, in most writings on the bar in the Jacksonian period we regularly learn that it was a period of legal decline because entrance requirements declined. All of this, of course, is based on the unlikely assumption that the pedestrian and rote law office, Blackstone-mouthing, pleading-copy, legal training of the period made anyone a better lawyer. Not surprisingly, some of the best judges of the period—most notably, John Marshall—were not regarded by their contemporaries as superior lawyers by any measure of technical mastery. Finally, this strand of argument degenerates still further in the hands of people . . . who come to measure the sophistication and skill of the bar in terms of the most self-serving and banal contemporaneous judgments of technical skill. I have read too many Bench & Bar biographies of the nineteenth century with their ultimate compliment to a brother lawyer—"he was the best special pleader of his time"—not to think that an historian's acceptance of the profession's standards of legal attainment in any historical period carries its own ideological baggage.

Thus far I have mentioned two major premises of Pound's work: adulation of the common law and hostility to codification; measuring legal attainment or sophistication of the bar in terms of narrow and self-serving technical categories. These two feed directly into a third— Pound's own special anti-Marxist medicine—"the received legal tradition."

Pound was undoubtedly correct in insisting in his work that the "received" or "taught" tradition in law had made the Anglo-American legal system to some extent autonomous of political and economic change. "An exclusively economic interpretation . . ." he wrote, "ignores the prevailing mode of thought of the time which often reflects an economic situation of the past when the taught ideal was formative" ("The Economic Interpretation of the Law of Torts," 53 *Harv. L. Rev.* 365, 382 (1940)).

Granted this is so, but Pound's writings usually convey the reassuring message that this crucial formative economic era can be located at some comfortable distance in the past. In the same article, where he emphasizes the point that the received tradition has often become functionally autonomous from the economic influence of an earlier period, he shows the special blindness of lawyer's legal history when dealing with more immediate events. The movement towards fault liability and its justification by writers such as Holmes was, he wrote, simply a result of the triumph of "common sense" (p. 376). While it should now be clear to us that the growth of fault liability in the nineteenth century was part of the system of legal thought devoted to reducing the costs of economic development, for Pound it was simply a better solution in terms of some unhistorical and disembodied intellectual criterion of "common sense."

Pound's invocation of "common sense" is historically part of the lawyer's self-serving and uncritical assumption that the process of "thinking like a lawyer" has been more or less historically constant. Thus, it is assumed that the basics of legal thought—with its canons of relevance, its

724

criteria of good and bad arguments and its rules of authority, construction and interpretation—are equivalent to Reason itself. Reason, finally, is assumed to be itself governed by historically unchanging criteria.

The result was that legal historians such as Pound conceived of legal history in terms of intellectually "right" and "wrong" solutions, no different in principle from scientific solutions. Never did he seriously articulate the criteria by which he rejoiced over the defeat of the codification movement, though it seems clear that his views were fundamentally political. Codification was democratic lawmaking. The rule of the common law maintained the separation between law and politics. The former conferred the primary lawmaking power on an untutored populace; the latter enabled the legal profession to control the scope and form of legal change.

Lawyer's legal history, however, is rarely willing either to acknowledge that both the internal demand of professionalization or the external demand of creating an ideological buffer zone between the claims of politics and those of law have shaped the received legal tradition itself. As a result, in most American legal history the received legal tradition is treated not as itself a contingent and changing product of specific historical struggles, but rather as a kind of meta-historical set of values within which social conflict has always taken place.

One of the most notorious examples of the dominant form of conservative legal history is Anton-Hermann Chroust's two volume study *The Rise of the Legal Profession in America* (1965), which relies heavily on Pound's earlier work. Writing on the postrevolutionary American bar, Chroust reiterates the conventional view that most of those "admitted to practice after . . . scanty preparation, on the whole proved to be little qualified for the profession" (II, 34). In support of this proposition he cites only the following from Clark's *Memoir of Jeremiah Mason:* "Most of the members of the bar were poorly educated, and some of vulgar manners and indifferent morals" (II, 34, n. 112). Should an historian accept such a suspiciously self-justificatory view of the world? For Chroust the legal profession of the nineteenth century is populated by "responsible and experienced professional men" on one hand and "sharpers and pettifoggers" on the other (II, 35). When we turn to the Codification Movement during the Jacksonian Period, Chroust observes that Frederick Robinson's famous 1834 attack on the common law "could be summarily dismissed by the legal profession as the rantings of an ill-informed and prejudiced rabble-rouser" (II, 60). Another attack on the common law is characterized by Chroust as made by "an ignorant but vociferous Jacksonian demagogue" (II, 71). The judgment of the profession, it seems, is the only acknowledged source of historical truth.

It is a staple of Pound's writing to classify various schools of jurisprudential thought historically. Yet, those familiar with his work will remember that these schools of jurisprudence seem to march through the centuries, one replacing the other, giving absolutely no clue of why they served to express the political, or cultural forces of the time.

For an example of the way in which Pound deals with jurisprudential change I offer a 1914 article called "The End of Law as Developed in Legal Rules and Doctrines" (27 *Harv. L. Rev.* 195). The principal argument is that there is some sort of inevitable and necessary unfolding of different stages of legal ideas. Stage one is "Archaic Law" of which he writes: "In the beginnings of law the idea is simply to keep the peace" (p. 198). Stage two, he calls "The Strict Law." Of this he writes: "In a second stage of legal development . . . law has definitely prevailed as the regulative agency of society and the state has prevailed as the organ of social control" (p. 204). Of the third stage he writes: "A stage of liberalization, which may be called the stage of equity or natural law, succeeds the strict law. . . . The watchword of the stage of strict law was certainty. The watchword of this stage is morality or some phrase of ethical import, such as good conscience . . . or natural law. The former insists on uniformity, the latter on morality; the former on form, the latter on justice in the ethical sense . . ." (p. 213). Never are we told why the second stage becomes the third or, indeed, which social forces gain and which lose by this transition. In fact, the specific content of the morality of this stage is never articulated.

Now on to the next stage. "As a result of the stiffening process," he writes, "by which the undue fluidity of law and the over-wide scope for discretion involved in the identification of law and morals are gradually corrected," there emerged a fourth stage called the "stage of matured legal systems" in which "the watchwords are equality and security" (pp. 220-21). Nowhere is the development of capitalism even acknowledged. Nowhere does Pound even suggest Bentham's explicit subordination of equality to security. All that we are told is that "the all-important legal institutions of this stage are property and contract" (p. 224). Finally, he writes: "Toward the end of the nineteenth century a tendency became manifest throughout the world to depart radically from the fundamental ideas which had governed the maturity of legal systems" (p. 225). The result is what he calls "The Socialization of Law." Yet, we are never told of the growth of democracy or, indeed, the emergence of socialism. In short, all of this is still another form of the attempt to explain legal change while maintaining the indispensable separation of law from politics on which the modern legal profession is founded.

In "The Scope and Purpose of Sociological Jurisprudence," (24 *Harv. L. Rev.* 591 (1911)), Pound offers us another example of his conception of how "the science of law" develops historically (pp. 612-13). First, there is an early theory of comparative law. "The comparative tendency is followed by a philosophical tendency." Why this occurs, we are never told. Then: "To this philosophical tendency, an analytical tendency succeeds by way of revolt." And why does the "revolt" occur and succeed? "Being . . . neither historically sound nor critically adequate, [the earlier theories] fall to the ground. . . ." Next, we learn of still "another phase of the revolt from the philosophical" tendency, which takes the form of "an historical tendency" and "completes the exposure of the specious explanations of the preceding period and insures the overthrow of pseudo-philosophy." Finally, having exposed centuries of illusion, Pound declares: "This done, there is room and often need for a true philosophical jurisprudence. . . ." And with the same sense of scientific inevitability with which he purported to explain jurisprudential change in the past, Pound now triumphantly predicted its future:

> We should expect a new school to arise from this breakdown of the older schools, and there are many signs that such an event has taken place. Jurists are coming together upon a new ground from many different starting points. . . . The rising and still formative school to which we may look chiefly henceforth for advance in juristic thought, may be styled the Sociological School. [P. 594.]

As in the case of Justice Holmes' "common sense" adoption of the "fault" principle, Pound basically conceived of the history of legal ideas as a "scientific" discovery of ever more "correct" theories of law. Only then could legal change be reconciled with the fundamental ideology of the American legal profession from the beginning of the nineteenth century: that law is a science discoverable by reason and that its scientific character is what distinguished law from politics. The distinction between law and politics is the primary intellectual premise of professionalization. It distinguishes reason and learning from will and power. It at once legitimizes professional craft and technique and separates it from more commonly accessible forms of political knowledge.

Once legal history attempts to penetrate the distinction between law and politics by seeing legal and jurisprudential change as a product of changing social forces, it begins to undermine the indispensable ideological premise of the legal profession—indeed of any profession—that its characteristic modes of reasoning and its underlying substantive doctrines may not be universal or necessary, but rather particular and contingent. The characteristic form of escape is characterized by Pound's legal history: to conceive of jurisprudential change either as equivalent to scientific discovery—thus defusing its social and political character by explaining it as a simple intellectual process—or occasionally, but only occasionally, to employ history in order to demonstrate that changes regarded as undesirable were illegitimate political acts of usurpation.

The main thrust of lawyer's legal history, then, is to pervert the real function of history by reducing it to the pathetic role of justifying the world as it is. In order to make this possible, history must be ransacked in order to sing hosannas to all of the existing pieties of professionalization. Thus, it must be that the common law tradition—the ultimate expression of the domination of the legal profession in the legal order—must be applauded. Its historical antagonist, the codification movement, is dismissed either as the political goal of a lunatic fringe led by a demagogic leader or, when all else is lost, as an unwholesome and untrustworthy democratic force. This last theme, of course, is dependent on first establishing a conception of law as essentially apolitical and scientific in character, which is indispensable for a forthright attack on the Codification Movement as democratic.

Consequently, it is the ideological character of professionalization that makes lawyer's legal history inevitably conservative. Professionalization has certain common characteristics. First, the emphasis on craft and technique as factors that distinguish professional knowledge from ordinary lay forms of knowledge. Second, distinctive methodologies and forms of reasoning which, in Coke's famous phrase, serve to distinguish the artificial reason of the professional from the natural reason of the layman. Finally, what specially characterizes the profession's conception of modern law—that is, law since the beginning of the seventeenth century—is the insistence on a radical separation between law and politics.

This last point, needless to say, would require volumes to develop adequately. But let me offer here a brief sketch of its significance as I see it. With the rise of the nation state and the increasing social conflict brought about by the breakdown of a stable feudal order, there emerged a decline of medieval natural law thinking and the assertion of the modern positivist conception of law as will. This conception of law threatened the existence of a distinctive legal profession, which, as Coke's invocation of "artificial reason" suggests, put forth claims to a special competence in legal matters. It was therefore especially important to offer an alternative legal ideology which would sharply distinguish law from power. In the nineteenth century, as Perry Miller's *The Life of the Mind in America* (1965) illustrates, the special form of legal reasoning that emphasized the distinction between law and politics was the assertion of the scientific character of legal thought. In one way or another that form of legal justification remains with us today, though it has degenerated into a particularly corrupt glorification of pure methodology summed up in the phrase "thinking like a lawyer."

Now what is the relationship between these claims to the scientific character of legal reasoning and the attitude toward legal history? First, let me sketch the relationship between the scientific claims of the natural sciences and the scientist's concept of the history of science. I quote from Thomas Kuhn's *The Structure of Scientific Revolutions:*

> . . . both the layman's and the practitioner's knowledge of science is based on textbooks and a few other types of literature derived from them. Textbooks, however, being pedagogic vehicles for the perpetuation of normal science, have to be rewritten in whole or in part whenever the language, problem-structure, or standards of normal science change. In short, they have to be rewritten in the aftermath of each scientific revolution, and once rewritten, they inevitably disguise not only the role but the very existence of the revolutions that produced them. Unless he has personally experienced a revolution in his own lifetime, the historical sense either of the working scientist or of the lay reader of textbooks literature extends only to the outcome of the most recent revolutions in the field.
>
> Textbooks thus begin by truncating the scientist's sense of his discipline's history and then proceed to supply a substitute for what they have eliminated. Characteristically, textbooks of science contain just a bit of history, either in an introductory chapter, or more often, in scattered references to the great heroes of an earlier age. From such references both students and professionals come to feel like participants in a long-standing historical tradition. Yet the textbook-derived tradition in which scientists come to sense their participation is one that, in fact, never existed. For reasons that are both obvious and highly functional, science textbooks (and too many of the older histories of science) refer only to that part of the work of past scientists that can easily be viewed as contributions to that statement and solution of the texts' paradigm problems. Partly by selection and partly by distortion, the scientists of earlier ages are implicitly represented as having worked upon the same set of fixed problems and in accordance with the same set of fixed canons that the most recent revolution in scientific theory and method has made seem scientific. No wonder that textbooks and the historical tradition they imply have to be rewritten after each scientific revolution. And no wonder that, as they are rewritten, science once again comes to seem largely cumulative. [Pp. 137-138, 2d ed. 1970.]

The parallels between lawyers' legal history and scientists' history of science seem incredibly striking. Both emphasize continuity in history in order to make present methods and forms of inquiry appear universal. Both use history in order to demonstrate that existing categories of thought are historically necessary and not contingent. Both, in short, use history to justify and glorify the present. Therefore, the dominant form of legal history, best exemplified by Pound, never conceives of legal change as the result of political struggle but only as a result of changes in the received tradition brought about as jurisprudential thought progressively unfolds new truths.

Yet, the parallel between law and science is not complete. The special problem of lawyers is not necessarily present in scientific inquiry. The modern lawyer's effort to distinguish law from politics and reason from power is a special case of professionalization. While the scientist can plausibly conceive of scientific change as the result of the application of pure reason, the lawyer knows that legal change is hardly the exclusive result of disembodied acts of reason discovering previously unknown truths. Thus, he is forced in some way to take a stand on historical movements for legal change. And it is here that lawyers' legal history ultimately assumes its conservative character.

However much the history of law is written in terms of internal criteria established by the legal profession, it is forced to evaluate those explicit political movements for legal change originating outside of the profession. In modern democratic societies, these movements have often involved attacks on the special claims of the legal profession to hold itself out as the possessors of a mysterious science, involving forms of reasoning and access to knowledge unavailable to ordinary men. And so long as the historian adopts the categories of the profession, he will be driven to denounce these movements as "demagogic." The result is that an elitist and antidemocratic politics pervades most of the traditional writings on American legal history, just as it appears in virtually all of the rhetorical literature of the legal profession throughout American history.

M. Shapiro & B. Shapiro, Interdisciplinary Aspects of American Legal History*

Along with the revitalization of the *Journal of Legal History,* the publication of *Law in American History* under the auspices of Harvard's Charles Warren Center for Studies in American History marks an extremely im-

* [Book Review (*Law in American History* (D. Fleming & B. Bailyn eds. 1971)), 4 *J. Interdisciplinary Hist.* 611 (1974). Reprinted by permission.

Martin Shapiro is currently Professor of Law at the University of California, Berkeley. He was previously Professor of Government at Harvard University. He is the author of *Law and Politics in the Supreme Court* (1964), *Freedom of Speech: The Supreme Court and Judicial Review* (1966), and *Supreme Court and Administrative Agencies* (1968).

Barbara Shapiro is presently Professor of Rhetoric at the University of California, Berkeley. She was previously Professor of History and Dean of the College at Wheaton College. She is the author of *John Wilkins: An Intellectual Biography, 1614-72* (1969) and has written several articles on law in seventeenth-century England.]

portant step in the revival of the long neglected practice of legal history in this country.

The volume opens with a brief invocation by Justice Byron R. White, followed by a characteristically exhortative introductory essay James Willard Hurst who, by prescription and example, almost single-handedly kept the fires of American legal history alive through many lean years. This is another of his prescriptions and runs along familiar lines.

The first substantive piece is Richard Maxwell Brown's "Legal and Behavioral Perspectives on American Vigilantism." As its title implies, it is an attempt at the newer, social-science-oriented legal analysis. Based on Packer's widely employed two models of the criminal process,[1] Brown's article tries to explain the support of many late nineteenth-century lawyers and judges for lynch law, solely on the grounds that they had adopted the crime control rather than the due process model of criminal law. The attempt illustrates many of the pitfalls of history as social science.

Precisely because he is burdened by Packer's very neat, dichotomous, and all inclusive model, Brown is led to the bizarre conclusion that the sporadic vigilantism of the West, the persistent pattern of lynching in the South, and the white cap night riding of rural America are all functionally identical developments that can be lumped together in causal explanations of social phenomena. Vigilantism, lynching, and white capping are all "extralegal," and they all purport to be aimed at crime control. Hence, they are one.

Some, although by no means all, Western vigilantism was, in fact, aimed at crime control under conditions in which formal legal institutions were gravely inadequate. Lynching, on the other hand, was a form of guerilla warfare directed *against* an adequate and fully functioning legal order, but one imposed on a conquered population. Packer's model simply does not fit. Southerners did not fear that formal legal institutions would not adequately punish rapists; instead, they took the opportunity of alleged rapes of white women by blacks to demonstrate to blacks that the old social order had survived the war, no matter what the new legal order said.

The white cap movement is still another distinct phenomenon. It was intimately associated in time, place, and personnel with that general wave of agrarian alienation and unrest which we associate with the word

1. Herbert L. Packer, "Two Models of the Criminal Process," *University of Pennsylvania Law Review,* 113 (1964), 1-68, reprinted in revised form in idem, *The Limits of Criminal Sanction* (Stanford, 1968), 149-173.

"populism." In reality, the Indiana white capper was a desperately discontented man who felt victimized by the big money powers. He could not strike out physically at those powers, although in his frustration he felt the need to strike out. But no matter how frustrated, it is a rare man who wishes to risk a beating in order to give one, or even to risk strong social disapproval. So he formed gangs, attacked isolated individuals, and chose his victims from among alleged wife-beaters and chicken thieves in order to provide a socially acceptable excuse for his deviant conduct. Again, Packer's model does not fit, nor was it intended to fit, this kind of reality.

Having lumped three such disparate phenomena into one, Brown then sets himself the task of explaining why a segment of the bar supported it—a task doomed to failure since the "it" is a "them." Here we encounter yet another problem in legal social science. Suppose we begin by describing vigilantism, lynching, and white capping as popular phenomena in the sense that each was supported by some substantial and distinct body of people. How elaborate an explanation would we need of the observed phenomenon that some politicians at some times served as spokesmen for vigilantes, lynchers, and white caps? Although the phenomenon Brown observes is this simple, his analysis of it is greatly complicated by his adherence to Packer's model. Because he begins with law, he does not pose the question: Why do democratic politicians support popular movements? Rather he asks why lawyers support lawlessness—a much tougher question. Nearly all of the lawless lawyers whom Brown turns up are, in reality, local politicians acting like local politicians. Where one's basic data are lawyer-politicians, it is highly unpersuasive to attempt elaborate legal explanations when simple political ones will do.

In a final attempt to link the legal profession and his three-in-one phenomenon, Brown cites a number of professional pleas for a return to corporal punishment and notes that the white caps whipped people. It is hard to know what to make of this kind of argument. Brown can show that a number of academic lawyers referred to vigilantism in various ways; but fastening on the exterior form of punishment will not do, at least not without some very persuasive explanation as to why this is a factor as relevant as the procedural context and purpose of punishment. Again, Packer's disjunction will not work. A lawyer who argues for severe punishments is, indeed, for crime control, but not necessarily at the cost of due process.

A similar set of problems troubles Charles A. Miller in his "Constitutional Law and the Rhetoric of Race." Miller is basically concerned with what the Supreme Court has said. He examines the logical consistency and fit to the external world of the Court's opinions. There is a long tradition of this sort of commentary (the patron saint is surely T. R. Powell), and this form of scholarship is the forte and typical mode of the academic lawyer who takes the Supreme Court as his special province.[2] As Miller practices it, the form is historical in the sense that it arranges the cases to be examined in chronological order and seeks to trace lines of doctrinal influence and development. Essentially, however, it is a form of literary criticism because the central focus is criticism of the product of a group of writers in the context of a traditional although constantly changing body of rules concerning the form, style, and content of the particular literary mode.

This tradition of Supreme Court scholarship is so eminent that it requires no general defense, although being neither history nor social science, it must either be law or *sui generis*. Miller himself, however, is in need of defense of his particular enterprise for two reasons. First, he chooses race-relations opinions that have been parsed and reparsed so often by the literary critics that there seems to be little room for a new analysis. Second, he is a political scientist, and the traditional analysis of cases is not currently in high repute in political science. Accordingly, Miller begins his essay by noting that he is not simply doing traditional case analysis, but, instead, is concerned with the "rhetoric" of the Court. Then, in a rather cursory way, he argues that rhetoric is itself a significant historical and political variable that influences and can explain real political phenomena. If he had dealt solely and systematically with rhetoric he would have had to face squarely the problem of the relevance of judicial rhetoric to the history and politics of the Court. But by sometimes focusing on the opinion as an act—that is, as a decision, command, or policy pronouncement of a government body enjoying some degree of political authority, legitimacy, and power—and sometimes focusing on the opinion as a literary creation, without clearly differentiating between the two, he makes it appear that he is relating rhetoric to action when in fact he is simply bouncing back and forth between them. As often as not, when Miller is in disagreement with the Court, it is over the policies that the justices have favored, not the language that they have used.

The crux of Miller's argument is expressed near the end of his piece:

> Through the language of constitutional interpretation the Court can exercise the prerogative of molding values, not merely the authority to make decisions. Because of their political significance, constitutional

2. See T. R. Powell, *Vagaries and Varieties in Constitutional Interpretation* (New York, 1956).

733

opinions and their language may exert influence well beyond the specific legal holdings. This has certainly been so with Supreme Court opinions on race. And since Court language in the past has signified so much with respect to race it is tempting to suggest that carefully controlled rhetoric may be even more influential in the future, this time on the "right" side.[197]

Even here he fudges by saying "constitutional opinions and their language." In fact, Miller has not shown that language molds values or public policies. He offers no convincing evidence against the counterproposition that it is always values and policies that mold judicial language and never vice versa. If the whole notion of rhetoric were dropped from Miller's contribution, it would vary not one iota in substance, but stand revealed as yet another exercise in good old "con law." In that amphibian status—somewhere between history and political science—it is not a bad or useless exercise.

David H. Flaherty's "Law and the Enforcement of Morals in Early America" is, except for the introduction and conclusion, conventional history. The data are the acts, structures, and official records of government, plus diaries and memoirs. The actual state of the law in a given historical period is reconstructed from the official data, while modest inferences about the fit of law to society are drawn from the unofficial data. In short, as straight history this piece faces no immediate methodological problems.

As history, however, it is subject to some *caveats* of substance, largely revolving around the author's shifting usage of the term "moral law." The structure of the piece is that of a pyramid. In its early sections moral law is used in the broad sense prevalent in the period: rationally derived standards of right and wrong. The moral law thus forbade all wrong conduct. Yet, as the article progresses, the author begins to use "moral" more and more in the contemporaneous sense of "morals" legislation: that is, essentially as the control of victimless and largely sexual or sumptuary conduct. As a result we do not get the evolution of moral law in early America but only the development of a rather narrow and arbitrarily chosen slice of it. For instance, the author deals with rape and bastardy. Only by emphasizing the sexual aspect of these offenses and underplaying their elements of violence and economic irresponsibility, however, can he maintain the integrity of his materials. If rape, why not battery; and if bastardy, who not non-support? By the end of the piece, morals virtually have been reduced to sexual morality. No critical rule exists forbidding a scholar from narrowing his focus, but we would hope in future that the life of the moral law in America with which Flaherty begins would be traced down the paths of murder and assault and theft and misappropriation, as well as down the rather dreary path of fornication.

One of Flaherty's principal tasks is to trace the decline in prosecution of the lesser sexual offenses. He attributes that decline, in part, to institutional factors such as the absence of church courts, and then rather vaguely to "the gradual secularization of society" (232). He tends to portray that secularization largely in terms of functional specialization: The state came to pursue only secular purposes, leaving religion to the churches. Ideological factors might have been given somewhat more weight. In the later period, the state does largely cease to prosecute many "minor" sexual offenses, but as much because they are perceived as minor as because the state no longer seeks to establish God's kingdom on earth. They are perceived as minor in part because offending God is now seen as a personal matter, not one that might draw the wrath of God on the whole community. Fornication could hardly be seen as victimless, and therefore minor, until the community gave up the notion that if it harbored fornicators, *it* might be the victim of divine retribution. More important, what had previously been viewed as the most serious of all offenses—an offense against God—came to be seen as only an offense against social mores. By concentrating on enforcement patterns, and saying relatively little about changes in moral philosophy, the author may have given us a bit too much of the tail and not enough of the dog. Curiously enough, although employing secularization as a general explanation of legal change, when seeking rationales for morals legislation he seems to rely disproportionately on the writings of clergymen, which may seriously overplay the religious as against the secular motives of the actual legislators.

Nevertheless, Flaherty's effort, particularly in relating colonial law to its English background and in tracing the evolution of a single legal concern at statutory and administrative levels, is successful. The substantive criticisms we have offered here concern little more than points of emphasis and selection.

It remains to be said that Flaherty's introduction and conclusion are the sort of mundane essays that most of us write when we seek to generalize about law, morals, and society. A specialist in legal theory might well find the introduction unsystematic, oversimplified, and lacking in philosophic rigor, and then conclude that for this very reason the bulk of the historical discussion is not really shaped (as it purports to be) to illuminate the Hart-Fuller-Devlin-Dworkin debate over the relation of morals to law. Those who find that debate a trifle scholastic may enjoy Flaherty's rather cavalier reduction of it to a rough-and-ready law-morals distinction. Nevertheless, we again encounter the dangers of falling over the edge of history.

Stanley N. Katz seems bent on avoiding those dangers in "The Politics of Law in Colonial America: Controversies over Changing Courts and Equity Law in the Eighteenth Century." His article is standard institutional history—changes in the official institutions of government as recorded in official documents (executive papers and legislative proceedings), plus reaction to and argument about such changes as recorded in historico-literary remains (memoirs, letters, petitions, etc.). The evidence is marshalled to support concise and significant conclusions. In view of the well-known and long-standing English agitation for the reform of Chancery, one might quickly jump to the conclusion that American anti-equity sentiment was little more than a reflection of movements in the metropolis. Katz shows that American concerns were less directed at the inefficiency of administration of the equity courts—the usual bone of contention in England—than at fundamental questions of political legitimacy and at practical issues of political power. Furthermore, unlike the typical English situation, opposition to equity was not necessarily defense of common law. The point is also made in passing, although perhaps it is more important than it appears, that the American bar, unlike the English, could not have provided sufficient personnel to staff two court systems. This piece is sound, safe, informative, and productive of important new data for theory-building.

At the level of theory, Katz is aware that his work must somehow be relevant to the endlessly controversial law-and-development literature. He chooses the less interesting but better part of valor by confining himself to very limited cause-and-effect hypotheses entirely within the range of the particular data he is handling and at the lowest possible level of generalization. His furthest theoretical venture is the proposition that "Equity, in this sense, may represent a sort of characteristically postadolescent stage of development in Anglo-American legal institutions" (263). But he eschews any desire to press this point. At the end of his essay the author writes, "The real challenge is not to learn about the relatively infrequent intersection of law and political crisis, but to find out how legal institutions affected daily life" (284). That, however, is not a challenge which he accepts in this particular piece.

Morton Horwitz's "The Emergence of an Instrumental Conception of American Law 1780-1820," certainly the most original and useful piece in the volume, illustrates the advantages of remaining within the boundaries of a single, well-defined mode of historical analysis. Although its findings are particularly relevant to the law-and-development controversy in social science, Horwitz confines himself exclusively to a pure history-of-ideas approach. He argues that in the course of working out a new rationale for common law after the Revolution had severed the roots of its legitimacy, American judges abandoned the eighteenth-century, natural-law concept of law. Instead of law as foreordained rule and immutable principle of right reason, they began to see law as an instrument to achieve policy goals. Once law was conceived in terms of the exercise of sovereign will, given the political context it naturally followed that popular sovereignty was the source of law. But if law were will, not reason, then common law was the judge's will, and the judges were legislators. Consequently, the judges required a rationale for their lawmaking activities in the context of popular sovereignty, and that rationale emerges as the duty of judges to change law in response to the needs of the citizenry.

As history of ideas, about the only quarrel one could have with Horwitz's presentation is that he tends to neglect the European background of these developments: He presents the shift to an instrumental view of law as an almost purely indigenous phenomenon rather than as an episode in the sweep of positivism across nineteenth-century Western civilization. The omission is surely not due to ignorance, far more probably to space; but, as a result, it is not clear to what extent Horwitz would wish in the last analysis to insist on the autonomy of American intellectual development.

Beyond its merit as history of ideas, the major point of interest in this piece is its assertion of the autonomy of law and, ultimately, of ideas from material forces. It is not only an exercise in the history of ideas, but a defense of history of ideas as an endeavor. Horwitz writes:

> In a whole variety of areas of law, ancient rules are reconsidered from a functional or purposive perspective, often before new or special economic or technological pressure for change in the law has emerged. [290] In short, an instrumental perspective on law does not simply emerge as a response to new economic forces in the nineteenth century. Rather, judges begin to use law in order to encourage social change even in areas where they had previously refrained from doing so. Our task, then, is to explain why it was only in the nineteenth century that the common law took on its innovating and transforming role in American society. This in turn forces us to ask whether an explanation for this fundamental shift in the conception of law between 1780 and 1820 can be found in more general changes in the political theory of the period. [291]

Ultimately, it seems probable that Horwitz is neither asserting a narrow autonomy for law nor an absolutist, anti-materialist position on the autonomy of ideas, but is only arguing that political as well as economic variables may be significant in shaping legal developments. Yet, his argument that legal change may precede and shape rather than respond to economic change is so important that it is regrettable that it is buttressed by only a few random examples.

Harry N. Scheiber is an economic historian, but his "The Road to Munn: Eminent Domain and the Concept of Public Purpose in the State Courts" is not economic history. At first glance it appears to be the most conventional, even trivial, constitutional law. The aim of the piece is to refute the conventional wisdom that Chief Justice Waite's propounding of the doctrine of business "affected with a public interest" in *Munn v. Illinois* was a random excursion into legal antiquarianism. Given the huge gaps in our knowledge of American law, it hardly seems wise to devote over seventy pages to this kind of footnote to history.

Indeed, as usually happens when we seek to discover what was "really" going on in a given justice's mind in a given opinion, Scheiber is not totally persuasive, even in his footnote. He is sometimes driven to arguments about what a conscientious judge would have felt compelled to have read, rather than what he can prove Waite had read, and to *ad hoc* parsing of the text of opinions to show that if read in just the right way, Waite must mean something different and better than he seems to say.

On the other hand Scheiber gives us something different and better than his mind reading of Waite—a full-scale doctrinal history of the "affected with a public interest" rule. Traditionally, constitutional law has proceeded by the explication of a Supreme Court opinion solely by reference to other Supreme Court constitutional opinions. Scheiber expands doctrinal analysis outward in two directions: first, to state court opinions in eminent domain cases and second, to nonconstitutional Supreme Court opinions in riparian law. As history of legal doctrine, this piece is a welcome and substantial advance over the general state of the art.

Fifty or sixty years ago, doctrinal history was a staple of the law reviews and the introductory chapters of standard legal texts and case books. Since then, this sort of work largely has been pushed out of law schools by the demands of vocational education in a period of rapidly expanding law. Is "legal history" to be a new sanctuary for the style of historical-doctrinal analysis that has become obsolete in the training of lawyers? If so, and if deprived of its justification as background for the practitioner, what justification is there for it?

This particular piece acutely raises the problem of justification. The economic historian cannot care much whether Waite plucked Lord

Hale's doctrine fresh or got it second hand.[3] To the general intellectual historian, or historian of ideas, the point appears either obvious or trivial —the doctrines were all over the place and whether a given judge on a given day got them around the house or on an antiquarian excursion hardly matters. Only that peculiar breed, the American constitutional historian, could care about the question of the specific doctrinal-rhetorical sources of one opinion in a "leading case" or use this question as the central vehicle for exploring the development of the law of economic regulation. Why should we seek to trace the growth of certain ideas and policies of economic regulation almost solely through the arrangement and rearrangement of case materials rather than through the broader searches of the typical intellectual or economic historian?

Robert Stevens' "Two Cheers for 1870: The American Law School" is not really a finished essay but rather a rough, preliminary draft of a book. Thus, much of the criticism offered here may eventually prove gratuitous. The draft is in five parts. The first is devoted to the development of legal education and the legal profession up to Christopher Langdell. As such, it is little more than a brief summary of secondary work that itself has been much criticized, as Stevens acknowledges, for its lack of research depth.

Sections II and III take up the rise, dominance, and partial erosion of the Harvard case method of legal education. These sections are good history of education in the sense of using historical materials to illuminate a major problem of educational policy: What should the law school curriculum look like? They contain important insights, particularly in establishing a perspective from which to view the case method and its relation to science and the social sciences. At the same time, they concern matters so central to the evolution of American intellectual history and American politics that they rise far above the level of trade concerns or guild history.

In these very sections, however, a rather undigested strain of guild history does begin to appear. Alongside the analysis of legal education as such begins an account of the efforts of the various legal professional associations to regulate the quality of law schools and admission to the bar. Surely, the content of legal education and the self-regulation of the profession are somehow interrelated topics, but the author himself never makes clear the connection. He merely oscillates between descriptions of the developments in these two areas. This strain of guild history

3. For Lord Hale's doctrine of "affected with a public interest" see Mathew Hale, "De Portibus Maris," in Francis Hargrave (ed.), *Collection of Tracts Relative to the Law of England* (London, 1787).

becomes increasingly prominent in Section IV which begins with an interesting analysis of the growing conflict in the 1920s between case law teaching and social science, but increasingly becomes a compendium of trade gossip. By Section V, devoted to the more or less current scene, we are at the level of an American Association of Law Schools panel paper on the state of legal education.

Basically what we have here is a law school teacher, concerned with current problems in legal education, doing an excursion into history to show that most of the problems and potentials of today's law schools have been historically determined. Many historians feel that this sort of task-oriented history is likely to lead to superficial scholarship. Even while remembering the preliminary nature of this work, there is much here to substantiate such a charge.

A major benefit of Steven's work is that it confirms and amplifies Horwitz's at so many points, although there may be some difference between them concerning when the change to instrumentalism occurred. It also helps us to deal with Jerold S. Auerbach's "Enmity and Amity: Law Teachers and Practitioners, 1900-1922," by inoculating us against Auerbach's seemingly romantic view of the academic lawyer. The piece falls into two parts. The first sketches the antagonism between academics and practitioners at the turn of the century. In depicting the law faculties of the period Auerbach provides a highly useful supplement to Stevens by more adequately linking developments in the law schools to those in the university at large and to the more general intellectual and political climate. He concludes that the antagonism he observes primarily resulted from ideological conflict between conservative practitioners and reform-minded academic lawyers.

As with Brown's piece, some suspicion arises when a rather complex and narrowly legal explanation is substituted for a more obvious and general one. Quite apart from specific legal ideologies, one normally expects some antagonism between the academic and practicing wings of any profession, as a direct result of functional specialization. If Auerbach had worked "outward" in the sociology of professions rather than "inward" into legal-professional lore, he would have found these same tensions in other learned professions. Given the intimate connection between law and politics, inevitably some of this kind of strain would manifest itself as practitioner suspicion of the political orthodoxy of law faculties, but this is far more likely to have been a secondary manifestation than a root source of the antagonism.

Auerbach's principal difficulty may be that he sticks essentially to the narrowest techniques of the intellectual historian. He pays a great deal of attention to what law professors wrote about themselves and almost none to actual law school teaching, as it might be reconstructed from contemporary catalogues, case and text books, student notes, and law reviews. He does not seem to see the incipient and then real and perhaps inherent conflict between the case method of teaching and the role of the law teacher as reformer. He himself quotes Pound to the effect that the new teaching method was one of "class-room logical acrobatics" rather than social planning (561). Stevens' picture of law faculties as handmaidens to the profession seems more convincing than Auerbach's portrayal of brave reformers clad in the armor of scientific expertise.

There is a link between the case method of teaching and the complaints of the practitioner against the academic that is far more direct than the route through law reform suggested by Auerbach. By its very nature, the case method of teaching is the criticism of judges. As Auerbach himself shows, much of practitioner discontent stemmed from the fear that the young lawyer might not maintain proper respect for the idols of the profession once he had watched a professor ruthlessly and often mockingly expose their feet of clay during classroom dissection of their opinions. Many of the great classroom performers who specialized in making both the opinion writers and the students look like fools were political conservatives. More often, they criticized judges for errors in craftsmanship and ignorance of the received law rather than for failure to innovate. It was not the ideologies but the irreverence of the law schools that most bothered practitioners.

Auerbach persuades us that some of the impetus toward law reform came from some members of law faculties, and that this reform sentiment was a factor in the hostility he discovers between academic and practitioner. It would be a great mistake, however, from his work to form a picture of the turn-of-the-century law schools as centers of scientific innovation and reform facing a hostile profession bent on saving the legal status quo from faculty assault.

Indeed, the second major portion of Auerbach's article increases our reluctance to give full measure to the first. Here the author persuasively makes the case that in the latter part of the period that he studied, the practitioner establishment and the elite segment of the law schools formed an alliance to upgrade legal education, based on the natural desire of law faculties to improve legal education and on the desire of the old practitioner establishment to erect barriers against entry of the newer immigrant groups into the profession. The faculty side of the faculty-practitioner relation *is* now explained by the functional differentiation of teachers rather than by their specific legal ideology. If conservative practitioners viewed law schools as nests of reform, how could they have turned so confidently, as Auerbach shows, to those very schools as

741

bastions for preserving the status quo against the onslaught of "foreign" legal ideas?

In concluding his analysis of the alliance between teachers and practitioners, Auerbach writes:

> Higher educational standards were the bridge between them. But teachers and practitioners crossed it moving in opposite directions. Pausing temporarily as they met, they created an illusion that they might travel together when in fact, before long, they would be further apart than ever before. [601]

Perhaps in subsequent work* Auerbach will be able to prove this hypothesis. If so, he will come much closer than he presently has to convincing us that differences in legal and political ideology are as important as he believes them to be in explaining the hostility he has discovered. But even at this point, his work, and that of Stevens, opens up relations between legal education and the public role of the legal profession that are profoundly important to both the political and intellectual historian.

John T. Elliff's "Aspects of Federal Civil Rights Enforcement: The Justice Department and the FBI, 1939-1964" is history as one brand of political scientist does it. In fact, it is a case study in the political dynamics of organizational decision-making. The case study method is widely used by political scientists as a substitute for laboratory experiments or comparative studies. From the point of view of social science, it is a poor method because it provides the investigator with absolutely no means of controlling or manipulating variables. Yet, the case study is widely employed because it is practicable and deals with real events in depth. For those historians who stress the uniqueness of historical events, the political scientist's case study may be viewed as a historical monograph to be judged by the traditional standards for such work.

Elliff does not quite tell us his purpose. At times it appears that his principal interest is that of a political scientist in organizational behavior —in explaining how policy outputs flow from the political relations between a set of sub-units of a complex organization, each with its own ideologies, clienteles, and institutional interests. If this is his major interest, then his choice of the relatively long time period, 1939-1964, is not altogether fortunate because it reduces him to a rather cursory analysis of each of the crucial political-organizational interactions that he examines. If the question is what makes men in organizations behave as they do, this sort of diachronic treatment does not provide the richness of detail that is the alleged compensatory advantage of case studies.

* [See G. Auerbach, *Unequal Justice* (1975).]

On the other hand, Elliff may simply be trying to tell the story of what the Justice Department did about civil rights enforcement from 1939 to 1964. As a political scientist he might need some excuse for telling such a story, because most political scientists do not believe that their business is story telling. As a historian, he may not need one. Yet, even as story telling, Elliff's work would not meet the highest historical standards because he works almost exclusively from the office files of the Attorney General and the Criminal and Civil Rights Divisions of the Justice Department. Thus, we get a kind of "company" or "official" history, although with the addition of critical and independent evaluation.

The great strength of the broad-brush diachronic method adopted here is to expose long-term continuities in the behavior of the F.B.I., both toward its organizational "superiors" and toward the outside world. For this reason, the study is of interest both to the general political historian and to the social scientist interested in organizations. But if this is the major value of the work, then the author's failure, no doubt through no fault of his own, to gain access to the F.B.I. files gravely accentuates the "company history" problem and, more important, renders his analysis of F.B.I. motivations and behavior incomplete.

The post-*Brown v. Board of Education* segments of the case study are the strongest and of greatest interest to students of organization. Elliff is particularly convincing in exposing the paradox that the F.B.I. was freest in its anti-civil rights position after a special Civil Rights Division had been created in order to place special emphasis on civil rights enforcement. Elliff's approach clearly brings out the long, consistent, and politically sophisticated campaign of J. Edgar Hoover to place the institutional interests of his agency above any and all policy goals of the political regime. Like most good case studies, this one abounds in discreet insights about people and events that will be extremely useful to others working in the area and may well provide more than sufficient excuse for the existence of the work quite apart from grand debates over the place of case studies in scholarly inquiry.

The volume as a whole raises a special problem for consideration: The place of political scientists in legal history. . . . In this setting "public law," as the law subfield of political science is generally called, is the natural companion of "political theory," (which is conceived of essentially as the history of political thought, and of American intellectual and political history). In the context of the interdisciplinary study of history, it is important to point out that the presence of the essays of three political scientists in this volume does not necessarily signal a new commitment by political scientists to legal history, but rather runs counter to the general movement of political science, and its law subfield, which is away from historical studies, and particularly away from the history of legal doctrines, and toward "behaviorism," comparative studies, and contemporary policy analysis.

If the . . . orientation of this volume renders it a very special case in political science, something of the same thing may be said for its more general place in the corpus of legal history. Although a Hurst essay leads the volume, the remainder gravely underrepresents the whole movement of legal history as historical sociology, which is the central thrust of Hurst's work and is to be seen so prominently in the work of his midwestern disciples. The result is a volume that is essentially based on intellectual and institutional history, legal-doctrinal, case law analysis, and the more conventional wing of political science. Precisely because this volume and the participants in it are likely to have a major influence in shaping the field, it may be necessary to enter the reminder that economics, sociology, and what are loosely called the behavioral sciences also have a role to play in the interdisciplinary study of legal history. . . .

Auerbach . . . is hampered by what is a striking general tendency of the whole volume: It concentrates heavily on what lawyers and judges and law professors said about law, and says very little about what the law and lawmakers were actually doing. Surely it is no criticism of historians to say that they stick to what the documents can tell them. Often nothing remains of history but what men wrote. But here, perhaps because these are initial efforts in a reviving field, there is a marked inclination to stick to the top of the documentation—to those writings most readily available for investigation—rather than to dig deep in order to reconstruct mundane realities as accurately as possible. We catch few glimpses of office records, student note books, old text books, or even the mass of routine, day-to-day cases.

In general, then, this volume shows an early state of the art for legal history and a spectrum that is quite familiar to those interested in interdisciplinary studies. At one extreme, we discover quick but limited pay-offs from turning conventional modes of investigation into legal areas, quite justifiably treating legal thought and institutions as comparable to other thought and institutions and amenable to comparable methods of investigation. At the other, we find that attempts at genuine interdisciplinary investigation are difficult and that the triad of law, history, and social science is particularly volatile. And finally, we discover assorted miscellaneous persons—law teachers interested in legal education, political scientists doing case studies, constitutional law scholars investigating doctrine—all who are contributing in rather asymmetrical ways to the growth of a reviving discipline.

White, The Appellate Opinion as
Historical Source Material*

. . . American legal history has recently piqued the curiosity of historians and legal scholars seeking to make connections between their respective disciplines. Underlying this interest is the assumption that the working materials of the legal profession—cases, statutes, treatises, and the like—reflect to some degree the changing patterns of American civilization and may fruitfully be viewed as indices of the general tone of American culture at various points in time. This assumption may seem hardly worth lingering over, especially to historians accustomed to noting the ways in which institutions and ideas in America have taken on distinctive forms during particular time periods. Yet the inclusion of appellate court decisions in the general category of materials considered "representative" of the style and substance of intellectual contributions at a given point in American history raises a number of troublesome problems in interdisciplinary communication. I am concerned here with identifying some of those problems and with proposing one methodological approach designed to alleviate them. Specifically, my focus is on the factors that distinguish appellate opinions from the general mass of recorded social phenomena available to the historian, the relationship between these factors and the development in the legal profession of a particular set of techniques for analyzing material, and some of the implications of this development for the potential scholar in legal history.

By focusing upon some of the problems in a historical treatment of appellate court decisions, I am, of course, eschewing the "rather ordinary matter" of legal history, which Hurst has found so stimulating for what he calls "issues of high politics."[1] This is not to suggest that appellate decision-making should necessarily be the central concern of legal historians. My emphasis upon appellate decisions stems primarily from the fact that they have traditionally been the core materials of legal education in America—the practice field, as it were, on which a set of professional analytical techniques have been tried out. An understanding of the factors distinguishing the appellate opinion from other published

* [1 *J. Interdisciplinary Hist.* 491 (1971). Reprinted by permission.

G. Edward White (1941–) is Associate Professor at the University of Virginia School of Law. He was educated at Amherst College (B.A. 1963), Yale University (M.A. 1964; Ph.D. 1967), and Harvard University (J.D. 1970). He was Law Clerk to Chief Justice Earl Warren, United States Supreme Court (1971-1972). He is the author of *The American Judicial Tradition* (1976) and *The Eastern Establishment and the Western Experience* (1968).]

1. James Willard Hurst, *Law and Social Progress in United States History* (Ann Arbor, 1960), 18.

sources of its time can therefore lead to an understanding of the distinctive ways in which the legal profession orders its source material and ultimately to some sense of the differing biases of the disciplines of law and history.

When a historian attempts to analyze past opinions of the Supreme Court or federal or state appellate courts, his first problem is normally to learn how to read the opinion, a process which requires not only mastering jargonistic terms such as respondent, demur, hold, or remand, but understanding, at least in a rudimentary sense, the manner in which social situations are transposed into legal cases. Consider, for example, the case of an intellectual historian examining a variety of documents with a view toward understanding the positions on matters of public policy taken by influential and articulate men of the period. Should he attempt to include the opinions of appellate judges among his sources, he will be confronted with the following complicating factors: First, judges, in their professional role, only decide *cases*—their statements are made in the framework of a dispute between two parties that has been couched in certain legal terms and which they are asked to resolve in those terms; second, each case, in the American judicial system, is considered to be a discrete set of facts, the resolution of which has conclusive significance only for that fact-situation or one identical to it; third, the judge's role is defined as that of an informed and impartial arbiter of disputes whose decision is allegedly based on the legal "merits" of a case rather than on any personal inclinations of his own.

Each of these factors has a restrictive effect on judicial language. The first confines it to words and phrases of legal significance: for example, was the defendant negligent (in a case involving an auto accident), did he lack the requisite intent (in a murder case), or was there consideration for a promise (in a case involving the making of a contract). The second factor creates a division, familiar to lawyers, between language used to decide the precise legal point at issue or to justify that decision, and language of a more general nature (dicta) whose import is far less clear. The third stimulates among the judiciary a process of self-conscious depersonalization of their function, which may ultimately result in abdication of the arbiter role, as when Justice Felix Frankfurter resolved not to participate in a case testing the power of the District of Columbia Transit Authority to forbid the playing of radios in buses in Washington, D.C., on the grounds that his feelings were too "strongly engaged as the victim of the practice in controversy."[2] As a consequence of these formal constraints, the tone and substance of an appellate decision at a particular

2. Public Utilities Comm. v. Pollack, 343 (U.S. 451 (1952).

time may more closely resemble those of another decision from a much earlier period than those of a contemporary non-legal document; in addition, the decision may conceal rather than reveal the social attitudes of an individual judge.

Thus the historian approaching appellate decisions may find that his understanding of the ebb and flow of political ideologies in American history is not an entirely useful guide to case analysis, because legal issues and judicial decisions are difficult to characterize in ideological terms. It is often difficult to assess, for example, whether or not a particular decision upholding the rights of an employee against his employer is a "liberal" one, even if it occurs at a time when "liberals" generally sided with employees in labor-management conflicts. Indeed, a historian's sense of the ideological currents of a particular time period may encourage him to impose a characterization on legal materials that they will not bear.

The process of appellate decision-making also has its effect upon the scholarship of individuals with legal training. The techniques employed in appellate courts, where counsel present opposing arguments on the legal issues in question and judges in their decisions pay considerable attention to the previous findings of other courts on similar or analogous issues, often find their way into less specialized efforts by legal scholars.

Pound, for example, has characterized the development of legal history in America as a process whereby social, political, and economic conditions of time and place create a "pressure of new demands" upon the "taught legal tradition" which results in "new reasoned applications of the technique in which . . . judges had been trained." Social phenomena, in Pound's view, are analogous to pieces of evidence presented in a brief or an oral argument: They are "fitted into the traditional [legal] system in their interpretation and application."[3] Pound emphasizes the existence of a distinctive self-perpetuating set of responses to experience —taught legal tradition—which can exist apart from, and at the same time order, its social context.

Pound's description of legal history suggests a second manifestation of the influence of the appellate court model upon legal scholarship: the prevalence of what might be called an advocate's worldview. Such a view sees society as being shaped by what two legal scholars have called "the compulsive force of human desires" and "the compulsive logic of the facts of interdependence." In this view "every human being wants what he wants as intensely as he wants it," but "every human being . . . has

3. Roscoe Pound, *The Formative Era of American Law* (Boston, 1938), 82, 83, 86.

747

to reckon with the fact that other people want what they want in the same way also."[4] Society is therefore a complex of potentially hostile but interdependent interests, the welfare of which depends on mutual accommodation. In this complex, the role of one who has mastered the techniques of advocacy—who has learned how to frame, argue, and resolve the conflicts of opposing interests—is enormously important for the promotion of social welfare. The apparatus of the legal profession thus becomes a force for social stability and tranquility: In a world where desires are compulsive and interdependence is inescapable, those who possess the techniques necessary to resolve disputes and issue mutually satisfactory authoritative directions are bulwarks against societal self-destruction.

In terms of legal history, this view has manifested itself in a juxtaposition of the continuity of a legal tradition and the diversity of its social context: Pound is again illustrative. Writing of the nineteenth century, he found that "the course of judicial decision has been characteristically steady and uniform . . . through five generations of rapid political, economic and social change, bringing about a communis opinio over the country as a whole on the overwhelming majority of legal questions, despite the most divergent . . . political, economic, social, and even racial conditions." "The outstanding phenomenon" of American legal history was, for Pound, "the extent to which a taught tradition . . . has stood out against all manner of economically or politically powerful interests."[5]

In the language of contemporary American historians, the above characterization emphasizes consensus within the legal profession and conflict among the rest of society. But this distinction is an artificial one: the fact that the legal profession is, to some extent, able to translate social pressures into terms (cases, briefs, opinions) which it can manipulate and resolve does not mean that it is isolated from those pressures which do not come within its boundaries; nor can those disputes settled through the processes of law necessarily be said to symbolize the alleviation of more general social grievances. . . .

A further effect of the appellate model upon legal scholarship, and consequently upon the writing of legal history by lawyers, can be seen in the techniques employed by the legal profession in dealing with authoritative legal statements (such as rules, precedents, and statutes) made in the past. The American legal system presumes such statements to represent, at the moment of their enactment, valid guidelines for the future as well as the present, but it allows that presumption to be overcome in the

4. Henry M. Hart and Albert Sacks, "The Legal Process" (unpub. ms., 1958), 114.
5. Pound, *The Formative Era*, 82, 83.

form of challenges to the validity of the statements; in this fashion the system remains responsive to social change. A major portion of the work of judges and advocates involves testing the applicability of past legal pronouncements to present situations and consequently reassessing the validity and relevance of the social assumptions and policies of a prior time. Presentmindedness, then, is built into legal training; indeed, that training tends to encourage skepticism toward directives enacted at too remote a time period (more recent precedents, other things being equal, are preferred in a litigation), and to provide ammunition, in the form of the techniques of advocacy, for attacking the precepts of the past. Hence the American legal historian with legal training faces a dilemma because the very techniques that aid him in analyzing legal materials, by reason of their presentist bias, tend to de-emphasize the historical dimensions of those materials.

In addition to affecting the language and methodology of its actors, the process of appellate decision-making in America makes use of the element of time in distinctive ways. In the first place, as Henry Hart and John McNaughton have pointed out, appellate decisions have a double time dimension: "at the moment of their making, they speak from the present to the future . . . at the moment of their application, they speak out of the past to the present."[6] Appellate judges are conscious that their decisions are retesting the validity of past precedents and laying down guidelines for future conduct—guidelines that will themselves be retested. This affects the character of appellate decisions as social documents. The opinions of appellate judges, in addition to being more self-constrained and depersonalized than letters, diaries, novels, treatises, newspapers, magazines, and other standard materials of social and intellectual historians, are more difficult to locate in time, because one of the functions of the opinion is to preserve, through generalized and indeterminate language, a sense of continuity between past, present, and future. The historian looking for "period" language or social attitudes in an appellate opinion has to reckon with this tendency.

A second time-related problem is that of cultural lag. The presence in appellate opinions of elements intended to convey a sense of continuity, plus the time delays imposed by backlogs in trial and appellate court dockets, can play havoc with attempts to match legal materials with historical trends. Take, for example, a trend considered significant by historians: the emergence of heavy industry in the Northeast after the Civil War. This phenomenon is generally felt to have had a substantial effect

6. Henry M. Hart and John McNaughton, "Evidence and Inference in the Law," *Daedalus,* LXXXVII (1958), 42, 43.

on the course of American civilization after 1865: One can find ample evidence of the impact of industrial life and its models of success, such as the "captain of industry," on the social theories of late nineteenth-century Americans. One might also expect rapid industrialization to be reflected in an extensive modification of prior legal doctrines in the latter portion of the nineteenth century, as the courts took cognizance of the inapplicability of legal principles formulated in a preindustrial age. Such modification did indeed take place, but in a haphazard and uneven fashion: In certain areas, such as nuisance, many courts merely reaffirmed notions of land use that had been formulated prior to the advent of industrialization.

The historian, on observing an apparent reluctance on the part of late-nineteenth-century courts to take immediate cognizance of social change, may be tempted to characterize the judiciary of the period as "conservative."[9] But such a characterization tends to ignore the function of time in the legal process. When economic and technological innovations result in different ways of using space, as they did in the latter portion of the nineteenth century, these new uses may or may not pose legal problems that need to be settled in the courts, for they may or may not have been anticipated by some prior legal directive. For example, municipal ordinances regulating horsedrawn traffic on city streets may be adequate for automobiles if their terminology is sufficiently broad to include both types of transportation under a general category such as "vehicles"; they may, however, prove inadequate if they make judgments about traffic regulation based on the assumption that all vehicular traffic is horsedrawn. The continued use in the courts, then, of rules and principles formulated in an earlier period in time is a natural product of a system that innovates, for the most part, through glosses on generalities rather than through abrupt departures from prior rules, and is not necessarily an indication of conservatism among the judiciary.[10] . . .

I have referred above to some of the ways in which the appellate model, with its emphasis upon the techniques of advocacy, has influenced the cast of scholarship in the legal profession. A more general manifestation of this influence may be seen in the differing use by legal scholars and historians of value judgments in an empirical presentation. A perusal of law reviews and historical journals shows that articles in the former generally take the form of argumentative propositions on an as-

9. For example, Robert G. McCloskey, *American Conservatism in the Age of Enterprise* (Chicago, 1951) and *The American Supreme Court* (Chicago, 1960).

10. For a different view, which sees lag as "present-minded pragmatism rather than long-term rational planning," see Lawrence M. Friedman and Jack Ladinsky, "Law and Social Change in the Progressive Era," in Katz and Kutler, *New Perspectives*, II, 195-200.

pect of public policy, with the author's empirical findings used in support of this argument, whereas articles in the latter are rarely argumentative in the same sense. Historians seem to be searching for some kind of objective reality in the past, piling information on top of previous information in an attempt to get closer to truth. Their arguments are directed at previous generalizations made by their predecessors on the basis of too limited or faulty evidence; their "revision" of these generalizations is presented as part of a continuing professional search for what "really" happened. This stance is in contrast, by and large, to that of legal scholars, who are interested not so much in what happened or is happening as in what should have happened or should happen.

This difference stems in part from the kinds of subjects to which the two disciplines address themselves. In large measure legal scholarship deals with unresolved contemporary problems for which more than one solution exists; the task is to assess the problem and discern the optimum solution. In this setting there is much to be said in support of an argumentative presentation. Historians, however, confront problems that, for better or worse, have been "solved"; the question for them is often why, given the complex of factors in operation at the time that the solution was reached, it should have taken the particular form that it did. An appropriate answer to this last question, it is generally assumed, requires scholarly detachment: If a historian is too outraged by a particular result (such as the imposition of martial law in Southern states in the Reconstruction period), he may in an assessment of that policy emphasize certain factors influencing its formulation (sadism and vindictiveness in the personalities of influential Congressmen) at the expense of others (the reluctance of Southern states to enfranchise freed Negroes).[11] A shorthand way of representing this phenomenon is to characterize the scholarly ideal of the historian as objectivity; by contrast, that of the legal scholar might be persuasiveness.

At the extremes, the disciplinary ideals appear very far apart: If one assumes that law is "a science not only of what is but what ought to be"[12] and that the legal system in America is an open-ended vehicle for policy debate, the formulation of a coherent set of social values appears to be a prerequisite for effective functioning within that system, and objectivity, in the sense of value-free detachment, an inappropriate stance. That is, if commentators on past legal decisions were precluded from persuading their audience that those decisions were "wrong" in the sense of

11. See Bernard A. Weisberger, "The Dark and Bloody Ground of Reconstruction Historiography," *Journal of Southern History,* XXV (1959), 427-447.
12. Hart and McNaughton, "Evidence and Inference," 42.

being inapplicable or irrelevant to present conditions, the system would lose its receptiveness to change. Yet, insofar as that persuasion reflects present-minded evaluations of past phenomena, it moves away from the historical ideal of objectivity.

The divergence of the disciplinary ideals is not so marked in American legal history. First, the process employed in American courts of testing past decisions against present circumstances insures that at some point most precedents will become "invalid" in the sense of having no authoritative applicability. At this point one could argue that the present-mindedness essential to a persuasive critique of the decision is no longer necessary: The decision has become a historical curiosity. Second, it may be fair to say that the degree to which scholars remain "curious" about a past decision once it has lost its authority depends on present circumstances; that is, the decision of a historian to study a particular topic or time period and his reaction to it are heavily influenced by the fashions of his own time. In this sense "objectivity" on the part of the historian is unrealizable and even unnecessary.

Nevertheless, the different modes of presentation and idealized objectives of legal scholars and historians can force the legal historian to walk an analytical tightrope. The orthodox method of scholarly criticism of appellate opinions by lawyers consists of a rigorous dissection of the internal logic of the opinion in order to expose (and perhaps question) its tacit assumptions. In this task, the critic is admittedly interested in determining whether the starting premises of the judge are valid; should he find them invalid, his role resembles that of a lobbyist. But the legal historian, if he takes this tack, has a rather different function, that of showing that there is a historical explanation for the premises on which the opinion rests: for example, prevailing beliefs concerning the sanctity of private property against encroachments by the State. Ideally, the fact that such beliefs may presently be in disrepute plays no part in the analysis, but it is a difficult task to employ the analytical methods of an argumentative mode of discourse to arrive at a "detached" result.

Thus far I have been concerned with raising some of the problems that historians might encounter in utilizing appellate opinions as source material. The question such an approach may raise is whether in the face of these difficulties historians should continue their well-established custom of paying scant or cursory attention to appellate cases, or whether some method of analysis intended to anticipate the problems can be formulated. In the remainder of this essay I shall sketch the form one such method might take.

The method seeks to emphasize both the distinctive professional characteristics of the judicial process and the extent to which judicial decision-making mirrors broader social and ideological trends in American culture. It rests on four assumptions about the judiciary in America: First, judges, because of their authoritative role, are subjected to certain constraints which are internalized in the form of approved techniques of judicial decision-making, such as following precedent, testing general doctrines in terms of particular fact-situations, and publishing formal, reasoned justifications of their results; second, they are subjected to a variety of extraprofessional pressures stemming from the fact that they hold elective or high appointive office; third, individual judges interpret their function by weighing their social and political inclinations against the constraints of their role, with the result that as many potential theories of judicial performance exist as there are individual judges; fourth, since the operational vehicle for formulating theories of performance is the opinion, and since opinions are published documents open to criticism by a judge's peers and by readers both within and without the legal profession, the wide range of potential interpretations of judicial performance becomes narrowed to certain interpretations that are fashionable at different points in time.

It is therefore possible to identify in American appellate decisions the presence of certain ratiocinative styles during various time periods. By ratiocinative style I mean the manner in which a judge rationalizes the end result of his opinion—the way in which he manipulates the various sources of authority and persuasion (precedent, "public policy," etc.) at his disposal. At some points in time judges place greater reliance on precedent or the authority of their office; at others they are more concerned with changing social conditions that question a precedent's import, or are more apt to downgrade their authority to pass on questions in the face of a judgment by another institutional body, such as a legislature or an administrative agency.

The presence of shifting ratiocinative styles in American appellate opinions is particularly suggestive in light of the fact that at least since the early nineteenth century the core elements of the appellate decision-making process have remained constant: that is, appellate courts have continually followed the principles of searching for applicable precedents (which has also been termed deciding "like cases alike"), depersonalizing the judicial function, and elaborating the reasons for their results. Despite this institutional constancy, there have been marked shifts in the manner of opinion-writing: A notable example is the replacement in the early twentieth century of what Pound termed "mechanical jurisprudence"—in which "the judicial function was taken to be one of discovery of the definitely appointed precept . . . by an absolute method admitting of no scope for anything but logical identification of the actual

753

precept . . . and mechanical application thereof"—with a style that de-emphasized syllogistic logic and judicial omniscience and emphasized attention to "prevalent moral and political theories and intuitions of public policy."[13]

If the process of appellate opinion-writing is thought of as subsuming a number of elements—the professional and extraprofessional constraints upon the judge, his temperamental inclinations, his consciousness of acceptable modes of presentation at given times—an analysis of that process would appear to raise a number of historical questions. To what extent can comparisons be made between the ratiocinative styles of appellate opinions in particular time periods and modes of discourse in other disciplines at the same time? To what extent can the weight given to precedents and the use of syllogistic logic be said to represent certain assumptions about the locus of institutional power in America at given times? If such assumptions can be identified, are they shared by political or social movements extant at the time? How, in short, do prevailing cultural attitudes at given points in the history of American civilization penetrate the self-contained and self-perpetuating appellate court system?

What I propose is a correlation of prevailing cultural attitudes and appellate ratiocinative styles at various times in American history. It is difficult, however, to evaluate "prevailing cultural attitudes" without having previously formulated some index of them; hence a more precise correlation might be between the decisions of appellate courts and political or ideological movements, such as "Jacksonian Democracy," or "progressivism," which had widespread appeal during a particular time span. The first step in such a correlation would be to characterize the social assumptions and modes of thought and expression that distinguished the "Jacksonians" or "progressives"; the next would be to inquire whether these assumptions and modes could be found in appellate opinions at roughly similar points in time, taking into account the factor of time lag in the courts. The inquiry would necessitate an analysis of the internal structure of the opinions and would hence give some attention to the distinctive characteristics of the appellate opinion as a primary source for historical research. The ultimate concern, however, would be to locate the opinion in a historical context.

13. Roscoe Pound, "Mechanical Jurisprudence," Columbia Law Review, VIII (1908), 605; *The Formative Era*, 111.

Chapter 9

Law and Anthropology

I. GENERAL NOTIONS

Dias, Jurisprudence*

The Anthropological Approach

Anthropological investigations into the nature of primitive and undeveloped systems of law are of modern origin and might be regarded as a product of the Historical School.† Pride of place will here be accorded to Sir Henry Maine (1822-1888), who was the first and still remains the greatest representative of the historical movement in England.[1] It is not easy to place Maine's contributions to the theory of law. He began his work with a mass of material already published on the history and development of Roman law by the German Historical School, and he was able to build upon that and also to bring to bear a more balanced view of history than is found in Savigny. Maine, however, went further. He was learned in English, Roman and Hindu laws and also had knowledge

---

*[Pp. 532-541 (Butterworth & Co., 4th ed. 1976). Reprinted by permission.

R. W. M. Dias was born in Ceylon in 1921 and was schooled there until the age of 17, when he entered Trinity Hall at Cambridge University. He served in the Royal Air Force after graduation, and then returned to Trinity Hall to teach law in 1946. He has been a lecturer at Cambridge from 1951 to the present time, a Fellow of Magdalene College since 1955, and a barrister of the English Bar since 1945.]

†[In previous text, the author discussed the Historical School, most notably represented by Savigny, Gierke, and Hegel.]

1. The opinion is ventured that neither Maitland nor Holdsworth have made the contributions to legal theory that were made by Maine.

of Celtic systems. In this respect he parts company with the German historians. Instead of stressing the uniqueness of national institutions, he brought to bear a scientific urge to unify, classify and generalise the evolution of different legal orders. Thus he inaugurated both the comparative and anthropological approaches to the study of law, and history in particular, which was destined to bear abundant fruit in the years to come.[2]

Maine set out to discover whether a pattern of legal development could be extracted from a comparative examination of different systems, especially between Roman law and the Common law. What he sought were laws of historical development. He was led to distinguish between what he called "static" and "progressive" societies. The early development of both types is roughly the same and falls, in his thesis, into four stages. The first stage is that of lawmaking by personal command, believed to be of divine inspiration, e.g., Themistes of ancient Greece, and the dooms of the Anglo-Saxon kings. The second stage occurs when those commands crystallise into custom. In the third stage the ruler is superseded by a minority who obtain control over the law, e.g., the pontiffs in ancient Rome. The fourth stage is the revolt of the majority against this oligarchic monopoly, and the publication of the law in the form of a code, e.g., the XII Tables in Rome.

"Static" societies, according to Maine, do not progress beyond this point. The characteristic feature of "progressive" societies is that these proceed to develop the law by three methods—fiction, equity, and finally legislation. Ample examples of the use of fiction are to be found in Roman and early English law. The operation of equity and legislation has been considered in the earlier chapters of this book.

As a general inference Maine believed that no human institution was permanent, and that change was not necessarily for the better. Unlike Savigny, he favoured legislation and codification. He recognised that the advance of civilisation demanded an increasing use of legislation, and he often contended that the confused state of English law was due to its pre-eminently judge-made character. Codification is an advanced form of legislative development, and represents the stage at which all the preceding phases of development are woven into a coherent whole. He also did not share Savigny's mystique of the *Volksgeist*.

Side by side with these doctrines Maine developed another thesis. In early societies, both "static" and "progressive," the standards permit

---

2. *Ancient Law* (Pollock's edition). At the time of its publication his knowledge of Hindu law was not as profound as it became later, for he only took up his Indian appointment in the following year.

a desirable flexibility in application. Rigidity develops at a post-primitive or "middle" period. Above all, it is generally agreed that even in primitive societies people do control their destinies, that they are by no means blindly subservient to law. The conscious purpose of achieving some end precedes the adaptation of human behaviour, and the adaptation of behaviour is followed by adaptation of the structure of social organisation.

Fourthly, it used to be accepted that law and religion were indistinguishable in primitive societies. This view has given way to an increased recognition of the secular character of primitive law. The exact extent to which law and religion were associated seems, however, to be in some doubt. Diamond, for example, criticises Maine most strongly for his assertion that they were indistinguishable; the assoction of the two, in his view, is a comparatively late development. Hoebel, on the other hand, defends Maine on this point. Hocart believed that the dualism between religion and the secular authority (the state) originated in a division of function between a "sky-king," who was the supreme regulator and as such responsible for law, and an "earth-king," who was charged with the task of dealing with evil and wrongdoing; the former was reflective and unimpassioned, the latter quick in decision and violent in action. The role of the "sky-king" would seem to have combined religion and law. Further, if Hocart is right there seems to be implicit in this the distinction between the primary, prescriptive patterns of conduct and the secondary machinery of sanction; which leads on to the next point.

Fifthly, it is likewise agreed among anthropologists that there is, at any rate as far as contemporary primitive societies are concerned, a phenomenon that can be isolated from religious and other social observances and for which the term "law" would be convenient. This consists of rules of behaviour concerning the relations of individuals *inter se* and of groups, i.e., primary patterns of conduct importing an "ought." Gluckman has shown that among the Barotse the laws consist mainly of positive injunctions, "You ought," rather than negative, "you ought not." These "oughts" of primitive law are distinguishable from others by the nature of the obligation to obey them. It was a cardinal point of Malinowski's thesis, supported by Hogbin, that obedience rests on the reciprocity of services. People do unto others what the law bids them do because they depend on some service in return as part of their mutual co-existence. It is spontaneous and incessant goodwill that promotes and preserves social existence. It might well be that the ceremonial with which these services are usually rendered underlines their obligatory character, but this is of minor significance. Moreover, it is obedience, not disobedience, that is contemplated by law, the primary rule, not sanction. But some mechanism there has to be for dealing with cases of conflict and breach. As long as obedience prevails there is no call for this machinery. Examples of its working are also of interest. For instance, the records kept by Gluckman of the judicial processes among the Barotse show that the main task is reconciliation rather than the ordering of sanctions, which implies that even at the secondary stage an attempt is made to ensure conformity with the primary pattern of conduct. Sanctions apply only when reconciliation has failed or is not possible. One form which these take is to abandon the wrongdoer to the avenger, who has the moral support of the community behind him. In other cases, compensation may be payable to the victim, and it is a matter of dispute whether vengeance preceded compensation or whether they existed side by side. This is why it is difficult to distinguish between civil and criminal wrongdoing in early societies. The question depended on whether the action was thought to affect the society or only the individual. In the result, the conclusion which most anthropologists have reached is that what is called "law" should be described in terms of its function and the attitude of the people towards it rather than in terms of form or enforcement. It would appear to be something compulsorily observed and certainly far from what is commanded or backed by sanction.

Lastly, another point, which has emerged from modern investigations, is the disposal of the belief in communism as the primitive form of society. This may be seen in many ways, particularly in the prevalence of jealously protected private ownership of socially productive weapons and institutions, such as spells, incantations and, above all, ritual.

So far not much has been said, save indirectly, of the organisation of government. In this connection the outstanding contribution of Hocart deserves mention, especially as his name is as yet little known among jurists. On the evidence collected from a large number of widely separated tribes in many parts of the world, Hocart came to the conclusion that the functions of modern government were gradually fitted into the framework of a machinery that was previously fulfilling other functions. In other words, the framework of government was there before there was any governing to be done. Man does not consciously seek government; he seeks life, and with that end in view he does one thing after another, evolving and adapting special procedures and techniques, till he finds himself governed. The means by which primitive societies sought life was ritual. The lives and well-being of individuals depended on the life and well-being of society. Ritual was therefore a social affair and society had to organise itself for it. The structure of ritual was such that different roles were assigned to different individuals and groups. In all this one may detect the origin of caste; the various castes that one finds, the fisher, the farmer, the launderer, the potter, etc., may not have derived from the trades that the people actually pursued, but from the roles they fulfilled in the ritual. There probably was some connection between trade and a role, for no doubt it was usual to assign to a person the role which he was fitted to fulfil whenever this was possible.

It was the organisation, founded on ritual, that was adapted for purposes of government. Since the king could not play every role simultaneously, he assigned to each chieftain a particular role which had a particular objective. The aim of the ritual was the control of nature so as to render it bounteous and abundant. The particular form which the ritual assumed in any given case depended on the aspect of nature which was to be controlled, whether sunshine or rain or harvest or game, etc. To the group that was identified with some aspect of nature was entrusted the ritual concerning it. It follows from this, first, that only the group that exclusively owned a particular ritual was competent to perform it; secondly, every ritual had its leader; thirdly, the performers did not merely imitate nature as it happened to be at the moment, but as they wanted it to behave, e.g., to shed rain at a time of drought—an "ought" not an "is"; fourthly, in order to control nature the performers had to become one with nature and identify themselves with it; and fifthly, such equivalence was accomplished by the "word," which thus acquired special significance.

There was always a tendency for rituals to coalesce in one person or group of persons. The greatest cumulator was the king, and this process of cumulation is centralisation. Even after the king had begun to fulfil several roles, his chiefs had to stand ready to lend their assistance if called on to do so. In the role of the sun the king became the supreme regulator of the world, and this regulative function assumed greater and greater importance and eventually became the mark of the king. The aim of the ritual, as has been remarked, was to make nature bounteous. It followed that nature should itself be amply provided before a generous return could be expected of it. The king being identified with nature, the prosperity of the people could only be achieved by making the king prosperous. Revenue and tribute were the means of making him so.

In these and various other ways Hocart discerned the outlines of government, the organs of which were fitted into the existing framework of ritual. It is not possible in this short space to pursue his demonstration further, nor to consider his parallel investigations into the meaning of ceremonial statements, doctrines and courtesies relating to monarchy even today. One thing which his analysis has endorsed is the prescriptive nature and function of primitive law.

Malinowski, Crime and Custom in Savage Society*

Conclusion and Forecast

. . . In modern anthropological jurisprudence, it is universally assumed that all custom is law to the savage and that he has no law but his custom. All custom again is obeyed automatically and rigidly by sheer inertia. There is no civil law or its equivalent in savage societies. The only relevant facts are the occasional breaches in defiance of custom—the crimes. There is no mechanism of enforcement of the primitive rules of conduct except the punishment of flagrant crime. Modern anthropology, therefore, ignores and sometimes even explicitly denies the existence of any social arrangements or of any psychological motives which make primitive man obey a certain class of custom for purely social reasons. According to Mr. Hartland and all the other authorities, religious sanctions, supernatural penalties, group responsibility and solidarity, taboo and magic are the main elements of jurisprudence in savagery.

All these contentions are, as I have already indicated, either directly mistaken or only partially true, or, at least, they can be said to place the reality of native life in a false perspective. . . .

The Melanesian of the region here treated has unquestionably the greatest respect for his tribal custom and tradition as such. Thus much may be conceded to the old views at the outset. All the rules of his tribe, trivial or important, pleasant or irksome, moral or utilitarian, are regarded by him with reverence and felt to be obligatory. But the force of custom, the glamour of tradition, if it stood alone, would not be enough to counteract the temptations of appetite or lust or the dictates of self-interest. The mere sanction of tradition—the conformism and conservatism of the "savage"—operates often and operates alone in enforcing manners, customary usage, private and public behaviour in all cases where some rules are necessary to establish the mechanism of common

---

* [From *Crime and Custom in Savage Society* 63-64, 64-68 (1926).

Bronislaw Malinowski (1884-1942), Polish by birth and British by choice, gained worldwide renown as a member of the Mond Anthropological Expedition to New Guinea and Melanesia in 1914. He served as Professor of Anthropology at London University until 1939, and as visiting professor at Yale until his death. *Crime and Custom in Savage Society* is one of Malinowski's outstanding contributions in the field of primitive law or legal anthropology. See also his article "A New Instrument for the Interpretation of Law," 51 *Yale L.J.* 1237 (1942). Other of his best-known works are: *The Family Among Australian Primitives* (1913); *Primitive Religion and Social Differentiation* (1915); *Sexual Life of Savages in Northwestern Melanesia* (1929). Two of his books have appeared posthumously: *Freedom and Civilization* (1944) and *The Dynamics of Culture Change* (1945).]

life and co-operation and to allow of orderly proceedings—but where there is no need to encroach on self-interest and inertia or to prod into unpleasant action or thwart innate propensities.

There are other rules, dictates and imperatives which require and possess their special type of sanction, besides the mere glamour of tradition. The natives in the part of Melanesia described have to conform, for example, to a very exacting type of religious ritual, especially at burial and in mourning. There are, again, imperatives of behaviour between relations. There exists finally the sanction of tribal punishment, due to a reaction in anger and indignation of the whole community. By this sanction human life, property, and, last though not least, personal honour are safeguarded in a Melanesian community, as well as such institutions as chieftainship, exogamy, rank and marriage, which play a paramount part in their tribal constitution.

Each class of rules just enumerated is distinguishable from the rest by its sanctions and by its relation to the social organization of the tribe and to its cultures. They do not form this amorphous mass of tribal usage or "cake of custom" of which we have been hearing so much. The last category, the fundamental rules safeguarding life, property and personality form the class which might be described as "criminal law"—very often over-emphasized by anthropologists and falsely connected with the problem of "government" and "central authority" and invariably torn out of its proper context of other legal rules. For—and here we come at last to the most important point—there exists a class of binding rules which control most aspects of tribal life, which regulate personal relations between kinsmen, clansmen and tribesmen, settle economic relations, the exercise of power and of magic, the status of husband and wife and of their respective families. These are the rules of a Melanesian community which correspond to our civil law.

. . . The binding forces of Melanesian civil law are to be found in the concatenation of the obligations, in the fact that they are arranged into chains of mutual services, a give and take extending over long periods of time and covering wide aspects of interest and activity. To this there is added the conspicuous and ceremonial manner in which most of the legal obligations have to be discharged. This binds people by an appeal to their vanity and self-regard, to their love of self-enhancement by display. Thus the binding force of these rules is due to the natural mental trend of self-interest, ambition and vanity, set into play by a special social mechanism into which the obligatory actions are framed.

With a wider and more elastic "minimum definition" of law, there is no doubt that new legal phenomena of the same type as those found in N. W. Melanesia will be discovered. There is no doubt that custom is not based only on a universal, undifferentiated, ubiquitous force, this mental inertia, though this unquestionably exists, and adds its quota to other constraint. There must be in all societies a class of rules too practical to be backed up by religious sanctions, too burdensome to be left to mere goodwill, too personally vital to individuals to be enforced by an abstract agency. This is the domain of legal rules, and I venture to foretell that reciprocity, systematic incidence, publicity and ambition will be found to be the main factors in the binding machinery of primitive law.

Hoebel, Primitive Law and Modern*

. . . Every people has its system of social control, some effective and some less so. And all but a few of the poorest have as a part of their control system a complex of behavior patterns and institutional mechanisms that we may properly treat as law. When this area of behavior we speak of as law is found in the culture of a preliterate people we call it primitive law. When it is found in the culture of contemporary or recent literate people, we call it modern.

. . . Not all social norms are legal norms. Some of them are non-legal (custom) and others are by-legal. But first, it is probably high time I make clear *what* should pass as legal.

A feature of all social norms, sub-legal and legal, is of course, regularity and expectancy. Norms are what people regularly do and what you count on them doing in the future. Legal norms have regularity, imperative authority, and, in addition, an element of officialdom. A norm, if it is legal, is a must. It is an imperative buttressed by coercive force to be called upon at need. Law has biting teeth, not always bared, but still having the power to rend and destroy, if necessary.

It is essential that we insist upon recognition of the absolute imperative, if we are to make the anthropological treatment of law meaningful and realistic. We must check the anthropological tendency to spread the

*[*Transactions of the New York Academy of Sciences*, Se. II, Vol. 5, (December, 1942), pp. 31, 36-40, 41. Reprinted by permission.

E. Adamson Hoebel (1906–   ) holds a Ph.D. in anthropology from Columbia University. He is currently Regents Professor of Anthropology at the University of Minnesota and has been a senior specialist at the East-West Center and a Fellow at the Center for Advanced Study in the Behavioral Sciences. Dr. Hoebel has published extensively in anthropological and law journals and serves on the editorial boards of the *Law and Society Review* and the *Natural Law Forum*. His major publications include *The Political Organization and Law-ways of the Comanche Indians, The Law of Primitive Man, The Cheyenne Way* (with K. N. Llewellyn), *The Comanches* (with Ernest Wallace), and *Anthropology*. With A. A. Schiller, he also translated from the Dutch and edited Haar's *Adat Law in Indonesia.*]

concept of law over the entire body of social control. To deny that law is limited to the operation of courts of the state is anthropologically sound, but to say that universal custom is law is evidence of muddy thinking. For example, Chapple and Coon's notion that a law is a symbolized "pattern of action for all the members of a group," while custom "is limited to the members of an institution or to part of an institution."[14] will get us nowhere in effecting an understanding of what is legal. Similarly vague and overbroad, Driberg has approached the analysis of law in East Africa with the idea that, "Law comprises all those rules of conduct which regulate the behavior of individuals and communities."[15] Gillin in his treatment of Carib law suggested an ephemeral extreme with the declaration that law, broadly considered, is simply that body of opinion within a group which regulates the behavior of the members of the group.[16] It may be happily noted that this custard pie concept of law does not make its way into the recent sociology by the team of Gillin and Gillin.[17]

Against these over-extended anthropological vagaries, consider the legal scientists' expression on the specificity of law. By the English analytical authority, Salmond, rules of law are said to be, "The principles enforced by the State through judicial authorities by physical force in the pursuit of justice whether attained or not."[18] From the great and liberal German, Jhering, we learn that, "Law without force is an empty name."[19] "A legal rule without coercion is a fire which does not burn, a light that does not shine."[20] From the "pure theorist," Kelsen, comes the insistence that law in essence is "an external compulsive order."[21] And from our own great genius of the law, Holmes, "The foundation of jurisdiction is physical power."[22]

We shall err if we do not follow the students of jurisprudence in their analysis of coercive sanction as an important element in law.

14. Elliot D. Chapple and Carleton S. Coon, *Principles of Anthropology,* (New York: Henry Holt & Co., 1942), page 658.

15. J. H. Driberg, "Primitive Law in East Africa," (*Africa,* vol. 1, 1928) page 65.

16. John Phillip Gillin, "Crime and Punishment among the Barama River Carib of British New Guiana," (*American Anthropologist,* vol. 36, 1934), page 140.

17. John Lewis Gillin and John Phillip Gillin, *Sociology,* (New York: The Macmillan Co., 1942). . . .

18. John William Salmond, *Jurisprudence,* (London: Sweet & Maxwell, 1924).

19. Rudolph von Jhering, *Law as a Means to an End,* (New York: The Macmillan Co., translated by Isaac Husick, 1924), page 190.

20. Ibid., page 241.

21. Hans Kelsen, "The Pure Theory of Law," (*The Law Quarterly Review,* vol. 50, 1934), page 48.

22. Oliver Wendell Holmes, McDonald v. Mabee, (United States Reports, vol. 243), page 90; (United States Supreme Court Reporter, vol. 37), page 343.

In addition, we must reach a clear understanding of the element of officialdom. To the orthodox political theorist, legal philosopher, or law-man the official element in law means a state operating through courts. Here the anthropologist has a justifiable say in demanding that the inter-pretation of state and courts be wide indeed. It was in response to the demands of anthropological facts that Professor Max Radin was led to observe in reference to the official element in law: "But there is an infal-lible test for recognizing whether an imagined course of conduct is law-ful or unlawful. This infallible test, in our system, is to submit the ques-tion to the judgment of a court. In other systems, exactly the same test will be used, but it is often more difficult to recognize the court. None the less, although difficult, it can be done in almost any system at any time."[23] The ambiguous court, difficult to find in some systems, i.e., primitive systems which operate without institutionalized courts manned by a selected personnel of specialists may be the people's court of overtly expressed acceptance or rejection of the claim of a litigant as laid before the bar of public opinion. Remember, in a small primitive community all litigation of claims gathers a crowd of spectators, whose approval or dis-approval of the substantive grounds for the claims advanced by each liti-gant is expressed in one way or another.

In a primitive system of law, the official element means that any thing done or commanded in terms of the law is done or commanded for the well-being of the community. This is wholly true even in systems of so-called private law, or self-help. The aggrieved husband, out to punish the adulterous transgressor of his private marital privilege-rights, if he proceeds in accordance with established and recognized rules, has at least the tacit backing of general social approval. This gives him for the occasion an implicit social authority, and his acts are thereby quasi-official. In a modern law system, in contrast to most primitive ones, only a duly authorized and properly installed state official has the power to exercise the coercive legal imperatives. In our civil law (the field of private wrongs, or torts) the aggrieved party must take the the initiative in instituting legal action, but judgment on his claim and the execution of the judgment are reserved for the legal authorities. The provision of judicial and police officials to protect the demand-rights of the private citizen is our token of the public interest in, and recognition of, the as-pect of general social well-being in the private claim of the aggrieved.

It is in this sense that the point is made that there is no absolute dis-tinction between private and criminal law in either primitive law or mod-

23. Max Radin, "A Restatement of Hohfeld," (*Harvard Law Review*, vol. 51, 1938), page 1145.

ern.[24] This is not intended to maintain, as Professor Lowie has interpreted the argument, that there is no value in distinguishing crime from tort. We must agree with him that "the crystalized sense of public wrong" and "procedure by an agent of the state" are not minor matters.[25] In fact, the whole sweep of law in its evolution from primitive to modern has been in the direction of the supersedure of private law by public. But primitive law, which consists predominantly of private law, can be understood only by recognizing and insisting on the importance of the fact that the private prosecutor of a tortious transgressor is an implicit public official *protempore, pro eo solo delicto.*

In recapitulation, that which is characteristic of law is: (a) regularity —a common feature of laws of science and all social norms, legal and non-legal; (b) imperative sanctions, law is a "must" with biting teeth; and (c) an element of officialdom—recognized acceptance of the procedure and the prosecutor as operating for good of the society as a whole.

. . . This leads us to the lesson which the study of primitive law has to offer for the future. Today we have International By-law but no International Law. On the international level primitive law prevails. And only the most incipient type of primitive law at that! What has passed as international law consists of no more than normative rules for the conduct of affairs between nations as they have been enunciated and agreed upon from time to time by means of treaties, pacts, and covenants. In addition, prevailing custom in international intercourse, recognized by tacit consensus or verbalized in arbitration and world court awards, provides the other main source of its substance. But this body of social norms for international intercourse is as yet no more than the by-laws of the sub-groups we call nations.

International law, so-called, has consisted of substantive rules without imperative legal sanctions.

Whatever the idealist may desire, force and the threat of force are the ultimate power in the determination of international behavior, as in law within the nation or tribe. But until force and the threat of force are brought under the socialized control of the world community, by and for the world society, they remain the instruments of social anarchy and not the sanction of world law.

The metamorphosis from primitive law to modern on the plane of international intercourse awaits the emergence of the consciousness of

24. Cf., Karl N. Llewellyn and E. Adamson Hoebel, *The Cheyenne Way: Conflict and Case Law in Primitive Jurisprudence,* (The University of Oklahoma Press, 1941), pages 47–50.

25. Robert H. Lowie, Review of *The Cheyenne Way. (American Anthropologist,* vol. 44, 1942), pages 478-479.

world community by all men. The immediate and unmistakable conclusion from the study of the anthropology of law is that this metamorphosis must and will be turned. The only question is—when? If fulfillment comes in our day, it shall be our happy destiny to participate in the greatest event in legal history.

Llewellyn & Hoebel, The Cheyenne Way*

We have no desire to insist on words, so let us leave it this way: Norms, "right ways," departure from which involves somebody's doing something about it, are significantly different from norms whose disregard has no such consequence. And the feature of something's being done about it, and done with felt propriety, the feature of who does something, and of what that something is—these are sufficiently significant in what a developed society conceives of as "law" to give some hope of being worth watching accurately in a less developed one. A person can watch them effectively, however, only in cases of departure, of dispute, of trouble.[4]

For, to repeat, the idea of "legality" carries with it the idea not only of right, but of remedy. It includes not only the idea of prescribed right conduct, but that of prescribed penalty (or type of penalty) for wrong. Part of the process of specializing law-stuff out of the vague general matrix of what-is-and-ought-to-be-done, into some more particularized recognizability, is the specializing out also of recognizably proper persons to deal with offenders; or of recognizably proper ways of dealing with offenders and of recognizable limits on proper dealing with them.

And at whatever moment, in any culture, such matters come to take on clarity enough to be *felt*, at that moment begins an eternal juristic struggle. It is the struggle between an institution as a structure and the life purpose of the institution. In the case of law-stuff it takes the form of a struggle between the recognized form, which limits at once arbitrariness, passion, and vision and the underlying function of justice and social wisdom, to serve which the form first came into being. Perfection of

*[Pp. 24, 26-29. From *The Cheyenne Way: Conflict and Case Law in Primitive Jurisprudence*, by K. N. Llewellyn and E. Adamson Hoebel. Copyright 1941 by the University of Oklahoma Press. Reprinted by permission.

For biographical information, see pages 212 and 762 supra.]

4. See E. A. Hoebel, The Political Organization and Law-Ways of the Comanche Indians (*Memoirs of the American Anthropological Association*, No. 54, 1940, Supplement to *American Anthropologist*, Volume 42, No. 3, Part 2), 45-49

the legal, unmitigated, is also perfection of legalism. And again the test of what is there lies only in the cases of trouble, dispute, breach, disturbance; for no "norms" for lay conduct, however explicit, and few "norms" for the conduct of tribunals or officials, give much light on the juristic "way" of the society. They tell little about whether the "norm" and the official are made to serve the people, or whether the people are made to serve the official or the "norm." The techniques of "use" of any legal form or rule are, if anything, more important than the form and rule themselves. The techniques of operation of the legal personnel, and the latter's manner of handling the techniques—these commonly cut further into the nature of a society's legal system than does the "law" itself. But they must be dug out of the cases in which actual troubles have been dealt with.

There is another point in which the case of trouble or disturbance seems crucial in the evidence it offers. "Law," as we see it, purports to speak for and lay down norms for the Entirety which is in question. If in a given society one can recognize, for instance, a tribe, various associations, a governmental staff, bands, and families, he recognizes thereby a number of subgroups—smaller entities within the great Entirety. No such subgrouping can fail to have its own order, and some disruptions within this smaller order are to be expected. We are as little inclined to treat the handling of such disruptions as per se pertaining to the law *of the tribe* as we are to disregard the possibility that they may so pertain. If a mother in a primitive culture may spank her naughty child without interference or ostracism by her neighbors or the authorities, then it seems probable that under tribal law she has leeway to do so. If most mothers do, then use of the leeway seems to be tribal practice, felt socially as right practice. If unreasonable or extreme spanking results in trouble, then questions emerge concerning how far the leeway accorded by tribal law extends. But the whole focus changes if a family is viewed as a unit. There may then be found utterly and radically different bodies of "law" prevailing among these small units, and generalization concerning what happens in "the" family or in "this type of association" will have its dangers. The total picture of law-stuff in any society includes, along with the Great Law-stuff of the Whole, the sublaw-stuff or bylaw-stuff of the lesser working units. The two are not the same, but they are both important. Both are needed to complete the picture, but they cannot be presented without confusion if they are not distinguished. Accurately seeing what entirety is involved in each given instance, and how far the revealed norm ranges throughout the society studied, is greatly furthered by focusing on the cases of trouble, and especially on who it is that takes action, and with what support of opinion or active aid. Description is in turn made materially easier by distinguishing tribal or societal law-stuff from the bylaw-stuff of any smaller grouping.

All the above matters go to the value of the case of trouble as a main road into inquiry, in terms of its offering objective evidence which furthers needed discriminations, in terms of its giving sharper context to the data; in terms of its affording material which can be *known* to be more than merely what "is done" in general living, or merely what men *say* ought to be done in general living.

There are, however, two other aspects of the study of cases of trouble which warrant no less attention. The first has to do with the relation of the culture to the individual. The second has to do with the living interaction of differing aspects of the culture.

The case of trouble may have for the individual a quality of crisis. The man and his society or his subgroup appear in dramatic relation at a moment of maximum pressure, each upon the other. The study of crises is not the study of the normal and the regular; let that be granted. Nonetheless, the study of series of such crises offers a possibility of study of a culture at work on and through its people, for which no schematization of "norms" can substitute. It offers an insight into the personality factors when those factors glow in the white heat of internal, as well as of external, conflict. And, as the good case lawyer knows, it offers for a schematization of norms a set of sure foundation points, each of which has stood the test of trial.

The case of trouble, again, is the case of doubt, or is that in which discipline has failed, or is that in which unruly personality is breaking through into new paths of action or of leadership, or is that in which an ancient institution is being tried against emergent forces. It is the case of trouble which makes, breaks, twists, or flatly establishes a rule, an institution, an authority. Not all such cases do so. There are also petty rows, the routine of law-stuff which exists among primitives as well as among moderns. For all that, if there be a portion of a society's life in which tensions of the culture come to expression, in which the play of variant urges can be felt and seen, in which emergent power-patterns, ancient security-drives, religion, politics, personality, and cross-purposed views of justice tangle in the open, that portion of the life will concentrate in the case of trouble or disturbance. Not only the making of new law and the effect of old, but the hold and the thrust of all other vital aspects of the culture, shine clear in the crucible of conflict.

The trouble-cases, sought out and examined with care, are thus the safest main road into the discovery of law. Their data are most certain. Their yield is richest. They are the most revealing.

Gluckman, Introduction: The Process of
Tribal Law*

. . . Up to the year 1940, reports on the settlement of disputes among tribal peoples were relatively meager, and few of them worked out a detailed analysis of how mediating, arbitral, or judicial procedure and logic were applied to a series of cases. In 1940 an anthropologist, E. A. Hoebel, published *The Political Organization and Law-ways of the Comanche Indians.* He acknowledges there the influence of his "stimulating association" with one of the most creative modern American jurists, Karl N. Llewellyn, whose recent death we mourn. In the following year they published in collaboration *The Cheyenne Way,* a study of how the Cheyenne handled what the authors called "trouble cases." They therein raised new problems and set new standards in the analysis of tribal law.[1] These monographs, and particularly the one on the Cheyenne, traced the course of each of over a hundred disputes from its inception, through its crisis and the reaction of tribal leaders both in terms of action and reasoning, to its settlement or petering out. The Cheyenne had the beginnings of the development of governmental authority, and both their chiefs and the six Soldier Societies in which men were grouped were able to seize jurisdiction in some disputes and compel the parties to submit to their adjudication and abide by their judgment. I cannot here

---

*[From *The Ideas in Barotse Jurisprudence* 1-7, 17-26 (1972).First published in 1965 by Yale University Press. Reprinted with minor amendment and a new preface in 1972 by Manchester University Press on behalf of the Institute for African Studies, University of Zambia. Reprinted here by permission.

Max Gluckman (1911-1975) held a D.Phil. in social anthropology from the University of Oxford, which he attended as a Rhodes Scholar after studying both social anthropology and law at the University of the Witwatersrand. He was director of the Rhodes-Livingstone Institute of Social Studies in British Central Africa, and a lecturer at Oxford; since 1949 he was professor of social anthropology at the University of Manchester. In addition, he directed work in India and in Britain, notably in the field of industrial sociology and did field research in Zululand, South Africa, and Barotseland, and Zambia, and more cursory studies among other tribes in Africa, as well as of soccer crowds in Britain. In recognition of his analysis of *The Judicial Process among the Barotse of Northern Rhodesia* (1955), the Yale Law School invited him to deliver the Storrs Lectures in Jurisprudence in 1963; these lectures were published as *The Ideas in Barotse Jurisprudence* (1965). Among his other books are *Economy of the Central Barotse Plain* (1940), *Essays on Lozi Land and Royal Property* (1943), *Administrative Organization of the Barotse Native Authorities* (1943), *Malinowski's Sociological Theories* (1948), *Custom and Conflict in Africa* (1954), and *Politics, Law and Ritual in Tribal Society* (1965).]

1. Among American anthropologists who have worked in the same way are Richardson on The Kiowa (1940), Lips on the Naskapi (1947), W. Smith and Roberts on the Zuni (1954), and Pospisil on the Kapauku (1958). Hoebel also wrote a general book, *The Law of Primitive Man* (1954), which concentrates largely on juristic method.

do justice to the richness of the data or the stimulating penetration of this work as it exhibits the increasing juristic skill of Cheyenne leaders, while emphasizing the extent to which they suffered under an "absence of legal form." In the authors' own concluding words,

> For all the prodigality of juristic ingenuity, not enough of its results were cumulated into easily accessible patterns to draw minor trouble-festers to a head, and so to get them settled. This shows again and again in smouldering irritations over points of fact. It shows in the hanging-on of minor grievances. It shows in protest suicides which had too little reason. It shows in the nondevelopment of pipe-settlement into all the cases where pipe-settlement with its power of true appeasement would have been good to have. Had the chiefs of their own initiative, for instance, picked up pipe-carrying as a usual matter, the efficiency of the whole legal system would have been stepped up immeasureably.

In result, Llewellyn and Hoebel see Cheyenne juristic method just before the tribe lost its independence as poised between a stage when individual litigants suffered because there were not adequate legal forms, and a stage when legalism might creep in "to obscure the fundamental juristic task, that of getting the right answer with the tools at hand." Instead of having authorities secure in their powers of jurisdiction, the Cheyenne had "pleading-by-action, with a spectator waiting tensely for the apt moment to step in." Overall they graphically conclude that the Cheyenne system was "in full flux—while the buffalo vanish[ed] and the white man move[d] inexorably in. Cheyenne law leaped to its glory as it set."[2]

I may perhaps be interpreting into this analysis the implication that in the simplest legal systems proceedings are informal, and it is not necessary for plaintiffs to prosecute their suits in set forms. There is not yet a restriction imposed by rules like *ubi remedium, ibi jus,* such as existed in the early Roman and Anglo-Saxon law, which influenced Maine's analysis. If Llewellyn and Hoebel in fact meant to state this as a general, though as yet unsubstantiated, generalization, my own view is that they were correct.[3]

In most of the tribes of Africa, procedure is not trammeled by forms of pleading. Even among the nations of West Africa, whose economies approached those of the states of the Western Mediterranean in that slave labor was employed on plantations, there were no specific procedures or writs for bringing suit in court. One went to court and reported

2. *The Cheyenne Way* (1941), pp. 339-40.
3. Professor Hoebel informs me that this interpretation of their thesis is correct.

one's distress. The Ashanti of Ghana had a specific procedure, but it was a device to found jurisdiction, not a mode of pleading. Ashanti was a federation of smaller federations. If two persons in discrete political groups came into dispute they took an oath by the name of the chief under whose common authority they both fell, and this empowered him with authority to inquire into who was the ritual offender and incidentally give judgment on the substantive issue.

The procedure seems similar to that in early Roman times when suit was brought before the praetor by the *legis actio per sacramentum*. Of this Jolowicz states that since *sacramentum,* which denoted the stake forfeited by the loser, "literally means 'oath' it is supposed that, originally at any rate, the parties each made an oath as to the justice of their claims, and that what the judge had to decide was which oath was justified, the loser forfeiting a certain sum as penalty for his false oath."[6]

In Ashanti and other tribal law this kind of ritual formalism is characteristic of an uncertain jurisdiction, and the ritual element in it cannot be taken to show that early law was, or tribal law is, dominated by magic and religion.[7] The kind of formalism which demanded that action be brought in set words and forms, if it is general, apparently develops on the other hand only with writing, in the hands of a trained bureaucracy.[8] I have not found indications, in what I would call the true tribal societies, that any action has been ruled out of court because it did not accord with some formality. I venture to suggest that had the Cheyenne authorities developed a more complete jurisdiction over disputes, they would not have been restricted by any straitjacket of legal forms. Among the Barotse we are dealing with a powerful kingship exercising its authority through a hierarchy of councils which acted as parliaments, executives, and courts of justice; yet their proceedings in court, while highly marked by a distinctive etiquette, had no special procedures to restrict the search for redress by the allegedly aggrieved. Anyone could plead any suit in whatever words he himself pleased.

I do not think that the festering troubles, the smoldering irritations over points of fact, and the hanging-on of minor grievances, or even perhaps the suicides committed in protest among the Cheyenne, can be entirely ascribed to what Llewellyn and Hoebel call "absence of legal form." Minor grievances hang on, and irritation over points of fact ran-

6. *Historical Introduction to Roman Law* (1939), pp. 182 f. See also Maine, *Ancient Law* (1861, 1909 ed.), pp. 384-85.

7. For sound criticism of Maine on this point see Seagle, *The Quest for Law* (1941), Chap. 10.

8. This is clearly stated by Seagle as generally true, ibid., Chap. 8; Diamond, *Primitive Law* (1935), Chap. 30, 31.

kles in all small-scale fields of social relations, such as characterize tribal societies. I distinguish a society as "tribal" by several interrelated characteristics: there are only relatively simple tools, so that each worker produces little beyond what he can himself consume of the basic primary goods; since a wealthy man cannot eat more than a certain amount of food, wear luxurious clothes when only materials like skin, barkcloth, and a little cotton are available, or live in a palace when habitations are made of skin, grass, mud, and similar materials, these societies are marked by a basically egalitarian standard of living; trade goods may travel from hand to hand in a series of exchanges over distances, but the total volume of trade is limited.

Two important general results flow from this situation. First, the wealthy and powerful do not form what might be called a separate "class," cut off from the poor by a quite different style of life. . . .

Second, the usual settlements of these societies are camps, hamlets, or villages of a number of closely related families—what Ehrlich called "genetic associations." . . .

Despite these variations, in all societies of this type a grouping of some kind of kinsmen and/or kinswomen, with their spouses and usually their children, tends to live together. As a group, sometimes through particular representatives, they own certain rights, (which I shall later discuss) of access to land, in which they have other rights as members of smaller units and as individuals. As we shall see, goods are appropriated by the individual who produces them, despite some collaboration in productive activities, but consumption involves considerable and constant sharing.[9] . . .

I remember sitting conversing with a number of my own followers round a campfire in the cold of a winter night just outside the Barotse capital, when a ragged, middle-aged woman came out of the darkness and crouched beside us. We found it impossible to get any coherent information about herself from her, and my people concluded that she was mad. Eventually they told her that she could not stay with us, since there were only men in our camp. She asked us: "Is there a chief who drives the poor away from his fire?" My men remarked: "She is not mad. She has sense [or reason—it is the same word in Barotse]." After feeding her and taking her to her true chief's protection in the capital, they sadly shook their heads over her and said she must have become a wanderer, driven somewhat, but only somewhat, out of her senses by trying to use magic to make her fellow-wife lose the affection of their common husband—magic which had turned against its user.

9. I have analyzed a whole series of studies which support and fill in this brief summary in my *Politics, Law and Ritual in Tribal Society* (1965), Chap. 2.

This story brings home the emphatically personal nature of the relationships in these societies and their stress on the obligations of generosity and hospitality, as well as on liability and responsibility, rather than on immunity and power. The situation is magnificently illustrated by one of the Cheyenne cases cited by Llewellyn and Hoebel. When the Cheyenne launched their attacks on the herds of buffalo, one of the six Soldier Societies to which all men belonged, acted as policemen for the hunt. No one was supposed to charge upon a herd until they gave a signal, in order that all members of the tribe might have an equal chance to hunt successfully. Two young men once violated the rule. When the Soldier Society chief saw them riding down on the buffalo, he ordered his soldiers to pursue and whip them. The first men to reach them shot their horses and others smashed their guns, while all whipped them. Their father and the chiefs reprimanded them. Then the chiefs relented and said to their men: "Look how these two boys are here in our midst. Now they have no horses and no weapons. What do you want to do about it?" The police, out of their own resources, thereupon re-equipped the wrongdoers.[11]

. . . Since most people in any tribe live in a complex of social relations of this kind, a large number of the disputes arising over both property and the fulfillment of obligations are between kinsmen, or at least between persons in a quasi-kinship with one another. These disputes are therefore inevitably very entangled. . . . Barotse law, like all bodies of law, consists of a large number of rules of different kinds, which are not necessarily related logically; and juristic skill, in the Barotse's estimation, consists in the ability to find and apply the rule that will most appropriately give justice in the case under trial.

The determination of which rule is appropriate, and how it shall be applied, in these cases between kinsfolk or other persons mutually obligated in terms of status, is markedly influenced by the extent to which the parties have fulfilled or broken moral obligations. In addition, the judges may be influenced, both in assessing evidence and in forming a conclusion on the merits of the case, by the manner in which the parties have respectively observed codes of etiquette or conformed to ritual prescriptions and other customary modes of behavior. I therefore found that I could not in practice write about the Barotse judicial process without using the word "law" to cover these kinds of rules and conventions, as well as the rules which the judges enforce more specifically. My feeling that I must use the word law loosely, to cover several ranges of rules and conventions as well as certain procedures to secure redress, was strengthened by the fact that the issue on which the judges were adjudi-

11. *The Cheyenne Way* (1941), pp. 112-13.

cating was clearly not the narrow application of a single rule, or a small number of rules, to a set of facts. They were instead judging the general issue: whether particular people had behaved as reasonable incumbents of specified social positions.

Mr. Justice Holmes has said that "all rights are consequences attached to filling some situation of fact."[20] Barotse judges determine as the relevant facts in these cases the respective social positions of the parties and then how far each party has conformed to the obligations of his position. To these facts they then attach consequences, first in deciding which is more in the right, and second in deciding what rights they can enforce on his behalf. It seemed to me that I could not separate all these highly relevant judgments on facts, or the approval and disapproval evoked in the judges, from what might be called the final adjudicating ruling of the court over issues where they had the power to enforce action, and call the latter "law" and the former merely "moral." Moreover I found that the judges, in coming to a decision on the merits of the parties as reasonable incumbents of specific positions, were working with certain general presumptions about what is fair and proper, or just. . . .

Argument over the application of the word law, which has so many meanings in our own language, caused another eminent anthropologist to struggle at length in order to persuade his government that a specific body of rules was recognized as law by the Nuba of the Anglo–Egyptian Sudan, since breach of these rules provoked some kind of forceful physical retaliation, although the Nuba had no courts. He then had to report that the newly established Nuba courts did not in practice enforce all or only these particular rules. Above all, since in these kinds of societies there is a regular fulfillment of obligations according to a known code, and on the whole if facts are clear people can judge who was in the right and who in the wrong, it seemed inappropriate to me that Evans-Pritchard should state that "in the strict sense of the word law, the Nuer have no law," in an essay largely devoted to an analysis of regularity under rule in their lives. It was particularly inappropriate, since in another book he wrote about their law and their legal relations, and of "recognition by the one [losing] party of the justice of the other side's case."

Clearly there is no single "strict sense" of the word law in our own language, or the equivalent word in other European languages. Schapera has set out fully the multiple meanings of the equivalent word in Bechuanaland, as has Bohannan for the Tiv of Nigeria. This may be true of most or even all languages. The Barotse use *mulao*, which everyone including Barotse has translated as "law," to cover the following.

20. *The Common Law* (1881), p. 340.

1. What in other contexts we might better translate as custom, traditional usage, manner, habit, innate propensity, or technical rule of craft.
2. Properly legislated statutes and orders of their councils.
3. Decisions of these councils acting as courts of trial on particular disputes.
4. Orders issued by anyone in authority to his subordinates.
5. Traditional rules and institutions found among many tribes, which they call "the laws of tribes" [or of nations].
6. Traditional rules and practices particular to a single tribe or group of tribes.
7. General ideas about justice, equity and fairness, equality, and truth, which they believe should inform governing and adjudicating and which they call "laws of humankind" or "laws of God."
8. Certain specific moral premises about the appropriate relations between categories of persons, some of which they believe to be general to all peoples and hence to be "laws of humankind" and some of which they consider particular to themselves: these are perhaps what Kohler would have called their "jural postulates."
9. Regularities in their environment and in the behavior of persons —our laws of nature—which they call also "laws of God"; for them these laws have a moral implication, since their operation can be disturbed by immoral action and even thought.

The word *mulao* is also used in a personified manner, as when a judge says, "The law binds me as well as you" [the accused]; or "I am here to speak the law," or "The law is greater than I am."

Characteristic of almost all these uses of the word among the Barotse is the general idea of regularity and order and of rightness—what ought to be—either existing or to be striven for. In addition, the idea of law always contains also for them the idea of reason and sense and principle, all of which they call *ngana*. The implications of this idea are worked out in all their trials, where the standards by which parties and witnesses frame evidence and by which judges cross-examine and give judgment are the standards of "the reasonable man" (*mutu yangana*), specified in particulars for incumbents of varied positions in social life. . . .

[In] *The Province and Function of Law* (1947) Stone ended by refusing to define law. Stone himself has drawn my attention to Ehrlich, and again to Savigny, in a friendly and encouraging commentary on my book. But I am after all an anthropologist. Indeed when I began to find illumination in what I may call modern jurisprudence, and surrounded myself with books to further my analysis, I had to be reminded that my first duty was to analyze and present my field data, which I have done. Perhaps with my minimal understanding of modern jurisprudential theories, I was not prevented from allowing Barotse lawyers to speak for themselves. For this reason, I continue here unlearnedly to summarize the Barotse process of law as I observed it.

I found a multiplicity of meanings and possibilities of application to the facts of social life inherent in all the key terms of Barotse law. Their word, which we might translate in its commonest usage as "custom," covers many rules and items of behavior. . . . [I]n Barotse both right and duty are covered usually by a single word, derived from a verbal form which we can translate as "ought." There are, however, other words that can be specifically applied to what we would call "power," "privilege," and "claim." "Ownership" covers a variety of different situations. Anthropologists are happily in the position where their only obligation is to study social life. They are not called upon to improve it. Hence I was able to accept that this multiplicity of meanings—what the philosophers call "open texture"[28]—of terms was an inherent attribute of legal concepts, and that my task was to study the range covered by each word and to investigate what the judges did with the word. If I may use a metaphor, I tried to work out how the judges manipulated the uncertainty of words to give logical judgments in terms of general rules so as to achieve what they believed to be justice in individual cases, while maintaining the certainty of law and yet coping with the radical changes which Barotse life was undergoing as their country was absorbed into an alien polity and economy.

I believe that I was able to demonstrate through a series of cases that the judges in fact succeeded in both these aims. In consequence, even though the Barotse felt that the outcome of any piece of litigation might be uncertain, they also insisted that they lived by a code of law that was well known and certain. I have spoken of a paradox in which "the 'certainty' of law resides in the 'uncertainty' of its basic concepts."[30] Independently, therefore, I stated for the Barotse what Stone said of all law, when he considered what jurisprudents had worked out, and wrote:

> The defence of legal "certainty" insofar as it assumes that certainty can be attained by continuing to adhere closely to logical development of the "principles of law," is defending what has never existed. The appearance of certainty and stability in legal rules and principles conceals existing uncertainty.

28. Hart, *The Concept of Law* (1961), passim. I repeat that Stone's most learned and penetrating discussion of all these problems in *The Province and Function of Law* (1946) has driven home to me my temerity in ever daring to write on the Barotse judicial process in such general terms, and emphasized how much I would have profited from reading the studies of Ehrlich and many other jurists I cannot cite.
30. *Judicial Process among the Barotse* (1955), p. 326.

Stone then quotes Cardozo, Ehrlich, and other jurists to the same effect.[31] My own discussion of how social conditions and changing interests, standards of morals, and measures of reasonableness in Barotseland controlled development of the law by judges had also been far better worked out by Western jurists.[32] Nevertheless I should like to continue presenting Barotse ideas as I saw them before I extended my learning a little.

At that time I was struck by a statement in an article, "Language and the Law," by Professor G. L. Williams, then of the University of London and now at Cambridge, that while lawyers on the whole "have appreciated the danger" of "the flatulencies that may gather round the unacknowledged puns of language," and "have been at pains to construct a moderately precise technical language . . . oddly enough, it is least precise in its most fundamental parts."[33] This is exactly what I had found among the Barotse. It seemed to follow that the most important ideas of any legal system might be the least precise, in having the most open texture, precisely because they had to cover the widest range of rules and processes of social control. I therefore attempted to arrange Barotse legal analysis in a hierarchy ranging from simple determinations such as whether people had left a village or been driven from it, through decisions that they were therefore in the wrong or in the right (guilty or innocent), to the consequence that they possessed rights in the case, to the ultimate decision that "law" supported them. As I did so I found that the outstanding characteristic at the upper levels of this hierarchy was that the concepts of substantive law were multireferential: they were applicable to a variety of different rules, processes, and situations of fact. . . .

I suggest also that legal concepts have two other attributes, whose importance has to be analyzed. Concepts are *absorbent* in that they can draw into themselves a variety of raw facts of very different kind. They are also *permeable,* in the sense that they are at any one time permeated by certain principles, presumptions, prejudices and postulates, which the judges hold to be beyond question. Many of our own legal concepts exist among the Barotse: law, property rights, marriage, and wrong, but they are permeated by quite different presumptions, derived from Barotse society as a whole. When the Barotse say, "If you are invited to a meal and a fish bone sticks in your throat, you cannot sue your host," their attitude agrees with that of the Romans, and ourselves, that *volenti non fit injuria.* But the situations to which they apply this doctrine differ

31. *Province and Function of Law* (1947), pp. 204-05.
32. Ibid., pp. 170-71, Chap. 21-23.
33. Williams, *Law Quarterly Review,* 61 (1945/46), 179.

widely from the situations to which we apply it, as ours differ from those of the Romans. Yet it is clear that common legal problems thus confront very different types of society. . . .

Pospisil, Legal Levels and Multiplicity of Legal Systems*

"Where there are subgroups that are discrete entities within the social entirety," Hoebel has observed, "there is political organization—a system of regulation of relations between groups, or members of different groups within the society at large." Since all human societies contain some sort of subgroups (e.g., families, clans, bands, communities, etc.), Hoebel's statement implies universality of political organization—a virtual absence of human societies without pertinent political structures. Moreover, this concept is of paramount importance for a proper presentation and analysis of any political and, consequently, any legal system because it emphasizes the relationship that necessarily exists between such a system and the conglomeration of a society's subgroups. Since the regulation of the network of interrelations that gives this conglomeration its particular structure is the essence of the society's political organization, no significant analysis of the politics or law can be made without a proper and consistent reference to the particular system of subgroups to which it pertains.

Yet there are numerous anthropological studies that fail to relate accounts of political and legal organizations to the segmentation systems of the pertinent societies. Although one invariably finds an exposition of the membership characteristics and functions of the subgroups, the individual natives are usually not portrayed as taking part in the various activities primarily as members of such groups. Presentations are so focused upon the role and status of the individual that he appears to

*[From *Anthropology of Law: A Comparative Theory* 97-107, 112, 119-120, 124-126 (Harper & Row 1971) (some footnotes omitted). Reprinted by permission.

Leopold Pospisil (1923–) is professor of anthropology and director of the Anthropology Division at the Peabody Museum, Yale University. He holds a Ph.D. in anthropology from Yale (1956), an M.A. from the University of Oregon (1952), and a J.U.C. (law degree) from the Charles University of Prague, Czechoslovakia. His major fields of interest are political structure and anthropology of law and social structure. He has conducted field research among the Hopi Indians (1952), Kapauku Papuans of New Guinea (1954-1955), Nunamiut Eskimo of Alaska (1957), and Tirolean mountain farmers (1962-1963, 1964, 1965, 1966, 1967). He has written three books: *Kapauku Papuans and Their Law* (1958), *Kapauku Papuan Economy* (1963), and *The Kapauku Papuans of West New Guinea* (1963), and has published in professional journals and symposia.]

participate directly in the life of the society as a whole. As a consequence, a misleading impression of a "monolithic society" consisting of inter-acting individuals, rather than a complex society composed of subgroups of different membership inclusiveness, is likely to be created. It is one of the basic premises of this chapter that social relations (relations of indi-viduals to ego) as well as societal relations (relations among the segments of a society) are equally important for a meaningful analysis of a political and legal system.

In purely legal matters the anthropology of law has also neglected societal structure (segmentation of the society into its constituent sub-groups;). . . . Law of a primitive people has been almost invariably de-scribed as an expression of a well-integrated single legal system with few, if any, inconsistencies and discrepancies in its content and application. If any of the most obvious deviations from the abstract "prevailing rule" is described, its existence is explained as a variation or aberration, or it is flatly denied legality and labeled "illegal." Had the importance of sub-groups for analysis of political organization, so well expressed in the above quotation from Hoebel, always been borne in mind by the anthro-pologist, his analysis of the power structure and social control of a society could not have been presented as a politically integrated system with a single, smoothed out, all-embracing legal system. Instead, careful analy-sis would have revealed marked differences in the judiciary activity and informal social control exercised by the authorities of the various sub-groups. Any human society, I postulate, does not possess a single consist-ent legal system, but as many such systems as there are functioning sub-groups. Conversely, every functioning subgroup of a society regulates the relations of its members by its own legal system, which is of necessity different, at least in some respects, from those of the other sub-groups. . . .

History of the Idea of the Multiplicity of Legal Systems Within a Society

Traditionally, law has been conceived as the property of a society as a whole. As a logical consequence, a given society was thought to have only one legal system that controlled the behavior of all its members. Without any investigation of the social controls that operate on the sub-society levels, subgroups (such as associations and residential and kin-ship groups) have been *a priori* excluded from the possibility of regulat-ing their members' behavior by systems of rules applied in specific decisions by leaders of these groups—systems that in their essential characteristics very closely parallel the all-embracing law of the society.

This attitude was undoubtedly caused by the tremendous influence the well-elaborated and unified law of the Roman Empire exerted upon the outlook of the European lawyer. Had classical Greece exercised such influence over the legal minds of our civilization, our traditional concept of law might have been much more flexible and, cross-culturally speaking, "realistic." Most of the early ethnographers did not escape the traditionalist influence. Their insistence upon seeing law exclusively on the society level resulted either in a description of a simple, pervasive legal system in the investigated society, or, if the society under scrutiny did not have a comprehensive political organization and the ethnographer was not sophisticated enough to look for law elsewhere, in a denial of the existence of law among that people. This denial of law in a society that lacks an overall political organization has been maintained, for example, even by authors who have entitled their works *Nuer Law,* or *Leadership and Law among the Eskimos of the Keewatin District Northwest Territories* (Howell 1954: p.225; van den Steenhoven 1962: p. 112).

The tendency to dissociate law from the structure of the society and its subgroups (society's segments) has unfortunately persisted until the present time and led Spencer to treat the laws of the Tagemiut and Nunamiut Eskimos as if they belonged to a single system. An extreme of this traditionalist tendency has possibly been reached by Berndt. In his book *Excess and Restraint* (1962), he treated law and social control as though they were unrelated to the societal structure in which they occurred and represented some sort of a supracultural material. He discussed the law of four linguistically and culturally different Papuan societies (Jate, Usurufa, Fore, and Kamano) as if it constituted a single consistent legal system. Accordingly, his cases of conflict and dispute were taken from wherever they occurred, lacking identification with the groups within which the controversies arose. As a result, the reader is often not even sure of the ethnic provenience of the litigants. Even if one is quite ethnocentric and biased by the tradition of the West, one can hardly argue that the legal systems of four different Papuan peoples are identical.

Even when the close relationship between law and societal structure has been suggested by an ethnographer, a subsequent report of the same society by another author may neglect the suggestion and follow the old traditional path. For example, in spite of Evans-Pritchard's outstanding account of the Nuer social organization, Howell's analysis of law of this Nilotic tribe became so heavily influenced by the traditionalist view that it disregarded confirmations of the relationship between the social control and the subgroups that Evans-Pritchard had made quite explicit. The latter contended, for instance, that "the structural interrelations of tribal segments are seen in the relativity of law, for Nuer law is relative like the structure itself" but this went apparently unnoticed by Howell, who concluded his study of Nuer law with the following summary:

> It is less confusing to adopt the hypothesis that the extent of the law is limited to social control which is maintained by organized legal sanctions and applied by some form of organized political mechanism. By this definition, the Nuer had no law, for, as we have already seen, there was in the past nothing in the nature of politically organized society. (1954: p. 225)

True enough, the Nuer had no law on the levels of the society or tribe. This had been recognized by Evans-Pritchard, who stated:

> In a strict sense Nuer have no law. . . . In Nuerland legislative, judicial, and executive functions are not vested in any persons or councils. Between members of different tribes there is no question of redress; and even within a tribe, in my experience, wrongs are not brought forward in what we would call a legal form, though compensation for damage (*ruok*) is sometimes paid. (1940: p. 162)

However, this is not the full story of the Nuer law for Evans-Pritchard, who acknowledges its existence in a significantly qualified way: "The first point to note about Nuer law is that it has not everywhere the same force within a tribe, but is relative to the position of persons in social structure, to the distance between them in the kinship, lineage, age set, and, above all, in the political systems." Indeed, when one turns to the Nuer tribal subgroups, for example to the individual settlements, one finds that "within a village differences between persons are discussed by the elders of the village and agreement is generally and easily reached and compensation paid, or promised, for all are related by kinship and common interests." In other words, while the Nuer society as a whole, or its individual tribes, are not legally organized, law does exist on a lower level in the Nuer villages, where the elders use it in their settlement of disputes. Thus, contrary to Howell's conclusion, the Nuer did not represent a society without law.

In her article on "Conflict Resolution in Two Mexican Communities" Laura Nader gives credit to Mauss and Malinowski for the idea that within a single society several legal systems may be operating, "complementing, supplementing, or conflicting with each other" (Nader 1963: p. 584). Unfortunately, although the implication of the existence of a multiplicity of legal systems within a society may be drawn from the work of both of these scholars, neither of them stated this idea clearly. Actually, each in his own way maintained the existence of a single system of law in the Eskimo and Trobriand societies. Mauss described two legal systems that operated in Eskimo nuclear and extended families. However, instead of showing the coexistence of these two systems, Mauss claimed that one followed the other in a rhythm dictated by the seasons: the legal system of the nuclear family controlled the behavior of the Eskimo during the summer; in the wintertime, when nuclear families established common residence and became an extended family, a legal system for the larger group was instituted. One may justifiably wonder what happened to the nuclear family in the wintertime? Did it dissolve in the extended family group which somehow redefined the relationships between the nuclear family members for the duration of the arctic winter? From my research among the Nunamiut Eskimo I know quite well that the contrary is the case: both legal systems coexisted, functioning side by side, mainly by virtue of differentiated jurisdiction. Actually, among the Nunamiut Eskimo two additional legal systems functioned simultaneously with those of the nuclear and the extended family: that of the band and that of the band faction. Mauss, although describing two legal systems within an Eskimo society, failed to break away from the traditionalist doctrine: although there were two systems, only one, according to Mauss, was operational at a given time.

In contrast to Mauss, Malinowski did describe two conflicting systems of social control in the Trobriand society, both of which functioned at the same time. However, although his book provided a chapter with the heading "Systems of Law in Conflict," the content did not correspond to the title. He defined law as duties and rights based upon the matrilineal principle, but the relations deriving from the conflicting patrilineal principle he called merely "usage." Actually, thus, it was matrilineal law and "patrilineal usage" that were in conflict rather than two legal systems: "So that here the usage, established but non-legal, not only takes great liberties with the law, but adds insult to injury by granting the usurper considerable advantages over the rightful owner." Consequently, Malinowski also failed to conceptualize multiple legal systems within the same society and link them to the pertinent societal structure.

Although the traditionalist view that law is monopolized by the state, or the "society as a whole," has made a profound impact upon sociology and anthropology and, as we have seen, still persists in many of the recent works on law in these two fields, its simplicity failed to satisfy some noteworthy legal scholars. In contrast to what one might expect, it is interesting to learn that credit for the nontraditionalist trend of thought which did not limit its inquiry to the level of state or society must be given to jurisprudence rather than to the social sciences.

In 1868 the legal scholar Otto von Gierke had already directed attention to the inner ordering of the *Genossenschaften* (associations), and he recognized in them the essential features of law. Eugen Ehrlich, one of his followers, writes:

> As a result of his labors, we may consider it established that, within the scope of the concept of the association, the law is an organization, that is to say, a rule which assigns to each and every member of the association his position in the community, whether it be of domination or of subjection (*Überordnung, Unterordnung*), and his duties; and that it is now quite impossible to assume that law exists within these associations chiefly for the purpose of deciding controversies that arise out of the communal relation. (1936: p. 24)

So great was the enthusiasm of von Gierke for the more or less autonomous entities of the society's subgroups that he tended to an extreme view, diametrically opposed to the traditionalists' individualist legal thought of the nineteenth century. He promoted the associations to entities that somehow became distinct from the sum total of the members and of their interests. He went so far as to advance the idea of existence of a mystical "group-will" that was distinct from the wills of the members of such a group. Although this extremism obscured social reality by neglecting the role of the individual and by making a group of people into almost a living beast (thus giving rise to the unfortunate "Durkheimean trend" in sociology and anthropology), his emphasis upon the legal importance of the society's subgroups (associations) proved most significant in the subsequent development of legal thought, represented especially by Ehrlich, a lawyer.

Following in the footsteps of von Gierke, Eugen Ehrlich refused to accept legal orthodoxy and to recognize the state's (or society's) monopoly on law. Indeed, he explicitly stated that "It is not an essential element of the concept of law that it be created by the state, nor that it constitute the basis for the decisions of the courts or other tribunals, nor that it be the basis of a legal compulsion consequent upon such a decision." To Ehrlich, law was "an ordering" of human behavior, in any group of interacting people, no matter how small or how complex. To Ehrlich human society was not composed of individuals who acted independently, but of people who of necessity acted always as members of some of the society's subgroups. Thus the people's behavior is not necessarily ordered by the all-comprising state law, but primarily by the "inner ordering of the associations"—Ehrlich's "living law." "The inner order of the associations of human beings," writes Ehrlich, "is not only the original, but also, down to the present time, the basic form of law." Excellently and prophetically, Ehrlich points out in his own words the basic interrelationship of law and societal structure: "All attempts that have been made until now to comprehend the nature of law have failed because the investigation was not based on the order of the associations but on the legal propositions. Thus Ehrlich actually laid the foundations for the modern anthropology of law, allowing law to be in existence also within those societies which were not legally unified or politically organized.

Ehrlich's genius unfortunately failed when he inquired into the nature of the inner ordering of the society's subgroups. Being influenced by Gierke's philosophy of "group-will," he conceived of law as of the principles contained in the actual behavior of the members of the associations. To him, people conformed to these principles because of some amorphous social pressure of the association as a whole. He reacted so thoroughly against the traditionalist conception of the monopolistic state law (created by the order and will of the legislator) that he failed to uncover within the associations formal or informal leaders who actually influenced and molded what he called "living law." His unfortunate assumption that the source of law was the actual behavior of the people themselves rather than principles contained in the decisions of the leaders of the various associations led him to generalize about the living law as if the behavior of people in all the associations within the same society were identical. Thus he actually telescoped the various legal systems and subsystems of the associations into a more or less generalized whole called "living law," which he contrasted with the statutory law of the state "the legal propositions." However, no matter what our criticisms of Ehrlich may be today, it goes without saying that he revolutionized thought in the field that may be quite properly called the science of law, showing the way to the social scientists who, as he was writing, were still blinded by the European state-law tradition.

In his work *Wirtschaft und Gesellschaft* (1922) Max Weber, without trying to generalize for the laws of the various associations on the society's level and without attempting to force these into a nonrealistic "living law" that would contrast with the legal systems of the state, expressed quite explicitly the idea of the existence of several legal systems within a given society. First, he defined law so broadly as to be applicable to the ordering systems within the various social subgroups; then,

> for the sake of terminological consistency, we categorically deny that "law" exists only where legal coercion is guaranteed by the political authority. There is no practical reason for such a terminology. A "legal order" shall rather be said to exist wherever coercive means, of a physical or psychological kind, are available; i.e., wherever they are at the disposal of one or more persons who hold themselves ready to use them for

this purpose in the case of certain events; in other words, whenever we find a consociation specifically dedicated to the purpose of "legal coercion." (Weber 1967: p. 17)

Second, to Weber the nature of the coercion mechanism of the various consociations was not some sort of a mystical group will or group opinion but an authority, in many ways comparable to that of the state: "It goes without saying that this kind of coercion may be extended to claims which the state does not guarantee at all; such claims are nevertheless based on *rights* even though they are guaranteed by authorities other than the state." Thus Weber saw no basic qualitative difference between the state legal system and those systems created and upheld by the various subgroups of the society. He maintained no basic dichotomy comparable to Ehrlich's state law versus living law. Consequently, there is little doubt that Weber's sober approach to his inquiry into the nature of legal phenomena, by rejecting the mysticism and unnecessary pilosophizing of his predecessors in favor of an empirical disclosure of social reality, marks a very significant advance in the field of the sociological jurisprudence.

However, it was not until the joint effort of a lawyer and an anthropologist produced *The Cheyenne Way* (Llewellyn and Hoebel: 1941), that the idea of multiplicity of legal systems within a society was formulated, and the relationship of the society's law to the legal systems of the subgroups (associations) was explicitly stated. According to the two authors, investigation of the all-embracing legal system of a society as a whole (the traditionalist law) does not offer a complete and workable conception of the legal order within that society. "What is loosely lumped as 'custom' [on the society's level] can become very suddenly a meaningful thing—one with edges—if the practices in question can be related to a particular grouping." In other words, if one changes one's point of reference from that of the society as a whole and focuses upon the individual subgroups,

> there may then be found utterly and radically different bodies of "law" prevailing among these small units, and generalization concerning what happens in "the" family or in "this type of association" *made on the society's level* will have its dangers. The total picture of law-stuff in any society includes, along with the Great Law-stuff of the Whole, the sublaw-stuff or bylaw-stuff of the lesser working units. (1941: p. 28)

Although the authors did not systematically explore and contrast the differences between the various legal systems of the Cheyenne society's subunits, the book clearly laid the theoretical groundwork of a field of inquiry for the anthropologists of the future. Hoebel's subsequent departure from the well-expressed relativity of law and custom is to be regretted. In his more recent work he seems to hold a position that is not consonant with the views expressed above, and the orthodox emphasis upon the whole society's monopoly of the law appears to be resurrected when he states: "There are, of course, as many forms of coercion as there are forms of power. Of these, only certain methods and forms are legal. Coercion by gangsters is not legal. Even physical coercion by a parent is not legal if it is too extreme." But, of course, this is true only if we take the society as a whole as the point of reference. According to the society's legal system, some regulatory means of its subgroups may indeed be "illegal."

Legal Systems and Legal Levels

In one of my early articles I defined the political structure of a society as "a configuration of analytically derived relationships of those purposive activities of individuals and groups of individuals which establish or maintain authority and determine its legislative, executive and judicial functions." While anthropologists may agree in principle with this definition in discussing political structure, in their actual work they have often tended to concentrate so much on the relationships between individuals (describing fully their various roles and statuses) that they have deemphasized or even neglected the relationships of a society's subgroups. Thus a smooth, relatively static and simple picture of legal structure has been presented. Were the emphasis on subgroups always borne in mind by the ethnographers they could hardly have proposed such a simplified view of the social reality. Instead, they would have described a configuration of semiautonomous or autonomous groups possessing leaders with different personalities, abilities, education, and experience. If the judgments or decisions of these subgroup leaders engaged the author's attention, he would have to consider that they were based upon the application of different legal systems administered by these various leaders.

In my quantitative investigation of the disputes among the Kapauku Papuans, Nunamiut Eskimo, and Tirolean peasants I found that the decisions of the leaders of the various subgroups bore all the necessary criteria of law (in the same way that modern state law does): the decisions were made by leaders who were regarded as jural authorities by their followers (that means that the leaders' decisions were actually complied with—criterion of authority); these decisions were meant to be applied to all "identical" (similar) cases decided in the future (criterion of the intention of universal application); they were provided with physical or psychological sanctions (criterion of sanction), and they settled disputes between parties represented by living people, the decision being based upon the right of one party to a certain behavior from the other party and, conversely, obligating the other party to such a behavior (criterion of *obligatio*). Consequently, the judgments and decisions of the authorities of the various subgroups were legal in the subgroups in which they were issued, being based upon their particular legal systems.

Because of these findings I reject the traditional presentation of law on the level of the society only and follow the unorthodox path of legal thought characterized by von Gierke, Ehrlich, Weber, Llewellyn, and Hoebel. Indeed, I go a step farther and claim categorically that "every functioning subgroup of a society has its own legal system which is necessarily different in some respects from those of the other subgroups." Also, I am more radical than Llewellyn and Hoebel in proposing to delete the words "bylaw stuff" and "sublaw stuff" from the vocabulary of my discussion and refer to the matter that forms the content of the systems of social control of the subgroups as what it really is—the law (*ius*). Consequently, the totality of the principles incorporated in the legal decisions of an authority of a society's subgroup constitutes that subgroup's legal system. Since the legal systems form a hierarchy reflecting the degrees of inclusiveness of the corresponding subgroups, the total of the legal systems of subgroups of the same type and inclusiveness (for example, family, lineage, community, political confederacy) I propose to call *legal level*. As there are inevitable differences between the laws of different legal levels, and because an individual, whether a member of an advanced or a primitive society, is simultaneously a member of several subgroups of different inclusiveness (for example, a Kapauku is a member of his household, sublineage, lineage, and political confederacy, all the groups being politically and legally organized), he is subject to all the different legal systems of the subgroups of which he is a member. Consequently, law in a given society differs among groups of the same inclusiveness (within the same legal level); thus different laws are applied to different individuals. Law also exhibits discrepancies between legal systems of subgroups of different inclusiveness (between different legal levels), with the consequence that the same individuals may be subject to several legal systems different in the content of their law to the point of contradiction. . . .*

The multiplicity of legal systems in civilized societies has long been realized and mentioned in the legal literature by such authors as von Gierke, Ehrlich, Weber, and Llewellyn; its validity need not be demon-

---

*[In the omitted portion, the author discusses the multiplicity of legal systems in the Kapauku tribe.]

strated. It suffices here merely to point out, in a very sketchy way, examples of multiplicity of legal systems in three civilizations—the West, the Chinese, the Inca—that are not related to each other by legal tradition.

In a Western society that is composed of autonomous or semiautonomous administrative units, such as the United States, there exist, besides the federal or national legal system that is applied to the whole society (nation), the legal systems of its component states, many provisions of which actually contradict and conflict with federal law and the constitution. Many of these flagrant contradictions have been maintained until the present, when some of them are being ruled out by the U.S. Supreme Court as unconstitutional (e.g. state laws pertaining to segregation and racial discrimination), while others are being carried on into the future. However, the multiplicity of legal systems does not end, according to von Gierke, Ehrlich, Weber et al., at the level of the states. These authors clearly recognize that the various associations within the states have also formal bodies of regulations which, in essence, belong in the field of law, especially when they are recognized as valid by the superimposed state law.

I would like to go even farther and acknowledge the existence of legal systems in any organized group and their subgroups within the state. Consequently and ultimately, even a small grouping such as the American family has a legal system administered by the husband, or wife, or both, as the case may be. Even there, in individual cases, the decisions and rules enforced by the family authorities may be contrary to the law of the state and might be deemed illegal. Indeed, there are ruthlessly enforced legal systems of groups whose existence and *raison d'être* are regarded by the state not only as illegal but even criminal. That criminal gangs such as Cosa Nostra have their rules, judicial bodies, and sanctions that are more severe than those of the state, is common knowledge. What is not realized is that their rules and judicial decisions embody the same types of criteria as does the state law (authority's decision, *obligatio*, intention of universal application, sanction). Therefore the principles contained in the gang leaders' decisions qualify to be regarded as parts of legal systems, although these would be illegal, criminal, and invalid according to the legal systems of the states. To disregard such systems, as is often done in the writings of legal scholars, reflects not a cool scientific introspect but a moral value judgment that has its place in philosophy but not in the sociology or anthropology of law. . . .*

---

*[In the omitted portion, the author discusses the multiplicity of legal systems in two other "civilized" systems, which were unrelated by legal tradition, the Chinese and the Inca.]

Dynamics of Legal Levels

The number and types of legal levels in a given society is, of course, not constant. Some types of political groupings within a society may disappear (for example, a collapse of a centralized government with a subsequent shift of sovereignty to the formerly unified provinces), and new types may be created. From the logical point of view new levels may be created by subdividing existing groups of a given level or by unifying them into more inclusive groups, thus superimposing in the existing hierarchy a new level upon the old one. In the recent history of Western civilization we find plenty of examples of segmentation of political groups into new types of units of a lower level. For example, by introducing the administrative and legislative dualism of Austria and Hungary, the once monolithic Habsburg Empire interposed a new ploitical and legal level between that of the Empire and its individual "lands."

Among the primitives, segmentation usually occurs in a gradual and informal way, as a response to some demographic, economic, or political pressure, rather than through an authoritative and formal act of a political nature. . . .

Conclusion

The essential feature of law is its existence in concrete legal decisions. Rules for behavior that are not applied in legal decisions and consequently not enforced, although appearing in codifications in the form of dead laws, do not belong in the realm of law proper for the simple reason that they do not exercise social control. The essential feature of legal decision, in turn, is that a third party (authority) possesses the privilege to pass it. Furthermore, in order to pass a legally relevant decision whose provisions can actually be enforced, the adjudicating authority has to have power over both parties to the dispute—he must have jurisdiction over both litigants. In anthropological or sociological language this means that all three, the two litigants as well as the authority, have to belong to the same social group in which the latter wields judicial power (has jurisdiction). Law thus pertains to specific groups with well-defined membership; it does not just "float around" in a human society at large.

Because of this fact we should not expect to find law pertaining to a society as a whole if the society is not politically organized (unified). That, of course, does not mean that law would be absent in such a society. Society, be it a tribe or a "modern" nation, is not an undifferentiated amalgam of people. It is rather a patterned mosaic of subgroups that belong to certain, usually well-defined (or definable) types with different memberships, composition, and degree of inclusiveness. Every such subgroup owes its existence in a large degree to a legal system that is its own and that regulates the behavior of its members. Offenses within such a group cannot go unpunished and disputes cannot be allowed to continue indefinitely lest they disrupt and destroy the social group. Thus the existence of social control, which we usually call law, is of vital necessity to any functioning social group or subgroup. As a consequence, in a given society there will be as many legal systems as there are functioning social units.

This multiplicity of legal systems, whose legal provisions necessarily differ from one to another, sometimes even to the point of contradiction, reflects precisely the pattern of the subgroups of the society—what I have termed "societal structure" (structure of a society). Thus, according to the inclusiveness and types of the pertinent groups, legal systems can be viewed as belonging to different legal levels that are superimposed one upon the other, the system of a more inclusive group being applied to members of all its constituent subgroups. As a consequence, an individual is usually exposed to several legal systems simultaneously —to be exact, to as many systems as there are subgroups of which he is a member. This conception of a society as a patterned mosaic structure of subgroups with their specific legal systems and with a dynamic center of power brings together phenomena and processes of a basically legal nature that otherwise would be put into nonlegal categories and treated as being qualitatively different. It helps us to understand why a man in one society is primarily a member of his kin group or village and only secondarily of the tribe or state, whereas in another society the most inclusive, politically organized unit (a tribe or a state) controls him most. A gangster's behavior is not "absolutely illegal"; while it is definitely so on the state or national legal level, it has to be, at the same time, regarded as legal from the viewpoint of the gang. The field of law, it is obvious, does not escape the spreading notion of relativity.

Reflecting upon the above data and their interpretation, I have arrived at this conclusion: the examples and discussion have made it abundantly clear that any penetrating analysis of law of a primitive or civilized society can be attained only by relating it to the pertinent societal structure and legal levels, and by a full recognition of the plurality of legal systems within a society. After all, law as a category of social phenomena cannot be considered (as it traditionally has been) unrelated to the rest of the organizing principles of a society.

Bohannan, The Differing Realms of the Law*

Anthropology, including legal anthropology, is faced with a problem that may be unique in social science: in order to present the results of our field research without seriously warping the ideas, we must undertake a second job of research, on the homologous institutions of our own society, and in the scientific disciplines that have investigated those institutions. This paper is an exercise in the anthropological investigation of jurisprudence. It investigates three things: (1) definitions that jurisprudence has used, and the anthropological usefulness of such definitions, (2) the "double institutionalization" of norms and customs that comprises all legal systems, and (3) some of the problems of the association between legal institutions and certain types of political organization.

Legal Language

It is likely that more scholarship has gone into defining and explaining the concept of "law" than any other concept still in central use in the social sciences. Efforts to delimit the subject matter of law—like efforts to define it—usually fall into one of several traps that are more easily seen than avoided. The most naive, on the one hand, beg the question and use "law" in what they believe to be its common-sense, dictionary, definition—apparently without looking into a dictionary to discover that the word "law" has six entries in Webster's second edition (1953), of which the first alone has thirteen separate meanings, followed by five columns of the word used in combinations. The most sophisticated scholars, on the other hand, have been driven to realize that, in relation to a noetic unity like law, which is not represented by anything except

*[67 *American Anthropologist,* Special Publication, *The Ethnography of Law* 33-37 (1965) (footnotes omitted). Reproduced by permission of the American Anthropological Association from the American Anthropologist vol. 67 (no. 6, pt. 2): 33-37, 1965.

Paul Bohannan (1920–   ) is the Stanley G. Harris Professor of Social Science at Northwestern University. He has degrees from the University of Arizona and Oxford and has taught at Oxford and Princeton as well as at Northwestern. During 1963-1964 he was a fellow at the Center for Advanced Studies in the Behavioral Sciences. He has done research among the Tiv of Nigeria, the Wanga of Kenya, and divorcees in San Francisco. His interest in law is peripheral to a more general interest in problems of aggression and social control. He is editor of the American Museum Sourcebooks in Anthropology, and author of *Justice and Judgment Among the Tiv* (1957), *Social Anthropology* (1963), *Africa and Africans* (1964), *Tiv Economy* (1968), *Divorce and After* (with Mark Glazer, 1970), and *High Points in Anthropology* (1973).

man's ideas about it, definition can mean no more than a set of mnemonics to remind the reader what has been talked about.

Three modern studies, two in jurisprudence and one in anthropology, all show a common trend.

Hart concludes that there are three "basic issues": (1) How is law related to order backed by threats? (2) What is the relation between legal obligation and moral obligation? (3) What are rules, and to what extent is law an affair of rules? Stone sets out seven sets of "attributes usually found associated with the phenomena commonly designated as law": Law is (1) a complex whole, (2) which always includes norms regulating human behavior, (3) that are social norms; (4) the complex whole is "orderly" and (5) the order is characteristically a coercive order (6) that is institutionalized (7) with a degree of effectiveness sufficient to maintain itself. Pospisil examines several attributes of the law—the attribute of authority, that of intention of universal application, that of *obligatio* (the right-obligation cluster), and that of sanction. In his view, the "legal" comprises a field in which custom, political decision, and the various attributes overlap, though each may be found extended outside that overlapping field, and there is no firm line, but rather a "zone of transition," between that which is unquestionably legal and that which is not.

It was Hermann Kantorowicz who pointed out that there are many subjects, including some of a nonlegal nature, that employ a concept of law. He proceeded to a more questionable point: that it was up to "general jurisprudence" to provide a background to make these differing concepts sensible. Kantorowicz' method for supplying such a jurisprudential background is very like Pospisil's in anthropology—examination of some characteristics of law that are vital to one or more of the more specific concepts. Law, he tells us, is characterized by having a body of rules that prescribe external conduct (it makes little immediate difference to the law how one feels about it—the law deals in deeds). These rules must be stated in such a way that the courts, or other adjudging bodies, can deal with them. Each of the rules contains a moralizing or "ought" element—and Kantorowicz fully recognizes that this "ought" element is culturally determined and may change from society to society and from era to era. Normative rules of this sort must, obviously, also be distinguished from factual uniformities by which men, sometimes with and sometimes without the help of courts and lawyers, govern their daily round of activity. Law is one of the devices by means of which men can reconcile their actual activities and behavior with the ideal principles that they have come to accept in a way that is not too painful or revolting to their sensibilities, and a way that allows ordered (which is to say predictable) social life to continue.

Double Institutionalization

Law must be distinguished from traditions and fashions and more specifically it must be differentiated from norm and from custom. A norm is a rule, more or less overt, which expresses "ought" aspects of relationships between human beings. Custom is a body of such norms— including regular deviations and compromises with norms—that is actually followed in practice much of the time.

All social institutions are marked by "customs" and these "customs" exhibit most of the stigmata cited by any definition of law. But there is one salient difference. Whereas custom continues to inhere in, and only in, these institutions which it governs (and which in turn govern it), law is specifically recreated, by agents of society, in a narrower and recognizable context—that is, in the context of the institutions that are legal in character and, to some degree at least, discrete from all others.

Just as custom includes norms, but is both greater and more precise than norms, so law includes custom, but is both greater and more precise. Law has the additional characteristic that it must be what Kantorowicz calls "justiciable," by which he means that the rules must be capable of reinterpretation, and actually must be reinterpreted, by one of the legal institutions of society so that the conflicts within nonlegal institutions can be adjusted by an "authority" outside themselves.

It is widely recognized that many peoples of the world can state more or less precise "rules" which are, in fact, the norms in accordance with which they think they ought to judge their conduct. In all societies there are allowable lapses from such rules, and in most there are more or less precise rules (sometimes legal ones) for breaking rules.

In order to make the distinction between law and other rules, it has been necessary to introduce furtively the word "institution." I use the word in Malinowski's sense.

A legal institution is one by means of which the people of a society settle disputes that arise between one another and counteract any gross and flagrant abuses of the rules (as we have considered them above) of at least some of the other institutions of society. Every on-going society has legal institutions in this sense, as well as a wide variety of nonlegal institutions.

In carrying out the task of settling difficulties in the nonlegal institutions, legal institutions face three kinds of tasks: (1) There must be specific ways in which difficulties can be disengaged from the institutions in which they arose and which they now threaten and then be engaged within the processes of the legal institution. (2) There must be ways in which the trouble can now be handled within the framework of the legal

793

institution, and (3) There must be ways in which the new solutions which thus emerge can be reengaged within the processes of the nonlegal institutions from which they emerged. It is seldom that any framework save a political one can supply these requirements.

There are, thus, at least two aspects of legal institutions that are not shared with other instititions of society. Legal institutions—and often they alone—must have some regularized way to interfere in the malfunctioning (and, perhaps, the functioning as well) of the nonlegal institutions in order to disengage the trouble-case. There must, secondly, be two kinds of rules in the legal institutions—those that govern the activities of the legal institution itself (called "adjectival law" by Austin and procedure by most modern lawyers), and those that are substitutes or modifications or restatements of the rules of the nonlegal institution that has been invaded (called "substantive law").

Listed above are only the minimal aspects that are all shared by all known legal institutions. There may be other aspects, as for example the commonly recognized fact that legal institutions on both the procedural and the substantive side can be in the fullest sense innovatory.

Seen in this light, a fairly simple distinction can be made between law and custom. Customs are norms or rules (more or less strict, and with greater or less support of moral, ethical, or even physical coercion) about the ways in which people must behave if social institutions are to perform their tasks and society is to endure. All institutions (including legal institutions) develop customs. Some customs, in some societies, are *re*institutionalized at another level: they are restated for the more precise purposes of legal institutions. When this happens, therefore, law may be regarded as a custom that has been restated in order to make it amenable to the activities of the legal institutions. In this sense, it is one of the most characteristic attributes of legal institutions that some of these "laws" are about the legal institutions themselves, although most are about the other institutions of society—the familial, economic, political, ritual, or whatever.

One of the reddest herrings ever dragged into the working of orderly jurisprudence was Malinowski's little book called *Crime and Custom in Savage Society*. It is unfortunately almost the only anthropological book that appears on the standard reading list used in many law schools, "The Dean's List," and it has had an undue and all but disastrous influence on the rapprochement between anthropology and jurisprudence. Malinowski's idea was a good one; he claimed that law is "a body of binding obligations regarded as right by one party and acknowledged as the duty by the other, kept in force by the specific mechanism of reciprocity and publicity inherent in the structure of . . . society." His error was in equating what he had defined with the law. It is not law that is "kept in force by . . . reciprocity and publicity." It is custom, as we have defined it here. Law is, rather, "a body of binding obligations regarded as right by one party and acknowledged as the duty by the other" *which has been reinstitutionalized within the legal institution so that society can continue to function in an orderly manner on the basis of rules so maintained.* In short, reciprocity is the basis of custom; but the law rests on the basis of this double institutionalization. Central in it is that some of the customs of some of the institutions of society are restated in such a way that they can be "applied" by an institution designed (or, at very least, utilized) specifically for that purpose.

One of the best ways to perceive the doubly institutionalized norms or "laws" is to break up the law into smaller components, capable of attaching to persons (either human individuals or corporate groups) and so to work in terms of "rights" and their reciprocal duties or "obligations." In terms of rights and duties, the relationships between law and custom, law and morals, law and anything else, can be seen in a new light. Whether in the realm of kinship or contract, citizenship or property rights, the relationships between people can be reduced to a series of prescriptions with the obligations and their correlative rights that emanate from these presumptions. In fact, if it is not carried too far and unduly formalized, thinking in terms of rights and obligations of persons (or role players) is a convenient and fruitful way of investigating much of the custom of many institutions. Legal rights are only those rights that attach to norms that have been doubly institutionalized; they provide a means for seeing the legal institutions from the standpoint of the persons engaged in them.

The phenomenon of double institutionalization of norms and therefore of legal rights has been recognized for a long time, but analysis of it has been only partially successful. Kantorowicz, for example, has had to create the concept of "justiciability" of the law. It would be better to say that legal rights have their material origins (either overtly or covertly) in the customs of nonlegal institutions but must be *overtly restated* for the specific purpose of enabling the legal institutions to perform their task.

A legal right (and, with it, a law) is the restatement, for the purpose of maintaining peaceful and just operation of the institutions of society, of some but never all of the recognized claims of the persons within those institutions; the restatement must be made in such a way that these claims can be more or less assured by the total community or its representatives. Only so can the moral, religious, political, and economic implications of law be fully explored.

●

Law is never a mere reflection of custom, however. Rather, law is always out of phase with society, specifically because of the duality of the statement and restatement of rights. Indeed, the more highly developed the legal institutions, the greater the lack of phase, which not only results from the constant reorientation of the primary institutions, but also is magnified by the very dynamic of the legal institutions themselves.

Thus, it is the very nature of law, and its capacity to "do something about" the primary social institutions, that creates the lack of phase. Moreover, even if one could assume perfect legal institutionalization, change within the primary institutions would soon jar the system out of phase again. What is less obvious is that if there were ever to be perfect phase between law and society, then society could never repair itself, grow and change, flourish or wane. It is the fertile dilemma of law that it must always be out of step with society, but that people must always (because they work better with fewer contradictions, if for no other reason) attempt to reduce the lack of phase. Custom must either grow to fit the law or it must actively reject it; law must either grow to fit the custom, or it must ignore or suppress it. It is in these very interstices that social growth and social decay take place.

Social catastrophe and social indignation are sources of much law and resultant changes in custom. With technical and moral change, new situations appear that must be "legalized." This truth has particular and somewhat different applications to developed and to less highly developed legal systems. On the one hand, in developed municipal systems of law in which means for institutionalizing behavior on a legal level are already traditionally concentrated in political decision-making groups such as legislatures, nonlegal social institutions sometimes take a very long time to catch up with the law. On the other hand, in less developed legal systems, it may be that little or no popular demand is made on the legal institutions, and therefore little real contact exists or can be made to exist between them and the primary institutions. Law can, as we have seen in another context, become one of the major innovators of society, the more effective the greater a people's dependence on it. . . .

Diamond, The Rule of Law Versus the Order of Custom*

I

We must distinguish the rule of law from the authority of custom. In a recent effort to do so (which I shall critically examine because it is so

*[From *The Rule of Law* 115-120 (R. P. Woolf ed., Simon & Schuster 1971). Reprinted

typical), Paul Bohannan contends . . . that laws result from "double" institutionalization.[1] He means by this the lending of a specific force, a cutting edge to the functioning of "customary" institutions: marriage, the family, religion. But, he tells us, the laws so emerging assume a character and dynamic of their own. They form a structured legal dimension of society; they do not merely reflect, but interact with given institutions. Therefore, Bohannan is led to maintain that laws are typically out of phase with society and it is this process which is both a symptom and cause of social change. Thus, the laws of marriage, to illustrate Bohannan's argument with the sort of concrete example his definition lacks, are not synonymous with the institution of marriage. They reinforce certain rights and obligations while neglecting others. Moreover, they subject partners defined as truant to intervention by an external, impersonal agency whose decisions are sanctioned by the power of the police.

Bohannan's sociological construction *does* have the virtue of denying the primacy of the legal order, and of implying that law is generic to unstable (or progressive) societies, but it is more or less typical of abstract efforts to define the eternal essence of the law, and it begs the significant questions. Law has no such essence but a definable historical nature. Thus, if we inquire into the structure of the contemporary institutions, which according to Bohannan stand in a primary relation to the law, we find that their customary content has drastically diminished. Paul Radin made the point as follows: "A custom is in no sense a part of our properly functioning culture. It belongs definitely to the past. At best, it is moribund. But customs are an integral part of the life of primitive peoples. There is no compulsive submission to them. They are not followed because the weight of tradition overwhelms a man. . . . A custom is obeyed because it is intimately intertwined with a vast living network of interrelations, arranged in a meticulous and ordered manner. They are tied up with all the mechanisms used in government."[2] And, "What is significant in this connection," as J. G. Peristiany indicates, "is not that common values should exist, but that they should be expressed although no common political organization corresponds to them."[3] No contemporary institution functions with the kind of autonomy that permits us to

---

by permission.

Stanley Diamond (1922–) is Professor of Anthropology, Graduate Faculty, at the New School for Social Research, and chairman of the anthropology program. He is author of *Primitive Views of the World* and *Transformation of East Africa.*]

1. Paul Bohannan. "Law," *International Encyclopedia of the Social Sciences.* New York, 1968, pp. 73-78.

2. Paul Radin. *The World of Primitive Man.* New York, 1953, p. 223.

3. J. G. Peristiany. *The Institutions of Primitive Society.* Glencove, Illinois, 1956, p. 45.

postulate a significant dialectic between law and custom. We live in a law-ridden society; law has cannibalized the institutions which it presumably reinforces or with which it interacts.

Accordingly, morality continues to be reduced to or confused with legality. We tend to assume that legal behavior is the measure of moral behavior, and it is a matter of some interest that a former Chief Justice of the Supreme Court proposed, with the best of intentions, that a federal agency be established in order to advise government employees, and those doing business with the government, concerning the legal/ethical propriety of their behavior. Any conflict of interest not legally enjoined would thus become socially or morally acceptable. These efforts to legislate conscience by an external political power are the antithesis of custom: customary behavior comprises precisely those aspects of social behavior which are traditional, moral, and religious, which are, in short, conventional and nonlegal. Put another way, custom *is* social morality.[4] The relation between custom and law is, basically, one of contradiction, not continuity.

The customary and the legal orders are historically, not logically related. They touch coincidentally; one does not imply the other. Custom, as most anthropologists agree, is characteristic of primitive society, and laws of civilization. Robert Redfield's dichotomy between the primitive "moral order" and the civilized "legal" or "technical" order remains a classic statement of the case.

"The dispute," writes William Seagle, "whether primitive societies have law or custom, is not merely a dispute over words. Only confusion can result from treating them as interchangeable phenomena. If custom is spontaneous and automatic, law is the product of organized force. Reciprocity is in force in civilized communities too but at least nobody confuses social with formal legal relationships."[5] Parenthetically, one should note that students of primitive society who use the term "customary law" blur the issue semantically, but nonetheless recognize the distinction.

It is this overall legalization of behavior in modern society which Bohannan slights. In fascist Germany, for example, laws flourished as never before. By 1941, more edicts had been proclaimed than in all the years of the Republic and the Third Reich. At the same time, ignorance of the law inevitably increased. In a sense, the very force of the law depends upon ignorance of its specifications, which is hardly recognized as

4. Sydney P. Simpson and Julius Stone. *Law and Society in Evolution*, Book I. Saint Paul, 1942, p. 2
5. William Seagle. *The History of Law*. Tudor, 1946, p. 35.

a mitigating circumstance. As Seagle states, law is not definite and certain while custom is vague and uncertain. Rather, the converse holds. Customary rules must be clearly known; they are not sanctioned by organized political force, hence serious disputes about the nature of custom would destroy the integrity of society. But laws may always be invented, and stand a good chance of being enforced: "Thus, the sanction is far more important than the rule in the legal system . . . but the tendency is to minimize the sanction and to admire the rule."[6]

In fascist Germany, customs did not become laws through a process of "double institutionalization." Rather, repressive laws, conjured up in the interests of the Nazi party and its supporters, cannibalized the institutions of German society. Even the residual customary authority of the family was assaulted: children were encouraged to become police informers, upholding the laws against their kin. "The absolute reign of law has often been synonymous with the absolute reign of lawlessness."[7] Certainly, Germany under Hitler was a changing society, if hardly a progressive one, but it was a special case of the general process in civilization through which the organs of the state have become increasingly irresistible. It will be recalled that Bohannan takes law as opposed to custom to be symptomatic of changing societies. But the historical inadequacy of his argument is exactly here: he does not intimate the overall direction of that change and therefore fails to clarify the actual relation between custom and law. Accordingly, the notion that social change is a function of the law, and vice versa, implies a dialectic that is out of phase with *historical* reality.

Plato understood this well enough when he conceived the problem of civilization as primarily one of *injustice,* which he did not scant by legalistic definition. His remedy was the thorough restructuring of society. Whether we admire his utopia or not, the *Republic* testifies to Plato's recognition that laws follow social change and reflect prevailing social relationships but are the cause of neither.

Curiously, this view of the relationship between law and society accords with the Marxist perspective on the history of culture. Customary societies are said to precede legal societies, an idea which, semantics aside, most students of historical jurisprudence would accept. But Marxists envision the future as being without laws as we know them, as a return to custom, so to speak, on a higher level, since the repressive and punitive functions of law will become superfluous. Conflicts of economic and political interest will be resolved through the equitable reordering

6. Ibid., pp. 19-20.
7. Ibid.

of institutions. Law for the Marxists and most classic students of historical jurisprudence is the cutting edge of the state—but the former, insisting on both a historical and normative view of man, define the state as the instrument of the ruling class, anticipating its dissolution with the abolition of classes, and the common ownership of the basic means of production. But whatever our view of the ultimate Marxist dynamic, law is clearly inseparable from the state. Sir Henry Maine equates the history of individual property with that of civilization: "Nobody is at liberty to attack several property and to say at the same time that he values civilization. The history of the two cannot be disentangled. Civilization is nothing more than the name for the . . . order . . . dissolved but perpetually reconstituting itself under a vast variety of solvent influences, of which infinitely the most powerful have been those which have, slowly, and, in some parts of the world much less perfectly than others, substituted several property for collective ownership."[8] In the words of Jeremy Bentham, "Property and law are born together and die together."

Law, thus, is symptomatic of the emergence of the state; the legal sanction is not simply the cutting edge of institutions at all times and in all places. The "double institutionalization" to which Bohannan refers is, where it occurs, primarily a historical process of unusual complexity. And it occurs in several modes. Custom—spontaneous, traditional, personal, commonly known, corporate, relatively unchanging—is the modality of primitive society; law is the instrument of civilization, of political society sanctioned by organized force, presumably above society at large, and buttressing a new set of social interests. Law and custom both involve the regulation of behavior but their characters are entirely distinct; no evolutionary balance has been struck between developing law and custom, traditional—or emergent.

II. ANTHROPOLOGICAL METHODS AS APPLIED TO THE LEGAL PROCESS

Bohannan, Ethnography and Comparison in Legal Anthropology*

Legal anthropology is, as I have remarked elsewhere, a small field in which the general quality of the work is extraordinarily high. For that

8. Sir Henry Maine. *Village Communities and Miscellanies.* New York, 1889, p. 230.
*[Reprinted from *Law in Culture and Society* 401-416, edited by Laura Nader, copy-

reason it serves well as a microcosm in which to examine some of the problems that plague the more inclusive subject of social anthropology.

One of the recurrent problems is social anthropology is the relationship of ethnography to what is usually called comparison. Differences of opinion about the nature of data and its organization into ethnography and its reorganization into "comparative studies" have been at the heart of much disparateness within the discipline. Within legal anthropology these differences have assumed inordinate proportions.

Given the present state of the art, I find that there are four main areas on which some light can be thrown. I want to take them up in order of increasing importance: the use of native terms in reporting ethnography; the idea of the "folk system" and the way in which unavoidable warping of native ideas can be kept track of; some of the kinds of intellectual gymnastics that have been called comparison; and the difference between the theory and culture of ethnography and the theory and culture of comparison.

In the material that Gluckman added to the second edition (1967) of his *The Judicial Process among the Barotse* (originally published in 1955), he quotes a sentence from Mary Douglas' review of his book . . . which seems to touch the kernel of the problem: . . . "It is in the juxtaposition of previously unconnected ideas that the act of interpretation is to be found."

With this idea in mind, the present article will be seen to deal with four contexts in which novel juxtapositions can be made, and the kind of interpretations that can justifiably be derived from each: the new juxtaposition that comes when an ethnographer struggles to present his ideas in English to his colleagues; the new juxtapositions that arise between the models of the ethnographer and the models of his subject people; the new juxtaposition of ethnographic models with one another when they come from different cultures; and the new juxtaposition of new ethnographic models with those already accepted as theory in the subject.

Native Terms

I have been told on a number of occasions that my Tiv ethnography makes extensive use of native terms in reporting. I always agree that this

right 1969, by permission of the Wenner-Gren Foundation for Anthropological Research, New York.

For biographical information, see page 791 supra.]

is true. Gluckman takes this position: "I consider that very many of these concepts can, without distortion after careful and perhaps lengthy description and discussion, be given English equivalents, at least out of courtesy to one's readers."

Thus, the overeasy statement would seem to be that an author either uses native terms and makes it tough on the reader but easy on himself, or else he uses no native terms and makes it tough on himself but easy on the reader. This seems to me to be an erroneous way—at least an oversimple way—of looking at the problem. No one doubts that it is difficult to read an ethnographic report that is studded with foreign words. No one questions the fact that one's material should be made as easy to read as possible.

The alternative to using native words is to put a gloss on English words. That means to expand or reduce the meaning such words carry in their own culture so that they can carry an accurate meaning from the subject culture.

It is my firm opinion that the power of the word is always greater than the power of the gloss. If the ethnographer is not concerned with some (unfortunately he cannot be concerned with all) of the delicate nuances of his culture, than he may write without either native terms or glosses, "using words as the dictionaries define them"—but I brand him the lesser ethnographer. It boils down to this question: is it more difficult for a reader to keep in mind a set of native terms or a set of glosses on English words—usages of ordinary English words that will apply in no other context than the immediate one? I agree with William Empson that to introduce such a gloss is either to make a word mean so much that it becomes too blunt or to create what he calls a "negative pregnancy" to the meaning of the word—to accept only one chunk out of its ordinary day-to-day meaning. Either procedure, but particularly the latter, is to insert a trap for the reader that no amount of skillful writing or careful reading can keep him from falling into, because he subconsciously reinserts the entire range of meaning.

The result is that good ethnography is hard to read, whichever method one opts for. It is my opinion that every ethnographer owes it to himself, the people he studies, and his colleagues not to blunt the edge of his material. He must, of course, translate as much as possible; he must gauge the point at which difficulty of reading becomes impossibility of reading. But there is an analogous point at which the gloss method leads to even greater difficulty, because it simulates understanding through the use of a familiar word. Such simulation leads—almost inevitably, I think—to an assumption of comparability of everything called by the same word—and this is a difficulty that is almost impossible to correct.

The most blatant examples come in the old-fashioned treatment of kinship terminology: translation of kinship terms is notoriously difficult. . . .

While we are on the matter of language, another question can be taken care of: is the "native language" a reasonable alternative to the language of jurisprudence? Here is, indeed, another red herring. . . . Hoebel stated that "The Tiv folk system idealizes the Tiv legal process, and it is just as erroneous to slip into an acceptance of Tiv thinking about their system as representing the real thing as it would be uncritically to carry over inappropriate Austinian conceptions to the distortion of Tiv ideas and behavior." Gluckman puts it in this way: "It seems to me that the refinements of English, and in general, European, jurisprudence provide us with a more suitable vocabulary despite its connotations, than do the languages of tribal law."

Both these statements miss the point. English jurisprudence has developed a vocabulary for talking about English law (and to a lesser extent talking about comparative law and conflicts). Tiv have not developed jurisprudence. Therefore, even to get these two matters onto a comparative level, the ethnographer must do for the Tiv what they have not done for themselves—find a "theory" of Tiv legal action, for what Gluckman aptly calls forensic action. Then the job of comparison can begin. Gluckman is no doubt right that a larger proportion of what we shall below call the culture of comparison will be derived from English jurisprudence than from Tiv (or any other) ethnography. But the two "languages" per se—English jurisprudence and the native language—are not equivalent entities. In short, when you juxtapose one with the other, you are not merely changing language—you are changing media.

Hoebel's statement above has an additional difficulty in the phrase "representing the real thing." One cannot represent the real thing any way except by a grossly ethnocentric viewpoint or else by some kind of technique, such as the folk system or ethnoscience, to get at something less ethnocentric. . . .

One's knowledge of ethnography and the institutions of other societies must comfortably inform the writing of any ethnographic tract the very while they are not made part of it. That is to say, if I report an institution from the Tiv that is totally similar to another institution that is described by someone else, I must neither omit to report it nor merely say that it is "like the Romans." I must describe it in Tiv terms, so that other scholars can make up their minds whether it is like the Romans. If the ideas that an ethnographer has discovered or has had to invent to explain the situation in another culture are helpful and actually do work, then any ethnographer must use them, or improve on them, and he is at fault if he does not. This is utterly different from the comparative method. It is merely utilizing the full culture of one's own profession (which Gluckman confuses with comparison). In short, Gluckman has treated what I have talked about as the folk system as if it were merely a first step toward some problem that he is interested in. In fact, it seems to me that it would never lead to the problem he is interested in, and he has therefore branded it as "unique" and as "cultural solipsism." That does not mean that it is "not comparative" so much as that he has an ego-centric concept of comparison.

Folk Systems

The idea of the "folk system" formalized in my book on Tiv law has been by and large generously received. . . . [I]t can be seen as a coarser and larger-scale tool, but not greatly different from what has since that time come to be called ethnoscience. The considerable thought that has gone into the epistemology of ethnography, usually under the rubric of componential analysis or ethnoscience, leads me to think a new state-ment about the folk system worth while.

Every cultural tradition is, in Nietzsche's phrase, "ein aus sich rol-lendes Rad"—a wheel rolling out of itself. No matter the origin of its cultural traits, or how internally inconsistent it may be, a cultural tradi-tion has a character that becomes "more so" as it develops. These charac-teristics must be understood anthropologically in terms of the concepts and processes in which they are played out and given substance.

. . . [W]e must be very careful in examining how we know what we know.

Gluckman has taken my plea for an understanding of Tiv ethnogra-phy in Tiv terms to be quite another point: that the various cultural tra-ditions are "unique" and have no similarities whatever, that every folk system must be different from every other folk system in all its details. It seems to me that I did not say anything so absurd. However, since a number of anthropologists have confused the admonition for analysis of a system in its own terms with a plea for uniqueness, it is worth mention-ing. Simply put, the proportion of the ideas or artifacts within a cultural tradition that at one level or another are also found in other cultures is quite a different matter from whether or not we interpret whatever is there in orderly accordance with some kind of overt conception of what it means to the actors in the situation. I learned this, while a graduate student, from a lecture, given by Professor Isaac Schapera, taking an-thropologists to task for not reporting the familiar. His particular target on that occasion was the lack of information in the standard ethnogra-phies about Christianity in many African communities otherwise well reported. He went on to outline that in every sphere of life ethnographers were disposed to give closer attention to exotic items. He ended with a moral about the degree to which this process undermined the ethnographic record.

Taking his idea to heart, I think that it is necessary both to report the familiar fully (and "familiar" can, in the culture of the anthropologist, mean anything extensively dealt with in the literature, not necessarily merely something in his own ethnic background) and, specifically, to see how it is utilized and conceptualized in the subject culture.

In short, whether or not an item is "unique" is the least interesting aspect of it, except in diffusion studies. The way in which it fits into the larger conceptual system of the people who use it is what is important. It seems to me that when one gets comparative at too early a stage, this particular job is given short shrift—always to the crippling of the ethnography.

There are much more important things to say about folk systems than to argue about whether their components are unique. . . . I want to restate some of these points about the nature of the folk system—and this takes us back to the subject of "the real thing" mentioned above.

Ayoub points out that the description of a folk system must be in the ideolect of the analyst, and that the key elements of that ideolect may or may not be taken over into the language in which he is writing. This is, of course, one facet of the primary difficulty of almost all ethnographic reporting—that it must be done in a foreign language and hence is subject to vast distortion by the reader as well as by the writer. As a result, Ayoub is quite right in saying that we can never report *the* folk system. In one sense, obviously, there is no such thing—there are only the observable and discussable "facts" of communication and purposive action among the people. However, if the anthropologist can get the ideas so straight that he can discuss them in detail with informants in their own language, and if it is indeed the ethnographer instead of the informant who has made the major adjustment for purposes of communication, then I think he has something that can reasonably be called a folk system.

I was overeager in *Justice and Judgment* to say that a folk system is what the people think and say. I will again state my revision: a folk system is what an ethnographer thinks and says that allows him to interact successfully with the people he is studying. . . . I have . . . talked about the "working misunderstanding." The ethnographer ends up with a model in terms of which he can interact with the people—and, because of the nature of communication, he cannot go beyond that (although still another ethnographer may go further by virtue of his being able to see both systems).

Thus, today the question of whether or not the folk system as reported is *the* folk system strikes me as the same kind of question as whether some particular performance of a symphony is *the* symphony. Obviously, whether we like it or not, different ethnographers will come back with differing interpretations of a culture. However, those interpretations are not necessarily, and usually not actually, at odds—they merely allow us a better opportunity to discover the possibilities of a complex score. We simply must get used to the fact that every ethnography is an interpretation of only part of a culture. No amount of "scientific" fol-de-rol can avoid this fact. The scientism may give an appearance of comparable data, but (as in ethnoscience) it does so at the expense of vastly reducing the dimensions of the part of the culture that is reported. Yet there is enough overlap for us to recognize the culture in question.

There is a further difficulty: what is "out there" changes rapidly, particularly in those societies that anthropologists have been studying for the last fifty years. The problem, when two ethnographers studying the same society are separated by as little as a decade, becomes not merely "What is the real thing?" but "What is the *same* thing?"

Ayoub has inserted a third system, the concrete system. The concrete system seems to be what is "really" out there. I did not originally utilize any such idea because it seemed to me obvious that what is out there is unknowable except in terms of somebody or other's perception of it. There can be a large number of perceptions of it, but the ones I am interested in are those that can be systematized as folk systems, in the communication sense mentioned above, and as analytical systems. One perfects a folk system by arguing with informants; one perfects an analytical system by arguing with anthropologists. To go back to the text from Mary Douglas, the new milieux in which one tries out one's interpretations are once and for all different, even though the subject matter is much the same.

There is, of course, no possibility of ever arriving at a "fact" that is uncolored by that ethnographic instrument, the perceiver of the fact. The concrete system necessarily remains a mystery. All we can do is to learn more about our sensory means of perception, and mechanical and other extrinsic extensions of them, and our own cultural prison. Communication to a degree is possible, and it is the wish of most parties in most situations to refine that degree.

Therefore the "concrete" system is the "reality," and we need say no more about it—indeed, we cannot say any more about it. The folk system is the ethnographer's action-oriented reading of the concrete, which is sufficiently "collective" as to allow him to interact successfully with the other people who utilize this system of symbols and culture traits. The analytical system is a scientific (whatever we may mean by that) reading of the folk system or of many folk systems.

Ayoub claims that the difficulty is compounded, because for analytical purposes there is a necessary melding of the folk system with the concrete. What he surely means is that there is a stage of his work when any ethnographer knows more about a culture than he understands about it. Certainly he sees actions and things that he interprets tentatively before he tests the folk interpretation. But that should not be confused with "reality"—it is merely a stage in learning.

Some Chimeras of Comparison

If the core of ethnography is the creation of theory around ideas that are "discoverable" in a folk system, what is the core of comparative anthropology? To put the question another way, if the core of ethnography is the juxtaposition of a set of native ideas with a set of ideas in what we shall call below the "culture of ethnography," what is the new juxtaposition to be achieved in comparative anthropology and what are its methods and its dangers?

As long ago as 1896, Franz Boas in an essay in the pages of *Science* pointed out some of the chimeras that lay waste the fields of anthropology in the name of comparative method. His primary target was the questionable doctrine of the psychic unity of mankind. He argued convincingly that such a doctrine, more or less based on the systematic misunderstanding of Bastian (and, a latter-day investigator might add, of Jung), harbors a lurking hypothesis that the same phenomena everywhere develop in the same manner, represent the same thing, and have the same meaning. As Boas noted "even the most cursory review shows that the same phenomena may develop in a multitude of ways." The question for the comparative method is "when are two things the same thing?"

Boas went on to deplore

> the fact that so many fundamental features of culture are universal, or at least occur in many isolated places, interpreted by the assumption that the same features must always have developed from the same causes, leads to the conclusion that there is one grand system according to which mankind has developed everywhere; that all the occurring variations are no more than minor details in this grand, uniform evolution. It is clear that this theory has for its logical basis the assumption that the same phenomena are always due to the same causes.

The original grand theory of evolution was (temporarily) eclipsed, but the psychic need of some social scientists for a single grand theory that would explain everything was not. Some anthropologists have a penchant for rejecting any proposition that they can find an exception to, whether that exception leads to a valid refutation of a position or proposition or not. This is what Potter has called the "But not in the south" technique of one-upsmanship. Indeed, one reason social science has garnered its reputation for never getting anywhere can be laid to some of its most vocal practitioners who demand that theory be universal and reject all theory that is not. I have never understood how they can think their own theories can pass muster better than others.

The "psychic unity of mankind" as an idea did not die—it merely took refuge in the creed of liberalism. And as such it covertly informs much of Professor Gluckman's work. In his first Lozi law book Gluckman states that "it is unfortunately still necessary to demonstrate that Africans . . . use of processes of inductive and deductive reasoning which are in essence similar to those of the West, even if the premises be different." He wants, in short, not merely to study a culture and social structure, but also to prove that Africans are as good as anybody else. The point is later made even more explicit: "I am delighted in every way that his report bears witness to some similarities of social life everywhere, and to the basic similarities of all human beings in very varied conditions." Of course one must recognize that Gluckman knew his book would be read by some whites in southern Africa who might want to refute that position, and one sees his difficulty in writing with two audiences in mind. Yet he has not negotiated this passage very well, and the febrile doctrine of psychic unity stands in a way of a thoroughgoing analysis of what is to be found in his notes and cases. . . .

Another, and almost exactly opposite, mistake is one that is marked by Nader when—casually, so perhaps she does not deserve the brunt— she suggests that mine is a "relativist" approach. "Relativism" has created almost as much misunderstanding in the anthropological profession as has "prelogical" or the "psychic unity of mankind." Nader writes: "[Bohannan] shirks the problems that such a relativist approach implies for comparison, but then he was not interested in comparison at the time."

"Relativism" seems a shorthand term for a doctrine that holds that there is no absolute. In that sense, surely every social scientist must be a relativist. But relativism also sometimes means to some people "anything goes." Only if we mean by it that no analysis can be made of any culture without some set of premises or other, and that such premises are themselves necessarily culture-bound to some degree, can we see the "relative" problem. The "correct" set of premises is that which informs the action as well as the analysis. Seen so, relativism is not merely the opposite of "absolutism" but is itself relative. Denying psychic unity or denying the omni-appropriateness of one set of assumptions (English juris-prudence, in the case at hand) does not mean that one is, for that reason, a relativist. "Relativism" is valid only if it means that every society, and hence every ethnography, must be understood on its own terms (which may or may not be unique—the point is irrelevant), and only if the the-ory is forged from the force of creative processes dealing with those terms.

Another "mythical beast" that sometimes masquerades under the name of "comparison" is backward translation. As we have already noted, translation from the language and culture of the subject people into the technical language and culture of anthropology is the task of every ethnographer. The danger is that, instead of starting with the cul-ture in question, we as ethnographers begin with our own anthropologi-cal language or even our mother tongues and find equivalents in the lan-guage or even our mother tongues and find equivalents in the language of the people we study. It appears to me that this is what lies behind the difficulty that has led to so much misunderstanding of Gluckman's posi-tion. In the new material to the second edition of *The Judicial Process,* he notes (2nd ed., 1967:376) that a "myth" has grown up about his methods, and he takes as his scapegoat a statement by Nader about his using the categories of Roman-Dutch law. I think he adequately defends himself here; however, in the course of the defense, he has missed what it was that led to the myth. It appears to me that instead of starting with Lozi ideas and seeking to translate them for his colleagues, he begins with his own rather considerable sophistication in jurisprudence and translates as much as possible of it into Lozi. The original flag quote of my book, from Sir Henry Maine, was selected to warn against such a danger. Gluckman does surprisingly well at the translation—but in doing so he misses some of the Lozi point. I am not impugning Gluck-man's cases or his documentation, which we all know to be the very best. I am, rather, saying that he fails to give us Lozi interpretation because his own interpretation enters too early. Here is one of the more obvious examples of Gluckman's backward translation:

> The key concept here, equivalent to *law* in which it is embraced, is trial
> by due process of law (*tatubo kamulao*). The process is based on hearing
> evidence (*bupaki*) which established proof (also *bupaki*) on the facts (*litaba*
> = also things). Evidence itself is reduced by concepts of relevance (*bu-
> paki bobuswanela*, appropriate or right evidence; *bupaki bobukena*, evi-
> dence which enters); of cogency (*bupaki bobutiile*, strong evidence); of
> credibility (*bupaki bobusepehala*); and of corroboration (*bupaki bobuye-
> mela*). These types of evidence are tested as direct, circumstantial, or
> hearsay. The concepts of evidence have a marked flexibility, as con-

trasted with those of substantive law. First, they are multiple in their referents: they cover evidence given in courts about actions committed,
the judge's knowledge of the social and physical world (judicial presumptions: *linto zelwaziba*, things we know), and the judge's inferences
from the evidence (*lisupo*, indications, probabilities). . . .

It is obvious, from the passage given above and from a number of
others that might be selected, that Gluckman is translating fundamentally Western ideas into Lozi instead of translating fundamentally Lozi
ideas into English. Please note that I did *not* say that the Lozi and the
English do not have fundamentally similar ideas, but only that by this
method of exposition there is no possible way for a reader to discover
whether they have or not.

Indeed, as Gluckman goes on, the combination of the unstated bias
of a belief in the psychic unity of mankind and such backward translation very nearly becomes an overt bias: "On the whole, it is true to say
that the Lozi judicial process corresponds with, more than it differs
from, the judicial process in Western society." Of course it does, or
Gluckman could not have defined it as judicial. That is not the significant aspect. A final example: "The judges' manipulation of these concepts is *implicit* in their assessment of the evidence of the parties against
the standard of 'the reasonable and upright man.'" I have italicized *implicit* to make my point. Implicit in what? In Lozi social action, perhaps—
in spite of Gluckman's protestations we cannot tell. . . .

Another bugbear of the comparativist is a tendency not to distinguish between cross-cultural and interdisciplinary. Gluckman deals with
the interdisciplinary problems of communication between law and anthropology under his rubric of "comparison." In *The Judicial Process*,
Chapter VII is called "Some Comparative Implications of the Lozi Judicial Process." There is almost nothing in that chapter that is cross-cultural, which is what most anthropologists since Tylor have meant by
"comparative." Rather, the chapter is an examination of some jurisprudential writers and the way that some of their problems can be illumi-
nated by Gluckman's readings of his Lozi cases. In *The Ideas of Barotse
Jurisprudence* Gluckman has added some cross-cultural material, still
under his rubric "comparative." In one of the best parts of the book—
that dealing with political power and treason—over half the passage
deals not with the Lozi at all, but with medieval Europe. But when he
does add the cross-cultural material, it is almost totally without his even
trying to retain control of it. Here is his own statement:

Wrongs in Barotse society arise out of aggressive actions by outsiders, or
out of failure to fulfill obligations of familial life between persons in spe-

cific status relationships. I shall argue that general ideas of wrong are again best understood in terms of reaction to those wrongs arising in status relations. To demonstrate my argument I begin not from the Barotse, and their governmental system with its courts, but from societies where redress was secured by self-help and where vengeance for the killing of a man was enjoined on his kinsmen.

From that statement he goes into a direct discussion of Maitland's article on the history of malice aforethought, and on to the Nuer; he gives an Ibo reference, and then back briefly to the Barotse, with sidelights on the Zulu, Kalinga, Ifugao, Marc Bloch's Middle Ages, Wales, the Yurok, England; back to Maitland's early England, to the Australian aborigines, the Cheyenne; and other subjects that it would be tedious to list and to read.

The point that Gluckman wants to make is that theory is where you find it and that most of it has been thought of already. I agree, but the point I want to make is that if wide-ranging materials are utilized in this way, a theory of comparative method becomes necessary, as well as (in this particular case) a theory of jurisprudence. Comparison must be done in a controlled way, with great awareness and sensitivity to the original meaning, and with a set of methods that allow us to utilize what we are doing toward some specific ends beyond merely buttressing a position.

As many another social anthropologist might, I have come up with a genealogy of the various methods that have been used for comparative purposes.

There are two fundamental types of comparison, which I have called "casual" and "controlled" comparison. Casual comparison is inserted by a writer in order to aid his reader in adjusting the ethnography at hand to the vicissitudes either of the reader's own culture or some other culture he already knows. There are two modes of casual comparison. One I have called "ethnocentric" if the comparative examples are taken only from the culture of the writer and reader. The other I have called "selected counter-illuminative information," because it is chosen out of a very wide range of possible ethnography specifically because it illuminates the case in hand. This latter is the type of comparison Gluckman has done in the section of his book mentioned just above.

"Controlled" comparison is more complex, and for purposes of the present exposition I have oversimplified it into two sorts. The simplest form is comparison with a standard extrinsic to the particular culture in hand. The source of this standard is of considerable moment insofar as the better it is chosen, the further one can go before bogging down. However, bogging down is, I think, the inevitable end. Ultimately one can say only that something is or is not like something else—that helps, but it is limited.

The "standard" method of comparison is similar to the "application" of "general theory." It is possible to take an idea . . . and utilize that idea as a general theory of law. That is to say, the "facts" of any system can be squeezed into any such classification with greater or lesser force required. That is, however, precisely the same mistake as forcing the data into the boxes of English jurisprudence. All these are way stations on the road to better understanding of legal anthropology; we can forge on from them only by new ethnography or new syntheses. The irony is that we never arrive at our goal—or, if we do arrive, it is at the wrong goal or else it proves to be trite. That is the fate of all science—Kingdom Come is a mirage, but the world of here and now must nevertheless be organized to deal with mirages.

The other method of controlled comparison is the method of controlled variables. These variables may either be derived from a "mass-theory," such as the *Outline of Cultural Materials* trait list, or they may be carefully selected and refined in the variation of the method Boas expounded and that Eggan later called "controlled comparison." The criteria for comparison either may be deduced or may be ethnographically derived. Again, to overstate for purposes of exposition, "deduced" criteria are a prioristic. The mode of "ethnographic derivation," on the contrary, is one that is similar to the linguist's mode of determining phonemes in any language: if there is a difference in meaning in two sounds, there are two phonemes and hence a legitimate distinction. The ethnographically derived criteria are all the legitimate distinctions that are made in the culture of the sample—they will not all be ethnographically relevant in all situations, although these distinctions may sometimes be instructive by their very ethnographic absence. Therefore, the "bank" of distinctions is constantly enriched by ethnography and must be simplified and arranged and theorized about by students of cross-cultural comparison. This category of "ethnographically derived criteria" resembles what might be called, in presently fashionable lingo, "comparative ethnoscience." It is the sort of thing that Goodenough is doing with residence patterns, and the sort of thing that Lévi-Strauss began (but did not finish) in *Les structures élémentaires de la parenté* (too early he turned one brilliantly delineated model into his standard—that of kinship based on a model of economic reciprocity—never getting to the other modes of economic distribution—redistribution and market —that also obviously function in the kinship sphere).

My objection to Gluckman's "comparative" is that he swings uneasily between what I have called the "single standard" and what I have called "selected counter-illuminative information." With the first he lays himself open to the possible charge of imprinting an *a priori* set of categories and concepts; with the second he lays himself open to the charge of selecting only the positive cases. Both may be unjust—but we cannot be sure.

The Culture of Ethnography and the Culture of Comparison

We have now brought ourselves squarely up against the main epistemological problems in anthropology. First of all, how can we secure the advantages of juxtaposing ideas and analyses from the corpus of ethnographic works with the materials of our own subject cultures without implying that these ideas are *in* the subject culture? Put another way, if we consider the ethnographic record as a subculture, how do we utilize that subculture in our comprehension of the culture we are reporting and analyzing? The second problem is no less difficult: what is the process by which we can derive from ethnography the variables that are to be used for controlled culture of comparison, utilizing the very material that is the substance of the culture of ethnography?

The key to the first problem, it seems to me, lies in exercising the greatest care in making our own assumptions overt and, perhaps most important of all, in not confusing the bizarre and unstructured totality of ethnography with some kind of logical construct. The organization of an ethnography, on the one hand, focuses on a people—and that includes the special ethnographies that focus on particular problems of a specific people. The organization of a comparative study, on the other hand, focuses on the logical interconnectedness of propositions. The fact that the cultural items may be the same must not be allowed to mislead us. What I am in fact saying, obviously, is that Gluckman is not comparative at all—he is merely calling on an admirably wide arc of the culture of ethnography.

It seems to me that the key to the second problem—how to create a controlled culture of comparison—lies all around us; it is included in a statement by Gluckman that he meant as a criticism: "If [Bohannan] were correct [about a folk system being raised to the level of an analytical system] we would have to be 'cultural solipsists,' unable to compare or to generalize widely—unless we were to develop a whole new independent language without national home."[1] Gluckman, both here and in his 1967

1. This investigation creates for me a direct confrontation with some of the statements that Max Gluckman has made in the last decade or so. I have not heretofore answered any of his statements. I do so now without polemic—and I do not read what he has said as polemic. We are using each other's statements as aids to express our own points of view the

813

"Reappraisal," thrusts this idea away as if one could not possibly have meant *that*. However, I did mean that, and it cannot be said better. In fact, the name of the "whole new independent language without national home" will probably be Fortran or some other computer language.

The question, obviously, is how we go about developing "an independent language without national home." I have suggested above that the data to be worked with in constructing a comparative system are the folk models that were found to be necessary to explain and describe specific cultures. The comparatists, from Tylor to Gluckman, want to compare substantive material; I want, rather, to compare viewpoints or theories of substantive material. So obviously, did Boas: "The comparative method, notwithstanding all that has been said and written in its praise, has been remarkably barren of definite results, and I believe it will not become fruitful until we renounce the vain endeavor to construct a uniform systematic history of the evolution of culture, and until we begin to make our comparisons on the broader and sounder basis which I ventured to outline." That is, on the basis of full and understood ethnographic accounts, each sufficiently theorized.[2]

In the creation of this "independent language without national home," there are certain things we cannot do. Whether it be a computer language or a "people language," we cannot assume that it will be without bias or known culture. I have already pointed out here that many cultures of completely different types share a good many ideas without that making them similar in origin, or use, or psychic proclivity. Obviously we cannot become biasless—rather, we must investigate our biases and institute controls for them. Obviously human beings cannot compare (or do anything else) without culture; rather, we must control the logic of the culture of comparison.

---

more clearly, for we do have some differences of opinion that I, at least, think of some importance to social anthropology. Arguments identical with this one are going on in economic anthropology, with a different cast of characters, and in psychological anthropology with a constantly shifting cast of characters. Obviously all this has something to do with communication among scholars who have basically different philosophical foundations. It is a healthy sign in a healthy discipline.

2. Although Boas is saying all the right things, he did not himself in his ethnography of the Kwakiutl do all the right things. His ethnography is full of detail, but there is very little ethnographic theory to inform it, which is one of the reasons that it takes so much effort to use it today. Boas' Kwakiutl material can be used—but only if one puts almost as much effort into it as Boas himself did. Had he been more willing to create a theory of the Kwakiutl, this would not be so, and Boas instead of Malinowski would be the father of modern field studies.

What, then, is the origin of the propositions in this new logical and independent language—this culture of comparison? We go to the ethnographies. In the best of all possible worlds, we include all of them (though some will, of course, prove useless). We must work somewhat in the linguist's mode of determining the basic phonemic system (by the comparison of controlled pairs), and then by a process that ultimately allows us to find axioms that enable us to deduce the specific folk systems (today this is called "generating" the system in a simulation project), and then by a process that allows us to compare the axioms of one society with those of another, and to investigate the ways in which they bunch, as vectors, and hence are culturally correlated.

These are the neologisms that Gluckman is waiting for. It will take about ten years, it seems to me. We must learn to put up with the theoretical "weightlessness" that comes from escaping from our own gravity.

Gluckman, Concepts in the Comparative Study of Tribal Law*

. . . Bohannan and I are agreed, in fact, that the first duty of an ethnographer is to record clearly the facts in the society he is studying. We are further agreed, as became apparent at the seminar which led to this present book, that we have then to devise terms to bring together for comparison parallel, similar, and different, conceptions and procedures in various "folk systems," and then to devise terms for yet more abstract analytical generalizations. This raises the question of what it is one is attempting to compare, and here it may well be that we are interested in divergent problems. Bohannan may be aiming to compare folk conceptions in themselves . . . [While] I am interested, like most social anthropologists, in specifying the folk conceptions of a particular people as clearly as I can and then trying to explain why they are as they are, and how they differ from the folk conceptions of others, in terms of economic and social backgrounds.

In practice it is almost impossible to write in English about a foreign system of law without using English words that may appear to import English "folk conceptions" (I think "conceptions" is here more accurate than "concepts"). . . .

*[Reprinted from *Law in Culture and Society* 354, 358, 364, 366-367, 371-373, edited by Laura Nader, copyright 1969, by permission of the Wenner-Gren Foundation for Anthropological Research, New York.

For biographical information, see page 769 supra.]

There are a number of conceptions in any one system that it is difficult to transpose into even general concepts in other systems. In these circumstances, careful description remains the first step; and then I consider it helpful to readers, and essential for comparative analysis, to give some kind of clear terminology, speaking for itself as much as possible, in the language of analysis. . . .

In this light I do not feel that my use of words in common as well as in technical use in English was misleading. . . .

I used English words because I was writing in English, and I have always felt that it is unfair to readers to ask them to carry in their heads a large number of vernacular terms. . . .

I feel therefore that everyone will agree with Bohannan that the first task in reporting a legal system is clearly to describe its "folk-concepts." I consider that, after careful and perhaps lengthy description and discussion, very many of these concepts can, without distortion, be given English equivalents, at least out of courtesy to one's readers. But some such step is essential at the next stage, when one essays comparative work. The problem must be tackled at several levels: first, delineation of the tribal conception; second, its comparison with other conceptions of similar type; third, determination of some general word, perhaps with a qualifying adjective, to arrive at a word for comparative analysis. In some cases it may be better to use neologisms. . . .

Failing the use of neologisms, a research worker writing in his own language is, in my opinion, entitled to try to specialize by stipulation the riches in the vocabulary of that language; and it seems to me that the refinements of English, and in general European, jurisprudence provide us with a more suitable vocabulary than do the languages of tribal law. It might be helpful to use heavy black type or block letters or other printing devices to mark when a word like "law" or "reasonable" is used for general analytic comparison as against reporting. . . .

Analytic Models

Having considered concepts, let me turn to models. An essay by Bohannan, "The Differing Realms of Law" (1965), emphasizes for me that too little thought has been given to the problem of how far the application of Western jurisprudential analytic models distorts other systems of law. Let us look at Bohannan's relation of what he calls "custom" to what he calls "legal," to see if there is a fundamental logical difference between his procedure and my procedure (following Western jurists) whereby I call "custom" a source of what I call "law" and hence of what I call "forensic" (formerly legal) rulings. Bohannan states that:

A norm is a rule, more or less overt, which expresses "ought" aspects of relationships between human beings. Custom is a body of such norms that is actually followed in practice much of the time. . . . A legal institution is one by means of which the people of a society settle disputes that arise between one another and counteract any gross and flagrant abuses of the rules . . . , of at least some of the other institutions of society. Every on-going society has legal institutions in this sense, as well as a wide variety of nonlegal institutions.

. . . Seen in this light, a fairly simple distinction can be made between law and custom. Customs are norms or rules (more or less strict, and with greater or less support of moral, ethical or even physical coercion) about the ways in which people must behave if social institutions are to perform their tasks and society is to endure. All institutions (including legal institutions) develop customs. Some customs, in some societies, are *re*institutionalized. When this happens, therefore, law may be regarded [the first time he stipulates how he will personally use one of these multivocal words] as a custom that has been restated in order to make it amenable to the activities of the legal institutions. In this sense, it is one of the most characteristic attributes of legal institutions that some of these "laws" are about the legal institutions themselves, although most are about the other institutions of society—the familial, economic, political, ritual, or whatever.

We might rephrase this: the customs of all institutions of society are liable to be involved in a dispute, which may be settled by a legal institution. In such circumstances, the legal institution restates [certain?] customs in the institution involved, that is, it reinstitutionalizes these. These customs can be called "law." Customs are therefore the source of law in legal institutions. We are then back with the standard jurisprudential approach, but with a difference.

The difference is that Bohannan sees the re-institutionalization into legal institutions of custom as occurring out of "familial, economic, political and ritual, or whatever" institutions (domains of life, Fortes calls them), and out of the legal institutions (or domain), into the legal institutions. He does not discriminate between types of custom. The Western jurisprudential approach, which I have followed to analyze the Barotse judicial process, not only discriminates between the domains of social relations, but also discriminates between the types of rules and regularities that are restated as "law" or as "legal" or as "forensic rulings" in the judicial process. I have described these, for the Barotse, as statutes, precedents, moral exemplifications, public policy, good morals, equity, natural law (called by the Barotse, laws of God), laws of nature (also called by the Barotse laws of God), and reasonableness. Bohannan might say that these are in fact Barotse ideas about the laws of public policy, ideas about good morals, ideas about the laws of nature, and hence that they can all be called "customs" in his definition of the word. To do so would in my opinion obscure the complicated balancing of these different types of rule—practice, principle, and the like—that is involved in a judicial process or a process of settlement, mediation, negotiation, and so forth. I therefore believe that the standard jurisprudential approach to this process is, *for certain problems,* more refined and fruitful than Bohannan's. His approach may be useful if we shift our interest to examine problems involved in the maintenance of norms within specific domains of social relationships, though I consider that even then we would have to bring in the jurisprudential discriminations for refined analysis. But my major point is that there is no difference between using the language of Western social anthropology and using the language of Western jurisprudence in tackling these sorts of problems. Theoretically, both are equally distorting, even while they may be illuminating. It is mere prejudice for social anthropologists to consider that the schemes that jurisprudents have used successfully for the analysis of Western law cannot be applied to clarify the law of another "folk-system." It is particularly prejudice if in fact their own systems of analysis can be reduced to exactly the same logical procedures. . . .

I do not say that an anthropologist who has not studied jurisprudence cannot study tribal law; such a statement would be nonsense. But jurisprudence, insofar as it is scientific, is a social science; and hence I consider that its concepts are propositions that must be taken into account for profitable analysis of certain problems in social anthropology. Use of the terms can be dangerous; but there is no adventure of ideas without risk.

Epstein, The Case Method in the Field of Law*

Few topics in the entire range of anthropological literature can have been so bedevilled by the problems of definition as that of primitive law. Indeed, so much of the discussion in this field has revolved around the terminological wrangles of jurists and anthropologists about the meaning of the term "law" that it would seem at times as though the criti-

*[From *The Craft of Social Anthropology* 205-215, 216-217, 217-219, 221-224, 229-230 (A. L. Epstein ed., Travistock Publications 1967). Reprinted by permission.

Arnold L. Epstein (1924–) received an LL.B. from Queen's University, Belfast, and a Ph.D. from the University of Manchester. He is presently a Professorial Fellow at Australian National University in Canberra. Previously he has been a Research Officer for the Rhodes-Livingston Institute, Lusaka, Simon Research Fellow at the University of Manches-

cal issues for debate were of a semantic rather than a sociological kind. Where we are dealing with so complex a social institution perhaps some argument about words is unavoidable—after all Western philosophers, theologians, and jurists have been discussing the nature of law for more than two millennia—but in the context of anthropological discourse much barren disputation could surely be avoided if the search for definition were more closely related to purpose and problem. It seems to me that much of the debate about primitive law has been reduced to fruitless verbal exchanges precisely because our concern with the topic has not been made sufficiently explicit. To take but one example: Elias has taken Evans-Pritchard to task for stating that "in the strict sense, Nuer have no law," pointing out that they do have obligatory rules of conduct. If the implication of Evans-Pritchard's statement is that the Nuer are a lawless people, then Elias's view must command one's sympathy. Yet it is also clear from the whole of Evans-Pritchard's account that he intended to say no such thing. The argument here between lawyer and anthropologist is essentially sterile because the proponents are at cross-purposes. Each seizes on a different facet as being the distinctive criterion of law so that no common ground of discourse is established, and the road is blocked to further discussion. The dilemma here arises from the way in which the problem is posed. The question whether the Nuer or the Athabascans have law can be answered only in terms of definitions, that is to say in terms of the presence or absence of certain formal criteria. If there is no consensus about these criteria the question cannot be satisfactorily answered. Many authorities, for example, have stressed the critical significance of courts in the definition of law. The presence or absence of law is thus readily measured by the presence or absence of forensic institutions. Yet anthropology is essentially a comparative discipline: it is concerned with the principles that underlie the workings of different kinds of society and different social systems. If the institution is to be taken as the point of departure for analysis, then, since not all societies possess courts, comparison is ruled out from the very beginning. If we are to work on a comparative basis and examine the phenomenon of law in the full range of human societes and cultures we have to look for universals: in short, our concern must be with process rather than form. As Elias

ter, Research Fellow at the Australian National University in Canberra, and Senior Lecturer in Social Anthropology at the University of Manchester. He has done fieldwork among the Bemba, on the Copperbelt of Zambia, and among the Tolai of New Britain. He is author of *The Administration of Justice and the Urban African*, and *Politics in an Urban African Community*, and has been a contributor to *Rhodes-Livingston Journal*, *Africa*, *Oceania*, *Southwestern Journal of Anthropology*, and a number of symposia.]

himself has remarked: "Institutions may differ, processes tend to be everywhere the same."

With what processes, then, are we concerned in the field of law? For anthropological purposes the more fruitful approach to the problem would appear to begin from the postulate that there is no human society known to us in which men do not quarrel and dispute with their fellows. Disputes are a universal feature of human social life. The central question thus becomes not do the Nuer have law, but, in any given society, in what ranges of social relationships do quarrels arise, what forms do they take, and by what means are they handled? Adopting this standpoint we may then go on to deduce a number of different aspects or facets that we may expect to find in all societies, albeit differing in form and degree, and which together in any one society make up the total complex phenomenon for which I shall henceforth reserve the broad term law. This mode of proceeding has the further advantage that, in delineating the aspects of law, we are also able to map out a number of problem areas and suggest topics for further research.

Disputes in any society arise in an endless variety of ways and for a multiplicity of reasons. But underlying every dispute is a sense of grievance that arises out of an assumed or alleged breach of entitlement. This is not to say that a breach of entitlement is always necessary to spark off a quarrel; it is merely to observe that, even where a quarrel has been deliberately courted by some hostile act in the furtherance of self-interest, the tendency is for the aggressor to justify himself by pointing to the other's breach of his entitlement. It is in this sense that one may speak of the logical priority of rules in the dispute process, since every breach implies the prior existence of more-or-less well-recognized norms that set out the expectations we may have of others' behaviour. Where these rules or standards may be enforced through the powers of coercion vested in a legitimate authority, I shall speak of jural rules or rules of law. This body of rules may be regarded as constituting the substantive law of a given community.

Grievances then erupt into quarrels whose source can be attributed by the actors to some breach of a rule or norm of conduct. The first step in redressing the situation must lie in determining whether and what norm has been infringed, and where responsibility lies. This implies in all societies the need for some form of inquisitorial procedure that will be regularly followed in certain given circumstances. In societies that have achieved a degree of centralized political control, the need will most commonly be met through the institution of courts. However, the court represents only one among a number of alternative solutions. In societies lacking forensic institutions, similar basic ends may be achieved by other procedures—divinatory seances, oaths and ordeals, song contests, moots and the like—the distinguishing features of which will be considered later.

The question of inquisitorial procedures is, of course, closely related to that of modes of redress and, indeed, both of these aspects frequently merge, as in our concept of trial. Nevertheless, two processes are involved which should be kept analytically distinct. A diviner's verdict or the findings of a coroner may be very suggestive, but redress and enforcement will have to be sought through other channels. Redress is essentially concerned with the ways in which the situation is readjusted when a breach or norm has been established: this is bound up with the nature and deployment of the system of sanctions within the society. In this context our concern is with law as an instrument of social control and its relation to other agencies working towards similar social ends.

Starting, then, from the idea of disputes, we have isolated three necessary ingredients or universal aspects of law—rules, procedures of inquiry and adjudication, and modes of redress and enforcement. There is, however, another matter that requires mention. Rules of conduct may be regarded as obligatory and binding, but it does not follow that they are invariably obeyed or remain valid for all time. They may be so ignored that they fall into desuetude; they may be amended or discarded and replaced by others. Jural procedures likewise are not automatic in their operation: they have to be initiated by acts of human will, and this may involve winning first the support of others; there is always the possibility, too, that such procedures may be abused and manipulated for personal ends. Hence discussion in this field cannot ignore the element of human aims, purposes, and values. Jurisprudence, it has been said, is a normative science: it is concerned with the realm not of the "is" but of the "ought," and what ought to be is determined by a community's scheme of values, including its concepts of equity and justice.

In delimiting these various aspects of law, I have at the same time been indicating a number of problem areas within the field, whose further exploration will be my main concern in the remainder of this essay. But by what methods shall we proceed? It may be expected that the approach of the jurist to the study of primitive law will reflect the biases and emphases of his own legal training, which in turn derive from the character of his national legal institutions. Thus the use of the case method, for example, is likely to be more congenial to the Anglo-American than to the Continental scholar. It is also congenial to the anthropologist. Since I have had some training in both disciplines, it is the one I shall adopt as the chief instrument of attack. In this regard I merely re-echo Hoebel when he remarks that the study of "primitive law, like common law, must draw its generalizations from particulars which are cases, cases, and more cases." But what is the case method, and what kind of material does its use involve? Incidents and episodes observed by the anthropologist and recorded in his notebooks are the very stuff from which he builds up his account of the social system; but they may also be used in the ethnographic analysis itself with telling effect to illustrate a general point. . . . Where the case method is employed, . . . the material is used not so much by way of illustration but as providing the raw data for analysis, the various strands in the skein of facts being teased out and dissected to reveal underlying principles and regularities. The kind and range of data that need to be collected will vary of course with the problem being investigated. In this essay I shall try to show the different uses to which the case method may be put and how, judiciously applied, it may help to illuminate each of the different sets of problems to which I draw attention.

Rules, Concepts, and Categories

. . . For the practising lawyer it is the rules of law, and the way in which these may be interpreted or manipulated, which are of primary interest. For many jurists likewise, the central task of jurisprudence appears as the analysis and systematic exposition of legal rules and precepts, and the deduction of the general principles and concepts that underlie them, and the way in which these may be built up into a logical and coherent scheme or system. There seems to be no intrinsic reason why the study of primitive law should not be approached in a similar way. But in fact this aspect of the study has aroused little theoretical enthusiasm among anthropologists, and it is noticeable that studies along these lines have usually been carried out in response to the request of a colonial administration, . . . or else by administrative officers who had received training in anthropology. . . .

Such studies appear to have arisen out of the felt needs expressed by colonial administrators for the proper recording of customary law. The desirability of carrying out such a task, at least in British territories, was implied to some extent in the policy of Indirect Rule, under which local tribal courts were recognized as an integral part of the territorial legal system, but the problems of applying an unwritten body of rules in rapidly changing circumstances had raised the issue more urgently. As J. P. Moffett, Local Courts Adviser to the Government of Tanganyika, put it in a foreword to Cory's book on Sukuma law and custom (1953, p. ix): " . . .one reason why the recording of customary law is so essential is to enable the courts to refer to a generally approved or an 'authorized version' of the law, sanctioned by chiefs and people. Without a written record there can be no certainty in the law, nor is it wise to bring about changes in the law (the necessity of which arises with increasing frequency) without that sure knowledge of it, and of its underlying principles, which only written law can give."

According to Allott, the eventual aim of this kind of study . . .must be the production of legal textbooks that can be cited in courts. I do not wish to deny the importance of producing such manuals: at the same time it seems to me that the goal stated is unnecessarily restricted and, in any case, cannot commit the anthropologist. I would argue rather that the recording of customary law is also important as a first step towards the systematic study of tribal systems of law, and so provides the basis for further inquiry into the connexions between legal ideas, concepts, and categories and social structure and culture.

But granted the ends, what of the means? The available accounts are not always very specific on this point, sometimes merely stating that the information was gathered by attending tribal courts and from local informants. However, for his study of the Sukuma, Cory gave a good deal of attention to the question. Cory was faced with the problem of local variation in Sukuma custom, and he was led to work mainly through an assembly of expert and authoritative spokesmen: questions were put to the gathering and the matter was debated and discussed until all agreed on the answer, which was then recorded. Such a method may be valuable for the recording of statements of custom, but I must confess to some doubts as to its adequacy when discussing the finer points of law. In my own fieldwork among the Bemba, and later in the African urban courts of the Copperbelt, I found that court members could expound the points involved in a case they had just been hearing with great command and infinite patience, but they were much less at home in the discussion of hypothetical issues which I would sometimes have to put to them. This was not because they were unintelligent or lacking in legal insight and imagination, but because their mode of legal thinking was particular rather than abstract: the rules of law they expounded were not conceived as logical entities; they were rather embedded in a matrix of social relationships which alone gave them meaning. Since rules and standards have to be applied in an endless variety of circumstances, this suggests that the use of case material for the extracting of rules and principles should take priority over the use of informants. Cory did indeed use such material, but only in a limited way, and mainly as a check on his informants. The result is, I feel, that at times he has fallen into the trap against which there have been ample warnings in the literature. As Julius Lips, for example, rightly cautioned (cited in Hoebel, 1961, p. 428): "Even a simple description of *facts* pertaining to law in a primitive tribe may, if we use our own legal terminology, cause a distortion of the legal content of primitive institutions." Thus in his discussion of divorce, Cory sets out at length the various grounds that may be adduced to sustain a suit for divorce in a Sukuma tribal court. He also notes that certain forms of behaviour, such as the cursing of his wife by a husband or vice versa, would not constitute adequate grounds for dissolving a marriage. Such statements, it seems to me, could be quite misleading to someone with a formal legal training, but lacking intimate knowledge of an African tribal court. Thus a magistrate or High Court judge, hearing such a suit on appeal from a local tribal court, and using such a handbook, might be inclined to interpret the statement of the rules in it in terms of his own technical concept of grounds of divorce: this would imply that a marriage could only be dissolved if a proper case was made out, whereas it appears from a case cited by Cory in another context that a Sukuma court may grant a divorce "without the petitioner giving any grounds for his demand."

The view that I am putting forward that when working on the descriptive level to formulate the body of rules of law we should proceed mainly through the analysis of cases has also been adopted by Pospisil in his monograph on the law of Kapauku Papuans. The method does have disadvantages. One may have to sit through many long disputes before a case comes up involving some novel or critical point on which one is anxious to have information and, indeed, the whole period of fieldwork may pass without such issues coming up for juridical discussion. In these circumstances, of course, there is no alternative but to make the best possible use of one's informants.

What kind of data then does this use of case material involve? Since Pospisil makes considerable use of cases in his exposition of Kapauku law, it may be helpful to examine his method in some detail. His procedure is to state the rules as these emerged out of discussions with his informants, and then to show how they were applied in particular circumstances. Thus the rules about homicide in Kapauku society follow closely Nadel's concept of the social range of offences, the penalty or mode of redress depending upon the social units involved. Hence, for example, killing outside the political unit is not punishable (rule 1*c*), though a war usually results. Case 4 is reported as follows:

Place: Mogu, South Kamu Valley.
Date: June or July, 1954.
Parties:
    (*a*) Defendant: Ti Jaj of Mogo
    (*b*) Murdered man: Pi Meb of Obaa
    (*c*) Authority: Ti Mab of Mogo

Facts: The defendant and Pi Meb had gone into the woods together. In the evening, the defendant returned alone and announced that the other man had fallen from a tree and died. However, he refused to lead the people to the place of the accident. About twenty people combed the forests and finally found the corpse bearing a deep wound in the face, apparently inflicted by a stick. Since the defendant was reluctant to bring the search party to the place, and because the body lay in a very soft terrain full of rotten leaves and moss, which could not account for the deep wound, the defendant was was charged with murder.

Outcome: The defendant and the murdered man were from two different political units. To prevent war, the authority ordered blood money to be paid to the Pi people of Obaa. Close relatives of the defendant delivered 180 Km and 240 Tm to the brothers of the victim. The defendant was reprimanded for several days, but he escaped any bodily injury.

This case is used by Pospisil to illustrate one aspect of the principle of liability for homicide among Kapaukans, and it may be seen how case summaries of this kind, particularly when presented in series, may be valuable in working out a tribal *corpus juris.* At the same time, the data presented in the case raise other questions of method. The approach through the cases argues some consistency in the application of the rules from dispute to dispute. Yet even where the rules are capable of fairly precise formulation, it does not follow that the outcome of their application to a given set of circumstances can be predicted with any degree of reliability. Pospisil's cases relate to different communities and to different points of time and his summaries do not indicate the circumstances surrounding a particular dispute. The implication of Case 4, for example, where the defendants were anxious to avoid war, is that either rule 1c was not followed to the letter or that it stands in need of further qualification. In point of fact, few disputes centre upon the application of a single unequivocal rule, and the more usual content of a dispute is a dialogue of norm and counter-norm. Thus the process of litigation commonly involves the clarification of issues hitherto obscure, a point made repeatedly by Llewellyn and Hoebel in their now classic study of Cheyenne law, and in particular in their discussion of the *Case of Wolf Lies Down.* If we wish to grasp the *ratio decidendi* of a case, the rule or principle that it exemplifies or embodies, then the summary should also include some reference to the arguments adduced.

The importance of this point emerges even more forcefully when we turn from consideration of the rules themselves to the search for the unifying principles that underlie the rules—the concepts and categories of tribal jurisprudence. In the Anglo-American system of law we are, of course, accustomed to distinguish between civil and criminal law, and within the civil law between tort and contract and other of the law's major branches. Within each of these, further conceptual sub-divisions are recognized. Clearly, it would be absurd to assume *a priori* that these are all universal categories. Beidelman, for example, makes the point that jural classification, like classification of kin, varies with each society and has to be considered on its own terms in each case, and he presents an interesting illustration of a Kaguru local court treating what we would call an unnatural offence with a sheep as an issue of sexual trespass upon another man's property rather than of bestiality *per se*. A similar point lies at the core of Bohannan's exposition of Tiv jural concepts. Bohannan's view is that, in using the categories of our own legal system to organize the raw social data from other societies, one commits a cardinal ethnographic error. Where the Tiv are concerned the error would be that such an arrangement is not part of their way of looking at things, and hence would be false. Bohannan's general line of approach is best seen in his discussion of debt (*injo*). He points out that the Tiv word *injo* covers a wider range of phenomena and social relations than the English word "debt" usually does, and it includes matters which to the modern lawyer would fall into the distinct categories of tort and contract.

With Bohannan's insistence on the need to avoid doing violence to indigenous concepts I am fully in sympathy and, at the descriptive level, I applaud his attempts to capture in English the full texture and scope of Tiv legal ideas. My misgivings are that the preoccupation with what is unique in Tiv culture, and the problems of translation that this poses, blind him to problems for comparative analysis. Bohannan appears to feel that he has made his point when he shows that the Tiv idea of *injo* does not fit readily into our own modern categories of tort and contract. To this one can only say that it would be very surprising if it did, for these concepts have been worked out and refined over many centuries of continuous social change and legal growth. On the other hand, if one looks back to earlier phases in the development of the Common Law, it is interesting to discover that no adequate distinction was then drawn between proprietary rights such as an action in debt and remedies for breach of contract, or for wrongs now called torts. Bohannan himself is thus led into methodological sin because of an over-concern with cultural forms rather than universal processes. Bohannan's technique is to allow the Tiv, so far as possible, to speak for themselves, and their jural concepts are elucidated through the best possible medium—the records of cases heard before Tiv tribunals. But there is another aspect to the use of case material that should not be overlooked. Cases are also concerned with the solution of specific human problems as these arise within a given society—and this is not a static process. Novel circumstances arise which call for new solutions. Hence, as I have suggested earlier, legal ideas have continuously to be clarified and re-defined and new concepts gradually evolved in the process. The process itself is most commonly to be observed in the arguments through which a dispute is conducted. In general, Bohannan pays inadequate attention to this aspect of disputes, and it may be for this reason that when in one case he does discuss the issue explicitly, he provides a shattering instance of what may be termed Tivnocentricity. In this case, the plaintiff, a woman, had been having some trouble driving her goats to market, so she left the nanny in the care of the defendant on the understanding that he would take it to the market-place for her the following day. The woman's complaint was that the man had not done this, and had in fact sold the nanny. She sought compensation for it and for the two kids that it would have borne in the meantime. The defendant, on the other hand, argued that it was really a case of "releasing livestock," that the nanny had died, and he was not responsible. Bohannan remarks that it would be possible to consider cases that concern "releasing livestock" as cases of breach of contract, but adds: "little purpose would be served by so doing, for Tiv do not have a concept 'contract.'" It may be noted that early English law similarly lacked the concept, and that a bench of early Common Law judges might have handled the case not very differently from the Tiv. Bohannan observes, moreover, how in presenting his case the defendant sought to change the norm involved, so that his action would seem to be in accordance with *some* norm. In this the defendant was, of course, presenting a problem that must be familiar to any bench, and if the argument was in this instance somewhat ingenuous, at least it indicated the path along which the development of legal ideas can take place. In short, what Bohannan has overlooked is that there are certain questions of a legal character that must arise in any human society: What kinds of injury are to be recognized as calling for the right to redress? How is the notion of obligation to be defined: of what kinds are they and to whom are they owed, and in what measure? What is the nature of liability, and how far shall it take account of intention, negligence, or accident? Different societies will offer different solutions to these questions, but at least by posing the problem in these terms we can go on to examine the way in which they are related to other aspects of the social system, and to note the sets of conditions under which refinements of legal doctrine occur and new concepts and categories emerge. In this task the study of cases, in which full attention is paid to the play of argument, is an essential tool. An English legal historian has remarked that in the present state of our knowledge we cannot tell how the forms of action grew up in early English law, and adds that probably we never shall. "The plea rolls if completely analysed might tell us, but only a record of the discussions in the Inns of Court and of Serjeant's Inn would probably settle the point: such a record almost certainly does not exist." In the same way, without the adequate recording of tribal case material, we are bound to remain in ignorance of many of the essential features of primitive jurisprudence.

Procedures of Inquiry and Adjudication

I began with the postulate that there is no human group known to us in which men do not have their differences of opinion and quarrels. Friction indeed appears to be an inescapable fact of social life; and not merely because of the individual's concern in promoting his own interests, but also because disputes so frequently have their sources in the arrangements and conflicting norms of society itself. Yet the waging of disputes, if left unchecked, is also apt to be a wasteful and disruptive activity that may obstruct the achievement of other human ends and purposes. The problem, therefore, is not to eliminate dissension and faction but to provide the means through which grievances can be legitimately aired and disputes properly conducted. One of the tasks of the anthropologist is the examination of the various solutions to this problem that have been devised in different societies, and the structural and cultural features with which they are associated.

There are really three aspects to the problem—the inquiry into guilt or responsibility for a particular event; the process of adjudication between conflicting claims; and the modes of redress and enforcement where a breach of entitlement has been established or assumed. These three aspects are closely interrelated: in any given society, therefore, the lines of distinction between them are likely to be blurred and a single procedural arrangement may well cover more than one aspect; alternatively, different procedures may be invoked depending on social context and situation. Thus among ourselves a court of law combines the functions of inquiry and adjudication, and imposes penalties or indicates the mode of redress, and only the actual enforcement is left to other agencies. In tribal communities, on the other hand, where mystical techniques are commonly employed to discover an unknown offender, the merger of functions may in some instances be even more complete. Among the Azande, for example, the *bagbuduma* magic resorted to in cases of homicide where the sorcerer is not known is "regarded as a judge which seeks out the person who is responsible for the death, and as an executioner which slays him." Nevertheless, the importance of the analytical distinctions remains. The Azande, who practise vengeance magic, also recognize divination as a quite distinct procedure, while in

English law cases of death in violent or suspicious circumstances are first made the subject of a coroner's inquest. In short, we have to deal with a range of solutions that fall along a continuum, each procedural device having its own distinctive characteristics, but also sharing to some extent the properties of others. . . .

But not all grievances relate to what is "hidden and unknown" and not all disputes have their sources in a crisis of moral choice. In many instances a man is aggrieved because he feels that he can point to a clear breach of entitlement, and claims to know or can at least guess who the offender is. Here the inquiry takes a different form: it is now more a question of establishing the degree of liability and how it should be apportioned. The appropriate procedure in these circumstances will be some form of hearing, conducted according to well-understood rules, in which the disputants submit their case for arbitrament or adjudication. The essential characteristic of this mode is that it is a contest conducted by way of argument about the norms of entitlement.

The court of law provides the most obvious instance of such a process, but it is also important to remember that adjudication may cover a range of procedures. These vary from society to society, and, even within the same society, the procedure to be adopted depending not only on the nature of the issues in dispute, but on the framework of social relationships within which the dispute arises. For purposes of cross-cultural comparison, clear analytical distinctions are essential. We need to know whether we are observing a judicial process, in which judgment follows the rational assessment of the evidence and the arguments adduced, a tribunal of arbitration, or something else, and this requires that the full conduct of the proceedings, as well as their social context, shall be made absolutely clear. . . .

What I am suggesting, then, is that each mode of procedure has to be regarded as possessing its own internal structure in which the physical setting, the personnel involved, the nature of the dispute, and the character of the hearing itself are all interrelated. In terms of fieldwork this means that we must note where the hearing takes place, whether in a court-house or yard or in an open space; what persons are involved and the capacities in which they are present or serve; when and under what circumstances the body is convened; what powers it has and how far these are limited by jurisdiction, by the right of appeal, or otherwise. But the central problem here is the nature of the adjudicatory process itself: the aims which the process is designed to serve, and the means by which they are achieved. . . .

Detailed analysis of case material can thus throw a great deal of light on the adjudicatory process: the form that juridical reasoning takes in different societies; the assumptions that the judges bring to their task; the way in which decisions are arrived at, and the extent to which they are acceptable to the litigants. But the method may also be used to illuminate a number of other problems, for example, the way in which courts are able to accommodate the law to changing social circumstances or such questions as the relationship of law to custom or morality. Thus in the case just cited we may see how custom enters into the field of legal action without losing its distinctive identity. In that instance it appears that in Bemba tribal custom the obligations to one's wife's kin are onerous, and not even a chief may always successfully evade them. But such customs are not in themselves legally enforceable. No Bemba, for example, could bring a case againat his son-in-law simply because the latter had failed to greet him in the customary fashion. On the other hand, should a more serious dispute arise at a later date, such as a case of divorce, then such incidents might well be recalled and would assume significance as throwing light on the total social relationship in question.

Analyses of these kinds impose special demands on the fieldworker. Involved here are such matters as the way in which the case is presented; the modes of interrogation and examination; the kinds of evidence that may be led and the ways in which it is assessed; the often unspoken assumptions that underlie the judges' approach to their task. All of this requires much more than a summary of the facts and arguments of a case. It demands careful and detailed recording of all that passes at the hearing, including where possible the murmured *obiter dicta* of the judges, as well as the reactions of the audience. This is at the best of times a laborious and time-consuming task, and even where the fieldworker has a fair degree of fluency in the vernacular the use of idiom and metaphor and elliptic references to persons, events, or topography make it all too easy to miss vital points in the cut and thrust of argument. I do not wholly share Bohannan's view that the only sensible gadget for doing anthropological field research is the human understanding and a notebook. Thus my objection to the use of a tape-recorder for recording cases is not so much that it introduces 'gadgetry' into fieldwork, but that under the usual conditions of field research it simply does not work, or raises more problems that it solves. I did not have a machine when I studied urban courts on the Copperbelt, where the circumstances would probably have been quite favourable, but I did experiment with one in the more conventional setting of my fieldwork on the island of Matupit, New Britain. Far from disturbing the flow of action I found on Matupit that as the disputants warmed to their task they forgot all about the presence of the machine, so that in the subsequent attempts at transcription little could be picked out above the din of altercation and mutual abuse.

The procedure I have myself adopted has been to train an assistant to record the case in the vernacular as it proceeded or, where this was not possible, to prepare a text on it as soon as possible thereafter. At the same time I myself took notes of the hearing, recording passages or phrases verbatim in the vernacular. The two records were then checked against each other, discussed and clarified, and combined in a final typed record of the case. In this form the record served as a springboard to further inquiry: points that remained obscure or aspects of the case that I wished to pursue further could be taken up with different informants. It scarcely needs adding that this method may also be extremely useful in paving the way for broader ethnographic inquiry. . . . [M]aterial on disputes can be used as a starting-point for gathering information on nearly every other subject.

Redress, Sanctions, and Social Control

In the previous section two aspects of the handling of disputes have been considered: the inquisitorial and the adjudicatory. It remains now to consider . . . the modes of redress by which entitlements are enforced, the validity of norms that have been broken are reaffirmed, and the situation created by breach readjusted. This raises at once a wider range of problems than those considered hitherto. Ideally, perhaps, adjudication and politics represent two distinct fields of action, but probably in no society does the dispute process provide an instance of their complete divorce from one another. Among ourselves, for example, the very decision to go to court may well be prompted by political considerations, and a court trial may on occasion simply provide the legal trappings for what is essentially a political contest. Nevertheless, for certain purposes it is legitimate to treat the political factor as marginal: in the analysis of the judicial process, for example, we are concerned with the principles that give structure and coherence to a hearing, not why the case was brought in the first place. But when we treat of law in its aspect of social control we move more directly into the realm of politics itself. In this context our concern with the use of case material also shifts. In the earlier analysis the case was treated, so to speak, as a system in itself from the analysis of which certain regularities of a legal or forensic order could be abstracted. In the present context the case remains the unit of analysis, but in its political aspect as an index of group relationships.

In few societies is there a precise or automatic correspondence between offence and remedy. In primitive societies in particular, . . . the reaction to a particular breach of norm is bound up very closely with the nature of the social units involved. Hence, . . . in societies that lack the organs of centralized government it is the political aspect of the dispute process, rather than the purely forensic, which is the more immediately striking. . . . [V]illage meetings were a regular feature of social life, and much of the business of these meetings was taken up with the hearing of cases. I have myself referred elsewhere to the "necessity of decision" as a primary characteristic of a court of law. The procedure for hearing cases on Matupit had much in common with what I knew of courts in Africa, so I was at first puzzled to find that many of the village meetings at which disputes over land were submitted for public arbitrament had to break up without arriving at any satisfactory resolution of the issues. The fact was that what I was observing was less a judicial hearing than part of an on-going political process. The disputants might point to the wrongs they had been done, and couch their arguments in terms of an appeal to jural norms and precedents, but it was also apparent that they were rival leaders canvassing support and recognition of their authority: such hearings provided a forum for a trial of political strength as between opposed groups and not merely for the adjudication of legal issues and a claim for redress as between individual litigants.

The treatment of disputes within a political frame of reference calls for quite a different kind of case material, and a different mode of analysis. I would argue further that, in the context of discussions of social control, the use of material on disputes that does not take full account of the political aspect is open to serious criticism. In the first place, cases become difficult to follow, often because the reported behaviour of the parties, when not related to an on-going set of relationships, appears as arbitrary and capricious. Secondly, the presence of interesting theoretical problems is obscured. . . .

Conclusion

. . . Gluckman has followed Stone and other jurists in recognizing that a term such as "law" has many referents, and that the search for a single meaning, valid for all purposes, is quite futile. Similarly, in this essay, I have treated law as a complex social phenomenon concerned with a series of problems with which all human groups would appear to be confronted, and for which solutions must be devised. Postulating disputes as a universal feature of social life, I have sought to delimit some of the aspects of law, suggesting how each of them presents a different set of problems for anthropological investigation and research. I then tried to show how the case method, employed both as a field technique and as a tool of analysis, and applied in different ways, may serve to illuminate these problems. The discussion has concentrated on law as a body of rules, as a set of procedures of inquiry and adjudication, and as an instrument of social control. Nor does this, of course, exhaust the topic. Law may also be regarded as embodying a system of values; moreover, as a social institution it is itself subject to evaluation. We are concerned here with the basic assumptions or postulates that underlie the social life of a community, and the ways in which the task and purpose of law may be perceived. These are not easy questions to handle, yet even here the value of taking disputes as a point of departure, and examining them from the different points of view outlined in this essay, should at least be apparent. Thus the very conditions that characterize the hearing of cases contain a statement about the culture of a group that tells us at the same time something of immediate relevance about the place of law within the community. The seeming casualness of the proceedings in some African tribal courts is in marked contrast to the august atmosphere of their English counterparts. But, as Elias has pointed out, such informality does not mean that the actual situation is chaotic; rather, it reflects how closely the work of the courts is bound up in the daily lives of the people. I was present on one occasion at the court of the Bemba Paramount Chief when a schoolboy came to complain of being unfairly punished by his teacher. The court members were evidently amused at the lad's precocity, but they maintained a strict judicial gravity, summoned the teacher to appear before them, and dealt with the case in the same way as all the others. The court, in short, is conceived of as a possession of the people, a forum to which all may submit their grievances in the expectation of receiving a full and proper hearing. It is clear, again, that in the hearings themselves the statements of the litigants, the questioning of witnesses, and the deliberations of the judges not only illustrate legal ideas but also provide us with texts that embody many of the basic premises of the group, both implicit and explicit. But we need not stop at this point. The Bemba have a saying, *mulandu taupwa,* a case never ends. It is not so much that quarrels are never wholly resolved, but rather that cases have their sources in the ceaseless flow of social life and, in turn, contribute to that flow. For certain analytical purposes we carve a sequence of events—which we call a case—out of its matrix and dissect it. But if we are to gain a deeper understanding of the role of law in society, and its relation to justice and other social values, it is not enough to concentrate attention simply on the dispute process. We need to know a great deal more about the impact of judicial decisions, and of the ways they are communicated and received. Perhaps to this end the study of the "case" needs finally to be reset in the framework of the on-going social process from which it was abstracted.

Chapter 10

Law and Economics

Tribe, Policy Science: Analysis or Ideology?*

. . . With the market as a central paradigm, [the] model takes as its starting point the idea of individual man as a rational maximizer of satisfactions operating self-interestedly (i.e., typically motivated neither by altruism nor by envy) in a world of relative scarcity. Problems of choice, whether individual or social, are perceived essentially as problems of marginal "trade-off" or "exchange" among desired outputs, attributes, or ingredients of welfare. Inasmuch as gains with respect to some outputs (or the welfare of some individuals) may occasionally be achieved at the expense of other outputs (or individuals), there arises quite naturally the notion of the production-possibility frontier (or transformation curve) as the locus of all those combinations of relevant outputs (or attributes or individual states of welfare) which have the property that no gain in any one output can be realized without some loss in another. To decide which point on the production-possibility frontier (the so-called "efficient set") he prefers to all others, a satisfaction-maximizing individual in effect constructs a set of indifference curves (or surfaces), each

*[*Philosophy & Public Affairs*, 2, no. 1, p. 66 (Fall 1972). Copyright © 1972 by Princeton University Press. Reprinted by permission of Princeton University Press.

Laurence H. Tribe (1941–   ) received his A.B. (1962) and J.D. (1966) from Harvard University. Upon graduation from law school, he was Law Clerk for Justice M. O. Tobriner, California Supreme Court (1966-1967), and for Mr. Justice Stewart, United States Supreme Court (1967-1968). Since 1968, he has been a faculty member at Harvard University School of Law, where he received his professorship in 1972. Especially interested in the relationship between law and technology, his published works include *Channeling Technology Through Law* (1973), *Environmental Protection* (with L. Jaffee, 1971), and *Technology—Processes of Assessment* (with H. Brooks and Technology Assessment Panel, 1969).]

defined by the property that the individual is indifferent among the combinations of outputs represented by the various points of any given indifference curve. The indifference curves are treated as varying continuously with each output, so that arbitrarily small increments of any output can be "traded off" for sufficiently small decrements of any other; and such continuous substitutability is assumed to hold over the entire range of each output, so that arbitrarily low levels of any given output (i.e., levels arbitrarily close to zero) can be compensated for by sufficiently high levels of another output. Having constructed his indifference curves in this way, the rational individual chooses that point on the production-possibility frontier which lies on the highest of all those of his indifference curves that intersect the frontier, typically a point of tangency.[7]

If a large number of satisfaction-maximizing individuals are put into a perfectly competitive market situation (that is, a situation where all participants have complete information, all can bargain at no cost, and none can independently influence group behavior), classical economic theory dictates that the individuals will adjust their patterns of production, and will trade among themselves the goods they have produced, until all have identical marginal rates of substitution for all goods; until that point is reached, exchanges will be made moving each individual to a higher indifference curve. Prices—or more accurately, relative prices —serve as a common denominator defining the relative values different individuals place on different alternatives, providing a measure of the ratio of the rates of substitution between alternatives.

. . . This technique, which marks the effective socialization of the policy sciences' market origins, assumes that it is possible for the policy analyst to estimate the quantities of benefits stemming from a (usually governmental) project under alternative designs, the quantities of things used up or reduced, and the prices that should be associated with both ends of this equation. Given this information, the analyst is to choose that design which maximizes the difference between benefits and costs. Put this way, the problem seems largely to be one of measurement, the conversion of costs and benefits into some common denominator; corre-

7. The situation may be described in another way. As an individual moves along the production-possibility frontier he continually gives up some of one alternative in order to produce more of another. The measure of this trade-off is the rate of transformation. As the slope of the curve changes, this rate changes also. At any point on the curve the rate is defined marginally, as the slope between two points separated by a distance tending toward zero. This slope is called the marginal rate of transformation. Much the same can be said for indifference curves; the corresponding terms are rate of substitution and marginal rate of substitution.

spondingly, the role of the analyst becomes that of simulator, determining the prices that would have been attached to the various goods if a perfectly competitive market had existed.

Alternatively, the analytical problem may be seen as one of determining which attributes of the various outcomes, among both costs and benefits, to take into account, and with what weights. Traditionally, the practice has been to focus on those costs and benefits accruing to the persons associated with the decision-maker, leaving "externalities" out of the analysis. Further . . . there has generally been an attempt to separate costs and benefits related to efficiency (those bearing on "total" welfare or income) from distributional and other supposedly "intangible" considerations. Whatever cannot be expressed in terms of the common-denominator metric at the heart of the analysis is either excluded from consideration, simply noted outside of the analysis itself for the decision-maker's possible use, or at most incorporated into the analysis in the form of a constraint—a qualitative requirement, subject to which the project is designed so as to maximize benefits minus costs.

Once the analysis focuses explicitly on the definition and weighting of the key attributes in a decision problem, it may take the form of an explicit definition of an "object function," a rule that associates with each outcome a single mathematically determined value by means of which it may be compared with other outcomes. In practice, an objective function is rarely used to develop a complete ranking of all alternatives; instead the rule is used to select an optimal alternative—one that either minimizes or maximizes the value of the objective function.[13] The complexity of the objective function depends upon the kind of policy analysis undertaken. For a cost-benefit analysis, the function may be of the apparently simple form: maximize "benefits" minus "costs." . . . Whatever the formal complexity, however, certain critical decisions—which attributes to regard as relevant and what weights to attach to each—must always be made by someone.

Thus far, the techniques explored assume complete information as to the outcomes of various alternatives. Indeed, largely because institutional arrangements to force a confrontation with the *lack* of complete

---

13. "Maximizing" may not be strictly correct; taking into account the extent of a decision maker's uncertainty and the high costs of fully evaluating all conceivable alternatives, he may do best simply by "satisficing" within a model of "bounded rationality." See Herbert A. Simon, *Models of Man: Social and Rational* (New York, 1967), pp. 241-260. This model employs a simplified objective function (perhaps classifying outcomes only as poor and good), a highly limited set of alternatives, and a sequential choice process including selection of the first "satisfactory" alternative encountered, adjusting the definition of "satisfactory" upward if the choice proves easy and downward if the choice proves difficult.

data have rarely been designed, the techniques are often employed with remarkable disregard for underlying uncertainties (of description or prediction) that render their conclusions indeterminate in critical respects. The theoretical apparatus for the inclusion of uncertainty, however, has not been lacking. Systematic efforts to incorporate uncertainty into policy analysis began with the publication in 1944 of von Neumann and Morgenstern's *Theory of Games and Economic Behavior,* which provided a technique whereby a decision-maker could assign numbers (so-called "utilities") . . . to the set of all outcomes under consideration in such a way that (a) in the absence of any uncertainty the utilities express the decision-maker's ordinal ranking of the outcomes; and (b) given uncertainty, the utilities so incorporate the decision-maker's attitude toward risk that, under certain axioms resembling those of classical economic theory, the decision-maker will choose alternatives in a way that maximizes the expected utility of his choice.[17] . . .

Taken together, the family of techniques considered here have all been conceived as ways of improving decision-making by broadening the role of logic and empirical inquiry. While policy analysts themselves have begun to qualify their claims by making increasingly explicit the interests and values they believe any particular analysis includes or excludes, other disciplines, attracted by the theoretical rigor that remains, seek to employ the policy sciences with an enthusiasm that stands in growing contrast to the analysts' own circumspection.

II. Through a Slide Rule Darkly

One of the most persistent beliefs about the techniques discussed above is a conviction of their transparency to considerations of value and their neutrality with respect to fundamental world views and to more or less ultimate ends. Although it is by now widely recognized that such techniques can be abused as tools in a disguised play for power, the myth endures that the techniques *in themselves* lack substantive content, that intrinsically they provide nothing beyond value-free devices for organizing thought in rational ways—methods for sorting out issues and objectively clarifying the empirical relationships among alternative actions and their likely consequences. The user of such techniques, the myth

17. To deal formally with probability assessments involving unique events, Bayesian decision theory . . . construes probability statements as expressing subjective degrees of confidence. Thus, to say that X attaches a subjective probability of 30 percent to proposition S means that X would be indifferent between (a) betting that S is true and (b) betting on a lottery (with the same stakes) having a known 30 percent chance of winning.

continues, may turn them to whatever ends he seeks. Ends and values, goals and ideologies are seen as mere "inputs" to a machinelike, and hence inherently unbiased, process of solving problems consistent with the facts known and the values posited. The machine itself, like all machines, is said to be subject to misuse but to have no imperatives of its own; only animistic thinking, we are told, can obscure its essential neutrality.

How are such claims to be approached? From the start, some degree of skepticism would seem appropriate, inasmuch as every other language (and the policy sciences are surely languages, at least in part) imposes its own categories and paradigms on the world of experience, every other system of thought its own tendencies on the world of aspiration. I am reminded here of a passage quoted by Michel Foucault, in which Borges refers to the assertion of a certain Chinese encyclopedia that "animals are divided into: (a) belonging to the Emperor, (b) embalmed, (c) tame, (d) sucking pigs, (e) sirens, (f) fabulous, (g) stray dogs, (h) included in the present classification, (i) frenzied, (j) innumerable, (k) drawn with a very fine camelhair brush, (l) et cetera, (m) having just broken the water pitcher, (n) that from a long way off look like flies." As Foucault observes, what we "apprehend in one great leap" in "the wonderment of this taxonomy" is not only "the exotic charm of another system of thought" but—even more pointedly—"the limitation of our own, the stark impossibility of thinking *that*."[18]

To each "system of thought," each distinctive approach to stating and solving problems, at least presumptively there should correspond important versions of Foucault's unthinkable—perspectives and possibilities hidden if not entirely obscured by the system's basic design and by its fundamental presuppositions. The policy sciences (and their analogues in law and other fields), one can hypothesize, are unlikely to be different in this respect. But because their language has not (yet) become fully our own—because it is still possible for most of us to stand outside their frame of reference—we are in a position to perceive, in rough outline, the ways in which the policy sciences structure our world: the gaps they leave and the distortions they promote in that world as we might otherwise perceive it, or as we might otherwise wish to approach it.

In attempting to understand the sort of lens through which the policy sciences view their subject matter, it is helpful to begin by noting the extreme importance that the social sciences as a whole (of which the policy sciences represent a subcategory) have long given to objectivity—to detached, deliberately impersonal, empirically verifiable, and purport-

18. Michel Foucault, *The Order of Things* (New York, 1970), p. xv.

edly value-free analysis. Undoubtedly deriving in part from insecurity about the intellectual credentials (and hence the political power) of social science, this compulsion to imitate the exact sciences has been coupled with the premise that in those fields the accepted methodology has in fact been a wholly impersonal one, resting on purely "objective" modes of relation between the observer and the object of observation. It is because of this premise, for example, that necessarily "personal" judgments about values have long been deemed improper (because "unscientific") subjects for economic discourse.[19]

This entire emphasis, however, is based on a profoundly misguided (albeit widely held) conception of how even the most "exact" of the sciences approaches the world. As Michael Polanyi convincingly showed some time ago, deeply personal appraisals play a crucial role in the evolution and testing of any scientific theory.[20] Polanyi's insight that such theories must rest on fundamental personal orientations toward the world—individual human appraisals of order, connection, probability that cannot be accounted for in purely empiricist, value-free terms[21]—parallels Russell's realization that the very existence of a meaningful science presupposes some knowledge independent of experience;[22] . . . Thus "the objectivist urge to depersonalize our intelligent mental processes,"[24] . . . may well be false to the biological character of knowing itself as well as to the historical truth of how bodies of scientific knowledge have in fact evolved. There are good reasons, therefore, to suppose that the social sciences' passion for objectivity (in the sense of impersonal, detached, and purely empirical modes of investigation) is seriously misplaced.

But one need not accept this analysis in order to study the consequences, for particular enterprises within the social sciences, of pursuing a relentlessly objectivist position. Even if one rejects, for example, Polanyi's epistemological attack on the disjunction of subjectivity and objectivity,[25] one can still find it worthwhile to explore the system of effects

19. See, e.g., Lionel Robbins, *An Essay on the Nature and Significance of Economic Science,* 2nd ed. (London, 1935), pp. 142-143, 148-149.

20. *Personal Knowledge* (Chicago, 1958). . . .

21. Even probability statements, as Polanyi stresses, can never be "strictly contradicted by experience" (*Personal Knowledge,* p. 21).

22. Bertrand Russell, *Human Knowledge: Its Scope and Limits* (New York, 1948), pp. 522, 524, 526-527.

24. *Personal Knowledge,* p. 257.

25. For Polanyi, the concept of "personal knowledge" transcends the objective-subjective dichotomy by embodying both an irreducibly nonobjective dimension, insofar as it rests on an individual's appraisal and passion, and an irreducibly nonsubjective dimension, insofar as it rests on a commitment to obey requirements acknowledged by the individual to be independent of the self (*Personal Knowledge,* p. 300).

that may follow from constructing a theory or a methodology upon that disjunction—to investigate the ways in which a self-consciously objectivist ideal may substantively structure the characteristics and the conclusions of a given mode of thought.[26]

The central claim of the policy sciences, of course, has been their asserted capacity to enlarge the role of explicit, logical reasoning, of empirical knowledge, and of consensual discourse in realms of decision-making otherwise dominated by supposedly less trustworthy sources of choice. Insofar as this claim rests on the sort of objectivist ideal I have been discussing, it presents a special case of the general question posed above: How might objectivism itself shape the conclusions of a theory or method in the social sciences?

Before attempting to address that question directly, I would make one further comment. When I describe the several respects in which I believe objectivism distorts the perspectives afforded by the policy sciences, I do not mean to assert that there is some sort of necessary or even "causal" connection between the objectivist ideal, on the one hand, and each of the categories of distortion I will outline, on the other. I mean to argue only that objectivism as an ideal is related in a natural and reciprocal way to the entire collection of distortions taken as a whole—that it provides a central vantage point from which to observe the system of which each individual category of distortions forms an important part.[27]

1. Collapsing Process into Result

From many perspectives, the *procedures* that shape individual and social activity have significance independent of the final products they generate. Yet the traditional approach of both moral philosophy and welfare economics has been to focus exclusively on the end results of social and institutional processes in assessing their value. Thus classical utilitarianism, for example, has asked simply whether a particular process or distribution produces the greatest net balance of satisfaction; still other teleological doctrines have asked whether a process maximizes

26. Obviously, more must be said to specify the exact functions and features of the "objectivist ideal" posited here. . . , but I trust that the general shape of the concept is clear enough for our purposes without further elaboration.

27. It might prove even more illuminating to view the system of distortions from the substantive perspective of the policy sciences' underlying axiom of individual satisfaction-maximizing behavior, but I leave that possibility for later study. Another and quite different approach to this entire subject (an approach I intend to explore in subsequent work) would be to investigate not so much the *consequences* of the policy sciences' axioms and criteria as the underlying *pattern* they reveal, to study how that pattern "interlocks" with other contemporaneously developed areas of thought (cf. Foucault's *The Order of Things*), and to examine what underlying *purposes* the pattern and its history reveal. . . .

841

some other independently defined good (in the case of Aristotelian or Nietzschean perfectionism, for instance, human excellence); and classical welfare economics has asked whether a process or distribution (that of the market, for example) is Pareto-optimal in the sense that its results could not be altered to the benefit of some without detriment to others. Such "end-result" theories have great appeal, for the notion of maximizing some desired end may seem the very essence of rationality.[28]. . .

The history of American legal thought in this regard is only superficially different. Early notions of law as the objective expression of transcendent reason, successfully attacked by legal realism and sociological jurisprudence, have been re-formed into less mechanical, but no less rationalist, theories of law as process—but as process typically justified either in purely formal, positivist terms or in terms of a supposed tendency to maximize aggregate satisfaction in the end, rather than in terms intrinsic to the process itself in its constitutive function of defining substantive human roles, rights, and relationships and structuring their evolution over time. Paradoxically enough, therefore, proceduralism in legal thought has served largely as an "economic" vehicle of concern for end-result maximization.

In the light of their intellectual origins in the same broad tradition, it should not be surprising that the policy sciences too have taken an end-result position, focusing almost exclusively on ultimate outcomes, with no independent concern for the *procedure* whereby those outcomes are produced or for the *history* out of which they evolve. This lack of concern for process comes about partly because procedures for choice must include processes to resolve conflicts among persons and their interests, and most policy analysts believe that methods which rank as "objective" within their intellectual heritage can never settle how true conflicts should be resolved. But other facts also appear to play a role. Thus, . . . the characteristic obsession of policy analysis with end results may stem in part from the difficulty of always treating procedures as purely instrumental—and the resulting difficulty of reducing them to variables chosen mechanically (i.e., in an objective, impersonal way) so as to maximize some appropriately defined objective function. Finally, there may be intrinsic difficulties of self-reference (akin to those encountered in set theory, logic, and transformational linguistics) that arise

28. Compare the discussion of the deep intuitive appeal of teleological theories in John Rawls, *A Theory of Justice* (Cambridge, Mass., 1971), pp. 24-25. I first criticized the tendency of economics and policy analysis to focus on results to the exclusion of process in "Trial by Mathematics: Precision and Ritual in the Legal Process," *Harvard Law Review* 84 (1971): 1329, 1381-1383, 1391-1392. End-result theories are, of course, natural outgrowths of all *instrumental* (means-end) concepts of the rational.

when an analytic technique is focused on a process of choice that, if fully specified, would include reliance on the technique itself, rather than entirely upon some "detachable" subject matter. It appears, therefore, that the objectivist ideal lies close to the source of a major distortion in the policy sciences' perspective.

Nor can it be doubted that the distortion is a significant one. In most areas of human endeavor—from performing a symphony to orchestrating a society—the processes and rules that constitute the enterprise and define the roles of its participants matter quite apart from any identifiable "end state" that is ultimately produced. Indeed, in many cases it is the process itself that matters *most* to those who take part in it. Thus, when coupled with the policy analyst's characteristically passive role in accepting problems as formulated by a client, the reduction of all process to result virtually assures that the advice offered by the analyst will often be wide of the mark. For example, if an agency asks "Where should we build this highway?" the best answer would often be "Don't ask me that; ask me to help you design a procedure for consultation and bargaining to help decide where." But the mode of thought engendered by objectivist policy science greatly reduces the probability that any such answer will be offered.[42]

2. Reducing Wholes and Blending Parts

Just as the policy sciences are driven (in part by the search for "objectivity") to collapse process into result, so too, and for closely linked reasons, they are driven to collapse results into structureless mass. Seeking to limit himself to matters about which he can be "completely objective," the policy analyst who must compare two alternative courses of action first focuses on the *consequences* of each alternative (the initial or "process" reduction) and then on *objectively comparable features* of those consequences (the second or "substance" reduction), a task that suggests either (1) finding a common denominator to which all can be reduced, or (2) at least establishing "substitution rates" or "exchange ratios" (e.g., in

42. On the rare occasions when such an answer is given, the persisting tendency of the policy sciences is to overlook the significance of procedure *as such,* treating a process of choice or coordination as nothing more than a machine for generating outcomes. To use an instructive parable suggested to me by Robert Nozick, if a policy analyst were consulted by the members of an orchestra who wished to coordinate their efforts to play a Brahms concerto, he might advise them to use a special stylus he had invented to etch the optimal outcome (the ideal "sound of music") on a plastic disk, completely missing the point that the processes of interaction, coordination, and participation according to defined rules are themselves of overriding importance to the players.

the form of smooth indifference curves) for the comparison by pairs of the key attributes of each consequence.[43]

To offer a crude but instructive analogy, the comparison of a particular painting by Rembrandt with one by Picasso (to help decide, for example, whether it would be desirable to sell one in order to buy the other) in terms true to the objectivist ideal might proceed first by disregarding the history of each work (the "process" reduction), in order to focus exclusively on what appears on the canvas; and second by considering each work (the "substance" reduction) as just so much paint of various specifiable colors, in order to focus on features that can be impersonally compared (e.g., the Picasso might contain more of certain pigments than the Rembrandt). Such "structural" features as balance, movement, composition, and the like would be left out of account; for how could one "objectively" compare or even "analyze" them?

As Rawls has demonstrated in the field of moral philosophy,[44] any teleological theory—needing a way to compare the diverse good of different individuals so that the total good might be maximized—must seek "a common denominator among the plurality of persons, an interpersonal currency as it were, by means of which the social ordering can be specified." The tendency of teleological theories, as Rawls shows, is thus to arrive at some form of hedonism, the maximization of the net balance of pleasure over pain, whether as the principle of rational action for an individual person or as the more extended principle of rational choice for a society of persons. The classical utilitarian, for example, can be best understood as conceiving of "separate individuals . . . as so many different lines along which rights and duties are to be assigned and scarce means of satisfaction allocated . . . so as to give the greatest fulfillment of wants. The nature of the decision . . . is not, therefore, materially different from that of an entrepreneur deciding how to maximize his profit by producing this or that commodity, or that of a consumer deciding how to maximize his satisfaction by the purchase of this or that collection of goods. In each case there is a single person whose system of desires determines the best allocation of limited means. The correct decision is essentially a question of efficient administration." Thus the classical utilitarian, seeking an objective basis for social choice, conflates all persons into one (often through the device of an imagined "impartial spectator") and all goods into the production of a single good—individ-

43. An assumption of continuous substitutability is implicit even in the least obviously market-oriented method, . . . but the characteristic invocation of the continuity axiom is itself significant, and the axiom is needed for many (although not all) of the typical applications of policy analysis techniques.

44. *A Theory of Justice*, pp. 559–60.

ual satisfaction—whose maximization over the sum of all persons becomes the sole end of rational policy. Such a vision is an inescapably ideological one and lies at the core of "cost-benefit" analysis, with "total net benefits" serving to replace the concept of total individual satisfaction.

I believe that Rawls is correct when he argues that this program is radically misconceived, and that "there is no [single] dominant end the pursuit of which accords with our considered judgments of value." But more than that, I believe that the entire conception of reducing complex structures to their separate parts, and then making key features of those parts comparable by establishing rates of exchange among them, is in many contexts a profoundly limiting and distorting mode of analysis. . . .

C. *Reductionism in the Policy Sciences.* . . . [T]he policy sciences appear to be driven, partly by the objectivist ideal, to reduce the outcomes of decision problems to structureless masses, expressing the results of alternative courses of action in terms of greater or lesser amounts of certain qualities among which standards of commensurability are clearly established. Moreover, we have seen both how pervasive this reductionist approach has been in our intellectual tradition and how unacceptable its conclusions can be when certain structural features or discontinuities are posited.

There is a strong tendency, in this general mode of thought, to treat any indication of discontinuous or structured attributes in one of two ways. The first response is simply to treat the matter in question as involving a qualitative constraint—which usually means relegating it to the status of a mere afterthought in any full analysis or, equally significant, regarding it as an externally (and often politically) "given" feature of the situation rather than one amenable to analysis and rational discussion.[82] The second response is to overlook or deny the existence of the discontinuity altogether, often confusing the assertion of discontinuity with an assertion of absolute dominance. For example, when it is argued that man may owe something to nature for reasons beyond his own future well-being, and that avoiding at least *some* incursions into nature may have lexical priority over certain other human goods, a frequent response is that man clearly owes *nothing* to nature as such, because it is implausible "that the preservation of every extant biological species is an

---

82. . . . At most the policy analyst may manipulate the objective function by estimating its value under each of several hypothetical constraints so as to convey a sense of what "price" imposing the constraints at various levels might entail; but this is not always attempted, and even it falls far short of a full examination of the structures in question and how they are formed.

absolute good to be set above any conceivable human benefit that might come as a by-product of its extinction."[84] This seems to me a non sequitur. It might well be the case that there is no species whose complete preservation should have lexical priority over all human goods; but it simply does not follow that *no* minimal level (or perhaps some "overall" level) of species survival or diversity should receive lexical priority over at least *some* kinds of human benefits. Nor would it seem peculiar to insist, for example, that a lower limit be established on especially cruel treatment of animals, whatever the economic gains this cruelty brings to persons in general. The formulation of an appropriate moral theory in this regard must await further developments, but it already seems clear that the objectivist tendency to deny discontinuities by reducing everything to varying levels of smoothly interchangeable attributes (inevitably related to human satisfaction) seriously limits the capacity of the policy sciences to accommodate certain kinds of values.

Three categories of values that are particularly vulnerable or "fragile" in this regard suggest themselves. The first category encompasses those values that are intrinsically incommensurable, in at least some of their salient dimensions, with the human satisfactions that are bound to play a central role in any policy analysis; here I would include values related to ecological balance, unspoiled wilderness, species diversity, and the like.

The second category encompasses values with inherently global, holistic, or structural features that cannot be reduced to any finite listing or combination of independent attributes. Here I would again include ecological balance but also urban aesthetics, community cohesion, and the like.

The third and final category encompasses values that have an "on-off" character, and usually also a deeply evocative and emotional aspect. Under this heading I would include such values as the integrity of the body (threatened, for example, by chemical intrusion) or the integrity of the community or neighborhood (threatened, for example by an influx of little-understood "outsiders").

Whenever values in any of these major categories appear to be involved, at least potentially, in a given problem, one should recognize that the techniques of policy analysis as currently conceived will tend either to filter them out of the investigation altogether or to treat them in ways inconsistent with their special character.[89]

84. Address by Dean Harvey Brooks, Harvard Division of Engineering and Applied Physics, "What Can Technology Do About Technology," delivered 14 October 1970 at the Industrial Research Institute, Washington, D.C.

89. It should be noted that I have not included as a separate category of values intrin-

I have elsewhere referred to a closely related phenomenon as the "dwarfing of soft variables," arguing that quantitative decision-making techniques are likely to bias conclusions in the direction of the considerations they can most readily incorporate. But the problem here goes deeper. It relates not merely to undervaluing certain factors but to *reducing entire problems to terms that misstate their underlying structure,* typically collapsing into the task of maximizing some simple quantity an enterprise whose ordering principle is not one of maximization at all.

3. Anesthetizing Moral Feeling

It is increasingly remarked that the antiseptic terminology of systems analysis and related techniques, particularly in their wartime applications but elsewhere as well (for instance in the economics of poverty), has helped to mask the moral reality of much that the techniques have touched. I say nothing new when I observe that talking of gruesomely burned human beings as part of a "body count" hideously masks the truth, just as talking of the . . . "trade-off between employment and inflation" conceals the anguish of joblessness, or talking of the "collapse mode in a world resource model" obscures what global starvation would mean.

What seems to be less often recognized, however, are two facts about this phenomenon. First, at least in most cases, it flows quite naturally not from any Orwellian desire to corrupt language in order to deceive, but from the policy sciences' objectivist ideal. To facilitate detached thought and impersonal deliberation, what more plausible path could there be than to employ a bloodless idiom, one as drained as possible of all emotion? Second, the phenomenon rests on an elementary fallacy: it presupposes that the task of identifying and naming categories can in fact be wholly neutral. . . . The very choice of so deliberately emotionless a category as "body count" in which to place the dead incorporates certain premises about the enterprise in which they died and encourages perceptions and criteria of success framed in the terms of the ideology those premises define. Objectivism thus tends to generate a pol-

---

sically refractory to the techniques of policy analysis those that are "hard to quantify" (to order cardinally) or "difficult to rank" (to arrange ordinally). It seems to me unhelpful to talk about values in such terms, inasmuch as what usually matters is not the *existence* of some sort of ordering relating to the value in question but its *significance.* The reason "ecological balance" tends to be filtered out by the policy scientist's lens is not that the number of birds, ferns, and trees cannot be determined but rather that the value in question is too "structural" in character to be captured by such enumerations.

icy jargon and a frame of reference that may be many things—but surely cannot be called "objective."

4. Narrowing the Role of Rationality

I would suggest, finally, that the objectivist ideal in policy analysis dangerously (and paradoxically) constricts the role played by rationality in the process of choice. The frame of mind engendered by the policy analyst's concern to remain fully objective and detached leads him, at least in the paradigm case, to formulate his function in terribly cramped terms. He insists that his proper role is essentially to answer questions of fact as formulated by a particular decision-maker who seeks the policy analyst's advice. Were he to go further, the analyst believes, he could fatally compromise his detachment and objectivity. Thus matters of value (as distinguished from fact) are beyond his province, and choosing what question to ask (as distinguished from providing an answer) is not his task. I am aware that deviations from this supposed "ideal" are not unknown in the practice of the policy sciences, but such deviations are typically regarded as instances of tempering objective analysis with "wisdom," "intuition," or "human sensitivity." As a general proposition, it remains true, despite these deviations, that the nether regions of values and question-formulation are treated by the policy sciences as beyond the reach of systematic intellectual inquiry, although their importance is rarely denied.

A. *Facts and Values.* As to the supposed fundamental distinction between fact and value in this context, one must recognize that it is an exceedingly troublesome one at best. "Values" as perceived by one who holds them are often nothing more than predictions referable to even more fundamental values.[93] "Facts" as perceived by one who believes in their truth are often inseparable from the values held by the believer, particularly when the facts in question refer to predictions of likely consequences in a highly uncertain environment. Moreover, both the relations within a set of values[94] and the internal structure of a particular

---

93. The values expressed by such notions as ecological balance, for example, represent for some not ultimate ends but hedges against risks to human well-being. See generally Sen, *Collective Choice and Social Welfare*, pp. 59-64. A similar point can be made as to the supposed distinction between means and ends.

94. For example, it might be that acting on value V_1 precludes subsequently realizing value V_2 but not the reverse—as where V_1 would permit the periodic use of a lake for toxic waste disposal and V_2 would permit the occasional use of the lake for swimming. See James Krier, "The Pollution Problem and Legal Institutions: A Conceptual Overview," *UCLA Law Review* 18 (1972): 429, 455-456. Or it might be that unless value V_3 is given priority over value V_4, values V_5 and V_6 cannot both be realized.

value are amenable to much the same sort of disciplined insight and rational inquiry that can characterize discussions of "factual" questions. Finally, and perhaps most importantly, the whole point of personal or social choice in many situations is not to implement a given system of values in the light of the perceived facts, but rather to define, and sometimes deliberately to reshape, the values—and hence the identity—of the individual or community that is engaged in the process of choosing. The decision-maker, in short, often chooses not merely how to achieve his ends, but what they are to be and who he is to become. The fact-value dichotomy and the perception of values as fixed rather than fluid thus impoverishes significantly the potential contribution of intellect to problems of choice.[95]

The analyst might reply that the sort of exploration of value structures contemplated here is not truly incompatible with objective, impersonal inquiry; and although this would take him well beyond the conventional conception of policy analysis, I cannot claim that objectivism, however misguided in other respects, would clearly preclude such a response. But I do believe that it would preclude any reply not ultimately referable to a posited dichotomy between facts and values and to a posited imperative that the two be treated differently.

So long as such a dichotomy is insistently maintained, however, the analyst's perspective will remain skewed. To offer one concrete if limited illustration, I would focus on the frequently stressed tenet of decision theorists that one of the analyst's main functions is to help the decision-maker separate clearly (1) how he feels about various possible outcomes of his decision (this preference being a matter of personal value) from (2) his best assessment of the probability of each such outcome (this probability being a matter of impersonal fact).[96] Such separation, it is said, represents an essential prerequisite for rational choice. But a strong argument can be made that in many contexts this very separation tends

95. Whatever else may be said of the axioms underlying the policy sciences, and indeed underlying most of what might be called secular, pluralistic liberal thought . . . , it should at least be observed here that the objectivist fact-value (or means-end) dichotomy implicit in their structure . . . leads to a deep internal inconsistency. Typically starting from the premise that human ends and moral values are wholly subjective and personal and hence not derivable from reality by the "objective" methods of analytic reason and empirical investigation, these theories purport to reach conclusions (sometimes utilitarian and sometimes contractarian) about how society *ought* to be organized or how social choices *should* be made (e.g., so as to maximize the sum of individual satisfactions); but if the starting premise is correct, then conclusions of this normative form can never be more than arbitrary expressions of personal preference, opaque to rational discourse—hardly the status to which they must aspire.

96. The "correct" probability is thought to be a matter of impersonal fact even though any particular assessment of it will invariably be personal and subjective. . . .

849

to obscure an essential feature of the choice that the decision-maker confronts. As I have tried to show elsewhere, for example, the value a rational person should attach to each of the several possible outcomes of a criminal trial depends in significant part on the probabilities of those outcomes as they appear to the jury at the time of decision; in particular, convicting an innocent person should be deemed a worse outcome when the jury feels very unsure of the person's guilt (but chooses to convict anyway) than when the jury feels fully confident of guilt (but simply happens to be mistaken). What is being done to the accused in the two cases differs just as surely as kicking a child differs from tripping over it, and the consequences for society of permitting each of these practices differs as well. Similarly, destroying a species of wildlife should probably be regarded as a worse outcome when it results from the disregard of a high known risk than when it results from the materialization of a highly unlikely contingency. The tradition in many legal systems of distinguishing among acts in terms of the mental state accompanying them (treating murder differently from manslaughter, for example) rests on this sort of proposition. Yet the objectivist's fact-value dichotomy, leading to an insistence on separating assessments of probability from the valuation of outcomes, tends to exclude this important dimension of human choice.[98]

The same result can be arrived at, incidentally, by a quite different route. Even if the analyst were to drop his demand that probabilities and preferences be assessed separately, his objectivist ideal might nonetheless impel him to focus on those features of a situation that seem reducible to empirically verifiable propositions to the exclusion of those that cannot easily be discussed in a purely empiricist frame. Thus the "outcomes" a policy analyst allows himself to discuss are likely to be events stripped of such personal elements as reasons and intentions—elements without which the events in question may lose much if not all of their significance.[99]

It should be noted here that this distortion is not the sort that can be compensated for by the decision-maker once he has received the policy analyst's supposedly "objective" input. For in the cases posited that input is fundamentally irrelevant, resting as it does on the decision-maker's values with respect to a radically misspecified set of outcomes. . . . The

98. I say "tends to exclude" rather than "excludes" because a sufficiently careful policy analyst could define the "outcomes" in question so as to include information about the associated probability assessments. The objectivist perspective does not preclude such a step, but does make it far less likely.

99. . . . Note how parallel is the economic tendency to equate goods with rights, ignoring the fact that the very concept of a right entails certain assumptions as to the *reasons given* for its recognition.

systematic truncations occasioned by the fact-value dichotomy . . . represent weaknesses that cannot be overcome without fundamentally loosening the constraints on analysis typically engendered by the objectivist ideal.

B. *Questions and Answers.* But even if those constraints were loosened, there would remain the analytic posture of answering the decision-maker's question rather than suggesting to the decision-maker what question he should have asked. The very title "policy *analysis*" reveals a great deal in this regard. For analysis is not *synthesis,* and deciding what question to address—choosing the problem to solve—seems very much a synthetic task, and in any event is a task that can hardly be carried out in a wholly mechanical, and hence assuredly "objective," manner.

The first danger arising from this sort of posture is the danger of all literal-minded devices: they grant what you asked for and not what you *meant* to ask for. Norbert Wiener recalls in this connection a tale in which an English working couple comes into possession of a talisman, a monkey's paw said to have been endowed by an Indian holy man with the virtue of granting its owner three wishes.[103] The couple first wish for £200; shortly thereafter a messenger arrives to inform them that their son has been killed in a factory accident and that his employer has offered £200 out of sympathy. Their second wish is that their son return; it is answered by a strange knocking at the door that the parents somehow know to be their son—but not in the flesh. The tale ends with the couple's third wish, that the ghost go away. The moral that Wiener draws from this tale is that all magic—including the "magic" of automation— "is singularly literal-minded, that if it grants you anything at all it grants what you ask for, not what you should have asked for or what you intend." The risk is that the resulting flaw in what you get may be less obvious than it was in the case of the monkey's paw—until it is too late. . . .

. . . Basic to that concept, certainly, is the requirement that the analyst accept as given the values of the decision-maker he is advising; to substitute others in the course of redefining or reformulating the problem put to the analyst by the decision-maker would violate the notion of detached, impersonal analysis so radically as to inaugurate an altogether different technique, if indeed it could be called a "technique" at all. This very fact, however, imposes severe limits on the sorts of values that the policy sciences can realistically be expected to serve. Quite obviously, the only values that can be served will be those strongly held by persons who seek a policy analyst's aid. The point may seem too trivial to make, but its consequences are anything but minor. For at least three

103. See Norbert Wiener, *God & Golem, Inc.,* (Cambridge, Mass., 1964), pp. 58-59.

categories of values and interests are likely to be excluded on this basis: those too widely diffused over space (or too incrementally affected over time) to be strongly championed by any single client of a policy analyst; those associated only with persons not yet existing (future generations); and those not associated with persons at all (for example, the "rights" of wild animals).

And more generally, one must expect that *all* values peripheral to those centrally held by the analyst's client will be understated by the analysis. In this sense, policy analysis is afflicted with congenital tunnel vision —tied as it must remain (if it is to be "objective") to the mission, often single-minded, of its user.

One might reply that this is not a problem at all, inasmuch as a multitude of tunnel-visioned analyses for a multitude of clients will somehow leave all important values properly accounted for.[108] But there is no adequate ground for assuming the operation of any such invisible hand,[109] at least with respect to collective goods, future interests, and values not congruent with any directly human concern. The only remaining reply would have to be that the use of policy analysis need not be limited to individual decision-makers with narrow interests to advance but can be extended instead to collective groups of decision-makers and to decision-makers representing a broad public constituency. But the consistency of any such extension with the intrinsically reductionist characteristics of the policy sciences remains at this point an open question, and we are at least entitled to be skeptical about the answer in light of what has been said above.

We have thus seen that an objectivist framework can significantly color the sorts of conclusions one should expect of the policy sciences, not only because of its reductionist and anesthetizing characteristics but also because of the dichotomy such a framework presupposes and tends to reinforce between fact and value and the passivity it tends to impose on the act of analysis itself.

. . . Ultimately the policy sciences—and the larger fabric of liberal thought of which much of contemporary economics, moral philosophy, and legal analysis are all integral parts—might stand revealed as the all but inevitable manifestations (and the all but invincible perpetuators) of the modern technocratic state. But that would require an investigation that has here been only begun.

. . . I believe that I have succeeded in making plausible the more

---

108. Cf. Charles Lindblom, *The Intelligence of Democracy* (New York, 1965).
109. The very *tendency* to assume it may betray the policy sciences' debt to their economic heritage.

modest claim that, in part because of their particular form of commitment to a posture of detached and impersonal objectivity, the policy sciences tend to partition and warp reality in certain patterned ways, generating a fairly understandable, and sometimes quite unfortunate, system of blind spots and distortions.

Posner, The Economic Approach to Law*

The hallmark of the "new" law and economics is the application of the theories and empirical methods of economics to the central institutions of the legal system, including the common law doctrines of negligence, contract, and property; the theory and practice of punishment; civil, criminal, and administrative procedure; the theory of legislation and of rulemaking; and law enforcement and judicial administration. Whereas the "old" law and economics confined its attention to laws governing explicit economic relationships, and indeed to a quite limited subset of such laws (the law of contracts, for example, was omitted), the "new" law and economics recognizes no such limitation on the domain of economic analysis of law.

The new law and economics dates from the early 1960's, when Guido Calabresi's first article on torts and Ronald Coase's article on social cost were published.[9] These were the first attempts to apply economic analysis in a *systematic* way to areas of law that did not purport to regulate economic relationships. . . .

II

Although the product of only a few man-years, the "new" law and economics literature is already too rich and complex to be summarized

*[53 *Texas L. Rev.* 757, 759-778 (1975). Reprinted by permission.

Richard A. Posner (1939–) was educated at Yale (B.A. 1959) and Harvard (LL.B. 1962). He was President of the Harvard Law Review (1961-1962) and Law Clerk for Justice William Brennan, Jr., United States Supreme Court (1962-1963). During the period 1963 to 1968, he held various legal posts for the federal government. In 1968 he taught at Stanford University, and from 1969 to the present he has been Professor of Law at the University of Chicago. A well-known authority on antitrust law, he is the author of *Antitrust: Cases, Economic Notes and Other Materials* (1974), *Economic Analysis of Law* (2d ed. 1977), and other works. Since 1970, he has been Editor of the *Journal of Legal Studies*.]

9. Calabresi, Some Thoughts on Risk Distribution and the Law of Torts, 70 *Yale L.J.* 499 (1961); Coase, The Problem of Social Cost, 3 *J. Law & Econ.* 1 (1960). Although the Coase article bears the date 1960, the issue of the *Journal of Law and Economics* in which it appears was not in fact published until 1962. The articles were written independently.

adequately in the compass of this article. I shall content myself with a few words on what it means to apply economics to law and indicate briefly the major findings that are emerging from current and recent studies.

The basis of an economic approach to law is the assumption that the people involved with the legal system act as rational maximizers of their satisfactions. Suppose the question is asked, when will parties to a legal dispute settle rather than litigate? Since this choice involves uncertainty —the outcome of the litigation is not known for sure in advance—the relevant body of economic theory is that which analyzes decision-making by rational maximizers under conditions of uncertainty. If we are willing to assume, at least provisionally, that litigants behave rationally, then this well-developed branch of economic theory[22] can be applied in straight-forward fashion to the litigation context to yield predictions with respect to the decision to litigate or settle; we discover, for example, that litigation should be more frequent the greater the stakes in the dispute or the uncertainty of the outcome. These predictions can be, and have been, compared with the actual behavior of litigants in the real world. The comparisons indicate that the economic model is indeed a fruitful one as applied to litigation behavior,[23] i.e., it enables us to explain the actual behavior we observe.

It may be argued that if economic theory only involves exploring the implications of assuming that people behave rationally, then lawyers can apply the theory perfectly well without the help of specialists. In this view, the economic approach to law just supplies a novel and confusing vocabulary in which to describe the familiar analytical activities of the lawyer. There is indeed a good deal of implicit economic analysis in legal thought—a point to which I shall return—and a good deal of economic theory does consist of elegantly formalizing the obvious and the trivial. But it is not true that all of the useful parts of economic theory are intuitively obvious to the intelligent lawyer. The logic of rational maximization is subtle, frequently complex, and very often counterintuitive.[24]

22. See G. Becker, Economic Theory 57-66 (1971).
23. See, e.g., Landes, An Economic Analysis of the Courts, 14 J. Law & Econ. 61 (1971).
24. Sam Peltzman's recent study of the effects of automobile safety regulations provides a good example. Peltzman, The Regulation of Automobile Safety, [83 J. Pol. Econ. 677-725 (1975)]. Intuitively, it seems obvious that a technically sound and reasonably well-enforced seat-belt requirement would reduce the number of deaths and injuries from automobile accidents. But as Peltzman shows, this intuition is unsound. By increasing the driver's safety, the seat belt, if used, reduces the cost of fast driving, which should, according to economic theory, lead to an increase in driving speed and therefore in the number of accidents, possibly offsetting the beneficial effect of the seat-belt requirement in reducing injuries to drivers and other vehicle occupants. In particular, there should be a sharp increase in pedestrian injuries, since their number will increase with faster driving and

854

That is . . . why the application of economics to law is more than the translation of the conventional wisdom of academic lawyers into a different jargon.

Now to some of the major findings of the "new" law and economics research. The first is that the participants in the legal process indeed behave as if they were rational maximizers:[25] criminals, contracting parties, automobile drivers, prosecutors, and others subject to legal constraints or involved in legal proceedings act in their relation to the legal system as intelligent (not omniscient) maximizers of their satisfactions. Like ordinary consumers, they economize by buying less of a good or commodity when its price rises and more when it falls. To be sure, the "good" and the "price" in the economic analysis of law are often unconventional, which is perhaps why it took so long for economists to claim the law as a part of economics. The "good" might be crimes to a criminal or trials to an aggrieved plaintiff, and the "price" might be a term of imprisonment discounted by the probability of conviction, or a court queue. But though the goods and prices may be somewhat unusual, and the purchasers may not fit one's preconceived idea of "economic man," there is a growing, and cumulatively rather persuasive, body of evidence supporting the proposition that the usual economic relations continue to hold in the formally noneconomic markets of the legal system. For example, it has been found that an increase in the expected punishment costs of crime—through an increase either in the severity of punishment or in the probability of its being imposed—will reduce the amount of crime[26]

---

there is no offsetting effect from seat-belt protection. Peltzman's study found, as his analysis predicted, a relative increase in pedestrian injuries and in automobile deaths and injuries due to the seat-belt requirement. The economic theory that underlies his study is straightforward, but it is unlikely that a noneconomist would have reasoned to a similar conclusion.

As another example, while the implicitly economic proposition, "punishment deters," is intuitive, another important proposition derived from the economic model of crime and punishment is not: a 1% increase in the probability of apprehension for murder will have a greater deterrent effect than a 1% increase in the conditional probability of conviction given apprehension, which in turn will have a greater deterrent effect than a 1% increase in the probability of execution given conviction. See Ehrlich, The Deterrent Effect of Capital Punishment: A Matter of Life and Death, [65 *Am. Econ. Rev.* 397-415 (1975)].

25. I say "as if" instead of "as" to indicate that the economist is not interested in the question whether and in what sense people may be said to be "rational." It is enough for purposes of economic analysis that the assumption of rationality has greater explanatory power than alternative assumptions. On the realism of economic assumptions, see M. Friedman, The Methodology of Positive Economics, in *Essays in Positive Economics* 3 (1953).

26. See Tullock, Does Punishment Deter Crime?, *Pub. Interest,* Summer 1974, at 103 (summary of recent studies).

and that a decrease in the trial queue will increase the number of trials,[27] all in accordance with the predictions of economic analysis.

In the type of research just described, the legal system is treated as a given and the question studied is how individuals or firms involved in the system react to the incentives that it imparts. A second important finding emerging from the recent law and economics research is that the legal system itself—its doctrines, procedures, and institutions—has been strongly influenced by a concern (more often implicit than explicit) with promoting economic efficiency.[28] The rules assigning property rights and determining liability, the procedures for resolving legal disputes, the constraints imposed on law enforcers, methods of computing damages and determining the availability of injunctive relief—these and other important elements of the legal system can best be understood as attempts, though rarely acknowledged as such, to promote an efficient allocation of resources.[29] The idea that the logic of the law is really economics is, of course, repulsive to many academic lawyers, who see in it an attempt by practitioners of an alien discipline to wrest their field from them. Yet the positive economic analysis of legal institutions is one of the most promising as well as most controversial branches of the new law and economics. It seeks to define and illuminate the basic character of the legal system, and it has made at least some progress toward that ambitious goal. One by-product of this research that has considerable pedagogical importance has been the assignment of precise economic explanations to a number of fundamental legal concepts that had previously puzzled students and their professors, such as "assumption of risk," "pain and suffering" as a category of tort damages, contract damages for loss of expectation, plea bargaining, and the choice between damages and injunctive relief.

27. See Landes, supra note 23. Landes also finds that the number of trials is increased by an increase either in the amount of subsidization of legal services or in the stakes involved in the dispute, again as predicted by economic analysis.

28. This insight is, of course, not entirely novel. See, e.g., J. Hurst, *Law and Social Process in United States History* 4 (1972). What is novel is the rigor and persistence with which the insight is being applied in the recent literature.

29. . . . . For some recent additions to the literature, see Ehrlich & Posner, An Economic Analysis of Legal Rulemaking, 3 *J. Legal Stud.* 257 (1974), and Landes & Posner, [The Private Enforcement of Law, 4 *J. Legal Stud.* 1 (1975)]. This literature is to be sharply distinguished from an older body of writings (summarized in 1 R. Pound, *Jurispridence* 199, 224, 228-31 (1959)) that argued that the rules of law were designed to promote the welfare of a particular economic class. See, e.g., Bohlen, The Rule in Rylands v. Fletcher, 59 *U. Pa. L. Rev.* 298, 318-19 (1911). For an effective critique of that approach, see Pound, The Economic Interpretation and the Law of Torts, 53 *Harv. L. Rev.* 365 (1940).

A third important finding in the law and economics literature is that economic analysis can be helpful in designing reforms of the legal system. Obviously there is some tension between this finding and the previous one. Were the legal system systematically and effectively designed to maximize economic efficiency, the role of normative economic analysis would be very small. In fact what one observes is areas of the law that seem to have a powerful and consistent economic logic—for example, most common-law fields—and others that seem quite perverse from an economic standpoint—in particular, many statutory fields. Some effort has been made to explain what appears to be a systematic difference in this regard between judge-made and statutory law by analyzing the different constraints of the judicial and legislative processes. This work is part of a larger effort to explain—in economic terms, of course—the behavior of political institutions. But this is not a well developed area of law and economics, and many anomalies remain. For example, while civil procedure reveals many economizing features, the failure to require that the losing party to a lawsuit reimburse the winner for his litigation expenses appears to be highly inefficient, and no economic explanation for this settled feature of American procedure has been suggested or is apparent. The tendency of government to use queueing rather than pricing to ration access to the courts and to other government services is another puzzle, since pricing is a cheaper method of rationing. So long as there remain important areas of the legal system that are not organized in accordance with the requirements of efficiency, the economist can play an important role in suggesting changes designed to increase the efficiency of the system. Of course, it is not for the economist, *qua* economist, to say whether efficiency should override other values in the event of a conflict.

A fourth important finding in the law and economics literature is that the quantitative study of the legal system is fruitful. It may seem odd to ascribe such a finding to the economic approach to law. Surely, it will be argued, quantitative analysis of the legal system long predates the economists' interest in the system, and the methods of statistical research are independent of the theories that generate the hypotheses to be tested by those methods. These points are correct but misleading. Economists have raised the level of quantitative research in the legal system very markedly, to the point where it is now plain, as it was not previously, that the statistical study of legal institutions has much to contribute to our knowledge. This is not to say that no worthwhile statistical studies of the legal system have ever been conducted by noneconomists. But the number of such studies is small, and in only a few years economists have produced a body of statistical studies that in number weighted by quality already, I believe, overshadows the noneconomic quantitative work.[37]

Several reasons may be suggested for the greater success of the economists in studying the legal system quantitatively. First, economists tend to be better trained in modern methods of quantitative analysis than other social scientists, let alone lawyers. A second point, related but distinct, is that economists appear to be more resourceful in discovering and using existing statistics on the legal system, and also more sensitive to the qualitative problems involved in drawing inferences from statistical data. These are perhaps simply aspects of being better trained, but they are distinct from simply possessing more powerful mathematical techniques.

I shall illustrate these points with two celebrated examples of noneconomic quantitative research on the legal system. One is the study by the University of Chicago Jury Project on the use of the jury in criminal cases.[38] Rather than attempt to mine the considerable existing data on the use of the criminal jury, the researchers conducted an elaborate mail survey to generate fresh data. Unfortunately, but typically, only a small fraction of the judges to whom the survey was mailed responded. No effort was made to establish the reasons for judges' not responding, and as a result there is no basis for a conclusion that the survey results are representative of the views of American judges. Moreover, the key question in the survey was a hypothetical one—how would the judge have decided the case if he, rather than the jury, had been the trier of fact—and the reliability of answers given to such questions is open to serious doubt.

My second example is Thorsten Sellin's study of the deterrent effect of capital punishment,[39] which was cited by a Supreme Court Justice in

37. See, e.g., Ehrlich, [The Deterrent Effect of Capital Punishment: A Question of Life and Death, 65 *Am. Economic Rev.* 397 (1975); The Deterrent Effect of Criminal Law Enforcement, 1 *J. Legal Stud.* 259 (1972)]; Ehrlich, Participation in Illegitimate Activities: A Theoretical and Empirical Investigation, 81 *J. Pol. Econ.* 521 (1973); Komesar, A Theoretical and Empirical Analysis of Victims of Crime, 2 *J. Legal Stud.* 301 (1973); Landes, [Legality and Reality: Some Evidence on Criminal Procedure, 3 *J. Legal Stud.* 287 (1974); and supra note 23]; Landes, The Economics of Fair Employment Laws, 76 *J. Pol. Econ.* 507 (1968); Peltzman, supra note 24; Peltzman, An Evaluation of Consumer Protection Legislation: The 1962 Drug Amendments, 81 *J. Pol. Econ.* 1049 (1973).

38. H. Kalven, Jr. & H. Zeisel, *The American Jury* (1966) (no significant differences in fact-finding were found between judges and juries).

39. T. Sellin, *The Death Penalty: A Report for the Model Penal Code Project of the Am. Law Inst.* (1959). It was presumably Sellin's work that led my distinguished colleague Norval Morris to conclude that "the existence or nonexistence of capital punishment is irrelevant to the murder, or attempted murder, rate. This is as well established as any other proposition in social science." N. Morris & G. Hawkins, *The Honest Politician's Guide to Crime Control* 75-76 (1970). For empirical evidence to the contrary, see Ehrlich, [The Deterrent Effect of

Furman v. Georgia[40] for the proposition that capital punishment has no incremental deterrent effect.[41] The heart of Sellin's study was a series of comparisons of murder rates in groups of contiguous states, one of which had abolished the death penalty while the other had not. He found that the murder rate was no lower in the states that retained the death penalty and concluded that the death penalty does not deter murder. Sellin's procedure, however, was fatally flawed by his failure to hold constant other factors besides punishment that might influence the murder rate. Only if the death penalty is the only determinant of the murder rate, or if the other determinants are identical in states having different execution rates, would it be proper to infer from Sellin's evidence that the death penalty had no deterrent effect. Sellin was at least dimly aware of this problem: this was what made him compare murder and execution rates in contiguous states. But relying on contiguity to hold the other relevant variables constant is inadequate. There is no reason to expect that states, because they happen to have a common border, are identical in all respects relevant to the murder rate save the use of capital punishment. Suppose, for example, that the arrest and conviction rate for murder was higher in a state which had abolished capital punishment than in a state that retained the death penalty, so that while a convicted murderer was punished less severely in the former state, the chances of his escaping punishment were lower than in the neighboring retentionist state. The net expected punishment cost for murder might be higher in the former and, if so, this would explain the lower murder rate there in terms wholly consistent with the proposition that the independent deterrent effect of capital punishment—holding probability of conviction and all other relevant variables constant—is positive.[42]

Capital Punishment: A Question of Life and Death, 65 *Am. Economic Rev.* 397 (1975); The Deterrent Effect of Criminal Law Enforcement, 1 *J. Legal Stud.* 259 (1972)]. A full critique of the Sellin study may be found in a paper by Professor Ehrlich which presents additional findings from his study of capital punishment. [See Ehrlich, Deterrence: Evidence & Inference, 85 *Yale L.J.* 209 (1975).]

40. 408 U.S. 238 (1972).

41. Id. at 348-53, 373-74 (Marshall, J., concurring). Justice Marshall's opinion was one of several concurring in the judgment invalidating existing death-penalty statutes; no opinion (other than the brief per curiam opinion announcing the judgment of the court) commanded the support of a majority of the Justices.

42. Sellin also conducted some before-and-after studies of murder rates in states that had abolished the death penalty. Finding no increase in the murder rate in these states, he again concluded that the death penalty had no deterrent effect. But this procedure was also fatally flawed by Sellin's failure to hold constant other factors affecting the murder rate besides the death penalty which might have been changing at the same time. Ehrlich, supra note 24, found a negative relationship between capital punishment and murder in a time-series study that did attempt to hold constant such other factors.

Part of Sellin's problem, perhaps, was that he had no theory as to why people commit murders or other crimes. This brings me to the third reason why economists have an advantage in quantitative research: it is very difficult to conduct such research without a theoretical framework. If one has no notion as to why people commit crimes, it is very difficult to know what factors to hold constant in order to determine the independent significance of the test variable (punishment or whatever). The economist, viewing the decision to participate in criminal activity as a standard problem in occupational choice,[43] has a clear a priori idea of what factors influence the rate of criminal participation and should therefore be included in a model of criminal activity. The empirical researcher who does not proceed from theory to the construction of a model identifying relevant variables has great trouble measuring the independent significance of the variable in which he is interested.

III

I have said something about the evolution of the law and economics field and about the salient findings that emerge from the completed research in the field. I would now like to discuss briefly the agenda of future research. It is a general, and in my opinion deplorable, characteristic of legal scholarship that normative analysis vastly preponderates over positive. Academic lawyers are in general happier preaching reform of the legal system than trying to understand how it operates. This is true of many lawyers having a bent for economics—one can read hundreds of pages of Guido Calabresi on the social control of accidents without learning anything about the methods of accident control that the society in fact employs—and of those economists who view the legal system from the dizzy heights of theoretical welfare economics. The result of the preference for normative analysis is that our knowledge of the legal system is remarkably meager, incomplete, and unsystematic—a situation which, ironically, makes it very difficult to propose sound reforms of the system.

The economic approach to law has enormous potential, as yet only slightly realized, for increasing our knowledge about the legal system. Economics is basically a positive science, and I have already remarked upon the economist's superior sophistication with respect to the assembly and analysis of data. The economic approach has already yielded both quantitative and qualitative insights into the operation of the legal

43. See Ehrlich, Participation in Illegitimate Activities: A Theoretical and Empirical Investigation, 81 *J. Pol. Econ.* 521 (1973).

system, and I shall try to indicate briefly some promising directions for additional research.

To begin with, there is a cluster of important topics relating to the operation of the court system. As William Landes and I discovered recently in the course of compiling a statistical history of the federal court system, there is a wealth of quantitative data available on the federal courts, some stretching back to 1873.[44] Since the data were not originally collected for purposes of economic analysis (often it is unclear for *what* purpose they were collected), there are distressing gaps and inconsistencies in the data series. Yet they appear to be sufficiently complete to enable us to estimate changes over time in the productivity of the federal courts; to assess the factors that determine judicial productivity; to measure court delay, identify its causes, and estimate the costs of eliminating it; to explain changes over time in the number of federal judges and the budget of the federal courts; to measure the demand for the federal courts as it is affected, for example, by the availability of a substitute service (i.e., the state courts) in areas of overlapping jurisdiction; to estimate the cost to the judicial system of different kinds of proceedings (e.g., jury trials versus court trials, and criminal trials versus guilty pleas); and to assess the impact on the judicial system of major procedural reforms such as the Federal Rules of Civil Procedure, the Criminal Justice Act, and the criminal procedure decisions of the "Warren Court."

Law-enforcement agencies could be studied similarly, and some beginnings in this direction have already been made.[45] Good candidates for future economic studies of law enforcement include the Internal Revenue Service, the Immigration and Naturalization Service, and the Wage and Hour Division of the Department of Labor—to name three chosen virtually at random. These studies would ask such questions as the following: What are the social costs of income-tax evasion? Are they equal to the revenue loss? What would be an optimum system of tax penalties? Would it involve greater or less use of the criminal sanction than at present? Does the marginal product of various forms of tax enforcement activity (e.g., individual and corporate taxpayer audits) exceed the marginal cost, and if so, can this result be defended?[46] What is the

44. Data are available on cases filed and terminated, trials, the size of judgments, appeals, backlogs, etc., by type of case and by district and circuit in which the case was filed. Also available are data on the judges and other personnel and on the budget of the federal court system.

45. See Posner, The Behavior of Administrative Agencies, 1 *J. Legal Stud.* 305 (1972); Posner, A Statistical Study of Antitrust Enforcement, 13 *J. Law & Econ*, 365 (1970); Stigler, The Process of Economic Regulation, 17 *Antitrust Bull.* 207 (1972).

46. For tentative affirmative answers to both of these questions, see Landes & Posner, supra note [29], at 36-37.

appropriate role, from an efficiency standpoint, of the paid tax informer? What factors determine the size, budget, and enforcement decisions of the Immigration and Naturalization Service? Are these decisions "discretionary," in the sense of arbitrary and perhaps invidious, or are they systematically designed to minimize the impact of foreign competition on the domestic labor market? Are they therefore sensitive to trends and patterns of unemployment? Does the Wage and Hour Division refrain from vigorously enforcing the minimum-wage law in industries where compliance with the law would have a seriously adverse effect on production?[47] What factors determine the number of inspectors hired by the Division to enforce the law? Is a staff of inspectors even necessary, or would it be more efficient if enforcement were left to the private sector, as is done in the enforcement of usury laws?

These types of questions are within the analytical competence of economics to answer, and adequate data to support reliable empirical answers appear to be available. Our knowledge of the law-enforcement process would be greatly enriched by a few more economic studies of specific enforcement programs and agencies.

Another promising area for empirical economic research on the legal system is international crime rates. Explaining differences in crime rates across countries is the acid test of the economic theory of crime and its control, for if, as so many people believe, cultural rather than economic variables predominate in criminal behavior, they will show up most clearly in a cross-country comparison. International comparisons may also prove highly illuminating with respect to the hypotheses concerning private versus public enforcement of criminal and civil law that Landes and I proposed in a recent paper,[48] for differences in the permissible scope of private prosecution appear to be much greater among than within countries. While on this topic, I want to mention one of many interesting subjects for an historical study of law and economics: the private prosecution of criminal offenses in England in the eighteenth and nineteenth centuries. In the earlier part of that period English criminal-law enforcement had all the essential features of the system of private law enforcement proposed by Becker and Stigler[49] and dis-

47. For some evidence on the amount of compliance with the minimum-wage law, see Ashenfelter & Smith, Compliance with the Minimum Wage Law, April 1974 (Princeton Econ. Dep't).

48. See Landes & Posner, supra note [29] (the article examines the scope of the public monopoly of enforcement and the rights of victims of crime to institute prosecutions).

49. Becker & Stigler, Law Enforcement, Malfeasance, and Compensation of Enforcers, 3 *J. Legal Stud.* 1 (1974).

cussed critically by Landes and me,[50] but the system was progressively abandoned—why?

Economists studying criminal punishment have been critical of the heavy emphasis in our society on punishment in the form of incarceration rather than fine.[51] Yet we have no systematic knowledge of the use of fines, the implicit rate of exchange between fines and time in prison, changes over time in the level of fines to adjust for inflation and other factors, and the collection of fines. This is another rich area for empirical research. Another area, in which work is just beginning, is the economics of the legal profession. The regulation of the profession, the returns to legal education, and the demand for lawyers and how it has been affected by direct and indirect public subsidization, including the passage of new laws, are important areas for study. The work on the profession may help to explain the puzzle I mentioned earlier as to why we have not adopted the English system of requiring the losing party in a lawsuit to reimburse the winner for his legal expenses. Is the explanation, perhaps, that lawyers are a more influential interest group here than in England and that they benefit from the American rule, which would appear to increase the amount of litigation?[52]

An entirely different area for future research is family law, broadly defined to include not only the laws relating to marriage, divorce, and adoption, but also the laws governing the transfer of wealth within the family and the taxation of the household. The rich economic literature on marriage, fertility, and other dimensions of "household production"[53] is waiting to be mined for insights into the legal regulation of the family.

These are only a few examples of the many topics that beckon the law and economics scholar. The problem is not to identify interesting questions in the positive economic analysis of the legal system; there is a vast body of untapped research topics in this field. The problem, to which I will return after discussing the criticisms that have been made of

50. Landes & Posner, supra note [29].

51. See Becker, [*The Economics of Discrimination* (2d ed. 1971); Crime and Punishment: An Economic Approach, 76 *J. Pol. Econ.* 169 (1968)].

52. The English rule deters litigation by (1) increasing the variance of the expected outcome of a lawsuit, and hence reducing the utility of litigation compared to settlement for the risk averse, and (2) penalizing more heavily errors in predicting the outcome of a lawsuit. See Posner, An Economic Approach to Legal Procedure and Judicial Administration, 2 *J. Legal Stud.* 399, 428 (1973).

53. See Proceedings of a Conference Sponsored by Nat'l Bureau of Economic Research and The Population Council, Marriage, Family Human Capital, and Fertility, 82 *J. Pol. Econ.* S1 (1974).

the law and economics work, is to establish the necessary environment for a demanding and sometimes expensive form of research.

IV

. . . The economic approach to law has aroused a good deal of antagonism among academic lawyers. Part of this is a natural hostility to competition but more is involved because many economists are also hostile to the economic analysis of law. It seems worthwhile, therefore, to attempt to answer the criticisms[54]—which I am convinced are unjustified, or at least premature.

One criticism that is silly but too frequently made to ignore is that since economists cannot explain this or that (e.g., our current recession *cum* inflation), they have nothing to say to lawyers about the legal system. Because economics is an incomplete and imperfect science, it is easy to poke fun at, just as it is easy to poke fun at medicine for the same reason. But it is as foolish to write off economics as it would be to write off medicine.

A closely related criticism of the economic approach to law is that since economics has its limitations—for example, there is no widely accepted economic theory of the optimum distribution of income and wealth—the lawyer can ignore or even reject the approach until these limitations are overcome. This is tantamount, however, to the absurd proposition that unless a method of analysis is at once universal and unquestioned it is unimportant. A variant of this criticism is made by some legal philosophers who argue that since the philosophical basis of economics is utilitarianism,[55] which they consider discredited, economics has no foundation and must collapse, carrying the economic approach to law with it. Admittedly, economics does not provide a basis for unconditional normative statements of the form, "because the most efficient method of controlling crime would be to cut off the ears and nose of a convicted felon and brand him on the forehead, society should adopt these penalties." What the economist might be able to say, by way of normative analysis, is that a policy such as mutilation of felons increases efficiency[56] and should therefore be adopted, unless its adoption would im-

54. Many of these criticisms are not yet in print. Some may be found in Leff, Economic Analysis of Law: Some Realism About Nominalism, 60 *Va. L. Rev.* 451 (1974).

55. See generally J. Bentham, An Introduction to the Principles of Morals and Legislation, in 1 *The Works of Jeremy Bentham* 1 (J. Bowring ed. 1843); J. S. Mill, *Utilitarianism* (S. Gorovitz ed. 1971).

56. This is a hypothetical example. I have no view as to whether mutilation would in fact be an efficient method of punishment.

pair some more important social value. The economist's ability to make conditional suggestions of this sort is not endangered by the debate over the merits of utilitarianism, unless the challenge to utilitarianism is a challenge to ascribing *any* value to promoting economic efficiency. Even more clearly, the economist's ability to enlarge our understanding of how the legal system actually operates is not undermined by the attacks on utilitarianism. If the participants in the legal process act as rational maximizers of their satisfactions, or if the legal process itself has been shaped by a concern with maximizing economic efficiency, the economist has a rich field of study whether or not a society in which people behave in such a way or institutions are shaped by such concerns can be described as "good."

Another common criticism of the economic approach to law is that the attempt to explain the behavior of legal institutions, and of the people operating or affected by them, on economic grounds must fail because, surely, much more than rational maximizing is involved in such behavior. The motivations of the violent criminal cannot be reduced to income maximization[57] nor the goals of the criminal justice system to minimizing the costs of crime and its control. This criticism reflects a fundamental misunderstanding of the nature of scientific inquiry. A scientific theory necessarily abstracts from the welter of experience that it is trying to explain, and is therefore necessarily "unrealistic" when compared directly to actual conditions. Newton's law of falling bodies is "unrealistic" in assuming that bodies fall in a vacuum, but it is still a useful theory because it correctly predicts the behavior of a wide variety of falling bodies in the real world. Similarly, an economic theory of law is certain not to capture the full complexity, richness, and confusion of the phenomena—criminal activity or whatever—that it seeks to illuminate. That lack of realism does not invalidate the theory; it is, indeed, the essential precondition of a theory.

The criticism also ignores an important lesson from the history of scientific progress: in general, a theory cannot be overturned by pointing out its defects or limitations but only by proposing a more inclusive, more powerful, and above all more useful theory.[60] Whatever its deficiencies, the economic theory of law seems, to this biased observer anyway, the best positive theory of law extant. It is true that anthropologists, sociologists, psychologists, political scientists, and other social scientists besides economists also do positive analysis of the legal system. But their

57. See generally *The Criminal in Society* 391-473 (L. Radzinowicz & M. Wolfgang ed. 1971).

60. This I take to be a central theme in T. Kuhn, *The Structure of Scientific Revolutions* (2d ed. 1970), and T. Kuhn, *The Copernican Revolution: Planetary Astronomy in the Development of Western Thought* (1957).

work is thus far insufficiently rich in theoretical and empirical content to afford serious competition to the economists. This is admittedly a rather presumptuous and sweeping judgment, and to some extent an uninformed one since I cannot claim a thorough familiarity with the works in these fields. Nonetheless, my impression, for what it is worth, is that these fields have produced neither systematic, empirical research on the legal system nor plausible, coherent, and empirically verifiable theories of the legal system. Legal anthropology, for example, appears to be almost purely descriptive; it has no theoretical content that I can discern. The literature of political science on the behavior of courts, administrative agencies, and other legal institutions is thin and unconvincing. The sociology of law is, by the testimony of one of its better practitioners, in a highly unsatisfactory state,[61] divided between excessively abstract generalizing about the legal system as a whole[62] and excessively particularistic, and thus far unproductive, preoccupation with possible treatments for deviant behavior.[63] I should add that there are many fine scholars who call themselves political scientists or sociologists and study the legal system, but their work seems to owe little or nothing to their nominal disciplines,[65] attesting to the theoretical poverty of these fields as applied to law.

Still another common criticism of the "new" law and economics is that it manifests a strongly conservative political bias.[66] Its practitioners have found, for example, that capital punishment has a deterrent effect[67] and that legislation designed to protect the consumer frequently ends up hurting him.[68] Findings such as these provide ammunition to the supporters of capital punishment and the opponents of consumerist legislation. The oddest thing about this criticism is that economic research that provides support for liberal positions is rarely acknowledged, at least by liberals, as manifesting political bias. The theory of public

---

61. See Black, The Mobilization of Law, 2 *J. Legal Stud.* 125 (1973).

62. E.g., R. Pound, *Jurisprudence* (1959); M. Weber, *Max Weber on Law in Economy and Society* (M. Rheinstein ed. 1954).

63. See Martinson, What Works?—Questions and Answers About Prison Reform, *Pub. Interest,* Spring 1974, at 22.

65. See, e.g., Levin, Urban Politics and Judicial Behavior, 1 *J. Legal Stud.* 193 (1972); Ross, Law, Science, and Accidents: The British Road Safety Act of 1967, 2 *J. Legal Stud.* 1 (1973).

66. Perhaps this is less accurately described as a "criticism" than as a reason for the distaste with which the subject is regarded in some quarters.

67. See Ehrlich, supra note 24.

68. See Peltzman, An Evaluation of Consumer Protection Legislation: The 1962 Drug Amendments, 81 *J. Pol. Econ.* 1049 (1973).

goods,[69] for example, could be viewed as one of the ideological under-
pinnings of the welfare state, but it is not so viewed. Evidently once a
viewpoint becomes dominant it ceases to be perceived as having ideological significance. In addition, the criticism overlooks recent findings concerning bail,[70] right to counsel and standard of proof in criminal cases,[71]
the application of the first amendment to broadcasting,[72] discrimination
against women,[73] the social costs of monopoly,[74] and others, that bolster
liberal viewpoints.

In any event, the criticism is wide of the mark. The law and economics scholars have been scrupulous—more scrupulous I would argue
than their critics[75]—in respecting the line between positive and normative analysis. Ehrlich has said that capital punishment deters, not that it is
a good thing. This is not to deny that positive economic analysis has normative implications. If a social institution is inefficient, someone to
whom efficiency is an important value may want to change it. But the
economist cannot, and the good economist does not, tell him that he
should adopt efficiency as an important or paramount value (although
the economist can tell him something about the costs of not doing so).
Finally, and I would have thought conclusively, the motivations and personal opinions of researchers ought to be irrelevant to the appraisal of
their work, as should be the political implications, if any, of that work.
The validity of research is independent of the motives behind it or the
uses to which it may be put.

Much of what I have just said is equally applicable to the attacks that
have been made on the economic approach to law from the Right by
economists like Buchanan and law professors like Epstein, who argue

69. See, e.g., R. Musgrave, *The Theory of Public Finance* 43-44 (1959). For a critical view
of the theory, see Demsetz, The Private Production of Public Goods, 13 *J. Law & Econ.*
293 (1970).

70. See Landes, supra note 23 (defendants should be compensated for pretrial deten-
tion if found innocent or be credited with sentence time if found guilty).

71. See Posner, An Economic Approach to Legal Procedure and Judicial Administration, 2 *J. Legal Stud.* 399 (1973) (providing counsel to indigent defendants and requiring a
standard of proof higher in criminal cases than in civil cases minimize the social costs of
crime, which include the costs of erroneous convictions).

72. See Coase, The Federal Communications Commission, 2 *J. Law & Econ.* 1 (1959);
Coase, The Market for Goods and the Market for Ideas, 64 *Am. Econ. Rev.* 384 (No. 2,
1974).

73. See Komesar, [Toward A General Theory of Personal Injury Loss, 3 *J. Legal Stud.*
457 (1974)] (the true value of a housewife to a household has been underestimated in personal injury cases).

74. See Posner, The Costs of Monopoly and Regulation, [83 *J. Pol. Econ.* 807 (1975)];
Tullock, [The Welfare Costs of Tariffs, Monopolies and Theft, 5 *W. Econ. J.* 224 (1967)].

75. See Posner, Economic Justice and the Economist, *Pub. Interest,* Fall 1973, at 109.

that if judges are permitted to impose legal obligations (e.g., to impose a duty on passers-by to render aid to people in distress) in order to increase efficiency, the freedom of the individual from the state will be impaired.[77] I welcome these criticisms because they demonstrate that the economic approach to law cannot be labeled in pat political terms, but I am not persuaded by them. Judges can hardly avoid using some criterion of social welfare in fashioning rules of decision, and efficiency is a more libertarian criterion than any other I know. In any event, these criticisms are limited to the use of economics in normative analysis and have no application to positive analysis, which I believe will ultimately be the more important contribution of economics to law.

Another criticism leveled against the economic approach is that it ignores "justice," which in these critics' view is and should be the central concern of the legal system and of the people who study it. In evaluating this criticism, it is necessary to distinguish different senses in which the word justice is used in reference to the legal system. It is sometimes used to mean "distributive justice," which can be defined very crudely as the "proper" degree of economic inequality. Although economists cannot tell you what that degree is, they have much to say that is extremely relevant to the debate over inequality[78]—about the actual amounts of inequality in different societies and in different periods, the difference between real economic inequality and inequalities in pecuniary income that merely compensate for cost differences[79] or reflect different positions in the life cycle,[80] and the costs of achieving greater real or nominal equality. I grant that distributive questions are important in the legal system— in tax policy and elsewhere—but I contend that economists have a great deal to say about them, more perhaps than those who speculate philosophically about the normative issues of distributive justice.

A second meaning of "justice," and the most common I would argue, is simply "efficiency." When we describe as "unjust" convicting a person without a trial, taking property without just compensation, or failing to require a negligent automobile driver to answer in damages to the victim of his carelessness, we can be interpreted as meaning simply

77. See Buchanan, Good Economics—Bad Law, 60 *Va. L. Rev.* 483 (1974) Epstein, A Theory of Strict Liability, 2 *J. Legal Stud.* 151, 189-204 (1973).

78. For a recent empirical study of income distribution, see B. Chiswick, *Income Inequality: Regional Analyses Within a Human Capital Framework* (1974).

79. Such as the greater danger, uncertainty, or investment in education of a particular occupation compared to alternatives.

80. Two people might have identical lifetime earnings, but unequal current incomes if they were of different ages in occupations where earnings vary with age.

that the conduct or practice in question wastes resources. It is no surprise that in a world of scarce resources, waste is regarded as immoral. There may be, however, more to notions of justice than a concern with efficiency, for many types of conduct widely condemned as unjust may well be efficient. It is not obviously inefficient to permit people to commit suicide, to discriminate on racial or religious grounds,[82] or to eat the weakest passenger in the lifeboat in circumstances of genuine desperation; nor is it obviously inefficient for society to permit abortions, to substitute torture for imprisonment, or to give convicted felons a choice between imprisonment and participation in dangerous medical experiments. Nevertheless, many people would regard all of these things as horribly unjust. I doubt, however, that such views are completely impervious to what an economic study might show. For example, would the objection to medical experimentation on convicts remain unshaken if it were shown persuasively that the social benefits of such experiments greatly exceeded the costs? Would the objections to capital punishment survive a convincing demonstration that capital punishment had a significantly greater deterrent effect than life imprisonment? All of these are studiable issues, and since no rational society can ignore the costs of its public policies, they are issues to which economics has great relevance. The demand for justice is not independent of its price.

My guess is that when the issue of justice is studied seriously and when the many pseudo-justice issues are eliminated,[83] it will turn out that society is in fact willing to pay a certain price in reduced efficiency for policies (e.g., forbidding racial and religious discrimination) that advance notions of justice, but that society does so to preserve intact the social fabric—to forestall rebellion and other forms of upheaval. I am suggesting, in short, that we will eventually develop a utilitarian theory of justice.

82. See, e.g., Arrow, The Theory of Discrimination, in *Discrimination in Labor Markets* 3 (O. Ashenfelter & A. Reese ed. 1973); Phelps, The Statistical Theory of Racism and Sexism, 62 *Am. Econ. Rev.* 659 (1972); Posner, The DeFunis Case and the Constitutionality of Preferential Treatment of Racial Minorities, 1974 *Sup. Ct. Rev.* 1.

83. The complaint of injustice often arises from a failure to consider a proposed policy carefully. For example, people instinctively recoil whenever I suggest doing away with prison sentences for antitrust violators. The proposal seemingly suggests a different law for the rich than for the poor. The point is in fact quite different. Since most antitrust violators are highly solvent and most common criminals are not, the former can be adequately deterred by monetary sanctions—which are cheaper for society to administer than imprisonment—and the latter cannot be. The proposal envisages setting antitrust fines at a level equal to or greater than the cost to the violator of being imprisoned, so that the substitution of fines for imprisonment would not reduce effective punishment costs to the violator.

Baker, The Ideology of the Economic Analysis of Law*†

I

Posner's entire approach is based on certain important, though traditional, definitions of "efficiency" and "value" (p. 4): "Efficiency . . . means exploiting economic resources in such a way that human satisfaction as measured by aggregate consumer willingness to pay for goods and services is maximized." "When resources are being used where their *value* is greatest, we may say that they are being employed efficiently." "Value too is defined by willingness to pay. Willingness to pay is in turn a function of the existing distribution of income and wealth in a society."[4]

The intuitive idea behind these market paradigm definitions of value and efficiency is quite simple. In a voluntary trade, both parties are better off than before the trade—"value" is increased. In monetary transactions, as long as a buyer is willing and able to pay an amount which a seller is willing to accept, value could be increased by the trade—that is, by his behavior each party indicates that he thinks his situation has improved. When no more such trades can be made, the situation is "efficient." Law, then, can be evaluated in terms of its contribution to achieving efficient allocations. For example, in the case of an alleged nuisance, the law could grant the right to the party to whom the right was most valuable (pp. 18, 94). Negligence rules could be designed to allocate rights and duties so that parties will use the cheapest methods of avoid-

* [*Philosophy & Public Affairs* 5, no. 1, p. 3 (Fall 1975). Copyright © 1975 by Princeton University Press. Reprinted by permission of Princeton University Press.

C. Edwin Baker (1947–) received his B.A. from Stanford (1969) and his J.D. from Yale (1972). He is now Assistant Professor of Law at the University of Oregon.]

† [This article is in response to Posner, *Economic Analysis of Law* (1st ed., Little, Brown and Company 1972).]

4. Posner's definition of efficiency is basically the same as one frequently used by welfare economists: efficiency is increased if a change results in someone being made better off and no one being made worse off. An optimal allocation occurs when no one could be made better off without someone being made worse off ("better off" and "worse off" being subjectively defined by the individual affected).

In a case where the gain to those made better off is more than enough to pay for the loss to those made worse off, such that if those hurt were actually compensated and the change with the payoff thus would meet the efficiency requirement, writers have disagreed about whether the payoff must actually be made. In his analysis of the law, Posner clearly adopts the position not requiring an actual payoff, in part because the legal question is usually not, Should X be taken from A and given to B? but, Who, A or B, does or should have a right to X? The economic solution is to recognize the right in the one who would be made more "better off," the one who would be willing to pay the most for the right.

ing economic costs (p. 69). Property rules could define rights such that transfers to the highest valued use are made easier (cheaper) (pp. 10-13). Contract rules could help to "minimize the breakdowns in the process of exchange" and reduce the costs of exchange (pp. 42, 44). Throughout his book, Posner attempts to clarify the understanding of the various ways legal rules can impede or promote the goals of increasing value and achieving efficiency.

Of course, an analysis in terms of operationalized definitions of efficiency and value is irrelevant unless efficiency and value measure something that concerns us. If Posner's measuring rod of human satisfaction, aggregate consumer willingness to pay, is accepted as a "correct" measure of human satisfaction,[5] then presumably anyone who accepts human satisfaction as a goal would accept efficiency as a goal. Posner modestly says that the "economist cannot tell us whether . . . consumer satisfaction should be the dominant value of society" (pp. 4-5). But presumably any utilitarian[6] would readily argue that it is and should be. Despite Posner's disclaimer, the book as a whole constantly uses efficiency as a standard of criticism,[7] and most readers will see that efficiency is used as a normative, and not merely as a technical standard. Although Posner does not try to demonstrate that "maximizing" human satisfaction should be our only goal, he may be right that most would accept it as the dominant goal. Thus, to the extent that human satisfaction is maximized by increasing efficiency, this implicit but continual use of efficiency as his policy guide appears warranted.

The relevance of efficiency for policy use implies one further argument. Both human satisfaction and value are measured by consumer willingness to pay. And as Posner points out, "willingness to pay is . . . a function of *the existing distribution* of income and wealth in a society" (p. 4). If the existing distribution is unjust, then maximizing human satisfaction on the basis of willingness to pay would presumably produce unjust results. More to the point, if "human satisfaction" could be increased by changing the existing distribution, then increasing effi-

5. Posner argues that increasing efficiency involves increasing human satisfaction (p. 2).

6. Posner states that "Bentham's utilitarianism . . . is another name for economic theory" (p. 356).

7. For example: "The right *should be* assigned to the party whose use is more valuable . . ."; "The limitation has an economic *justification*." "If the analysis . . . is correct, the *ultimate question* for decision in many lawsuits is, *what allocation* of resources *would maximize efficiency*"; "There is abundant evidence that legislative regulation . . . brings about less efficient results than the market–common law system. . . . The crucial question is whether this *failure* is accidental and easily remediable. . . ." Posner, pp. 18, 250, 320, 329 (emphasis mine).

ciency, which is operationally tied to the existing distribution, would not be the unambiguous route to maximizing human satisfaction.[8] The utilitarian or the "rational maximizer"[9] would not necessarily be concerned to promote efficiency. (If the efficiency results from an actual trade or if payments are made such that no one is made worse off while someone is made better off, then presumably human satisfaction is increased—but not necessarily by as much as it would be increased from an "inefficient" change in the distribution. Moreover, if in a dispute the legal rule is to assign the right to the party who would pay the most for the awarded right, this "potentially" *efficient move,* by itself creating the distribution, *may decrease human satisfaction*—depending on the specific effect on distribution.) Thus, in order to use efficiency as an adequate guide for increasing satisfaction, Posner must assert either that human satisfaction would not be increased by changing the existing distribution or, at least, that there is no reason to believe that an identifiable type change in distribution could be expected to increase human satisfaction. In fact, Posner makes such assertions. Although he argues that the "economist cannot tell us whether the existing distribution of income and wealth is just" (p. 4), he also asserts that "there is no theoretical [economic?] basis for [the] conclusion" that a "transfer of money from a wealthy man to a poor one is likely to increase the sum of the two men's total utilities" (p. 216). This claim, that no theoretical basis exists for believing that a specific type change in distribution would increase human satisfaction, is crucial for the argument which concludes that shifting resources to the most highly valued use increases human satisfaction. . . .

Legal rules allocate rights and duties on the basis of relevant characteristics of a situation. Typically, legal disputes in actual cases concern the parties' divergent claims of right or denials of duty. The court decision frequently affects efficiency. The award may create an efficient or inefficient situation, may affect the difficulty (cost) of the behavior necessary to reach an efficient situation, or may affect the incentive for efficiency generating behavior. If the relevant cost-causing behavior of the parties has been completed, the specific decision may not directly affect efficiency; however, as a guide to future behavior, the rule announced

---

8. If compensation takes place when a change occurs, such that everybody is better off, then human satisfaction is presumably increased. But the increase may not be as much as would occur from a change in distribution. If compensation *is not paid* (it is normally not paid to the losing claimant in cases in which Posner's criteria are used to determine the assignment of a right), the "efficient" award may decrease human satisfaction as compared to an inefficient solution which "improved" the distribution.

9. "Economics is the science of human choice. . . . It explores and tests the implications of the assumption that man is a rational maximizer of his ends in life, his satisfactions. . . ." Posner, p. 1.

can. For example, the rule may define rights and duties so as to promote efficiency by recognizing the right in the party for whom the right is most valuable or by placing liabilities on the party who is best situated to minimize costs. In addition to its efficiency effect, the legal decision is inevitably distributive—someone is awarded the right (or the money for its violation) and someone else is not. Likewise, the rule embodies a distributive principle. The rule announces that in such a situation someone does and someone else does not have a certain right. (In this sense, the economic analysis of the legal dispute *cannot* take the distribution as given since the dispute is over what the distribution is.) The distributive effect is inevitable. The court may award the right to the party who would be better off even if he gave the losing party the amount the losing party would have paid for the right—however, the payment is not made; in fact, making the payment would be equivalent to awarding the right to the other party (who "valued" it less) and then forcing a sale—in the other words, choosing a different distribution. . . .

Since "rights" are more valuable in some hands or in some uses than in others, and since law (and non-legal practices) defines the consequences of various methods of transfer or change (and of attempted transfers), law can be analyzed by asking whether it encourages or frustrates movement to more valued uses. Posner confronted this task. He analyzed law against the standard of encouraging movement to more valued uses (efficiency), given his definition of value. But not only can the goal of maximizing "value" be critized, the concept of "value" can be examined. Any given set of rules can be criticized by viewing its effect on some kind of value. Conversely, any set of rules can be viewed as defining or illustrating some specific notion of value, although some specific notions will be so far from our own that we would consider the defining rules "irrational." Disputes about the meaning of "value" are possible; nothing inherent in the human condition forces us to say that value is a totally subjective notion and that it must mean solely the satisfaction of present individual desires. Nor are we required to assume that value is properly defined on the basis of the given distribution of wealth. These disputes over the meaning of "value" may take the form of controversies about what rules of ownership and change are best or most acceptable. . . .

II

One of the most important uses of Posner's economic analysis is in determining how rights should be allocated and where liability should be imposed. In this context of rights allocation and liability rules, two central biases of Posner's operational definitions of value and efficiency, a bias in favor of the rich and a bias in favor of the exploitative or productive use of resources will be examined. More specifically, a demonstration of the following set of propositions will be attempted.

Posner's approach:

I. *Favors the claimant of the right whose use is productive over one whose use is consumptive.*

II. *Favors the rich claimant whose use is consumptive over the poor claimant whose use is consumptive.*

And from these propositions, the following corollaries could be formulated:

A. As a general matter, the rich are favored directly by Proposition II and indirectly by Proposition I to the extent that the rich own a disproportionate share of the productive assets, or, more strictly, to the extent that the rich are more likely to be willing and able to buy a right for productive use.[13]

B. A person favored in a previous case is progressively more likely to be favored in the next case because:

a. if he wants a right for consumptive use, he will be richer because of a previous grant, and because he is richer, the right claimed will be more valuable to him. (Follows from Proposition II above.)

b. given that the rich are more likely to want a right for productive use (see A above), the one who is richer because of a previous gain will be the one more likely to claim the right for productive use, and thus will be favored by the effect of Proposition I.

c. if a party's gain of a claimed right in a previous case had the effect of making his productive resources (e.g., labor) more valuable to him, then a right not to have his productive resources interfered with or damaged would be more valuable to him because of the previous gain.

To say that Posner's definition of value favors certain groups implies an alternative, coherent definition of value (or a replacement for the concept) which by comparison does not favor those groups. And the

---

13. This favoritism for the rich depends on the contingent assumption that the rich are more able and willing to buy the right and implement it in productive use—a reasonable assumption. In a capitalist system, the favoritism is less clearly toward the rich as a group, but, almost by definition, is toward the capitalists. Of course, most of the rich might be tied into that group; but if, for instance, a landed gentry existed, its position might be prejudiced.

label "bias" indicates that no convincing reason has been advanced for choosing this definition rather than some alternative. . . .

. . . A demonstration of this insufficiency must await an exact statement of how Posner's economic approach would direct that rights and liabilities be assigned. At first, the economic directive for assigning property rights appears clear. In cases of conflicting property uses, "the right should be assigned to the party whose use is more valuable—the party . . . for whom discontinuance of the interference would be more costly" (p. 18).[14]

Who is the "party whose use is more valuable?" The most "obvious answer," and the only answer consistent with Posner's definition of value (pp. 4; 68, n.3), is the party who, given the existing distribution of wealth, is willing (and able) to pay the most for the right (hereinafter called the *situation ante* approach because the criteria used is willingness to pay *before* the assignment). Absent his precise definition of value based on willingness to pay given the existing distribution, three alternative analytic identifications[15] of the party whose use is most valuable surely would have been suggested: (1) the party who, if he had the right, would require the highest price from the purchaser (hereinafter called the *situation post* approach because the criteria used presupposes an assignment); (2) the party who, if he had the right, would not sell it to the other party who wanted the right; or (3) the party who, if he did not have the right, would buy it from the other party—assuming, for the obvious answer and the three alternatives, that there are no transaction costs.[16] Posner suggests (p. 18) that the third alternative would have the same economic effect as the "obvious answer." In fact, if Posner's assertion— "that the initial assignment of legal rights does not affect which use ultimately prevails" (p. 17)—were true, then Posner's answer and the three alternatives would all be equivalent. And it is precisely this "theorem" that (assuming there are no transaction costs) the ultimate use of resources will be the same regardless of how rights to control their use are

14. This assignment promotes efficiency by eliminating the need for market transactions which are not costless. Thus, resources are not wasted getting the right to the holder for whom it is most valuable. . . .

15. These methods of measuring value are all congruent with typical assumptions of the economic model used here. For example, all are consistent with efficiency—granting to the party whose use is most valuable by any of these definitions results in a situation which cannot be improved by trades. All three are "market" definitions of values. However, they differ in their assumptions about what the initial distribution of wealth *is*—illustrating the inescapability of the distributive problem and the impossibility of merely taking the initial distribution as given.

16. Transaction costs include all the costs of making the trade. No transaction costs would be the equivalent of a frictionless market.

initially distributed, which Coase is generally credited with having established in his now-classic article, "The Problem of Social Cost."[18]

But Coase's analysis is subject to an important qualification, a qualification which is vital for understanding the biases implicit in Posner's, and much legal-economic, analysis. The initial assignment of a right can affect the wealth of the parties which in turn can affect the parties' "valuation" of the right, and thus affects the ultimate use of the resource. An extreme example, given by Posner, of the initial assignment determining the use which ultimately prevails is the case of a "right to a barrel of water as between two dying men in a desert" (pp. 17-18, n.1). In this case, the third alternative allocation rule—e.g., assign to the party who would buy it from the other party if the other party had the right—is indeterminate. Neither party would buy because neither party would sell. The bias of Posner's approach also begins to show. If the barrel of water is assigned to the one for whom it is most valuable, the one willing and able to pay the most for it, the water would be assigned to the richer of the two men. But the analysis is moving too fast. Why would the initial assignment—contrary to the standard reading of Coase—make a difference?

The initial assignment normally affects the relative wealth of the parties. An assignment of the right to the barrel of water (or a right to be free from pollution or a right of property owners not to have their property damaged by sparks from trains) increases the wealth of the party assigned the right. As Posner notes, the distributive effects of the original assignment will affect the general demand for various goods and services if the parties do not spend their money in identical ways—and hence will affect the use of resources (pp. 17-18, n.1). In addition, since a person's wealth affects how much that person is willing and able to pay for a specific desired right, the effect on a person's wealth of the initial assignment of that right will influence how much the person "values" the right. In these cases, the initial assignment may determine who "values" the right the most.

Two investigations suggest themselves. First, in what cases (all, some, none) does the wealth of the party influence how much he is willing and able to pay for the right in question? Second, what are the typical

18. [A typical restatement of the Coase argument is made by George Stigler: "The Coase theorem [is] that the manner in which legal rights were assigned would have no effect whatever upon methods of production. The same amount of smoke would be released from the factory's chimney whether the factory owner or the householder was legally responsible for the smoke damages." "The Law and Economics of Public Policy: A Plea to Scholars," *Journal of Legal Studies* 1:1, 11-12.]

implications of the assumption about wealth embodied by the different definitions of value?

Proposition I: Productive Claimant Favored Over Consumptive Claimant

The initial assignment of the right, and thus the wealth of the party, quite clearly determined which of the dying men in the desert ultimately possessed the one barrel of water. However, in Coase's example of the farmer whose crops are damaged by a rancher's straying cattle or a train's sparks, the effect of the property or liability rule on the wealth of the parties appeared not to influence the ultimate use of the economic resources. The crucial distinction is that in the first case the right was desired for consumptive uses, in the second case for productive uses.

Normally, as a person's wealth increases, the amount he will be willing and able to pay for a right or good which he wants for himself, and not merely in order to convert into more income, will increase. The "value" of a right to a person who desired it for consumptive use would be greater if the right has already been assigned to him, given that: (1) he is wealthier because of the assignment, (2) value is defined in terms of willingness to pay, (3) and he is more willing to pay when he is wealthier.

However, the wealth of a person should not affect how much he values a right which he desires solely for its productive use. In a perfect, costless market, goods or rights desired solely for their productive use will be purchased up to the price at which they just give a return for the money and will be sold at any price down to the point equal to the return from their productive use. The maximum purchase price and minimum selling price converge. Thus, although the original assignment may affect the wealth of the parties, in the case of productive use, it would not affect the amount they would be willing to pay for the right (assuming demand for the produced goods does not change). This distinction between productive and consumptive uses is the basis for our first claim, Proposition 1, concerning the bias of Posner's approach. The economic goal is to assign the right to the party for whom the right is most valuable. Posner, by looking to willingness to pay given the existing distribution, that is, the amount the party would pay for a right not already possessed, has picked a time to consider value when the value to the party who wants the right for a consumptive use is lowest, . . . thus making it less likely that the right will be "most valuable" to that consuming party. For example, . . . householders who want clean air for their enjoyment but will only pay 9 (units of money) for the right to clean air, if they already possessed the right, might be unwilling to sell it for less than 11 (as they are wealthier for possessing the right). Measuring value as the amount one would be willing to pay favors the factory owner who would buy or sell the right to pollute for 10.

Assigning the right to either the factory or to the householder achieves an efficient result: no change would result in everyone being better off without making someone worse off. Nevertheless, Posner's method of "valuation" produces a specific efficient result; figuring value as the amount one would require to sell the right if one possessed it (e.g., alternative 1 above) would produce a characteristically different "efficient" result. No neutral efficiency analysis exists which can avoid or segregate the distributive question; in the legal dispute the value maximizing award depends on what initial distribution is assumed while the content of the initial distribution is the precise issue in dispute. (Requiring the winning party to make payments to the losing party or to a third party, e.g., the state, does not remove the distributive issue but merely implies certain answers to it.) Theoretically, some specific initial distribution is adopted for purposes of evaluation. The one chosen indicates what favoritism is adopted.

Proposition II: Rich Consumptive Claimants Favored Over Poor Consumptive Claimants

Next we can ask if any groups or types of consumptive claimants are more or less favored by Posner's *situation ante* method of measuring "value." However, first we need a more precise inquiry into when and why an increase in wealth will increase the amount a person "values"—is willing to pay for—a right or good. A change in a person's wealth could be expected to result in some change in his individual "demand" function. In the normal situation, an increase in wealth would cause his demand function to shift upwards—i.e. he would demand more at the given price or be willing, if necessary, to pay a higher price for the same amount. However, this will not always happen. Sometimes an increase in wealth will not increase the amount a person is willing to pay for a right. For example, suppose Alex, whose income is X, is able to devote five dollars to entertainment. His other uses of X are fairly fixed so he does as well as he can with five dollars. Although Alex would much prefer to go to the seven-dollar football game than to the five dollar movie, given his entertainment budget, he decides to purchase the movie ticket. But then suppose someone gives him a movie ticket. Alex may offer to sell the movie ticket for four dollars so that he can buy the seven-dollar football ticket, and have two dollars left for a beer and a hot dog. (For another, more extreme case, consider the effect on the "value" of cat food—sometimes used as human food—of an increase in personal wealth.)

878

The movie-ticket case presents a right (one admission to the movie) which is valued less when the person's wealth is increased. In the man-in-the-desert situation the right (to the barrel of water) is valued more as wealth increases—and thus involves the opposite effect. In the movie-ticket case, the desire for the movie ticket declined because greater wealth made available more desired uses of time and resources; in the water in the desert case, the desire for water remained the same (although its "value" increased) when the person had more money. This difference suggests that, when predicting the influence of an increase of wealth on the value of a good, one should consider how the increase will affect the "utility" or desire for that good. If the desire remains the same, the value would increase with an increase in wealth. If the desire or utility decreases at the same or a faster rate than the utility of wealth decreased, the value would remain the same or decline. Two slightly different schemata exemplify decreasing desire or utility. First, more expensive goods may become attainable which substitute for the originally desired good—thus providing an alternative, but preferred, satisfaction of a need. Second, the needs that a person wants to satisfy may change. (Often either schema could apply depending upon the abstractness of the concept of need.) More generally, greater satisfaction of some desires may make the satisfaction of a given desire less important. The crucial factors determining the effect of the increase in wealth on the "utility" or desire for a specific "good" or right—the effect on demand—appear to be the persistence of the need or the availability of superior, but more expensive, substitutes for the good (change in desires, change in satisfiers of desire).

The argument for Proposition I assumed that if the wealth of the consumer was increased he would value the right more. When this generally valid proposition holds, the increase in value is directly related to the increase in wealth. The larger the proportional increase in wealth, the larger will be the proportional increase in value. Since the award of the right would provide a greater proportional increase in the wealth of a poor person than of a rich person, an initial assumption that each claimant has the right increases the "measured" value of the right for the poor person more than it does for the rich person. . . .

. . . However, this will only be true in the normal case where the increase in wealth does not decrease the desire for, or "utility" of, the right. To assert that Posner's analysis as applied to law exhibits these biases is to assert that in the most frequent or important cases of application, an increase of wealth (of the amount resulting from possessing the right in question) will have what I shall call the *normal effect*, that is, will increase the value of the right for consumptive claimants. The validity of this essentially empirical assertion is beyond the scope of this paper.

However, a general characterization of when the normal effect does and does not hold provides a basis for an informed guess as to the legal situations in which the propositions and the corresponding biases hold.

As noted above, for some specific consumables the normal effect may not hold because of the availability of superior alternative goods or because of a change in desires that accompanies the increase in wealth. In cases where the "right" in dispute relates to one's personal capacities, one's identity, or the constant feature of one's environment the normal effect should normally apply. The *value* of health, a basic education, the vote, control over or guaranteed availability of some instruments of production—e.g., future income and provision for the exercise of personal capacities—the quality of the environment, personal relations, "free" time, liberty, and items of intrinsic personal value can be expected to increase as one's wealth increases, although in some cases the specific items filling some of these needs may change.

I merely hypothesize that the normal effect holds in most cases where the content of the legal rule is disputed or where the rule requires a direct application of a utility analysis. For example, I would assume this generally to be true in most pollution and nuisance cases; in individual rights cases, e.g. free speech, right to counsel, right of entry into the judicial process, right to vote, rights relating to education (these, although not controversies between consumptive claimants, are cases where the poorer the claimant the more he is prejudiced by a welfare analysis applying a *situation ante* measure of value); in tort cases where part of the injury is to a "consumptive" rather than a productive interest; in many land use decisions; and in decisions articulating safety standards.

An example may clarify how measuring value in terms of willingness and ability to pay given the existing distribution favors the richer consumptive claimant. Assume that a city is deciding whether to use an open space for high intensity recreation (e.g. basketball courts, swimming area) favored by poor youth or for a fee-charging golf course favored by rich. Assume that the total cost to the city of either use is the same and that there are no negotiation costs (or other transaction costs). Then if the rich were willing to offer the city $5,000 to make a golf course but that the poor youth could only scrape together $4,500 for their offer, would "value" be increased by using the land as a golf course? Presumably, Posner would say yes. But if granted the right to have the land used for high intensity recreation, the poor youth might not give up the right for less than $7,000 while the rich, whose wealth would be little changed by being granted the right to have the land used for golf, would be willing to sell the right for a little more than $5,000. Adopting the *situation post* perspective clearly favors the poor for whom the right constitutes a larger proportionate addition of wealth. Alternatively, Posner's *situation ante* approach favors the rich—and, thus, illustrates Proposition II. It must be emphasized that both the *situation ante* and the *situation post* approach to defining value involve a bias, at least until the favoritism implicit in the adopted definition is justified. Neither definition is objectively accurate. Neither indicates how, in fact, human satisfaction would be maximized. More importantly, the specification of the concept of value is not merely an economic problem.

The foregoing discussion has explained and illustrated the first two propositions—namely, that the *situation ante* definition of value favors the productive user and the richer consumption claimant. Illustrations of these propositions in the context of legal disputes and judicial rule-making are plentiful.[28] However, several examples in the context of legislative decision-making may clarify the argument.

The military draft (assuming the right to "buy" out by paying for a replacement) illustrates both propositions. For the drafting unit, which wants labor (productive use),[29] the value of the right to draft should equal the amount possessing the right reduces its costs for achieving its goals (e.g. military protection). Consider two people, one rich and the other poor who are certain of being drafted if the draft exists, who are of equal value to the drafting agency and whose earnings would be equally affected by being drafted. Both have a consumptive desire not to be drafted. (The consumptive desire may be due to a preference for other employment or a dislike of regimentation, a desire for personal freedom or a dislike of the values implicit in military involvement.) The amount either would pay to avoid draft liability would be some amount *less* than the amount he would require for giving up a right to be free from the draft (assuming he had such a right). The individual is wealthier if he initially has a right to be free from the draft and thus is better able to stay out, illustrating Proposition I. The draft situation also illustrates Proposition II, a general bias in favor of the rich as compared with the poor consumptive claimant. When the maximum each is willing to pay to avoid liability is the same, that amount typically represents a greater concern for freedom from draft liability for the poor person than for the rich person. The rich claimant who would only pay $500 not to be regi-

28. Mishan suggests that the outstanding diseconomies resulting from permissive laws are "air and water pollution, noise, visual disturbance, [and] destruction of natural beauty." Mishan, "Pareto Optimality [and the Law," 19 *Oxford Economic Papers* 225], 278.

29. "Productive" from the perspective of the drafting agency. Always, a productive use eventually creates something of consumptive use. The entire military product is of consumptive value for society. Assuming a given budget, the amount for which the drafting agency would pay for or sell the power to draft should converge.

mented would normally require only a little more than $500 to accept the regimentation. However, the poor claimant who could scrape together only $500 to escape regimentation may require $1,000 before he would "voluntarily" accept it. Assuming nonpossession prejudices the poor more than the rich. . . .

In analyzing the basic biases implicit in Posner's approach and in suggesting why they are not more often recognized, we have observed (1) that, even in the frictionless world of perfect markets, the initial assignment would affect the final resource use and (2) that the traditional formulas for making the initial assignment involve characteristic types of favoritism. An examination of some of Posner's applications of his own approach has shown that in selected cases,* he appears to make mistakes which generally favor the same groups which his general methodology favors. . . .

Klevorick, Law and Economic Theory: An Economist's View†

Taking stock of the realized and potential contributions of any area of intellectual endeavor is a difficult task. The assessment process is even more difficult if the field is relatively young and if it is interdisciplinary. Such is the case with law and economic theory. In this paper, I will attempt to give my view, as a participant in the law and economics enterprise, of the types of contributions economic theory can make to law—to legal decision making, to the study and development of legal doctrine, and to the study and analysis of legal structure. These views should be understood as simply *an* economist's view. I make no attempt to describe what must be a wide spectrum of views held by economists working in the area, and I certainly make no pretense to present the views of the lawyers engaged in this joint enterprise.

The first kind of contribution an economic theorist can make in law arises when economic concepts become important in understanding some aspect of a particular legal case. Although the overall question raised by the case may not be economic in nature, at some point an un-

* [At pp. 21-27, which are omitted.]

† [65 *Am. Economic Rev.* 237 (1975). Reprinted by permission of the American Economic Association.

Alvin K. Klevorick (1943–) studied at Amherst College (B.A. 1963) and at Princeton University (M.A. 1965; Ph.D. 1967). He began his academic career as Assistant Professor of Economics at Yale University in 1967. He was Visiting Lecturer of Law at Yale Law School (1972-1973), and has been a regular member of the Law School faculty thereafter.]

derstanding of how markets work, how markets value commodities, services, and assets, and how individuals interact in their economic roles may become critical in deciding the ultimate disposition of the case. One can take an example as basic as the valuation of a capital asset. Suppose, for example, that through some set of circumstances (which we will not inquire into now), A has destroyed B's widget-making machine. The latter has no sentimental attachment to his machine, but values it only for the widgets it enables him to produce and sell. Without inquiring how the court reaches this position, suppose the court decides to award B an amount in damages equal to the value of the machine A has destroyed. An economist armed with his understanding of how markets value capital assets should be able to help the court in deciding the appropriate amount for B to receive in damages, given the court's decision that B should be compensated for the loss he has incurred because of A's destruction of the machine. An economist should also be able to help the court if B returns, as some real-world plaintiffs have, and asks for compensation, *in addition to* the amount the court has already awarded him, for the loss of profits he will incur until he can replace his widget-making machine with the new one he has just ordered.

In such a situation, the economist essentially plays the role of technician. He takes the problem facing the legal decision maker framed the way the legal decision maker has posed it, and he brings his expertise to bear in dealing with a specific part of the case. The economist draws upon his understanding of the way in which particular functions of society are performed, and he uses that understanding to shed light on specific issues in a given case. It is not a terribly imaginative role, but it is undoubtedly a terribly important one.

The second type of contribution an economist can make to law might be described as the economist in the role of "supertechnician." Once again, the economist takes the problem as set by the lawyer or by the legal decision maker, but in this instance the entire structure of the problem area has economic roots. The objectives and design of the institutions and doctrine are explicitly stated in economic terms, and the economist is called upon to evaluate and give advice about the best ways to achieve the specified objective(s). Most of the traditional areas of interaction between law and economics would fall, I think, into this category. They include, for example, the areas of antitrust law, public utility regulation, and labor law. When the issues at hand concern the most efficient way, or at least more efficient ways, of structuring an industry or a sector of the economy or the relationship between economic agents, the question comes ready-made for the economist to make an important contribution.

One particularly important function the economist can play in his role as supertechnician is to question whether the legal decision maker's general approach in a particular area actually helps to achieve the end the legal decision maker has in mind. For example, putting aside for the moment the multiplicity of reasons and rationales that might lie behind the institution of public utility regulation, suppose the legal decision maker asserts and believes that the primary objective of a system of public utility regulation is efficiency in the economist's strictly defined sense. The economist should be able to point out the kinds of characteristics commonly associated with natural monopoly and the kinds of characteristics which might suggest the need for special concern about the efficient functioning of an industry. He can help to focus the discussion to see whether the industry for which regulation has been proposed is indeed a natural monopoly. If the answer is yes, the economist can—and should—then suggest to the decision maker the variety of possible responses to the natural monopoly situation, responses ranging from having the natural monopoly privately owned and unregulated, to the general type of public utility regulation we have today, to an alternative type of regulation, or, finally, to public enterprise.

One thing the economist should do is provide the decision maker with an evaluation of the advantages and disadvantages of each of these alternative approaches. He should frame the discussion so that it encompasses not only the direct impacts each of these systems will have on the efficiency of the sector or industry whose regulation is being contemplated, but also the side effects or indirect effects that such regulation might have on this industry and its consumers and on other industries and other consumers in the economy. It would also seem to be incumbent upon the economist to try, to whatever extent possible, to indicate the income- (or wealth-) distributional impacts of such a regulatory policy. For although we have assumed (for the sake of this discussion) that the averred and true goal of the decision maker's use of regulation is to achieve efficiency, there are undoubtedly some tradeoffs between efficiency and distribution in the choice of a response to the natural monopoly problem, and the economist is particularly well suited to the task of pointing out what kinds of tradeoffs exist. Of course, while most of my discussion is concerned with the role of the economic theorist, the kinds of judgments that would be important, indeed critical, in such a balancing act are empirical judgments (and empirical guesses if hard data do not exist concerning these alternative costs and benefits). But even the theorist can help, and should help, to focus the discussion at the level of a comparative institutional analysis—a comparison of the alternative systems available for trying to achieve the given objectives.

In the context of this role as supertechnician, the economic theorist can also have a considerable input in designing the particular legal structure that is eventually chosen to cope with the given legal problem. For example, in the public utility area the economic theorist may be able to indicate which kinds of regulatory structures are most likely to achieve the goal of efficiency. He would be able to delineate, from an efficiency point of view, which kinds of issues are best handled using automatic adjustment clauses and which types of issues are best thrashed out in an alternative procedural setting.

In sum, when the economic theorist acts as a supertechnician for the lawyer, he draws on his expertise in analyzing a problem posed by the lawyer, just as he did in the role I described as economist as technician. But now the problem he is addressing is in its own terms economic in nature.

The third role I see for the economic theorist in the joint enterprise of law and economics is one that has come to flourish quite recently. Put briefly, it envisions the economist or economic theorist as the propounder of a new vocabulary, a new analytical structure for viewing a traditional legal problem. In contrast to the economist's approach in the first two categories of interaction I discussed, in this third role he no longer takes the problem as framed by the lawyer. Rather he takes the general problem area with which the lawyer is concerned—say, torts, or property, or procedure—and poses in his own terms—that is, in economic terms—the problem he sees the legal structure or legal doctrine confronting. He provides, thereby, a different way of looking at the legal issue which yields alternative explanations of how current law came to be what it is and new proposals for new law.

In the area of torts, for example, some economic theorists have posed the problem facing society as minimization of the expected social costs of accidents, taking account of: the costs incurred when accidents occur and the probabilities that such accidents will occur; the relationship between those accident costs and probabilities and the steps people take to avoid accidents; the costs of the resources devoted to avoiding accidents; and the costs of any administrative structure used to make decisions about the optimal level and allocation of these several kinds of costs among members of society. Economic theorists have used this type of framework to discuss and evaluate the traditional negligence rules, to provide a critique of the fault system of accident law, and to evaluate new proposals for automobile accident law, for example, no-fault plans. To take another example, the design of a system of civil procedure, criminal procedure, and judicial administration has been formulated by some lawyer-economists as the problem of minimizing the sum of the social costs of resources devoted to such procedural systems and administrative mechanisms plus the error costs of those procedures. This framework has then been used to evaluate various specific aspects of procedure and judicial administration: for example, the discovery rules of the Federal Rules of Civil Procedure, the bail system, the existence of plea bargaining, and the use of the jury.

This third role is probably the most exciting one the economic theorist can currently play. This form of interaction with the lawyer appears to be the most creative and the most challenging. Hence, it is interesting to ask whether particular kinds of problems confront the economist when he presents a new vocabulary or a new structure for analyzing a legal problem. I think two such problems are particularly important—one arises from a constraint imposed by the economist's tools while the other is a limitation imposed by the lawyer's formulation of the problem area.

The constraint imposed by the economist's tools is perhaps seen best in the context of a concrete example. Consider the problem of designing a set of liability rules for accident law in the world in which we live today. It should be clear that any attempt to analyze reality, to make meaningful statements about it, requires some abstraction from the richness of the phenomena being studied. The lawyer's world view is an abstraction just as the economist's is. The economic theorist's approach is to begin with the simplest possible model which captures important structural elements of the problem and to analyze that model as carefully as possible. As a theorist, I think this is a wise strategy. Having analyzed the simplest model, one might then proceed by relaxing some of the unrealistic assumptions which made one's first construction so tractable. For example, one might assume at the first step that all accident costs are, in fact, known to all parties making decisions about what levels of care to exercise. The second level of analysis might involve a relaxation of that assumption and a recognition that some parties will not be fully aware of these costs. The single (certain) values individuals attached to accident costs in the first model might now be replaced by subjective probability distributions people have about the accident costs that will be incurred.

Now suppose that in the simplest model several different liability rules would each yield the full-information social optimum by leading individual decision makers to attain the social-cost-minimizing combination of care levels. As one relaxes the assumptions of the model, the set of liability rules that will achieve the social optimum will undoubtedly become smaller. Further relaxations of the original assumptions—further gropings toward a more realistic representation of the world and people's decision-making processes—will undoubtedly reduce even further the number of liability rules that yield the social-cost-minimizing solution. Indeed, it is most likely that before long the set of socially optimal liability rule structures will become empty. In short, there is no first-best solution in the real world or, for that matter, in the most complicated, yet tractable model we may construct.

The question then is: If the economic theorist is going to use his theoretical analysis to make policy recommendations, how should he proceed? It would be tempting simply to consider those policies that were socially optimal in, say, the next-to-the-most complicated model he had. The problem with this, of course, is that the order in which the theorist relaxes his original assumptions to arrive at the most complicated model he analyzes—that is, the path that leads to the continually shrinking set of socially optimal policies—has no particular normative justification. He could follow an alternative complicating path which might well generate an alternative second-best policy.

The realization that we are making decisions in a second-best (indeed, an nth-best) setting does not imply that the theorist's models and analyses should be dispensed with or ignored. Nor should the second-best nature of the decision problem be used by the economist as an excuse for avoiding statements of a policy nature. To evaluate alternative policies, however, the theoretical model must be used in conjunction with careful, empirically rooted judgments (guesses?) about which of the theorist's original simplifying assumptions are most likely to affect the applicability of his model's results. And the order in which the theorist relaxes these assumptions in building successively more realistic models need not reflect the empirical importance of the various assumptions. Hence, there is no reason to evaluate second-best policies by simply removing, in reverse order, the complications introduced to obtain the most realistic model.

The theorist can contribute in two ways to the comparative institutional analysis the law and economics enterprise should produce in such situations. First, by providing a new and different way of looking at the traditional legal issue, he will, hopefully, provide clarification and new insights into that issue. Second, he will provide an indication of the kinds of empirical guesses that are needed in order to use his theoretical investigation for policy formulation in the world in which lawyers actually operate.

A different, but equally important, difficulty arises when the economic theorist provides a new vocabulary for a problem which the lawyer poses in a form not really amenable to economic analysis. While the theorist might be tempted to show how his analytical structures can be applied to particular issues in such areas, it is simply the case that his tools are inappropriate to the overall task. I have particularly in mind those areas in which lawyers or legal scholars have framed the legal question in process-oriented rather than outcome-oriented terms, that is, as a question about how a decision will be made rather than about what the decision will be. Questions of institutional competence, questions of whether a particular issue is one that should be taken up by legislatures or by courts, are questions which are not easily comprehended within the economist's framework.

The issue as posed by the lawyer in such cases does not seem to be rooted in the search for some neatly defined social optimum—be it the maximum of a social welfare function or the minimum of some social cost function. The problem is not framed as the search for an *efficient* way of reaching a decision or deriving a structure of rules, but rather as the determination of the *"appropriate"* way of reaching a decision or the *"appropriate"* institution to use to decide the particular issue. And the question of appropriateness is most likely to be resolved by appeals to history, to political theories of democracy, and to sociological theories of the role expectations of different members of the society. This is not to say that the economist's analytical structures cannot provide some help in examining these questions. In particular, when the lawyer appeals to political theories of democracy to help decide which institution is appropriate, he may well benefit from consideration of voting models and other models of the political process developed by theoretical economists and political scientists working in the area of public choice. The point simply is that when the lawyer or legal scholar has framed the problem in process terms, focusing on the appropriateness of one institution rather than another to perform a particular function or to make a particular decision, the lawyer is least likely to be receptive to the economist's vocabulary, rooted as that is in terms of a search for efficient structures, for efficient decision-making processes, and the like.

To be sure, questions of relative institutional competence can be stated in economic terms. One can talk about which institution has a comparative advantage in performing which function. We can ask whether courts or legislatures are "better" at developing liability rules, whether courts or administrative agencies are "better" at determining the value of a fair rate of return to a public utility, whether legislatures or courts are "better situated" to decide which interests are fundamental and which interests are not (alternatively, which wants are merit wants), or whether the judiciary or the legislature or the executive is the appropriate institution to decide if and when prior restraint over publication should be exercised. One can use the terminology of economics and talk about the costs and benefits of using one institution rather than the other. But when the legal scholar has posed the problem in process terms, the analytical structure the economist offers for the given legal issue may not prove very helpful to the lawyer.

Let me try to illustrate this point with two examples. The first concerns freedom of speech. I believe that the economist (or the lawyer-economist) can contribute to our understanding of and deliberation about the appropriate scope for freedom of speech by taking seriously a concept which many Justices and legal scholars have invoked in their discussions of First Amendment freedom of speech issues: the marketplace of ideas. The economist can contribute by taking such references to the marketplace of ideas as something more than simply rhetoric—as, instead, an attempt to invoke what appears to the lawyer to be an appropriate analogy. Then, by bringing to bear his understanding of the ways in which markets work, of the potential sources of market failure, and of the possible responses to such market failures—all within a comparative institutional analysis framework—the economist may provide intcrest-ing observations (at least in efficiency terms) about possible arguments justifying and opposing limitations on freedom of speech in specific situations.

Exploiting the analogy of the market-place of ideas, the economist can, I believe, provide a clarifying view of some aspects of the development of legal doctrine in the First Amendment area, for example, "the clear and present danger" test and its development and application in the case law. But suppose the legal scholar's formulation of the First Amendment issue takes the form of the question: Which institution or which branch of government is the *appropriate* one to determine the scope of First Amendment rights? For example, suppose that the majority of a duly elected legislature believes that advocacy of a particular political phiosophy poses an imminent danger to the nation. The legislature enacts a statute making advocacy of the particular political views a criminal act. The legal scholar might ask: How deferential should a court be to the legislature's judgment if a suit is brought challenging the law? The economist's analysis and interpretation of the development of judicial doctrine may not be very helpful to the lawyer or legal scholar in answering this question.

The second example concerns whether juries in criminal trials should be representative, whether they should represent a cross section of the community. Here I think the economist can help in evaluating how effective representativeness of the jury is in furthering perform-ance of the jury's fact-finding function. He can suggest and explicate the analogy between the selection of a jury and the selection of a portfolio of assets by an investor. Pursuing this analogy, with the consequent delineation of the similarity between representativeness of a jury and diversification of an investment portfolio, the economist can draw upon portfolio selection theory to suggest the kinds of circumstances under which representativeness would make the jury a more effective fact-finding body and the types of situations in which reresentativeness would not serve that end. I think that introduction of the economist's vocabulary in this discussion is interesting and helpful. But if the question of jury representativeness is framed not in the instrumental sense of achieving some further objective, like fact finding, but rather in more process-oriented terms, which would have a representative jury as the *appropriate* type to decide criminal cases, then the economist's vocabulary is much less likely to clarify and illuminate the issues for the lawyer.

We come now to the question of what happens after the economist has proposed a new vocabulary for viewing a traditional area of legal concern. One possibility, of course, is that the new vocabulary will simply be rejected, and I have tried to indicate at least one reason why that may occur. A second possibility is that the new vocabulary, the new way of viewing the problem, will come to displace the old. While I regard this outcome as highly unlikely, it nevertheless suggests the major danger that I see, and that I hope will be averted, in the application of economic theory to legal problems: namely, a type of intellectual imperialism on the part of the economic theorist or the lawyer-economist. It is the danger that, having created or at least suggested a new vocabulary for viewing the legal issue, the economic theorist or the lawyer-economist will develop—or even worse, try to generate in others—a form of tunnel vision in which he sees the new vocabulary as the only "reasonable" one for viewing the area. While I firmly believe that economics can make a contribution to law and that economic theory in particular can make such a contribution, I do not believe that the analytical grid the economic theorist imposes on the legal problem is the only one worth examining.

The most likely result of the economist's suggestion of a new analytical structure is the coexistence of his new approach to the problem with other, perhaps more traditional, approaches to it. For example, thinking of civil procedure as designed to minimize the sum of the direct costs and error costs of procedure will come to coexist with an understanding of certain elements of procedure as generating or guaranteeing a sense of fairness in the way our legal system operates. Our system of tort law will be understood both in terms of minimization of the social costs of accidents and in terms of noneconomically based ideas of causation and reciprocity.

Economic theory's contribution to law is likely to be greatest if, in proposing new analytical structures for traditional legal issues, the economist or lawyer-economist takes a constructive eclectic view and welcomes the contributions other social scientists may be able to make to our understanding of these areas. For psychologists, historians, sociologists, and others can also suggest new and potentially useful approaches to legal issues, approaches which will undoubtedly complement the economist's with its relative inattention to a variety of questions—like historical development, the formation of individual and social tastes, and so on. The economic theorist's new formulation essentially provides a new metaphor for viewing the particular area of legal concern. But the economist's suggested metaphor is only one among many, and in attempting to understand, to analyze, and to aid in the development of the law, an approach which draws upon the variety of ways the several social sciences analyze human behavior is likely to be the most helpful and the most successful.

Heller, The Importance of Normative Decision-Making: The Limitations of Legal Economics as a Basis for a Liberal Jurisprudence —as Illustrated by the Regulation of Vacation Home Development*

IV. The Social Basis of Legal Economics

. . . Economic jurisprudence is becoming the new core doctrine of liberal legal thought because: (1) it affords a more complete explanation of the contemporary role of the modern state than did pre-existing legal philosophy, and (2) it appears to offer a value free or procedural theory of social justice. The argument [here] is that while legal econnomic analysis can aid in the rationalization of existing legal concepts, it cannot at the present time fulfill its second promise. To fully understand why and to what extent economic analysis ought to be accepted by the law today, it is necessary to refer to earlier liberal political economics and the historical conditions that spawned it. Specifically, it is here suggested that although an economic theory of law could have been the basis of a self-contained theory of justice during the period of the liberal order characterized by economic growth and substantial communal agreement about social values, the change in historical conditions since that time must cause us to reevaluate the relationship of law and economics. If our hopeful reliance on an inherently limited decisionmaking technique is

* [1976 *Wis. L. Rev.* 385, 468-473. Reprinted by permission of the copyright owner, the Wisconsin Law Review.

Thomas C. Heller (1944–) received his A.B. from Princeton (1965) and an LL.B. from Yale (1968). He is Associate Professor of Law at the University of Wisconsin.]

merely symptomatic of more basic weaknesses in liberal social theory, then it is ultimately those flaws which must be addressed. To the extent that it is accepted that liberal theory is currently inadequate, the quest for an ideal of social justice must revert to direct consideration of the problems of substantive moral philosophies from which liberalism has struggled to escape.

In accordance with earlier theories of law, economics would be entirely inappropriate to describe legal phenomena. To the natural lawyers whose thought made up the pre-liberal jurisprudence, the sphere of the legal was normative and wholly separate from that of the social sciences. The concept of law as an autonomous discipline was continued in the legal conceptualism which dominated the late nineteenth and early twentieth centuries.[206] Law was conceived to be a system of general and abstract rules which formed a consistent or integrated order apart from external political or economic considerations. Lawyers were like logicians who manipulated the tenets of a self-contained philosophy sufficient to resolve the problems presented it. The paradigmatic forms of law were the contract and property doctrines, and they offered a universalized structure for transactions in private markets. Law in this perspective was disjunctively opposed to the multitude of particularized regulatory acts which have characterized the modern public sector.

The traditional role of law was limited; it was a creature very different from the administrative leviathan which has appeared in Western capitals.[207] Legal conceptualism, which cannot account for the activities of the emergent public sector, can be described as an immature form of a more general liberal theory of law. Hidden in the jurisprudence of conceptualism was its implicit tie to the early beliefs of economic theory that freely operating and efficient markets could be organized with only formal legal norms. There is no complete inconsistency between legal economics and the doctrines of legal conceptualism. In fact, it remains appropriate for the operation of the decentralized sectors of the economy where efficient markets continue to function.[209] However, the internalization of cost-benefit principles within the private transactions and the historical lack of publicly managed resource allocation produce only

206. Trubek, Max Weber on Law and the Rise of Capitalism, 1972 *Wis. L. Rev.* 720, 730-31; J. Merryman, *The Civil Law Tradition* 65-73 (1969); Woodward, The Limits of Legal Realism: An Historical Perspective, 54 *Va. L. Rev.* 689, 711-17 (1968). For a fuller description of the emergence of this form of thought see J. Dawson, *The Oracles of the Law* 148-262 (1968), and R. Unger, *Knowledge and Politics* 67-100 (1975).

207. F. von Hayek, *The Road to Serfdom* (1944).

209. It has also become clear that much received legal doctrine was at least consistent with, if not the product of, an implicit past reliance on cost-benefit principles. Posner, A Theory of Negligence, 1 *J. Legal Studies* 29 (1971).

the appearance that law is autonomous and separate from economics. A theory of law which restricts its range of inquiry to the relatively less important private sector in an increasingly regulated economy will not be intellectually sufficient.

Today, rather than ignoring or resisting governmental intervention as a legal reality, economic jurisprudence makes it the essence of a coherent theory of the comprehensive role of law in the contemporary state. Concepts such as imperfect competition, external economics and information failure have made ongoing regulatory controls a central element in the relationship between state and society. An economic theory of law first rejects the idea that the law is comprised of a fixed set of general rules and affirms the conceptual unity of law and regulation under a single legitimate principle of allocative choice. Second, economics provides a functional analysis of social institutions that can be used to study innovative conflicts and to criticize confused concepts of received legal doctrine. Economic jurisprudence is compelling because it affords a more complete and consistent reflection of the principles of liberal social theory than did the formal categories of legal thought which preceded it.[210]

The search for a better jurisprudential method is also stimulated by a growing sense of crisis about the regulatory state. The expansion of governmental intervention in the market has been accompanied by a perception that public decisionmakers are prone to biased policy solutions. We seek a theory which both acknowledges the role of government and yet imposes limits on arbitrary official behavior which can ultimately delegitimize the concept of law. Discretion in the sovereign is the essential problem of jurisprudence in any system which rejects the idea that law is a philosophical order, independent of political objectives, and possessed of an internal logic that mandates specific results. The American legal realist and related positivist movements, which temporarily filled the void left by legal conceptualism, simply avoided defining the substance of correct decisions by describing a sovereign discretion in the courts or the legislature.[211] No jurisprudence which recognizes an authority with

210. The critical implications of legal economics, which are an important source of its value, are also a major reason it is resisted. The residual forms of conceptualism are familiar to those educated to them. In addition, the supposed autonomy of the law has insulated its practitioners from the encroachments of economics and other foreign considerations. There is an economic jurisprudence, unfortunately, a false threat to the legal profession which is uncertain of its possible obsolescence.

211. See H. Hart, *The Concept of Law* (1961). Realism provided the first critique of conceptualism by showing, not that the doctrine was rationally insufficient, but that it did not eliminate discretionary behavior. It remained, however, essentially a critical or negative movement with a fundamental inability to recreate a true positivist jurisprudence like the current movement to legal economics. . . .

discretionary power can explain the principles which ought to resolve innovative legal conflicts.[212] Nor can it provide a conceptual image of a proper decision against which public policies can be either criticized or supported. It is because economics offers more than the guinea stamp of the state that it has attracted such attention.

What is not as evident is why the solutions of economic analysis actually merit legal recognition. The answer to this normative question is obscured because the concept of economic science has undergone evolutionary change. The dominant contemporary position holds that economics is only an instrumental technique of formal rationality, independent of any particular social context. Economic methods are universally applicable tools which indicate how any individual or group may maximize aggregate welfare given any subjectively defined set of preferences within an initial resource constraint.[213] At the individual level, economics rationally organizes consumption and investment decisions within a predetermined budget. At the social level, welfare analysis optimizes resource use within any given distribution of wealth or relative to any specified social welfare function.[214] As a pure positivist science, economics is wholly value free. It approves no objectives or ends and is concerned only with the instrumental effectiveness with which they are pursued.[215]

The economic is a necessary component of all policy analysis since it predicts the allocative and distributive effects caused by the responses of rational utility maximizers to suggestions of change. It functions as a technical tool which constrains legal choice by describing the unintended and self-defeating consequences of particular rules and their consistency with other elements of the legal system. It would not be correct, however, to attempt to construct an autonomous and complete jurisprudence on such a base. The selection of a utility function to be maximized

212. Discretion in an ordinary language sense means the right to make a decision which may not be called into account. A discretionary decision may be based on taste, random choice, whimsy or principle. It is then diametrically opposed to a rational legal decision which ought to be the product of a mandatory application of legitimated decision principles. The hallmark of a modern legal system is that decisions can be mistaken and redressed when they are not consistent with articulated and implicit principles of decision. Since discretionary behavior is beyond criticism, there is no corresponding right of critique. See K. Davis, *Discretionary Justice* 4-5 (1945), and Dworkin, The Model of Rules, 35 *U. Chi. L. Rev.* 14 (1967).

213. F. von Mises, *The Epistemological Basis of Economics* 139-82 (1960).

214. D. Winch, *Analytical Welfare Economics* 175-200 (1971).

215. Economics is a positivist science in the sense that it recognizes scientific knowledge only in the realm of means and is agnostic in the matter of ends. This is a position not limited to liberal economics but general to the development of Western social science. . . .

and the choice of a distribution within which to work are wholly exogenous acts which must be resolved on non-economic, normative grounds. Since from an economic viewpoint these are discretionary choices, formal legal economics can provide no escape from the jurisprudential problem. Nor would the use of aggregative techniques offer more than the most minimal legitimation for policy solutions determined ultimately by non-economic principles.

It is no criticism of current economics that it does not pretend to be a self-contained logic of social choice. Careful economics is especially aware of its own limitations. On the other hand, there is little to explain the attraction of such a science for theorists seeking non-discretionary and legitimate legal answers. Such a method of arriving at unique and just solutions would be available only if the procedures of economic analysis evolved and were applied in a social system organized by normatively desirable principles of distribution. Economics, like law, is a universal element of social organization.[216] However, the specific content of the discipline varies with the conditions of the social order in which it exists. The definition of economics as a generalized technique provides no account of the historical milieu in which modern economics grew and flourished. In historical terms, our legal and economic theories can be understood as institutionalized reflections of the liberal paradigm of social organization. The aggregative methodologies of market economics

---

216. In each distinct social order the purpose of the law is to prevent all actions inconsistent with the implicit normative principles or virtual constitution which structures the system. Every social theory justifies and distinguishes itself through the act of defining boundaries between legitimate and non-legitimate behavior. If the order is to persist, it must continually make plain and reinforce the principles which recommend it. Legality is a functional requisite of each social entity because it is the mode of critique of arbitrary actions and policies which result from improper application of mandatory procedures of choice. However, legal rules will vary with each social theory. Law as a form is a universal element of social organization; but, its content is derived directly from the virtual constitution of each different order.

This view of law as a moment of a unified system of social thought sees law as a relativist, but not a positivist order. It is relativist because the social entity of which it is a part is historically defined and limited. The content of law is not defined across cultures. Thus jurisprudence is also anti-positivist since it does not define law as the product of any specific institution. Law is not what the courts, legislature, party or church say that it is. Rather, it is defined in relation to social principles which can be conceived as a virtual constitution, more or less written, depending on the problems which call forth articulation. In contrast, a specific rule represents the remediable attempt of an interpretative agency to render these principles less general so that they may be applied to specific fact situations. The law is that network of rights, duties, and remedies which would functionally exist in any normatively integrated association and would be institutionally enforced in an ideal application of those normative principles.

were developed and accepted because they were means for rational, skeptical, self-interested individuals to equitably acquire the potential gains of cooperative industry. Although the current conception of economic science centers only upon the rational ordering of preferences and the radical separation of values and techniques, this is but a universalized form which has been abstracted from a specific form of social theory we can call a liberal utopia. Economic technique per se provides no definitive logic of social choice.

Chapter 11

Law and Sociology

Jones, An Invitation to Jurisprudence*

. . . A social environment would be intolerable without the existence of efficacious institutions for peace-keeping and dispute-settlement, but genuine "social tranquility" has further requirements and overtones. By almost anybody's definition, a good society is, among other things, a society in which creativity is unhobbled by constant apprehensions, diversity flourishes without group or class hostility, and inevitable social change is accepted not as something terrifying but as something to be planned for. We are brought, then, to three other of law's social ends-in-view: (1) the maintenance of a reasonable security of individual expectations, (2) the resolution of conflicting social interests, and (3) the channeling of social change. I am not suggesting for a moment that this is a complete tally of law's tasks in society. No such catalogue could be attempted in a lecture ten times as long as this one, and, in the time we have, we shall not be able to do more than touch on the three listed tasks. Nonetheless, the three do go, as Contracts scholars used to say, "to the essence" of law in society and are items that must be taken into account in any serious attempt at evaluation of a questioned legal rule or legal institution.

Security of Expectations

Life in society is limited and unimaginative if men and women cannot plan their future conduct with reasonable assurance that the rules

---

* [74 *Colum. L. Rev.* 1023, 1026-1043 (1974). (Footnotes omitted.) Reprinted by permission.

For biographical information, see page 702 supra.]

will not be changed after a commitment or investment, of effort or money, is made. Crusty old Jeremy Bentham, whose ideas on man and society retain a surprising freshness for those who will read him without textbook preconceptions, put "security," in the sense of security of individual expectations, at the first place in his hierarchy of law's social values. In Bentham's view, even constitutional liberty is an "expectation" —that one's freedom will not be interfered with arbitrarily by public power-holders—and property, contract and reparation for injury are founded not in natural right or human will, as earlier legal philosophers had it, but on expectation, and the securing of this expectation can only be the work of law. "Without law," wrote Bentham, "there is no security, and therefore no abundance, not even a certainty of subsistence; and, in such a state of things, the only equality which could obtain would be equality of poverty."

The maintenance of reasonable security of expectations has seemed so compelling as one of law's ends-in-view that there is a whole armory of legal ideas and legal institutions designed to provide it: constitutional provisions like the guarantee against *ex post facto* criminal laws, judicial policies like that embodied in the emerging doctrine of prospective operation of overruling decisions, and, indeed, the principle of *stare decisis* with its special force, as you will have observed, in the "reliance areas" of the law where it is realistic to assume that action was taken on the strength of known judicial precedents.

In our society, and particularly as concerns larger commercial, industrial and property interests, lawyers—legal counselors—are the principal agents for the engineering of expectations. The counselor in his law office is the retailer of the legal system for those who know when to turn to him, and can afford to consult him, to make it as sure as such things can be that the expectations arising from contracts, settlements, wills, negotiations and transactions will, in the course of time, be realized in fact. I suggest—although this may be a new way of looking at the phenomenon—that the vast programs of the 1960's to provide legal services for poor people and for people of modest means be examined in the same perspective. Are not these programs, when extended from courtroom advocacy to office counseling, an effort to give the expectations of the less fortunately placed members of our society a security comparable to that heretofore enjoyed only by the well-to-do? Office counseling for the poor lacks the drama of a criminal defense or a consumers' class action, but the need is great and the opportunities for service hardly yet tapped. Who knows, perhaps there will not be too many lawyers after all.

For, make no mistake about it, security of expectations is not just a rich man's value. It can be even more important to a poor person or a person of moderate means. If I have twenty substantial property or contractual interests, and one goes sour on me, I may be angered or inconvenienced, but I am not impoverished. But if I have only one or two more humble expectations—a pension, seniority in my job, the promise of a small legacy, an assurance of child support payments, or a low-rent long-term lease on my apartment—disappointment of that expectation can be disastrous. When you read *Kirksey v. Kirksey* in your Contracts course, did you wonder what in God's name ever happened to the widow, Sister Antillico, and her small children after the court decision came down that her brother-in-law's promise to "let you have a place to raise your family" was legally worthless? That should have been your first reaction if you think of law not as a game but as a means of social ends. One can quarrel with Bentham's stubborn insistence that "the cultivation of 'security'" is "the main object of law"—that is, with his placement of security above even equality and subsistence as values to be served by law-government. But is any assessment of a judicial decision or legislative enactment a complete assessment if it fails to ask Bentham's question: will this decision or statute promote or undermine security of individual expectations?

The Resolution of Conflicting Social Interests

Card-carrying jurisprudents like me are fond of seeking out the areas of agreement, the shared values and communities of interest, that supposedly underlie every legal and political system. This high-minded endeavor is subject to a certain limitation: the need for law arises not when people agree on what should be done for the good of all but when their interests, demands and aspirations come into collision. A great truth of political philosophy is condensed in Judge Learned Hand's description of democracy as "a political contrivance by which the group conflicts inevitable in all society find a relatively harmless outlet in the give and take of legislative compromise." How then are we to characterize law? Hand's answer is again no-nonsense and unsentimental: "the law is no more than the formal expression of that tolerable compromise that we call justice, without which the rule of the tooth and claw must prevail."

The theme that law's central task is the containment and management of inevitable group conflicts runs through the writings of the late Roscoe Pound, whom we think of as the founder of at least the American version of what has become known as "sociological jurisprudence." Contemporary law students are sometimes put off by Pound's style, which can be heavy and unduly taxonomic, but the best of his work—as in his long and, I think, classic study, *A Survey of Social Interests*—stands like a rock against the efforts of jurisprudential revisionists to belittle it. In Pound's theory of social interests, legal institutions—legislatures, administrative commissions and courts—are interpreted as, above all, agencies for the balancing and weighing of the competing group demands that arise in any society:

> Looked at functionally, the law is an attempt to satisfy, to reconcile, to harmonize, to adjust these overlapping and often conflicting claims and demands . . . so as to give effect to the greatest total of interests or to the interests that weigh most in our civilization, with the least sacrifice of the scheme of interests as a whole.

Manifestly, it is in the legislatures, national and state, that the great conflicts of group interest are typically fought out or bargained out and, at least provisionally, resolved. But in the universe of Pound's "sociological jurisprudence," even constitutional adjudication is thought of as far less the formal application of constitutional principles than the responsible weighing of the competing group interests—debtors and creditors, employers and employees, majorities and minorities—that can come to courts as well as legislatures. When one asked Pound whether a recent Supreme Court decision was a "good" decision or a "bad" one, the old gentleman—for so I remember him with gratitude and considerable awe—had a way of answering not in terms of the correctness or incorrectness of the Court's application of constitutional precedents or doctrine but in terms of how thoughtfully and disinterestedly the Court had weighed the conflicting social interests involved in the case and how fair and durable its adjustment of the interest-conflicts promised to be. Try this approach to legal evaluation on the next ten cases you read, in Constitutional Law or any other course. You may become conscious of analytical dimensions beyond any you had originally seen in the controversy.

The existence of law in a vast and pluralistic society will not and cannot bring about a perfect harmony of competing demands, convictions and aspirations. We ask too much of law—and something we would not want anyway—if we look to law to prevent the occurrence of social controversy and the airing of social grievances. "Trouble" cases will continue to arise; indeed, experience in every country I know anything about demonstrates that there are many more open and expressed conflicts of interest in a society in which law prevails than in a feudal or otherwise closed system in which appeal to law can be made only by the stronger or better placed. The rule of law has as its practical and achievable end-in-view the maintenance of a balance—sometimes a delicate balance—in which competing interest-group claims are voiced, listened to and weighed through peaceful political or judicial procedures and decided authoritatively and with the consent, however grudging, of the disappointed parties.

So, whether we are entirely happy about it or not, compromise—the reasoned accommodation of opposed interests—is a central and indispensable technique in the legislative and judicial resolution of competing social interests. All-or-nothing people are at times useful catalysts, but they are never effective legal reformers. If sociological jurisprudence has a message for today and tomorrow, it may be that those who have the power and responsibility for the resolution of competing social interests reach the soundest decisions when they listen—really listen, which is the hardest thing in the world for a law-trained person to do—to the inevitably extreme demands of all the contending social factions and then strive for the way of "tolerable" adjustment and ultimate social reconciliation. A compromise, to be durable, must be fair. To resolve deeply felt conflicting social interests on a winner-take-all basis, as has been done so often in legal history, is to forget that winners and losers are going to have to live in the same society for a long, long time.

The Channeling of Social Change

In this opening lecture, I want to do everything I can to put my own deeply held standards of legal evaluation on the line, and not obscure them with fancy phrases or surreptitiously introduced "ultimate" or "ideal" ends. So, at the risk of wearying you, I will restate the central hypothesis that is going to run through these three John Dewey Lectures. A legal rule or a legal institution is a *good* rule or institition when—that is, to the extent that—it contributes to the establishment and preservation of a social environment in which the quality of human life can be spirited, improving and unimpaired. If this be granted, it follows that any account of the social ends to which law is means must proceed from a view or concept of the social world as it is and can reasonably be expected to become.

I have no credentials as a social prophet, but there is one thing we can be quite sure about: tomorrow's society will be different from today's in its material conditions and moral attitudes, just as today's society is far different from that of fifty or even twenty-five years ago. "Nothing steadfastly *is*," said Heraclitus, "Everything is becoming," and these words express a truth that lawyers, no less than philosophers and theologians, must understand and learn to live with. This is not to say that change is always and necessarily progress; history records about as many social changes for the worse as for the better. Change is simply predictable, inevitable and ceaseless as the basic social fact. In the words of the old song, "We don't know where we're going, but we're on our way."

This sets one of law's most important ends-in-view. Law, thought of merely as a body of doctrine and aggregate of institutions, is neither for social change nor against it. What law does—or can do when its legislators, judges and practicing lawyers are socially aware and professionally resourceful—is to provide institutions and procedures for the channeling of inevitable social change in ways that make sought reforms effective with the minimum possible impairment of law's other ends-in-view: the public peace, just dispute-settlement, reasonable security of expectations and tolerable adjustment of conflicting social interests. Law's principles, institutions and procedures are there to be drawn on for the social task at hand, but they have to be used. The channeling of social change can be accomplished only through continuing acts of creative and informed intuition by men and women who combine genuine mastery of legal techniques with equally profound understanding of social forces.

It has become a truism that law must be kept up to date, responsive to the continuing processes of social change. Present-day judges are very much aware that concepts and categories received from law's past—privity of contract, sovereign immunity, "fault" in divorce actions and many more—may not order contemporary phenomena effectively and justly. It is not that these concepts were necessarily wrong when they were handed down; we are, I think, too quick to assume that. It is simply that, whatever their original justification, they offer the wrong answers for today's problems. One hates, in a way, to see old friends like negligence, consideration and "state action" withering away in vitality and influence, but, to borrow a phrase from Justice Roger Traynor, "the number they have called is no longer in service."

To say that law must be kept responsive to changing social conditions and social attitudes is, however, to state only half of the equation. The relation between law and social change is reciprocal, for law, in its turn, can have a molding effect on social development. The imperatives of the legal order carry at least prima facie rightness for most members of society. More often than not, a legal principle, if soundly conceived and resolutely enforced, becomes a kind of self-fulfilling prophecy and creates the social climate necessary for its acceptance. When wisely and imaginatively employed, law is far more than an instrument of command; it is organized society's principal resource for the engineering of that widespread and supportive public assent—the true consent of the governed—without which great social initiatives never really get off the ground. I have been wondering lately if this is not the most important way in which law operates—or can be drawn on—for the sound and effective channeling of social change.

And so we have touched base with five of law's most visible ends-in-view: preservation of the public peace and safety, the settlement of individual disputes, the maintenance of security of expectations, the resolution of conflicting social interests, and the channeling of social change. This is no complete inventory of law's tasks, nor is it a neat set of mutually exclusive teleological pigeonholes. There are manifest overlappings —for example, the resolution of conflicting social interests is one of the ways in which law helps to channel the forces of social change—and some of law's ends-in-view can come into collision with others, as when law's adjustment to social change involves some unavoidable impairment of the security, of individual expectations. In law as in ethics, the hardest task is often not the identification of values but the assignment of priorities when, in a specific problem context, one value cannot be fully served without some sacrifice of another. But even and particularly when values cut across one another, disinterested and informed judgment on legal and social problems requires that each of the competing ends-in-view be understood in its full claim as an aspect or dimension of what law is *for*: the creation and preservation of a social environment in which, to the degree manageable in a complex and imperfect world, the quality of human life can be spirited, improving and unimpaired.

II. Judicial Decision-Making: Sources and Methods

In the first of these John Dewey Lectures, we looked, very generally and therefore impressionistically, at some of the social ends to which law is means. Today we continue the same inquiry, but with a narrower focus. We shall be looking not at law generally but at law's distinctive institution, the courts, and specifically at the sources and methods of judicial decision-making. But it is, I insist, the same inquiry, and the same standards of evaluation apply. Judicial decisions, like other legal phenomena, must be appraised in terms of their consequences, that is, in terms of their service—or disservice—to the achievement of law's social ends-in-view.

We have already rejected the notion that law generally is a form of art for art's sake; we must be on our guard not to think of judicial decision-making that way. The temptations towards an arty, in-group frame of evaluative reference are greater in the analysis and appraisal of appellate decisions than in any other area of legal functioning. Court adjudication is our home stadium, whether we be law students, legal scholars, or practicing lawyers. We know the rules that govern play there. We admire, and properly, the resourceful tactic, the brilliant strategy, the masterful case synthesis in a brief or a judicial opinion. One can forget, as I have often forgotten during my lifetime love affair with the common law judicial process, that there is a world outside the appellate courtroom, and that judge-made law, like all other law, is "good" and "bad" according to its impact in that world.

Today's discussion is billed as "Judicial Decision-Making: Sources and Methods." At the outset, unavoidably, we have to define a few terms. In a legal system characterized, as ours is, by the principle of stare decisis, judicial decisions, at least those reached by appellate courts, have a twofold function: first, they are settlements of concrete disputes then before the court, and, second, they operate, through the doctrine of precedent, as general law or, more precisely, as sources of the general law. Thus when the Court of Appeals of New York, in Cardozo's day, decided *MacPherson v. Buick Motor Co.,* the effect of the decision went beyond settlement of the particular controversy between Mr. MacPherson and the Buick Motor Company and controlled, or greatly influenced, the outcome of countless future claims against automobile manufacturers and, as it turned out, manufacturers generally.

For purposes of analysis, we treat these two effects separately. Let us call the first, more direct, effect "judicial dispute-settlement" and call the second, more dispersed, effect "judicial law-making." Please bear in mind—because I do not want to be misunderstood—that I do not use the term "judicial law-making" in any pejorative sense. I am not saying that judge-made law is always or even usually made out of whole cloth, and "judicial law-making," as I shall be using the term, includes not only the announcement of an entirely new rule but also the authoritative clarification—even the reenunciation—of a rule that might have been gleaned by close analysis of the older materials. My suggestion is simply that it is useful, analytically, to distinguish between "dispute-settlement," which relates to the parties then before the court, and "law-making," which relates to a decision's potential impact, as general law, on others.

To be sure, these two functions or effects of appellate judicial decisions are related operationally. A particular dispute may be settled against the personal inclination of the participating judges—although rather less often than is commonly supposed—because, as judges often put it, "the opinion will not write," that is, because deciding the case as the judge or judges might "like" to decide it simply cannot be squared with an honest interpretation of the authoritative legal sources. And, as every student of the judicial process soon learns, a particularly appealing claim—that factually attractive "test case" institutional advocates are al-

ways looking for—can lead to the announcement, in justification of the
result reached, of an awkward, subsequently embarrassing general rule.
But, with this reservation, the emphasis of today's discussion will be on
the "law-making" aspect, as heretofore defined, of judicial decisions. Judicial decision-making in its more immediate, dispute-settling dimension
will be taken up in my third lecture, "The Problem of Justice in the Settlement of Disputes."

We move now to our inquiry into the materials and methods of judicial decision-making—to the material sources, one might say, of judge-
made law. I propose that we start this inquiry with the analyses provided
by John Dewey, who, for my money, wrote more instructively about the
judicial process than any other philosopher before him or since, and by
Oliver Wendell Holmes, Jr., the founding father of what has become
known as American Legal Realism, a jurisprudential faith to which I
have faithfully subscribed since my conversion to it many years ago by
the late Karl N. Llewellyn.

The Dewey-Holmes Dialogue

Dewey and Holmes never met, as far as I know, but their ideas,
taken together, provide considerable insight into the intellectual atmosphere of the years between the two World Wars, when they were both
toweringly influential figures. Insight is provided into our own times,
too, because Dewey and Holmes retain their influence, either as masters
to be cited or as high-visibility targets to shoot at. Had I ever been able to
persuade my Law School colleagues to let me teach Jurisprudence as a
first year course, an early exercise in that course would have been a comparison of Holmes's greatest essay, *The Path of the Law*, published in
1897, with Dewey's remarkable short article, *Logical Method and Law*,
published in 1924 and inspired, I like to remember, by Dewey's collaboration with Edwin W. Patterson in Columbia's graduate seminar in legal
philosophy. This exercise in intercultural comparison was never imposed on a first year class—perhaps for fear of violating the constitutional ban on cruel and unusual punishments—but I am going to take a
few minutes to do it now, because I know of no better way to get us to the
heart of what I want to say about judicial law-making.

In his book, *Social Thought in America*, the late Morton White used
Holmes and Dewey as two of his five exemplars of what he called "the
revolt against formalism" in Twentieth Century American social theory.
But White did not get fully into what amounted to almost a dialogue—
or, at least, a mutual admiration society—between the great pragmatist
philosopher and the Great Dissenter. For Dewey, Holmes was the para-

digm of the civilized, self- and socially conscious judge. Dewey's *Logical Method and Law* is, in one aspect, an admiring commentary on Holmes's jurisprudential ideas, and there are more references to Holmes in Dewey's books than to all other judges combined. "One of our greatest American philosophers," Dewey once wrote of Holmes, and this was no casual observation.

Holmes, for his part, was well along in years before he began reading Dewey's philosophy, but Dewey's ideas hit the grand old Justice where he lived. Nor is it surprising that the legal scholar, who had stated on the first page of his great study of English legal history that "[t]he life of the law has not been logic: it has been experience," hastened to buy a copy of Dewey's *Experience and Nature* and, despite his Bostonian distaste for Dewey's literary style, read it through three times over a four year period. References to Dewey soon begin to appear in Holmes's letters to his most intimate correspondent, Sir Frederick Pollock. Thus, Holmes writes:

> I certainly thought Dewey's [approach] an advance on Berkeley and Hume . . . I found him very hard reading. Still his view of the universe came home to me closer than any other that I know.

And, a year later to Pollock:

> But although Dewey's book [*Experience and Nature*] is incredibly ill written, it seemed to me after several rereadings to have a feeling of intimacy with the inside of the cosmos that I found unequaled. So methought God would have spoken had He been inarticulate but keenly desirous to tell you how it was.

If you know anything about Holmes, you will see at once that this is the most profound compliment he ever paid to anyone in his long life.

Given the world view they shared, we would expect to find striking affinities in what Dewey and Holmes had to say about judicial decision-making. And we certainly find these affinities, with one qualification that must be noted. Dewey, a sophiscated observer of the judicial process but not a working judge, is writing normatively, that is, about what he considers to be *good* judicial thinking. Holmes, although this point is usually missed by both his critics and his admirers, is writing for the most part descriptively, about how judges—most judges—*do* think and how their conventional modes of thinking can, on occasion, get them and society into trouble.

First, then, to Dewey's norms of sound judicial thinking; the summary that follows is essentially an abridgment in Dewey's own words. A "reasoned or rational" judicial decision is "the outcome of inquiry, comparison of alternatives, weighing of [the social] facts." When is one decisional alternative to be chosen over the other? When it is the one that will do more "to secure orderly methods in behalf of . . . social welfare." Thus, judicial logic must be a logic relative to the social consequences of a chosen rule rather than to its doctrinal antecedents. The general rules found in the precedents are by no means to be ignored in this process—after all, they are "statements of generic ways in which it has been found helpful" to treat type-situations in the past—but it is to be kept in mind that these inherited rules are "working hypotheses" and need constantly to be retested by the way they are actually working out in society. This kind of judicial thinking—choice among law-making alternatives in terms of practical social consequences—is, says Dewey, "the indispensable prerequisite of steady, secure and intelligent . . . social advance by means of law."

If Holmes read *Logical Method and Law,* as I am sure he did, he must have agreed fully with Dewey's normative prescription that judicial logic should be a logic relative to social consequences, that judicial law-making should be based on reasoned, deliberate weighing of the likely, social consequences of fixing the new rule one way or another. But Holmes was making a further and somewhat different point, and that is that judges *are* influenced by their notions of what sound social policy ought to be, whether or not they are fully conscious, or even conscious at all, of this powerful influence on their action. The key passage in understanding Holmes is, I think, the following from *The Path of the Law:*

> The language of judicial decision is mainly the language of logic. And the logical method and form flatter that longing for certainty and for repose which is in every human mind. But certainty generally is illusion, and repose is not the destiny of man. Behind the logical form lies a judgment as to the relative worth and importance of competing legislative grounds, often an inarticulate and unconscious judgment, it is true, and yet the very root and nerve of the whole proceeding.

To make his point clear beyond possible misunderstanding, Holmes continues:

> I think that the judges themselves have failed adequately to recognize their duty of weighing considerations of social advantage. The duty is inevitable, and the result of the often proclaimed judicial aversion to deal with such considerations is simply to leave the very ground and foundation of judgments inarticulate, and often unconscious, as I have said.

In short, Dewey's message is that considerations of social advantage *should be* controlling in judicial law-making; the Holmes gloss on this is that such considerations *are* controlling, inevitably, on the law-making activities of the judge, whether or not the judge is conscious of where his social perceptions or social prejudices are taking him. Thus the good judge, according to Holmes, is one who knows exactly what he is doing, and has to be doing, in this decisional context and so considers definitely and explicitly the social considerations on which the rules courts lay down must be justified.

Our comparison of Dewey and Holmes reveals, at most, a difference of perspective or emphasis. Certainly Dewey and Holmes, as men of reason, share the conviction that the marksman deliberately aiming at an explicitly identified target—one thinks of judges like Stanley Fuld and Roger Traynor—will hit the bullseye far more often than someone who fires his gun by intuition or on half-understood impulse. And I am pretty sure that neither Dewey nor Holmes would have quarrelled with the approach to legal evaluation stated in my first lecture, and now applied to judicial decision-making; the courts, too, serve law's social ends in view when—and to the extent that—judges reach their law-making conclusions by way of a disinterested and informed weighing of the probable consequences of their action on the prevailing quality of human life in society.

The "Serious Business" of the Courts—And Why It Is Inevitable

It is about now that I shall begin to run into objections. Many learned lawyers and law scholars would cheerfully accept my pragmatist-utilitarian approach as a standard for the evaluation of legislation—the Securities and Exchange Act, say, or the 1969 Tax Reform Act—but would sharply challenge the propriety of applying that approach to judicial decision-making. A critic steeped in the older, pre-Realist jurisprudence would have denied that judges ever "make" law at all. The judiciary "may truly be said to have neither force nor will, but merely judgment," wrote Alexander Hamilton in the *Federalist Papers,* which comes close to saying that judges are not decision-*makers* and never have to do more than announce judgments foreordained for them by "the law."

Hardly anyone thinks of the judicial process that way any more. The objection to my evaluative hypothesis would be put today in more sophisticated terms, perhaps something like this: "Is it fair, even realistic, to evaluate judicial decisions in terms of their likely social consequences, since courts, unlike legislative law-makers, are restricted in the choices they can make and so cannot give primary place to considerations of social advantage?" There is substance to this question, and it must be answered carefully. Judicial decision-making is, indeed, limited or conditioned in many important ways. First, judges are "generally bound"—as the phrase goes—by the authoritative sources of the legal order, the rules laid down for their guidance by statutes and past judicial precedents. Second, judges are committed to certain traditional and established methods—what Pound called their "received technique"—in the use of these authoritative sources. And, third, courts and judges have a limited political and social function, the bounds of which are hard to define with precision but are sensed and respected by all judges worthy of the name and find shorthand expression in such concepts as "fidelity to law," "judicial restraint," and—as I think most instructive—Karl Llewellyn's notion of the "steadying factors" that make appellate judicial decisions "reckonable."

I agree fully and cordially that the factors just mentioned—the authoritative sources, received techniques and limited political function of the judiciary—differentiate judicial law-making from legislative law-making as, say, a painter working with the pigments and in the visual tradition of the Renaissance might be contrasted with a contemporary avant-garde artist, who is likely to execute any design that comes into his mind and with any materials that come to hand. These special ground rules for judicial decision-making are considerations to be kept in mind in appraising the social consequences of judicial decisions, but they in no way rule out the pragmatist-utilitarian approach to evaluation of judicial law-making. We can surely take one important step without encountering serious objection from anybody. However arguable my evaluative hypothesis may be as applied to any single case, certainly a body of judge-made law, a whole line of judicial decisions in an area like manufacturer's liability or holder in due course, must be appraised in terms of how it is working in society. What other standard of evaluation comes to mind, aside from the long outmoded notion of *elegantia juris*?

And let me record one concession to narrow the range of possible disagreement. I am not saying that the courts are undirected, uncontrolled by the precedents and statutes, in all the cases that come before them or even in most of them. Many, perhaps most, of the controversies that reach the appellate courts can be disposed of without much more than a reference to existing rules and precedents. Some lawyers and judges of experience will say that three-fourths of the cases that come to court leave the judges no room, no leeway, for alternative decisions— and so no occasion to weigh the social considerations. I would put the figure far lower, but there is no reason to insist on that for our present purposes. On any account of the judicial process, even the most conservative, there is a substantial incidence of cases in which the rule can be set, and justified with all traditional case-law proprieties, either way. Whatever this incidence may be—a fifth, a fourth, or a third—it is indisputable that judicial decision-making involves, at certain times anyway, the inescapability of choice between alternatives, and so of social responsibility for choice. And, as Thomas Paine might have put it, these are the times that try judges' souls. Or, as Cardozo said in his more measured way:

> It is when the colors do not match, when the references in the index fail, when there is no decisive precedent, that the serious business of the judge begins.

In what remains of this second lecture, I am going to use Cardozo's phrase, "serious business," as shorthand for "decision uncontrolled by the formal legal sources." A court has to *make* law in such a "serious business" case because, by assumption, there is no controlling pre-existing law to "discover." How would we have the court proceed in this problem context other than by a disinterested and informed weighing of the probable consequences of its new or now-modified rule in the social environment in which the chosen rule will have its impact?

What is there about law's sources and methods that gives rise to these "serious business" problems, that leaves open these frequent occasions in which the decision is uncontrolled by precedent or statute? Why, in a developed and massively documented legal system, are there so many decisional situations in which the judges find no mandate—and little guidance—in the law's formal and authoritative sources? The explanation is familiar learning to most of you from Legal Method and your other first semester courses; let me simply refresh your recollections a bit and go on from what you have already learned. Consider, first, the case law, the law of judicial precedents. Its propositions, unlike those in the natural sciences, do not constitute a logically cohesive and unified deductive system; they are, at most, an aggregate, and an incomplete one. Unprovided-for cases are forever arising as social change brings new problems, or new facets of old problems, in its wake. A search of the authorities often discloses the existence of conflicting precedents, and the deciding court, in this confusion of doctrinal voices, must decide which, if either of them, is to be the rule for the future. And it is not always as easy as it might seem to distill a *rule* from a judicial opinion, which is, in a way, like trying to condense a parable into a proverb.

The judge's "received" techniques do relatively little to eliminate this irreducible element of ambiguity in the case-law sources. A court *may* employ the holding-dictum distinction to narrow the binding authority of a precedent from an apparent yard to an adjudged millimetre or *may,* with equal professional propriety, accept the past case as sufficiently persuasive authority for the broadest proposition expressed in its opinion. A precedent is not fully authoritative beyond its "material facts," but—to paraphrase Chief Justice Hughes—the material facts of a past controversy are what the present court says they were. And stare decisis, although a powerful legal policy, is not an absolute bar to reconsideration of even the most firmly established case-law rule; flat overrulings of once hallowed precedents are no longer the rare occurrences they were fifty or even twenty years ago. John Dewey's characterization of case-law principles as "working hypotheses" is more than an ideal to be sought; it is a quite accurate statement of the status these principles actually have in contemporary appellate litigation. Precedents always guide—structure, in a sense—appellate judicial decisions, but they do not always control them, and never in "serious business" cases.

The problems that compel judicial creativity are not, I suggest, vastly different as concerns judicial application of the statute law. Statutory ambiguity is but an instance of the difficulties, familiar in every discipline from theology to sociology, which inevitably attend any effort to apply general propositions to the wayward and infinitely varied concrete facts of human experience. As Chief Judge Charles Breitel has written:

> Because perfect generalization for the future is impossible, no generalization is complete. Aware of this impossibility, legislatures often do no more than purport to lay down the most general statements of law, intending that the courts and other law-applying agencies shall creatively adapt the general principle to specific cases.

How different is that, really, from the task of the courts in their development of case-law doctrine?

Along with this irreducible element of ambiguity in the legislative sources, we have—perhaps we must have—a variety of often conflicting methods, "received" techniques, of statutory interpretation. There are about as many ways of interpreting a statute as there are of skinning a cat. When one reads a succession of statutory interpretation decisions, it is not enough to note that the same court, in its progress, interpreted one statute according to its "plain meaning"—"plain" to the court, that is, if not to anybody else—the next statute broadly and generously in accordance with its manifest purpose as exhibited in the extrinsic sources, and the third quite narrowly, in line with one or another ancient maxim. The serious analyst must go a step farther and ask *why*—that is, for what substantial reason of sought public policy—did the court in each case use the particular interpretative technique it chose to apply? That inquiry is likely to be the genuinely enlightening one. And our immediate hypothesis holds; statutes, too, guide and structure judicial search and inquiry, but they do not always control it, and certainly not in "serious business" cases.

The Construction of Law-Making Judgments: What the Courts Need Most and How They Are to Get It

Why is it so hard to tell, on a first reading of the court's opinion in a "serious business" case, that the controversy was originally a stand-off, as concerns formal legal doctrine, and was decided as it was chiefly in accordance with the court's views—informed judgment, intuitive impression or largely unconscious predilection, depending on judge or judges involved—of what is sound public policy? The source of the analytical difficulty is in the syllogistic form characteristic of judicial opinions, which operates, as often as not, to obscure policy decision in a wrapping of essentially secondary doctrinal explanations. For courts must not only reach decisions, they also have to justify them, and, as John Dewey wrote a long time ago, there is always danger that the logic of justification will overpower and conceal the logic of search and inquiry by which a decision was actually arrived at.

Once we have this clearly in mind, it becomes too evident for serious question that the day-to-day decision-making of the courts involves processes far more challenging and creative than pre-Realist legal philosophy had supposed. In "serious business" situations, the positive law is not a command to the judge but, at most, an authorization of alternative decisions. Judges, by and large, are reluctant lawmakers, but the role is thrust upon even the most modest of them by the realities of their function. The case must be decided, one way or the other. Unlike the pure social scientist, the judge cannot withhold his action until all the returns are in. There is no hiding place from the political and moral obligation to decide.

So we are brought to the final and show-down question. If judges are to reach their decisions by way of a genuinely informed evaluation of the probable consequences of their action on the quality of human life in society, where do they get the data they need to accomplish that design? Courts, unlike legislative committees, hold no investigative hearings and have miniscule research staffs—a law clerk or two per judge, and these largely occupied with library research. If considerations of social advantage or disadvantage are to be brought clearly to judicial attention, it must be through the adversary system, yet the adversary system, in most cases, works far less effectively to present the social consequences dimension of a controversy than its more purely "legal," or legalistic, side.

Important steps have been taken recently to reduce the inequality of legal representation that made the adversary system as unbalanced as it was, for example, at the time the early employer's liability cases came to be decided, but it is still true that a vastly better advocate can overpower his opponent and, except in a very strong court, make the worse policy alternative appear to be the better. Even when the opposed advocates are equal in ability and resourcefulness, the conventions of appellate advocacy—holdovers, perhaps, from pre-Realist jurisprudence—are such that far more attention will be given to doctrinal "antecedents" than to likely social "consequences." My impression—which may be a bit unfair because I have not been regularly active in the appellate courts for many years—is that most briefs and oral arguments do not go much farther than efforts to persuade the court that the statutes or precedents relied on by the other side are not controlling on the court. If both sides succeed in this endeavor, as is likely in a close case, all that has been accomplished is a kind of clearing of the deck. The court has not been helped much on what it really wants to know: "Where do we go from here?"

One who would appraise the soundness of the social policy judgments that are, and have to be, made in the courts must consider also the actual and potential usefulness, to this end, of legal scholarship: the treatises, studies, casebooks and law reviews. Legal scholarship is less doctrine-bound, more nearly "law in society" oriented, than it was when I began law teaching in the late 1930's, but it is still not as helpful as it should be on "social consequences" issues. This is partly due to out-of-date but surviving notions that law is somehow an autonomous and self-contained discipline, partly due to the circumstance that what I call "efficacy research"—field studies of how legal precepts are actually working out in society—takes longer and costs incomparably more than analytical work in a law library.

Perhaps a new generation of legal scholars will come to the aid of the law and the courts in this respect. But somehow I doubt it. My impression, which again may be unfair, is that our younger, more "activist," law scholars are fully as infatuated with doctrines and concepts as we were in my day. The only visible change is that the concepts are different. When entirely new and quite prickly issues of public policy demand authoritative decision, the typical young law scholar, like most of us years ago, can find more final answers, more certain and revealed truth, in an obscure text from the Constitution than Rabbi Joshua ben Perahya could find in a passage from the Torah. Surely it is not that easy. The urgent need of the courts is for social facts, not super-refined doctrinal exegesis. Picasso could say *"Je ne cherche pas, je trouve,"* but lawyers and legal scholars are in a very different line of business.

When pressed with the question of where a judge is to get the social data he needs for instrumentally sound decisions, Judge Cardozo had only this answer: "[H]e must get his knowledge . . . from experience and study and reflection; in brief, from life itself." We smile at this, perhaps, yet there is great truth in the answer, because it underlines the vast importance of wise and disinterested judicial selection; the judge-made law can never be much better than the judges who make it. But a more socially imaginative style of appellate advocacy and a legal scholarship better balanced between the law library and the social out-of-doors could help make good judges better at weighing social alternatives and the inevitable poor judges a little better at it than they would otherwise be. That is the only way of insuring in the long run of things, that the courts —stumbling occasionally, as we all do—will make their full potential contribution towards realization of law's social ends-in-views. . . .

Zeisel, Reflections on Experimental Techniques in the Law*

Much of the law's reasoning turns on the effects of the rules it creates or enforces. Normally these effects are alleged or implied, but rarely proven. Yet during the last decades, first the natural sciences and, learning from them, the social sciences have developed techniques of experimentation that would allow firmer determinations of what a rule of law does or does not accomplish.

The basic tool (and also the paradigm for retrospective analysis) is the controlled experiment. Its essence is simple: The objects or people on which the experiment is to be performed are divided randomly, that is, by some lottery device, into two groups; the experimental treatment is then applied to the one group and withheld from the other, the control group. If an effect is found in the experimental group that is absent from the control group, it can be attributed to the experimental treatment, since at the time of the prior random selection the two groups had

---

* [2 *J. Legal Stud.* 107 (1973) (some footnotes omitted). Reprinted by permission from The Journal of Legal Studies, Vol. 2, No. 1.

For biographical information, see page 317 supra.]

been strictly comparable, and in fact interchangeable. And randomization assures that whatever the outcome of the experiment, it is possible to calculate the degree of certainty that can be attached to it.

Several controlled legal experiments have been or are being conducted, as we shall see; but sometimes the controlled experiment, employed in its pure form for legal investigations, encounters obstacles on the part of the law. Since by definition it gives something to one group and withholds it from another, it would seem to violate the basic guarantee of equality before the law. For example, while one might want to know what difference it makes to the fate of a defendant if he can afford to hire his own counsel, one can hardly undertake an experiment in which one group of defendants is assured of individual counsel and the other group compelled to accept a public defender. To take another example, one might like to know what effects it has on the future of convicted defendants if instead of being sent to prison they are put on probation, or vice versa. An attempt to answer this question through a controlled experiment in which these two types of sentence were assigned randomly might again encounter objections.

Several circumstances, nevertheless, argue in favor of the experiment, even in legally sensitive areas. First, it is by no means certain that the experimental treatment makes any difference; the uncertainty may in fact be the reason for the experiment. Second, discrimination in an experiment is by definition only temporary; after it is concluded and the best solution is found, the solution will be applied to all.[3] Finally, there are areas at the fringe of the law where random assignment is more tolerable because the right involved is not sufficiently important to merit special protection.

Certain modifications have been developed that make controlled experimentation tolerable even in sensitive areas. They operate in three dimensions: abandonment of direct control of the experimental treatment in favor of the indirect experiment, simulation of part of the experimental design, and the use of natural experimental conditions.

The Indirect Experiment

The essence of the indirect experiment is that it removes direct control over the experimental variable from the investigator while maintaining the controlled character of the experiment, albeit at a price. Three examples follow.

3. For a more elaborate statement see The Case for the Official Experiment, in Hans Zeisel, Harry Kalven, Jr. & Bernard Buchholz, *Delay in the Court* ch. 21 (1959).

1. The first of the indirect experiments concerned a procedural device designed to reduce the trial load of the courts. Normally, a claimant in our civil courts presents his case both as to liability and size of damages; he is followed by the defendant who presents evidence in rebuttal of both claims. After the parties have had their say the jury retires and decides whether the defendant is liable for damages, and if so how large these damages should be. The question of damages thus becomes relevant only if liability is found. It was proposed to try the liability issue in its entirety first and ask the jury to decide whether the defendant owed anything at all. Only if liability was affirmed would the trial continue, and in that event the jury would render a second verdict on the amount of damages. Since liability is found in only slightly more than half of all cases, this mode of trial was expected to dispense with about half of all damage litigation. The U.S. District Court for Northern Illinois was sufficiently intrigued by this idea to permit by rule the conduct of split trials, and asked the University of Chicago Law School to assess its effect on the workload of the court.

The ideal design for this investigation would have been random assignment of cases to the traditional and split mode of trial. But this the judges, quite properly, considered their decision to make. Once random assignment is replaced by deliberate judicial decisions, the difficulties begin. Suppose the judges decided, sensibly enough, to order a split trial whenever they believed that the jury was likely to deny liability. Such a principle of selection would make it impossible to compare the duration of the split trials with that of the normal ones, because we would know that the split trials concerned different kinds of cases to begin with.

At first glance, the lack of a control group seemed to vitiate the experiment. But by slightly shifting the focus of the inquiry, it was possible to save the integrity of the experiment. As the cases come to the court they are randomly assigned to the individual judges. This means that the cases coming before Judge A would not differ, in the long run, from the cases coming before Judge B. And it so happened that the various judges of the court made differential use of the split rule, in that some used it for almost all their cases. some for hardly any, and some for varying proportions in between. If it were true that the application of the split trial rule saved time, the judges who applied the rule more often should require on the average less trial time than those who applied it less often.

This turned out to be the case, as [Table 1] shows.[5]

5. Hans Zeisel & Thomas Callahan, Split Trials and Time Saving: A Statistical Analysis, 76 *Harv. L. Rev.* 1606 (1963).

TABLE 1
Proportion of Split Trials and Average Trial Time in
Personal Injury Trials

Judge	Proportion of Cases Tried under Split Trial (Per Cent)	Average Length of All Trials Before This Judge (Days)	Number of Trials Before This Judge*
A	89	3.2	(26)
B	51	3.3	(41)
C	38	3.5	(26)
D	14	3.8	(22)
E	7	3.9	(27)
F	7	4.3	(14)

* Only judges with more than 10 trials were included.

The regression line based on these data indicated that if a judge were to conduct all trials under the split trial rule, his average trial time would be cut by about 20 per cent. This would be, then, the amount of time that could be saved through general application of the split trial rule.

This particular experimental design, however, contained a hidden flaw. Conceivably, the judges who tried their cases in general more expeditiously might also have made more frequent use of the split trial rule. Such self-selection could have biased the results of the experiment. Supplemental evidence was therefore adduced. It was clear that any savings had to come from the elimination of the damage trial, so the frequency of damage trials was determined both for the regular and for the split trials, as shown in [Table 2].

TABLE 2
Disposition of Cases in Regular and Split Trials

	Regular Trials (Per Cent)	Separate Trials (Per Cent)
Complete trial on liability and damages	76	15
Trial ended in liability verdict	—	58
(a) Because verdict was for defendant	—	43
(b) Because damages were settled after verdict on liability	—	15
Other dispositions (settlement during trial, directed verdicts)	24	27
	100%	100%

The dispositions of the two groups of cases differ drastically: 76 per cent of all regular cases go through a complete trial as against only 15 per cent of the split trials. In 58 per cent of the split cases, trial of the damage issue was avoided *because* of the intermediate liability verdict. In 43 per cent of the cases the trial simply ended when liability was denied and in another 15 per cent there was no trial of the damages because the case was settled after the jury had found liability. The convergence of the two sets of data left no room for doubting the efficacy of the split trial rule.

2. A similar problem arose when the courts of New Jersey decided to appraise the value of what has become known as pretrial. In most of our courts civil suits (occasionally also criminal cases) before they come to trial are scheduled for pretrial. There, counsel for both sides, occasionally with their clients present, meet with the judge to present briefly the issues under dispute and air the possibilities of a settlement. Tradition has it that the pretrial facilitates settlement and hence is a most desirable means of reducing the trial load and thereby the congestion of our metropolitan courts.

But analysis of the available evidence raised doubts as to whether pretrial in fact saved court time since, to begin with it, it uses up court time. We suggested that a controlled experiment could provide the answer. At the time, the New Jersey courts had a rule that made pretrial obligatory. . . .

Again, the ideal experimental design was simple: randomly assigning one part of the cases to pretrial, omitting pretrial with the other part. But there was concern as to the constitutionality of a procedure that denied the right to pretrial to a group of litigants who could not be distinguished on the merits from the members of the group to which pretrial was granted.

A compromise was agreed upon that allowed random assignment of one half of the cases to obligatory pretrial and the other half to optional pretrial, where pretrial would be held only if at least one of the litigants requested it.

This design, which allowed the litigants and counsel to have a pretrial whenever they wanted it, had from the experimenter's viewpoint two short-comings. It blunted the objective of the experiment by comparing obligatory with optional pretrial, and therefore allowed no direct inference as to the effect of pretrial itself. And, of course, if all litigants in the optional group had opted for pretrial, we would have learned nothing.

The experiment was conducted and 2954 cases assigned randomly to the two groups. Only about one-half of all litigants in the optional group asked for pretrial, compared with the obligatory group where all cases were pretried. The results of the experiment were as follows:

	Obligatory Pretrial	Optional Pretrial
Suits settled before they reached the trial stage	76%	78%

The conclusion emerged simple and clean: contrary to the widely held belief, obligatory pretrial failed to increase the settlement ratio; there were just as many settlements without it. From the point of view of reducing the number of trials, obligatory pretrial was found to be a waste of time, and the State of New Jersey forthwith changed its rule and made pretrial optional.

3. The third experiment had a major impact on the criminal law. It revolutionized one of its most solid traditions: the practice of setting bail for arraigned defendants. Bail is set, as a matter of constitutional right, for virtually all defendants. If they can post it, they are set free; if not, they must remain in jail. Whether or not they *can* post it as a rule depends—since criminal defendants seldom have substantial sums of money—on the bondsman who, against a premium of some ten per cent, will or will not take the risk of providing the demanded bail.

The system has been criticized because it favors the well-to-do and the criminal accused who work for the well-to-do, because it surrenders the actual power of decision to the bondsman, and because it keeps an inordinate proportion of defendants in jail, many of whom are subsequently acquitted. Nevertheless, the system stood fast until the creation of a foundation which conducted a controlled experiment with the cooperation of the New York judiciary and the assistance of New York University Law School. All defendants arraigned in the felony court of Manhattan were interviewed to assess the risk of their failing to appear at their trial if the court freed them without requiring bail. On the basis of these interviews, the defendants were classified into two groups: those for whom such a release without bail could be recommended to the court, and those for whom such a recommendation could not be made. The recommendable group was then divided at random in half. For one of the halves the recommendation to release the defendant without bail was actually transmitted to the arraignment judge; with respect to the other half, the judge was told nothing. In all cases the judge made the ultimate decision as to bail, in the one group guided by the recommendation, in the other group without such guidance. In this latter group only 14 per cent of all defendants were freed without bail, as against 60 per cent in the recommended one-half. The remaining question was whether at the time of trial a larger proportion of the group of which 60 per cent had been freed without bail would fail to appear in court than of the group where only 14 per cent were freed without bail. When trial time came, in both groups not more than one per cent of all defendants deliberately failed to appear. The experiment demonstrated that the number of defendants released without bail could be approximately quadrupled without increasing the likelihood of defendant's not appearing at the trial.

The aftermath of this experiment was dramatic. The City of New York adopted the interviewing procedure as a permanent feature of the criminal justice system; and today most major cities and many rural areas have adopted the interviewing procedure and with it the practice of release without bail. The experiment had fallen on unusually fertile soil. Everyone—except the bondsmen—stood to profit from the liberalization: the municipalities by saving money on jails; the defendants by being spared unnecessary hardship; not least, the ends of justice were advanced at a point where the traditional approach was ripe for reform.

In all three of these experiments the direct control over the experimental variable had been left to the judges or the litigants: The decision whether or not to hold a pretrial was left to the litigants; the decision whether or not to order a split trial was left to the judge; and so was the decision whether or not to release a defendant without bail. But because of the prior random assignment of the cases to experimental and control groups, all three studies retained their character as controlled experiments. Two disadvantages result from such indirect control. The first is a lack of directness in the measurement. The New Jersey experiment permitted no direct observation of the effect of pretrial itself; it measured only the difference between obligatory and optional pretrial. More importantly, the lack of direct control could have vitiated the experiment. If all litigants in the optional group had insisted on pretrial, if all judges in the split trial experiment had made use of it with the same frequency, and if the judges in the bail experiment had paid no heed to the Vera interviewers' recommendations, there would have been no difference between experimental and control group and hence no experiment.

This shift in the goal, coupled with the risk of failure, are the price to be paid for the privilege of conducting an experiment in an area where the law cannot surrender certain decisions.

We may note here in passing that the same difficulty and the same solution offer themselves where the experiment involves decisions that for other than legal reasons cannot be imposed on the subjects, such as submission to an experimental medical treatment. Here too, the indirect experiment has found its place.[9]

Simulation

If indirect experimentation is one line along which the experimenter can meet the concerns of the law half-way, simulation is the other. The three experimental sequences we now turn to fall into that category. They were not undertaken by the law itself, although assisted at crucial points by the judiciary or the litigants. They all came out of the University of Chicago Law School study of the American jury.

The first sequence concerned the broad issue of the difference it would make if all cases now going to the jury were decided by a judge sitting without a jury. The second experiment was designed to explore the jury's handling of the defense of insanity, if instructed under differing rules of law. The third experiment set out to determine whether in civil cases different juries in different parts of the country, given an identical set of facts, award different amounts of damages.

1. The question of the difference between jury and judge verdicts would seem to demand a controlled experiment, where every case is tried twice, once with and once without a jury—an obviously impossible solution. Yet this is almost precisely the experiment that was performed, if one permits the "two trials" to take place simultaneously, since every jury trial takes place also before a judge, the one who presides over it. Hence, all that had to be done was to ask a nationwide sample of trial judges to reveal, for a sample of their trials, how the jury had decided the case and how he, the judge, would have decided it without a jury.

The results of this study, in criminal cases, have been published in *The American Jury*, where [Table 3] summarizes the pattern of agreement and disagreement between jury and judge.[10]

It appears that judge and jury agree in (13 + 62 =) 75 percent of all cases; and of the 24 per cent disagreement cases the jury is on the defendant's side in (17 + 5 =) 22 per cent, and on the prosecutor's side only in (1 + 2 =) 3 per cent. The survey asked, of course, for information beyond the two verdicts; the questionnaire contained some fifty-odd questions aimed at a detailed description of the case, so that we could

9. Cf., e.g., The National Diet Heart Study (37 *Circulation*, Suppl. No. 1, March 1968) in which three different sets of diets (in the form of actual grocery baskets) were given to three randomly determined groups with the expectation that they would be used. The final decision, of course, remained with the consumers.

10. Harry Kalven, Jr. & Hans Zeisel, *The American Jury* 56 (1966).

TABLE 3
Agreement and Disagreement Between Jury and Judge in Criminal Trials
(as % of all trials)

	Jury		
Judge would have:	Acquitted	Convicted	Hung
acquitted	13	2	1
convicted	17	62	5

Total = 100%
Number of Trials (3576)

▧ Agreement

understand the reasons why the jury differed from the judge in the one out of four cases where they disagreed. And it is, of course, the adequacy or inadequacy of these reasons on which the merit of the jury verdict rests.

2. The second experiment in which simulation played a major part concerned the competing insanity instructions. In the Anglo-American system the defense of insanity has been embodied for more than a century in the so-called M'Naghten rule, under which the defendant is acquitted either if he did not know what he was doing or if he did not know that what he was doing was wrong. In recent years, the rule has come under increasing criticism, primarily from psychiatrists, and in 1954 the U.S. Court of Appeals for the District of Columbia established a new rule in the case of one Durham. Under the Durham rule, the defense of insanity was established if the criminal act was shown to be the "product of a mental disease or a mental defect."

For some time, the two rules competed for the favor of the nation's judiciary and it was of obvious interest to learn what difference the rule made in actual outcomes.[11] The "law" in a criminal jury trial becomes

11. In the meantime the U.S. Court of Appeals for the District of Columbia Circuit has modified the *Durham* rule, first in McDonald v. United States, 312 F.2d 847 (1962), and more recently in Brawner v. United States, 471 F.2d 969 (1972). The new rule, conforming to that adopted by other federal courts of appeals, is that of the American Law Institute's Model Penal Code and provides that "a person is not responsible for criminal conduct if . . . as a result of mental disease or defect he lacks substantial capacity to appreciate the wrongfulness of his conduct or to conform his conduct to the requirements of the law."

operative through the judge's instruction to the jury, in which the judge spells out the conditions under which the jury is to either acquit or convict the defendant. The question, therefore, as to what difference the law makes means what difference it makes to the jury whether the judge instructs it according to the rule in M'Naghten or according to Durham. The rule may affect a variety of facets of the trial, but obviously the main question is how the two rules affect the defendant's chances of acquittal.

To test the issue,[12] two trial records were composed, a case of housebreaking, a simplified version of the original Durham trial; and an incest case, also an abbreviated version of an actual trial. In both trials the accused's only defense was insanity. The trial evidence was acted out and, with the other elements of the trial, put on recording tape. Three main variants of each case were produced. The tapes were identical except for that part of the judge's instruction that dealt with the defense of insanity and for the concomitant psychiatric testimony. In one version the instruction and psychiatric testimony were according to M'Naghten; in the second according to Durham; and in the third the instruction left it to the jurors' own judgment as to whether the evidence in the cases supported a defense of insanity, thus forcing the jury to establish its own law of insanity.

Each of the three versions was then taken into two major metropolitan courts and presented to some 100 juries in turn. A judge called the jurors into his court room and asked them to cooperate in the experiment; by doing so, they were advised, they would oblige the court and also discharge their turn of jury duty. The jurors would then listen to the taped trial and afterwards deliberate and find a verdict. [Table 4 shows] the outcome of the experiment in terms of the jurors' vote on their first ballot, prior to the beginning of the deliberation.

In both trials, the Durham rule elicited a higher percentage of acquittals by reason of insanity than the M'Naghten rule. That the percentages under Durham are very close to those obtained under the "No

TABLE 4
Percentage of Jurors Voting "Not Guilty-Insane" on First Ballot

	M'Naghten	Durham	No Rule
Housebreaking	57 (120)	65 (120)	76 (120)
Incest	24 (240)	36 (312)	34 (264)
		( ) = Number of jurors	

12. Rita James Simon, *The Jury and the Defense of Insanity* (1967).

Rule" instruction suggested—as indeed it has been argued—that Durham comes close to being no rule.

3. The last one in this series of experiments involved a complete simulation. Nevertheless, it was probably a very reliable experiment. There is a notion abroad among lawyers that juries in some parts of the country are likely to award larger damages, for a given injury claim, than juries elsewhere. But there was no precise knowledge concerning either the geographic pattern or the degree of variation.

Since there are some sixty thousand civil jury trials held each year in the United States, it seemed tempting simply to compare the awards made in various jurisdictions. But this proved unprofitable partly because such trial statistics were unavailable, but primarily because the variety of injury cases coming before the courts is so great that to compare "average" award levels would be largely meaningless. Instead, a controlled experiment was designed by submitting simulated cases to the representatives of major insurance companies in various parts of the country. Five personal injury claims were composed by slightly modifying and simplifying five actual personal injury reports. They were written up in précis form such as is normally submitted to claim adjusters. The cases were submitted to the claim adjusters with this question: "How much, judging from your experience, would you expect a jury in your court to award for this case?" The question was asked for a number of courts, which constituted a probability sample of regions and community sizes of the United States. To offset personal differences, the requests were submitted to three adjusters in each community, one from each of the three insurance companies that cooperated in the experiment. [Table 5] gives the average of the (3 adjusters × 5 awards =) 15 awards in terms of deviations from the national average, summarized for major census regions and city sizes.

Awards for identical claims vary between roughly 80 per cent of the national average in the rural South and Midwest to roughly 120 per cent

TABLE 5
Geographic Variation of Jury Awards for Identical Claims
(In per cent deviation from the national average = 100)

City Size	Region			
	West	*Midwest*	*South*	*East*
Large	+20	+2	0	+19
Medium	+8	−11	−9	+10
Rural	0	−21	−15	−6

of that average in the large cities on the East and West coast. Translated into a formula, the table says: add 10 per cent to the average if the trial takes place on the East or West coast and another 10 per cent if it is conducted in a large city; subtract 10 per cent if it is conducted in the South or Midwest and another 10 per cent if it takes place in a rural area. The variations were found to correlate highly with the average per capita income of the community.

As these examples illustrate, simulation opens another line of compromise where the experimenter can pacify the law's basic concerns. However, simulation is a more serious deviation from the ideal experiment than the "indirect experiment" is, because its impact cannot be readily measured but must instead be assessed intuitively and through circumstantial evidence.

In the case of the judge-jury study, the element of simulation was relatively minor, the presiding judge's "verdict" being merely the one "he would have rendered had he tried the case without a jury." For a number of reasons we believe this simulation was highly realistic. Presumably the judge, in general, would find it more comfortable to report agreement with the jury, so if he reports disagreement we can accept his statement. In addition, the experiment required that his disagreement be corroborated in a variety of ways. If he would have convicted, he is asked to state the sentence he would have imposed; he also gives reasons for his disagreement. Most importantly, it was felt that the judge in the course of a jury trial could not help arriving at his own conclusion as to guilt or innocence, so that our question did not ask the judge to *make* a decision but only to report a judgment he had made anyway.

In the verdict-variation experiment, the simulation, although total, was also almost perfect. The submitted précis contained exactly the type of information a claim adjuster is normally called to act upon, and the judgment he was asked to make—what a jury in his area would be likely to do with such a case—was the very judgment that the claim adjuster is paid to make accurately.

The simulation in the insanity experiment was more complex. In a taped trial that had been condensed to about one hour, the added instruction by the judge forms a relatively larger part of the total trial than it would in a real one. Moreover, to have only the audio tape probably reduces the impact of the trial itself more than it reduces the impact of the judge's instructions. Thus, it is quite possible that the simulation exaggerated the relative importance of the instructions, thereby producing larger experimental differences than a real trial would have produced. On the other hand, the jurors were real, they were sitting in a real court house, and the recordings of their deliberations leave no doubt about their seriousness. Some of the juries took many hours to return a verdict, there were fights and agonizing as with real juries, and some cases even ended in hung juries.

The fact remains that the impairment created by simulation is difficult to assess. At a certain point, therefore, one might prefer to have less simulation even if it means giving up some of the rigor of the experimental design. Here too, it is useful to recall the frequent reliance of the biological sciences on simulation, in the use of animals in experiments designed to test human reactions.

The Natural Experiment

The third escape route from legal constraints is to make use of what may be termed the "natural experiment." Here, there is no need for the experimenter to arrange for random assignment because random assignment has been part of the judicial process itself. A good example is provided by studies comparing judging or sentencing practices of different judges. Whenever a court assigns its cases randomly among its judges, the analyst may attribute with confidence differences in sentences to differences between judges, since the groups of cases that come before one or the other judge are as comparable as an experimenter could make them.[16] Our judge-jury study had elements of a natural experiment in that the rules of criminal procedure require jury and judge to be exposed to the same "experimental treatment," which is to say that both see exactly the same trial.

Randomization will not always be explicit. In some situations, natural events may be relied upon to provide random exposure. An example is the interesting curve describing the relationship of driving accidents of women to their menstrual cycle [see Figure 5].

The graph indicates sharply increased accidents on the days before and during the menses. This should be a natural experiment, unless women on the crucial days drive more frequently or under more hazardous conditions, a highly implausible assumption.[17]

Because the natural experiment is far less costly than the artifically controlled experiment, the analyst is often tempted to bestow on natural events, without further proof, the character of a controlled experiment.

16. The pioneering study was Frederick Joseph Gaudet, Individual Differences in the Sentencing Tendencies of Judges, 32 *Archives of Psychology,* No. 230 (1938). Our split-trial study also relied on such random assignment.

17. Actually the bi-modal curve is the composite of two separate uni-modal curves. For reasons not quite known, nulliparous women have their accident peak before, parous women during, their menses. Cf. Katharina Dalton, *The Premenstrual Syndrome* 89 (1964).

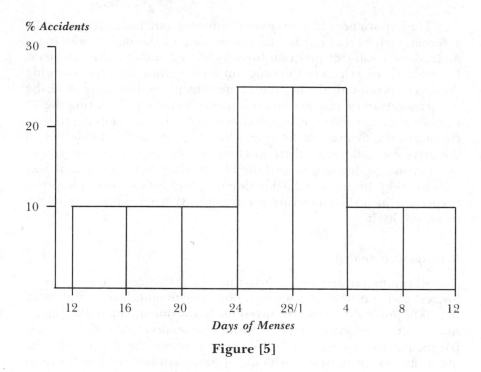

% Accidents

Days of Menses

Figure [5]

For instance, when it became important to learn how criminal jury verdicts would be affected if the law were to allow majority verdicts instead of insisting on unanimity, it was natural to compare jury verdicts from Oregon (the only state that allowed majority verdicts) with verdicts from other states. The frequency of hung juries in Oregon turned out to be three per cent as against five per cent in other states.[18] Acceptance of the comparison implied that the cases and the jurors in Oregon and in other states are as comparable *as if* they had been randomly assigned. Or, to put the implication differently, had one conducted an experiment in Oregon, by assigning all jury trials at random to majority rule and unanimity rule proceedings, one would have found the same three and five per cent frequencies of hung juries. But if the cases in Oregon are different from the cases that come to trial in other states, or if Oregon jurors are for some reason more likely to agree with one another, we would attribute falsely to the difference in voting rules what in fact was the result of different types of cases or different types of jurors in the Oregon courts.

18. Harry Kalven, Jr. & Hans Zeisel, The American Jury: Notes for an English Controversy, 57 *The Round Table*, No. 226, at 158 (April 1967); Hans Zeisel, . . . And Then There Were None: The Diminution of the Federal Jury, 38 *U. Chi. L. Rev.* 710 (1971).

The importance of a randomized control group is well illustrated by a recent analysis that did not have one. One of the major cities has a methadone treatment program for which drug addicts may volunteer. To evaluate the effects of the program on the crime rate, the following data were produced: during the 12 months prior to admission to the program the arrest rate per 100 volunteers had been 70; during the 12 months after admission, it had declined to 40. It was tempting to conclude that the methadone treatment was responsible for the decline in the arrest rates. But since there was no control group of volunteers who by random assignment were excluded from admission, there was no way of separating the arrest reduction due to the addict's motive to improve (expressed in his volunteering for treatment) from the effects of the treatment itself.

Retrospective Analysis

Situations created by explicit random assignment (e.g., cases to judges) and situations in which random assignment, however likely in fact, is unproven are radically different. In the one situation, the analyst may assign emerging differences without hesitation to the different experimental treatments (e.g., differences between the judges). In the other situation he must start with the opposite assumption: that the cases in the compared groups *may not* have been interchangeable prior to the experimental exposure, that differences in the result may be due not to the difference in treatment but to differences that existed before the experimental treatment began. For example, sentences given to defendants convicted in jury trials are on the average higher than those given in bench trials in the same court system. But it would be incorrect to conclude from this comparison alone that judges reward defendants who waive their right to jury trial with a lower sentence. The cases that are tried before a jury are on the average more serious to begin with; hence cases tried to a judge cannot be compared to cases tried to a jury as if they had been assigned randomly to these two modes of trial.

The technique of retrospective analysis (where prior natural randomization is the rare exception) is an attempt to arrange comparisons in a way that comes as close as possible to the comparison that would have been obtained through randomization, which would have made the two groups prior to the experimental treatment interchangeable. The analysis tries to approach this goal by breaking the overall group down into smaller segments which, one hopes, approach comparability. Instead of comparing sentences in *all* jury trials with those in *all* bench trials, one would compare such sentences separately for each particular crime category and for defendants of specified sex, age, and prior criminal record. One would compare, for instance, white, male defendants, under 25 years of age, without prior criminal record found guilty of auto theft—after a jury trial—with white, male defendants under 25, without prior record, found guilty of auto theft—after a bench trial.

The drawback of this procedure of fractioned analysis is that however far it is carried (always the size of the sample sets limits), it never attains certainty. There is no way of knowing for sure that all hidden factors that might render a causal inference spurious have been eliminated.

Retrospective analysis encounters still another difficulty that the controlled experiment eliminates. Technically known as the identification problem, it is the difficulty of determining (in retrospect) the temporal sequence of two factors. Suppose, for instance, that one were to find that in states in which the proportion of crimes in which the criminal is apprehended is high, the crime rate tends to be low. One might be tempted to conclude that it is the higher probability of apprehension that is responsible for the lower crime rate. But it could be the other way around: the fewer crimes, the more attention the police can pay to each, hence the greater the chances of apprehension. Or, the observed relationship between the two factors may reflect a mixture of both these effects. A controlled experiment that, at a certain point in time, increased the police forces in some areas but not others would resolve the problem.

Retrospective study uses essentially the same modes of analysis as the controlled experiment. They both use cross-tabulation if the distinguishing factors are attributes (classifications that differ not in gradations but in kind: male-female; black-white; Judge A vs. Judge B; jury vs. judge, etc.). They both use regression analysis if the factors allow for gradation (age, income, apprehension rates, crime rates, etc.).

Whatever technique is used, retrospective analysis must reckon with the two difficulties discussed above—the identification problem, and the required interchangeability prior to the experimental exposure. Because it bypasses both these difficulties the controlled experiment, where feasible, is the preferred research device.

The Problem of Extrapolation and Some Cautionary Conclusions

The controlled experiment would seem to suffer from a peculiar limitation; by its nature, it is an operation with specific limits in time, space and operating conditions. Hence, there is always the question as to how far its results can be extrapolated, that is, applied to other places, other times, and other conditions.

Would the pretrial experiment, if conducted in Illinois instead of New Jersey, have yielded the same result? Would jury reactions to the defense of insanity in a murder trial be the same as in a case involving burglary or incest? There are no general rules for answering such questions; each situation requires its own assessment. The limitations of the controlled experiment are the price to be paid for the power of its analytical resolution. The endeavor must always be to choose a clearly, not necessarily narrowly, defined experimental variable, and then test it under as many environmental conditions as possible.

The limiting circumstances of controlled experiments are not a problem peculiar to the law or the social sciences in general; they hold for the so-called natural sciences as well. All one can say is that the judgment on how far a particular finding can be extrapolated will be the more correct the more developed the particular area of scientific endeavor is. That is why extrapolations in physics or chemistry can be made with greater confidence than, for instance, in biology, and in biology with greater confidence than in the social sciences.

Reading this report on a variety of legal experiments may create in some readers' minds the expectation that the law is rapidly approaching a stage where a great many of its premises will be tested through controlled experimentation. The law is very far from such a stance, and it would be a mistake to expect such a development.

There are many legal and practical constraints that set limits to experimentation. Both the costs of experimentation and the time it requires will often prove insurmountable obstacles: legislators and courts are usually in a hurry and short of money. There is also the ever-present danger that even a generously designed experiment may run into unforeseen barriers and thereby end inconclusively or fail altogether. There is also the occasional danger that an effect attributed to the experimental treatment was in fact caused by the subjects' awareness of being part of an experiment, the so-called Hawthorne effect named after a famous first example.[21] Even if the experiment succeeds, it seldom answers the "ultimate question." It provides as a rule only part of the answer, and there is always the question of just how valuable that part is. . . .

There is one particular place in the law where the controlled experiment should play an increasingly important role. Occasionally, when a legal innovation is instituted, there is some lingering doubt as to whether

21. A study conducted in the Hawthorne, Chicago works of the Western Electric Company. F. J. Roethiisberger & W. F. Dickson, *Management and the Worker* (1939).

it will work. Often such a tentative innovation is even labeled "experimental" in the sense of a try-out. For instance, before Great Britain abolished capital punishment permanently, it suspended it for a trial period of several years to see what would happen. But "to see what would happen" is very different from building an experimental design into the innovation in order to enable a precise evaluation of the enacted rule.

Whenever the expected consequences of a rule are at issue, the lawmaker should at least consider the possibilities of a controlled experiment. Even if, for any number of good reasons, he should decide not to undertake the experiment, the mere process of thinking through such a possible experimental design will have been useful. The growing vogue of insistence on "evaluation" of innovating projects, so that the funding agency may learn what has been accomplished, will help. Eventually it will lead to building into such projects the elements of controlled experimentation.

Controlled experimentation, of course, is but one of the approaches, and in a sense the sharpest one, exploring legal issues empirically. The borderline between the prospective experiment and retrospective analysis, as we have seen, is blurred; there is a spectrum rather than a dichotomy, especially when one considers the trade-offs created by simulations. In the end, the law's attitude toward experimentation is necessarily but part of its more general attitude toward systematically collected, scientifically analyzed data. And in this perspective the signs are encouraging.

Selznick, Law, Society, and Moral Evolution*

. . . A number of themes in the sociology of law have a central place in our discussion:
  (1) the relevance of legal theory to private, non-state institutions;
  (2) the nature of legality, and its social foundations;
  (3) incipient and inchoate law;
  (4) legal cognition, including the changing content and social function of legal abstractions;
  (5) the relation between law and politics. . . .

* [Chapter 1, "Law, Society, and Moral Evolution," from *Law, Society, and Industrial Justice,* by Philip Selznick, © 1969 by the Russell Sage Foundation, New York. Reprinted by permission.
  For biographical information, see page 640 supra.]

Law as Generic

If we are to study justice in industry, or in any other specialized institution, we must first be clear that law is found in many settings; it is not uniquely associated with the state. We need a concept of law that is sufficiently general to embrace legal experience within "private" associations, but not so general as to make law lose its distinctive character or become equivalent to social control.

Definitions and concepts. Although we need an appropriate concept of law, we have no wish to argue for a special and restrictive definition; we do not propose stringent criteria to limit how the word "law" may be used. In our discussion we try to bear in mind the difference between how a term is defined and how we conceive a phenomenon.

In the logic of social inquiry, "concept" has a peculiar status. When we speak of the concept of totalitarianism or mass society or alienation or culture or socialization, we have in mind something more than a handy definition. The concept is open-ended, subject to debate and revision, accessible to empirical judgment. That is so because "concept" shades into "theory." Indeed, to explicate a concept is to state a theory.

Social science is best served when definitions are "weak" and concepts are "strong."[2] A weak definition is inclusive; its conditions are easily met. A strong concept is more demanding in that, for example, it may identify attributes that are latent as well as manifest, or offer a model of what the phenomenon is like in a fully developed (or deteriorated) state. Accordingly, in what follows the word law is used in a way that is general enough to embrace all legal experience, however various or rudimentary. At the same time, law and legal process are understood as pointing to a larger achievement and a greater elaboration.

The centrality of authority. Contemporary jurisprudence is reasonably comfortable with law conceived as a generic phenomenon. This appears clearly in the writings of H. L. A. Hart and Lon Fuller.[3] Although they disagree sharply in other ways, both offer a theory of law detached from the concept of the state, that is, the organized political community. Moreover, both reject coercion as a touchstone of the distinctively legal.

Neither public government as usually understood nor "orders backed by threats" are central to the idea of law. Rather, *rule* and *authority* bring law into focus. A legal system is known by the existence of authoritative rules. Thus Hart argues that, in stepping "from the pre-legal to the legal world," a society develops social rules for curing the

2. This point was suggested by Gertrude Jaeger Selznick.
3. H. L. A. Hart, *The Concept of Law* (Oxford: Oxford University Press, 1961); Lon L. Fuller, *The Morality of Law* (New Haven: Yale University Press, 1964).

defects of a social order based on unofficial norms.[4] A regime of unofficial norms has a number of inherent limitations, including the difficulty of resolving uncertainties as to the existence or scope of a norm. In a pre-legal setting, no criterion or procedure is available for settling such issues. The distinctively legal emerges with the development of "secondary rules," that is, rules of authoritative determination. These rules, selectively applied, raise up the unofficial norms and give them a legal status.

It follows that a "rule is something more than an observed regularity of conduct, more also than a social prescription or norm. A rule is a special kind of norm—one that bears some warrant of validity.[5] It therefore tends to be formal, explicit, deliberately instituted. It is in some sense official.

The special work of law is to identify claims and obligations that merit official validation and enforcement. This may consist of nothing more than the establishment of a public record, say, of land holdings or clan prerogatives, invested with a special claim upon the community's respect as a guide to action. When institutions emerge that do this work we can speak of a legal order. These institutions need not be specialized. They may have no resource for coercive enforcement. It is essential only that their determinations affecting rights and duties are accepted as authoritative.

This approach may be compared with the sociological theory of Max Weber, who attempted to distinguish law from other modes of social control by offering a rather austere "operational" definition. Weber agreed that not every normative order is a legal order. The distinctively legal emerges when "there exists a 'coercive apparatus,' i.e., that there are one or more persons whose special task it is to hold themselves ready to apply specially provided means of coercion (legal coercion) for the purpose of norm enforcement."[6] A legal norm is known by the probability that it will be enforced by a specialized staff. Weber's definition is meant to exclude all value judgments in the assessment of what is or is not law.

Although he emphasized coercion, Weber was careful to point out that the latter may be psychological, not necessarily physical. The threat of physical force is not essential to legal action, for coercion may consist in public reprimand or boycott. This is important because Weber does

4. Hart, op. cit., 91.
5. As we use it at this point, "rule" does not necessarily carry a connotation of specificity; it includes authoritative "principles."
6. Max Rheinstein (ed.), *Max Weber on Law in Economy and Society* (Cambridge, Mass.: Harvard University Press, 1954), 13.

not limit the idea of law to the political community, which may assume a monopoly of legitimate violence. His definition allows for what he called "extra-state" law, such as ecclesiastical law, or the law of any other corporate group binding on its members. So long as coercive means are available, exercised by a specialized staff within the group, the requirements for the existence of a legal order are fulfilled.

Weber's treatment seems very matter-of-fact and tough-minded. There is no reference to ideals or standards. Nevertheless, we should note that he speaks, not of coercion alone, but of a coercive "apparatus" and of "specially provided means for the purpose of norm enforcement." These qualifications are crucial, for Weber clearly does not mean that *any* group dedicated to the suppression of deviance becomes *eo ipso* an instrument of law. He must mean that such a group is specially *constituted,* that it acts authoritatively.

In much of his work, Weber saw quite clearly the intimate relation of the legal and authoritative. His theory of authority and legitimacy, for example, contrasts the charismatic, the traditional, and the "rational legal," thus placing law in a context of evolving forms of authority.[7] In that analysis, Weber assimilates fully developed law to a system of governance by rules. He sees the distinctively legal obligation as running to an impersonal order that exhibits a strain toward rationality. When Weber did not speak of the concept of law abstractly, but actually used it, especially in his theory of bureaucracy, he greatly modified the significance of coercion.

Of course, coercion is an important and often indispensable *resource* for law. But so is education, symbolism, and the appeal to reason. Coercion does not make law, though it may indeed establish an order out of which law may emerge. In the authoritative use of coercion, whether by private or public agencies, the legal element is not the coercion itself but the invocation of authority.

This point bears closely on the distinction between law and the state. We associate the state with coercion because it is the state, the organized political community, that has the main responsibility for maintaining public order. Whether coercion used to that end is *lawful* is always an open question.

The view of law sketched here assimilates the theory of law to the theory of authority. This postulate governs both a minimal definition of law and a more elaborated concept. Rules of authoritative determination may take many forms and call upon many different resources. They may

7. Max Weber, *Theory of Social and Economic Organization* (New York: Oxford University Press, 1947), Chap. 3.

be blunt, crude, and "undeveloped." To bring law within the theory of authority does not require us to hold that only a "pure" or developed legal order deserves to be classified as such.

We should see law as endemic in all institutions *that rely for social control on formal authority and rule-making.* Law so understood is analytically distinct from the narrower view of public government, but it is also distinct from the broader idea of social control. The middle ground we seek is occupied by Fuller, for example, when he interprets law as "the enterprise of subjecting human conduct to the governance of rules."[8] The phrase "governance of rules" must be understood as shorthand for a system of order that contains specialized mechanisms for certifying rules as authoritative and for safeguarding rule-making and rule-applying from the intrusion of other forms of direction and control.

Fuller argues explicitly that law should not be equated with public government.

> A view that seeks to understand law in terms of the activity that sustains it, instead of considering only the formal sources of its authority, may sometimes suggest a use of words that violates the normal expectations of language. This inconvenience may, I suggest, be offset by the capacity of such a view to make us perceive essential similarities. It may help us to see that the imperfectly achieved systems of law within a labor union or a university may often cut more deeply into the life of a man than any court judgment ever likely to be rendered against him. On the other hand, it may also help us to realize that all systems of law, big and little, are subject to the same infirmities.[9]

To equate law and the state impoverishes sociological analysis, because the concept of law should be available for study of any setting in which human conduct is subject to explicit rule-making; and when we deny the place of law in specialized institutions *we withhold from the private setting the funded experience of the political community in matters of governance.*

Law as a Realm of Value

To say that law is generic is a necessary first step in applying legal theory to specialized institutions. Our second step invokes the perspective of moral evolution. We want to ask what it means to "legalize" an institution, that is, to infuse its mode of governance with the aspirations

8. Fuller, op. cit., 106.
9. Ibid., 129.

and constraints of a legal order. To do this, we should first understand the view that law is intimately associated with the realization of values.

In the discussion of law there is an ever-renewed conflict between those who see it as a functional necessity and others who invest it with hope and promise. The former accept law as given, as fact, at best as an instrument of practical problem-solving. For the legal idealist, on the other hand, law connotes a larger moral achievement.

When law is conceived as a functional necessity, the focus tends to be on order and control. Law is summoned by elementary urgencies: keep the peace, settle disputes, suppress deviance. Authority pays its way, and redeems its coercive sins, if it can establish tranquillity, facilitate cooperative action, and uphold the mores, whatever they may be. This might be called the *minimalist* view of what law is and does. For it, "justice" is not a compelling symbol and at an extreme may even be scorned as the refuge of hopelessly muddled men.

It should be noted that order and control are values of a sort. They are certainly "things prized," and would satisfy almost any minimum definition of value, such as "the object of any interest." But order and control are values in a weak sense. They cannot of themselves sustain personal or group identity. They do not readily serve as vehicles of loyalty and commitment.

The alternative is to think of law as instituting a *kind* of order and a *kind* of social control. This approach asks more of a legal system and yields a richer sense of value. The contribution of law to social order is not lost, *but a closer concern for the continuum of means and ends appears.* Where there is fidelity to law, order is not to be purchased at any price. Rather, law imposes limits on social control. For example, the commitment of police to lawfulness is always to some extent a restraint on the means they can use to prevent crime or apprehend criminals.[10] The greater the self-consciousness about law, and the more law is looked to for the vindication of rights, the more apparent is a tension between law and order.

A normative concept of law, or of any similar phenomenon, turns attention from necessity to fulfillment. Instead of concentrating on the minimum functions of law, or on the minimum conditions that signify its emergence, the emphasis shifts to law's civilizing potential. A logically similar problem appears when the idea of "education" is discussed. A minimalist concept of education is content to equate it with the transmission of skills, including social skills, and of a received tradition. A more

10. See Herbert Packer, "Two Models of the Criminal Process," 113 *University of Pennsylvania Law Review* 1 (1964).

expansive and normative view embraces the contribution of education to moral sensibility.[11]

A superficially attractive way of resolving the conceptual ambiguity would restrict law, education, friendship, or literature in minimalist terms, then specify additional attributes that warrant the designation "good" law, "good" education, "good" literature, "good" friendship, and so forth. This solution has merit, but it is defective if the normative attributes are taken to be mere subjective preferences. For that lends an arbitrary cast to the phenomenon's "high state" or "excellence," as if this were a matter of likes and dislikes and had no intrinsic relation to the natural characteristics or the social dynamics of the institution or relationship. Although a definition of law should be spacious and inclusive, it ought to contain a theoretical warrant for treating at least a *strain* toward legal development as objectively grounded. This is accomplished when law is defined as a system of authoritative rules and decision-making.

A normative theory of law or friendship specifies *latent* values that inhere in the phenomenon. These values serve as resources for critical evaluation, not from the standpoint of the observer's preferences, but in the light of the inner order of the phenomenon, including what the participants are likely to experience as deprivation or satisfaction.

We perceive latent values in the world of fact when we recognize, for example, that fatherhood, sexuality, leadership, friendship, and many other phenomena have a natural potential for "evaluation." This potential is not an abstract possibility but an empirical likelihood founded in conditions that are routinely generated by the experience or relationship. Biological parenthood, for example, is invested with value because ths satisfactions associated with parenthood—satisfactions that are biologically functional—are not fully realized unless a guiding ideal emerges. Arbitrary social convention plays a part in this envaluation, but only a part. The same holds true for the dialectic of sex and satisfaction. The union of sex and love is by no means inevitable, but it is a value latent in human mating. That such values are subject to distortion, and are always incompletely realized, is not in itself a denial of their latency. On the contrary, to the extent that problems are set by such natural aspirations, whether or not they are fulfilled, their empirical significance is confirmed.

11. For a discussion of normative concepts in social science, see Ernest Nagel, *The Structure of Science* (New York: Harcourt, Brace & World, 1961), 490-495; see also Gertrude Jaeger and Philip Selznick, "A Normative Theory of Culture," *American Sociological Review,* 29 (October, 1964), 653-669.

The transition from necessity to fulfillment has its echoes in contemporary social and psychological theory. "Functional analysis" is a way of studying social structure or personality by examining items of behavior or other social units for the work they do in sustaining or undermining a going concern or system. What is apparently or manifestly propaganda may be latently a way of contributing to group cohesion by keeping members busy; a mode of punishment sustains the common conscience; selective recruitment of administrative personnel undermines an established policy or bolsters a shaky elite. Functional analysis is most familiar in the study of personality where a great many items of perception and behavior become meaningful only when their contribution to the maintenance of personal adjustment, including neurotic adjustment, is understood.

In such interpretations, there is a strong and understandable tendency to identify what is required for the maintenance of a system with what is required for the *bare survival* of a group or individual. The very term "survival" suggests that what is at stake is the biological extinction of the individual or the complete dissolution of the group. In fact, however, systems may decay despite the continuity of individual or group life. If a man extricates himself from neurotic dependence on some other person or activity, then a system has changed. If an organization maintains its personnel and budget, and even its formal identity, but transforms its effective goals, capabilities, commitments, and role in the community, then too a system has changed. To be sure, some systems are indispensable if life is to exist at all; but other systems are required if a certain *kind* of life is to survive. In social science the most important analyses have to do not with the bare continuity of life but with certain kinds and levels of organization.

The idea that law connotes a special kind of order is implicitly accepted when we pay our respects to "the rule of law." In English *a* rule of law is a specific norm or guide to decision. The phrase is meant to be descriptive and value-free. But *the* rule of law is a more connotative and value-laden idea. It refers to aspirations that distinguish a developed legal order from a system of subordination to naked power.

The Ideal of Legality

The impulse to create a legal order is, in the first instance, a practical one. From the standpoint of the rulers, power is made more secure when it is legitimate; from the standpoint of the ruled, fears of oppression are allayed. Thus legalization is rooted in the problems of collective life. It is not, in its primitive forms, an expression of social idealism. It is obvious, moreover, that communities survive and even flourish without going very far toward legalization. We do not suppose that the values associated with law must necessarily be realized. Other values, for example, religious or aesthetic values, may define a world more appealing.

To understand what legalization entails for the life of a political community or a specialized institution, however, we should consider its ideal or developed state. In what follows we shall briefly explicate what is meant by "legality," which we take to be a synonym for "rule of law."

The essential element in the rule of law is the restraint of official power by rational principles of civic order. Where this ideal exists, no power, including the democratic majority, is immune from criticism or entirely free to follow its own bent, however well-intentioned it may be. Legality imposes an environment of constraint, of tests to be met, standards to be observed, ideals to be fulfilled.

Legality has to do mainly with *how* policies and rules are made and applied rather than with their content. The vast majority of rules, including judge-made rules, spell out policy choices, choices not uniquely determined by the requirements of legality. Whether contracts must be supported by consideration; whether a defendant in an accident case should be spared liability because of plaintiff's contributory negligence; whether minors should be relieved of legal consequences that might otherwise apply to their actions—these and a host of other issues treated in the common law are basically matters of general public policy. For practical and historical reasons, a great many of these policy matters are decided by the courts in the absence of, or as a supplement to, legislative determination. In making these decisions, and in devising substantive rules, the courts are concerned with dimensions of justice that go beyond the ideal of legality. Legality is a part of justice, but only a part.

Nevertheless, there are times when the ideal of legality does determine the content of a legal rule or doctrine. This occurs when the purpose of the rule is precisely to implement that ideal, the most obvious illustration being the elaboration of procedural rules of pleading and evidence. In addition, principles of statutory interpretation, including much of constitutional law, directly serve the aim of creating and sustaining the "legal state." Some of these rules are "merely" procedural, chosen because some device was necessary, for which some other procedure might readily be substituted. Others are vital to the protection of just those substantial rights which the ideal of legality is meant to protect. These include primarily all that we term civil rights, the rights of members of a polity to act as full citizens and to be free of oppressive and arbitrary official power. Again, it is not the aim of this ideal to protect

939

the individual against *all* power, but only against the misuse of power by those whose actions have the color of authority. Later we shall argue that in modern society we must extend our notions of who it is that acts "officially."

The effort to see in law a set of standards, an internal basis for criticism and reconstruction, leads us to a true *Grundnorm*—the idea that a legal order faithful to itself seeks *progressively to reduce the degree of arbitrariness in positive law and its administration.* By "positive law" we mean those public obligations that have been defined by duly constituted mechanisms, such as a legislature, court, administrative agency, or referendum. This is not the whole of law, for by the latter we must mean the entire body of authoritative materials—"precepts, techniques, and ideals"[12]—that guide official decision-making. Law is "positive" when a particular conclusion has been reached by some authorized body—a conclusion expressed in a determinate rule or judgment.

Plainly, positive law includes an arbitrary element. For him who must obey it, it is to some extent brute fact and brute command. But this arbitrary element, while necessary and inevitable, is repugnant to the ideal of legality. Therefore the proper aim of the legal order, and the special contribution of legal scholarship, is to minimize the arbitrary element in legal norms and decisions. This objective may be compared to the scientific ideal of "reducing the degree of empiricism," that is, the number of theoretically ungrounded factual generalizations within the corpus of scientific knowledge.

If the reduction of arbitrariness is central to legality, three corollaries may be suggested:

1. Legality is a variable achievement. A developed legal order is the product of continuing effort and posits values that are always incompletely fulfilled. We can unblushingly speak of more or less legality, meaning nothing more obscure than that some systems of rules, and some modes of decision, are less arbitrary than others. A major topic in legal sociology is the study of empirical conditions that reduce or exacerbate the arbitrary element in making or applying rules. For example, studies of police discretion locate systematic sources of arbitrary decision in the handling of juveniles; "treatment" is seen as a cover for unsupervised control; the low visibility of decisions in administrative agencies tends to encourage self-serving discretion.

---

12. See Roscoe Pound, *Jurisprudence* (St. Paul: West Publishing Co., 1959), II, 107: "Law in the sense we are considering is made up of precepts, techniques and ideals: A body of authoritative precepts, developed and applied by an authoritative technique in the light of or on the background of authoritative traditional ideals."

This is not to suggest that the notion of "arbitrary" is completely clear, or that it has a simple meaning. Rules are made arbitrarily when appropriate interests are not consulted and when there is no clear relation between the rule enunciated and the official end to be achieved. Rules are arbitrary when they reflect confused policies, are based on ignorance or error, and when they suggest no inherent principles of criticism. Discretion is arbitrary when it is whimsical, or governed by criteria extraneous to legitimate means or ends. All of this is a matter of degree. Few decisions are completely arbitrary, yet we may compare the more and the less.

The reduction of arbitrariness cannot be equated with the elaboration of formal rules and procedures. "Formal justice" equalizes parties and makes decisions predictable; it is therefore a major contribution to the mitigation of arbitrary rule. But legal "correctness" has its own costs. Like any other technology, it is vulnerable to the divorce of means and ends. When this occurs, legality degenerates into legalism. Substantive justice is undone when there is too great a commitment to upholding the autonomy and integrity of the legal process. Rigid adherence to precedent and mechanical application of rules hamper the capacity of the legal system to take account of new interests and circumstances, or to adapt to social inequality. Formal justice tends to serve the status quo. It therefore may be experienced as arbitrary by those whose interests are dimly perceived or who are really outside "the system."

Formal attributes of equality or certainty may run counter to the continuities of culture and social organization. One student of the role of British law in India has noted:

> The common law proceeds on the basis of equality before the law while indigenous dispute-settling finds it unthinkable to separate the parties from their statuses and relations. The common law gives a clear-cut "all or none" decision, while indigenous processes seek a face-saving solution agreeable to all parties; the common law deals only with a single isolated offense or transaction, while the indigenous system sees this as arbitrarily leaving out the underlying dispute of which this may be one aspect; the common law has seemingly arbitrary rules of evidence, which do not permit that which is well-known to be proved and that which is not can be proved; the common law then seems abrupt and overly decisive, distant, expensive, and arbitrary.[13]

13. Marc Galanter, "Hindu Law and the Development of the Modern Indian Legal System" (mimeo; prepared for delivery at the 1964 Annual Meeting of the American Political Science Association), 25. On the relation between formal and substantive justice, see Max Weber's discussion in Rheinstein [op. cit. supra note 6], 224 ff.

The limits of formalism suggest that the reduction of arbitrariness requires a union of formal and substantive justice.

Properly understood, the concept of legality is more critical than celebrationist. To say that legality is a variable achievement is to leave room for the conclusion that, at any given time, the system of positive law is "congealed injustice."[14] An affirmative approach to legal values need not accept the defensive rhetoric of men in power. On the contrary, it offers principles of criticism to evaluate the shortcomings of the existing system of rules and practices.

2. *Legality extends to administration as well as adjudication.* Wherever there is official conduct, the possibility of arbitrary decision arises. That conduct may be far removed from rule-making or adjudication, at least in spirit or purpose. It may be a practical effort to get a job done. Yet the question of legitimacy—of power exercised *in the light* of governing norms—is always appropriate. Furthermore, the problem of arbitrariness is at issue whenever rights are determined, something that may occur quite incidentally, in the course of administrative decision and policy-making. Thus any official decision, whether it be a purchase, a hiring, a deployment of police power, or any other active effort to accomplish a defined social purpose, may be criticized in the name of legality.

It has been said that "reliance on the action of abstract rules governing the relations between individuals . . . is the essential basis of the Rule of Law."[15] That formulation is too sweeping, for it limits the legal ideal to the adjudicative mode. It precludes a law-governed, arbitrariness-minimizing sphere of administrative action.

In adjudication, whether conducted by an administrative agency or a court, there is a quest for and application of rules that are logically, if not historically, prior to the case at hand. It is not a rule tailored to the needs and circumstances of a particular plaintiff or defendant, with the idea of achieving a particular outcome. The same rule is applied to every member of a legally defined class of cases. A particular case cannot be handled, without risk to legality, unless it belongs to a category, unless it can be so classified that a general rule, applicable to the entire class of cases, can be invoked.

The application of general rules does not prelude "tempering justice with mercy," taking account of special strengths or weaknesses, or any other effort to adapt the administration of justice to the actual cir-

14. Howard Zinn, *Disobedience and Democracy: Nine Fallacies on Law and Order* (New York: Vintage Books, 1968), 4.

15. F. A. Hayek, *The Political Ideal of the Rule of Law* (Cairo: National Bank of Egypt, 1955), 32.

cumstances before the court or administrative tribunal. In principle, this is only a matter of specifying more closely the category to which the case belongs, often by combining a set of applicable concepts or doctrines, for example, that a contract made by a minor is voidable but that unjust enrichment will not be allowed. The only important criterion is: Would another litigant in the same circumstances be judged according to the same criteria?

Thus, in the determination of rights, "discretion" is compatible with the rule of law when it remains essentially judicial rather than administrative. Like any other discretion, judicial discretion involves a certain freedom of choice. The choice, however, is of a special kind. From among many possible ways of classifying the events at hand, the court selects that particular classification which will fix the rights and obligations of the parties. To this end, judicial discretion may carpenter doctrines and otherwise rework the legal materials. But the objective remains: Find a rule or a rule-set that will do justice in a special class of situations.

Administrative discretion is of another order.[16] The administrator (where he is not really a judge) is also interested in diagnosing and classifying the world. But he properly looks to an end-in-view, the refashioning of human or other resources so that a particular outcome will be achieved. A judge becomes an administrator when his objective is to reform a criminal, avert a strike, or abate a nuisance. For then his aim is not justice but accomplishment, not fairness but therapy.

Administration may be controlled by law, but its special place in the division of labor is to get the work of society done, not to realize the ideals of legality. Adjudication also gets work done, in settling disputes, but this is secondary and not primary. The primary function of adjudication is to discover the legal coordinates of a particular situation. That is a far cry from manipulating the situation to achieve a desired outcome.

This line of reasoning suggests that administration, even in a developed legal order, is distinguished from adjudication by a weaker commitment to the ideal of legality. It does not follow, however, that legality is foreign to the ethos of administration. Its relevance appears in two ways. First, there is a common commitment to objective and impersonal

---

16. In his *Administrative Law Treatise* (St. Paul: West Publishing Co., 1958), K. C. Davis assimilates the administrative process to adjudication by defining an "administrative agency" as "a governmental authority other than a court and other than a legislative body, which affects the rights of private parties through either adjudication or rule-making" (I, 1). He suggests a distinction between the "executive process" and the "administrative process" (ibid., 57). It seems better to maintain the more conventional usage and see administration as fundamentally task-oriented.

decision-making. Second, administration can contain within it machinery that approximates adjudication when rights are affected.

Objective decisions call for *universalistic* rather than *particularistic* criteria of assessment—a distinction that is as subtle in logic as it is precarious in experience. The model of particularism is found in ties of common association—religious, political, kinship, friendship, even conspiratorial. The claim of a particular individual to be treated in a distinctive way is recognized. The prototypical case is nepotism. However, the nepotistic response may be made in the light of a general norm governing how one should treat a relative or friend. The tension is created by competing norms, not by a difference between decision in the light of what is general as distinguished from what is specific. The norm of particularism is subversive of objective and impartial judgment because it introduces extraneous, person-centered criteria of decision into settings where there should be a sovereignty of institutional purpose.

Universalism is as pertinent to administration as it is to adjudication. Universalism asks only that criteria of decision transcend the special interests of persons or groups. Situations may be dealt with according to the special requirements, and specific outcomes may be sought, but the integrity of official decision is retained so long as there is an objective relation between the course of decision-making and the requirements of institutional purpose. The official can then give reasons for his actions and expose them to criticism in the light of publicly acknowledged ends.

3. Legality applies to public participation as well as to the conduct of officials. If legality aspires to minimize the arbitrary element in law, then public participation must itself be subject to scrutiny and criticism. Positive law is a product of both will and reason; the mixture is variable and unstable. Although positive law cannot be *merely* an expression of social power, neither is it free of that element. The actions of an electorate and the decisions of a legislature may conform to procedural standards and yet contain strong arbitrary elements. Some statutes are passed under the heavy pressures of special interests or in a mood of panic, confusion, or unreason. And the quality of decision by a popular majority may be marred and distorted under conditions of collective excitement, irrelevant symbolism, or misinformation. When the public acts officially, or influences official conduct, it may do so arbitrarily. Legality recognizes the arbitrary element in law, and even protects some of those elements, such as the right of a legitimate decider to prevail for the time being despite some acting out of power or whim. But the larger aspiration of a community dedicated to law is to enlarge the role of reason and fairness in all public decision.

The general public contributes to legality, not only through the quality of democratic decision-making, but also insofar as it has the competence, and recognizes the duty, of criticizing authority. To be sure, there must be public respect for law, and appropriate self-restraint, but in a vital legal order something more is wanted than submission to constituted authority. A military establishment places very great emphasis on obedience to lawful commands, yet such a setting is hardly a model of institutionalized legality. So too, a conception of law as the manifestation of awesome authority encourages feelings of deference and is compatible with much arbitrary rule. In a community that aspires to a high order of legality obedience to law is not submissive compliance. The obligation to obey the law is closely tied to the defensibility of the rules themselves and of the official decisions that enforce them.

Thus understood, legality has a strong affinity with the ideal of political democracy. This is most readily manifest in democracy's dependence on limited governmental authority, and on the possibility of appeal, beyond majority will, for the protection of minority rights and the free creation of new majorities. But there is also an affinity of fundamental values—above all, to the role of reason in official judgment. Legality does not require the machinery of democratic decision-making. But it does require that the civic participant be treated as a "legal man," a right-and-duty bearing entity invested with the presumption of competence and guaranteed access to tribunals that are committed to the impartial assessment of evidence and argument.

4. Legality is an affirmative ideal. The rule of law is a practical ideal, which is to say it rests in part on pessimistic premises regarding the nature of man and society. "Free government," wrote Thomas Jefferson, "is founded in jealousy, and not in confidence, it is jealousy, and not confidence, which prescribes limited constitutions, to bind down those whom we are obliged to trust with power; . . . in questions of power, then, let no more be heard of confidence in man, but bind him down from mischief by the chains of the Constitution."[17] The assumption is that no man, no group of men, is to be trusted with unlimited power. No amount of wisdom or good will can justify a transfer of untrammeled power to mortal men.

This view does not require the belief that any man, given the chance, would misuse power; rather, the premise is that there is a sufficient *risk* of such misuse to forbid *reliance upon* the idealism and good will

17. See E. D. Warfield, *The Kentucky Resolutions of 1798* (New York: G. P. Putnam's Sons, 1887), 157-158.

of men in authority. Nor does Jefferson's pessimism necessarily deny that power and authority can be ennobling, summoning ordinary men to political and moral heights.

Legality begins as a principle of constraint, but it promises more than a way of moderating the uses of power. The "progressive reduction of arbitrariness" knows no near stopping-place. The closer we look at that process, the more we realize that it calls for an affirmative view of what it means to participate in a legal order, whether as citizen, judge, or executive. In its richest connotation, legality evokes the Greek view of a social order founded in reason, whose constitutive principle is justice.[18]

The Morality of Cooperation

We can better understand the human foundations of legality and the values it expresses, if we examine some relevant aspects of moral development. The latter must be understood as a natural process, a kind of maturation. One phase of moral development is social and psychological —the reconstruction of the self, of interpersonal relations, and of orientations toward authority. Another phase is institutional—the creation of new social forms, new modes of participation, new ways of exercising authority.

The theory of moral development is hardly a well-established part of modern psychology and sociology. Nevertheless, a number of classic studies have dealt with this theme, and have done so in ways that are pertinent to the rule of law. Perhaps most closely relevant are the theories of Emile Durkheim, Jean Piaget, George H. Mead, and Max Weber. Durkheim and Piaget explicitly adopted a naturalist view of types and stages of morality, and they saw the import of their theories for conceptions of law and for modes of participation in the legal order.

In his *Division of Labor in Society*[19] Durkheim distinguished two types of social solidarity, "mechanical" and "organic," the latter representing a later stage of development. Mechanical solidarity is based on likeness and a sense of common identity. People are bound together by the fact that they have been brought up to act and think alike, follow similar life routines and share a "common conscience." The main source of cohesion is symbolic experience. This solidarity is "mechanical," Durkheim thought, because it resembles "the cohesion which unites the elements of an inanimate body, as opposed to that which makes a unit out of a living

18. See Werner Jaeger, "Praise of Law," in Paul Sayre (ed.), *Interpretations of Modern Legal Philosophers* (New York: Oxford University Press, 1947), 352-375.

19. George Simpson (trans.), *Emile Durkheim on the Division of Labor in Society* (New York: The Macmillan Company, 1933). First published in French in 1893.

body."[20] Organic solidarity, on the other hand, is based on differentiation, analogous to a complex living body with specialized organs, each dependent on the others, and the whole dependent on the functional integration of the parts. Social differentiation makes people and groups interdependent; this outcome is organic solidarity.

In the stage of mechanical solidarity, social control through law is largely a matter of upholding the symbolic order. Group identity is reaffirmed by punishing deviants who violate what is sacred to the group. To enforce and reassert the common conscience, the community resorts to *punitive* law and *repressive* sanctions.

With the development of organic solidarity, another type of law becomes predominant. This is *restitutive* law, which is the law of cooperation. Its purpose is to restore social equilibrium by making a man whole, that is, compensating him for losses incurred when someone fails to discharge his lawful obligations. The classic branch of restitutive law is the law of contracts. The contract is, wrote Durkheim, "*par excellence, the juridical expression of cooperation.*"[21]

Each type of solidarity, and each of the two types of law, is associated with a distinctive "morality." Repressive law is a manifestation of communal morality and is suffused with the spirit of constraint. Restitutive law is the morality of cooperation; it binds together specialized groups or occupations, rather than whole communities. In organic solidarity Durkheim saw a rational basis for law and one that was compatible with personal autonomy.

Mechanical solidarity presumes that individuals are the same; organic solidarity presumes that they are different. "The first is possible only insofar as the individual personality is absorbed into the collective personality; the second is possible only if each one has a sphere of action which is peculiar to him; that is, a personality."[22] Thus restitutive law encourages autonomy as it facilitates cooperative action.

A strikingly similar model, using entirely different materials, was put forward by the Swiss psychologist Jean Piaget in *The Moral Judgment of the Child.* Piaget studied the responses of children to issues of punishment and fairness. He began with the premise that "all morality consists in a system of rules, and the essence of morality is to be sought for in the respect which the individual acquires for these rules."[23] As a result of this

20. Ibid., 130.
21. Ibid., 123.
22. Ibid., 131.
23. Jean Piaget, *The Moral Judgment of the Child* (New York: Free Press, 1965), 13. First published in 1932.

focus on rules, the theme of the study became the child's conception of justice.

Piaget distinguished two types of rules, coercive and rational. The former are based on respect for authority, and compliance is won by punishment. Characteristically, the child's obedience to a coercive rule does not depend on understanding its purpose. The rule is a received and external fact. Rational rules, on the other hand, are founded in a sense of fairness, mutuality, and respect for the ends the rule is meant to serve. A regime of coercive rules is a "morality of constraint"; a regime of rational rules is a "morality of cooperation."[24]

The two types of morality are stages on life's way. A first period, roughly until the age of eight, is characterized by submission to authority and externality of rules. It is a stage of "strict law,"[25] in which the bare fact of infraction, regardless of context or intent, warrants severe punishment. In the second stage (ages nine to twelve) the commitment to retribution declines. There is a greater awareness of reciprocity, equal treatment, and mutual respect among peers, as well as an increased capacity to distinguish a just rule from one that is merely authoritative.

> [The younger children] do not attempt to understand the psychological context; deeds and punishments are for them simply so much material to be brought into some kind of balance, and this kind of moral mechanics, this materialism of retributive justice, so closely akin to the moral realism studied before, makes them insensible to the human side of the problem. . . . [C]hildren who put retributive justice above distributive are those who adopt the point of view of adult constraint, while those who put equality of treatment above punishment are those who, in their relations with other children, or more rarely in the relations between themselves and adults, have learnt better to understand psychological situations and to judge according to norms of a new moral type.[26]

In Piaget's theory moral evolution is marked by changes in personality, rules, and social relations. At stage one the child is "egocentric" rather than autonomous. He is basically a "loner," unable to engage in genuine cooperation; his play is characteristically mechanical and imitative; at the same time, he is dominated by respect for adult wishes. At this stage the child does not distinguish his own perspectives from the perspectives of others, and the psychological bases for criticism of authority have not been laid.

The transition to stage two sees the child increasing his freedom from adult constraint. He looks to the peer group for satisfaction and

24. Ibid., 335.
25. See Pound, op. cit. [supra note 12], I, 382-406.
26. Piaget, op. cit. [supra note 23], 267f.

guidance. In the peer group an awareness of cooperation takes hold. Group participation encourages a more generalized, less egocentric approach to the world and, at the same time, helps the child to discover the boundaries that separate him from others. According to Piaget, cooperation presumes the participation of autonomous individuals, and as the child's own autonomy grows he gains respect for the autonomy of others. Thus the morality of cooperation is a morality of rational rules, interdependent activities, and autonomous individuals.

Piaget's two stages correspond closely to Durkheim's. Mechanical solidarity creates a morality of constraint; organic solidarity yields a morality of cooperation. Each posits a growth or rationality, social differentiation, and personal autonomy. On the other hand, in a lengthy commentary on Durkheim, Piaget argues that the French sociologist lost his early insight, expressed in *The Division of Labor in Society,* that there are two moralities, one based on conformity to established norms, the other arising out of the necessities and opportunities of the division of labor. In his later writings on education, Durkheim seemed to recognize only one source of moral development—acceptance of authority.[27]

Of course, any theory of determinate "stages" of moral development is highly vulnerable, but more recent studies conducted to test Piaget's hypotheses have confirmed the basic findings, especially his theory that "the child's earliest morality is oriented to obedience, punishment, and impersonal forces, and that it progresses toward more internal and subjective values."[28] Some specific conclusions, such as the importance Piaget gave to the peer group in producing the morality of cooperation, have not been upheld.[29]

27. Saul Geiser suggests that the cleavage between Durkheim and Piaget is fundamental, and epistemological. For Durkheim, social facts are characterized by externality and constraint. "This postulate gives little weight to *subjective understanding* as a determinant of the nature of social objects, including rules. For Piaget, the child's understanding of the rules is crucial; it is this that changes in the course of psychological development." (Private communication.) At the same time, we should recognize that objective circumstances, including forms of cooperation, have much to do with the kinds of rules and sanctions that emerge in a given setting.

28. Lawrence Kohlberg, "Development of Moral Character and Moral Ideology," in Martin L. Hoffman (ed.), *Review of Child Development Research* (New York: Russell Sage Foundation, 1964), 399.

29. While holding to the idea of development, Kohlberg and other current students of moral growth are chary of determinate stages. They emphasize that the two moralities coexist and compete. In analysis, it is difficult to avoid the language of "stages," though they should not be applied mechanically, or taken as mutually exclusive progressions. See Roger Brown, *Social Psychology* (New York: Free Press, 1965), 241-242, 403ff., 409. For a related analysis, see Jane Loevinger, "The Meaning and Measurement of Ego Development," *American Psychologist,* 21 (1966), 195-206. Seven "stages" or "milestones" of ego development are discussed, 198-200.

The idea that a morality of cooperation replaces a more primitive morality of constraint finds supportive resonance in the theories of George H. Mead, the American philosopher and social psychologist. The concept of moral evolution is less explicit in Mead's writings, but it is not far to seek. In *Mind, Self, and Society* Mead located moral development in the transition from a regime of "significant others" to a consciousness of the "generalized other."[30] The young child internalizes the attitudes and expectations of his parents and of other individuals who dominate his life. These significant others have a direct, personal impact on the child's conception of himself and of his world. Gradually, however, the child learns a different form of social participation. He begins to grasp the meaning of cooperation and to govern his actions by his understanding of group activity. In time he can take the point of view of the group, not by mechanically following an assigned course of conduct but by recognizing how rules are related and how they contribute to the playing of a game or the achievement of a goal. The generalized other is this perspective of cooperative group life.

For Mead, moral evolution could be discerned (1) in the capacity for rational participation in rule-governed, organized social activity; (2) in the growth of personal autonomy, mitigating the over-determined, oversocialized self; and (3) in the enlargement of the self as parochial perspectives are overcome and the individual can adopt the standpoint of ever-larger communities and universal values. Here again, the interdependence of rational rules, cooperation, and personal autonomy is stressed.

At the institutional level, the most persuasive theories of moral evolution center on the emergence of rational forms of social organization. Here the major figure is Max Weber. Weber located that evolution in a determinate set of social processes, especially the rise of economic calculation and bureaucratization, and he kept close to the historical data. Weber would have resisted the notion that his historical sociology contains a theory of moral evolution, for he understood the ambiguities of rationality, and he was reluctant to compromise the "objectivity" of social science. Nevertheless, he did trace a pattern of change in which a received morality of constraint—traditional norms and forms of authority—was replaced by a new morality founded in the requirements of rational action. A basic feature of that morality was the reduction of arbitrariness in official conduct.

We shall have more to say about Weber's theory of rationality and

---

30. George H. Mead, *Mind, Self, and Society* (Chicago: University of Chicago Press, 1934), 154.

legality. . . . At this point it may be noted that Weber's uneasiness about the moral worth of rationality was warranted, and points to an important limitation of his theory as a way of identifying the social foundations of legality. In his analysis of bureaucracy Weber adopted what Edmond Cahn once called the "official perspective."[31] Regularity and rationality were summoned by the needs of the administrative system, and the latter was typically a device for implementing the legitimate commands and policies of higher authority. Weber had no rich sense of group process, nor much feeling for psychological reality. He did not see rationality as the outcome of group conflict and accommodation within a framework of evolving, responsive purpose; nor did he fully appreciate the potential for human growth in self-affirming participation.

Other currents in the theory of organization, in some cases heavily influenced by American pragmatism, have given great weight to the morality of cooperation. The writings of Mary Parker Follett and Chester I. Barnard, for example, insist that the efficient and effective organization must be viewed as a "cooperative system." In such a system authority is not self-justifying. It is founded in practical necessity, subject to reconstruction as new constraints and opportunities appear, disciplined by the "authority of the situation," and responsible to organizational purposes.

Miss Follett once wrote that administrative wisdom lies in depersonalizing the giving of orders, thus separating authority from domination:

> One *person* should not give orders to another *person*, but both should agree to take their orders from the situation. . . . Our job is not how to get people to obey orders, but how to devise methods by which we can best *discover* the order integral to a particular situation. When that is found, the employee can issue it to the employer, as well as the employer to the employee. This often happens easily and naturally. My cook or my stenographer points out the law of the situation, and I, if I recognize it as such, accept it, even although it may reverse some "order" I have given.[32]

In the morality of cooperation authority is situational, problematic, and responsive.

31. See Edmond Cahn, "Law in the Consumer Perspective," 112 *University of Pennsylvania Law Review* 1-21 (November, 1963).

32. Henry C. Metcalf and L. Urwick (eds.), *Dynamic Administration: The Collected Papers of Mary Parker Follett* (New York: Harper & Row, Publishers, 1942), 59. Barnard's theory, in a sense less dynamic and less sensitive to the creative needs and potentials of lower-level participants, is contained in Chester I. Barnard, *The Functions of the Executive* (Cambridge, Mass.: Harvard University Press, 1938).

For Piaget, and for the American pragmatists, the morality of cooperation is the font of genuine rationality. Rationality is most securely based, and most fully achieved, if it emerges from below and is not merely a system imposed from above. How the morality of cooperation contributes to that end may be restated as follows:

1. Personal autonomy and competence. The individual is not a submissive, reactive participant in a regime of mechanical solidarity. He is capable of making his own assessments, transcending egocentric boundaries, and criticizing authority. He sees his obligation as deriving from personal and group requirements, and from his autonomously made commitments. In short, he is a responsible and rational actor.

2. Norms rooted in experience. In the morality of constraint the system of norms is received, pre-ordained, and prescriptive. Codes of conduct are transmitted by authority figures who claim unqualified deference. In such a system the paradigmatic legal act is the suppression of deviance.

The morality of cooperation, on the other hand, looks to norms that arise out of group experience. It is a morality of participation, of finding your own way, of meeting today's needs with today's resources. It is a philosophy of the present. The outcome of group learning may be a rediscovery of truths long since revealed, but the moral effect is to make each generation its own master. In the morality of cooperation the paradigmatic legal act is the reconstruction of received precepts to facilitate action and vindicate emergent rights.

3. Dialogue and problem-solving. Genuine cooperation is something more than the bare coordination of activities. Individual and group differences are recognized, not erased. And the reconciliation of those differences is not won by a demand for conformity. Rather, the guiding norm is joint problem-solving based on effective communication and openness to new perspectives. A problem-solving orientation in group affairs is not easily won, especially when authority and subordination are at stake. There must be a willingness to address issues on their merits, to make realistic assessments rather than conjure up imagined risks, to avoid standing pat on traditional thoughtways or prerogatives. The ethos of problem-solving is, therefore, strongly opposed to a morality of constraint, which imposes solutions and limits alternatives.

The congruence of a legal ethic and the morality of cooperation needs no laboring. If legality abhors arbitrary judgment and constraint, presses for justifications, invokes the authority of agreed-upon purpose, and values the competent participant, so too does the morality of cooperation. To be sure, not everything fits so neatly. One aspect of legality— legal continuity and the valuing of received precepts—is insecurely footed in a morality of cooperation. We shall return to that issue in a moment. At this point we may note some implications of the view that the morality of cooperation is a phase of human development, arises from personal and group experience, and is more than modestly congruent with the requirements of a developed legal order:

(1) The affirmative ideal of legality is no mere subjective preference. It rests on a natural foundation and has objective worth. It may lose out in competition with other values, or be blocked by the absence of congenial conditions, but the legal ethic finds its warrant in the contribution it can make to human growth and self-realization.

(2) If the morality of cooperation has the place we give it, then we may expect the emergence of legality—in explicit aspiration and institutional form, as well as in supporting circumstance—where rational forms of social organization prevail. Rational systems do not necessarily produce a full morality of cooperation, but they encourage it, the more so as the need for effective participation grows. Moreover, the rationality of the system tends to diminish arbitrariness, including the authority of what is historically given, and to enhance the authority of purpose. When the ethic of cooperation makes sense historically as the preferred way of organizing human relations, a dynamic toward legality is created. For this reason, we see legalization as a peculiarly salient issue for the modern special-purpose organization.

(3) The two moralities suggest contrasting images of the legal order: (a) as a mechanism for upholding what is settled and established, and especially what is sanctified by tradition; (b) as a mechanism for problem-solving, guided by a commitment to rationality, personal autonomy, and rather general social ideals. The former encourages the use of law to enforce conformity and resist change; the latter sees law as a resource for facilitating change while maintaining core values.

The Emergent Polity

It is obvious that the two moralities, and their legal correlates, persist and compete. There is no question of a morality of cooperation fully supplanting a morality of constraint, if only because no enduring social system can entirely dispense with received precepts. With the ascendance of the morality of cooperation, however, *the received precept is generalized.* The authoritative starting-point shifts from the specific norm to the more general concept or ideal, from the prescriptive regulation to the guiding principle.[33]

33. The transition from due process conceived as a set of fixed norms to a "flexible" due process illustrates this point. . . . See also John T. Noonan, Jr., "*Tokos* and *Atokion:* An Examination of Natural Law Reasoning Against Usury and Against Contraception," 10 *Natural Law Forum* 215-235 (1965), tracing a similar shift in Catholic doctrine.

In his lectures on the growth of the law, Cardozo took it for granted that "principles," no less than specific rules or judgments, are part of the law:

> "The general body of doctrine and tradition" from which the judgments derived, and "by which we criticize them" [here he was quoting Pound] must be ranked as law also, not merely because it is the chief object of our study, but because also the limits which it imposes upon a judge's liberty of choice are not purely advisory, but involve in greater or less degree an element of coercive power. . . . What permits us to say that the principles are law is the force or persuasiveness of the prediction that they will or ought to be applied. Even when the conclusion upon a special state of facts is in doubt, as in the case of the manufacturer of the Buick car, there is little doubt that the conclusion will be drawn from a stock of principles and rules which will be treated as invested with legal obligation. The court will not roam at large, and light upon one conclusion or another as the result of favor or caprice. This stock of rules and principles is what for most purposes we mean by law.[34]

Cardozo accepted Justice Holmes' view that law is revealed in the prediction of "what the courts will do in fact," but he added the civilizing emphasis that the *grounds* of the prediction, when confirmed, should be considered part of the law. The explication of principles that guide judicial decision is a discovery of law, not in the strict sense of positive law, but as part of a larger body of authoritative materials. We should also note that Cardozo, in the passage just quoted, speaks of principles that "ought to be" applied, thereby suggesting that legal principles are something more than empirical summaries of what judges do.

Even a cursory look at the legal order will remind us that a great deal more is included than rules. Legal ideas, variously and unclearly labeled "concepts," "principles," and "doctrines," have a vital place in authoritative decision. "Detrimental reliance," "attractive nuisance," "reasonable doubt," "exhaustion of remedies," "agency," are among the many familiar concepts which purport to grasp some truth and provide a foundation for the elaboration of specific rules. In addition, of course, there are even more general ideas stating the necessary conditions of "ordered liberty" or that guilt is individual rather than collective. It would be wrong to speak of these as merely a "source" of law; they are too closely woven into the fabric of legal thought and have too direct a role in decision-making.[35]

34. Benjamin N. Cardozo, *The Growth of the Law* (New Haven: Yale University Press, 1924), 36f., 43.

35. See Roscoe Pound, "Hierarchy of Sources and Forms in Different Systems of Law," 7 *Tulane Law Review* 475-487 (June, 1933); also Graham Hughes, "Rules, Policy and Decision-Making," 77 *Yale Law Journal* 411-439 (January, 1968).

If principles and concepts are in some important sense part of the law, it does not follow that the legal world is a heavenly city of abstract ideas. On the contrary, the development and application of these materials requires a continuing assessment of human situations. The transition from general principle to specific rule requires a confrontation of social reality. *Ex facto ius oritur*—the law springs from the fact. The maxim reminds us that a preoccupation with ideas and ideals, however essential to the legal process, will be sterile indeed if it is not supplemented by more pragmatic and empirical concerns.

One way of seeing the interplay of principle and fact in law is to take seriously the difference between general values and specific norms. Science as an enterprise may be known by ideals of rigor and self-correction, but the norms of proper inquiry must vary with the content and maturity of the discipline. Democracy seeks the rational, self-preserving consent of the governed, but under certain circumstances maximizing the number of voters, or relying on techniques of direct rather than representative government may undermine rather than further the democratic ideal. The norms derive, not from the ideals of the system alone, but also from knowledge of what men and institutions are like. Only thus can we know what norms are required to fulfill the ideal.

The same logic applies, and with special force, in the legal order. The concept of legality does not settle the rules of pleading, evidence, or judicial discretion. Legality is a master ideal, not a specific set of injunctions. This ideal is to be realized in history, not outside of it; and history makes its own demands, offers its own opportunities. Even when we know the meaning of legality we must still work out the relation between general principles and the changing structure of society. New circumstances do not necessarily alter principles, but they may and do require that new rules of law be formulated and old ones changed.

In this perspective, the achievement of legality is seen as the refinement of basic principles, their application in depth, and their extension to new social settings. As this evolution takes place, however, *the line between the legal and the political is blurred.* Indeed, that line is obscured at two points: (a) when law emerges and (b) when its distinctive mission is fulfilled. For the legal order stands midway between "power politics" and "polity." In its early stages law emerges from and depends upon the assertion of power and the contest of wills; it confirms the outcome of the struggle and, at the same time, provides a moderating framework and a sublimating symbolism. In dialectical imagery, force is the thesis, law the disciplining antithesis. But as a system of discipline law has its own shortcomings. Standing alone, it cannot fulfill its own promise as an affirmative ideal. The latent historical outcome—the renewing synthesis—is the absorption of legal ideals into the political order and, at

955

the same time, the creation of supportive institutions, values, and modes of thought.

Black, Comment, The Boundaries of Legal Sociology*

I

Contemporary sociology of law is characterized by a confusion of science and policy. Its analysis proceeds in the disembodied tongue of science, in the language of "system," "structure," "pattern," and "organization," or in the vocabulary of technique, of "needs," "functions," and "viability." Rarely does the language impart emotion, indignation, or even personal involvement on the part of the investigator. But while legal sociology is presented in this scientific language and scientific tone, normative considerations—the "ought" and the "just"—become subtly implicated.

Although legal sociologists typically criticize one another according to the usual scientific standards of methodological precision and theoretical validity, they frequently become preoccupied with the "policy implications" of their research. Occasionally, in assessing one another, they shed the mantle of science and become unabashedly political. Recently, for instance, a sociologist characterized the literature of legal sociology as bourgeois, liberal, pluralist, and meliorist.[2] He went on to argue that a more radical sociology is required, one that is "more critical in its premises and farther-reaching in its proposals."[3] Whether liberal or radical, however, legal sociologists tend to share a style of discourse that deserves attention and comment.

It is my contention that a purely sociological approach to law should involve not an assessment of legal policy, but rather, a scientific analysis of legal life *as a system of behavior*. The ultimate contribution of this enterprise would be a general theory of law, a theory that would predict

---

* [81 *Yale L.J.* 1086-1100 (1972). Reprinted by permission of The Yale Law Journal and Fred B. Rothman & Company from The Yale Law Journal, Vol. 81, pp. 1086-1100.

Donald Black (1941–) is presently Associate Professor of Sociology at Yale University.]

2. Currie, Book Review, 81 *Yale L.J.* 134 (1971), reviewing *Law and the Behavioral Sciences* (L. Friedman & S. Macaulay eds. 1969) and *Society and the Legal Order* (R. Schwartz & J. Skolnick eds. 1970). These two collections of the legal sociology literature not only collect representative materials but also attempt to explain the relevance of the materials, thereby providing excellent examples of the style of discourse now dominating the field.

3. Id. at 145.

and explain every instance of legal behavior. While such a general theory may never be attained, efforts to achieve it should be central to the sociology of law. By contrast, the core problems of legal policymaking are problems of value. Such value considerations are as irrelevant to a sociology of law as they are to any other scientific theory of the empirical world.

Invoking the language of science and relying upon its aura of respectability, sociologists move, in a special and almost imperceptible way, beyond science and deal with questions of legal evaluation. Because they confuse scientific questions with policy questions, they severely retard the development of their field. At best, they offer an applied sociology of law—at worst, sheer ideology.

After examining the type of discourse that passes for a sociology of law and noting its apparent shortcomings, I shall discuss more directly the nature and aims of a pure sociology of law.

II

With one phrase, *legal effectiveness,* we capture the major thematic concern of contemporary sociology of law. The wide range of work that revolves around the legal-effectiveness theme displays a common strategy of problem formulation, namely a comparison of legal reality to a legal ideal of some kind. Typically a gap is shown between law-in-action and law-in-theory. Often the sociologist then goes on to suggest how the reality might be brought closer to the ideal. Law is regarded as ineffective and in need of reform owing to the disparity between the legal reality and the ideal.[4]

Legal-effectiveness studies differ from one another, however, in the kinds of legal ideals against which their findings are measured. At one extreme are "impact studies" that compare reality to legal ideals with a very plain and specific operational meaning. Here the legal measuring rod is likely to be a statute whose purpose is rather clearly discernible or a judicial decision unambiguously declarative of a specific policy. The *Miranda* decision, for example, requiring the police to apprise suspects of their legal rights before conducting an in-custody interrogation, has a

---

4. Because research in legal sociology consistently shows these disparities, the field has become identified with debunkery and the unmasking of law. In legal scholarship this debunking spirit goes back to the legal realism movement which has haunted American law schools since it emerged around the turn of the century. Much legal sociology, then, is a new legal realism, appearing in the prudent garb of social science, armed with sophisticated research methods, new language, and abstract theoretical constructs.

core meaning about which consensus is quite high.[5] Soon after *Miranda* was handed down by the Supreme Court, research was initiated to evaluate the degree of police compliance with the decision.[6] When the core meaning of a decision thus is clear, this type of research can be expected to show whether or not a decision has, in fact, been implemented.

Sociologists, however, may launch these implementation studies where legislation or judicial opinion is considerably more ambiguous than in *Miranda*. In such instances, the "impact" may be difficult to measure. What must be done, for example, to implement *In re Gault*?[7] Though it is generally recognized that *Gault* guarantees to juvenile suspects constitutional rights previously accorded only to adults, the extent of these juvenile rights is not at all clear. Hence it becomes difficult, perhaps impossible, to identify the degree to which *Gault* has been implemented.[9]

Finally, the sociologist may attempt to compare legal reality to an ideal grounded in neither statutory nor case law. Here the investigator assesses his empirical materials against standards of justice such as "the rule of law," "arbitrariness," "legality," or a concept of "due process" not explicitly anchored in the due process clause of the Constitution. Jerome Skolnick, for instance, asserts that the police employ the informer system in narcotics enforcement "irrespective of the constraints embodied in principles of due process."[10] But there is no indication of where Skolnick locates these principles. Presumably he realizes that no court in the United States has declared the practice illegal, and there is no reason to think such a decision is likely in the near future. In another study, Skolnick investigates plea-bargaining in the courtroom, concluding that the cooperation underlying this practice "deviates" from some unarticulated adversarial ideal.[12] Similarly, Leon Mayhew, in arguing that the Massachusetts Commission Against Discrimination failed to define discrimination adequately and thereby ignored much illegal conduct, provides neither a legal argument nor an empirical referent for

5. Miranda v. Arizona, 384 U.S. 436 (1966).

6. See, e.g., Project, Interrogations in New Haven: The Impact of Miranda, 76 *Yale L.J.* 1519 (1967).

7. 387 U.S. 1 (1967).

9. See, e.g., Lefstein, Stapleton, & Teitelbaum, In Search of Juvenile Justice: Gault and its Implementation 3 *L. & Soc. Rev.* 491 (1969), in which these problems of operationalization are evident.

10. J. Skolnick, *Justice Without Trial* 138 (1966).

12. Skolnick, Social Control in the Adversary System, 11 *J. Conflict Resolution* 52 (1967).

his interpretation of the Commission's proper mission.[13] In short, then, some studies in legal sociology seem to move beyond the law when they measure legal reality against an ideal.

At its most useful, legal-effectiveness research may be valuable to people in a position to reform the legal order. In this sense it consists of studies in *applied* sociology of law. This would appear to be particularly true of those investigations that relate empirical findings to legal ideals which are clearly expressed in the written law. Such research might provide legal reformers with a kind of leverage for change, though the mere evidence of a gap between law-in-action and law-in-theory would not in itself overwhelm all resistance to change. Who can imagine a study, after all, that would not discover such a gap? Little is more predictable about the law than that these gaps exist.

However, legal-effectiveness research sometimes moves beyond applied sociology. When legal reality is compared to an ideal with no identifiable empirical referent, such as "the rule of law" or "due process," the investigator may inadvertently implant his personal ideals as the society's legal ideals. At this point social science ceases and advocacy begins. The value of legal-effectiveness research of this kind is bound to be precarious, for it involves, perhaps unwittingly, moral judgment at the very point where it promises scientific analysis.

III

As I have described it, the sociology of law significantly resembles a broader style of thought that has come to be known as *technocratic* thought, or, to use an earlier term, scientism. In the technocratic worldview, every problem—factual, moral, political, or legal—reduces to a question of technique. A good technique is one that works, and what works can be learned through science. Any problem that cannot be solved in this way is no problem at all, hardly worthy of our attention. In theory, moreover, every problem can be solved if only the appropriate expertise is applied to it. Among the key words in the technocratic vocabulary are efficiency and, one I noted earlier, effectiveness. It is a style of thought in some respects akin to pragmatism, but it is a pragmatism with unstated goals, a search for the most rational way to go somewhere that is never clearly specified. Rather, we must infer what these goals are,

13. L. Mayhew, *Law and Equal Opportunity* (1969), reviewed, Black, Book Review, 40 *Soc. Inquiry* 179 (1970). See Mayhew, Teleology and Values in the Social System: Reply to Donald J. Black, 40 *Soc. Inquiry* 182 (1970).

and that is how some technocratic approaches come to be known as liberal and bourgeois, others as radical and critical. Technocrats do not make political arguments in the usual sense; they do not moralize. They simply want to get the job done.

The technocratic style dominates much discussion of social controversy at the higher reaches of American life. We are given to understand that scientific research will reveal whether marijuana should be legalized, that the Vietnam War was a miscalculation, and that economic analysis will determine the most "rational" tax program. The new nations of Africa and Asia are studied to determine what their modernization "requires." Riots, violence, and pornography give rise to government study commissions and research grants for the universities. Moral problems of every sort are translated into problems of knowledge and science, of know-how. To discuss the criminal in the moral terms of right and wrong comes to be seen as primitive and unschooled; medical terminology is introduced into the discussion of the treatment of criminal offenders. In the name of science and progress, what was once seen as evil is studied and treated, not condemned.

The logic of this technocratic mentality has helped to catapult sociology to a position of some prominence in these times of rapid social change and conflict. Sociology, it is thought, will point the way to solutions to the many problems before us. The sociologists themselves have shown little reluctance to accept this responsibility. The typical sociologist knows almost nothing about moral or social philosophy, but if public policy is no more than a matter of scientific technique, why should he? In a technocratic era, moral philosophy is an oddity in the real world of action, a quaint remnant of the nineteenth century, something for the undergraduates.

IV

Law can be seen as a thing like any other in the empirical world. It is crucial to be clear that from a sociological standpoint, law consists in observable acts, not in rules as the concept of rule or norm is employed in both the literature of jurisprudence and in every-day legal languages.[15] From a sociological point of view, law is not what lawyers regard as bind-

15. Hence this sociological concept of law is very different from and not logically incompatible with the legal positivism of Hans Kelsen and his "pure theory of law." See, e.g., H. Kelsen, *General Theory of Law and State* (1945). Similarly, to take another well-known example, a sociological approach does not conflict with the rule-oriented jurisprudence of H. L. A. Hart in *The Concept of Law* (1961).

ing or obligatory precepts, but rather, for example, the observable dispositions of judges, policemen, prosecutors, or administrative officials. Law is like any other thing in the sense that it is as amenable to the scientific method as any other aspect of reality. No intellectual apparatus peculiar to the study of law is required. At the same time, a social science of law true to positivism, the conventional theory of science, cannot escape the limitations inherent in scientific thought itself. Perhaps a word should be said about these limitations.

Within the tradition of positivist philosophy, three basic principles of scientific knowledge can be noted. First, science can know only phenomena and never essences. The quest for the one correct concept of law or for anything else "distinctively legal" is therefore inherently unscientific.[19] The essence of law is a problem for jurisprudence, not science. Second, every scientific idea requires a concrete empirical referent of some kind. A science can only order experience, and has no way of gaining access to non-empirical domains of knowledge. Accordingly, insofar as such ideals as justice, the rule of law, and due process are without a grounding in experience, they have no place in the sociology of law. Third, value judgments cannot be discovered in the empirical world and for that reason are without cognitive meaning in science.[21]

It is for this last reason that science knows nothing and can know nothing about the effectiveness of law. Science is incapable of an evaluation of the reality it confronts. To measure the effectiveness of law or of anything else for that matter, we must import standards of value that are foreign to science. What is disturbing about the contemporary literature on legal effectiveness then is not that it evaluates law, but rather, that its evaluations and proposals are presented as scientific findings. Far from denying this confusion, Philip Selznick has gone so far in the opposite direction as to claim that "nothing we know today precludes an effort to define 'ends proper to man's nature' and to discover objective standards of moral judgment."[25]

It is apparent by now that my critique of contemporary legal sociol-

19. Philip Selznick, one of the most ambitious and influential students of legal effectiveness, considers the "cardinal weakness" of the sociological approach to law to be its "failure to offer a theory of the distinctively legal." Selznick, The Sociology of Law, 9 *International Encyclopedia of the Social Sciences* 51 (D. L. Sills ed. 1968).

21. Some legal sociologists are willing to tolerate an obfuscation of factual and normative discourse. Selznick, for instance, while conceding that the separation of fact and value has some merit, nevertheless suggests that this distinction is meant for "unsophisticated minds." We must, he continues, unlearn this "easy and reassuring" formula from our "intellectual youth." Selznick finds a natural-law approach more appropriate for the mature thinker. Selznick, Sociology and Natural Law, 6 *Natural L.F.* 86 (1961).

25. Selznick, supra note 21, at 93-94.

ogy is premised on the notion that sociology is a scientific enterprise and, as such, can be distinguished from moral philosophy, jurisprudence, or any other normatively oriented study—in other words, that the study of fact can be distinguished from the study of value. This is not to say that I am unaware of the criticisms that have been levied against a purely value-free social science. But while accepting these criticisms, I cannot understand the conclusion that the effort to develop an objective science of man should be abandoned.

It is important to understand precisely how values become involved in social science. One widely recognized intrusion of values occurs at the first stage of scientific inquiry: the choice of the problem for study. The values of the investigator may determine, for example, whether he selects a problem with great relevance for public policy or one of wholly academic interest. This intrusion of values was long ago noted by Max Weber, perhaps the most illustrious proponent of value-free sociology. Weber contended that the role of values in the choice of a problem is unavoidable and should be faced squarely, but he insisted that the problem, once selected, could and should be pursued "non-evaluatively."[26]

But I would go further than Weber and grant that these value orientations may bias the analysis of the problem as well as its selection. Though various methodological techniques have been developed to minimize the effects of these biases, good social science still requires a disciplined disengagement on the part of the investigator—so disciplined, in fact, that it may rarely be achieved. Various arguments can be made to the effect that bias is built into social science at its very foundations. For example, the claim has been made that every social science study necessarily implicates the investigator in the perspective of an actual hierarchical position, seeing social life from either the social top or the bottom, and is therefore inherently biased.[27] For purposes of discussion I grant even this. Similarly it is arguable that all social science is, beyond science, a form of ideology, if only because it is by its nature an instance of social behavior subject to the scrutiny of the very discipline of which it is a part. Sociology, that is, can be analyzed sociologically. Sociology does not occur in a vacuum and is undoubtedly influenced by social forces. Accordingly, sociology may be viewed as ideology supporting either the defenders of the status quo or their opponents.[28]

26. See M. Weber, *The Methodology of the Social Sciences* 21-22 (E. A. Shils & H. A. Finch transls. 1949). For a direct attack on Weber's approach to these questions, see Gouldner, Anti-Minotaur: The Myth of a Value-Free Sociology, 9 *Soc. Problems* 199 (1962).

27. Becker, Whose Side Are We On?, 14 *Soc. Problems* 239 (1967).

28. This is a major theme of a recent critique of sociological theory. See A. Gouldner, *The Coming Crisis of Western Sociology* (1970).

Finally, because much social science can be interpreted in an ideological framework, its theories and findings can be used as weapons in the arena of public policymaking. The polemical impact of social science may be particularly great at this historical moment, given the enormous prestige of science in modern society. Not only do these theories and findings feed into existing policy debates, but they also can stimulate controversy and change by drawing attention to empirical situations that might otherwise be unknown or ignored by policy-makers and social critics. Thus social science performs—willingly or not—an intelligence function in the political process.[29] Because of such political ramifications, the argument has been put forward that the sociologist remains responsible for the consequences of his work. Only by making an explicit moral commitment can the social scientist hope to protect himself and others from the unintended consequences of his work.[30] It is apparent that social science resonates into the realm of ideology, thereby raising serious questions about the scholar's responsibilities to his fellow man.

In several senses, then, values enter into the activity of social science. While values may play a similar role in science of all kinds, it can at least be admitted that their role is especially visible and dramatic when man is studying himself. Values may be all the more prominent in the study of man's moral life, of which legal sociology is one branch. The major arguments against the possibility of a pure science of man, in short, seem to have some merit.[31] But the crucial question is what all of this implies for

29. It should be clear that the policy impact of science is never direct but is always mediated by normative analysis, whether explicit or implicit. Policy cannot be deduced from scientific propositions alone. All of this is dramatically illustrated by the relation between the Marxian theory and public policy. Surely no theory of social science has had more impact upon the world. It has been an important weapon in ideological debate, and it has alerted policymakers and the public to the situation of the working class and the role of class conflict in social change. Yet as a scientific theory the Marxian analysis of society and history has no logical implications for political action. Without passing judgment upon the exploitation and growing misery of the proletariat, one could just as well sit back passively and watch history unfold as join the revolution. Both responses are logically independent of the theory.

30. R. Dahrendorf, Values and Social Science: The Value Dispute in Perspective, in *Essays in the Theory of Society* 17 (1968).

31. Of course in this brief discussion I cannot begin to review the sizable literature on the subject. Perhaps I should note, however, one criticism of the value-neutral strategy that bears directly on the study of law—one, moreover, that seems to me to be wholly without merit. This criticism asserts that the study of normative life, because it is normative, requires a partially normative approach on the part of the investigator if he is to comprehend its empirical character. The investigator must take the normative view of the participants if he is to understand their normative behavior. Selznick, for instance, suggests that the sociologist should make an "assessment" of the degree to which a normative system reaches

the traditional distinction between fact and value. I say it implies nothing. In fact, much of the criticism of value-free sociology itself rests upon observable patterns of value impact upon social science and for that reason relies upon the fact-value distinction for its own validity.

We have seen that a social scientist may be affected by values in the choice of his problem and may be biased in his approach to it. Critics of a value-free social science assert that these psychological effects, along with the ideological character of social science when viewed as the object of analysis itself, undermine the validity of social science. But this is to confuse the origins and uses of a scientific statement with its validity. *The fact that scientific statements are influenced by values does not make them value statements.* The psychological and social influence of values on scientific inquiry has no logical implications for the validity of a scientific proposition. Its validity is determined only by empirical verification. A value statement, by contrast, is not subject to such a test.[33] How, for example, is the following statement to be empirically verified: "Democratic process is an ultimate good"? The fact that we can distinguish between scientific propositions and such value statements is all we need to assert the possibility of social science. In short, values may affect social science profoundly, but that is no reason to abandon the enterprise.[34]

---

an ideal "from the standpoint of the normative system being studied" though "the student of a normative system need not have any personal commitment to the desirability of that system." Selznick, supra note 21, at 88. In the study of law, therefore, it seems we must include an assessment of legal reality in terms of the ideals of the legal system we study.

In my view this argument incorrectly assumes that such normative ideals can be identified at a wholly empirical level. I do not believe, for example, that the degree of conformity of law with, let us say, a constitutional ideal, is a wholly empirical question. The nature of the ideal is itself a normative question, a question of normative interpretation. In the study of law such interpretation is the heart of legal scholarship, and from a positivist standpoint that activity is, at its core, normative rather than scientific. It advances an "ought" as the proper measure of reality, and it does not matter whether or not the interpreter himself subscribes to the "ought." It remains an unavoidably normative judgment. In effect, then, Selznick's view is that in order to understand normative life we must *be* normative. This view, I believe, is a non sequitur.

33. Although not subject to empirical verification, a value statement may be subject to other criteria such as its logical status in relation to a more general axiological principle.

34. My critique of contemporary legal sociology arises from a very conventional conception of scientific method, a conception associated with the broader tradition of positivist thought. I have not made and do not intend to make a philosophical defense of this tradition. I wish only to advocate a sociology of law true to basic positivist principles as they have come to be understood in the history of the philosophy of science.

V

The proper concern of legal sociology should be the development of a general theory of law. A general theory involves several key elements that may not at first be obvious. To say that a theory of law is general means that it seeks to order law wherever it is found. It seeks to discover the principles and mechanisms that predict empirical patterns of law, whether these patterns occur in this day or the past, regardless of the substantive area of law involved and regardless of the society. By contrast, the contemporary study of law is ideographic, very concrete and historical. Legal scholars tend to rebel at the suggestion of a general theory of their subject matter. Nevertheless, unless we seek generality in our study of law, we abandon hope for a serious sociology of law.

If the sweep of legal sociology is to be this broad, a correspondingly broad concept of law is required. I like to define law simply as *governmental social control*.[35] This is one possibility among many consistent with a positivist strategy. It is a concept easily employed in cross-societal analysis, encompassing any act by a political body that concerns the definition of social order or its defense. At the same time it excludes such forms of social control as popular morality and bureaucratic rules in private organizations. It is more inclusive than an American lawyer might deem proper, but more selective than anthropological concepts which treat law as synonymous with normative life and dispute settlement of every description, governmental or otherwise. If we are to have a manageable subject matter, our concept must construe law as one among a larger

35. I mention this only as a means of delineating the subject matter of legal sociology. A definition of the subject matter is a prerequisite to any scientific inquiry. Just as a physicist must first define motion before he can describe its characteristics, a sociologist of religion, for example, must first define the pattern of social behavior that constitutes religion before he can proceed with his research. This does not mean that there is only one proper definition. Law itself has been defined non-normatively in a variety of ways. See, e.g., M. Weber, *The Theory of Social and Economic Organization* 127 (T. Parsons ed. & transl. 1964): "An order will be called *law* when conformity with it is upheld by the probability that deviant action will be met by physical or psychic sanctions aimed to compel conformity or to punish disobedience, and applied by a group of men especially empowered to carry out this function."

I have chosen "governmental social control" as a definition of law for the reasons that follow in the text. I should add, however, that for me the choice of a particular sociological concept of law is not at all critical to my larger aim, since my ultimate interest goes beyond law per se to all forms of social control. For me, the study of law is preliminary and subordinate to the more general study of social control systems of all kinds. Therefore, if my concept of law is too narrow or too broad it does not matter *theoretically*, since it will in any case be relevant to a sociology of social control.

array of social control systems. And if we are to have a strategically detached approach, our concept must be value neutral. We need a theoretical structure applicable to the law of the Nazis as well as American law, to revolutionary law and colonial law as well as the cumbersome law of traditional China. What do these systems share, and how can we explain the differences among them?

Ultimately a theory is known and judged by its statements about the world. These statements both guide and follow empirical research. They propose uniformities in the relation between one part of reality and another. Thus a general theory of law is addressed to the relation between law and other aspects of social life, including, for instance, other forms of social control, social stratification, the division of labor, social integration, group size, and the structure and substance of social networks. . . .

VI

We should be clear about the relation between sociological and legal scholarship. There is, properly speaking, no conflict of professional jurisdiction between the two. A legal problem is a problem of value and is forever beyond the reach of sociology. Jurisdictional conflict arises only when the sociologist makes policy recommendations in the name of science: In matters of legal policy, the lawyer must rely on his own wits.

But a more significant matter than jurisdictional clarity is the relation between pure and applied sociology of law. My view, hardly novel, is that the quality of applied science depends upon the quality of pure science. Just as major advances in mechanical and chemical engineering have been made possible by theoretical formulations in pure physics and chemistry, so legal engineering ultimately requires a general theory of how legal systems behave as natural phenomena. The case for a pure sociology of law does not rest solely on its social usefulness, but if utility is at issue, then in the long run the type of work I advocate is crucial. At present, applied sociology of law has little to apply. What more serious claim could be brought against it?

Nonet, For Jurisprudential Sociology*

. . . Given its past accomplishments, "pure sociology" would seem a high-risk and very speculative intellectual investment. We should of course tolerate, and even encourage, the few who may try it. But it does not follow we should allow it to become a program for the rest of us. On

* [10 *Law & Soc. Rev.* 525, 529-531, 537, 543-545, (1976) (footnote omitted). The Law

the contrary, experience recommends . . . [that] just as other branches of sociology need to be informed by the normative thought on which they comment, so *sociology of law must be jurisprudentially informed* (Principle I). Even if a "pure sociology" of law were to develop, we should still want to invest most of our resources in more tangibly fruitful ventures. The reason for that is the relatively low yield of purely theoretical work of any kind, in all sociology and all philosophy, in jurisprudence as well as in sociology of law. Hence another tenet . . . (also, regrettably, the least observed): *sociology of law must have redeeming value for policy.* Never let any project stand on its theoretical merits alone (Principle II). . . .

If one agrees with Black (as I do) that debunking is too limited, too unpromising, and too easy a goal for sociological inquiry, perhaps the alternative is not to dismiss or ignore the role of values, rules, and other normative elements in legal phenomena, but rather to take them more seriously. This is part of the program H. L. A. Hart proposed for jurisprudence. It is also what Selznick proposed for legal sociology when, for similar reasons but in different words, he argued against the anti-formalist (read: rule-skeptical) mood that had pervaded the field and its immediate parents, i.e. legal realism and sociological jurisprudence. . . . Although Auerbach criticized a statement drawn from that argument, . . . judging from what he advocates elsewhere in the paper, I cannot imagine that Auerbach could have disagreed with the main thrust of Selznick's essay, and with another basic tenet . . . which is: *the sociology of law must take legal ideas seriously.* (Principle III. Corollary: sociologists who want to study law should become legally literate.) Perhaps a difference between Auerbach and Selznick was that the former had greater confidence in the promise of legal realism, and the good sense of social science, than the latter could muster. In fact, legal realism was fraught with ambiguity in its posture towards legal ideas. On the one hand, it hoped to make legal thought more purposive, more policy-oriented, more aware of consequences, and hence, more informed by the problems of law in action. On the other hand, its impatience towards legal formalism suggested a more radical critique of the inherent impotence of any legal thought. It was inevitable that such a perspective appeal to social scientists bent on demystification. Besides, it is all too comforting

---

& Society Review is the official publication of the Law and Society Association, which holds the copyright to the article. Reprinted by permission.

Philippe Nonet (1939–) is a colleague at the Center for the Study of Law and Society, Berkeley, California, and a member of the Department of Sociology at the University of California, Berkeley.]

for the student of sociology to think he can study "pure" legal "behavior" (without bothering to learn about the complicated and obscure arguments that occupy lawyers), and still hope to capture all that "really" matters about the legal order. . . .

According to Black, clarity of meaning is what distinguishes narrow, specific policies (the kind of standards by which "applied" sociology evaluates legal behavior) from larger, more general ends (such as due-process, the Rule of Law, and other such standards which are the concern of jurisprudence, moral, and political philosophy, and by which illegitimate evaluative sociology assesses legal "reality"). To draw the line on that ground is to reduce scientific inquiry to the role of a bureaucratic investigation of compliance. As defined, "applied" legal sociology is perhaps less difficult than jurisprudential sociology. It is certainly not more scientific; on the contrary, it retreats from a major scientific responsibility of policy reasearch, that is, the clarification of purpose. Whatever meaning a specific policy may have, it owes that meaning to some larger purpose(s) or interest(s) it helps achieve in a particular context. Therefore, to evaluate the implementation of a policy is inevitably to further determine (clarify) what the pursuit of some larger ends requires (means) in the context under study. Research can, of course, determine whether the racial composition of classrooms meets the quantitative guidelines established by court decrees in school integration cases. But all judicial, bureaucratic, and "affirmative action" authorities to the contrary notwithstanding, that information alone would be meaningless, as full compliance with the guidelines is as compatible with increased racial conflict and poorer education, as it is with exactly opposite achievements. Good policy research would require that compliance with the guidelines be assessed in light of the ends of education and racial justice. This kind of assessment is precisely what we wish bureaucracies did more often, when we criticize them for transforming means (rules and routines of all kinds) into ends. Thus clarity, or rather the progressive clarification of values, is a *purpose, not a condition,* of policy research, as it is of jurisprudence and jurisprudential sociology. For this reason, a fourth tenet (Principle IV) . . . is: *The sociology of law must integrate jurisprudential and policy analysis.* . . .

Unfortunately, jurisprudence is no alternative to "pure" sociology. To prefer it would only be to choose another set of blinders. In fact, jurisprudence and pure sociology are deeply involved with one another: there is no better match for a sociology that denies the normative aspects of legal phenomena, than a legal philosophy blind to factual issues in the analysis of normative ideas. To Black, jurisprudence is as "logically" incapable of failing for lack of knowledge, as sociology is of failing for philosophical naiveté. What can disturb such a solid and comfortable relation of mutually respectful ignorance?

Perhaps sociology can do so, if it returns to its historic intellectual task: that is, to enlarge the intellectual horizons of legal, political, economic, and other modes of normative thought; to broaden the concerns of these disciplines beyond the limits of their *specialized* institutional domains; to blur, not to draw, "boundaries," as between fact and value, law and politics, economy and society, policy and administration; to help all kinds of social thought recognize the relevance of facts, problems, interests, and values, of which they would not otherwise take account. Philosophy shared that intellectual responsibility until positivism sterilized it. Must sociology go through the same crisis? And if it must, where will that responsibility be assumed?

We need a jurisprudential sociology, a social science of law that speaks to the problems, and is informed by the ideas, of jurisprudence. Such a sociology recognizes the continuities of analytical, descriptive and evaluative theory. Analytical issues—e.g., the role of coercion in law; the relation of law to the state; the interplay of law and politics; the distinction between law and morality; the place of rules, principles, purpose, and knowledge in legal judgment; the tension between procedural and substantive justice;—are taken as pointing to variable aspects of legal phenomena. The extent to which the law is coercive, vulnerable to politics, purposive, or open to social knowledge, is subject to variations that require empirical inquiry. At the same time, those jurisprudential-sociological variables condition the ends law can pursue, and the resources it can muster to serve those ends. To study such questions as: the kinds of sanctions and remedies that are available to legal institutions; the principles and structures of authority that characterize various legal processes; the way law receives and interprets political and moral values; the administrative resources legal agencies can deploy; the authority of purpose in legal reasoning;—is also to assess the competences and limitations of different kinds of legal orders or legal institutions. Whatever knowledge is gained about these problems should contribute to formulating principles of institutional design, and guides for the diagnosis of institutional troubles.

There is nothing arcane or novel about jurisprudential sociology. In fact, as I pointed out at the beginning of my argument, and as a glance at the index of this Review would confirm, most socio-legal studies are informed by concerns for legal values or legal policy—normative concerns whose rational pursuit would require close observance of the principles of jurisprudential sociology. If the social study of law had remained free to be true to its purposes, and to be responsive to the requirements of its research tasks, all its practitioners would hold the truth of those principles to be self-evident. Unfortunately, since the ascent of bureaucratic orthodoxy in the social sciences, confessing that truth, and resisting the ritual, pseudo-scientific rigors of "pure sociology," exposes one to excommunication, to being expelled out of "the boundaries of legal sociology." The practice of jurisprudential sociology is alive; it has only been driven underground.

Chapter 12

Law and Politics

I. GOVERNING THE GOVERNORS

Wilson, The Bureaucracy Problem*

The federal bureaucracy, whose growth and problems were once only the concern of the Right, has now become a major concern of the Left, the Center, and almost all points in between. Conservatives once feared that a powerful bureaucracy would work a social revolution. The Left now fears that this same bureaucracy is working a conservative reaction. And the Center fears that the bureaucracy isn't working at all.

Increasing federal power has always been seen by conservatives in terms of increasing *bureaucratic* power. If greater federal power merely meant, say, greater uniformity in government regulations—standardized trucking regulations, for example, or uniform professional licensing practices—a substantial segment of American businessmen would probably be pleased. But growing federal power means increased discretion vested in appointive officials whose behavior can neither be antici-

* [From *The Public Interest,* No. 6 (Winter 1967), pp. 3-9. © 1967 by National Affairs, Inc. Reprinted by permission.

James Q. Wilson (1931–　) is Professor of Government at Harvard University. His publications include *Political Organization* (1973), *Thinking About Crime* (1975), and *Varieties of Police Behavior: The Management of Law and Order in Eight Communities* (1968). He is the editor of *Metropolitan Enigma: Inquiries into the Nature and Dimensions of America's Urban Crisis* (1968), and *Urban Renewal: The Record and the Controversy* (1967).]

pated nor controlled. The behavior of state and legal bureaucrats, by contrast, can often be anticipated *because* it can be controlled by businessmen and others.

Knowing this, liberals have always resolved most questions in favor of enhancing federal power. The "hacks" running local administrative agencies were too often, in liberal eyes, the agents of local political and economic forces—businessmen, party bosses, organized professions, and the like. A federal bureaucrat, because he was responsible to a national power center and to a single President elected by a nationwide constituency, could not so easily be bought off by local vested interests; in addition, he would take his policy guidance from a President elected by a process that gave heavy weight to the votes of urban, labor, and minority groups. The New Deal bureaucrats, especially those appointed to the new, "emergency" agencies, were expected by liberals to be free to chart a radically new program and to be competent to direct its implementation.

It was an understandable illusion. It frequently appears in history in the hopes of otherwise intelligent and far-sighted men. Henry II thought his clerks and scribes would help him subdue England's feudal barons; how was he to know that in time they would become the agents of Parliamentary authority directed at stripping the king of his prerogatives? And how were Parliament and its Cabinet ministers, in turn, to know that eventually these permanent undersecretaries would become an almost self-governing class whose day-to-day behavior would become virtually immune to scrutiny or control? Marxists thought that Soviet bureaucrats would work for the people, despite the fact that Max Weber had pointed out why one could be almost certain they would work mostly for themselves. It is ironic that among today's members of the "New Left," the "Leninist problem"—i.e., the problem of over-organization and of self-perpetuating administrative power—should become a major preoccupation.

This apparent agreement among polemicists of the Right and Left that there is a bureaucracy problem accounts, one suspects, for the fact that nonbureaucratic solutions to contemporary problems seem to command support from both groups. The negative income tax as a strategy for dealing with poverty is endorsed by economists of such different persuasions as Milton Friedman and James Tobin, and has received favorable consideration among members of both the Goldwater brain trust and the Students for a Democratic Society. Though the interests of the two groups are somewhat divergent, one common element is a desire to scuttle the social workers and the public welfare bureaucracy, who are usually portrayed as prying busy-bodies with pursed lips and steel-rimmed glasses ordering midnight bedchecks in public housing projects. (Police officers who complain that television makes them look like fools in the eyes of their children will know just what the social workers are going through.)

Now that everybody seems to agree that we ought to do something about the problem of bureaucracy, one might suppose that something would get done. Perhaps a grand reorganization, accompanied by lots of "systems analysis," "citizen participation," "creative federalism," and "interdepartmental coordination." Merely to state this prospect is to deny it.

There is not one bureaucracy problem, there are several, and the solution to each is in some degree incompatible with the solution to every other. First, there is the problem of accountability or control—getting the bureaucracy to serve agreed-on national goals. Second is the problem of equity—getting bureaucrats to treat like cases alike and on the basis of clear rules, known in advance. Third is the problem of efficiency —maximizing output for a given expenditure, or minimizing expenditures for a given output. Fourth is the problem of responsiveness—inducing bureaucrats to meet, with alacrity and compassion, those cases which can never be brought under a single national rule and which, by common human standards of justice or benevolence, seem to require that an exception be made or a rule stretched. Fifth is the problem of fiscal integrity—properly spending and accounting for public money.

Each of these problems mobilizes a somewhat different segment of the public. The problem of power is the unending preoccupation of the President and his staff, especially during the first years of an administration. Equity concerns the lawyers and the courts, though increasingly the Supreme Court seems to act as if it thinks its job is to help set national goals as a kind of auxiliary White House. Efficiency has traditionally been the concern of businessmen who thought, mistakenly, that an efficient government was one that didn't spend very much money. (Of late, efficiency has come to have a broader and more accurate meaning as an optimal relationship between objectives and resources. Robert McNamara has shown that an "efficient" Department of Defense costs a lot more money than an "inefficient" one; his disciples are now carrying the message to all parts of a skeptical federal establishment.) Responsiveness has been the concern of individual citizens and of their political representatives, usually out of wholly proper motives, but sometimes out of corrupt ones. Congress, especially, has tried to retain some power over the bureaucracy by intervening on behalf of tens of thousands of immigrants, widows, businessmen, and mothers-of-soldiers, hoping that the collective effect of many individual interventions would be a bureaucracy that, on large matters as well as small, would do Congress's will.

973

(Since Congress only occasionally has a clear will, this strategy only works occasionally.) Finally, fiscal integrity—especially its absence—is the concern of the political "outs" who want to get in and thus it becomes the concern of "ins" who want to keep them out.

Obviously the more a bureaucracy is responsive to its clients—whether those clients are organized by radicals into Mothers for Adequate Welfare or represented by Congressmen anxious to please constituents—the less it can be accountable to presidential directives. Similarly, the more equity, the less responsiveness. And a preoccupation with fiscal integrity can make the kind of program budgeting required by enthusiasts of efficiency difficult, if not impossible.

Indeed, of all the groups interested in bureaucracy, those concerned with fiscal integrity usually play the winning hand. To be efficient, one must have clearly stated goals, but goals are often hard to state at all, much less clearly. To be responsive, one must be willing to run risks, and the career civil service is not ordinarily attractive to people with a taste for risk. Equity is an abstraction, of concern for the most part only to people who haven't been given any. Accountability is "politics," and the bureaucracy itself is the first to resist that (unless, of course, it is the kind of politics that produces pay raises and greater job security). But an absence of fiscal integrity is welfare chiseling, sweetheart deals, windfall profits, conflict of interest, malfeasance in high places—in short, corruption. Everybody recognizes *that* when he sees it, and none but a few misguided academics have anything good to say about it. As a result, fiscal scandal typically becomes the standard by which a bureaucracy is judged (the FBI is good because it hasn't had any, the Internal Revenue Service is bad because it has) and thus the all-consuming fear of responsible executives.

If it is this hard to make up one's mind about how one wants the bureaucracy to behave, one might be forgiven if one threw up one's hands and let nature take its course. Though it may come to that in the end, it is possible—and important—to begin with a resolution to face the issue squarely and try to think through the choices. Facing the issue means admitting what, in our zeal for new programs, we usually ignore: *There are inherent limits to what can be accomplished by large hierarchical organizations.*

The opposite view is more often in vogue. If enough people don't like something, it becomes a problem; if the intellectuals agree with them, it becomes a crisis; any crisis must be solved; if it must be solved, then it can be solved—and creating a new organization is the way to do it. If the organization fails to solve the problem (and when the problem is a fundamental one, it will almost surely fail), then the reason is "politics," or "mismanagement," or "incompetent people," or "meddling," or "socialism," or "inertia."

Some problems cannot be solved and some government functions cannot, in principle, be done well. Notwithstanding, the effort must often be made. The rule of reason should be to try to do as few undoable things as possible. It is regrettable, for example, that any country must have a foreign office, since none can have a good one. The reason is simple: it is literally impossible to have a "policy" with respect to *all* relevant matters concerning *all* foreign countries, much less a consistent and reasonable policy. And the difficulty increases with the square of the number of countries, and probably with the cube of the speed of communications. The problem long ago became insoluble and any sensible Secretary of State will cease trying to solve it. He will divide his time instead between *ad hoc* responses to the crisis of the moment and appearances on Meet the Press.

The answer is not, it must be emphasized, one of simply finding good people, though it is at least that. Most professors don't think much of the State Department, but it is by no means clear that a department made up only of professors would be any better, and some reason to believe that it would be worse. One reason is that bringing in "good outsiders," especially good outsiders from universities, means bringing in men with little experience in dealing with the substantive problem but many large ideas about how to approach problems "in general." General ideas, no matter how soundly based in history or social science, rarely tell one what to do tomorrow about the visit from the foreign trade mission from Ruritania or the questions from the Congressional appropriations subcommittee.

Another reason is that good people are in very short supply, even assuming we knew how to recognize them. Some things literally cannot be done—or cannot be done well—because there is no one available to do them who knows how. *The supply of able, experienced executives is not increasing nearly as fast as the number of problems being addressed by public policy.* All the fellowships, internships, and "mid-career training programs" in the world aren't likely to increase that supply very much, simply because the essential qualities for an executive—judgment about men and events, a facility for making good guesses, a sensitivity to political realities, and an ability to motivate others—are things which, if they can be taught at all, cannot be taught systematically or to more than a handful of apprentices at one time.

This constraint deserves emphasis, for it is rarely recognized as a constraint at all. Anyone who opposed a bold new program on the grounds that there was nobody around able to run it would be accused of being a pettifogger at best and a reactionary do-nothing at worst. Everywhere except in government, it seems, the scarcity of talent is accepted as a fact of life. Nobody (or almost nobody) thinks seriously of setting up a great new university overnight, because anybody familiar with the university business knows that, for almost any professorship one would want to fill, there are rarely more than five (if that) really top-flight people in the country, and they are all quite happy—and certainly well-paid—right where they are. Lots of new business ideas don't become profit-making realities because good business executives are both hard to find and expensive to hire. The government—at least publicly—seems to act as if the supply of able political executives were infinitely elastic, though people setting up new agencies will often admit privately that they are so frustrated and appalled by the shortage of talent that the only wonder is why disaster is so long in coming. Much would be gained if this constraint were mentioned to Congress *before* the bill is passed and the hopes aroused, instead of being mentioned afterward as an excuse for failure or as a reason why higher pay scales for public servants are an urgent necessity. "Talent is Scarcer Than Money" should be the motto of the Budget Bureau.

If administrative feasibility is such a critical issue, what can be done about it? Not a great deal. If the bureaucracy problem is a major reason why so many programs are in trouble, it is also a reason why the problem itself cannot be "solved." But it can be mitigated—though not usually through the kinds of expedients we are fond of trying: Hoover Commissions, management studies, expensive consultants, co-ordinating committees, "czars," and the like. The only point at which very much leverage can be gained on the problem *is when we decide what it is we are trying to accomplish.* When we define our goals, we are implicitly deciding how much, or how little, of a bureaucracy problem we are going to have. A program with clear objectives, clearly stated, is a program with a fighting chance of coping with each of the many aspects of the bureaucracy problem. Controlling an agency is easier when you know what you want. Equity is more likely to be assured when over-all objectives can be stated, at least in part, in general rules to which people in and out of the agency are asked to conform. Efficiency is made possible when you know what you are buying with your money. Responsiveness is never easy or wholly desirable; if every person were treated in accordance with his special needs, there would be no program at all. (The only system that meets the responsiveness problem squarely is the free market.) But at least with clear objectives we would know what we are giving up in those cases when responsiveness seems necessary, and thus we would be able to decide how much we are willing to tolerate. And fiscal integrity is just as easy to insure in a system with clear objectives as in one with fuzzy ones;

in the former case, moreover, we are less likely to judge success simply in terms of avoiding scandal. We might even be willing to accept a little looseness if we knew what we were getting for it.

The rejoinder to this argument is that there are many government functions which, by their nature, can never have clear objectives. I hope I have made it obvious by now that I am aware of that. We can't stop dealing with foreign nations just because we don't know what we want; after all, they may know what *they* want, and we had better find out. My argument is advanced, not as a panacea—there is no way to avoid the problem of administration—but as a guide to choice in those cases where choice is open to us, and as a criterion by which to evaluate proposals for coping with the bureaucracy problem.

Dealing with poverty—at least in part—by giving people money seems like an obvious strategy. Governments are very good at taking money from one person and giving it to another; the goals are not particularly difficult to state; measures are available to evaluate how well we are doing in achieving a predetermined income distribution. There may be many things wrong with this approach, but administrative difficulty is not one of them. And yet, paradoxically, it is the last approach we will probably try. We will try everything else first—case work, counseling, remedial education, community action, federally financed mass protests to end "alienation," etc. And whatever else might be said in their favor, the likelihood of smooth administration and ample talent can hardly be included.

Both the White House and the Congress seem eager to do something about the bureaucracy problem. All too often, however, the problem is described in terms of "digesting" the "glut" of new federal programs—as if solving administrative difficulties had something in common with treating heartburn. Perhaps those seriously concerned with this issue will put themselves on notice that they ought not to begin with the pain and reach for some administrative bicarbonate of soda; they ought instead to begin with what was swallowed and ask whether an emetic is necessary. *Coping with the bureaucracy problem is inseparable from rethinking the objectives of the programs in question.* Administrative reshuffling, budgetary cuts (or budgetary increases), and congressional investigation of lower-level boondoggling will not suffice and are likely, unless there are some happy accidents, to make matters worse. Thinking clearly about goals is a tough assignment for a political system that has been held together in great part by compromise, ambiguity, and contradiction. And if a choice must be made, any reasonable person would, I think, prefer the system to the clarity. But now that we have decided to intervene in such a wide range of human affairs, perhaps we ought to reassess that particular trade-off.

Wright, Beyond Discretionary Justice

See page 328 supra.

Rostow, The Democratic Character of Judicial Review*

A theme of uneasiness, and even of guilt, colors the literature about judicial review. Many of those who have talked, lectured, and written about the Constitution have been troubled by a sense that judicial review is undemocratic. Why should a majority of nine Justices appointed for life be permitted to outlaw as unconstitutional the acts of elected officials or of officers controlled by elected officials? Judicial review, they have urged, is an undemocratic shoot on an otherwise respectable tree. It should be cut off, or at least kept pruned and inconspicuous. The attack has gone further. Reliance on bad political doctrine, they say, has produced bad political results. The strength of the courts has weakened other parts of the government. The judicial censors are accused of causing laxness and irresponsibility in the state and national legislatures, and political apathy in the electorate. At the same time, we are warned, the participation of the courts in this essentially political function will inevitably lead to the destruction of their independence and thus compromise all other aspects of their work.

I

The idea that judicial review is undemocratic is not an academic issue of political philosophy. Like most abstractions, it has far-reaching practical consequences. I suspect that for some judges it is the mainspring of decision, inducing them in many cases to uphold legislative and executive action which would otherwise have been condemned. Par-

* [66 *Harv. L. Rev.* 193-200 (1952). Copyright 1952 by The Harvard Law Review Association. Reprinted by permission.

Eugene V. Rostow (1913–) was educated at Yale University (A.B. 1933; LL.B. 1937) and Cambridge University (M.A. 1959; LL.D. 1962). After two years in private practice in New York City, Rostow began his academic career at Yale in 1938. He has served in several government positions, most recently as Under Secretary of State for Political Affairs (1966-1969). He was Dean of the Yale University School of Law (1955-1965). His works include *Law, Power, and the Pursuit of Peace* (1968); *Planning for Freedom* (1959); *Sovereign Prerogative* (1962); *Is Law Dead* (ed. 1971); and *Peace in the Balance* (1972).]

ticularly in the multiple opinions of recent years, the Supreme Court's self-searching often boils down to a debate within the bosoms of the Justices over the appropriateness of judicial review itself.

The attack on judicial review as undemocratic rests on the premise that the Constitution should be allowed to grow without a judicial check. The proponents of this view would have the Constitution mean what the President, the Congress, and the state legislatures say it means.[2] In this way, they contend, the electoral process would determine the course of constitutional development, as it does in countries with plenipotentiary parliaments.

But the Constitution of the United States does not establish a parliamentary government, and attempts to interpret American government in a parliamentary perspective break down in confusion or absurdity. One may recall, in another setting, the anxious voice of the *Washington Post* urging President Truman to resign because the Republican Party had won control of the Congress in the 1946 elections.

It is a grave oversimplification to contend that no society can be democratic unless its legislature has sovereign powers. The social quality of democracy cannot be defined by so rigid a formula. Government and politics are after all the arms, not the end, of social life. The purpose of the Constitution is to assure the people a free and democratic society. The final aim of that society is as much freedom as possible for the individual human being. The Constitution provides society with a mechanism of government fully competent to its task, but by no means universal in its powers. The power to govern is parcelled out between the states and the nation and is further divided among the three main branches of all governmental units. By custom as well as constitutional practice, many vital aspects of community life are beyond the direct reach of government—for example, religion, the press, and, until recently at any rate, many phases of educational and cultural activity. The separation of powers under the Constitution serves the end of democracy in society by limiting the roles of the several branches of government and protecting the citizen, and the various parts of the state itself, against encroach-

2. Many writers have distinguished the authority of the Supreme Court to deny effect to an unconstitutional act of the Congress or the President from its duty under Article VI to declare unconstitutional provisions of state constitutions or statutes, although Article VI declares even federal statutes to be "the supreme Law of the Land" only when made in pursuance of the Constitution. Holmes, Law and the Court, in *Collected Legal Papers* 291, 295-96 (1920); Jackson, *The Struggle for Judicial Supremacy* 15 et seq. (1941); Thayer, The Origin and Scope of the American Doctrine of Constitutional Law, in *Legal Essays* 1, 35-41 (1908); Thayer, *John Marshall* 61-65 (1901); Haines, *The American Doctrine of Judicial Supremacy* 131-35, 511-12 (2d ed. 1932).

ments from any source. The root idea of the Constitution is that man can be free because the state is not.

The power of constitutional review, to be exercised by some part of the government, is implicit in the conception of a written constitution delegating limited powers. A written constitution would promote discord rather than order in society if there were no accepted authority to construe it, at the least in cases of conflicting action by different branches of government or of constitutionally unauthorized governmental action against individuals. The limitation and separation of powers, if they are to survive, require a procedure for independent mediation and construction to reconcile the inevitable disputes over the boundaries of constitutional power which arise in the process of government. British Dominions operating under written constitutions have had to face the task pretty much as we have, and they have solved it in similar ways. Like institutions have developed in other federal systems.

So far as the American Constitution is concerned, there can be little real doubt that the courts were intended from the beginning to have the power they have exercised. The Federalist Papers are unequivocal; the Debates as clear as debates normally are. The power of judicial review was commonly exercised by the courts of the states, and the people were accustomed to judicial construction of the authority derived from colonial charters.[3] Constitutional interpretation by the courts, Hamilton said, does not

by any means suppose a superiority of the judicial to the legislative power. It only supposes that the power of the people is superior to both; and that where the will of the legislature, declared in its statutes, stands in opposition to that of the people, declared in the Constituition, the judges ought to be governed by the latter rather than the former. They ought to regulate their decisions by the fundamental laws, rather than by those which are not fundamental.[4]

Hamilton's statement is sometimes criticized as a verbal legalism.[5] But it has an advantage too. For much of the discussion has complicated the problem without clarifying it. Both judges and their critics have

3. The evidence is reviewed in Thayer, The Origin and Scope of the American Doctrine of Constitutional Law, in *Legal Essays* 1, 3-7 (1908); Beard, *The Supreme Court and the Constitution* (1912); and Haines, op. cit. supra note 2, at 44-59, 88-121. A useful bibliography appears in Dodd, *Cases on Constitutional Law* 8-18 (3d ed. 1941).

4. *The Federalist*, No. 78 at 506 (Modern Library ed. 1937).

5. See Thayer, *John Marshall* 96 (1901); Thayer, The Origin and Scope of the American Doctrine of Constitutional Law, in *Legal Essays*, 1, 12-15 (1908); Haines, op. cit. supra note 2, at 518-27.

wrapped themselves so successfully in the difficulties of particular cases that they have been able to evade the ultimate issue posed in the Federalist Papers.

Whether another method of enforcing the Constitution could have been devised, the short answer is that no such method has developed. The argument over the constitutionality of judicial review has long since been settled by history. The power and duty of the Supreme Court to declare statutes or executive action unconstitutional in appropriate cases is part of the living Constitution. "The course of constitutional history," Mr. Justice Frankfurter . . . remarked, has cast responsibilities upon the Supreme Court which it would be "stultification" for it to evade.[6] The Court's power has been exercised differently at different times: sometimes with reckless and doctrinaire enthusiasm; sometimes with great deference to the status and responsibilities of other branches of the government; sometimes with a degree of weakness and timidity that comes close to the betrayal of trust. But the power exists, as an integral part of the process of American government. The Court has the duty of interpreting the Constitution in many of its most important aspects, and especially in those which concern the relations of the individual and the state. The political proposition underlying the survival of the power is that there are some phases of American life which should be beyond the reach of any majority, save by constitutional amendment. In Mr. Justice Jackson's phrase, "One's right to life, liberty, and property, to free speech, a free press, freedom of worship and assembly, and other fundamental rights may not be submitted to vote; they depend on the outcome of no elections."[7] Whether or not this was the intention of the Founding Fathers, the unwritten Constitution is unmistakable.

If one may use a personal definition of the crucial word, this way of policing the Constitution is not undemocratic. True, it employs appointed officials, to whom large powers are irrevocably delegated. But democracies need not elect all the officers who exercise crucial authority in the name of the voters. Admirals and generals can win or lose wars in the exercise of their discretion. The independence of judges in the administration of justice has been the pride of communities which aspire to be free. Members of the Federal Reserve Board have the lawful power to plunge the country into depression or inflation. The list could readily be extended. Government by referendum or town meeting is not the only possible form of democracy. The task of democracy is not to have the people vote directly on every issue, but to assure their ultimate responsi-

6. Rochin v. California, 342 U.S. 165, 173 (1952).
7. West Virginia State Board of Educ. v. Barnette, 319 U.S. 624, 638 (1943).

bility for the acts of their representatives, elected or appointed. For judges deciding ordinary litigation, the ultimate responsibility of the electorate has a special meaning. It is a responsibility for the quality of the judges and for the substance of their instructions, never a responsibility for their decisions in particular cases. It is hardly characteristic of law in democratic society to encourage bills of attainder, or to allow appeals from the courts in particular cases to legislatures or to mobs. Where the judges are carrying out the function of constitutional review, the final responsibility of the people is appropriately guaranteed by the provisions for amending the Constitution itself, and by the benign influence of time, which changes the personnel of courts. Given the possibility of constitutional amendment, there is nothing undemocratic in having responsible and independent judges act as important constitutional mediators. Within the narrow limits of their capacity to act, their great task is to help maintain a pluralist equilibrium in society. They can do much to keep it from being dominated by the states or the Federal Government, by Congress or the President, by the purse or the sword.

In the execution of this crucial but delicate function, constitutional review by the judiciary has an advantage thoroughly recognized in both theory and practice. The power of the courts, however final, can only be asserted in the course of litigation. Advisory opinions are forbidden, and reefs of self-limitation have grown up around the doctrine that the courts will determine constitutional questions only in cases of actual controversy, when no lesser ground of decision is available, and when the complaining party would be directly and personally injured by the assertion of the power deemed unconstitutional. Thus the check of judicial review upon the elected branches of government must be a mild one, limited not only by the detachment, integrity, and good sense of the Justices, but by the structural boundaries implicit in the fact that the power is entrusted to the courts. Judicial review is inherently adapted to preserving broad and flexible lines of constitutional growth, not to operating as a continuously active factor in legislative or executive decisions.

The division and separation of governmental powers within the American federal system provides the community with ample power to act, without compromising its pluralist structure. The Constitution formalizes the principle that a wide dispersal of authority among the institutions of society is the safest foundation for social freedom. It was accepted from the beginning that the judiciary would be one of the chief agencies for enforcing the restraints of the Constitution. In a letter to Madison, Jefferson remarked of the Bill of Rights:

> In the arguments in favor of a declaration of rights, you omit one which
> has great weight with me; the legal check which it puts into the hands of

the judiciary. This is a body, which, if rendered independent and kept strictly to their own department, merits great confidence for their learning and integrity. In fact, what degree of confidence would be too much, for a body composed of such men as Wythe, Blair and Pendleton? On characters like these, the *"civium ardor prava pubentium"* would make no impression.[8]

Jefferson, indeed, went further. He regretted the absence in the Constitution of a direct veto power over legislation entrusted to the judiciary, and wished that no legislation could take effect for a year after its final enactment.[9] Within such constitutional limits, Jefferson believed, American society could best achieve its goal of responsible self-government. "I have no fear," he wrote, "but that the result of our experiment will be, that men may be trusted to govern themselves without a master."[10]

Democracy is a slippery term. I shall make no effort at a formal definition here. Certainly as a matter of historical fact some societies with parliamentary governments have been and are "democratic" by standards which Americans would accept, although it is worth noting that almost all of them employ second chambers, with powers at least of delay, and indirect devices for assuring continuity in the event of a parliamentary collapse, either through the crown or some equivalent institution, like the presidency in France. But it would be scholastic pedantry to define democracy in such a way as to deny the title of "democrat" to Jefferson, Madison, Lincoln, Brandeis, and others who have found the American constitutional system, including its tradition of judicial review, well adapted to the needs of a free society.[11] As Mr. Justice Brandeis said,

> the doctrine of the separation of powers was adopted by the Convention of 1787, not to promote efficiency but to preclude the exercise of arbitrary power. The purpose was, not to avoid friction, but, by means of

8. Jefferson, *Life and Selected Writings* 462 (Modern Library ed. 1944). This passage, Griswold comments, "suggests that while [Jefferson] relied on the Court to safeguard the Bill of Rights, he was also counting on the bill to ensure a long-run democratic tendency on the part of the Court. History has borne out the acumen of this thought. . . . The Court's vested responsibility for our civil liberties has kept it anchored to democratic fundamentals through all kinds of political weather." A. W. Griswold, Jefferson's Republic—The Rediscovery of Democratic Philosophy, *Fortune,* April, 1950, p. 111, at 130. Later in life, of course, Jefferson strongly differed with many of the decisions and opinions of the Supreme Court and expressed his disagreement in terms which sometimes seemed to repudiate the constitutionality of judicial review itself.

9. Jefferson, *Life and Selected Writings* 437, 441, 460 (Modern Library ed. 1944).

10. 6 *The Writings of Thomas Jefferson* 151 (Lipscomb and Bergh ed. 1904).

11. See, e.g., Lincoln, First Inaugural Address, in 6 *Messages and Papers of the Presidents* 5-12 (Richardson ed. 1897); Wilson, *Constitutional Government in the United States* c. 6 (1911).

the inevitable friction incident to the distribution of governmental powers among three departments, to save the people from autocracy.[12]

It is error to insist that no society is democratic unless it has a government of unlimited powers, and that no government is democratic unless its legislature has unlimited powers. Constitutional review by an independent judiciary is a tool of proven use in the American quest for an open society of widely dispersed powers. In a vast country, of mixed population, with widely different regional problems, such an organization of society is the surest base for the hopes of democracy.

Bickel, The Least Dangerous Branch*

The Counter-Majoritarian Difficulty

The root difficulty is that judicial review is a counter-majoritarian force in our system. There are various ways of sliding over this ineluctable reality. Marshall did so when he spoke of enforcing, in behalf of "the people," the limits that they have ordained for the institutions of a limited government. And it has been done ever since in much the same fashion by all too many commentators. Marshall himself followed Hamilton, who in the 78th *Federalist* denied that judicial review implied a superiority of the judicial over the legislative power—denied, in other words, that judicial review constituted control by an unrepresentative minority of an elected majority. "It only supposes," Hamilton went on, "that the power of the people is superior to both; and that where the will of the legislature, declared in its statutes, stands in opposition to that of the people, declared in the Constitution, the judges ought to be governed by the latter rather than the former." But the word "people" so used is an abstraction. Not necessarily a meaningless or a pernicious one by any means; always charged with emotion, but nonrepresentational—

---

12. Myers v. United States, 272 U.S. 52, 293 (1926) (dissenting opinion).

* [Pp. 16-28 (1962). From *The Least Dangerous Branch* by Alexander M. Bickel, copyright © by The Bobbs-Merrill Company, Inc., reprinted by permission of the publisher.

Alexander M. Bickel (1924-1974) was educated at the City College of New York (B.S. 1947) and Harvard University (LL.B. 1949). He was Law Clerk to Justice Felix Frankfurter, United States Supreme Court (1952-1953), and served in various other governmental positions from 1949 until he became a Research Associate at Harvard in 1954. In 1956 Bickel left Harvard to join the faculty of Yale Law School. He became Chancellor Kent Professor of Law and Legal History in 1966. He is the author of numerous influential works, including *The Least Dangerous Branch—The Supreme Court at the Bar of Politics* (1962), *Politics and the Warren Court* (1965), and *Reform and Continuity* (1971).]

an abstraction obscuring the reality that when the Supreme Court declares unconstitutional a legislative act or the action of an elected executive, it thwarts the will of representatives of the actual people of the here and now, it exercises control, not in behalf of the prevailing majority, but against it. That, without mystic overtones, is what actually happens. It is an altogether different kettle of fish, and it is the reason the charge can be made that judicial review is undemocratic.

Most assuredly, no democracy operates by taking continuous nose counts on the broad range of daily governmental activities. Representative democracies—that is to say, all working democracies—function by electing certain men for certain periods of time, then passing judgment periodically on their conduct of public office. It is a matter of a laying on of hands, followed in time by a process of holding to account—all through the exercise of the franchise. The elected officials, however, are expected to delegate some of their tasks to men of their own appointment, who are not directly accountable at the polls. The whole operates under public scrutiny and criticism—but not at all times or in all parts. What we mean by democracy, therefore, is much more sophisticated and complex than the making of decisions in town meeting by a show of hands. It is true also that even decisions that have been submitted to the electoral process in some fashion are not continually resubmitted, and they are certainly not continually unmade. Once run through the process, once rendered by "the people" (using the term now in its mystic sense, because the reference is to the people in the past), myriad decisions remain to govern the present and the future despite what may well be fluctuating majorities against them at any given time. A high value is put on stability, and that is also a counter-majoritarian factor. Nevertheless, although democracy does not mean constant reconsideration of decisions once made, it does mean that a representative majority has the power to accomplish a reversal. This power is of the essence, and no less so because it is often merely held in reserve.

I am aware that this timid assault on the complexities of the American democratic system has yet left us with a highly simplistic statement, and I shall briefly rehearse some of the reasons. But nothing in the further complexities and perplexities of the system, which modern political science has explored with admirable and ingenious industry, and some of which it has tended to multiply with a fertility that passes the mere zeal of the discoverer—nothing in these complexities can alter the essential reality that judicial review is a deviant institution in the American democracy.

It is true, of course, that the process of reflecting the will of a popular majority in the legislature is deflected by various inequalities of representation and by all sorts of institutional habits and characteristics, which perhaps tend most often in favor of inertia. Yet it must be remembered that statutes are the product of the legislature and the executive acting in concert, and that the executive represents a very different constituency and thus tends to cure inequities of over- and underrepresentation. Reflecting a balance of forces in society for purposes of stable and effective government is more intricate and less certain than merely assuring each citizen his equal vote. Moreover, impurities and imperfections, if such they be, in one part of the system are no argument for total departure from the desired norm in another part. A much more important complicating factor—first adumbrated by Madison in the 10th *Federalist* and lately emphasized by Professor David B. Truman and others[13] —is the proliferation and power of what Madison foresaw as "faction," what Mr. Truman calls "groups," and what in popular parlance has always been deprecated as the "interests" or the "pressure groups."

No doubt groups operate forcefully on the electoral process, and no doubt they seek and gain access to an effective share in the legislative and executive decisional process. Perhaps they constitute also, in some measure, an impurity or imperfection. But no one has claimed that they have been able to capture the governmental process except by combining in some fashion, and thus capturing or constituting (are not the two verbs synonymous?) a majority. They often tend themselves to be majoritarian in composition and to be subject to broader majoritarian influences. And the price of what they sell or buy in the legislature is determined in the biennial or quadrennial electoral marketplace. It may be, as Professor Robert A. Dahl has written, that elections themselves, and the political competition that renders them meaningful, "do not make for government by majorities in any very significant way," for they do not establish a great many policy preferences. However, "they are a crucial device for controlling leaders." And if the control is exercised by "groups of various types and sizes, all seeking in various ways to advance their goals," so that we have "minorities rule" rather than majority rule, it remains true nevertheless that only those minorities rule which can command the votes of a majority of individuals in the legislature who can command the votes of a majority of individuals in the electorate. In one fashion or another, both in the legislative process and at elections, the minorities must coalesce into a majority. Although, as Mr. Dahl says, "it is fashionable in some quarters to suggest that everything believed about democratic politics prior to World War I, and perhaps World War

13. See D. B. Truman, *The Governmental Process* (New York: Knopf, 1951).

II, was nonsense," he makes no bones about his own belief that "the radical democrats who, unlike Madison, insist upon the decisive importance of the election process in the whole grand strategy of democracy are essentially correct."[14]

The insights of Professor Truman and other writers into the role that groups play in our society and our politics have a bearing on judicial review. They indicate that there are other means than the electoral process, though subordinate and subsidiary ones, of making institutions of government responsive to the needs and wishes of the governed. Hence one may infer that judicial review, although not responsible, may have ways of being responsive. But nothing can finally depreciate the central function that is assigned in democratic theory and practice to the electoral process; nor can it be denied that the policy-making power of representative institutions, born of the electoral process, is the distinguishing characteristic of the system. Judicial review works counter to this characteristic.

It therefore does not follow from the complex nature of a democratic system that, because admirals and generals and the members, say, of the Federal Reserve Board or of this or that administrative agency are not electorally responsible, judges who exercise the power of judicial review need not be responsible either, and in neither case is there a serious conflict with democratic theory.[15] For admirals and generals and the like are most often responsible to officials who are themselves elected and through whom the line runs directly to a majority. What is more significant, the policies they make are or should be interstitial or technical only and are reversible by legislative majorities. Thus, so long as there has been a meaningful delegation by the legislature to administrators, which is kept within proper bounds, the essential majority power is there, and it is felt to be there—a fact of great consequence. Nor will it do to liken judicial review to the general lawmaking function of judges. In the latter aspect, judges are indeed something like administrative officials, for their decisions are also reversible by any legislative majority—and not infrequently they are reversed. Judicial review, however, is the power to apply and construe the Constitution, in matters of the greatest moment, against the wishes of a legislative majority, which is, in turn, powerless to affect the judicial decision.

14. R. A. Dahl, *A Preface to Democratic Theory* (Chicago: University of Chicago Press, 1956), pp. 125, 132. (Copyright 1956 by the University of Chicago.)

15. See E. V. Rostow, "The Democratic Character of Judicial Review," 66 *Harvard Law Review* 193, 195 (1952).

"For myself," said the late Judge Learned Hand,

> it would be most irksome to be ruled by a bevy of Platonic Guardians, even if I knew how to choose them, which I assuredly do not. If they were in charge, I should miss the stimulus of living in a society where I have, at least theoretically, some part in the direction of public affairs. Of course I know how illusory would be the belief that my vote determined anything; but nevertheless when I go to the polls I have a satisfaction in the sense that we are all engaged in a common venture. If you retort that a sheep in the flock may feel something like it; I reply, following Saint Francis, "My brother, the Sheep."[16]

This suggests not only the democratic value that inheres in obtaining the broad judgment of a majority of the people in the community and thus tending to produce better decisions. Judge Hand, if anything, rather deprecated the notion that the decisions will be better, or are affected at all. Some might think that he deprecated it beyond what is either just or realistic when he said that the belief that his vote determined anything was illusory. Hardly altogether. But the strong emphasis is on the related idea that coherent, stable—and *morally supportable*—government is possible only on the basis of consent, and that the secret of consent is the sense of common venture fostered by institutions that reflect and represent us and that we can call to account.

It has been suggested[17] that the Congress, the President, the states, and the people (in the sense of current majorities) have from the beginning and in each generation acquiesced in, and thus consented to, the exercise of judicial review by the Supreme Court. In the first place, it is said that the Amending Clause of the Constitution has been employed to reverse the work of the Court only twice, perhaps three times; and it has never been used to take away or diminish the Court's power. But the Amending Clause itself incorporates an extreme minority veto. The argument then proceeds to draw on the first Judiciary Act, whose provisions regarding the jurisdiction of the federal courts have been continued in effect to this day. Yet we have seen that the Judiciary Act can be read as a grant of the power to declare federal statutes unconstitutional only on the basis of a previously and independently reached conclusion that such a power must exist. And even if the Judiciary Act did grant this power, as it surely granted the power to declare state actions unconstitu-

16. L. Hand, *The Bill of Rights* (Cambridge: Harvard University Press, 1958), pp. 73-74.

17. See, e.g., C. L. Black, Jr. *The People and the Court* (New York: Macmillan, 1960), pp. 23 et seq., 210 et seq.

tional, it amounted to an expression of the opinion of the first Congress that the Constitution implies judicial review. It is, in fact, extremely likely that the first Congress thought so. That is important; but it merely adds to the historical evidence on the point, which, as we have seen, is in any event quite strong. Future Congresses and future generations can only be said to have acquiesced in the belief of the first Congress that the Constitution implies this power. And they can be said to have become resigned to what follows, which is that the power can be taken away only by constitutional amendment. That is a very far cry from consent to the power on its merits, as a power freely continued by the decision or acquiescence of a majority in each generation. The argument advances not a step toward justification of the power on other than historical grounds.

A further, crucial difficulty must also be faced. Besides being a counter-majoritarian check on the legislature and the executive, judicial review may, in a larger sense, have a tendency over time seriously to weaken the democratic process. Judicial review expresses, of course, a form of distrust of the legislature. "The legislatures," wrote James Bradley Thayer at the turn of the century,

> are growing accustomed to this distrust and more and more readily inclined to justify it, and to shed the considerations of constitutional restraints,—certainly as concerning the extract extent of these restrictions,—turning that subject over to the courts; and what is worse, they insensibly fall into a habit of assuming that whatever they could constitutionally do they may do,—as if honor and fair dealing and common honesty were not relevant to their inquiries. The people, all this while, become careless as to whom they send to the legislature; too often they cheerfully vote for men whom they would not trust with an important private affair, and when these unfit persons are found to pass foolish and bad laws, and the courts step in and disregard them, the people are glad that these few wiser gentlemen on the bench are so ready to protect them against their more immediate representatives. . . . [I]t should be remembered that the exercise of it [the power of judicial review], even when unavoidable, is always attended with a serious evil, namely, that the correction of legislative mistakes comes from the outside, and the people thus lose the political experience, and the moral education and stimulus that comes from fighting the question out in the ordinary way, and correcting their own errors. The tendency of a common and easy resort to this great function, now lamentably too common, is to dwarf the political capacity of the people, and to deaden its sense of moral responsibility. It is no light thing to do that.[18]

18. J. B. Thayer, *John Marshall* (Boston: Houghton Mifflin, 1901), pp. 103-104, 106-107.

To this day, in how many hundreds of occasions does Congress enact a measure that it deems expedient, having essayed consideration of its constitutionality (that is to say, of its acceptability on principle), only to abandon the attempt in the declared confidence that the Court will correct errors of principle, if any? It may well be, as has been suggested,[19] that any lowering of the level of legislative performance is attributable to many factors other than judicial review. Yet there is no doubt that what Thayer observed remains observable. It seemed rather a puzzle, for example, to a scholar who recently compared British and American practices of legislative investigation. Professor Herman Finer wrote, with what might have seemed to Thayer charming ingenuousness:

> Is it not a truly extraordinary phenomenon that in the United States, where Congress is not a sovereign body, but subordinate to a constitution, there appear to be less restraints upon the arbitrary behavior of members in their . . . rough handling of the civil rights of the citizen during investigations. . . ? Though Parliament is sovereign and can legally do anything it likes, its practices are kinder, more restrained, and less invasive of the rights of those who come under its investigative attention. The student is forced to pause and reflect upon this remarkable reversal of demeanor and status.[20]

Finally, another, though related, contention has been put forward. It is that judicial review runs so fundamentally counter to democratic theory that in a society which in all other respects rests on that theory, judicial review cannot ultimately be effective. We pay the price of a grave inner contradiction in the basic principle of our government, which is an inconvenience and a dangerous one; and in the end to no good purpose, for when the great test comes, judicial review will be unequal to it. The most arresting expression of this thought is in a famous passage from a speech of Judge Learned Hand, a passage, Dean Eugene V. Rostow has written, "of Browningesque passion and obscurity," voicing a "gloomy and apocalyptic view."[21] Absent the institution of judicial review, Judge Hand said:

> I do not think that anyone can say what will be left of those [fundamental principles of equity and fair play which our constitutions enshrine]; I do not know whether they will serve only as counsels; but this much I think I do know—that a society so riven that the spirit of moderation is

19. See Rostow, op. cit. supra n. 15, at p. 201.
20. H. Finer, "Congressional Investigations: The British System," 18 *University of Chicago Law Review* 521, 522 (1951).
21. Rostow, op. cit. supra n. 15, at p. 205.

gone, no court *can* save; that a society where that spirit flourishes, no court *need* save; that in a society which evades its responsibility by thrusting upon the courts the nurture of that spirit, that spirit in the end will perish.[22]

Over a century before Judge Hand spoke, Judge Gibson of Pennsylvania, in his day perhaps the ablest opponent of the establishment of judicial review, wrote: "Once let public opinion be so corrupt as to sanction every misconstruction of the Constitution and abuse of power which the temptation of the moment may dictate, and the party which may happen to be predominant will laugh at the puny efforts of a dependent power to arrest it in its course."[23] And Thayer also believed that "under no system can the power of courts go far to save a people from ruin; our chief protection lies elsewhere."[24]

The Moral Approval of the Lines: Principle

Such, in outline, are the chief doubts that must be met if the doctrine of judicial review is to be justified on principle. Of course, these doubts will apply with lesser or greater force to various forms of the exercise of the power. For the moment the discussion is at wholesale, and we are seeking a justification on principle, quite aside from supports in history and the continuity of practice. The search must be for a function which might (indeed, must) involve the making of policy, yet which differs from the legislative and executive functions; which is peculiarly suited to the capabilities of the courts; which will not likely be performed elsewhere if the courts do not assume it; which can be so exercised as to be acceptable in a society that generally shares Judge Hand's satisfaction in a "sense of common venture"; which will be effective when needed; and whose discharge by the courts will not lower the quality of the other departments' performance by denuding them of the dignity and burden of their own responsibility. It will not be possible fully to meet all that is said against judicial review. Such is not the way with questions of government. We can only fill the other side of the scales with countervailing judgments on the real needs and the actual workings of our society and, of course, with our own portions of faith and hope. Then we may estimate how far the needle has moved.

22. L. Hand, "The Contribution of an Independent Judiciary to Civilization," in I. Dilliard, ed., *The Spirit of Liberty* (New York: Knopf, 1953), pp. 155-65.

23. Eakin v. Raub, 12 S. & R. 330, 343, 355 (1825).

24. J. B. Thayer, "The Origin and Scope of the American Doctrine of Constitutional Law," in *Legal Essays* (Boston: The Boston Book Co., 1908), pp. 1, 39.

The point of departure is a truism; perhaps it even rises to the unassailability of a platitude. It is that many actions of government have two aspects: their immediate, necessarily intended, practical effects, and their perhaps unintended or unappreciated bearing on values we hold to have more general and permanent interest. It is a premise we deduce not merely from the fact of a written constitution but from the history of the race, and ultimately as a moral judgment of the good society, that government should serve not only what we conceive from time to time to be our immediate material needs but also certain enduring values. This in part is what is meant by government under law. But such values do not present themselves ready-made. They have a past always, to be sure, but they must be continually derived, enunciated, and seen in relevant application. And it remains to ask which institution of our government —if any single one in particular—should be the pronouncer and guardian of such values.

Men in all walks of public life are able occasionally to perceive this second aspect of public questions. Sometimes they are also able to base their decisions on it; that is one of the things we like to call acting on principle. Often they do not do so, however, particularly when they sit in legislative assemblies. There, when the pressure for immediate results is strong enough and emotions ride high enough, men will ordinarily prefer to act on expediency rather than take the long view. Possibly legislators—everything else being equal—are as capable as other men of following the path of principle, where the path is clear or at any rate discernible. Our system, however, like all secular systems, calls for the evolution of principle in novel circumstances, rather than only for its mechanical application. Not merely respect for the rule of established principles but the creative establishment and renewal of a coherent body of principled rules—that is what our legislatures have proven themselves ill equipped to give us.

Initially, great reliance for principled decision was placed in the Senators and the President, who have more extended terms of office and were meant to be elected only indirectly. Yet the Senate and the President were conceived of as less closely tied to, not as divorced from, electoral responsibility and the political marketplace. And so even then the need might have been felt for an institution which stands altogether aside from the current clash of interests, and which, insofar as is humanly possible, is concerned only with principle. We cannot know whether, as Thayer believed, our legislatures are what they are because we have judicial review, or whether we have judicial review and consider it necessary because legislatures are what they are. Yet it is arguable also that the partial separation of the legislative and judicial functions—and it is not meant to be absolute—is beneficial in any event, because it makes it possible for the desires of various groups and interests concerning immediate results to be heard clearly and unrestrainedly in one place. It may be thought fitting that somewhere in government, at some stage in the process of law-making, such felt needs should find unambiguous expression. Moreover, and more importantly, courts have certain capacities for dealing with matters of principle that legislatures and executives do not possess. Judges have, or should have, the leisure, the training, and the insulation to follow the ways of the scholar in pursuing the ends of government. This is crucial in sorting out the enduring values of a society, and it is not something that institutions can do well occasionally, while operating for the most part with a different set of gears. It calls for a habit of mind, and for undeviating institutional customs. Another advantage that courts have is that questions of principle never carry the same aspect for them as they did for the legislature or the executive. Statutes, after all, deal typically with abstract or dimly foreseen problems. The courts are concerned with the flesh and blood of an actual case. This tends to modify, perhaps to lengthen, everyone's view. It also provides an extremely salutary proving ground for all abstractions; it is conducive, in a phrase of Holmes, to thinking things, not words, and thus to the evolution of principle by a process that tests as it creates.

Their insulation and the marvelous mystery of time give courts the capacity to appeal to men's better natures, to call forth their aspirations, which may have been forgotten in the moment's hue and cry. This is what Justice Stone called the opportunity for "the sober second thought."[26] Hence it is that the courts, although they may somewhat dampen the people's and the legislatures' efforts to educate themselves, are also a great and highly effective educational institution. Judge Gibson, in the very opinion mentioned earlier, highly critical as he was, took account of this. "In the business of government," he wrote, "a recurrence to first principles answers the end of an observation at sea with a view to correct the dead reckoning; and, for this purpose, a written constitution is an instrument of inestimable value. It is of inestimable value also, in rendering its principles familiar to the mass of the people. . . ."[27] The educational institution that both takes the observation to correct the dead reckoning and makes it known is the voice of the Constitution: the Supreme Court exercising judicial review. The Justices, in Dean Rostow's phrase, "are inevitably teachers in a vital national

26. H. F. Stone, "The Common Law in the United States," 50 *Harvard Law Review* 4, 25 (1936).

27. Eakin v. Raub, supra n. 23, at p. 354.

seminar."[28] No other branch of the American government is nearly so well equipped to conduct one. And such a seminar can do a great deal to keep our society from becoming so riven that no court will be able to save it. Of course, we have never quite been that society in which the spirit of moderation is so richly in flower that no court need save it.

Thus, as Professor Henry M. Hart, Jr., has written, and as surely most of the profession and of informed laity believe; for if not this, what and why?—thus the Court appears "predestined in the long run, not only by the thrilling tradition of Anglo-American law but also by the hard facts of its position in the structure of American institutions, to be a voice of reason, charged with the creative function of discerning afresh and of articulating and developing impersonal and durable principles. . . ."[29] This line of thought may perhaps blunt, if it does not meet, the force of all the arguments on the other side. No doubt full consistency with democratic theory has not been established. The heart of the democratic faith is government by the consent of the governed. The further premise is not incompatible that the good society not only will want to satisfy the immediate needs of the greatest number but also will strive to support and maintain enduring general values. I have followed the view that the elected institutions are ill fitted, or not so well fitted as the courts, to perform the latter task. This rests on the assumption that the people themselves, by direct action at the ballot box, are surely incapable of sustaining a working system of general values specifically applied. But that much we assume throughout, being a representative, deliberative democracy. Matters of expediency are not generally submitted to direct referendum. Nor should matters of principle, which require even more intensive deliberation, be so submitted. Reference of specific policies to the people for initial decision is, with few exceptions, the fallacy of the misplaced mystics, or the way of those who would use the forms of democracy to undemocratic ends. It is not the way in which working democracies live. But democracies do live by the idea, central to the process of gaining the consent of the governed, that the majority has the ultimate power to displace the decision-makers and to reject any part of their policy. With that idea, judicial review must achieve some measure of consonance.

Democratic government under law—the slogan pulls in two opposed directions, but that does not keep it from being applicable to an

28. Rostow, op. cit. supra n. 15, at p. 208.
29. H. M. Hart, Jr., "Foreword: The Time Chart of the Justices," 73 *Harvard Law Review* 84, 99 (1959).

operative polity. If it carries the elements of explosion, it doesn't contain a critical mass of them. Yet if the critical mass is not to be reached, there must be an accommodation, a degree of concord between the diverging elements. Having been checked, should the people persist; having been educated, should the people insist, must they not win over every fundamental principle save one—which is the principle that they must win? Are we sufficiently certain of the permanent validity of any other principle to be ready to impose it against a consistent and determined majority, and could we do so for long? Have not the people the right of peaceable revolution, as assuredly, over time, they possess the capacity for a bloody one?

The premise of democracy is egalitarian, and, as Professor Herbert J. Muller has written, every bright sophomore knows how to punch holes in it. Yet, as Mr. Muller goes on to say, there is "no universal standard of superiority," there are no sure scales in which to weigh all the relevant virtues and capacities of men, and many a little man may rightly claim to be a better citizen than the expert or the genius. Moreover, and most significantly, "all men are in fact equal in respect of their common structure and their common destiny." Hence, to repeat the insight of Judge Hand, government must be their common venture. Who will think it moral ultimately to direct the lives of men against the will of the greater number of them? Or wise? "Man's historical experience should sober the revolutionaries who know the certain solution to our problems, and sober as well the traditionalists whose solution is a return to the ancient faiths, which have always failed in the past."[30]

To bring judicial review into concord with such presuppositions requires a closer analysis of the actual operation of the process in various circumstances. The preliminary suggestions may be advanced that the rule of principle imposed by the Court is seldom rigid, that the Court has ways of persuading before it attempts to coerce, and that, over time, sustained opinion running counter to the Court's constitutional law can achieve its nullification, directly or by desuetude. It may further be that if the process is properly carried out, an aspect of the current—not only the timeless, mystic—popular will finds expression in constitutional adjudication. The result may be a tolerable accommodation with the theory and practice of democracy.

30. H. J. Muller, *The Uses of the Past* (New York: Oxford University Press, 1957), pp. 364-65, 367.

M. R. Cohen, Constitutional and Natural Rights in 1789 and Since*

Sentiment, Symbol, and Direction

. . . Since Plato there have never been absent those who believe that the great mass of the people are unreasoning beasts that must be controlled by inoculating them with myths or fictions (unfeeling skeptics call them pious frauds.) I do not wish to discuss here the advantage of controlling the will of a democratic majority by the judgment of a few elderly gentlemen who are removed from popular clamor. But it is curious to note that it is those Americans who are at heart distrustful of democracy who speak of the courts as standing between us and dictatorship, and yet their arguments are precisely those which the adherents of Hitler and Mussolini use against the frailty of democratically representative or elective government. This is a question of political philosophy beyond the range of this article. If, however, there are any principles of political science which enlightened experience makes clear, they are (1) that the worst form of government is that which separates power from responsibility, and (2) that the weakest government is that which has relatively little access to the sources of information. And does not the fiction that the courts only follow the words of the Constitution in fact relieve them of the responsibility for the fatal results of their decisions? And is it not also true that this fiction that the courts decide only questions of law prevents us from organizing the courts so that they could have the opportunity of making adequate investigation into the actual facts on which they have to pass? Do we want our judges to be not only irresponsible to any earthly power, but also independent of adequate knowledge of the social consequences of their decisions?

II. LAW AS SOCIAL CONTRACT

Hobbes, Leviathan

See page 1 supra.

---

* [From *The Faith of a Liberal* 192, by Morris R. Cohen. Copyright, 1946, by Henry Holt and Company, Inc. Used by permission of the publishers. Originally published in 1 *Nat. Law. Guild Q.*, 92 (1938).

For biographical information, see page 81 supra.]

Locke, Two Treatises of Government*

Chapter II. Of the State of Nature

. . . 14. It is often asked, as a mighty objection, "Where are, or ever were, there any men, in such a state of nature?" To which it may suffice, as an answer at present: that since all princes, and rulers of independent governments, all thro' the world, are in a state of nature, it is plain the world never was, nor ever will be, without numbers of men in that state. I have named all governors of independent communities, whether they are, or are not, in league with others. For it is not every compact, that puts an end to the state of nature between men, but only this one, of agreeing together mutually to enter into one community, and make one body politick; other promises and compacts men may make, one with another, and yet still be in the state of nature. The promises and bargains for truck &c. between the two men in the desert island, mentioned by Garcilasso de la Vega, in his history of Peru, or between a Swiss and an Indian in the woods of America, are binding to them, tho' they are perfectly in a state of nature, in reference to one another. For truth, and keeping of faith, belongs to men as men, and not as members of society.

M. R. Cohen, The Meaning of Human History†

Chapter 8. The Institutional Approach to History

2. The Institutions of Civilization

. . . (3)*The Social Contract.* It has been a good many years, I think, since any political philosopher has referred to the theory of the social contract except to refute it. The theory which played so large a part in the political thinking of Hobbes, Locke, Rousseau and Kant, which has

---

* [*Works of John Locke* (6th ed. 1759), Vol. 2, Book 2, Ch. 2 ("Of the State of Nature"), p. 171. First published 1698.

John Locke (1632-1704) centered his philosophy on the analysis of the extent and capabilities of the human mind, and is generally credited as the initiator of the empiricist movement. One of his most important works is *An Essay Concerning Human Understanding.* One of the early exponents of the concept of social contract, Locke greatly influenced the development of American democracy.]

†[Pp. 238-245. La Salle, Ill.: Open Court Publishing Co., 1947. Reprinted by permission.

For biographical information, see page 81 supra.]

its historic roots in the Epicurean conception of government drawing its justification from the consent of the governed, and in the Biblical conception of a covenant between a people and its Lord, and which had so large a role in the shaping of American institutions, has been the butt of attacks from many quarters for more than a centruy. Hume, Bentham, Hegel and nearly all Anglo-American political scientists since Austin have dealt mercilessly with the theory of the social contract. These critics have generally construed the theory in absolute historical terms. The theory of the social contract as portrayed by its critics is either a myth or a bit of historical falsification. According to this conception, once upon a time there was a state of nature in which there was a "war of all against all" and life was "nasty, brutish and short." The people therefore came together and entered into a contract to give up certain practices inconvenient to each other, to conform to laws based upon common consent, and to obey a personal or impersonal sovereign.

Conceiving of the social contract theory in these terms, critics of the theory have asked: "Where are these contracts? In what language are they written? What are their terms? How are they enforced?" These are usually asked as rhetorical questions, for if those who have asked such questions were anxious to know the answers they would not have much trouble in finding actual contracts setting up governments. Consider, for instance, the government of one of the first colonies which united to form this nation. The Mayflower compact declares:

> In ye name of God Amen. We whose names are underwritten, the loyall subjects of our dread soveraigne lord King James, by ye grace of God, of great Britaine, Franc, & Ireland king, defender of ye faith, &c.
> Haveing undertaken, for ye glorie of God, and advancemente of ye christian faith and honour of our king & countrie, a voyage to plant ye first colonie in ye Northerne parts of Virginia. Doe by these presents solemnly & mutualy in ye presence of God, and one of another, covenant, & combine our selves togeather into a civill body politick; for our better ordering, & preservation & furtherance of ye ends aforesaid; and by vertue hearof to enacte, constitute, and frame such just & equall lawes, ordinances, Acts, constitutions, & offices, from time to time, as shall be thought most meete & convenient for ye generall good of ye colonie: Unto which we promise all due submission and obedience. In witnes whereof we have hereunder subscribed our names at Cap-Codd ye .11. of November, in ye year of ye raigne of our soveraigne lord king James of England, France, & Ireland ye eighteenth, and of Scotland ye fiftie fourth, Ano: Dom. 1620. (*Bradford's History "Of Plimoth Plantation," From the Original Manuscript.* Boston, 1898. Plate facing p. 110.)

Consider too, the Constitution of the United States which begins with the preamble:

> We, the people of the United States, in order to form a more perfect Union, establish justice, insure domestic tranquility, provide for the common defence, promote the general welfare, and secure the blessings of liberty to ourselves and our posterity, do ordain and establish this Constitution for the United States of America.

In form, as well as in spirit, the Constitution of the United States is a contract. It carries the signatures of thirty-nine signers and one witness, includes a provision for the ratification of the act of these thirty-nine agents by the electorates of the various independent American states, and carries the proviso that no state should be bound by the agreement except in consideration of eight other ratifications.

Numerous other historical examples might be cited of government originating in formal compacts. Certainly the whole conception of feudal government is based on this notion. The man who finds the freedom of anarchy too oppressive will select as powerful and reasonable a sovereign as he can find in the neighborhood and enter into a compact offering fealty in exchange for protection, surrendering an interest in land, and receiving the right to call upon the lord's laws, courts and arms. Depending upon the variety of the tenure the tenant may undertake to contribute agricultural produce or services, to render military service, or to say a certain number of prayers each year for the soul of his lord. Such an exchange of rights and obligations agreed to by both parties strictly exemplifies the notion of the social compact as an historical fact.

This, however, is answering the critics of the social contract theory in terms of their own misconception of the theory. Actually, the theory of the social contract as developed by Hobbes, Locke, Rousseau, and Kant was put forward not as an explanation of remote historical origins but as a scheme for interpreting contemporary processes of government.

A similar answer may be made to many of the critics of the philosophy of natural law, as I have elsewhere suggested: [2]

> This argument assumes that the old doctrine of natural law rested on a belief in the actual existence of human beings in a state of nature prior to organized society; and as history has not shown that such a state ever existed, natural law falls to the ground. To this very simple argument

2. M. R. Cohen, *Reason and Nature,* pp. 402-403.

the reply is that the old doctrines of natural law rested on no such foundation. Even Rousseau disclaims it in his maturer work, as is well known to those who take the unusual course of actually reading his *Contrat Social*. When Grotius, Hobbes, and their followers speak of a state of nature they do not as a rule mean to refer to a past event. The "state of nature" is a term of logical or psychologic analysis, denoting that which would or does exist apart from civil authority. It is logically, not chronologically, prior to the "civil state." Similarly the "social contract" is not a past event, but a concept of a continuous social transformation.

This comes out most clearly in Kant, who discusses the whole matter on purely ethical postulates. That Hobbes, also, kept free from historical assumptions is clearly brought out by Dunning, *Political Theories*, Vol. 2. There are two or three passages in Locke and one, at least, in Kant—not to mention Rousseau's immature discourse—in which the "state of nature" is spoken of in the past tense. But these lapses into the common way of speaking cannot be shown to have had any influence on the general ideas of Locke or Kant.

Government is not something which was created once and for all in a remote past. Rather, like language, it is something that grows by piecemeal accretion and development. A social contract theory, therefore, ought to enable us to understand not how government first arose in the unknown past, but rather how it is arising today. Every international treaty, every new type of government regulation, every new statute, administrative policy, or judicial decision is an element in the process through which government comes into being. We have government today in many fields where there was no government half a century ago. If a theory of government should explain not what happened in an unknown past, but what is happening before our eyes in the world about us, I think the social contract theory fills the role a little more adequately then most of us have been inclined to suppose.

Consider, for example, what happens when a corporation is created. Clearly, a corporation involves a governmental relation among individuals and between these individuals and a state or nation. Just as the feudal vassal promised fealty to his lord, submission to the jurisdiction of the lord's courts, and material contributions of one sort or another in exchange for the protections of sovereignty, so the modern corporation promises submission to the law and jurisdiction of the charter-issuing state and makes payments to that state in exchange for the protection which the state offers in shielding the incorporators from liability for what would otherwise be their just debts. Here, certainly, is a fragment of government arising out of contract and one can hardly attain a realistic understanding of modern corporate development without viewing the process of incorporation in the light of economic concepts of competition and bargaining. A would-be corporation shops for a sovereign in much the same way that it shops for its office supplies. States like Delaware, Arizona and South Dakota have for many decades actively competed for the business of incorporating.[3] One may still say, if one wishes, that the validity of corporation law is derived from the sovereign out of which the law issues. But the fact of the matter is that the corporation laws of some states are mostly dead letters, because people will not incorporate in those states. It takes at least two parties to make government. Without such mutual consent there is no government.

The same sort of competition for patronage that we find among the states with regard to the transaction of incorporation can be found in a variety of other governmental relations, of which divorce, taxation, money lending and insurance may serve as striking examples.

What is true among the states of the nation is to a certain extent true of international relations generally. Despite all its professions of patriotic nationalism capital combats every project for increased taxation or industrial control with the threat to run away from the country and to find greener pastures abroad. In general, we find that a government which promises stability and protection of private property will attract a large share of the world's financial dealings to its sovereignty. This may involve the actual location of factories and stores, or it may involve the location of financial offices and operations, or it may involve a purely formal choice of sovereigns, as where a contract of sale between a Frenchman and an American specifies that French law is to control the interpretation and enforcement of the contract. The competition of sovereigns to attract business and capital is to a certain extent paralleled by the competition for the allegiance of human beings. The nation that promises freedom and opportunity to its nationals will attract men and women who value freedom and opportunity. The oath of allegiance required of would-be citizens is certainly a part of a social contract in which loyalty is a promissory consideration for the counterpromises of protection which may be found in the constitution and laws of the sovereign. While the native-born citizen is generally exempted from such oaths or pledges, unless he holds public office or serves in the army or goes to public school, our courts have regarded the mutual obligations of the nation and the native citizen as constituting an implied contract, and there is much substance in this assumption so long as men are free to renounce their national allegiance and to exercise what Congress has referred to as the "natural right" of expatriation.

The competition between states and nations for allegiance and jurisdiction is paralleled by the competition between governmental and non-

3. See W. Z. Ripley, *Main Street and Wall Street.*

governmental institutions, e.g., the church, the business corporation, the labor union, and the family. If people prefer the authority of the state to that of the family or the church, the scope of government is broadened. In the converse situation the scope of government may be narrowed. The more a state offers that cannot be obtained more reasonably from another state or another institution, the more it can demand and secure in return from its subjects. The measure of fealty and homage that a government can expect from any group in its population is not unrelated to the services and contributions that government makes to that group.

The fact that government is permeated by the form of the command tends to obscure the very large degree to which government actually rests upon the consent of the governed, upon the acceptance of authority, upon the free choice of sovereigns, upon the common agreements and compromises reached by conflicting groups within a society and formalized as treaties of peace on the statute books of the Nation. Government by simple majority rule is practical only in moments of great stress. No community can stand the social cost of coercing forty-nine percent of its citizens to do something they do not wish to do, except on very rare occasions.

I do not mean to deny that there is a coercive element in all government. It may equally be said that there is a coercive element in all human relations and particularly in all commercial relations. But government is also, in large part, a series of consensual transactions subject to the laws of supply and demand, diminishing returns, monopoly price, and all the other laws that govern the exchange of services and commodities. Whether we look at government in the realms where its achievements are solid or in the realms of industrial and international anarchy where government is a hope rather than an achievement, we can find, I think, keys to understanding in the hypothesis that government is the outcome or product of interpersonal and intergroup agreements. This, rather than the explanation of a mythical past, is the real contribution which the social contract theory has made to the contemporary problems of many earlier ages. I see no reason why it may not make as great a contribution to the understanding of our own contemporary history.

Rawls, A Theory of Justice*

. . . Let us assume, to fix ideas, that a society is a more or less self-sufficient association of persons who in their relations to one another

* [Pp. 4-5, 11-13, 14-15, 60-63, 136-142, 150-156, 302 (1971). Reprinted by permission

recognize certain rules of conduct as binding and who for the most part act in accordance with them. Suppose further that these rules specify a system of cooperation designed to advance the good of those taking part in it. Then, although a society is a cooperative venture for mutual advantage, it is typically marked by a conflict as well as by an identity of interests. There is an identity of interests since social cooperation makes possible a better life for all than any would have if each were to live solely by his own efforts. There is a conflict of interests since persons are not indifferent as to how the greater benefits produced by their collaboration are distributed, for in order to pursue their ends they each prefer a larger to a lesser share. A set of principles is required for choosing among the various social arrangements which determine this division of advantages and for underwriting an agreement on the proper distributive shares. These principles are the principles of social justice: they provide a way of assigning rights and duties in the basic institutions of society and they define the appropriate distribution of the benefits and burdens of social cooperation.

Now let us say that a society is well-ordered when it is not only designed to advance the good of its members but when it is also effectively regulated by a public conception of justice. That is, it is a society in which (1) everyone accepts and knows that the others accept the same principles of justice, and (2) the basic social institutions generally satisfy and are generally known to satisfy these principles. In this case while men may put forth excessive demands on one another, they nevertheless acknowledge a common point of view from which their claims may be adjudicated. If men's inclination to self-interest makes their vigilance against one another necessary, their public sense of justice makes their secure association together possible. Among individuals with disparate aims and purposes a shared conception of justice establishes the bonds of civic friendship; the general desire for justice limits the pursuit of other ends. One may think of a public conception of justice as constituting the fundamental charter of a well-ordered human association. . . .

---

of the author and publishers from *A Theory of Justice* by John Rawls, Cambridge, Mass.: The Belknap Press of Harvard University Press, Copyright © 1971 by the President and Fellows of Harvard College.

John Rawls (1921–   ) was educated at Princeton University (A.B. 1943; Ph.D. 1950) and Cornell University (postgraduate 1947-1948). A former Fulbright Fellow at Oxford, Rawls has been a faculty member of M.I.T. and Harvard University. He has been Professor of Philosophy at Harvard since 1962.]

3. The Main Idea of the Theory of Justice

My aim is to present a conception of justice which generalizes and carries to a higher level of abstraction the familiar theory of the social contract as found, say, in Locke, Rousseau, and Kant.[4] In order to do this we are not to think of the original contract as one to enter a particular society or to set up a particular form of government. Rather, the guiding idea is that the principles of justice for the basic structure of society are the object of the original agreement. They are the principles that free and rational persons concerned to further their own interests would accept in an initial position of equality as defining the fundamental terms of their association. These principles are to regulate all further agreements; they specify the kinds of social cooperation that can be entered into and the forms of government that can be established. This way of regarding the principles of justice I shall call justice as fairness.

Thus we are to imagine that those who engage in social cooperation choose together, in one joint act, the principles which are to assign basic rights and duties and to determine the division of social benefits. Men are to decide in advance how they are to regulate their claims against one another and what is to be the foundation charter of their society. Just as each person must decide by rational reflection what constitutes his good, that is, the system of ends which it is rational for him to pursue, so a group of persons must decide once and for all what is to count among them as just and unjust. The choice which rational men would make in this hypothetical situation of equal liberty, assuming for the present that this choice problem has a solution, determines the principles of justice.

In justice as fairness the original position of equality corresponds to the state of nature in the traditional theory of the social contract. This original position is not, of course, thought of as an actual historical state of affairs, much less as a primitive condition of culture. It is understood as a purely hypothetical situation characterized so as to lead to a certain conception of justice.[5] Among the essential features of this situation is

4. As the text suggests, I shall regard Locke's *Second Treatise of Government*, Rousseau's *The Social Contract*, and Kant's ethical works beginning with *The Foundations of the Metaphysics of Morals* as definitive of the contract tradition. For all of its greatness, Hobbes's *Leviathan* raises special problems. A general historical survey is provided by J.W. Gough, *The Social Contract*, 2nd ed. (Oxford, The Clarendon Press, 1957), and Otto Gierke, *Natural Law and the Theory of Society*, trans. with an introduction by Ernest Barker (Cambridge, The University Press, 1934). A presentation of the contract view as primarily an ethical theory is to be found in G. R. Grice, *The Grounds of Moral Judgment* (Cambridge, The University Press, 1967). See also §19, note 30.

5. Kant is clear that the original agreement is hypothetical. See *The Metaphysics of Morals*, pt. I (*Rechtslehre*), especially §§47, 52; and pt. II of the essay "Concerning the Com-

that no one knows his place in society, his class position or social status, nor does any one know his fortune in the distribution of natural assets and abilities, his intelligence, strength, and the like. I shall even assume that the parties do not know their conceptions of the good or their special psychological propensities. The principles of justice are chosen behind a veil of ignorance. This ensures that no one is advantaged or disadvantaged in the choice of principles by the outcome of natural chance or the contingency of social circumstances. Since all are similarly situated and no one is able to design principles to favor his particular condition, the principles of justice are the result of a fair agreement or bargain. For given the circumstances of the original position, the symmetry of everyone's relations to each other, this initial situation is fair between individuals as moral persons, that is, as rational beings with their own ends and capable, I shall assume, of a sense of justice. The original position is, one might say, the appropriate initial status quo, and thus the fundamental agreements reached in it arc fair. This explains the propriety of the name "justice as fairness": it conveys the idea that the principles of justice are agreed to in an initial situation that is fair. The name does not mean that the concepts of justice and fairness are the same, any more than the phrase "poetry as metaphor" means that the concepts of poetry and metaphor are the same.

Justice as fairness begins, as I have said, with one of the most general of all choices which persons might make together, namely, with the choice of the first principles of a conception of justice which is to regulate all subsequent criticism and reform of institutions. Then, having chosen a conception of justice, we can suppose that they are to choose a constitution and a legislature to enact laws, and so on, all in accordance with the principles of justice initially agreed upon. Our social situation is just if it is such that by this sequence of hypothetical agreements we would have contracted into the general system of rules which defines it. Moreover, assuming that the original position does determine a set of principles (that is, that a particular conception of justice would be chosen), it will then be true that whenever social institutions satisfy these principles those engaged in them can say to one another that they are cooperating on terms to which they would agree if they were free and equal persons whose relations with respect to one another were fair.

---

mon Saying: This May Be True in Theory but It Does Not Apply in Practice," in *Kant's Political Writings,* ed. IIans Reiss and trans. by H. B. Nisbet (Cambridge, The University Press, 1970), pp. 73-87. See Georges Vlachos, *La Pensée politique de Kant* (Paris, Presses Universitaires de France, 1962), pp. 326-335; and J. G. Murphy, *Kant: The Philosophy of Right* (London, Macmillan, 1970), pp. 109-112, 133-136, for a further discussion.

They could all view their arrangements as meeting the stipulations which they would acknowledge in an initial situation that embodies widely accepted and reasonable constraints on the choice of principles. The general recognition of this fact would provide the basis for a public acceptance of the corresponding principles of justice. No society can, of course, be a scheme of cooperation which men enter voluntarily in a literal sense; each person finds himself placed at birth in some particular position in some particular society, and the nature of this position materially affects his life prospects. Yet a society satisfying the principles of justice as fairness comes as close as a society can to being a voluntary scheme, for it meets the principles which free and equal persons would assent to under circumstances that are fair. In this sense its members are autonomous and the obligations they recognize self-imposed. . . .

I shall maintain instead that the persons in the initial situation would choose two rather different principles: the first requires equality in the assignment of basic rights and duties, while the second holds that social and economic inequalities, for example inequalities of wealth and authority, are just only if they result in compensating benefits for everyone, and in particular for the least advantaged members of society. These principles rule out justifying institutions on the grounds that the hardships of some are offset by a greater good in the aggregate. It may be expedient but it is not just that some should have less in order that others may prosper. But there is no injustice in the greater benefits earned by a few provided that the situation of persons not so fortunate is thereby improved. The intuitive idea is that since everyone's well-being depends upon a scheme of cooperation without which no one could have a satisfactory life, the division of advantages should be such as to draw forth the willing cooperation of everyone taking part in it, including those less well situated. Yet this can be expected only if reasonable terms are proposed. The two principles mentioned seem to be a fair agreement on the basis of which those better endowed, or more fortunate in their social position, neither of which we can be said to deserve, could expect the willing cooperation of others when some workable scheme is a necessary condition of the welfare of all.[6] Once we decide to look for a conception of justice that nullifies the accidents of natural endowment and the contingencies of social circumstance as counters in quest for political and economic advantage, we are led to these principles. They express the result of leaving aside those aspects of the social world that seem arbitrary from a moral point of view. . . .

6. For the formulation of this intuitive idea I am indebted to Allan Gibbard.

11. Two Principles of Justice

I shall now state in a provisional form the two principles of justice that I believe would be chosen in the original position. . . .

> The first statement of the two principles reads as follows.
> First: each person is to have an equal right to the most extensive basic liberty compatible with a similar liberty for others.
> Second: social and economic inequalities are to be arranged so that they are both (a) reasonably expected to be to everyone's advantage, and (b) attached to positions and offices open to all.

There are two ambiguous phrases in the second principle, namely "everyone's advantage" and "open to all." Determining their sense more exactly will lead to a second formulation of the principle in §13. The final version of the two principles is given in §46; §39 considers the rendering of the first principle.

By way of general comment, these principles primarily apply, as I have said, to the basic structure of society. They are to govern the assignment of rights and duties and to regulate the distribution of social and economic advantages. As their formulation suggests, these principles presuppose that the social structure can be divided into two more or less distinct parts, the first principle applying to the one, the second to the other. They distinguish between those aspects of the social system that define and secure the equal liberties of citizenship and those that specify and establish social and economic inequalities. The basic liberties of citizens are, roughly speaking, political liberty (the right to vote and to be eligible for public office) together with freedom of speech and assembly; liberty of conscience and freedom of thought; freedom of the person along with the right to hold (personal) property; and freedom from arbitrary arrest and seizure as defined by the concept of the rule of law. These liberties are all required to be equal by the first principle, since citizens of a just society are to have the same basic rights.

The second principle applies, in the first approximation, to the distribution of income and wealth and to the design of organizations that make use of differences in authority and responsibility, or chains of command. While the distribution of wealth and income need not be equal, it must be to everyone's advantage, and at the same time, positions of authority and offices of command must be accessible to all. One applies the second principle by holding positions open, and then, subject to this constraint, arranges social and economic inequalities so that everyone benefits.

These principles are to be arranged in a serial order with the first principle prior to the second. This ordering means that a departure from the institutions of equal liberty required by the first principle cannot be justified by, or compensated for, by greater social and economic advantages. The distribution of wealth and income, and the hierarchies of authority, must be consistent with both the liberties of equal citizenship and equality of opportunity.

It is clear that these principles are rather specific in their content, and their acceptance rests on certain assumptions that I must eventually try to explain and justify. A theory of justice depends upon a theory of society in ways that will become evident as we proceed. For the present, it should be observed that the two principles (and this holds for all formulations) are a special case of a more general conception of justice that can be expressed as follows.

> All social values—liberty and opportunity, income and wealth, and the bases of self-respect—are to be distributed equally unless an unequal distribution of any, or all, of these values is to everyone's advantage.

Injustice, then, is simply inequalities that are not to the benefit of all. Of course, this conception is extremely vague and requires interpretation.

As a first step, suppose that the basic structure of society distributes certain primary goods, that is, things that every rational man is presumed to want. These goods normally have a use whatever a person's rational plan of life. For simplicity, assume that the chief primary goods at the disposition of society are rights and liberties, powers and opportunities, income and wealth. (Later on in Part Three the primary good of self-respect has a central place.) These are the social primary goods. Other primary goods such as health and vigor, intelligence and imagination, are natural goods; although their possession is influenced by the basic structure, they are not so directly under its control. Imagine, then, a hypothetical initial arrangement in which all the social primary goods are equally distributed: everyone has similar rights and duties, and income and wealth are evenly shared. This state of affairs provides a benchmark for judging improvements. If certain inequalities of wealth and organizational powers would make everyone better off than in this hypothetical starting situation, then they accord with the general conception.

Now it is possible, at least theoretically, that by giving up some of their fundamental liberties men are sufficiently compensated by the resulting social and economic gains. The general conception of justice imposes no restrictions on what sort of inequalities are permissible; it only requires that everyone's position be improved. We need not suppose anything so drastic as consenting to a condition of slavery. Imagine instead that men forego certain political rights when the economic returns are significant and their capacity to influence the course of policy by the exercise of these rights would be marginal in any case. It is this kind of exchange which the two principles as stated rule out; being arranged in serial order they do not permit exchanges between basic liberties and economic and social gains. The serial ordering of principles expresses an underlying preference among primary social goods. When this preference is rational so likewise is the choice of these principles in this order.

In developing justice as fairness I shall, for the most part, leave aside the general conception of justice and examine instead the special case of the two principles in serial order. The advantage of this procedure is that from the first the matter of priorities is recognized and an effort made to find principles to deal with it. One is led to attend throughout to the conditions under which the acknowledgment of the absolute weight of liberty with respect to social and economic advantages, as defined by the lexical order of the two principles, would be reasonable. Offhand, this ranking appears extreme and too special a case to be of much interest; but there is more justification for it than would appear at first sight. . . . Furthermore, the distinction between fundamental rights and liberties and economic and social benefits marks a difference among primary social goods that one should try to exploit. It suggests an important division in the social system. Of course, the distinctions drawn and the ordering proposed are bound to be at best only approximations. There are surely circumstances in which they fail. But it is essential to depict clearly the main lines of a reasonable conception of justice; and under many conditions anyway, the two principles in serial order may serve well enough. When necessary we can fall back on the more general conception. . . .

24. The Veil of Ignorance

The idea of the original position is to set up a fair procedure so that any principles agreed to will be just. The aim is to use the notion of pure procedural justice as a basis of theory. Somehow we must nullify the effects of specific contingencies which put men at odds and tempt them to exploit social and natural circumstances to their own advantage. Now in order to do this I assume that the parties are situated behind a veil of ignorance. They do not know how the various alternatives will affect their own particular case and they are obliged to evaluate principles solely on the basis of general considerations.[11]

It is assumed, then, that the parties do not know certain kinds of particular facts. First of all, no one knows his place in society, his class position or social status; nor does he know his fortune in the distribution of natural assets and abilities, his intelligence and strength, and the like. Nor, again, does anyone know his conception of the good, the particulars of his rational plan of life, or even the special features of his psychology such as his aversion to risk or liability to optimism or pessimism. More than this, I assume that the parties do not know the particular circumstances of their own society. That is, they do not know its economic or political situation, or the level of civilization and culture it has been able to achieve. The persons in the original position have no information as to which generation they belong. These broader restrictions on knowledge are appropriate in part because questions of social justice arise between generations as well as within them, for example, the question of the appropriate rate of capital saving and of the conservation of natural resources and the environment of nature. There is also, theoretically anyway, the question of a reasonable genetic policy. In these cases too, in order to carry through the idea of the orginal position, the parties must not know the contingencies that set them in opposition. They must choose principles the consequences of which they are prepared to live with whatever generation they turn out to belong to.

As far as possible, then, the only particular facts which the parties know is that their society is subject to the circumstances of justice and whatever this implies. It is taken for granted, however, that they know the general facts about human society. They understand political affairs and the principles of economic theory; they know the basis of social organization and the laws of human psychology. Indeed, the parties are presumed to know whatever general facts affect the choice of the principles of justice. There are no limitations on general information, that is, on general laws and theories, since conceptions of justice must be adjusted to the characteristics of the systems of social cooperation which they are to regulate, and there is no reason to rule out these facts. It is, for example, a consideration against a conception of justice that, in view of the laws of moral psychology, men would not acquire a desire to act

11. The veil of ignorance is so natural a condition that something like it must have occurred to many. The closest explicit statement of it known to me is found in J. C. Harsanyi, "Cardinal Utility in Welfare Economics and in the Theory of Risk-Taking," *Journal of Political Economy*, vol. 61 (1953). Harsanyi uses it to develop a utilitarian theory, as I discuss below in §§27-28.

upon it even when the institutions of their society satisfied it. For in this case there would be difficulty in securing the stability of social cooperation. It is an important feature of a conception of justice that it should generate its own support. That is, its principles should be such that when they are embodied in the basic structure of society men tend to acquire the corresponding sense of justice. Given the principles of moral learning, men develop a desire to act in accordance with its principles. In this case a conception of justice is stable. This kind of general information is admissible in the original position. . . .

Thus there follows the very important consequence that the parties have no basis for bargaining in the usual sense. No one knows his situation in society nor his natural assets, and therefore no one is in a position to tailor principles to his advantage. We might imagine that one of the contractees threatens to hold out unless the others agree to principles favorable to him. But how does he know which principles are especially in his interests? The same holds for the formation of coalitions: if a group were to decide to band together to the disadvantage of the others, they would not know how to favor themselves in the choice of principles. Even if they could get everyone to agree to their proposal, they would have no assurance that it was to their advantage, since they cannot identify themselves either by name or description. . . .

The restrictions on particular information in the original position are, then, of fundamental importance. Without them we would not be able to work out any definite theory of justice at all. We would have to be content with a vague formula stating that justice is what would be agreed to without being able to say much, if anything, about the substance of the agreement itself. The formal constraints of the concept of right, those applying to principles directly, are not sufficient for our purpose. The veil of ignorance makes possible a unanimous choice of a particular conception of justice. Without these limitations on knowledge the bargaining problem of the original position would be hopelessly complicated. Even if theoretically a solution were to exist, we would not, at present anyway, be able to determine it. . . .

Now the reasons for the veil of ignorance go beyond mere simplicity. We want to define the original position so that we get the desired solution. If a knowledge of particulars is allowed, then the outcome is biased by arbitrary contingencies. As already observed, to each according to his threat advantage is not a principle of justice. If the original position is to yield agreements that are just, the parties must be fairly situated and treated equally as moral persons. The arbitrariness of the world must be corrected for by adjusting the circumstances of the initial contractual situation. Moreover, if in choosing principles we required

1011

unanimity even when there is full information, only a few rather obvious cases could be decided. A conception of justice based on unanimity in these circumstances would indeed be weak and trivial. But once knowledge is excluded, the requirement of unanimity is not out of place and the fact that it can be satisfied is of great importance. It enables us to say of the preferred conception of justice that it represents a genuine reconciliation of interests. . . .

It will be recalled that the general conception of justice as fairness requires that all primary social goods be distributed equally unless an unequal distribution would be to everyone's advantage. No restrictions are placed on exchanges of these goods and therefore a lesser liberty can be compensated for by greater social and economic benefits. Now looking at the situation from the standpoint of one person selected arbitrarily, there is no way for him to win special advantages for himself. Nor, on the other hand, are there grounds for his acquiescing in special disadvantages. Since it is not reasonable for him to expect more than an equal share in the division of social goods, and since it is not rational for him to agree to less, the sensible thing for him to do is to acknowledge as the first principle of justice one requiring an equal distribution. Indeed, this principle is so obvious that we would expect it to occur to anyone immediately.

Thus, the parties start with a principle establishing equal liberty for all, including equality of opportunity, as well as an equal distribution of income and wealth. But there is no reason why this acknowledgment should be final. If there are inequalities in the basic structure that work to make everyone better off in comparison with the benchmark of initial equality, why not permit them? The immediate gain which a greater equality might allow can be regarded as intelligently invested in view of its future return. If, for example, these inequalities set up various incentives which succeed in eliciting more productive efforts, a person in the original position may look upon them as necessary to cover the costs of training and to encourage effective performance. One might think that ideally individuals should want to serve one another. But since the parties are assumed not to take an interest in one another's interests, their acceptance of these inequalities is only the acceptance of the relations in which men stand in the circumstances of justice. They have no grounds for complaining of one another's motives. A person in the original position would, therefore, concede the justice of these inequalities. Indeed, it would be shortsighted of him not to do so. He would hesitate to agree to these regularities only if he would be dejected by the bare knowledge or perception that others were better situated; and I have assumed that the parties decide as if they are not moved by envy. In order to make the principle regulating inequalities determinate, one looks at the system

1012

from the standpoint of the least advantaged representative man. Inequalities are permissible when they maximize, or at least all contribute to, the long-term expectations of the least fortunate group in society.

Now this general conception imposes no constraints on what sorts of inequalities are allowed, whereas the special conception, by putting the two principles in serial order (with the necessary adjustments in meaning), forbids exchanges between basic liberties and economic and social benefits. I shall not try to justify this ordering here. . . . [R]oughly, the idea underlying this ordering is that if the parties assume that their basic liberties can be effectively exercised, they will not exchange a lesser liberty for an improvement in economic well-being. It is only when social conditions do not allow the effective establishment of these rights that one can concede their limitation; and these restrictions can be granted only to the extent that they are necessary to prepare the way for a free society. The denial of equal liberty can be defended only if it is necessary to raise the level of civilization so that in due course these freedoms can be enjoyed. Thus in adopting a serial order we are in effect making a special assumption in the original position, namely, that the parties know that the conditions of their society, whatever they are, admit the effective realization of the equal liberties. The serial ordering of the two principles of justice eventually comes to be reasonable if the general conception is consistently followed. This lexical ranking is the long-run tendency of the general view. For the most part I shall assume that the requisite circumstances for the serial order obtain.

It seems clear from these remarks that the two principles are at least a plausible conception of justice. The question, though, is how one is to argue for them more systematically. Now there are several things to do. One can work out their consequences for institutions and note their implications for fundamental social policy. In this way they are tested by a comparison with our considered judgments of justice. . . . But one can also try to find arguments in their favor that are decisive from the standpoint of the original position. In order to see how this might be done, it is useful as a heuristic device to think of the two principles as the maximin solution to the problem of social justice. There is an analogy between the two principles and the maximin rule for choice under uncertainty.[18] This is evident from the fact that the two principles are those a person would choose for the design of a society in which his enemy is to

18. An accessible discussion of this and other rules of choice under uncertainty can be found in W. J. Baumol, *Economic Theory and Operations Analysis,* 2nd ed. (Englewood Cliffs, N.J., Prentice-Hall Inc., 1965), ch. 24. Baumol gives a geometric interpretation of these rules, including the diagram used in §13 to illustrate the difference principle. See pp. 558-562. See also R. D. Luce and Howard Raiffa, *Games and Decisions* (New York, John Wiley and Sons, Inc., 1957), ch. XIII, for a fuller account.

assign him his place. The maximin rule tells us to rank alternatives by their worst possible outcomes: we are to adopt the alternative the worst outcome of which is superior to the worst outcomes of the others. The persons in the original position do not, of course, assume that their initial place in society is decided by a malevolent opponent. As I note below, they should not reason from false premises. The veil of ignorance does not violate this idea, since an absence of information is not misinformation. But that the two principles of justice would be chosen if the parties were forced to protect themselves against such a contingency explains the sense in which this conception is the maximin solution. And this analogy suggests that if the original position has been described so that it is rational for the parties to adopt the conservative attitude expressed by this rule, a conclusive argument can indeed be constructed for these principles. Clearly the maximin rule is not, in general, a suitable guide for choices under uncertainty. But it is attractive in situations marked by certain special features. My aim, then, is to show that a good case can be made for the two principles based on the fact that the original position manifests these features to the fullest possible degree, carrying them to the limit, so to speak.

Consider the gain-and-loss table below. It represents the gains and losses for a situation which is not a game of strategy. There is no one playing against the person making the decision; instead he is faced with several possible circumstances which may or may not obtain. Which circumstances happen to exist does not depend upon what the person choosing decides or whether he announces his moves in advance. The numbers in the table are monetary values (in hundreds of dollars) in comparison with some initial situation. The gain (g) depends upon the individual's decision (d) and the circumstances (c). Thus $g = f(d,c)$. Assuming that there are three possible decisions and three possible circumstances, we might have [the] gain-and-loss [values shown in Table 6]. The maximin rule requires that we make the third decision. For in this case the worst that can happen is that one gains five hundred dollars,

	Circumstances		
Decisions	c_1	c_2	c_3
d_1	−7	8	12
d_2	−8	7	14
d_3	5	6	8

[Table 6]

which is better than the worst for the other actions. If we adopt one of these we may lose either eight or seven hundred dollars. Thus, the choice of d_3 maximizes $f(d,c)$ for that value of c, which for a given d, minimizes f. The term "maximin" means the *maximum minimorum;* and the rule directs our attention to the worst that can happen under any proposed course of action, and to decide in the light of that.

Now there appear to be three chief features of situations that give plausibility to this unusual rule.[19] First, since the rule takes no account of the likelihoods of the possible circumstances, there must be some reason for sharply discounting estimates of these probabilities. Offhand, the most natural rule of choice would seem to be to compute the expectation of monetary gain for each decision and then to adopt the course of action with the highest prospect. . . . Thus it must be, for example, that the situation is one in which a knowledge of likelihoods is impossible, or at best extremely insecure. In this case it is unreasonable not to be skeptical of probabilistic calculations unless there is no other way out, particularly if the decision is a fundamental one that needs to be justified to others.

The second feature that suggests the maximin rule is the following: the person choosing has a conception of the good such that he cares very little, if anything, for what he might gain above the minimum stipend that he can, in fact, be sure of by following the maximin rule. It is not worthwhile for him to take a chance for the sake of a further advantage, especially when it may turn out that he loses much that is important to him. This last provision brings in the third feature, namely, that the rejected alternatives have outcomes that one can hardly accept. The situation involves grave risks. Of course these features work most effectively in combination. The paradigm situation for following the maximin rule is when all three features are realized to the highest degree. This rule does not, then, generally apply, nor of course is it self-evident. Rather, it is a maxim, a rule of thumb, that comes into its own in special circumstances. Its application depends upon the qualitative structure of the possible gains and losses in relation to one's conception of the good, all this against a background in which it is reasonable to discount conjectural estimates of likelihoods.

It should be noted, as the comments on the gain-and-loss table say, that the entries in the table represent monetary values and not utilities. This difference is significant since for one thing computing expectations on the basis of such objective values is not the same thing as computing

19. Here I borrow from William Fellner, *Probability and Profit* (Homewood, Ill., R. D. Irwin, Inc., 1965), pp. 140-142, where these features are noted.

expected utility and may lead to different results. The essential point though is that in justice as fairness the parties do not know their conception of the good and cannot estimate their utility in the ordinary sense. In any case, we want to go behind de facto preferences generated by given conditions. Therefore expectations are based upon an index of primary goods and the parties make their choice accordingly. The entries in the example are in terms of money and not utility to indicate this aspect of the contract doctrine.

Now, as I have suggested, the original position has been defined so that it is a situation in which the maximin rule applies. In order to see this, let us review briefly the nature of this situation with these three special features in mind. To begin with, the veil of ignorance excludes all but the vaguest knowledge of likelihoods. The parties have no basis for determining the probable nature of their society, or their place in it. Thus they have strong reasons for being wary of probability calculations if any other course is open to them. They must also take into account the fact that their choice of principles should seem reasonable to others, in particular their descendants, whose rights will be deeply affected by it. There are further grounds for discounting that I shall mention as we go along. For the present it suffices to note that these considerations are strengthened by the fact that the parties know very little about the gain-and-loss table. Not only are they unable to conjecture the likelihoods of the various possible circumstances, they cannot say much about what the possible circumstances are, much less enumerate them and foresee the outcome of each alternative available. Those deciding are much more in the dark than the illustration by a numerical table suggests. It is for this reason that I have spoken of an analogy with the maximin rule.

. . . I now wish to give the final statement of the two principles of justice for institutions. For the sake of completeness, I shall give a full statement including earlier formulations.

First Principle
> Each person is to have an equal right to the most extensive total system of equal basic liberties compatible with a similar system of liberty for all.

Second Principle
> Social and economic inequalities are to be arranged so that they are both:
> > (a) to the greatest benefit of the least advantaged, consistent with the just savings principle, and
> > (b) attached to offices and positions open to all under conditions of fair equality of opportunity.

First Priority Rule (The Priority of Liberty)

The principles of justice are to be ranked in lexical order and therefore liberty can be restricted only for the sake of liberty. There are two cases:

(a) a less extensive liberty must strengthen the total system of liberty shared by all;

(b) a less then equal liberty must be acceptable to those with the lesser liberty. . . .

General Conception

All social primary goods—liberty and opportunity, income and wealth, and the bases of self-respect—are to be distributed equally unless an unequal distribution of any or all of these goods is to the advantage of the least favored.

T. Nagel, Rawls on Justice*

A Theory of Justice[1] is a rich, complicated, and fundamental work. It offers an elaborate set of arguments and provides many issues for discussion. This review will focus on its contribution to the more abstract portions of ethical theory.

The book contains three elements. One is a vision of men and society as they should be. Another is a conception of moral theory. The third is a construction that attempts to derive principles expressive of the vision, in accordance with methods that reflect the conception of moral theory. In that construction Rawls has pursued the contractarian tradition in moral and political philosophy. His version of the social contract, a hypothetical choice situation called the original position, was first presented in 1958 and is here developed in great and explicit detail. The aim is to provide a way of treating the basic problems of social choice, for which no generally recognized methods of precise solution exist, through the proxy of a specially constructed parallel problem of individual choice, which can be solved by the more reliable intuitions and decision procedures of rational prudence.

---

* [82 *Philosophical Rev.* 220-234 (1973). Reprinted by permission.

Thomas Nagel (1937–) was educated at Cornell University (B.A. 1958), Oxford University (B.Phil. 1960), and Harvard University (Ph.D. 1963). He was Assistant Professor at the University of California, Berkeley, from 1963 until 1966. Since 1966, he has been a member of the Philosophy Department at Princeton University. He is the author of *Philosophy and Altruism* (1970).]

1. John Rawls, *A Theory of Justice* (Cambridge, Mass., Harvard University Press, 1971), pp. xv, 607. All page references to *Theory* will appear in text in parentheses.

If this enterprise is to succeed, and the solution to the clearer prudential problem is to be accepted as a solution to the more obscure moral one, then the alleged correspondence between the two problems must bear a great deal of weight. Critics of the theory have tended to take issue with Rawls over what principles would be chosen in the original position, but it is also necessary to examine those features of the position that are thought to support the most controversial choices and to ask why the results of a decision taken under these highly specific and rather peculiar conditions should confirm the justice of the principles chosen. This doctrine of correspondence is both fundamental and obscure, and its defense is not easy to extract from the book. A proper treatment of the subject will have to cover considerable ground, and it is probably best to begin with Rawls' moral epistemology.

Rawls believes that it will be more profitable to investigate the foundations of ethics when there are more substantive ethical results to seek the foundations of. Nevertheless, in Section 9 he expounds a general position that helps to explain his method of proceeding. Ethics, he says, cannot be derived from self-evident axioms nor from definitions, but must be developed, like any other scientific subject, through the constant interaction between theoretical construction and particular observation. In this case the particular observations are not experiments but substantive moral judgments. It is a bit like linguistics: ethics explores our moral sense as grammar explores out linguistic competence.[2]

Intuitionism attempts to capture the moral sense by summarizing our particular moral intuitions in principles of maximum generality, relying on further intuitions to settle conflicts among those principles. This is not what Rawls means. He intends rather that the underlying principles should possess intuitive moral plausibility of their own, and that the total theory should not merely summarize but illuminate and make plausible the particular judgments that it explains. Moreover, its intrinsic plausibility may persuade us to modify or extend our intuitions, thereby achieving greater theoretical coherence. Our knowledge of contingent facts about human nature and society will play a substantial part in the process.

When this interplay between general and particular has produced a relatively stable outcome, and no immediate improvements on either

---

2. This seems to me a false analogy, because the intuitions of native speakers are decisive as regards grammar. Whatever native speakers agree on is English, but whatever ordinary men agree in condemning is not necessarily wrong. Therefore the intrinsic plausibility of an ethical theory can impel a change in our moral intuitions. Nothing corresponds to this in linguistics (*pace* Rawls' suggestion on p. 49), where the final test of a theory is its ability to explain the data.

level suggest themselves, then our judgments are said to be in a state of *reflective equilibrium*. Its name implies that the state is always subject to change, and that our current best approximation to the truth will eventually be superseded. The indefinite article in Rawls' title is significant: he believes that all present moral theories "are primitive and have grave defects" (p. 52). His own results are provisional: "I doubt," he says (p. 581), "that the principles of justice (as I have defined them) will be the preferred conception on anything resembling a complete list."

If the principles and judgments of a theory are controversial and do not command immediate intuitive assent, then the support they receive from the underlying moral conception assumes special importance. To a certain extent that conception may reveal itself directly in the basic principles of the theory, but it is more clearly visible when the theory contains a model or construction that accounts for the principles and for their relation to one another. Alternative theories of justice are intuitively represented by different models (utilitarianism, for example, by the impartial sympathetic observer). Rawls' model is the original position, and the principles it is used to support are controversial. To enhance their appeal, the construction must express an intuitive idea that has independent plausibility. Before turning to the model itself, it will be useful to review briefly the substantive conclusions of the theory, identifying their controversial elements and thus the respects in which they are most in need of independent support.

Rawls' substantive doctrine is a rather pure form of egalitarian liberalism, whose controversial elements are its egalitarianism, its anti-perfectionism and anti-meritocracy, the primacy it gives to liberty, and the fact that it is more egalitarian about liberty than about other goods. The justice of social institutions is measured not by their tendency to maximize the sum or average of certain advantages, but by their tendency to counteract the natural inequalities deriving from birth, talent, and circumstance, pooling those resources in the service of the common good. The common good is measured in terms of a very restricted, basic set of benefits to individuals: personal and political liberty, economic and social advantages, and self-respect.

The justice of institutions depends on their conformity to two principles. The first requires the greatest equal liberty compatible with a like liberty for all. The second (the difference principle) permits only those inequalities in the distribution of primary economic and social advantages that benefit everyone, in particular the worst-off. Liberty is prior in the sense that it cannot be sacrificed for economic and social advantages, unless they are so scarce or unequal as to prevent the meaningful exercise of equal liberty until material conditions have improved.

The view is firmly opposed to mere equality of opportunity, which allows too much influence to the morally irrelevant contingencies of birth and talent; it is also opposed to counting a society's advanced cultural or intellectual achievements among the gains which can make sacrifice of the more primary goods just. What matters is that everyone be provided with the basic conditions for the realization of his own aims, regardless of the absolute level of achievement that may represent.

When the social and political implications of this view are worked out in detail, as is done in Part Two of the book, it is extremely appealing, but far from self-evident. In considering its theoretical basis, one should therefore ask whether the contractarian approach, realized in terms of the original position, depends on assumptions any less controversial than the substantive conclusions it is adduced to support.

The notion that a contract is the appropriate model for a theory of social justice depends on the view that it is fair to require people to submit to procedures and institutions only if, given the opportunity, they could in some sense have agreed in advance on the principles to which they must submit. That is why Rawls calls the theory "justice as fairness." (Indeed, he believes that a similar contractual basis can be found for the principles of individual morality, yielding a theory of rightness as fairness.) The fundamental attitude toward persons on which justice as fairness depends is a respect for their autonomy or freedom.[3] Since social institutions are simply there and people are born into them, submission cannot be literally voluntary, but (p. 13) "A society satisfying the principles of justice as fairness comes as close as a society can to being a voluntary scheme, for it meets the principles which free and equal persons would assent to under circumstances that are fair."

Before considering whether the original position embodies these conditions, we must ask why respect for the freedom of others, and the desire to make society as near to voluntary as possible, should be taken as the mainspring of the sense of justice. That gives liberty a position of

3. Expanding on this point, Rawls submits that his view is susceptible to a Kantian interpretation, but the details of the analogy are not always convincing. See, e.g., the claim on p. 253 that the principles of justice are categorical imperatives, because the argument for them does not assume that the parties to the agreement have particular ends, but only that they desire those primary goods that it is rational to want whatever else one wants. First of all, the desire for those primary goods is not itself the motive for obeying the principles of justice in real life, but only for choosing them in the original position. Secondly, imperatives deriving from such a desire would be hypothetical and assertoric in Kant's system, not categorical. But since our adherence to the two principles is supposed to be motivated by a sense of justice growing out of gratitude for the benefits received from just institutions, the imperatives of justice as fairness would in fact appear to be hypothetical and problematic (*Foundation of the Metaphysics of Morals*, pp. 415-416 of the Prussian Academy Edition).

great importance from the very beginning, an importance that it retains in the resulting substantive theory. But we must ask how the respect for autonomy by itself can be expected to yield further results as well.

When one justifies a policy on the ground that the affected parties would have (or even have) agreed to it, much depends on the reasons for their agreement. If it is motivated by ignorance or fear or helplessness or a defective sense of what is reasonable, then actual or possible prior agreement does not sanction anything. In other cases, prior agreement for the right reasons can be obtained or presumed, but it is not the agreement that justifies what has been agreed to, but rather whatever justifies the agreement itself. If, for example, certain principles would be agreed to because they are just, that cannot be what makes them just. In many cases the appeal to hypothetical prior agreement is actually of this character. It is not a final justification, not a mark of respect for autonomy, but merely a way of recalling someone to the kind of *moral* judgment he would make in the absence of distorting influences derived from his special situation.

Actual or presumable consent can be the *source* of a justification only if it is already accepted that the affected parties are to be treated as certain reasons would incline each of them to want to be treated. The circumstances of consent are designed to bring those reasons into operation, suppressing irrelevant considerations, and the fact that the choice would have been made becomes a further reason for adhering to the result.

When the interests of the parties do not naturally coincide, a version of consent may still be preserved if they are able to agree in advance on a procedure for settling conflicts. They may agree unanimously that the procedure threats them equally in relevant respects, though they would not be able to agree in advance to any of the particular distributions of advantages that it might yield. (An example would be a lottery to determine the recipient of some indivisible benefit.)

For the result of such a choice to be morally acceptable, two things must be true: (a) the choice must be unanimous; (b) the circumstances that make unanimity possible must not undermine the equality of the parties in other respects. Presumably they must be deprived of some knowledge (for example, of who will win the lottery) in order to reach agreement, but it is essential that they not be unequally deprived (as would be the case, for example, if they agreed to submit a dispute to an arbitrator who, unknown to any of them, was extremely biased).

The more disparate the conflicting interests to be balanced, however, the more information the parties must be deprived of to insure unanimity, and doubts begin to arise whether any procedure can be relied on to treat everyone equally in respect of the relevant interests. There is then a real question whether hypothetical choice under conditions of ignorance, as a representation of consent, can by itself provide a moral justification for outcomes that could not be unanimously agreed to if they were known in advance.

Can such a procedure be used to justify principles for evaluating the basic structure of social institutions? Clearly the preferences of individuals are so divergent that they would not voluntarily agree on a common set of principles if all were given an equal voice. According to the theory of the original position, the appeal to prior agreement can be utilized, nevertheless, by requiring the hypothetical choice to be made on the basis of reasons that all men have in common, omitting those which would lead them to select different principles and institutions. By restricting the basis of the hypothetical agreements in this way, however, one may lose some of its justifying power. We must therefore look carefully at the conditions imposed on a choice in the original position. Since Rawls does not, in any case, offer abstract argument for the contractarian approach, its defense must be found in its application.

The original position is supposed to be the most philosophically favored interpretation of a hypothetical initial *status quo* in which fundamental agreements would be fair. The agreements can then be appealed to in disputes over the justice of institutions. The parties have an equal voice and they choose freely: in fact, they can all arrive independently at the same conclusions. Each of us, moreover, can enter the original position at any time simply by observing its rather special restrictions on arguments, and choosing principles from that point of view.

All this is possible because the grounds of choice are severely restricted as follows. The parties are mutually disinterested—that is, neither altruistic nor envious. About their own desires they know only what is true of everyone: that they have some life plan or conception of the good and a personal commitment to certain other individuals. Whatever the details, they know these interests can be advanced by the employment of very basic primary goods under conditions of liberty. They also possess general knowledge about eonomics, politics, and sociology and they know that the circumstances of justice, conflicting interests and moderate scarcity, obtain. Finally, they believe that they have a sense of justice which will help them to adhere to the principles selected, but they know enough about moral psychology to realize that their choices must take into account the strains of commitment which will be felt when the principles are actually adopted, and the importance of choosing principles that will, when put into application, evoke their own support and thereby acquire psychological stability. Everything else—their talents, their social position, even the general nature or stage of development of their particular society—is covered over with a thick veil of ignorance on the ground that it is morally irrelevant. The choice should not be influenced by social and natural contingencies that would lead some parties to press for special advantages, or give some of them special bargaining power.

Rawls contends (p. 21) that these restrictions "collect together into one conception a number of conditions on principles that we are ready upon due consideration to recognize as reasonable . . . One argues," he says (p. 18), "from widely accepted but weak premises to more specific conclusions. Each of the presumptions should by itself be natural and plausible; some of them may seem innocuous or even trivial. The aim of the contract approach is to establish that taken together they impose significant bounds on acceptable principles of justice."

I do not believe that the assumptions of the original position are either weak or innocuous or uncontroversial. In fact, the situation thus constructed may not be fair. Rawls says that the aim of the veil of ignorance is "to rule out those principles that it would be rational to propose for acceptance, however little the chance of success, only if one knew certain things that are irrelevant from the standpoint of justice" (p. 18). Let us grant that the parties should be equal and should not be in possession of information which would lead them to seek advantages on morally irrelevant grounds like race, sex, parentage, or natural endowments. But they are deprived also of knowledge of their particular conception of the good. It seems odd to regard that as morally irrelevant from the standpoint of justice. If someone favors certain principles because of his conception of the good, he will not be seeking special advantages for himself so long as he does not know who in the society he is. Rather he will be opting for principles that advance the good for everyone, as defined by that conception. (I assume a conception of the good is just that, and not simply a system of tastes or preferences.) Yet Rawls appears to believe that it would be as unfair to permit people to press for the realization of their conception of the good as to permit them to press for the advantage of their social class.

It is true that men's different conceptions of the good divide them and produce conflict, so allowing this knowledge to the parties in the original position would prevent unanimity. Rawls concludes that the information must be suppressed and a common idea substituted which will permit agreement without selecting any particular conception of the good. This is achieved by means of the class of primary goods that it is supposedly rational to want whatever else one wants. Another possible conclusion, however, is that the model of the original position will not

1023

work because in order to secure spontaneous unanimity and avoid the necessity of bargaining one must suppress information that is morally relevant, and moreover suppress it in a way that does not treat the parties equally.

What Rawls wishes to do, by using the notion of primary goods, is to provide an Archimedean point, as he calls it, from which choice is possible without unfairness to any of the fuller conceptions of the good that lead people to differ. A *theory* of the good is presupposed, but it is ostensibly neutral between divergent particular conceptions, and supplies a least common denominator on which a choice in the original position can be based without unfairness to any of the parties. Only later, when the principles of justice have been reached on this basis, will it be possible to rule out certain particular interests or aims as illegitimate because they are unjust. It is a fundamental feature of Rawls' conception of the fairness of the original position that it should not permit the choice of principles of justice to depend on a particular conception of the good over which the parties may differ.

The construction does not, I think, accomplish this, and there are reasons to believe that it cannot be successfully carried out. Any hypothetical choice situation which requires agreement among the parties will have to impose strong restrictions on the grounds of choice, and these restrictions can be justified only in terms of a conception of the good. It is one of those cases in which there is no neutrality to be had, because neutrality needs as much justification as any other position.

Rawls' minimal conception of the good does not amount to a weak assumption: it depends on a strong assumption of the sufficiency of that reduced conception for the purposes of justice. The refusal to rank particular conceptions of the good implies a very marked tolerance for individual inclinations. Rawls is opposed not only to teleological conceptions according to which justice requires adherence to the principles that will maximize the good. He is also opposed to the natural position that even in a nonteleological theory what is just must depend on what is good, at least to the extent that a correct conception of the good must be used in determining what counts as an advantage and what as a disadvantage, and how much, for purposes of distribution and compensation. I interpret him as saying that the principles of justice are objective and interpersonally recognizable in a way that conceptions of the good are not. The refusal to rank individual conceptions and the reliance on primary goods are intended to insure this objectivity.

Objectivity may not be so easily achieved.[4] The suppression of

4. For the ideas in this paragraph I am indebted to Mary Gibson.

knowledge required to achieve unanimity is not equally fair to all the parties, because the primary goods are not equally valuable in pursuit of all conceptions of the good. They will serve to advance many different individual life plans (some more efficiently than others), but they are less useful in implementing views that hold a good life to be readily achievable only in certain well-defined types of social structure, or only in a society that works concertedly for the realization of certain higher human capacities and the suppression of baser ones, or only given certain types of economic relations among men. The model contains a strong individualistic bias, which is further strengthened by the motivational assumptions of mutual disinterest and absence of envy. These assumptions have the effect of discounting the claims of conceptions of the good that depend heavily on the relation between one's own position and that of others (though Rawls is prepared to allow such considerations to enter in so far as they affect self-esteem). The original position seems to presuppose not just a neutral theory of the good, but a liberal, individualistic conception according to which the best that can be wished for someone is the unimpeded pursuit of his own path, provided it does not interfere with the rights of others. The view is persuasively developed in the later portions of the book, but without a sense of its controversial character.

Among different life plans of this general type the construction is neutral. But given that many conceptions of the good do not fit into the individualistic pattern, how can this be described as a fair choice situation for principles of justice? Why should parties in the original position be prepared to commit themselves to principles that may frustrate or contravene their deepest convictions, just because they are deprived of the knowledge of those convictions?

There does not seem to be any way of redesigning the original position to do away with a restrictive assumption of this kind. One might think it would be an improvement to allow the parties full information about eveyone's preferences and conception of the good, merely depriving them of the knowledge of who they were. But this, as Rawls points out (pp. 173-4), would yield no result at all. For either the parties would retain their conceptions of the good and, choosing from different points of view, would not reach unanimity, or else they would possess no aims of their own and would be asked to choose in terms of the aims of all the people they might be—an unintelligible request which provides no basis for a unified choice, in the absence of a dominant conception. The reduction to a common ground of choice is therefore essential for the model to operate at all, and the selection of that ground inevitably represents a strong assumption.

Let us now turn to the argument leading to the choice of the two principles in the original position as constructed. The core of this argument appears in Sections 26-9, intertwined with an argument against the choice of the principle of average utility. Rawls has gone to some lengths to defend his controversial claim that in the original position it is rational to adopt the maximin rule which leads one to choose principles that favor the bottom of the social hierarchy, instead of accepting a greater risk at the bottom in return for the possibility of greater benefits at the top (as might be prudentially rational if one had an equal chance of being anyone in the society).

Rawls states (p. 154) that three conditions which make maximin plausible hold in the original position to a high degree. (1) "There must be some reason for sharply discounting estimates of . . . probabilities." (2) "The person choosing has a conception of the good such that he cares very little, if anything, for what he might gain above the minimum stipend that he can, in fact, be sure of by following the maximin rule." (3) "The rejected alternatives have outcomes that one can hardly accept." Let us consider these in turn.

The first condition is very important, and the claim that it holds in the original position is not based simply on a general rejection of the principle of insufficient reason (that is, the principle that where probabilities are unknown they should be regarded as equal). For one could characterize the original position in such a way that the parties would be prudentially rational to choose as if they had an equal chance of being anyone in the society, and the problem is to see why this would be an inappropriate representation of the grounds for a choice of principles.

One factor mentioned by Rawls is that the subject matter of the choice is extremely serious, since it involves institutions that will determine the total life prospects for the parties and those close to them. It is not just a choice of alternatives for a single occasion. Now this would be a reason for a conservative choice even if one knew the relative probabilities of different outcomes. It would be irresponsible to accept even a small risk of dreadful life prospects for oneself and one's descendants in exchange for a good chance of wealth or power. But what is needed is an account of why probabilities should be totally discounted, and not just with regard to the most unacceptable outcomes. The difference principle, for example, is supposed to apply at all levels of social development, so it is not justified merely by the desire to avoid grave risks. The fact that total life prospects are involved does not seem an adequate explanation. There must be some reason against allowing probabilities (proportional, for instance, to the number of persons in each social position) to enter into the choice of distributions above an acceptable minimum. Let me stress that I am posing a question not about decision theory but about the design of the original position and the comprehensiveness of the veil of ignorance. Why should it be thought that a just solution will be reached only if these considerations are suppressed?

Their suppression is justified, I think, only on the assumption that the proportions of people in various social positions are regarded as morally irrelevant, and this must be because it is not thought acceptable to sum advantages and disadvantages over persons, so that a loss for some is compensated by a gain for others. This aspect of the design of the original position appears, therefore, to be motivated by the wish to avoid extending to society as a whole the principle of rational choice for one man. Now this is supposed to be one of the *conclusions* of the contract approach, not one of its presuppositions. Yet the constraints on choice in Rawls' version of the original position are designed to rule out the possibility of such an extension,[5] by requiring that probabilities be discounted. I can see no way to avoid presupposing some definite view on this matter in the design of a contract situation. If that is true, then a contract approach cannot give any particular view very much support.

Consider next the second condition. Keeping in mind that the parties in the original position do not know the stage of development of their society, and therefore do not know what minimum will be guaranteed by a maximin strategy, it is difficult to understand how an individual can know that he "cares very little, if anything, for what he might gain above the minimum." The explanation Rawls offers (p. 156) seems weak. Even if parties in the original position accept the priority of liberty, and even if the veil of ignorance leaves them with a skeletal conception of the good, it seems impossible that they should care very little for increases in primary economic and social goods above what the difference principle guarantees at any given stage of social development.

Finally, the third condition, that one should rule out certain possibilities as unacceptable, is certainly a ground for requiring a social minimum and the priority of basic personal liberties, but it is not a ground for adopting the maximin rule in that general form needed to justify the choice of the difference principle. That must rely on stronger egalitarian premises.[6]

5. I.e. they do not just refuse to assume that the extension is acceptable: they assume that it is unacceptable.

6. A factor not considered in Rawls' argument, which suggests that the difference principle may be too weak, is the following. If differential social and economic benefits are allowed to provide incentives, then the people at the top will tend to be those with certain talents and abilities, and the people at the bottom, even though they are better off than they would be otherwise, will tend to lack those qualities. Such a consistent schedule of

Some of these premises reveal themselves in other parts of the argument. For example, the strongly egalitarian idea that sacrifice at the bottom is always worse than sacrifice at the top plays a central role in the appeal to strains of commitment and psychological stability. It is urged against the utilitarian alternative to the difference principle, for example, that the sacrifices utilitarianism might require would be psychologically unacceptable.

> The principles of justice apply to the basic structure of the social system and to the determination of life prospects. What the principle of utility asks is precisely a sacrifice of these prospects. We are to accept the greater advantages of others as a sufficient reason for lower expectations over the whole course of our life. This is surely an extreme demand, In fact, when society is conceived as a system of cooperation designed to advance the good of its members, it seems quite incredible that some citizens should be expected, on the basis of political principles, to accept lower prospects of life for the sake of others [p. 178].

Notice that if we substitute the words "difference principle" for "principle of utility," we get an argument that might be offered against the difference principle by someone concentrating on the sacrifices it requires of those at the top of the social order. They must live under institutions that limit their life prospects unless an advantage to them also benefits those beneath them. The only difference between the two arguments is in the relative position of the parties and of their sacrifices.[7] It is of course a vital difference, but that depends on a moral judgment—namely, that sacrifices which lessen social inequality are acceptable while sacrifices which increase inequality are not.

This appeal to psychological stability and the strains of commitment therefore adds to the grounds of choice in the original position a moral view that belongs to the substance theory. The argument may receive

---

rewards inevitably affects people's sense of their intrinsic worth, and any society operating on the difference principle will have a meritocratic flavor. This is very different from the case where an unequal distribution that benefits the worst off is not visibly correlated with any independent qualities. Rawls does suggest (p. 546) that "excusable envy" may be given its due in the operation of the difference principle by including self-esteem among the primary goods. But he does not stress the *bases* of income inequality. The phenomenon I have described is not *envy*. Rawls is too willing to rely on equal liberty as the support of self-esteem; this leads him to underrate the effect of differential rewards on people's conception of themselves. A reward that is consistently attached to a certain quality stops being perceived as mere good luck.

7. Exactly the same sacrifice could, after all, be either at the bottom or at the top, depending on the stage of advancement of the society.

some support from Rawls' idea about the natural development of moral sentiments, but they in turn are not independent of his ethical theory. If a hypothetical choice in the original position must be based on what one can expect to find morally acceptable in real life, then that choice is not the true ground of acceptability.[8]

Another strong conclusion of the theory is the priority of equal liberty, expressed in the lexical ordering of the two principles. The argument for *equal* liberty as a natural goal is straightforward. No analogue of the difference principle can apply permanently to liberty because it cannot be indefinitely increased. There will come a point at which increases in the liberty of the worst off can be achieved not by further increasing the liberty of the best off, but only by closing the gap. If one tries to maximize for everyone what really has a maximin, the result is equality.

The priority of liberty over other goods, however, is chosen in the original position on the basis of a judgment that the fundamental interest in determining one's plan of life assumes priority once the most basic material needs have been met, and that further increases in other goods depend for their value primarily on the ability to employ them under conditions of maximum liberty. "Thus the desire for liberty is the chief regulative interest that the parties must suppose they all will have in common in due course. The veil of ignorance forces them to abstract from the particulars of their plans of life thereby leading to this conclusion. The serial ordering of the two principles then follows" (p. 543). The parties also reflect that equal liberty guarantees them all a basic self-esteem against the background of which some differences in social position and wealth will be acceptable. Here again an explicitly liberal conception of individual good is used to defend a choice in the original position.

I have attempted to argue that the presumptions of the contract

---

8. A similar objection could be made to Rawls' claim that the difference principle provides a condition of reciprocal advantage that allows everyone to cooperate willingly in the social order. Obviously, those at the bottom could not prefer any other arrangement, but what about those at the top? Rawls says the following:"To begin with, it is clear that the well-being of each depends on a scheme of social cooperation without which no one could have a satisfactory life. Secondly, we can ask for the willing cooperation of everyone only if the terms of the scheme are reasonable. The difference principle, then, seems to be a fair basis on which those better endowed, or more fortunate in their social circumstances, could expect others to collaborate with them when some workable arrangement is a necessary condition of the good of all" (p. 103). But if some scheme of social cooperation is necessary for *anyone* to have a satisfactory life, everyone will benefit from a wide range of schemes. To assume that the worst off need further benefits to cooperate willingly while the best off do not is simply to repeat the egalitarian principle.

method Rawls employs are rather strong, and that the original position therefore offers less independent support to his conclusions than at first appears. The egalitarian liberalism which he develops and the conception of the good on which it depends are extremely persuasive, but the original position serves to model rather than to justify them. The contract approach allied with a non-liberal conception of the good would yield different results, and some conceptions of the good are incompatible with a contract approach to justice altogether. I believe that Rawls' conclusions can be more persuasively defended by direct moral arguments for liberty and equality, some of which he provides and some of which are indirectly represented in his present position. He remarks that it is worth

> noting from the outset that justice as fairness, like other contract views, consists of two parts: (1) an interpretation of the initial situation and of the problem of choice posed there, and (2) a set of principles which, it is argued, would be agreed to. One may accept the first part of the theory (or some variant thereof), but not the other, and conversely [p. 15].

He suggests that the principles are more likely to be rejected than their contractual basis, but I suspect the reverse. It seems to me likely that over the long term this book will achieve its permanent place in the literature of political theory because of the substantive doctrine that it develops so eloquently and persuasively. The plausibility of the results will no doubt be taken to confirm the validity of the method, but such inferences are not always correct. It is possible that the solution to the combinatorial problems of social choice can be reached by means of self-interested individual choice under carefully specified conditions of uncertainty, but the basis of such a solution has yet to be discovered. . . .

R. M. Dworkin, The Original Position*

B. The Contract

I come, then, to . . . the use [Rawls] makes of the old idea of a social contract. I distinguish, as does Rawls, the general idea that an imaginary contract is an appropriate device for reasoning about justice, from

* [40 *U. Chi. L. Rev.* 500, 519-528 (1973). © 1973 by The University of Chicago. Reprinted by permission.

For biographical information, see page 145 supra.]

the more specific features of the original position, which count as a particular application of that general idea. Rawls thinks that all theories that can be seen to rest on a hypothetical social contract of some sort are related and are distinguished as a class from theories that cannot; he supposes, for example, that average utilitarianism, which can be seen as the product of a social contract on a particular interpretation, is more closely related to his own theory than either is to classical utilitarianism, which cannot be seen as the product of a contract on any interpretation. . . .

Rawls says that the contract is a powerful argument for his principles because it embodies philosophical principles that we accept, or would accept if we thought about them. We want to find out what these principles are, and we may put our problem this way. The two principles comprise a theory of justice that is built up from the hypothesis of a contract. But the contract cannot sensibly be taken as the fundamental premise or postulate of that theory, for the reasons I described in the first part of this article. It must be seen as a kind of halfway point in a larger argument, as itself the product of a deeper political theory that argues for the two principles *through* rather than *from* the contract. We must therefore try to identify the features of a deeper theory that would recommend the device of a contract as the engine for a theory of justice, rather than the other theoretical devices Rawls mentions, like the device of the impartial spectator.

We shall find the answer, I think, if we attend to and refine the familiar distinction philosophers make between two types of moral theories, which they call teleogical theories and deontological theories. I shall argue that any deeper theory that would justify Rawls's use of the contract must be a particular form of deontological theory, a theory that takes the idea of rights so seriously as to make them fundamental in political morality. I shall try to show how such a theory would be distinguished, as a type, from other types of political theories, and why only such a theory could give the contract the role and prominence Rawls does.

I must begin this argument, however, by explaining how I shall use some familiar terms. (1) I shall say that some state of affairs is a *goal* within a particular political theory if it counts in favor of a political act, within that theory, that the act will advance or preserve that state of affairs, and counts against an act that it will retard or threaten it. Goals may be relatively specific, like full employment or respect for authority, or relatively abstract, like improving the general welfare, advancing the power of a particular nation, or creating a utopian society according to a particular concept of human goodness or of the good life. (2) I shall say that an individual has a *right* to a particular political act, within a political

1031

theory, if the failure to provide that act, when he calls for it, would be unjustified within that theory even if the goals of the theory would, on the balance, be disserviced by that act. The strength of a particular right, within a particular theory, is a function of the degree of disservice to the goals of the theory, beyond a mere disservice on the whole, that is necessary to justify refusing an act called for under the right. In the popular political theory apparently prevailing in the United States, for example, individuals have rights to free public speech on political matters and to a certain minimum standard of living, but neither right is absolute and the former is much stronger than the latter. (3) I shall say that an individual has a *duty* to act in a particular way, within a political theory, if a political decision constraining such act is justified within that theory notwithstanding that no goal of the system would be served by that decision. A theory may provide, for example, that individuals have a duty to worship God, even though it does not stipulate any goal served by requiring them to do so.[17]

The three concepts I have described work in different ways, but they all serve to justify or to condemn, at least pro tanto, particular political decisions. In each case, the justification provided by citing a goal, a right, or a duty is in principle complete, in the sense that nothing need be added to make the justification effective, if it is not undermined by some competing considerations. But, though such a justification is in this sense complete, it need not, within the theory, be ultimate. It remains open to ask why the particular goal, right, or duty is itself justified, and the theory may provide an answer by deploying a *more basic* goal, right, or duty that is served by accepting this less basic goal, right, or duty as a complete justification in particular cases.

A particular goal, for example, might be justified as contributing to a more basic goal; thus, full employment might be justified as contributing to greater average welfare. Or a goal might be justified as serving a more basic right or duty; a theory might argue, for example, that improving the gross national product, which is a goal, is necessary to enable the state to respect the rights of individuals to a decent minimum standard of living, or that improving the efficiency of the police process is necessary to enforce various individual duties not to sin. On the other hand, rights and duties may be justified on the ground that, by acting as a complete justification on particular occasions, they, in fact serve more fundamental goals; the duty of individuals to drive carefully may be jus-

---

17. I do not count, as goals, the goal of respecting rights or enforcing duties. In this and other apparent ways my use of the terms I define is narrower than ordinary language permits.

tified, for example, as serving the more basic goal of improving the general welfare. This form of justification does not, of course, suggest that the less basic right or duty itself justifies political decisions only when these decisions, considered one by one, advance the more basic goal. The point is rather the familiar one of rule utilitarianism, that treating the right or duty as a complete justification in particular cases, without reference to the more basic goal, will in fact advance the goal in the long run.

So goals can be justified by other goals or by rights or duties, and rights or duties can be justified by goals. Rights and duties can also be justified, of course, by other, more fundamental duties or rights. Your duty to respect my privacy, for example, may be justified by my right to privacy. I do not mean merely that rights and duties may be correlated, as opposite sides of the same coin. That may be so when, for example, a right and the corresponding duty are justified as serving a more fundamental goal, as when your right to property and my corresponding duty not to trespass are together justified by the more fundamental goal of socially efficient land use. In many cases, however, corresponding rights and duties are not correlative, but one is derivative from the other, and it makes a difference which is derivative from which. There is a difference between the idea that you have a duty not a lie to me because I have a right not to be lied to, and the idea that I have a right that you not lie to me because you have a duty not to tell lies. In the first case I justify a duty by calling attention to a right; if I intend any further justification it is the right that I must justify, and I cannot do so by calling attention to the duty. In the second case it is the other way around. The difference is important because, as I shall shortly try to show, a theory that takes rights as fundamental is a theory of a different character from one that takes duties as fundamental.

Political theories will differ from one another, therefore, not simply in the particular goals, rights, and duties each sets out, but also in the way each connects the goals, rights, and duties it employs. In a well-formed theory some consistent set of these, internally ranked or weighted, will be taken as fundamental or ultimate within the theory. It seems reasonable to suppose that any particular theory will give ultimate pride of place to just one of these concepts; it will take some overriding goal, or some set of fundamentals rights, or some set of transcendent duties, as fundamental, and show other goals, rights, and duties as subordinate and derivative.[18]

We may therefore make a tentative initial classification of the politi-

18. But an "intuitionist" theory, as Rawls uses that term, need not.

cal theories we might produce, on the constructive model, as deep theories that might contain a contract as an intermediate device. Such a theory might be *goal-based*, in which case it would take some goal, like improving the general welfare, as fundamental; it might be *right-based*, taking some right, like the right of all men to the greatest possible overall liberty as fundamental; or it might be *duty-based*, taking some duty like the duty to obey God's will as set forth in the Ten Commandments, as fundamental. It is easy to find examples of pure, or nearly pure, cases of each of these types of theory. Utilitarianism is, as my example suggested, a goal-based theory; Kant's categorical imperatives compose a duty-based theory; and Tom Paine's theory of revolution is right-based.

Theories within each of these types are likely to share certain very general characteristics. The types may be contrasted, for example, by comparing the attitudes they display towards individual choice and conduct. Goal-based theories are concerned with the welfare of any particular individual only in so far as this contributes to some state of affairs stipulated as good quite apart from his choice of that state of affairs. This is plainly true of totalitarian goal-based theories, like fascism, that take the interest of a political organization as fundamental. It is also true of the various forms of utilitarianism, because, though they count up the impact of political decisions on distinct individuals, and are in this way concerned with individual welfare, they merge these impacts into overall totals or averages and take the improvement of these totals or averages as desirable quite apart from the decision of any individual that it is. It is also true of perfectionist theories, like Aristotle's, that impose upon individuals an ideal of excellence and take the goal of politics to be the culture of such excellence.

Right-based and duty-based theories, on the other hand, place the individual at the center, and take his decision or conduct as of fundamental importance. But the two types put the individual in a different light. Duty-based theories are concerned with the moral quality of his acts, because they suppose that it is wrong, without more, for an individual to fail to meet certain standards of behavior. Kant thought that it was wrong to tell a lie no matter how beneficial the consequences, not because having this practice promoted some goal, but just because it was wrong. Right-based theories are, in contrast, concerned with the independence rather than the conformity of individual action. They presuppose and protect the value of individual thought and choice. Both types of theory make use of the idea of moral rules, codes of conduct to be followed, on individual occasions, without consulting self-interest. Duty-based theories treat such codes of conduct as of the essence, whether set by society to the individual or by the individual to himself. The man at

1034

their center is the man who must conform to such a code, or be punished or corrupted if he does not. Right-based theories, however, treat codes of conduct as instrumental, perhaps necessary to protect the rights of others, but having no essential value in themselves. The man at their center is the man who benefits from others' compliance, not the man who leads the life of virtue by complying himself.

We should, therefore, expect that the different types of theories would be associated with different metaphysical or political temperaments, and that one or another would be dominant in certain sorts of political economy. Goal-based theories, for example, seem especially compatible with homogeneous societies, or those at least temporarily united by an urgent, overriding goal, like self-defense or economic expansion. We should also expect that these differences between types of theory would find echoes in the legal systems of the communities they dominate. We should expect, for example, that a lawyer would approach the question of punishing moral offenses through the criminal law in a different way if his inchoate theory of justice were goal-, right- or duty-based. If his theory were goal-based he would consider the full effect of enforcing morality upon his overriding goal. If this goal were utilitarian, for example, he would entertain, though he might, in the end, reject, Lord Devlin's arguments that the secondary effects of punishing immorality may be beneficial.[19] If his theory were duty-based, on the other hand, he would see the point of the argument, commonly called retributive, that since immorality is wrong the state must punish it even if it harms no one. If his theory were right-based, however, he would reject the retributive argument, and judge the utilitarian argument against the background of his own assumption that individual rights must be served even at some cost to the general welfare.

All this is, of course, superficial and trivial as ideological sociology. My point is only to suggest that these differences in the character of a political theory are important quite apart from the details of position that might distinguish one theory from another of the same character. It is for this reason that the social contract is so important a feature of Rawls's methodology. It signals that his deep theory is a right-based theory, rather than a theory of either of the other two types.

The social contract provides every potential party with a veto: unless he agrees, no contract is formed. The importance, and even the existence, of this veto is obscured in the particular interpretation of the contract that constitutes the original position. Since no one knows anything about himself that would distinguish him from anyone else, he cannot

19. See Dworkin, Lord Devlin and the Enforcement of Morals, 75 *Yale L.J.* 986 (1966).

rationally pursue any interest that is different. In these circumstances nothing turns on each man having a veto, or, indeed, on there being more than one potential party to the contract in the first place. But the original position is only one interpretation of the contract, and in any other interpretation in which the parties do have some knowledge with which to distinguish their situation or ambitions from those of others, the veto that the contract gives each party becomes crucial. The force of the veto each individual has depends, of course, upon his knowledge, that is to say, the particular interpretation of the contract we in the end choose. But the fact that individuals should have any veto at all is in itself remarkable.

It can have no place in a purely goal-based theory, for example. I do not mean that the parties to a social contract could not settle on a particular social goal and make that goal henceforth the test of the justice of political decisions. I mean that no goal-based theory could make a contract the proper device for deciding upon a principle of justice in the first place; that is, the deep theory we are trying to find could not itself be goal-based.

The reason is straightforward. Suppose some particular overriding goal, like the goal of improving the average welfare in a community, or increasing the power and authority of a state, or creating a utopia according to a particular conception of the good, is taken as fundamental within a political theory. If any such goal is fundamental, then it authorizes such distribution of resources, rights, benefits, and burdens within the community as will best advance that goal, and condemns any other. The contract device, however, which supposes each individual to pursue his own interest and gives each a veto on the collective decision, applies a very different test to determine the optimum distribution. It is designed to produce the distribution that each individual deems in his own best interest, given his knowledge under whatever interpretation of the contract is specified, or at least to come as close to that distribution as he thinks he is likely to get. The contract, therefore, offers a very different test of optimum distribution than a direct application of the fundamental goal would dictate. There is no reason to suppose that a system of individual vetoes will produce a good solution to a problem in which the fairness of a distribution, considered apart from the contribution of the distribution to an overall goal, is meant to count for nothing.

It might be, of course, that a contract would produce the result that some fundamental goal dictates. Some critics, in fact, think that men in the original position, Rawls's most favored interpretation of the contract, would choose a theory of justice based on principles of average utility, that is, just the principles that a deep theory stipulating the fundamental goal of average utility would produce.[20] But if this is so, it is either because of coincidence or because the interpretation of the contract has been chosen to produce this result; in either case the contract is supererogatory, because the final result is determined by the fundamental goal and the contract device adds nothing.

One counterargument is available. Suppose it appears that the fundamental goal will in fact be served only if the state is governed in accordance with principles that all men will see to be, in some sense, in their own interest. If the fundamental goal is the aggrandizement of the state, for example, it may be that this goal can be reached only if the population does not see that the government acts for this goal, but instead supposes that it acts according to principles shown to be in their individual interests through a contract device; only if they believe this will they work in the state's interest at all. We cannot ignore this devious, if unlikely, argument, but it does not support the use that Rawls makes of the contract. The argument depends upon a deception, like Sidgewick's famous argument that utilitarianism can best be served by keeping the public ignorant of that theory.[21] A theory that includes such a deception is ineligible on the constructivist model we are pursuing, because our aim, on that model, is to develop a theory that unites our convictions and can serve as a program for public action; publicity is as much a requirement of our deep theory as of the conception of justice that Rawls develops within it.

So a goal-based deep theory cannot support the contract, except as a useless and confusing appendage. Neither can a duty-based deep theory, for much the same reasons. A theory that takes some duty or duties to be fundamental offers no ground to suppose that just institutions are those seen to be in everyone's self-interest under some description. I do not deny, again, that the parties to the contract may decide to impose certain duties upon themselves and their successors, just as they may decide to adopt certain goals, in the exercise of their judgment of their own self-interest. Rawls describes the duties they would impose upon themselves under his most favored interpretation, the original position, and calls these natural duties. But this is very different from supposing that the deep theory, which makes this decision decisive of what these duties are, can itself be duty-based.

It is possible to argue, of course, as many philosophers have, that a man's self-interest lies in doing his duty under the moral law, either be-

20. John Mackie presented a forceful form of this argument to an Oxford seminar in the fall of 1972.
21. H. Sidgewick, *The Methods of Ethics* 489 ff. (7th ed. 1907).

cause God will punish him otherwise, or because fulfilling his role in the natural order is his most satisfying activity, or, as Kant thought, because only in following rules he could consistently wish universal can he be free. But that says a man's duties define his self-interest, and not the other way round. It is an argument not for deciding upon a man's particular duties by letting him consult his own interest, but rather for his setting aside any calculations of self-interest, except calculations of duty. It could not, therefore, support the role of a Rawlsian contract in a duty-based deep theory.

It is true that if a contract were a feature of a duty-based deep theory, an interpretation of the contract could be chosen that would dissolve the apparent conflict between self-interest and duty. It might be a feature of the contract situation, for example, that all parties accepted the idea just mentioned, that their self-interest lay in ascertaining and doing their duty. This contract would produce principles that accurately described their duties, at least if we add the supposition that they are proficient, for some reason, in discovering what their duties are. But then, once again, we have made the contract supererogatory, a march up the hill and then back down again. We would have done better simply to work out principles of justice from the duties the deep theory takes as fundamental.

The contract does, however, make sense in a right-based deep theory. Indeed, it seems a natural development of such a theory. The basic idea of a right-based theory is that distinct individuals have interests that they are entitled to protect if they so wish. It seems natural, in developing such a theory, to try to identify the institutions an individual would veto in the exercise of whatever rights are taken as fundamental. The contract is an excellent device for this purpose, for at least two reasons. First, it allows us to distinguish between a veto in the exercise of these rights and a veto for the sake of some interest that is not so protected, a distinction we can make by adopting an interpretation of the contract that reflects our sense of what these rights are. Second, it enforces the requirements of the constructive model of argument. The parties to the contract face a practical problem; they must devise a constitution from the options available to them, rather than postponing their decision to a day of later moral insight, and they must devise a program that is both practical and public in the sense I have described.

It seems fair to assume, then, that the deep theory behind the original position must be a right-based theory of some sort. There is another way to put the point, which I have avoided until now. It must be a theory that is based on the concept of rights that are *natural,* in the sense that they are not the product of any legislation, or convention, or hypothetical contract. I have avoided that phrase because it has, for many people, disqualifying metaphysical associations. They think that natural rights are supposed to be spectral attributes worn by primitive men like amulets, which they carry into civilization to ward off tyranny. Mr. Justice Black, for example, thought it was a sufficient refutation of a judicial philosophy he disliked simply to point out that it seemed to rely on this preposterous notion.[23]

But on the constructive model, at least, the assumption of natural rights is not a metaphysically ambitious one. It requires no more than the hypothesis that the best political program, within the sense of that model, is one that takes the protection of certain individual choices as fundamental, and not properly subordinated to any goal or duty or combination of these. This requires no ontology more dubious or controversial than any contrary choice of fundamental concepts would be and, in particular, no more than the hypothesis of a fundamental goal that underlies the various popular utilitarian theories would require. Nor is it disturbing that a Rawlsian deep theory makes these rights natural rather than legal or conventional. Plainly, any right-based theory must presume rights that are not simply the product of deliberate legislation or explicit social custom, but are independent grounds for judging legislation and custom. On the constructive model, the assumption that rights are in this sense natural is simply one assumption to be made and examined for its power to unite and explain our political convictions, one basic programatic decision to submit to this test of coherence and experience.

Nozick, Anarchy, State, and Utopia*

Protective Associations

. . . In a state of nature an individual may himself enforce his rights, defend himself, exact compensation, and punish (or at least try

---

23. Griswold v. Connecticut, 381 U.S. 479, 507 (1964) (dissenting opinion).

* [Pp. 12-14, 15-17, 110-113 (1974). Excerpted from *Anarchy, State, and Utopia*, by Robert Nozick, © 1974 by Basic Books, Inc., Publishers, New York. Reprinted by permission.

Robert Nozick (1938–) was educated at Columbia University (A.B. 1959) and Princeton University (A.M. 1961; Ph.D. 1963). He was a member of the Philosophy Department at Princeton (1962-1965), Fulbright Scholar at Oxford University (1963-1964), Assistant Professor of Philosophy at Harvard University (1965-1967), and Associate Professor of Philosophy at Rockefeller University (1967-1969) before becoming Professor of Philosophy at Harvard in 1969. His book, *Anarchy, State, and Utopia* (1974), received a National Book Award in 1975.]

his best to do so). Others may join with him in his defense, at his call. They may join with him to repulse an attacker or to go after an aggressor because they are public spirited, or because they are his friends, or because he has helped them in the past, or because they wish him to help them in the future, or in exchange for something. Groups of individuals may form mutual-protection associations: all will answer the call of any member for defense or for the enforcement of his rights. In union there is strength. Two inconveniences attend such simple mutual-protection associations: (1) everyone is always on call to serve a protective function (and how shall it be decided who shall answer the call for those protective functions that do not require the services of all members?); and (2) any member may call out his associates by saying his rights are being, or have been, violated. Protective associations will not want to be at the beck and call of their cantankerous or paranoid members, not to mention those of their members who might attempt, under the guise of self-defense, to use the association to violate the rights of others. Difficulties will also arise if two different members of the same association are in dispute, each calling upon his fellow members to come to his aid.

A mutual-protection association might attempt to deal with conflict among its own members by a policy of nonintervention. But this policy would bring discord within the association and might lead to the formation of subgroups who might fight among themselves and thus cause the breakup of the association. This policy would also encourage potential aggressors to join as many mutual-protection associations as possible in order to gain immunity from retaliatory or defensive action, thus placing a great burden on the adequacy of the initial screening procedure of the association. Thus protective associations (almost all of those that will survive which people will join) will not follow a policy of nonintervention; they will use some procedure to determine how to act when some members claim that other members have violated their rights. Many arbitrary procedures can be imagined (for example, act on the side of that member who complains first), but most persons will want to join associations that follow some procedure to find out which claimant is correct. When a member of the association is in conflict with nonmembers, the association also will want to determine in some fashion who is in the right, if only to avoid constant and costly involvement in each member's quarrels, whether just or unjust. The inconvenience of everyone's being on call, whatever their activity at the moment or inclinations or comparative advantage, can be handled in the usual manner by division of labor and exchange. Some people will be *hired* to perform protective functions, and some entrepreneurs will go into the business of selling protective services. Different sorts of protective policies would be offered, at different prices, for those who may desire more extensive or elaborate protection.[4]

An individual might make more particular arrangements or commitments short of turning over to a private protective agency all functions of detection, apprehension, judicial determination of guilt, punishment, and exaction of compensation. Mindful of the dangers of being the judge in his own case, he might turn the decision as to whether he has indeed been wronged, and to what extent, to some other neutral or less involved party. In order for the occurrence of the social effect of justice's being seen to be done, such a party would have to be generally respected and thought to be neutral and upright. Both parties to a dispute may so attempt to safeguard themselves against the appearance of partiality, and both might even agree upon the *same* person as the judge between them, and agree to abide by his decision. (Or there might be a specified process through which one of the parties dissatisfied with the decision could appeal it.) But, for obvious reasons, there will be strong tendencies for the above-mentioned functions to converge in the same agent or agency. . . .

4. We shall see (p. 18) how money may exist in a state of nature without an explicit agreement that establishes a medium of exchange. Private protective services have been proposed and discussed by various writers in the individualist-anarchist tradition. For background, see Lysander Spooner, *No Treason: The Constitution of No Authority* (1870), *Natural Law,* and *A Letter to Grover Cleveland on His False Inaugural Address; The Usurpation and Crimes of Lawmakers and Judges, and the Consequent Poverty, Ignorance, and Servitude of the People* (Boston: Benjamin R. Tucker, 1886), all republished in *The Collected Works of Lysander Spooner,* 6 vols. (Weston, Mass.: M & S Press, 1971). Benjamin R. Tucker discusses the operation of a social system in which all protective functions are privately supplied in *Instead of a Book* (New York, 1893), pp. 14, 25, 32-33, 36, 43, 104, 326-329, 340-341, many passages of which are reprinted in his *Individual Liberty,* ed. Clarence Lee Swartz (New York, 1926). It cannot be overemphasized how lively, stimulating, and interesting are the writings and arguments of Spooner and Tucker, so much so that one hesitates to mention any secondary source. But see also James J. Martin's able and interesting *Men Against The State: The Expositors of Individualist Anarchism in America, 1827-1908* for a description of the lives and views of Spooner, Tucker, and other writers in their tradition. See also the more extended discussion of the private protection scheme in Francis Tandy, *Voluntary Socialism* (Denver: F. D. Tandy, 1896), pp. 62-78. A critical discussion of the scheme is presented in John Hospers, *Libertarianism* (Los Angeles: Nash, 1971), chap. 11. A recent proponent is Murray N. Rothbard, who in *Power and Market* (Menlo Park, Calif.: Institute for Humane Studies, Inc., 1970), pp. 1-7, 120-123, briefly describes how he believes the scheme might operate and attempts to meet some objections to it. The most detailed discussion I know is in Morris and Linda Tannehill, *The Market for Liberty* (Lansing, Mich.: privately printed, 1970), especially pp. 65-115. Since I wrote this work in 1972, Rothbard has more extensively presented his views in *For a New Liberty* (New York: Macmillan, 1973), chaps. 3 and 11, and David Friedman has defended anarcho-capitalism with gusto in *The Machinery of Freedom* (New York: Harper & Row, 1973), pt. III. Each of these works is well worth reading, but neither leads me to revise what I say here.

The Dominant Protective Association

Initially, several different protective associations or companies will offer their services in the same geographical area. What will occur when there is a conflict between clients of different agencies? Things are relatively simple if the agencies reach the same decision about the disposition of the case. (Though each might want to exact the penalty.) But what happens if they reach different decisions as to the merits of the case, and one agency attempts to protect its client while the other is attempting to punish him or make him pay compensation? Only three possibilities are worth considering:

> 1. In such situations the forces of the two agencies do battle. One of the agencies always wins such battles. Since the clients of the losing agency are ill protected in conflicts with clients of the winning agency, they leave their agency to do business with the winner.
> 2. One agency has its power centered in one geographical area, the other in another. Each wins the battles fought close to its center of power, with some gradient being established. People who deal with one agency but live under the power of the other either move closer to their own agency's home headquarters of shift their patronage to the other protective agency. (The border is about as conflictful as one between states.)

In neither of these two cases does there remain very much geographical interspersal. Only one protective agency operates over a given geographical area.

> 3. The two agencies fight evenly and often. They win and lose about equally, and their interspersed members have frequent dealings and disputes with each other. Or perhaps without fighting or after only a few skirmishes the agencies realize that such battling will occur continually in the absence of preventive measures. In any case, to avoid frequent, costly, and wasteful battles the two agencies, perhaps through their executives, agree to resolve peacefully those cases about which they reach differing judgments. They agree to set up, and abide by the decisions of, some third judge or court to which they can turn when their respective judgments differ. (Or they might establish rules determining which agency has jurisdiction under which circumstances.)[8] Thus emerges a system of appeals courts and agreed upon rules about jurisdiction and the conflict of laws. Though different agencies operate, there is one unified federal judicial system of which they all are components.

8. For an indication of the complexity of such a body of rules, see American Law Institute, *Conflict of Laws; Second Restatement of the Law,* Proposed Official Draft, 1967-1969.

In each of these cases, almost all the persons in a geographical area are under some common system that judges between their competing claims and *enforces* their rights. Out of anarchy, pressed by spontaneous groupings, mutual-protection associations, division of labor, market pressures, economies of scale, and rational self-interest there arises something very much resembling a minimal state or a group of geographically distinct minimal states. Why is this market different from all other markets? Why would a virtual monopoly arise in this market without the government intervention that elsewhere creates and maintains it?[9] The worth of the product purchased, protection against others, is *relative:* it depends upon how strong the others are. Yet unlike other goods that are comparatively evaluated, maximal competing protective services cannot coexist; the nature of the service brings different agencies not only into competition for customers' patronage, but also into violent conflict with each other. Also, since the worth of the less than maximal product declines disproportionately with the number who purchase the maximal product, customers will not stably settle for the lesser good, and competing companies are caught in a declining spiral. Hence the three possibilities we have listed.

Our story above assumes that each of the agencies attempts in good faith to act within the limits of Locke's law of nature.[10] But one "protective association" might aggress against other persons. Relative to Locke's law of nature, it would be an outlaw agency. What actual counterweights would there be to its power? (What actual counterweights are there to the power of a state?) Other agencies might unite to act against it. People might refuse to deal with the outlaw agency's clients, boycotting them to reduce the probability of the agency's intervening in their own affairs. This might make it more difficult for the outlaw agency to get clients; but this boycott will seem an effective tool only on very optimistic assumptions about what cannot be kept secret, and about the costs to an individual of partial boycott as compared to the benefits of receiving the more extensive coverage offered by an "outlaw" agency. If the "outlaw" agency simply is an *open* aggressor, pillaging, plundering, and extorting under no plausible claim of justice, it will have a harder time than states. For the state's claim to legitimacy induces its citizens to believe they have

9. See Yale Brozen, "Is Government the Source of Monopoly?" *The Intercollegiate Review,* 5, no. 2 (1968-69), 67-78; Fritz Machlup, *The Political Economy of Monopoly* (Baltimore: Johns Hopkins Press, 1952).

10. Locke assumed that the preponderant majority, though not all, of the persons living in the state of nature would accept the law of nature. See Richard Ashcroft, "Locke's State of Nature," *American Political Science Review,* September 1968, pp. 898-915, especially pt. I.

some duty to obey its edicts, pay its taxes, fight its battles, and so on; and so some persons cooperate with it voluntarily. An openly aggressive agency could not depend upon, and would not receive, any such voluntary cooperation, since persons would view themselves simply as its victims rather than as its citizens.[11] . . .

Protecting Others

If the protective agency deems the independents' procedures for enforcing their own rights insufficiently reliable or fair when applied to its clients, it will prohibit the independents from such self-help enforcement. The grounds for this prohibition are that the self-help enforcement imposes risks of danger on its clients. Since the prohibition makes it impossible for the independents credibly to threaten to punish clients who violate their rights, it makes them unable to protect themselves from harm and seriously disadvantages the independents in their daily activities and life. Yet it is perfectly possible that the independents' activities including self-help enforcement could proceed without anyone's rights being violated (leaving aside the question of procedural rights). According to our principle of compensation . . . in these circumstances those persons promulgating and benefiting from the prohibition must compensate those disadvantaged by it. The clients of the protective agency, then, must compensate the independents for the disadvantages imposed upon them by being prohibited self-help enforcement of their own rights against the agency's clients. Undoubtedly, the least expensive way to compensate the independents would be to *supply* them with protective services to cover those situations of conflict with the paying customers of the protective agency. This will be less expensive than leaving them unprotected against violations of their rights (by not punishing any client who does so) and then attempting to pay them afterwards to cover their losses through having (and being in a position in which they were exposed to having) their rights violated. If it were *not* less expensive, then instead of buying protective services, people would save their money and use it to cover their losses perhaps by jointly pooling their money in an insurance scheme.

Must the members of the protective agency *pay* for protective services (vis-à-vis its clients) for the independents? Can they insist that the independents purchase the services themselves? After all, using self-help

---

11. See Morris and Linda Tannehill, *The Market for Liberty;* on the importance of voluntary cooperation to the functioning of governments see, for example, Adam Roberts, ed., *Civilian Resistance as National Defense* (Baltimore: Penguin Books, 1969) and Gene Sharp, *The Politics of Non-Violent Action* (Boston: Porter Sargent, 1973).

procedures would not have been without costs for the independent. The principle of compensation does not require those who prohibit an epileptic from driving to pay his full cost of taxis, chauffeurs, and so on. If the epileptic were allowed to run his own automobile, this too would have its costs: money for the car, insurance, gasoline, repair bills, and aggravation. In compensating for disadvantages imposed, the prohibitors need pay only an amount sufficient to compensate for the disadvantages of the prohibition *minus* an amount representing the costs the prohibited party would have borne were it not for the prohibition. The prohibitors needn't pay the complete costs of taxis; they must pay only the amount which when combined with the costs to the prohibited party of running his own private automobile is sufficient for taxis. They may find it less expensive to compensate in kind for the disadvantages they impose than to supply monetary compensation; they may engage in some activity that removes or partially lessens the disadvantages, compensating in money only for the net disadvantages remaining.

If the prohibitor pays to the person prohibited monetary compensation equal to an amount that covers the disadvantages imposed *minus* the costs of the activity where it permitted, this amount may be insufficient to enable the prohibited party to overcome the disadvantages. If his costs in performing the prohibited action would have been monetary, he can combine the compensation payment with this money unspent and purchase the equivalent service. But if his costs would not have been directly monetary but involve energy, time, and the like, as in the case of the independent's self-help enforcement of rights, then this monetary payment of the difference will not by itself enable the prohibited party to overcome the disadvantage by purchasing the equivalent of what he is prohibited. If the independent has other financial resources he can use without disadvantaging himself, then this payment of the difference will suffice to leave the prohibited party undisadvantaged. But *if* the independent has no such other financial resources, a protective agency may *not* pay him an amount *less* than the cost of its least expensive protective policy, and so leave him only the alternatives of being defenseless against the wrongs of its clients or having to work in the cash market to earn sufficient funds to total the premium on a policy. For this financially pressed prohibited individual, the agency must make up the difference between the *monetary* costs to him of the unprohibited activity and the amount necessary to purchase an overcoming or counter-balancing of the disadvantage imposed. The prohibitor must completely supply enough, in money or in kind, to overcome the disadvantages. No compensation need be provided to someone who would not be disadvantaged by buying protection for himself. For those of scanter resources, to whom the unprohibited activity had no monetary costs, the agency must

1045

provide the difference between the resources they can spare without dis-advantage and the cost of protection. For someone for whom it had some monetary costs, the prohibitor must supply the additional mone-tary amount (over and above what they can spare without disadvantage) necessary to overcome the disadvantages. If the prohibitors compensate in kind, they may *charge* the financially pressed prohibited party for this, up to the monetary costs to him of his unprohibited activity provided this amount is not greater than the price of the good. As the only effec-tive supplier, the dominant protective agency must offer in compensa-tion the difference between its own fee and monetary costs to this pro-hibited party of self-help enforcement. It almost always will receive this amount back in partial payment for the purchase of a protection policy. It goes without saying that these dealings and prohibitions apply only to those using unreliable or unfair enforcement procedures.

Thus the dominant protective agency must supply the independ-ents—that is, everyone it prohibits from self-help enforcement against its clients on the grounds that their procedures of enforcement are unre-liable or unfair—with protective services against its clients; it may have to provide some persons services for a fee that is less than the price of these services. These persons may, of course, choose to refuse to pay the fee and so do without these compensatory services. If the dominant pro-tective agency provides protective services in this way for independents, won't this lead people to leave the agency in order to receive its services without paying? Not to any great extent, since compensation is paid only to those who would be disadvantaged by purchasing protection for themselves, and only in the amount that will equal the cost of an unfancy policy when added to the sum of the monetary costs of self-help protec-tion plus whatever amount the person comfortably could pay. Further-more, the agency protects these independents it compensates only against its own paying clients on whom the independents are forbidden to use self-help enforcement. The more free riders there are, the more desirable it is to be a client always protected by the agency. This factor, along with the others, acts to reduce the number of free riders and to move the equilibrium toward almost universal participation.

Plattner, The New Political Theory*

. . . Nozick believes that the task of justifying the minimal state against anarchist objections can be accomplished by showing that such a

* ["The New Political Theory" by Marc Plattner, from *The Public Interest,* No. 40 (Sum-

state may arise from a situation of anarchy without violating anyone's rights. The initial situation of anarchy from which he begins is explicitly based upon Locke's state of nature, and acknowledges all the "inconveniences" that Locke found in such a situation. But Nozick refuses to accept Locke's "remedy" for these inconveniences—a civil government established on the basis of a social contract. Instead, he provides what he calls an "invisible-hand" explanation of the origin of the state—i.e., one in which a state arises without anyone actually having the objective of establishing it.

This "invisible-hand" explanation (which features entrepreneurs who sell "protection policies" to the inhabitants of the state of nature) is, to say the least, much more incredible than Locke's depiction of the social contract, and obviously is not meant to be a genuinely historical account. It encompasses a bewildering assortment of assumptions. At certain stages it assumes that people will routinely violate others' rights. At other stages it supposes that people will act with remarkable restraint. In some places it is meant to describe what would happen; in other places it is meant to describe only what *should* (if people act morally) happen. Because this explanation is so convoluted and laborious, the first part of *Anarchy, State, and Utopia* makes for difficult—and often tedious— reading.

Now, why does Nozick go to such lengths to provide this purely hypothetical invisible-hand explanation—as opposed to a contract explanation—of the origin of the state? Surprisingly, that is not such an easy question to answer. He does indeed have some words of high praise for the genre of invisible-hand explanations: They have "a certain lovely quality," are "specially satisfying," "yield greater understanding," and are "more satisfying" (pp. 18, 19) than explanations that account for phenomena on the basis of people's intentions. Perhaps I simply lack the professional philosopher's lofty appreciation of the aesthetic quality of certain kinds of arguments, but all this fails to convince that an extremely complicated and utterly implausible account of something should be preferred to a relatively simple and straightforward one.

Of course, the reason for Nozick's presenting the invisible-hand explanation would be obvious enough if the Lockean contract explanation were shown to be morally impermissible—i.e., necessarily to violate people's rights. But Nozick never shows this. Indeed, given his principles, he

mer 1975), pp. 119, 121-122. © 1975 by National Affairs, Inc. Reprinted by permission.

Marc F. Plattner (1945–) is Consulting Editor of *The Public Interest* and a member of the staff of the Twentieth Century Fund.]

cannot show it. Locke's social contract is formed by a group of men in the state of nature, each of whom "by consenting with others to make one body politic under one government, puts himself under an obligation to every one of that society to submit to the determination of the majority and to be concluded by it." Now, there is absolutely no reason why a group of men in Nozick's state of nature would not be perfectly within their rights to do the same. In fact, according to Nozick's "nonpaternalistic" version of the rights of man, they would even be able legitimately to contract themselves into total subjection to a despot. For if an individual may sell himself into slavery, why could a group of men not do the same?

It is clear, of course, why Nozick *wants* to avoid a contract teaching —a contract teaching easily lends itself to the justification of a more than minimal state. But it is not sufficient to his libertarian purpose for Nozick merely to offer an alternate derivation of the state from a state of nature. *To make good his claim that the more than minimal state cannot be justified, he would have to demonstrate that the derivation of the state by a Lockeantype contract is morally impermissible. And this he fails to do. . . .*

Scanlon, Nozick on Rights, Liberty, and Property*†

In *Anarchy, State, and Utopia*[1] Robert Nozick approaches political philosophy within a framework which at first sight seems both familiar and congenial to contemporary liberal thought. It is a framework which emphasizes individual rights and the derivation of political obligation from consent. The conclusions of the book, however, are liberal in the nineteenth-century sense of the term. Nozick holds that the only legitimate state is the minimal state, whose activities are confined to the protection of individuals and their property and to the enforcement of contracts. This state is unique among social organizations in having the right to force residents to pay for its services whether or not they have consented to do so. Citizens may band together for whatever other purposes they may desire—to provide education, to aid the needy, to organize so-

* [*Philosophy & Public Affairs* 6, no. 1 (Fall 1976). Copyright © 1976 by Princeton University Press. Reprinted by permission of Princeton University Press.

Thomas Scanlon (1940–) is Associate Professor of Philosophy at Princeton University, and is the author of articles on political philosophy and logic.]

† I am grateful to Dennis Thompson for helpful comments. NEH Fellowship support is also gratefully acknowledged.

1. (New York, 1974). Page numbers in the text refer to this book.

cial insurance schemes—but such schemes must be purely voluntary, and the state must enforce anyone's right not to be compelled to contribute to them.

Nozick reaches these conclusions by adhering as closely as possible to the idea that, in economic life as in politics, all valid obligations derive from consent. Of course, consent alone cannot be theoretically basic. Something must determine the conditions under which acquiescence counts as morally binding consent. In addition, the obligations and entitlements one person acquires through voluntary agreements can affect the alternatives open to others who have not been parties to these agreements. Something must determine when such side effects make an agreement void. In Nozick's theory these conditions and limits are set by a skeletal framework of rights derived from Locke. The minimal role allowed to the state and the great scope left to voluntary agreement and consent in his theory are direct consequences of the particular character of these rights. . . .

The contrast between Nozick's and Rawls' views on political obligation illustrates the important difference between two types of consent theory. In theories of the first type, actual consent has a fundamental role as the source of legitimacy of social institutions. Theories of the second type start from the assumption that the institutions with which political philosophy is concerned are fundamentally nonvoluntary. These institutions are held to be legitimate if they satisfy appropriate conditions, and the idea of hypothetical consent enters as a metaphorical device used in the formulation and defense of these conditions. Questions of actual consent arise only as internal questions of liberty, that is, as questions about what options acceptable institutions must leave open to those living under them. The difference between these two theories is magnified by the fact that the idea of consent involves choice against some background of alternatives. If what is at issue is initial consent to institutions from without, then the relevant background is that of this pre-institutional condition. It is only this viewpoint that makes the "baseline" of conditions in the state of nature seem relevant. By contrast, since the questions raised through the device of the hypothetical contract are questions about the justifiability of social institutions to people who find themselves living under them, the relevant background is given by the alternatives actually available to people in societies and the values that such people attach to these alternatives. This is not to say that the values assigned to various choices and prospects by people in a given society are always morally determinative. They may be set aside if they can be shown to be artifactual in a way that makes them morally suspect. But there is no temptation, on this view, to take the standards of some earlier (for example, pretechnological) age as relevant to the acceptability of contemporary institutions.

The idea that respect for individual liberty requires that consent be a necessary condition for all obligations beyond the requirements of a minimal framework of rights arises in the same way as the idea that makes subjective preference seem the only acceptable basis for ethically significant judgments of relative well being. Further, the two views involve similar mistakes. Welfare economists and those who support subjective versions of utilitarianism are moved by the belief that the interests of the affected parties are the bases on which social policies should be appraised and by the belief that it is unacceptable to "impose" on these parties, as the relevant account of their interests, a system of values that they do not share. The response to these beliefs is generally to bring individual preferences into a theory at the foundational level, making them the basis for all judgments of relative value. A few restrictions on what can count as admissible preferences may be allowed in the form of requirements of consistency, transitivity, and so on, but anything beyond such purely formal restrictions is seen as a threat. When a theory is constructed in this way, so that it treats almost all preferences at face value regardless of their origins or content, its conclusions can be substantially affected by the social conditions which influence prevailing preferences and their relative strengths. This robs the theory of an important kind of critical power and, in addition, makes it an uncertain guardian of even those values of individual autonomy which it set out to protect. Many different conditions are important for the development of autonomous preferences, and the ability of individuals to give effect to their preferences in their own lives and in the determination of social policy depends on a variety of power and liberties. To give appropriate recognition to the value of individual autonomy a theory must assign appropriate weights to all these factors in balancing them against each other and against other competing considerations. Autonomy is not adequately recognized simply by letting these weights and all others be determined by whatever constellation of individual preferences happens to prevail at the point at which the theory is applied.

Similar problems arise for a view which, acting out of a desire to safeguard individual liberty, brings consent in at the foundational level as the basis of almost all obligations, and allows it to be restricted by only a minimum of "imposed" moral requirements. The consequences such a theory can endorse are unacceptably open to determination by factors affecting the relative bargaining strength of various individuals, for example, variations in the demand for and scarcity of particular talents and resources. In particular, the ability of individuals to exercise the kind of control over their lives that freedom from imposed obligations is supposed to secure will be to an unacceptable degree merely a function of their bargaining strength. As in the previous case, the conclusion to be drawn here is that individual liberty is not adequately protected simply by bringing consent in as the foundation of obligation. An adequate theory must take into account the various ways—other than merely by being morally free to withhold one's services—in which individuals may be enabled to exercise control over their own lives and their common institutions (or disabled from doing so).

Preference-based theories of social welfare and consent-based theories of obligation can be seen as, respectively, teleological and deontological responses to similar intuitive ideas. The two are brought together when utility is taken as the basis of arguments for the efficiency of the free market. Each also derives support from a form of skepticism about the existence of an ethically significant, objective basis for the comparison and balancing of the interests of different individuals.[10]

The two forms of consent theory correspond to two differing views of rights. Either view may recognize rights as a basis for individual claims against social institutions. Thus both see some rights as "natural" in the sense of having validity that does not derive from positive law or social institutions. On the first view, however, the rights that are the basis for moral criticism and defense of social institutions are seen as "natural rights" in the stronger sense that they are the very same rights which individuals possess and can claim against one another in a state of nature. On the second view, rights represent general judgments about the conditions of legitimacy of social institutions, for example, judgments of the form "Any institutions granting *that* power are morally unacceptable." Exactly which such generalizations seem true and important—what things are rights and what these rights encompass—are matters that will change as social conditions change. Some of these rights concern things that would be of no relevance, or only a very different and more limited kind of relevance, in a state of nature. (Rights to freedom of expression, due process of law and political participation seem to have this character.)

It is central to Nozick's argument that the rights with which he is concerned are claimed to be natural rights in the stronger sense. The objections I have raised to his examples almost all demand that he consider the consequences of enforcement of absolute property and contract rights and that he explain why the loss of liberty this involves for

10. In Nozick's case the skepticism concerns the ethical significance of such balancing, not its epistemological basis.

some people is not worse than that which is involved in the alternative systems which he deplores. Such objections suppose that the property rights enforced by the minimal state and those embodied in socialist institutions are two alternative social systems open to the same kind of objections and needing the same kind of defense. Nozick rejects this symmetrical picture. In his view, the particular property rights protected by the minimal state are not licensed or created by it and consequently do not need to be defended as part of its justification. These rights are ones that individuals have quite independently of the social institutions in which they live. In enforcing these rights the minimal state is only doing for them what they were already entitled to do for themselves. Consequently it is not doing anything that could be held to infringe anyone's liberty. . . .

III. THE ROLE OF GOVERNMENT

Hare, Rawls' Theory of Justice*

. . . We next have to examine the conclusions that Rawls thinks it does lead to. He thinks that the POPs† would, in choosing their principles, "maximin"—that is to say, choose the course which has the best worst outcome. They will seek to maximize the welfare of the least-advantaged representative members of their society. It is important to distinguish this strategy from another, which I will call the "insurance" strategy; for Rawls uses arguments in favour of maximining which are really only arguments in favour of insuring against utter calamity (cf. 156/30, 163/18, 176/23). We insure our houses against fire because we think that a certain outcome, namely having one's house burnt down and having no money to buy another, is so calamitous that we should rule it out. This is not at all the same strategy as maximining. If the POL‡ society were going to be affluent enough to provide a more than

* [23 *Philosophical Quarterly* 144, 248-250 (1973). (References are to the original Rawls edition.) Reprinted by permission.

R. M. Hare (1919–) is Professor of Philosophy at Corpus Christi College at Oxford University. He is the author of *Freedom and Reason, The Language of Morals, Applications of Moral Philosophy, Essays on Philosophical Method, Practical Inferences,* and *Essays on the Moral Concepts.*]

† ["People in the original position."]

‡ ["People in ordinary life."]

just acceptable standard of living for even the least advantaged, the insurance strategy would allow the POPs to purchase a very great gain for the more advantaged at the cost of a small loss for the least advantaged; but the maximin strategy would forbid this. Maximiners would end up refusing to let the man with, say, ten thousand pounds a year have any more if the man with the minimum income of nine thousand pounds received in consequence a pound or two less; but the follower of the insurance strategy would by that time have lost interest.

POPs following an insurance strategy would fix a minimum and frame their principles of justice to secure that. They would not have to know whether the minimum was feasible; all they would have to do would be to say that below it, the interests of the more advantaged were always to be sacrificed to those of the less (as in wartime rationing). Rawls has not actually given us anything to determine what minimum the POPs would fix (might they not differ on this?). But neither has he given us anything to determine the minimum which he himself requires for his argument. It is what they "can be sure of by following the maximin rule" (154/30); but how do they know what this amounts to? And if they do not know, how can they tell that anything less is "intolerable" (156/24)?

The POP game is in effect played by imagining ourselves in the original position and then choosing principles of justice. Rawls' POPs come to the decisions that they come to simply because they are replicas of Rawls himself with what altruism he has removed and a veil of ignorance clapped over his head. It is not surprising, therefore, that they reach conclusions which he can accept. If I myself play this game, I import into the original position *my* prejudices and inclinations, which in some respects are different from Rawls'. I have some inclination to insure against the worst calamities, in so far as this is possible.[7] But I have no inclination to maximin, once the acceptable minimum is assured; after that point I feel inclined to take chances in the hope of maximizing

---

7. It is a difficult question (too difficult for discussion here) to what extent an insurance strategy on the part of the POPs is compatible with utilitarianism. Utilitarian POPs could insure against calamities if the premium were such as to maximize their expectation of utility, and this is what many *POLs* try to do. To be willing to pay a high premium may simply be an indication that one attaches a high negative value to the calamity in question, and less value to the possible affluence one is sacrificing. The diminishing marginal utility of affluence is relevant here. So, on the other hand, is the sheer impossibility of insuring against some of the worst calamities (for example, that of being a person whose temperament simply prevents him being happy). A utilitarian POP might well achieve the results of an insurance strategy without the strategy, if he assigned a high acceptance-utility to a level-one (*prima facie*) principle enjoining *compassion*—a sentiment which is perhaps better able than "justice as fairness" to make us look after the unfortunate.

my expectation of welfare as I do in actual life (for example, I do not entirely refrain from investing my spare cash because I might lose it). And in certain cases I do not feel inclined to maximin even in very reduced circumstances. If, when I was a prisoner of war, a benevolent and trustworthy Japanese officer had said that he would play poker with me and, if I won enough, allow me to buy myself a ticket home through neutral territory with a safe conduct, then I should have accepted the invitation, in order to give myself a chance, however small, of freedom (the priority of liberty!) rather than forgo this chance and husband my money to buy smokes with as I languished on the Burma railway.

Thus the maximin strategy does not appeal to me as *in general* a good one for choices under uncertainty. Even Rawls does not go so far as to claim that. He states three features of situations which give "plausibility" to the maximin strategy (154/11). The first is the ignorance of objective probabilities; but we have seen that the imposition of this condition is entirely arbitrary. The second is that the chooser has to have "a conception of the good such that he cares very little, if anything, for what he might gain above the minimum stipend" (154/28); but this condition is clearly inapplicable, for the POPs "do not know their conception of the good" (155/15).[8] The third feature is that some outcomes are "intolerable" (156/24); but this justifies only insurance, not maximining. It looks, therefore, as if Rawls has not succeeded in making his choice of strategy even "plausible." But in spite of this he says "the original position has been defined so that it is a situation in which the maximin rule applies" (155/22). We can only say "Amen."

I do not claim to have shown that the maximin strategy is a bad one for POPs, only that Rawls has given no good reason for holding that it is a good one. The truth is that it is a wide open question how the POPs would choose; he has reduced the information available to them and about them so much that it is hard to say *what* they would choose, unless his own intuitions supply the lack. Rawls, however, has one recourse, and that is that the results of his theory have to tally with his "considered judgments." But they do not tally with mine. A maximin strategy would (and in Rawls does) yield principles of justice according to which it would always be just to impose any loss, however great, upon a better-off group in order to bring a gain, however small, to the least advantaged group, however affluent the latter's starting point. If intuitions are to be used,

---

8. They therefore make do with assumptions about "primary goods" (which seem in this passage, though not always, all to have monetary values). The fate of a man who was made miserable because he lacked something which he valued very much, but which was not on Rawls' list of primary goods, is therefore not even insured against.

this is surely counterintuitive; at least, not many of us are as egalitarian as that. . . .

Nozick, Anarchy, State, and Utopia*

. . . The term "distributive justice" is not a neutral one. Hearing the term "distribution," most people presume that some thing or mechanism uses some principle or criterion to give out a supply of things. Into this process of distributing shares some error may have crept. So it is an open question, at least, whether *re*distribution should take place; whether we should do again what has already been done once, though poorly. However, we are not in the position of children who have been given portions of pie by someone who now makes last minute adjustments to rectify careless cutting. There is no *central* distribution, no person or group entitled to control all the resources, jointly deciding how they are to be doled out. What each person gets, he gets from others who give to him in exchange for something, or as a gift. In a free society, diverse persons control different resources, and new holdings arise out of the voluntary exchanges and actions of persons. There is no more a distributing or distribution of shares than there is a distributing of mates in a society in which persons choose whom they shall marry. . . .

The Entitlement Theory

The subject of justice in holdings consists of three major topics. The first is the *original acquisition of holdings,* the appropriation of unheld things. This includes the issues of how unheld things may come to be held, the process, or processes, by which unheld things may come to be held, the things that may come to be held by these processes, the extent of what comes to be held by a particular process, and so on. We shall refer to the complicated truth about this topic, which we shall not formulate here, as the principle of justice in acquisition. The second topic concerns the *transfer of holdings* from one person to another. By what processes may a person transfer holdings to another? How may a person acquire a holding from another who holds it? Under this topic come general descriptions of voluntary exchange, and gift and (on the other

* [Pp. 149-150, 150-153, 153-155, 159-160, 185-186, 195-199 (1974). Footnotes renumbered. Excerpted from *Anarchy, State, and Utopia,* by Robert Nozick, © 1974 by Basic Books, Inc., Publishers, New York. Reprinted by permission.
For biographical information, see page 1039 supra.]

hand) fraud, as well as reference to particular conventional details fixed upon in a given society. The complicated truth about this subject (with placeholders for conventional details) we shall call the principle of justice in transfer. (And we shall suppose it also includes principles governing how a person may divest himself of a holding, passing it into an unheld state.)

If the world were wholly just, the following inductive definition would exhaustively cover the subject of justice in holdings.

1. A person who acquires a holding in accordance with the principle of justice in acquisition is entitled to that holding.
2. A person who acquires a holding in accordance with the principle of justice in transfer, from someone else entitled to the holding, is entitled to the holding.
3. No one is entitled to a holding except by (repeated) applications of 1 and 2.

The complete principle of distributive justice would say simply that a distribution is just if everyone is entitled to the holdings they possess under the distribution.

A distribution is just if it arises from another just distribution by legitimate means. The legitimate means of moving from one distribution to another are specified by the principle of justice in transfer. The legitimate first "moves" are specified by the principle of justice in acquisition.[1] Whatever arises from a just situation by just steps is itself just. The means of change specified by the principle of justice in transfer preserve justice. As correct rules of inference are truth-preserving, and any conclusion deduced via repeated application of such rules from only true premises is itself true, so the means of transition from one situation to another specified by the principle of justice in transfer are justice-preserving, and any situation actually arising from repeated transitions in accordance with the principle from a just situation is itself just. The parallel between justice-preserving transformations and truth-preserving transformations illuminates where it fails as well as where it holds. That a conclusion could have been deduced by truth-preserving means from premises that are true suffices to show its truth. That from a just situation a situation *could* have arisen via justice-preserving means does

---

1. Applications of the principle of justice in acquisition may also occur as part of the move from one distribution to another. You may find an unheld thing now and appropriate it. Acquisitions also are to be understood as included when, to simplify, I speak only of transitions by transfers.

not suffice to show its justice. The fact that a thief's victims voluntarily *could* have presented him with gifts does not entitle the thief to his ill-gotten gains. Justice in holdings is historical; it depends upon what actually has happened. We shall return to this point later.

Not all actual situations are generated in accordance with the two principles of justice in holdings: the principle of justice in acquisition and the principle of justice in transfer. Some people steal from others, or defraud them, or enslave them, seizing their product and preventing them from living as they choose, or forcibly exclude others from competing in exchanges. None of these are permissible modes of transition from one situation to another. And some persons acquire holdings by means not sanctioned by the principle of justice in acquisition. The existence of past injustice (previous violations of the first two principles of justice in holdings) raises the third major topic under justice in holdings: the rectification of injustice in holdings. If past injustice has shaped present holdings in various ways, some identifiable and some not, what now, if anything, ought to be done to rectify these injustices? What obligations do the performers of injustice have toward those whose position is worse than it would have been had the injustice not been done? Or, than it would have been had compensation been paid promptly? How, if at all, do things change if the beneficiaries and those made worse off are not the direct parties in the act of injustice, but, for example, their descendants? Is an injustice done to someone whose holding was itself based upon an unrectified injustice? How far back must one go in wiping clean the historical slate of injustices? What may victims of injustice permissibly do in order to rectify the injustices being done to them, including the many injustices done by persons acting through their government? I do not know of a thorough or theoretically sophisticated treatment of such issues.[2] Idealizing greatly, let us suppose theoretical investigation will produce a principle of rectification. This principle uses historical information about previous situations and injustices done in them (as defined by the first two principles of justice and rights against interference), and information about the actual course of events that flowed from these injustices, until the present, and it yields a description (or descriptions) of holdings in the society. The principle of rectification presumably will make use of its best estimate of subjunctive information about what would have occurred (or a probability distribution over what might have occurred, using the expected value) if the injustice had not taken place.

---

2. See, however, the useful book by Boris Bittker, *The Case for Black Reparations* (New York: Random House, 1973).

If the actual description of holdings turns out not to be one of the descriptions yielded by the principle, then one of the descriptions yielded must be realized.[3] . . .

Historical Principles and End-Result Principles

The general outlines of the entitlement theory illuminate the nature and defects of other conceptions of distributive justice. The entitlement theory of justice in distribution is *historical;* whether a distribution is just depends upon how it came about. In contrast, *current time-slice principles* of justice hold that the justice of a distribution is determined by how things are distributed (who has what) as judged by some *structural* principle(s) of just distribution. A utilitarian who judges between any two distributions by seeing which has the greater sum of utility and, if the sums tie, applies some fixed equality criterion to choose the more equal distribution, would hold a current time-slice principle of justice. As would someone who had a fixed schedule of trade-offs between the sum of happiness and equality. According to a current time-slice principle, all that needs to be looked at, in judging the justice of a distribution, is who ends up with what; in comparing any two distributions one need look only at the matrix presenting the distributions. No further information need be fed into a principle of justice. It is a consequence of such principles of justice that any two structurally identical distributions are equally just. (Two distributions are structurally identical if they present the same profile, but perhaps have different persons occupying the particular slots. My having ten and your having five, and my having five and your having ten are structurally identical distributions.) Welfare economics is the theory of current time-slice principles of justice. The subject is conceived as operating on matrices representing only current information about distribution. This, as well as some of the usual conditions (for example, the choice of distribution is invariant under relabeling of columns), guarantees that welfare economics will be a current time-slice theory, with all of its inadequacies.

Most persons do not accept current time-slice principles as constituting the whole story about distributive shares. They think it relevant in

3. If the principle of rectification of violations of the first two principles yields more than one description of holdings, then some choice must be made as to which of these is to be realized. Perhaps the sort of considerations about distributive justice and equality that I argue against play a legitimate role in *this* subsidiary choice. Similarly, there may be room for such considerations in deciding which otherwise arbitrary features a statute will embody, when such features are unavoidable because other considerations do not specify a precise line; yet a line must be drawn.

assessing the justice of a situation to consider not only the distribution it embodies, but also how that distribution came about. If some persons are in prison for murder or war crimes, we do not say that to assess the justice of the distribution in the society we must look only at what this person has, and that person has, and that person has, . . . at the current time. We think it relevant to ask whether someone did something so that he *deserved* to be punished, deserved to have a lower share. Most will agree to the relevance of further information with regard to punishments and penalties. Consider also desired things. One traditional socialist view is that workers are entitled to the product and full fruits of their labor; they have earned it; a distribution is unjust if it does not give the workers what they are entitled to. Such entitlements are based upon some past history. No socialist holding this view would find it comforting to be told that because the actual distribution *A* happens to coincide structurally with the one he desires, *D, A* therefore is no less just than *D;* it differs only in that the "parasitic" owners of capital receive under *A* what the workers are entitled to under *D,* and the workers receive under *A* what the owners are entitled to under *D,* namely very little. This socialist rightly, in my view, holds onto the notions of earning, producing, entitlement, desert, and so forth, and he rejects current time-slice principles that look only to the structure of the resulting set of holdings. (The set of holdings resulting from what? Isn't it implausible that how holdings are produced and come to exist has no effect at all on who should hold what?) His mistake lies in his view of what entitlements arise out of what sorts of productive processes.

We construe the position we discuss too narrowly by speaking of *current* time-slice principles. Nothing is changed if structural principles operate upon a time sequence of current time-slice profiles and, for example, give someone more now to counterbalance the less he has had earlier. A utilitarian or an egalitarian or any mixture of the two over time will inherit the difficulties of his more myopic comrades. He is not helped by the fact that *some* of the information others consider relevant in assessing a distribution is reflected, unrecoverably, in past matrices. Henceforth, we shall refer to such unhistorical principles of distributive justice, including the current time-slice principles, as *end-result principles* or *end-state principles.*

In contrast to end-result principles of justice, *historical principles* of justice hold that past circumstances or actions of people can create differential entitlements or differential deserts to things. An injustice can be worked by moving from one distribution to another structurally identical one, for the second, in profile the same, may violate people's entitlements or deserts; it may not fit the actual history.

Patterning

. . . To think that the task of a theory of distributive justice is to fill in the blank in "to each according to his _____" is to be predisposed to search for a pattern; and the separate treatment of "from each according to his _____" treats production and distribution as two separate and independent issues. On an entitlement view these are *not* two separate questions. Whoever makes something, having bought or contracted for all other held resources used in the process (transferring some of his holdings for these cooperating factors), is entitled to it. The situation is *not* one of something's getting made, and there being an open question of who is to get it. Things come into the world already attached to people having entitlements over them. From the point of view of the historical entitlement conception of justice in holdings, those who start afresh to complete "to each according to his _____" treat objects as if they appeared from nowhere, out of nothing. A complete theory of justice might cover this limit case as well; perhaps here is a use for the usual conceptions of distributive justice.[4]

So entrenched are maxims of the usual form that perhaps we should present the entitlement conception as a competitor. Ignoring acquisition and rectification, we might say:

> From each according to what he chooses to do, to each according to what he makes for himself (perhaps with the contracted aid of others) and what others choose to do for him and choose to give him of what they've been given previously (under this maxim) and haven't yet expended or transferred.

This, the discerning reader will have noticed, has its defects as a slogan. So as a summary and great simplification (and not as a maxim with any independent meaning) we have:

> *From each as they choose, to each as they are chosen.*

. . . Why does social cooperation *create* the problem of distributive justice. Would there be no problem of justice and no need for a theory of justice, if there was no social cooperation at all, if each person got his share solely by his own efforts? If we suppose, as Rawls seems to, that

---

4. Varying situations continuously from that limit situation to our own would force us to make explicit the underlying rationale of entitlements and to consider whether entitlement considerations lexicographically precede the considerations of the usual theories of distributive justice, so that the *slightest* strand of entitlement outweighs the considerations of the usual theories of distributive justice.

this situation does *not* raise questions of distributive justice, then in virtue of what facts about social cooperation do these questions of justice emerge? What is it about social cooperation that gives rise to issues of justice? It cannot be said that there will be conflicting claims only where there is social cooperation; that individuals who produce independently and (initially) fend for themselves will not make claims of justice on each other. If there were ten Robinson Crusoes, each working alone for two years on separate islands, who discovered each other and the facts of their different allotments by radio communication via transmitters left twenty years earlier, could they not make claims on each other, supposing it were possible to transfer goods from one island to the next?[5] Wouldn't the one with least make a claim on ground of need, or on the ground that his island was naturally poorest, or on the ground that he was naturally least capable of fending for himself? Mightn't he say that justice demanded he be given some more by the others, claiming it unfair that he should receive so much less and perhaps be destitute, perhaps starving? He might go on to say that the different individual noncooperative shares stem from differential natural endowments, which are not deserved, and that the task of justice is to rectify these arbitrary facts and inequities. Rather than its being the case that no one *will* make such claims in the situation lacking social cooperation, perhaps the point is that such claims clearly would be without merit. Why would they clearly be without merit? In the social noncooperation situation, it might be said, each individual deserves what he gets unaided by his own efforts; or rather, no one else can make a claim *of justice* against this holding. It is pellucidly clear in this situation who is entitled to what, so no theory of justice is needed. On this view social cooperation introduces a muddying of the waters that makes it unclear or indeterminate who is entitled to what. Rather than saying that no theory of justice applies to this noncooperative case, (wouldn't it be unjust if someone stole another's products in the noncooperative situation?), I would say that it is a clear case of application of the correct theory of justice: the entitlement theory. . . .

Rawls would have us imagine the worse-endowed persons say something like the following: "Look, better endowed: you gain by cooperating with us. If you want our cooperation you'll have to accept reasonable terms. We suggest these terms: We'll cooperate with you only if we get *as much as possible*. That is, the terms of our cooperation should give us that maximal share such that, if it was tried to give us more, we'd end up with

5. See Milton Friedman, *Capitalism and Freedom* (Chicago: University of Chicago Press, 1962), p. 165.

less." How generous these proposed terms are might be seen by imagining that the better endowed make the almost symmetrical opposite proposal: "Look, worse endowed: you gain by cooperating with *us*. If you want our coöperation you'll have to accept reasonable terms. We propose these terms: We'll cooperate with you so long as *we* get as much as possible. That is, the terms of our cooperation should give us the maximal share such that, if it was tried to give us more, we'd end up with less." If these terms seem outrageous, as they are, why don't the terms proposed by those worse endowed seem the same? Why shouldn't the better endowed treat this latter proposal as beneath consideration, supposing someone to have the nerve explicitly to state it?

Rawls devotes much attention to explaining why those less well favored should not complain at receiving less. His explanation, simply put, is that because the inequality works for his advantage, someone less well favored shouldn't complain about it; he receives *more* in the unequal system than he would in an equal one. (Though he might receive still more in another unequal system that placed someone else below him.) But Rawls discusses the question of whether those *more* favored will or should find the terms satisfactory *only* in the following passage, where *A* and *B* are any two representative men with *A* being the more favored:

> The difficulty is to show that *A* has no grounds for complaint. Perhaps he is required to have less than he might since his having more would result in some loss to *B*. Now what can be said to the more favored man? To begin with, it is clear that the well-being of each depends on a scheme of social cooperation without which no one could have a satisfactory life. Secondly, we can ask for the willing cooperation of everyone only if the terms of the scheme are reasonable. The difference principle, then, seems to be a fair basis on which those better endowed, or more fortunate in their social circumstances, could expect others to collaborate with them when some workable arrangement is a necessary condition of the good of all.[6]

What Rawls imagines being said to the more favored men does *not* show that these men have no grounds for complaint, nor does it at all diminish the weight of whatever complaints they have. That the well-being of all depends on social cooperation without which no one could have a satisfactory life could also be said to the less well endowed by someone proposing any other principle, including that of maximizing the position of the best endowed. Similarly for the fact that we can ask for the willing cooperation of everyone only if the terms of the scheme are reasonable.

6. Rawls, *Theory of Justice*, p. 103.

The question is: What terms *would be* reasonable? What Rawls imagines being said thus far merely sets up his problem; it doesn't distinguish his proposed difference principle from the almost symmetrical counterproposal that we imagined the better endowed making, or from any other proposal. Thus, when Rawls continues, "The difference principle, then, seems to be a fair basis on which those best endowed, or more fortunate in their social circumstances, could expect others to collaborate with them when some workable arrangement is a necessary condition of the good of all," the presence of the "then" in his sentence is puzzling. Since the sentences which precede it are neutral between his proposal and any other proposal, the conclusion that the difference principle presents a fair basis for cooperation *cannot* follow from what precedes it in this passage. Rawls is merely repeating that it seems reasonable; hardly a convincing reply to anyone to whom it doesn't seem reasonable.[7] Rawls has

7. I treat Rawls' discussion here as one concerning better- and worse-endowed individuals who know they are so. Alternatively, one might imagine that *these* considerations are to be weighed by someone in the original position. ("If I turn out to be better endowed then . . . ; if I turn out to be worse endowed then. . . .") But this construal will not do. Why would Rawls bother saying, "The two principles . . . seem to be a fair agreement on the basis of which those better endowed or more fortunate in their social position could expect the willing cooperation of others" (*Theory of Justice*, p. 15). Who is doing the expecting when? How is this to be translated into subjunctives to be contemplated by someone in the original position? Similarly, questions arise about Rawls' saying, "The difficulty is to show that *A* has no grounds for complaint. Perhaps he is required to have less than he might since his having more would result in some loss to *B*. *Now what can be said to the more favored man?* . . . The difference principle then seems to be a fair basis on which those better endowed . . . could expect others to collaborate with them . . ." (*Theory of Justice*, p. 103, my italics). Are we to understand this as: someone in the original position wonders what to say to himself as he then thinks of the possibility that he will turn out to be one of the better endowed? And does he then say that the difference principle *then* seems a fair basis for cooperation despite the fact that, and even while, he is contemplating the possibility that he is better endowed? Or does he say then that even later if and when he knows he is better endowed the difference principle will seem fair to him at that later time? And when are we to imagine him possibly complaining? Not while in the original position, for then he is agreeing to the difference principle. Nor does he worry, while in the process of deciding in the original position, that he will complain later. For he knows that he will have no cause to complain later at the effects of whatever principle he himself rationally will choose soon in the original position. Are we to imagine him complaining against himself? And isn't the answer to any later complaint, "You agreed to it (or you would have agreed to it if so originally positioned)"? What "difficulty" does Rawls concern himself with here? Trying to squeeze it into the original position makes it completely mysterious. And what is thinking of what is a "fair agreement" (sect. 3) or a "fair basis" (p. 103) doing here anyway, in the midst of the rational self-interested calculations of persons in the original position, who do not then knowingly possess, or at any rate utilize, particular moral notions?

I see no coherent way to incorporate how Rawls treats and speaks of the issue of the terms of cooperation between the better and the worse endowed into the structure and

not shown that the more favored man *A* has no grounds for complaint at being required to have less in order that another *B* might have more than he otherwise would. And he can't show this, since *A does* have grounds for complaint. Doesn't he?

The Original Position and End-Result Principles

How can it have been supposed that these terms offered by the less well endowed are fair? Imagine a social pie somehow appearing so that *no one* has any claim at all on any portion of it, no one has any more of a claim than any other person; yet there must be unanimous agreement on how it is to be divided. Undoubtedly, apart from threats or holdouts in bargaining, an equal distribution would be suggested and found plausible as a solution. (It is, in Schelling's sense, a focal point solution.) If *somehow* the size of the pie wasn't fixed, and it was realized that pursuing an equal distribution somehow would lead to a smaller total pie than otherwise might occur, the people might well agree to an unequal distribution which raised the size of the least share. But in any actual situation, wouldn't this realization reveal something about differential claims on parts of the pie? Who is it that could make the pie larger, and would do it if given a larger share, but not if given an equal share under the scheme of equal distribution? To whom is an incentive to be provided to make this larger contribution? (There's no talk here of inextricably entangled joint product; it's known *to whom* incentives are to be offered, or at least to whom a bonus is to be paid after the fact.) Why doesn't this identifiable differential contribution lead to some differential entitlement?

If things fell from heaven like manna, and no one had any special entitlement to any portion of it, and no manna would fall unless all agreed

perspective of the original position. Therefore my discussion considers Rawls here as addressing himself to individuals *outside* the original position, either to better-endowed individuals or to his readers, to convince *them* that the difference principle which Rawls extracts from the original position is fair. It is instructive to compare how Rawls imagines justifying the social order to a person in the worst-off group in an unequal society. Rawls wants to tell this person that the inequalities work out to his advantage. This is told to someone who knows who he is: "The social order can be justified to everyone, and in particular to those who are least favored" (p. 103). Rawls does not want to say, "You would have gambled, and you lost," or any such thing, even "You chose it then in the original position"; nor does he wish merely to address someone in the original position. He also wants a consideration apart from the original position that will convince someone who knows of his inferior position in an unequal society. To say, "You have less in order that I may prosper," would *not* convince someone who knows of his inferior position, and Rawls rightly rejects it, even though its subjunctive analogue for someone in the original position, if we could make sense of this, would not be without force.

to a particular distribution, and somehow the quantity varied depending on the distribution, then it is plausible to claim that persons placed so that they couldn't make threats, or hold out for specially large shares, would agree to the difference principle rule of distribution. But is *this* the appropriate model for thinking about how the things people produce are to be distributed? Why think the same results should obtain for situations where there *are* differential entitlements as for situations where there are not?

A procedure that founds principles of distributive justice on what rational persons who know nothing about themselves or their histories would agree to *guarantees that end-state principles of justice will be taken as fundamental.* Perhaps some historical principles of justice are derivable from end-state principles, as the utilitarian tries to derive individual rights, prohibitions on punishing the innocent, and so forth, from *his* end-state principle; perhaps such arguments can be constructed even for the entitlement principle. But no historical principle, it seems, could be agreed to in the first instance by the participants in Rawls' original position. For people meeting together behind a veil of ignorance to decide who gets what, knowing nothing about any special entitlements people may have, will treat anything to be distributed as manna from heaven.[8]

Devlin, Law, Democracy and Morality

See page 540 supra.

Mill, On Liberty*

Chapter I. Introductory

The subject of this essay is not the so-called "liberty of the will," so unfortunately opposed to the misnamed doctrine of philosophical necessity; but civil, or social liberty: the nature and limits of the power which

---

8. Do the people in the original position ever wonder whether *they* have the *right* to decide how everything is to be divided up? Perhaps they reason that since they are deciding this question, they must assume they are entitled to do so; and so particular people can't have particular entitlements to holdings (for then they wouldn't have the right to decide together on how all holdings are to be divided); and hence everything legitimately may be treated like manna from heaven.

* [Chapters I, II, III, and IV (1859). Some text omitted.

John Stuart Mill (1806-1873), a British philosopher and economist, is well known for his writings on logic and scientific methodology and his essays on social and political life.

can be legitimately exercised by society over the individual. A question seldom stated, and hardly ever discussed in general terms, but which profoundly influences the practical controversies of the age by its latent presence, and is likely soon to make itself recognized as the vital question of the future. It is so far from being new that, in a certain sense, it has divided mankind almost from the remotest ages; but in the stage of progress into which the more civilized portions of the species have now entered, it presents itself under new conditions and requires a different and more fundamental treatment. . . .

The object of this essay is to assert one very simple principle, as entitled to govern absolutely the dealings of society with the individual in the way of compulsion and control, whether the means used be physical force in the form of legal penalties or the moral coercion of public opinion. That principle is that the sole end for which mankind are warranted, individually or collectively, in interfering with the liberty of action of any of their number is self-protection. That the only purpose for which power can be rightfully exercised over any member of a civilized community, against his will, is to prevent harm to others. His own good, either physical or moral, is not a sufficient warrant. He cannot rightfully be compelled to do or forbear because it will be better for him to do so, because it will make him happier, because, in the opinions of others, to do so would be wise or even right. These are good reasons for remonstrating with him, or reasoning with him, or persuading him, or entreating him, but not for compelling him or visiting him with any evil in case he do otherwise. To justify that, the conduct from which it is desired to deter him must be calculated to produce evil to someone else. The only part of the conduct of anyone for which he is amenable to society is that which concerns others. In the part which merely concerns himself, his independence is, of right, absolute. Over himself, over his own body and mind, the individual is sovereign. . . .

It is proper to state that I forego any advantage which could be derived to my argument from the idea of abstract right, as a thing independent of utility. . . .

Mill never attended a school or university, but began the study of Greek at age three and mastered the equivalent of a university degree in classics by age twelve. Mill began a debating society of utilitarians at age sixteen and wrote approximately 50 articles promoting utilitarianism by age twenty. Primary sources on John Stuart Mill are his *Autobiography, Collected Works,* and *John Stuart Mill and Harriet Taylor: Their Correspondence* (F. A. Hayek ed. 1951).]

Chapter II. Of the Liberty of Thought and Discussion

. . . For the interest, therefore, of truth and justice it is far more important to restrain this employment of vituperative language than the other; and, for example if it were necessary to choose, there would be much more need to discourage offensive attacks on infidelity than on religion. It is, however, obvious that law and authority have no business with restraining either, while opinion ought, in every instance, to determine its verdict by the circumstances of the individual case—condemning everyone, on whichever side of the argument he places himself, in whose mode of advocacy either want of candour, or malignity, bigotry, or intolerance of feeling manifest themselves; but not inferring these vices from the side which a person takes, though it be the contrary side of the question to our own; and giving merited honour to everyone, whatever opinion he may hold, who has calmness to see and honesty to state what his opponents and their opinions really are, exaggerating nothing to their discredit, keeping nothing back which tells, or can be supposed to tell, in their favour. This is the real morality of public discussion; and if often violated, I am happy to think that there are many controversialists who to a great extent observe it, and a still greater number who conscientiously strive towards it.

Chapter III. Of Individuality, as One of the Elements of Well-Being

. . . No one pretends that actions should be as free as opinions. On the contrary, even opinions lose their immunity when the circumstances in which they are expressed are such as to constitute their expression a positive instigation to some mischievous act. An opinion that corn dealers are starvers of the poor, or that private property is robbery, ought to be unmolested when simply circulated through the press, but may justly incur punishment when delivered orally to an excited mob assembled before the house of a corn dealer, or when handed about among the same mob in the form of a placard. Acts, of whatever kind, which without justifiable cause do harm to others may be, and in the more important cases absolutely require to be, controlled by the unfavourable sentiments, and, when needful, by the active interference of mankind. The liberty of the individual must be thus far limited; he must not make himself a nuisance to other people. But if he refrains from molesting others in what concerns them, and merely acts according to his own inclination and judgement in things which concern himself, the same reasons which show that opinion should be free prove also that he should be allowed, without molestation, to carry his opinions into practice at his own cost. That mankind are not infallible; that their truths, for the most part, are only half-truths; that unity of opinion, unless resulting from the fullest and freest comparison of opposite opinions, is not desirable, and diversity not an evil, but a good, until mankind are much more capable than at present of recognizing all sides of the truth, are principles applicable to men's modes of action not less than to their opinions. As it is useful that while mankind are imperfect there should be different opinions, so it is that there should be different experiments of living; that free scope should be given to varieties of character, short of injury to others; and that the worth of different modes of life should be proved practically, when anyone thinks fit to try them. It is desirable, in short, that in things which do not primarily concern others, individuality should assert itself. Where not the person's own character but the traditions or customs of other people are the rule of conduct, there is wanting one of the principal ingredients of human happiness, and quite the chief ingredient of individual and social progress.

In maintaining this principle, the greatest difficulty to be encountered does not lie in the appreciation of means towards an acknowledged end, but in the indifference of persons in general to the end itself. If it were felt that the free development of individuality is one of the leading essentials of well-being; that it is not only a co-ordinate element with all that is designated by the terms civilization, instruction, education, culture, but is itself a necessary part and condition of all those things, there would be no danger that liberty should be under-valued, and the adjustment of the boundaries between it and social control would present no extraordinary difficulty. But the evil is that individual spontaneity is hardly recognized by the common modes of thinking as having any intrinsic worth, or deserving any regard on its own account. The majority, being satisfied with the ways of mankind as they now are (for it is they who make them what they are), cannot comprehend why those ways should not be good enough for everybody; and what is more, spontaneity forms no part of the ideal of the majority of moral and social reformers, but is rather looked on with jealousy, as a troublesome and perhaps rebellious obstruction to the general acceptance of what these reformers, in their own judgment, think would be best for mankind. . . .

. . . No one would assert that people ought not to put into their mode of life, and into the conduct of their concerns, any impress whatever of their own judgement or of their own individual character. On the other hand, it would be absurd to pretend that people ought to live as if nothing whatever had been known in the world before they came into it; as if experience had as yet done nothing towards showing that one mode of existence, or of conduct, is preferable to another. Nobody denies that people should be so taught and trained in youth as to know and benefit by the ascertained results of human experience. But it is the privilege and proper condition of a human being, arrived at the maturity of his faculties, to use and interpret experience in his own way. It is for him to find out what part of recorded experience is properly applicable to his own circumstances and character. The traditions and customs of other people are, to a certain extent, evidence of what their experience has taught *them*—presumptive evidence, and as such, have a claim to his deference; but, in the first place, their experience may be too narrow, or they may have not interpreted it rightly. Secondly, their interpretation of experience may be correct, but unsuitable to him. Customs are made for customary circumstances and customary characters; and his circumstances or his character may be uncustomary. Thirdly, though the customs be both good as customs and suitable to him, yet to conform to custom merely *as* custom does not educate or develop in him any of the qualities which are the distinctive endowment of a human being. The human faculties of perception, judgement, discriminative feeling, mental activity, and even moral preference are exercised only in making a choice. He who does anything because it is the custom makes no choice. He gains no practice either in discerning or in desiring what is best. The mental and moral, like the muscular, powers are improved only by being used. The faculties are called into no exercise by doing a thing merely because others do it, no more than by believing a thing only because others believe it. If the grounds of an opinion are not conclusive to the person's own reason, his reason cannot be strengthened, but is likely to be weakened, by his adopting it: and if the inducements to an act are not such as are consentaneous to his own feelings and character (where affection, or the rights of others, are not concerned), it is so much done towards rendering his feelings and character inert and torpid instead of active and energetic.

He who lets the world, or his own portion of it, choose his plan of life for him has no need of any other faculty than the ape-like one of imitation. He who chooses his plan for himself employs all his faculties. He must use observation to see, reasoning and judgement to foresee, activity to gather materials for decision, discrimination to decide, and when he has decided, firmness and self-control to hold to his deliberate decision. And these qualities he requires and exercises exactly in proportion as the part of his conduct which he determines according to his own judgement and feelings is a large one. It is possible that he might be guided in some good path, and kept out of harm's way, without any of these things. But what will be his comparative worth as a human being?

It really is of importance, not only what men do, but also what manner of men they are that do it. Among the works of man which human life is rightly employed in perfecting and beautifying, the first in importance surely is man himself. Supposing it were possible to get houses built, corn grown, battles fought, causes tried, and even churches erected and prayers said by machinery—by automatons in human form—it would be a considerable loss to exchange for these automatons even the men and women who at present inhabit the more civilized parts of the world, and who assuredly are but starved specimens of what nature can and will produce. Human nature is not a machine to be built after a model, and set to do exactly the work prescribed for it, but a tree, which requires to grow and develop itself on all sides, according to the tendency of the inward forces which make it a living thing.

It will probably be conceded that it is desirable people should exercise their understandings, and that an intelligent following of custom, or even occasionally an intelligent deviation from custom, is better than a blind and simply mechanical adhesion to it. To a certain extent it is admitted that our understanding should be our own; but there is not the same willingness to admit that our desires and impulses should be our own likewise, or that to possess impulses of our own, and of any strength, is anything but a peril and a snare. Yet desires and impulses are as much a part of a perfect human being as beliefs and restraints; and strong impulses are only perilous when not properly balanced, when one set of aims and inclinations is developed into strength, while others, which ought to coexist with them, remain weak and inactive. It is not because men's desires are strong that they act ill; it is because their consciences are weak. There is no natural connection between strong impulses and a weak conscience. The natural connection is the other way. To say that one person's desires and feelings are stronger and more various than those of another is merely to say that he has more of the raw material of human nature and is therefore capable, perhaps of more evil, but certainly of more good. Strong impulses are but another name for energy. Energy may be turned to bad uses; but more good may always be made of an energetic nature than of an indolent and impassive one. Those who have most natural feeling are always those whose cultivated feelings may be made the strongest. The same strong susceptibilities which make the personal impulses vivid and powerful are also the source from whence are generated the most passionate love of virtue and the sternest self-control. It is through the cultivation of these that society both does its duty and protects its interests, not by rejecting the stuff of which heroes are made, because it knows not how to make them. A person whose desires and impulses are his own—are the expression of his own nature, as it has been developed and modified by his own culture—is said to have a character. One whose desires and impulses are not his own has no character, no more than a steam engine has a character. If, in addition to being his own, his impulses are strong and are under the government of a strong will, he has an energetic character. Whoever thinks that individuality of desires and impulses should not be encouraged to unfold itself must maintain that society has no need of strong natures—is not the better for containing many persons who have much character—and that a high general average of energy is not desirable.

In some early states of society, these forces might be, and were, too much ahead of the power which society then possessed of disciplining and controlling them. There has been a time when the element of spontaneity and individuality was in excess, and the social principle had a hard struggle with it. The difficulty then was to induce men of strong bodies or minds to pay obedience to any rules which required them to control their impulses. To overcome this difficulty, law and discipline, like the Popes struggling against the Emperors, asserted a power over the whole man, claiming to control all his life in order to control his character—which society had not found any other sufficient means of binding. But society has now fairly got the better of individuality; and the danger which threatens human nature is not the excess, but the deficiency, of personal impulses and preferences. Things are vastly changed since the passions of those who were strong by station or by personal endowment were in a state of habitual rebellion against laws and ordinances, and required to be rigorously chained up to enable the persons within their reach to enjoy any particle of security. In our times, from the highest class of society down to the lowest, everyone lives as under the eye of a hostile and dreaded censorship. Not only in what concerns others, but in what concerns only themselves, the individual or the family do not ask themselves, what do I prefer? or, what would suit my character and disposition? or, what would allow the best and highest in me to have fair play and enable it to grow and thrive? They ask themselves, what is suitable to my position? what is usually done by persons of my station and pecuniary circumstances? or (worse still) what is usually done by persons of a station and circumstances superior to mine? I do not mean that they choose what is customary in preference to what suits their own inclination. It does not occur to them to have any inclination except for what is customary. Thus the mind itself is bowed to the yoke: even in what people do for pleasure, conformity is the first thing thought of; they like in crowds; they exercise choice only among things commonly done; peculiarity of taste, eccentricity of conduct are

shunned equally with crimes, until by dint of not following their own nature they have no nature to follow: their human capacities are withered
and starved; they become incapable of any strong wishes or native pleasures, and are generally without either opinions or feelings of home
growth, or properly their own. Now is this, or is it not, the desirable condition of human nature? . . .

Having said that the individuality is the same thing with development, and that it is only the cultivation of individuality which produces,
or can produce, well-developed human beings, I might here close the
argument; for what more or better can be said of any condition of
human affairs than that it brings human beings themselves nearer to the
best thing they can be? Or what worse can be said of any obstruction to
good than that it prevents this? Doubtless, however, these considerations
will not suffice to convince those who most need convincing; and it is
necessary further to show that these developed human beings are of
some use to the undeveloped—to point out to those who do not desire
liberty, and would not avail themselves of it, that they may be in some
intelligible manner rewarded for allowing other people to make use of it
without hindrance.

In the first place, then, I would suggest that they might possibly
learn something from them. It will not be denied by anybody that originality is a valuable element in human affairs. There is always need of
persons not only to discover new truths and point out when what were
once truths are true no longer, but also to commence new practices and
set the example of more enlightened conduct and better taste and sense
in human life. This cannot well be gainsaid by anybody who does not
believe that the world has already attained perfection in all its ways and
practices. It is true that this benefit is not capable of being rendered by
everybody alike; there are but few persons, in comparison with the
whole of mankind, whose experiments, if adopted by others, would be
likely to be any improvement on established practice. But these few are
the salt of the earth; without them, human life would become a stagnant
pool. Not only is it they who introduce good things which did not before
exist; it is they who keep the life in those which already exist. If there
were nothing new to be done, would human intellect cease to be necessary? Would it be a reason why those who do the old things should forget
why they are done, and do them like cattle, not like human beings?
There is only too great a tendency in the best beliefs and practices to
degenerate into the mechanical; and unless there were a succession of
persons whose ever-recurring originality prevents the grounds of those
beliefs and practices from becoming merely traditional, such dead matter would not resist the smallest shock from anything really alive, and
there would be no reason why civilization should not die out, as in the

1072

Byzantine Empire. Persons of genius, it is true, are, and are always likely to be, a small minority; but in order to have them, it is necessary to preserve the soil in which they grow. Genius can only breathe freely in an *atmosphere* of freedom. Persons of genius are, *ex vi termini*,[20] more individual than any other people—less capable, consequently, of fitting themselves, without hurtful compression, into any of the small number of moulds which society provides in order to save its members the trouble of forming their own character. If from timidity they consent to be forced into one of these moulds, and to let all that part of themselves which cannot expand under the pressure remain unexpanded, society will be little the better for their genius. If they are of a strong character and break their fetters, they become a mark for the society which has not succeeded in reducing them to commonplace, to point out with solemn warning as "wild," "erratic," and the like—much as if one should complain of the Niagara river for not flowing smoothly between its banks like a Dutch canal.

I insist thus emphatically on the importance of genius and the necessity of allowing it to unfold itself freely both in thought and in practice, being well aware that no one will deny the position in theory, but knowing also that almost everyone, in reality, is totally indifferent to it. People think genius a fine thing if it enables a man to write an exciting poem or paint a picture. But in its true sense, that of originality in thought and action, though no one says that it is not a thing to be admired, nearly all, at heart, think that they can do very well without it. Unhappily this is too natural to be wondered at. Originality is the one thing which unoriginal minds cannot feel the use of. They cannot see what it is to do for them: how should they? If they could see what it would do for them, it would not be originality. The first service which originality has to render them is that of opening their eyes: which being once fully done, they would have a chance of being themselves original. Meanwhile, recollecting that nothing was ever done which someone was not the first to do, and that all good things which exist are the fruits of originality, let them be modest enough to believe that there is something still left for it to accomplish, and assure themselves that they are more in need of originality, the less they are conscious of the want.

Chapter IV. Of the Limits to the Authority of Society over the Individual

What, then, is the rightful limit to the sovereignty of the individual over himself? Where does the authority of society begin? How much of human life should be assigned to individuality, and how much to society?

20. By definition.

Each will receive its proper share if each has that which more particularly concerns it. To individuality should belong the part of life in which it is chiefly the individual that is interested; to society, the part which chiefly interests society.

Though society is not founded on a contract, and though no good purpose is answered by inventing a contract in order to deduce social obligations from it, everyone who receives the protection of society owes a return for the benefit, and the fact of living in society renders it indispensable that each should be bound to observe a certain line of conduct towards the rest. This conduct consists, first, in not injuring the interests of one another, or rather certain interests which, either by express legal provision or by tacit understanding, ought to be considered as rights; and secondly, in each person's bearing his share (to be fixed on some equitable principle) of the labours and sacrifices incurred for defending the society or its members from injury and molestation. These conditions society is justified in enforcing at all costs to those who endeavour to withhold fulfilment. Nor is this all that society may do. The acts of an individual may be hurtful to others or wanting in due consideration for their welfare, without going to the length of violating any of their constituted rights. The offender may then be justly punished by opinion, though not by law. As soon as any part of a person's conduct affects prejudicially the interests of others, society has jurisdiction over it, and the question whether the general welfare will or will not be promoted by interfering with it becomes open to discussion. But there is no room for entertaining any such question when a person's conduct affects the interests of no persons besides himself, or needs not affect them unless they like (all the persons concerned being of full age and the ordinary amount of understanding). In all such cases, there should be perfect freedom, legal and social, to do the action and stand the consequences.

It would be a great misunderstanding of this doctrine to suppose that it is one of selfish indifference which pretends that human beings have no business with each other's conduct in life, and that they should not concern themselves about the well-doing or well-being of one another, unless their own interest is involved. Instead of any diminution, there is need of a great increase of disinterested exertion to promote the good of others. But disinterested benevolence can find other instruments to persuade people to their good than whips and scourges, either of the literal or the metaphorical sort. I am the last person to undervalue the self-regarding virtues; they are only second in importance, if even second, to the social. It is equally the business of education to cultivate both. But even education works by conviction and persuasion as well as by compulsion, and it is by the former only that, when the period of education is passed, the self-regarding virtues should be inculcated. Human beings owe to each other help to distinguish the better from the worse, and encouragement to choose the former and avoid the latter. They should be forever stimulating each other to increased exercise of their higher faculties and increased direction of their feelings and aims towards wise instead of foolish, elevating instead of degrading, objects and contemplations. But neither one person, nor any number of persons, is warranted in saying to another human creature of ripe years that he shall not do with his life for his own benefit what he chooses to do with it. He is the person most interested in his own well-being: the interest which any other person, except in cases of strong personal attachment, can have in it is trifling compared with that which he himself has; the interest which society has in him individually (except as to his conduct to others) is fractional and altogether indirect, while with respect to his own feelings and circumstances the most ordinary man or woman has means of knowledge immeasurably surpassing those that can be possessed by anyone else. The interference of society to overrule his judgement and purposes in what only regards himself must be grounded on general presumptions which may be altogether wrong and, even if right, are as likely as not to be misapplied to individual cases, by persons no better acquainted with the circumstances of such cases than those are who look at them merely from without. In this department, therefore, of human affairs, individuality has its proper field of action. In the conduct of human beings towards one another it is necessary that general rules should for the most part be observed in order that people may know what they have to expect; but in each person's own concerns his individual spontaneity is entitled to free exercise. Considerations to aid his judgement, exhortations to strengthen his will, may be offered to him, even obtruded on him, by others; but he himself is the final judge. All errors which he is likely to commit against advice and warning are far outweighed by the evil of allowing others to constrain him to what they deem his good. . . .

The distinction here pointed out between the part of a person's life which concerns only himself and that which concerns others, many persons will refuse to admit. How (it may be asked) can any part of the conduct of a member of society be a matter of indifference to the other members? No person is an entirely isolated being; it is impossible for a person to do anything seriously or permanently hurtful to himself without mischief reaching at least to his near connections, and often far beyond them. If he injures his property, he does harm to those who directly or indirectly derived support from it, and usually diminishes, by a greater or less amount, the general resources of the community. If he deteriorates his bodily or mental faculties, he not only brings evil upon all who depended on him for any portion of their happiness, but disqualifies himself for rendering the services which he owes to his fellow creatures generally, perhaps becomes a burden on their affection or benevolence; and if such conduct were very frequent hardly any offence that is committed would detract more from the general sum of good. Finally, if by his vices or follies a person does no direct harm to others, he is nevertheless (it may be said) injurious by his example, and ought to be compelled to control himself for the sake of those whom the sight or knowledge of his conduct might corrupt or mislead.

And even (it will be added) if the consequences of misconduct could be confined to the vicious or thoughtless individual, ought society to abandon to their own guidance those who are manifestly unfit for it? If protection against themselves is confessedly due to children and persons under age, is not society equally bound to afford it to persons of mature years who are equally incapable of self-government? If gambling, or drunkenness, or incontinence, or idleness, or uncleanliness are as injurious to happiness, and as great a hindrance to improvement, as many or most of the acts prohibited by law, why (it may be asked) should not law, so far as is consistent with practicability and social convenience, endeavour to repress these also? And as a supplement to the unavoidable imperfections of law, ought not opinion at least to organize a powerful police against these vices and visit rigidly with social penalties those who are known to practise them? There is no question here (it may be said) about restricting individuality, or impeding the trial of new and original experiments in living. The only things it is sought to prevent are things which have been tried and condemned from the beginning of the world until now—things which experience has shown not to be useful or suitable to any person's individuality. There must be some length of time and amount of experience after which a moral or prudential truth may be regarded as established; and it is merely desired to prevent generation after generation from falling over the same precipice which has been fatal to their predecessors.

I fully admit that the mischief which a person does to himself may seriously affect, both through their sympathies and their interests, those nearly connected with him and, in a minor degree, society at large. When, by conduct of this sort, a person is led to violate a distinct and assignable obligation to any other person or persons, the case is taken out of the self-regarding class and becomes amenable to moral disapprobation in the proper sense of the term. If, for example, a man, through intemperance or extravagance, becomes unable to pay his debts, or, having undertaken the moral responsibility of a family, becomes from the same cause incapable of supporting or educating them, he is deservedly reprobated and might be justly punished; but it is for the breach of duty to his family or creditor, not for the extravagance. If the resources which ought to have been devoted to them had been diverted from them for the most prudent investment, the moral culpability would have been the same. George Barnwell murdered his uncle to get money for his mistress, but if he had done it to set himself up in business, he would equally have been hanged.[25] Again, in the frequent case of a man who causes grief to his family by addiction to bad habits, he deserves reproach for his unkindness or ingratitude; but so he may for cultivating habits not in themselves vicious, if they are painful to those with whom he passes his life, or who from personal ties are dependent on him for their comfort. Whoever fails in the consideration generally due to the interests and feelings of others, not being compelled by some more imperative duty, or justified by allowable self-preference, is a subject of moral disapprobation for that failure, but not for the cause of it, nor for the errors, merely personal to himself, which may have remotely led to it. In like manner, when a person disables himself, by conduct purely self-regarding, from the performance of some definite duty incumbent on him to the public, he is guilty of a social offence. No person ought to be punished simply for being drunk; but a soldier or a policeman should be punished for being drunk on duty. Whenever, in short, there is a definite damage, or a definite risk of damage, either to an individual or to the public, the case is taken out of the province of liberty and placed in that of morality or law.

But with regard to the merely contingent or, as it may be called, constructive injury which a person causes to society by conduct which neither violates any specific duty to the public, nor occasions perceptible hurt to any assignable individual except himself, the inconvenience is one which society can afford to bear, for the sake of the greater good of human freedom. If grown persons are to be punished for not taking proper care of themselves, I would rather it were for their own sake than under pretence of preventing them from impairing their capacity or rendering to society benefits which society does not pretend it has a right

25. *The London Merchant, or The History of George Barnwell,* a play by George Lillo based on a popular ballad, was first produced at Drury Lane in 1731. Shown in various versions in the 18th and 19th centuries, it was also published as a short story in 1829. It was a morality play about a young apprentice of London who, under the corrupting influence of a woman of the town, was induced first to rob his master and then to murder his uncle.

to exact. But I cannot consent to argue the point as if society had no means of bringing its weaker members up to its ordinary standard of rational conduct, except waiting till they do something irrational, and then punishing them, legally or morally, for it. Society has had absolute power over them during all the early portion of their existence; it has had the whole period of childhood and nonage in which to try whether it could make them capable of rational conduct in life. The existing generation is master both of the training and the entire circumstances of the generation to come; it cannot indeed make them perfectly wise and good, because it is itself so lamentably deficient in goodness and wisdom; and its best efforts are not always, in individual cases, its most successful ones; but it is perfectly well able to make the rising generation, as a whole, as good as, and a little better than, itself. If society lets any considerable number of its members grow up mere children, incapable of being acted on by rational consideration of distant motives, society has itself to blame for the consequences. Armed not only with all the powers of education, but with the ascendancy which the authority of a received opinion always exercises over the minds who are least fitted to judge for themselves, and aided by the *natural* penalties which cannot be prevented from falling on those who incur the distaste or the contempt of those who know them—let not society pretend that it needs, besides all this, the power to issue commands and enforce obedience in the personal concerns of individuals in which, on all principles of justice and policy, the decision ought to rest with those who are to abide the consequences. Nor is there anything which tends more to discredit and frustrate the better means of influencing conduct than a resort to the worse. If there be among those whom it is attempted to coerce into prudence or temperance any of the material of which vigorous and independent characters are made, they will infallibly rebel against the yoke. No such person will ever feel that others have a right to control him in his concerns, such as they have to prevent him from injuring them in theirs; and it easily comes to be considered a mark of spirit and courage to fly in the face of such usurped authority and do with ostentation the exact opposite of what it enjoins, as in the fashion of grossness which succeeded, in the time of Charles II, to the fanatical moral intolerance of the Puritans. With respect to what is said of the necessity of protecting society from the bad example set to others by the vicious or the self-indulgent, it is true that bad example may have a pernicious effect, especially the example of doing wrong to others with impunity to the wrongdoer. But we are now speaking of conduct which, while it does no wrong to others, is supposed to do great harm to the agent himself; and I do not see how those who believe this can think otherwise than that the example, on the whole, must be more salutary than hurtful, since, if it displays the misconduct, it displays also the painful or degrading consequences which, if the conduct is justly censured, must be supposed to be in all or most cases attendant on it.

But the strongest of all the arguments against the interference of the public with purely personal conduct is that, when it does interfere, the odds are that it interferes wrongly and in the wrong place. On questions of social morality, of duty to others, the opinion of the public, that is, of an overruling majority, though often wrong, is likely to be still oftener right, because on such questions they are only required to judge of their own interests, of the manner in which some mode of conduct, if allowed to be practised, would affect themselves. But the opinion of a similar majority, imposed as a law on the minority, on questions of self-regarding conduct is quite as likely to be wrong as right, for in these cases public opinion means, at the best, some people's opinion of what is good or bad for other people, while very often it does not even mean that—the public, with the most perfect indifference, passing over the pleasure or convenience of those whose conduct they censure and considering only their own preference. There are many who consider as an injury to themselves any conduct which they have a distaste for, and resent it as an outrage to their feelings; as a religious bigot, when charged with disregarding the religious feelings of others, has been known to retort that they disregard his feelings by persisting in their abominable worship or creed. But there is no parity between the feeling of a person for his own opinion and the feeling of another who is offended at his holding it, no more than between the desire of a thief to take a purse and the desire of the right owner to keep it. And a person's taste is as much his own peculiar concern as his opinion or his purse. It is easy for anyone to imagine an ideal public which leaves the freedom and choice of individuals in all uncertain matters undisturbed and only requires them to abstain from modes of conduct which universal experience has condemned. But where has there been seen a public which set any such limit to its censorship? Or when does the public trouble itself about universal experience? In its interferences with personal conduct it is seldom thinking of anything but the enormity of acting or feeling differently from itself; and this standard of judgement, thinly disguised, is held up to mankind as the dictate of religion and philosophy by nine-tenths of all moralists and speculative writers. These teach that things are right because they are right; because we feel them to be so. They tell us to search in our own minds and hearts for laws of conduct binding on ourselves and on all others. What can the poor public do but apply these instructions and make their own personal feelings of good and evil, if they are tolerably unanimous in them, obligatory on all the world?

The evil here pointed out is not one which exists only in theory; and it may perhaps be expected that I should specify the instances in which the public of this age and country improperly invests its own preferences with the character of moral laws. I am not writing an essay on the aberrations of existing moral feeling. That is too weighty a subject to be discussed parenthetically, and by way of illustration. Yet examples are necessary to show that the principle I maintain is of serious and practical moment, and that I am not endeavouring to erect a barrier against imaginary evils. And it is not difficult to show, by abundant instances, that to extend the bounds of what may be called moral police until it encroaches on the most unquestionably legitimate liberty of the individual is one of the most universal of all human propensities. . . .

. . . [T]here are, in our own day, gross usurpations upon the liberty of private life actually practised, and still greater ones threatened with some expectation of success, and opinions propounded which assert an unlimited right in the public not only to prohibit by law everything which it thinks wrong, but, in order to get at what it thinks wrong, to prohibit a number of things which it admits to be innocent.

Under the name of preventing intemperance, the people of one English colony, and of nearly half the United States, have been interdicted by law from making any use whatever of fermented drinks, except for medical purposes, for prohibition of their sale is in fact, as it is intended to be, prohibition of their use.[27] And though the impracticability of executing the law has caused its repeal in several of the States which had adopted it, including the one from which it derives its name, an attempt has notwithstanding been commenced, and is prosecuted with considerable zeal by many of the professed philanthropists, to agitate for a similar law in this country. The association, or "Alliance," as it terms itself, which has been formed for this purpose, has acquired some notoriety through the publicity given to a correspondence between its secretary and one of the very few English public men who hold that a politician's opinion ought to be founded on principles.[28] Lord Stanley's share in this

27. The law prohibiting the sale of liquor was first enacted in the state of Maine in 1851—hence known as the "Maine Law."

28. The United Kingdom Alliance was founded in 1852. In 1856 The Times published an exchange of letters between Samuel Pope, the secretary of the Alliance, and Lord Stanley (later Lord Derby, the 15th Earl). Mill's tribute to Stanley is all the more interesting because Stanley was a Conservative; his father, the Earl of Derby, was then leader of the Conservative Party.

correspondence is calculated to strengthen the hopes already built on him by those who know how rare such qualities as are manifested in some of his public appearances unhappily are among those who figure in political life. The organ of the Alliance, who would "deeply deplore the recognition of any principle which could be wrested to justify bigotry and persecution," undertakes to point out the "broad and impassable barrier" which divides such principles from those of the association. "All matters relating to thought, opinion, conscience, appear to me," he says, "to be without the sphere of legislation; all pertaining to social act, habit, relation, subject only to a discretionary power vested in the State itself, and not in the individual, to be within it." No mention is made of a third class, different from either of these, viz., acts and habits which are not social, but individual; although it is to this class, surely, that the act of drinking fermented liquors belongs. Selling fermented liquors, however, is trading, and trading is a social act. But the infringement complained of is not on the liberty of the seller, but on that of the buyer and consumer; since the State might just as well forbid him to drink wine as purposely make it impossible for him to obtain it. The secretary, however, says, "I claim, as a citizen, a right to legislate whenever my social rights are invaded by the social act of another." And now for the definition of these "social rights": "If anything invades my social rights, certainly the traffic in strong drink does. It destroys my primary right of security by constantly creating and stimulating social disorder. It invades my right of equality by deriving a profit from the creation of a misery I am taxed to support. It impedes my right to free moral and intellectual development by surrounding my path with dangers and by weakening and demoralizing society, from which I have a right to claim mutual aid and intercourse." A theory of "social rights" the like of which probably never before found its way into distinct language: being nothing short of this—that it is the absolute social right of every individual that every other individual shall act in every respect exactly as he ought; that whosoever fails thereof in the smallest particular violates my social right and entitles me to demand from the legislature the removal of the grievance. So monstrous a principle is far more dangerous than any single interference with liberty; there is no violation of liberty which it would not justify; it acknowledges no right to any freedom whatever, except perhaps to that of holding opinions in secret, without ever disclosing them; for the moment an opinion which I consider noxious passes anyone's lips, it invades all the "social rights" attributed to me by the Alliance. The doctrine ascribes to all mankind a vested interest in each other's moral, intellectual, and even physical perfection, to be defined by each claimant according to his own standard.

G. Dworkin, Paternalism*

I

By paternalism I shall understand roughly the interference with a person's liberty of action justified by reasons referring exclusively to the welfare, good, happiness, needs, interests or values of the person being coerced. One is always well-advised to illustrate one's definitions by examples but it is not easy to find "pure" examples of paternalistic interferences. For almost any piece of legislation is justified by several different kinds of reasons and even if historically a piece of legislation can be shown to have been introduced for, purely paternalistic motives, it may be that advocates of the legislation with an anti-paternalistic outlook can find sufficient reasons justifying the legislation without appealing to the reasons which were originally adduced to support it. Thus, for example, it may be that the original legislation requiring motorcyclists to wear safety helmets was introduced for purely paternalistic reasons. But the Rhode Island Supreme Court recently upheld such legislation on the grounds that it was "not persuaded that the legislature is powerless to prohibit individuals from pursuing a course of conduct which could conceivably result in their becoming public charges," thus clearly introducing reasons of a quite different kind. Now I regard this decision as being based on reasoning of a very dubious nature but it illustrates the kind of problem one has in finding examples. The following is a list of the kinds of interferences I have in mind as being paternalistic.

II

1. Laws requiring motorcyclists to wear safety helmets when operating their machines.
2. Laws forbidding persons from swimming at a public beach when lifeguards are not on duty.
3. Laws making suicide a criminal offense.

* [From *Morality and the Law* pp. 107–126 (R. A. Wasserstrom ed. 1971). Reprinted by permission.

Gerald Dworkin (1937–) is Associate Professor, University of Illinois at Chicago Circle. He was previously a member of the Philosophy Department at Massachusetts Institute of Technology. He is the editor of *Determinism, Free Will and Moral Responsibility* (1970) and a co-editor with Judith Jarvis Thomson of an anthology entitled *Ethics* (1969). He has also published articles in various philosophical, psychological, and legal journals.]

4. Laws making it illegal for women and children to work at certain types of jobs.
5. Laws regulating certain kinds of sexual conduct, e.g., homosexuality among consenting adults in private.
6. Laws regulating the use of certain drugs which may have harmful consequences to the user but do not lead to anti-social conduct.
7. Laws requiring a license to engage in certain professions with those not receiving a license subject to fine or jail sentence if they do engage in the practice.
8. Laws compelling people to spend a specified fraction of their income on the purchase of retirement annuities. (Social Security)
9. Laws forbidding various forms of gambling (often justified on the grounds that the poor are more likely to throw away their money on such activities than the rich who can afford to).
10 Laws regulating the maximum rates of interest for loans.
11. Laws against duelling.

In addition to laws which attach criminal or civil penalties to certain kinds of action there are laws, rules, regulations, decrees, which make it either difficult or impossible for people to carry out their plans and which are also justified on paternalistic grounds. Examples of this are:

1. Laws regulating the types of contracts which will be upheld as valid by the courts, e.g. (an example of Mill's to which I shall return) no man may make a valid contract for perpetual involuntary servitude.
2. Not allowing as a defense to a charge of murder or assault the consent of the victim.
3. Requiring members of certain religious sects to have compulsory blood transfusions. This is made possible by not allowing the patient to have recourse to civil suits for assault and battery and by means of injunctions.
4. Civil commitment procedures when these are specifically justified on the basis of preventing the person being committed from harming himself. (The D.C. Hospitalization of the Mentally Ill Act provides for involuntary hospitalization of a person who "is mentally ill, and because of that illness, is likely to injure *himself* or others if allowed to remain at liberty." The term injure in this context applies to unintentional as well as intentional injuries.)
5. Putting fluorides in the community water supply.

All of my examples are of existing restrictions on the liberty of individuals. Obviously one can think of interferences which have not yet

1083

been imposed. Thus one might ban the sale of cigarettes, or require that people wear safety-belts in automobiles (as opposed to merely having them installed) enforcing this by not allowing motorists to sue for injuries even when caused by other drivers if the motorist was not wearing a seat-belt at the time of the accident.

I shall not be concerned with activities which though defended on paternalistic grounds are not interferences with the liberty of persons, e.g. the giving of subsidies in kind rather than in cash on the grounds that the recipients would not spend the money on the goods which they really need, or not including a $1000 deductible provision in a basic protection automobile insurance plan on the ground that the people who would elect it could least afford it. Nor shall I be concerned with measures such as "truth-in-advertising" acts and the Pure Food and Drug legislation which are often attacked as paternalistic but which should not be considered so. In these cases all that is provided—it is true by the use of compulsion—is information which it is presumed that rational persons are interested in having in order to make wise decisions. There is no interference with the liberty of the consumer unless one wants to stretch a point beyond good sense and say that his liberty to apply for a loan without knowing the true rate of interest is diminished. It is true that sometimes there is sentiment for going further than providing information, for example when laws against usurious interest are passed preventing those who might wish to contract loans at high rates of interest from doing so, and these measures may correctly be considered paternalistic.

III

Bearing these examples in mind let me return to a characterization of paternalism. I said earlier that I meant by the term, roughly, interference with a person's liberty for his own good. But as some of the examples show the class of persons whose good is involved is not always identical with the class of persons whose freedom is restricted. Thus in the case of professional licensing it is the practitioner who is directly interfered with and it is the would-be patient whose interests are presumably being served. Not allowing the consent of the victim to be a defense to certain types of crime primarily affects the would-be aggressor but it is the interests of the willing victim that we are trying to protect. Sometimes a person may fall into both classes as would be the case if we banned the manufacture and sale of cigarettes and a given manufacturer happened to be a smoker as well.

Thus we may first divide paternalistic interferences into "pure" and "impure" cases. In "pure" paternalism the class of persons whose freedom is restricted is identical with the class of persons whose benefit is intended to be promoted by such restrictions. Examples: the making of suicide a crime, requiring passengers in automobiles to wear seat-belts, requiring a [Jehovah's Witness] to receive a blood transfusion. In the case of "impure" paternalism in trying to protect the welfare of a class of persons we find that the only way to do so will involve restricting the freedom of other persons besides those who are benefitted. Now it might be thought that there are no cases of "impure" paternalism since any such case could always be justified on non-paternalistic grounds, i.e. in terms of preventing harms to others. Thus we might ban cigarette manufacturers from continuing to manufacture their product on the grounds that we are preventing them from causing illness to others in the same way that we prevent other manufacturers from releasing pollutants into the atmosphere, thereby causing danger to the members of the community. The difference is, however, that in the former but not the latter case the harm is of such a nature that it could be avoided by those individuals affected if they so chose. The incurring of the harm requires, so to speak, the active co-operation of the victim. It would be mistaken theoretically and hypocritical in practice to assert that our interference in such cases is just like our interference in standard cases of protecting others from harm. At the very least someone interfered with in this way can reply that no one is complaining about his activities. It may be that impure paternalism requires arguments or reasons of a stronger kind in order to be justified since there are persons who are losing a portion of their liberty and they do not even have the solace of having it be done "in their own interest." Of course in some sense, if paternalistic justifications are ever correct then we are protecting others, we are preventing some from injuring others, but it is important to see the differences between this and the standard case.

Paternalism then will always involve limitations on the liberty of some individuals in their own interest but it may also extend to interferences with the liberty of parties whose interests are not in question.

IV

Finally, by way of some more preliminary analysis, I want to distinguish paternalistic interferences with liberty from a related type with which it is often confused. Consider, for example, legislation which forbids employees to work more than, say, 40 hours per week. It is sometimes argued that such legislation is paternalistic for if employees desired such a restriction on their hours of work they could agree among themselves to impose it voluntarily. But because they do not the society imposes its own conception of their best interests upon them by the use of coercion. Hence this is paternalism.

Now it may be that some legislation of this nature is, in fact, paternalistically motivated. I am not denying that. All I want to point out is that there is another possible way of justifying such measures which is not paternalistic in nature. It is not paternalistic because as Mill puts it in a similar context such measures are "required not to overrule the judgment of individuals respecting their own interest, but to give effect to that judgment: they being unable to give effect to it except by concert, which concert again cannot be effectual unless it receives validity and sanction from the law."[2]

The line of reasoning here is a familiar one first found in Hobbes and developed with great sophistication by contemporary economists in the last decade or so. There are restrictions which are in the interests of a class of persons taken collectively but are such that the immediate interest of each individual is furthered by his violating the rule when others adhere to it. In such cases the individuals involved may need the use of compulsion to give effect to their collective judgment of their own interest by guaranteeing each individual compliance by the others. In these cases compulsion is not used to achieve some benefit which is not recognized to be a benefit by those concerned, but rather because it is the only feasible means of achieving some benefit which *is* recognized as such by all concerned. This way of viewing matters provides us with another characterization of paternalism in general. Paternalism might be thought of as the use of coercion to achieve a good which is not recognized as such by those persons for whom the good is intended. Again while this formulation captures the heart of the matter—it is surely what Mill is objecting to in *On Liberty*—the matter is not always quite like that. For example when we force motorcyclists to wear helmets we are trying to promote a good—the protection of the person from injury—which is surely recognized by most of the individuals concerned. It is not that a cyclist doesn't value his bodily integrity; rather, as a supporter of such legislation would put it, he either places, perhaps irrationally, another value or good (freedom from wearing a helmet) above that of physical well-being or, perhaps, while recognizing the danger in the abstract, he either does not fully appreciate it or he underestimates the likelihood of its occurring. But now we are approaching the question of possible justi-

2. J. S. Mill, *Principles of Political Economy* (New York: P. F. Collier and Sons, 1900), p. 442.

fications of paternalistic measures and the rest of this essay will be devoted to that question.

V

I shall begin for dialectical purposes by discussing Mill's objections to paternalism and then go on to discuss more positive proposals.

An initial feature that strikes one is the absolute nature of Mill's prohibitions against paternalism. It is so unlike the carefully qualified admonitions of Mill and his fellow Utilitarians on other moral issues. He speaks of self-protection as the *sole* end warranting coercion, of the individual's own goals as *never* being a sufficient warrant. Contrast this with his discussion of the prohibition against lying in *Util.*

> Yet that even this rule, sacred as it is, admits of possible exception, is acknowledged by all moralists, the chief of which is where the with-holding of some fact . . . would save an individual . . . from great and unmerited evil.[3]

The same tentativeness is present when he deals with justice.

> It is confessedly unjust to break faith with any one: to violate an engagement, either express or implied, or disappoint expectations raised by our own conduct, at least if we have raised these expectations knowingly and voluntarily. Like all the other obligations of justice already spoken of, this one is not regarded as absolute, but as capable of being overruled by a stronger obligation of justice on the other side.[4]

This anomaly calls for some explanation. The structure of Mill's argument is as follows:

(1) Since restraint is an evil the burden of proof is on those who propose such restraint.
(2) Since the conduct which is being considered is purely self-regarding, the normal appeal to the protection of the interests of others is not available.
(3) Therefore we have to consider whether reasons involving reference to the individual's own good, happiness, welfare, or interests are sufficient to overcome the burden of justification.

3. Mill, *Utilitarianism* and *On Liberty*, p. 174.
4. Ibid., p. 299.

(4) We either cannot advance the interests of the individual by compulsion, or the attempt to do so involves evil which outweigh the good done.

(5) Hence the promotion of the individual's own interests does not provide a sufficient warrant for the use of compulsion.

Clearly the operative premise here is (4) and it is bolstered by claims about the status of the individual as judge and appraiser of his welfare, interests, needs, etc.

> With respect to his own feelings and circumstances, the most ordinary man or woman has means of knowledge immeasurably surpassing those that can be possessed by any one else.[5]

> He is the man most interested in his well-being: the interest which any other person, except in cases of strong personal attachment, can have in it, is trifling, compared to that which he himself has.[6]

These claims are used to support the following generalizations concerning the utility of compulsion for paternalistic purposes.

> The interferences of society to overrule his judgment and purposes in what only regards himself must be grounded on general presumptions; which may be altogether wrong, and even if right, are as likely as not to be misapplied to individual cases.[7]

> But the strongest of all the arguments against the interference of the public with purely personal conduct is that when it does interfere, the odds are that it interferes wrongly and in the wrong place.[8]

> All errors which the individual is likely to commit against advice and warning are far outweighed by the evil of allowing others to constrain him to what they deem his good.[9]

Performing the utilitarian calculation by balancing the advantages and disadvantages we find that:

> Mankind are greater gainers by suffering each other to live as seems good to themselves, than by compelling each other to live as seems good to the rest.[10]

5. Ibid., p. 207.
6. Ibid., p. 206.
7. Ibid., p. 207.
8. Ibid., p. 214.
9. Ibid., p. 207.
10. Ibid., p. 138.

From which follows the operative premise (4).

This classical case of a utilitarian argument with all the premises spelled out is not the only line of reasoning present in Mill's discussion. There are asides, and more than asides, which look quite different and I shall deal with them later. But this is clearly the main channel of Mill's thought and it is one which has been subjected to vigorous attack from the moment it appeared—most often by fellow Utilitarians. The link that they have usually seized on is, as Fitzjames Stephen put it, the absence of proof that the "mass of adults are so well acquainted with their own interests and so much disposed to pursue them that no compulsion or restraint put upon them by any others for the purpose of promoting their interest can really promote them."[11] Even so sympathetic a critic as Hart is forced to the conclusion that:

> In Chapter 5 of his essay Mill carried his protests against paternalism to lengths that may now appear to us as fantastic. . . . No doubt if we no longer sympathise with this criticism this is due, in part, to a general decline in the belief that individuals know their own interest best.[12]

> Mill endows the average individual with "too much of the psychology of a middle-aged man whose desires are relatively fixed, not liable to be artificially stimulated by external influences; who knows what he wants and what gives him satisfaction of happiness; and who pursues these things when he can."[13]

Now it is interesting to note that Mill himself was aware of some of the limitations on the doctrine that the individual is the best judge of his own interests. In his discussion of government intervention in general (even where the intervention does not interfere with liberty but provides alternative institutions to those of the market) after making claims which are parallel to those just discussed, e.g.

> People understand their own business and their own interests better, and care for them more, than the government does, or can be expected to do.[14]

11. J. F. Stephen, *Liberty, Equality, Fraternity* (New York: Henry Holt & Co., n.d.), p. 24.
12. H. L. A. Hart, *Law, Liberty and Morality* (Stanford: Stanford University Press, 1963), p. 32.
13. Ibid., p. 33.
14. Mill, *Principles*, II, 448.

He goes on to an intelligent discussion of the "very large and conspicuous exceptions" to the maxim that:

> Most persons take a juster and more intelligent view of their own interest, and of the means of promoting it than can either be prescribed to them by a general enactment of the legislature, or pointed out in the particular case by a public functionary.[15]

Thus there are things

> of which the utility does not consist in ministering to inclinations, nor in serving the daily uses of life, and the want of which is least felt where the need is greatest. This is peculiarly true of those things which are chiefly useful as tending to raise the character of human beings. The uncultivated cannot be competent judges of cultivation. Those who most need to be made wiser and better, usually desire it least, and, if they desired it, would be incapable of finding the way to it by their own lights.
>   . . . . A second exception to the doctrine that individuals are the best judges of their own interest, is when an individual attempts to decide irrevocably now what will be best for his interest at some future and distant time. The presumption in favor of individual judgment is only legitimate, where the judgment is grounded on actual, and especially on present, personal experience; not where it is formed antecedently to experience, and not suffered to be reversed even after experience has condemned it.[16]

The upshot of these exceptions is that Mill does not declare that there should never be government interference with the economy but rather that

> . . . in every instance, the burden of making out a strong case should be thrown not on those who resist but on those who recommend government interference. Letting alone, in short, should be the general practice: every departure from it, unless required by some great good, is a certain evil.[17]

In short, we get a presumption not an absolute prohibition. The question is why doesn't the argument against paternalism go the same way?

I suggest that the answer lies in seeing that in addition to a purely utilitarian argument Mill uses another as well. As a Utilitarian Mill has to

15. Ibid., II, 458.
16. Ibid., II, 459.
17. Ibid., II, 451.

show, in Fitzjames Stephen's words, that:

> Self-protection apart, no good object can be attained by any compulsion
> which is not in itself a greater evil than the absence of the object which
> the compulsion obtains.[18]

To show this is impossible; one reason being that it isn't true. Preventing
a man from selling himself into slavery (a paternalistic measure which
Mill himself accepts as legitimate), or from taking heroin, or from driving a car without wearing seat-belts may constitute a lesser evil than allowing him to do any of these things. A consistent Utilitarian can only
argue against paternalism on the grounds that it (as a matter of fact)
does not maximize the good. It is always a contingent question that may
be refuted by the evidence. But there is also a non-contingent argument
which runs through *On Liberty*. When Mill states that "there is a part of
the life of every person who has come to years of discretion, within
which the individuality of that person ought to reign uncontrolled either
by any other person or by the public collectively" he is saying something
about what it means to be a person, an autonomous agent. It is because
coercing a person for his own good denies this status as an independent
entity that Mill objects to it so strongly and in such absolute terms. To be
able to choose is a good that is independent of the wisdom of what is
chosen. A man's "mode of laying out his existence is the best, not because
it is the best in itself, but because it is his own mode."[19]

> It is the privilege and proper condition of a human being, arrived at the
> maturity of his faculties, to use and interpret experience in his own
> way.[20]

As further evidence of this line of reasoning in Mill consider the one
exception to his prohibition against paternalism.

> In this and most civilised countries, for example, an engagement by
> which a person should sell himself, or allow himself to be sold, as a slave,
> would be null and void; neither enforced by law nor by opinion. The
> ground for thus limiting his power of voluntarily disposing of his own
> lot in life, is apparent, and is very clearly seen in this extreme case. The
> reason for not interfering, unless for the sake of others, with a person's
> voluntary acts, is consideration for his liberty. His voluntary choice is

18. Stephen, p. 49.
19. Mill, *Utilitarianism* and *On Liberty*, p. 197.
20. Ibid., p. 186.

evidence that what he so chooses is desirable, or at least endurable, to him, and his good is on the whole best provided for by allowing him to take his own means of pursuing it. But by selling himself for a slave, he abdicates his liberty; he foregoes any future use of it beyond that single act. He therefore defeats, in his own case, the very purpose which is the justification of allowing him to dispose of himself. He is no longer free; but is thenceforth in a position which has no longer the presumption in its favour, that would be afforded by his voluntarily remaining in it. The principle of freedom cannot require that he should be free not to be free. It is not freedom to be allowed to alienate his freedom.[21]

Now leaving aside the fudging on the meaning of freedom in the last line it is clear that part of this argument is incorrect. While it is true that *future* choices of the slave are not reasons for thinking that what he chooses then is desirable for him, what is at issue is limiting his immediate choice; and since this choice is made freely, the individual may be correct in thinking that his interests are best provided for by entering such a contract. But the main consideration for not allowing such a contract is the need to preserve the liberty of the person to make future choices. This gives us a principle—a very narrow one—by which to justify some paternalistic interferences. Paternalism is justified only to preserve a wider range of freedom for the individual in question. How far this principle could be extended, whether it can justify all the cases in which we are inclined upon reflection to think paternalistic measures justified remains to be discussed. What I have tried to show so far is that there are two strains of argument in Mill—one a straight-forward Utilitarian mode of reasoning and one which relies not on the goods which free choice leads to but on the absolute value of the choice itself. The first cannot establish any absolute prohibition but at most a presumption and indeed a fairly weak one given some fairly plausible assumptions about human psychology; the second while a stronger line of argument seems to me to allow on its own grounds a wider range of paternalism than might be suspected. I turn now to a consideration of these matters.

VI

We might begin looking for principles governing the acceptable use of paternalistic power in cases where it is generally agreed that it is legitimate. Even Mill intends his principles to be applicable only to mature individuals, not those in what he calls "non-age." What is it that justifies

21. Ibid., pp. 235-236.

us in interfering with children? The fact that they lack some of the emotional and cognitive capacities required in order to make fully rational decisions. It is an empirical question to just what extent children have an adequate conception of their own present and future interests but there is not much doubt that there are many deficiencies. For example it is very difficult for a child to defer gratification for any considerable period of time. Given these deficiencies and given the very real and permanent dangers that may befall the child it becomes not only permissible but even a duty of the parent to restrict the child's freedom in various ways. There is however an important moral limitation on the exercise of such parental power which is provided by the notion of the child eventually coming to see the correctness of his parent's interventions. Parental paternalism may be thought of as a wager by the parent on the child's subsequent recognition of the wisdom of the restrictions. There is an emphasis on what could be called future-oriented consent—on what the child will come to welcome, rather than on what he does welcome.

The essence of this idea has been incorporated by idealist philosophers into various types of "real-will" theory as applied to fully adult persons. Extensions of paternalism are argued for by claiming that in various respects, chronologically mature individuals share the same deficiencies in knowledge, capacity to think rationally, and the ability to carry out decisions that children possess. Hence in interfering with such people we are in effect doing what they would do if they were fully rational. Hence we are not really opposing their will, hence we are not really interfering with their freedom. The dangers of this move have been sufficiently exposed by Berlin in his Two Concepts of Liberty. I see no gain in theoretical clarity nor in practical advantage in trying to pass over the real nature of the interferences with liberty that we impose on others. Still the basic notion of consent is important and seems to me the only acceptable way of trying to delimit an area of justified paternalism.

Let me start by considering a case where the consent is not hypothetical in nature. Under certain conditions it is rational for an individual to agree that others should force him to act in ways in which, at the time of action, the individual may not see as desirable. If, for example, a man knows that he is subject to breaking his resolves when temptation is present, he may ask a friend to refuse to entertain his requests at some later stage.

A classical example is given in the Odyssey when Odysseus commands his men to tie him to the mast and refuse all future orders to be set free, because he knows the power of the Sirens to enchant men with their songs. Here we are on relatively sound ground in later refusing Odysseus' request to be set free. He may even claim to have changed his mind but since it is just such changes that he wished to guard against we are entitled to ignore them.

A process analogous to this may take place on a social rather than individual basis. An electorate may mandate its representatives to pass legislation which when it comes time to "pay the price" may be unpalatable. I may believe that a tax increase is necessary to halt inflation though I may resent the lower pay check each month. However in both this case and that of Odysseus the measure to be enforced is specifically requested by the party involved and at some point in time there is genuine consent and agreement on the part of those persons whose liberty is infringed. Such is not the case for the paternalistic measures we have been speaking about. What must be involved here is not consent to specific measures but rather consent to a system of government, run by elected representatives, with an understanding that they may act to safeguard our interests in certain limited ways.

I suggest that since we are all aware of our irrational propensities, deficiencies in cognitive and emotional capacities and avoidable and unavoidable ignorance it is rational and prudent for us to in effect take out "social insurance policies." We may argue for and against proposed paternalistic measures in terms of what fully rational individuals would accept as forms of protection. Now, clearly since the initial agreement is not about specific measures we are dealing with a more-or-less blank check and therefore there have to be carefully defined limits. What I am looking for are certain kinds of conditions which make it plausible to suppose that rational men could reach agreement to limit their liberty even when other men's interests are not affected.

Of course as in any kind of agreement schema there are great difficulties in deciding what rational individuals would or would not accept. Particularly in sensitive areas of personal liberty, there is always a danger of the dispute over agreement and rationality being a disguised version of evaluative and normative disagreement.

Let me suggest types of situations in which it seems plausible to suppose that fully rational individuals would agree to having paternalistic restrictions imposed upon them. It is reasonable to suppose that there are "goods" such as health which any person would want to have in order to pursue his own good—no matter how that good is conceived. This is an argument that is used in connection with compulsory education for children but it seems to me that it can be extended to other goods which have this character. Then one could agree that the attainment of such goods should be promoted even when not recognized to be such, at the moment, by the individuals concerned.

An immediate difficulty that arises stems from the fact that men are always faced with competing goods and that there may be reasons why even a value such as health—or indeed life—may be overridden by competing values. Thus the problem with the Christian Scientist and blood transfusions. It may be more important for him to reject "impure substances" than to go on living. The difficult problem that must be faced is whether one can give sense to the notion of a person irrationally attaching weights to competing values.

Consider a person who knows the statistical data on the probability of being injured when not wearing seat belts in an automobile and knows the types and gravity of the various injuries. He also insists that the inconvenience attached to fastening the belt every time he gets in and out of the car outweighs for him the possible risks to himself. I am inclined in this case to think that such a weighing is irrational. Given his life-plans which we are assuming are those of the average person, his interests and commitments already undertaken, I think it is safe to predict that we can find inconsistencies in his calculations at some point. I am assuming that this is not a man who for some conscious or unconscious reasons is trying to injure himself nor is he a man who just likes to "live dangerously." I am assuming that he is like us in all the relevant respects but just puts an enormously high negative value on inconvenience—one which does not seem comprehensible or reasonable.

It is always possible, of course to assimilate this person to creatures like myself. I, also, neglect to fasten my seat belt and I concede such behavior is not rational but not because I weigh the inconvenience differently from those who fasten the belts. It is just that having made (roughly) the same calculation as everybody else I ignore it in my actions. [Note: a much better case of weakness of the will than those usually given in ethics texts.] A plausible explanation for this deplorable habit is that although I know in some intellectual sense what the probabilities and risks are I do not fully appreciate them in an emotionally genuine manner.

We have two distinct types of situation in which a man acts in a non-rational fashion. In one case he attaches incorrect weights to some of his values; in the other he neglects to act in accordance with his actual preferences and desires. Clearly there is a stronger and more persuasive argument for paternalism in the latter situation. Here we are really not—by assumption—imposing a good on another person. But why may we not extend our interference to what we might call evaluative delusions? After all in the case of cognitive delusions we are prepared, often, to act against the expressed will of the person involved. If a man believes that when he jumps out the window he will float upwards—Robert Nozick's example—would not we detain him, forcibly if necessary? The reply will be that this man doesn't wish to be injured and if we could convince him that he is mistaken as to the consequences of his action he would not wish to perform the action. But part of what is involved in claiming that a man who doesn't fasten his seat-belts is attaching an irrational weight to the inconvenience of fastening them is that if he were to be involved in an accident and severely injured he would look back and admit that the inconvenience wasn't as bad as all that. So there is a sense in which if I could convince him of the consequences of his action he also would not wish to continue his present course of action. Now the notion of consequences being used here is covering a lot of ground. In one case it's being used to indicate what will or can happen as a result of a course of action and in the other it's making a prediction about the future evaluation of the consequences—in the first sense—of a course of action. And whatever the difference between facts and values—whether it be hard and fast or soft and slow—we are genuinely more reluctant to consent to interferences where evaluative differences are the issue. Let me now consider another factor which comes into play in some of these situations which may make an important difference in our willingness to consent to paternalistic restrictions.

Some of the decisions we make are of such a character that they produce changes which are in one or another way irreversible. Situations are created in which it is difficult or impossible to return to anything like the initial stage at which the decision was made. In particular some of these changes will make it impossible to continue to make reasoned choices in the future. I am thinking specifically of decisions which involve taking drugs that are physically or psychologically addictive and those which are destructive of one's mental and physical capacities.

I suggest we think of the imposition of paternalistic interferences in situations of this kind as being a kind of insurance policy which we take out against making decisions which are far-reaching, potentially dangerous and irreversible. Each of these factors is important. Clearly there are many decisions we make that are relatively irreversible. In deciding to learn to play chess I could predict in view of my general interest in games that some portion of my free-time was going to be pre-empted and that it would not be easy to give up the game once I acquired a certain competence. But my whole life-style was not going to be jeopardized in an extreme manner. Further it might be argued that even with addictive drugs such as heroin one's normal life plans would not be seriously interfered with if an inexpensive and adequate supply were readily available. So this type of argument might have a much narrower scope than appears to be the case at first.

A second class of cases concerns decisions which are made under extreme psychological and sociological pressures. I am not thinking here

of the making of the decision as being something one is pressured into—
e.g. a good reason for making duelling illegal is that unless this is done
many people might have to manifest their courage and integrity in ways
in which they would rather not do so—but rather of decisions such as
that to commit suicide which are usually made at a point where the individual is not thinking clearly and calmly about the nature of his decision.
In addition, of course, this comes under the previous heading of all-too-
irrevocable decision. Now there are practical steps which a society could
take if it wanted to decrease the possibility of suicide—for example not
paying social security benefits to the survivors or as religious institutions
do, not allowing such persons to be buried with the same status as natural deaths. I think we may count these as interferences with the liberty of
persons to attempt suicide and the question is whether they are justifiable.

Using my argument schema the question is whether rational individuals would consent to such limitations. I see no reason for them to
consent to an absolute prohibition but I do think it is reasonable for
them to agree to some kind of enforced waiting period. Since we are all
aware of the possibility of temporary states, such as great fear or depression, that are inimical to the making of well-informed and rational
decisions, it would be prudent for all of us if there were some kind of
institutional arrangement whereby we were restrained from making a
decision which is (all too) irreversible. What this would be like in practice
is difficult to envisage and it may be that if no practical arrangements
were feasible then we would have to conclude that there should be no
restriction at all on this kind of action. But we might have a "cooling off"
period, in much the same way that we now require couples who file for
divorce to go through a waiting period. Or, more far-fetched, we might
imagine a Suicide Board composed of a psychologist and another member picked by the applicant. The Board would be required to meet and
talk with the person proposing to take his life, though its approval would
not be required.

A third class of decisions—these classes are not supposed to be dis-
joint—involves dangers which are either not sufficiently understood or
appreciated correctly by the persons involved. Let me illustrate, using
the example of cigarette smoking, a number of possible cases.

1. A man may not know the facts—e.g. smoking between 1 and 2 packs
   a day shortens life expectancy 6.2 years, the costs and pain of the illness caused by smoking, etc.
2. A man may know the facts, wish to stop smoking, but not have the
   requisite will-power.
3. A man may know the facts but not have them play the correct role in

his calculation because, say, he discounts the danger psychologically because it is remote in time and/or inflates the attractiveness of other consequences of his decision which he regards as beneficial.

In case 1 what is called for is education, the posting of warnings, etc. In case 2 there is no theoretical problem. We are not imposing a good on someone who rejects it. We are simply using coercion to enable people to carry out their own goals. (Note: There obviously is a difficulty in that only a subclass of the individuals affected wish to be prevented from doing what they are doing.) In case 3 there is a sense in which we are imposing a good on someone since given his current appraisal of the facts he doesn't wish to be restricted. But in another sense we are not imposing a good since what is being claimed—and what must be shown or at least argued for—is that an accurate accounting on his part would lead him to reject his current course of action. Now we all know that such cases exist, that we are prone to disregard dangers that are only possibilities, that immediate pleasures are often magnified and distorted.

If in addition the dangers are severe and far-reaching we could agree to allowing the state a certain degree of power to intervene in such situations. The difficulty is in specifying in advance, even vaguely, the class of cases in which intervention will be legitimate.

A related difficulty is that of drawing a line so that it is not the case that all ultra-hazardous activities are ruled out, e.g. mountain-climbing, bull-fighting, sports-car racing, etc. There are some risks—even very great ones—which a person is entitled to take with his life.

A good deal depends on the nature of the deprivation—e.g. does it prevent the person from engaging in the activity completely or merely limit his participation—and how important to the nature of the activity is the absence of restriction when this is weighed against the role that the activity plays in the life of the person. In the case of automobile seat belts, for example, the restriction is trivial in nature, interferes not at all with the use or enjoyment of the activity, and does, I am assuming, considerably reduce a high risk of serious injury. Whereas, for example, making mountain climbing illegal prevents completely a person engaging in an activity which may play an important role in his life and his conception of the person he is.

In general the easiest cases to handle are those which can be argued about in the terms which Mill thought to be so important—a concern not just for the happiness or welfare, in some broad sense, of the individual but rather a concern for the autonomy and freedom of the person. I suggest that we would be most likely to consent to paternalism in those instances in which it preserves and enhances for the individual his ability to rationally consider and carry out his own decisions.

I have suggested in this essay a number of types of situations in which it seems plausible that rational men would agree to granting the legislative powers of a society the right to impose restrictions on what Mill calls "self-regarding" conduct. However, rational men knowing something about the resources of ignorance, ill-will and stupidity available to the law-makers of a society—a good case in point is the history of drug legislation in the United States—will be concerned to limit such intervention to a minimum. I suggest in closing two principles designed to achieve this end.

In all cases of paternalistic legislation there must be a heavy and clear burden of proof placed on the authorities to demonstrate the exact nature of the harmful effects (or beneficial consequences) to be avoided (or achieved) and the probability of their occurrence. The burden of proof here is twofold—what lawyers distinguish as the burden of going forward and the burden of persuasion. That the authorities have the burden of going forward means that it is up to them to raise the question and bring forward evidence of the evils to be avoided. Unlike the case of new drugs where the manufacturer must produce some evidence that the drug has been tested and found not harmful, no citizen has to show with respect to self-regarding conduct that it is not harmful or promotes his best interests. In addition the nature and cogency of the evidence for the harmfulness of the course of action must be set at a high level. To paraphrase a formulation of the burden of proof for criminal proceedings—better 10 men ruin themselves than one man be unjustly deprived of liberty.

Finally I suggest a principle of the least restrictive alternative. If there is an alternative way of accomplishing the desired end without restricting liberty then although it may involve great expense, inconvenience, etc. the society must adopt it.